RAPID REVIEW

Weygandt, Kieso, Kimmel

Financial Accounting, Fifth Edition

PLANT ASSETS (Chapter 10)

Presentation

Tangible Assets	Intangible Assets
Property, plant, and equipment	Intangible assets (Patents, copyrights, trademarks, franchises, goodwill)
Natural resources	

Computation of Annual Depreciation Expense

Straight-line	$\frac{\text{Cost} - \text{Salvage value}}{\text{Useful life (in years)}}$
Units-of-activity	$\frac{\text{Depreciable cost}}{\text{Useful life (in units)}} \times$ Units of activity during year
Declining-balance	Book value at beginning of year × Declining balance rate* *Declining-balance rate = 1 ÷ Useful life (in years)

Note: If depreciation is calculated for partial periods, the straight-line and declining-balance methods must be adjusted for the relevant proportion of the year. Multiply the annual depreciation expense by the number of months expired in the year divided by 12 months.

BONDS (Chapter 11)

Premium	Market interest rate < Contractual interest rate
Face Value	Market interest rate = Contractual interest rate
Discount	Market interest rate > Contractual interest rate

Computation of Annual Bond Interest Expense

Interest expense = Interest paid (payable) + Amortization of discount
(OR − Amortization of premium)

Straight-line amortization	$\frac{\text{Bond discount (premium)}}{\text{Number of interest periods}}$	
Effective-interest amortization (preferred) method)	Bond interest expense	Bond interest paid
	Carrying value of bonds at beginning of period × Effective interest rate	Face amount of bonds × Contractual interest rate

STOCKHOLDERS' EQUITY (Chapter 12)

No-Par Value vs. Par Value Stock Journal Entries

No-Par Value	Par Value
Cash Common Stock	Cash Common Stock (par value) Paid-in Capital in Excess of Par Value

Comparison of Dividend Effects

	Cash	Common Stock	Retained Earnings
Cash dividend	↓	No effect	↓
Stock dividend	No effect	↑	↓
Stock split	No effect	No effect	No effect

Debits and Credits to Retained Earnings

Retained Earnings	
Debits (Decreases)	Credits (Increases)
1. Net loss 2. Prior period adjustments for overstatement of net income 3. Cash dividends and stock dividends 4. Some disposals of treasury stock	1. Net income 2. Prior period adjustments for understatement of net income

INVESTMENTS (Chapter 13)

Comparison of Long-Term Bond Investment and Liability Journal Entries

Event	Investor	Investee
Purchase / issue of bonds	Debt Investments Cash	Cash Bonds Payable
Interest receipt / payment	Cash Interest Revenue	Interest Expense Cash

Comparison of Cost and Equity Methods of Accounting for Long-Term Stock Investments

Event	Cost	Equity
Acquisition	Stock Investments Cash	Stock Investments Cash
Investee reports earnings	No entry	Stock Investments Investment Revenue
Investee pays dividends	Cash Dividend Revenue	Cash Stock Investments

STATEMENT OF CASH FLOWS (Chapter 14)

Cash flows from operating activities (**indirect method**)

Net income			
Add:	Decreases in current assets	$ X	
	Increases in current liabilities	X	
	Amortization and depreciation	X	
	Losses on disposals of assets	X	
Deduct:	Increases in current assets	(X)	
	Decreases in current liabilities	(X)	
	Gains on disposals of assets	(X)	
Cash provided (used) by operating activities			$ X

Cash flows from operating activities (**direct method**)

Cash receipts (Examples: from sales of goods and services to customers, from receipts of interest and dividends on loans and investments)	$ X	
Cash payments (Examples: to suppliers, for operating expenses, for interest, for taxes)	(X)	
Cash provided (used) by operating activities		$ X

IRREGULAR ITEMS (Chapter 15)

Presentation of Non-Typical Items

Prior period adjustments	Statement of retained earnings (adjustment of beginning retained earnings)
Changes in accounting principle	Income statement (cumulative effect adjustment presented just above "Net income")
Discontinued operations	Income statement (presented separately after "Income from continuing operations")
Extraordinary items	Income statement (presented separately after "Income before extraordinary items")

eGrade Plus

with EduGen

www.wiley.com/college/weygandt

Based on the Activities You Do Every Day

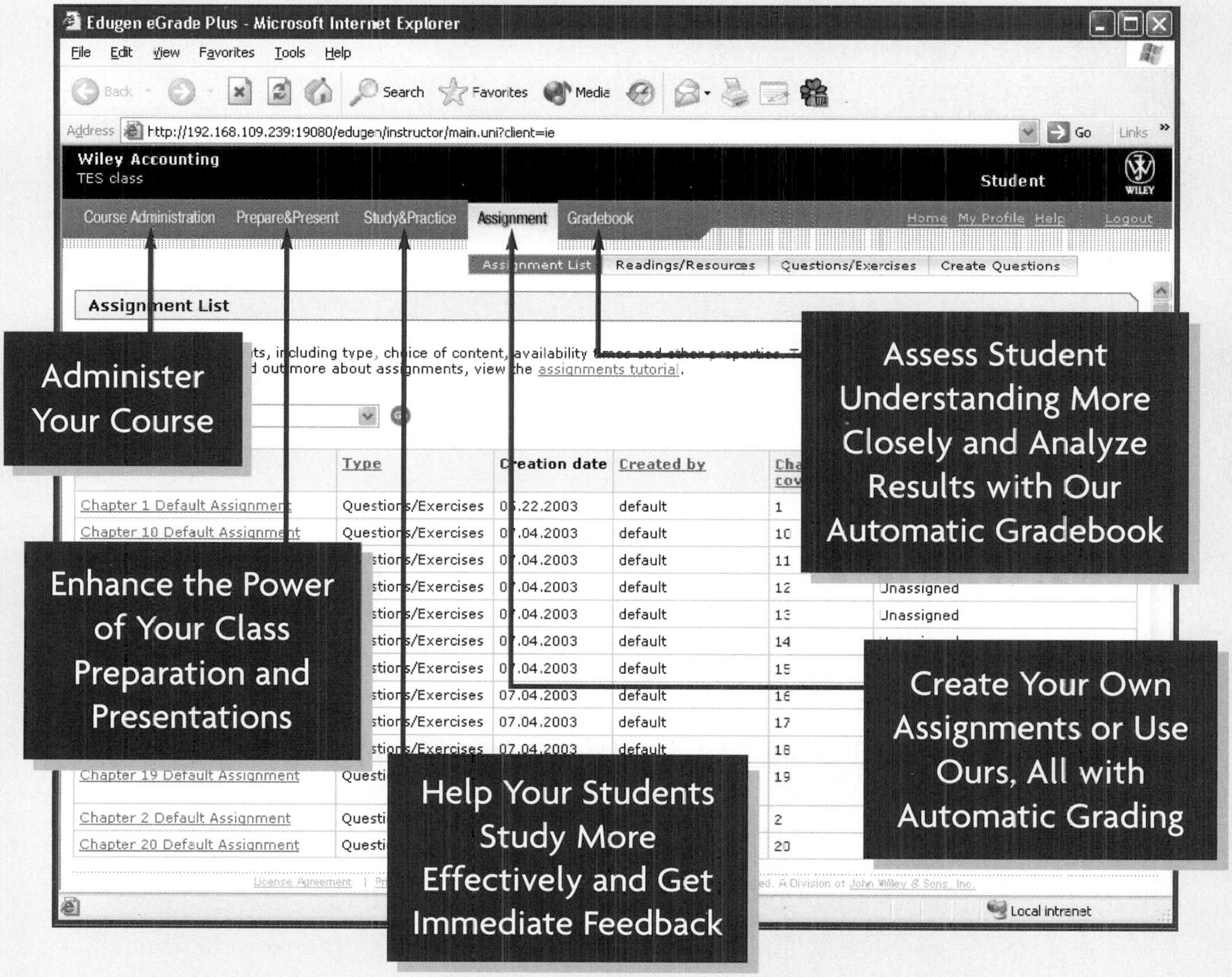

All the content and tools you need, all in one location, in an easy-to-use browser format.

Choose the resources you need, or rely on the arrangement supplied by us.

Now, many of Wiley's Book Companion Sites are available with EduGen, allowing you to create your own teaching and learning environment. Upon adoption of EduGen, you can begin to customize your course with the resources shown here. eGrade Plus with EduGen integrates text and media and keeps all of a book's online resources in one easily accessible location. eGrade Plus integrates two resources: homework problems for students and a multimedia version of this Wiley text. With eGrade Plus, each problem is linked to the relevant section of the multimedia book.

Administer Your Course

Course Administration tools allow you to manage your class and integrate your Wiley website resources with most Course Management Systems, allowing you to keep all of your class materials in one location.

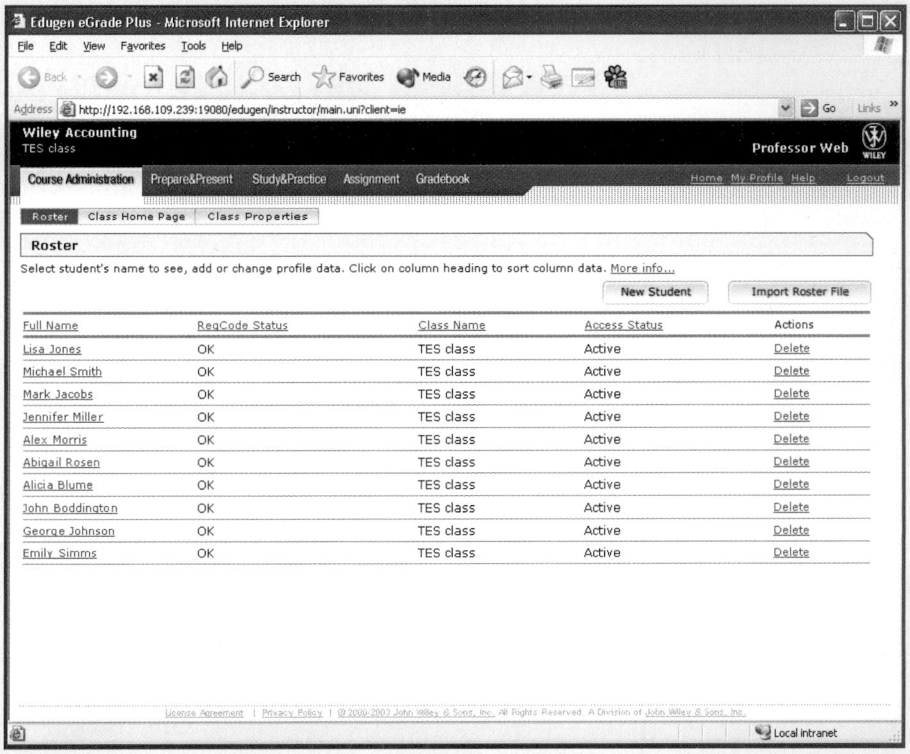

Enhance the Power of Your Class Preparation and Presentations

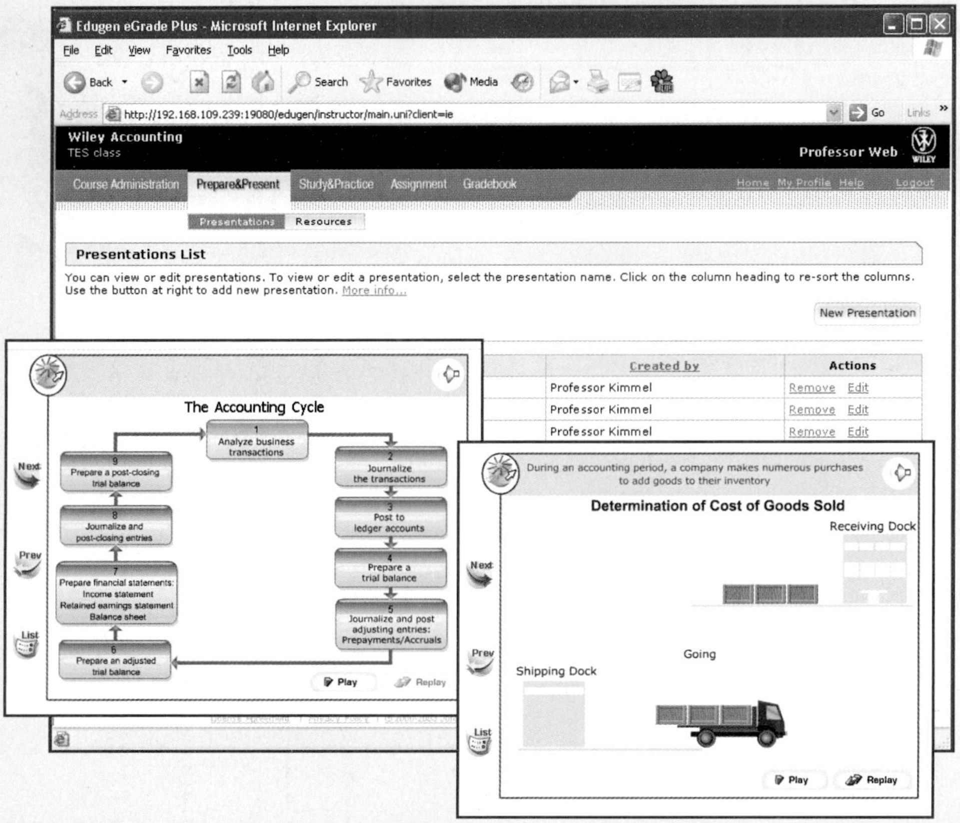

A **"Prepare and Present" tool** contains all of the Wiley-provided resources, such as **a multimedia version of the text, interactive chapter reviews, web-based tutorials, videos**, and **PowerPoint slides**, making your preparation time more efficient. You may easily adapt, customize, and add to Wiley content to meet the needs of your course.

Create Your Own Assignments or Use Ours, All with Automatic Grading

An **"Assignment"** area allows you to create **student homework** and **quizzes** that utilize **Wiley-provided question banks**, and an **electronic version of the text**. One of the most powerful features of Wiley's premium websites is that student assignments will be automatically graded and recorded in your gradebook. This will not only save you time but will provide your students with immediate feedback on their work.

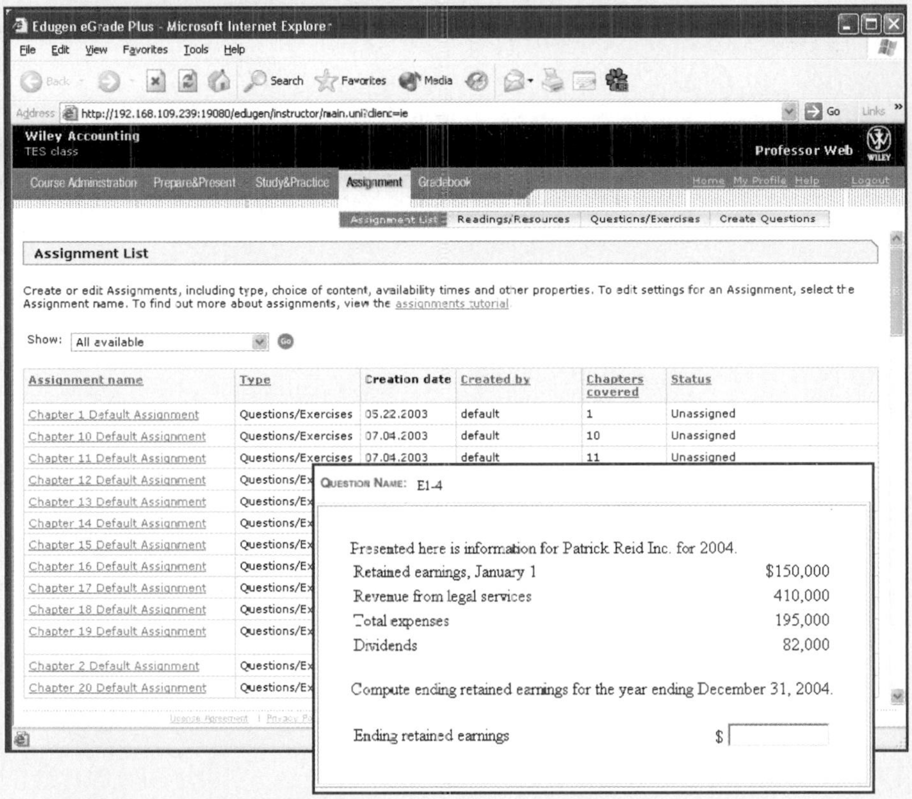

Assess Student Understanding More Closely

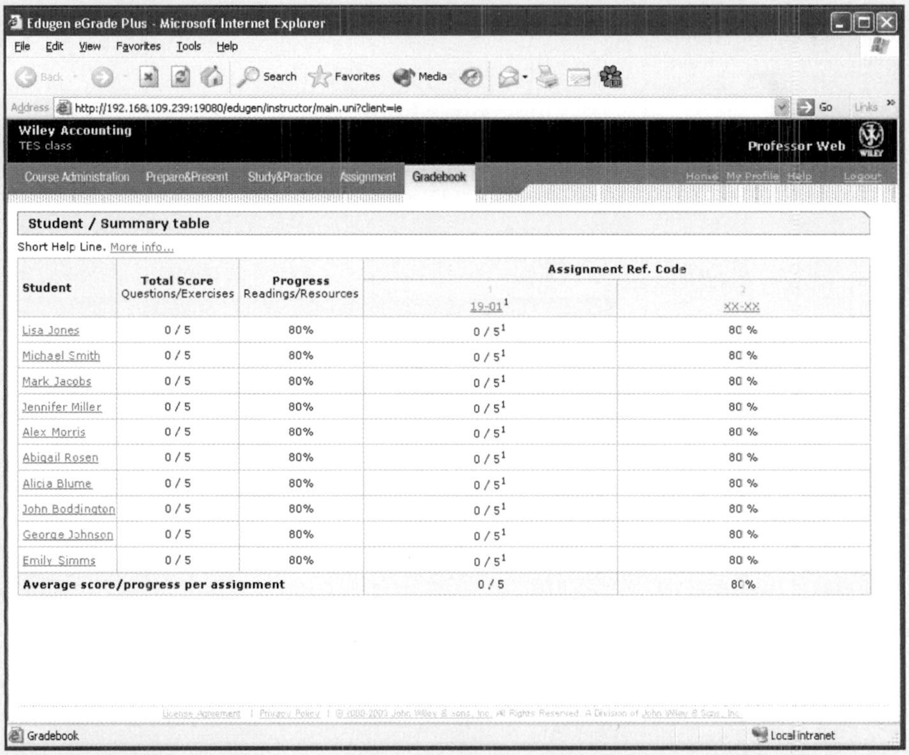

An **Instructor's Gradebook** will keep track of your students' progress and allow you to analyze individual and overall class results to determine their progress and level of understanding.

Students,

eGrade Plus with EduGen Allows You to:

Study More Effectively

Get Immediate Feedback When You Practice on Your Own

Our website links directly to **electronic book content**, so that you can review the text while you study and complete homework online. Additional resources include **interactive chapter reviews, web-based tutorials**, and **self-assessment quizzing**.

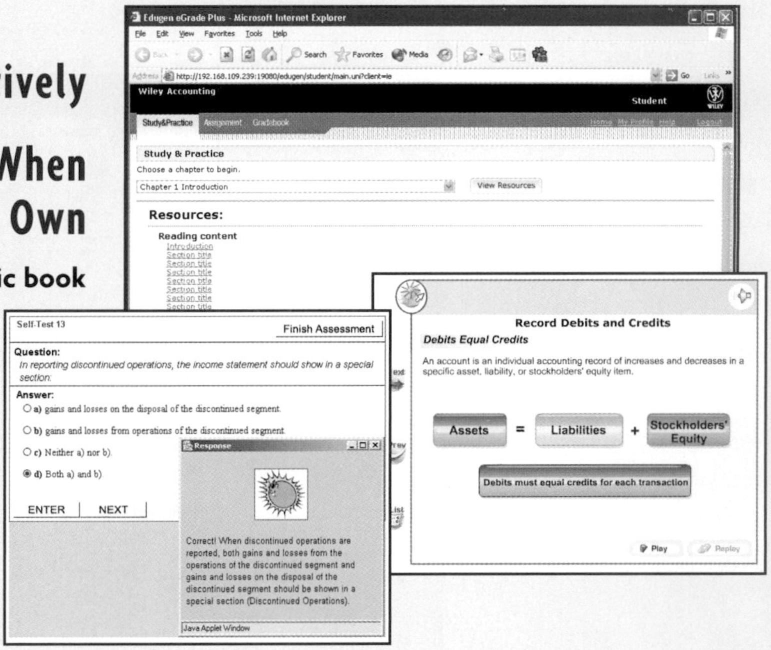

Complete Assignments / Get Help with Problem Solving

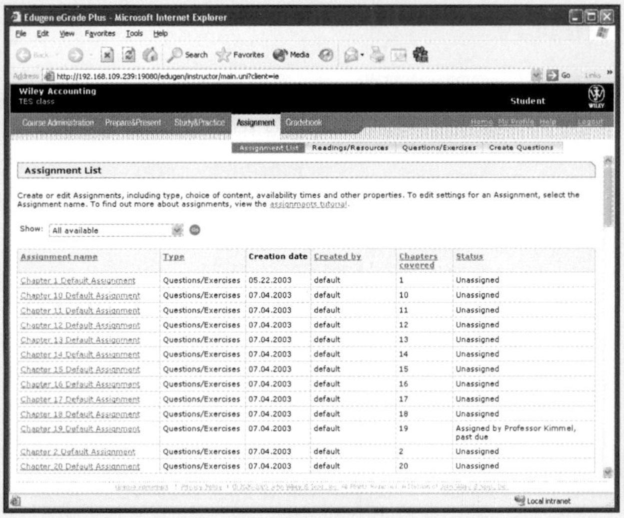

An **"Assignment"** area keeps all your assigned work in one location, making it easy for you to stay on task. In addition, many homework problems contain a **link** to the relevant section of the **electronic book**, providing you with a text explanation to help you conquer problem-solving obstacles as they arise.

Keep Track of How You're Doing

A **Personal Gradebook** allows you to view your results from past assignments at any time.

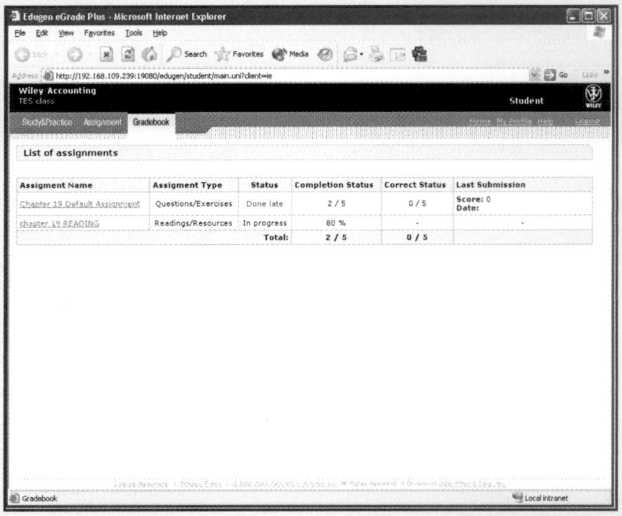

5TH EDITION

Financial Accounting

Jerry J. Weygandt *PhD, CPA*
ARTHUR ANDERSEN ALUMNI PROFESSOR OF ACCOUNTING
University of Wisconsin
Madison, Wisconsin

Donald E. Kieso *PhD, CPA*
KPMG EMERITUS PROFESSOR OF ACCOUNTING
Northern Illinois University
DeKalb, Illinois

Paul D. Kimmel *PhD, CPA*
ASSOCIATE PROFESSOR OF ACCOUNTING
University of Wisconsin—Milwaukee
Milwaukee, Wisconsin

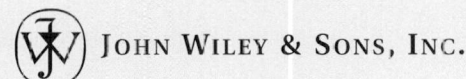

JOHN WILEY & SONS, INC.

Dedicated to
the **Wiley sales representatives**
who sell our books and service our adopters
in a professional and ethical manner

and to
Enid, Donna, and Merlynn

PUBLISHER *Susan Elbe*
ASSOCIATE PUBLISHER *Jay O'Callaghan*
SENIOR MARKETING MANAGER *Steve Herdegen*
PROJECT EDITOR *David Kear*
OUTSIDE DEVELOPMENT EDITOR *Ann Torbert*
SUPPLEMENTS EDITOR *Ed Brislin*
PRODUCTION SERVICES MANAGER *Jeanine Furino*
COVER DESIGNER *David Levy*
SENIOR DESIGNER *Kevin Murphy*
PHOTO EDITOR *Sara Wight*
ILLUSTRATION EDITOR *Sandra Rigby*
PRODUCTION MANAGEMENT *Suzanne Ingrao/Ingrao Associates*
MEDIA EDITOR *Allison Morris*
COVER PHOTO *©David Madison/Stone/Getty Images*

This book was set in Times Ten by *The GTS Companies*, York, PA Campus and printed and bound by Von Hoffmann Press. The cover was printed by Von Hoffmann Press.

This book is printed on acid-free paper.

The specimen financial statements. Appendix A and Appendix B, are printed with permission of PepsiCo, Inc., and The Coca-Cola Company.

Pepsi is a registered trademark of PepsiCo, Inc. Used with permission.

ISBN: 0-471-65527-9

Printed in the United States of America

10 9 8 7 6 5 4 3 2 1

About the Authors

Jerry J. Weygandt, PhD, CPA, is Arthur Andersen Alumni Professor of Accounting at the University of Wisconsin—Madison. He holds a Ph.D. in accounting from the University of Illinois. Articles by Professor Weygandt have appeared in the *Accounting Review, Journal of Accounting Research, Accounting Horizons, Journal of Accountancy,* and other academic and professional journals. These articles have examined such financial reporting issues as accounting for price-level adjustments, pensions, convertible securities, stock option contracts, and interim reports. Professor Weygandt is author of other accounting and financial reporting books and is a member of the American Accounting Association, the American Institute of Certified Public Accountants, and the Wisconsin Society of Certified Public Accountants. He has served on numerous committees of the American Accounting Association and as a member of the editorial board of the *Accounting Review;* he also has served as President and Secretary-Treasurer of the American Accounting Association. In addition, he has been actively involved with the American Institute of Certified Public Accountants and has been a member of the Accounting Standards Executive Committee (AcSEC) of that organization. He has served on the FASB task force that examined the reporting issues related to accounting for income taxes and is presently a trustee of the Financial Accounting Foundation. Professor Weygandt has received the Chancellor's Award for Excellence in Teaching and the Beta Gamma Sigma Dean's Teaching Award. He is on the board of directors of M & I Bank of Southern Wisconsin and the Dean Foundation. He is the recipient of the Wisconsin Institute of CPA's Outstanding Educator's Award and the Lifetime Achievement Award. In 2001 he received the American Accounting Association's Outstanding Accounting Educator Award.

Donald E. Kieso, PhD, CPA, received his bachelor's degree from Aurora University and his doctorate in accounting from the University of Illinois. He has served as chairman of the Department of Accountancy and is currently the KPMG Emeritus Professor of Accountancy at Northern Illinois University. He has public accounting experience with Price Waterhouse & Co. (San Francisco and Chicago) and Arthur Andersen & Co. (Chicago) and research experience with the Research Division of the American Institute of Certified Public Accountants (New York). He has done postdoctorate work as a Visiting Scholar at the University of California at Berkeley and is a recipient of NIU's Teaching Excellence Award and four Golden Apple Teaching Awards. Professor Kieso is the author of other accounting and business books and is a member of the American Accounting Association, the American Institute of Certified Public Accountants, and the Illinois CPA Society. He has served as a member of the Board of Directors of the Illinois CPA Society, the AACSB's Accounting Accreditation Committees, the State of Illinois Comptroller's Commission, as Secretary-Treasurer of the Federation of Schools of Accountancy, and as Secretary-Treasurer of the American Accounting Association. Professor Kieso is currently serving on the Board of Trustees and Executive Committee of Aurora University, as a member of the Board of Directors of Kishwaukee Health System, and as Treasurer and Director of Valley West Community Hospital. From 1989 to 1993 he served as a charter member of the national Accounting Education Change Commission. He is the recipient of the Outstanding Accounting Educator Award from the Illinois CPA Society, the FSA's Joseph A. Silvoso Award of Merit, the NIU Foundation's Humanitarian Award for Service to Higher Education, a Distinguished Service Award from the Illinois CPA Society, and in 2003 an honorary doctorate from Aurora University.

Paul D. Kimmel, PhD, CPA, received his bachelor's degree from the University of Minnesota and his doctorate in accounting from the University of Wisconsin. He is an Associate Professor at the University of Wisconsin—Milwaukee, and has public accounting experience with Deloitte & Touche (Minneapolis). He was the recipient of the UWM School of Business Advisory Council Teaching Award, the Reggie Taite Excellence in Teaching Award, and a three-time winner of the Outstanding Teaching Assistant Award at the University of Wisconsin. He is also a recipient of the Elijah Watts Sells Award for Honorary Distinction for his results on the CPA exam. He is a member of the American Accounting Association and has published articles in *Accounting Review, Accounting Horizons, Issues in Accounting Education, Journal of Accounting Education,* as well as other journals. His research interests include accounting for financial instruments and innovation in accounting education. He has published papers and given numerous talks on incorporating critical thinking into accounting education, and helped prepare a catalog of critical thinking resources for the Federated Schools of Accountancy.

To the Instructor

In the previous editions of *Financial Accounting,* we sought to create a book about business that made the subject clear and fascinating to beginning students. And that is still our passion: to provide a link between accounting principles, student learning, and the real world.

Student Empowerment and Success

In our effort to create an even more effective text, we surveyed the market, talked personally with instructors, and held focus groups with professors and students. We heard again and again that the biggest challenges students face are to become motivated, to learn how to study, and to manage their tasks. We have been gratified to learn that our textbook has helped empower students to meet these challenges and that it has been rated highest in customer satisfaction by both instructors and students.

We have responded to this information by making the pedagogical framework of the Fifth Edition of *Financial Accounting* even stronger and the presentation even clearer. We continue to give students the tools and the motivation they need to succeed in subsequent accounting courses and in their future business careers.

Goals and Features of the Fifth Edition

The Fifth Edition of *Financial Accounting* provides an opportunity to improve a textbook that has set high standards for quality. Users and reviewers continue to comment positively on the writing style, the use of real-world examples, pedagogical features, and the fact that the textbook is not only about accounting but about business as well. The primary purpose of this revision was to maintain these successful features and improve on them.

In the Real World, Accounting Matters

Since we wrote the fourth edition *of Financial Accounting,* a lot has happened in the real world of business and corporate accounting. The U.S. economy witnessed the collapse of the high-tech industry, a falling stock market along with employee layoffs, and the bankruptcies of numerous well-known corporations. Accounting scandals and corporate misdeeds made headlines on a weekly basis for over three years.

Companies like **WorldCom**, **Enron**, and **Global Crossing** restated current and prior years' earnings by billions of dollars and went into bankruptcy, employees lost jobs, and stockholders lost billions. One of the world's largest and most respected public accounting firms was found guilty of obstructing justice in the Enron case, went out of business, and ceased to exist within a matter of months thereafter.

As a result of a rash of accounting irregularities and erroneous corporate reporting, new laws—notably the Sarbanes-Oxley Act of 2002—have been passed, and the structure of the accounting and auditing professions have been altered. What became evident to the whole world is that **accounting matters!** The losses of money and jobs, and the imprisonment and fining of corporate officers due to accounting misstatements and improprieties proved that accounting is important. Good and accurate accounting is essential in the real world of business.

In response to these recent real-world events, in this fifth edition of *Financial Accounting,* we are emphasizing the theme "Accounting Matters!" The label "Accounting Matters!" appears on our chapter-opening real-world Feature Stories and on the three or four business insight boxes in every chapter. These real-world stories are reinforced with critical thinking questions that encourage students to think about how the situation described in the boxed story relates to the chapter content. Guideline answers to the Accounting Matters! questions are presented at the end of the chapter. The "Accounting Matters! features are highlighted throughout the book by the gold "Accounting Matters!" label or gold icon in the margin.

Accounting Matters!

Organizational and Content Changes

In this new edition, we simplified the presentation of inventory in Chapters 5 and 6 by making the following changes: We moved the coverage of recording transactions under the periodic method to Appendix A of Chapter 5; moved the comparison of the perpetual journal entries with the periodic journal entries to Appendix B of Chapter 5; and inserted in Chapter 5 a brief new section on determining cost of goods sold under the periodic method.

Chapter 10 has been simplified by moving exchanges of plant assets to an appendix to the chapter. We also simplified Chapter 12 by deleting some topics (convertible and callable preferred stock, computation of book value per share with preferred stock) and by moving others (discontinued operations, extraordinary items, change in accounting principle) elsewhere (to Chapter 15).

Chapter 11 on long-term debt now includes a chapter-end appendix on the present value concepts and computations related to bond pricing. Discussions of both the effective-interest and the straight-line amortization methods have been placed in end-of-chapter appendices, allowing the instructor the flexibility of covering one or the other, both, or neither. This normally difficult chapter also has been simplified by the deletion of two topics: issuance of bonds between interest dates, and bond sinking funds.

Coverage of the statement of cash flows (Chapter 14) has been rewritten and streamlined by covering all cash flow activities and transactions in a one-year extended illustration rather than over two years. The chapter has been further simplified in the analysis section by deleting three cash-basis ratios and concentrating only on free cash flow.

To give students the opportunity to follow an extended real-world example, we have integrated references to PepsiCo, Inc.'s financial statements throughout the book, including Review It questions, ratio presentations, and end-of-chapter assignment problems. PepsiCo's 2003 annual report is included in Appendix A at the end of the book. Comparative Analysis Problems at the end of each chapter require students to compute and compare financial data and ratios of PepsiCo, Inc. with those of The Coca-Cola Company, whose financial statements are presented in Appendix B.

For another opportunity to follow an extended problem, we have added to each chapter a continuing problem for a single (hypothetical) company, Cookie Creations. This new problem appears at the end of each chapter as the last Broadening Your Perspective assignment, under the heading "Continuing Cookie Chronicle." This new problem will enable you and your students to follow throughout the book the accounting operations for a single company.

We also made design enhancements throughout the text. These include a crisper look to our illustrations, along with cleaner, more open margin space. Also new to this edition, the accounting equation presented in the margins next to journal entries has been supplemented with illustrative cash flow effects (increase/decrease/no effect) and a description of the effect on stockholders' equity.

Simplified Presentation

As in the previous edition, we continue to simplify and condense the textual material. To achieve this goal, the text was reviewed and carefully edited to ensure its clarity and exposition. The changes that were made can be characterized into four types, as described below.

CONDENSATIONS AND DELETIONS. We either condensed or deleted material that was better suited for more advanced-level courses, along with concepts and procedures that are little used. We made these decisions after gathering a great deal of information from instructors on how they teach the course and what they think today's beginning accounting students need to know.

ORGANIZATIONAL CHANGES AND REVISIONS. The most significant organizational changes and revisions were made to simplify chapters or to provide instructors with greater flexibility of coverage. The chapters most affected are the inventory coverage in Chapters 5 and 6, long-term debt (bonds) coverage in Chapter 11, stockholders' equity in Chapter 12, and cash flow coverage in Chapter 14.

ADDITIONS. In a very few cases, we added new material to the textbook. These topics had to pass a strict test to warrant their inclusion: they were added only if they represented a major concept, issue, or procedure that a beginning student should understand.

UPDATES. This edition was subject to comprehensive updating to ensure that it is relevant and fresh. Updating involved replacing business or ethics insights boxes, problem material, real-world examples cited in the text, infographic illustrations, and chapter-opening Feature Stories.

A chapter-by-chapter summary of these changes is provided on this and the next three pages.

Key Changes in Each Chapter

In every chapter throughout, we have added critical thinking questions to the Accounting Matters! boxed items, and guideline answers to those questions at the end of the chapter. We also have added the Continuing Cookie Chronicle problem as the last item in every Broadening Your Perspective section. In addition, we made the following key changes in the chapters.

Chapter 1 ***Accounting Matters!***

- New AM! Feature Story on PepsiCo, Inc. Recent financial scandals and accounting misdeeds are addressed in the Feature Story as well as in the chapter.
- A new section titled "Why Study Accounting?" defends the importance of accounting and its contributions to our economic system.
- The section on the accounting profession and careers in accounting has been moved to an appendix of the chapter.
- New Accounting Matters! (AM!)—International Insight about the lack of confidence Chinese investors have in their financial reports.
- Deleted two Insight items.
- Adapted Financial Reporting Problem to PepsiCo, Inc., and Comparative Analysis Problem to PepsiCo versus Coca-Cola.
- Added new Research Case.
- Added new Interpreting Financial Statements case using Xerox Corporation.
- Revised all brief exercises, exercises, and problems.

Chapter 2 ***The Recording Process***

- New AM!—Business Insight about companies' mistakes in their accounting records (Hanover Compressor, Bank One, and Waste Management Co.).
- Deleted two Insight items.
- Adapted Financial Reporting Problem to PepsiCo, Inc., and Comparative Analysis Problem to PepsiCo versus Coca-Cola.
- Added new Interpreting Financial Statements case using Motorola, Inc.
- Added new Global Focus case using Doman Industries Ltd.
- Revised all brief exercises, exercises, and problems.

Chapter 3 ***Adjusting the Accounts***

- Reorganized adjusting entry illustrations.
- New AM!—Business Insight covering exceptionally large outlays by companies for advertising.
- Adapted Financial Reporting Problem to PepsiCo, Inc., and Comparative Analysis Problem to PepsiCo versus Coca-Cola.
- Added new Interpreting Financial Statements case using Chieftain International, Inc.
- Revised some brief exercises, and all exercises and problems.

Chapter 4 ***Completion of the Accounting Cycle***

- Reduced the number of Insight items from five to three.
- Revised and updated all real-world illustrations of classified balance sheet presentations.
- Adapted Financial Reporting Problem to PepsiCo, Inc., and Comparative Analysis Problem to PepsiCo versus Coca-Cola.
- Added new Research Case.
- Added new Global Focus case about Lign Multiwood, a Swedish company.
- Revised some brief exercises, and all exercises and problems.

Chapter 5 ***Accounting for Merchandising Operations***

- Revised and updated the AM! Feature Story on Buy.com.
- Reorganized the chapter to include the computation of cost of goods sold under the periodic inventory system.
- Moved transaction accounting under the periodic inventory system, including the comparison of perpetual and periodic entries, from Chapter 6 to an appendix of Chapter 5.
- Reduced the number of Insight items from five to three.
- Adapted Financial Reporting Problem to PepsiCo, Inc., and Comparative Analysis Problem to PepsiCo versus Coca-Cola.
- Added new Research Case.
- Added new Interpreting Financial Statements case using Zany Brainy, Inc.
- Revised all brief exercises, exercises, and problems.

Chapter 6 ***Inventories***

- Simplified this chapter by moving to Chapter 5 the coverage of the periodic inventory system, including the appendix comparing the perpetual and periodic entries.
- Adapted Financial Reporting Problem to PepsiCo, Inc., and Comparative Analysis Problem to PepsiCo versus Coca-Cola.
- Added new Research Case.
- Added new Interpreting Financial Statements case using Cooper Tire and Rubber Co.
- Revised all brief exercises, exercises, and problems.

Chapter 7 ***Accounting Principles***

- Deleted two Insight items.
- Revised some brief exercises and all exercises and problems.
- Revised the Comprehensive Problem.

Chapter 8 ***Internal Control and Cash***

- Deleted five Insight items.
- New AM!—Ethics Insight on "dumb frauds."
- New AM!—International Insight on "internal control achieved by Egyptian scribes."
- Adapted Financial Reporting Problem to PepsiCo, Inc., and Comparative Analysis Problem to PepsiCo versus Coca-Cola.
- Added a new Research Case.
- Updated Interpreting Financial Statements case about Microsoft and Oracle.
- Added new Global Focus case about KPMG's global survey on fraud.
- Added a second Ethics Case.
- Revised some brief exercises, and all exercises and problems.

Chapter 9 ***Accounting for Receivables***

- New AM!—Business Insight on decisions by suppliers not to ship goods to Kmart after it filed for bankruptcy protection.
- Deleted two Insight items.
- Adapted Comparative Analysis Problem to PepsiCo versus Coca-Cola.
- Added new Research Case.
- Added new Interpreting Financial Statements case using The Scotts Company.
- Added new Exploring the Web assignment on factoring.
- Revised all brief exercises, exercises, and problems.

Chapter 10 ***Plant Assets, Natural Resources, and Intangible Assets***

- Revised and updated intangible asset topics—patents, copyrights, trademarks, franchises, and goodwill.
- Coverage of exchange of plant assets moved to end-of-chapter appendix.
- New AM!—Ethics Insight on WorldCom's improper booking of expenses as capital expenditures.
- New AM!—Business Insight on cybersquatters and Internet domain names.
- Added Comprehensive Problem covering Chapters 6–10.
- Adapted Financial Reporting Problem to PepsiCo, Inc., and Comparative Analysis Problem to PepsiCo versus Coca-Cola.
- Added new Research Case.
- Added new Interpreting Financial Statements using Bob Evans Farms, Inc.
- Revised most brief exercises, and all exercises and problems.

Chapter 11 ***Liabilities***

- Shortened and simplified the chapter by moving amortization of bond premium and discount (both effective interest and straight-line methods) to appendixes of the chapter.
- Added an appendix to the chapter on "Present Value Concepts Related to Bond Pricing."
- Deleted coverage of issuing bonds between interest dates.
- Deleted coverage of bond sinking funds.
- Deleted two Insight items.
- Adapted Financial Reporting Problem to PepsiCo, Inc., and Comparative Analysis Problem to PepsiCo versus Coca-Cola.
- Added new Research Case.
- Added new Interpreting Financial Statements case using Lufkin Industries and CNH Global N. V.
- Added a second Global Focus case about the Tokyo Stock Exchange.
- Revised all brief exercises, exercises, and problems.

Chapter 12 ***Corporations: Organization, Stock Transactions, Dividends, and Retained Earnings***

- Updated various aspects of the AM! Feature Story.
- Updated numerous illustrations.
- Deleted coverage of convertible preferred stock.
- Deleted coverage of callable preferred stock.
- Deleted computation of book value per share when a company has preferred stock.
- Deleted four Insight items.
- Shortened and simplified coverage of book value.
- New AM!—Ethics Insight about Enron's collapse.
- Shortened and simplified the chapter by moving coverage of (1) discontinued operations, (2) extraordinary items, and (3) change in accounting principle to Chapter 15.
- Shortened coverage of earnings per share by deleting the coverage of "EPS and Irregular Items."
- New AM!—Business Insight about investors' renewed interest in dividends.
- Adapted Financial Reporting Problem to PepsiCo, Inc., and Comparative Analysis Problem to PepsiCo versus Coca-Cola.
- Added new Research Case.
- Added new Interpreting Financial Statement case using Marriott Corporation.
- Added a new Global Focus on American depositary receipts (ADRs).
- Added new Group Decision Case.
- Revised all brief exercises, exercises, and problems.

Chapter 13 ***Investments***

- Revised and updated the AM! Feature Story.
- Updated numerous illustrations.
- Adapted Financial Reporting Problem to PepsiCo, Inc., and Comparative Analysis Problem to PepsiCo versus Coca-Cola.
- Added new Interpreting Financial Statements case using Delta Air Lines, Inc.
- Revised all brief exercises, exercises, and problems.

Chapter 14 ***The Statement of Cash Flows***

- Revised, shortened, and edited coverage of both the indirect and the direct methods of preparing the operating activities section.
- Condensed the coverage from two years' of transactions to one year of transactions for both the indirect and direct methods.
- New AM!—Ethics Insight covering misguided cash flow reporting by WorldCom, Inc. and Dynegy, Inc.
- Revised analysis section to cover only free cash flow; three cash-basis ratios were deleted.
- Adapted Financial Reporting Problem to PepsiCo, Inc., and Comparative Analysis Problem to PepsiCo versus Coca-Cola.
- Added new Research Case.
- Added new Global Focus case using Elan Corporation.
- Revised all brief exercises, exercises, and problems.

Chapter 15 ***Financial Statement Analysis***

- Added coverage on "Earning Power and Irregular Items" including discontinued operations, extraordinary items, change in accounting principle, and comprehensive income.
- Simplified the chapter by reducing the ratio analysis coverage from 16 ratios to 13 ratios. (Deleted three cash-basis ratios.)
- Updated real-world data in the comparative ratio analysis section.
- Adapted Financial Reporting Problem to PepsiCo, Inc., and Comparative Analysis Problem to PepsiCo versus Coca-Cola.
- Added new Research Case.
- Added second Group Decision Case.
- Revised all brief exercises, exercises, and problems.

TOOLS FOR STUDENT SUCCESS

Tools for Student Success

Financial Accounting, Fifth Edition, provides many proven pedagogical tools to help students learn accounting concepts and procedures and apply them to the business world. This pedagogical framework emphasizes the processes that students undergo as they learn. Turn to the **Student Owner's Manual** on page xxiii to see all of the learning tools in detail. These tools help students learn how to use the textbook, understand the context, learn the material, "put it all together," develop skills through practice, and expand and apply knowledge. Here are a few key features.

Learning How to Use the Textbook

- The **Student Owner's Manual**, p. xxiii, and notes in blue in Chapter 1, explain to students how to take advantage of the text's learning tools to help achieve success in the course.
- A **Learning Styles Quiz**, p. xxxii, and **Learning Styles Chart**, pp. xxxiii–xxxiv, include tips on in-class and at-home learning strategies.
- **The Navigator** guides students through each chapter by pulling all of the learning tools together into a learning system. **The Navigator** box on the chapter-opening page lays out a study framework, and throughout the chapter, **Navigator** icons prompt students to use the learning aids and to set priorities as they study.

Understanding the Context

- **Concepts for Review**, listed at the beginning of each chapter, identify concepts from previous chapters that will apply in the chapter to come.
- **Study Objectives**, listed at the beginning of each chapter, reappear in the margins and again in the **Summary of Study Objectives**.
- An **Accounting Matters! Feature Story** helps students picture how the chapter topic relates to the real world of accounting and business and serves as a recurrent example.
- A **Chapter Preview** links the AM! Feature Story to the major topics of the chapter and provides a road map to the chapter.

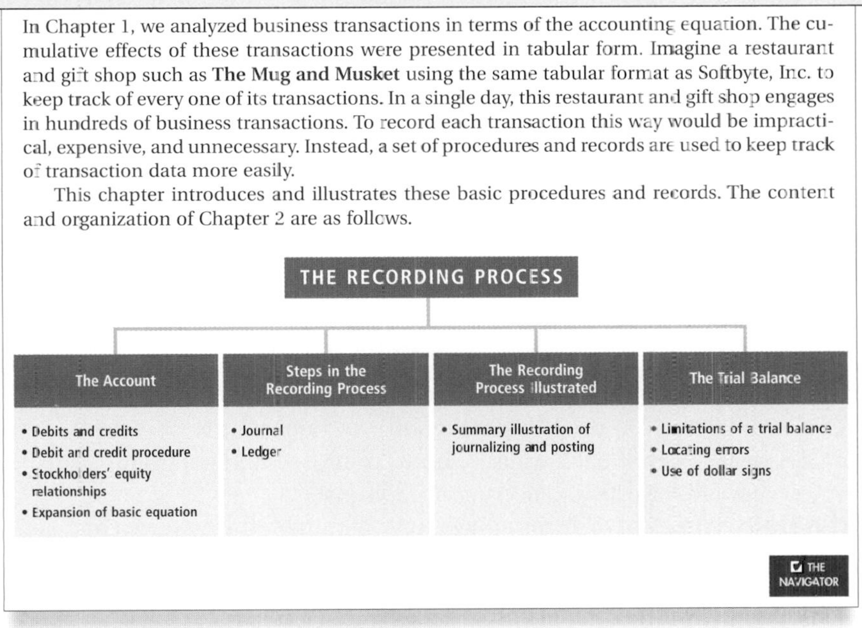

In Chapter 1, we analyzed business transactions in terms of the accounting equation. The cumulative effects of these transactions were presented in tabular form. Imagine a restaurant and gift shop such as **The Mug and Musket** using the same tabular format as Softbyte, Inc. to keep track of every one of its transactions. In a single day, this restaurant and gift shop engages in hundreds of business transactions. To record each transaction this way would be impractical, expensive, and unnecessary. Instead, a set of procedures and records are used to keep track of transaction data more easily.

This chapter introduces and illustrates these basic procedures and records. The content and organization of Chapter 2 are as follows.

Learning the Material

- Emphasis on accounting experiences of **real companies and business situations throughout**.

DELL

DELL INC.
(in millions)

Stockholders' equity	
Common stock, 2,681,000,000 shares	$1,479
Retained earnings	3,394
Total stockholders' equity	$4,873

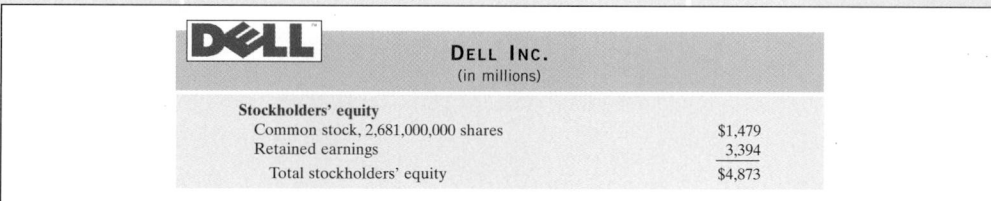

- **Accounting Matters!** boxes give students glimpses into how real companies use accounting in practice. ***E-Business Insights*** report on how technology is affecting business transactions. Critical thinking questions at the end of the boxes help students link the story to chapter content. Guideline answers appear at the end of the chapter, to provide feedback to students' study efforts.

ACCOUNTING MATTERS! e Business Insight

It can cost a lot to convert from traditional business to e-commerce. For example, when **Borders**, the second largest seller of books, went online, it had to build an entirely new $15 million distribution center. The reason? It previously shipped large orders of books to its stores. Instead, it now has to distribute tiny orders to individual customers. The distribution costs of online sales can be surprisingly high—as much as 15 percent of sales.

? The *distribution costs* of online sales can be greater than for traditional in-store sales. What costs may be less for online sales?

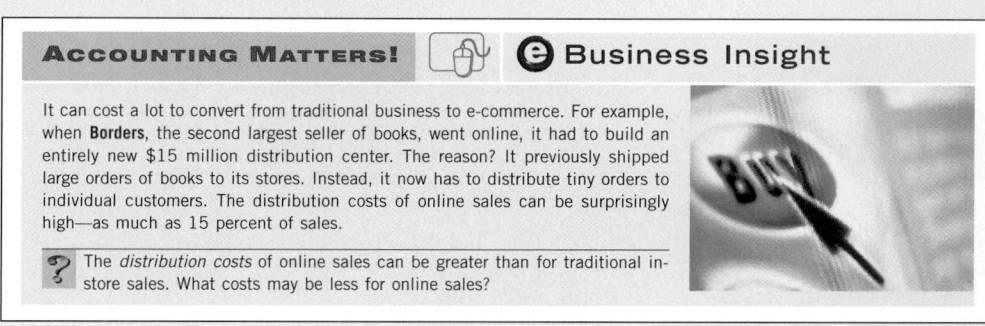

- **Color illustrations**, including **infographics**, help students visualize and apply accounting concepts to the real world.
- **Before You Go On** sections provide learning checks **(Review It)** and mini demonstration problems **(Do It)**. Questions marked with the **PepsiCo** logo send students to find information in PepsiCo's 2003 annual report printed in and packaged with the book.

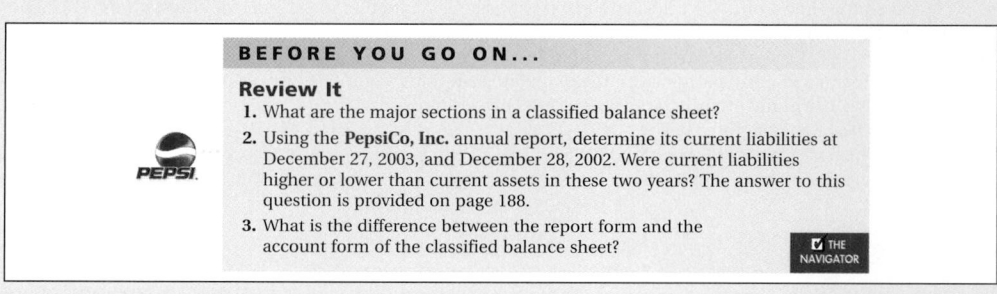

BEFORE YOU GO ON...

Review It

1. What are the major sections in a classified balance sheet?
2. Using the **PepsiCo, Inc.** annual report, determine its current liabilities at December 27, 2003, and December 28, 2002. Were current liabilities higher or lower than current assets in these two years? The answer to this question is provided on page 188.
3. What is the difference between the report form and the account form of the classified balance sheet?

PEPSI

THE NAVIGATOR

A	=	L	+	SE
+3,430				−70 Rev
−3,500				

Cash Flows
+3,430

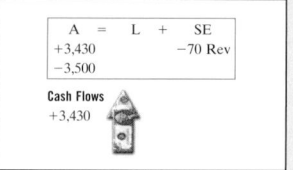

- **Accounting Equation analyses** in the margin next to key journal entries reinforce understanding of the impact of an accounting transaction on the financial statements. They indicate the **stockholders' equity** account that is affected, and also report the **cash effect** of each transaction to reinforce understanding of the difference between cash effects and accrual accounting.
- **Helpful Hints, Alternative Terminology**, and highlighted **Key terms and concepts** help focus students on key concepts as they study the material.
- **Ethics Notes** help sensitize students to some of the ethical issues of accounting.

TOOLS FOR STUDENT SUCCESS

Putting It Together

At the end of each chapter are several features useful for review and reference.

- A **Demonstration Problem** with an **Action Plan** gives students another opportunity to refer to a detailed solution to a representative problem before they do homework assignments. The Web icon indicates that an interactive version of the Demonstration Problem is available online with eGrade Plus.

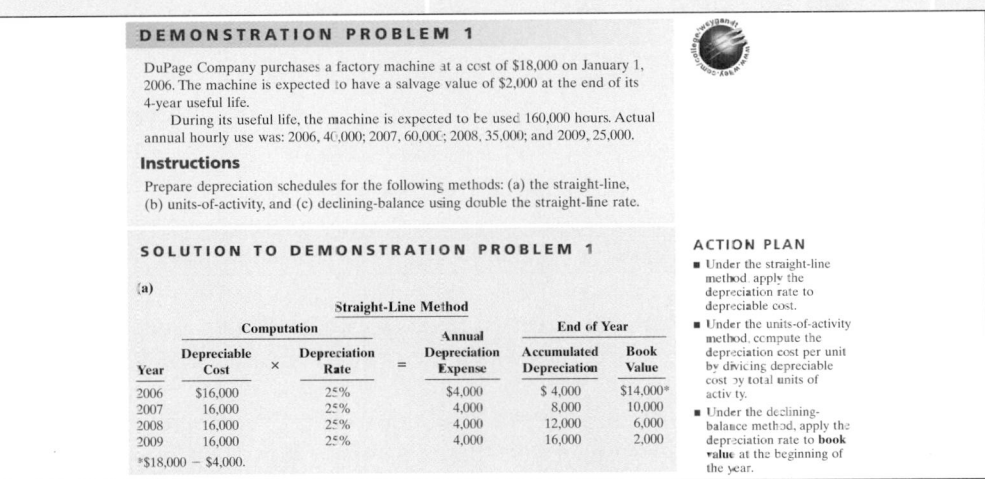

DEMONSTRATION PROBLEM 1

DuPage Company purchases a factory machine at a cost of $18,000 on January 1, 2006. The machine is expected to have a salvage value of $2,000 at the end of its 4-year useful life.

During its useful life, the machine is expected to be used 160,000 hours. Actual annual hourly use was: 2006, 40,000; 2007, 60,000; 2008, 35,000; and 2009, 25,000.

Instructions

Prepare depreciation schedules for the following methods: (a) the straight-line, (b) units-of-activity, and (c) declining-balance using double the straight-line rate.

SOLUTION TO DEMONSTRATION PROBLEM 1

(a)

Straight-Line Method

	Computation					End of Year	
Year	Depreciable Cost	×	Depreciation Rate	=	Annual Depreciation Expense	Accumulated Depreciation	Book Value
2006	$16,000		25%		$4,000	$ 4,000	$14,000*
2007	16,000		25%		4,000	8,000	10,000
2008	16,000		25%		4,000	12,000	6,000
2009	16,000		25%		4,000	16,000	2,000

*$18,000 − $4,000.

ACTION PLAN

- Under the straight-line method, apply the depreciation rate to depreciable cost.
- Under the units-of-activity method, compute the depreciation cost per unit by dividing depreciable cost by total units of activity.
- Under the declining-balance method, apply the depreciation rate to **book value** at the beginning of the year.

- A **Summary of Study Objectives** reviews the main points of the chapter.
- A **Glossary** of key terms gives definitions with page references to the text.

Developing Skills Through Practice

Each chapter is supported by a full complement of homework material. **Self-Study Questions, Questions, Brief Exercises, Exercises**, and two sets of **Problems** are all keyed to the Study Objectives. Certain exercises and problems, marked with a pencil icon, help students practice business writing skills. ***Check figures*** for selected Problems appear in the students' textbook. In addition:

- **Comprehensive Problems** in 5 chapters give students the opportunity to put to use concepts covered across multiple chapters.
- Certain Exercises and Problems can be solved using the **Excel** and **Peachtree supplements** that are available to accompany the text and are identified by these icons.
- Others can be solved with the **General Ledger Software** available with the text and are marked with this icon.

Peachtree®

Instructions

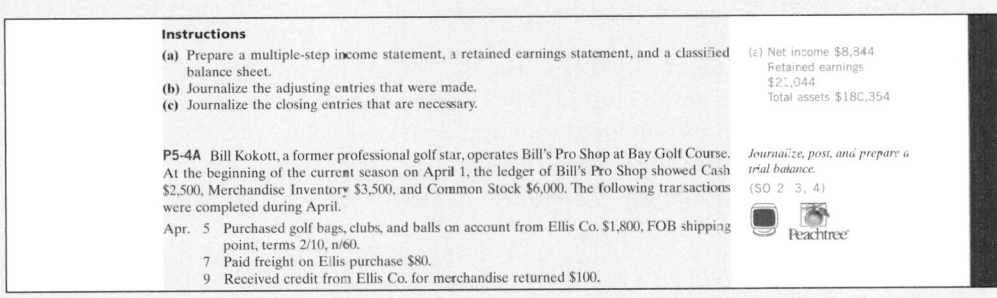

(a) Prepare a multiple-step income statement, a retained earnings statement, and a classified balance sheet.
(b) Journalize the adjusting entries that were made.
(c) Journalize the closing entries that are necessary.

(a) Net income $8,344
Retained earnings $21,044
Total assets $180,354

P5-4A Bill Kokott, a former professional golf star, operates Bill's Pro Shop at Bay Golf Course. At the beginning of the current season on April 1, the ledger of Bill's Pro Shop showed Cash $2,500, Merchandise Inventory $3,500, and Common Stock $6,000. The following transactions were completed during April.

Journalize, post, and prepare a trial balance.
(SO 2, 3, 4)
Peachtree®

Apr. 5 Purchased golf bags, clubs, and balls on account from Ellis Co. $1,800, FOB shipping point, terms 2/10, n/60.
7 Paid freight on Ellis purchase $80.
9 Received credit from Ellis Co. for merchandise returned $100.

Expanding and Applying Knowledge

The **Broadening Your Perspective** section at the end of each chapter offers a wealth of resources for those instructors who want to broaden the learning experience by bringing in more real-world decision making, analysis, and critical thinking activities.

> **BROADENING YOUR PERSPECTIVE**
>
> **Financial Reporting and Analysis**
>
> ■ **FINANCIAL REPORTING PROBLEM: PepsiCo**
>
> **BYP3-1** The financial statements of **PepsiCo** are presented in Appendix A at the end of this textbook.
>
> **Instructions**
>
> **(a)** Using the consolidated financial statements and related information, identify items that may result in adjusting entries for prepayments.
>
> **(b)** Using the consolidated financial statements and related information, identify items that may result in adjusting entries for accruals.
>
> **(c)** Using the Selected Financial Data and Five-Year Summary, what has been the trend since 1999 for net income?

- A **Financial Reporting Problem** directs students to study various aspects of the financial statements of PepsiCo, Inc., which are printed in Appendix A and packaged with the book.
- A **Comparative Analysis Problem** offers the opportunity to compare and contrast the financial reporting of PepsiCo, with that of a competitor, The Coca-Cola Company, whose financial statements are excerpted in Appendix B.
- **Research Cases** lead students to articles recently published in popular business periodicals. Students are asked to read the article and answer analytic questions about key topics and concepts.
- **Interpreting Financial Statements** problems offer minicases that ask students to read parts of financial statements of actual companies and use the decision tools of the chapter to interpret them.
- **A Global Focus** cases ask students to apply concepts presented in the chapter to specific situations faced by actual international companies.
- **Exploring the Web** exercises guide students to Internet sites from which they can mine and analyze information related to the chapter topic.
- **Group Decision Cases** help promote group collaboration and build decision-making and business communication skills by requiring teams of students to evaluate a manager's decision.
- **Communication Activities** provide practice in written communication and presentation skills much in demand among employers.
- **Ethics Cases** ask students to analyze situations, identify the stakeholders and the ethical issues involved, and decide on an appropriate course of action. By means of a marginal icon, we have identified these cases as an Accounting Matters! feature.
- **Continuing Cookie Chronicle case** follows a small, growing company through its accounting activities.
- **Answers to Accounting Matters! Questions** suggest guideline answers for the critical thinking questions at the ends of the Accounting Matters! boxes. These answers encourage students to use the questions and provide feedback to that effort.
- **Answers to PepsiCo Review It Questions** appear next.
- Finally, **Answers to Self-Study Questions** enable students to check their understanding of key concepts in the chapter.

Accounting Matters!

Accounting Matters!

Active Teaching and Learning Supplementary Material

Financial Accounting, Fifth Edition, features a full range of teaching and learning resources. Driven by the same principles of the textbook, these materials provide a consistent and well-integrated learning system. This hands-on, real-world package guides *instructors* through the process of active learning and gives them the tools to create an interactive learning environment. With its emphasis on activities, exercises, and the Internet, the package encourages *students* to take an active role in the course and prepares them for decision making in a real-world context.

Weygandt's Integrated Technology Solutions

Helping Teachers Teach and Students Learn

www.wiley.com/college/weygandt

For Instructors

The *Financial Accounting* companion Web site provides a seamless integration of text and media and keeps all of a book's online resources in one easily accessible location.

***Financial Accounting* Web site** at *www.wiley.com/college/weygandt*. On this Web site instructors will find electronic versions of the **Solutions Manual, Instructor's Manual, Test Bank, Computerized Test Bank, PowerPoint** presentations, and other resources. In addition, portions of the *Financial Accounting* Web site are available with **eGradePlus**, a new online resource that integrates text and media and allows you to customize your course with the following tools:

- A **Course Administration** tool helps instructors manage their course and integrate Wiley Web site resources with course management systems, thereby helping instructors keep all class materials in one location.
- A **Prepare and Present** tool contains all instructor resources. Instructors can easily adapt, customize, and add to this content to meet the needs of their particular course.
- An **Assignment** area is one of the most powerful features of the *Financial Accounting* Web site. It allows instructors to assign online homework and quizzes comprised of end-of-chapter textbook questions. Instructors save time as results are automatically graded and recorded in an instructor gradebook. Students benefit from the option to receive immediate feedback on their work, allowing them to quickly determine their understanding of course content.
- An **Instructor's Gradebook** will keep track of student progress and allow instructors to analyze individual and overall understanding of course concepts.

For Students

The *Financial Accounting* student Web site provides a wealth of support materials that will help students develop their conceptual understanding of class material and increase their ability to solve problems. On this Web site students will find Excel templates, PowerPoint presentations, Web quizzing, and other resources. In addition, portions of the student Web site are available in a premium version where students will find the following resources:

- **Study and Practice** resources that can include select interactive, end-of-chapter problems linked directly to the text e-book. Additional resources include interactive interactive chapter reviews, Demonstration Problem Web-based tutorials, and other problem-solving resources.
- An **Assignment** area contains all homework assignments in one location. Many homework problems contain a link to the relevant sections of the e-book, providing students with context-sensitive help.
- A **Personal Gradebook** allows each student to view their results from past assignments at any time.

Instructor Active Teaching Aids

An extensive support package, including print and technology tools, helps you maximize your teaching effectiveness. We offer useful supplements for instructors with varying levels of experience and instructional circumstances.

Instructor's Resource System on CD-ROM

The Instructor's Resource CD (IR CD) provides all instructor support material in an electronic format that is easy to navigate and use. The IR CD contains an electronic version of instructor print supplements that can be used in the classroom, for printing out material, for uploading to your own Website, or for downloading and modifying. The IR CD gives you the flexibility to access and prepare instructional material based on your individual needs.

Solutions Manual

The Solutions Manual contains detailed solutions to all exercises and problems in the textbook and suggested answers to the questions and cases. Each chapter includes an assignment classification table, an assignment characteristics table, and a Bloom's taxonomy table. Print is large and bold for easy readability in lecture settings, and instructors may duplicate portions of the manual without paying a permissions fee. The Solutions Manual has been carefully verified by a team of independent accuracy checkers. (The *Solutions Manual* is also available at *www.wiley.com/college/weygandt* and on the IR CD.)

Solutions Transparencies

Packaged in an organizer box with chapter file folders, these transparencies feature detailed solutions to all exercises and problems in the textbook as well as suggested answers to the Broadening Your Perspectives activities. They feature large, bold type for better projection and easy readability in large classroom settings.

Instructor's Manual

The Instructor's Manual is a comprehensive set of resources for preparing and presenting an active learning course. Included in each chapter are chapter reviews and lecture outlines with teaching tips. In addition to an assignment classification table, an assignment characteristics table, and a list of study objectives, each chapter contains a 20-minute quiz. Illustrations at the end of each chapter include diagrams, graphs, and exercises that can be used as classroom handouts or overhead transparencies. (Also available at *www.wiley.com/college/weygandt* and on the IR CD.)

Teaching Transparencies

The Instructor's Manual illlustrations are printed on these 4-color acetate transparencies. Designed to support and clarify concepts in the text, the Teaching Transparencies will enhance lectures.

Test Bank

The Test Bank is a comprehensive testing package that allows instructors to tailor examinations according to study objectives, learning skills, and content. The Text Bank contains over 3,000 examination questions and exercises. Examination questions focus on computations, concepts, decision-making, and the real-world environment. Actual financial statements are used throughout to provide a relevant context for questions. For each chapter of the Test Bank, there is a summary of questions by study objectives and a summary of objectives by questions (linking test items to study objectives), and an indication of question placement according to Bloom's taxonomy. Exercises are identified by estimated completion time. New to this edition are brief exercises and more computational multiple-choice questions.

In addition to a final exam, the Test Bank provides an achievement test for every two chapters in the textbook and a comprehensive exam for every three to five chapters of the text. The tests, which are easy to photocopy and distribute to students, consist of problems and exercises as well as multiple-choice, matching, and true/false questions. (Also available at *www.wiley.com/college/weygandt* and on the IR CD.)

Computerized Test Bank

The Test Bank is also available for use with IBM and IBM-compatible computers running Windows 3.1 or higher. This Computerized Test Bank offers a number of valuable options that allow instructors to create multiple versions of the same test. Instructors can scramble the order of questions and the order of answer-choices within a multiple-choice question. The computerized test bank also allows instructors to customize test questions by modifying existing problems or adding new questions. (Available at *www.wiley.com/college/weygandt* and on the IR CD.)

PowerPoint Presentations

This PowerPoint lecture aid contains a combination of key concepts, images, and problems from the textbook for use in the classroom. Designed according to the organization of the material in the textbook, this series of electronic transparencies can be used to visually reinforce accounting principles. (Available at *www.wiley.com/college/weygandt* and on the IR CD.)

WebCT and Blackboard

WebCT or Blackboard offers an integrated set of course management tools that enable instructors to easily design, develop, and manage Web-based and Web-enhanced courses.

The Wiley *Financial Accounting* WebCT and Blackboard courses contain the basic course management shell with all online resources for students. This shell allows the professor to present all or part of a course online and helps the student organize the course material, understand key concepts, and access additional tools. The Wiley WebCT or Blackboard course can be customized to fit an individual professor's needs. For more information, see *www.wiley.com/college/solutions.*

Solutions Manuals for Practice Sets

Solutions Manuals for the following practice sets and study aids are available online and on the Instructor's Resource CD:

- Peachtree Workbook
- Excel Templates
- University Bookstore Practice Set
- Custom Party Associates Practice Set

Business Extra Select

Wiley's Business Extra Select program is a simple, integrated, online custom-publishing process that allows you to combine content from Wiley's leading business publications with copyright-cleared content from such respected sources as *Fortune*, *The Economist,* the *Wall Street Journal, Harvard Business School* cases, and much more. In just a few simple steps you can help your students make the connection between the concepts you teach in your class and their real-world applications!

Faculty Resource Network

The Faculty Resource Network is a group of peers ready to support the use of online course management tools and discipline-specific software/learning systems in the classroom. They will help you apply innovative classroom techniques, implement specific software packages, and tailor the technology experience to the specific needs of each individual class. The Faculty Resource Network also provides you with virtual training sessions led *by* faculty *for* faculty. All you need to participate in a virtual seminar is a high-speed Internet access and a phone line. For more information about the Faculty Resource Network, please contact your Wiley representative or go to *www.FacultyResourceNetwork.com.*

Student Active Learning Aids

The Financial Accounting Web site

The ***Financial Accounting* Web site**, *www.wiley.com/college/weygandt,* provides a wealth of support materials that will help students develop their understanding of course concepts and increase their ability to solve problems. On this Web site students will find **Web Quizzing, Excel files, PowerPoint presentations**, and other resources. In addition, portions of the student Web site are available with **eGradePlus**, an online study aid where students will find **Interactive Homework Questions** assigned by their instructors, a personal gradebook, and much more.

Study Guide

The Study Guide is a comprehensive review of *Financial Accounting* and a powerful tool when used in the classroom and in preparation for exams. Each chapter of the Study Guide includes a chapter review consisting of 20 to 30 key points; a demonstration problem linked to study objectives in the textbook; and additional opportunities for students to practice their knowledge and skills through true/false, multiple-choice, and matching questions and exercises linked to study objectives. Detailed solutions and explanations to all exercises provide students with immediate feedback.

Working Papers

Working Papers are templates customized for each end-of-chapter exercise, problem, and case. A convenient resource for organizing and completing homework assignments, they demonstrate how to correctly set up solution formats.

Excel Working Papers

Available on CD-ROM, these Excel-formatted forms can be used for all end-of-chapter exercises, problems, and cases. The Excel Working Papers provide students with the option of printing forms and completing them manually, or entering data electronically and then printing out a completed form. By entering data electronically, students can paste homework to a new file and e-mail the worksheet to their instructor.

Wiley General Ledger Software

General Ledger Software is a computerized ledger program that allows students to solve selected end-of-chapter ledger problems that are identified by an icon in the margin of the text. Because many features are automated, the software package saves students time in answering end-of-chapter ledger problems. Modeled after professional accounting software packages, Wiley General Ledger Software prepares students for the "real world."

Peachtree Complete® Accounting Workbook

Peachtree

This workbook teaches students how to effectively use Peachtree Complete® Accounting Software, an accounting tool used by accounting professionals. End-of-chapter problems denoted by the Peachtree icon can be solved using this supplementary software package.

Solving Financial Accounting Problems Using Excel

The Excel templates and accompanying workbook allow students to complete select end-of-chapter exercises and problems identified by a spreadsheet icon in the margin of the main text. A useful introduction to computers, the electronic spreadsheets also enhance students' accounting skills.

Practice Sets

The *Financial Accounting* practice sets expose students to a real-world simulation of maintaining a complete set of accounting records for a business. As they integrate the business events, accounting concepts, procedures, and records covered within the textbook, students will find that practice sets reinforce the concepts and procedures learned. The practice sets have been designed to meet a variety of skill levels and can be used at various places throughout the course. Each of the practice sets has been revised to reflect changes made to the Fifth Edition of the textbook.

- **University Bookstore—A Corporate Practice Set.** This corporate practice set exposes students to a real-world simulation of maintaining a complete set of accounting records for a business. Students work with a bond transaction, and are also asked to complete a financial analysis of the company. The practice set can be worked either independently or in a group. The set includes few transactions, and thus reinforces students' analytical skills and creative problem solving.
- **Custom Party Associates Practice Set.** This practice set focuses on a company that specializes in party planning and supplies, which offers students elements of both service- and merchandising-company transactions. Custom Party Associates is uniquely set up as both a proprietorship and a corporation, offering flexibility in teaching approaches. The practice set requires a bank reconciliation, contains both accounts payable and accounts receivable subsidiary ledgers, focuses on the perpetual inventory system, includes two employee pay periods for which employee records are maintained, and involves property, plant, and equipment transactions.

Financial Accounting Tutor (FacT) CD

FacT is a self-paced CD-Rom designed to review financial accounting concepts. It uses simple examples that introduce concepts gradually and reveal the logic underlying the accounting process. Discussions and examples are followed by brief, interactive problems that provide immediate feedback.

Acknowledgments

From the first edition of this textbook and through the years since, we have benefited greatly from feedback provided by numerous instructors, reviewers, and ancillary authors and proofers. We offer our thanks to those many people for their criticism, constructive suggestions, and innovative ideas. We are indebted to the following people for their contributions to the most recent editions of the book.

Reviewers and Focus Group Participants

Sheila Ammons, *Austin Community College*
Matt Anderson, *Michigan State University*
Yvonne Baker, *Cincinnati State Tech Community College*
Peter Battelle, *University of Vermont*
Michael Blackett, *National American University*
David Boyd, *Arkansas State University*
Leon Button, *Scottsdale Community College*
David Carr, *Austin Community College*
Andy Chen, *Northeast Illinois University*
Trudy Chiaravelli, *Lansing Community College*
Edward J. Corcoran, *Community College of Philadelphia*
Kennth Couvillion, *San Joaquin Delta College*
Thomas Davies, *University of South Dakota*
Peggy DeJong, *Kirkwood Community College*
Kevin Dooley, *Kapi'olani Community College*
Edmond Douville, *Indiana University Northwest*
Pamela Druger, *Augustana College*
John Eagan, *Erie Community College*
Jeff Edwards, *Portland Community College*
Richard Ellison, *Middlesex Community College*
Richard Ghio, *San Joaquin Delta College*
Jeannie Harrington, *Middle Tennessee State University*
William Harvey, *Henry Ford Community College*
Zach Holmes, *Oakland Community College*
Paul Holt, *Texas A&M—Kingsville*
Verne Ingram, *Red Rocks Community College*
Mark Johnston, *Washtenaw Community College*
Shirly Kleiner, *Johnson County Community College*
Jo Koehn, *Central Missouri State University*
Doug Laufer, *Metropolitan State College of Denver*
Robert Laycock, *Montgomery College*
James Lukawitz, *University of Memphis*
Maureen McBeth, *College of DuPage*
Janice Mardon, *Green River Community College*
Jerry Martens, *Community College of Aurora*
John Marts, *University of North Carolina—Wilmington*
Shea Mears, *Des Moines Area Community College*
Pam Meyer, *University of Louisiana—Lafayette*
Kathy S. Moffeit, *Southwest Texas State University*
Robin Nelson, *Community College of Southern Nevada*
George Palz, *Erie Community College*
Bill Rencher, *Seminole Community College*
Carla Rich, *Pensacola Junior College*
Renee Rigoni, *Monroe Community College*
Patricia Robinson, *Johnson & Wales University*
Jill Russell, *Camden County College*
Ken Sinclair, *Lehigh University*
Alice Sineath, *Forsyth Tech Community College*
Jeff Slater, *North Shore Community College*
James Smith, *Ivy Tech State College*
Carol Springer, *Georgia State University*
Lynda Thompson, *Massasoit Community College*
Sue Van Boven, *Paradise Valley Community College*
Christian Widmer, *Tidewater Community College*

Ancillary Authors, Contributors, and Proofers

Our special thanks also go to the ancillary authors, contributors, and proofers who worked on the Fifth Edition:

John Borke, *University of Wisconsin—Platteville:* Text and Solutions Manual proofer

Larry R. Falcetto, *Emporia State University:* Instructor's Manual and Check Figures author, text and Solutions Manual proofer

Patricia Fedje, *Minot State University:* Custom Party Associates Practice Set author

Kurt Hull, *University of California—Los Angeles:* PowerPoint author, QuickBooks Practice Set author

Candace Humphrey, *Northeast Iowa Community College:* University Bookstore Practice Set author

Duglas W. Kieso, *Aurora University:* Study Guide author

Laura McNally: eGrade author and proofer

Sally Nelson, *Northeast Iowa Community College:* University Bookstore Practice Set author

Rex Schildhouse, *University of Phoenix, San Diego:* Excel Templates and Workbook author

Teresa Speck, *St. Mary's University:* Text and Solutions Manual proofer

Lynn Stallworth, *Southeastern Louisiana University:* Test Bank author

Sheila Viel, *University of Wisconsin—Milwaukee:* Problem material contributor and text proofer

Dick D. Wasson, *Southwestern College:* Working Papers and Excel Working Papers author

Finally, special thanks to Wayne Higley of Buena Vista University for his technical proofing.

We appreciate the exemplary support and professional commitment given us by publisher and vice president Susan Elbe, associate publisher Jay O'Callaghan, marketing manager Steve Herdegen, associate editor Ed Brislin, program assistant Brian Kamins, program assistant Kristin Babroski, media editor Allie Morris, vice president of higher education production and manufacturing Ann Berlin, development editor Ann Torbert, production manager Jeanine Furino, designer Dawn Stanley, illustration editor Sandra Rigby, photo editor Sara Wight, project manager Suzanne Ingrao of Ingrao Associates, permissions assistant Yolanda Pagano, product manager Carole Kuhn at TechBooks, and project manager Karin Vonesh at Elm Street Publishing Services. They provided innumerable services that helped this project take shape.

Finally, our thanks for the support provided by Will Pesce, President and Chief Executive Officer, and Bonnie Lieberman, Senior Vice President of the College Division.

We thank PepsiCo, Inc. and The Coca-Cola Company for permitting us the use of their 2003 Annual Reports for our specimen financial statements and accompanying notes.

Suggestions and comments from users—instructors and students alike—will be appreciated.

Jerry J. Weygandt
Madison, Wisconsin
Donald E. Kieso
DeKalb, Illinois
Paul D. Kimmel
Milwaukee, Wisconsin

Student Owner's Manual
How to Use the Study Aids in This Book

Chapter 1

Accounting Matters!

THE NAVIGATOR ✓	
Understand **Concepts for Review**	❑
Read **Feature Story**	❑
Scan **Study Objectives**	❑
Read **Preview**	❑
Read text and answer **Before You Go On** p. 8 ❑ p. 14 ❑ p. 21 ❑ p. 25 ❑	
Work **Demonstration Problem**	
Review **Summary of Study Objectives**	
Answer **Self-Study Questions**	
Complete **Assignments**	

CONCEPTS FOR REVIEW

Before studying this chapter, you should know or, if necessary, review:

- How to use the study aids in this book.
  (Student Owner's Manual, pages xxv–xxxii)
- How you learn best.
  (Student Owner's Manual, pages xxv–xxxii)
- The nature of the special student supplements that accompany this textbook.
  (Student Owner's Manual, pages xxv–xxxii)

THE NAVIGATOR

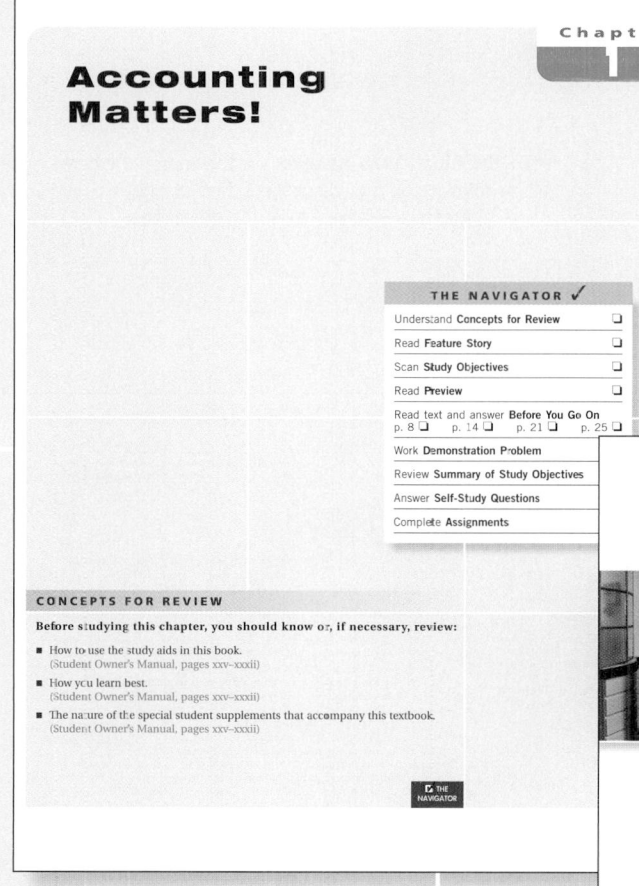

THE NAVIGATOR is a learning system designed to guide you through each chapter and help you succeed in learning the material. It consists of (1) a checklist at the beginning of the chapter, which outlines text features and study aids you will need, and (2) a series of check boxes that prompt you to use the learning aids in the chapter ◀ and set priorities as you study.

▼ The **ACCOUNTING MATTERS! FEATURE STORY** helps you picture how the chapter topic relates to the real world of accounting and business. References to the Feature Story throughout the chapter will help you put new ideas in context, organize them, and remember them. Note that the names of **REAL COMPANIES** are highlighted in red here and in the chapter text.

ACCOUNTING MATTERS! FEATURE STORY

Financial Reporting: A Matter of Trust In recent years the financial press has been full of articles about financial scandals and accounting misdeeds. It started with **Enron,** but then spread to **Xerox, Qwest, Global Crossing,** and **WorldCom,** among others. Many of the articles expressed concern that as an increasing number of misdeeds came to public attention, a mistrust of financial reporting in general was developing. These articles made clear just how important accounting and financial reporting are to the U.S. and world financial markets and to society as a whole. Without financial reports, managers would not be able to evaluate how well their company is doing or to make decisions about the best way to make their company grow in the future. Without financial reports, investors and lenders could not make informed decisions about how to allocate their funds. There is no doubt that a sound, well-functioning economy depends on accurate and dependable financial reporting—accounting matters!

In order to make financial decisions as either an investor or a manager, you need to know how to read financial reports. In this book you will learn about financial reporting and some basic tools used to evaluate financial reports. In the first chapter we introduce you to the real financial statements of a company whose products most of you probably are familiar with—**PepsiCo, Inc.** We have chosen the financial statements of PepsiCo because they are a good example from the real world. An appendix to this textbook contains the statements in their entirety, and a copy of the PepsiCo, Inc. 2003 Annual Report accompanies this text.

PepsiCo manufactures Pepsi-Cola, the number two soft drink beverage in the world. PepsiCo also manufactures the number one bottled water (Aquafina), the number one sports drink (Gatorade), the number one ready-to-drink tea (Lipton), and the number one ready-to-drink coffee (Frappuccino). In addition, PepsiCo is the largest manufacturer of snack foods in the world. Its Frito-Lay chips dominate the U.S. market with 59% of all snack-chip sales and the world market with over 32%. In all, PepsiCo ranks among the world's largest packaged goods and beverage companies, with over $25 billion in sales, $23 billion in assets, and 140,000 employees. PepsiCo is not only large; it is also quite profitable, ranking twenty-eighth among all U.S. companies, with $3.3 billion in net income.

www.pepsico.com

THE NAVIGATOR

STUDY OBJECTIVES

After studying this chapter, you should be able to:

1. Explain what accounting is.
2. Identify the users and uses of accounting.
3. Understand why ethics is a fundamental business concept.
4. Explain the meaning of generally accepted accounting principles and the cost principle.
5. Explain the meaning of the monetary unit assumption and the economic entity assumption.
6. State the basic accounting equation, and explain the meaning of assets, liabilities, and stockholders' equity.
7. Analyze the effects of business transactions on the basic accounting equation.
8. Understand what the four financial statements are and how they are prepared.

THE NAVIGATOR

▲ **CONCEPTS FOR REVIEW,** listed at the beginning of the chapter, are the accounting concepts learned in previous chapters that you will need to know in order to understand the topics you are about to learn. Page references point you to the earlier material, if you need to review before reading the chapter.

▶ **STUDY OBJECTIVES** at the beginning of each chapter give you a framework for learning the specific concepts covered in the chapter. Each study objective reappears in the margin where the concept is discussed. Finally, you can review the study objectives in the **SUMMARY** at the end of the chapter text.

PREVIEW OF CHAPTER 2

In Chapter 1, we analyzed business transactions in terms of the accounting equation. The cumulative effects of these transactions were presented in tabular form. Imagine a restaurant and gift shop such as **The Mug and Musket** using the same tabular format as Softbyte, Inc. to keep track of every one of its transactions. In a single day, this restaurant and gift shop engages in hundreds of business transactions. To record each transaction this way would be impractical, expensive, and unnecessary. Instead, a set of procedures and records are used to keep track of transaction data more easily.

This chapter introduces and illustrates these basic procedures and records. The content and organization of Chapter 2 are as follows.

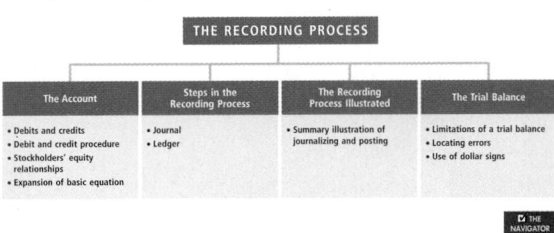

THE RECORDING PROCESS

The Account	Steps in the Recording Process	The Recording Process Illustrated	The Trial Balance
• Debits and credits • Debit and credit procedure • Stockholders' equity relationships • Expansion of basic equation	• Journal • Ledger	• Summary illustration of journalizing and posting	• Limitations of a trial balance • Locating errors • Use of dollar signs

THE NAVIGATOR

◀ The **PREVIEW** links the Feature Story with the major topics of the chapter and describes the purpose of the chapter. It then outlines the topics that are discussed. This narrative and visual preview helps you organize the information you are learning.

The Account

An **account** is an individual accounting record of increases and decreases in a specific asset, liability, or stockholders' equity item. For example, Softbyte, Inc. (the company discussed in Chapter 1) would have separate accounts for Cash, Accounts Receivable, Accounts Payable, Service Revenue, Salaries Expense, and so on. In its simplest form, an account consists of three parts: (1) the title of the account, (2) a left or debit side, and (3) a right or credit side. Because the alignment of these parts of an account resembles the letter T, it is referred to as a **T account**. The basic form of an account is shown in Illustration 2-1.

STUDY OBJECTIVE 1

Explain what an account is and how it helps in the recording process.

◀ **STUDY OBJECTIVES** reappear in the margins where the related topic is discussed. End-of-chapter assignments are keyed to study objectives.

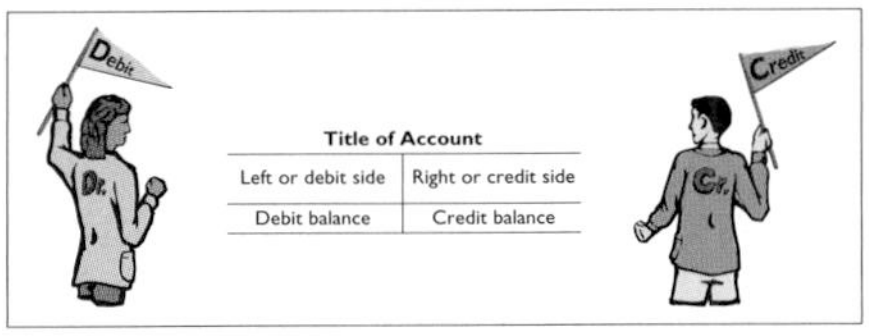

Illustration 2-1
Basic form of account

Illustration 10-14
Double-declining-balance depreciation schedule

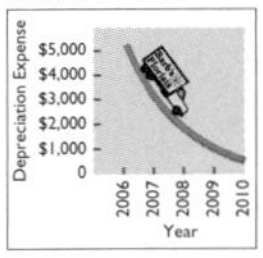

BARB'S FLORISTS

	Computation					End of Year	
Year	**Book Value Beginning of Year**	×	**Depreciation Rate**	=	**Annual Depreciation Expense**	**Accumulated Depreciation**	**Book Value**
2006	$13,000		40%		**$5,200**	$ 5,200	$7,800
2007	7,800		40		**3,120**	8,320	4,680
2008	4,680		40		**1,872**	10,192	2,808
2009	2,808		40		**1,123**	11,315	1,685
2010	1,685		40		**685***	12,000	**1,000**

*Computation of $674 ($1,685 × 40%) is adjusted to $685 in order for book value to equal salvage value.

HELPFUL HINT

The method recommended for an asset that is expected to be more productive in the first half of its useful life is the declining-balance method.

You can see that the delivery equipment is 69% depreciated ($8,320 ÷ $12,000) at the end of the second year. Under the straight-line method it would be depreciated 40% ($4,800 ÷ $12,000) at that time. Because the declining-balance method produces higher depreciation expense in the early years than in the later years, it is considered an **accelerated-depreciation method**.

The declining-balance method is compatible with the matching principle. The higher depreciation expense in early years is matched with the higher benefits received in these years. On the other hand, lower depreciation expense is recognized in later years when the asset's contribution to revenue is less. Also, some assets lose usefulness rapidly because of obsolescence. In these cases, the declining-balance method provides a more appropriate depreciation amount.

When an asset is purchased during the year, the first year's declining-balance depreciation must be prorated on a time basis. For example, if Barb's Florists had purchased the truck on April 1, 2006, depreciation for 2006 would become $3,900 ($13,000 × 40% × 9/12). The book value at the beginning of 2007 is then $9,100 ($13,000 − $3,900), and the 2007 depreciation is $3,640 ($9,100 × 40%). Subsequent computations would follow from those amounts.

▲
▶ **COLOR ILLUSTRATIONS,** such as **INFOGRAPHICS,** help you visualize and apply information as you study. They reinforce important concepts and often contain material that may appear on exams.

▶ **HELPFUL HINTS** in the margins are like having an instructor with you as you read. They further clarify concepts being discussed.

The Basics of Adjusting Entries **105**

The asset Accounts Receivable shows that $200 is owed by clients at the balance sheet date. The balance of $10,600 in Service Revenue represents the total revenue earned during the month ($10,000 + $400 + $200). **If the adjusting entry is not made, the following will all be understated: assets and stockholders' equity on the balance sheet, and revenues and net income on the income statement.**

On November 10, Pioneer receives cash of $200 for the services performed in October. Thus, the following entry is made.

ALTERNATIVE TERMINOLOGY

Accrued revenues are also called *accrued receivables.*

Nov. 10	Cash	200	
	Accounts Receivable		200
	(To record cash collected on account)		

A	=	L	+	SE
+200				
−200				

Cash Flows
+200

The subsequent collection of revenue from clients will be recorded with a debit (increase) to Cash and a credit (decrease) to Accounts Receivable.

Accrued Expenses

As indicated on page 97, expenses incurred but not yet paid or recorded at the statement date are called **accrued expenses**. Interest, rent, taxes, and salaries can be accrued expenses. Accrued expenses result from the same causes as accrued revenues. In fact, an accrued expense on the books of one company is an accrued revenue to another company. For example, the $200 accrual of fees by Pioneer is an accrued expense to the client that received the service.

Adjustments for accrued expenses are needed for two purposes: (1) to record the obligations that exist at the balance sheet date, and (2) to recognize the expenses that apply to the current accounting period. Prior to adjustment, both liabilities and expenses are understated. Therefore, as shown in Illustration 3-13, **an adjusting entry for accrued expenses results in an increase (a debit) to an expense account and an increase (a credit) to a liability account**.

ALTERNATIVE TERMINOLOGY

Accrued expenses are also called *accrued liabilities.*

◀ **ALTERNATIVE TERMINOLOGY** notes present synonymous terms that you may come across in practice.

◀ **ACCOUNTING EQUATION ANALYSES** appear in the margin next to key journal entries. They will help you understand the impact of an accounting transaction on the financial statements, on the stockholders' equity accounts, and on the company's cash flows.

▶ **FINANCIAL STATEMENTS** appear regularly throughout the book. Those from actual companies are identified by a logo or photo. Often, numbers or categories are highlighted in red to draw your attention to key information.

▶ **KEY TERMS** and concepts are printed in blue where they are first explained in the text. They are listed and defined again in the end-of-chapter **GLOSSARY.**

DECKERS outdoor corporation

DECKERS OUTDOOR CORPORATION
Balance Sheet (partial)

Current liabilities	
Notes payable	$ 3,951,000
Accounts payable	12,916,000
Allowance for returns	1,255,000
Salaries and commissions payable	2,342,000
Taxes payable	732,000
Other current liabilities	912,000
Total current liabilities	$22,108,000

Illustration 4-22
Current liabilities section

Users of financial statements look closely at the relationship between current assets and current liabilities. This relationship is important in evaluating a company's **liquidity**—its ability to pay obligations that are expected to become due within the next year or operating cycle. When current assets exceed current liabilities at the balance sheet date, the likelihood for paying the liabilities is favorable. When the reverse is true, short-term creditors may not be paid, and the company may ultimately be forced into bankruptcy.

Long-Term Liabilities

Obligations expected to be paid after one year or an operating cycle, whichever is longer, are classified as **long-term liabilities**. Liabilities in this category include bonds payable, mortgages payable, long-term notes payable, lease liabilities, and obligations under employee pension plans. Many companies report long-term debt maturing after one year as a single amount in the balance sheet. They then show the details of the debt in the notes that accompany the financial statements. Others list the various sources of long-term liabilities. In its balance sheet, **Brunswick Corporation** reported the following.

ALTERNATIVE TERMINOLOGY

Long-term liabilities are also called *long-term debt* or *noncurrent liabilities.*

BRUNSWICK CORPORATION
Balance Sheet (partial)
(in millions)

Long-term liabilities	
Notes payable	$437.2
Bonds payable	124.4
Guaranteed debt	15.5
Other long-term debt	12.4
Total long-term liabilities	$589.5

Illustration 4-23
Long-term liabilities section

ACCOUNTING MATTERS! Ethics Insight

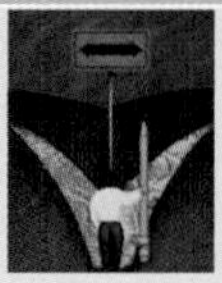

Companies would rather report steadily increasing profits than fluctuating profits. To "smooth" earnings, companies sometimes shift the reporting of revenues or expenses between periods. A recent *Wall Street Journal* article reported that **Microsoft Corp.** agreed to settle Securities and Exchange Commission charges that it misstated its earnings in some years by illegally maintaining different "reserve" accounts for such expenses as marketing and obsolete inventory. The settlement did not require Microsoft to pay a fine. Microsoft accepted the commission's order without admitting or denying wrongdoing and agreed not to commit accounting violations. "The SEC said Microsoft maintained undisclosed reserve accounts totaling between $200 million and $900 million between 1994 and 1998 and didn't maintain proper internal controls to document them or substantiate their size." The SEC said that the improper use of these reserve accounts resulted in "material inaccuracies" in the financial reports filed with the SEC.

Source: Rebecca Buckman, "Microsoft, SEC Settle Probe Into Earnings Misstatements," *Wall Street Journal Online* (June 4, 2002).

? What accounting principles do you think Microsoft violated? What did the SEC mean by "material inaccuracies"? Why would a company prefer to report steadily increasing profits rather than fluctuating profits?

◀ **ACCOUNTING MATTERS!** examples give you more glimpses into how actual companies make decisions using accounting information. These high-interest boxes are classified by three types of issues—business, **ETHICS**, international, and e-business. The e-business insights report on how technology is affecting business transactions.

◀ **QUESTIONS** at the end of the box encourage you to make further connections between the story in the box and the chapter topics.

▶ **"STATEMENT PRESENTATION AND ANALYSIS" SECTIONS** in seven chapters demonstrate how the topic of the chapter is presented in financial statements and then show the financial ratios used to evaluate its use by the company. A summary of the financial ratios used in the book is shown on the book's back endpaper.

▶ Names of **REAL COMPANIES** used as examples in the text are shown in red.

▶ **KEY FORMULAS** that you will need to know and use are boxed off.

LAX CORPORATION
Balance Sheet (partial)

Long-term liabilities		
Bonds payable 10% due in 2012	$1,000,000	
Less: Discount on bonds payable	80,000	$ 920,000
Mortgage notes payable, 11%, due in 2018 and secured by plant assets		500,000
Lease liability		540,000
Total long-term liabilities		$1,960,000

Illustration 11-20
Balance sheet presentation of long-term liabilities

Analysis

Long-term creditors and stockholders are interested in a company's long-run solvency. Of particular interest is the company's ability to pay interest as it comes due and to repay the face value of the debt at maturity. Debt to total assets and times interest earned are two ratios that provide information about debt-paying ability and long-run solvency.

The **debt to total assets ratio** measures the percentage of the total assets provided by creditors. It is computed, as shown in the formula below, by dividing total debt (both current and long-term liabilities) by total assets. The higher the percentage of debt to total assets, the greater the risk that the company may be unable to meet its maturing obligations.

The **times interest earned ratio** indicates the company's ability to meet interest payments as they come due. It is computed by dividing income before income taxes and interest expense by interest expense.

To illustrate these ratios, we will use data from **Johnson & Johnson**'s 2003 annual report. The company had total liabilities of $21,394 million, total assets of $48,263 million, interest expense of $207 million, income taxes of $3,111 million, and net income of $7,197 million. Johnson & Johnson's debt to total assets ratio and times interest earned ratio are shown below, along with their computations.

Total Debt	÷	**Total Assets**	=	**Debt to Total Assets**
$21,394	÷	$48,263	=	**44.3%**
Income before Income Taxes and Interest Expense	÷	**Interest Expense**	=	**Times Interest Earned**
$7,197 + $3,111 + $207	÷	$207	=	**50.8 times**

Illustration 11-21
Debt to total assets and times interest earned ratios, with computations

Johnson & Johnson has a relatively low debt to total assets percentage of 44.3%. Its interest coverage of 50.8 times appears extremely safe.

BEFORE YOU GO ON...

Review It

1. What are the four types of adjusting entries?
2. What is the effect on assets, stockholders' equity, expenses, and net income if a prepaid expense adjusting entry is not made?
3. What is the effect on liabilities, stockholders' equity, revenues, and net income if an unearned revenue adjusting entry is not made?
4. Using **PepsiCo**'s Consolidated Statement of Income, what was the amount of depreciation expense for 2003 and 2002? (See Note 4 to the financial statements.) The answer to this question is provided on page 137.

Do It

The ledger of Hammond, Inc. on March 31, 2006, includes the following selected accounts before adjusting entries.

	Debit	Credit
Prepaid Insurance	3,600	
Office Supplies	2,800	
Office Equipment	25,000	
Accumulated Depreciation—Office Equipment		5,000
Unearned Revenue		9,200

An analysis of the accounts shows the following.

1. Insurance expires at the rate of $100 per month.
2. Supplies on hand total $800.
3. The office equipment depreciates $200 a month.
4. One-half of the unearned revenue was earned in March.

Prepare the adjusting entries for the month of March.

ACTION PLAN

- Make adjusting entries at the end of the period for revenues earned and expenses incurred in the period.
- Don't forget to make adjusting entries for prepayments. Failure to adjust for prepayments leads to overstatement of the asset or liability and related understatement of the expense or revenue.

SOLUTION

1. Insurance Expense	100	
Prepaid Insurance		100
(To record insurance expired)		
2. Office Supplies Expense	2,000	
Office Supplies		2,000
(To record supplies used)		
3. Depreciation Expense	200	
Accumulated Depreciation—Office Equipment		200
(To record monthly depreciation)		
4. Unearned Revenue	4,600	
Service Revenue		4,600
(To record revenue for services provided)		

Related exercise material: *BE3-3, BE3-4, BE3-5, BE3-6, E3-2, E3-3, E3-4, E3-5, E3-6, E3-7, E3-8, and E3-9.*

THE NAVIGATOR

◀ **BEFORE YOU GO ON** sections follow each key topic. ***REVIEW IT*** questions prompt you to stop and review the key points you have just studied. If you cannot answer these questions, you should go back and read the section again.

REVIEW IT questions marked with the PepsiCo icon direct you to find information in PepsiCo, Inc.'s 2003 Annual Report, printed in Appendix A. Answers appear at the end of the chapter.

Brief ***DO IT*** exercises ask you to put to work your newly acquired knowledge. They outline an **ACTION PLAN** necessary to complete the exercise, and they show a **SOLUTION.**

▶ A **DEMONSTRATION PROBLEM** is the final step before you begin homework. These sample problems provide you with an **ACTION PLAN** in the margin that lists the strategies needed to approach and solve the problem. The **SOLUTION** demonstrates both the form and content of complete answers.

The **WEB ICON** indicates that an interactive version of the Demonstration Problem is available online. The **PEACHTREE ICON** indicates that the Demonsration Problem can be solved using Peachtree Complete Accounting® software.

DEMONSTRATION PROBLEM

In its first year of operations, DeMarco Company had the following selected transactions in stock investments that are considered trading securities.

June 1 Purchased for cash 600 shares of Sanburg common stock at $24 per share, plus $300 brokerage fees.
July 1 Purchased for cash 800 shares of Cey common stock at $33 per share, plus $600 brokerage fees.
Sept. 1 Received a $1 per share cash dividend from Cey Corporation.
Nov. 1 Sold 200 shares of Sanburg common stock for cash at $27 per share, less $150 brokerage fees.
Dec. 15 Received a $0.50 per share cash dividend on Sanburg common stock.

At December 31, the fair values per share were: Sanburg $25 and Cey $30.

Instructions

(a) Journalize the transactions.
(b) Prepare the adjusting entry at December 31 to report the securities at fair value.

SOLUTION TO DEMONSTRATION PROBLEM

(a) June 1	Stock Investments	14,700	
	Cash		14,700
	(To record purchase of 600 shares of Sanburg common stock)		
July 1	Stock Investments	27,000	
	Cash		27,000
	(To record purchase of 800 shares of Cey common stock)		
Sept. 1	Cash	800	
	Dividend Revenue		800
	(To record receipt of $1 per share cash dividend from Cey Corporation)		
Nov. 1	Cash	5,250	

ACTION PLAN

- Include the price paid plus brokerage fees in the cost of the investment.
- Compute the gain or loss on sales as the difference between net selling price and the cost of the securities.
- Base the adjustment to fair value on the total difference between the cost and the fair value of the securities.

SUMMARY OF STUDY OBJECTIVES

1. **Explain the time period assumption.** The time period assumption assumes that the economic life of a business can be divided into artificial time periods.
2. **Explain the accrual basis of accounting.** Accrual-basis accounting means that events that change a company's financial statements are recorded in the periods in which the events occur, rather than in the periods in which the company receives or pays cash.
3. **Explain why adjusting entries are needed.** Adjusting entries are made at the end of an accounting period. They ensure that revenues are recorded in the period in which they are earned and that expenses are recognized in the period in which they are incurred.
4. **Identify the major types of adjusting entries.** The major types of adjusting entries are prepaid expenses, unearned revenues, accrued revenues, and accrued expenses.
5. **Prepare adjusting entries for prepayments.** Prepayments are either prepaid expenses or unearned revenues. Adjusting entries for prepayments are required at the statement date to record the portion of the prepayment that represents the expense incurred or the revenue earned in the current accounting period.
6. **Prepare adjusting entries for accruals.** Accruals are either accrued revenues or accrued expenses. Adjusting entries for accruals are required to record revenues earned and expenses incurred in the current accounting period that have not been recognized through daily entries.
7. **Describe the nature and purpose of an adjusted trial balance.** An adjusted trial balance shows the balances of all accounts, including those that have been adjusted, at the end of an accounting period. Its purpose is to show the effects of all financial events that have occurred during the accounting period.

THE NAVIGATOR

▶ The **SUMMARY OF STUDY OBJECTIVES** reviews the main points related to the Study Objectives. It provides you with another opportunity to review what you have learned as well as to see how the key topics within the chapter fit together.

GLOSSARY

Account A record of increases and decreases in specific asset, liability, or stockholders' equity items. (p. 47).

Chart of accounts A list of accounts and the account numbers that identify their location in the ledger. (p. 60).

Common stock Issued in exchange for the owners' investment paid in to the corporation. (p. 50).

Compound entry A journal entry that involves three or more accounts. (p. 56).

Credit The right side of an account. (p. 48).

Debit The left side of an account. (p. 48).

Dividend A distribution by a corporation to its stockholders on a pro rata (equal) basis. (p. 50).

Double-entry system A system that records in appropriate accounts the dual effect of each transaction. (p. 48).

General journal The most basic form of journal. (p. 55).

General ledger A ledger that contains all asset, liability, and stockholders' equity accounts. (p. 57).

Journal An accounting record in which transactions are initially recorded in chronological order. (p. 55).

Journalizing The entering of transaction data in the journal. (p. 55).

Ledger The entire group of accounts maintained by a company. (p. 57).

Posting The procedure of transferring journal entries to the ledger accounts. (p. 59).

Retained earnings Net income that is retained in the business. (p. 50).

Simple entry A journal entry that involves only two accounts. (p. 56).

T account The basic form of an account. (p. 47).

Three-column form of account A form with columns for debit, credit, and balance amounts in an account. (p. 59).

Trial balance A list of accounts and their balances at a given time. (p. 6...

◀ The **GLOSSARY** defines all the **KEY TERMS** and **CONCEPTS** introduced in the chapter. Page references help you find any terms you need to study further. The **WEB ICON** tells you that you can review these terms interactively on the Web site.

APPENDIX EXCHANGE OF PLANT ASSETS

STUDY OBJECTIVE 10

Explain how to account for the exchange of plant assets.

Plant assets may also be disposed of through exchange. Exchanges can be for either similar or dissimilar assets. Because exchanges of similar assets are more common, they are discussed here. An exchange of similar assets occurs, for example, when old office furniture is exchanged for new office furniture. In an exchange of similar assets, the new asset performs the **same function** as the old asset.

In exchanges of similar plant assets, it is necessary to determine two things: (1) the cost of the asset acquired, and (2) the gain or loss on the asset given up. Because a noncash asset is given up in the exchange, cost is the **cash equivalent price** paid. That is, cost is the fair market value of the asset given up plus the cash paid. The gain or loss on disposal is the **difference between the fair market value and the book value of the asset given up**. These determinations are explained and illustrated below.

Loss Treatment

A loss on the exchange of similar assets is recognized immediately. To illustrate, assume that Roland Company exchanged old office equipment for new office equipment. The book value of the old equipment is $26,000 (cost $70,000 less accumulated depreciation $44,000). Its fair market value is $10,000, and cash of $81,000 is paid. The cost of the new office equipment, $91,000, is computed as follows.

Illustration 10A-1
Computation of cost of new office equipment

Fair market value of old office equipment	$10,000
Cash	81,000
Cost of new office equipment	**$91,000**

▶ In some chapters, **APPENDIXES** that follow the **GLOSSARY** offer expanded coverage of accounting procedures or further discussion of certain topics.

SELF-STUDY QUESTIONS

Self-Study/Self-Test

Answers are at the end of the chapter.

(SO 1) 1. Which of the following statements about an account is true?
a. In its simplest form, an account consists of two parts.
b. An account is an individual accounting record of increases and decreases in specific asset, liability, and stockholders' equity items.
c. There are separate accounts for specific assets and liabilities but only one account for stockholders' equity items.
d. The left side of an account is the credit or decrease side.

(SO 2) 2. Debits:
a. increase both assets and liabilities.
b. decrease both assets and liabilities.
c. increase assets and decrease liabilities.
d. decrease assets and increase liabilities.

(SO 2) 3. A revenue account:
a. is increased by debits.
b. is decreased by credits.
c. has a normal balance of a debit.
d. is increased by credits.

(SO 2) 4. Accounts that normally have debit balances are:
a. assets, expenses, and revenues.
b. assets, expenses, and common stock.
c. assets, liabilities, and dividends.
d. assets, dividends, and expenses.

(SO 3) 5. Which of the following is *not* part of the recording process?
a. Analyzing transactions.
b. Preparing a trial balance.
c. Entering transactions in a journal.
d. Posting transactions.

(SO 4) 6. Which of the following statements about a journal is false?
a. It is not a book of original entry.
b. It provides a chronological record of transactions.
c. It helps to locate errors because the debit and credit amounts for each entry can be readily compared.
d. It discloses in one place the complete effect of a transaction.

7. A ledger: (SO 5)
a. contains only asset and liability accounts.
b. should show accounts in alphabetical order.
c. is a collection of the entire group of accounts maintained by a company.
d. is a book of original entry.

8. Posting: (SO 6)
a. normally occurs before journalizing.
b. transfers ledger transaction data to the journal.
c. is an optional step in the recording process.
d. transfers journal entries to ledger accounts.

9. A trial balance: (SO 7)
a. is a list of accounts with their balances at a given time.
b. proves the mathematical accuracy of journalized transactions.
c. will not balance if a correct journal entry is posted twice.
d. proves that all transactions have been recorded.

10. A trial balance will not balance if: (SO 7)
a. a correct journal entry is posted twice.
b. the purchase of supplies on account is debited to Supplies and credited to Cash.
c. a $100 cash dividend by the corporation is debited to Dividends for $1,000 and credited to Cash for $100.
d. a $450 payment on account is debited to Accounts Payable for $45 and credited to Cash for $45.

THE NAVIGATOR

◀ **SELF-STUDY QUESTIONS** provide a practice test, keyed to Study Objectives, that gives you an opportunity to check your knowledge of important topics. Answers appear at the end of the chapter. The **WEB ICON** tells you that you can answer these **SELF-STUDY QUESTIONS** interactively on the book's Web site. There is an additional **SELF-TEST** at the Web site that can further help you master the material.

QUESTIONS

1. Why is an account referred to as a T account?
2. "The terms *debit* and *credit* mean increase and decrease, respectively." Do you agree? Explain.
3. Britney Spears, a fellow student, contends that the double-entry system means each transaction must be recorded twice. Is Britney correct? Explain.
4. Julia Roberts, a beginning accounting student, believes debit balances are favorable and credit balances are unfavorable. Is Julia correct? Discuss.
5. State the rules of debit and credit as applied to (a) asset accounts, (b) liability accounts, and (c) stockholders' equity.
6. What is the normal balance for each of the following accounts? (a) Accounts Receivable. (b) Cash. (c) Dividends. (d) Accounts Payable. (e) Service Revenue. (f) Salaries Expense. (g) Common Stock.
7. Indicate whether each of the following accounts is an asset, a liability, or a stockholders' equity account and whether it would have a debit or credit balance: (a) Accounts Receivable, (b) Accounts Payable, (c) Equipment, (d) Dividends, (e) Supplies.
8. For the following transactions, indicate the account debited and the account credited.
...sed on account.
12. (a) When entering a transaction in the journal, should the debit or credit be written first?
(b) Which should be indented, the debit or credit?
13. Describe a compound entry, and provide an example.
14. (a) Should business transaction debits and credits be recorded directly in the ledger accounts?
(b) What are the advantages of first recording transactions in the journal and then posting to the ledger?
15. The account number is entered as the last step in posting the amounts from the journal to the ledger. What is the advantage of this step?
16. Journalize the following business transactions.
(a) Tom Cruise invests $12,000 in the business in exchange for shares of common stock.
(b) Insurance of $720 is paid for the year.
(c) Supplies of $900 are purchased on account.
(d) Cash of $3,000 is received for services rendered.
17. (a) What is a ledger? (b) Why is a chart of accounts important?
18. What is a trial balance and what are its purposes?
19. Joe Alverez is confused about how accounting information flows through the accounting system. He believes the flow of information is as follows.
(a) D... ...ledger

▶ **QUESTIONS** allow you to explain your understanding of concepts and relationships from the chapter. Use them to help prepare for class discussion and tests.

▶ **BRIEF EXERCISES** help you focus on one Study Objective at a time and thus help you build confidence in your basic skills and knowledge.

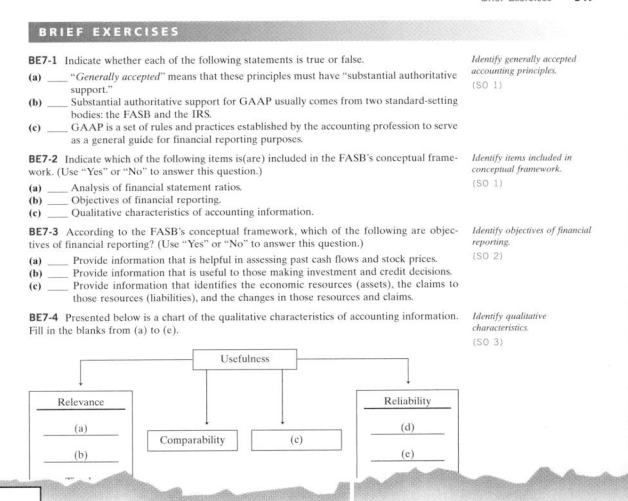

Brief Exercises 317

BRIEF EXERCISES

BE7-1 Indicate whether each of the following statements is true or false.

Identify generally accepted accounting principles. (SO 1)

(a) ____ *"Generally accepted"* means that these principles must have "substantial authoritative support."
(b) ____ Substantial authoritative support for GAAP usually comes from two standard-setting bodies: the FASB and the IRS.
(c) ____ GAAP is a set of rules and practices established by the accounting profession to serve as a general guide for financial reporting purposes.

BE7-2 Indicate which of the following items is(are) included in the FASB's conceptual framework. (Use "Yes" or "No" to answer this question.)

Identify items included in conceptual framework. (SO 1)

(a) ____ Analysis of financial statement ratios.
(b) ____ Objectives of financial reporting.
(c) ____ Qualitative characteristics of accounting information.

BE7-3 According to the FASB's conceptual framework, which of the following are objectives of financial reporting? (Use "Yes" or "No" to answer this question.)

Identify objectives of financial reporting. (SO 2)

(a) ____ Provide information that is helpful in assessing past cash flows and stock prices.
(b) ____ Provide information that is useful to those making investment and credit decisions.
(c) ____ Provide information that identifies the economic resources (assets), the claims to those resources (liabilities), and the changes in those resources and claims.

BE7-4 Presented below is a chart of the qualitative characteristics of accounting information. Fill in the blanks from (a) to (e).

Identify qualitative characteristics. (SO 3)

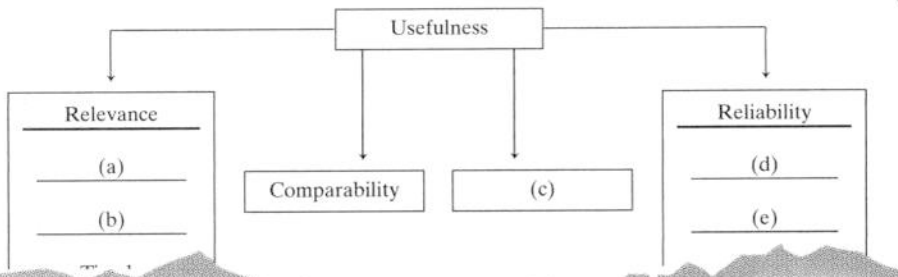

EXERCISES

Prepare entries for interest-bearing notes. (SO 2)

E11-1 On June 1, Padillio Company borrows $70,000 from First Bank on a 6-month, $70,000, 12% note.

Instructions
(a) Prepare the entry on June 1.
(b) Prepare the adjusting entry on June 30.
(c) Prepare the entry at maturity (December 1), assuming monthly adjusting entries have been made through November 30.
(d) What was the total financing cost (interest expense)?

Journalize sales and related taxes. (SO 3)

E11-2 In providing accounting services to small businesses, you encounter the following situations pertaining to cash sales.

1. Sue Jackson Company rings up sales and sales taxes separately on its cash register. On April 10, the register totals are sales $25,000 and sales taxes $1,500.
2. Person Company does not segregate sales and sales taxes. Its register total for April 15 is $20,330, which includes a 7% sales tax.

Instructions
Prepare the entry to record the sales transactions and related taxes for each client.

Journalize unearned subscription revenue. (SO 3)

E11-3 Nevin Company publishes a monthly sports magazine, *Fishing Preview*. Subscriptions to the magazine cost $20 per year. During November 2006, Nevin sells 9,000 subscriptions beginning with the December issue. Nevin prepares financial statements quarterly and recognizes subscription revenue earned at the end of the quarter. The company uses the accounts Unearned Subscriptions and Subscription Revenue.

Instructions
(a) Prepare the entry in November for the receipt of the subscriptions.
(b) Prepare the adjusting entry at December 31, 2006, to record subscription revenue earned in December 2006.
(c) Prepare the adjusting entry at March 31, 2007, to record subscription revenue earned in first quarter of 2007.

Comp... alternatives of ...

E11-4 Southeast Airlines is considering ... alternatives for the financing of a purchase ... fleet of airplanes. These t...

◀ **EXERCISES,** which are more difficult than Brief Exercises, help you continue to build confidence in your ability to use the material learned in the chapter.

▼ **SPREADSHEET EXERCISES** and **PROBLEMS,** identified by an icon, are selected problems that can be solved using the spreadsheet software *Solving Principles of Accounting Problems Using Excel.*

PROBLEMS: SET A

P5-1A Phantom Book Warehouse distributes hardback books to retail stores and extends credit terms of 2/10, n/30 to all of its customers. At the end of May, Phantom's inventory consisted of 240 books purchased at $1,200. During the month of June the following merchandising transactions occurred.

Journalize purchase and sales transactions under a perpetual inventory system. (SO 2, 3)

June 1 Purchased 160 books on account for $5 each from Ex Libris Publishers, FOB destination, terms 2/10, n/30. The appropriate party also made a cash payment of $50 for the freight on this date.
3 Sold 120 books on account to Readers-R-Us for $10 each.
6 Received $50 credit for 10 books returned to Ex Libris Publishers.
9 Paid Ex Libris Publishers in full, less discount.
15 Received payment in full from Readers-R-Us.
17 Sold 120 books on account to Bargain Books for $10 each.
20 Purchased 110 books on account for $5 each from Bookem Publishers, FOB destination, terms 2/15, n/30. The appropriate party also made a cash payment of $50 for the freight on this date.
24 Received payment in full from Bargain Books.
26 Paid Bookem Publishers in full, less discount.
28 Sold 110 books on account to Read-n-Weep Bookstore for $10 each.
30 Granted Read-n-Weep Bookstore $150 credit for 15 books returned costing $75.

Phantom Book Warehouse's chart of accounts includes the following: No. 101 Cash, No. 112 Accounts Receivable, No. 120 Merchandise Inventory, No. 201 Accounts Payable, No. 401 Sales, No. 412 Sales Returns and Allowances, No. 414 Sales Discounts, No. 505 Cost of Goods Sold.

Instructions
...urnalize the transactions for the month of June for Phantom Book Warehouse using a per...tual inventory system.

▶ Each **PROBLEM** helps you pull together and apply several concepts from the chapter. Two sets of **PROBLEMS—A** and **B**—are keyed to the same Study Objectives and provide additional opportunities for practice.

Problems: Set B 575

PROBLEMS: SET B

P12-1B Keeler Corporation was organized on January 1, 2006. It is authorized to issue 10,000 shares of 8%, $100 par value preferred stock, and 500,000 shares of no-par common stock with a stated value of $3 per share. The following stock transactions were completed during the first year.

Journalize stock transactions, post, and prepare paid-in capital section. (SO 2, 4, 7)

Peachtree

Jan. 10 Issued 80,000 shares of common stock for cash at $4 per share.
Mar. 1 Issued 5,000 shares of preferred stock for cash at $105 per share.
Apr. 1 Issued 24,000 shares of common stock for land. The asking price of the land was $90,000. The fair market value of the land was $85,000.
May 1 Issued 80,000 shares of common stock for cash at $4.50 per share.
Aug. 1 Issued 10,000 shares of common stock to attorneys in payment of their bill of $40,000 for services provided in helping the company organize.
Sept. 1 Issued 10,000 shares of common stock for cash at $5 per share.
Nov. 1 Issued 1,000 shares of preferred stock for cash at $109 per share.

Instructions
(a) Journalize the transactions.
(b) Post to the stockholders' equity accounts. (Use J5 as the posting reference.)
(c) Prepare the paid-in capital section of stockholders' equity at December 31, 2006.

(c) Total paid-in capital $1,489,000

P12-2B Goldberg Corporation had the following stockholders' equity accounts on January 1, 2006: Common Stock ($5 par) $500,000, Paid-in Capital in Excess of Par Value $200,000, and Retained Earnings $100,000. In 2006, the company had the following treasury stock transactions.

Journalize and post treasury stock transactions, and prepare stockholders' equity section. (SO 3, 7)

Mar. 1 Purchased 5,000 shares at $8 per share.
June 1 Sold 1,000 shares at $12 per share.
Sept. 1 Sold 2,000 shares at $10 per share.
Dec. 1 Sold 1,000 shares at $6 per share.

Goldberg Corporation uses the cost method of accounting for treasury stock. In 2006, the company reported net income of $40,000.

Instructions
(a) Journalize the treasury stock transactions, and prepare the closing entry at December 31, 2006, for net income.
(b) Open accounts for (1) Paid-in Capital from Treasury Stock, (2) Treasury Stock, and (3) Retained Earnings. Post to these accounts using J10 as the posting reference.
(c) Prepare the stockholders' equity section for Goldberg Corporation at December 31, 2006.

(b) Treasury Stock $8,000
(c) Total stockholders' equity $838,000

P12-3B The stockholders' equity accounts of Port Corporation on Janu...

◀ Problems marked with the **PEACHTREE** icon can be worked using *Peachtree Complete Accounting® Software*. A separate student workbook that includes the software is available for purchase.

◀ **GENERAL LEDGER PROBLEMS,** identified by a blue computer screen icon, are selected problems that can be solved using the *General Ledger Software* package.

◀ **CHECK FIGURES** in the margin provide key numbers to let you know you're on the right track.

▶ **COMPREHENSIVE PROBLEMS** in 5 chapters give you the opportunity to put to use concepts covered across multiple chapters.

COMPREHENSIVE PROBLEM: CHAPTERS 11 TO 13

PART I

Megan Bergeron and her two colleagues, Jesse Ortiz and Tara Sheley, are personal trainers at an upscale health spa/resort in Tampa, Florida. They want to start a health club that specializes in health plans for people in the 50+ age range. The growing population in this age range and strong consumer interest in the health benefits of physical activity have convinced them they can profitably operate their own club. In addition to many other decisions, they need to determine what type of business organization they want. Jesse believes there are more advantages to the corporate form than a partnership, but he hasn't yet convinced Megan and Tara. They have come to you, a small business consulting specialist, seeking information and advice regarding the choice of starting a partnership versus a corporation.

Instructions

(a) Prepare a memo (dated May 26, 2005) that describes the advantages and disadvantages of both partnerships and corporations. Advise Megan, Jesse, and Tara regarding which organizational form you believe would better serve their purposes. Make sure to include reasons supporting your advice.

▶ Certain Exercises and Problems, marked with a pencil icon, help you practice **BUSINESS WRITING SKILLS**, which are much in demand among employers.

232 CHAPTER 5 Accounting for Merchandising Operations

BROADENING YOUR PERSPECTIVE

Financial Reporting and Analysis

■ **FINANCIAL REPORTING PROBLEM: PepsiCo, Inc.**

BYP5-1 The financial statements of **PepsiCo, Inc.** are presented in Appendix A at the end of this textbook.

Instructions

Answer the following questions using the Consolidated Statement of Income.

(a) What was the percentage change in (1) sales and in (2) net income from 2001 to 2002 and from 2002 to 2003?
(b) What was the company's gross profit rate in 2001, 2002, and 2003?
(c) What was the company's percentage of net income to net sales in 2001, 2002, and 2003? Comment on any trend in this percentage.

■ **COMPARATIVE ANALYSIS PROBLEM: PepsiCo vs. Coca-Cola**

BYP5-2 **PepsiCo's** financial statements are presented in Appendix A. **The Coca-Cola Company's** financial statements are presented in Appendix B.

Instructions

(a) Based on the information contained in these financial statements, determine each of the following for each company.
(1) Gross profit for 2003.
(2) Gross profit rate for 2003.
(3) Operating income for 2003.
(4) Percent change in operating income from 2002 to 2003.
(b) What conclusions concerning the relative profitability of the two companies can be drawn from these data?

■ **RESEARCH CASE**

BYP5-3 The January 25, 2001, issue of the *Wall Street Journal* includes an article by Nick Wingfield titled "**Webvan** Seeks to Refine Customers in Hopes of Surviving Cash Crunch."

Instructions

Read the article and answer the following questions.

(a) Describe in a few sentences Webvan's business plan.
(b) What was the biggest challenge to Webvan's survival?
(c) What was Webvan's gross profit rate (also called gross margin)? On the average $100 sale of goods, what was its gross profit? How did Webvan's gross profit rate compare to that of a traditional grocer?
(d) What operating expenses did Webvan have that a traditional grocer wouldn't have?
(e) According to the article, what were some things that Webvan could try to do to improve its profitability?

■ **INTERPRETING FINANCIAL STATEMENTS**

BYP5-4 **Zany Brainy, Inc.** was a specialty retailer of toys, games, books, and multimedia products for kids. As of the end of the fiscal year 2000, the company operated 188 stores in 34 states. On May 15, 2001, the company filed voluntary Chapter 11 bankruptcy. It went out of business in 2003. Provided below is financial information for the 2 years prior to the company's decision to file for bankruptcy, as well as information for a large competitor, **Toys R Us**.

◀ The **BROADENING YOUR PERSPECTIVE** section helps you pull together various concepts from the chapter and apply them to real-world business situations.

◀ In the **FINANCIAL REPORTING PROBLEM** you study various aspects of the financial statements of PepsiCo, Inc., which are printed in Appendix A.

◀ A **COMPARATIVE ANALYSIS PROBLEM** offers the opportunity to compare and contrast the financial reporting of PepsiCo with a competitor, The Coca-Cola Company.

◀ A **RESEARCH CASE** directs you to published articles in business periodicals for further study and analysis of key topics.

◀ **INTERPRETING FINANCIAL STATEMENTS** asks you to read parts of financial statements of real companies, interpret this information, and apply concepts from the chapter to specific situations faced by these companies.

▶ **A GLOBAL FOCUS** asks you to analyze financial statements of foreign or international companies and to interpret the information in comparison to what you know about domestic U.S. companies.

■ **A GLOBAL FOCUS**

BYP13-5 **Xerox Corporation** has a 50% investment interest in a joint venture with the Japanese corporation Fuji, called **Fuji Xerox**. Xerox accounts for this investment using the equity method. The following additional information regarding this investment was taken from a recent Xerox annual report (in millions).

Investment in Fuji Xerox per balance sheet	$ 1,354
Fuji Xerox net income	108
Xerox total assets	30,024
Xerox total liabilities	25,167
Fuji Xerox total assets	6,279
Fuji Xerox total liabilities	3,757

Instructions

(a) What alternative approaches are available for accounting for long-term investments in stock? Discuss whether Xerox is correct in using the equity method to account for this investment.
(b) Under the equity method, how does Xerox report its investment in Fuji Xerox? If Xerox owned a majority of Fuji Xerox, it then would have to consolidate Fuji Xerox instead of using the equity method. Discuss how this would change Xerox's financial statements. That is, in what way and by how much would assets and liabilities change?
(c) The use of 50% joint ventures is becoming a fairly common practice. Why might companies like Xerox prefer to participate in a joint venture rather than own a majority share?

■ **EXPLORING THE WEB**

BYP13-6 The **American Association of Individual Investors (AAII)** provides considerable useful information and services for people interested in investing.

Address: www.aaii.org/invbas/, or go to www.wiley.com/college/weygandt

Steps

1. Go to the site shown above.
2. Choose Glossary.

Instructions

Find the definition of the following terms.

(a) Ask price.
(b) Margin.
(c) Prospectus.
(d) Yield.

▶ **EXPLORING THE WEB** exercises guide you to Web sites where you can find and analyze information related to the chapter topic.

Critical Thinking

■ **GROUP DECISION CASE**

BYP7-7 Presented below are key figures and relationships from the financial statements of a prominent company in each of three different industries for two recent fiscal years.

	Manufacturing		Mining/Oil		Merchandising	
	2003	2004	2003	2004	2003	2004
From the balance sheets:						
Total assets (millions)	$11,079	$11,083	$33,884	$35,089	$8,524	$9,485
Current ratio	1.72	1.73	1.14	1.12	1.51	1.56
Working capital (millions)	$2,390	$2,349	$1,037	$1,072	$1,236	$1,452
Debt to total assets ratio	0.45	0.43	0.59	0.58	0.72	0.72
Profitability:						
Total sales (millions)	$13,021	$13,340	$31,916	$41,540	$14,739	$16,115
Profit margin percentage	10.0%	8.7%	0.8%	5.2%	2.8%	1.9%
Return on assets	11.8%	10.4%	0.7%	6.1%	4.8%	3.2%
Return on common equity	21.4%	18.3%	1.8%	15.0%	20.1%	13.5%
Earnings per common share	$5.91	$5.26	$0.73	$6.10	$5.20	$3.72
From the annual reports:						
End-of-year stock price	$67.75	$72.63	$85.75	$95.25	$56.50	$62.00

Instructions
With the class divided into groups, answer the following.

(a) The benchmark for the current ratio is generally 2:1. None of these companies has a ratio that high, yet all three are well regarded firms. Why might a current ratio less than 2:1 *not* signal a problem?
(b) The merchandising company acquired a chain of well-known department stores just prior to 2003. Apart from such major acquisitions, what else might contribute to differing debt total assets ratios? Consider industry-specific as well as company-specific consideration

◀ The **GROUP DECISION CASE** helps you build decision-making skills by analyzing accounting information in a less structured situation. These cases require teams of students to evaluate a manager's decision, or they lead to a decision among alternative courses of action. They also give practice in building business communication skills.

▶ **COMMUNICATION ACTIVITIES** help you build business communication skills by asking you to engage in real-world business situations using writing, speaking, or presentation skills.

▶ In the **ETHICS CASES**, you will reflect on typical ethical dilemmas, analyze the stakeholders and the issues involved, and decide on an appropriate course of action.

■ **COMMUNICATION ACTIVITY**

BYP1-8 Erin Danielle, the accountant for Bloomington Company, has been trying to get the balance sheet to balance. The company's balance sheet is as follows.

BLOOMINGTON COMPANY
Balance Sheet
For the Month Ended December 31, 2006

Assets		Liabilities	
Equipment	$22,500	Common stock	$23,000
Cash	9,000	Accounts receivable	(6,000)
Supplies	2,000	Dividends	(2,000)
Accounts payable	(8,000)	Notes payable	10,500
	$25,500		$25,500

Instructions
Explain to Erin Danielle in a memo why the original balance sheet is incorrect, and what should be done to correct it.

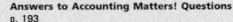

■ **ETHICS CASE**

Accounting Matters!

BYP1-9 After numerous campus interviews, Jeff Hunter, a senior at Great Northern College, received two office interview invitations from the Baltimore offices of two large firms. Both firms offered to cover his out-of-pocket expenses (travel, hotel, and meals). He scheduled the interviews for both firms on the same day, one in the morning and one in the afternoon. At the conclusion of each interview, he submitted to both firms his total out-of-pocket expenses for the trip to Baltimore: mileage $98 (280 miles at $0.35), hotel $130, meals $36, parking and tolls $18, for a total of $282. He believes this approach is appropriate. If he had made two trips, his cost would have been two times $282. He is also certain that neither firm knew he had visited the other on that same trip. Within ten days Jeff received two checks in the mail, each in the amount of $282.

Instructions
(a) Who are the stakeholders (affected parties) in this situation?
(b) What are the eth... sues in this case?
...on?

Accounting Matters!

■ **CONTINUING COOKIE CHRONICLE**

(*Note:* This is a continuation of the Cookie Chronicle from Chapters 1 and 2. From the information gathered through Chapter 2, follow the instructions below using the general ledger accounts you have already prepared.)

BYP3-10 It is the end of November and Natalie has been in touch with her grandmother. Her grandmother asked Natalie for financial statements because she believes it's important that Natalie, at some point in time, repay the loan she received from her. Natalie also feels that it's important to know the financial position of her business each month.

The following additional information will help you prepare Cookie Creations' financial statements:

1. A count reveals that $75 of brochures and posters remain at the end of November.
2. A count reveals that $25 of baking supplies were used during November.
3. Natalie estimates that all of her baking equipment will have a useful life of 5 years or months. (Assume Natalie decides to record a full month's worth of depreciation regardl of when the equipment was obtained by the business.)
4. Natalie's grandmother has decided to charge interest of 6% on the note payable extend on November 16. The loan plus interest is to be repaid in 24 months. (Assume that hal month of interest accrued during November.)
5. On November 30, a friend of Natalie's asks her to teach a class at the neighborhood scho Natalie agrees and teaches a group of 35 first-grade students how to make holiday cooki The next day Natalie prepares an invoice for $250 and leaves it with the school princip The principal says it will be paid sometime in December.
6. Natalie receives a cell phone bill for $50. She uses h... ...hone only for busin... The is for services provided during Nov...

◀ The **CONTINUING COOKIE CHRONICLE** follows the accounting operations for a single company, Cookie Creations, throughout the book.

▶ **ANSWERS TO ACCOUNTING MATTERS! QUESTIONS** repeats the critical thinking questions at the ends of **ACCOUNTING MATTERS!** boxes and suggest guideline answers.

▶ **ANSWERS TO *REVIEW IT* QUESTIONS** based on the PepsiCo financial statements appear here.

▶ **ANSWERS TO SELF-STUDY QUESTIONS** provide feedback on your understanding of concepts.

▶ After you complete your homework assignments, it's a good idea to go back to **THE NAVIGATOR** checklist at the start of the chapter to see if you have used all the chapter's study aids.

Answers to Accounting Matters! Questions

Accounting Matters!

p. 193
Q: How is a grocery store's accounting equation changed by the computer's bar-code actions?
A: Cash and Sales Revenue would increase; Inventory would decrease; and Cost of Goods Sold would increase.
p. 197
Q: The *distribution costs* of online sales can be greater than for traditional in-store sales. What costs may be less for online sales?
A: The costs of a sales force, store rent or depreciation, utilities, and other store operating expenses may decrease for online sales.
p. 199
Q: How does management know the amount of sales returns?
A: The activity in the contra sales account, Sales Returns and Allowances, communicates to management excessive returns.
Q: Would returns for a floral supply company have a greater negative impact on earnings than returns for a department store?
A: The negative impact of returned sales is probably greater for a floral supply company than for a department store because of the perishable nature of the inventory and the higher labor cost to prepare shipments.
p. 205
Q: Why have investors and analysts demanded more accuracy in isolating "Other gains and losses" from operating items?
A: Greater accuracy in the classification of operating versus nonoperating ("Other gains and losses") items permits investors and analysts to judge the real operating margin, the results of continuing operations, and management's ability to control operating expenses.

Answer to PepsiCo Review It Question 1, p. 208
For **PepsiCo**, the 2003 gross profit rate is 54.1% ($14,592 ÷ $26,971). The 2002 gross profit rate was 54.2% ($13,615 ÷ $25,112). The rate therefore decreased by 0.1% from 2002 to 2003.

Answers to Self-Study Questions
1. c **2.** a **3.** c **4.** b **5.** c **6.** d **7.** b **8.** c **9.** d **10.** d **11.** a ***12.** b ***13.** a

REMEMBER to go back to the Navigator box on the chapter-opening page and check off your completed work.

How Do I Learn Best?

This questionnaire aims to find out something about your preferences for the way you work with information. You will have a preferred learning style, and one part of that learning style is your preference for the intake and the output of ideas and information.

Circle the letter of the answer that best explains your preference. Circle more than one if a single answer does not match your perception. Leave blank any question that does not apply.

1. You are about to give directions to a person who is standing with you. She is staying in a hotel in town and wants to visit your house later. She has a rental car. Would you
- **a.** draw a map on paper?
- **b.** tell her the directions?
- **c.** write down the directions (without a map)?
- **d.** pick her up at the hotel in your car?

2. You are not sure whether a word should be spelled "dependent" or "dependant." Do you
- **c.** look it up in the dictionary?
- **a.** see the word in your mind and choose by the way it looks?
- **b.** sound it out in your mind?
- **d.** write both versions down on paper and choose one?

3. You have just received a copy of your itinerary for a world trip. This is of interest to a friend. Would you
- **b.** call her immediately and tell her about it?
- **c.** send her a copy of the printed itinerary?
- **a.** show her on a map of the world?
- **d.** share what you plan to do at each place you visit?

4. You are going to cook something as a special treat for your family. Do you
- **d.** cook something familiar without the need for instructions?
- **a.** thumb through the cookbook looking for ideas from the pictures?
- **c.** refer to a specific cookbook where there is a good recipe?

5. A group of tourists has been assigned to you to find out about wildlife reserves or parks. Would you
- **d.** drive them to a wildlife reserve or park?
- **a.** show them slides and photographs?
- **c.** give them pamphlets or a book on wildlife reserves or parks?
- **b.** give them a talk on wildlife reserves or parks?

6. You are about to purchase a new CD player. Other than price, what would most influence your decision?
- **b.** The salesperson telling you what you want to know.
- **c.** Reading the details about it.
- **d.** Playing with the controls and listening to it.
- **a.** Its fashionable and upscale appearance.

7. Recall a time in your life when you learned how to do something like playing a new board game. Try to avoid choosing a very physical skill, e.g., riding a bike. How did you learn best? By
- **a.** visual clues—pictures, diagrams, charts?
- **c.** written instructions?
- **b.** listening to somebody explaining it?
- **d.** doing it or trying it?

8. You have an eye problem. Would you prefer that the doctor
- **b.** tell you what is wrong?
- **a.** show you a diagram of what is wrong?
- **d.** use a model to show what is wrong?

9. You are about to learn to use a new program on a computer. Would you
- **d.** sit down at the keyboard and begin to experiment with the program's features?
- **c.** read the manual that comes with the program?
- **b.** call a friend and ask questions about it?

10. You are staying in a hotel and have a rental car. You would like to visit friends whose address/location you do not know. Would you like them to
- **a.** draw you a map on paper?
- **b.** tell you the directions?
- **c.** write down the directions (without a map)?
- **d.** pick you up at the hotel in their car?

11. Apart from price, what would most influence your decision to buy a particular book?
- **d.** You have used a copy before.
- **b.** A friend talking about it.
- **c.** Quickly reading parts of it.
- **a.** The appealing way it looks.

12. A new movie has arrived in town. What would most influence your decision to go (or not go)?
- **b.** You heard a radio review about it.
- **c.** You read a review about it.
- **a.** You saw a preview of it.

13. Do you prefer a lecturer or teacher who likes to use
- **c.** a textbook, handouts, readings?
- **a.** flow diagrams, charts, graphs?
- **d.** field trips, labs, practical sessions?
- **b.** discussion, guest speakers?

	a.	b.	c.	d.
Count your choices:	❑	❑	❑	❑
	V	A	R	K

Now match the letter or letters you have recorded most to the same letter or letters in the Learning Styles Chart. You may have more than one learning style preference—many people do. Next to each letter in the chart are suggestions that will refer you to different learning aids throughout this text.

Learning Styles Chart

V *Visual*

INTAKE: TO TAKE IN THE INFORMATION	TO MAKE A STUDY PACKAGE	TEXT FEATURES THAT MAY HELP YOU THE MOST	OUTPUT: TO DO WELL ON EXAMS
• Pay close attention to charts, drawings, and handouts your instructor uses. • Underline. • Use different colors. • Use symbols, flow charts, graphs, different arrangements on the page, white space.	Convert your lecture notes into "page pictures." To do this: • Use the "Intake" strategies. • Reconstruct images in different ways. • Redraw pages from memory. • Replace words with symbols and initials. • Look at your pages.	**The Navigator** **Accounting Matters! Feature Story** **Preview** **Infographics/Illustrations Photos** **Accounting Matters! boxes** **Accounting Equation Analyses** **Key Terms in blue** **Words in bold** **Demonstration Problem** **Action Plan** **Questions/Exercises/Problems** **Financial Reporting Problem** **Comparative Analysis Problem** **Interpreting Financial Statements** **A Global Focus** **Exploring the Web**	• Recall your "page pictures." • Draw diagrams where appropriate. • Practice turning your visuals back into words.

A *Aural*

INTAKE: TO TAKE IN THE INFORMATION	TO MAKE A STUDY PACKAGE	TEXT FEATURES THAT MAY HELP YOU THE MOST	OUTPUT: TO DO WELL ON EXAMS
• Attend lectures and tutorials. • Discuss topics with students and instructors. • Explain new ideas to other people. • Use a tape recorder. • Leave spaces in your lecture notes for later recall. • Describe overheads, pictures, and visuals to somebody who was not in class.	You may take poor notes because you prefer to listen. Therefore: • Expand your notes by talking with others and with information from your textbook. • Tape record summarized notes and listen. • Read summarized notes out loud. • Explain your notes to another "aural" person.	**Preview** **Infographics/Illustrations** **Accounting Matters! boxes** **Review It/Do It/Action Plan** **Summary of Study Objectives** **Glossary** **Demonstration Problem** **Action Plan** **Self-Study Questions** **Questions/Exercises/Problems** **Financial Reporting Problem** **Comparative Analysis Problem** **Exploring the Web** **Group Decision Case** **Communication Activity** **Ethics Case**	• Talk with the instructor. • Spend time in quiet places recalling the ideas. • Practice writing answers to old exam questions. • Say your answers out loud.

R Reading/Writing

INTAKE: TO TAKE IN THE INFORMATION	TO MAKE A STUDY PACKAGE	TEXT FEATURES THAT MAY HELP YOU THE MOST	OUTPUT: TO DO WELL ON EXAMS
• Use lists and headings. • Use dictionaries, glossaries, and definitions. • Read handouts, textbooks, and supplementary library readings. • Use lecture notes.	• Write out words again and again. • Reread notes silently. • Rewrite ideas and principles into other words. • Turn charts, diagrams, and other illustrations into statements.	**The Navigator** **Accounting Matters! Feature Story** **Study Objectives** **Preview** **Review It/Do It/Action Plan** **Summary of Study Objectives** **Glossary** **Self-Study Questions** **Questions/Exercises/Problems** **Writing Problems** **Financial Reporting Problem** **Comparative Analysis Problem** **Research Case** **Interpreting Financial Statements** **A Global Focus** **Exploring the Web** **Group Decision Case** **Communication Activity** **Continuing Cookie Chronicle**	• Write exam answers. • Practice with multiple-choice questions. • Write paragraphs, beginnings and endings. • Write your lists in outline form. • Arrange your words into hierarchies and points.

K Kinesthetic

INTAKE: TO TAKE IN THE INFORMATION	TO MAKE A STUDY PACKAGE	TEXT FEATURES THAT MAY HELP YOU THE MOST	OUTPUT: TO DO WELL ON EXAMS
• Use all your senses. • Go to labs, take field trips. • Listen to real-life examples. • Pay attention to applications. • Use hands-on approaches. • Use trial-and-error methods.	You may take poor notes because topics do not seem concrete or relevant. Therefore: • Put examples in your summaries. • Use case studies and applications to help with principles and abstract concepts. • Talk about your notes with another "kinesthetic" person. • Use pictures and photographs that illustrate an idea.	**The Navigator** **Accounting Matters! Feature Story** **Preview** **Infographics/Illustrations** **Review It/Do It/Action Plan** **Summary of Study Objectives** **Demonstration Problem/ Action Plan** **Self-Study Questions** **Questions/Exercises/Problems** **Financial Reporting Problem** **Comparative Analysis Problem** **A Research Case** **Interpreting Financial Statements** **A Global Focus** **Exploring the Web** **Group Decision Case** **Communication Activity** **Continuing Cookie Chronicle**	• Write practice answers. • Role-play the exam situation.

www.wiley.com/college/weygandt

For all learning styles: Be sure to use the book's Web site to enhance your understanding of the concepts and procedures of the text. In addition, see the next page (p. xxxiv) for a list of Student Supplements available with this textbook.

Student Supplements That Help You Get the Best Grade You Can

The Financial Accounting Web site

The book's Web site at *www.wiley.com/college/weygandt* provides a wealth of materials that will help you develop conceptual understanding and increase your ability to solve problems. For example, you will find PowerPoint presentations and Web quizzing. Be sure to check the site often.

Study Guide

The Study Guide is a comprehensive review of accounting. It guides you through chapter content, tied to study objectives. It provides resources for use during lectures and also is **an excellent tool when preparing for exams.** Each chapter of the Study Guide includes a chapter review (20 to 30 key points); a demonstration problem; and for extra practice, true/false, multiple-choice, and matching questions, and additional exercises, with solutions.

Working Papers

Working Papers are partially completed accounting forms for all end-of-chapter exercises, problems, and cases. They are a convenient resource for organizing and completing homework assignments, and they demonstrate how to correctly set up solution formats. Also available on CD-ROM are *Excel Working Papers,* which are Excel-formatted, partially completed accounting forms.

General Ledger Software

The General Ledger Software program allows you to use a computerized accounting system to solve the end-of-chapter text problems that are identified by the icon shown here.

Peachtree Complete® Accounting

A workbook and accompanying CD teach you how to use Peachtree Complete® Accounting Software. Selected problems in the book, denoted by the Peachtree icon, can be solved using this software package.

Solving Accounting Principles Problems Using Excel

A manual guides you step-by-step from an introduction to computers and Excel, to completion of preprogrammed spreadsheets, to design of your own spreadsheets. Accompanying spreadsheet templates allow you to complete selected end-of-chapter exercises and problems, identified by the icon shown here.

Practice Sets

Practice sets expose you to real-world simulations of maintaining a complete set of accounting records for a business. They integrate the business events, accounting concepts, procedures, and records covered within the textbook, and they reinforce the concepts and procedures learned. Two different practice sets are available: University Bookstore and Custom Party Associates.

Financial Accounting Tutor (FacT) CD

This self-paced CD-ROM is designed to review financial accounting concepts. It uses simple examples that introduce concepts gradually and reveal the logic underlying the accounting process. Discussions and examples are followed by brief, interactive problems that provide immediate feedback.

For more information on any of these student supplements, check with your professor or bookstore, or go to the Wiley Web site at *www.wiley.com/college/weygandt.*

Brief Contents

Detailed Contents

Chapter 1

Accounting Matters!

The Navigator is a learning system designed to prompt you to use the learning aids in the chapter and set priorities as you study.

THE NAVIGATOR ✓

- Understand **Concepts for Review** ❑
- Read **Feature Story** ❑
- Scan **Study Objectives** ❑
- Read **Preview** ❑
- Read text and answer **Before You Go On** p. 8 ❑ p. 14 ❑ p. 21 ❑ p. 25 ❑
- Work **Demonstration Problem** ❑
- Review **Summary of Study Objectives** ❑
- Answer **Self-Study Questions** ❑
- Complete **Assignments** ❑

CONCEPTS FOR REVIEW

Concepts for Review highlight concepts from your earlier reading that you need to understand before starting the new chapter

Before studying this chapter, you should know or, if necessary, review:

- How to use the study aids in this book. (Student Owner's Manual, pages xxiii–xxx)
- How you learn best. (Student Owner's Manual, pages xxxi–xxxii)
- The nature of the special student supplements that accompany this textbook. (Student Owner's Manual, page xxxiv)

☑ THE NAVIGATOR

The Feature Story helps you picture how the chapter topic relates to the real world of accounting and business. You will find references to the story throughout the chapter.

ACCOUNTING MATTERS! FEATURE STORY

Financial Reporting: A Matter of Trust

In recent years the financial press has been full of articles about financial scandals and accounting misdeeds. It started with **Enron,** but then spread to **Xerox**, **Qwest**, **Global Crossing**, and **WorldCom**, among others. Many of the articles expressed concern that as an increasing number of misdeeds came to public attention, a mistrust of financial reporting in general was developing. These articles made clear just how important accounting and financial reporting are to the U.S. and world financial markets and to society as a whole. Without financial reports, managers would not be able to evaluate how well their company is doing or to make decisions about the best way to make their company grow in the future. Without financial reports, investors and lenders could not make informed decisions about how to allocate their funds. There is no doubt that a sound, well-functioning economy depends on accurate and dependable financial reporting—accounting matters!

In order to make financial decisions as either an investor or a manager, you need to know how to read financial reports. In this book you will learn about financial reporting and some basic tools used to evaluate financial reports. In the first chapter we introduce you to the real financial statements of a company whose products most of you probably are familiar with—**PepsiCo, Inc.** We have chosen the financial statements of PepsiCo because they are a good example from the real world. An appendix to this textbook contains the statements in their entirety, and a copy of the PepsiCo, Inc. 2003 Annual Report accompanies this text.

PepsiCo manufactures Pepsi-Cola, the number two soft drink beverage in the world. PepsiCo also manufactures the number one bottled water (Aquafina), the number one sports drink (Gatorade), the number one ready-to-drink tea (Lipton), and the number one ready-to-drink coffee (Frappuccino). In addition, PepsiCo is the largest manufacturer of snack foods in the world. Its Frito-Lay chips dominate the U.S. market with 59% of all snack-chip sales and the world market with over 32%. In all, PepsiCo ranks among the world's largest packaged goods and beverage companies, with over $25 billion in sales, $23 billion in assets, and 140,000 employees. PepsiCo is not only large; it is also quite profitable, ranking twenty-eighth among all U.S. companies, with $3.3 billion in net income.

www.pepsico.com

Chapter-opening vignettes end with the Internet addresses of the companies cited in the story to help you connect with these real businesses and explore them further.

THE NAVIGATOR

STUDY OBJECTIVES

After studying this chapter, you should be able to:

Study Objectives give you a framework for learning the specific concepts covered in the chapter.

1. Explain what accounting is.
2. Identify the users and uses of accounting.
3. Understand why ethics is a fundamental business concept.
4. Explain the meaning of generally accepted accounting principles and the cost principle.
5. Explain the meaning of the monetary unit assumption and the economic entity assumption.
6. State the basic accounting equation, and explain the meaning of assets, liabilities, and stockholders' equity.
7. Analyze the effects of business transactions on the basic accounting equation.
8. Understand what the four financial statements are and how they are prepared.

THE NAVIGATOR

PREVIEW OF CHAPTER 1

The opening story about **PepsiCo, Inc.** highlights the importance of having good financial information to make effective business decisions. Whatever one's pursuits or occupation, the need for financial information is inescapable. You cannot earn a living, spend money, buy on credit, make an investment, or pay taxes without receiving, using, or dispensing financial information. Good decision making depends on good information.

The purpose of this chapter is to show you that accounting is the system used to provide useful financial information. The content and organization of Chapter 1 are as follows.

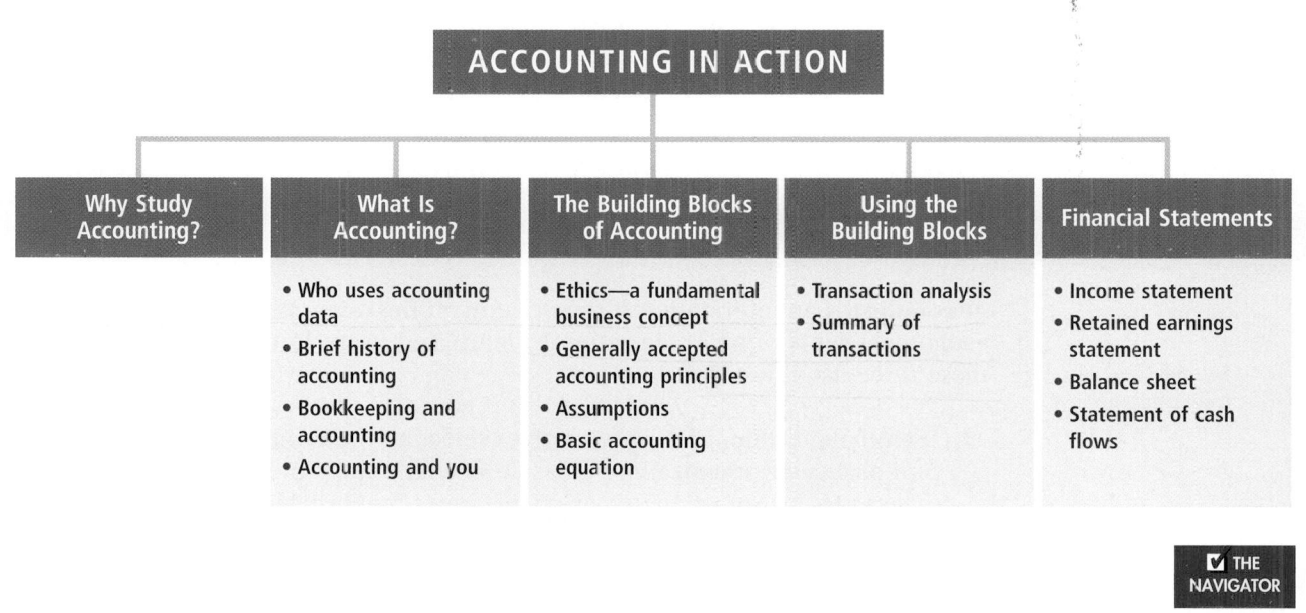

ACCOUNTING IN ACTION

- **Why Study Accounting?**
- **What Is Accounting?**
  - Who uses accounting data
  - Brief history of accounting
  - Bookkeeping and accounting
  - Accounting and you
- **The Building Blocks of Accounting**
  - Ethics—a fundamental business concept
  - Generally accepted accounting principles
  - Assumptions
  - Basic accounting equation
- **Using the Building Blocks**
  - Transaction analysis
  - Summary of transactions
- **Financial Statements**
  - Income statement
  - Retained earnings statement
  - Balance sheet
  - Statement of cash flows

☑ THE NAVIGATOR

*The **Preview** describes and outlines the major topics and subtopics you will see in the chapter.*

Why Study Accounting?

Accounting Matters!

As indicated in the Feature Story, accounting scandals and corporate misdeeds made headlines on a weekly basis for over two years. **WorldCom**'s $3.8 billion restatement of inflated earnings contributed to losses to shareholders of $179.3 billion and to job losses of 17,000. **Enron**'s variety of schemes that inflated income by $586 million, leading to financial restatements and bankruptcy, caused investor losses of $66.4 billion and job losses of 6,100. **Xerox Corp.**, using "accounting tricks" to fool investors, restated five years of earnings to reclassify more than $6 billion in revenue.

Numerous proposals to improve business practices and accounting oversights have come from federal agencies and regulators, the investment community, and the accounting profession. As a consequence, new laws have been passed to legislate business behavior as well as accounting and auditing practices. The Sarbanes-Oxley Act, signed into law in July of 2002, increases the resources for the government to combat fraud and to curb poor reporting practices, and it introduces sweeping changes to the structure of the accounting and auditing professions.

One thing is very evident from these recent embarrassing, illegal, or unethical business events: **Accounting is important**. **Good accounting is essential** to sound business and investing decisions. **Bad accounting cannot be tolerated**. At the slightest hint of a company's accounting improprieties, investors sell their stock and batter its stock price.

Recent events show that **accounting matters** and prove the worth of studying, understanding, and using the accounting process and accounting information. This textbook is your introduction to accounting as a valuable tool of business record keeping, communication, and analysis. Make the most of this course—it will serve you for a lifetime in ways you cannot now imagine.

What Is Accounting?

STUDY OBJECTIVE 1

Explain what accounting is.

Accounting is an information system that **identifies**, **records**, and **communicates** the economic events of an organization to interested users. Let's take a closer look at these three activities.

__Essential terms__ are printed in blue when they first appear, and are defined in the end-of-chapter glossary.

1. **Identifying** economic events involves selecting the **economic activities relevant to a particular organization**. The sale of snack chips by **PepsiCo**, the providing of services by **Sprint**, the payment of wages by **Ford Motor Company**, and the collection of ticket and broadcast money and the payment of expenses by major league sports teams are examples of economic events.
2. Once identified, economic events are **recorded** to provide a history of the organization's financial activities. Recording consists of keeping a **systematic**, **chronological diary of events**, measured in dollars and cents. In recording, economic events are also classified and summarized.
3. The identifying and recording activities are of little use unless the information is **communicated** to interested users. Financial information is communicated through **accounting reports**, the most common of which are called **financial statements**. To make the reported financial information meaningful, accountants report the recorded data in a standardized way. Information resulting from similar transactions is accumulated and totaled. For example, all sales transactions of **PepsiCo** are accumulated over a certain period of time and reported as one amount in the company's financial statements. Such data are said to be reported **in the aggregate**. By presenting the recorded data in the aggregate, the accounting process simplifies a multitude of transactions and makes a series of activities understandable and meaningful.

__References__ throughout the chapter tie the accounting concepts you are learning to the story that opened the chapter.

A vital element in communicating economic events is the accountant's ability to **analyze** and **interpret** the reported information. Analysis involves the use of ratios, percentages, graphs, and charts to highlight significant financial trends and relationships. Interpretation involves **explaining the uses**, **meaning**, **and limitations of reported data**. Appendix A of this textbook illustrates the financial statements and accompanying notes and graphs from **PepsiCo, Inc.**; Appendix B illustrates the financial statements of **The Coca-Cola Company**. We refer to these statements at various places throughout the text. At this point, they probably strike you as complex and confusing. By the end of this course, you'll be surprised at your ability to understand and interpret them.

The accounting process may be summarized as shown in Illustration 1-1.

Illustration 1-1
Accounting process

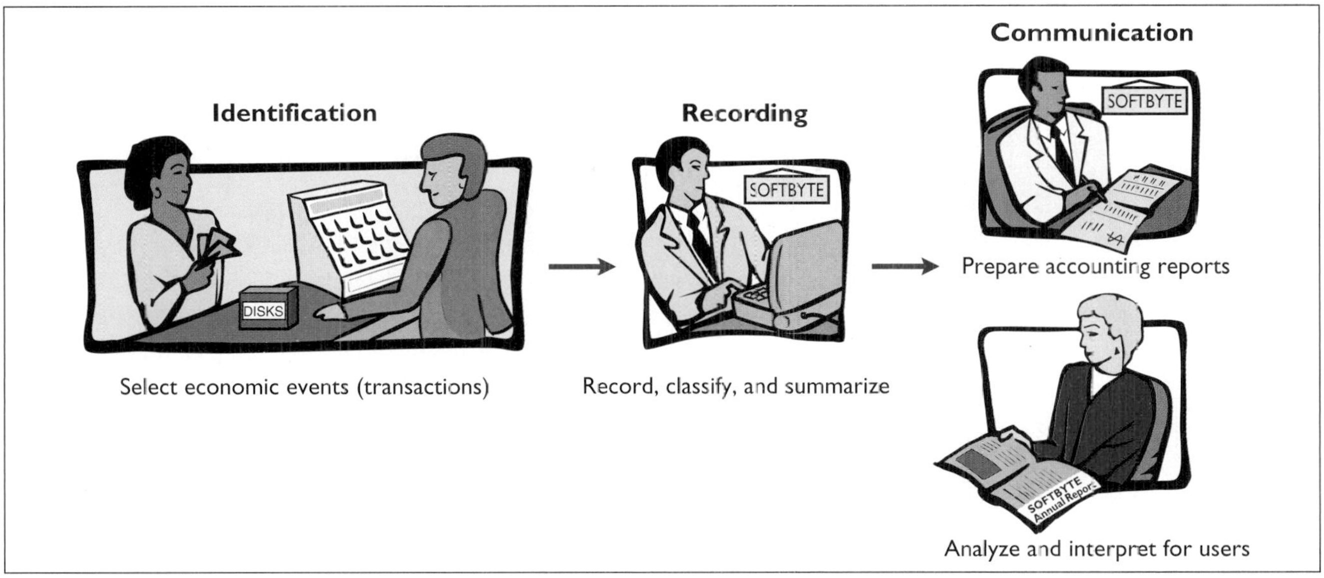

Accounting should consider the needs of the users of financial information. Therefore, you should know who these users are and something about their needs for information.

Who Uses Accounting Data?

Because it communicates financial information, accounting is often called "the language of business." The information that a user of financial information needs depends upon the kinds of decisions the user makes. The differences in the decisions divide the users of financial information into two broad groups: internal users and external users.

STUDY OBJECTIVE 2

Identify the users and uses of accounting.

Internal Users

Internal users of accounting information are managers who plan, organize, and run a business. These include **marketing managers, production supervisors, finance directors, and company officers**. In running a business, managers must answer many important questions, as shown in Illustration 1-2 (page 6).

To answer these and other questions, users need detailed information on a timely basis. For internal users, accounting provides **internal reports**. Examples are financial comparisons of operating alternatives, projections of income from new sales campaigns, and forecasts of cash needs for the next year. In addition, summarized financial information is presented in the form of financial statements.

Helpful Hints *help clarify concepts or items being discussed.*

HELPFUL HINT

The IRS requires businesses to retain records that can be audited. Also, the Foreign Corrupt Practices Act requires public companies to keep records.

External Users

There are several types of **external users** of accounting information. **Investors** (owners) use accounting information to make decisions to buy, hold, or sell stock. **Creditors** such as suppliers and bankers use accounting information to evaluate the risks of granting credit or lending money. Some questions that may be asked by investors and creditors about a company are shown in Illustration 1-3 (page 6).

The information needs and questions of other external users vary considerably. **Taxing authorities**, such as the Internal Revenue Service, want to know whether the

Illustration 1-2
Questions asked by internal users

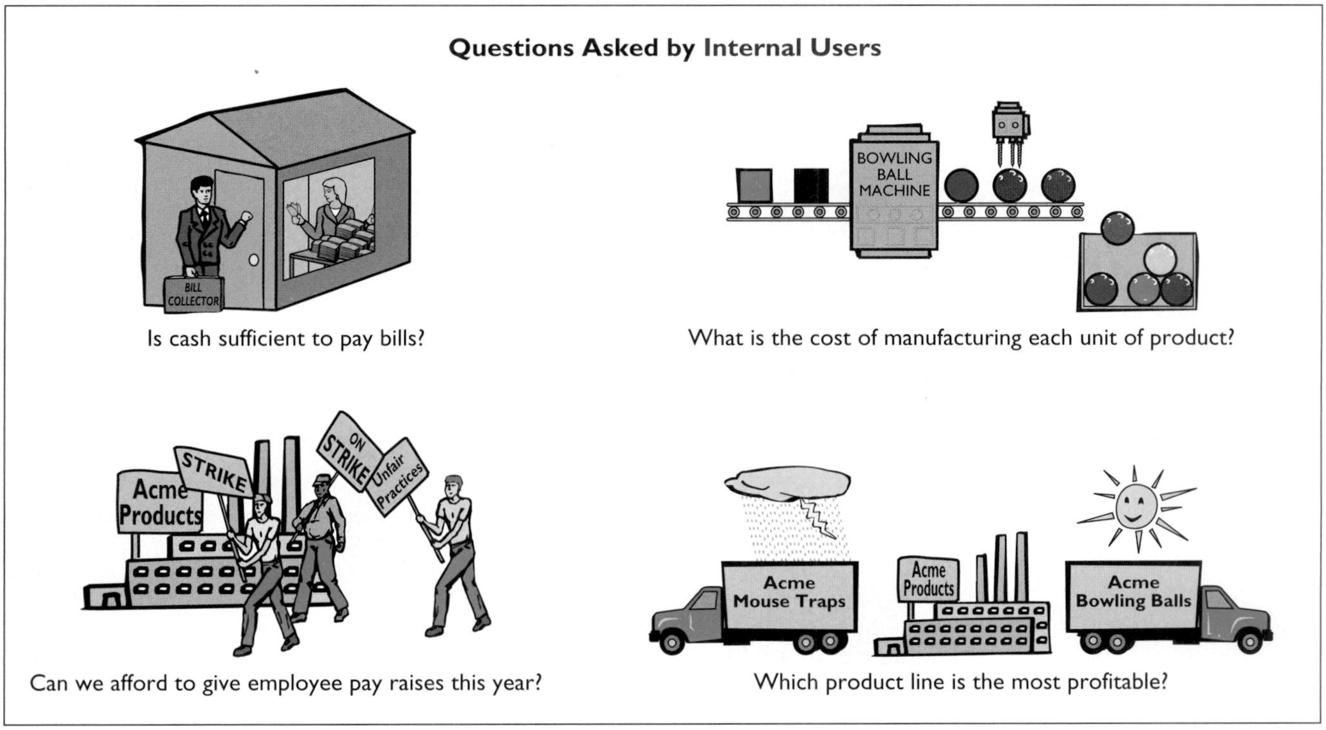

Illustration 1-3
Questions asked by external users

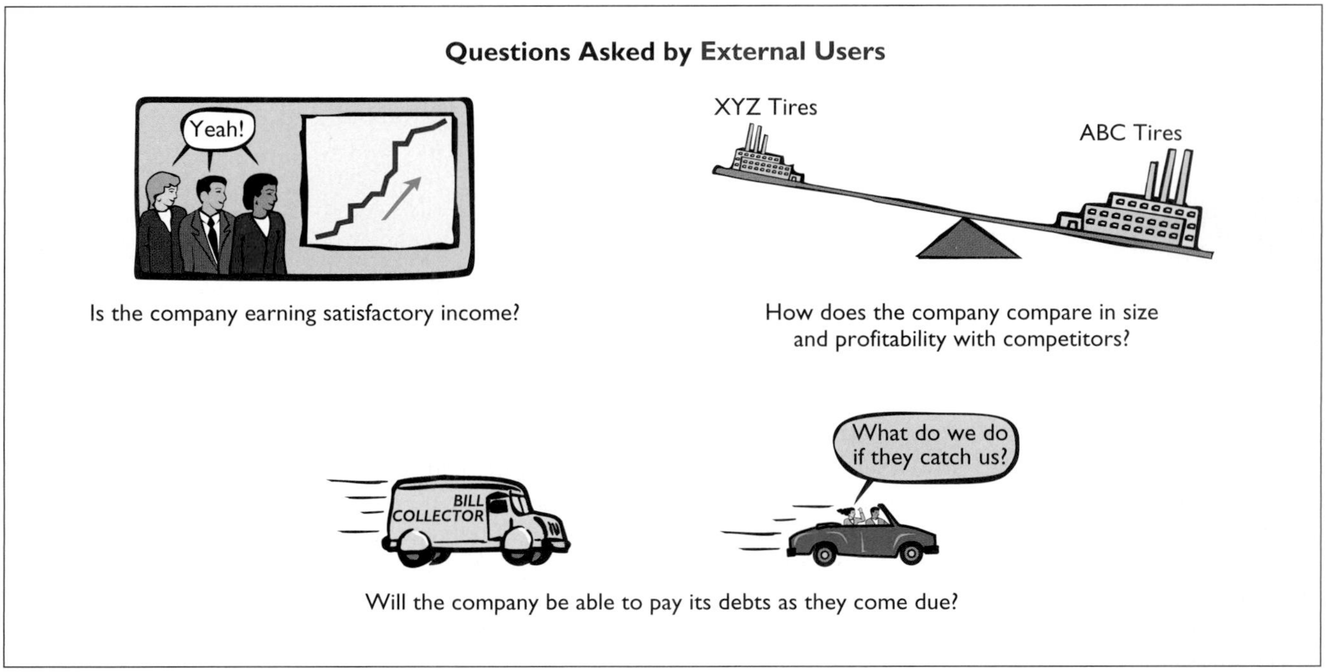

company complies with the tax laws. **Regulatory agencies**, such as the Securities and Exchange Commission and the Federal Trade Commission, want to know whether the company is operating within prescribed rules. **Customers** are interested in whether a company will continue to honor product warranties and support its product lines. **Labor unions** want to know whether the owners can pay increased wages and benefits. **Economic planners** use accounting information to forecast economic activity.

Accounting Matters! *examples illustrate important and interesting accounting situations in business. Each example is followed by a relevant question; a "guideline answer" is at the very end of the chapter.*

ACCOUNTING MATTERS! International Insight

Concern over the quality and integrity of financial reporting is not limited to the United States. Recently the Chinese Ministry of Finance reprimanded a large accounting firm for preparing fraudulent financial reports for a number of its publicly traded companies. Afterward, the state-run news agency noted that investors and analysts actually felt that the punishment of the firm was not adequate. In fact, a 2001 survey of investors in China found that less than 10% had full confidence in companies' annual reports. As a result of these concerns the Chinese Institute of Certified Public Accountants vowed to strengthen its policing of its members.

? What has been done in the United States to improve the quality and integrity of financial reporting and to build investor confidence in financial reports?

Brief History of Accounting

The **origins of accounting** are generally attributed to the work of Luca Pacioli, an Italian Renaissance mathematician. Pacioli was a close friend and tutor to Leonardo da Vinci and a contemporary of Christopher Columbus. In his 1494 text *Summa de Arithmetica, Geometria, Proportione et Proportionalite,* Pacioli described a system to ensure that financial information was recorded efficiently and accurately.

With the advent of the **industrial age** in the nineteenth century and, later, the emergence of large corporations, a separation of the owners from the managers of businesses took place. As a result, the need to report the financial status of the enterprise became more important, to ensure that managers acted in accord with owners' wishes. Also, transactions between businesses became more complex, making necessary improved approaches for reporting financial information.

Our economy has now evolved into a post-industrial age—**the information age**—in which many "products" are information services. The computer has been the driver of the information age.

Distinguishing Between Bookkeeping and Accounting

Many individuals mistakenly consider bookkeeping and accounting to be the same. This confusion is understandable because the accounting process **includes the bookkeeping function**. However, accounting also includes much more. **Bookkeeping usually involves only the recording of economic events**. It is therefore just one part of the accounting process. In total, **accounting involves the entire process of identifying, recording, and communicating economic events**.

Accounting may be further divided into financial accounting and managerial accounting. **Financial accounting** is the field of accounting that provides economic and financial information for investors, creditors, and other external users. **Managerial accounting** provides economic and financial information for managers and other internal users. Financial accounting is covered in this textbook.

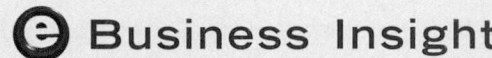

ACCOUNTING MATTERS! **e Business Insight**

E-business involves much more than simply selling goods over the Internet. According to Lou Gerstner, **IBM**'s CEO, "e-business is all about cycle time, speed, globalization, enhanced productivity, reaching new customers, and sharing knowledge across institutions for competitive advantage." Many accountants are involved in designing and implementing computer systems, including systems for e-business. In fact, in recent years e-business consulting has been one of the largest areas of growth for large accounting firms.

? What qualifies accountants to design and implement computer systems and to serve as e-business consultants?

Accounting and You

E-Business Insight examples show how e-business technology has expanded the services provided by accountants.

One question frequently asked by students of accounting is, "How will the study of accounting help me?" It should help you a great deal, because a working knowledge of accounting is desirable for virtually every field of endeavor. Some examples of how accounting is used in other careers include:

General management: Imagine running **General Motors**, a major hospital, a school, a **McDonald's** franchise, a bike shop. All general managers need to understand accounting data in order to make wise business decisions.

Marketing: A marketing specialist develops strategies to help the sales force be successful. But making a sale is meaningless unless it is a profitable sale. Marketing people must be sensitive to costs and benefits, which accounting helps them quantify and understand.

Finance: Do you want to be a banker, an investment analyst, a stock broker? These fields rely heavily on accounting. In all of them you will regularly examine and analyze financial statements. In fact, it is difficult to get a good job in a finance function without two or three courses in accounting.

Real estate: The most prevalent career in real estate is that of a broker, a person who sells real estate. Because a third party—the bank—is almost always involved in financing a real estate transaction, brokers must understand the numbers involved: Can the buyer afford to make the payments to the bank? Does the cash flow from an industrial property justify the purchase price? What are the tax benefits of the purchase?

Accounting Matters!

Accounting is useful even for occupations you might think completely unrelated. If you become a doctor, a lawyer, a social worker, a teacher, an engineer, an architect, or an entrepreneur—you name it—a working knowledge of accounting is relevant. You will need to understand financial reports in any enterprise you are associated with.

Before You Go On questions at the end of major text sections offer an opportunity to stop and reexamine the key points you have studied.

BEFORE YOU GO ON...

Review It

1. What is accounting?
2. What is meant by analysis and interpretation?
3. Who uses accounting information? Identify specific internal and external users of accounting information.

4. To whom are the origins of accounting generally attributed?
5. What is the difference between bookkeeping and accounting?
6. How can you use your accounting knowledge?

THE NAVIGATOR

The Building Blocks of Accounting

Every profession develops a body of theory consisting of principles, assumptions, and standards. Accounting is no exception. Just as a doctor follows certain standards in treating a patient's illness, an accountant follows certain standards in reporting financial information. For these standards to work, a fundamental business concept is followed—ethical behavior.

Ethics—A Fundamental Business Concept

STUDY OBJECTIVE 3

Understand why ethics is a fundamental business concept.

Wherever you make your career—whether in accounting, marketing, management, finance, government, or elsewhere—your actions will affect other people and organizations. The standards of conduct by which one's actions are judged as right or wrong, honest or dishonest, fair or not fair, are **ethics**. Imagine trying to carry on a business or invest money if you could not depend on the individuals you deal with to be honest. If managers, customers, investors, co-workers, and creditors all consistently lied, effective communication and economic activity would be impossible. Information would have no credibility.

Fortunately most individuals in business are ethical. Their actions are both legal and responsible, and they consider the organization's interests in their decision making.

To sensitize you to ethical situations and to give you practice at solving ethical dilemmas, we have included in the book three types of ethics materials: (1) marginal notes that provide helpful hints for developing ethical sensitivity, (2) Ethics in Accounting boxes that highlight ethics situations and issues, and (3) at the end of the chapter, an ethics case simulating a business situation. In the process of analyzing these ethics cases and your own ethical experiences, you should apply the three steps outlined in Illustration 1-4.

Illustration 1-4
Steps in analyzing ethics cases

Solving an Ethical Dilemma

1. Recognize an ethical situation and the ethical issues involved.
Use your personal ethics to identify ethical situations and issues. Some businesses and professional organizations provide written codes of ethics for guidance in some business situations.

2. Identify and analyze the principal elements in the situation.
Identify the *stakeholders*—persons or groups who may be harmed or benefited. Ask the question: What are the responsibilities and obligations of the parties involved?

3. Identify the alternatives, and weigh the impact of each alternative on various stakeholders.
Select the most ethical alternative, considering all the consequences. Sometimes there will be one right answer. Other situations involve more than one right solution; these situations require an evaluation of each and a selection of the best alternative.

Generally Accepted Accounting Principles

The accounting profession has developed standards that are generally accepted and universally practiced. This common set of standards is called **generally accepted accounting principles (GAAP)**. These standards indicate how to report economic events.

STUDY OBJECTIVE 4

Explain the meaning of generally accepted accounting principles and the cost principle.

Two organizations are primarily responsible for establishing generally accepted accounting principles. The first is the **Financial Accounting Standards Board (FASB)**. This private organization establishes broad reporting standards of general applicability as well as specific accounting rules. The second standards-setting group is the **Securities and Exchange Commission (SEC)**. The SEC is a governmental agency that requires companies to file financial reports following generally accepted accounting principles. In situations where no principles exist, the SEC often mandates that certain guidelines be used. In general, the FASB and the SEC work hand in hand to assure that timely and useful accounting principles are developed.

One important principle is the **cost principle**, which states that assets should be recorded at their cost. **Cost is the value exchanged at the time something is acquired.** If you buy a house today, the cost is the amount you pay for it, say $200,000. If you sell the house in two years for $230,000, the sales price is its **market value**—the value determined by the market for homes at that time. At the time of acquisition, cost and fair market value are the same. In subsequent periods, cost and fair market value may vary, **but the cost amount continues to be used in the accounting records**.

To see the importance of the cost principle, consider the following example. At one time, **Greyhound Corporation** had 128 bus stations nationwide that cost approximately $200 million. The current market value of the stations is now close to $1 billion. But, until the bus stations are actually sold, estimates of their market values are subjective—they are informed estimates. So, under the cost principle, the bus stations are recorded and reported at $200 million, not $1 billion.

ALTERNATIVE TERMINOLOGY

The cost principle is often referred to as the *historical cost principle.*

As the Greyhound example indicates, cost has an important advantage over other valuations: Cost is **reliable**. The values exchanged at the time something is acquired generally can be **objectively measured** and can be **verified**. Critics argue that cost is often not relevant and that market values provide more useful information. Despite this shortcoming, cost continues to be used in the financial statements because of its reliability.

Assumptions

STUDY OBJECTIVE 5

Explain the meaning of the monetary unit assumption and the economic entity assumption.

In developing generally accepted accounting principles, certain basic assumptions are made. These assumptions provide a foundation for the accounting process. Two main assumptions are the **monetary unit assumption** and the **economic entity assumption**.

Monetary Unit Assumption

The **monetary unit assumption** requires that only transaction data that can be expressed in terms of money be included in the accounting records. This assumption enables accounting to quantify (measure) economic events. The monetary unit assumption is vital to applying the cost principle discussed earlier. This assumption does prevent some relevant information from being included in the accounting records. For example, the health of the owner, the quality of service, and the morale of employees would not be included because they cannot be quantified in terms of money.

An important part of the monetary unit assumption is the added assumption that the unit of measure remains sufficiently constant over time. However, the assumption of a stable monetary unit has been challenged because of the significant decline in the purchasing power of the dollar. For example, what used to cost $1 in 1960 costs over $4 in 2005. In such situations, adding, subtracting, or comparing 1960 dollars with 2005 dollars is highly questionable. The profession has recognized this problem and encourages companies to disclose the effects of changing prices.

Economic Entity Assumption

An economic entity can be any organization or unit in society. It may be a business enterprise (such as **General Electric Company**), a governmental unit (the state of Ohio), a municipality (Seattle), a school district (St. Louis District 48), or a church (Southern Baptist). The **economic entity assumption** requires that the activities of the entity be kept separate and distinct from the activities of its owner and all other economic entities. To illustrate, Sally Rider, owner of Sally's Boutique, should keep her personal living costs separate from the expenses of the Boutique. **PepsiCo**, **The Coca-Cola Company**, and **Cadbury-Schweppes** are segregated into separate economic entities for accounting purposes.

We will generally discuss the economic entity assumption in relation to a business enterprise, which may be organized as a proprietorship, partnership, or corporation.

PROPRIETORSHIP. A business owned by one person is generally a **proprietorship**. The owner is often the manager/operator of the business. Small service-type businesses (plumbing companies, beauty salons, and auto repair shops), farms, and small retail stores (antique shops, clothing stores, and used-book stores) are often sole proprietorships. **Usually only a relatively small amount of money (capital) is necessary to start in business as a proprietorship. The owner (proprietor) receives any profits, suffers any losses, and is personally liable for all debts of the business.** There is no legal distinction between the business as an economic unit and the owner, but the accounting records of the business activities are kept separate from the personal records and activities of the owner.

HELPFUL HINT

Approximately 70% of U. S. companies are proprietorships; however, they account for only 6.5% of gross revenues. Corporations, on the other hand, are approximately 19% of all companies, but account for 90% of the revenues. Obviously, proprietorships, though numerous, tend to be small.

PARTNERSHIP. A business owned by two or more persons associated as partners is a **partnership**. In most respects a partnership is like a proprietorship except that more than one owner is involved. Typically a partnership agreement (written or oral) sets forth such terms as initial investment, duties of each partner, division of net income (or net loss), and settlement to be made upon death or withdrawal of a partner. Each partner generally has unlimited personal liability for the debts of the partnership. **Like a proprietorship, for accounting purposes the partnership affairs must be kept separate from the personal activities of the partners.** Partnerships are often used to organize retail and service-type businesses, including professional practices (lawyers, doctors, architects, and certified public accountants).

CORPORATION. A business organized as a separate legal entity under state corporation law and having ownership divided into transferable shares of stock is a **corporation**. The holders of the shares (stockholders) **enjoy limited liability**; that is, they are not personally liable for the debts of the corporate entity. Stockholders **may transfer all or part of their shares to other investors at any time** (i.e., sell their shares). The ease with which ownership can change adds to the attractiveness of investing in a corporation. Because ownership can be transferred without dissolving the corporation, the corporation **enjoys an unlimited life.**

Although the combined number of proprietorships and partnerships in the United States is more than four times the number of corporations, the revenue produced by corporations is nine times greater. Most of the largest enterprises in the United States—for example, **ExxonMobil**, **General Motors**, **Wal-Mart**, **Citigroup**, and **PepsiCo, Inc.**—are corporations.

STUDY OBJECTIVE 6

State the basic accounting equation, and explain the meaning of assets, liabilities, and stockholders' equity.

Basic Accounting Equation

Other essential building blocks of accounting are the categories into which economic events are classified. The two basic elements of a business are what it owns

This ***icon*** *informs you of additional resources available at the textbook's Web site.*

www.wiley.com/college/weygandt

Accounting Cycle Tutorial—Analyzing Business Transactions

and what it owes. **Assets** are the resources owned by a business. For example, PepsiCo's competitor **The Coca-Cola Company** has total assets of approximately $24.5 billion. Liabilities and stockholders' equity are the rights or claims against these resources. Thus, a company such as Coca-Cola Company that has $24.5 billion of assets also has $24.5 billion of claims against those assets. Claims of those to whom money is owed (creditors) are called **liabilities**. Claims of owners are called **stockholders' equity**. For example, Coca-Cola Company has liabilities of $12.7 billion and stockholders' equity of $11.8 billion. This relationship of assets, liabilities, and stockholders' equity can be expressed as an equation as follows.

Illustration 1-5
The basic accounting equation

Assets	=	Liabilities	+	Stockholders' Equity

This relationship is referred to as the **basic accounting equation**. Assets must equal the sum of liabilities and stockholders' equity. Because creditors' claims must be paid before ownership claims if a business is liquidated, liabilities are shown before stockholders' equity in the basic accounting equation.

The accounting equation applies to all **economic entities** regardless of size, nature of business, or form of business organization. It applies to a small proprietorship such as a corner grocery store as well as to a giant corporation such as **Kellogg** or **General Mills**. The equation provides the **underlying framework** for recording and summarizing the economic events of a business enterprise.

Let's look in more detail at the categories in the basic accounting equation.

Assets

Cash
Supplies
Equipment

As noted above, **assets** are resources owned by a business. They are used in carrying out such activities as production, consumption, and exchange. The common characteristic possessed by all assets is the capacity to provide future services or benefits. In a business enterprise, that service potential or future economic benefit eventually results in cash inflows (receipts) to the enterprise.

For example, the enterprise Campus Pizza owns a delivery truck that provides economic benefits from its use in delivering pizzas. Other assets of Campus Pizza are tables, chairs, jukebox, cash register, oven, mugs and silverware, and, of course, cash.

Liabilities

Accts. Pay.
Notes Pay. (Long-Term)
Wages Pay.
Taxes Pay.

Liabilities are claims against assets. That is, **liabilities are existing debts and obligations**. For example, businesses of all sizes usually borrow money and purchase merchandise on credit. Campus Pizza, for instance, purchases cheese, sausage, flour, and beverages on credit from suppliers. These obligations are called **accounts payable**. Campus Pizza also has a **note payable** to First National Bank for the money borrowed to purchase the delivery truck. Campus Pizza may also have **wages payable** to employees and **sales and real estate taxes payable** to the local government. All of these persons or entities to whom Campus Pizza owes money are its **creditors**.

Most claims of creditors attach to the entity's **total** assets rather than to the specific assets provided by the creditor. Creditors may legally force the liquidation of a business that does not pay its debts. In that case, the law requires that creditor claims be paid before ownership claims.

Stockholders' Equity

The ownership claim on total assets is known as **stockholders' equity**. It is equal to total assets minus total liabilities. Here is why: The assets of a business are supplied or claimed by either creditors or stockholders. To determine what belongs to stockholders, we therefore subtract creditors' claims—the liabilities—from assets. The remainder—stockholders' equity—is the stockholders' claim on the assets of the business. It is often referred to as **residual equity** (that is, the equity "left over" after creditors' claims are satisfied). The stockholders' equity section of a corporation's balance sheet consists of (1) paid-in (contributed) capital and (2) retained earnings (earned capital).

HELPFUL HINT

In some places accountants use the term *owner's equity* and in others *owners' equity*. *Owner's* refers to one owner (the case with a sole proprietorship), and *owners'* refers to multiple owners (the case with partnerships). The term *stockholders' equity* refers to ownership in corporations.

PAID-IN CAPITAL. **Paid-in capital** is the term used to describe the total amount paid in by stockholders. The principal source of paid-in capital is the investment of cash and other assets in the corporation by stockholders in exchange for capital stock. Corporations may issue several classes of stock, but the stock representing ownership interest is common stock.

RETAINED EARNINGS. The **retained earnings** section of the balance sheet is determined by three items: revenues, expenses, and dividends.

Revenues. **Revenues are the gross increases in stockholders' equity resulting from business activities entered into for the purpose of earning income.** Generally, revenues result from the sale of merchandise, the performance of services, the rental of property, and the lending of money.

Revenues usually result in an increase in an asset. They may arise from different sources and are identified by various names depending on the nature of the business. Campus Pizza, for instance, has two categories of sales revenues—pizza sales and beverage sales. Other titles for and sources of revenue common to many businesses are: sales, fees, services, commissions, interest, dividends, royalties, and rent.

HELPFUL HINT

The effect of revenues is positive—an increase in stockholders' equity coupled with an increase in assets or a decrease in liabilities.

Expenses. **Expenses are the decreases in stockholders' equity that result from operating the business.** They are the cost of assets consumed or services used in the process of earning revenue. Expenses represent actual or expected cash outflows (payments). Like revenues, expenses take many forms and are identified by various names depending on the type of asset consumed or service used. For example, Campus Pizza recognizes the following types of expenses: cost of ingredients (meat, flour, cheese, tomato paste, mushrooms, etc.); cost of beverages; wages expense; utilities expense (electric, gas, and water expense); telephone expense; delivery expense (gasoline, repairs, licenses, etc.); supplies expense (napkins, detergents, aprons, etc.); rent expense; interest expense; and property tax expense. When revenues exceed expenses, **net income** results. When expenses exceed revenues, a **net loss** results.

HELPFUL HINT

The effect of expenses is negative—a decrease in stockholders' equity coupled with a decrease in assets or an increase in liabilities.

Dividends. When a company is successful, it generates net income. **Net income** represents an increase in net assets which are then available to distribute to stockholders. The distribution of cash or other assets to stockholders is called a **dividend**. Dividends reduce retained earnings. However, dividends are not an expense of a corporation. A corporation first determines its revenues and expenses and then computes net income or net loss. At this point, a corporation may decide to distribute a dividend.

In summary, the principal sources (increases) of stockholders' equity are (1) investments by stockholders and (2) revenues from business' operations. In contrast, reductions (decreases) in stockholders' equity are a result of (1) expenses and (2) dividends. These relationships are shown in Illustration 1-6 on the next page.

Illustration 1-6
Increases and decreases in stockholders' equity

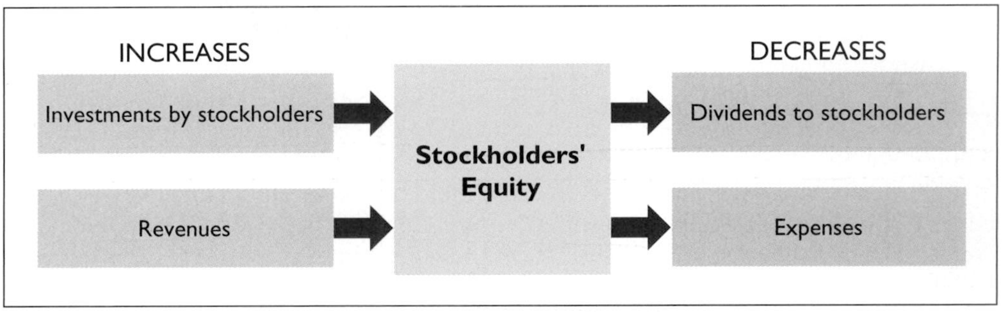

__Review It__ questions marked with this icon require that you use PepsiCo's Annual Report.

Sometimes __Review It__ questions stand alone; other times they are accompanied by practice exercises.
The __Do It__ exercises, like the one here, ask you to put newly acquired knowledge to work. They outline the __Action Plan__ necessary to complete the exercise and show a __Solution__.

BEFORE YOU GO ON...

Review It

1. Why is ethics a fundamental business concept?
2. What are generally accepted accounting principles? Give an example.
3. Explain the monetary unit and the economic entity assumptions.
4. The accounting equation is: Assets = Liabilities + Stockholders' Equity. Replacing the words in that equation with dollar amounts, what is **PepsiCo's** accounting equation at December 27, 2003? (The answer to this question is provided on page 44.)
5. What are assets, liabilities, and stockholders' equity?

Do It

Classify the following items as issuance of stock (I), dividends (D), revenues (R), or expenses (E). Then indicate whether the following items increase or decrease stockholders' equity: (1) rent expense, (2) service revenue, (3) dividends, and (4) salaries expense.

ACTION PLAN

- Review the rules for changes in stockholders' equity: Investments and revenues increase stockholders' equity. Expenses and dividends decrease stockholders' equity.
- Understand the sources of revenue: the sale of merchandise, performance of services, rental of property, and lending of money.
- Understand what causes expenses: the consumption of assets or services.
- Recognize that dividends are distributions of cash or other assets to stockholders.

SOLUTION

1. Rent expense is classified as an expense (E); it decreases stockholders' equity.
2. Service revenue is classified as revenue (R); it increases stockholders' equity.
3. Dividends is classified as dividends (D); it decreases stockholders' equity.
4. Salaries expense is classified as an expense (E); it decreases stockholders' equity.

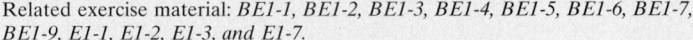

Related exercise material: *BE1-1, BE1-2, BE1-3, BE1-4, BE1-5, BE1-6, BE1-7, BE1-9, E1-1, E1-2, E1-3, and E1-7.*

THE NAVIGATOR

Using the Building Blocks

STUDY OBJECTIVE 7

Analyze the effects of business transactions on the basic accounting equation.

Transactions (often referred to as business transactions) are the economic events of an enterprise that are recorded. Transactions may be identified as external or internal. **External transactions involve economic events between the company and some outside enterprise.** For example, Campus Pizza's purchase of cooking equipment from a supplier, payment of monthly rent to the landlord, and sale of pizzas to customers are external transactions. **Internal transactions are economic events that occur entirely within one company.** The use of cooking and cleaning supplies illustrates internal transactions for Campus Pizza.

A company may carry on many activities that do not in themselves represent business transactions. Hiring employees, answering the telephone, talking with customers, and placing orders for merchandise are examples. Some of these activities, however, may lead to business transactions: Employees will earn wages, and merchandise will be delivered by suppliers. Each event must be analyzed to find out if it has an effect on the components of the basic accounting equation. If it does, it will be recorded in the accounting process. Illustration 1-7 demonstrates the transaction identification process.

Illustration 1-7
Transaction identification process

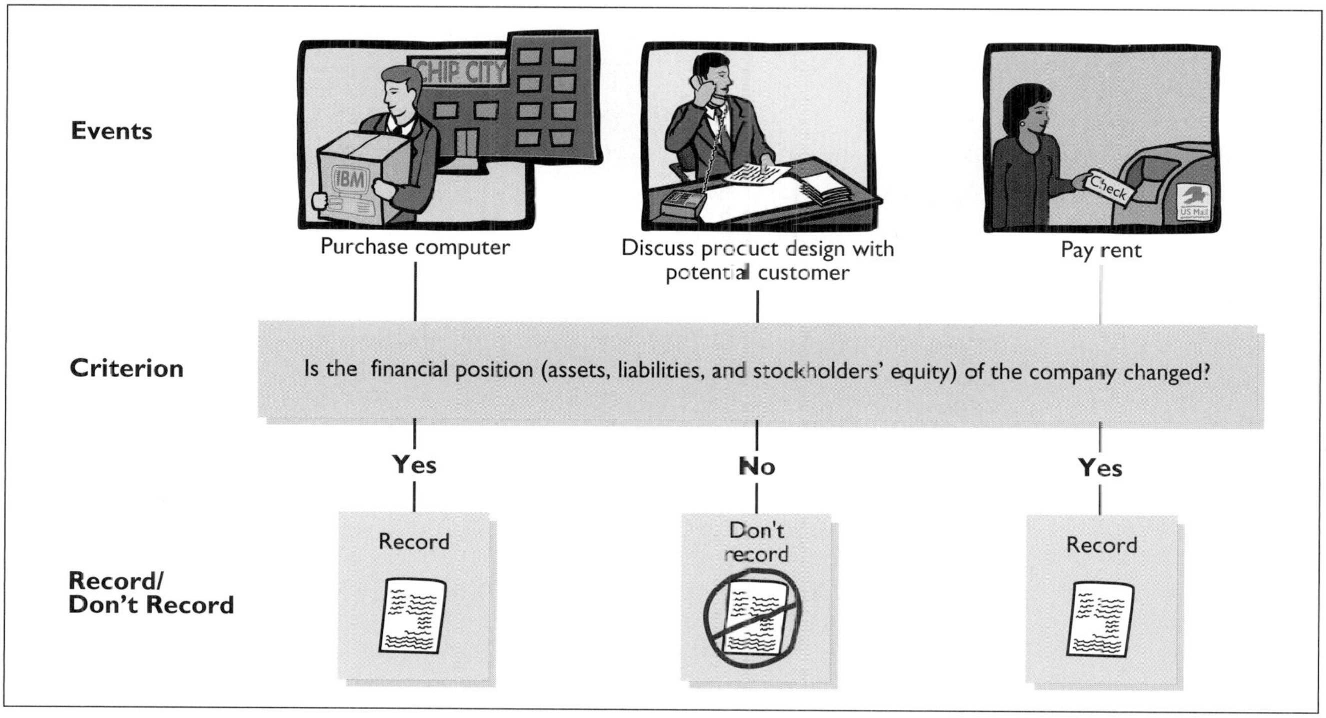

The equality of the basic equation must be preserved. Therefore, each transaction must have a dual effect on the equation. For example, if an asset is increased, there must be a corresponding:

1. Decrease in another asset, or
2. Increase in a specific liability, or
3. Increase in stockholders' equity.

It follows that two or more items could be affected when an asset is increased. For example, as one asset is increased $10,000, another asset could decrease $6,000 and a specific liability could increase $4,000. Any change in a liability or ownership claim is subject to similar analysis.

Transaction Analysis

The following examples are business transactions for a new computer programming business during its first month of operations. You will want to study these transactions until you are sure you understand them. They are not difficult, but they are important to your success in this course. The ability to analyze transactions in terms of the basic accounting equation is essential for an understanding of accounting.

TRANSACTION (1). INVESTMENT BY STOCKHOLDERS. Ray and Barbara Neal decide to open a computer programming company that they incorporate as Softbyte, Inc. They invest $15,000 cash in the business in exchange for $15,000 of common stock. The common stock indicates the ownership interest that the Neals have in Softbyte, Inc. The transaction results in an equal increase in both assets and stockholders' equity. In this case, there is an increase in the asset Cash of $15,000, and an increase in Common Stock of $15,000.

The effect of this transaction on the basic equation is shown below. Recorded to the right of Common Stock is the reason why stockholders' equity changed, i.e., investment.

	Assets	=	**Liabilities**	+	**Stockholders' Equity**	
	Cash	=			Common Stock	
(1)	**+$15,000**	=			**+$15,000**	**Investment**

Observe that the equality of the basic equation has been maintained. Note also that the source of the increase in stockholders' equity is indicated, to make clear that the increase is an investment rather than revenue from operations. Why does this matter? Because investments by stockholders do not represent revenues; they are excluded in determining net income. Therefore, it is necessary to make clear that the increase is an investment rather than revenue from operations. Additional investments (i.e., investments made by stockholders after the corporation has been initially formed) have the same effect on stockholders' equity as the initial investment.

TRANSACTION (2). PURCHASE OF EQUIPMENT FOR CASH. Softbyte, Inc. purchases computer equipment for $7,000 cash. This transaction results in an equal increase and decrease in total assets, though the composition of assets is changed: Cash is decreased $7,000, and the asset Equipment is increased $7,000. The specific effect of this transaction and the cumulative effect of the first two transactions are:

		Assets			=	**Liabilities**	+	**Stockholders' Equity**
		Cash	+	Equipment	=			Common Stock
	Old Bal.	$15,000						$15,000
(2)		**−7,000**		**+$ 7,000**				
	New Bal.	$ 8,000	+	$ 7,000	=			$15,000
			$15,000					

Observe that total assets are still $15,000 and stockholders' equity also remains at $15,000, the amount of the original investment.

TRANSACTION (3). PURCHASE OF SUPPLIES ON CREDIT. Softbyte, Inc. purchases for $1,600 from Acme Supply Company computer paper and other supplies expected to last several months. Acme agrees to allow Softbyte to pay this bill next month, in October. This transaction is often referred to as a purchase on account or a credit purchase. Assets are increased by the transaction because of the expected future benefits of using the paper and supplies, and liabilities are increased by the amount due Acme Company. The asset Supplies is increased $1,600, and the liability Accounts Payable is increased by the same amount. The effect on the equation is:

		Assets					=	Liabilities	+	Stockholders' Equity
		Cash	+	Supplies	+	Equipment	=	Accounts Payable	+	Common Stock
	Old Bal.	$8,000				$7,000				$15,000
(3)				+$1,600				+$1,600		
	New Bal.	$8,000	+	$1,600	+	$7,000	=	$1,600	+	$15,000
				$16,600					$16,600	

Total assets are now $16,600. This total is matched by a $1,600 creditor's claim and a $15,000 stockholders' claim.

TRANSACTION (4). SERVICES RENDERED FOR CASH. Softbyte, Inc. receives $1,200 cash from customers for programming services it has provided. This transaction represents Softbyte's principal revenue-producing activity. Recall that **revenue increases stockholders' equity**. Both assets and stockholders' equity are, therefore, increased. In this transaction, Cash is increased $1,200, and Retained Earnings is increased $1,200. The new balances in the equation are:

		Assets					=	Liabilities	+	Stockholders' Equity			
		Cash	+	Supplies	+	Equipment	=	Accounts Payable	+	Common Stock	+	Retained Earnings	
	Old Bal.	$8,000		$1,600		$7,000		$1,600		$15,000			
(4)		+1,200										+$1,200	**Service Revenue**
	New Bal.	$9,200	+	$1,600	+	$7,000	=	$1,600	+	$15,000	+	$1,200	
				$17,800						$17,800			

The two sides of the equation balance at $17,800. Note that stockholders' equity is increased when revenues are earned. The source of the increase in stockholders' equity is indicated as Service Revenue. Service revenue is included in determining Softbyte, Inc's. net income.

TRANSACTION (5). PURCHASE OF ADVERTISING ON CREDIT. Softbyte, Inc. receives a bill for $250 from the *Daily News* for advertising the opening of its business but postpones payment of the bill until a later date. This transaction results in an increase in liabilities and a decrease in stockholders' equity. The specific items involved are Accounts Payable and Retained Earnings. The effect on the equation is:

		Assets					=	Liabilities	+	Stockholders' Equity			
		Cash	+	Supplies	+	Equipment	=	Accounts Payable	+	Common Stock	+	Retained Earnings	
	Old Bal.	$9,200		$1,600		$7,000		$1,600		$15,000		$1,200	
(5)								**+250**				**−250**	**Advertising Expense**
	New Bal.	$9,200	+	$1,600	+	$7,000	=	$1,850	+	$15,000	+	$ 950	
				$17,800						$17,800			

The two sides of the equation still balance at $17,800. Observe that Retained Earnings is decreased when the expense is incurred, and the specific cause of the decrease (Advertising Expense) is noted. Expenses do not have to be paid in cash at the time they are incurred. When payment is made at a later date, the liability Accounts Payable will be decreased and the asset Cash will be decreased [see Transaction (8)]. The cost of advertising is considered an expense, as opposed to an asset, because the benefits have been used. This expense is included in determining net income.

TRANSACTION (6). SERVICES RENDERED FOR CASH AND CREDIT. Softbyte, Inc. provides programming services of $3,500 for customers. Cash of $1,500 is received from customers, and the balance of $2,000 is billed to customers on account. This transaction results in an equal increase in assets and stockholders' equity. Three specific items are affected: Cash is increased $1,500; Accounts Receivable is increased $2,000; and Retained Earnings is increased $3,500. The new balances are as follows.

		Assets							=	Liabilities	+	Stockholders' Equity			
		Cash	+	Accounts Receivable	+	Supplies	+	Equipment	=	Accounts Payable	+	Common Stock	+	Retained Earnings	
	Old Bal.	$ 9,200				$1,600		$7,000		$1,850		$15,000		$ 950	
(6)		**+1,500**		**+$2,000**										**+3,500**	**Service Revenue**
	New Bal.	$10,700	+	$2,000	+	$1,600	+	$7,000	=	$1,850	+	$15,000	+	$4,450	
				$21,300								$21,300			

Why increase Retained Earnings by $3,500 when only $1,500 has been collected? Because the inflow of assets resulting from the earning of revenues does not have to be in the form of cash. Remember that stockholders' equity is increased when revenues are earned; in Softbyte's case revenues are earned when the service is provided. When collections on account are received at a later date, Cash will be increased and Accounts Receivable will be decreased [see Transaction (9)].

TRANSACTION (7). PAYMENT OF EXPENSES. Expenses paid in cash for September are store rent $600, salaries of employees $900, and utilities $200. These payments result in an equal decrease in assets and stockholders' equity. Cash is decreased $1,700 and Retained Earnings is decreased by the same amount. The effect of these payments on the equation is:

	Assets				=	Liabilities +	Stockholders' Equity		
	Cash +	Accounts Receivable	+ Supplies +	Equipment =		Accounts Payable +	Common Stock +	Retained Earnings	
Old Bal.	$10,700	$2,000	$1,600	$7,000		$1,850	$15,000	$4,450	
(7)	**−1,700**							**−600**	**Rent Expense**
								−900	**Salaries Expense**
								−200	**Utilities Expense**
New Bal.	$ 9,000 +	$2,000	+ $1,600 +	$7,000	=	$1,850	+ $15,000 +	$2,750	
		$19,600					$19,600		

The two sides of the equation now balance at $19,600. Three lines are required in the analysis to indicate the different types of expenses that have been incurred.

TRANSACTION (8). PAYMENT OF ACCOUNTS PAYABLE. Softbyte, Inc. pays its *Daily News* advertising bill of $250 in cash. Remember that the bill was previously recorded [in Transaction (5)] as an increase in Accounts Payable and a decrease in Retained Earnings. Thus, this payment "on account" decreases the asset Cash by $250 and also decreases the liability Accounts Payable by $250. The effect of this transaction on the equation is:

	Assets				=	Liabilities +	Stockholders' Equity	
	Cash +	Accounts Receivable	+ Supplies	+ Equipment	=	Accounts Payable +	Common Stock +	Retained Earnings
Old Bal.	$9,000	$2,000	$1,600	$7,000		$1,850	$15,000	$2,750
(8)	**−250**					**−250**		
New Bal.	$8,750 +	$2,000	+ $1,600 +	$7,000	=	$1,600 +	$15,000 +	$2,750
		$19,350					$19,350	

Observe that the payment of a liability related to an expense that has previously been incurred does not affect stockholders' equity. The expense was recorded in Transaction (5) and should not be recorded again. Neither Common Stock nor Retained Earnings changes as a result of this transaction.

TRANSACTION (9). RECEIPT OF CASH ON ACCOUNT. The sum of $600 in cash is received from customers who have previously been billed for services [in Transaction (6)]. This transaction does not change total assets, but it changes the composition of those assets. Cash is increased $600 and Accounts Receivable is decreased $600. The new balances are:

	Assets				=	Liabilities +	Stockholders' Equity	
	Cash +	Accounts Receivable	+ Supplies	+ Equipment	=	Accounts Payable +	Common Stock +	Retained Earnings
Old Bal.	$8,750	$2,000	$1,600	$7,000		$1,600	$15,000	$2,750
(9)	**+600**	**−600**						
New Bal.	$9,350 +	$1,400	+ $1,600 +	$7,000	=	$1,600 +	$15,000 +	$2,750
		$19,350					$19,350	

Note that a collection on account for services previously billed and recorded does not affect stockholders' equity. Revenue was already recorded in Transaction (6) and should not be recorded again.

TRANSACTION (10). DIVIDENDS. The corporation pays a dividend of $1,300 in cash to Ray and Barbara Neal, the stockholders of Softbyte, Inc. This transaction results in an equal decrease in assets and stockholders' equity. Both Cash and Retained Earnings are decreased $1,300, as shown below.

	Assets				=	Liabilities +	Stockholders' Equity		
	Cash +	Accounts Receivable +	Supplies +	Equipment	=	Accounts Payable +	Common Stock +	Retained Earnings	
Old Bal.	$9,350	$1,400	$1,600	$7,000		$1,600	$15,000	$2,750	
(10)	**−1,300**							**−1,300**	**Dividends**
New Bal.	$8,050 +	$1,400 +	$1,600 +	$7,000	=	$1,600 +	$15,000 +	$1,450	
	$18,050					$18,050			

Note that the dividend reduces retained earnings, which is part of stockholders' equity. Dividends are not expenses. Like stockholders' investments, dividends are excluded in determining net income.

Summary of Transactions

The transactions of Softbyte, Inc. are summarized in Illustration 1-8. The transaction number, the specific effects of the transaction, and the balances after each

Illustration 1-8
Tabular summary of Softbyte, Inc. transactions

	Assets				=	Liabilities +	Stockholders' Equity		
Transaction	Cash +	Accounts Receivable +	Supplies +	Equipment	=	Accounts Payable +	Common Stock +	Retained Earnings	
(1)	+$15,000				=		+ $15,000		**Investment**
(2)	−7,000			+$7,000					
	8,000		+	7,000	=		15,000		
(3)			+$1,600			+$1,600			
	8,000		+ 1,600 +	7,000	=	1,600 +	15,000		
(4)	+1,200							+1,200	**Service Revenue**
	9,200		+ 1,600 +	7,000	=	1,600 +	15,000 +	1,200	
(5)						+250		−250	**Advert. Expense**
	9,200		+ 1,600 +	7,000	=	1,850 +	15,000 +	950	
(6)	+1,500	+$2,000						+3,500	**Service Revenue**
	10,700 +	2,000 +	1,600 +	7,000	=	1,850 +	15,000 +	4,450	
(7)	−1,700							−600	**Rent Expense**
								−900	**Salaries Expense**
								−200	**Utilities Expense**
	9,000 +	2,000 +	1,600 +	7,000	=	1,850 +	15,000 +	2,750	
(8)	−250					−250			
	8,750 +	2,000 +	1,600 +	7,000	=	1,600 +	15,000 +	2,750	
(9)	+600	−600							
	9,350 +	1,400 +	1,600 +	7,000	=	1,600 +	15,000 +	2,750	
(10)	−1,300							−1,300	**Dividends**
	$ 8,050 +	$1,400 +	$1,600 +	$7,000	=	$1,600 +	$15,000 +	$1,450	
	$18,050					$18,050			

transaction are indicated. The illustration demonstrates a number of significant facts:

1. Each transaction must be analyzed in terms of its effect on:
   (a) the three components of the basic accounting equation.
   (b) specific types (kinds) of items within each component.
2. The two sides of the equation must always be equal.
3. The causes of each change in the stockholders' claim on assets must be indicated in the Common Stock and Retained Earnings columns.

There! You made it through transaction analysis. If you feel a bit shaky on any of the transactions, it might be a good idea at this point to get up, take a short break, and come back again for a 10- to 15-minute review of the transactions, to make sure you understand them before you go on to the next section.

BEFORE YOU GO ON...

Review It

1. What is an example of an external transaction? What is an example of an internal transaction?
2. If an asset increases, what are the three possible effects on the basic accounting equation?

Do It

A tabular analysis of the transactions made by Roberta Mendez & Co., a certified public accounting firm, for the month of August is shown below. Each increase and decrease in stockholders' equity is explained.

	Assets			=	Liabilities	+	Stockholders' Equity			
	Cash	+	Office Equipment	=	Accounts Payable	+	Common Stock	+	Retained Earnings	
1.	+25,000						+25,000			Investment
2.			+7,000		+7,000					
3.	+8,000								+8,000	Service Revenue
4.	−850								−850	Rent Expense

Describe each transaction that occurred for the month.

ACTION PLAN

- Analyze the tabular analysis to determine the nature and effect of each transaction.
- Keep the accounting equation always in balance.
- Remember that a change in an asset will require a change in another asset, a liability, or in stockholders' equity.

SOLUTION

1. Stockholders purchased additional shares of stock for $25,000 cash.
2. The company purchased $7,000 of office equipment on credit.
3. The company received $8,000 of cash in exchange for services performed.
4. The company paid $850 for this month's rent.

Related exercise material: *BE1-4, BE1-5, BE1-6, BE1-7, E1-2, E1-3, E1-4, E1-6, and E1-7.*

THE NAVIGATOR

Financial Statements

STUDY OBJECTIVE 8

Understand what the four financial statements are and how they are prepared.

After transactions are identified, recorded, and summarized, four financial statements are prepared from the summarized accounting data:

1. An **income statement** presents the revenues and expenses and resulting net income or net loss of a company for a specific period of time.
2. A **retained earnings statement** summarizes the changes in retained earnings for a specific period of time.
3. A **balance sheet** reports the assets, liabilities, and stockholders' equity of a business enterprise at a specific date.
4. A **statement of cash flows** summarizes information concerning the cash inflows (receipts) and outflows (payments) for a specific period of time.

HELPFUL HINT

The income statement, retained earnings statement, and statement of cash flows are all for a *period* of time, whereas the balance sheet is for a *point* in time.

Each statement provides management, stockholders, and other interested parties with relevant financial data.

The financial statements of Softbyte, Inc. and their interrelationships are shown in Illustration 1-9 (page 23). The statements are interrelated: **(1) Net income of $2,750 shown on the income statement is added to the beginning balance of retained earnings in the retained earnings statement. (2) Retained earnings of $1,450 at the end of the reporting period shown in the retained earnings statement is reported on the balance sheet. (3) Cash of $8,050 on the balance sheet is reported on the statement of cash flows.**

HELPFUL HINT

There is only one group of notes for the whole set of financial statements, rather than separate sets of notes for each financial statement.

Also, every set of financial statements is accompanied by explanatory notes and supporting schedules that are an integral part of the statements. Examples of these notes and schedules are illustrated in later chapters of this textbook.

Be sure to carefully examine the format and content of each statement. The essential features of each are briefly described in the following sections.

Income Statement

ALTERNATIVE TERMINOLOGY

The income statement is sometimes referred to as the *statement of operations, earnings statement,* or *profit and loss statement.*

The primary focus of the income statement is to report the success or profitability of the company's operations over a specific period of time. For example, Softbyte, Inc.'s income statement is dated "For the Month Ended September 30, 2006." It is prepared from the data appearing in the retained earnings column of Illustration 1-8. The heading of the statement identifies the company, the type of statement, and the time period covered by the statement.

On the income statement, revenues are listed first, followed by expenses. Finally net income (or net loss) is determined. Although practice varies, we have chosen in our illustrations and homework solutions to list expenses in order of magnitude. Alternative formats for the income statement will be considered in later chapters.

Note that investment and dividend transactions between the stockholders and the business are not included in the measurement of net income. For example, the cash dividend from Softbyte, Inc. was not regarded as a business expense, as explained earlier. This type of transaction is considered a reduction of retained earnings which causes a decrease in stockholders' equity.

Retained Earnings Statement

Softbyte, Inc.'s retained earnings statement reports the changes in retained earnings for a specific period of time. The time period is the same as that covered by the income statement ("For the Month Ended September 30, 2006"). Data for the preparation of the retained earnings statement are obtained from the retained earnings column of the tabular summary (Illustration 1-8) and from the income statement in Illustration 1-9.

Illustration 1-9
Financial statements and their interrelationships

SOFTBYTE, INC.
Income Statement
For the Month Ended September 30, 2006

Revenues		
Service revenue		$4,700
Expenses		
Salaries expense	$900	
Rent expense	600	
Advertising expense	250	
Utilities expense	200	
Total expenses		1,950
Net income		**$2,750**

SOFTBYTE, INC.
Retained Earnings Statement
For the Month Ended September 30, 2006

Retained earnings, September 1	$ 0
Add: Net income	**2,750**
	2,750
Less: Dividends	1,300
Retained earnings, September 30	**$1,450**

SOFTBYTE, INC.
Balance Sheet
September 30, 2006

Assets

Cash		**$ 8,050**
Accounts receivable		1,400
Supplies		1,600
Equipment		7,000
Total assets		$18,050

Liabilities and Stockholders' Equity

Liabilities		
Accounts payable		$ 1,600
Stockholders' equity		
Common stock	**$15,000**	
Retained earnings	**1,450**	**16,450**
Total liabilities and stockholders' equity		$18,050

SOFTBYTE, INC.
Statement of Cash Flows
For the Month Ended September 30, 2006

Cash flows from operating activities		
Cash receipts from revenues		$3,300
Cash payments for expenses		(1,950)
Net cash provided by operating activities		1,350
Cash flows from investing activities		
Purchase of equipment		(7,000)
Cash flows from financing activities		
Sale of common stock	$15,000	
Payment of cash dividends	(1,300)	13,700
Net increase in cash		8,050
Cash at the beginning of the period		0
Cash at the end of the period		**$8,050**

HELPFUL HINT

The heading of each statement identifies the company, the type of statement, and the specific date or time period covered by the statement.

HELPFUL HINT

The four financial statements are prepared in the sequence shown, for the following reasons: Net income is computed first and is needed to determine the ending balance in retained earnings. The ending balance in retained earnings is needed in preparing the balance sheet. The cash shown on the balance sheet is needed in preparing the statement of cash flows.

HELPFUL HINT

Note that final sums are double-underlined, and negative amounts are presented in parentheses.

The beginning retained earnings amount is shown on the first line of the statement. Then, net income and dividends are identified. The retained earnings ending balance is the final amount on the statement. The information provided by this statement indicates the reasons why retained earnings increased or decreased during the period. If there is a net loss, it is deducted with dividends in the retained earnings statement.

Balance Sheet

Softbyte, Inc.'s balance sheet reports the assets, liabilities, and stockholders' equity at a specific date (September 30, 2006). The balance sheet is prepared from the column headings and the month-end data shown in the last line of the tabular summary (Illustration 1-8).

Observe that the assets are listed at the top, followed by liabilities and stockholders' equity. Total assets must equal total liabilities and stockholders' equity. In the Softbyte, Inc. illustration, only one liability, accounts payable, is reported on the balance sheet. In most cases, there will be more than one liability. When two or more liabilities are involved, a customary way of listing is as follows.

Illustration 1-10
Presentation of liabilities

Liabilities	
Notes payable	$10,000
Accounts payable	63,000
Salaries payable	18,000
Total liabilities	$91,000

The balance sheet is like a snapshot of the company's financial condition at a specific moment in time (usually the month-end or year-end).

ACCOUNTING MATTERS! Business Insight

Why do companies choose the particular year-ends that they do? Not every company uses December 31 as the accounting year-end. Many companies choose to end their accounting year when inventory or operations are at a low. This is advantageous because compiling accounting information requires much time and effort by managers, so they would rather do it when they aren't as busy operating the business. Also, inventory is easier and less costly to count when it is low. Some companies whose year-ends differ from December 31 are **Delta Air Lines**, June 30; **Walt Disney Productions**, September 30; **Kmart Corp.**, January 31; and **Dunkin Donuts, Inc.**, October 31.

? What year-end would you likely use if you owned a ski resort and ski rental business? What if you owned a college bookstore? Why choose those year-ends?

Statement of Cash Flows

The primary purpose of a statement of cash flows is to provide financial information about the cash receipts and cash payments of an enterprise for a specific period of time. **The statement of cash flows reports (1) the cash effects of a company's operations during a period, (2) its investing transactions, (3) its financing transactions, (4) the net increase or decrease in cash during the period, and (5) the cash amount at the end of the period.**

Reporting the sources, uses, and net increase or decrease in cash is useful because investors, creditors, and others want to know what is happening to a company's most liquid resource. The statement of cash flows, therefore, provides answers to the following simple but important questions:

1. Where did the cash come from during the period?
2. What was the cash used for during the period?
3. What was the change in the cash balance during the period?

A statement of cash flows for Softbyte, Inc., is provided in Illustration 1-9.

As shown in the statement, cash increased $8,050 during the period: Net cash flow provided from operating activities increased cash $1,350. Cash flow from investing transactions decreased cash $7,000. And cash flow from financing transactions increased cash $13,700. At this time, you need not be concerned with how these amounts are determined. Chapter 14 will examine in detail how the statement is prepared.

HELPFUL HINT

Investing activities pertain to investments made by the company, not investments made by the stockholders.

HELPFUL HINT

The cash at the end of the period reported in the statement of cash flows equals the cash reported in the balance sheet.

BEFORE YOU GO ON...

Review It

1. What are the income statement, retained earnings statement, balance sheet, and statement of cash flows?
2. How are the financial statements interrelated?

THE NAVIGATOR

Web icons *next to end-of-chapter materials indicate that you can find additional study resources on the book's Web site.*

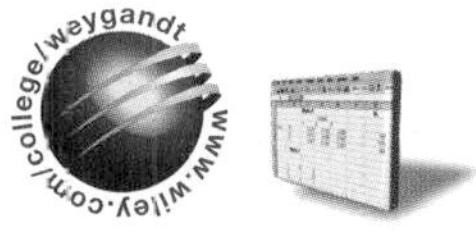

Demonstration Problems *are a final review of the chapter.* ***The Action Plan*** *(next page) gives tips about how to approach the problem, and the* ***Solution*** *(next page) demonstrates both the form and content of complete answers.*

DEMONSTRATION PROBLEM

Legal Services, Inc. was incorporated on July 1, 2006. During the first month of operations, the following transactions occurred.

1. Stockholders invested $10,000 in cash in exchange for shares of stock.
2. Paid $800 for July rent on office space.
3. Purchased office equipment on account, $3,000.
4. Provided legal services to clients for cash, $1,500 (use Service Revenue).
5. Borrowed $700 cash from a bank on a note payable.
6. Performed legal services for client on account, $2,000.
7. Paid monthly expenses: salaries $500; utilities $300; and telephone $100.

Instructions

(a) Prepare a tabular summary of the transactions.
(b) Prepare the income statement, retained earnings statement, and balance sheet at July 31 for Legal Services, Inc.

ACTION PLAN

- Remember that assets must equal liabilities and stockholders' equity after each transaction.
- Investments and revenues increase stockholders' equity.
- Dividends and expenses decrease stockholders' equity.
- The income statement shows revenues and expenses for a period of time.
- The retained earnings statement shows the changes in retained earnings for a period of time.
- The balance sheet reports assets, liabilities, and stockholders' equity at a specific date.

This would be a good time to return to the ***Student Owner's Manual*** *at the beginning of the book (or look at it for the first time if you skipped it before), to read about the various types of assignment materials that appear at the end of each chapter. Knowing the purpose of the different assignments will help you appreciate what each contributes to your accounting skills and competencies.*

SOLUTION TO DEMONSTRATION PROBLEM

(a)

	Assets			= Liabilities		+ Stockholders' Equity		
Transaction	Cash	+ Accounts Receivable	+ Equipment	= Notes Payable	+ Accounts Payable	+ Common Stock	+ Retained Earnings	
(1)	+$10,000					+$10,000		Investment
(2)	−800						−$800	Rent Expense
	9,200			=		10,000 +	−800	
(3)			+$3,000		+$3,000			
	9,200		+ 3,000 =		3,000 +	10,000 +	−800	
(4)	+1,500						+1,500	Service Revenue
	10,700		+ 3,000 =		3,000 +	10,000 +	700	
(5)	+700			+$700				
	11,400		+ 3,000 =	700 +	3,000 +	10,000 +	700	
(6)		+$2,000					+2,000	Service Revenue
	+11,400 +	2,000 +	3,000 =	700 +	3,000 +	10,000 +	2,700	
(7)	−900						−500	Salaries Expense
							−300	Utilities Expense
							−100	Telephone Expense
	$10,500 +	$2,000 +	$3,000 =	$700 +	$3,000 +	$10,000 +	$1,800	
		$15,500				$15,500		

(b)

LEGAL SERVICES, INC.
Income Statement
For the Month Ended July 31, 2006

Revenues		
Service revenue		$3,500
Expenses		
Rent expense	$800	
Salaries expense	500	
Utilities expense	300	
Telephone expense	100	
Total expenses		1,700
Net income		$1,800

LEGAL SERVICES, INC.
Retained Earnings Statement
For the Month Ended July 31, 2006

Retained earnings, July 1	$ -0-
Add: Net income	1,800
Retained earnings, July 31	$1,800

LEGAL SERVICES, INC.
Balance Sheet
July 31, 2006

Assets

Cash	$10,500
Accounts receivable	2,000
Equipment	3,000
Total assets	$15,500

Liabilities and Stockholders' Equity

Liabilities		
Notes payable		$ 700
Accounts payable		3,000
Total liabilities		3,700
Stockholders' equity		
Common stock	$10,000	
Retained earnings	1,800	11,800
Total liabilities and stockholders' equity		$15,500

THE NAVIGATOR

SUMMARY OF STUDY OBJECTIVES

1. **Explain what accounting is.** Accounting is an information system that identifies, records, and communicates the economic events of an organization to interested users.
2. **Identify the users and uses of accounting.** The major users and uses of accounting are: (a) Management uses accounting information in planning, controlling, and evaluating business operations. (b) Investors (owners) decide whether to buy, hold, or sell their financial interests on the basis of accounting data. (c) Creditors (suppliers and bankers) evaluate the risks of granting credit or lending money on the basis of accounting information. Other groups that use accounting information are taxing authorities, regulatory agencies, customers, labor unions, and economic planners.
3. **Understand why ethics is a fundamental business concept.** Ethics are the standards of conduct by which actions are judged as right or wrong. If you cannot depend on the honesty of the individuals you deal with, effective communication and economic activity would be impossible, and information would have no credibility.
4. **Explain the meaning of generally accepted accounting principles and the cost principle.** Generally accepted accounting principles are a common set of standards used by accountants. The cost principle states that assets should be recorded at their cost.
5. **Explain the meaning of the monetary unit assumption and the economic entity assumption.** The monetary unit assumption requires that only transaction data capable of being expressed in terms of money be included in the accounting records. The economic entity assumption requires that the activities of each economic entity be kept separate from the activities of its owners and other economic entities.
6. **State the basic accounting equation, and explain the meaning of assets, liabilities, and stockholders' equity.** The basic accounting equation is:

   Assets = Liabilities + Stockholders' Equity

   Assets are resources owned by a business. Liabilities are creditorship claims on total assets. Stockholders' equity is the ownership claim on total assets.
7. **Analyze the effects of business transactions on the basic accounting equation.** Each business transaction must have a dual effect on the accounting equation. For example if an individual asset is increased, there must be a corresponding (1) decrease in another asset, or (2) increase in a specific liability, or (3) increase in stockholders' equity.
8. **Understand what the four financial statements are and how they are prepared.** An income statement presents the revenues and expenses of a company for a specified period of time. A retained earnings statement summarizes the changes in retained earnings that have occurred for a specific period of time. A balance sheet reports the assets, liabilities, and stockholders' equity of a business at a specific date. A statement of cash flows summarizes information about the cash inflows (receipts) and outflows (payments) for a specific period of time.

THE NAVIGATOR

GLOSSARY

www.wiley.com/college/weygandt

Accounting The information system that identifies, records, and communicates the economic events of an organization to interested users. (p. 4).

Assets Resources owned by a business. (p. 12).

Balance sheet A financial statement that reports the assets, liabilities, and stockholders' equity at a specific date. (p. 22).

Basic accounting equation Assets = Liabilities + Stockholders' Equity. (p. 12).

Bookkeeping A part of accounting that involves only the recording of economic events. (p. 7).

Corporation A business organized as a separate legal entity under state corporation law having ownership divided into transferable shares of stock. (p. 11).

Cost principle An accounting principle that states that assets should be recorded at their cost. (p. 10).

Dividend A distribution by a corporation to its stockholders on a pro rata (equal) basis. (p. 13).

Economic entity assumption An assumption that requires that the activities of the entity be kept separate and distinct from the activities of its owners and all other economic entities. (p. 11).

Ethics The standards of conduct by which one's actions are judged as right or wrong, honest or dishonest, fair or not fair. (p. 9).

Expenses The cost of assets consumed or services used in the process of earning revenue. (p. 13).

Financial accounting The field of accounting that provides economic and financial information for investors, creditors, and other external users. (p. 7).

Financial Accounting Standards Board (FASB) A private organization that establishes generally accepted accounting principles. (p. 10).

Generally accepted accounting principles (GAAP) Common standards that indicate how to report economic events. (p. 9).

Income statement A financial statement that presents the revenues and expenses and resulting net income or net loss of a company for a specific period of time. (p. 22).

Liabilities Creditorship claims on total assets. (p. 12).

Managerial accounting The field of accounting that provides economic and financial information for managers and other internal users. (p. 7).

Monetary unit assumption An assumption stating that only transaction data that can be expressed in terms of money be included in the accounting records. (p. 10).

Net income The amount by which revenues exceed expenses. (p. 13).

Net loss The amount by which expenses exceed revenues. (p. 13).

Partnership An association of two or more persons to carry on as co-owners of a business for profit. (p. 11).

Proprietorship A business owned by one person. (p. 11).

Retained earnings statement A financial statement that summarizes the changes in retained earnings for a specific period of time. (p. 22).

Revenues The gross increase in stockholders' equity resulting from business activities entered into for the purpose of earning income. (p. 13).

Securities and Exchange Commission (SEC) A governmental agency that requires companies to file financial reports in accordance with generally accepted accounting principles. (p. 10).

Statement of cash flows A financial statement that provides information about the cash inflows (receipts) and cash outflows (payments) of an entity for a specific period of time. (p. 22).

Stockholders' equity The ownership claim on total assets of a corporation. (p. 13).

Transactions The economic events of the enterprise that are recorded by accountants. (p. 15).

APPENDIX THE ACCOUNTING PROFESSION

The Accounting Profession

www.wiley.com/college/weygandt

Careers in Accounting

STUDY OBJECTIVE 9

Identify the three major fields of the accounting profession and potential accounting careers.

What would you do if you join the accounting profession? You probably would work in one of three major fields—public accounting, private accounting, or not-for-profit accounting.

Public Accounting

In **public accounting**, you would offer expert service to the general public in much the same way that a doctor serves patients and a lawyer serves clients. A major portion of public accounting involves **auditing**. In this area, a certified public accountant (CPA) examines the financial statements of companies and expresses an opinion as to the fairness of presentation. When the presentation is fair, users consider the statements to be **reliable**. For example, **PepsiCo** investors would demand audited financial statements before extending it financing.

Taxation is another major area of public accounting. The work performed by tax specialists includes tax advice and planning, preparing tax returns, and representing clients before governmental agencies such as the Internal Revenue Service.

A third area in public accounting is **management consulting**. It ranges from the installing of basic accounting systems to helping companies determine whether they should use the space shuttle for high-tech research and development projects.

Private Accounting

Instead of working in public accounting, you might choose to be an employee of a business enterprise. In **private** (or **managerial**) **accounting**, you would be involved in one of the following activities.

1. **General accounting**—recording daily transactions and preparing financial statements and related information.
2. **Cost accounting**—determining the cost of producing specific products.
3. **Budgeting**—assisting management in quantifying goals concerning revenues, costs of goods sold, and operating expenses.
4. **Accounting information systems**—designing both manual and computerized data processing systems.
5. **Tax accounting**—preparing tax returns and doing tax planning for the company.
6. **Internal auditing**—reviewing the company's operations to see if they comply with management policies and evaluating the efficiency of operations.

You can see that within a specific company, private accountants perform as wide a variety of duties as the public accountant.

Illustration 1A-1 presents the general career paths in public and private accounting.

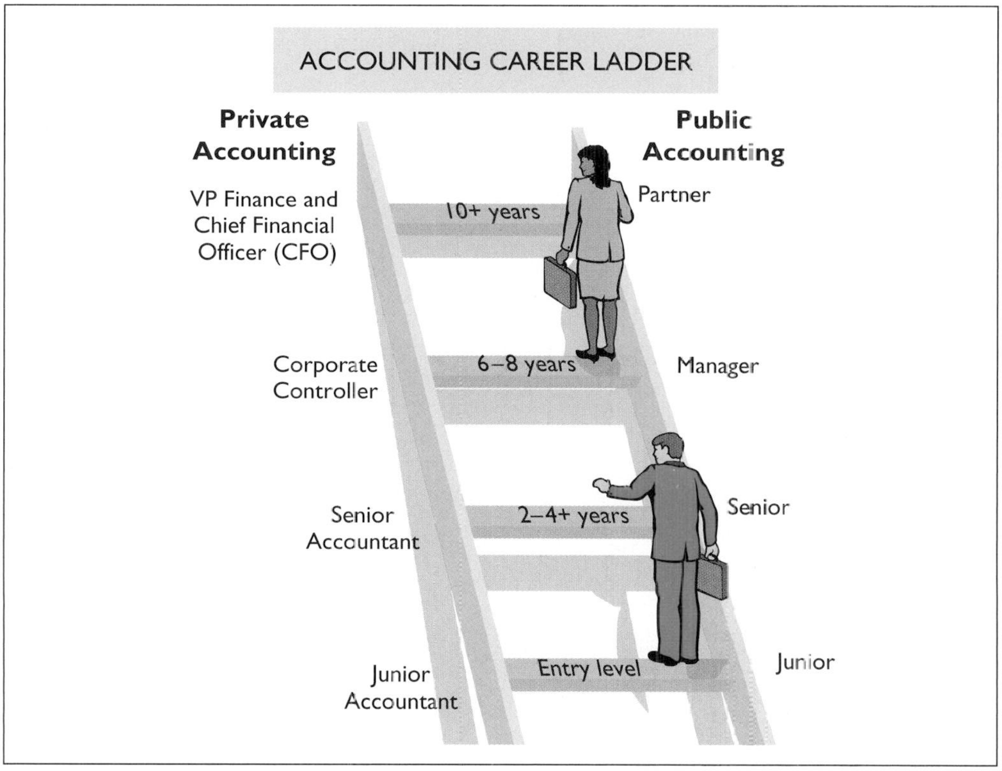

Illustration 1A-1
Career paths in public and private accounting

Not-for-Profit Accounting

Like businesses that exist to make a profit, not-for-profit organizations also need sound financial reporting and control. Donors to such organizations as the **United Way**, the **Ford Foundation**, and the **Red Cross** want information about how well the organization has met its financial objectives and whether continued support is justified. Hospitals, colleges, and universities must make decisions about allocating funds.

Another area of not-for-profit accounting is government accounting. Local, state, and federal governmental units provide financial information to legislators, citizens, employees, and creditors. At the federal level, the largest employers of accountants are the **Internal Revenue Service**, the **General Accounting Office**, the **Federal Bureau of Investigation**, and the **Securities and Exchange Commission**.

ACCOUNTING MATTERS! Business Insight

"Help Wanted: Forensic CPAs." Tom Taylor's job at the **FBI** has changed. He used to pack a .357 magnum; now he wields a No. 2 pencil and a notebook computer. Taylor, age 37, for two years an FBI agent, is a forensic accountant, somebody who sniffs through company books to ferret out white-collar crime. Demand for this service has surged in the past few years. In one recent year, a recruiter for San Diego's **Robert Half International**, a headhunting firm, had requests for more than 1,000 such "snoops."

Qualifications for forensic accountants: a CPA with FBI, IRS, or similar government experience. Interestingly, despite its macho image, the FBI has long hired mostly accountants and lawyers as agents.

? Why would the FBI and the IRS want to hire accountants?

SUMMARY OF STUDY OBJECTIVE FOR APPENDIX

9. **Identify the three major fields of the accounting profession and potential accounting careers.** The accounting profession is comprised of three major fields: public accounting, private accounting, and not-for-profit accounting. In public accounting one may pursue a career in auditing, taxation, or management consulting. In private or managerial accounting, one may pursue a career in cost accounting, budgeting, general accounting, accounting information systems, tax accounting, or internal auditing. In not-for-profit accounting one may pursue a career at hospitals, universities, and foundations, or in local, state, and federal governmental units.

GLOSSARY FOR APPENDIX

www.wiley.com/college/weygandt

Auditing The examination of financial statements by a certified public accountant in order to express an opinion as to the fairness of presentation. (p. 28).

Management consulting An area of public accounting involving financial planning and control and the development of accounting and computer systems. (p. 29).

Private (or managerial) accounting An area of accounting within a company that involves such activities as cost accounting, budgeting, and accounting information systems. (p. 29).

Public accounting An area of accounting in which the accountant offers expert service to the general public. (p. 28).

Taxation An area of public accounting involving tax advice, tax planning, and preparation of tax returns. (p. 28).

*__Note:__ All asterisked Questions relate to material in the appendix to the chapter.

SELF-STUDY QUESTIONS

Self-Study/Self-Test

Answers are at the end of the chapter.

(SO 1) **1.** Which of the following is *not* a step in the accounting process?
- **a.** identification.
- **b.** verification.
- **c.** recording.
- **d.** communication.

(SO 2) **2.** Which of the following statements about users of accounting information is *incorrect*?
- **a.** Management is an internal user.
- **b.** Taxing authorities are external users.
- **c.** Present creditors are external users.
- **d.** Regulatory authorities are internal users.

(SO 4) **3.** Generally accepted accounting principles are:
- **a.** the guidelines used to resolve ethical dilemmas.
- **b.** established by the Internal Revenue Service.
- **c.** primarily established by the Financial Accounting Standards Board and the Securities Exchange Commission.
- **d.** truths derived from the laws of nature.

(SO 4) **4.** The cost principle states that:
- **a.** assets should be initially recorded at cost and adjusted when the market value changes.
- **b.** activities of an entity be kept separate and distinct from its owner.
- **c.** assets should be recorded at their cost.
- **d.** only transaction data capable of being expressed in terms of money should be included in the accounting records.

(SO 5) **5.** Which of the following statements about basic assumptions is *incorrect*?
- **a.** Basic assumptions are the same as accounting principles.
- **b.** The economic entity assumption states that there should be a particular unit of accountability.
- **c.** The monetary unit assumption enables accounting to measure economic events.
- **d.** An important part of the monetary unit assumption is the stable monetary unit assumption.

6. Net income will result during a time period when: (SO 6)
- **a.** assets exceed liabilities.
- **b.** assets exceed revenues.
- **c.** expenses exceed revenues.
- **d.** revenues exceed expenses.

7. Performing services on account will have the following effects on the basic accounting equation: (SO 7)
- **a.** increase assets and decrease stockholders' equity.
- **b.** increase assets and increase stockholders' equity.
- **c.** increase assets and increase liabilities.
- **d.** increase liabilities and increase stockholders' equity.

8. As of December 31, 2005, Tetrick Company has assets of $3,500 and stockholders' equity of $2,000. What are the liabilities for Tetrick Company as of December 31, 2005? (SO 7)
- **a.** $1,500.
- **b.** $1,000.
- **c.** $2,500.
- **d.** $2,000.

9. On the last day of the period, Jim Otto Company buys a $700 machine on credit. This transaction will affect the: (SO 8)
- **a.** income statement only.
- **b.** balance sheet only.
- **c.** income statement and retained earnings statement only.
- **d.** income statement, retained earnings statement, and balance sheet.

10. The financial statement that reports assets, liabilities, and stockholders' equity is the: (SO 8)
- **a.** income statement.
- **b.** retained earnings statement.
- **c.** balance sheet.
- **d.** statement of cash flows.

***11.** Services provided by a public accountant include: (SO 9)
- **a.** auditing, taxation, and management consulting.
- **b.** auditing, budgeting, and management consulting.
- **c.** auditing, budgeting, and cost accounting.
- **d.** internal auditing, budgeting, and management consulting.

QUESTIONS

1. "Accounting is ingrained in our society and is vital to our economic system." Do you agree? Explain.
2. Identify and describe the steps in the accounting process.
3. (a) Who are internal users of accounting data?
   (b) How does accounting provide relevant data to these users?
4. What uses of financial accounting information are made by (a) investors and (b) creditors?
5. "Bookkeeping and accounting are the same." Do you agree? Explain.
6. Jackie Remmers Inc. purchased land for $81,000 cash on December 10, 2005. At December 31, 2006, the land's value has increased to $95,000. What amount should be reported for land on Jackie Remmers' balance sheet at December 31, 2006? Explain.
7. What is the monetary unit assumption? What impact does inflation have on the monetary unit assumption?
8. What is the economic entity assumption?
9. What are the three basic forms of business organizations for profit-oriented enterprises?

10. Teresa Speck is the owner of a successful printing shop. Recently her business has been increasing, and Teresa has been thinking about changing the organization of her business from a proprietorship to a corporation. Discuss some of the advantages Teresa would enjoy if she were to incorporate her business.

11. What is the basic accounting equation?

12. (a) Define the terms assets, liabilities, and stockholders' equity. (b) What items affect stockholders' equity?

13. Which of the following items are liabilities of Richard Westphal Company?
   (a) Cash.
   (b) Accounts payable.
   (c) Inventory.
   (d) Accounts receivable.
   (e) Supplies.
   (f) Equipment.
   (g) Salaries payable.
   (h) Service revenue.
   (i) Rent expense.

14. Can a business enter into a transaction in which only the left side of the basic accounting equation is affected? If so, give an example.

15. Are the following events recorded in the accounting records? Explain your answer in each case.
   (a) The president of a corporation dies.
   (b) Supplies are purchased on account.
   (c) An employee is fired.

16. Indicate how the following business transactions affect the basic accounting equation.
   (a) Paid cash for janitorial services.
   (b) Purchased equipment for cash.
   (c) Invested cash in the business for stock.
   (d) Paid accounts payable in full.

17. Listed below are some items found in the financial statements of Jan Way Inc. Indicate in which financial statement the following items would appear.
   (a) Advertising expense.
   (b) Equipment.
   (c) Service revenue.
   (d) Cash.
   (e) Common stock.
   (f) Wages payable.

18. In February 2005, Maggie Sharrer invested $12,000 in Gardentech, Inc. Gardentech's accountant, Jori Aloisio, recorded this receipt as an increase in cash and revenues. Is this treatment appropriate? Why or why not?

19. "A company's net income appears directly on the income statement and the retained earnings statement, and it is included indirectly in the company's balance sheet." Do you agree? Explain.

20. Rebecca Sherrick Inc. had a stockholders' equity balance of $164,000 at the beginning of the period. At the end of the accounting period, the stockholders' equity balance was $198,000.
   (a) Assuming no additional investment or distributions during the period, what is the net income for the period?
   (b) Assuming an additional investment of $8,000 but no distributions during the period, what is the net income for the period?

21. Summarized operations for the Alica Cosky Co. for the month of July are as follows.

   Revenues earned: for cash $45,000; on account $95,000.

   Expenses incurred: for cash $26,000; on account $43,000.

   Indicate for Alica Cosky Co. (a) the total revenues, (b) the total expenses, and (c) net income for the month of July.

BRIEF EXERCISES

Use basic accounting equation. (SO 6)

BE1-1 Presented below is the basic accounting equation. Determine the missing amounts.

	Assets	=	Liabilities	+	Stockholders' Equity
(a)	$90,000		$50,000		?
(b)	?		$45,000		$70,000
(c)	$94,000		?		$65,000

Use basic accounting equation. (SO 6)

BE1-2 Given the accounting equation, answer each of the following questions.

(a) The liabilities of Shumway Company are $100,000 and the stockholders' equity is $232,000. What is the amount of Shumway Company's total assets?

(b) The total assets of Becky Company are $190,000 and its stockholders' equity is $80,000. What is the amount of its total liabilities?

(c) The total assets of Norris Co. are $600,000 and its liabilities are equal to one half of its total assets. What is the amount of Norris Co.'s stockholders' equity?

Use basic accounting equation. (SO 6)

BE1-3 At the beginning of the year, Gonzales Company had total assets of $870,000 and total liabilities of $500,000. Answer the following questions.

(a) If total assets increased $150,000 during the year and total liabilities decreased $80,000, what is the amount of stockholders' equity at the end of the year?

(b) During the year, total liabilities increased $100,000 and stockholders' equity decreased $70,000. What is the amount of total assets at the end of the year?

(c) If total assets decreased $80,000 and stockholders' equity increased $120,000 during the year, what is the amount of total liabilities at the end of the year?

BE1-4 Presented below are three business transactions. On a sheet of paper, list the letters (a), (b), (c) with columns for assets, liabilities, and stockholders' equity. For each column, indicate whether the transactions increased (+), decreased (–), or had no effect (NE) on assets, liabilities, and stockholders' equity.

Determine effect of transactions on basic accounting equation. (SO 7)

(a) Purchased supplies on account.
(b) Received cash for providing a service.
(c) Paid expenses in cash.

BE1-5 Follow the same format as BE1-4 above. Determine the effect on assets, liabilities, and stockholders' equity of the following three transactions.

Determine effect of transactions on basic accounting equation. (SO 7)

(a) Invested cash in the business.
(b) Paid a cash dividend.
(c) Received cash from a customer who had previously been billed for services provided.

BE1-6 Classify each of the following items as asset (A), liability (L), revenue (R), or expense (E).

Determine effect of transactions on stockholders' equity. (SO 7)

_______**(a)** Advertising expense	_______**(e)** Cash
_______**(b)** Commission revenue	_______**(f)** Rent revenue
_______**(c)** Insurance expense	_______**(g)** Utilities expense
_______**(d)** Office equipment	_______**(h)** Accounts payable

BE1-7 Presented below are three transactions. Mark each transaction as affecting common stock (C), dividends (D), revenue (R), expense (E), or not affecting stockholders' equity (NSE).

Determine effect of transactions on basic stockholders' equity. (SO 7)

_______**(a)** Received cash for services performed.
_______**(b)** Paid cash to purchase equipment.
_______**(c)** Paid employee salaries.

BE1-8 In alphabetical order below are balance sheet items for Gomez Company at December 31, 2006. Prepare a balance sheet, following the format of Illustration 1-9.

Prepare a balance sheet. (SO 8)

Accounts payable	$85,000
Accounts receivable	$72,500
Cash	$44,000
Common stock	$31,500

BE1-9 Indicate whether each of the following items is an asset (A), liability (L), or part of stockholders' equity (SE).

Identify assets, liabilities, and stockholders' equity. (SO 6)

_______**(a)** Accounts receivable	_______**(d)** Office supplies
_______**(b)** Salaries payable	_______**(e)** Common stock
_______**(c)** Equipment	_______**(f)** Notes payable

BE1-10 Indicate whether the following items would appear on the income statement (IS), balance sheet (BS), or retained earnings statement (RE).

Determine where items appear on financial statements. (SO 8)

_______**(a)** Notes payable	_______**(d)** Cash
_______**(b)** Advertising expense	_______**(e)** Service revenue
_______**(c)** Common stock	

EXERCISES

E1-1 Robinson Cleaners has the following balance sheet items.

Classify accounts as assets, liabilities, and stockholders' equity. (SO 6)

Accounts payable	Accounts receivable
Cash	Notes payable
Cleaning equipment	Salaries payable
Cleaning supplies	Common stock

Instructions

Classify each item as an asset, liability, or stockholders' equity.

E1-2 Selected transactions for Green Acres Lawn Care Company are listed below.

Analyze the effect of transactions. (SO 6, 7)

1. Made cash investment to start business.
2. Paid monthly rent.

3. Purchased equipment on account.
4. Billed customers for services performed.
5. Paid dividends.
6. Received cash from customers billed in (4).
7. Incurred advertising expense on account.
8. Purchased additional equipment for cash.
9. Received cash from customers when service was performed.

Instructions

List the numbers of the above transactions and describe the effect of each transaction on assets, liabilities, and stockholders' equity. For example, the first answer is: (1) Increase in assets and increase in stockholders' equity.

Analyze the effect of transactions on assets, liabilities, and stockholders' equity.
(SO 6, 7)

E1-3 Rollins Computer Timeshare Company entered into the following transactions during May 2006.

1. Purchased computer terminals for $21,500 from Digital Equipment on account.
2. Paid $4,000 cash for May rent on storage space.
3. Received $15,000 cash from customers for contracts billed in April.
4. Provided computer services to Fisher Construction Company for $3,000 cash.
5. Paid Northern States Power Co. $11,000 cash for energy usage in May.
6. Stockholders invested an additional $32,000 in the business.
7. Paid Digital Equipment for the terminals purchased in (1) above.
8. Incurred advertising expense for May of $1,200 on account.

Instructions

Indicate with the appropriate letter whether each of the transactions above results in:

(a) an increase in assets and a decrease in assets.
(b) an increase in assets and an increase in stockholders' equity.
(c) an increase in assets and an increase in liabilities.
(d) a decrease in assets and a decrease in stockholders' equity.
(e) a decrease in assets and a decrease in liabilities.
(f) an increase in liabilities and a decrease in stockholders' equity.
(g) an increase in stockholders' equity and a decrease in liabilities.

Analyze transactions and compute net income.
(SO 7)

E1-4 An analysis of the transactions made by J. L. Kang & Co., a certified public accounting firm, for the month of August is shown below. Each increase and decrease in stockholders' equity is explained.

	Cash	+	Accounts Receivable	+	Supplies	+	Office Equipment	=	Accounts Payable	+	Stockholders' Equity	
1.	+$15,000										+$15,000	Investment
2.	−2,000						+$5,000		+$3,000			
3.	−750				+$750							
4.	+2,600		+$3,700								+6,300	Service Revenue
5.	−1,500								−1,500			
6.	−1,000										−1,000	Dividends
7.	−650										−650	Rent Expense
8.	+450		−450									
9.	−3,900										−3,900	Salaries Expense
10.									+500		−500	Utilities Expense

Instructions

(a) Describe each transaction that occurred for the month.
(b) Determine how much stockholders' equity increased for the month.
(c) Compute the amount of net income for the month.

Prepare an income statement, retained earnings statement, and a balance sheet.
(SO 8)

E1-5 An analysis of transactions for J. L. Kang & Co. was presented in E1–4.

Instructions

Prepare an income statement and retained earnings statement for August and a balance sheet at August 31, 2006.

Determine net income (or loss).
(SO 7)

E1-6 The Kimm Company had the following assets and liabilities on the dates indicated.

December 31	Total Assets	Total Liabilities
2005	$380,000	$250,000
2006	$460,000	$310,000
2007	$590,000	$400,000

Kimm began business on January 1, 2005, with an investment of $100,000.

Instructions

From an analysis of the change in stockholders' equity during the year, compute the net income (or loss) for:

(a) 2005, assuming Kimm paid $15,000 in dividends for the year.

(b) 2006, assuming stockholders made an additional investment of $50,000 and Kimm paid no dividends in 2006.

(c) 2007, assuming stockholders made an additional investment of $15,000 and Kimm paid dividends of $30,000 in 2007.

Analyze financial statements items.
(SO 6, 7)

E1-7 Two items are omitted from each of the following summaries of balance sheet and income statement data for two corporations for the year 2006, Craig Corporation and Holly Enterprises.

	Craig Corporation	Holly Enterprises
Beginning of year:		
Total assets	$ 97,000	$129,000
Total liabilities	85,000	(c)
Total stockholders' equity	(a)	75,000
End of year:		
Total assets	160,000	180,000
Total liabilities	120,000	50,000
Total stockholders' equity	40,000	130,000
Changes during year in stockholders' equity:		
Additional investment	(b)	25,000
Dividends	24,000	(d)
Total revenues	215,000	100,000
Total expenses	175,000	55,000

Instructions

Determine the missing amounts.

Prepare income statement and retained earnings statement.
(SO 8)

E1-8 The following information relates to Karin Weigel Co. for the year 2006.

Common stock, January 1, 2006	$ 48,000	Advertising expense	$ 1,800
Dividends during 2006	5,000	Rent expense	10,400
Service revenue	62,500	Utilities expense	3,100
Salaries expense	28,000		

Instructions

After analyzing the data, prepare an income statement and a retained earnings statement for the year ending December 31, 2006. Beginning retained earnings was $10,000.

Correct an incorrectly prepared balance sheet.
(SO 8)

E1-9 Lynn Close is the bookkeeper for Sanculi Company. Lynn has been trying to get the balance sheet of Sanculi Company to balance. Sanculi's balance sheet is as follows.

SANCULI COMPANY
Balance Sheet
December 31, 2006

Assets		Liabilities	
Cash	$16,500	Accounts payable	$20,000
Supplies	8,000	Accounts receivable	(8,500)
Equipment	46,000	Common stock	50,000
Dividends	8,500	Retained earnings	17,500
Total assets	$79,000	Total liabilities and stockholders' equity	$79,000

Instructions
Prepare a correct balance sheet.

Compute net income and prepare a balance sheet.
(SO 8)

E1-10 Griswold Inc., a public camping ground near the Boundary Waters Canoe Area, has compiled the following financial information as of December 31, 2006.

Revenues during 2006—camping fees	$192,000	Notes payable	$ 45,000
Revenues during 2006—general store	65,000	Expenses during 2006	180,000
Accounts payable	11,000	Supplies	2,500
Cash	7,000	Common stock	50,000
Original cost of equipment	109,000	Retained earnings	?
Market value of equipment	150,000		

Instructions
(a) Determine Griswold's net income for 2006.
(b) Prepare a balance sheet for Griswold as of December 31, 2006.

Prepare an income statement.
(SO 8)

E1-11 Presented below is financial information related to the 2006 operations of Debra-Joan Cruise Company.

Maintenance expense	$ 97,000
Property tax expense (on dock facilities)	10,000
Salaries expense	142,000
Advertising expense	3,500
Ticket revenue	335,000

Instructions
Prepare the 2006 income statement for Debra-Joan Cruise Company.

Prepare a retained earnings statement.
(SO 8)

E1-12 Presented below is information related to Douglas, Inc.

Retained earnings, January 1, 2006	$150,000
Legal service revenue earned—2006	420,000
Total expenses—2006	212,000
Dividends—2006	52,000

Instructions
Prepare the 2006 retained earnings statement for Douglas, Inc.

PROBLEMS: SET A

Analyze transactions and compute net income.
(SO 6, 7)

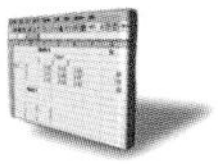

P1-1A On April 1, Matrix Travel Agency was established. The following transactions were completed during the month.

1. Stockholders invested $10,000 cash, receiving stock in exchange.
2. Paid $400 cash for April office rent.
3. Purchased office equipment for $2,500 cash.
4. Incurred $300 of advertising costs in the *Chicago Tribune,* on account.
5. Paid $600 cash for office supplies.
6. Earned $7,500 for services rendered: $1,000 cash is received from customers, and the balance of $6,500 is billed to customers on account.
7. Paid $200 cash dividend.
8. Paid *Chicago Tribune* amount due in transaction (4).
9. Paid employees' salaries $2,200.
10. Received $5,000 in cash from customers who have previously been billed in transaction (6).

Instructions
(a) Prepare a tabular analysis of the transactions using the following column headings: Cash, Accounts Receivable, Supplies, Office Equipment, Accounts Payable, Common Stock, and Retained Earnings.

(b) From an analysis of the Retained Earnings column, compute the net income or net loss for April.

Analyze transactions and prepare income statement, retained earnings statement, and balance sheet.

(SO 6, 7, 8)

P1-2A Mandy Arnold opened a law office, Mandy Arnold, Attorney at Law, on July 1, 2006. On July 31, the balance sheet showed Cash $4,000, Accounts Receivable $1,500, Supplies $500, Office Equipment $5,000, Accounts Payable $4,200, Common Stock $6,000, and Retained Earnings $800. During August the following transactions occurred.

1. Collected $1,400 of accounts receivable.
2. Paid $2,700 cash on accounts payable.
3. Earned revenue of $7,500 of which $3,000 is collected in cash and the balance is due in September.
4. Purchased additional office equipment for $1,000, paying $400 in cash and the balance on account.
5. Paid salaries $3,000, rent for August $900, and advertising expenses $350.
6. Paid dividends of $550.
7. Received $2,000 from Standard Federal Bank—money borrowed on a note payable.
8. Incurred utility expenses for month on account $250.

Check figures next to some Problems give you an intermediate solution, to let you know if you are on the right track.

Instructions

(a) Prepare a tabular analysis of the August transactions beginning with July 31 balances. The column headings should be as follows: Cash + Accounts Receivable − Supplies + Office Equipment = Notes Payable + Accounts Payable + Common Stock + Retained Earnings.

(a) Ending retained earnings $3,250

(b) Prepare an income statement for August, a retained earnings statement for August, and a balance sheet at August 31.

(b) Net income $3,000
Total assets $13,600

Prepare income statement, retained earnings statement, and balance sheet.

(SO 8)

P1-3A Divine Cosmetics Co., a company that provides skin care treatment, was started on June 1 with an investment of $26,200 cash. Following are the assets and liabilities of the company at June 30 and the revenues and expenses for the month of June.

Cash	$10,000	Notes Payable	$13,000
Accounts Receivable	4,000	Accounts Payable	1,200
Service Revenue	5,500	Supplies Expense	1,600
Cosmetic Supplies	2,000	Gas and Oil Expense	800
Advertising Expense	500	Utilities Expense	300
Equipment	25,000		

No additional investments were made by stockholders in June, but a dividend of $1,700 in cash was paid during the month.

Instructions

(a) Prepare an income statement and retained earnings statement for the month of June and a balance sheet at June 30, 2006.

(b) Prepare an income statement and retained earnings statement for June assuming the following data are not included above: (1) $800 of revenue was earned and billed but not collected at June 30, and (2) $100 of gas and oil expense was incurred but not paid.

(a) Net income $2,300
Total assets $41,000
(b) Net income $3,000

Analyze transactions and prepare financial statements.

(SO 7, 8)

P1-4A Laura Stiner started her own consulting firm, Stiner Consulting, Inc. on May 1, 2006. The following transactions occurred during the month of May.

May 1 Stiner invested $8,000 cash in the business.
2 Paid $800 for office rent for the month.
3 Purchased $500 of supplies on account.
5 Paid $50 to advertise in the *County News.*
9 Received $3,000 cash for services provided.
12 Paid a $700 cash dividend.
15 Performed $3,300 of services on account.
17 Paid $3,000 for employee salaries.
20 Paid for the supplies purchased on account on May 3.
23 Received a cash payment of $2,000 for services provided on account on May 15.
26 Borrowed $5,000 from the bank on a note payable.
29 Purchased office equipment for $2,400 on account.
30 Paid $150 for utilities.

(a) Ending retained earnings $1,600

Instructions

(a) Show the effects of the previous transactions on the accounting equation using the following format.

		Assets				Liabilities		Stockholders' Equity	
Date	Cash +	Accounts Receivable +	Supplies +	Office Equipment =		Notes Payable +	Accounts Payable +	Common Stock +	Retained Earnings

Include explanations for any changes in the Retained Earnings account in your analysis.

(b) Net income $2,300
(c) Cash $12,800

(b) Prepare an income statement for the month of May.
(c) Prepare a balance sheet at May 31, 2006.

Determine financial statement amounts and prepare retained earnings statement.
(SO 7, 8)

P1-5A Financial statement information about four different companies is as follows.

	Winger Company	Selara Company	Delta Company	Hindi Company
January 1, 2006				
Assets	$ 75,000	$ 90,000	(g)	$150,000
Liabilities	50,000	(d)	75,000	(j)
Stockholders' equity	(a)	50,000	54,000	100,000
December 31, 2006				
Assets	(b)	117,000	180,000	(k)
Liabilities	55,000	62,000	(h)	80,000
Stockholders' equity	40,000	(e)	100,000	140,000
Stockholders' equity changes in year				
Additional investment	(c)	8,000	10,000	15,000
Dividends	10,000	(f)	12,000	10,000
Total revenues	350,000	400,000	(i)	500,000
Total expenses	335,000	385,000	360,000	(l)

Instructions

(a) Determine the missing amounts. (*Hint:* For example, to solve for (a), Assets – Liabilities = Stockholders' equity = $25,000.)
(b) Prepare the retained earnings statement for Winger Company. Assume that the beginning balance of retained earnings was zero.
(c) Write a memorandum explaining the sequence for preparing financial statements and the interrelationship of the retained earnings statement to the income statement and balance sheet.

PROBLEMS: SET B

Analyze transactions and compute net income.
(SO 6, 7)

P1-1B McInnes's Repair Inc. was started on May 1. A summary of May transactions is presented below.

1. Stockholders' invested $10,000 cash to start the repair company.
2. Purchased equipment for $5,000 cash.
3. Paid $400 cash for May office rent.
4. Paid $500 cash for supplies.
5. Incurred $250 of advertising costs in the *Beacon News* on account.
6. Received $3,100 in cash from customers for repair service.
7. Paid dividends of $1,000 in cash.
8. Paid part-time employee salaries $1,000.
9. Paid utility bills $140.
10. Provided repair service on account to customers $850.
11. Collected cash of $120 for services billed in transaction (10).

(a) Total retained earnings $1,160

Instructions

(a) Prepare a tabular analysis of the transactions, using the following column headings: Cash, Accounts Receivable, Supplies, Equipment, Accounts Payable, Common Stock, and Retained Earnings. Revenue is called Service Revenue.

(b) From an analysis of the Retained Earnings column, compute the net income or net loss for May.

(b) Net income $2,160

P1-2B On August 31, the balance sheet of Nashville Corporation showed Cash $9,000, Accounts Receivable $1,700, Supplies $600, Office Equipment $6,000, Accounts Payable $3,600, Common Stock $13,000, and Retained Earnings $700. During September the following transactions occurred.

Analyze transactions and prepare income statement, retained earnings statement, and balance sheet.

(SO 6, 7, 8)

1. Paid $2,900 cash on accounts payable.
2. Collected $1,300 of accounts receivable.
3. Purchased additional office equipment for $2,100, paying $800 in cash and the balance on account.
4. Earned revenue of $6,300, of which $2,500 is paid in cash and the balance is due in October.
5. Paid dividends of $600.
6. Paid salaries $1,700, rent for September $900, and advertising expense $300.
7. Incurred utilities expense for month on account $170.
8. Received $10,000 from Capital Bank–money borrowed on a note payable.

Instructions

(a) Prepare a tabular analysis of the September transactions beginning with August 31 balances. The column headings should be as follows: Cash + Accounts Receivable + Supplies + Office Equipment = Notes Payable + Accounts Payable + Common Stock + Retained Earnings.

(a) Ending retained earnings $3,330

(b) Prepare an income statement for September, a retained earnings statement for September, and a balance sheet at September 30, 2006.

(b) Net income $3,230
Total assets $28,500

P1-3B On May 1, Skyward Flying School Inc., a company that provides flying lessons, was started with an investment of $45,000 cash in the business. Following are the assets and liabilities of the company on May 31, 2006, and the revenues and expenses for the month of May.

Prepare income statement, retained earnings statement, and balance sheet.

(SO 8)

Cash	$ 6,500	Notes Payable	$30,000
Accounts Receivable	7,200	Rent Expense	1,200
Equipment	64,000	Repair Expense	400
Lesson Revenue	8,600	Fuel Expense	2,500
Advertising Expense	500	Insurance Expense	400
		Accounts Payable	800

No additional investments were made in May, but dividends of $1,700 were paid during the month.

Instructions

(a) Prepare an income statement and a retained earnings statement for the month of May and a balance sheet at May 31.

(a) Net income $3,600
Total assets $77,700

(b) Prepare an income statement and a retained earnings statement for May assuming the following data are not included above: (1) $900 of revenue was earned and billed but not collected at May 31, and (2) $1,500 of fuel expense was incurred but not paid.

(b) Net income $3,000

P1-4B Pat Donahue started his own delivery service, Donahue Deliveries, Inc. on June 1, 2006. The following transactions occurred during the month of June.

Analyze transactions and prepare financial statements.

(SO 7, 8)

June	1	Stockholders invested $10,000 cash in the business.
	2	Purchased a used van for deliveries for $10,000. Pat paid $2,000 cash and signed a note payable for the remaining balance.
	3	Paid $500 for office rent for the month.
	5	Performed $2,400 of services on account.
	9	Paid $200 in cash dividends.
	12	Purchased supplies for $150 on account.
	15	Received a cash payment of $750 for services provided on June 5.
	17	Purchased gasoline for $100 on account.
	20	Received a cash payment of $1,500 for services provided.
	23	Made a cash payment of $500 on the note payable.
	26	Paid $250 for utilities.
	29	Paid for the gasoline purchased on account on June 17.
	30	Paid $1,000 for employee salaries.

Instructions

(a) Show the effects of the previous transactions on the accounting equation using the following format.

	Assets							=	Liabilities			+	Stockholders' Equity		
Date	Cash	+	Accounts Receivable	+	Supplies	+	Delivery Van	=	Notes Payable	+	Accounts Payable	+	Common Stock	+	Retained Earnings

Include explanations for any changes in the Retained Earnings account in your analysis.

(b) Net income $2,050
(c) Cash $7,700

(b) Prepare an income statement for the month of June.
(c) Prepare a balance sheet at June 30, 2006.

Determine financial statement amounts and prepare retained earnings statement.
(SO 7, 8)

P1-5B Financial statement information about four different companies is as follows.

	Karma Company	Molly Company	McCain Company	Bodie Company
January 1, 2006				
Assets	$ 89,000	$110,000	(g)	$170,000
Liabilities	50,000	(d)	75,000	(f)
Stockholders' equity	(a)	60,000	40,000	90,000
December 31, 2006				
Assets	(b)	147,000	200,000	(k)
Liabilities	55,000	75,000	(h)	80,000
Stockholders' equity	60,000	(e)	130,000	160,000
Stockholders' equity changes in year				
Additional investment	(c)	15,000	10,000	15,000
Dividends	25,000	(f)	14,000	20,000
Total revenues	350,000	420,000	(i)	520,000
Total expenses	320,000	385,000	342,000	(l)

Instructions

(a) Determine the missing amounts. (*Hint:* For example, to solve for (a), Assets − Liabilities = Stockholders' Equity = $39,000.)
(b) Prepare the retained earnings statement for Karma Company. Assume that the beginning balance of retained earnings was zero.
(c) Write a memorandum explaining the sequence for preparing financial statements and the interrelationship of the retained earnings statement to the income statement and balance sheet.

BROADENING YOUR PERSPECTIVE

Financial Reporting and Analysis

■ FINANCIAL REPORTING PROBLEM: PepsiCo

PEPSI

BYP1-1 The actual financial statements of **PepsiCo**, as presented in the company's 2003 Annual Report, are contained in Appendix A (at the back of the textbook).

Instructions

Refer to PepsiCo's financial statements and answer the following questions.

(a) What were PepsiCo's total assets at December 27, 2003? At December 28, 2002?
(b) How much cash (and cash equivalents) did PepsiCo have on December 27, 2003?
(c) What amount of accounts payable and other current liabilities did PepsiCo report on December 27, 2003? On December 28, 2002?
(d) What were PepsiCo net sales in 2001? In 2002? In 2003?
(e) What is the amount of the change in PepsiCo's net income from 2002 to 2003?

■ COMPARATIVE ANALYSIS PROBLEM: PepsiCo vs. Coca-Cola

BYP1-2 **PepsiCo**'s financial statements are presented in Appendix A. **Coca-Cola**'s financial statements are presented in Appendix B.

Instructions

(a) Based on the information contained in these financial statements, determine the following for each company.

(1) Total assets at December 27, 2003, for PepsiCo, and for Coca-Cola, at December 31, 2003.

(2) Accounts (notes) receivable, net at December 27, 2003, for PepsiCo and at December 31, 2003, for Coca-Cola.

(3) Net sales for year ended in 2003.

(4) Net income for year ended in 2003.

(b) What conclusions concerning the two companies can be drawn from these data?

■ RESEARCH CASE

BYP1-3 The February 6, 2002, issue of the *Wall Street Journal* includes an article by Steve Liesman, Jonathan Weil, and Michael Schroeder titled "Accounting Debacles Spark Calls for Change: Here's the Rundown."

Instructions

Read the article and answer the following questions.

(a) What concern is raised by the fact that some audit firms receive significant payments from their audit clients for non-audit work, such as consulting? What solutions have been proposed in response to this potential problem?

(b) At the time of this article, who policed the accounting profession? What alternative has the Securities and Exchange Commission (SEC) proposed?

(c) What criticisms have been made of the primary accounting standards-setting group, the Financial Accounting Standards Board (FASB)?

(d) In what ways, and from what groups, is the SEC demanding more disclosure?

■ INTERPRETING FINANCIAL STATEMENTS

BYP1-4 The year 2000 was not a particularly pleasant year for the managers of **Xerox Corporation**, or its shareholders. The company's stock price had already fallen in the previous year from $60 per share to $30. Just when it seemed things couldn't get worse, Xerox's stock fell to $4 per share. The data below were taken from the December 31, 2000, statement of cash flows of Xerox. All dollars are in millions.

Cash used in operating activities		$ (663)
Cash used in investing activities		(644)
Financing activities		
Dividends paid	$ (587)	
Net cash received from issuing debt	3,498	
Cash provided by financing activities		2,911

Instructions

Analyze the information above, and then answer the following questions.

(a) If you were a creditor of Xerox, what reaction might you have to the above information?

(b) If you were an investor in Xerox, what reaction might you have to the above information?

(c) If you were evaluating the company as either a creditor or a stockholder, what other information would you be interested in seeing?

(d) Xerox decided to pay a cash dividend in 2000. This dividend was approximately equal to the amount paid in 1999. Discuss the issues that were probably considered in making this decision.

■ A GLOBAL FOCUS

BYP1-5 Today companies must compete in a global economy. **Nestlé**, a Swiss company, is the largest food company in the world. If you were interested in broadening your investment portfolio, you might consider investing in Nestlé. However, investing in international companies can pose some additional challenges. Consider the following excerpts from the notes to Nestlé's financial statements.

NESTLÉ
Notes to the Financial Statements (partial)

(a) The Group accounts comply with International Accounting Standards (IAS) issued by the International Accounting Standards Committee (IASC) and with the Standards Interpretations issued by the Standards Interpretation Committee of the IASC (SIC).
(b) The accounts have been prepared under the historical cost convention and on an accrual basis. All significant consolidated companies have a 31st December accounting year end. All disclosures required by the 4th and 7th European Union company law directives are provided.
(c) On consolidation, assets and liabilities of Group companies denominated in foreign currencies are translated into Swiss francs at year-end rates. Income and expense items are translated into Swiss francs at the annual average rates of exchange or, where known or determinable, at the rate on the date of the transaction for significant items.

Instructions
Discuss the implications of each of these items in terms of the effect it might have (positive or negative) on your ability to compare Nestlé to a U.S. food company such as **Tootsie Roll** or **Hershey Foods**. (*Hint:* In preparing your answer review the discussion of principles and assumptions in financial reporting on pages 10 and 11.)

■ EXPLORING THE WEB

BYP1-6 This exercise will familiarize you with skill requirements, job descriptions, and salaries for accounting careers.

Address: www.careers-in-accounting.com, or go to www.wiley.com/college/weygandt

Instructions
Go to the site shown above. Answer the following questions.

(a) What are the three broad areas of accounting (from "Skills and Talents Required")?
(b) List eight skills required in accounting.
(c) How do the three accounting areas differ in terms of these eight required skills?
(d) Explain one of the key job functions (options) in accounting.
(e) Based on the *Smart Money* survey, what is the salary range for a junior staff accountant with Deloitte & Touche?

Critical Thinking

■ GROUP DECISION CASE

BYP1-7 Lucy and Nick Lars, local golf stars, opened the Chip-Shot Driving Range on March 1, 2005, by investing $20,000 of their cash savings in the business. A caddy shack was constructed for cash at a cost of $6,000, and $800 was spent on golf balls and golf clubs. The Lars leased five acres of land at a cost of $1,000 per month and paid the first month's rent. During the first month, advertising costs totaled $750, of which $150 was unpaid at March 31, and $400 was paid to members of the high-school golf team for retrieving golf balls. All revenues from customers were deposited in the company's bank account. On March 15, Lucy and Nick received a dividend of $800 in cash. A $100 utility bill was received on March 31 but was not paid. On March 31, the balance in the company's bank account was $15,100.

Lucy and Nick thought they had a pretty good first month of operations. But, their estimates of profitability ranged from a loss of $4,900 to net income of $1,650.

Instructions
With the class divided into groups, answer the following.

(a) How could the Lars have concluded that the business operated at a loss of $4,900? Was this a valid basis on which to determine net income?
(b) How could the Lars have concluded that the business operated at a net income of $1,650? (*Hint:* Prepare a balance sheet at March 31.) Was this a valid basis on which to determine net income?
(c) Without preparing an income statement, determine the actual net income for March.
(d) What was the revenue earned in March?

■ COMMUNICATION ACTIVITY

BYP1-8 Erin Danielle, the accountant for Bloomington Company, has been trying to get the balance sheet to balance. The company's balance sheet is as follows.

BLOOMINGTON COMPANY
Balance Sheet
For the Month Ended December 31, 2006

Assets		Liabilities	
Equipment	$22,500	Common stock	$23,000
Cash	9,000	Accounts receivable	(6,000)
Supplies	2,000	Dividends	(2,000)
Accounts payable	(8,000)	Notes payable	10,500
	$25,500		$25,500

Instructions
Explain to Erin Danielle in a memo why the original balance sheet is incorrect, and what should be done to correct it.

■ ETHICS CASE

Accounting Matters!

BYP1-9 After numerous campus interviews, Jeff Hunter, a senior at Great Northern College, received two office interview invitations from the Baltimore offices of two large firms. Both firms offered to cover his out-of-pocket expenses (travel, hotel, and meals). He scheduled the interviews for both firms on the same day, one in the morning and one in the afternoon. At the conclusion of each interview, he submitted to both firms his total out-of-pocket expenses for the trip to Baltimore: mileage $98 (280 miles at $0.35), hotel $130, meals $36, parking and tolls $18, for a total of $282. He believes this approach is appropriate. If he had made two trips, his cost would have been two times $282. He is also certain that neither firm knew he had visited the other on that same trip. Within ten days Jeff received two checks in the mail, each in the amount of $282.

Instructions
(a) Who are the stakeholders (affected parties) in this situation?
(b) What are the ethical issues in this case?
(c) What would you do in this situation?

■ CONTINUING COOKIE CHRONICLE

Accounting Matters!

BYP1-10 Natalie Koebel spent much of her childhood learning the art of cookie making from her grandmother. They passed many happy hours together, mastering every type of cookie imaginable and later devising new recipes that were both healthy and delicious. Now in college, Natalie is investigating various possibilities for starting her own business as part of the requirements for an Entrepreneurship class she is taking.

Because of her extensive knowledge, Natalie has settled on the idea of a cookie-making school. She will start it on a part-time basis and offer her services in peoples' homes. She will offer group sessions (which will probably be more entertainment than education for the participants) and individual lessons. Natalie also has decided to include children in her target market. The first difficult decision is to come up with the perfect name for her business. In the end, she selects "Cookie Creations" and then moves on to more important issues.

Instructions

(a) What form of business organization—proprietorship, partnership, or corporation—do you recommend Natalie use for her business? Discuss the advantages and disadvantages of each form, and give your reasons for choosing the form of business organization you recommend.

(b) Will Natalie need accounting information? If yes, what information will she need and why? How often will she need this information?

(c) Identify specific asset, liability, and equity accounts that Cookie Creations will likely use to record its business transactions.

(d) Should Natalie open a separate bank account for the business? Why or why not?

(e) Natalie expects she will have to use her car to drive to people's homes and to pick up supplies, but she also needs to use her car for personal reasons (to get to school, for example). She recalls from her first-year accounting course something about keeping business and personal assets separate. She wonders what she should do for accounting purposes. What do you recommend?

Accounting Matters!

Answers to Accounting Matters! Questions

p. 7

Q: What has been done in the United States to improve the quality and integrity of financial reporting and to build investor confidence in financial reports?

A: New laws have been passed to legislate fair business behavior as well as accounting and auditing practices. Specifically, the Sarbanes-Oxley Act, signed into law in July 2002, increases the resources for the government to combat fraud and to curb poor reporting practices. The Act also introduces sweeping changes to the structure and practices of the accounting and auditing professions and increases the responsibility of corporate boards and officers.

p. 8

Q: What qualifies accountants to design and implement computer systems and to serve as e-business consultants?

A: Accountants, as the providers of financial information, are educated to identify, record, and communicate economic events and activities and their results. Computers are an integral part of the accounting process as the recorders and generators of financial data. Most accountants therefore use computers and have sufficient knowledge about computer systems to serve as e-business consultants.

p. 24

Q: What year-end would you likely use if you owned a ski resort and ski rental business?

A: Probable choices for a ski resort would be between May 31 or August 31.

Q: What if you owned a college bookstore?

A: For a college bookstore, a likely year-end would be June 30.

Q: Why choose those year-ends?

A: The optimum accounting year-end, especially for seasonal businesses, is when inventory and activities are lowest.

p. 30

Q: Why would the FBI and the IRS want to hire accountants?

A: The FBI, the IRS, and similar governmental agencies hire accountants for their skills as forensic auditors in examining accounting records and systems to detect fraud and other white-collar crimes.

Answer to PepsiCo Review It Question 4, p. 14

PepsiCo's accounting equation is:

Assets	=	Liabilities	+	Stockholders' Equity
$25,327,000,000	=	$13,453,000,000	+	$11,874,000,000

(Stockholders' equity includes preferred stock.)

Answers to Self-Study Questions

1. b **2.** d **3.** c **4.** c **5.** a **6.** d **7.** b **8.** a **9.** b **10.** c ***11.** a

REMEMBER to go back to the Navigator box on the chapter-opening page and check off your completed work.

Chapter 2

The Recording Process

THE NAVIGATOR ✓	
Understand **Concepts for Review**	❑
Read **Feature Story**	❑
Scan **Study Objectives**	❑
Read **Preview**	❑
Read text and answer **Before You Go On** p. 53 ❑ p. 56 ❑ p. 67 ❑ p. 71 ❑	
Work **Demonstration Problem**	❑
Review **Summary of Study Objectives**	❑
Answer **Self-Study Questions**	❑
Complete **Assignments**	❑

CONCEPTS FOR REVIEW

Before studying this chapter, you should know or, if necessary, review:

- What are assets, liabilities, common stock, retained earnings, dividends, revenues, and expenses.
  (Ch. 1, pp. 12–13)
- Why assets equal liabilities plus stockholders' equity.
  (Ch. 1, p. 12)
- What transactions are and how they affect the basic accounting equation.
  (Ch. 1, pp. 15–21)

✓ THE NAVIGATOR

Accounting Matters! **FEATURE STORY**

No Such Thing as a Perfect World

When she got a job doing the accounting for **Forster's Restaurants**, Tanis Anderson had almost finished her business administration degree at Simon Fraser University. But even after Tanis completed her degree requirements, her education still continued—this time, in the real world.

Tanis's responsibilities include paying the bills, tracking food and labor costs, and managing the payroll for **The Mug and Musket**, a popular destination restaurant in Surrey, British Columbia. "My title is Director of Finance," she laughs, "but really that means I take care of whatever needs doing!"

The use of judgment is a big part of the job. As Tanis says, "I learned all the fundamentals in my business classes, but school prepares you for a perfect world, and there is no such thing."

She feels fortunate that her boss understands her job is a learning experience as well as a responsibility. "Sometimes he's let me do something he knew perfectly well was a mistake so I can learn something through experience," she admits.

To help others gain the benefits of her real-world learning, Tanis is always happy to help students in the area who want to use Forster's as the subject of a project or report. "It's the least I can do," she says.

THE NAVIGATOR

STUDY OBJECTIVES

After studying this chapter, you should be able to:

1. Explain what an account is and how it helps in the recording process.
2. Define debits and credits and explain how they are used to record business transactions.
3. Identify the basic steps in the recording process.
4. Explain what a journal is and how it helps in the recording process.
5. Explain what a ledger is and how it helps in the recording process.
6. Explain what posting is and how it helps in the recording process.
7. Prepare a trial balance and explain its purposes.

THE NAVIGATOR

PREVIEW OF CHAPTER 2

In Chapter 1, we analyzed business transactions in terms of the accounting equation. The cumulative effects of these transactions were presented in tabular form. Imagine a restaurant and gift shop such as **The Mug and Musket** using the same tabular format as Softbyte, Inc. to keep track of every one of its transactions. In a single day, this restaurant and gift shop engages in hundreds of business transactions. To record each transaction this way would be impractical, expensive, and unnecessary. Instead, a set of procedures and records are used to keep track of transaction data more easily.

This chapter introduces and illustrates these basic procedures and records. The content and organization of Chapter 2 are as follows.

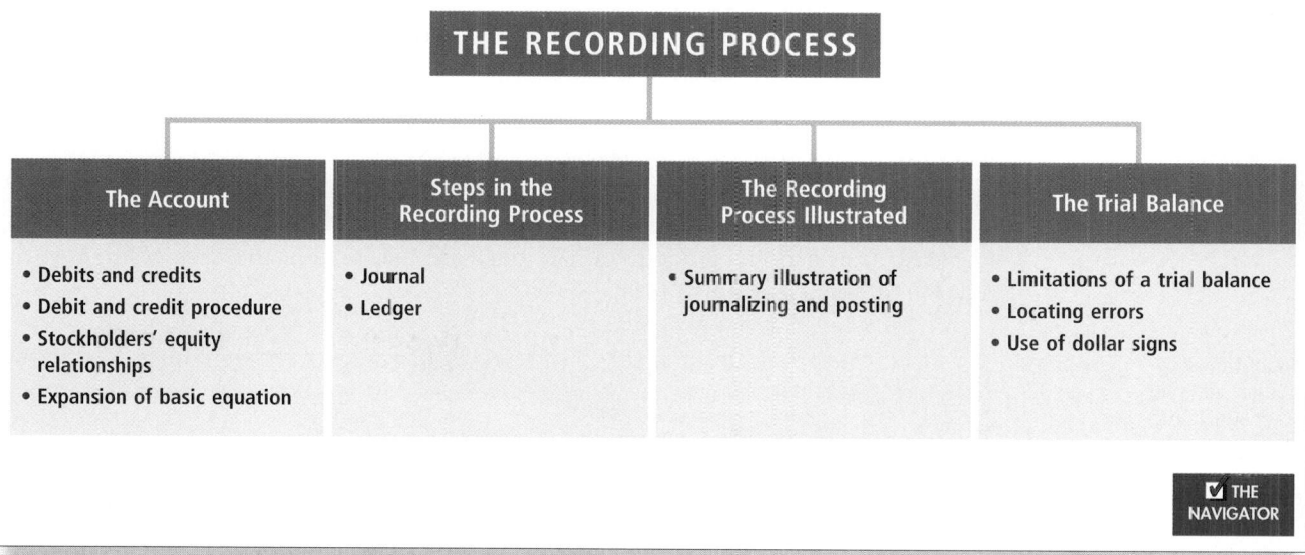

THE RECORDING PROCESS

The Account
- Debits and credits
- Debit and credit procedure
- Stockholders' equity relationships
- Expansion of basic equation

Steps in the Recording Process
- Journal
- Ledger

The Recording Process Illustrated
- Summary illustration of journalizing and posting

The Trial Balance
- Limitations of a trial balance
- Locating errors
- Use of dollar signs

THE NAVIGATOR

The Account

STUDY OBJECTIVE 1

Explain what an account is and how it helps in the recording process.

An **account** is an individual accounting record of increases and decreases in a specific asset, liability, or stockholders' equity item. For example, Softbyte, Inc. (the company discussed in Chapter 1) would have separate accounts for Cash, Accounts Receivable, Accounts Payable, Service Revenue, Salaries Expense, and so on. In its simplest form, an account consists of three parts: (1) the title of the account, (2) a left or debit side, and (3) a right or credit side. Because the alignment of these parts of an account resembles the letter T, it is referred to as a **T account**. The basic form of an account is shown in Illustration 2-1.

Title of Account

Left or debit side	Right or credit side
Debit balance	Credit balance

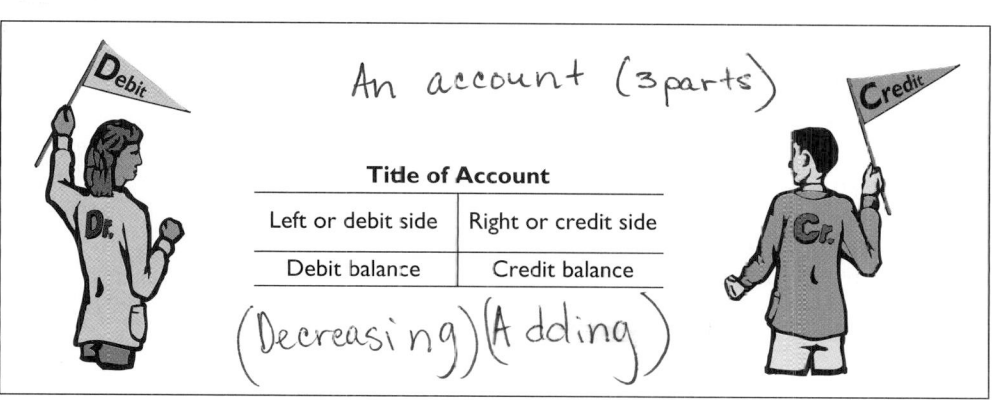

Illustration 2-1
Basic form of account

www.wiley.com/college/weygandt

Accounting Cycle Tutorial—Recording Business Transactions

The T account is a standard shorthand in accounting that helps make clear the effects of transactions on individual accounts. We will use it often throughout this book to explain basic accounting relationships. (Note that when we are referring to a specific account, we capitalize its name.)

Debits and Credits

STUDY OBJECTIVE 2

Define debits and credits and explain how they are used to record business transactions.

Today, the term **debit** indicates left, and **credit** indicates right. They are commonly abbreviated as Dr. for debit and Cr. for credit.[1] These terms come from Latin words that originally meant "debtor" and "creditor." Today they are directional signals. They indicate which side of a T account a number will be recorded on. Entering an amount on the left side of an account is called **debiting** the account; making an entry on the right side is **crediting** the account.

The procedure of having debits on the left and credits on the right is an accounting custom, or rule (like the custom of driving on the right-hand side of the road in the United States). **This rule applies to all accounts.** When the totals of the two sides are compared, an account will have a **debit balance** if the total of the debit amounts exceeds the credits. An account will have a **credit balance** if the credit amounts exceed the debits.

The recording of debits and credits in an account is shown in Illustration 2-2 for the cash transactions of Softbyte. The data are taken from the cash column of the tabular summary in Illustration 1-8.

Illustration 2-2
Tabular summary compared to account form

Tabular Summary

Cash
$15,000
−7,000
1,200
1,500
−1,700
−250
600
−1,300
$ 8,050

Account Form

Cash			
(Debits)	15,000	**(Credits)**	7,000
	1,200		1,700
	1,500		250
	600		1,300
Balance **(Debit)**	8,050		

In the tabular summary every positive item represents a receipt of cash; every negative amount represents a payment of cash. Notice that in the account form the increases in cash are recorded as debits, and the decreases in cash are recorded as credits. Having increases on one side and decreases on the other helps in determining the total of each side of the account as well as the overall balance in the account. The account balance, a debit of $8,050, indicates that Softbyte, Inc. has had $8,050 more increases than decreases in cash.

Debit and Credit Procedure

HELPFUL HINT

Debits must equal credits for each transaction.

In Chapter 1 you learned the effect of a transaction on the basic accounting equation. Remember that each transaction must affect two or more accounts to keep the basic accounting equation in balance. In other words, for each transaction **debits must equal credits** in the accounts. The equality of debits and credits provides the basis for the **double-entry system** of recording transactions.

Under the double-entry system the dual (two-sided) effect of each transaction is recorded in appropriate accounts. This universally used system provides a logical

[1] These terms and their abbreviations come from the Latin words *debere* (Dr.) and *credere* (Cr.).

method for recording transactions. It also offers a means of proving the accuracy of the recorded amounts. If every transaction is recorded with equal debits and credits, then the sum of all the debits to the accounts must equal the sum of all the credits.

The double-entry system for determining the equality of the accounting equation is much more efficient than the plus/minus procedure used in Chapter 1. There, it was necessary after each transaction to compare total assets with total liabilities and stockholders' equity to determine the equality of the two sides of the accounting equation.

Assets and Liabilities

We know that both sides of the basic equation (Assets = Liabilities + Stockholders' Equity) must be equal. It follows that increases and decreases in assets and liabilities must be recorded opposite from each other. In Illustration 2-2, increases in cash—an asset—were entered on the left side, and decreases in cash were entered on the right side. Therefore, increases in liabilities must be entered on the right or credit side, and decreases in liabilities must be entered on the left or debit side. The effects that debits and credits have on assets and liabilities are summarized as follows.

Debits	Credits
Increase assets	Decrease assets
Decrease liabilities	Increase liabilities

Illustration 2-3
Debit and credit effects—assets and liabilities

Debits to a specific asset account should exceed the credits to that account. Credits to a liability account should exceed debits to that account. **The normal balance of an account is on the side where an increase in the account is recorded.** Thus, asset accounts normally show debit balances, and liability accounts normally show credit balances. The normal balances can be diagrammed as follows.

HELPFUL HINT
The normal balance for an account is always the same as the increase side.

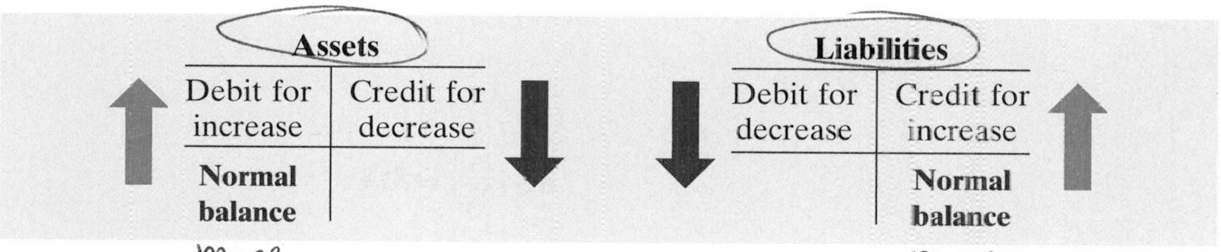

Illustration 2-4
Normal balances—assets and liabilities

Knowing the normal balance in an account may help you trace errors. For example, a credit balance in an asset account such as Land or a debit balance in a liability account such as Accounts Payable would indicate recording errors. Occasionally, an abnormal balance may be correct. The Cash account, for example, will have a credit balance when a company has overdrawn its bank balance (i.e., written a "bad" check).

Stockholders' Equity

As indicated in Chapter 1, there are five subdivisions of stockholders' equity: common stock, retained earnings, dividends, revenues, and expenses. In a double-entry system, accounts are kept for each of these subdivisions, as explained below.

COMMON STOCK. **Common stock** is issued in exchange for the owners' investment paid into the corporation. The Common Stock account is increased by credits and decreased by debits. When cash is invested in the business in exchange for shares of the corporation's stock, Cash is debited and Common Stock is credited.

The rules of debit and credit for the Common Stock account are stated as follows.

Illustration 2-5
Debit and credit effect—common stock

Debits	Credits
Decrease common stock	Increase common stock

The normal balance in this account may be diagrammed as follows.

Illustration 2-6
Normal balance—common stock

Common Stock	
Debit for decrease	Credit for increase
	Normal balance

more credit

HELPFUL HINT

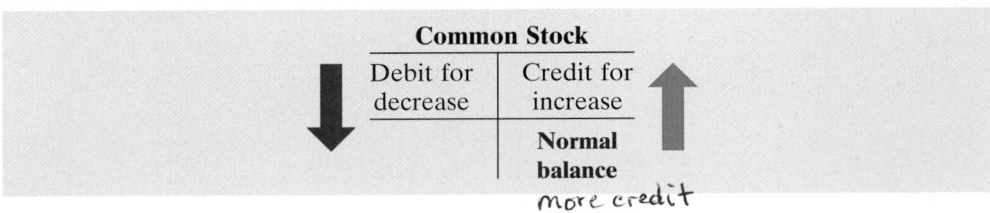

The rules for debit and credit and the normal balance of common stock are the same as for liabilities.

RETAINED EARNINGS. **Retained earnings** is net income that is retained in the business. It represents the portion of stockholders' equity that has been accumulated through the profitable operation of the business. Retained earnings is increased by credits (net income) and decreased by debits (dividends or net losses) as shown below.

Illustration 2-7
Debit and credit effect and normal balance—retained earnings

Retained Earnings	
Debit for decrease	Credit for increase
	Normal balance

more credit

DIVIDENDS. A **dividend** is a distribution by a corporation to its stockholders on a pro rata (equal) basis. The most common form of a distribution is a **cash dividend**. Dividends can be declared (authorized) only by the board of directors. They are a reduction of the stockholders' claims on retained earnings. The Dividends account is increased by debits and decreased by credits, with a normal debit balance as shown in Illustration 2-8.

Illustration 2-8
Debit and credit effect and normal balance—dividends

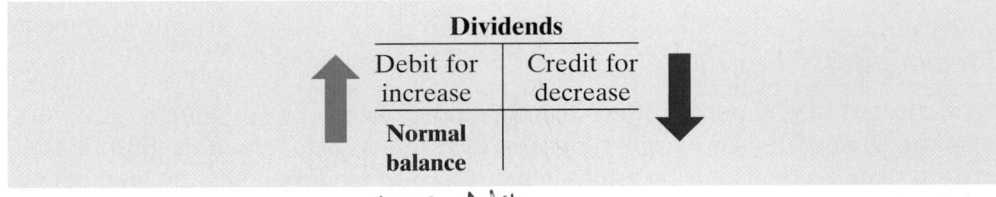

Dividends	
Debit for increase	Credit for decrease
Normal balance	

more Debit

Revenues and Expenses

Remember that the ultimate purpose of earning revenues is to benefit the stockholders of the business. When revenues are earned, stockholders' equity is increased. Revenues are a subdivision of stockholders' equity that provides information as to **why** stockholders' equity increased. Revenue accounts are increased by credits and decreased by debits. Accordingly, **the effect of debits and credits on revenue accounts is identical to their effect on stockholders' equity**.

Expenses have the opposite effect: expenses decrease stockholders' equity. Since expenses are the negative factor in computing net income, and revenues are the positive factor, it is logical that the increase and decrease sides of expense accounts should be the reverse of revenue accounts. Thus, expense accounts are increased by debits and decreased by credits.

The effect of debits and credits on revenues and expenses may be stated as follows.

HELPFUL HINT

Because revenues increase stockholders' equity, a revenue account has the same debit and credit rules as does the common stock account. Conversely, expenses have the opposite effect.

Debits	Credits
Decrease revenues	Increase revenues
Increase expenses	Decrease expenses

Illustration 2-9
Debit and credit effects—revenues and expenses

Credits to revenue accounts should exceed the debits, and debits to expense accounts should exceed credits. Thus, revenue accounts normally show credit balances, and expense accounts normally show debit balances. The normal balances may be diagrammed as follows.

Revenues	
Debit for decrease ↓	Credit for increase ↑
	Normal balance

Expenses	
Debit for increase ↑	Credit for decrease ↓
Normal balance	

Illustration 2-10
Normal balances—revenues and expenses

ACCOUNTING MATTERS! Business Insight

The Chicago Cubs baseball team has the following major revenue and expense accounts.

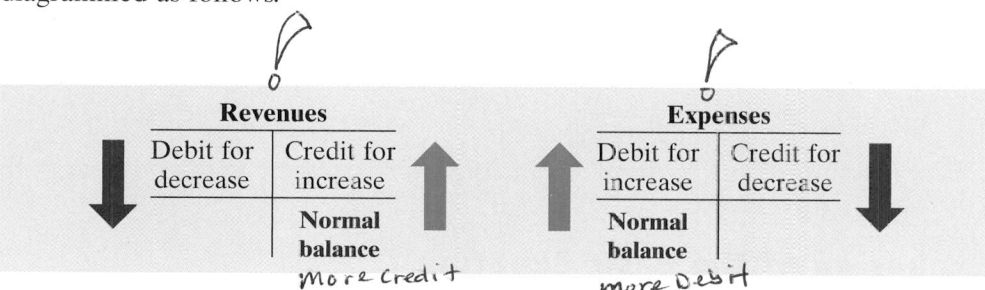

Revenues	Expenses
Admissions (ticket sales)	Players' salaries
Concessions	Administrative salaries
Television and radio	Travel
Advertising	Ballpark maintenance

? Do you think that the Chicago Bears (football team) would be likely to have the same major revenue and expense accounts as the Cubs? Do you think that Chicago-based Wrigley Company would be likely to have the same major revenue and expense accounts? Why or why not?

Stockholders' Equity Relationships

As indicated in Chapter 1, common stock and retained earnings are reported in the stockholders' equity section of the balance sheet. Dividends are reported on the retained earnings statement. Revenues and expenses are reported on the income statement. Dividends, revenues, and expenses are eventually transferred to retained earnings at the end of the period. As a result, a change in any one of these three items affects stockholders' equity. The relationships related to stockholders' equity are shown in Illustration 2-11.

Illustration 2-11
Stockholders' equity relationships

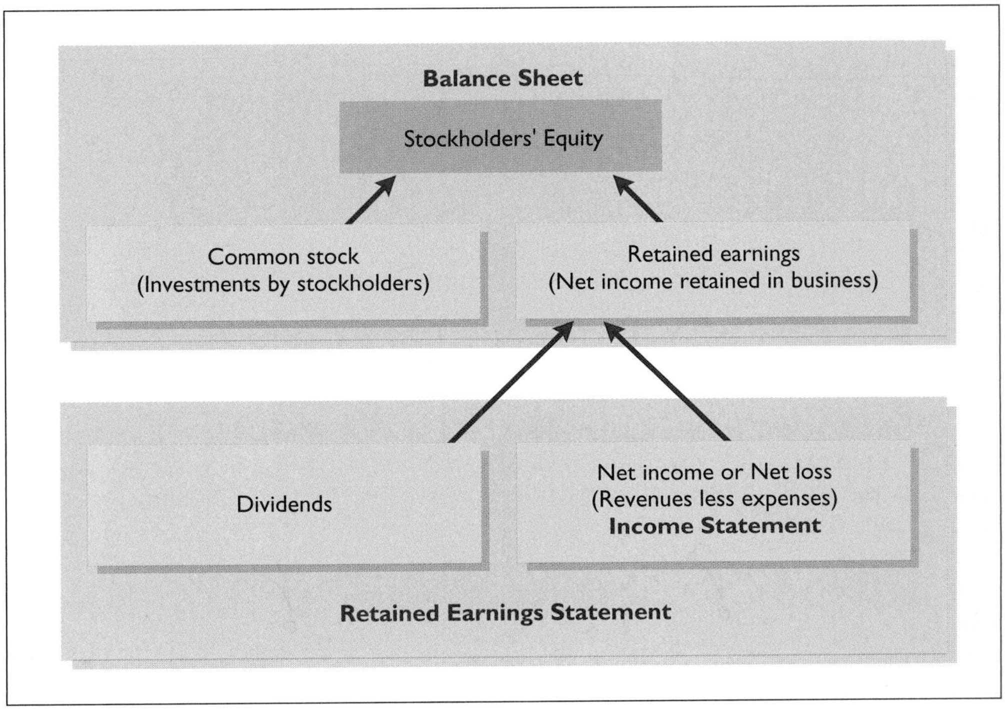

Expansion of the Basic Equation

You have already learned the basic accounting equation. Illustration 2-12 expands this equation to show the accounts that comprise stockholders' equity. In addition, the debit/credit rules and effects on each type of account are illustrated. Study this diagram carefully. It will help you understand the fundamentals of the double-entry system. Like the basic equation, the expanded basic equation must be in balance (total debits equal total credits).

Illustration 2-12
Expanded basic equation and debit/credit rules and effects

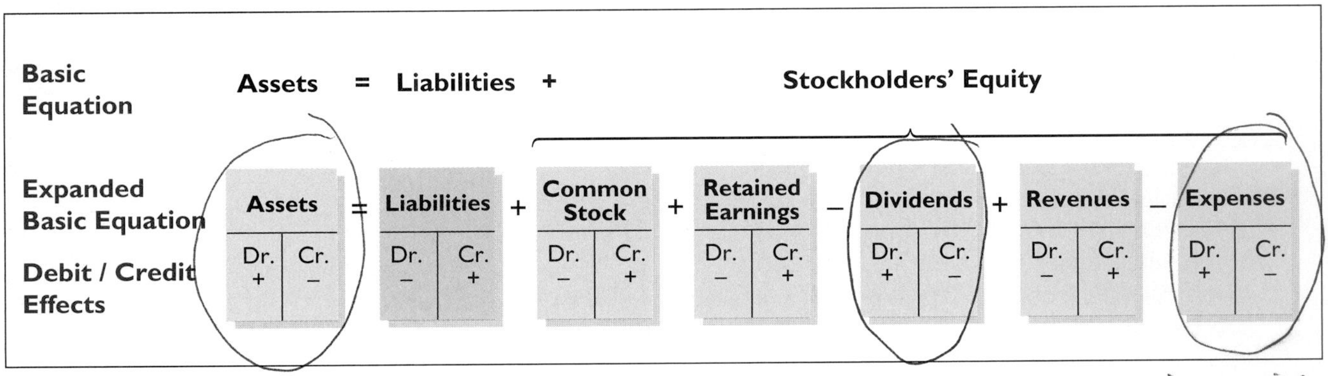

BEFORE YOU GO ON...

Review It

1. What do the terms debit and credit mean?
2. What are the debit and credit effects on assets, liabilities, and stockholders' equity?
3. What are the debit and credit effects on revenues, expenses, and dividends?
4. What are the normal balances for **PepsiCo**'s Cash, Accounts Payable, and Interest Expense accounts? The answers to this question are provided on page 90.

Do It

Kate Browne, president of Hair It Is, Inc., has just rented space in a shopping mall in which she will open and operate a beauty salon. Long before opening day and before purchasing equipment, hiring assistants, and remodeling the space, Kate has been advised to set up a double-entry set of accounting records in which to record all of her business transactions.

Identify the balance sheet accounts that Hair It Is, Inc., will likely need to record the transactions needed to establish and open the business. Also, indicate whether the normal balance of each account is a debit or a credit.

ACTION PLAN

- Determine the types of accounts needed: Kate will need asset accounts for each type of asset she invests in the business, and liability accounts for any debts she incurs.
- Understand the types of stockholders' equity accounts: Only Common Stock will be needed when Kate begins the business. Other stockholders' equity accounts will be needed later.

SOLUTION Hair It Is, Inc., would likely need the following accounts to record the transactions needed to ready the beauty salon for opening day: Cash (debit balance); Equipment (debit balance); Supplies (debit balance); Accounts Payable (credit balance); Notes Payable (credit balance), if the business borrows money; and Common Stock (credit balance).

Related exercise material: *BE2-1, BE2-2, E2-1, and E2-3.*

THE NAVIGATOR

Steps in the Recording Process

STUDY OBJECTIVE 3

Identify the basic steps in the recording process.

In practically every business, the basic steps in the recording process are:

1. Analyze each transaction for its effects on the accounts.
2. Enter the transaction information in a journal (book of original entry).
3. Transfer the journal information to the appropriate accounts in the ledger (book of accounts).

Although it is possible to enter transaction information directly into the accounts without using a journal, few businesses do so.

The sequence of events in the recording process begins with the transaction. Evidence of the transaction is provided by a **business document**, such as a sales slip, a check, a bill, or a cash register tape. This evidence is analyzed to determine the effects of the transaction on specific accounts. The transaction is then entered in the journal. Finally, the journal entry is transferred to the designated accounts in the ledger. The sequence of events in the recording process is shown in Illustration 2-13.

Illustration 2-13
The recording process

The basic steps in the recording process occur repeatedly. The analysis of transactions was illustrated in Chapter 1. Further examples will be given in this and later chapters. The other steps in the recording process are explained in the next sections.

ACCOUNTING MATTERS! Business Insight

While most companies record transactions very carefully, the reality is that sometimes even the most careful companies make mistakes in their accounting records. For example, **Hanover Compressor** at one time announced that it was restating its financial results for an error that had been made in each of the previous five years. It had accidentally omitted the cost of compressors manufactured at one of its plants, causing the cost of its inventory to be misstated. **Bank One Corporation** was fined $1.8 million by banking regulators because regulators felt that its accounting system was unreliable and caused the bank to violate certain minimum banking requirements. Finally, before a major overhaul of its accounting system, the financial records of **Waste Management Company** were in such disarray that of the company's 57,000 employees, 10,000 were receiving pay slips that were in error.

? In order to prepare and issue financial statements, these companies' accounting equations (debit and credits) must have been in balance at year-end. How could these errors or misstatements have occurred?

The Journal

STUDY OBJECTIVE 4

Explain what a journal is and how it helps in the recording process.

Transactions are initially recorded in chronological order in **journals** before being transferred to the accounts. Thus, the journal is referred to as the book of original entry. For each transaction the journal shows the debit and credit effects on specific accounts. (In a computerized system, "journals" are now kept as files, and "accounts" are recorded in computer databases.)

Companies may use various kinds of journals, but every company has the most basic form of journal, a **general journal**. Typically, a general journal has spaces for dates, account titles and explanations, references, and two amount columns. Whenever we use the term journal in this textbook without a modifying adjective, we mean the general journal.

The journal makes several significant contributions to the recording process:

1. It discloses in one place the complete effects of a transaction.
2. It provides a chronological record of transactions.
3. It helps to prevent or locate errors because the debit and credit amounts for each entry can be readily compared.

Journalizing

Entering transaction data in the journal is known as **journalizing**. Separate journal entries are made for each transaction. A complete entry consists of: (1) the date of the transaction, (2) the accounts and amounts to be debited and credited, and (3) a brief explanation of the transaction.

Illustration 2-14 shows the technique of journalizing, using the first two transactions of Softbyte, Inc. These transactions were: September 1, stockholders invested $15,000 cash in the corporation in exchange for shares of stock, and computer equipment was purchased for $7,000 cash. The number J1 indicates that these two entries are recorded on the first page of the general journal.

Illustration 2-14
Technique of journalizing

GENERAL JOURNAL — J1

Date	Account Titles and Explanation	Ref.	Debit	Credit
2006				
Sept. 1	Cash		15,000	
	Common Stock			15,000
	(Issued shares of stock for cash)			
1	Computer Equipment		7,000	
	Cash			7,000
	(Purchased equipment for cash)			

The standard form and content of journal entries are as follows.

1. The date of the transaction is entered in the Date column. The date recorded should include the year, month, and day of the transaction.
2. The debit account title (that is, the account to be debited) is entered first at the extreme left margin of the column headed "Account Titles and Explanation," and the amount of the debit is recorded in the Debit column.
3. The credit account title (that is, the account to be credited) is indented and entered on the next line in the column headed "Account Titles and Explanation," and the amount of the credit is recorded in the Credit column.
4. A brief explanation of the transaction is given on the line below the credit account title.

5. A space is left between journal entries. The blank space separates individual journal entries and makes the entire journal easier to read.
6. The column titled Ref. (which stands for reference) is left blank when the journal entry is made. This column is used later when the journal entries are transferred to the ledger accounts. At that time, the ledger account number is placed in the Reference column to indicate where the amount in the journal entry was transferred.

No Ref. #

It is important to use correct and specific account titles in journalizing. Since most accounts appear later in the financial statements, wrong account titles lead to incorrect financial statements. Some flexibility exists initially in selecting account titles. The main criterion is that each title must appropriately describe the content of the account. For example, the account title used for the cost of delivery trucks may be Delivery Equipment, Delivery Trucks, or Trucks. Once a company chooses the specific title to use, all later transactions involving the account should be recorded under that account title.[2]

If an entry involves only two accounts, one debit and one credit, it is considered a **simple entry**. Some transactions, however, require more than two accounts in journalizing. When three or more accounts are required in one journal entry, the entry is referred to as a **compound entry**. To illustrate, assume that on July 1, Butler Company purchases a delivery truck costing $14,000 by paying $8,000 cash and the balance on account (to be paid later). The compound entry is as follows.

Illustration 2-15
Compound journal entry

GENERAL JOURNAL J1

Date	Account Titles and Explanation	Ref.	Debit	Credit
2006				
July 1	Delivery Equipment		14,000	
	Cash			8,000
	Accounts Payable			6,000
	(Purchased truck for cash with balance on account)			

HELPFUL HINT

Assume you find this compound entry:

Wages Expense 700
Cash 1,200
Rent Expense 400
(Paid cash for wages and rent) Is the entry correct? No. It is incorrect in form because both debits should be listed before the credit. It is incorrect in content because the debit amounts do not equal the credit amount.

In a compound entry, the total debit and credit amounts must be equal. Also, the standard format requires that all debits be listed before the credits.

BEFORE YOU GO ON...

Review It

1. What is the sequence of the steps in the recording process?
2. What contribution does the journal make to the recording process?
3. What is the standard form and content of a journal entry made in the general journal?

[2] In homework problems, when specific account titles are given, they should be used. When account titles are not given, you may select account titles that identify the nature and content of each account. The account titles used in journalizing should not contain explanations such as Cash Paid or Cash Received.

Do It

In establishing her beauty salon, Hair It Is, Inc., Kate Browne as president and sole stockholder engaged in the following activities.

1. Opened a bank account in the name of Hair It Is, Inc., and deposited $20,000 of her own money in this account in exchange for shares of common stock.
2. Purchased equipment on account (to be paid in 30 days) for a total cost of $4,800.
3. Interviewed three applicants for the position of beautician.

In what form (type of record) should Hair It Is, Inc., record these three activities? Prepare the entries to record the transactions.

ACTION PLAN

- Understand which activities need to be recorded and which do not. Any that have economic effects should be recorded in a journal.
- Analyze the effects of transactions on asset, liability, and stockholders' equity accounts.

SOLUTION Each transaction that is recorded is entered in the general journal. The three activities would be recorded as follows.

1. Cash	20,000	
Common Stock		20,000
(Issued shares of stock for cash)		
2. Equipment	4,800	
Accounts Payable		4,800
(Purchased equipment on account)		
3. No entry because no transaction has occurred.		

Related exercise material: *BE2-3, BE2-5, BE2-6, E2-2, E2-4, E2-6, E2-7, and E2-8.*

THE NAVIGATOR

The Ledger

STUDY OBJECTIVE 5

Explain what a ledger is and how it helps in the recording process.

The entire group of accounts maintained by a company is called the **ledger**. The ledger keeps in one place all the information about changes in specific account balances.

Companies may use various kinds of ledgers, but every company has a general ledger. A **general ledger** contains all the assets, liabilities, and stockholders' equity accounts, as shown in Illustration 2-16.

Illustration 2-16 The general ledger

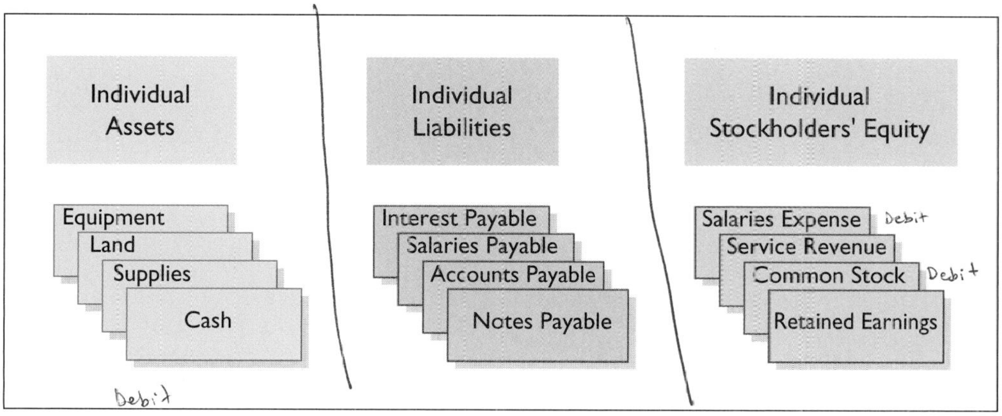

A business can use a looseleaf binder or card file for the ledger. Each account is kept on a separate sheet or card. Whenever the term ledger is used in this textbook without a modifying adjective, it means the general ledger.

The ledger should be arranged in the order in which accounts are presented in the financial statements, beginning with the balance sheet accounts. First in order are the asset accounts, followed by liability accounts, stockholders' equity accounts, revenues, and expenses. Each account is numbered for easier identification.

The ledger provides management with the balances in various accounts. For example, the Cash account shows the amount of cash that is available to meet current obligations. Amounts due from customers can be found by examining Accounts Receivable, and amounts owed to creditors can be found by examining Accounts Payable.

ACCOUNTING MATTERS! **Business Insight**

In his autobiography Sam Walton described the double-entry accounting system he began the **Wal-Mart** empire with: "We kept a little pigeonhole on the wall for the cash receipts and paperwork of each [Wal-Mart] store. I had a blue binder ledger book for each store. When we added a store, we added a pigeonhole. We did this at least up to twenty stores. Then once a month, the bookkeeper and I would enter the merchandise, enter the sales, enter the cash, and balance it."

Source: Sam Walton, *Made in America* (New York: Doubleday, 1992), p. 53.

? Why did Sam Walton keep separate pigeonholes and blue binders for each store? Why bother to keep separate records for each store?

Standard Form of Account

The simple T-account form used in accounting textbooks is often very useful for illustration purposes. However, in practice, the account forms used in ledgers are much more structured. A widely used form is shown in Illustration 2-17, using assumed data from a cash account.

Illustration 2-17
Three-column form of account

CASH — No. 101

Date	Explanation	Ref.	Debit	Credit	Balance
2006					
June 1			25,000		25,000
2				8,000	17,000
3			4,200		21,200
9			7,500		28,700
17				11,700	17,000
20				250	16,750
30				7,300	9,450

This form is often called the **three-column form of account** because it has three money columns—debit, credit, and balance. The balance in the account is determined after each transaction. Note that the explanation space and reference columns are used to provide special information about the transaction.

Posting

STUDY OBJECTIVE 6

Explain what posting is and how it helps in the recording process.

The procedure of transferring journal entries to the ledger accounts is called **posting**. Posting involves the following steps.

1. In the ledger, enter in the appropriate columns of the account(s) debited the date, journal page, and debit amount shown in the journal.
2. In the reference column of the journal, write the account number to which the debit amount was posted.
3. In the ledger, enter in the appropriate columns of the account(s) credited the date, journal page, and credit amount shown in the journal.
4. In the reference column of the journal, write the account number to which the credit amount was posted.

These four steps are diagrammed in Illustration 2-18 using the first journal entry of Softbyte, Inc. The boxed numbers indicate the sequence of the steps.

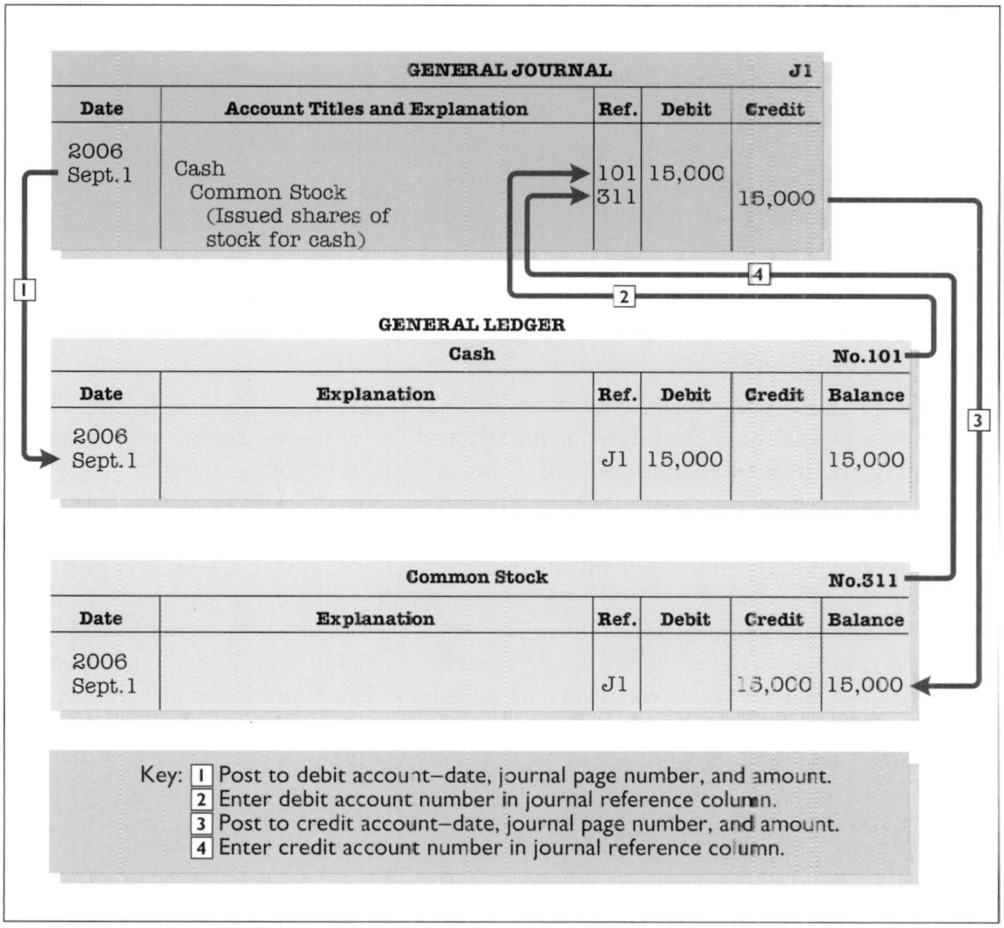

Illustration 2-18
Posting a journal entry

HELPFUL HINT

How can one tell whether all postings have been completed? Answer: Scan the reference column of the journal to see whether there are any blanks opposite account titles. If there are no blanks, all postings have been made.

Posting should be performed in chronological order. That is, all the debits and credits of one journal entry should be posted before proceeding to the next journal entry. Postings should be made on a timely basis to ensure that the ledger is up to date.[3]

The reference column **in the journal** serves several purposes. The numbers in this column indicate the entries that have been posted. After the last entry has been posted, this column should be scanned to see that all postings have been made.

The reference column **of a ledger account** indicates the journal page from which the transaction was posted. The explanation space of the ledger account is used infrequently because an explanation already appears in the journal. It generally is used only when detailed analysis of account activity is required.

ACCOUNTING MATTERS! **e Business Insight**

Determining what to record is the most critical (and for most businesses the most expensive) point in the accounting process. In computerized systems, after this phase is completed, the input and all further processing just boil down to merging files and generating reports. Programmers and management information system types with good accounting backgrounds (such as they should gain from a good principles of accounting textbook) are better able to develop effective computerized systems.

? What do accountants call those things that are first recorded at "the most critical . . . point in the accounting process"? What is the name of the "book" into which those things are first recorded? What does the accountant call the group of accounts into which the individual entries are posted (merged and filed)?

Chart of Accounts

The number and type of accounts used differ for each enterprise. The number of accounts depends on the amount of detail desired by management. For example, the management of one company may want one account for all types of utility expense. Another may keep separate expense accounts for each type of utility, such as gas, electricity, and water. Similarly, a small corporation like Softbyte, Inc. will have fewer accounts than a corporate giant like **Ford Motor Company**. Softbyte, Inc. may be able to manage and report its activities in twenty to thirty accounts, while Ford requires thousands of accounts to keep track of its worldwide activities.

Most companies have a **chart of accounts** that lists the accounts and the account numbers that identify their location in the ledger. The numbering system used to identify the accounts usually starts with the balance sheet accounts and follows with the income statement accounts.

[3] In homework problems, it will be permissible to journalize all transactions before posting any of the journal entries.

In this and the next two chapters, we will be explaining the accounting for Pioneer Advertising Agency Inc. (a service enterprise). Accounts 101–199 indicate asset accounts; 200–299 indicate liabilities; 300–399 indicate stockholders' equity accounts; 400–499, revenues; 600–799, expenses; 800–899, other revenues; and 900–999, other expenses.

The chart of accounts for Pioneer Advertising Agency Inc. is shown in Illustration 2-19. Accounts shown in red are used in this chapter; accounts shown in black are explained in later chapters.

You will notice that there are gaps in the numbering system of the chart of accounts for Pioneer Advertising Agency Inc. Gaps are left to permit the insertion of new accounts as needed during the life of the business.

Illustration 2-19
Chart of accounts for Pioneer Advertising Agency Inc.

PIONEER ADVERTISING AGENCY INC.
Chart of Accounts

Assets	Stockholders' Equity
101 Cash	**311 Common Stock**
112 Accounts Receivable	320 Retained Earnings
126 Advertising Supplies	**332 Dividends**
130 Prepaid Insurance	350 Income Summary
157 Office Equipment	
158 Accumulated Depreciation—Office Equipment	**Revenues**
	400 Service Revenue
Liabilities	**Expenses**
200 Notes Payable	631 Advertising Supplies Expense
201 Accounts Payable	711 Depreciation Expense
209 Unearned Revenue	722 Insurance Expense
212 Salaries Payable	**726 Salaries Expense**
230 Interest Payable	**729 Rent Expense**
	905 Interest Expense

The Recording Process Illustrated

Illustrations 2-20 through 2-29 show the basic steps in the recording process, using the October transactions of the Pioneer Advertising Agency Inc. Its accounting period is a month. A basic analysis and a debit-credit analysis precede the journalizing and posting of each transaction. For simplicity, the T-account form is used in the illustrations instead of the standard account form.

Study the transaction analyses in Illustrations 2-20 through 2-29 carefully. **The purpose of transaction analysis is first to identify the type of account involved, and then to determine whether a debit or a credit to the account is required.** You should always perform this type of analysis before preparing a journal entry. Doing so will help you understand the journal entries discussed in this chapter as well as more complex journal entries to be described in later chapters.

Keep in mind that every journal entry affects one or more of the following items: assets, liabilities, stockholders' equity, revenues, or expenses. By becoming skilled at transaction analysis, you will be able to recognize quickly the impact of any transaction on these five items.

Illustration 2-20
Investment of cash by stockholders

Transaction	October 1, stockholders invest $10,000 cash in an advertising venture to be known as the Pioneer Advertising Agency Inc.
Basic Analysis	The asset Cash is increased $10,000, and stockholders' equity (specifically, Common Stock) is increased $10,000.
Debit – Credit Analysis	Debits increase assets: debit Cash $10,000. Credits increase stockholders' equity: credit Common Stock $10,000

Journal Entry

Oct. 1	Cash	101	10,000	
	Common Stock	311		10,000
	(Issued shares of stock for cash)			

Posting

Cash	101
Oct. 1, 10,000	

Common Stock	311
	Oct. 1, 10,000

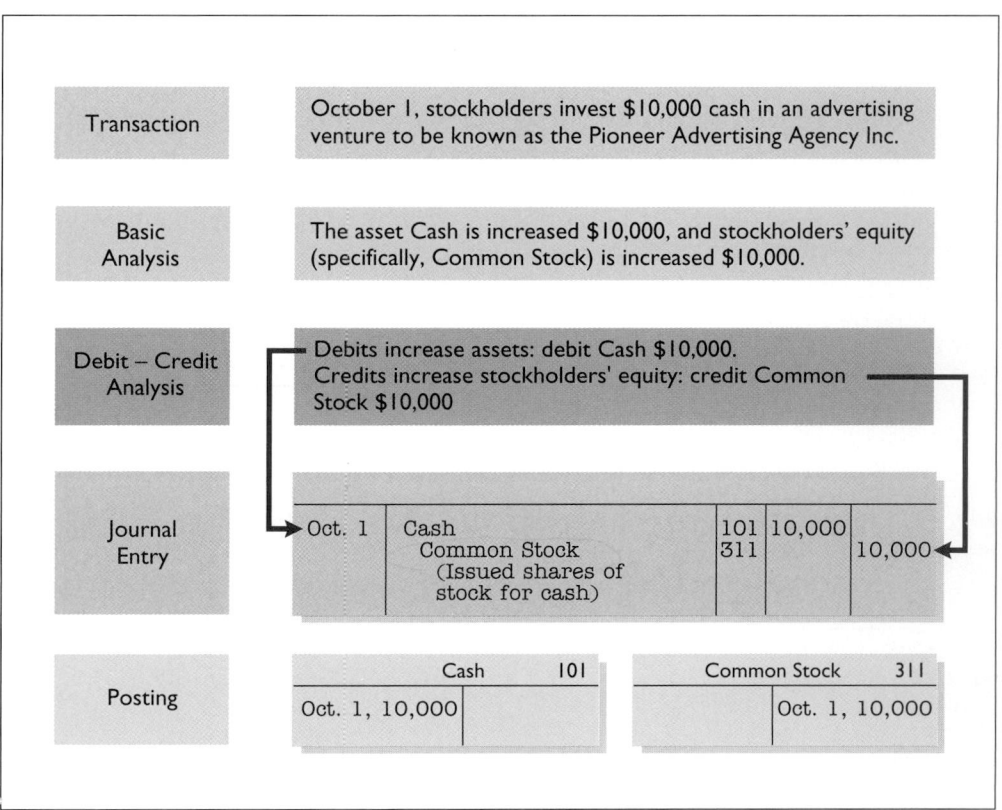

Illustration 2-21
Purchase of office equipment

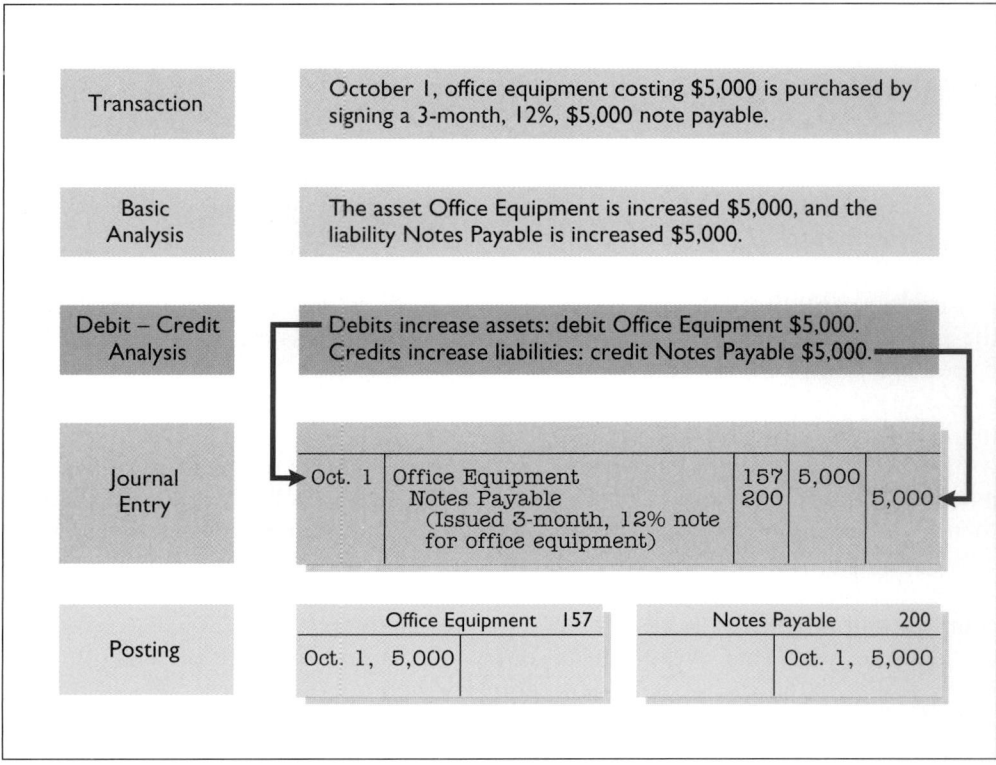

Transaction	October 1, office equipment costing $5,000 is purchased by signing a 3-month, 12%, $5,000 note payable.
Basic Analysis	The asset Office Equipment is increased $5,000, and the liability Notes Payable is increased $5,000.
Debit – Credit Analysis	Debits increase assets: debit Office Equipment $5,000. Credits increase liabilities: credit Notes Payable $5,000.

Journal Entry

Oct. 1	Office Equipment	157	5,000	
	Notes Payable	200		5,000
	(Issued 3-month, 12% note for office equipment)			

Posting

Office Equipment	157
Oct. 1, 5,000	

Notes Payable	200
	Oct. 1, 5,000

Illustration 2-22
Receipt of cash for future service

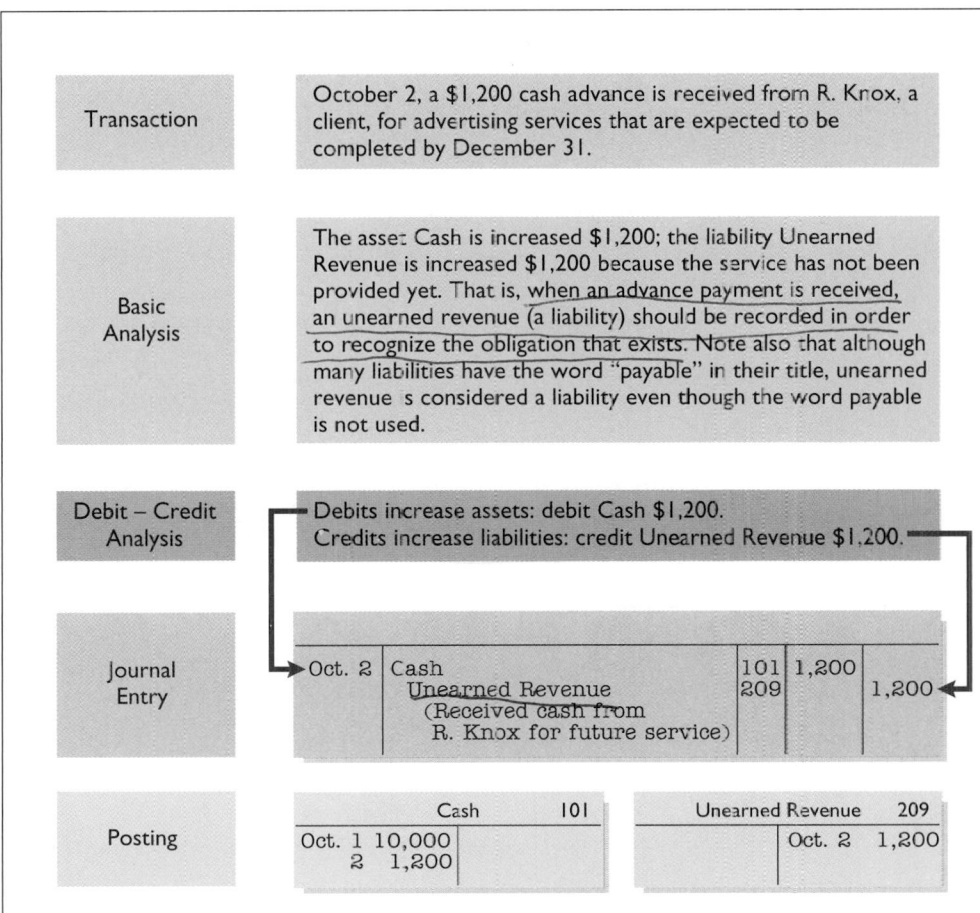

Transaction	October 2, a $1,200 cash advance is received from R. Knox, a client, for advertising services that are expected to be completed by December 31.
Basic Analysis	The asset Cash is increased $1,200; the liability Unearned Revenue is increased $1,200 because the service has not been provided yet. That is, when an advance payment is received, an unearned revenue (a liability) should be recorded in order to recognize the obligation that exists. Note also that although many liabilities have the word "payable" in their title, unearned revenue is considered a liability even though the word payable is not used.
Debit – Credit Analysis	Debits increase assets: debit Cash $1,200. Credits increase liabilities: credit Unearned Revenue $1,200.

Journal Entry

Oct. 2	Cash	101	1,200	
	Unearned Revenue	209		1,200
	(Received cash from R. Knox for future service)			

Posting

Cash		101
Oct. 1	10,000	
2	1,200	

Unearned Revenue		209
	Oct. 2	1,200

HELPFUL HINT

When the revenue is earned, the Unearned Revenue account is debited (decreased), and a revenue account is credited (increased).

Illustration 2-23
Payment of monthly rent

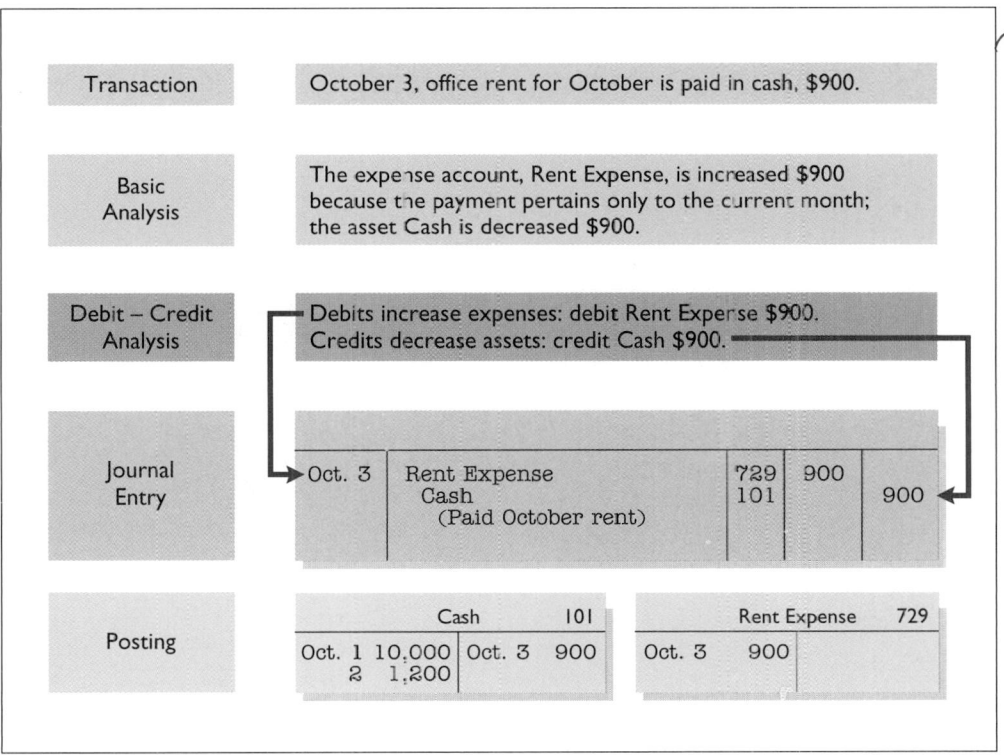

Transaction	October 3, office rent for October is paid in cash, $900.
Basic Analysis	The expense account, Rent Expense, is increased $900 because the payment pertains only to the current month; the asset Cash is decreased $900.
Debit – Credit Analysis	Debits increase expenses: debit Rent Expense $900. Credits decrease assets: credit Cash $900.

Journal Entry

Oct. 3	Rent Expense	729	900	
	Cash	101		900
	(Paid October rent)			

Posting

Cash			101
Oct. 1	10,000	Oct. 3	900
2	1,200		

Rent Expense		729
Oct. 3	900	

Illustration 2-24
Payment for insurance

Transaction

October 4, $600 is paid for a one-year insurance policy that will expire next year on September 30.

Basic Analysis

The asset Prepaid Insurance is increased $600 because the payment extends to more than the current month; the asset Cash is decreased $600. Note that payments of expenses that will benefit more than one accounting period are identified as prepaid expenses or prepayments. When a payment is made, an asset account is debited in order to show the service or benefit that will be received in the future.

Debit – Credit Analysis

Debits increase assets: debit Prepaid Insurance $600.
Credits decrease assets: credit Cash $600.

Journal Entry

Oct. 4	Prepaid Insurance	130	600	
	Cash	101		600
	(Paid one-year policy; effective date October 1)			

Posting

Cash 101

Oct. 1	10,000	Oct. 3	900
2	1,200	4	600

Prepaid Insurance 130

Oct. 4	600		

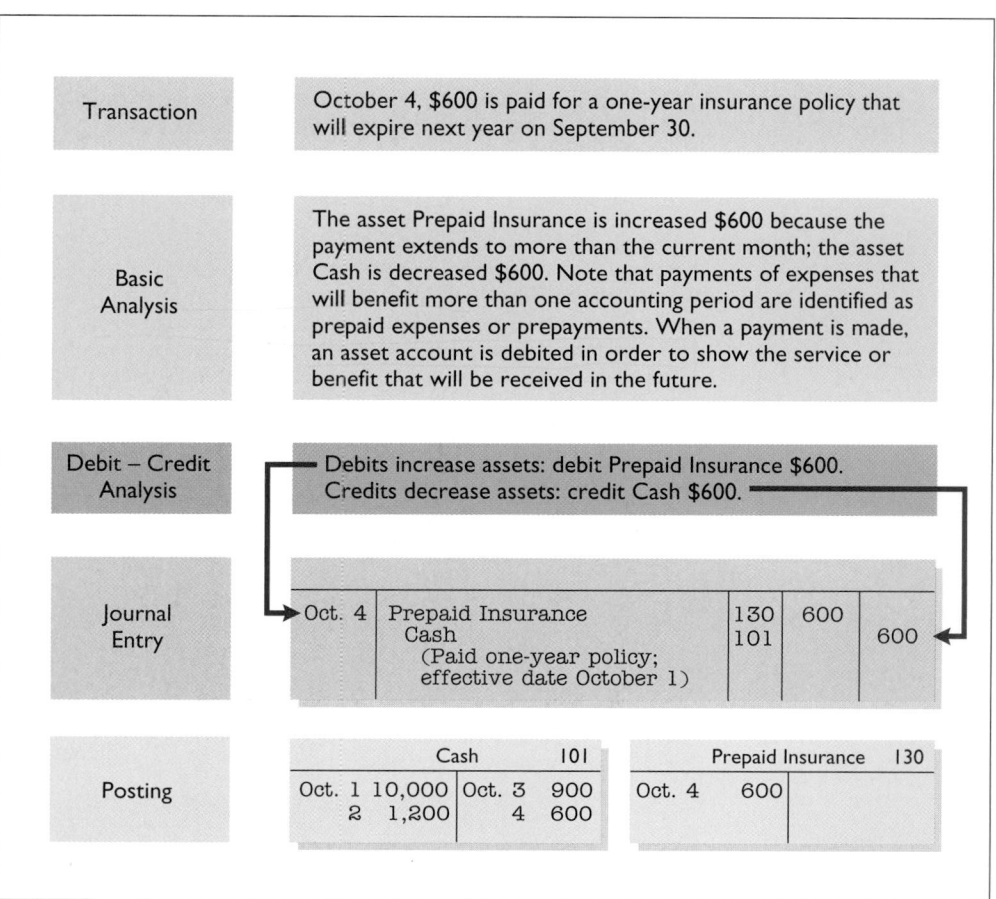

Illustration 2-25
Purchase of supplies on credit

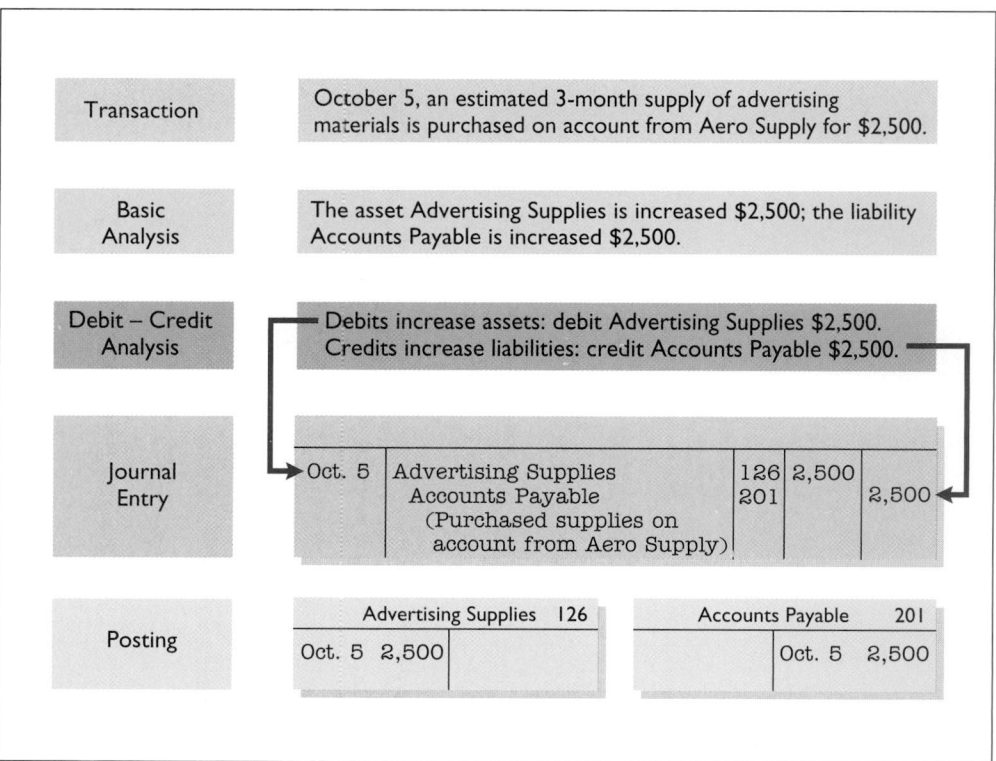

Transaction

October 5, an estimated 3-month supply of advertising materials is purchased on account from Aero Supply for $2,500.

Basic Analysis

The asset Advertising Supplies is increased $2,500; the liability Accounts Payable is increased $2,500.

Debit – Credit Analysis

Debits increase assets: debit Advertising Supplies $2,500.
Credits increase liabilities: credit Accounts Payable $2,500.

Journal Entry

Oct. 5	Advertising Supplies	126	2,500	
	Accounts Payable	201		2,500
	(Purchased supplies on account from Aero Supply)			

Posting

Advertising Supplies 126

Oct. 5	2,500		

Accounts Payable 201

		Oct. 5	2,500

Illustration 2-26
Hiring of employees

Transaction	October 9, hire four employees to begin work on October 15. Each employee is to receive a weekly salary of $500 for a 5-day work week, payable every 2 weeks—first payment made on October 26.
Basic Analysis	A business transaction has not occurred. There is only an agreement between the employer and the employees to enter into a business transaction beginning on October 15. Thus, a debit–credit analysis is not needed because there is no accounting entry. (See transaction of October 26 for first entry.)

Illustration 2-27
Declaration and payment of dividend by corporation

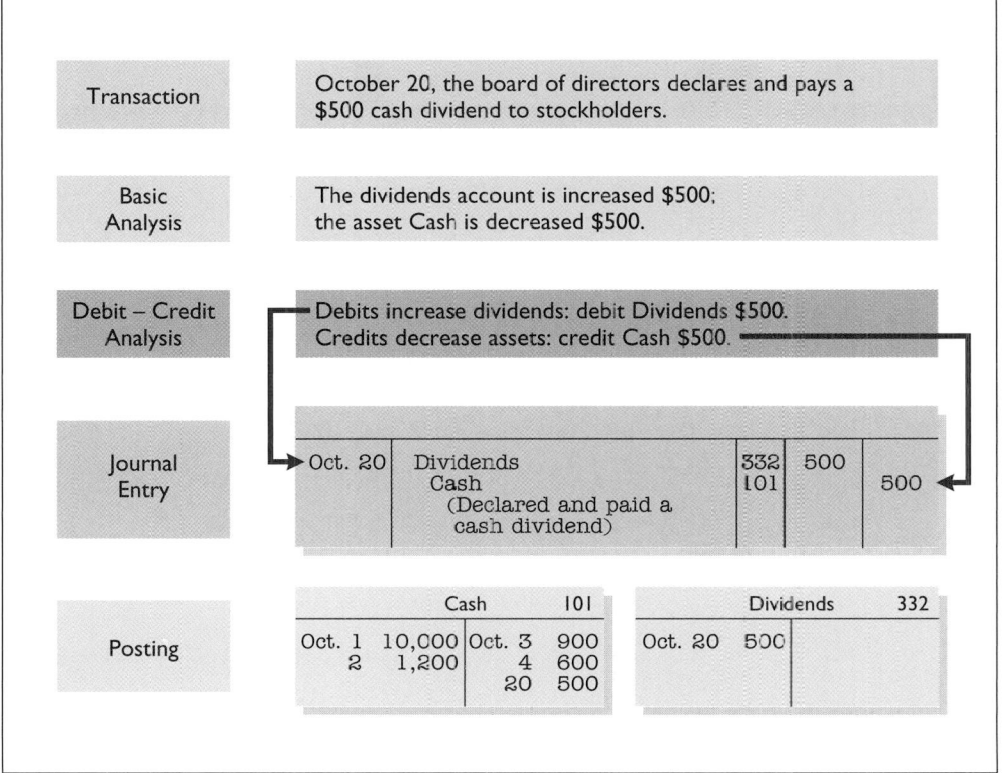

Transaction	October 20, the board of directors declares and pays a $500 cash dividend to stockholders.
Basic Analysis	The dividends account is increased $500; the asset Cash is decreased $500.
Debit – Credit Analysis	Debits increase dividends: debit Dividends $500. Credits decrease assets: credit Cash $500.

Journal Entry

Oct. 20	Dividends	332	500	
	Cash	101		500
	(Declared and paid a cash dividend)			

Posting

Cash 101

Oct. 1	10,000	Oct. 3	900
2	1,200	4	600
		20	500

Dividends 332

Oct. 20	500		

Illustration 2-28
Payment of salaries

Transaction	October 26, employee salaries of $4,000 are owed and paid in cash. (See October 9 transaction.)
Basic Analysis	The expense account Salaries Expense is increased $4,000; the asset Cash is decreased $4,000.
Debit – Credit Analysis	Debits increase expenses: debit Salaries Expense $4,000. Credits decrease assets: credit Cash $4,000.

Journal Entry

Oct. 26	Salaries Expense	726	4,000	
	Cash	101		4,000
	(Paid salaries to date)			

Posting

Cash			101
Oct. 1	10,000	Oct. 3	900
2	1,200	4	600
		20	500
		26	4,000

Salaries Expense			726
Oct. 26	4,000		

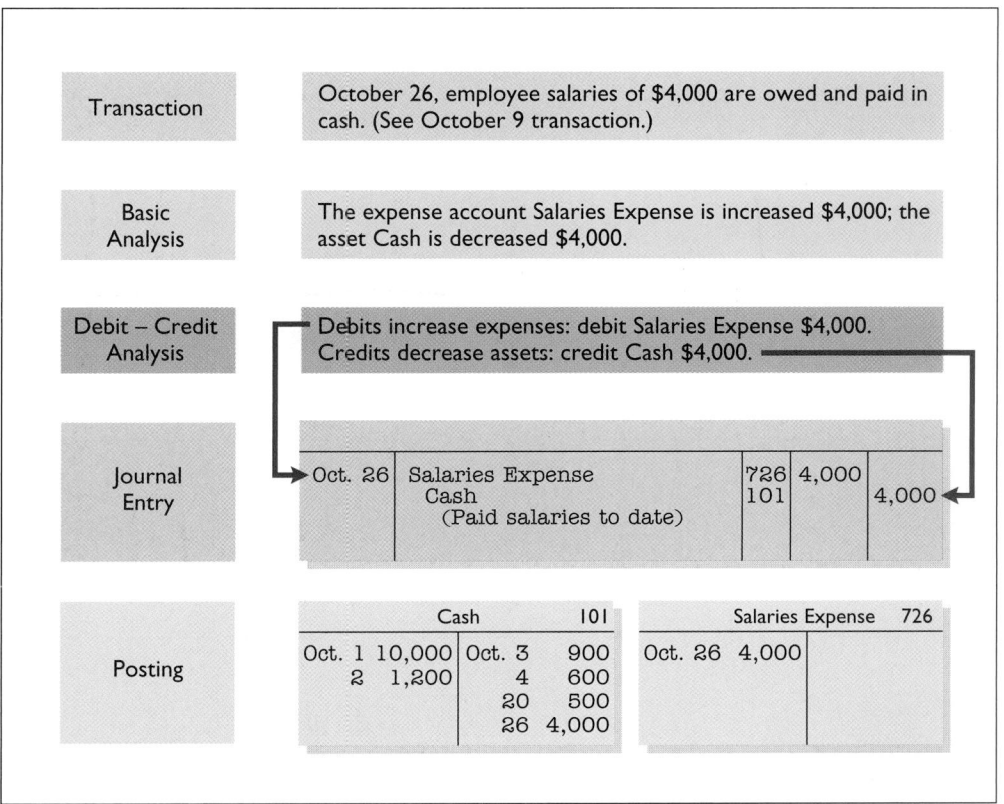

Illustration 2-29
Receipt of cash for services provided

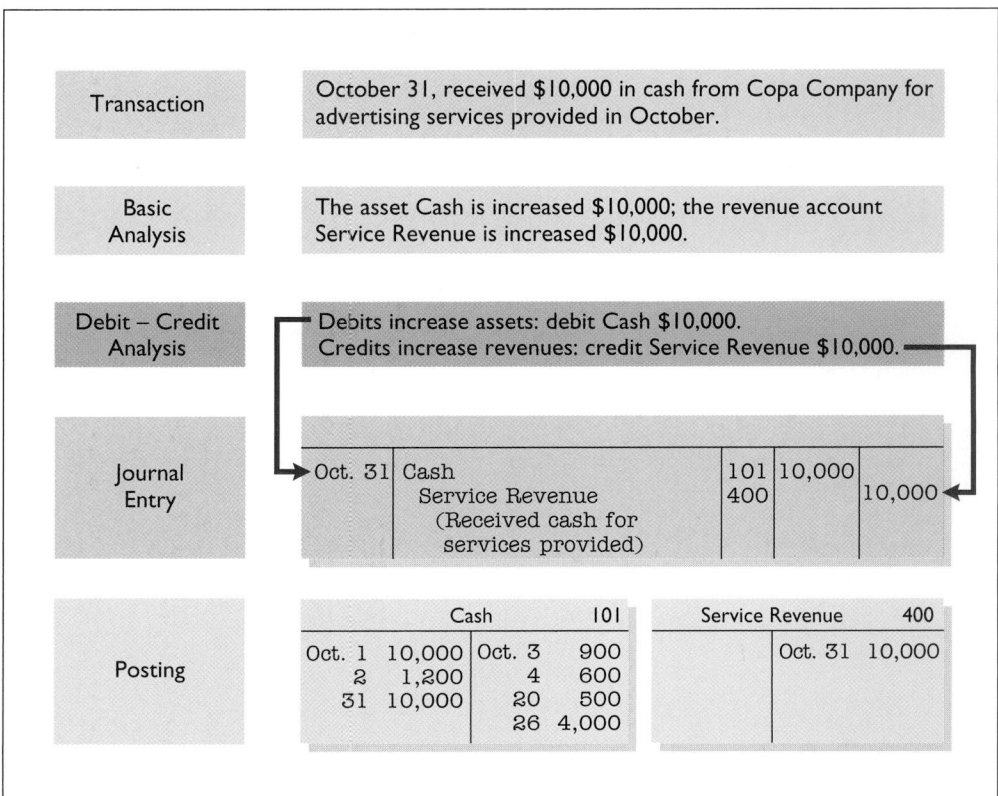

Transaction	October 31, received $10,000 in cash from Copa Company for advertising services provided in October.
Basic Analysis	The asset Cash is increased $10,000; the revenue account Service Revenue is increased $10,000.
Debit – Credit Analysis	Debits increase assets: debit Cash $10,000. Credits increase revenues: credit Service Revenue $10,000.

Journal Entry

Oct. 31	Cash	101	10,000	
	Service Revenue	400		10,000
	(Received cash for services provided)			

Posting

Cash			101
Oct. 1	10,000	Oct. 3	900
2	1,200	4	600
31	10,000	20	500
		26	4,000

Service Revenue			400
		Oct. 31	10,000

BEFORE YOU GO ON...

Review It

1. How does journalizing differ from posting?
2. What is the purpose of the (a) ledger and (b) chart of accounts?
3. Why are gaps left in the chart of accounts numbering system?

Do It

Hair It Is, Inc. recorded the following transactions in a general journal during the month of March.

Cash	2,280	
Service Revenue		2,280
Wages Expense	400	
Cash		400
Utilities Expense	92	
Cash		92

Post these entries to the general ledger accounts. Determine the ending balance in the Cash account. The beginning balance in cash on March 1 was $600.

ACTION PLAN

- Recall that posting involves transferring the journalized debits and credits to specific accounts in the ledger.
- Determine the ending balance by netting the total debits and credits.

SOLUTION

Cash

3/1	600	400
	2,280	92
3/31 Bal.	2,388	

Service Revenue

	2,280

Wages Expense

400	

Utilities Expense

92	

Related exercise material: *BE2-7, BE2-8, E2-5, and E2-8.*

THE NAVIGATOR

Summary Illustration of Journalizing and Posting

The journal for Pioneer Advertising Agency Inc. for October is shown in Illustration 2-30. The ledger is shown in Illustration 2-31, on page 69, with all balances in color.

Illustration 2-30
General journal entries

GENERAL JOURNAL — Page J1

Date	Account Titles and Explanation	Ref.	Debit	Credit
2006				
Oct. 1	Cash	101	10,000	
	Common Stock	311		10,000
	(Issued shares of stock for cash)			
1	Office Equipment	157	5,000	
	Notes Payable	200		5,000
	(Issued 3-month, 12% note for office equipment)			
2	Cash	101	1,200	
	Unearned Revenue	209		1,200
	(Received cash from R. Knox for future services)			
3	Rent Expense	729	900	
	Cash	101		900
	(Paid October rent)			
4	Prepaid Insurance	130	600	
	Cash	101		600
	(Paid one-year policy; effective date October 1)			
5	Advertising Supplies	126	2,500	
	Accounts Payable	201		2,500
	(Purchased supplies on account from Aero Supply)			
20	Dividends	332	500	
	Cash	101		500
	(Declared and paid a cash dividend)			
26	Salaries Expense	726	4,000	
	Cash	101		4,000
	(Paid salaries to date)			
31	Cash	101	10,000	
	Service Revenue	400		10,000
	(Received cash for services provided)			

Illustration 2-31
General ledger

General Ledger

Cash — No. 101

Date	Explanation	Ref.	Debit	Credit	Balance
2006					
Oct. 1		J1	10,000		10,000
2		J1	1,200		11,200
3		J1		900	10,300
4		J1		600	9,700
20		J1		500	9,200
26		J1		4,000	5,200
31		J1	10,000		**15,200**

Advertising Supplies — No. 126

Date	Explanation	Ref.	Debit	Credit	Balance
2006					
Oct. 5		J1	2,500		**2,500**

Prepaid Insurance — No. 130

Date	Explanation	Ref.	Debit	Credit	Balance
2006					
Oct. 4		J1	600		**600**

Office Equipment — No. 157

Date	Explanation	Ref.	Debit	Credit	Balance
2006					
Oct. 1		J1	5,000		**5,000**

Notes Payable — No. 200

Date	Explanation	Ref.	Debit	Credit	Balance
2006					
Oct. 1		J1		5,000	**5,000**

Accounts Payable — No. 201

Date	Explanation	Ref.	Debit	Credit	Balance
2006					
Oct. 5		J1		2,500	**2,500**

Unearned Revenue — No. 209

Date	Explanation	Ref.	Debit	Credit	Balance
2006					
Oct. 2		J1		1,200	**1,200**

Common Stock — No. 311

Date	Explanation	Ref.	Debit	Credit	Balance
2006					
Oct. 1		J1		10,000	**10,000**

Dividends — No. 332

Date	Explanation	Ref.	Debit	Credit	Balance
2006					
Oct. 20		J1	500		**500**

Service Revenue — No. 400

Date	Explanation	Ref.	Debit	Credit	Balance
2006					
Oct. 31		J1		10,000	**10,000**

Salaries Expense — No. 726

Date	Explanation	Ref.	Debit	Credit	Balance
2006					
Oct. 26		J1	4,000		**4,000**

Rent Expense — No. 729

Date	Explanation	Ref.	Debit	Credit	Balance
2006					
Oct. 3		J1	900		**900**

The Trial Balance

STUDY OBJECTIVE 7
Prepare a trial balance and explain its purposes.

A **trial balance** is a list of accounts and their balances at a given time. Customarily, a trial balance is prepared at the end of an accounting period. The accounts are listed in the order in which they appear in the ledger; debit balances are listed in the left column and credit balances in the right column.

The primary purpose of a trial balance is to prove (check) that the debits equal the credits after posting. In other words, the sum of the debit account balances in the trial balance should equal the sum of the credit account balances. **If the debits and credits do not agree, the trial balance can be used to uncover errors in journalizing and posting. In addition, it is useful in the preparation of financial statements,** as will be explained in the next two chapters.

The steps for preparing a trial balance are:

1. List the account titles and their balances.
2. Total the debit and credit columns.
3. Prove the equality of the two columns.

The trial balance prepared from Pioneer Advertising's ledger is shown below.

Illustration 2-32
A trial balance

PIONEER ADVERTISING AGENCY INC.
Trial Balance
October 31, 2006

	Debit	Credit
Cash	$15,200	
Advertising Supplies	2,500	
Prepaid Insurance	600	
Office Equipment	5,000	
Notes Payable		$ 5,000
Accounts Payable		2,500
Unearned Revenue		1,200
Common Stock		10,000
Dividends	500	
Service Revenue		10,000
Salaries Expense	4,000	
Rent Expense	900	
	$28,700	**$28,700**

HELPFUL HINT

To sum a column of figures is sometimes referred to as *to foot* the column. The column is then said to be *footed.*

HELPFUL HINT

A trial balance is so named because it is a test to see if the sum of the debit balances equals the sum of the credit balances.

Note that the total debits ($28,700) equal the total credits ($28,700). Account numbers are sometimes shown to the left of the account titles in the trial balance.

A trial balance is a necessary checkpoint for uncovering certain types of errors before you proceed to other steps in the accounting process. For example, if only the debit portion of a journal entry has been posted, the trial balance would bring this error to light.

Limitations of a Trial Balance

A trial balance does not guarantee freedom from recording errors, however. **It does not prove that all transactions have been recorded or that the ledger is correct.** Numerous errors may exist even though the trial balance columns agree. For example, the trial balance may balance even when (1) a transaction is not journalized, (2) a correct journal entry is not posted, (3) a journal entry is posted twice, (4) incorrect accounts are used in journalizing or posting, or (5) offsetting errors are made in recording the amount of a transaction. In other words, as long as equal debits and credits are posted, even to the wrong account or in the wrong amount, the total debits will equal the total credits.

ETHICS NOTE

Auditors are required to differentiate *errors* from *irregularities* when evaluating the accounting system. An error is the result of an unintentional mistake; as such, it is neither ethical nor unethical. An irregularity, on the other hand, is an intentional misstatement, which is viewed as unethical.

Locating Errors

The procedure for preparing a trial balance is relatively simple. However, if the trial balance does not balance, locating an error in a manual system can be time-consuming, tedious, and frustrating. Errors generally result from mathematical mistakes, incorrect postings, or simply transcribing data incorrectly.

What do you do if you are faced with a trial balance that does not balance? First determine the amount of the difference between the two columns of the trial balance. After this amount is known, the following steps are often helpful:

1. If the error is $1, $10, $100, or $1,000, re-add the trial balance columns and re-compute the account balances.
2. If the error is divisible by 2, scan the trial balance to see whether a balance equal to half the error has been entered in the wrong column.
3. If the error is divisible by 9, retrace the account balances on the trial balance to see whether they are incorrectly copied from the ledger. For example, if a balance was $12 and it was listed as $21, a $9 error has been made. Reversing the order of numbers is called a transposition error.
4. If the error is not divisible by 2 or 9 (for example, $365), scan the ledger to see whether an account balance of $365 has been omitted from the trial balance, and scan the journal to see whether a $365 posting has been omitted.

Use of Dollar Signs

Note that dollar signs do not appear in the journals or ledgers. Dollar signs are usually used only in the trial balance and the financial statements. Generally, a dollar sign is shown only for the first item in the column and for the total of that column. A single line is placed under the column of figures to be added or subtracted; the total amount is double underlined to indicate the final sum.

HELPFUL HINT

We have avoided the use of cents in the text to save you time and effort.

BEFORE YOU GO ON...

Review It

1. What is a trial balance and what is its primary purpose?
2. How is a trial balance prepared?
3. What are the limitations of a trial balance?

THE NAVIGATOR

DEMONSTRATION PROBLEM

Bob Sample and other student investors opened the Campus Laundromat Inc. on September 1, 2006. During the first month of operations the following transactions occurred.

Sept. 1 Stockholders invested $20,000 cash in the business.
2 Paid $1,000 cash for store rent for the month of September.
3 Purchased washers and dryers for $25,000, paying $10,000 in cash and signing a $15,000, 6-month, 12% note payable.
4 Paid $1,200 for one-year accident insurance policy.
10 Received bill from the *Daily News* for advertising the opening of the laundromat $200.
20 Declared and paid a cash dividend to stockholders $700.
30 Determined that cash receipts for laundry fees for the month were $6,200.

The chart of accounts for the company is the same as for Pioneer Advertising Agency Inc. except for the following: No. 154 Laundry Equipment and No. 610 Advertising Expense.

Instructions

(a) Journalize the September transactions. (Use **J1** for the journal page number.)
(b) Open ledger accounts and post the September transactions.
(c) Prepare a trial balance at September 30, 2006.

ACTION PLAN

- Make separate journal entries for each transaction.
- In journalizing, make sure debits equal credits.
- In journalizing, use specific account titles taken from the chart of accounts.
- Provide appropriate description of journal entry.
- Arrange ledger in statement order, beginning with the balance sheet accounts.
- Post in chronological order.
- Use numbers in the reference column to indicate the amount has been posted.
- In the trial balance, list accounts in the order in which they appear in the ledger.
- List debit balances in the left column, and credit balances in the right column.

SOLUTION TO DEMONSTRATION PROBLEM

(a) GENERAL JOURNAL **J1**

Date	Account Titles and Explanation	Ref.	Debit	Credit
2006				
Sept. 1	Cash	101	20,000	
	Common Stock	311		20,000
	(Stockholders invested cash in business)			
2	Rent Expense	729	1,000	
	Cash	101		1,000
	(Paid September rent)			
3	Laundry Equipment	154	25,000	
	Cash	101		10,000
	Notes Payable	200		15,000
	(Purchased laundry equipment for cash and 6-month, 12% note payable)			
4	Prepaid Insurance	130	1,200	
	Cash	101		1,200
	(Paid one-year insurance policy)			
10	Advertising Expense	610	200	
	Accounts Payable	201		200
	(Received bill from *Daily News* for advertising)			
20	Dividends	332	700	
	Cash	101		700
	(Declared and paid a cash dividend)			
30	Cash	101	6,200	
	Service Revenue	400		6,200
	(Received cash for laundry fees earned)			

(b) GENERAL LEDGER

Cash No. 101

Date	Explanation	Ref.	Debit	Credit	Balance
2006					
Sept. 1		J1	20,000		20,000
2		J1		1,000	19,000
3		J1		10,000	9,000
4		J1		1,200	7,800
20		J1		700	7,100
30		J1	6,200		13,300

Prepaid Insurance No. 130

Date	Explanation	Ref.	Debit	Credit	Balance
2006					
Sept. 4		J1	1,200		1,200

Laundry Equipment No. 154

Date	Explanation	Ref.	Debit	Credit	Balance
2006					
Sept. 3		J1	25,000		25,000

Notes Payable No. 200

Date	Explanation	Ref.	Debit	Credit	Balance
2006					
Sept. 3		J1		15,000	15,000

Accounts Payable No. 201

Date	Explanation	Ref.	Debit	Credit	Balance
2006					
Sept. 10		J1		200	200

Common Stock No. 311

Date	Explanation	Ref.	Debit	Credit	Balance
2006					
Sept. 1		J1		20,000	20,000

Dividends No. 332

Date	Explanation	Ref.	Debit	Credit	Balance
2006					
Sept. 20		J1	700		700

Service Revenue — No. 400

Date	Explanation	Ref.	Debit	Credit	Balance
2006					
Sept. 30		J1		6,200	6,200

Advertising Expense — No. 610

Date	Explanation	Ref.	Debit	Credit	Balance
2006					
Sept. 10		J1	200		200

Rent Expense — No. 729

Date	Explanation	Ref.	Debit	Credit	Balance
2006					
Sept. 2		J1	1,000		1,000

(c)

CAMPUS LAUNDROMAT INC.
Trial Balance
September 30, 2006

	Debit	Credit
Cash	$13,300	
Prepaid Insurance	1,200	
Laundry Equipment	25,000	
Notes Payable		$15,000
Accounts Payable		200
Common Stock		20,000
Dividends	700	
Service Revenue		6,200
Advertising Expense	200	
Rent Expense	1,000	
	$41,400	$41,400

THE NAVIGATOR

SUMMARY OF STUDY OBJECTIVES

1. **Explain what an account is and how it helps in the recording process.** An account is a record of increases and decreases in a specific asset, liability, or stockholders' equity item.
2. **Define debits and credits and explain how they are used to record business transactions.** The terms debit and credit are synonymous with left and right. Assets, dividends, and expenses are increased by debits and decreased by credits. Liabilities, common stock, retained earnings, and revenues are increased by credits and decreased by debits.
3. **Identify the basic steps in the recording process.** The basic steps in the recording process are: (a) analyze each transaction in terms of its effects on the accounts, (b) enter the transaction information in a journal, (c) transfer the journal information to the appropriate accounts in the ledger.
4. **Explain what a journal is and how it helps in the recording process.** The initial accounting record of a transaction is entered in a journal before the data are entered in the accounts. A journal (a) discloses in one place the complete effects of a transaction, (b) provides a chronological record of transactions, and (c) prevents or locates errors because the debit and credit amounts for each entry can be readily compared.
5. **Explain what a ledger is and how it helps in the recording process.** The entire group of accounts maintained by a company is referred to as the ledger. The ledger keeps in one place all the information about changes in specific account balances.
6. **Explain what posting is and how it helps in the recording process.** Posting is the procedure of transferring journal entries to the ledger accounts. This phase of the recording process accumulates the effects of journalized transactions in the individual accounts.
7. **Prepare a trial balance and explain its purposes.** A trial balance is a list of accounts and their balances at a given time. Its primary purpose is to prove the equality of debits and credits after posting. A trial balance also uncovers errors in journalizing and posting and is useful in preparing financial statements.

THE NAVIGATOR

GLOSSARY

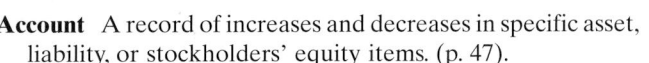

Account A record of increases and decreases in specific asset, liability, or stockholders' equity items. (p. 47).

Chart of accounts A list of accounts and the account numbers that identify their location in the ledger. (p. 60).

Common stock Issued in exchange for the owners' investment paid in to the corporation. (p. 50).

Compound entry A journal entry that involves three or more accounts. (p. 56).

Credit The right side of an account. (p. 48).

Debit The left side of an account. (p. 48).

Dividend A distribution by a corporation to its stockholders on a pro rata (equal) basis. (p. 50).

Double-entry system A system that records in appropriate accounts the dual effect of each transaction. (p. 48).

General journal The most basic form of journal. (p. 55).

General ledger A ledger that contains all asset, liability, and stockholders' equity accounts. (p. 57).

Journal An accounting record in which transactions are initially recorded in chronological order. (p. 55).

Journalizing The entering of transaction data in the journal. (p. 55).

Ledger The entire group of accounts maintained by a company. (p. 57).

Posting The procedure of transferring journal entries to the ledger accounts. (p. 59).

Retained earnings Net income that is retained in the business. (p. 50).

Simple entry A journal entry that involves only two accounts. (p. 56).

T account The basic form of an account. (p. 47).

Three-column form of account A form with columns for debit, credit, and balance amounts in an account. (p. 59).

Trial balance A list of accounts and their balances at a given time. (p. 69).

SELF-STUDY QUESTIONS

Self-Study/Self-Test

Answers are at the end of the chapter.

(SO 1) **1.** Which of the following statements about an account is true?
- **a.** In its simplest form, an account consists of two parts.
- **b.** An account is an individual accounting record of increases and decreases in specific asset, liability, and stockholders' equity items.
- **c.** There are separate accounts for specific assets and liabilities but only one account for stockholders' equity items.
- **d.** The left side of an account is the credit or decrease side.

(SO 2) **2.** Debits:
- **a.** increase both assets and liabilities.
- **b.** decrease both assets and liabilities.
- **c.** increase assets and decrease liabilities.
- **d.** decrease assets and increase liabilities.

(SO 2) **3.** A revenue account:
- **a.** is increased by debits.
- **b.** is decreased by credits.
- **c.** has a normal balance of a debit.
- **d.** is increased by credits.

(SO 2) **4.** Accounts that normally have debit balances are:
- **a.** assets, expenses, and revenues.
- **b.** assets, expenses, and common stock.
- **c.** assets, liabilities, and dividends.
- **d.** assets, dividends, and expenses.

(SO 3) **5.** Which of the following is *not* part of the recording process?
- **a.** Analyzing transactions.
- **b.** Preparing a trial balance.
- **c.** Entering transactions in a journal.
- **d.** Posting transactions.

(SO 4) **6.** Which of the following statements about a journal is false?
- **a.** It is not a book of original entry.
- **b.** It provides a chronological record of transactions.
- **c.** It helps to locate errors because the debit and credit amounts for each entry can be readily compared.
- **d.** It discloses in one place the complete effect of a transaction.

7. A ledger: (SO 5)
- **a.** contains only asset and liability accounts.
- **b.** should show accounts in alphabetical order.
- **c.** is a collection of the entire group of accounts maintained by a company.
- **d.** is a book of original entry.

8. Posting: (SO 6)
- **a.** normally occurs before journalizing.
- **b.** transfers ledger transaction data to the journal.
- **c.** is an optional step in the recording process.
- **d.** transfers journal entries to ledger accounts.

9. A trial balance: (SO 7)
- **a.** is a list of accounts with their balances at a given time.
- **b.** proves the mathematical accuracy of journalized transactions.
- **c.** will not balance if a correct journal entry is posted twice.
- **d.** proves that all transactions have been recorded.

10. A trial balance will not balance if: (SO 7)
- **a.** a correct journal entry is posted twice.
- **b.** the purchase of supplies on account is debited to Supplies and credited to Cash.
- **c.** a $100 cash dividend by the corporation is debited to Dividends for $1,000 and credited to Cash for $100.
- **d.** a $450 payment on account is debited to Accounts Payable for $45 and credited to Cash for $45.

THE NAVIGATOR

QUESTIONS

1. Why is an account referred to as a T account?
2. "The terms *debit* and *credit* mean increase and decrease, respectively." Do you agree? Explain.
3. Britney Spears, a fellow student, contends that the double-entry system means each transaction must be recorded twice. Is Britney correct? Explain.
4. Julia Roberts, a beginning accounting student, believes debit balances are favorable and credit balances are unfavorable. Is Julia correct? Discuss.
5. State the rules of debit and credit as applied to (a) asset accounts, (b) liability accounts, and (c) stockholders' equity.
6. What is the normal balance for each of the following accounts? (a) Accounts Receivable. (b) Cash. (c) Dividends. (d) Accounts Payable. (e) Service Revenue. (f) Salaries Expense. (g) Common Stock.
7. Indicate whether each of the following accounts is an asset, a liability, or a stockholders' equity account and whether it would have a debit or credit balance: (a) Accounts Receivable, (b) Accounts Payable, (c) Equipment, (d) Dividends, (e) Supplies.
8. For the following transactions, indicate the account debited and the account credited.
   (a) Supplies are purchased on account.
   (b) Cash is received on signing a note payable.
   (c) Employees are paid salaries in cash.
9. Presented below is a series of accounts. Indicate whether these accounts generally will have (a) debit entries only, (b) credit entries only, (c) both debit and credit entries.
   (1) Cash.
   (2) Accounts Receivable.
   (3) Dividends.
   (4) Accounts Payable.
   (5) Salaries Expense.
   (6) Service Revenue.
10. What are the basic steps in the recording process?
11. What are the advantages of using the journal in the recording process?
12. (a) When entering a transaction in the journal, should the debit or credit be written first?
    (b) Which should be indented, the debit or credit?
13. Describe a compound entry, and provide an example
14. (a) Should business transaction debits and credits be recorded directly in the ledger accounts?
    (b) What are the advantages of first recording transactions in the journal and then posting to the ledger?
15. The account number is entered as the last step in posting the amounts from the journal to the ledger. What is the advantage of this step?
16. Journalize the following business transactions.
    (a) Tom Cruise invests $12,000 in the business in exchange for shares of common stock.
    (b) Insurance of $720 is paid for the year.
    (c) Supplies of $900 are purchased on account.
    (d) Cash of $3,000 is received for services rendered.
17. (a) What is a ledger? (b) Why is a chart of accounts important?
18. What is a trial balance and what are its purposes?
19. Joe Alverez is confused about how accounting information flows through the accounting system. He believes the flow of information is as follows.
    (a) Debits and credits posted to the ledger.
    (b) Business transaction occurs.
    (c) Information entered in the journal.
    (d) Financial statements are prepared.
    (e) Trial balance is prepared.
    Indicate to Joe the proper flow of the information.
20. Two students are discussing the use of a trial balance. They wonder whether the following errors, each considered separately, would prevent the trial balance from balancing.
    (a) The bookkeeper debited Cash for $600 and credited Wages Expense for $600 for payment of wages.
    (b) Cash collected on account was debited to Cash for $800 and Service Revenue was credited for $80.
    What would you tell them?

BRIEF EXERCISES

BE2-1 For each of the following accounts indicate (a) the effect of a debit or a credit on the account and (b) the normal balance.

Indicate debit and credit effects and normal balance.

(SO 2)

1. Accounts Payable.
2. Advertising Expense.
3. Service Revenue.
4. Accounts Receivable.
5. Common Stock.
6. Dividends.

Identify accounts to be debited and credited.
(SO 2)

BE2-2 Transactions for the Kaustav Sen Company for the month of June are presented below. Identify the accounts to be debited and credited for each transaction.

June 1 Kaustav Sen invests $4,000 cash in exchange for shares of common stock in a small welding corporation.
2 Purchases equipment on account for $900.
3 $800 cash is paid to landlord for June rent.
12 Bills J. Kronsnoble $300 for welding work done on account.

Journalize transactions.
(SO 4)

BE2-3 Using the data in BE2-2, journalize the transactions. (You may omit explanations.)

Identify and explain steps in recording process.
(SO 3)

BE2-4 Tim Weber, a fellow student, is unclear about the basic steps in the recording process. Identify and briefly explain the steps in the order in which they occur.

Indicate basic and debit-credit analysis.
(SO 2)

BE2-5 J. A. Motzek Inc. has the following transactions during August of the current year. Indicate (a) the effect on the accounting equation and (b) the debit-credit analysis illustrated on pages 62–66 of the text.

Aug. 1 Opens an office as a financial advisor, investing $5,000 in cash in exchange for common stock.
4 Pays insurance in advance for 6 months, $1,800 cash.
16 Receives $800 from clients for services provided.
27 Pays secretary $1,000 salary.

Journalize transactions.
(SO 4)

BE2-6 Using the data in BE2-5, journalize the transactions. (You may omit explanations.)

Post journal entries to T accounts.
(SO 6)

BE2-7 Selected transactions for the Gilles Company are presented in journal form below. Post the transactions to T accounts. Make one T account for each item and determine each account's ending balance.

J1

Date	Account Titles and Explanation	Ref.	Debit	Credit
May 5	Accounts Receivable		6,000	
	Service Revenue			6,000
	(Billed for services provided)			
12	Cash		2,400	
	Accounts Receivable			2,400
	(Received cash in payment of account)			
15	Cash		3,000	
	Service Revenue			3,000
	(Received cash for services provided)			

Post journal entries to standard form of account.
(SO 6)

BE2-8 Selected journal entries for the Gilles Company are presented in BE2-7. Post the transactions using the standard form of account.

Prepare a trial balance.
(SO 7)

BE2-9 From the ledger balances given below, prepare a trial balance for the P. J. Farve Company at June 30, 2006. List the accounts in the order shown on page 61 of the text. All account balances are normal.

Accounts Payable $9,000, Cash $6,800, Common Stock $20,000, Dividends $1,200, Equipment $17,000, Service Revenue S6,000, Accounts Receivable $3,000, Salaries Expense $6,000, and Rent Expense $1,000.

Prepare a correct trial balance.
(SO 7)

BE2-10 An inexperienced bookkeeper prepared the following trial balance. Prepare a correct trial balance, assuming all account balances are normal.

CHENG CORPORATION
Trial Balance
December 31, 2006

	Debit	Credit
Cash	$16,800	
Prepaid Insurance		$3,500
Accounts Payable		3,000
Unearned Revenue	4,200	
Common Stock		13,000
Dividends		4,500
Service Revenue		25,600
Salaries Expense	18,600	
Rent Expense		2,400
	$39,600	$52,000

EXERCISES

E2-1 Selected transactions for H. Burns, Inc., an interior decorating firm, in its first month of business, are as follows.

Identify debits, credits, and normal balances.

(SO 2)

Jan. 2 Invested $15,000 cash in business in exchange for common stock.
3 Purchased used car for $4,000 cash for use in business.
9 Purchased supplies on account for $500.
11 Billed customers $1,800 for services performed.
16 Paid $200 cash for advertising.
20 Received $700 cash from customers billed on January 11.
23 Paid creditor $300 cash on balance owed.
28 Declared and paid a $1,000 cash dividend.

Instructions

For each transaction indicate the following.

(a) The basic type of account debited and credited (asset, liability, stockholders' equity).
(b) The specific account debited and credited (cash, rent expense, service revenue, etc.).
(c) Whether the specific account is increased or decreased.
(d) The normal balance of the specific account.

Use the following format, in which the January 2 transaction is given as an example.

	Account Debited				Account Credited			
Date	**(a) Basic Type**	**(b) Specific Account**	**(c) Effect**	**(d) Normal Balance**	**(a) Basic Type**	**(b) Specific Account**	**(c) Effect**	**(d) Normal Balance**
Jan. 2	Asset	Cash	Increase	Debit	Stockholders' Equity	Common Stock	Increase	Credit

E2-2 Data for H. Burns, Inc., interior decorating, are presented in E2-1.

Journalize transactions.

(SO 4)

Instructions

Journalize the transactions using journal page J1. (You may omit explanations.)

E2-3 Presented below is information related to Robbins Real Estate Agency, Inc.

Analyze transactions and determine their effect on accounts.

(SO 2)

Oct. 1 Lynn Robbins begins business as a real estate agent with a cash investment of $20,000 in exchange for common stock.
2 Hires an administrative assistant.
3 Purchases office furniture for $1,900, on account.
6 Sells a house and lot for B. Kidman; bills B. Kidman $3,200 for realty services provided.
27 Pays $700 on the balance related to the transaction of October 3.
30 Pays the administrative assistant $2,000 in salary for October.

Instructions

Prepare the debit-credit analysis for each transaction as illustrated on pages 62–66.

Journalize transactions.
(SO 4)

E2-4 Transaction data for Robbins Real Estate Agency are presented in E2-3.

Instructions

Journalize the transactions. (You may omit explanations.)

Post journal entries and prepare a trial balance.
(SO 6, 7)

E2-5 Selected transactions from the journal of Roberta Mendez, investment broker, are presented below.

Date	Account Titles and Explanation	Ref.	Debit	Credit
Aug. 1	Cash		3,000	
	Common Stock			3,000
	(Investment of cash for stock)			
10	Cash		2,400	
	Service Revenue			2,400
	(Received cash for services provided)			
12	Office Equipment		5,000	
	Cash			1,000
	Notes Payable			4,000
	(Purchased office equipment for cash and notes payable)			
25	Accounts Receivable		1,600	
	Service Revenue			1,600
	(Billed for services provided)			
31	Cash		900	
	Accounts Receivable			900
	(Receipt of cash on account)			

Instructions

(b) Trial balance totals $11,000

(a) Post the transactions to T accounts.
(b) Prepare a trial balance at August 31, 2006.

Journalize transactions from account data and prepare a trial balance.
(SO 4, 7)

E2-6 The T accounts below summarize the ledger of Padre Landscaping Company at the end of the first month of operations.

Cash — No. 101

4/1	10,000	4/15	600
4/12	900	4/25	1,500
4/29	400		
4/30	1,000		

Unearned Revenue — No. 205

		4/30	1,000

Accounts Receivable — No. 112

4/7	3,200	4/29	400

Common Stock — No. 311

		4/1	10,000

Supplies — No. 126

4/4	1,800		

Service Revenue — No. 400

		4/7	3,200
		4/12	900

Accounts Payable — No. 201

4/25	1,500	4/4	1,800

Salaries Expense — No. 726

4/15	600		

Instructions

(b) Trial balance totals $15,400

(a) Prepare the complete general journal entries (including explanations) from which the postings to Cash were made.
(b) Prepare a trial balance at April 30, 2006.

E2-7 Presented below is the ledger for Maxim Co.

Journalize transactions from account data and prepare a trial balance.

(SO 4, 7)

Cash No. 101

10/1	5,000	10/4	400
10/10	650	10/12	1,500
10/10	3,000	10/15	250
10/20	500	10/30	300
10/25	2,000	10/31	500

Accounts Receivable No. 112

10/6	800	10/20	500
10/20	940		

Supplies No. 126

10/4	400		

Furniture No. 149

10/3	2,000		

Notes Payable No. 200

		10/10	3,000

Accounts Payable No. 201

10/12	1,500	10/3	2,000

Common Stock No. 311

		10/1	5,000
		10/25	2,000

Dividends No. 332

10/30	300		

Service Revenue No. 407

		10/6	800
		10/10	650
		10/20	940

Store Wages Expense No. 628

10/31	500		

Rent Expense No. 729

10/15	250		

Instructions

(a) Reproduce the journal entries for the transactions that occurred on October 1, 10, and 20, and provide explanations for each.

(b) Determine the October 31 balance for each of the accounts above, and prepare a trial balance at October 31, 2006.

(b) Trial balance totals $12,890

E2-8 Selected transactions for Neve Campbell Company during its first month in business are presented below.

Prepare journal entries and post using standard account form.

(SO 4, 6)

Sept.	1	Invested $10,000 cash in the business in exchange for common stock.
	5	Purchased equipment for $12,000 paying $6,000 in cash and the balance on account.
	25	Paid $3,000 cash on balance owed for equipment.
	30	Declared and paid a $500 cash dividend.

Campbell's chart of accounts shows: No. 101 Cash, No. 157 Equipment, No. 201 Accounts Payable, No. 311 Common Stock, No. 332 Dividends.

Instructions

(a) Journalize the transactions on page J1 of the journal.

(b) Post the transactions using the standard account form.

E2-9 The bookkeeper for Stan Tucci Equipment Repair made a number of errors in journalizing and posting, as described below.

Analyze errors and their effects on trial balance.

(SO 7)

1. A credit posting of $400 to Accounts Receivable was omitted.
2. A debit posting of $750 for Prepaid Insurance was debited to Insurance Expense.
3. A collection from a customer of $100 in payment of its account owed was journalized and posted as a debit to Cash $100 and a credit to Service Revenue $100.
4. A credit posting of $300 to Property Taxes Payable was made twice.
5. A cash purchase of supplies for $250 was journalized and posted as a debit to Supplies $25 and a credit to Cash $25.
6. A debit of $495 to Advertising Expense was posted as $459.

Instructions

For each error:

(a) Indicate whether the trial balance will balance.
(b) If the trial balance will not balance, indicate the amount of the difference.
(c) Indicate the trial balance column that will have the larger total.

Consider each error separately. Use the following form, in which error (1) is given as an example.

Error	(a) In Balance	(b) Difference	(c) Larger Column
(1)	No	$400	debit

Prepare a trial balance.
(SO 2, 7)

E2-10 The accounts in the ledger of Speedy Delivery Service contain the following balances on July 31, 2006.

Accounts Receivable	$10,642	Prepaid Insurance	$ 1,968
Accounts Payable	8,396	Repair Expense	961
Cash	?	Service Revenue	10,610
Delivery Equipment	49,360	Dividends	700
Gas and Oil Expense	758	Common Stock	40,000
Insurance Expense	523	Salaries Expense	4,428
Notes Payable	26,450	Salaries Payable	815
		Retained Earnings	4,636

Instructions

Prepare a trial balance with the accounts arranged as illustrated in the chapter and fill in the missing amount for Cash.

Trial balance totals $90,907

PROBLEMS: SET A

Journalize a series of transactions.
(SO 2, 4)

P2-1A Surepar Miniature Golf and Driving Range was opened on March 1 by Bill Affleck. The following selected events and transactions occurred during March:

Mar. 1 Invested $60,000 cash in the business in exchange for common stock.
3 Purchased Lee's Golf Land for $38,000 cash. The price consists of land $23,000, building $9,000, and equipment $6,000. (Make one compound entry.)
5 Advertised the opening of the driving range and miniature golf course, paying advertising expenses of $1,600.
6 Paid cash $1,480 for a one-year insurance policy.
10 Purchased golf clubs and other equipment for $2,600 from Parton Company payable in 30 days.
18 Received $800 in cash for golf fees earned.
19 Sold 100 coupon books for $15 each. Each book contains 10 coupons that enable the holder to play one round of miniature golf or to hit one bucket of golf balls.
25 Declared and paid $1,000 cash dividend.
30 Paid salaries of $600.
30 Paid Parton Company in full.
31 Received $500 cash for fees earned.

Bill Affleck uses the following accounts: Cash; Prepaid Insurance; Land; Buildings; Equipment; Accounts Payable; Unearned Revenue; Common Stock; Dividends; Golf Revenue; Advertising Expense; and Salaries Expense.

Instructions

Journalize the March transactions.

Journalize transactions, post, and prepare a trial balance.
(SO 2, 4, 6, 7)

Peachtree

P2-2A Judi Dench is a licensed architect. During the first month of the operation of her company, Judi Dench, Inc., the following events and transactions occurred.

April 1 Stockholders invested $25,000 cash in exchange for common stock.
1 Hired a secretary-receptionist at a salary of $300 per week payable monthly.
2 Paid office rent for the month $800.
3 Purchased architectural supplies on account from Halo Company $1,500.

10 Completed blueprints on a carport and billed client $900 for services.
11 Received $500 cash advance from R. Welk for the design of a new home.
20 Received $1,500 cash for services completed and delivered to P. Donahue.
30 Paid secretary-receptionist for the month $1,500.
30 Paid $600 to Halo Company for accounts payable due.

Judi uses the following chart of accounts: No. 101 Cash, No. 112 Accounts Receivable, No. 126 Supplies, No. 201 Accounts Payable, No. 205 Unearned Revenue, No. 311 Common Stock, No. 400 Service Revenue, No. 726 Salaries Expense, and No. 729 Rent Expense.

Instructions

(a) Journalize the transactions.
(b) Post to the ledger accounts.
(c) Prepare a trial balance on April 30, 2006.

Trial balance totals $28,800

P2-3A Chambers Brokerage Services Inc. was formed on May 1, 2006. The following transactions took place during the first month.

Journalize transactions, post, and prepare a trial balance and financial statements.

(SO 2, 4, 6, 7)

Transactions on May 1:

1. Stockholders invested $120,000 cash in the company in exchange for stock.
2. Hired two employees to work in the warehouse. They will each be paid a salary of $2,000 per month.
3. Signed a 2-year rental agreement on a warehouse; paid $36,000 cash in advance for the first year. (*Hint*: The portion of the cost related to May 2006 is an expense for this month.)
4. Purchased furniture and equipment costing $70,000. A cash payment of $20,000 was made immediately; the remainder will be paid in 6 months.
5. Paid $3,000 cash for a one-year insurance policy on the furniture and equipment. (*Hint:* The portion of the cost related to May 2006 is an expense for this month.)

Transactions during the remainder of the month:

6. Purchased basic office supplies for $1,000 cash.
7. Purchased more office supplies for $3,000 on account.
8. Total revenues earned were $30,000—$10,000 cash and $20,000 on account.
9. Paid $800 to suppliers for accounts payable due.
10. Received $5,000 from customers in payment of accounts receivable.
11. Received utility bills in the amount of $400, to be paid next month.
12. Paid the monthly salaries of the two employees, totalling $4,000.

Instructions

(a) Prepare journal entries to record each of the events listed.
(b) Post the journal entries to T accounts.
(c) Prepare a trial balance as of May 31, 2006.
(d) Prepare an income statement and a retained earnings statement for Chambers Brokerage Services for the month ended May 31, 2006, and a balance sheet as of May 31, 2006.

Trial balance totals $202,600

P2-4A The trial balance of Ron Salem Co. shown below does not balance.

Prepare a correct trial balance.

(SO 7)

RON SALEM CO.
Trial Balance
June 30, 2006

	Debit	Credit
Cash		$ 3,840
Accounts Receivable	$ 3,231	
Supplies	800	
Equipment	3,000	
Accounts Payable		2,666
Unearned Revenue	2,200	
Common Stock		9,000
Dividends	800	
Service Revenue		2,380
Salaries Expense	3,400	
Office Expense	910	
	$14,341	$17,886

Each of the listed accounts has a normal balance per the general ledger. An examination of the ledger and journal reveals the following errors.

1. Cash received from a customer in payment of its account was debited for $570, and Accounts Receivable was credited for the same amount. The actual collection was for $750.
2. The purchase of a printer on account for $340 was recorded as a debit to Supplies for $340 and a credit to Accounts Payable for $340.
3. Services were performed on account for a client for $890. Accounts Receivable was debited for $890, and Service Revenue was credited for $89.
4. A debit posting to Salaries Expense of $367 was omitted.
5. A payment of a balance due for $309 was credited to Cash for $309 and credited to Accounts Payable for $390.
6. The payment of a $500 cash dividend was debited to Salaries Expense for $500 and credited to Cash for $500.

Instructions

Trial balance totals $16,348

Prepare a correct trial balance. (*Hint:* It helps to prepare the correct journal entry for the transaction described and compare it to the mistake made).

Journalize transactions, post, and prepare a trial balance.

(SO 2, 4, 6, 7)

Peachtree

P2-5A The Russo Theater will begin operations in March. The Russo will be unique in that it will show only triple features of sequential theme movies. As of March 1, the ledger of Russo showed: No. 101 Cash $16,000; No. 140 Land $42,000; No. 145 Buildings (concession stand, projection room, ticket booth, and screen) $18,000; No. 157 Equipment $16,000; No. 201 Accounts Payable $12,000; and No. 311 Common Stock $80,000. During the month of March the following events and transactions occurred.

Mar.	2	Rented the three *Star Wars* movies (*Star Wars, The Empire Strikes Back,* and *The Return of the Jedi*) to be shown for the first 3 weeks of March. The film rental was $9,000; $3,000 was paid in cash and $6,000 will be paid on March 10.
	3	Ordered the first three *Star Trek* movies to be shown the last 10 days of March. It will cost $300 per night.
	9	Received $6,500 cash from admissions.
	10	Paid balance due on *Star Wars* movies rental and $3,000 on March 1 accounts payable.
	11	Russo Theater contracted with M. Brewer Company to operate the concession stand. Brewer is to pay 10% of gross concession receipts (payable monthly) for the right to operate the concession stand.
	12	Paid advertising expenses $800.
	20	Received $7,200 cash from customers for admissions.
	20	Received the *Star Trek* movies and paid the rental fee of $3,000.
	31	Paid salaries of $4,800.
	31	Received statement from M. Brewer showing gross receipts from concessions of $8,000 and the balance due to Russo Theater of $800 ($8,000 × 10%) for March. Brewer paid one-half the balance due and will remit the remainder on April 5.
	31	Received $12,000 cash from customers for admissions.

In addition to the accounts identified above, the chart of accounts includes: No. 112 Accounts Receivable, No. 405 Admission Revenue, No. 406 Concession Revenue, No. 610 Advertising Expense, No. 632 Film Rental Expense, and No. 726 Salaries Expense.

Instructions

(a) Enter the beginning balances in the ledger. Insert a check mark (✓) in the reference column of the ledger for the beginning balance.

(b) Journalize the March transactions.

(c) Post the March journal entries to the ledger. Assume that all entries are posted from page 1 of the journal.

Trial balance totals $115,500

(d) Prepare a trial balance on March 31, 2006.

PROBLEMS: SET B

P2-1B Frontier Park Inc. was started on April 1 by C. J. Amaro and associates. The following selected events and transactions occurred during April.

Journalize a series of transactions.

(SO 2, 4)

Apr. 1 Stockholders invested $50,000 cash in the business in exchange for common stock.
4 Purchased land costing $30,000 for cash.
8 Incurred advertising expense of $1,800 on account.
11 Paid salaries to employees $1,500.
12 Hired park manager at a salary of $4,000 per month, effective May 1.
13 Paid $1,500 cash for a one-year insurance policy.
17 Declared and paid a $600 cash dividend.
20 Received $5,700 in cash for admission fees.
25 Sold 100 coupon books for $25 each. Each book contains 10 coupons that entitle the holder to one admission to the park.
30 Received $8,900 in cash admission fees.
30 Paid $900 on balance owed for advertising incurred on April 8.

Amaro uses the following accounts: Cash; Prepaid Insurance; Land; Accounts Payable; Unearned Admission Revenue; Common Stock; Dividends; Admission Revenue; Advertising Expense; and Salaries Expense.

Instructions

Journalize the April transactions.

P2-2B Kara Shin is a licensed CPA. During the first month of operations of her company, Shin Corp., the following events and transactions occurred.

Journalize transactions, post, and prepare a trial balance.

(SO 2, 4, 6, 7)

May 1 Stockholders invested $20,000 cash in exchange for common stock.
2 Hired a secretary-receptionist at a salary of $1,000 per month.
3 Purchased $1,500 of supplies on account from Read Supply Company.
7 Paid office rent of $900 cash for the month.
11 Completed a tax assignment and billed client $2,100 for services provided.
12 Received $3,500 advance on a management consulting engagement.
17 Received cash of $1,200 for services completed for H. Arnold Co.
31 Paid secretary-receptionist $1,000 salary for the month.
31 Paid 40% of balance due Read Supply Company.

Kara uses the following chart of accounts: No. 101 Cash, No. 112 Accounts Receivable, No. 126 Supplies, No. 201 Accounts Payable, No. 205 Unearned Revenue, No. 311 Common Stock, No. 400 Service Revenue, No. 726 Salaries Expense, and No. 729 Rent Expense.

Instructions

(a) Journalize the transactions.
(b) Post to the ledger accounts.
(c) Prepare a trial balance on May 31, 2006.

Trial balance totals $27,700

P2-3B Mark Hockenberry owns and manages Byte Repair Service, Inc., which had the following trial balance on December 31, 2005 (the end of its fiscal year).

Journalize and post transactions, prepare a trial balance, and determine elements of financial statements.

(SO 2, 4, 6, 7)

BYTE REPAIR SERVICE, INC.
Trial Balance
December 31, 2005

Cash	$ 8,000	
Accounts Receivable	15,000	
Parts Inventory	13,000	
Prepaid Rent	3,000	
Shop Equipment	21,000	
Accounts Payable		$19,000
Common Stock		30,000
Retained Earnings		11,000
	$60,000	$60,000

Summarized transactions for January 2006 were as follows:

1. Advertising costs, paid in cash, $1,000.
2. Additional repair parts inventory acquired on account $4,000.
3. Miscellaneous expenses, paid in cash, $2,000.
4. Cash collected from customers in payment of accounts receivable $13,000.
5. Cash paid to creditors for accounts payable due $15,000.
6. Repair parts used during January $4,000. (*Hint*: Debit this to Repair Parts Expense.)
7. Repair services performed during January: for cash $5,000; on account $9,000.
8. Wages for January, paid in cash, $3,000.
9. Rent expense for January recorded. However, no cash was paid out for rent during January. A rent payment had been made for 4 months, in advance, on December 1, 2005, in the amount of $4,000.
10. Dividends paid during January were $2,000.

Instructions

(a) Explain why the December 31, 2005, balance in the Prepaid Rent account is $3,000. (Refer to the Trial Balance and item (9) above.)

(b) Open T accounts for each of the accounts listed in the trial balance, and enter the opening balances for 2006.

(c) Prepare journal entries to record each of the January transactions.

(d) Post the journal entries to the accounts in the ledger. (Add accounts as needed.)

Trial balance totals $63,000

(e) Prepare a trial balance as of January 31, 2006.

(f) Determine the total assets as of January 31, 2006. (It is not necessary to prepare a balance sheet. Simply list the relevant amounts from the trial balance and calculate the total.)

(g) Determine the net income or loss for the month of January 2006. (It is not necessary to prepare an income statement. Simply list the relevant amounts from the trial balance, and calculate the amount of the net income or loss.)

Prepare a correct trial balance.
(SO 7)

P2-4B The trial balance of the Garland Company shown below does not balance.

GARLAND COMPANY
Trial Balance
May 31, 2006

	Debit	Credit
Cash	$3,850	
Accounts Receivable		$2,750
Prepaid Insurance	700	
Equipment	12,000	
Accounts Payable		4,500
Property Taxes Payable	560	
Common Stock		11,700
Service Revenue	8,690	
Salaries Expense	4,200	
Advertising Expense		1,100
Property Tax Expense	800	
	$30,800	$20,050

Your review of the ledger reveals that each account has a normal balance. You also discover the following errors.

1. The totals of the debit sides of Prepaid Insurance, Accounts Payable, and Property Tax Expense were each understated $100.
2. Transposition errors were made in Accounts Receivable and Service Revenue. Based on postings made, the correct balances were $2,570 and $8,960, respectively.
3. A debit posting to Salaries Expense of $200 was omitted.
4. A $1,000 cash dividend by the corporation was debited to Common Stock for $1,000 and credited to Cash for $1,000.
5. A $520 purchase of supplies on account was debited to Equipment for $520 and credited to Cash for $520.

6. A cash payment of $450 for advertising was debited to Advertising Expense for $45 and credited to Cash for $45.
7. A collection from a customer for $420 was debited to Cash for $420 and credited to Accounts Payable for $420.

Instructions

Prepare a correct trial balance. Note that the chart of accounts includes the following: Dividends and Supplies. (*Hint:* It helps to prepare the correct journal entry for the transaction described and compare it to the mistake made.)

Trial balance totals $26,720

P2-5B The Lake Theater opened on April 1. All facilities were completed on March 31. At this time, the ledger showed: No. 101 Cash $6,000; No. 140 Land $10,000; No. 145 Buildings (concession stand, projection room, ticket booth, and screen) $8,000; No. 157 Equipment $6,000; No. 201 Accounts Payable $2,000; No. 275 Mortgage Payable $8,000; and No. 311 Common Stock $20,000. During April, the following events and transactions occurred.

Journalize transactions, post, and prepare a trial balance.
(SO 2, 4, 6, 7)

Apr. 2 Paid film rental of $800 on first movie.
3 Ordered two additional films at $1,000 each.
9 Received $1,800 cash from admissions.
10 Made $2,000 payment on mortgage and $1,000 for accounts payable due.
11 Lake Theater contracted with R. Zarle Company to operate the concession stand. Zarle is to pay 17% of gross concession receipts (payable monthly) for the right to operate the concession stand.
12 Paid advertising expenses $300.
20 Received one of the films ordered on April 3 and was billed $1,000. The film will be shown in April.
25 Received $5,200 cash from admissions.
29 Paid salaries $1,600.
30 Received statement from R. Zarle showing gross concession receipts of $1,000 and the balance due to The Lake Theater of $170 ($1,000 × 17%) for April. Zarle paid one-half of the balance due and will remit the remainder on May 5.
30 Prepaid $900 rental on special film to be run in May.

In addition to the accounts identified above, the chart of accounts shows: No. 112 Accounts Receivable, No. 136 Prepaid Rentals, No. 405 Admission Revenue, No. 406 Concession Revenue, No. 610 Advertising Expense, No. 632 Film Rental Expense, and No. 726 Salaries Expense.

Instructions

(a) Enter the beginning balances in the ledger as of April 1. Insert a check mark (✓) in the reference column of the ledger for the beginning balance.
(b) Journalize the April transactions.
(c) Post the April journal entries to the ledger. Assume that all entries are posted from page 1 of the journal.
(d) Prepare a trial balance on April 30, 2006.

Trial balance totals $35,170

BROADENING YOUR PERSPECTIVE

Financial Reporting and Analysis

■ FINANCIAL REPORTING PROBLEM: PepsiCo

BYP2-1 The financial statements of **PepsiCo** are presented in Appendix A. The statements contain the following selected accounts, stated in millions of dollars.

Accounts Payable	$5,213	Income Taxes Payable	$ 611
Accounts Receivable	2,830	Interest Expense	163
Property, Plant, and Equipment	7,828	Inventory	1,412

Instructions

(a) Answer the following questions.
 (1) What is the increase and decrease side for each account?
 (2) What is the normal balance for each account?

(b) Identify the probable other account in the transaction and the effect on that account when:
 (1) Accounts Receivable is decreased.
 (2) Accounts Payable is decreased.
 (3) Inventory is increased.

(c) Identify the other account(s) that ordinarily would be involved when:
 (1) Interest Expense is increased.
 (2) Property, Plant, and Equipment is increased.

■ COMPARATIVE ANALYSIS PROBLEM: PepsiCo vs. Coca-Cola

BYP2-2 **PepsiCo**'s financial statements are presented in Appendix A. **Coca-Cola**'s financial statements are presented in Appendix B.

Instructions

(a) Based on the information contained in the financial statements, determine the normal balance of the listed accounts for each company.

PepsiCo	Coca-Cola
1. Inventory	**1.** Accounts Receivable
2. Property, Plant, and Equipment	**2.** Cash and Cash Equivalents
3. Accounts Payable	**3.** Cost of Goods Sold
4. Interest Expense	**4.** Sales (revenue)

(b) Identify the other account ordinarily involved when:
 (1) Accounts Receivable is increased.
 (2) Wages Payable is decreased.
 (3) Property, Plant, and Equipment is increased.
 (4) Interest Expense is increased.

■ RESEARCH CASE

BYP2-3 Several commonly available indexes enable individuals to locate articles from numerous business publications and periodicals. Articles can generally be searched for by company name or by subject matter. Four common indexes are the *Wall Street Journal Index, Business Abstracts* (formerly *Business Periodicals Index*), *Predicasts F&S Index,* and *ABI/Inform.*

Instructions

Use one of these resources to find a list of articles about **Best Buy**, **Circuit City**, or **Tweeter Home Entertainment**. Choose an article from this list that you believe would be of interest to an investor or creditor of this company. Read the article and answer the following questions. (*Note:* Your library may have either hard-copy or CD-ROM versions of these indexes.)

(a) What is the article about?
(b) What company-specific information is included in the article?
(c) Is the article related to anything you read in this chapter?
(d) Identify any accounting-related issues discussed in the article.

■ INTERPRETING FINANCIAL STATEMENTS

BYP2-4 The following selected accounts are excerpted from the 2003 financial statements of **Motorola, Inc.** (in millions).

Cash and Cash Equivalents	$ 7,877
Inventories	2,792
Notes Payable	896
Selling, General, and Administrative Expenses	4,073
Sales Revenue	27,058
Dividends	372
Common Stock	7,017
Income Tax Expense	400

Instructions

(a) What is the increase and decrease side for each of Motorola's accounts?
(b) What is the normal balance for each account?
(c) List those accounts that appear on Motorola's balance sheet.
(d) List those accounts that appear on Motorola's income statement.
(e) On what financial statement does Dividends appear?

■ A GLOBAL FOCUS

BYP2-5 **Doman Industries Ltd.**, whose products are sold in 30 countries worldwide, is an integrated Canadian forest products company.

Doman sells the majority of its lumber products in the United States and a significant amount of its pulp products in Asia. Doman also has loans from other countries. For example, the company borrowed US $160 million at an annual interest rate of 12%. Doman must repay this loan, and interest, in U.S. dollars.

One of the challenges global companies face is to make themselves attractive to investors from other countries. This is difficult to do when different accounting rules in different countries blur the real impact of earnings. For example, in 1998 Doman reported a loss of $2.3 million, using Canadian accounting rules. Had it reported under U.S. accounting rules, its loss would have been $12.1 million.

Many companies that want to be more easily compared with U.S. and other global competitors have switched to U.S. accounting principles. **Canadian National Railway**, **Corel**, **Cott**, **Inco**, and the **Thomson Corporation** are but a few examples of large Canadian companies whose financial statements are now presented in U.S. dollars, which adhere to U.S. GAAP, or are reconciled to U.S. GAAP.

Instructions

(a) Identify advantages and disadvantages that companies should consider when switching to U.S. reporting standards.
(b) Suppose you wish to compare Doman Industries to a U.S.-based competitor. Do you believe the use of country-specific accounting policies would hinder your comparison? If so, explain how.
(c) Suppose you wish to compare Doman Industries to a Canadian-based competitor. If the companies chose to apply generally acceptable Canadian accounting policies differently, how could this affect your comparison of their financial results?
(d) Do you see any significant distinction between comparing statements prepared using generally accepted accounting principles of different countries and comparing statements prepared using generally accepted accounting principles of the same country (e.g., U.S.) but that apply the principles differently?

■ EXPLORING THE WEB

BYP2-6 Much information about specific companies is available on the World Wide Web. Such information includes basic descriptions of the company's location, activities, industry, financial health, and financial performance.

www.wiley.com/college/weygandt

Address: biz.yahoo.com/i, or go to www.wiley.com/college/weygandt

Steps

1. Type in a company name, or use index to find company name.
2. Choose **Profile**. Perform instructions (a)–(c) below.
3. Click on the company's specific industry to identify competitors. Perform instructions (d)–(g) below.

Instructions

Answer the following questions.

(a) What is the company's industry?
(b) What was the company's total sales?
(c) What was the company's net income?
(d) What are the names of four of the company's competitors?
(e) Choose one of these competitors.
(f) What is this competitor's name? What were its sales? What was its net income?
(g) Which of these two companies is larger by size of sales? Which one reported higher net income?

Critical Thinking

■ GROUP DECISION CASE

BYP2-7 Amy Torbert is president of Hollins Riding Academy Inc. The academy's primary sources of revenue are riding fees and lesson fees, which are paid on a cash basis. Hollins also boards horses for owners, who are billed monthly for boarding fees. In a few cases, boarders pay in advance of expected use. For its revenue transactions, the academy maintains the following accounts: No. 1 Cash, No. 5 Boarding Accounts Receivable, No. 27 Unearned Boarding Revenue, No. 51 Riding Revenue, No. 52 Lesson Revenue, and No. 53 Boarding Revenue.

The academy owns 10 horses, a stable, a riding corral, riding equipment, and office equipment. These assets are accounted for in accounts No. 11 Horses, No. 12 Building, No. 13 Riding Corral, No. 14 Riding Equipment, and No. 15 Office Equipment.

For its expenses, the academy maintains the following accounts: No. 6 Hay and Feed Supplies, No. 7 Prepaid Insurance, No. 21 Accounts Payable, No. 60 Salaries Expense, No. 61 Advertising Expense, No. 62 Utilities Expense, No. 63 Veterinary Expense, No. 64 Hay and Feed Expense, and No. 65 Insurance Expense.

Hollins makes periodic payments of cash dividends to stockholders. To record stockholders' equity in the business and dividends, three accounts are maintained: No. 50 Common Stock, No. 51 Retained Earnings, and No. 52 Dividends.

During the first month of operations an inexperienced bookkeeper was employed. Amy Torbert asks you to review the following eight entries of the 50 entries made during the month. In each case, the explanation for the entry is correct.

May 1	Cash	18,000	
	Common Stock		18,000
	(Invested $18,000 cash in exchange for stock)		
5	Cash	250	
	Riding Revenue		250
	(Received $250 cash for lessons provided)		
7	Cash	500	
	Boarding Revenue		500
	(Received $500 for boarding of horses beginning June 1)		
14	Riding Equipment	80	
	Cash		800
	(Purchased desk and other office equipment for $800 cash)		
15	Salaries Expense	400	
	Cash		400
	(Issued dividend checks to stockholders)		
20	Cash	148	
	Riding Revenue		184
	(Received $184 cash for riding fees)		
30	Veterinary Expense	75	
	Accounts Payable		75
	(Received bill of $75 from veterinarian for services rendered)		
31	Hay and Feed Expense	1,500	
	Cash		1,500
	(Purchased an estimated 2 months' supply of feed and hay for $1,500 on account)		

Instructions

With the class divided into groups, answer the following.

(a) Identify each journal entry that is correct. For each journal entry that is incorrect, prepare the entry that should have been made by the bookkeeper.

(b) Which of the incorrect entries would prevent the trial balance from balancing?

(c) What was the correct net income for May, assuming the bookkeeper reported net income of $4,500 after posting all 50 entries?

(d) What was the correct cash balance at May 31, assuming the bookkeeper reported a balance of $12,475 after posting all 50 entries (and the only errors occurred in the items listed above)?

■ COMMUNICATION ACTIVITY

BYP2-8 Shandler's Maid Company offers home cleaning service. Two recurring transactions for the company are billing customers for services rendered and paying employee salaries. For example, on March 15, bills totaling $5,000 were sent to customers and $2,000 was paid in salaries to employees.

Instructions

Write a memo to your instructor that explains and illustrates the steps in the recording process for each of the March 15 transactions. Use the format illustrated in the text under the heading, "The Recording Process Illustrated" (p. 61).

■ ETHICS CASE

Accounting Matters!

BYP2-9 Sara Rankin is the assistant chief accountant at Hokey Company, a manufacturer of computer chips and cellular phones. The company presently has total sales of $20 million. It is the end of the first quarter. Sara is hurriedly trying to prepare a general ledger trial balance so that quarterly financial statements can be prepared and released to management and the regulatory agencies. The total credits on the trial balance exceed the debits by $1,000. In order to meet the 4 p.m. deadline, Sara decides to force the debits and credits into balance by adding the amount of the difference to the Equipment account. She chose Equipment because it is one of the larger account balances; percentage-wise, it will be the least misstated. Sara "plugs" the difference! She believes that the difference will not affect anyone's decisions. She wishes that she had another few days to find the error but realizes that the financial statements are already late.

Instructions

(a) Who are the stakeholders in this situation?
(b) What are the ethical issues involved in this case?
(c) What are Sara's alternatives?

■ CONTINUING COOKIE CHRONICLE

Accounting Matters!

(*Note:* The Continuing Cookie Chronicle was started in Chapter 1 and will continue in each chapter.)

BYP2-10 After researching the different forms of business organization, Natalie Koebel decides to operate "Cookie Creations" as a corporation. She then starts the process of getting the business running. In November 2005, the following activities occur.

Nov. 8 Natalie invests $500 in exchange for common stock.
9 She creates promotional materials: a brochure and a poster for advertising the company and the services available.
11 Natalie pays $95 to have the brochures and posters printed. She plans to distribute these as opportunities arise.
13 She buys baking supplies, for $125 cash.
14 Natalie starts to gather some baking equipment to take with her when teaching the cookie classes. She has an excellent top-of-the-line food processor and mixer that originally cost her $550. Natalie decides to start using it only in her new business. She estimates that the equipment is currently worth $300.
16 Natalie realizes that her initial cash investment is not enough. Her grandmother lends $2,000 cash, for which Natalie signs a note payable in the name of the business, Cookie Creations.
17 She buys more baking equipment for $900 cash.
20 She books her first class for November 29 for $100. One of her mother's friends needed a novel idea for her young daughter's birthday party.
25 Natalie books a second class for December 4 for $125. She receives $25 cash in advance as a down payment.
29 She teaches her first class, booked on November 20, and collects the $100 cash.

30 Natalie's brother designs a Web site for Cookie Creations that will be used for advertising. She agrees to pay her brother $600 for his work, payable at the end of December. (Because the Web site is expected to have a useful life of 2 years before upgrades are needed, it should be treated as an asset.)

30 Natalie pays $1,200 for a one-year insurance policy that will expire on December 1, 2006.

Instructions

(a) Prepare journal entries to record the November transactions.

(b) Post the journal entries to general ledger accounts.

(c) Prepare a trial balance at November 30, 2005.

Accounting Matters!

Answers to Accounting Matters! Questions

p. 51

Q: Do you think that the Chicago Bears would be likely to have the same major revenue and expense accounts as the Cubs?

A: Because their businesses are similar—professional sports—many of the revenue and expense accounts for the baseball and football teams might be similar.

Q: Do you think that Chicago-based Wrigley Company would be likely to have the same major revenue and expense accounts? Why or why not?

A: No, many of the Wrigley Company's revenue and expense accounts would be different from those of the sports teams. Companies use specific accounts that most accurately track the key activities and transactions of the business, in order to maintain control over those transactions and to inform owners and creditors.

p. 54

Q: In order to prepare and issue financial statements, these companies' accounting equations (debit and credits) must have been in balance at year-end. How could these errors or misstatements have occurred?

A: A company's accounting equation (its books) can be in balance yet its financial statements have errors or misstatements because of the following: entire transactions were not recorded; transactions were recorded at wrong amounts; transactions were recorded in the wrong accounts; transactions were recorded in the wrong accounting period. Audits of financial statements uncover some, but obviously not all, errors or misstatements.

p. 58

Q: Why did Sam Walton keep separate pigeonholes and blue binders for each store?

A: Using separate pigeonholes and binders permitted Sam to accumulate and track the performance of each individual store easily.

Q: Why bother to keep separate records for each store?

A: Keeping separate records for each store provided Walton with more information (about performance of individual stores and managers) and greater control.

p. 60

Q: What do accountants call those things that are first recorded at "the most critical . . . point in the accounting process"?

A: The things recorded are *transactions*.

Q: What is the name of the "book" into which those things are first recorded?

A: The "book" into which transactions are first recorded is a *journal*. (In computerized systems, the journal is an electronic file—not a separate book.)

Q: What does the accountant call the group of accounts into which the individual entries are posted (merged and filed)?

A: The transaction entries are posted (merged and filed) into a group of accounts called a *ledger*.

Answer to PepsiCo Review It Question 4, p. 53

Normal balances for **PepsiCo** (or any company) are: Cash—debit; Accounts Payable—credit; Interest Expense—debit.

Answers to Self-Study Questions

1. b **2.** c **3.** d **4.** d **5.** b **6.** a **7.** c **8.** d **9.** a **10.** c

REMEMBER to go back to the Navigator box on the chapter-opening page and check off your completed work.

Chapter 3

Adjusting the Accounts

THE NAVIGATOR ✓

- Understand **Concepts for Review** ❑
- Read **Feature Story** ❑
- Scan **Study Objectives** ❑
- Read **Preview** ❑
- Read text and answer **Before You Go On** p. 96 ❑ p. 103 ❑ p. 108 ❑ p. 113 ❑
- Work **Demonstration Problem** ❑
- Review **Summary of Study Objectives** ❑
- Answer **Self-Study Questions** ❑
- Complete **Assignments** ❑

CONCEPTS FOR REVIEW

Before studying this chapter, you should know or, if necessary, review:

- What a double-entry system is. (Ch. 2, p. 48)
- How to increase or decrease assets, liabilities, and stockholders' equity using debit and credit procedures. (Ch. 2, pp. 48–51)
- How to journalize a transaction. (Ch. 2, pp. 55–56)
- How to post a journal entry. (Ch. 2, pp. 59–60)
- How to prepare a trial balance. (Ch. 2, pp. 69–70)

✓ THE NAVIGATOR

ACCOUNTING MATTERS! FEATURE STORY

Timing Is Everything

In Chapter 1 you learned a neat little formula: Net income = Revenues − Expenses. And in Chapter 2 you learned some nice, orderly rules for recording corporate revenue and expense transactions. Guess what? Things are not really that nice and neat. In fact, it is often difficult to determine in what time period some revenues and expenses should be reported. And, in measuring net income, timing is everything.

There are rules that give guidance on these issues. But occasionally these rules are overlooked, misinterpreted, or even intentionally ignored. Consider the following examples.

- **McKesson HBOC**, one of the largest prescription drug distributors, at one time restated its first-quarter earnings because $26.2 million included in healthcare software sales weren't final and should not have been recorded. This negative surprise caused McKesson's share price to plummet 48 percent overnight, from $65.75 to $34.50, wiping out $9 billion in the market value of its stock.
- **Cambridge Biotech Corp.**, which develops vaccines and diagnostic tests for humans and animals, said that it reported revenue from transactions that "don't appear to be bona fide."
- **Media Vision Technology Inc.**, a maker of sound and animation equipment for computers, was accused of operating a "phantom" warehouse to hide inventory for returned products already recorded as sales.
- **Penguin USA**, a book publisher, said that it understated expenses in a number of years because it failed to report expenses for discounts given to customers for paying early.

In each case, accrual accounting concepts were violated. That is, revenues or expenses were not recorded in the proper period, which had a substantial impact on reported income. Their timing was off! Accounting matters!

☑ THE NAVIGATOR

STUDY OBJECTIVES

After studying this chapter, you should be able to:

1. Explain the time period assumption.
2. Explain the accrual basis of accounting.
3. Explain why adjusting entries are needed.
4. Identify the major types of adjusting entries.
5. Prepare adjusting entries for prepayments.
6. Prepare adjusting entries for accruals.
7. Describe the nature and purpose of an adjusted trial balance.

☑ THE NAVIGATOR

PREVIEW OF CHAPTER 3

In Chapter 2 we examined the recording process through the preparation of the trial balance. Before we will be ready to prepare financial statements from the trial balance, additional steps need to be taken. The timing mismatch between revenues and expenses of the four companies mentioned in our Feature Story illustrates the types of situations that make these additional steps necessary. For example, long-lived assets purchased or constructed in prior accounting years are being used to produce goods and provide services in the current year. What portion of these assets' costs, if any, should be recognized as an expense of the current period? Before financial statements can be prepared, this and other questions relating to the recognition of revenues and expenses must be answered. With the answers in hand, we can then adjust the relevant account balances.

The content and organization of Chapter 3 are as follows.

ADJUSTING THE ACCOUNTS

Timing Issues	The Basics of Adjusting Entries	The Adjusted Trial Balance and Financial Statements
• Time period assumption • Fiscal and calendar years • Accrual- vs. cash-basis accounting • Recognizing revenues and expenses	• Types of adjusting entries • Adjusting entries for prepayments • Adjusting entries for accruals • Summary	• Preparing the adjusted trial balance • Preparing financial statements

THE NAVIGATOR

Timing Issues

STUDY OBJECTIVE 1

Explain the time period assumption.

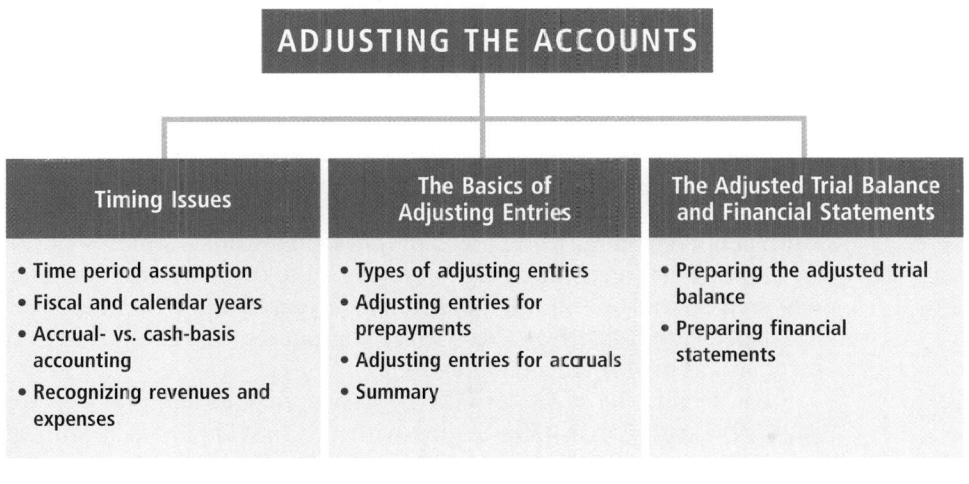

No adjustments would be necessary if we could wait to prepare financial statements until a company ended its operations. At that point, we could easily determine its final balance sheet and the amount of lifetime income it earned. The following anecdote illustrates one way to compute lifetime income.

> A grocery store owner from the old country kept his accounts payable on a spindle, accounts receivable on a note pad, and cash in a cigar box. His daughter, having just passed the CPA exam, chided the father: "I don't understand how you can run your business this way. How do you know what your profits are?"
>
> "Well," the father replied, "when I got off the boat 40 years ago, I had nothing but the pants I was wearing. Today your brother is a doctor, your sister is a college professor, and you are a CPA. Your mother and I have a nice car, a

well-furnished house, and a lake home. We have a good business, and everything is paid for. So, you add all that together, subtract the pants, and there's your profit."

Time Period Assumption

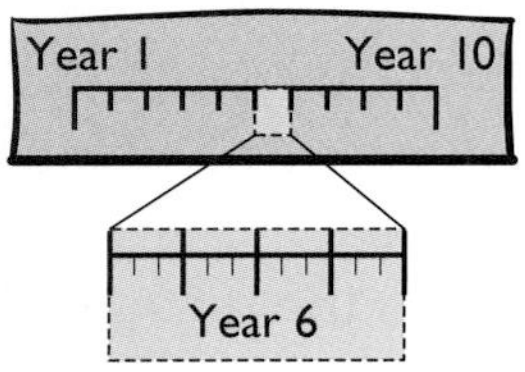

Selecting an Accounting Time Period

Although the old grocer may be correct in his evaluation, it is impractical to wait so long for the results of operations. All entities, from the corner grocery, to a global company like **Kellogg**, to your college or university, find it desirable and necessary to report the results of their activities more frequently. For example, management usually wants monthly financial statements, and the Internal Revenue Service requires all businesses to file annual tax returns. Therefore, **accountants divide the economic life of a business into artificial time periods**. This convenient assumption is referred to as the **time period assumption**.

ALTERNATIVE TERMINOLOGY

The time period assumption is also called the *periodicity assumption.*

Many business transactions affect more than one of these arbitrary time periods. For example, Farmer Brown's milking machine bought in 2001 and the airplanes purchased by **Delta Air Lines** five years ago are still in use today. Therefore we must determine the relevance of each business transaction to specific accounting periods. Doing so may involve subjective judgments and estimates.

Fiscal and Calendar Years

Both small and large companies prepare financial statements periodically in order to assess their financial condition and results of operations. **Accounting time periods are generally a month, a quarter, or a year.** Monthly and quarterly time periods are called **interim periods**. Most large companies are required to prepare both quarterly and annual financial statements.

An accounting time period that is one year in length is referred to as a **fiscal year**. A fiscal year usually begins with the first day of a month and ends twelve months later on the last day of a month. The accounting period used by most businesses coincides with the **calendar year** (January 1 to December 31). As discussed in Chapter 1 (page 24), though, some companies use a fiscal year that differs from the calendar year. Sometimes a company's year-end will vary from year to year. For example, **PepsiCo**'s fiscal year ends on the last Saturday in December, which was December 28 in 2002 and December 27 in 2003.

Accrual- vs. Cash-Basis Accounting

STUDY OBJECTIVE 2

Explain the accrual basis of accounting.

What you will learn in this chapter is **accrual-basis accounting**. Under the accrual basis, transactions that change a company's financial statements are recorded **in the periods in which the events occur**. For example, using the accrual basis to determine net income means recognizing revenues when earned (rather than when the cash is received). It also means recognizing expenses when incurred (rather than when paid). Information presented on an accrual basis reveals relationships likely to be important in predicting future results. Under accrual accounting, revenues are recognized when services are performed, so trends in revenues are thus more meaningful for decision-making.

An alternative to the accrual basis is the cash basis. Under **cash-basis accounting**, revenue is recorded when cash is received, and an expense is recorded when cash is paid. The cash basis often leads to misleading financial statements. It fails to record revenue that has been earned but for which the cash has not been received. Also, expenses are not matched with earned revenues. **Cash-basis accounting is not in accordance with generally accepted accounting principles (GAAP).**

Most companies use accrual-basis accounting. Individuals and some small companies use cash-basis accounting. The cash basis is justified for small businesses because they often have few receivables and payables. Accountants are sometimes asked to convert cash-basis records to the accrual basis. As you might expect, extensive adjusting entries are required for this task.

Recognizing Revenues and Expenses

Determining the amount of revenues and expenses to be reported in a given accounting period can be difficult. To help in this task, accountants have developed two principles as part of generally accepted accounting principles (GAAP): the revenue recognition principle and the matching principle.

The **revenue recognition principle** dictates that revenue be recognized in the accounting period in which it is earned. **In a service enterprise, revenue is considered to be earned at the time the service is performed.** To illustrate, assume that a dry cleaning business cleans clothing on June 30 but customers do not claim and pay for their clothes until the first week of July. Under the revenue recognition principle, revenue is earned in June when the service is performed, rather than in July when the cash is received. At June 30, the dry cleaner would report a receivable on its balance sheet and revenue in its income statement for the service performed.

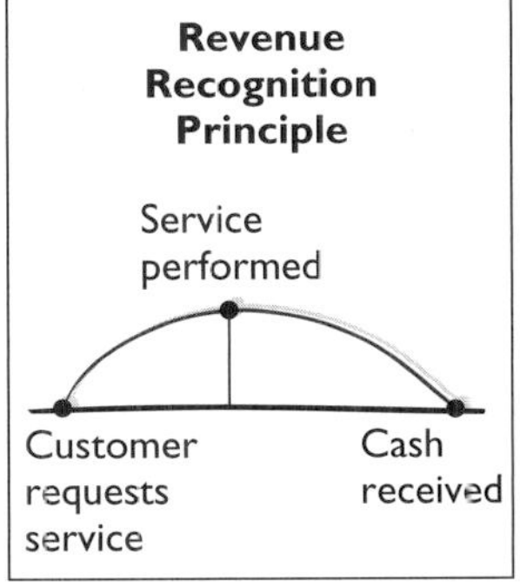

Accountants follow the approach of "let expenses follow revenues." That is, expense recognition is tied to revenue recognition. In the preceding example, this principle means that the salary expense incurred in performing the cleaning service on June 30 should be reported in the income statement for the same period in which the service revenue is recognized. The critical issue in expense recognition is when the expense makes its contribution to revenue. This may or may not be the same period in which the expense is paid. If the salary incurred on June 30 is not paid until July, the dry cleaner would report salaries payable on its June 30 balance sheet. The practice of expense recognition is referred to as the **matching principle** because it dictates that efforts (expenses) be matched with accomplishments (revenues).

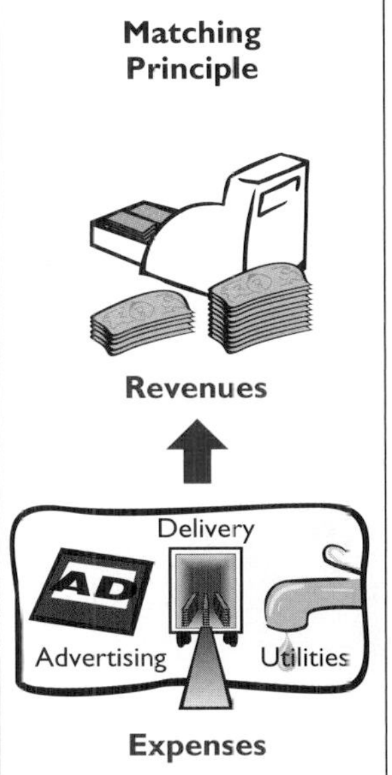

Once the economic life of a business has been divided into artificial time periods, the revenue recognition and matching principles can be applied. This one assumption and two principles thus provide guidelines as to when revenues and expenses should be reported. These relationships are shown in Illustration 3-1 (page 96).

ACCOUNTING MATTERS! Business Insight

Suppose you are a filmmaker like George Lucas and spend $11 million to produce a film such as *Star Wars*. Over what period should the cost be expensed? It should be expensed over the economic life of the film. But what is its economic life? The filmmaker must estimate how much revenue will be earned from box office sales, video sales, television, and games and toys—a period that could be less than a year or more than 20 years, as is the case for **Twentieth Century Fox**'s *Star Wars*. Originally released in 1977, and rereleased in 1997, domestic revenues total nearly $500 million for *Star Wars* and continue to grow.

Source: Star Trek Newsletter, 22.

? What accounting principle does this example illustrate? How will financial results be affected if the expenses are recognized over a period that is *less than* that used for revenues? What if the expenses are recognized over a period that is *longer than* that used for revenues?

Illustration 3-1
GAAP relationships in revenue and expense recognition

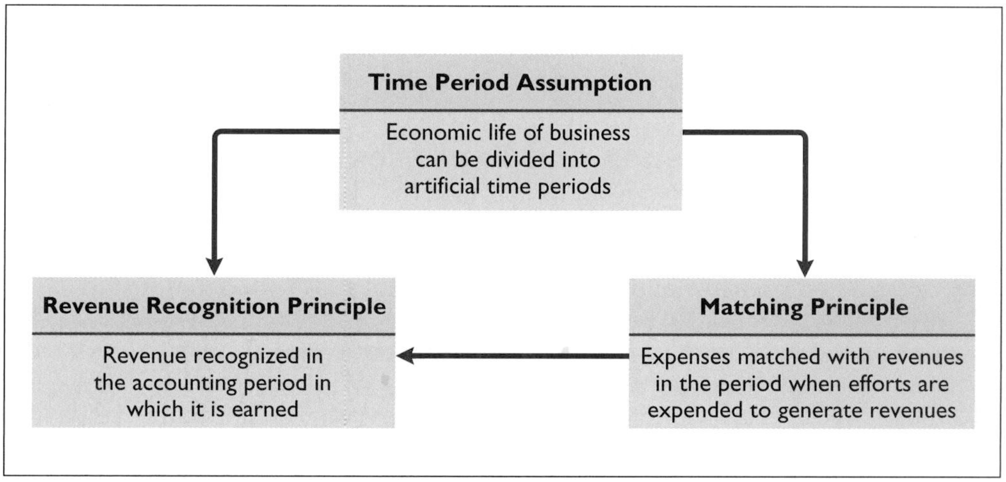

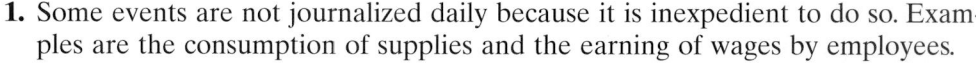

BEFORE YOU GO ON...

Review It

1. What is the relevance of the time period assumption to accounting?
2. What are the revenue recognition and matching principles?

THE NAVIGATOR

The Basics of Adjusting Entries

STUDY OBJECTIVE 3

Explain why adjusting entries are needed.

In order for revenues to be recorded in the period in which they are earned, and for expenses to be recognized in the period in which they are incurred, adjusting entries are made at the end of the accounting period. In short, **adjusting entries are needed to ensure that the revenue recognition and matching principles are followed.**

Adjusting entries make it possible to report on the balance sheet the appropriate assets, liabilities, and stockholders' equity at the statement date and to report on the income statement the proper net income (or loss) for the period. However, the trial balance—the first pulling together of the transaction data—may not contain up-to-date and complete data. This is true for the following reasons.

Accounting Cycle Tutorial—Making Adjusting Entries

1. Some events are not journalized daily because it is inexpedient to do so. Examples are the consumption of supplies and the earning of wages by employees.
2. Some costs are not journalized during the accounting period because they expire with the passage of time rather than through recurring daily transactions. Examples are equipment deterioration, and rent and insurance.
3. Some items may be unrecorded. An example is a utility service bill that will not be received until the next accounting period.

Adjusting entries are required every time financial statements are prepared. The starting point is an analysis of each account in the trial balance to determine whether it is complete and up-to-date. The analysis requires a thorough understanding of the company's operations and the interrelationship of accounts. Preparing adjusting entries is often an involved process. The company may need to make inventory counts of supplies and repair parts. It may need to prepare supporting schedules of insurance policies, rental agreements, and other contractual commitments. Adjustments are often prepared after the balance sheet date. However, the adjusting entries are dated as of the balance sheet date.

HELPFUL HINT

Adjusting entries are needed to enable financial statements to be in conformity with GAAP.

Types of Adjusting Entries

STUDY OBJECTIVE 4

Identify the major types of adjusting entries.

Adjusting entries can be classified as either prepayments or accruals. Each of these classes has two subcategories as shown in Illustration 3-2.

Illustration 3-2
Categories of adjusting entries

Prepayments

1. **Prepaid Expenses.** Expenses paid in cash and recorded as assets before they are used or consumed.
2. **Unearned Revenues.** Cash received and recorded as liabilities before revenue is earned.

Accruals

1. **Accrued Revenues.** Revenues earned but not yet received in cash or recorded.
2. **Accrued Expenses.** Expenses incurred but not yet paid in cash or recorded.

Specific examples and explanations of each type of adjustment are given on the following pages. Each example is based on the October 31 trial balance of Pioneer Advertising Agency Inc. from Chapter 2, reproduced in Illustration 3-3.

Illustration 3-3
Trial balance

PIONEER ADVERTISING AGENCY INC.
Trial Balance
October 31, 2006

	Debit	Credit
Cash	$15,200	
Advertising Supplies	2,500	
Prepaid Insurance	600	
Office Equipment	5,000	
Notes Payable		$ 5,000
Accounts Payable		2,500
Unearned Revenue		1,200
Common Stock		10,000
Retained Earnings		–0–
Dividends	500	
Service Revenue		10,000
Salaries Expense	4,000	
Rent Expense	900	
	$28,700	**$28,700**

We assume that Pioneer Advertising uses an accounting period of one month. Thus, monthly adjusting entries will be made. The entries will be dated October 31.

Adjusting Entries for Prepayments

STUDY OBJECTIVE 5

Prepare adjusting entries for prepayments.

As indicated earlier, prepayments are either prepaid expenses or unearned revenues. Adjusting entries for prepayments are required to record the portion of the prepayment that represents the **expense incurred or the revenue earned** in the current accounting period.

If an adjustment is needed for prepayments, the asset and liability are overstated and the related expense and revenue are understated before the adjustment. For example, in the trial balance, the balance in the asset Advertising Supplies shows only supplies purchased. This balance is overstated; a related expense account, Advertising Supplies Expense, is understated because the cost of supplies used has not

HELPFUL HINT

Remember that credits decrease assets and increase revenues. Debits increase expenses and decrease liabilities.

been recognized. Thus the adjusting entry for prepayments will **decrease a balance sheet account** (Advertising Supplies) and **increase an income statement account** (Advertising Supplies Expense).

Prepaid Expenses

As stated on page 97, expenses paid in cash and recorded as assets before they are used or consumed are called **prepaid expenses** or **prepayments**. When a cost is prepaid, an asset account is debited to show the service or benefit that will be received in the future. Prepayments often occur in regard to insurance, supplies, advertising, and rent. In addition, prepayments are made when buildings and equipment are purchased.

Prepaid expenses expire either with the passage of time (e.g., rent and insurance) or through use and consumption (e.g., supplies). The expiration of these costs does not require daily journal entries, which would be unnecessary and impractical. Instead, it is customary to postpone recognizing cost expirations until financial statements are prepared. At each statement date, adjusting entries are made for two purposes: (1) to record the expenses that apply to the current accounting period, and (2) to show the unexpired costs in the asset accounts.

Prior to adjustment, assets are overstated and expenses are understated. Therefore, as shown in Illustration 3-4, **an adjusting entry for prepaid expense results in an increase (debit) to an expense account and a decrease (credit) to an asset account**.

Illustration 3-4
Adjusting entries for prepaid expenses

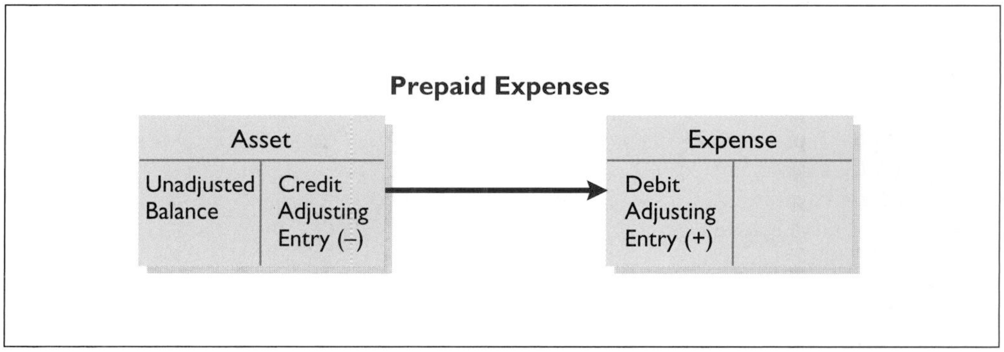

SUPPLIES. Businesses use various types of supplies. For example, a CPA firm will have **office supplies** such as stationery, envelopes, and accounting paper. An advertising firm will have **advertising supplies** such as graph paper, video film, and poster paper. Supplies are generally debited to an asset account when they are acquired. In the course of operations, supplies are depleted, but recognition of supplies used is deferred until the adjustment process. At that point, a physical inventory (count) of supplies is taken. The difference between the balance in the Supplies (asset) account and the cost of supplies on hand represents the supplies used (expense) for the period.

Pioneer Advertising Agency Inc. purchased advertising supplies costing $2,500 on October 5. A debit (increase) was made to the asset Advertising Supplies. This account shows a balance of $2,500 in the October 31 trial balance. An inventory count at the close of business on October 31 reveals that $1,000 of supplies are still on hand. Thus, the cost of supplies used is $1,500 ($2,500 – $1,000), and the following adjusting entry is made.

***Equation analyses** summarize the effects of the transaction on the accounting equation.*

EQUATION ANALYSIS				
A	=	L	+	SE
−1,500				−1,500 Exp

Cash Flows
no effect

Oct. 31	Advertising Supplies Expense	1,500	
	Advertising Supplies		1,500
	(To record supplies used)		

After the adjusting entry is posted, the two supplies accounts show:

Illustration 3-5
Supplies accounts after adjustment

Advertising Supplies				Advertising Supplies Expense			
10/5	2,500	10/31 **Adj.**	**1,500**	10/31 **Adj.**	**1,500**		
10/31 Bal.	1,000						

The asset account Advertising Supplies now shows a balance of $1,000, which is the cost of supplies on hand at the statement date. In addition, Advertising Supplies Expense shows a balance of $1,500, which equals the cost of supplies used in October. **If the adjusting entry is not made, October expenses will be understated and net income overstated by $1,500. Also, both assets and stockholders' equity will be overstated by $1,500 on the October 31 balance sheet.**

ACCOUNTING MATTERS! Business Insight

In the past, the costs of media advertising for burgers, bleaches, athletic shoes, and such products were sometimes recorded as assets and expensed in subsequent periods as sales took place. The reasoning behind this treatment was that long ad campaigns provided benefits over multiple accounting periods. Today this treatment is no longer allowed. Instead, advertising costs must be expensed when the advertising takes place. The issue is important because the outlays for advertising can be substantial. Recent big spenders: **Coca-Cola** spent $2 billion, **PepsiCo, Inc.** $1.7 billion, **Campbell Soup Company** $1.7 billion, and **JCPenney Company** $947 million.

? Why do you think current accounting rules require that the cost of long ad campaigns be expensed rather than recorded as an asset?

INSURANCE. Most companies have fire and theft insurance on merchandise and equipment, personal liability insurance for accidents suffered by customers, and automobile insurance on company cars and trucks. The cost of insurance protection is determined by the payment of insurance premiums. The minimum term of coverage is usually one year, but three- to five-year terms are available and offer lower annual premiums. Insurance premiums normally are charged to the asset account Prepaid Insurance when paid. At the financial statement date it is necessary to debit (increase) Insurance Expense and credit (decrease) Prepaid Insurance for the cost that has expired during the period.

Insurance

Oct.4
Insurance purchased; record asset

Insurance Policy			
Oct $50	Nov $50	Dec $50	Jan $50
Feb $50	March $50	April $50	May $50
June $50	July $50	Aug $50	Sept $50
I YEAR $600			

Oct.31
Insurance expired; record insurance expense

On October 4, Pioneer Advertising Agency Inc. paid $600 for a one-year fire insurance policy. The effective date of coverage was October 1. The premium was charged to Prepaid Insurance when it was paid, and this account shows a balance of $600 in the October 31 trial balance. Analysis reveals that $50 ($600 ÷ 12) of insurance expires each month. Thus, the following adjusting entry is made.

Oct. 31	Insurance Expense	50	
	Prepaid Insurance		50
	(To record insurance expired)		

A	=	L	+	SE
−50				−50 Exp

Cash Flows
no effect

After the adjusting entry is posted, the accounts show:

Illustration 3-6
Insurance accounts after adjustment

Prepaid Insurance				Insurance Expense			
10/4	600	10/31 **Adj.**	**50**	10/31 **Adj.**	**50**		
10/31 Bal.	550						

The asset Prepaid Insurance shows a balance of $550. This amount represents the unexpired cost for the remaining eleven months of coverage. The $50 balance in Insurance Expense is equal to the insurance cost that has expired in October. **If this adjustment is not made, October expenses will be understated by $50 and net income overstated by $50. Also, both assets and stockholders' equity will be overstated by $50 on the October 31 balance sheet.**

Depreciation

Oct.2

Office equipment purchased; record asset

Office Equipment			
Oct $40	Nov $40	Dec $40	Jan $40
Feb $40	March $40	April $40	May $40
June $40	July $40	Aug $40	Sept $40
Depreciation = $480/year			

Oct.31

Depreciation recognized; record depreciation expense

DEPRECIATION. A business enterprise typically owns productive facilities such as buildings, equipment, and vehicles. Because these assets provide service for a number of years, each is recorded as an asset, rather than an expense, in the year it is acquired. As explained in Chapter 1, such assets are recorded at cost, as required by the cost principle. The term of service is referred to as the **useful life**.

According to the matching principle, a portion of the cost of a long-lived asset should be reported as an expense during each period of the asset's useful life. **Depreciation** is the allocation of the cost of an asset to expense over its useful life in a rational and systematic manner.

Need for Depreciation Adjustment. From an accounting standpoint, acquiring productive facilities is viewed essentially as a long-term prepayment for services. The need for periodic adjusting entries for depreciation is, therefore, the same as that for other prepaid expenses: to recognize the cost that has expired (expense) during the period and to report the unexpired cost (asset) at the end of the period.

At the time an asset is acquired, its useful life cannot be known with certainty. The asset may be useful for a longer or shorter time than expected, depending on such factors as actual use, deterioration due to the elements, or obsolescence. Thus, you should recognize that **depreciation is an estimate** rather than a factual measurement of the cost that has expired. A common procedure in computing depreciation expense is to divide the cost of the asset by its useful life. For example, if cost is $10,000 and useful life is expected to be 10 years, annual depreciation is $1,000.[1]

For Pioneer Advertising, depreciation on the office equipment is estimated to be $480 a year, or $40 per month. Accordingly, depreciation for October is recognized by the following adjusting entry.

A	=	L	+	SE
−40				−40 Exp

Cash Flows
no effect

Oct. 31	Depreciation Expense	40	
	Accumulated Depreciation—Office Equipment		40
	(To record monthly depreciation)		

After the adjusting entry is posted, the accounts show:

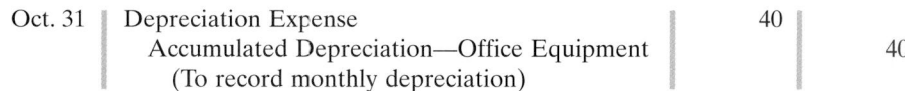

Illustration 3-7
Accounts after adjustment for depreciation

Office Equipment

	Debit		Credit
10/1	5,000		

Accumulated Depreciation—Office Equipment

	Debit		Credit
		10/31 **Adj.**	40

Depreciation Expense

	Debit		Credit
10/31 **Adj.**	40		

The balance in the accumulated depreciation account will increase $40 each month. After journalizing and posting the adjusting entry at November 30, the balance will be $80; at December 31, $120; and so on.

HELPFUL HINT

All contra accounts have increases, decreases, and normal balances opposite to the account to which they relate.

Statement Presentation. Accumulated Depreciation—Office Equipment is a contra asset account. A **contra asset account** is one that is offset against an asset account on the balance sheet. This accumulated depreciation account appears just after Office Equipment on the balance sheet. Its normal balance is a credit. An alternative would be to credit (decrease) Office Equipment directly for the depreci-

[1]Additional consideration is given to computing depreciation expense in Chapter 10.

ation each month. But use of the contra account provides disclosure of **both the original cost** of the equipment **and the total cost that has expired to date**. In the balance sheet, Accumulated Depreciation—Office Equipment is deducted from the related asset account as follows.

Office equipment	$5,000	
Less: Accumulated depreciation—office equipment	40	**$4,960**

Illustration 3-8
Balance sheet presentation of accumulated depreciation

The difference between the cost of any depreciable asset and its related accumulated depreciation is referred to as the **book value** of that asset. In Illustration 3-8, the book value of the equipment at the balance sheet date is $4,960. You should realize that the book value is generally different from the market value (the price at which the asset could be sold in the marketplace). The reason the two are different is that depreciation is a means of cost allocation, not a matter of valuation.

ALTERNATIVE TERMINOLOGY

Book value is sometimes referred to as *carrying value* or *unexpired cost*.

Depreciation expense also identifies that portion of the asset's cost that has expired in October. As in the case of other prepaid adjustments, the omission of this adjusting entry would cause total assets, total stockholders' equity, and net income to be overstated and depreciation expense to be understated.

If the company owns additional equipment, such as delivery or store equipment, or if it has buildings, depreciation expense is recorded on each of those items. Related accumulated depreciation accounts also are established, such as: Accumulated Depreciation—Delivery Equipment; Accumulated Depreciation—Store Equipment; and Accumulated Depreciation—Buildings.

Unearned Revenues

As stated on page 97, cash received and recorded as liabilities before revenue is earned is called **unearned revenues**. Such items as rent, magazine subscriptions, and customer deposits for future service may result in unearned revenues. Airlines such as **United**, **American**, and **Delta** treat receipts from the sale of tickets as unearned revenue until the flight service is provided. Similarly, college tuition received prior to the start of a semester is considered unearned revenue. Unearned revenues are the opposite of prepaid expenses. Indeed, unearned revenue on the books of one company is likely to be a prepayment on the books of the company that has made the advance payment. For example, if identical accounting periods are assumed, a landlord will have unearned rent revenue when a tenant has prepaid rent.

Unearned Revenues

Oct.2

Thank you in advance for your work
I will finish by Dec. 31
$1,200

Cash is received in advance; liability is recorded

Oct.31
Some service has been provided; some revenue is recorded

When the payment is received for services to be provided in a future accounting period, an unearned revenue account (a liability) should be credited (increased) to recognize the obligation that exists. Later, unearned revenues are earned by providing service to a customer. It may not be practical to make daily journal entries as the revenue is earned. In such cases, recognition of earned revenue is delayed until the end of the period. Then an adjusting entry is made to record the revenue that has been earned and to show the liability that remains. Typically, prior to adjustment, liabilities are overstated and revenues are understated. Therefore, as shown in Illustration 3-9 (page 102), **the adjusting entry for unearned revenues results in a decrease (a debit) to a liability account and an increase (a credit) to a revenue account.**

ALTERNATIVE TERMINOLOGY

Unearned revenue is sometimes referred to as *deferred revenue.*

Pioneer Advertising Agency Inc. received $1,200 on October 2 from R. Knox for advertising services expected to be completed by December 31. The payment was credited to Unearned Revenue; this account shows a balance of $1,200 in the October 31 trial balance. Analysis reveals that $400 of those fees was earned in October. The following adjusting entry is made.

Oct. 31	Unearned Revenue	400	
	Service Revenue		400
	(To record revenue for services provided)		

A	=	L	+	SE
		−400		+400 Rev

Cash Flows
no effect

Illustration 3-9
Adjusting entries for unearned revenues

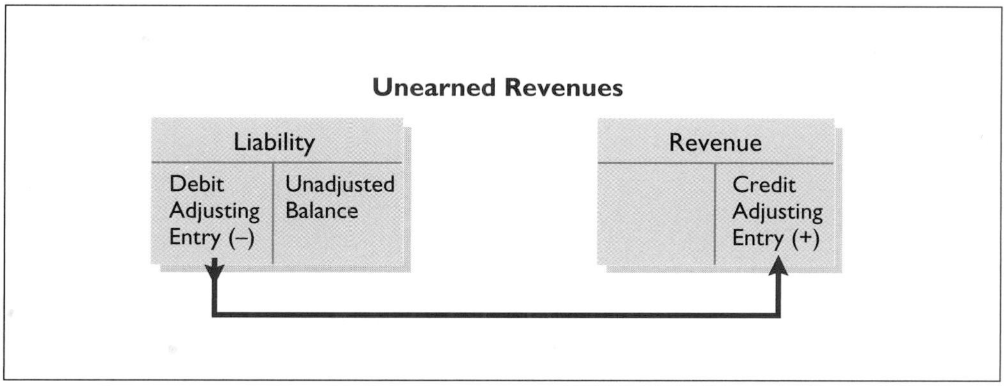

After the adjusting entry is posted, the accounts show:

Illustration 3-10
Revenue accounts after prepayments adjustment

Unearned Revenue				Service Revenue			
10/31 **Adj.**	**400**	10/2	1,200			10/31 Bal.	10,000
		10/31 Bal.	800			31 **Adj.**	**400**

The liability Unearned Revenue now shows a balance of $800. This amount represents the remaining prepaid advertising services to be performed in the future. At the same time, Service Revenue shows total revenue of $10,400 earned in October. **If this adjustment is not made, revenues and net income would be understated by $400 in the income statement. Also, liabilities would be overstated and stockholders' equity would be understated by $400 on the October 31 balance sheet.**

ACCOUNTING MATTERS! Ethics Insight

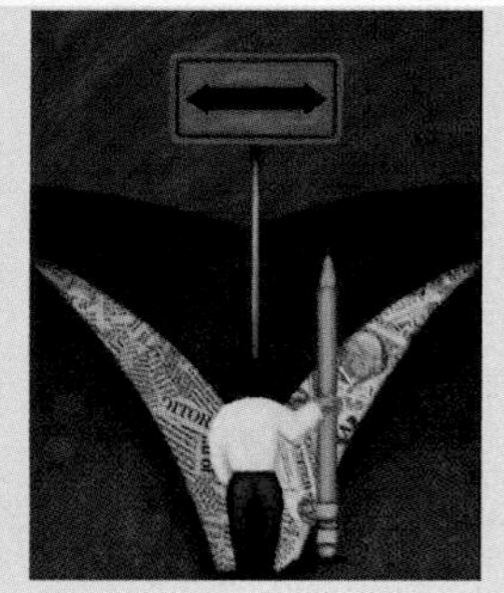

Companies would rather report steadily increasing profits than fluctuating profits. To "smooth" earnings, companies sometimes shift the reporting of revenues or expenses between periods. A recent *Wall Street Journal* article reported that **Microsoft Corp.** agreed to settle Securities and Exchange Commission charges that it misstated its earnings in some years by illegally maintaining different "reserve" accounts for such expenses as marketing and obsolete inventory. The settlement did not require Microsoft to pay a fine. Microsoft accepted the commission's order without admitting or denying wrongdoing and agreed not to commit accounting violations. "The SEC said Microsoft maintained undisclosed reserve accounts totaling between $200 million and $900 million between 1994 and 1998 and didn't maintain proper internal controls to document them or substantiate their size." The SEC said that the improper use of these reserve accounts resulted in "material inaccuracies" in the financial reports filed with the SEC.

Source: Rebecca Buckman, "Microsoft, SEC Settle Probe Into Earnings Misstatements," *Wall Street Journal Online* (June 4, 2002).

? What accounting principles do you think Microsoft violated? What did the SEC mean by "material inaccuracies"? Why would a company prefer to report steadily increasing profits rather than fluctuating profits?

BEFORE YOU GO ON...

Review It

1. What are the four types of adjusting entries?
2. What is the effect on assets, stockholders' equity, expenses, and net income if a prepaid expense adjusting entry is not made?
3. What is the effect on liabilities, stockholders' equity, revenues, and net income if an unearned revenue adjusting entry is not made?
4. Using **PepsiCo**'s Consolidated Statement of Income, what was the amount of depreciation expense for 2003 and 2002? (See Note 4 to the financial statements.) The answer to this question is provided on page 137.

PEPSI.

Do It

The ledger of Hammond, Inc. on March 31, 2006, includes the following selected accounts before adjusting entries.

	Debit	Credit
Prepaid Insurance	3,600	
Office Supplies	2,800	
Office Equipment	25,000	
Accumulated Depreciation—Office Equipment		5,000
Unearned Revenue		9,200

An analysis of the accounts shows the following.

1. Insurance expires at the rate of $100 per month.
2. Supplies on hand total $800.
3. The office equipment depreciates $200 a month.
4. One-half of the unearned revenue was earned in March.

Prepare the adjusting entries for the month of March.

ACTION PLAN

- Make adjusting entries at the end of the period for revenues earned and expenses incurred in the period.
- Don't forget to make adjusting entries for prepayments. Failure to adjust for prepayments leads to overstatement of the asset or liability and related understatement of the expense or revenue.

SOLUTION

1. Insurance Expense	100	
Prepaid Insurance		100
(To record insurance expired)		
2. Office Supplies Expense	2,000	
Office Supplies		2,000
(To record supplies used)		
3. Depreciation Expense	200	
Accumulated Depreciation—Office Equipment		200
(To record monthly depreciation)		
4. Unearned Revenue	4,600	
Service Revenue		4,600
(To record revenue for services provided)		

Related exercise material: *BE3-3, BE3-4, BE3-5, BE3-6, E3-2, E3-3, E3-4, E3-5, E3-6, E3-7, E3-8, and E3-9.*

THE NAVIGATOR

STUDY OBJECTIVE 6

Prepare adjusting entries for accruals.

Adjusting Entries for Accruals

The second category of adjusting entries is **accruals**. Adjusting entries for accruals are required to record revenues earned and expenses incurred in the current accounting period that have not been recognized through daily entries.

An accrual adjustment is needed when various accounts are understated: the revenue account and the related asset account, and/or the expense account and the related liability account. Thus, the adjusting entry for accruals will **increase both a balance sheet and an income statement account**.

Accrued Revenues

Oct.31

Revenue and receivable are recorded for unbilled services

Nov.

Cash is received; receivable is reduced

Accrued Revenues

As explained on page 97, revenues earned but not yet received in cash or recorded at the statement date are **accrued revenues**. Accrued revenues may accumulate (accrue) with the passing of time, as in the case of interest revenue and rent revenue. Or they may result from services that have been performed but are neither billed nor collected, as in the case of commissions and fees. The former are unrecorded because the earning of interest and rent does not involve daily transactions. The latter may be unrecorded because only a portion of the total service has been provided.

An adjusting entry is required for two purposes: (1) to show the receivable that exists at the balance sheet date, and (2) to record the revenue that has been earned during the period. Prior to adjustment both assets and revenues are understated. Therefore, as shown in Illustration 3-11, **an adjusting entry for accrued revenues results in an increase (a debit) to an asset account and an increase (a credit) to a revenue account**.

Illustration 3-11
Adjusting entries for accrued revenues

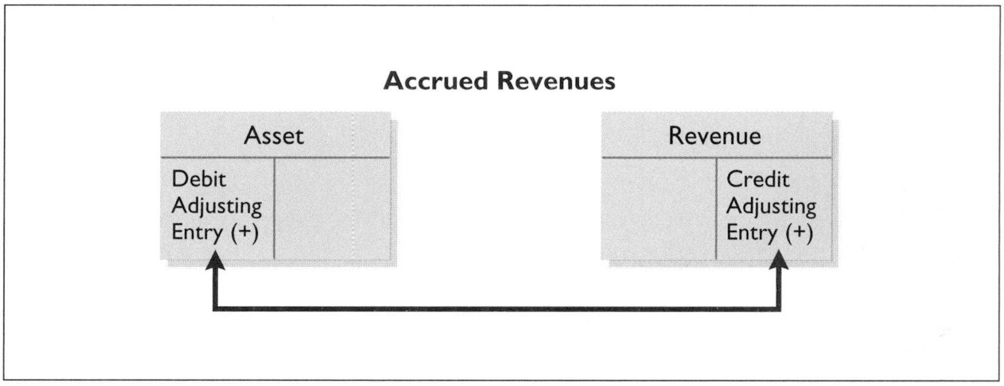

In October Pioneer Advertising Agency Inc. earned $200 for advertising services that have not been recorded. The following adjusting entry is made on October 31.

A	=	L	+	SE
+200				+200 Rev

Cash Flows
no effect

Oct. 31	Accounts Receivable	200	
	Service Revenue		200
	(To record revenue for services provided)		

After the adjusting entry is posted, the accounts show:

Illustration 3-12
Receivable and revenue accounts after accrual adjustment

Accounts Receivable			Service Revenue	
10/31 **Adj.**	**200**		10/31	10,000
			31	400
			31 **Adj.**	**200**
			10/31 Bal.	10,600

The asset Accounts Receivable shows that $200 is owed by clients at the balance sheet date. The balance of $10,600 in Service Revenue represents the total revenue earned during the month ($10,000 + $400 + $200). **If the adjusting entry is not made, the following will all be understated: assets and stockholders' equity on the balance sheet, and revenues and net income on the income statement.**

On November 10, Pioneer receives cash of $200 for the services performed in October. Thus, the following entry is made.

Nov. 10	Cash	200	
	Accounts Receivable		200
	(To record cash collected on account)		

A	=	L	+	SE
+200				
−200				

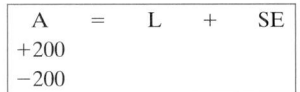

Cash Flows
+200

The subsequent collection of revenue from clients will be recorded with a debit (increase) to Cash and a credit (decrease) to Accounts Receivable.

ALTERNATIVE TERMINOLOGY

Accrued revenues are also called *accrued receivables.*

Accrued Expenses

As indicated on page 97, expenses incurred but not yet paid or recorded at the statement date are called **accrued expenses**. Interest, rent, taxes, and salaries can be accrued expenses. Accrued expenses result from the same causes as accrued revenues. In fact, an accrued expense on the books of one company is an accrued revenue to another company. For example, the $200 accrual of fees by Pioneer is an accrued expense to the client that received the service.

Adjustments for accrued expenses are needed for two purposes: (1) to record the obligations that exist at the balance sheet date, and (2) to recognize the expenses that apply to the current accounting period. Prior to adjustment, both liabilities and expenses are understated. Therefore, as shown in Illustration 3-13, **an adjusting entry for accrued expenses results in an increase (a debit) to an expense account and an increase (a credit) to a liability account.**

ALTERNATIVE TERMINOLOGY

Accrued expenses are also called *accrued liabilities.*

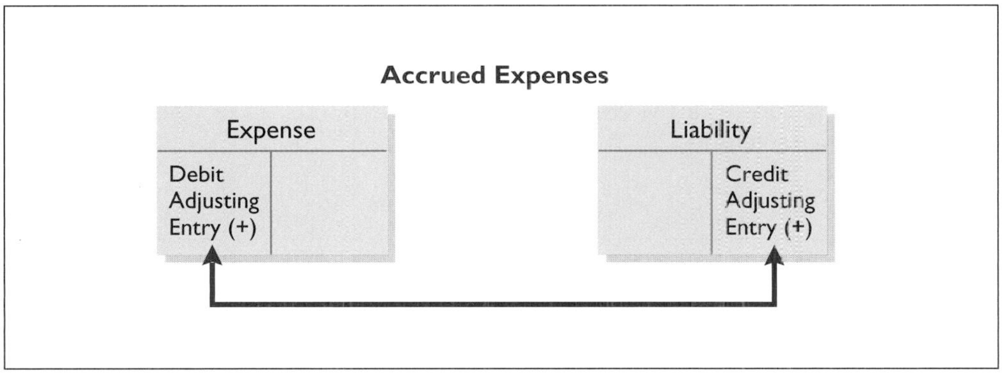

Illustration 3-13
Adjusting entries for accrued expenses

ACCRUED INTEREST. Pioneer Advertising Agency Inc. signed a $5,000, 3-month note payable on October 1. The note requires interest at an annual rate of 12%. The amount of the interest accumulation is determined by three factors: (1) the face value of the note, (2) the interest rate, which is always expressed as an annual rate, and (3) the length of time the note is outstanding. In this instance, the total interest due on the $5,000 note at its due date 3 months hence is $150 ($5,000 × 12% × 3/12), or $50 for one month. The formula for computing interest and its application to Pioneer Advertising Agency Inc. for the month of October[2] are shown in Illustration 3-14 (page 106). Note that the time period is expressed as a fraction of a year.

HELPFUL HINT

Interest is a cost of borrowing money that accumulates with the passage of time.

[2]The computation of interest will be considered in more depth in later chapters.

Illustration 3-14
Formula for computing interest

Face Value of Note	×	Annual Interest Rate	×	Time in Terms of One Year	=	Interest
$5,000	×	12%	×	1/12	=	**$50**

The accrued expense adjusting entry at October 31 is:

A	=	L	+	SE
		+50		−50 Exp

Cash Flows
no effect

Oct. 31	Interest Expense	50	
	Interest Payable		50
	(To record interest on notes payable)		

After this adjusting entry is posted, the accounts show:

Illustration 3-15
Interest accounts after adjustment

Interest Expense			Interest Payable		
10/31 **Adj.**	**50**			10/31 **Adj.**	**50**

Interest Expense shows the interest charges for the month. The amount of interest owed at the statement date is shown in Interest Payable. It will not be paid until the note comes due at the end of 3 months. The Interest Payable account is used instead of crediting (increasing) Notes Payable. The reason for using the two accounts is to disclose the two types of obligations (interest and principal) in the accounts and statements. **If this adjusting entry is not made, liabilities and interest expense will be understated, and net income and stockholders' equity will be overstated.**

ACCRUED SALARIES. Some types of expenses are paid for after the services have been performed. Examples are employee salaries and commissions. At Pioneer Advertising Agency Inc. salaries were last paid on October 26; the next payday is November 9. As shown in the calendar in Illustration 3-16, three working days remain in October (October 29–31).

Illustration 3-16
Calendar showing Pioneer's pay periods

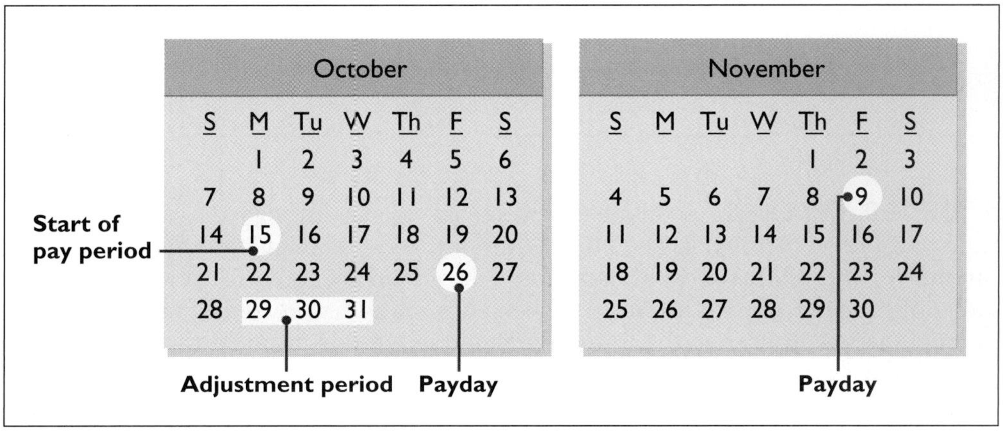

At October 31, the salaries for the last three days of the month represent an accrued expense and a related liability. The employees receive total salaries of $2,000

for a five-day work week, or $400 per day. Thus, accrued salaries at October 31 are $1,200 ($400 × 3). The adjusting entry is:

Oct. 31	Salaries Expense	1,200	
	Salaries Payable		1,200
	(To record accrued salaries)		

A	=	L	+	SE
		+1,200		−1,200 Exp

Cash Flows
no effect

After this adjusting entry is posted, the accounts show:

Illustration 3-17
Salary accounts after adjustment

Salaries Expense			Salaries Payable		
10/26	4,000			10/31 **Adj.**	**1,200**
31 **Adj.**	**1,200**				
10/31 Bal.	5,200				

After this adjustment, the balance in Salaries Expense of $5,200 (13 days × $400) is the actual salary expense for October. (The employees started work on October 15.) The balance in Salaries Payable of $1,200 is the amount of the liability for salaries owed as of October 31. **If the $1,200 adjustment for salaries is not recorded, Pioneer's expenses will be understated $1,200, and its liabilities will be understated $1,200.**

At Pioneer Advertising, salaries are payable every two weeks. The next payday is November 9, when total salaries of $4,000 will again be paid. The payment will consist of $1,200 of salaries payable at October 31 plus $2,800 of salaries expense for November (seven working days as shown in the November calendar × $400). Therefore, the following entry is made on November 9.

Nov. 9	Salaries Payable	1,200	
	Salaries Expense	2,800	
	Cash		4,000
	(To record November 9 payroll)		

A	=	L	+	SE
−4,000		−1,200		−2,800 Exp

Cash Flows
−4,000

This entry does two things: (1) It eliminates the liability for Salaries Payable that was recorded in the October 31 adjusting entry. (2) It records the proper amount of Salaries Expense for the period between November 1 and November 9.

ACCOUNTING MATTERS! e Business Insight

In many computer systems, the adjusting process is handled like any other transaction, with the accountant inputting the adjustment at the time required. The main difference between adjusting entries and regular transactions is that with adjusting entries, one part of the computer system may perform the required calculation for such items as depreciation or interest and then "feed" these figures to the journalizing process. Such systems are also able to display information before and after changes are made.

? If a computer performs adjusting entries, what role does the accountant play? Why might management be interested in "information before and after changes"?

BEFORE YOU GO ON...

Review It

1. If an accrued revenue adjusting entry is not made, what is the effect on assets, stockholders' equity, revenues, and net income?
2. If an accrued expense adjusting entry is not made, what is the effect on liabilities, stockholders' equity, expenses, and net income?

Do It

Calvin and Hobbs are the new owners of Micro Computer Services Inc. At the end of August 2006, their first month of ownership, Calvin and Hobbs are trying to prepare monthly financial statements. They have the following information for the month.

1. At August 31, Micro Computer owed employees $800 in salaries that will be paid on September 1.
2. On August 1, Micro Computer borrowed $30,000 from a local bank on a 15-year note. The annual interest rate is 10%.
3. Service revenue unrecorded in August totaled $1,100.

Prepare the adjusting entries needed at August 31, 2006.

ACTION PLAN

- Make adjusting entries at the end of the period for revenues earned and expenses incurred in the period.
- Don't forget to make adjusting entries for accruals. Adjusting entries for accruals will increase both a balance sheet and an income statement account.

SOLUTION

1. Salaries Expense	800	
Salaries Payable		800
(To record accrued salaries)		
2. Interest Expense	250	
Interest Payable		250
(To record interest)		
($30,000 × 10% × 1/12 = $250)		
3. Accounts Receivable	1,100	
Service Revenue		1,100
(To record revenue for services provided)		

Related exercise material: *BE3-7, E3-2, E3-3, E3-4, E3-5, E3-6, E3-7, E3-8, and E3-9.*

THE NAVIGATOR

Summary of Basic Relationships

The four basic types of adjusting entries are summarized in Illustration 3-18. Take some time to study and analyze the adjusting entries shown in the summary. Be sure to note that **each adjusting entry affects one balance sheet account and one income statement account**.

Illustration 3-18
Summary of adjusting entries

Type of Adjustment	Reason for Adjustment	Accounts before Adjustment	Adjusting Entry
1. Prepaid expenses	Prepaid expenses originally recorded in asset accounts have been used.	Assets overstated Expenses understated	Dr. Expenses Cr. Assets
2. Unearned revenues	Unearned revenues initially recorded in liability accounts have been earned.	Liabilities overstated Revenues understated	Dr. Liabilities Cr. Revenues
3. Accrued revenues	Revenues have been earned but not yet received in cash or recorded.	Assets understated Revenues understated	Dr. Assets Cr. Revenues
4. Accrued expenses	Expenses have been incurred but not yet paid in cash or recorded.	Expenses understated Liabilities understated	Dr. Expenses Cr. Liabilities

The journalizing and posting of adjusting entries for Pioneer Advertising Agency Inc. on October 31 are shown in Illustrations 3-19 and 3-20. All adjustments are identified in the ledger by the reference J2 because they have been journalized on page 2 of the general journal. A center caption entitled "Adjusting Entries" may be inserted between the last transaction entry and the first adjusting entry to identify these entries. When reviewing the general ledger in Illustration 3-20 (on the next page), note that the adjustments are highlighted in color.

Illustration 3-19
General journal showing adjusting entries

GENERAL JOURNAL — J2

Date	Account Titles and Explanation	Ref.	Debit	Credit
2006	Adjusting Entries			
Oct. 31	Advertising Supplies Expense	631	1,500	
	Advertising Supplies	126		1,500
	(To record supplies used)			
31	Insurance Expense	722	50	
	Prepaid Insurance	130		50
	(To record insurance expired)			
31	Depreciation Expense	711	40	
	Accumulated Depreciation—Office Equipment	158		40
	(To record monthly depreciation)			
31	Unearned Revenue	209	400	
	Service Revenue	400		400
	(To record revenue for services provided)			
31	Accounts Receivable	112	200	
	Service Revenue	400		200
	(To record revenue for services provided)			
31	Interest Expense	905	50	
	Interest Payable	230		50
	(To record interest on notes payable)			
31	Salaries Expense	726	1,200	
	Salaries Payable	212		1,200
	(To record accrued salaries)			

HELPFUL HINT

(1) Adjusting entries should not involve debits or credits to cash.
(2) Evaluate whether the adjustment makes sense. For example, an adjustment to recognize supplies used should increase supplies expense.
(3) Double-check all computations.

Illustration 3-20
General ledger after adjustment

GENERAL LEDGER

Cash — No. 101

Date	Explanation	Ref.	Debit	Credit	Balance
2006					
Oct. 1		J1	10,000		10,000
2		J1	1,200		11,200
3		J1		900	10,300
4		J1		600	9,700
20		J1		500	9,200
26		J1		4,000	5,200
31		J1	10,000		15,200

Accounts Receivable — No. 112

Date	Explanation	Ref.	Debit	Credit	Balance
2006					
Oct. 31	**Adj. entry**	**J2**	**200**		**200**

Advertising Supplies — No. 126

Date	Explanation	Ref.	Debit	Credit	Balance
2006					
Oct. 5		J1	2,500		2,500
31	**Adj. entry**	**J2**		**1,500**	**1,000**

Prepaid Insurance — No. 130

Date	Explanation	Ref.	Debit	Credit	Balance
2006					
Oct. 4		J1	600		600
31	**Adj. entry**	**J2**		**50**	**550**

Office Equipment — No. 157

Date	Explanation	Ref.	Debit	Credit	Balance
2006					
Oct. 1		J1	5,000		5,000

Accumulated Depreciation—Office Equipment — No. 158

Date	Explanation	Ref.	Debit	Credit	Balance
2006					
Oct. 31	**Adj. entry**	**J2**		**40**	**40**

Notes Payable — No. 200

Date	Explanation	Ref.	Debit	Credit	Balance
2006					
Oct. 1		J1		5,000	5,000

Accounts Payable — No. 201

Date	Explanation	Ref.	Debit	Credit	Balance
2006					
Oct. 5		J1		2,500	2,500

Unearned Revenue — No. 209

Date	Explanation	Ref.	Debit	Credit	Balance
2006					
Oct. 2		J1		1,200	
31	**Adj. entry**	**J2**	**400**		**800**

Salaries Payable — No. 212

Date	Explanation	Ref.	Debit	Credit	Balance
2006					
Oct. 31	**Adj. entry**	**J2**		**1,200**	**1,200**

Interest Payable — No. 230

Date	Explanation	Ref.	Debit	Credit	Balance
2006					
Oct. 31	**Adj. entry**	**J2**		**50**	**50**

Common Stock — No. 311

Date	Explanation	Ref.	Debit	Credit	Balance
2006					
Oct. 1		J1		10,000	10,000

Retained Earnings — No. 320

Date	Explanation	Ref.	Debit	Credit	Balance
2006					

Dividends — No. 332

Date	Explanation	Ref.	Debit	Credit	Balance
2006					
Oct. 20		J1	500		500

Service Revenue — No. 400

Date	Explanation	Ref.	Debit	Credit	Balance
2006					
Oct. 31		J1		10,000	10,000
31	**Adj. entry**	**J2**		**400**	**10,400**
31	**Adj. entry**	**J2**		**200**	**10,600**

Advertising Supplies Expense — No. 631

Date	Explanation	Ref.	Debit	Credit	Balance
2006					
Oct. 31	**Adj. entry**	**J2**	**1,500**		**1,500**

Depreciation Expense — No. 711

Date	Explanation	Ref.	Debit	Credit	Balance
2006					
Oct. 31	**Adj. entry**	**J2**	**40**		**40**

Insurance Expense — No. 722

Date	Explanation	Ref.	Debit	Credit	Balance
2006					
Oct. 31	**Adj. entry**	**J2**	**50**		**50**

Salaries Expense — No. 726

Date	Explanation	Ref.	Debit	Credit	Balance
2006					
Oct. 26		J1	4,000		4,000
31	**Adj. entry**	**J2**	**1,200**		**5,200**

Rent Expense — No. 729

Date	Explanation	Ref.	Debit	Credit	Balance
2006					
Oct. 3		J1	900		900

Interest Expense — No. 905

Date	Explanation	Ref.	Debit	Credit	Balance
2006					
Oct. 31	**Adj. entry**	**J2**	**50**		**50**

The Adjusted Trial Balance and Financial Statements

STUDY OBJECTIVE 7

Describe the nature and purpose of an adjusted trial balance.

After all adjusting entries have been journalized and posted, another trial balance is prepared from the ledger accounts. This is called an **adjusted trial balance**. Its purpose is to **prove the equality** of the total debit balances and the total credit balances in the ledger after all adjustments have been made. The accounts in the adjusted trial balance contain all data that are needed for the preparation of financial statements.

Preparing the Adjusted Trial Balance

The adjusted trial balance for Pioneer Advertising Agency Inc. is presented in Illustration 3-21. It has been prepared from the ledger accounts in Illustration 3-20. The amounts affected by the adjusting entries are highlighted in color. Compare these amounts to those in the unadjusted trial balance in Illustration 3-3 on page 97.

Illustration 3-21
Adjusted trial balance

PIONEER ADVERTISING AGENCY INC.
Adjusted Trial Balance
October 31, 2006

	Dr.	Cr.
Cash	$15,200	
Accounts Receivable	**200**	
Advertising Supplies	**1,000**	
Prepaid Insurance	**550**	
Office Equipment	5,000	
Accumulated Depreciation—Office Equipment		$ **40**
Notes Payable		5,000
Accounts Payable		2,500
Unearned Revenue		**800**
Salaries Payable		**1,200**
Interest Payable		**50**
Common Stock		10,000
Retained Earnings		–0–
Dividends	500	
Service Revenue		**10,600**
Salaries Expense	**5,200**	
Advertising Supplies Expense	**1,500**	
Rent Expense	900	
Insurance Expense	**50**	
Interest Expense	**50**	
Depreciation Expense	**40**	
	$30,190	$30,190

Preparing Financial Statements

Financial statements can be prepared directly from the adjusted trial balance. Illustrations 3-22 and 3-23 show the interrelationships of data in the adjusted trial balance and the financial statements.

As shown in Illustration 3-22, the income statement is first prepared from the revenue and expense accounts. The retained earnings statement is derived from the retained earnings and dividends accounts and the net income (or net loss) shown in the income statement. As shown in Illustration 3-23, the balance sheet is then prepared from the asset and liability accounts, the common stock account, and the ending retained earnings balance as reported in the retained earnings statement.

Illustration 3-22
Preparation of the income statement and retained earnings statement from the adjusted trial balance

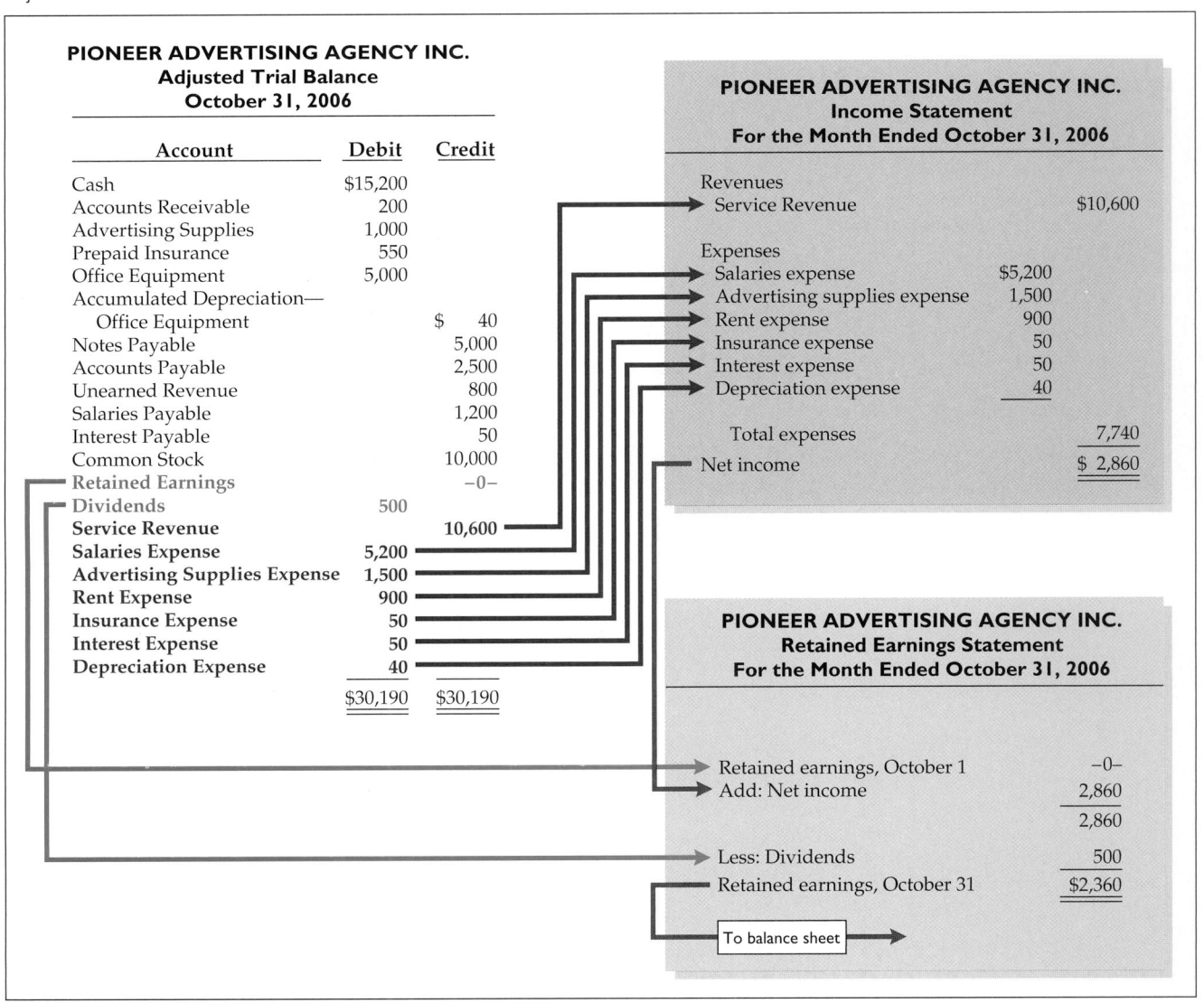

PIONEER ADVERTISING AGENCY INC.
Adjusted Trial Balance
October 31, 2006

Account	Debit	Credit
Cash	$15,200	
Accounts Receivable	200	
Advertising Supplies	1,000	
Prepaid Insurance	550	
Office Equipment	5,000	
Accumulated Depreciation—Office Equipment		$ 40
Notes Payable		5,000
Accounts Payable		2,500
Unearned Revenue		800
Salaries Payable		1,200
Interest Payable		50
Common Stock		10,000
Retained Earnings		–0–
Dividends	500	
Service Revenue		**10,600**
Salaries Expense	**5,200**	
Advertising Supplies Expense	**1,500**	
Rent Expense	**900**	
Insurance Expense	**50**	
Interest Expense	**50**	
Depreciation Expense	**40**	
	$30,190	$30,190

PIONEER ADVERTISING AGENCY INC.
Income Statement
For the Month Ended October 31, 2006

Revenues		
Service Revenue		$10,600
Expenses		
Salaries expense	$5,200	
Advertising supplies expense	1,500	
Rent expense	900	
Insurance expense	50	
Interest expense	50	
Depreciation expense	40	
Total expenses		7,740
Net income		$ 2,860

PIONEER ADVERTISING AGENCY INC.
Retained Earnings Statement
For the Month Ended October 31, 2006

Retained earnings, October 1	–0–
Add: Net income	2,860
	2,860
Less: Dividends	500
Retained earnings, October 31	$2,360

To balance sheet

PIONEER ADVERTISING AGENCY INC.
Adjusted Trial Balance
October 31, 2006

Account	Debit	Credit
Cash	$15,200	
Accounts Receivable	200	
Advertising Supplies	1,000	
Prepaid Insurance	550	
Office Equipment	5,000	
Accumulated Depreciation—Office Equipment		$ 40
Notes Payable		5,000
Accounts Payable		2,500
Unearned Revenue		800
Salaries Payable		1,200
Interest Payable		50
Common Stock		10,000
Retained Earnings		–0–
Dividends	500	
Service Revenue		10,600
Salaries Expense	5,200	
Advertising Supplies Expense	1,500	
Rent Expense	900	
Insurance Expense	50	
Interest Expense	50	
Depreciation Expense	40	
	$30,190	$30,190

PIONEER ADVERTISING AGENCY INC.
Balance Sheet
October 31, 2006

Assets		
Cash		$15,200
Accounts receivable		200
Advertising supplies		1,000
Prepaid insurance		550
Office equipment	$5,000	
Less: Accumulated depreciation	40	4,960
Total assets		$21,910
Liabilities and Stockholders' Equity		
Liabilities		
Notes payable		$ 5,000
Accounts payable		2,500
Unearned revenue		800
Salaries payable		1,200
Interest payable		50
Total liabilities		9,550
Stockholders' equity		
Common stock		10,000
Retained earnings		2,360
Total liabilities and stockholders' equity		$21,910

Balance at Oct. 31 from Retained Earnings Statement in Illustration 3-22

Illustration 3-23
Preparation of the balance sheet from the adjusted trial balance

BEFORE YOU GO ON...

Review It

1. What is the purpose of an adjusted trial balance?
2. How is an adjusted trial balance prepared?

THE NAVIGATOR

DEMONSTRATION PROBLEM

Green Thumb Lawn Care Inc. began operating on April 1. At April 30, the trial balance shows the following balances for selected accounts.

Prepaid Insurance	$ 3,600
Equipment	28,000
Notes Payable	20,000
Unearned Revenue	4,200
Service Revenue	1,800

Analysis reveals the following additional data.

1. Prepaid insurance is the cost of a 2-year insurance policy, effective April 1.
2. Depreciation on the equipment is $500 per month.
3. The note payable is dated April 1. It is a 6-month, 12% note.

(*continued from p. 113*)

4. Seven customers paid for the company's 6 months' lawn service package of $600 beginning in April. These customers were serviced in April.
5. Lawn services provided other customers but not billed at April 30 totaled $1,500.

Instructions

Prepare the adjusting entries for the month of April. Show computations.

ACTION PLAN

- Note that adjustments are being made for one month.
- Make computations carefully.
- Select account titles carefully.
- Make sure debits are made first and credits are indented.
- Check that debits equal credits for each entry.

SOLUTION TO DEMONSTRATION PROBLEM

General Journal **J1**

Date	Account Titles and Explanation	Ref.	Debit	Credit
	Adjusting Entries			
Apr. 30	Insurance Expense		150	
	Prepaid Insurance			150
	(To record insurance expired: $3,600 ÷ 24 = $150 per month)			
30	Depreciation Expense		500	
	Accumulated Depreciation—Equipment			500
	(To record monthly depreciation)			
30	Interest Expense		200	
	Interest Payable			200
	(To record interest on notes payable: $20,000 × 12% × 1/12 = $200)			
30	Unearned Revenue		700	
	Service Revenue			700
	(To record service revenue: $600 ÷ 6 = $100; $100 per month × 7 = $700)			
30	Accounts Receivable		1,500	
	Service Revenue			1,500
	(To record revenue for services provided)			

THE NAVIGATOR

SUMMARY OF STUDY OBJECTIVES

1. **Explain the time period assumption.** The time period assumption assumes that the economic life of a business can be divided into artificial time periods.
2. **Explain the accrual basis of accounting.** Accrual-basis accounting means that events that change a company's financial statements are recorded in the periods in which the events occur, rather than in the periods in which the company receives or pays cash.
3. **Explain why adjusting entries are needed.** Adjusting entries are made at the end of an accounting period. They ensure that revenues are recorded in the period in which they are earned and that expenses are recognized in the period in which they are incurred.
4. **Identify the major types of adjusting entries.** The major types of adjusting entries are prepaid expenses, unearned revenues, accrued revenues, and accrued expenses.
5. **Prepare adjusting entries for prepayments.** Prepayments are either prepaid expenses or unearned revenues. Adjusting entries for prepayments are required at the statement date to record the portion of the prepayment that represents the expense incurred or the revenue earned in the current accounting period.
6. **Prepare adjusting entries for accruals.** Accruals are either accrued revenues or accrued expenses. Adjusting entries for accruals are required to record revenues earned and expenses incurred in the current accounting period that have not been recognized through daily entries.
7. **Describe the nature and purpose of an adjusted trial balance.** An adjusted trial balance shows the balances of all accounts, including those that have been adjusted, at the end of an accounting period. Its purpose is to show the effects of all financial events that have occurred during the accounting period.

THE NAVIGATOR

GLOSSARY

Accrual-basis accounting Accounting basis in which transactions that change a company's financial statements are recorded in the periods in which the events occur. (p. 94).

Accrued expenses Expenses incurred but not yet paid in cash or recorded. (p. 105).

Accrued revenues Revenues earned but not yet received in cash or recorded. (p. 104).

Adjusted trial balance A list of accounts and their balances after all adjustments have been made. (p. 111).

Adjusting entries Entries made at the end of an accounting period to ensure that the revenue recognition and matching principles are followed. (p. 96).

Book value The difference between the cost of a depreciable asset and its related accumulated depreciation. (p. 101).

Calendar year An accounting period that extends from January 1 to December 31. (p. 94).

Cash-basis accounting Accounting basis in which revenue is recorded when cash is received and an expense is recorded when cash is paid. (p. 94).

Contra asset account An account that is offset against an asset account on the balance sheet. (p. 100).

Depreciation The allocation of the cost of an asset to expense over its useful life in a rational and systematic manner. (p. 100).

Fiscal year An accounting period that is one year in length. (p. 94).

Interim periods Monthly or quarterly accounting time periods. (p. 94).

Matching principle The principle that efforts (expenses) be matched with accomplishments (revenues). (p. 95).

Prepaid expenses Expenses paid in cash and recorded as assets before they are used or consumed. (p. 98).

Revenue recognition principle The principle that revenue be recognized in the accounting period in which it is earned. (p. 95).

Time period assumption An assumption that the economic life of a business can be divided into artificial time periods. (p. 94).

Unearned revenues Cash received and recorded as liabilities before revenue is earned. (p. 101).

Useful life The length of service of a productive facility. (p. 100).

APPENDIX ALTERNATIVE TREATMENT OF PREPAID EXPENSES AND UNEARNED REVENUES

STUDY OBJECTIVE 8

Prepare adjusting entries for the alternative treatment of prepayments.

In our discussion of adjusting entries for prepaid expenses and unearned revenues, we illustrated transactions for which the initial entries were made to balance sheet accounts. In the case of prepaid expenses, the prepayment was debited to an asset account. In the case of unearned revenue, the cash received was credited to a liability account. Some businesses use an alternative treatment: (1) At the time an expense is prepaid, it is debited to an expense account. (2) At the time of a receipt for future services, it is credited to a revenue account. The circumstances that justify such entries and the different adjusting entries that may be required are described below. The alternative treatment of prepaid expenses and unearned revenues has the same effect on the financial statements as the procedures described in the chapter.

Prepaid Expenses

Prepaid expenses become expired costs either through the passage of time (e.g., insurance) or through consumption (e.g., advertising supplies). If, at the time of purchase, the company expects to consume the supplies before the next financial statement date, **it may be more convenient initially to debit (increase) an expense account rather than an asset account.**

Assume that Pioneer Advertising Agency Inc. expects that all of the supplies purchased on October 5 will be used before the end of the month. A debit of $2,500 to Advertising Supplies Expense (rather than to the asset account Advertising Supplies) on October 5 will eliminate the need for an adjusting entry on October 31, if all the supplies are used. At October 31, the Advertising Supplies Expense account will show a balance of $2,500, which is the cost of supplies used between October 5 and October 31.

But what if the company does not use all the supplies, and an inventory of $1,000 of advertising supplies remains on October 31? Obviously, an adjusting entry is needed. Prior to adjustment, the expense account Advertising Supplies Expense is overstated $1,000, and the asset account Advertising Supplies is understated $1,000. Thus the following adjusting entry is made.

A	=	L	+	SE
+1,000				+1,000 Exp

Cash Flows
no effect

Oct. 31	Advertising Supplies	1,000	
	Advertising Supplies Expense		1,000
	(To record supplies inventory)		

After posting the adjusting entry, the accounts show:

Illustration 3A-1
Prepaid expense accounts after adjustment

Advertising Supplies

10/31 Adj.	**1,000**		

Advertising Supplies Expense

10/5	2,500	10/31 Adj.	**1,000**
10/31 Bal.	**1,500**		

After adjustment, the asset account Advertising Supplies shows a balance of $1,000, which is equal to the cost of supplies on hand at October 31. In addition, Advertising Supplies Expense shows a balance of $1,500, which is equal to the cost of supplies used between October 5 and October 31. If the adjusting entry is not made, expenses will be overstated and net income will be understated by $1,000 in the October income statement. Also, both assets and stockholders' equity will be understated by $1,000 on the October 31 balance sheet.

A comparison of the entries and accounts for advertising supplies is shown in Illustration 3A-2.

Illustration 3A-2
Adjustment approaches—a comparison

Prepayment Initially Debited to Asset Account (per chapter)				Prepayment Initially Debited to Expense Account (per appendix)			
Oct. 5	Advertising Supplies	2,500		Oct. 5	Advertising Supplies Expense	2,500	
	Accounts Payable		2,500		Accounts Payable		2,500
Oct. 31	Advertising Supplies Expense	1,500		Oct. 31	Advertising Supplies	1,000	
	Advertising Supplies		1,500		Advertising Supplies Expense		1,000

After posting the entries, the accounts appear as follows.

Illustration 3A-3
Comparison of accounts

(per chapter) Advertising Supplies

10/5	2,500	10/31 Adj.	**1,500**
10/31 Bal.	**1,000**		

(per appendix) Advertising Supplies

10/31 Adj.	**1,000**		

(per chapter) Advertising Supplies Expense

10/31 Adj.	**1,500**		

(per appendix) Advertising Supplies Expense

10/5	2,500	10/31 Adj.	**1,000**
10/31 Bal.	**1,500**		

Note that the account balances under each alternative are the same at October 31: Advertising Supplies $1,000, and Advertising Supplies Expense $1,500.

Unearned Revenues

Unearned revenues become earned either through the passage of time (e.g., unearned rent) or through providing the service (e.g., unearned fees). Similar to the case for prepaid expenses, a revenue account may be credited (increased) when cash is received for future services.

To illustrate, assume that Pioneer Advertising Agency Inc. received $1,200 for future services on October 2. The services were expected to be performed before October 31.[3] In such a case, Service Revenue is credited. If revenue is in fact earned before October 31, no adjustment is needed.

However, if at the statement date $800 of the services have not been performed, an adjusting entry is required. The revenue account Service Revenue is overstated $800, and the liability account Unearned Revenue is understated $800. Thus, the following adjusting entry is made.

HELPFUL HINT

The required adjusted balances here are Service Revenue $400 and Unearned Revenue $800.

Oct. 31	Service Revenue	800	
	Unearned Revenue		800
	(To record unearned revenue)		

A	=	L	+	SE
		+800		−800 Rev

Cash Flows
no effect

After posting the adjusting entry, the accounts show:

Illustration 3A-4
Unearned revenue accounts after adjustment

Unearned Revenue				Service Revenue			
		10/31 **Adj.**	**800**	10/31 **Adj.**	**800**	10/2	1,200
						10/31 **Bal.**	**400**

The liability account Unearned Revenue shows a balance of $800. This is equal to the services that will be provided in the future. In addition, the balance in Service Revenue equals the services provided in October. If the adjusting entry is not made, both revenues and net income will be overstated by $800 in the October income statement. Also, liabilities will be understated by $800, and stockholders' equity will be overstated by $800 on the October 31 balance sheet.

A comparison of the entries and accounts for service revenue earned and unearned is shown in Illustration 3A-5.

Illustration 3A-5
Adjustment approaches—a comparison

Unearned Revenue Initially Credited to Liability Account (per chapter)				Unearned Revenue Initially Credited to Revenue Account (per appendix)			
Oct. 2	Cash	1,200		Oct. 2	Cash	1,200	
	Unearned Revenue		1,200		Service Revenue		1,200
Oct. 31	Unearned Revenue	400		Oct. 31	Service Revenue	800	
	Service Revenue		400		Unearned Revenue		800

[3]This example focuses only on the alternative treatment of unearned revenues. In the interest of simplicity, the entries to Service Revenue pertaining to the immediate earning of revenue ($10,000) and the adjusting entry for accrued revenue ($200) have been ignored.

After posting the entries, the accounts appear as follows.

Illustration 3A-6
Comparison of accounts

(per chapter)

Unearned Revenue

Debit		Credit	
10/31 **Adj.**	**400**	10/2	1,200
		10/31 **Bal.**	**800**

Service Revenue

Debit		Credit	
		10/31 **Adj.**	**400**

(per appendix)

Unearned Revenue

Debit		Credit	
		10/31 **Adj.**	**800**

Service Revenue

Debit		Credit	
10/31 **Adj.**	**800**	10/2	1,200
		10/31 **Bal.**	**400**

Note that the balances in the accounts are the same under the two alternatives: Unearned Revenue $800, and Service Revenue $400.

Summary of Additional Adjustment Relationships

The use of alternative adjusting entries requires additions to the summary of basic relationships presented earlier in Illustration 3-18. The additions are shown in color in Illustration 3A-7.

Alternative adjusting entries **do not apply** to accrued revenues and accrued expenses because **no entries occur before these types of adjusting entries are made**. Therefore, the entries in Illustration 3-18 (see page 109) for these two types of adjustments remain unchanged.

Illustration 3A-7
Summary of basic relationships for prepayments

Type of Adjustment	Reason for Adjustment	Account Balances before Adjustment	Adjusting Entry
1. Prepaid expenses	(a) Prepaid expenses initially recorded in asset accounts have been used.	Assets overstated Expenses understated	Dr. Expenses Cr. Assets
	(b) Prepaid expenses initially recorded in expense accounts have not been used.	**Assets understated** **Expenses overstated**	**Dr. Assets** **Cr. Expenses**
2. Unearned revenues	(a) Unearned revenues initially recorded in liability accounts have been earned.	Liabilities overstated Revenues understated	Dr. Liabilities Cr. Revenues
	(b) Unearned revenues initially recorded in revenue accounts have not been earned.	**Liabilities understated** **Revenues overstated**	**Dr. Revenues** **Cr. Liabilities**

SUMMARY OF STUDY OBJECTIVE FOR APPENDIX

8. **Prepare adjusting entries for the alternative treatment of prepayments.** Prepayments may be initially debited to an expense account. Unearned revenues may be credited to a revenue account. At the end of the period, these accounts may be overstated. The adjusting entries for prepaid expenses are a debit to an asset account and a credit to an expense account. Adjusting entries for unearned revenues are a debit to a revenue account and a credit to a liability account.

*Note: All asterisked Questions, Exercises, and Problems relate to material in the appendix to the chapter.

SELF-STUDY QUESTIONS

Self-Study/Self-Test www.wiley.com/college/weygandt

Answers are at the end of the chapter.

(SO 1) **1.** The time period assumption states that:

a. revenue should be recognized in the accounting period in which it is earned.
b. expenses should be matched with revenues.
c. the economic life of a business can be divided into artificial time periods.
d. the fiscal year should correspond with the calendar year.

(SO 2) **2.** The principle or assumption dictating that efforts (expenses) be matched with accomplishments (revenues) is the:

a. matching principle.
b. cost principle.
c. periodicity assumption.
d. revenue recognition principle.

(SO 2) **3.** One of the following statements about the accrual basis of accounting is *false*. That statement is:

a. Events that change a company's financial statements are recorded in the periods in which the events occur.
b. Revenue is recognized in the period in which it is earned.
c. This basis is in accord with generally accepted accounting principles.
d. Revenue is recorded only when cash is received, and expense is recorded only when cash is paid.

(SO 3) **4.** Adjusting entries are made to ensure that:

a. expenses are recognized in the period in which they are incurred.
b. revenues are recorded in the period in which they are earned.
c. balance sheet and income statement accounts have correct balances at the end of an accounting period.
d. all of the above.

(SO 4) **5.** Each of the following is a major type (or category) of adjusting entries *except:*

a. prepaid expenses.
b. accrued revenues.
c. accrued expenses.
d. earned revenues.

(SO 5) **6.** The trial balance shows Supplies $1,350 and Supplies Expense $0. If $750 of supplies are on hand at the end of the period, the adjusting entry is:

a. Supplies	600	
Supplies Expense		600
b. Supplies	750	
Supplies Expense		750
c. Supplies Expense	750	
Supplies		750
d. Supplies Expense	600	
Supplies		600

7. Adjustments for unearned revenues: (SO 5)

a. decrease liabilities and increase revenues.
b. have an assets and revenues account relationship.
c. increase assets and increase revenues.
d. decrease revenues and decrease assets.

8. Adjustments for accrued revenues: (SO 6)

a. have a liabilities and revenues account relationship.
b. have an assets and revenues account relationship.
c. decrease assets and revenues.
d. decrease liabilities and increase revenues.

9. Kathy Siska earned a salary of $400 for the last week of September. She will be paid on October 1. The adjusting entry for Kathy's employer at September 30 is: (SO 6)

a. No entry is required.

b. Salaries Expense	400	
Salaries Payable		400
c. Salaries Expense	400	
Cash		400
d. Salaries Payable	400	
Cash		400

10. Which of the following statements is *incorrect* concerning the adjusted trial balance? (SO 7)

a. An adjusted trial balance proves the equality of the total debit balances and the total credit balances in the ledger after all adjustments are made.
b. The adjusted trial balance provides the primary basis for the preparation of financial statements.
c. The adjusted trial balance lists the account balances segregated by assets and liabilities.
d. The adjusted trial balance is prepared after the adjusting entries have been journalized and posted.

***11.** The trial balance shows Supplies $0 and Supplies Expense $1,500. If $700 of supplies are on hand at the end of the period, the adjusting entry is: (SO 8)

a. Debit Supplies $800 and credit Supplies Expense $800.
b. Debit Supplies Expense $800 and credit Supplies $800.
c. Debit Supplies $700 and credit Supplies Expense $700.
d. Debit Supplies Expense $700 and credit Supplies $700.

THE NAVIGATOR

QUESTIONS

1. (a) How does the time period assumption affect an accountant's analysis of business transactions?
(b) Explain the terms *fiscal year, calendar year*, and *interim periods*.

2. State two generally accepted accounting principles that relate to adjusting the accounts.

3. Joe Thomas, a lawyer, accepts a legal engagement in March, performs the work in April, and is paid in May. If

Thomas's law firm prepares monthly financial statements, when should it recognize revenue from this engagement? Why?

4. Why do accrual-basis financial statements provide more useful information than cash-basis statements?
5. In completing the engagement in (3) above, Thomas incurs $4,500 of expenses in April, which are paid in May. How much expense should be deducted from revenues in the month the revenue is recognized? Why?
6. "Adjusting entries are required by the cost principle of accounting." Do you agree? Explain.
7. Why may a trial balance not contain up-to-date and complete financial information?
8. Distinguish between the two categories of adjusting entries, and identify the types of adjustments applicable to each category.
9. What is the debit/credit effect of a prepaid expense adjusting entry?
10. "Depreciation is a valuation process that results in the reporting of the fair market value of the asset." Do you agree? Explain.
11. Explain the differences between depreciation expense and accumulated depreciation.
12. Corts Company purchased equipment for $18,000. By the current balance sheet date, $7,000 had been depreciated. Indicate the balance sheet presentation of the data.
13. What is the debit/credit effect of an unearned revenue adjusting entry?
14. A company fails to recognize revenue earned but not yet received. Which of the following accounts are involved in the adjusting entry: (a) asset, (b) liability, (c) revenue, or (d) expense? For the accounts selected, indicate whether they would be debited or credited in the entry.
15. A company fails to recognize an expense incurred but not paid. Indicate which of the following accounts is debited and which is credited in the adjusting entry: (a) asset, (b) liability, (c) revenue, or (d) expense.
16. A company makes an accrued revenue adjusting entry for $900 and an accrued expense adjusting entry for $600. How much was net income understated prior to these entries? Explain.
17. On January 9, a company pays $6,000 for salaries, of which $2,000 was reported as Salaries Payable on December 31. Give the entry to record the payment.
18. For each of the following items before adjustment, indicate the type of adjusting entry (prepaid expense, unearned revenue, accrued revenue, and accrued expense) that is needed to correct the misstatement. If an item could result in more than one type of adjusting entry, indicate each of the types.
    (a) Assets are understated.
    (b) Liabilities are overstated.
    (c) Liabilities are understated.
    (d) Expenses are understated.
    (e) Assets are overstated.
    (f) Revenue is understated.
19. One-half of the adjusting entry is given below. Indicate the account title for the other half of the entry.
    (a) Salaries Expense is debited.
    (b) Depreciation Expense is debited.
    (c) Interest Payable is credited.
    (d) Supplies is credited.
    (e) Accounts Receivable is debited.
    (f) Unearned Service Revenue is debited.
20. "An adjusting entry may affect more than one balance sheet or income statement account." Do you agree? Why or why not?
21. Why is it possible to prepare financial statements directly from an adjusted trial balance?

*22. Moon Company debits Supplies Expense for all purchases of supplies and credits Rent Revenue for all advanced rentals. For each type of adjustment, give the adjusting entry.

BRIEF EXERCISES

Indicate why adjusting entries are needed.
(SO 3)

BE3-1 The ledger of Lim Company includes the following accounts. Explain why each account may require adjustment.

(a) Prepaid Insurance
(b) Depreciation Expense
(c) Unearned Revenue
(d) Interest Payable

Identify the major types of adjusting entries.
(SO 4)

BE3-2 Lopez Company accumulates the following adjustment data at December 31. Indicate **(a)** the type of adjustment (prepaid expense, accrued revenues and so on), and **(b)** the accounts before adjustment (overstated or understated).

1. Supplies of $100 are on hand.
2. Services provided but not recorded total $900.
3. Interest of $200 has accumulated on a note payable.
4. Rent collected in advance totaling $800 has been earned.

BE3-3 Gleason Advertising Company's trial balance at December 31 shows Advertising Supplies $6,700 and Advertising Supplies Expense $0. On December 31, there are $1,700 of supplies on hand. Prepare the adjusting entry at December 31, and using T accounts, enter the balances in the accounts, post the adjusting entry, and indicate the adjusted balance in each account.

Prepare adjusting entry for supplies.

(SO 5)

BE3-4 At the end of its first year, the trial balance of Easton Company shows Equipment $30,000 and zero balances in Accumulated Depreciation—Equipment and Depreciation Expense. Depreciation for the year is estimated to be $6,000. Prepare the adjusting entry for depreciation at December 31, post the adjustments to T accounts, and indicate the balance sheet presentation of the equipment at December 31.

Prepare adjusting entry for depreciation.

(SO 5)

BE3-5 On July 1, 2006, Orlow Co. pays $12,000 to Pizner Insurance Co. for a 3-year insurance contract. Both companies have fiscal years ending December 31. For Orlow Co., journalize and post the entry on July 1 and the adjusting entry on December 31.

Prepare adjusting entry for prepaid expense.

(SO 5)

BE3-6 Using the data in BE3-5, journalize and post the entry on July 1 and the adjusting entry on December 31 for Pizner Insurance Co. Pizner uses the accounts Unearned Insurance Revenue and Insurance Revenue.

Prepare adjusting entry for unearned revenue.

(SO 5)

BE3-7 The bookkeeper for Wooster Company asks you to prepare the following accrued adjusting entries at December 31.

Prepare adjusting entries for accruals.

(SO 6)

1. Interest on notes payable of $400 is accrued.
2. Services provided but not recorded total $1,250.
3. Salaries earned by employees of $900 have not been recorded.

Use the following account titles: Service Revenue, Accounts Receivable, Interest Expense, Interest Payable, Salaries Expense, and Salaries Payable.

BE3-8 The trial balance of Wow Company includes the following balance sheet accounts. Identify the accounts that require adjustment. For each account that requires adjustment, indicate **(a)** the type of adjusting entry (prepaid expenses, unearned revenues, accrued revenues, and accrued expenses) and **(b)** the related account in the adjusting entry.

Analyze accounts in an unadjusted trial balance.

(SO 4)

Accounts Receivable	Interest Payable
Prepaid Insurance	Unearned Service Revenue
Accumulated Depreciation—Equipment	

BE3-9 The adjusted trial balance of Lucille Corporation at December 31, 2006, includes the following accounts: Retained Earnings $15,600; Dividends $6,000; Service Revenue $38,400; Salaries Expense $16,000; Insurance Expense $2,000; Rent Expense $4,000; Supplies Expense $1,500; and Depreciation Expense $1,100. Prepare an income statement for the year.

Prepare an income statement from an adjusted trial balance.

(SO 7)

BE3-10 Partial adjusted trial balance data for Lucille Corporation is presented in BE3-9. The balance in Retained Earnings is the balance as of January 1. Prepare a retained earnings statement for the year assuming net income is $13,800 for the year.

Prepare a retained earnings statement from an adjusted trial balance.

(SO 7)

***BE3-11** Basler Company records all prepayments in income statement accounts. At April 30, the trial balance shows Supplies Expense $3,100, Service Revenue $9,200, and zero balances in related balance sheet accounts. Prepare the adjusting entries at April 30 assuming **(a)** $1,000 of supplies on hand and **(b)** $2,000 of service revenue should be reported as unearned.

Prepare adjusting entries under alternative treatment of prepayments.

(SO 8)

EXERCISES

E3-1 On numerous occasions, proposals have surfaced to put the federal government on the accrual basis of accounting. This is no small issue. If this basis were used, it would mean that billions of dollars in unrecorded liabilities would have to be booked, and the federal deficit would increase substantially.

Distinguish between cash and accrual basis of accounting.

(SO 2)

Instructions

(a) What is the difference between accrual-basis accounting and cash-basis accounting?
(b) Why would politicians prefer the cash basis over the accrual basis?
(c) Write a letter to your senator explaining why the federal government should adopt the accrual basis of accounting.

Identify types of adjustments and account relationships.

(SO 4, 5, 6)

E3-2 Shumway Company accumulates the following adjustment data at December 31.

1. Services provided but not recorded total $750.
2. Store supplies of $450 have been used.
3. Utility expenses of $225 are unpaid.
4. Unearned revenue of $260 has been earned.
5. Salaries of $900 are unpaid.
6. Prepaid insurance totaling $350 has expired.

Instructions

For each of the above items indicate the following.

(a) The type of adjustment (prepaid expense, unearned revenue, accrued revenue, or accrued expense).

(b) The accounts before adjustment (overstatement or understatement).

Prepare adjusting entries from selected account data.

(SO 5, 6, 7)

E3-3 The ledger of Welch Rental Agency Inc. on March 31 of the current year includes the following selected accounts before adjusting entries have been prepared.

	Debit	Credit
Prepaid Insurance	$ 3,600	
Supplies	2,800	
Equipment	25,000	
Accumulated Depreciation—Equipment		$ 8,400
Notes Payable		20,000
Unearned Rent		12,000
Rent Revenue		60,000
Interest Expense	–0–	
Wages Expense	14,000	

An analysis of the accounts shows the following.

1. The equipment depreciates $300 per month.
2. One-third of the unearned rent was earned during the quarter.
3. Interest of $500 is accrued on the notes payable.
4. Supplies on hand total $1,100.
5. Insurance expires at the rate of $200 per month.

Instructions

Prepare the adjusting entries at March 31, assuming that adjusting entries are made quarterly. Additional accounts are: Depreciation Expense, Insurance Expense, Interest Payable, and Supplies Expense.

Prepare adjusting entries.

(SO 5, 6, 7)

E3-4 Greg Mabasa, D.D.S., opened a dental practice on January 1, 2006. During the first month of operations the following transactions occurred.

1. Performed services for patients who had dental plan insurance. At January 31, $875 of such services was earned but not yet recorded.
2. Utility expenses incurred but not paid prior to January 31 totaled $630.
3. Purchased dental equipment on January 1 for $80,000, paying $20,000 in cash and signing a $60,000, 3-year note payable. The equipment depreciates $400 per month. Interest is $500 per month.
4. Purchased a one-year malpractice insurance policy on January 1 for $21,000.
5. Purchased $1,600 of dental supplies. On January 31, determined that $600 of supplies were on hand.

Instructions

Prepare the adjusting entries on January 31. Account titles are: Accumulated Depreciation—Dental Equipment, Depreciation Expense, Service Revenue, Accounts Receivable, Insurance Expense, Interest Expense, Interest Payable, Prepaid Insurance, Supplies, Supplies Expense, Utilities Expense, and Utilities Payable.

Prepare adjusting entries.

(SO 5, 6, 7)

E3-5 The trial balance for Pioneer Advertising Agency Inc., is shown in Illustration 3-3 (p. 97). In lieu of the adjusting entries shown in the text at October 31, assume the following adjustment data.

1. Advertising supplies on hand at October 31 total $850.
2. Expired insurance for the month is $100.

3. Depreciation for the month is $50.
4. Unearned revenue earned in October totals $600.
5. Services provided but not recorded at October 31 are $450.
6. Interest accrued at October 31 is $70.
7. Accrued salaries at October 31 are $1,200.

Instructions

Prepare the adjusting entries for the items above.

Prepare correct income statement.

(SO 2, 5, 6, 7)

E3-6 The income statement of Olympic Corp. for the month of July shows net income of $1,400 based on Service Revenue $5,500, Wages Expense $2,300, Supplies Expense $1,200, and Utilities Expense $600. In reviewing the statement, you discover the following.

1. Insurance expired during July of $400 was omitted.
2. Supplies expense includes $300 of supplies that are still on hand at July 31.
3. Depreciation on equipment of $150 was omitted.
4. Accrued but unpaid wages at July 31 of $300 were not included.
5. Services provided but unrecorded totaled $1,000.

Instructions

Prepare a correct income statement for July 2006.

Analyze adjusted data.

(SO 4, 5, 6, 7)

E3-7 A partial adjusted trial balance of Ruiz Company at January 31, 2006, shows the following.

RUIZ COMPANY
Adjusted Trial Balance
January 31, 2006

	Debit	Credit
Supplies	$ 850	
Prepaid Insurance	2,400	
Salaries Payable		$ 800
Unearned Revenue		750
Supplies Expense	950	
Insurance Expense	400	
Salaries Expense	1,800	
Service Revenue		2,000

Instructions

Answer the following questions, assuming the year begins January 1.

(a) If the amount in Supplies Expense is the January 31 adjusting entry, and $650 of supplies was purchased in January, what was the balance in Supplies on January 1?
(b) If the amount in Insurance Expense is the January 31 adjusting entry, and the original insurance premium was for one year, what was the total premium and when was the policy purchased?
(c) If $3,000 of salaries was paid in January, what was the balance in Salaries Payable at December 31, 2005?
(d) If $1,600 was received in January for services performed in January, what was the balance in Unearned Revenue at December 31, 2005?

Journalize basic transactions and adjusting entries.

(SO 5, 6, 7)

E3-8 Selected accounts of Engle Company are shown below.

Supplies Expense

7/31	800		

Supplies

7/1 Bal.	1,100	7/31	800
7/10	200		

Salaries Payable

		7/31	1,200

Accounts Receivable

7/31	500		

Unearned Revenue

7/31	900	7/1 Bal.	1,500
		7/20	750

(*continued from p. 123*)

Salaries Expense		
7/15	1,200	
7/31	1,200	

Service Revenue		
	7/14	2,000
	7/31	900
	7/31	500

Instructions

After analyzing the accounts, journalize **(a)** the July transactions and **(b)** the adjusting entries that were made on July 31. (*Hint:* July transactions were for cash.)

Prepare adjusting entries from analysis of trial balances.

(SO 5, 6, 7)

Peachtree

E3-9 The trial balances before and after adjustment for Villa Company at the end of its fiscal year are presented below.

VILLA COMPANY
Trial Balance
August 31, 2006

	Before Adjustment		After Adjustment	
	Dr.	**Cr.**	**Dr.**	**Cr.**
Cash	$10,400		$10,400	
Accounts Receivable	8,800		9,400	
Office Supplies	2,300		700	
Prepaid Insurance	4,000		2,500	
Office Equipment	14,000		14,000	
Accumulated Depreciation—Office Equipment		$ 3,600		$ 4,900
Accounts Payable		5,800		5,800
Salaries Payable		–0–		1,100
Unearned Rent		1,500		600
Common Stock		10,000		10,000
Retained Earnings		5,600		5,600
Service Revenue		34,000		34,600
Rent Revenue		11,000		11,900
Salaries Expense	17,000		18,100	
Office Supplies Expense	–0–		1,600	
Rent Expense	15,000		15,000	
Insurance Expense	–0–		1,500	
Depreciation Expense	–0–		1,300	
	$71,500	$71,500	$74,500	$74,500

Instructions

Prepare the adjusting entries that were made.

Prepare financial statements from adjusted trial balance.

(SO 7)

Peachtree

E3-10 The adjusted trial balance for Villa Company is given in E3-9.

Instructions

Prepare the income statement and a retained earnings statement for the year and the balance sheet at August 31.

Record transactions on accrual basis; convert revenue to cash receipts.

(SO 5, 6)

E3-11 The following data are taken from the comparative balance sheets of Midway Billiards Club, which prepares its financial statements using the accrual basis of accounting.

December 31	2006	2005
Fees receivable from members	$12,000	$ 9,000
Unearned fees revenue	17,000	20,000

Fees are billed to members based upon their use of the club's facilities. Unearned fees arise from the sale of gift certificates, which members can apply to their future use of club facilities. The 2006 income statement for the club showed that fees revenue of $153,000 was earned during the year.

Instructions

(*Hint:* You will probably find it helpful to use T accounts to analyze these data.)

(a) Prepare journal entries for each of the following events that took place during 2006.

(1) Fees receivable from 2005 were all collected.
(2) Gift certificates outstanding at the end of 2005 were all redeemed.
(3) An additional $35,000 worth of gift certificates were sold during 2006. A portion of these were used by the recipients during the year; the remainder were still outstanding at the end of 2006.
(4) Fees for 2006 for services provided to members were billed to members.
(5) Fees receivable for 2006 (i.e., those billed in item [4] above) were partially collected.

(b) Determine the amount of cash received by the club, with respect to fees, during 2006.

Journalize transactions and adjusting entries using appendix.
(SO 8)

***E3-12** At Concord Company, prepayments are debited to expense when paid, and unearned revenues are credited to revenue when received. During January of the current year, the following transactions occurred.

Jan. 2 Paid $2,400 for fire insurance protection for the year.
10 Paid $1,700 for supplies.
15 Received $6,100 for services to be performed in the future.

On January 31, it is determined that $1,500 of the services fees have been earned and that there are $800 of supplies on hand.

Instructions

(a) Journalize and post the January transactions. (Use T accounts.)
(b) Journalize and post the adjusting entries at January 31.
(c) Determine the ending balance in each of the accounts.

PROBLEMS: SET A

Prepare adjusting entries, post to ledger accounts, and prepare an adjusted trial balance.
(SO 5, 6, 7)

P3-1A Vektek Consulting Inc. began operating on May 1, 2006. The trial balance at May 31 is as follows.

VEKTEK CONSULTING, INC.
Trial Balance
May 31, 2006

Account Number		Debit	Credit
101	Cash	$ 7,700	
110	Accounts Receivable	4,000	
120	Prepaid Insurance	2,400	
130	Supplies	1,500	
135	Office Furniture	12,000	
200	Accounts Payable		$ 3,500
230	Unearned Service Revenue		3,000
311	Common Stock		19,100
320	Retained Earnings		–0–
400	Service Revenue		6,000
510	Salaries Expense	3,000	
520	Rent Expense	1,000	
		$31,600	$31,600

In addition to those accounts listed on the trial balance, the chart of accounts for Vektek Consulting Inc. also contains the following accounts and account numbers: No. 136 Accumulated Depreciation—Office Furniture, No. 210 Travel Payable, No. 220 Salaries Payable, No. 320 Retained Earnings, No. 530 Depreciation Expense, No. 540 Insurance Expense, No. 550 Travel Expense, and No. 560 Supplies Expense.

Other data:

1. $500 of supplies have been used during the month.
2. Travel expense incurred but not paid on May 31, 2006, $200.
3. The insurance policy is for 2 years.

4. $1,000 of the balance in the unearned service revenue account remains unearned at the end of the month.
5. May 31 is a Wednesday, and employees are paid on Fridays. Vektek Consulting Inc. has two employees, who are paid $500 each for a 5-day work week.
6. The office furniture has a 5-year life with no salvage value. It is being depreciated at $200 per month for 60 months.
7. Invoices representing $1,000 of services performed during the month have not been recorded as of May 31.

Instructions

(a) Prepare the adjusting entries for the month of May. Use J4 as the page number for your journal.
(b) Post the adjusting entries to the ledger accounts. Enter the totals from the trial balance as beginning account balances and place a check mark in the posting reference column.
(c) Prepare an adjusted trial balance at May 31, 2006.

(c) Adj. trial balance $33,600

Prepare adjusting entries, post, and prepare adjusted trial balance, and financial statements.
(SO 5, 6, 7)

Peachtree®

P3-2A The Thayer Motel Inc. opened for business on May 1, 2006. Its trial balance before adjustment on May 31 is as follows.

THAYER MOTEL INC.
Trial Balance
May 31, 2006

Account Number		Debit	Credit
101	Cash	$ 2,500	
126	Supplies	1,900	
130	Prepaid Insurance	2,400	
140	Land	15,000	
141	Lodge	70,000	
149	Furniture	16,800	
201	Accounts Payable		$ 5,300
208	Unearned Rent		4,600
275	Mortgage Payable		35,000
311	Common Stock		60,000
332	Dividends	1,000	
429	Rent Revenue		9,200
610	Advertising Expense	500	
726	Salaries Expense	3,000	
732	Utilities Expense	1,000	
		$114,100	$114,100

In addition to those accounts listed on the trial balance, the chart of accounts for Thayer Motel also contains the following accounts and account numbers: No. 142 Accumulated Depreciation—Lodge, No. 150 Accumulated Depreciation—Furniture, No. 212 Salaries Payable, No. 230 Interest Payable, No. 320 Retained Earnings, No. 619 Depreciation Expense—Lodge, No. 621 Depreciation Expense—Furniture, No. 631 Supplies Expense, No. 718 Interest Expense, and No. 722 Insurance Expense.

Other data:

1. Insurance expires at the rate of $200 per month.
2. A count of supplies shows $900 of unused supplies on May 31.
3. Annual depreciation is $2,400 on the lodge and $3,000 on furniture.
4. The mortgage interest rate is 12%. (The mortgage was taken out on May 1.)
5. Unearned rent of $2,500 has been earned.
6. Salaries of $800 are accrued and unpaid at May 31.

Instructions

(a) Journalize the adjusting entries on May 31.

(b) Prepare a ledger using the three-column form of account. Enter the trial balance amounts and post the adjusting entries. (Use J1 as the posting reference.)

(c) Prepare an adjusted trial balance on May 31.

(d) Prepare an income statement and a retained earnings statement for the month of May and a balance sheet at May 31.

(c) Adj. trial balance $115,700
(d) Net income $4,400
Ending retained earnings balance $3,400
Total assets $106,950

P3-3A Mendoza Co. was organized on July 1, 2006. Quarterly financial statements are prepared. The unadjusted and adjusted trial balances as of September 30 are shown below.

Prepare adjusting entries and financial statements.

(SO 5, 6, 7)

MENDOZA CO.
Trial Balance
September 30, 2006

	Unadjusted		Adjusted	
	Dr.	**Cr.**	**Dr.**	**Cr.**
Cash	$ 6,700		$ 6,700	
Accounts Receivable	400		600	
Prepaid Rent	1,500		900	
Supplies	1,200		1,000	
Equipment	15,000		15,000	
Accumulated Depreciation—Equipment				$ 850
Notes Payable		$ 5,000		5,000
Accounts Payable		1,510		1,510
Salaries Payable				400
Interest Payable				50
Unearned Rent		900		500
Common Stock		14,000		14,000
Retained Earnings		–0–		–0–
Dividends	600		600	
Commission Revenue		14,000		14,200
Rent Revenue		400		800
Salaries Expense	9,000		9,400	
Rent Expense	900		1,500	
Depreciation Expense			850	
Supplies Expense			200	
Utilities Expense	510		510	
Interest Expense			50	
	$35,810	$35,810	$37,310	$37,310

Instructions

(a) Journalize the adjusting entries that were made.

(b) Prepare an income statement and a retained earnings statement for the 3 months ending September 30 and a balance sheet at September 30.

(c) If the note bears interest at 12%, how many months has it been outstanding?

(b) Net income $2,490
Ending retained earnings $1,890
Total assets $23,350

P3-4A A review of the ledger of Khan Company at December 31, 2006, produces the following data pertaining to the preparation of annual adjusting entries.

Prepare adjusting entries

(SO 5, 6)

1. Prepaid Insurance $9,800. The company has separate insurance policies on its buildings and its motor vehicles. Policy B4564 on the building was purchased on July 1, 2005, for $6,000. The policy has a term of 3 years. Policy A2958 on the vehicles was purchased on January 1, 2006, for $4,800. This policy has a term of 2 years.

1. Insurance expense $4,400

2. Unearned Subscriptions $49,000. The company began selling magazine subscriptions in 2006 on an annual basis. The magazine is published monthly. The selling price of a subscription is $50. A review of subscription contracts reveals the following.

2. Subscription revenue $7,000

Subscription Date	Number of Subscriptions
October 1	200
November 1	300
December 1	480
	980

3. Interest expense $1,200

3. Notes Payable $40,000. This balance consists of a note for 6 months at an annual interest rate of 9%, dated September 1.

4. Salaries expense $2,940

4. Salaries Payable $0. There are eight salaried employees. Salaries are paid every Friday for the current week. Five employees receive a salary of $500 each per week, and three employees earn $800 each per week. December 31 is a Wednesday. Employees do not work weekends. All employees worked the last 3 days of December.

Instructions

Prepare the adjusting entries at December 31, 2006.

Journalize transactions and follow through accounting cycle to preparation of financial statements.

(SO 5, 6, 7)

P3-5A On November 1, 2006, the account balances of Samone Equipment Repair Corp. were as follows. Trial Balance

No.	Debits		No.	Credits	
101	Cash	$ 2,790	154	Accumulated Depreciation	$ 500
112	Accounts Receivable	2,510	201	Accounts Payable	2,100
126	Supplies	2,000	209	Unearned Service Revenue	1,400
153	Store Equipment	10,000	212	Salaries Payable	500
			311	Common Stock	10,000
			320	Retained Earnings	2,800
		$17,300			$17,300

During November the following summary transactions were completed.

Nov. 8 Paid $1,100 for salaries due employees, of which $600 is for November.
10 Received $1,200 cash from customers on account.
12 Received $1,400 cash for services performed in November.
15 Purchased store equipment on account $3,000.
17 Purchased supplies on account $500.
20 Paid creditors on account $2,500.
22 Paid November rent $300.
25 Paid salaries $1,000.
27 Performed services on account and billed customers for services provided $700.
29 Received $550 from customers for future service.

Adjustment data consist of:

1. Supplies on hand $1,000.
2. Accrued salaries payable $500.
3. Depreciation for the month is $120.
4. Unearned service revenue of $1,150 is earned.

Instructions

(a) Enter the November 1 balances in the ledger accounts.
(b) Journalize the November transactions.
(c) Post to the ledger accounts. Use J1 for the posting reference. Use the following accounts: No. 407 Service Revenue, No. 615 Depreciation Expense, No. 631 Supplies Expense, No. 726 Salaries Expense, and No. 729 Rent Expense.
(d) Prepare a trial balance at November 30.
(e) Journalize and post adjusting entries.
(f) Prepare an adjusted trial balance.
(g) Prepare an income statement and a retained earnings statement for November and a balance sheet at November 30.

(d) Trial balance $20,450
(f) Adj. trial balance $21,070
(g) Net loss $770; Ending retained earnings $2,030; Total assets $16,430

***P3-6A** Salzer Graphics Company was organized on January 1, 2006, by Jill Salzer. At the end of the first 6 months of operations, the trial balance contained the following accounts.

Prepare adjusting entries, adjusted trial balance, and financial statements using appendix.

(SO 5, 6, 7, 8)

Peachtree

Debits		Credits	
Cash	$ 9,500	Notes Payable	$ 20,000
Accounts Receivable	14,000	Accounts Payable	9,000
Equipment	45,000	Common Stock	22,000
Insurance Expense	1,800	Retained Earnings	–0–
Salaries Expense	30,000	Graphic Revenue	52,100
Supplies Expense	3,700	Consulting Revenue	6,000
Advertising Expense	1,900		
Rent Expense	1,500		
Utilities Expense	1,700		
	$109,100		$109,100

Analysis reveals the following additional data.

1. The $3,700 balance in Supplies Expense represents supplies purchased in January. At June 30, $1,300 of supplies was on hand.
2. The note payable was issued on February 1. It is a 12%, 6-month note.
3. The balance in Insurance Expense is the premium on a one-year policy, dated March 1, 2006.
4. Consulting fees are credited to revenue when received. At June 30, consulting fees of $1,100 are unearned.
5. Graphic revenue earned but unrecorded at June 30 totals $2,000.
6. Depreciation is $3,000 per year.

Instructions

(a) Journalize the adjusting entries at June 30. (Assume adjustments are recorded every 6 months.)

(b) Prepare an adjusted trial balance.

(c) Prepare an income statement and a retained earnings statement for the 6 months ended June 30 and a balance sheet at June 30.

(b) Adj. trial balance $113,600

(c) Net income $18,400
Ending retained earnings $18,400
Total assets $71,500

PROBLEMS: SET B

P3-1B Joey Cuono started his own consulting firm, Cuono Company, on June 1, 2006. The trial balance at June 30 is as follows.

Prepare adjusting entries, post to ledger accounts, and prepare adjusted trial balance.

(SO 5, 6, 7)

CUONO COMPANY
Trial Balance
June 30, 2006

Account Number		Debit	Credit
101	Cash	$ 7,150	
110	Accounts Receivable	6,000	
120	Prepaid Insurance	3,000	
130	Supplies	2,000	
135	Office Equipment	15,000	
200	Accounts Payable		$ 4,500
230	Unearned Service Revenue		4,000
311	Common Stock		21,750
320	Retained Earnings		–0–
400	Service Revenue		7,900
510	Salaries Expense	4,000	
520	Rent Expense	1,000	
		$38,150	$38,150

In addition to those accounts listed on the trial balance, the chart of accounts for Cuono Company also contains the following accounts and account numbers: No. 136 Accumulated Depreciation—Office Equipment, No. 210 Utilities Payable, No. 220 Salaries Payable, No. 530 Depreciation Expense, No. 540 Insurance Expense, No. 550 Utilities Expense, and No. 560 Supplies Expense.

Other data:

1. Supplies on hand at June 30 are $1,100.
2. A utility bill for $150 has not been recorded and will not be paid until next month.
3. The insurance policy is for a year.
4. $2,500 of unearned service revenue has been earned at the end of the month.
5. Salaries of $1,500 are accrued at June 30.
6. The office equipment has a 5-year life with no salvage value. It is being depreciated at $250 per month for 60 months.
7. Invoices representing $2,000 of services performed during the month have not been recorded as of June 30.

Instructions

(a) Prepare the adjusting entries for the month of June. Use J3 as the page number for your journal.

(b) Post the adjusting entries to the ledger accounts. Enter the totals from the trial balance as beginning account balances and place a check mark in the posting reference column.

(c) Adj. trial balance $42,050

(c) Prepare an adjusted trial balance at June 30, 2006.

Prepare adjusting entries, post, and prepare adjusted trial balance, and financial statements.

(SO 5, 6, 7)

P3-2B Spring River Resort Inc. opened for business on June 1 with eight air-conditioned units. Its trial balance before adjustment on August 31 is as follows.

SPRING RIVER RESORT INC.
Trial Balance
August 31, 2006

Account Number		Debit	Credit
101	Cash	$ 19,600	
126	Supplies	3,300	
130	Prepaid Insurance	6,000	
140	Land	25,000	
143	Cottages	125,000	
149	Furniture	26,000	
201	Accounts Payable		$ 6,500
208	Unearned Rent		7,400
275	Mortgage Payable		80,000
311	Common Stock		100,000
320	Retained Earnings		–0–
332	Dividends	5,000	
429	Rent Revenue		80,000
622	Repair Expense	3,600	
726	Salaries Expense	51,000	
732	Utilities Expense	9,400	
		$273,900	$273,900

In addition to those accounts listed on the trial balance, the chart of accounts for Spring River Resort also contains the following accounts and account numbers: No. 112 Accounts Receivable, No. 144 Accumulated Depreciation—Cottages, No. 150 Accumulated Depreciation—Furniture, No. 212 Salaries Payable, No. 230 Interest Payable, No. 620 Depreciation Expense—Cottages, No. 621 Depreciation Expense—Furniture, No. 631 Supplies Expense, No. 718 Interest Expense, and No. 722 Insurance Expense.

Other data:

1. Insurance expires at the rate of $400 per month.
2. A count on August 31 shows $900 of supplies on hand.
3. Annual depreciation is $3,600 on cottages and $2,400 on furniture.
4. Unearned rent of $4,100 was earned prior to August 31.

5. Salaries of $400 were unpaid at August 31.
6. Rentals of $800 were due from tenants at August 31. (Use Accounts Receivable.)
7. The mortgage interest rate is 9% per year. (The mortgage was taken out on August 1.)

Instructions

(a) Journalize the adjusting entries on August 31 for the 3-month period June 1–August 31.
(b) Prepare a ledger using the three-column form of account. Enter the trial balance amounts and post the adjusting entries. (Use J1 as the posting reference.)
(c) Prepare an adjusted trial balance on August 31.
(d) Prepare an income statement and a retained earnings statement for the 3 months ending August 31 and a balance sheet as of August 31.

(c) Adj. trial balance $277,200
(d) Net income $14,800
Ending retained earnings balance $9,800
Total assets $200,600

P3-3B Costello Advertising Agency Inc. was founded by John Costello in January of 2005. Presented below are both the adjusted and unadjusted trial balances as of December 31, 2005.

Prepare adjusting entries and financial statements.

(SO 5, 6, 7)

COSTELLO ADVERTISING AGENCY INC.

Trial Balance
December 31, 2005

	Unadjusted		Adjusted	
	Dr.	Cr.	Dr.	Cr.
Cash	$ 11,000		$ 11,000	
Accounts Receivable	20,000		23,500	
Art Supplies	8,600		5,000	
Prepaid Insurance	3,350		2,500	
Printing Equipment	60,000		60,000	
Accumulated Depreciation		$ 28,000		$ 33,000
Accounts Payable		5,000		5,000
Interest Payable		–0–		150
Notes Payable		5,000		5,000
Unearned Advertising Fees		7,200		5,600
Salaries Payable		–0–		1,300
Common Stock		20,000		20,000
Retained Earnings		5,500		5,500
Dividends	12,000		12,000	
Advertising Revenue		58,600		63,700
Salaries Expense	10,000		11,300	
Insurance Expense			850	
Interest Expense	350		500	
Depreciation Expense			5,000	
Art Supplies Expense			3,600	
Rent Expense	4,000		4,000	
	$129,300	$129,300	$139,250	$139,250

Instructions

(a) Journalize the annual adjusting entries that were made.
(b) Prepare an income statement and a retained earnings statement for the year ending December 31, 2005, and a balance sheet at December 31.
(c) Answer the following questions.
   (1) If the note has been outstanding 6 months, what is the annual interest rate on that note?
   (2) If the company paid $14,500 in salaries in 2006, what was the balance in Salaries Payable on December 31, 2005?

(b) Net income $38,450
Ending retained earnings $31,950
Total assets $69,000
(c) (1) 6%
(2) $4,500

P3-4B A review of the ledger of Bellingham Corporation at December 31, 2006, produces the following data pertaining to the preparation of annual adjusting entries.

Preparing adjusting entries.

(SO 5, 6)

1. Salaries expense $2,200

1. Salaries Payable $0. There are eight salaried employees. Salaries are paid every Friday for the current week. Five employees receive a salary of $800 each per week, and three employees earn $500 each per week. December 31 is a Tuesday. Employees do not work weekends. All employees worked the last 2 days of December.

2. Rent revenue $74,000

2. Unearned Rent $324,000. The company began subleasing office space in its new building on November 1. At December 31, the company had the following rental contracts that are paid in full for the entire term of the lease.

Date	Term (in months)	Monthly Rent	Number of Leases
Nov. 1	6	$4,000	5
Dec. 1	6	$8,500	4

3. Advertising expense $5,200

3. Prepaid Advertising $15,600. This balance consists of payments on two advertising contracts. The contracts provide for monthly advertising in two trade magazines. The terms of the contracts are as follows.

Contract	Date	Amount	Number of Magazine Issues
A650	May 1	$6,000	12
B974	Oct. 1	9,600	24

The first advertisement runs in the month in which the contract is signed.

4. Interest expense $5,250

4. Notes Payable $100,000. This balance consists of a note for one year at an annual interest rate of 9%, dated June 1.

Instructions

Prepare the adjusting entries at December 31, 2006. (Show all computations.)

Journalize transactions and follow through accounting cycle to preparation of financial statements.

(SO 5, 6, 7)

P3-5B On September 1, 2006, the account balances of Beck Equipment Repair Corp. were as follows.

No.	Debits		No.	Credits	
101	Cash	$ 4,880	154	Accumulated Depreciation	$ 1,500
112	Accounts Receivable	3,520	201	Accounts Payable	3,400
126	Supplies	2,000	209	Unearned Service Revenue	1,400
153	Store Equipment	15,000	212	Salaries Payable	500
			311	Common Stock	10,000
			320	Retained Earnings	8,600
		$25,400			$25,400

During September the following summary transactions were completed.

Sept. 8 Paid $1,400 for salaries due employees, of which $900 is for September.
10 Received $1,200 cash from customers on account.
12 Received $3,400 cash for services performed in September.
15 Purchased store equipment on account $3,000.
17 Purchased supplies on account $1,200.
20 Paid creditors $4,500 on account.
22 Paid September rent $500.
25 Paid salaries $1,050.
27 Performed services on account and billed customers for services provided $1,200.
29 Received $650 from customers for future service.

Adjustment data consist of:

1. Supplies on hand $1,700.
2. Accrued salaries payable $400.
3. Depreciation is $200 per month.
4. Unearned service revenue of $1,450 is earned.

Instructions

(a) Enter the September 1 balances in the ledger accounts.
(b) Journalize the September transactions.
(c) Post to the ledger accounts. Use J1 for the posting reference. Use the following accounts: No. 407 Service Revenue, No. 615 Depreciation Expense, No. 631 Supplies Expense, No. 726 Salaries Expense, and No. 729 Rent Expense.

(d) Prepare a trial balance at September 30.
(e) Journalize and post adjusting entries.
(f) Prepare an adjusted trial balance.
(g) Prepare an income statement and a retained earnings statement for September and a balance sheet at September 30.

(d) Trial balance $29,850
(f) Adj. trial balance $30,450
(g) Net income $1,500
Ending retained earnings $10,100
Total assets $24,200

BROADENING YOUR PERSPECTIVE

Financial Reporting and Analysis

■ FINANCIAL REPORTING PROBLEM: PepsiCo

BYP3-1 The financial statements of **PepsiCo** are presented in Appendix A at the end of this textbook.

Instructions

(a) Using the consolidated financial statements and related information, identify items that may result in adjusting entries for prepayments.
(b) Using the consolidated financial statements and related information, identify items that may result in adjusting entries for accruals.
(c) Using the Selected Financial Data and Five-Year Summary, what has been the trend since 1999 for net income?

■ COMPARATIVE ANALYSIS PROBLEM: PepsiCo vs. Coca-Cola

BYP3-2 **PepsiCo**'s financial statements are presented in Appendix A. **Coca-Cola**'s financial statements are presented in Appendix B.

Instructions

Based on information contained in these financial statements, determine the following for each company.

(a) Net increase (decrease) in property, plant, and equipment (net) from 2002 to 2003.
(b) Increase (decrease) in selling, general, and administrative expenses from 2002 to 2003.
(c) Increase (decrease) in long-term debt (obligations) from 2002 to 2003.
(d) Increase (decrease) in net income from 2002 to 2003.
(e) Increase (decrease) in cash and cash equivalents from 2002 to 2003.

■ RESEARCH CASE

BYP3-3 The North American Industry Classification System (NAICS), a new classification system for organizing economic data, has recently replaced the separate standard classification systems previously used by Canada, the United States, and Mexico. NAICS provides a common standard framework for the collection of economic and financial data for all three nations.

Instructions

At your library, find the *NAICS Manual,* and answer the following.

(a) The NAICS numbering system uses five levels of detail to identify company activities. What do the first two digits identify? The fourth digit? The sixth digit?
(b) Identify the sector, subsector, industry group, NAICS industry, and U.S. industry represented by the code 513322.

■ INTERPRETING FINANCIAL STATEMENTS

BYP3-4 **Chieftain International, Inc.** is an oil and natural gas exploration and production company. A recent balance sheet reported $208 million in assets with only $4.6 million in liabilities, all of which were short-term accounts payable.

During the year, Chieftain expanded its holdings of oil and gas rights, drilled 37 new wells, and invested in expensive 3-D seismic technology. The company generated $19 million cash from operating activities and paid no dividends. It had a cash balance of $102 million at the end of the year.

Instructions

(a) Name at least two advantages to Chieftain from having no long-term debt. Can you think of disadvantages?
(b) What are some of the advantages to Chieftain from having this large a cash balance? What is a disadvantage?
(c) Why do you suppose Chieftain has the $4.6 million balance in accounts payable, since it appears that it could have made all its purchases for cash?

■ A GLOBAL FOCUS

BYP3-5 **Hoescht Marion Roussel (HMR)** is one of the world's largest research-based pharmaceutical companies. It is headquartered in Frankfurt, Germany. It conducts research in Germany, France, and the United States. Its financial statements are based on the International Accounting Standards of the International Accounting Standards Committee.

Instructions

Answer each of the following questions.

(a) The statement of cash flows reports interest paid during a recent year of $344 million, while the income statement reports interest expense of $721 million. What might explain this difference? Give an example of the journal entry that you would expect to see that would cause this difference (ignore amounts).
(b) Among its liabilities, the company reports provisions for litigation and environmental protection. What types of litigation and environmental protection costs might this company incur? What are the possible points in time that litigation costs might be expensed? At what point do you think these costs should be expensed on the income statement in order to provide proper matching of revenues and expenses? What challenges to matching does litigation present?
(c) The notes to the company's financial statements state that the company records revenues "at the time of shipment of products or performance of services." Is this consistent with the revenue recognition practices described in this chapter? What considerations might you want to take into account in determining whether this is the appropriate approach to recognize revenues?

■ EXPLORING THE WEB

www.wiley.com/college/weygandt

BYP3-6 A wealth of accounting-related information is available via the Internet. For example the Rutgers Accounting Web offers access to a great variety of sources.

Address: www.rutgers.edu/accounting, or go to www.wiley.com/college/weygandt

Steps: Click on **Accounting Resources**. (*Note*: Once on this page, you may have to click on the **text only** box to access the available information.)

Instructions

(a) List the categories of information available through the **Accounting Resources** page.
(b) Select any one of these categories and briefly describe the types of information available.

Critical Thinking

■ GROUP DECISION CASE

BYP3-7 The Happy Travel Court was organized on April 1, 2005, by Alice Henry. Alice is a good manager but a poor accountant. From the trial balance prepared by a part-time bookkeeper, Alice prepared the following income statement for the quarter that ended March 31, 2006.

HAPPY TRAVEL COURT
Income Statement
For the Quarter Ended March 31, 2006

Revenues		
Travel court rental revenue		$90,000
Operating expenses		
Advertising	$ 5,200	
Wages	29,800	
Utilities	900	
Depreciation	800	
Repairs	4,000	
Total operating expenses		40,700
Net income		$49,300

Alice knew that something was wrong with the statement because net income had never exceeded $20,000 in any one quarter. Knowing that you are an experienced accountant, she asks you to review the income statement and other data.

You first look at the trial balance. In addition to the account balances reported above in the income statement, the ledger contains the following additional selected balances at March 31, 2006.

Supplies	$ 6,200
Prepaid Insurance	7,200
Notes Payable	12,000

You then make inquiries and discover the following.

1. Travel court rental fees include advanced rentals for summer month occupancy $20,000.
2. There were $1,300 of supplies on hand at March 31.
3. Prepaid insurance resulted from the payment of a one-year policy on January 1, 2006.
4. The mail on April 1, 2006, brought the following bills: advertising for week of March 24, $110; repairs made March 10, $260; and utilities, $180.
5. There are four employees, who receive wages totaling $350 per day. At March 31, 2 days' wages have been incurred but not paid.
6. The note payable is a 3-month, 10% note dated January 1, 2006.

Instructions

With the class divided into groups, answer the following.

(a) Prepare a correct income statement for the quarter ended March 31, 2006.

(b) Explain to Alice the generally accepted accounting principles that she did not recognize in preparing her income statement and their effect on her results.

■ COMMUNICATION ACTIVITY

BYP3-8 In reviewing the accounts of Karibeth Corp. at the end of the year, you discover that adjusting entries have not been made.

Instructions

Write a memo to Kari Beth Renfro, the president of Karibeth Corp., that explains the following: the nature and purpose of adjusting entries, why adjusting entries are needed, and the types of adjusting entries that may be made.

■ ETHICS CASE

Accounting Matters!

BYP3-9 Santa Fe Company is a pesticide manufacturer. Its sales declined greatly this year due to the passage of legislation outlawing the sale of several of Santa Fe's chemical pesticides. In the coming year, Santa Fe will have environmentally safe and competitive chemicals to replace these discontinued products. Sales in the next year are expected to greatly exceed any prior year's. The decline in sales and profits appears to be a one-year aberration. But even so, the company president fears a large dip in the current year's profits. He believes that such a dip could cause a significant drop in the market price of Santa Fe's stock and make the company a takeover target.

To avoid this possibility, the company president calls in Diane Leto, controller, to discuss this period's year-end adjusting entries. He urges her to accrue every possible revenue and to defer as many expenses as possible. He says to Diane, "We need the revenues this year, and next year can easily absorb expenses deferred from this year. We can't let our stock price be hammered down!" Diane didn't get around to recording the adjusting entries until January 17, but she dated the entries December 31 as if they were recorded then. Diane also made every effort to comply with the president's request.

Instructions

(a) Who are the stakeholders in this situation?
(b) What are the ethical considerations of (1) the president's request and (2) Diane's dating the adjusting entries December 31?
(c) Can Diane accrue revenues and defer expenses and still be ethical?

Accounting Matters!

■ CONTINUING COOKIE CHRONICLE

(*Note:* This is a continuation of the Cookie Chronicle from Chapters 1 and 2. From the information gathered through Chapter 2, follow the instructions below using the general ledger accounts you have already prepared.)

BYP3-10 It is the end of November and Natalie has been in touch with her grandmother. Her grandmother asked Natalie for financial statements because she believes it's important that Natalie, at some point in time, repay the loan she received from her. Natalie also feels that it's important to know the financial position of her business each month.

The following additional information will help you prepare Cookie Creations' financial statements:

1. A count reveals that $75 of brochures and posters remain at the end of November.
2. A count reveals that $25 of baking supplies were used during November.
3. Natalie estimates that all of her baking equipment will have a useful life of 5 years or 60 months. (Assume Natalie decides to record a full month's worth of depreciation regardless of when the equipment was obtained by the business.)
4. Natalie's grandmother has decided to charge interest of 6% on the note payable extended on November 16. The loan plus interest is to be repaid in 24 months. (Assume that half a month of interest accrued during November.)
5. On November 30, a friend of Natalie's asks her to teach a class at the neighborhood school. Natalie agrees and teaches a group of 35 first-grade students how to make holiday cookies. The next day Natalie prepares an invoice for $250 and leaves it with the school principal. The principal says it will be paid sometime in December.
6. Natalie receives a cell phone bill for $50. She uses her cell phone only for business. The bill is for services provided during November and is due December 15.

Instructions

Using the information that you have gathered through Chapter 2, and based on the new information above, do the following:

(a) Prepare and post the adjusting journal entries.
(b) Prepare an adjusted trial balance.
(c) Prepare an income statement and statement of retained earnings for the month ended November 30, 2005, and a balance sheet as at November 30, 2005.

Accounting Matters!

?

Answers to Accounting Matters! Questions

p. 95

Q: What accounting principle does this example illustrate?

A: This situation demonstrates the difficulty of properly *matching expenses to revenues.*

Q: How will financial results be affected if the expenses are recognized over a period that is *less than* that used for revenues?

A: If the expenses are recognized over a period that is *less than* that used for revenues, earnings will be understated during the early years and overstated during the later years.

Q: What if the expenses are recognized over a period that is *longer than* that used for revenues?
A: If the expenses are recognized over a period that is *longer than* that used for revenues, earnings will be overstated during the early years and understated in later years. In either case, management and stockholders could be misled.

p. 99

Q: Why do you think current accounting rules require that the cost of long ad campaigns be expensed rather than recorded as an asset?
A: The costs of ad campaigns are expensed because it is too difficult to estimate and measure the projected benefits of these expenses over multiple accounting periods. The current rule standardizes accounting practice for these costs and curbs some of the accounting abuses that had been occurring for advertising costs.

p. 102

Q: What accounting principles do you think Microsoft violated?
A: Microsoft probably violated the revenue recognition and matching principles.
Q: What did the SEC mean by "material inaccuracies"?
A: By using the term "material inaccuracies," the SEC was indicating that the inaccuracies were large enough to influence financial decisions of Microsoft's investors or creditors.
Q: Why would a company prefer to report steadily increasing profits rather than fluctuating profits?
A: Investors and creditors usually consider companies with fluctuating earnings to be riskier than those with steadily increasing profits, an evaluation that can have a negative impact on stock price.

p. 107

Q: If a computer performs adjusting entries, what role does the accountant play?
A: The accountant focuses on *analysis and interpretation* of financial results.
Q: Why might management be interested in "information before and after changes"?
A: Comparing "before" and "after" results can assist management in deciding between alternatives for adjustments before final financial statements are produced.

Answer to PepsiCo Review It Question 4, p. 103

Per Note 4, **PepsiCo**'s 2003 depreciation expense is $1,020 million; 2002 depreciation expense is $929 million.

Answers to Self-Study Questions

1. c **2.** a **3.** d **4.** d **5.** d **6.** d **7.** a **8.** b **9.** b **10.** c ***11.** c

REMEMBER to go back to the Navigator box on the chapter-opening page and check off your completed work.

Chapter 4

Completion of the Accounting Cycle

THE NAVIGATOR ✓

- Understand **Concepts for Review** ❑
- Read **Feature Story** ❑
- Scan **Study Objectives** ❑
- Read **Preview** ❑
- Read text and answer **Before You Go On** p. 147 ❑ p. 157 ❑ p. 164 ❑
- Work **Demonstration Problem** ❑
- Review **Summary of Study Objectives** ❑
- Answer **Self-Study Questions** ❑
- Complete **Assignments** ❑

CONCEPTS FOR REVIEW

Before studying this chapter, you should know or, if necessary, review:

- How to apply the revenue recognition and matching principles. (Ch. 3, pp. 95–96)
- How to make adjusting entries. (Ch. 3, pp. 97–108)
- How to prepare an adjusted trial balance. (Ch. 3, p. 111)
- How to prepare a balance sheet, income statement, and retained earnings statement. (Ch. 3, pp. 112–113)

☑ THE NAVIGATOR

ACCOUNTING MATTERS! FEATURE STORY

Everyone Likes to Win

When Ted Castle was a hockey coach at the University of Vermont, his players were self-motivated by their desire to win. Hockey was a game you either won or lost. But at **Rhino Foods, Inc.**, a specialty-bakery-foods company he founded in Burlington, Vermont, he discovered that manufacturing-line workers were not so self-motivated. Ted thought, what if he turned the food-making business into a game, with rules, strategies, and trophies?

Ted knew that in a game knowing the score is all-important. He felt that only if the employees know the score—know exactly how the business is doing daily, weekly, monthly—could he turn food-making into a game. But Rhino is a closely held, family-owned business, and its financial statements and profits were confidential. Should Ted open Rhino's books to the employees?

A consultant he was working with put Ted's concerns in perspective. The consultant said, "Imagine you're playing touch football. You play for an hour or two, and the whole time I'm sitting there with a book, keeping score. All of a sudden I blow the whistle, and I say, 'OK, that's it. Everybody go home.' I close my book and walk away. How would you feel?" Ted opened his books and revealed the financial statements to his employees.

The next step was to teach employees the rules and strategies of how to win at making food. The first lesson: "Your opponent at Rhino is expenses. You must cut and control expenses." Ted and his staff distilled those lessons into daily scorecards (production reports and income statements) that keep Rhino's employees up-to-date on the game. At noon each day, Ted posts the previous day's results at the entrance to the production room. Everyone checks whether they made or lost money on what they produced the day before. And it's not just an academic exercise; there's a bonus check for each employee at the end of every four-week "game" that meets profitability guidelines. Everyone can be a winner!

Rhino has flourished since the first game. Employment has increased from 20 to 130 people, while both revenues and profits have grown dramatically.

☑ THE NAVIGATOR

STUDY OBJECTIVES

After studying this chapter, you should be able to:

1. Prepare a work sheet.
2. Explain the process of closing the books.
3. Describe the content and purpose of a post-closing trial balance.
4. State the required steps in the accounting cycle.
5. Explain the approaches to preparing correcting entries.
6. Identify the sections of a classified balance sheet.

☑ THE NAVIGATOR

PREVIEW OF CHAPTER 4

As was true at **Rhino Foods, Inc.**, financial statements can help employees understand what is happening in the business. In Chapter 3, we prepared financial statements directly from the adjusted trial balance. However, with so many details involved in the end-of-period accounting procedures, it is easy to make errors. Locating and correcting errors can cost much time and effort. One way to minimize errors in the records and to simplify the end-of-period procedures is to use a work sheet.

In this chapter we will explain the role of the work sheet in accounting as well as the remaining steps in the accounting cycle, especially the closing process, again using Pioneer Advertising Agency Inc. as an example. Then we will consider (1) correcting entries and (2) classified balance sheets. The content and organization of Chapter 4 are as follows.

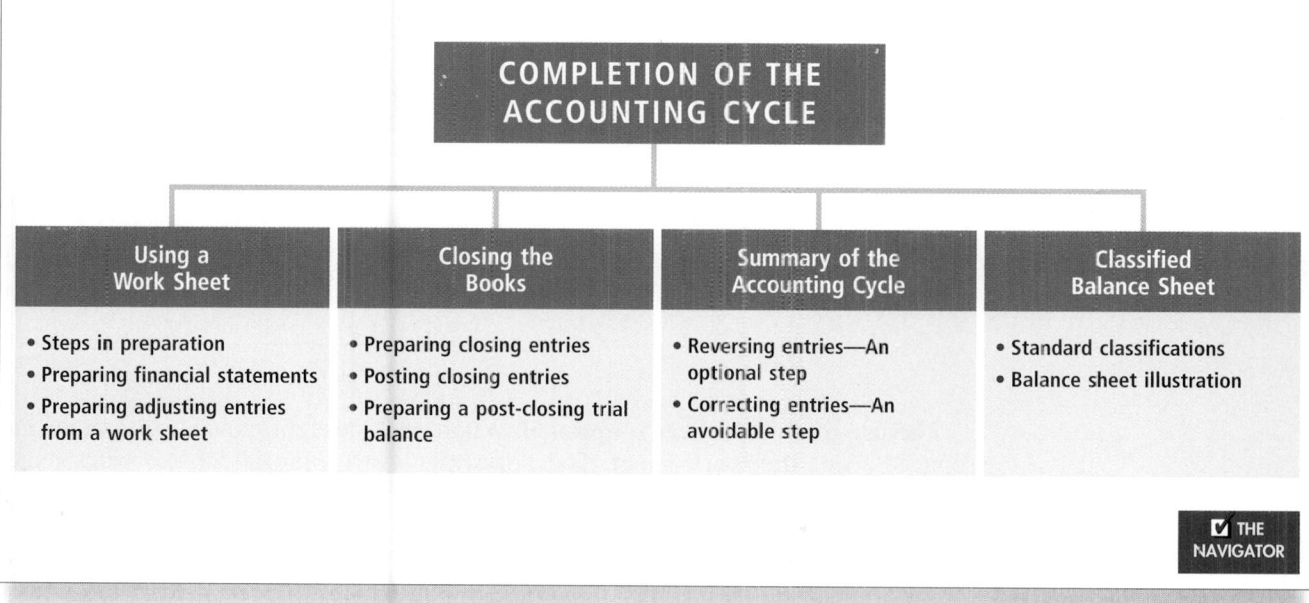

COMPLETION OF THE ACCOUNTING CYCLE

Using a Work Sheet
- Steps in preparation
- Preparing financial statements
- Preparing adjusting entries from a work sheet

Closing the Books
- Preparing closing entries
- Posting closing entries
- Preparing a post-closing trial balance

Summary of the Accounting Cycle
- Reversing entries—An optional step
- Correcting entries—An avoidable step

Classified Balance Sheet
- Standard classifications
- Balance sheet illustration

THE NAVIGATOR

Using a Work Sheet

STUDY OBJECTIVE 1

Prepare a work sheet.

A **work sheet** is a multiple-column form that may be used in the adjustment process and in preparing financial statements. As its name suggests, the work sheet is a working tool. **A work sheet is not a permanent accounting record**; it is neither a journal nor a part of the general ledger. The work sheet is merely a device used to make it easier to prepare adjusting entries and the financial statements. In small companies with relatively few accounts and adjustments, a work sheet may not be needed. In large companies with numerous accounts and many adjustments, it is almost indispensable.

The basic form of a work sheet and the procedure (five steps) for preparing it are shown in Illustration 4-1 (page 142). Each step must be performed in the prescribed sequence.

Illustration 4-1
Form and procedure for a work sheet

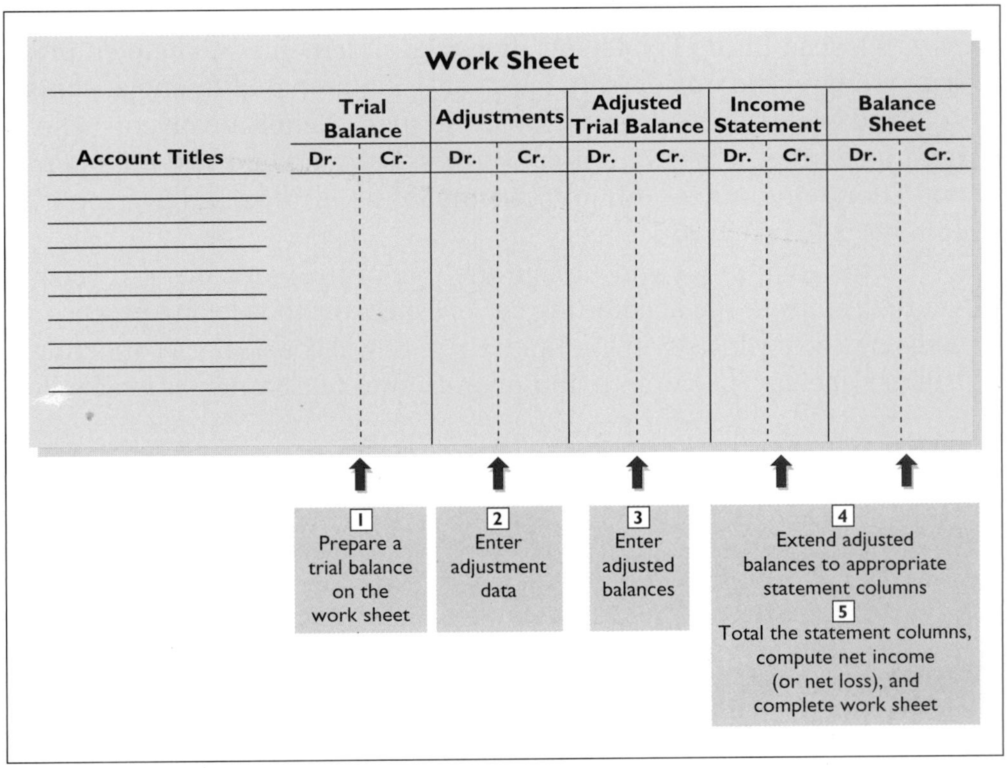

The use of a work sheet is optional. When one is used, financial statements are prepared from the work sheet. The adjustments are entered in the work sheet columns and are then journalized and posted after the financial statements have been prepared. Thus, management and other interested parties can receive the financial statements at an earlier date when a work sheet is used.

Steps in Preparing a Work Sheet

We will use the October 31 trial balance and adjustment data of Pioneer Advertising in Chapter 3 to illustrate the preparation of a work sheet. Each step of the process is described below and demonstrated in Illustrations 4-2 and 4-3A, B, C, and D following page 143.

Step 1. Prepare a Trial Balance on the Work Sheet

All ledger accounts with balances are entered in the account titles space. Debit and credit amounts from the ledger are entered in the trial balance columns. The work sheet trial balance for Pioneer Advertising Agency Inc. is shown in Illustration 4-2 on page 144.

Step 2. Enter the Adjustments in the Adjustments Columns

Turn over the first transparency, Illustration 4-3A. When a work sheet is used, all adjustments are entered in the adjustments columns. In entering the adjustments, applicable trial balance accounts should be used. If additional accounts are needed, they are inserted on the lines immediately below the trial balance totals. Each adjustment is indexed and keyed; this practice facilitates the journalizing of the adjusting entry in the general journal. **The adjustments are not journalized until after the work sheet is completed and the financial statements have been prepared.**

The adjustments for Pioneer Advertising Agency Inc. are the same as the adjustments presented in Illustration 3-19 on page 109. They are keyed in the adjustments columns of the work sheet as follows.

(a) An additional account Advertising Supplies Expense is debited $1,500 for the cost of supplies used, and Advertising Supplies is credited $1,500.

(b) An additional account Insurance Expense is debited $50 for the insurance that has expired, and Prepaid Insurance is credited $50.

(c) Two additional depreciation accounts are needed. Depreciation Expense is debited $40 for the month's depreciation, and Accumulated Depreciation—Office Equipment is credited $40.

(d) Unearned Revenue is debited $400 for services provided, and Service Revenue is credited $400.

(e) An additional account Accounts Receivable is debited $200 for services provided but not billed, and Service Revenue is credited $200.

(f) Two additional accounts relating to interest are needed. Interest Expense is debited $50 for accrued interest, and Interest Payable is credited $50.

(g) Salaries Expense is debited $1,200 for accrued salaries, and an additional account Salaries Payable is credited $1,200.

Note in the illustration that after all the adjustments have been entered, the adjustments columns are totaled and the equality of the column totals is proved.

Step 3. Enter Adjusted Balances in the Adjusted Trial Balance Columns

Turn over the second transparency, Illustration 4-3B. The adjusted balance of an account is obtained by combining the amounts entered in the first four columns of the work sheet for each account. For example, the Prepaid Insurance account in the trial balance columns has a $600 debit balance and a $50 credit in the adjustments columns. The result is a $550 debit balance recorded in the adjusted trial balance columns. **For each account on the work sheet, the amount in the adjusted trial balance columns is the account balance that will appear in the ledger after the adjusting entries have been journalized and posted.** The balances in these columns are the same as those in the adjusted trial balance in Illustration 3-21 (page 111).

After all account balances have been entered in the adjusted trial balance columns, the columns are totaled and their equality is proved. The agreement of the column totals facilitates the completion of the work sheet. If these columns are not in agreement, the financial statement columns will not balance and the financial statements will be incorrect.

Step 4. Extend Adjusted Trial Balance Amounts to Appropriate Financial Statement Columns

HELPFUL HINT

Every adjusted trial balance amount must be extended to one of the four statement columns.

Turn over the third transparency, Illustration 4-3C. The fourth step is to extend adjusted trial balance amounts to the income statement and balance sheet columns of the work sheet. Balance sheet accounts are entered in the appropriate balance sheet debit and credit columns. For instance, Cash is entered in the balance sheet debit column, and Notes Payable is entered in the credit column. Accumulated Depreciation is extended to the balance sheet credit column. The reason is that accumulated depreciation is a contra-asset account with a credit balance.

Because the work sheet does not have columns for the retained earnings statement, the balances in Common Stock and Retained Earnings, if any, are extended to the balance sheet credit column. In addition, the balance in Dividends is extended to the balance sheet debit column because it is a stockholders' equity account with a debit balance.

The expense and revenue accounts such as Salaries Expense and Service Revenue are entered in the appropriate income statement columns.

All of these extensions are shown in Illustration 4-3C.

(**Note:** Text continues on page 145, following acetate overlays.)

Illustration 4-2
Preparing a trial balance

PIONEER ADVERTISING AGENCY INC
Work Sheet
For the Month Ended October 31, 2006

	Trial Balance		Adjustments		Adjusted Trial Balance		Income Statement		Balance Sheet	
Account Titles	Dr.	Cr.	Dr.	Cr.	Dr.	Cr.	Dr.	Cr.	Dr.	Cr.
Cash	15,200									
Advertising Supplies	2,500									
Prepaid Insurance	600									
Office Equipment	5,000									
Notes Payable		5,000								
Accounts Payable		2,500								
Unearned Revenue		1,200								
Common Stock		10,000								
Dividends	500									
Service Revenue		10,000								
Salaries Expense	4,000									
Rent Expense	900									
Totals	28,700	28,700								

Include all accounts with balances from ledger.

Trial balance amounts are taken directly from ledger accounts.

Step 5. Total the Statement Columns, Compute the Net Income (or Net Loss), and Complete the Work Sheet

Turn over the fourth transparency, Illustration 4-3D. Each of the financial statement columns must be totaled. The net income or loss for the period is then found by computing the difference between the totals of the two income statement columns. If total credits exceed total debits, net income has resulted. In such a case, as shown in Illustration 4-3D, the words "Net Income" are inserted in the account titles space. The amount then is entered in the income statement debit column and the balance sheet credit column. **The debit amount balances the income statement columns, and the credit amount balances the balance sheet columns.** In addition, the credit in the balance sheet column indicates the increase in stockholders' equity resulting from net income.

If, instead, total debits in the income statement columns exceed total credits, a net loss has occurred. The amount of the net loss is entered in the income statement credit column and the balance sheet debit column.

After the net income or net loss has been entered, new column totals are determined. The totals shown in the debit and credit income statement columns will match. The totals shown in the debit and credit balance sheet columns will also match. If either the income statement columns or the balance sheet columns are not equal after the net income or net loss has been entered, an error has been made in the work sheet. The completed work sheet for Pioneer Advertising Agency Inc. is shown in Illustration 4-3D.

ACCOUNTING MATTERS! e Business Insight

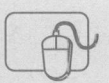

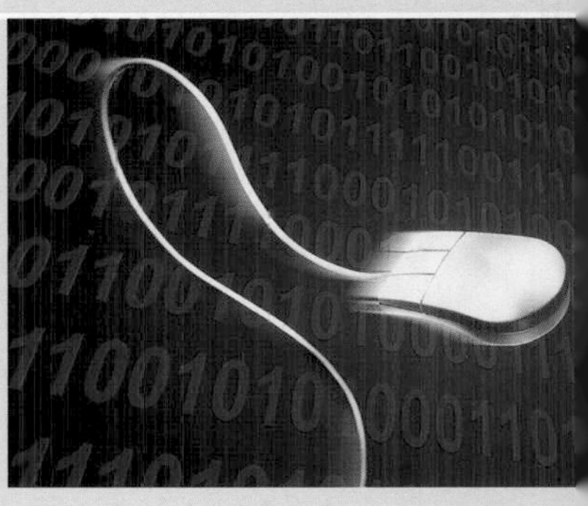

The work sheet can be computerized using an electronic spreadsheet program. The Excel supplement for this textbook is one of the most popular versions of such spreadsheet packages. With a program like Excel, you can produce any type of work sheet (accounting or otherwise) that you could produce with paper and pencil on a columnar pad. The tremendous advantage of an electronic work sheet over the paper-and-pencil version is the ability to change selected data easily. When data are changed, the computer updates the balance of your computations instantly. More specific applications of electronic spreadsheets will be noted as we proceed.

? What are the advantages of an electronic worksheet over a pencil-and-paper version?

Preparing Financial Statements from a Work Sheet

www.wiley.com/college/weygandt

Accounting Cycle Tutorial—Preparing Financial Statements and Closing the Books

After a work sheet has been completed, all the data that are required for the preparation of financial statements are at hand. The income statement is prepared from the income statement columns. The balance sheet and retained earnings statement are prepared from the balance sheet columns. The financial statements prepared from the work sheet for Pioneer Advertising Agency Inc. are shown in Illustration 4-4 (page 146). At this point, adjusting entries have not been journalized and posted. Therefore, the ledger does not support all financial statement amounts.

The amount shown for common stock on the work sheet does not change from the beginning to the end of the period unless additional stock is issued by the company during the period. Because there was no balance in Pioneer's retained earnings, the account is not listed on the work sheet. Only after dividends and net income (or loss) are posted to retained earnings does this account have a balance at the end of the first year of the business.

Illustration 4-4
Financial statements from a work sheet

PIONEER ADVERTISING AGENCY INC.
Income Statement
For the Month Ended October 31, 2006

Revenues		
Service revenue		$10,600
Expenses		
Salaries expense	$5,200	
Advertising supplies expense	1,500	
Rent expense	900	
Insurance expense	50	
Interest expense	50	
Depreciation expense	40	
Total expenses		7,740
Net income		$ 2,860

PIONEER ADVERTISING AGENCY INC.
Retained Earnings Statement
For the Month Ended October 31, 2006

Retained earnings, October 1	$ –0–
Add: Net income	2,860
	2,860
Less: Dividends	500
Retained earnings, October 31	$2,360

PIONEER ADVERTISING AGENCY INC.
Balance Sheet
October 31, 2006

Assets		
Cash		$15,200
Accounts receivable		200
Advertising supplies		1,000
Prepaid insurance		550
Office equipment	$5,000	
Less: Accumulated depreciation	40	4,960
Total assets		$21,910
Liabilities and Stockholders' Equity		
Liabilities		
Notes payable		$ 5,000
Accounts payable		2,500
Interest payable		50
Unearned revenue		800
Salaries payable		1,200
Total liabilities		9,550
Stockholders' equity		
Common stock		10,000
Retained earnings		2,360
Total liabilities and stockholders' equity		$21,910

Using a work sheet, financial statements can be prepared before adjusting entries are journalized and posted. **However, the completed work sheet is not a substitute for formal financial statements.** Data in the financial statement columns of the work sheet are not properly arranged for statement purposes. Also, as noted above, the financial statement presentation for some accounts differs from their statement columns on the work sheet. **A work sheet is essentially a working tool of the accountant; it is not distributed to management and other parties.**

Preparing Adjusting Entries from a Work Sheet

A work sheet is not a journal, and it cannot be used as a basis for posting to ledger accounts. To adjust the accounts, it is necessary to journalize the adjustments and post them to the ledger. **The adjusting entries are prepared from the adjustments columns of the work sheet.** The reference letters in the adjustments columns and the explanations of the adjustments at the bottom of the work sheet help identify the adjusting entries. However, writing the explanation to the adjustments at the bottom of the work sheet is not required. As indicated previously, the journalizing and posting of adjusting entries **follows** the preparation of financial statements when a work sheet is used. The adjusting entries on October 31 for Pioneer Advertising Agency Inc. are the same as those shown in Illustration 3-19 (page 109).

BEFORE YOU GO ON...

Review It

1. What are the five steps in preparing a work sheet?
2. How is net income or net loss shown in a work sheet?
3. How does a work sheet relate to preparing financial statements and adjusting entries?

Do It

Susan Elbe is preparing a work sheet. Explain to Susan how the following adjusted trial balance accounts should be extended to the financial statement columns of the work sheet: Cash; Accumulated Depreciation; Accounts Payable; Dividends; Service Revenue; and Salaries Expense.

ACTION PLAN

- Extend asset balances to the balance sheet debit column. Extend liability balances to the balance sheet credit column. Extend accumulated depreciation to the balance sheet credit column.
- Extend the Dividends account to the balance sheet debit column.
- Extend expenses to the income statement debit column.
- Extend revenue accounts to the income statement credit column.

SOLUTION

Income statement debit column—Salaries Expense
Income statement credit column—Service Revenue
Balance sheet debit column—Cash; Dividends
Balance sheet credit column—Accumulated Depreciation; Accounts Payable

As indicated in the e-Business Insight box on page 145, the work sheet is an ideal application for electronic spreadsheet software like Microsoft Excel.

Related exercise material: *BE4-1, BE4-2, BE4-3, E4-1, E4-2, E4-4, and E4-5.*

THE NAVIGATOR

Closing the Books

STUDY OBJECTIVE 2

Explain the process of closing the books.

At the end of the accounting period, the accounts are made ready for the next period. This is called **closing the books**. In closing the books, it is necessary to distinguish between temporary and permanent accounts. **Temporary** or **nominal accounts** relate only to a given accounting period. They include all income statement accounts and dividends. All temporary accounts are closed. In contrast, **permanent** or **real accounts** relate to one or more future accounting periods. They consist of all balance sheet accounts, including common stock and retained earnings. Permanent accounts are not closed. Instead, their balances are carried forward into the next accounting period. Illustration 4-5 identifies the accounts in each category.

Illustration 4-5
Temporary versus permanent accounts

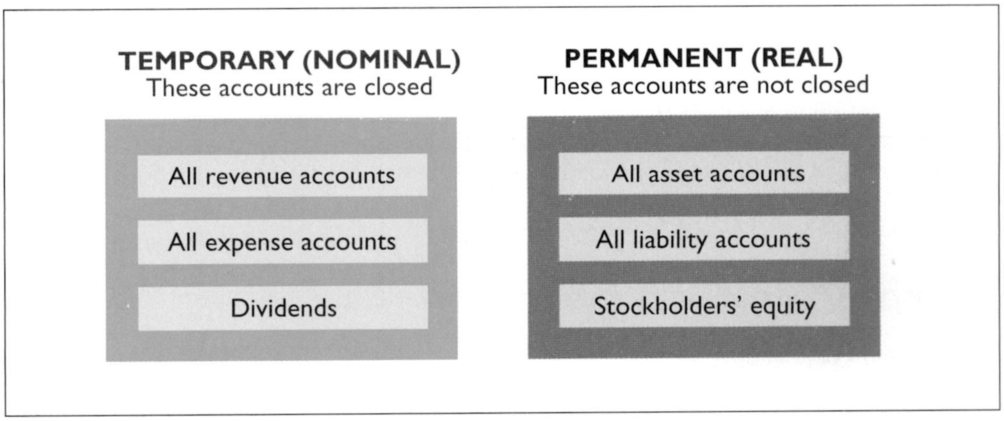

HELPFUL HINT

A contra asset account, such as accumulated depreciation, is a permanent account also.

Preparing Closing Entries

At the end of the accounting period, the temporary account balances are transferred to the permanent stockholders' equity account, Retained Earnings, through the preparation of closing entries. **Closing entries** formally recognize in the ledger the transfer of net income (or net loss) and Dividends to Retained Earnings as shown in the retained earnings statement. **These entries also produce a zero balance in each temporary account. These accounts are then ready to be used to accumulate data in the next accounting period separate from the data of prior periods.** Permanent accounts are not closed.

Journalizing and posting closing entries is a required step in the accounting cycle. (See Illustration 4-12 on page 155.) This step is performed after financial statements have been prepared. In contrast to the steps in the cycle that you have already studied, closing entries are generally journalized and posted **only at the end of a company's annual accounting period**. This practice facilitates the preparation of annual financial statements because all temporary accounts will contain data for the entire year.

In preparing closing entries, each income statement account could be closed directly to Retained Earnings. However, to do so would result in excessive detail in the Retained Earnings account. Instead, the revenue and expense accounts are closed to another temporary account, **Income Summary**; only the net income or net loss is transferred from this account to Retained Earnings.

HELPFUL HINT

When the work sheet is used, revenue and expense account data are found in the income statement columns, and Dividends is in the balance sheet debit column.

Closing entries are journalized in the general journal. A center caption entitled Closing Entries, inserted in the journal between the last adjusting entry and the first closing entry, identifies these entries. Then the closing entries are posted to the ledger accounts.

Closing entries may be prepared directly from the adjusted balances in the ledger, from the income statement and balance sheet columns of the work sheet, or from the income and retained earnings statements. Separate closing entries could be prepared for each nominal account, but the following four entries accomplish the desired result more efficiently:

1. Debit each revenue account for its balance, and credit Income Summary for total revenues.
2. Debit Income Summary for total expenses, and credit each expense account for its balance.
3. Debit Income Summary and credit Retained Earnings for the amount of net income.
4. Debit Retained Earnings for the balance in the Dividends account, and credit Dividends for the same amount.

The four entries are referenced in the diagram of the closing process shown in Illustration 4-6 and in the journal entries in Illustration 4-7 (page 150). The posting of closing entries is shown in Illustration 4-8 (page 151).

HELPFUL HINT

Dividends is closed directly to Retained Earnings and *not* to Income Summary because Dividends is not an expense.

Illustration 4-6
Diagram of closing process—corporation

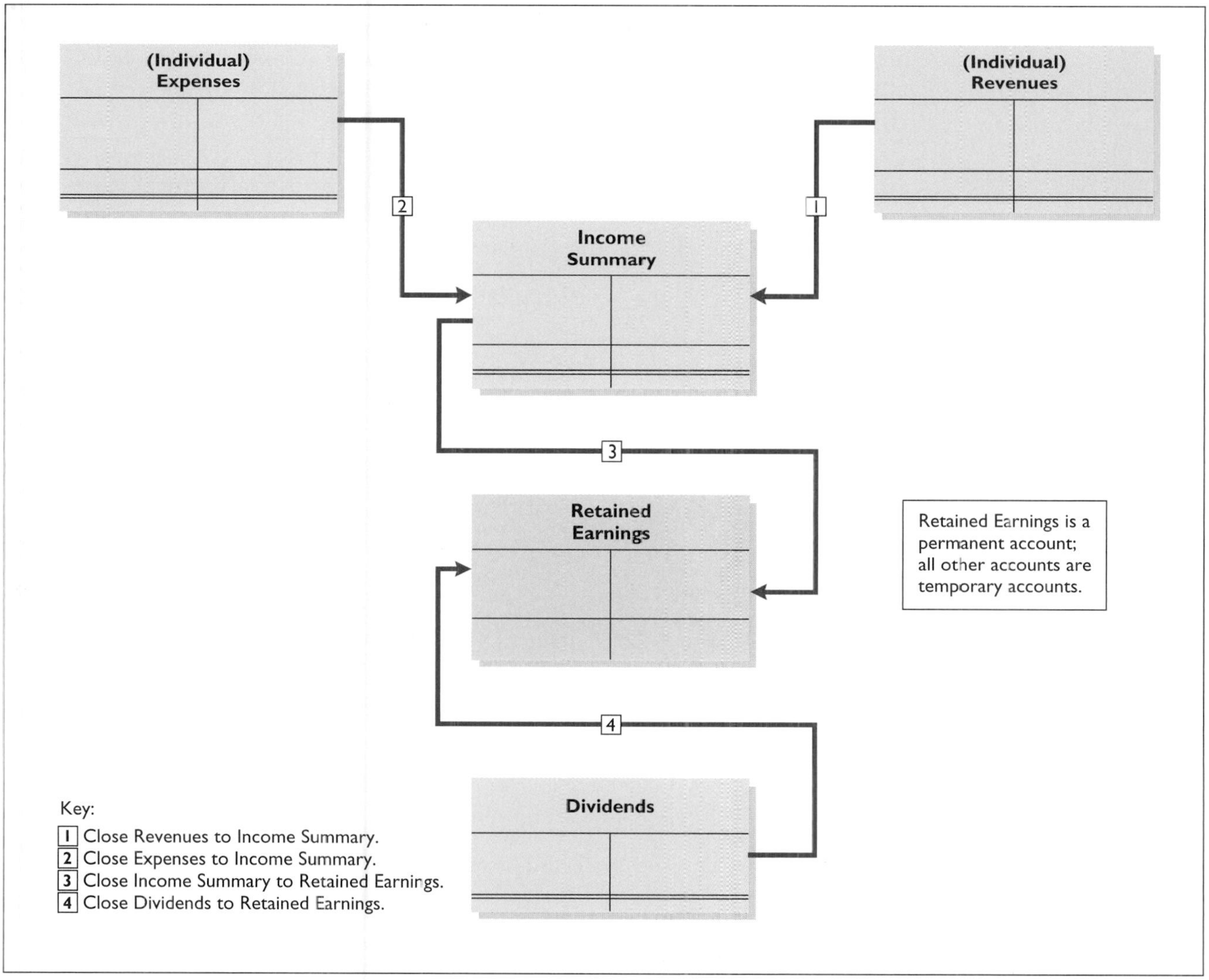
(Individual) Expenses
(Individual) Revenues
Income Summary
Retained Earnings
Dividends
1
2
3
4
Retained Earnings is a permanent account; all other accounts are temporary accounts.
Key:
1 Close Revenues to Income Summary.
2 Close Expenses to Income Summary.
3 Close Income Summary to Retained Earnings.
4 Close Dividends to Retained Earnings.

If a net loss has occurred, entry (3) credits Income Summary and debits Retained Earnings.

ACCOUNTING MATTERS! **Business Insight**

Until Sam Walton had opened twenty Wal-Mart stores, he used what he called the "ESP method" of closing the books. ESP was a pretty basic method: If the books didn't balance, Walton calculated the amount by which they were off and entered that amount under the heading ESP—which stood for "Error Some Place." As Walton noted, "It really sped things along when it came time to close those books."

Source: Sam Walton, *Made in America* (New York: Doubleday, 1992), p. 53.

? How did Sam Walton know the "books didn't balance"? In what circumstances today might the ESP method be acceptable?

Closing Entries, Illustrated

In practice, closing entries are generally prepared only at the end of a company's annual accounting period. However, to illustrate the journalizing and posting of closing entries, we will assume that Pioneer Advertising Agency Inc. closes its books monthly. The closing entries at October 31 are shown in Illustration 4-7.

Illustration 4-7
Closing entries journalized

GENERAL JOURNAL **J3**

Date	Account Titles and Explanation	Ref.	Debit	Credit
	Closing Entries			
	(1)			
Oct. 31	Service Revenue	400	10,600	
	Income Summary	350		10,600
	(To close revenue account)			
	(2)			
31	Income Summary	350	7,740	
	Advertising Supplies Expense	631		1,500
	Depreciation Expense	711		40
	Insurance Expense	722		50
	Salaries Expense	726		5,200
	Rent Expense	729		900
	Interest Expense	905		50
	(To close expense accounts)			
	(3)			
31	Income Summary	350	2,860	
	Retained Earnings	320		2,860
	(To close net income to retained earnings)			
	(4)			
31	Retained Earnings	320	500	
	Dividends	332		500
	(To close dividends to retained earnings)			

HELPFUL HINT

Income Summary is a very descriptive title: total revenues are closed to Income Summary, total expenses are closed to Income Summary, and the balance in the Income Summary is a net income or net loss.

Note that the amounts for Income Summary in entries (1) and (2) are the totals of the income statement credit and debit columns, respectively, in the work sheet.

A couple of cautions in preparing closing entries: (1) Avoid unintentionally doubling the revenue and expense balances rather than zeroing them. (2) Do not close Dividends through the Income Summary account. **Dividends are not expenses, and they are not a factor in determining net income.**

Posting Closing Entries

The posting of the closing entries and the ruling of the accounts are shown in Illustration 4-8. Note that all temporary accounts have zero balances after posting the closing entries. In addition, you should realize that the balance in Retained Earnings represents the accumulated undistributed earnings of the corporation at the end of the accounting period. This balance is shown on the balance sheet and is the ending amount reported on the retained earnings statement, as shown in Illustration 4-4. **The Income Summary account is used only in closing.** No entries are journalized and posted to this account during the year.

As part of the closing process, the **temporary accounts**—revenues, expenses, and Dividends—in T-account form are totaled, balanced, and double-ruled, as shown in Illustration 4-8. The **permanent accounts**—assets, liabilities, and stockholders' equity (Common Stock and Retained Earnings)—are not closed. A single rule is drawn beneath the current-period entries, and the account balance carried forward to the next period is entered below the single rule. (For example, see Retained Earnings.)

HELPFUL HINT

The balance in Income Summary before it is closed must equal the net income or net loss for the period.

Illustration 4-8
Posting of closing entries

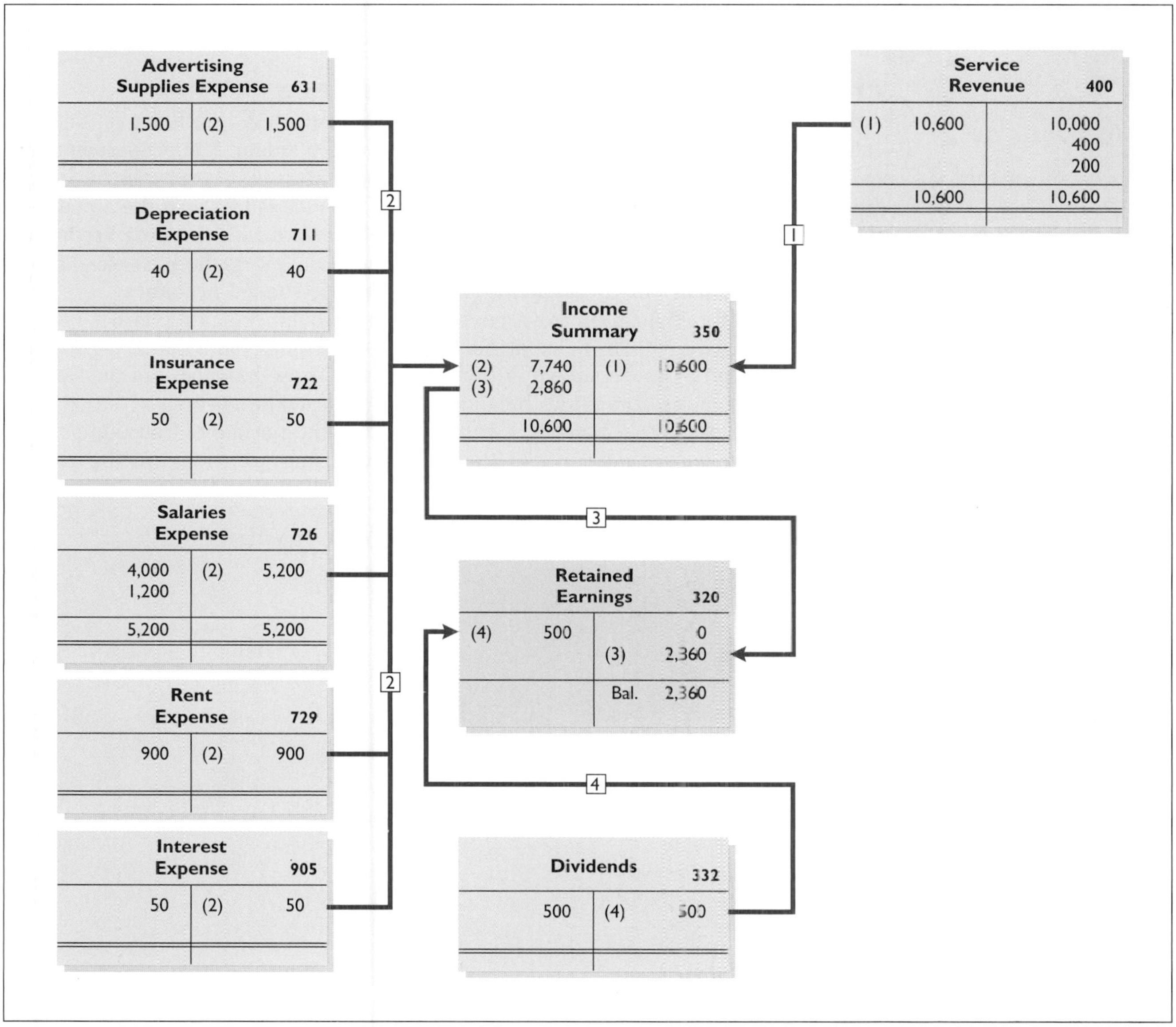

ACCOUNTING MATTERS! **e Business Insight**

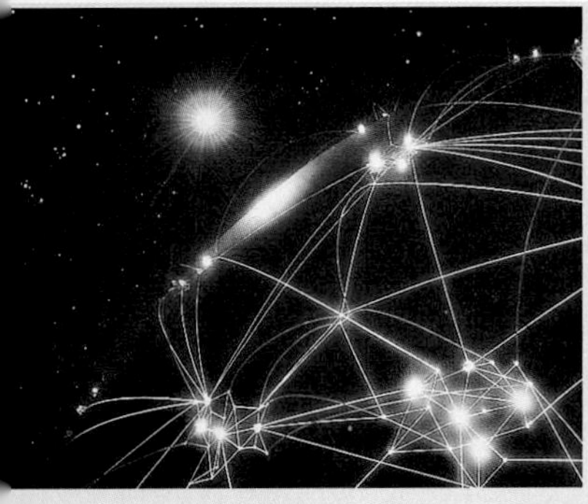

Technology has dramatically changed the accounting process. When Larry Carter became chief financial officer of **Cisco Systems**, closing the quarterly accounts would take up to ten days. Within four years he got it down to two days and halved the cost of finance, to 1 percent of sales. He since has made the "one-day virtual close"—closing within a day on any day in the quarter—a reality at Cisco.

This is not just showing off. Knowing exactly where you are all of the time, says Mr. Carter, allows you to respond faster than your competitors. But it also means that the 600 people who used to spend 10 days a quarter tracking transactions can now be more usefully employed on things such as mining data for business intelligence to find new business opportunities.

Source: Excerpted from "Business and the Internet," *The Economist* (June 26, 1999), p. 12.

? If you do not have the IT resources to do a "virtual close," can the net income or net loss be known without "closing the books"?

Preparing a Post-Closing Trial Balance

STUDY OBJECTIVE 3

Describe the content and purpose of a post-closing trial balance.

After all closing entries have been journalized and posted, another trial balance, called a **post-closing trial balance**, is prepared from the ledger. The post-closing trial balance lists permanent accounts and their balances after closing entries have been journalized and posted. **The purpose of this trial balance is to prove the equality of the permanent account balances that are carried forward into the next accounting period.** Since all temporary accounts will have zero balances, **the post-closing trial balance will contain only permanent—that is, balance sheet—accounts.**

The procedure for preparing a post-closing trial balance again consists entirely of listing the accounts and their balances. The post-closing trial balance for Pioneer Advertising Agency Inc. is shown in Illustration 4-9. These balances are the same as those reported in the company's balance sheet in Illustration 4-4.

The post-closing trial balance is prepared from the permanent accounts in the ledger. The permanent accounts of Pioneer Advertising are shown in the general

Illustration 4-9
Post-closing trial balance

HELPFUL HINT

Will total debits in a post-closing trial balance equal total assets on the balance sheet? Answer: No. Accumulated depreciation is deducted from assets on the balance sheet but added to the credit balance total in a post-closing trial balance.

PIONEER ADVERTISING AGENCY INC.
Post-Closing Trial Balance
October 31, 2006

	Debit	Credit
Cash	$15,200	
Accounts Receivable	200	
Advertising Supplies	1,000	
Prepaid Insurance	550	
Office Equipment	5,000	
Accumulated Depreciation—Office Equipment		$ 40
Notes Payable		5,000
Accounts Payable		2,500
Unearned Revenue		800
Salaries Payable		1,200
Interest Payable		50
Common Stock		10,000
Retained Earnings		2,360
	$21,950	**$21,950**

ledger in Illustration 4-10 below. Remember that the balance of each permanent account is computed after every posting. Therefore, no additional work on these accounts is needed as part of the closing process.

A post-closing trial balance provides evidence that the journalizing and posting of closing entries have been properly completed. It also shows that the accounting equation is in balance at the end of the accounting period. However, like the trial balance, it does not prove that all transactions have been recorded or that the ledger is correct. For example, the post-closing trial balance will balance if a transaction is not journalized and posted or if a transaction is journalized and posted twice.

The remaining accounts in the general ledger are temporary accounts (shown in Illustration 4-11 on page 154). After the closing entries are correctly posted, each temporary account has a zero balance. These accounts are double-ruled to finalize the closing process.

Illustration 4-10
General ledger, permanent accounts

(Permanent Accounts Only)

GENERAL LEDGER

Cash — No. 101

Date	Explanation	Ref.	Debit	Credit	Balance
2006					
Oct. 1		J1	10,000		10,000
2		J1	1,200		11,200
3		J1		900	10,300
4		J1		600	9,700
20		J1		500	9,200
26		J1		4,000	5,200
31		J1	10,000		**15,200**

Accounts Receivable — No. 112

Date	Explanation	Ref.	Debit	Credit	Balance
2006					
Oct. 31	Adj. entry	J2	**200**		**200**

Advertising Supplies — No. 126

Date	Explanation	Ref.	Debit	Credit	Balance
2006					
Oct. 5		J1	2,500		2,500
31	Adj. entry	J2		**1,500**	**1,000**

Prepaid Insurance — No. 130

Date	Explanation	Ref.	Debit	Credit	Balance
2006					
Oct. 4		J1	600		600
31	Adj. entry	J2		**50**	**550**

Office Equipment — No. 157

Date	Explanation	Ref.	Debit	Credit	Balance
2006					
Oct. 1		J1	5,000		**5,000**

Accumulated Depreciation—Office Equipment — No. 158

Date	Explanation	Ref.	Debit	Credit	Balance
2006					
Oct. 31	Adj. entry	J2		**40**	**40**

Notes Payable — No. 200

Date	Explanation	Ref.	Debit	Credit	Balance
2006					
Oct. 1		J1		5,000	**5,000**

Accounts Payable — No. 201

Date	Explanation	Ref.	Debit	Credit	Balance
2006					
Oct. 5		J1		2,500	**2,500**

Unearned Revenue — No. 209

Date	Explanation	Ref.	Debit	Credit	Balance
2006					
Oct. 2		J1		1,200	1,200
31	Adj. entry	J2	400		**800**

Salaries Payable — No. 212

Date	Explanation	Ref.	Debit	Credit	Balance
2006					
Oct. 31	Adj. entry	J2		**1,200**	**1,200**

Interest Payable — No. 230

Date	Explanation	Ref.	Debit	Credit	Balance
2006					
Oct. 31	Adj. entry	J2		**50**	**50**

Common Stock — No. 311

Date	Explanation	Ref.	Debit	Credit	Balance
2006					
Oct. 1		J1		10,000	10,000

Retained Earnings — No. 320

Date	Explanation	Ref.	Debit	Credit	Balance
2006					
Oct. 1					–0–
31	**Closing entry**	**J3**		**2,860**	**2,860**
31	**Closing entry**	**J3**	**500**		**2,360**

Note. The permanent accounts for Pioneer Advertising Agency Inc. are shown here; the temporary accounts are shown in Illustration 4-11. Both permanent and temporary accounts are part of the general ledger; they are segregated here to aid in learning.

Illustration 4-11
General ledger, temporary accounts

(Temporary Accounts Only)

GENERAL LEDGER

Dividends No. 332

Date	Explanation	Ref.	Debit	Credit	Balance
2006					
Oct. 20		J1	500		500
31	**Closing entry**	**J3**		**500**	**–0–**

Income Summary No. 350

Date	Explanation	Ref.	Debit	Credit	Balance
2006					
Oct. 31	**Closing entry**	**J3**		**10,600**	**10,600**
31	**Closing entry**	**J3**	**7,740**		**2,860**
31	**Closing entry**	**J3**	**2,860**		**–0–**

Service Revenue No. 400

Date	Explanation	Ref.	Debit	Credit	Balance
2006					
Oct. 31		J1		10,000	10,000
31	Adj. entry	J2		**400**	10,400
31	Adj. entry	J2		**200**	10,600
31	**Closing entry**	**J3**	**10,600**		**–0–**

Advertising Supplies Expense No. 631

Date	Explanation	Ref.	Debit	Credit	Balance
2006					
Oct. 31	Adj. entry	J2	**1,500**		1,500
31	**Closing entry**	**J3**		**1,500**	**–0–**

Depreciation Expense No. 711

Date	Explanation	Ref.	Debit	Credit	Balance
2006					
Oct. 31	Adj. entry	J2	**40**		40
31	**Closing entry**	**J3**		**40**	**–0–**

Insurance Expense No. 722

Date	Explanation	Ref.	Debit	Credit	Balance
2006					
Oct. 31	Adj. entry	J2	**50**		50
31	**Closing entry**	**J3**		**50**	**–0–**

Salaries Expense No. 726

Date	Explanation	Ref.	Debit	Credit	Balance
2006					
Oct. 26		J1	4,000		4,000
31	Adj. entry	J2	**1,200**		5,200
31	**Closing entry**	**J3**		**5,200**	**–0–**

Rent Expense No. 729

Date	Explanation	Ref.	Debit	Credit	Balance
2006					
Oct. 3		J1	900		900
31	**Closing entry**	**J3**		**900**	**–0–**

Interest Expense No. 905

Date	Explanation	Ref.	Debit	Credit	Balance
2006					
Oct. 31	Adj. entry	J2	**50**		50
31	**Closing entry**	**J3**		**50**	**–0–**

Note: The temporary accounts for Pioneer Advertising Agency Inc. are shown here; the permanent accounts are shown in Illustration 4-10. Both permanent and temporary accounts are part of the general ledger; they are segregated here to aid in learning.

Summary of the Accounting Cycle

STUDY OBJECTIVE 4

State the required steps in the accounting cycle.

The required steps in the accounting cycle are shown in Illustration 4-12 on page 155. From the graphic you can see that the cycle begins with the analysis of business transactions and ends with the preparation of a post-closing trial balance. The steps in the cycle are performed in sequence and are repeated in each accounting period.

Steps 1–3 may occur daily during the accounting period, as explained in Chapter 2. Steps 4–7 are performed on a periodic basis, such as monthly, quarterly, or annually. Steps 8 and 9, closing entries, and a post-closing trial balance, are usually prepared only at the end of a company's **annual** accounting period.

There are also two optional steps in the accounting cycle. As you have seen, a work sheet may be used in preparing adjusting entries and financial statements. In addition, reversing entries may be used, as explained in the following section.

Reversing Entries—An Optional Step

Some accountants prefer to reverse certain adjusting entries at the beginning of a new accounting period. A **reversing entry** is made at the beginning of the next

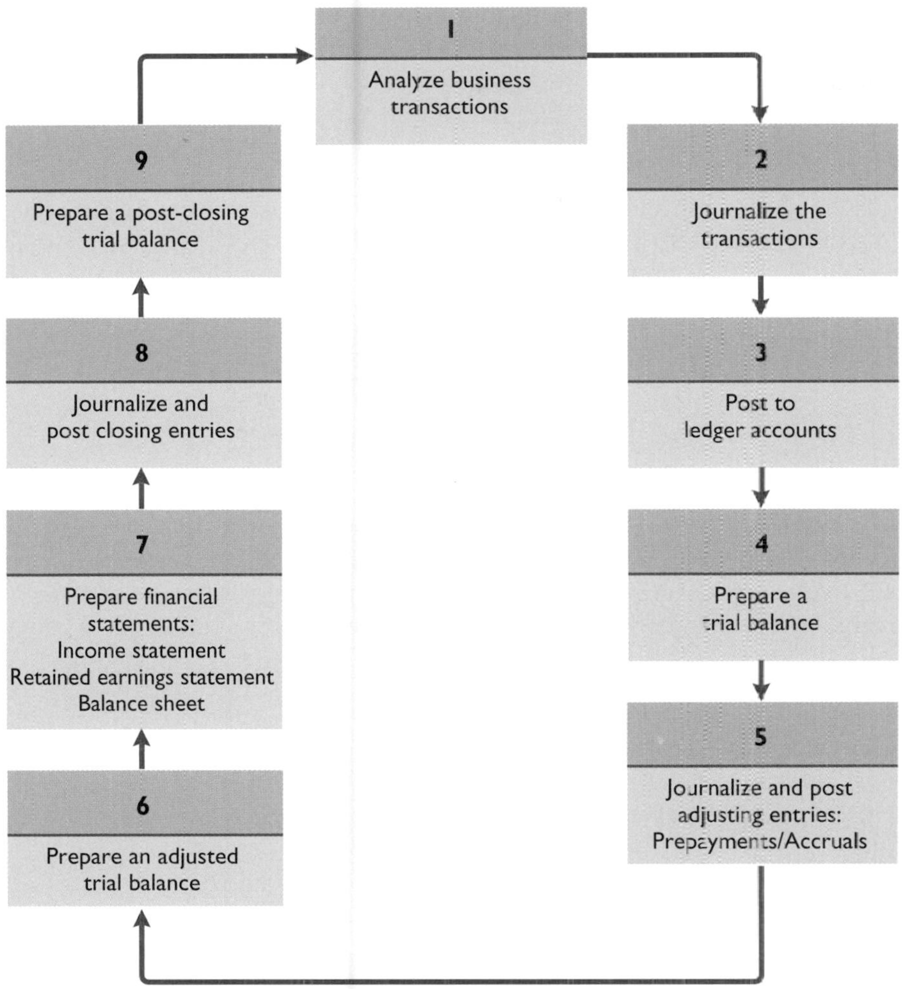

Optional steps: If a work sheet is prepared, steps 4, 5, and 6 are incorporated in the work sheet. If reversing entries are prepared, they occur between steps 9 and 1 as discussed on page 154.

Illustration 4-12
Steps in the accounting cycle

accounting period. It is the exact opposite of the adjusting entry made in the previous period. **The preparation of reversing entries is an optional bookkeeping procedure that is not a required step in the accounting cycle.** Therefore, we have chosen to cover this topic in an appendix at the end of the chapter.

STUDY OBJECTIVE 5

Explain the approaches to preparing correcting entries.

Correcting Entries—An Avoidable Step

Unfortunately, errors may occur in the recording process. Errors should be corrected **as soon as they are discovered** by journalizing and posting **correcting entries**. If the accounting records are free of errors, no correcting entries are necessary.

You should recognize several differences between correcting entries and adjusting entries. First, adjusting entries are an integral part of the accounting cycle. Correcting entries, on the other hand, are unnecessary if the records are free of errors. Second, **adjustments are journalized and posted only at the end of an accounting period. In contrast, correcting entries are made whenever an error is discovered.** Finally, adjusting entries always affect at least one balance sheet account and one income statement account. In contrast, correcting entries may involve any combination of accounts in need of correction. **Correcting entries must be posted before closing entries.**

ETHICS NOTE

Citigroup once reported a correcting entry reducing reported revenue by $23 million, while firing 11 employees. Company officials did not specify why the employees had apparently intentionally inflated the revenue figures, although it was noted that their bonuses were tied to their unit's performance.

To determine the correcting entry, it is useful to compare the incorrect entry with the correct entry. Doing so helps identify the accounts and amounts that should—and should not—be corrected. After comparison, a correcting entry is made to correct the accounts. This approach is illustrated in the following two cases.

Case 1

On May 10, a $50 cash collection on account from a customer is journalized and posted as a debit to Cash $50 and a credit to Service Revenue $50. The error is discovered on May 20, when the customer pays the remaining balance in full.

Illustration 4-13
Comparison of entries

Incorrect Entry (May 10)			Correct Entry (May 10)		
Cash	50		Cash	50	
Service Revenue		50	Accounts Receivable		50

A comparison of the incorrect entry with the correct entry reveals that the debit to Cash $50 is correct. However, the $50 credit to Service Revenue should have been credited to Accounts Receivable. As a result, both Service Revenue and Accounts Receivable are overstated in the ledger. The following correcting entry is required.

Illustration 4-14
Correcting entry

A	=	L	+	SE
−50				−50 Rev

Cash Flows
no effect

Correcting Entry

May 20	Service Revenue	50	
	Accounts Receivable		50
	(To correct entry of May 10)		

Case 2

On May 18, office equipment costing $450 is purchased on account. The transaction is journalized and posted as a debit to Delivery Equipment $45 and a credit to Accounts Payable $45. The error is discovered on June 3, when the monthly statement for May is received from the creditor.

Illustration 4-15
Comparison of entries

Incorrect Entry (May 18)			Correct Entry (May 18)		
Delivery Equipment	45		Office Equipment	450	
Accounts Payable		45	Accounts Payable		450

A comparison of the two entries shows that three accounts are incorrect. Delivery Equipment is overstated $45; Office Equipment is understated $450; and Accounts Payable is understated $405. The correcting entry is:

Illustration 4-16
Correcting entry

A	=	L	+	SE
+450				
−45		+405		

Cash Flows
no effect

Correcting Entry

June 3	Office Equipment	450	
	Delivery Equipment		45
	Accounts Payable		405
	(To correct entry of May 18)		

Instead of preparing a correcting entry, **it is possible to reverse the incorrect entry and then prepare the correct entry**. This approach will result in more entries and postings than a correcting entry, but it will accomplish the desired result.

ACCOUNTING MATTERS! Business Insight

Yale Express, a short-haul trucking firm, turned over much of its cargo to local truckers for delivery completion. Yale collected the entire delivery charge and, when billed by the local trucker, sent payment for the final phase to the local trucker. Yale used a cutoff period of 20 days into the next accounting period in making its adjusting entries for accrued liabilities. That is, it waited 20 days to receive the local truckers' bills to determine the amount of the unpaid but incurred delivery charges as of the balance sheet date.

On the other hand, **Republic Carloading**, a nationwide, long-distance freight forwarder, frequently did not receive transportation bills from truckers to whom it passed on cargo until months after the year-end. In making its year-end adjusting entries, Republic waited for months in order to include all of these outstanding transportation bills.

When Yale Express merged with Republic Carloading, Yale's vice president employed the 20-day cutoff procedure for both firms. As a result, millions of dollars of Republic's accrued transportation bills went unrecorded. When the erroneous procedure was detected and correcting entries were made, these and other errors changed a reported profit of $1.14 million into a loss of $1.88 million!

? What might Yale Express's vice president have done to produce more accurate financial statements without waiting months for Republic's outstanding transportation bills?

BEFORE YOU GO ON...

Review It

1. How do permanent accounts differ from temporary accounts?
2. What four different types of entries are required in closing the books?
3. What is the content and purpose of a post-closing trial balance?
4. What are the required and optional steps in the accounting cycle?

Do It

The work sheet for Hancock Corporation shows the following in the financial statement columns: Common Stock $98,000, Dividends $15,000, Retained Earnings $42,000, and Net Income $18,000. Prepare the closing entries at December 31 that affect stockholders' equity.

ACTION PLAN

- Remember to make closing entries in the correct sequence.
- Make the first two entries to close revenues and expenses.
- Make the third entry to close net income to retained earnings.
- Make the final entry to close dividends to retained earnings.

SOLUTION

Dec. 31	Income Summary	18,000	
	Retained Earnings		18,000
	(To close net income to retained earnings)		
31	Retained Earnings	15,000	
	Dividends		15,000
	(To close dividends to retained earnings)		

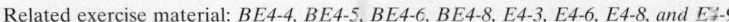

Related exercise material: *BE4-4, BE4-5, BE4-6, BE4-8, E4-3, E4-6, E4-8, and E4-9.*

THE NAVIGATOR

Classified Balance Sheet

STUDY OBJECTIVE 6

Identify the sections of a classified balance sheet.

The financial statements illustrated up to this point were purposely kept simple. We classified items as assets, liabilities, and stockholders' equity in the balance sheet, and as revenues and expenses in the income statement. **Financial statements, however, become more useful to management, creditors, and potential investors when the elements are classified into significant subgroups.** In the remainder of this chapter, we will introduce you to the primary balance sheet classifications. The classified income statement will be presented in Chapter 5. The classified financial statements are what Ted Castle, owner of **Rhino Foods, Inc.**, gave to his employees to understand what was happening in the business.

Standard Classifications

A **classified balance sheet** usually contains these standard classifications:

Illustration 4-17
Standard balance sheet classifications

Assets	Liabilities and Stockholders' Equity
Current assets	Current liabilities
Long-term investments	Long-term liabilities
Property, plant, and equipment	Stockholders' equity
Intangible assets	

These sections help the financial statement user determine such matters as (1) the availability of assets to meet debts as they come due and (2) the claims of short- and long-term creditors on total assets. A classified balance sheet also makes it easier to compare companies in the same industry, such as **GM**, **Ford**, and **DaimlerChrysler** in the automobile industry. Each of the sections is explained next.

A complete set of specimen financial statements for **PepsiCo, Inc.** is shown in Appendix A at the back of the book.

Current Assets

Current assets are cash and other resources that are reasonably expected to be realized in cash or sold or consumed in the business within one year of the balance sheet date or the company's operating cycle, whichever is longer. For example, accounts receivable are current assets because they will be realized in cash through collection within one year. A prepayment such as supplies is a current asset because of its expected use or consumption in the business within one year.

The **operating cycle** of a company is the average time that is required to go from cash to cash in producing revenues. The term "cycle" suggests a circular flow, which in this case, starts and ends with cash. For example, in municipal transit companies, the operating cycle would tend to be short since services are provided entirely on a cash basis. On the other hand, the operating cycle in manufacturing companies is longer: they purchase goods and materials, manufacture and sell products, bill customers, and collect cash. This is a cash to cash cycle that may extend for several months. Most companies have operating cycles of less than one year. More will be said about operating cycles in later chapters.

In a service enterprise, it is customary to recognize four types of current assets: (1) cash, (2) short-term investments such as U.S. government bonds, (3) receivables (notes receivable, accounts receivable, and interest receivable), and (4) prepaid expenses (insurance and supplies). **These items are listed in the order of liquidity.** That is, they are listed in the order in which they are expected to be converted into cash. This arrangement is illustrated below in the presentation of **UAL, Inc. (United Airlines)**.

Illustration 4-18
Current assets section

UNITED AIRLINES

UAL, INC, (UNITED AIRLINES)
Balance Sheet (partial)
(in millions)

Current assets	
Cash	$1,348
Short-term investments	388
Receivables	788
Aircraft fuel, spare parts, and supplies	310
Prepaid expenses	219
Other current assets	326
Total current assets	$3,379

A company's current assets are important in assessing the company's short-term debt-paying ability, as explained later in the chapter.

HELPFUL HINT

Long-term investments are investments made *by* the business—not investments by the owner or stockholders *in* the business.

Long-Term Investments

Like current assets, **long-term investments** are resources that can be realized in cash. However, the conversion into cash is not expected within one year or the operating cycle, whichever is longer. In addition, long-term investments are not intended for use or consumption within the business. This category, often just called "investments," normally includes stocks and bonds of other corporations. **Yahoo! Inc.** reported the following in its balance sheet.

Illustration 4-19
Long-term investments section

YAHOO!

YAHOO! INC.
Balance Sheet (partial)

Long-term investments	
Long-term investments in marketable securities	$763,408

ALTERNATIVE TERMINOLOGY

Property, plant, and equipment are sometimes referred to as *plant assets* or *fixed assets.*

Property, Plant, and Equipment

Property, plant, and equipment are tangible resources of a relatively permanent nature that are used in the business and not intended for sale. This category includes land, buildings, machinery and equipment, delivery equipment, and furniture and fixtures. Assets subject to depreciation should be reported at cost less accumulated depreciation. This practice is illustrated in the following presentation of **Delta Air Lines**.

DELTA AIR LINES, INC.
Balance Sheet (partial)
(in millions)

Property, plant, and equipment			
Flight equipment	$20,295		
Less: Accumulated depreciation	6,109	$14,186	
Ground property and equipment	4,841		
Less: Accumulated depreciation	2,503	2,338	$16,524

Illustration 4-20
Property, plant, and equipment section

Intangible Assets

Intangible assets are noncurrent resources that do not have physical substance. They are recorded at cost, and this cost is expensed over the useful life of the intangible asset. Intangible assets include patents, copyrights, and trademarks or trade names that give the holder **exclusive right** of use for a specified period of time. Their value to a company is generally derived from the rights or privileges granted by governmental authority.

In its balance sheet, **The Walt Disney Company** reported the following.

THE WALT DISNEY COMPANY
Balance Sheet (partial)
(in millions)

Intangible assets		
Patents, trademarks, and other intangibles	$ 2,776	
Goodwill	17,083	19,859

Illustration 4-21
Intangible assets section

Current Liabilities

Listed first in the liabilities and stockholders' equity section of the balance sheet are current liabilities. **Current liabilities** are obligations that are reasonably expected to be paid from existing current assets or through the creation of other current liabilities. As in the case of current assets, the time period for payment is one year or the operating cycle, whichever is longer. Current liabilities include (1) debts related to the operating cycle, such as accounts payable and wages and salaries payable, and (2) other short-term debts, such as bank loans payable, interest payable, taxes payable, and current maturities of long-term obligations (payments to be made within the next year on long-term obligations).

The arrangement of items within the current liabilities section has evolved through custom rather than from a prescribed rule. Notes payable is usually listed first, followed by accounts payable. Other items are then listed in any order. The current liabilities section adapted from the balance sheet of **Deckers Outdoor Corporation** is as follows.

Illustration 4-22
Current liabilities section

DECKERS outdoor corporation

DECKERS OUTDOOR CORPORATION
Balance Sheet (partial)

Current liabilities	
Notes payable	$ 3,951,000
Accounts payable	12,916,000
Allowance for returns	1,255,000
Salaries and commissions payable	2,342,000
Taxes payable	732,000
Other current liabilities	912,000
Total current liabilities	$22,108,000

Users of financial statements look closely at the relationship between current assets and current liabilities. This relationship is important in evaluating a company's **liquidity**—its ability to pay obligations that are expected to become due within the next year or operating cycle. When current assets exceed current liabilities at the balance sheet date, the likelihood for paying the liabilities is favorable. When the reverse is true, short-term creditors may not be paid, and the company may ultimately be forced into bankruptcy.

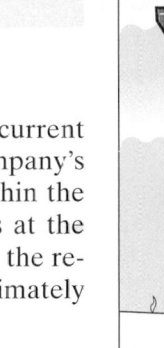

Long-Term Liabilities

Obligations expected to be paid after one year or an operating cycle, whichever is longer, are classified as **long-term liabilities**. Liabilities in this category include bonds payable, mortgages payable, long-term notes payable, lease liabilities, and obligations under employee pension plans. Many companies report long-term debt maturing after one year as a single amount in the balance sheet. They then show the details of the debt in the notes that accompany the financial statements. Others list the various sources of long-term liabilities. In its balance sheet, **Brunswick Corporation** reported the following.

ALTERNATIVE TERMINOLOGY

Long-term liabilities are also called *long-term debt* or *noncurrent liabilities.*

Illustration 4-23
Long-term liabilities section

BRUNSWICK CORPORATION
Balance Sheet (partial)
(in millions)

Long-term liabilities	
Notes payable	$437.2
Bonds payable	124.4
Guaranteed debt	15.5
Other long-term debt	12.4
Total long-term liabilities	$589.5

Stockholders' (Owners') Equity

The content of the owners' equity section varies with the form of business organization. In a proprietorship, there is one capital account. In a partnership, there is a capital account for each partner. For a corporation, owners' (stockholders') equity is divided into two accounts—Common Stock and Retained Earnings. As previously indicated, investments of capital in the business by the stockholders are recorded in the Common Stock account. Income retained for use in the business is recorded in the Retained Earnings account. These two accounts are combined and reported as **stockholders' equity** on the balance sheet.

In its balance sheet, **Dell Computer Corporation** recently reported its stockholders' equity section as follows.

Illustration 4-24
Stockholders' equity section

DELL INC.
(in millions)

Stockholders' equity	
Common stock, 2,681,000,000 shares	$1,479
Retained earnings	3,394
Total stockholders' equity	$4,873

Classified Balance Sheet Illustrated

An unclassified, report form balance sheet of Pioneer Advertising Agency Inc. was presented in Illustration 4-4 on page 146. Using the same adjusted trial balance accounts at October 31, 2006, we can prepare the classified balance sheet shown in Illustration 4-25. For illustrative purposes, assume that $1,000 of the notes payable is due currently and $4,000 is long term.

The balance sheet is most often presented in **report form**, with assets listed above liabilities and stockholders' equity. The balance sheet may also be presented in **account form**: the assets section is placed on the left and the liabilities and stockholders' equity sections on the right, as shown in Illustration 4-25.

Illustration 4-25
Classified balance sheet in account form

PIONEER ADVERTISING AGENCY INC.
Balance Sheet
October 31, 2006

Assets			Liabilities and Stockholders' Equity		
Current assets			Current liabilities		
Cash		$15,200	Notes payable		$ 1,000
Accounts receivable		200	Accounts payable		2,500
Advertising supplies		1,000	Unearned revenue		800
Prepaid insurance		550	Salaries payable		1,200
Total current assets		16,950	Interest payable		50
Property, plant, and equipment			Total current liabilities		5,550
Office equipment	$5,000		Long-term liabilities		
Less: Accumulated depreciation	40	4,960	Notes payable		4,000
Total assets		$21,910	Total liabilities		9,550
			Stockholders' equity		
			Common stock	$10,000	
			Retained earnings	2,360	
			Total stockholders' equity		12,360
			Total liabilities and stockholders' equity		$21,910

Another, more complete example of a classified balance sheet is presented in report form in Illustration 4-26.

Illustration 4-26
Classified balance sheet in report form

FRANKLIN CORPORATION
Balance Sheet
October 31, 2006

Assets

Current assets			
Cash		$ 6,600	
Short-term investments		2,000	
Accounts receivable		7,000	
Inventories		4,000	
Supplies		2,100	
Prepaid insurance		400	
Total current assets			$22,100
Long-term investments			
Investment in stock of Walters Corp.		5,200	
Investment in real estate		2,000	7,200
Property, plant, and equipment			
Land		10,000	
Office equipment	$ 24,000		
Less: Accumulated depreciation	5,000	19,000	29,000
Intangible assets			
Patents			3,100
Total assets			$61,400

Liabilities and Stockholders' Equity

Current liabilities		
Notes payable	$11,000	
Accounts payable	2,100	
Salaries payable	1,600	
Unearned revenue	900	
Interest payable	450	
Total current liabilities		$16,050
Long-term liabilities		
Notes payable	1,300	
Mortgage payable	10,000	
Total long-term liabilities		11,300
Total liabilities		27,350
Stockholders' equity		
Common stock	20,000	
Retained earnings	14,050	
Total stockholders' equity		34,050
Total liabilities and stockholders' equity		$61,400

BEFORE YOU GO ON...

Review It

1. What are the major sections in a classified balance sheet?
2. Using the **PepsiCo, Inc.** annual report, determine its current liabilities at December 27, 2003, and December 28, 2002. Were current liabilities higher or lower than current assets in these two years? The answer to this question is provided on page 188.
3. What is the difference between the report form and the account form of the classified balance sheet?

THE NAVIGATOR

DEMONSTRATION PROBLEM

At the end of its first month of operations, Watson Answering Service, Inc., has the following unadjusted trial balance.

WATSON ANSWERING SERVICE, INC.
August 31, 2006
Trial Balance

	Debit	Credit
Cash	$ 5,400	
Accounts Receivable	8,800	
Prepaid Insurance	2,400	
Supplies	1,300	
Equipment	60,000	
Notes Payable		$40,000
Accounts Payable		2,400
Common Stock		30,000
Dividends	1,000	
Service Revenue		10,900
Salaries Expense	3,200	
Utilities Expense	800	
Advertising Expense	400	
	$83,300	$83,300

Other data consist of the following:

1. Insurance expires at the rate of $200 per month.
2. There are $1,000 of supplies on hand at August 31.
3. Monthly depreciation on the equipment is $900.
4. Interest of $500 on the notes payable has accrued during August.

Instructions

(a) Prepare a work sheet.
(b) Prepare a classified balance sheet assuming $35,000 of the notes payable are long-term.
(c) Journalize the closing entries.

ACTION PLAN

- In completing the work sheet, be sure to (a) key the adjustments, (b) start at the top of the adjusted trial balance columns and extend adjusted balances to the correct statement columns, and (c) enter net income (or net loss) in the proper columns.
- In preparing a classified balance sheet, know the contents of each of the sections.
- In journalizing closing entries, remember that there are only four entries and that dividends are closed to retained earnings.

SOLUTION TO DEMONSTRATION PROBLEM

(a)

WATSON ANSWERING SERVICE, INC.
Work Sheet
For the Month Ended August 31, 2006

Account Titles	Trial Balance Dr.	Trial Balance Cr.	Adjustments Dr.	Adjustments Cr.	Adjusted Trial Balance Dr.	Adjusted Trial Balance Cr.	Income Statement Dr.	Income Statement Cr.	Balance Sheet Dr.	Balance Sheet Cr.
Cash	5,400				5,400				5,400	
Accounts Receivable	8,800				8,800				8,800	
Prepaid Insurance	2,400			(a) 200	2,200				2,200	
Supplies	1,300			(b) 300	1,000				1,000	
Equipment	60,000				60,000				60,000	
Notes Payable		40,000				40,000				40,000
Accounts Payable		2,400				2,400				2,400
Common Stock		30,000				30,000				30,000
Dividends	1,000				1,000				1,000	
Service Revenue		10,900				10,900		10,900		
Salaries Expense	3,200				3,200		3,200			
Utilities Expense	800				800		800			
Advertising Expense	400				400		400			
Totals	83,300	83,300								
Insurance Expense			(a) 200		200		200			
Supplies Expense			(b) 300		300		300			
Depreciation Expense			(c) 900		900		900			
Accumulated Depreciation—Equipment				(c) 900		900				900
Interest Expense			(d) 500		500		500			
Interest Payable				(d) 500		500				500
Totals			1,900	1,900	84,700	84,700	6,300	10,900	78,400	73,800
Net Income							4,600			4,600
Totals							10,900	10,900	78,400	78,400

Explanation: (a) Insurance expired, (b) Supplies used, (c) Depreciation expensed, (d) Interest accrued.

(b)

WATSON ANSWERING SERVICE, INC.
Balance Sheet
August 31, 2006

Assets

Current assets		
Cash		$ 5,400
Accounts receivable		8,800
Prepaid insurance		2,200
Supplies		1,000
Total current assets		17,400
Property, plant, and equipment		
Equipment	$60,000	
Less: Accumulated depreciation—equipment	900	59,100
Total assets		$76,500

Liabilities and Stockholders' Equity

Current liabilities		
Notes payable		$ 5,000
Accounts payable		2,400
Interest payable		500
Total current liabilities		7,900
Long-term liabilities		
Notes payable		35,000
Total liabilities		42,900
Stockholders' equity		
Common stock	$30,000	
Retained earnings	3,600*	
Total stockholders' equity		33,600
Total liabilities and stockholders' equity		$76,500

*Net income of $4,600 less dividends of $1,000.

(c)

Aug. 31	Service Revenue	10,900	
	Income Summary		10,900
	(To close revenue account)		
31	Income Summary	6,300	
	Salaries Expense		3,200
	Depreciation Expense		900
	Utilities Expense		800
	Interest Expense		500
	Advertising Expense		400
	Supplies Expense		300
	Insurance Expense		200
	(To close expense accounts)		
31	Income Summary	4,600	
	Retained Earnings		4,600
	(To close net income to retained earnings)		
31	Retained Earnings	1,000	
	Dividends		1,000
	(To close dividends to retained earnings)		

THE NAVIGATOR

SUMMARY OF STUDY OBJECTIVES

1. **Prepare a work sheet.** The steps in preparing a work sheet are: (a) prepare a trial balance on the work sheet, (b) enter the adjustments in the adjustments columns, (c) enter adjusted balances in the adjusted trial balance columns, (d) extend adjusted trial balance amounts to appropriate financial statement columns, and (e) total the statement columns, compute net income (or net loss), and complete the work sheet.

2. **Explain the process of closing the books.** Closing the books occurs at the end of an accounting period. The process is to journalize and post closing entries and then rule and balance all accounts. In closing the books, separate entries are made to close revenues and expenses to Income Summary, Income Summary to Retained Earnings, and Dividends to Retained Earnings. Only temporary accounts are closed.

3. **Describe the content and purpose of a post-closing trial balance.** A post-closing trial balance contains the balances in permanent accounts that are carried forward to the next accounting period. The purpose of this trial balance is to prove the equality of these balances.

4. **State the required steps in the accounting cycle.** The required steps in the accounting cycle are: (a) analyze business transactions, (b) journalize the transactions, (c) post to ledger accounts, (d) prepare a trial balance, (e) journalize and post adjusting entries, (f) prepare an adjusted trial

balance, (g) prepare financial statements, (h) journalize and post closing entries, and (i) prepare a post-closing trial balance.

5. **Explain the approaches to preparing correcting entries.** One approach for determining the correcting entry is to compare the incorrect entry with the correct entry. After comparison, a correcting entry is made to correct the accounts. An alternative to a correcting entry is to reverse the incorrect entry and then prepare the correct entry.

6. **Identify the sections of a classified balance sheet.** In a classified balance sheet, assets are classified as current assets; long-term investments; property, plant, and equipment; and intangibles. Liabilities are classified as either current or long-term. There is also an owners' equity section, which varies with the form of business organization.

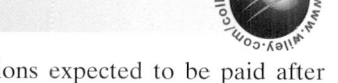

THE NAVIGATOR

GLOSSARY

Classified balance sheet A balance sheet that contains a number of standard classifications or sections. (p. 158).

Closing entries Entries made at the end of an accounting period to transfer the balances of temporary accounts to a permanent stockholders' equity account, Retained Earnings. (p. 148).

Correcting entries Entries to correct errors made in recording transactions. (p. 155).

Current assets Cash and other resources that are reasonably expected to be realized in cash or sold or consumed in the business within one year or the operating cycle, whichever is longer. (p. 158).

Current liabilities Obligations reasonably expected to be paid from existing current assets or through the creation of other current liabilities within the next year or operating cycle, whichever is longer. (p. 160).

Income Summary A temporary account used in closing revenue and expense accounts. (p. 148).

Intangible assets Noncurrent resources that do not have physical substance. (p. 160).

Liquidity The ability of a company to pay obligations that are expected to become due within the next year or operating cycle. (p. 161).

Long-term investments Resources not expected to be realized in cash within the next year or operating cycle. (p. 159).

Long-term liabilities Obligations expected to be paid after one year. (p. 161).

Operating cycle The average time required to go from cash to cash in producing revenues. (p. 158).

Permanent (real) accounts Balance sheet accounts whose balances are carried forward to the next accounting period. (p. 148).

Post-closing trial balance A list of permanent accounts and their balances after closing entries have been journalized and posted. (p. 152).

Property, plant, and equipment Assets of a relatively permanent nature that are being used in the business and not intended for sale. (p. 159).

Reversing entry An entry made at the beginning of the next accounting period that is the exact opposite of the adjusting entry made in the previous period. (p. 154).

Stockholders' equity The ownership claim of shareholders on total assets as represented by common stock and retained earnings. (p. 162).

Temporary (nominal) accounts Revenue, expense, and Dividends accounts whose balances are transferred to Retained Earnings at the end of an accounting period. (p. 148).

Work sheet A multiple-column form that may be used in the adjustment process and in preparing financial statements. (p. 141).

APPENDIX REVERSING ENTRIES

STUDY OBJECTIVE 7

Prepare reversing entries.

After the financial statements are prepared and the books are closed, it is often helpful to reverse some of the adjusting entries before recording the regular transactions of the next period. Such entries are called reversing entries. **A reversing entry is made at the beginning of the next accounting period and is the exact opposite of the adjusting entry made in the previous period.** The recording of reversing entries is an **optional** step in the accounting cycle.

The purpose of reversing entries is to simplify the recording of a subsequent transaction related to an adjusting entry. In Chapter 3, you may recall, the payment of salaries after an adjusting entry resulted in two debits: one to Salaries Payable and the other to Salaries Expense. With reversing entries, the entire subsequent payment can be debited to Salaries Expense. **The use of reversing entries does not change the amounts reported in the financial statements. What it does is simplify the recording of subsequent transactions.**

Illustration of Reversing Entries

Reversing entries are most often used to reverse two types of adjusting entries: accrued revenues and accrued expenses. They are seldom made for prepaid expenses and unearned revenues. To illustrate the optional use of reversing entries for accrued expenses, we will use the salaries expense transactions for Pioneer Advertising Agency Inc. The transaction and adjustment data are as follows.

1. October 26 (initial salary entry): $4,000 of salaries earned between October 15 and October 26 are paid.
2. October 31 (adjusting entry): Salaries earned between October 29 and October 31 are $1,200. These will be paid in the November 9 payroll.
3. November 9 (subsequent salary entry): Salaries paid are $4,000. Of this amount, $1,200 applied to accrued wages payable and $2,800 was earned between November 1 and November 9.

The comparative entries with and without reversing entries are shown in Illustration 4A-1.

Illustration 4A-1
Comparative entries—not reversing vs. reversing

When Reversing Entries Are Not Used (per chapter)				When Reversing Entries Are Used (per appendix)			
	Initial Salary Entry				**Initial Salary Entry**		
Oct. 26	Salaries Expense	4,000		**Oct. 26**	**Salaries Expense**	**4,000**	
	Cash		4,000		**Cash**		**4,000**
	Adjusting Entry				Adjusting Entry		
Oct. 31	Salaries Expense	1,200		**Oct. 31**	**Salaries Expense**	**1,200**	
	Salaries Payable		1,200		**Salaries Payable**		**1,200**
	Closing Entry				Closing Entry		
Oct. 31	Income Summary	5,200		**Oct. 31**	**Income Summary**	**5,200**	
	Salaries Expense		5,200		**Salaries Expense**		**5,200**
	Reversing Entry				Reversing Entry		
Nov. 1	No reversing entry is made.			**Nov. 1**	**Salaries Payable**	**1,200**	
					Salaries Expense		**1,200**
	Subsequent Salary Entry				Subsequent Salary Entry		
Nov. 9	Salaries Payable	1,200					
	Salaries Expense	2,800		**Nov. 9**	**Salaries Expense**	**4,000**	
	Cash		4,000		**Cash**		**4,000**

The first three entries are the same whether or not reversing entries are used. The last two entries are different. The November 1 **reversing entry** eliminates the $1,200 balance in Salaries Payable that was created by the October 31 adjusting entry. The reversing entry also creates a $1,200 credit balance in the Salaries Expense account. As you know, it is unusual for an expense account to have a credit balance. The balance is correct in this instance, though, because it anticipates that the entire amount of the first salary payment in the new accounting period will be debited to Salaries Expense. This debit will eliminate the credit balance, and the resulting debit balance in the expense account will equal the salaries expense incurred in the new accounting period ($2,800 in this example).

When reversing entries are made, all cash payments of expenses can be debited to the expense account. This means that on November 9 (and every payday) Salaries Expense can be debited for the amount paid without regard to any accrued salaries payable. Being able to make the same entry each time simplifies the recording process: Subsequent transactions can be recorded as if the related adjusting entry had never been made.

The posting of the entries with reversing entries is shown in Illustration 4A-2.

Illustration 4A-2
Postings with reversing entries

Salaries Expense

10/26 Paid	4,000	10/31 Closing	5,200
31 Adjusting	1,200		
	5,200		5,200
11/9 Paid	4,000	**11/1 Reversing**	**1,200**

Salaries Payable

11/1 Reversing	**1,200**	10/31 Adjusting	1,200

Reversing entries may also be made for accrued revenue adjusting entries. For Pioneer Advertising, the adjusting entry was: Accounts Receivable (Dr.) $200 and Service Revenue (Cr.) $200. Thus, the reversing entry on November 1 is:

Nov. 1	Service Revenue	200	
	Accounts Receivable		200
	(To reverse October 31 adjusting entry)		

A	=	L	+	SE
−200				−200 Rev

Cash Flows
no effect

When the accrued fees are collected, Cash is debited and Service Revenue is credited.

SUMMARY OF STUDY OBJECTIVE FOR APPENDIX

7. **Prepare reversing entries.** Reversing entries are the opposite of the adjusting entries made in the preceding period. They are made at the beginning of a new accounting period to simplify the recording of later transactions related to the adjusting entries. In most cases, only accrued adjusting entries are reversed.

*__Note:__ All asterisked Questions, Exercises, and Problems relate to material in the appendix to the chapter.

SELF-STUDY QUESTIONS

Self-Study/Self-Test www.wiley.com/college/weygandt

Answers are at the end of the chapter.

(SO 1) 1. Which of the following statements is *incorrect* concerning the work sheet?
  - **a.** The work sheet is essentially a working tool of the accountant.
  - **b.** The work sheet cannot be used as a basis for posting to ledger accounts.
  - **c.** The work sheet is distributed to management and other interested parties.
  - **d.** Financial statements can be prepared directly from the work sheet before journalizing and posting the adjusting entries.

2. In a work sheet, net income is entered in the following columns: (SO 1)
  - **a.** income statement (Dr) and balance sheet (Dr).
  - **b.** income statement (Dr) and balance sheet (Cr).
  - **c.** income statement (Cr) and balance sheet (Dr).
  - **d.** income statement (Cr) and balance sheet (Cr).

3. An account that will have a zero balance after closing entries have been journalized and posted is: (SO 2)
  - **a.** Unearned Revenue.
  - **b.** Advertising Supplies.
  - **c.** Prepaid Insurance.
  - **d.** Rent Expense.

(SO 2) 4. When a net loss has occurred, Income Summary is:
 a. credited and retained earnings is debited.
 b. debited and retained earnings is credited.
 c. debited and common stock is credited.
 d. credited and common stock is debited.

(SO 2) 5. The closing process involves separate entries to close (1) expenses, (2) dividends, (3) revenues, and (4) net income (or loss). The correct sequencing of the entries is:
 a. (4), (3), (2), (1)
 b. (1), (2), (3), (4)
 c. (3), (2), (1), (4)
 d. (3), (1), (4), (2)

(SO 3) 6. Which type of accounts will appear in the post-closing trial balance?
 a. Temporary (nominal) accounts.
 b. Permanent (real) accounts.
 c. Accounts shown in the income statement columns of a work sheet.
 d. None of the above.

(SO 4) 7. All of the following are required steps in the accounting cycle *except*:
 a. preparing a work sheet.
 b. journalizing and posting closing entries.
 c. preparing an adjusted trial balance.
 d. preparing a post-closing trial balance.

(SO 5) 8. Cash of $100 received at the time the service was rendered was journalized and posted as a debit to Cash $100 and a credit to Accounts Receivable $100. Assuming the incorrect entry is not reversed, the correcting entry is:
 a. debit Service Revenue $100 and credit Accounts Receivable $100.
 b. debit Cash $100 and credit Service Revenue $100.
 c. debit Accounts Receivable $100 and credit Service Revenue $100.
 d. debit Accounts Receivable $100 and credit Cash $100.

9. In a classified balance sheet, assets are usually classified using the following categories: (SO 6)
 a. current assets; long-term assets; property, plant, and equipment; and intangible assets.
 b. current assets; long-term investments; property, plant, and equipment; and other assets.
 c. current assets; long-term investments; property, plant, and equipment; and intangible assets.
 d. current assets; long-term investments; tangible assets; and intangible assets.

10. Current assets are listed: (SO 6)
 a. by importance.
 b. by liquidity.
 c. by longevity.
 d. alphabetically.

*11. On December 31, Sondgeroth Corporation correctly made an adjusting entry to recognize $2,000 of accrued salaries payable. On January 8 of the next year, total salaries of $3,500 were paid. Assuming the correct reversing entry was made on January 1, the entry on January 8 will result in a credit to Cash $3,500, and the following debit(s): (SO 7)
 a. Salaries Payable $3,500.
 b. Salaries Expense $3,500.
 c. Salaries Payable $2,000 and Salaries Expense $1,500.
 d. Salaries Payable $1,500 and Salaries Expense $2,000.

☑ THE NAVIGATOR

QUESTIONS

1. "A work sheet is a permanent accounting record and its use is required in the accounting cycle." Do you agree? Explain.

2. Explain the purpose of the work sheet.

3. What is the relationship, if any, between the amount shown in the adjusted trial balance column for an account and that account's ledger balance?

4. If a company's revenues are $125,000 and its expenses are $113,000, in which financial statement columns of the work sheet will the net income of $12,000 appear? When expenses exceed revenues, in which columns will the difference appear?

5. Why is it necessary to prepare formal financial statements if all of the data are in the statement columns of the work sheet?

6. Identify the account(s) debited and credited in each of the four closing entries, assuming the company has net income for the year.

7. Describe the nature of the Income Summary account and identify the types of summary data that may be posted to this account.

8. What are the content and purpose of a post-closing trial balance?

9. Which of the following accounts would not appear in the post-closing trial balance? Interest Payable; Equipment; Depreciation Expense; Dividends, Unearned Revenue; Accumulated Depreciation—Equipment; and Service Revenue.

10. Distinguish between a reversing entry and an adjusting entry. Are reversing entries required?

11. Indicate, in the sequence in which they are made, the three required steps in the accounting cycle that involve journalizing.

12. Identify, in the sequence in which they are prepared, the three trial balances that are often used to report financial information about a company.

13. How do correcting entries differ from adjusting entries?

14. What standard classifications are used in preparing a classified balance sheet?

15. What is meant by the term "operating cycle?"

16. Define current assets. What basis is used for arranging individual items within the current assets section?

17. Distinguish between long-term investments and property, plant, and equipment.

18. How do current liabilities differ from long-term liabilities?

19. (a) What is the term used to describe the owner's equity section of a corporation? (b) Identify the two owner's equity accounts in a corporation and indicate the purpose of each.

20. How does a report form balance sheet differ from an account form balance sheet?

***21.** Sang Nam Company prepares reversing entries. If the adjusting entry for interest payable is reversed, what type of an account balance, if any, will there be in Interest Payable and Interest Expense after the reversing entry is posted?

***22.** At December 31, accrued salaries payable totaled $4,500. On January 10, total salaries of $8,000 are paid. (a) Assume that reversing entries are made at January 1. Give the January 10 entry, and indicate the Salaries Expense account balance after the entry is posted. (b) Repeat part (a) assuming reversing entries are not made.

BRIEF EXERCISES

BE4-1 The steps in using a work sheet are presented in random order below. List the steps in the proper order by placing numbers 1–5 in the blank spaces.

List the steps in preparing a work sheet.
(SO 1)

(a) _____ Prepare a trial balance on the work sheet.
(b) _____ Enter adjusted balances.
(c) _____ Extend adjusted balances to appropriate statement columns.
(d) _____ Total the statement columns, compute net income (loss), and complete the work sheet.
(e) _____ Enter adjustment data.

BE4-2 The ledger of Keo Company includes the following unadjusted balances: Prepaid Insurance $4,000, Service Revenue $58,000, and Salaries Expense $25,000. Adjusting entries are required for **(a)** expired insurance $1,200; **(b)** services provided $1,100, but unbilled and uncollected; and **(c)** accrued salaries payable $800. Enter the unadjusted balances and adjustments into a work sheet and complete the work sheet for all accounts. *Note:* You will need to add the following accounts: Accounts Receivable, Salaries Payable, and Insurance Expense.

Prepare partial work sheet.
(SO 1)

BE4-3 The following selected accounts appear in the adjusted trial balance columns of the work sheet for Cesar Company: Accumulated Depreciation, Depreciation Expense, Common Stock, Dividends, Service Revenue, Supplies, and Accounts Payable. Indicate the financial statement column (income statement Dr., balance sheet Cr., etc.) to which each balance should be extended.

Identify work sheet columns for selected accounts.
(SO 1)

BE4-4 The ledger of Rowen Company contains the following balances: Common Stock $30,000; Dividends $2,000; Service Revenue $50,000; Salaries Expense $23,000; and Supplies Expense $4,000. Prepare the closing entries at December 31.

Prepare closing entries from ledger balances.
(SO 2)

BE4-5 Using the data in BE4-4, enter the balances in T accounts, post the closing entries, and rule and balance the accounts.

Post closing entries; rule and balance T accounts.
(SO 2)

BE4-6 The income statement for Mosquera Golf Club for the month ending July 31 shows Green Fee Revenue $14,600, Salaries Expense $8,200, Maintenance Expense $2,500, and Net Income $3,900. Prepare the entries to close the revenue and expense accounts. Post the entries to the revenue and expense accounts, and complete the closing process for these accounts using the three-column form of account.

Journalize and post closing entries using the three-column form of account.
(SO 2)

BE4-7 Using the data in BE4-3, identify the accounts that would be included in a post-closing trial balance.

Identify post-closing trial balance accounts.
(SO 3)

BE4-8 The steps in the accounting cycle are listed in random order below. List the steps in proper sequence, assuming no work sheet is prepared, by placing numbers 1–9 in the blank spaces.

List the required steps in the accounting cycle in sequence.
(SO 4)

(a) _____ Prepare a trial balance.
(b) _____ Journalize the transactions.
(c) _____ Journalize and post closing entries.
(d) _____ Prepare financial statements.
(e) _____ Journalize and post adjusting entries.
(f) _____ Post to ledger accounts.
(g) _____ Prepare a post-closing trial balance.
(h) _____ Prepare an adjusted trial balance.
(i) _____ Analyze business transactions.

Prepare correcting entries.
(SO 5)

BE4-9 At Rafeul Huda Company, the following errors were discovered after the transactions had been journalized and posted. Prepare the correcting entries.

1. A collection on account from a customer for $780 was recorded as a debit to Cash $780 and a credit to Service Revenue $780.
2. The purchase of store supplies on account for $1,580 was recorded as a debit to Store Supplies $1,850 and a credit to Accounts Payable $1,850.

Prepare the current assets section of a balance sheet.
(SO 6)

BE4-10 The balance sheet debit column of the work sheet for Kren Company includes the following accounts: Accounts Receivable $12,500; Prepaid Insurance $3,600; Cash $18,400; Supplies $5,200, and Short-term Investments $6,700. Prepare the current assets section of the balance sheet, listing the accounts in proper sequence.

Prepare reversing entries.
(SO 7)

***BE4-11** At October 31, Prasad Company made an accrued expense adjusting entry of $1,200 for salaries. Prepare the reversing entry on November 1, and indicate the balances in Salaries Payable and Salaries Expense after posting the reversing entry.

EXERCISES

Complete work sheet
(SO 1)

E4-1 The adjusted trial balance columns of the work sheet for Cajon Company are as follows.

CAJON COMPANY
Work Sheet (partial)
For the Month Ended April 30, 2006

	Adjusted Trial Balance		Income Statement		Balance Sheet	
Account Titles	**Dr.**	**Cr.**	**Dr.**	**Cr.**	**Dr.**	**Cr.**
Cash	14,752					
Accounts Receivable	7,840					
Prepaid Rent	2,280					
Equipment	23,050					
Accumulated Depreciation		4,921				
Notes Payable		5,700				
Accounts Payable		5,672				
Common Stock		25,000				
Retained Earnings		8,960				
Dividends	3,650					
Service Revenue		12,590				
Salaries Expense	9,840					
Rent Expense	760					
Depreciation Expense	671					
Interest Expense	57					
Interest Payable		57				
Totals	62,900	62,900				

Instructions
Complete the work sheet.

Prepare financial statements from work sheet.
(SO 1, 6)

E4-2 Work sheet data for Cajon Company are presented in E4-1. No common stock was issued during April.

Instructions
Prepare an income statement, a retained earnings statement, and a classified balance sheet.

Journalize and post closing entries and prepare a post-closing trial balance
(SO 2, 3)

E4-3 Work sheet data for Cajon Company are presented in E4-1.

Instructions
(a) Journalize the closing entries at April 30.
(b) Post the closing entries to Income Summary and Retained Earnings. Use T accounts.
(c) Prepare a post-closing trial balance at April 30.

E4-4 The adjustments columns of the work sheet for Munoz Company are shown below.

Prepare adjusting entries from a work sheet and extend balance to work sheet columns.

(SO 1)

Account Titles	Adjustments Debit	Adjustments Credit
Accounts Receivable	600	
Prepaid Insurance		400
Accumulated Depreciation		900
Salaries Payable		500
Service Revenue		600
Salaries Expense	500	
Insurance Expense	400	
Depreciation Expense	900	
	2,400	2,400

Instructions

(a) Prepare the adjusting entries.

(b) Assuming the adjusted trial balance amount for each account is normal, indicate the financial statement column to which each balance should be extended.

E4-5 Selected work sheet data for Jane Freeman Company are presented below.

Derive adjusting entries from work sheet data.

(SO 1)

Account Titles	Trial Balance Dr.	Trial Balance Cr.	Adjusted Trial Balance Dr.	Adjusted Trial Balance Cr.
Accounts Receivable	?		34,000	
Prepaid Insurance	26,000		18,000	
Supplies	7,000		?	
Accumulated Depreciation		12,000		?
Salaries Payable		?		5,000
Service Revenue		88,000		95,000
Insurance Expense			?	
Depreciation Expense			10,000	
Supplies Expense			4,000	
Salaries Expense	?		49,000	

Instructions

(a) Fill in the missing amounts.

(b) Prepare the adjusting entries that were made.

E4-6 The adjusted trial balance of Lanza Company at the end of its fiscal year is:

Journalize and post closing entries and prepare a post-closing trial balance.

(SO 2, 3)

LANZA COMPANY
Adjusted Trial Balance
July 31, 2006

No.	Account Titles	Debits	Credits
101	Cash	$ 14,840	
112	Accounts Receivable	8,780	
157	Equipment	15,900	
167	Accumulated Depreciation		$ 5,400
201	Accounts Payable		4,220
208	Unearned Rent Revenue		1,800
311	Common Stock		20,000
320	Retained Earnings		25,200
332	Dividends	16,000	
404	Commission Revenue		67,000
429	Rent Revenue		6,500
711	Depreciation Expense	4,000	
720	Salaries Expense	55,700	
732	Utilities Expense	14,900	
		$130,120	$130,120

Instructions

(a) Prepare the closing entries using page J15.

(b) Post to Retained Earnings and No. 350 Income Summary accounts. (Use the three-column form.)

(c) Prepare a post-closing trial balance at July 31.

Prepare financial statements.
(SO 6)

E4-7 The adjusted trial balance for Lanza Company is presented in E4-6.

Instructions

(a) Prepare an income statement and a retained earnings statement for the year. There were no issuances of stock during the year.

(b) Prepare a classified balance sheet at July 31.

Prepare closing entries.
(SO 2)

E4-8 Selected accounts for Roth Salon are presented below. All June 30 postings are from closing entries.

Salaries Expense

6/10	3,200	6/30	8,800
6/28	5,600		

Service Revenue

6/30	16,100	6/15	7,700
		6/24	8,400

Dividends

6/15	2,500	6/30	2,500

Supplies Expense

6/12	600	6/30	1,300
6/24	700		

Rent Expense

6/1	3,000	6/30	3,000

Retained Earnings

6/30	2,500	6/30	3,000
		Bal.	500

Instructions

(a) Prepare the closing entries that were made.

(b) Post the closing entries to Income Summary.

Prepare correcting entries.
(SO 5)

E4-9 Kogan Company has an inexperienced accountant. During the first 2 weeks on the job, the accountant made the following errors in journalizing transactions. All entries were posted as made.

1. A payment on account of $830 to a creditor was debited to Accounts Payable $380 and credited to Cash $380.
2. The purchase of supplies on account for $560 was debited to Equipment $56 and credited to Accounts Payable $56.
3. A $400 cash dividend was debited to Salaries Expense $400 and credited to Cash $400.

Instructions

Prepare the correcting entries.

Prepare a classified balance sheet.
(SO 6)

E4-10 The adjusted trial balance for Rego Bowling Alley Inc. at December 31, 2006, contains the following accounts.

Debits		**Credits**	
Building	$128,800	Common Stock	$100,000
Accounts Receivable	14,520	Retained Earnings	15,000
Prepaid Insurance	4,680	Accumulated Depreciation—Building	45,600
Cash	18,040	Accounts Payable	12,300
Equipment	62,400	Mortgage Payable	94,780
Land	64,000	Accumulated Depreciation—Equipment	18,720
Insurance Expense	780	Interest Payable	2,600
Depreciation Expense	7,360	Bowling Revenues	14,180
Interest Expense	2,600		$303,180
	$303,180		

Instructions

(a) Prepare a classified balance sheet; assume that $13,600 of the mortgage payable will be paid in 2007.

(b) Comment on the liquidity of the company.

Prepare closing and reversing entries.

(SO 2, 4, 7)

*__E4-11__ On December 31, the adjusted trial balance of Garg Employment Agency shows the following selected data.

Accounts Receivable	$24,000	Commission Revenue	$92,000
Interest Expense	7,800	Interest Payable	1,500

Analysis shows that adjusting entries were made to (1) accrue $4,200 of commission revenue and (2) accrue $1,500 interest expense.

Instructions

(a) Prepare the closing entries for the temporary accounts at December 31.

(b) Prepare the reversing entries on January 1.

(c) Post the entries in (a) and (b). Rule and balance the accounts. (Use T accounts.)

(d) Prepare the entries to record (1) the collection of the accrued commissions on January 10 and (2) the payment of all interest due ($2,700) on January 15.

(e) Post the entries in (d) to the temporary accounts.

PROBLEMS: SET A

Prepare a work sheet, financial statements, and adjusting and closing entries.

(SO 1, 2, 3, 6)

P4-1A The trial balance columns of the work sheet for Undercover Roofing Inc. at March 31, 2006, are as follows.

UNDERCOVER ROOFING INC.
Work Sheet
For the Month Ended March 31, 2006

Account Titles	Trial Balance Dr.	Trial Balance Cr.
Cash	2,500	
Accounts Receivable	1,800	
Roofing Supplies	1,100	
Equipment	6,000	
Accumulated Depreciation—Equipment		1,200
Accounts Payable		1,400
Unearned Revenue		300
Common Stock		5,000
Retained Earnings		2,000
Dividends	600	
Service Revenue		3,000
Salaries Expense	700	
Miscellaneous Expense	200	
	12,900	12,900

Other data:

1. A physical count reveals only $140 of roofing supplies on hand.
2. Depreciation for March is $200.
3. Unearned revenue amounted to $130 after adjustment on March 31.
4. Accrued salaries are $350.

Instructions

(a) Enter the trial balance on a work sheet and complete the work sheet.

(b) Prepare an income statement and a retained earnings statement for the month of March and a classified balance sheet at March 31. No additional issuances of stock occured in March.

(c) Journalize the adjusting entries from the adjustments columns of the work sheet.

(d) Journalize the closing entries from the financial statement columns of the work sheet.

(a) Adjusted trial balance $13,450
(b) Net income $ 760
Total assets $9,040

Complete work sheet; prepare financial statements, closing entries, and post-closing trial balance.

(SO 1, 2, 3, 6)

P4-2A The adjusted trial balance columns of the work sheet for Eagle Company, owned by Alfred Eagle, are as follows.

EAGLE COMPANY
Work Sheet
For the Year Ended December 31, 2006

Account No.	Account Titles	Adjusted Trial Balance Dr.	Adjusted Trial Balance Cr.
101	Cash	13,600	
112	Accounts Receivable	15,400	
126	Supplies	2,000	
130	Prepaid Insurance	2,800	
151	Office Equipment	34,000	
152	Accumulated Depreciation—Office Equipment		8,000
200	Notes Payable		20,000
201	Accounts Payable		6,000
212	Salaries Payable		3,500
230	Interest Payable		800
311	Common Stock		20,000
320	Retained Earnings		5,000
332	Dividends	10,000	
400	Service Revenue		88,000
610	Advertising Expense	12,000	
631	Supplies Expense	5,700	
711	Depreciation Expense	8,000	
722	Insurance Expense	5,000	
726	Salaries Expense	42,000	
905	Interest Expense	800	
	Totals	151,300	151,300

Instructions

(a) Net income $14,500
(b) Current assets $33,800; Current liabilities $20,300
(e) Post-closing trial balance $67,800

(a) Complete the work sheet by extending the balances to the financial statement columns.
(b) Prepare an income statement, a retained earnings statement, and a classified balance sheet. (*Note:* $10,000 of the notes payable become due in 2007.) No additional issuances of stock occured during 2006.
(c) Prepare the closing entries. Use J14 for the journal page.
(d) Post the closing entries. Use the three-column form of account. Income Summary is No. 350.
(e) Prepare a post-closing trial balance.

Prepare financial statements, closing entries, and post-closing trial balance.

(SO 1, 2, 3, 6)

P4-3A The completed financial statement columns of the work sheet for Lathrop Company are shown below and on the next page.

LATHROP COMPANY
Work Sheet
For the Year Ended December 31, 2006

Account No.	Account Titles	Income Statement Dr.	Income Statement Cr.	Balance Sheet Dr.	Balance Sheet Cr.
101	Cash			17,400	
112	Accounts Receivable			13,500	
130	Prepaid Insurance			3,500	
157	Equipment			26,000	
167	Accumulated Depreciation				5,600
201	Accounts Payable				11,300
212	Salaries Payable				3,000
311	Common Stock				20,000
320	Retained Earnings				16,000
332	Dividends			14,000	
400	Service Revenue		64,000		
622	Repair Expense	2,000			
711	Depreciation Expense	2,600			
722	Insurance Expense	2,200			

Account No.	Account Titles	Income Statement Dr.	Income Statement Cr.	Balance Sheet Dr.	Balance Sheet Cr.
726	Salaries Expense	37,000			
732	Utilities Expense	1,700			
	Totals	45,500	64,000	74,400	55,900
	Net Income	18,500			18,500
		64,000	64,000	74,400	74,400

Instructions

(a) Prepare an income statement, a retained earnings statement, and a classified balance sheet.
(b) Prepare the closing entries. No additional shares of stock were issued during the year.
(c) Post the closing entries and rule and balance the accounts. Use T accounts. Income Summary is account No. 350.
(d) Prepare a post-closing trial balance.

(a) Ending retained earnings $20,500
Total current assets $34,400
(d) Post-closing trial balance $60,400

P4-4A Nish Kumar Management Services Inc. began business on January 1, 2006, with a capital investment of $120,000. The company manages condominiums for owners (Service Revenue) and rents space in its own office building (Rent Revenue). The trial balance and adjusted trial balance columns of the work sheet at the end of the first year are as follows.

Complete work sheet; prepare classified balance sheet, entries, and post-closing trial balance.

(SO 1, 2, 3, 6)

Peachtree

NISH KUMAR MANAGEMENT SERVICES INC.
Work Sheet
For the Year Ended December 31, 2006

Account Titles	Trial Balance Dr.	Trial Balance Cr.	Adjusted Trial Balance Dr.	Adjusted Trial Balance Cr.
Cash	14,500		14,500	
Accounts Receivable	23,600		23,600	
Prepaid Insurance	3,100		1,400	
Land	56,000		56,000	
Building	106,000		106,000	
Equipment	49,000		49,000	
Accounts Payable		10,400		10,400
Unearned Rent Revenue		5,000		2,800
Mortgage Payable		100,000		100,000
Common Stock		120,000		120,000
Retained Earnings		–0–		–0–
Dividends	20,000		20,000	
Service Revenue		75,600		75,600
Rent Revenue		24,000		26,200
Salaries Expense	30,000		30,000	
Advertising Expense	17,000		17,000	
Utilities Expense	15,800		15,800	
Totals	335,000	335,000		
Insurance Expense			1,700	
Depreciation Expense—Building			2,500	
Accumulated Depreciation—Building				2,500
Depreciation Expense—Equipment			3,900	
Accumulated Depreciation—Equipment				3,900
Interest Expense			9,000	
Interest Payable				9,000
Totals			350,400	350,400

Instructions

(a) Prepare a complete work sheet.
(b) Prepare a classified balance sheet. (*Note*: $10,000 of the mortgage payable is due for payment next year.)
(c) Journalize the adjusting entries.
(d) Journalize the closing entries.
(e) Prepare a post-closing trial balance.

(a) Net income $21,900
(b) Total current assets $39,500
(e) Post-closing trial balance $250,500

Complete all steps in accounting cycle.
(SO 1, 2, 3, 4, 6)

Peachtree

P4-5A Eve Tsai opened Tsai's Window Washing Corp. on July 1, 2006. During July the following transactions were completed.

July	1	Issued $12,000 of common stock for $12,000 cash.
	1	Purchased used truck for $6,000, paying $3,000 cash and the balance on account.
	3	Purchased cleaning supplies for $1,300 on account.
	5	Paid $1,200 cash on one-year insurance policy effective July 1.
	12	Billed customers $2,500 for cleaning services.
	18	Paid $1,000 cash on amount owed on truck and $800 on amount owed on cleaning supplies.
	20	Paid $1,200 cash for employee salaries.
	21	Collected $1,400 cash from customers billed on July 12.
	25	Billed customers $3,000 for cleaning services.
	31	Paid gas and oil for month on truck $200.
	31	Declared and paid $900 cash dividend.

The chart of accounts for Tsai's Window Washing Corp. contains the following accounts: No. 101 Cash, No. 112 Accounts Receivable, No. 128 Cleaning Supplies, No. 130 Prepaid Insurance, No. 157 Equipment, No. 158 Accumulated Depreciation—Equipment, No. 201 Accounts Payable, No. 212 Salaries Payable, No. 311 Common Stock, No. 320 Retained Earnings, No. 332 Dividends, No. 350 Income Summary, No. 400 Service Revenue, No. 633 Gas & Oil Expense, No. 634 Cleaning Supplies Expense, No. 711 Depreciation Expense, No. 722 Insurance Expense, and No. 726 Salaries Expense.

Instructions

(a) Journalize and post the July transactions. Use page J1 for the journal and the three-column form of account.

(b) Trial balance $20,000

(b) Prepare a trial balance at July 31 on a work sheet.

(c) Adjusted trial balance $22,300

(c) Enter the following adjustments on the work sheet and complete the work sheet.
   (1) Services provided but unbilled and uncollected at July 31 were $1,500.
   (2) Depreciation on equipment for the month was $200.
   (3) One-twelfth of the insurance expired.
   (4) An inventory count shows $600 of cleaning supplies on hand at July 31.
   (5) Accrued but unpaid employee salaries were $600.

(d) Journalize and post adjusting entries. Use page J2 for the journal.

(e) Net income $4,000; Total assets $18,200

(e) Prepare the income statement and a retained earnings statement for July and a classified balance sheet at July 31.

(f) Journalize and post closing entries and complete the closing process. Use page J3 for the journal.

(g) Post-closing trial balance $18,400

(g) Prepare a post-closing trial balance at July 31.

Analyze errors and prepare correcting entries and trial balance.
(SO 5)

P4-6A Tom Brennan, CPA, was retained by 24/7 Cable Inc. to prepare financial statements for April 2006. Brennan accumulated all the ledger balances per 24/7's records and found the following.

24/7 CABLE INC.
Trial Balance
April 30, 2006

	Debit	Credit
Cash	$ 4,100	
Accounts Receivable	3,200	
Supplies	800	
Equipment	10,600	
Accumulated Depreciation		$ 1,350
Accounts Payable		2,100
Salaries Payable		500
Unearned Revenue		890
Common Stock		10,000
Retained Earnings		2,900
Service Revenue		5,450
Salaries Expense	3,300	
Advertising Expense	400	
Miscellaneous Expense	290	
Depreciation Expense	500	
	$23,190	$23,190

Tom Brennan reviewed the records and found the following errors.

1. Cash received from a customer on account was recorded as $870 instead of $780.
2. A payment of $65 for advertising expense was entered as a debit to Miscellaneous Expense $65 and a credit to Cash $65.
3. The first salary payment this month was for $1,900, which included $500 of salaries payable on March 31. The payment was recorded as a debit to Salaries Expense $1,900 and a credit to Cash $1,900. (No reversing entries were made on April 1.)
4. The purchase on account of a printer costing $290 was recorded as a debit to Supplies and a credit to Accounts Payable for $290.
5. A cash payment of repair expense on equipment for $95 was recorded as a debit to Equipment $59 and a credit to Cash $59.

Instructions

(a) Prepare an analysis of each error showing (1) the incorrect entry, (2) the correct entry, and (3) the correcting entry. Items 4 and 5 occurred on April 30, 2006.

(b) Prepare a correct trial balance.

Trial balance $22,690

PROBLEMS: SET B

P4-1B Sherlock Holmes began operations as a private investigator on January 1, 2006. The trial balance columns of the work sheet for Sherlock Holmes P.I. at March 31 are as follows.

Prepare work sheet, financial statements, and adjusting and closing entries.

(SO 1, 2, 3, 6)

SHERLOCK HOLMES P.I.
Work Sheet
For the Quarter Ended March 31, 2006

	Trial Balance	
Account Titles	**Dr.**	**Cr.**
Cash	11,400	
Accounts Receivable	5,620	
Supplies	1,050	
Prepaid Insurance	2,400	
Equipment	30,000	
Notes Payable		10,000
Accounts Payable		12,350
Common Stock		20,000
Dividends	600	
Service Revenue		13,620
Salaries Expense	2,200	
Travel Expense	1,300	
Rent Expense	1,200	
Miscellaneous Expense	200	
	55,970	55,970

Other data:

1. Supplies on hand total $680.
2. Depreciation is $1,000 per quarter.
3. Interest accrued on 6-month note payable, issued January 1, $300.
4. Insurance expires at the rate of $200 per month.
5. Services provided but unbilled at March 31 total $830.

Instructions

(a) Enter the trial balance on a work sheet and complete the work sheet.

(b) Prepare an income statement and a retained earnings statement for the quarter and a classified balance sheet at March 31. Stockholders purchased $20,000 of common stock for cash at the beginning of the quarter ended March 31, 2006.

(c) Journalize the adjusting entries from the adjustments columns of the work sheet.

(d) Journalize the closing entries from the financial statement columns of the work sheet.

(a) Adjusted trial balance $58,100
(b) Net income $ 7,280
Total assets $49,330

Complete work sheet; prepare financial statements, closing entries, and post-closing trial balance.

(SO 1, 2, 3, 6)

P4-2B The adjusted trial balance columns of the work sheet for Mr. Watson Company are as follows.

MR. WATSON COMPANY
Work Sheet
For the Year Ended December 31, 2006

Account No.	Account Titles	Adjusted Trial Balance Dr.	Adjusted Trial Balance Cr.
101	Cash	20,800	
112	Accounts Receivable	16,200	
126	Supplies	2,300	
130	Prepaid Insurance	4,400	
151	Office Equipment	44,000	
152	Accumulated Depreciation—Office Equipment		18,000
200	Notes Payable		20,000
201	Accounts Payable		8,000
212	Salaries Payable		2,600
230	Interest Payable		1,000
311	Common Stock		20,000
320	Retained Earnings		16,000
332	Dividends	12,000	
400	Service Revenue		79,800
610	Advertising Expense	12,000	
631	Supplies Expense	3,700	
711	Depreciation Expense	6,000	
722	Insurance Expense	4,000	
726	Salaries Expense	39,000	
905	Interest Expense	1,000	
	Totals	165,400	165,400

Instructions

(a) Net income $14,100
(b) Current assets $43,700
Current liabilities $21,600
(e) Post-closing trial balance $87,700

(a) Complete the work sheet by extending the balances to the financial statement columns.
(b) Prepare an income statement, a retained earnings statement, and a classified balance sheet. $10,000 of the notes payable become due in 2007. No additional issuances of stock occured during 2006.
(c) Prepare the closing entries. Use J14 for the journal page.
(d) Post the closing entries. Use the three-column form of account. Income Summary is account No. 350.
(e) Prepare a post-closing trial balance.

Prepare financial statements, closing entries, and post-closing trial balance.

(SO 1, 2, 3, 6)

P4-3B The completed financial statement columns of the work sheet for Hubbs Company are shown below and on page 181.

HUBBS COMPANY
Work Sheet
For the Year Ended December 31, 2006

Account No.	Account Titles	Income Statement Dr.	Income Statement Cr.	Balance Sheet Dr.	Balance Sheet Cr.
101	Cash			10,200	
112	Accounts Receivable			7,500	
130	Prepaid Insurance			1,800	
157	Equipment			28,000	
167	Accumulated Depreciation				8,600
201	Accounts Payable				11,700
212	Salaries Payable				3,000
311	Common Stock				20,000
320	Retained Earnings				14,000

Account No.	Account Titles	Income Statement Dr.	Income Statement Cr.	Balance Sheet Dr.	Balance Sheet Cr.
332	Dividends			7,200	
400	Service Revenue		44,000		
622	Repair Expense	3,400			
711	Depreciation Expense	2,800			
722	Insurance Expense	1,200			
726	Salaries Expense	35,200			
732	Utilities Expense	4,000			
	Totals	46,600	44,000	54,700	57,300
	Net Loss		2,600	2,600	
		46,600	46,600	57,300	57,300

Instructions

(a) Prepare an income statement, a retained earnings statement, and a classified balance sheet. Stockholders made additional purchases of common stock of $4,000 during 2006.

(a) Net loss $2,600
Total assets $38,900

(b) Prepare the closing entries.

(c) Post the closing entries and rule and balance the accounts. Use T accounts. Income Summary is account No. 350.

(d) Prepare a post-closing trial balance.

(d) Post-closing trial balance $47,500

P4-4B London Amusement Park Inc. has a fiscal year ending on September 30. Selected data from the September 30 work sheet are presented below.

Complete work sheet; prepare classified balance sheet, entries, and post-closing trial balance.

(SO 1, 2, 3, 6)

LONDON AMUSEMENT PARK INC.
Work Sheet
For the Year Ended September 30, 2006

	Trial Balance Dr.	Trial Balance Cr.	Adjusted Trial Balance Dr.	Adjusted Trial Balance Cr.
Cash	41,400		41,400	
Supplies	18,600		1,200	
Prepaid Insurance	31,900		3,900	
Land	80,000		80,000	
Equipment	120,000		120,000	
Accumulated Depreciation		36,200		42,200
Accounts Payable		14,600		14,600
Unearned Admissions Revenue		3,700		1,000
Mortgage Payable		50,000		50,000
Common Stock		100,000		100,000
Retained Earnings		9,700		9,700
Dividends	14,000		14,000	
Admissions Revenue		277,500		280,200
Salaries Expense	105,000		105,000	
Repair Expense	30,500		30,500	
Advertising Expense	9,400		9,400	
Utilities Expense	16,900		16,900	
Property Taxes Expense	18,000		21,000	
Interest Expense	6,000		10,000	
Totals	491,700	491,700		
Insurance Expense			28,000	
Supplies Expense			17,400	
Interest Payable				4,000
Depreciation Expense			6,000	
Property Taxes Payable				3,000
Totals			504,700	504,700

Instructions

(a) Net income $36,000
(b) Total current assets $46,500
(e) Post-closing trial balance $246,500

(a) Prepare a complete work sheet.
(b) Prepare a classified balance sheet. (*Note*: $10,000 of the mortgage payable is due for payment in the next fiscal year.)
(c) Journalize the adjusting entries using the work sheet as a basis.
(d) Journalize the closing entries using the work sheet as a basis.
(e) Prepare a post-closing trial balance.

Complete all steps in accounting cycle.
(SO 1, 2, 3, 4, 6)

P4-5B Mike Young opened Young's Carpet Cleaners Inc. on March 1. During March, the following transactions were completed.

Mar.	1	Issued $10,000 of common stock for $10,000 cash.
	1	Purchased used truck for $6,000, paying $3,000 cash and the balance on account.
	3	Purchased cleaning supplies for $1,200 on account.
	5	Paid $1,800 cash on one-year insurance policy effective March 1.
	14	Billed customers $2,800 for cleaning services.
	18	Paid $1,500 cash on amount owed on truck and $500 on amount owed on cleaning supplies.
	20	Paid $1,800 cash for employee salaries.
	21	Collected $1,400 cash from customers billed on March 14.
	28	Billed customers $2,500 for cleaning services.
	31	Paid gas and oil for month on truck $200.
	31	Declared and paid $700 cash dividend.

The chart of accounts for Young's Carpet Cleaners Inc. contains the following accounts: No. 101 Cash, No. 112 Accounts Receivable, No. 128 Cleaning Supplies, No. 130 Prepaid Insurance, No. 157 Equipment, No. 158 Accumulated Depreciation—Equipment, No. 201 Accounts Payable, No. 212 Salaries Payable, No. 311 Common Stock, No. 320 Retained Earnings, No. 332 Dividends, No. 350 Income Summary, No. 400 Service Revenue, No. 633 Gas & Oil Expense, No. 634 Cleaning Supplies Expense, No. 711 Depreciation Expense, No. 722 Insurance Expense, and No. 726 Salaries Expense.

Instructions

(b) Trial balance $17,500
(c) Adjusted trial balance $18,950
(e) Net income $ 2,500
Total assets $14,500
(g) Post-closing trial balance $14,750

(a) Journalize and post the March transactions. Use page J1 for the journal and the three-column form of account.
(b) Prepare a trial balance at March 31 on a work sheet.
(c) Enter the following adjustments on the work sheet and complete the work sheet.
   (1) Earned but unbilled revenue at March 31 was $700.
   (2) Depreciation on equipment for the month was $250.
   (3) One-twelfth of the insurance expired.
   (4) An inventory count shows $600 of cleaning supplies on hand at March 31.
   (5) Accrued but unpaid employee salaries were $500.
(d) Journalize and post adjusting entries. Use page J2 for the journal.
(e) Prepare the income statement and a retained earnings statement for March and a classified balance sheet at March 31.
(f) Journalize and post closing entries and complete the closing process. Use page J3 for the journal.
(g) Prepare a post-closing trial balance at March 31.

COMPREHENSIVE PROBLEM: CHAPTERS 2 TO 4

Mary Coleman opened Mary's Maids Cleaning Service Inc. on July 1, 2006. During July, the following transactions were completed.

July	1	Issued $14,000 of common stock for $14,000 cash.
	1	Purchased a used truck for $10,000, paying $3,000 cash and the balance on account.
	3	Purchased cleaning supplies for $800 on account.
	5	Paid $2,400 on a one-year insurance policy, effective July 1.
	12	Billed customers $3,800 for cleaning services.
	18	Paid $1,000 of amount owed on truck, and $400 of amount owed on cleaning supplies.
	20	Paid $1,600 for employee salaries.

21 Collected $1,400 from customers billed on July 12.
25 Billed customers $2,500 for cleaning services.
31 Paid gas and oil for the month on the truck, $400.
31 Declared and paid a $600 cash dividend.

The chart of accounts for Mary's Maids Cleaning Service Inc. contains the following accounts: No. 101 Cash, No. 112 Accounts Receivable, No. 128 Cleaning Supplies, No. 130 Prepaid Insurance, No. 157 Equipment, No. 158 Accumulated Depreciation—Equipment, No. 201 Accounts Payable, No. 212 Salaries Payable, No. 311 Common Stock, No. 320 Retained Earnings, No. 332 Dividends, No. 350 Income Summary, No. 400 Service Revenue, No. 633 Gas & Oil Expense, No. 634 Cleaning Supplies Expense, No. 711 Depreciation Expense, No. 722 Insurance Expense, and No. 726 Salaries Expense.

Instructions

(a) Journalize and post the July transactions. Use page J1 for the journal.
(b) Prepare a trial balance at July 31 on a work sheet.
(c) Enter the following adjustments on the work sheet, and complete the work sheet.
  (1) Earned but unbilled fees at July 31 were $1,300.
  (2) Depreciation on equipment for the month was $200.
  (3) One-twelfth of the insurance expired.
  (4) An inventory count shows $300 of cleaning supplies on hand at July 31.
  (5) Accrued but unpaid employee salaries were $500.
(d) Journalize and post the adjusting entries. Use page J2 for the journal.
(e) Prepare the income statement and a retained earnings statement for July, and a classified balance sheet at July 31, 2006.
(f) Journalize and post the closing entries, and complete the closing process. Use page J3 for the journal.
(g) Prepare a post-closing trial balance at July 31.

(b) Trial balance totals $26,700

(e) Net income $4,200
Total assets $24,500

(g) Trial balance totals $24,700

BROADENING YOUR PERSPECTIVE

Financial Reporting and Analysis

■ FINANCIAL REPORTING PROBLEM: PepsiCo

BYP4-1 The financial statements of **PepsiCo, Inc.** are presented in Appendix A at the end of this textbook.

Instructions

Answer the following questions using the Consolidated Balance Sheet and the Notes to Consolidated Financial Statements section.

(a) What were PepsiCo's total current assets at December 27, 2003 and December 28, 2002?
(b) Are assets that PepsiCo included under current assets listed in proper order? Explain.
(c) How are PepsiCo's assets classified?
(d) What are "cash equivalents"?
(e) What were PepsiCo's total current liabilities at December 27, 2003 and December 28, 2002?

■ COMPARATIVE ANALYSIS PROBLEM: PepsiCo vs. Coca-Cola

BYP4-2 **PepsiCo**'s financial statements are presented in Appendix A. **Coca-Cola**'s financial statements are presented in Appendix B.

Instructions

(a) Based on the information contained in these financial statements, determine each of the following for PepsiCo at December 27, 2003, and for Coca-Cola at December 31, 2003.
  (1) Total current assets.
  (2) Net amount of property, plant, and equipment (land, buildings, and equipment).
  (3) Total current liabilities.
  (4) Total stockholders' (shareholders') equity.
(b) What conclusions concerning the companies' respective financial positions can be drawn?

■ RESEARCH CASE

BYP4-3 The February 21, 2002, issue of the *Wall Street Journal* includes an article by Ken Brown titled "Creative Accounting: Four Areas to Buff Up a Company's Picture."

Instructions

Read the article and do the following.

Although the title says "four areas," it actually describes five ways that companies inappropriately manipulate their financial statements. Describe each of these five methods. For each method, give an example of a company that has been accused of using the method, and describe what that specific company was accused of.

■ INTERPRETING FINANCIAL STATEMENTS

BYP4-4 **Laser Recording Systems**, founded in 1981, produces disks for use in the home market. The following is an excerpt from Laser Recording Systems financial statements (all dollars in thousands).

LASER RECORDING SYSTEMS
Management Discussion

Accrued liabilities increased to $1,642 at January 31, from $138 at the end of the previous fiscal year. Compensation and related accruals increased $195 due primarily to increases in accruals for severance, vacation, commissions, and relocation expenses. Accrued professional services increased by $137 primarily as a result of legal expenses related to several outstanding contractual disputes. Other expenses increased $35, of which $18 was for interest payable.

Instructions

(a) Can you tell from the discussion whether Laser Recording Systems has prepaid its legal expenses and is now making an adjustment to the asset account Prepaid Legal Expenses, or whether the company is handling the legal expense via an accrued expense adjustment?

(b) Identify each of the adjustments Laser Recording Systems is discussing as one of the four types of possible adjustments discussed in Chapter 3. How is net income ultimately affected by each of the adjustments?

(c) What journal entry did Laser Recording make to record the accrued interest?

■ A GLOBAL FOCUS

BYP4-5 **Lign Multiwood** is a Swedish forest products company. Its statements conform with the standards of the Swedish Standards Board. Its financial statements are presented to have minimal difference in methods with member countries of the European Union. The balance sheet presented on page 185 is from its 2000 annual report.

Instructions

List all differences that you notice between Lign Multiwood's balance sheet presentation (format and terminology) and the presentation of U.S. companies shown in the chapter: For differences in terminology, list the corresponding terminology used by U.S. companies.

■ EXPLORING THE WEB

www.wiley.com/college/weygandt

BYP4-6 Numerous companies have established home pages on the Internet, e.g., **Boston Beer Company (www.samadams.com)** and **Kodak (www.kodak.com).**

Instructions

Examine the home pages of any two companies and answer the following questions.

(a) What type of information is available?

(b) Is any accounting-related information presented?

(c) Would you describe the home page as informative, promotional, or both? Why?

LIGN MULTIWOOD
Balance Sheet
at December 31
(Swedish kronor)

ASSETS	2000	1999
Fixed assets		
Intangible fixed assets		
Balanced expenses for development work	28 407 064	12 056 864
Licence rights	1 200 000	600 000
	29 607 064	12 656 864
Material fixed assets		
Machinery and other technical plant	33 608 189	34 606 812
Fittings & fixtures, tools and installations	564 952	163 020
	34 173 141	34 769 832
Financial fixed assets		
Other long-term securities holdings	165 000	165 000
Deferred tax claim	3 042 000	1 129 000
	3 207 000	1 294 000
Total fixed assets	66 987 205	48 720 696
Current assets		
Stocks held, etc.		
Stocks of test materials	554 000	116 924
	554 000	116 924
Short-term receivables		
Customer receivables	727 159	652 662
Other receivables	1 099 197	711 979
Prepaid costs and accrued income	2 479 411	1 620 467
	4 305 767	2 985 108
Cash in hand and on deposit	17 965 269	40 755 806
Total current assets	22 825 036	43 857 838
TOTAL ASSETS	89 812 241	92 578 534
EQUITY CAPITAL AND LIABILITIES		
Equity capital		
Tied equity capital		
Share capital	2 825 740	2 825 740
Tied reserves	56 745 410	56 745 410
	59 571 150	59 571 150
Accumulated loss		
Balanced loss	−2 801 000	− 598 000
Year's profit/loss	−4 933 000	−2 203 000
	−7 734 000	−2 801 000
	51 837 150	56 770 150
Minority interest	40 000	40 000
Long-term liabilities		
Other liabilities	33 619 451	34 162 457
	33 619 451	34 162 457
Short-term liabilities		
Accounts payable	2 151 435	1 232 505
Other liabilities	959 044	64 099
Accrued costs and prepaid income	1 205 161	309 323
	4 315 640	1 605 927
TOTAL EQUITY CAPITAL AND LIABILITIES	89 812 241	92 578 534

Critical Thinking

GROUP DECISION CASE

BYP4-7 Everclean Janitorial Service Inc. was started 2 years ago by Laurie Merar. Because business has been exceptionally good, Laurie decided on July 1, 2006, to expand operations by acquiring an additional truck and hiring two more assistants. To finance the expansion, Laurie obtained on July 1, 2006, a $25,000, 10% bank loan, payable $10,000 on July 1, 2007, and the balance on July 1, 2008. The terms of the loan require the borrower to have $10,000 more current assets than current liabilities at December 31, 2006. If these terms are not met, the bank loan will be refinanced at 15% interest. At December 31, 2006, the accountant for Everclean Janitorial Service Inc. prepared the balance sheet shown below.

Laurie presented the balance sheet to the bank's loan officer on January 2, 2007, confident that the company had met the terms of the loan. The loan officer was not impressed. She said, "We need financial statements audited by a CPA." A CPA was hired and immediately realized that the balance sheet had been prepared from a trial balance and not from an adjusted trial balance. The adjustment data at the balance sheet date consisted of the following.

(1) Earned but unbilled janitorial services were $5,700.
(2) Janitorial supplies on hand were $2,800.
(3) Prepaid insurance was a 3-year policy dated January 1, 2006.
(4) December expenses incurred but unpaid at December 31, $700.
(5) Interest on the bank loan was not recorded.
(6) The amounts for property, plant, and equipment in the balance sheet were reported net of accumulated depreciation (cost less accumulated depreciation). These amounts were $4,000 for cleaning equipment and $5,000 for delivery trucks as of January 1, 2006. Depreciation for 2006 was $2,000 for cleaning equipment and $5,000 for delivery trucks.

EVERCLEAN JANITORIAL SERVICE INC.
Balance Sheet
December 31, 2006

Assets		**Liabilities and Stockholders' Equity**		
Current assets		Current liabilities		
Cash	$ 6,500	Notes payable		$10,000
Accounts receivable	9,000	Accounts payable		2,500
Janitorial supplies	5,200	Total current liabilities		12,500
Prepaid insurance	4,800	Long-term liability		
Total current assets	25,500	Notes payable		15,000
Property, plant, and equipment		Total liabilities		27,500
Cleaning equipment (net)	22,000	Stockholders' equity		
Delivery trucks (net)	34,000	Common stock	$40,000	
Total property, plant, and equipment	56,000	Retained earnings	14,000	54,000
Total assets	$81,500	Total liabilities and stockholders' equity		$81,500

Instructions

With the class divided into groups, answer the following.

(a) Prepare a correct balance sheet.
(b) Were the terms of the bank loan met? Explain.

COMMUNICATION ACTIVITY

BYP4-8 The accounting cycle is important in understanding the accounting process.

Instructions

Write a memo to your instructor that lists the steps of the accounting cycle in the order they should be completed. End with a paragraph that explains the optional steps in the cycle.

■ ETHICS CASE

Accounting Matters!

BYP4-9 As the controller of Take No Prisoners Perfume Company, you discover a misstatement that overstated net income in the prior year's financial statements. The misleading financial statements appear in the company's annual report which was issued to banks and other creditors less than a month ago. After much thought about the consequences of telling the president, Rocky Balboa, about this misstatement, you gather your courage to inform him. Rocky says, "Hey! What they don't know won't hurt them. But, just so we set the record straight, we'll adjust this year's financial statements for last year's misstatement. We can absorb that misstatement better in this year than in last year anyway! Just don't make such a mistake again."

Instructions

(a) Who are the stakeholders in this situation?
(b) What are the ethical issues in this situation?
(c) What would you do as a controller in this situation?

■ CONTINUING COOKIE CHRONICLE

Accounting Matters!

(Note: The Continuing Cookie Chronicle was started in Chapter 1 and continued in Chapters 2 and 3.)

BYP4-10 Natalie is gearing up for the holiday season. During the month of December, the following transactions happen.

Dec. 1 Natalie hires an assistant to help with cookie making and to do some administrative duties. Natalie and her assistant agree on an hourly rate of $8.
4 Natalie teaches the class that was booked on November 25 and receives the balance outstanding.
8 She collects the amount due from the neighborhood school that was accrued at the end of November, 2005.
10 She receives $625 in advance from the local school board for five classes that are to be given during December and January.
15 She pays for the cell phone bill accrued in the adjusting journal entries in November 2005.
16 Natalie issues a check to her brother for payment of the Web site he set up in November 2005.
18 She receives a deposit of $50 on a cookie class that is scheduled for early January.
24 Natalie adds up all of the additional revenue for the classes taught during the month. She has not had time to account for each class individually. She determines that during the period December 1 to 24 she taught $3,500 worth of cookie-making classes. For these classes, she has collected $3,000 in cash and sent out invoices for $500. (This is in addition to the December 4 and the December 10 transactions.)
24 Natalie adds up all of the sugar, flour, and chocolate chips she purchased during the month. In total she paid $1,250 for these baking supplies.
24 Natalie issues a check to her assistant for $800. Her assistant worked approximately 100 hours from the time she started working for Natalie until December 24.
24 Because Natalie has had such a busy December doing school work and giving lessons, she decides to take the rest of the month off.
24 Cash dividends on $500 are paid.

As at December 31, the following adjusting entry data are available:

1. A count reveals that $50 of brochures and posters remain at the end of December.
2. Another month's worth of depreciation needs to be recorded on the baking equipment purchased in November. (The baking equipment has a useful life of 5 years or 60 months.)
3. One month's worth of amortization needs to be recorded for the Web site. (Recall that the Web site has a useful life of 2 years or 24 months.)
4. An additional month's worth of interest on her grandmother's loan needs to be accrued. (Recall that the interest rate is 6%.)
5. One month's worth of insurance has expired.
6. Natalie is unexpectedly telephoned on December 28 to give a cookie class at the neighborhood community center. In January, she invoices the center for $375. The invoice will be paid some time in early January.

7. A count on December 31 reveals that $1,000 of baking supplies were used during December.
8. Natalie receives her cell phone bill, $75. The bill is for services provided during the month of December and is due January 15. (Recall that the cell phone is only used for business.)
9. Because the cookie-making class on December 28 is for such a large group of children, Natalie's assistant helps out. Her assistant works 7 hours at a rate of $8 per hour.
10. An analysis of the unearned revenue account reveals that two of the five classes paid for by the local school board on December 10 have still not been taught by the end of December. The $50 deposit received on December 18 for another class also remains unearned.

Instructions

Using the information that you have gathered through Chapter 3, the general ledger accounts already prepared, and the new information above, do the following.

(a) Prepare and post the December 2005 transactions. (Use the general ledger accounts that you prepared in Chapter 3.)
(b) Prepare a trial balance as at December 31, 2005.
(c) Prepare and post adjusting journal entries for the month of December.
(d) Prepare an adjusted trial balance as at December 31, 2005.
(e) Prepare an income statement and a retained earnings for the 2 months ended December 31, 2005, and a classified balance sheet as at December 31, 2005.
(f) Prepare and post closing entries as at December 31, 2005.
(g) Prepare a post-closing trial balance.

Accounting Matters!

Answers to Accounting Matters! Questions

p. 145

Q: What are the advantages of an electronic worksheet over a pencil-and-paper version?

A: Preparation of an electronic worksheet on a computer is faster and easier, and also generally more accurate and flexible, than a manually produced pencil-and-paper version. Ability to prepare electronic worksheets is a competency that is expected of today's accountants.

p. 150

Q: How did Sam Walton know the "books didn't balance"?

A: Using the trial balance and the adjusted trial balance, Sam could see that the debits and credits either balanced or did not balance. Also, the accounting equation did not balance (Assets ≠ Liabilities + Common Stock + Retained Earnings − Dividends + Revenues − Expenses).

p. 150

Q: In what circumstances today might the ESP method be acceptable?

A: The ESP method might be acceptable today in looking at interim (e.g., month's end) results. It might also be used by sole proprietors who determine that they do not want to "spend dollars looking for pennies." However, the ESP method cannot be used by companies who must report the results of operations to regulators or the public.

p. 152

Q: If you do not have the IT resources to do a "virtual close," can the net income or net loss be known without "closing the books"?

A: The net income or net loss can be determined by preparing an income statement from the adjusted trial balance without formally closing the books—that is, without closing (balancing and ruling) every revenue and expense account.

p. 157

Q: What might Yale Express's vice president have done to produce more accurate financial statements without waiting months for Republic's outstanding transportation bills?

A: Yale's vice president could have engaged his accountants and auditors to prepare an adjusting entry based on an estimate of the outstanding transportation bills. (The estimate could have been made considering past experience and the current volume of business.)

Answers to PepsiCo Review It Question 2, p. 164

PepsiCo's current liabilities in 2003 were $6,415 million. Current liabilities in 2002 were $6,052 million. In both 2003 and 2002, current liabilities were less than current assets.

Answers to Self-Study Questions

1. c **2.** b **3.** d **4.** a **5.** d **6.** b **7.** a **8.** c **9.** c **10.** b **11.** b

REMEMBER to go back to the Navigator box on the chapter-opening page and check off your completed work.

Chapter 5

Accounting for Merchandising Operations

THE NAVIGATOR ✓

- Understand **Concepts for Review** ❑
- Read **Feature Story** ❑
- Scan **Study Objectives** ❑
- Read **Preview** ❑
- Read text and answer **Before You Go On** p. 200 ❑ p. 203 ❑ p. 208 ❑ p. 209 ❑
- Work **Demonstration Problem** ❑
- Review **Summary of Study Objectives** ❑
- Answer **Self-Study Questions** ❑
- Complete **Assignments** ❑

CONCEPTS FOR REVIEW

Before studying this chapter, you should know or, if necessary, review:

- How to close revenue, expense, and dividends accounts. (Ch. 4, pp. 148–151)
- The steps in the accounting cycle. (Ch. 4, pp. 154–155)

THE NAVIGATOR

ACCOUNTING MATTERS! FEATURE STORY

Selling Dollars for 85 Cents

For most of the last decade **Wal-Mart** has set the rules of the retail game. Entrepreneur Scott Blum, founder and CEO of **Buy.com**, has a different game plan. He is selling consumer products at or below cost. Buy.com is trying to create an outlet synonymous with low prices—in the hope of becoming the leading e-commerce portal on the Internet. He plans to make up the losses from sales by selling advertising on the company's Web site and a magazine to be mailed to Buy.com customers.

As if the idea of selling below cost weren't unusual enough, Blum has added another twist to merchandising: Unlike **Amazon.com**, he doesn't want to handle inventory. So he has wholesalers and distributors ship the products directly to his Web site customers.

Buy.com's slogan, "The lowest prices on earth," may be the most eye-catching sales pitch ever. The company is ruthlessly committed to being the price leader—even if it means losing money on every sale. Its own computers search competitors' Web sites to make sure that Buy.com has the lowest prices on the Internet. When Amazon.com, in June 2002, reduced its minimum-purchase order for free shipping to $49 (from $99), Buy.com one-upped that move a day later by offering free shipping with no minimum purchase.

eToys, **Pets.com**, and **Cyberian Outpost** all went under during the dot-com wreck of 2000–2001, and Amazon.com, after seven years, had yet to turn a profit. Only **eBay**, an auction site, is consistently profitable. Still, Scott Blum stretches for a bigger portion of a $50 billion online sales market by being the low-cost e-tailer.

Consider the implications if Buy.com is successful: Buy.com's success could change the very way wholesalers and distributors view their businesses. Its success may have an impact on all kinds of retailers—starting with Buy.com itself. If Buy.com proves that the ad space on a product order form—its Web site—is almost as valuable as the product being ordered, another virtual reseller is sure to enter the market with even lower prices.

Of course, there is one big winner if Buy.com succeeds: you. It has never been a better time to be a customer.

www.buy.com

Source: Quentin Hardy, "The Death and Life of Buy.com," *Forbes* (January 21, 2002), pp. 86–89.

☑ THE NAVIGATOR

STUDY OBJECTIVES

After studying this chapter, you should be able to:

1. Identify the differences between a service enterprise and a merchandiser.
2. Explain the entries for purchases under a perpetual inventory system.
3. Explain the entries for sales revenues under a perpetual inventory system.
4. Explain the steps in the accounting cycle for a merchandiser.
5. Distinguish between a multiple-step and a single-step income statement.
6. Explain the computation and importance of gross profit.
7. Determine cost of goods sold under a periodic system.

☑ THE NAVIGATOR

PREVIEW OF CHAPTER 5

As indicated in the Feature Story, **Wal-Mart** is a gigantic merchandiser with over a 60% share of the retail sales market. Like traditional merchandisers such as **Sears Roebuck**, it generates revenues by selling goods to customers rather than performing services. Merchandisers that purchase and sell directly to consumers—such as **Kmart**, **Safeway**, and **Toys "R" Us**—are called **retailers**. In contrast, merchandisers that sell to retailers are known as **wholesalers**. For example, retailer **Walgreens** might buy goods from wholesaler **McKesson**; **Office Depot** might buy office supplies from wholesaler **United Stationers**.

The steps in the accounting cycle for a merchandiser are the same as the steps for a service enterprise. But merchandisers use additional accounts and entries that are required in recording merchandising transactions.

The content and organization of Chapter 5 are as follows.

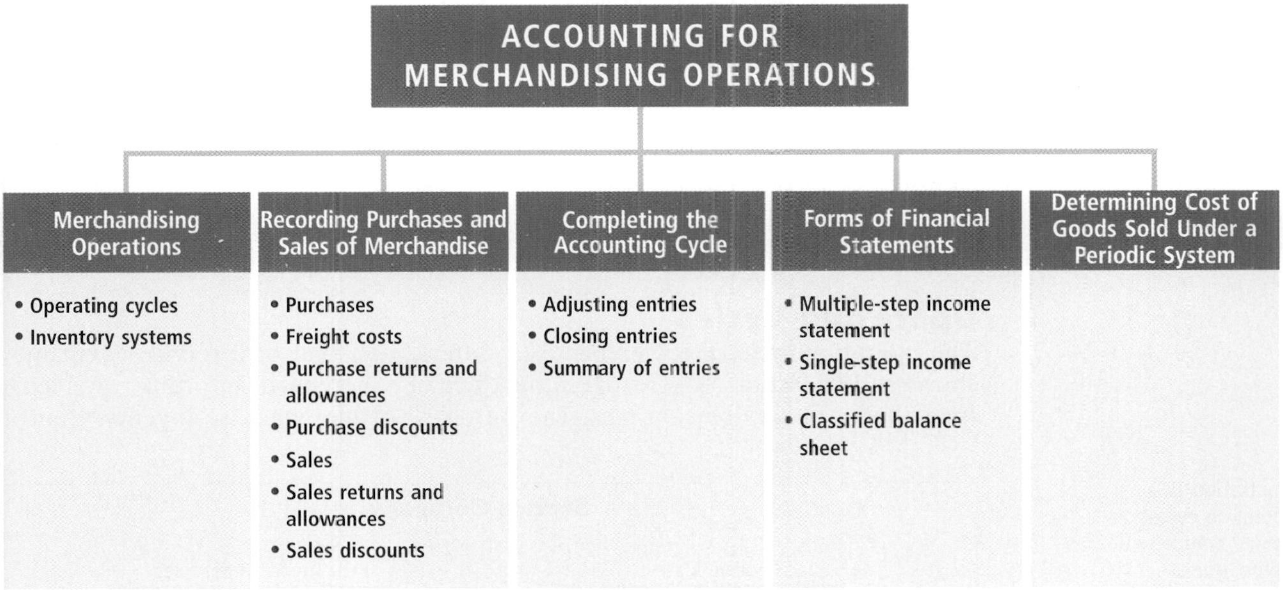

THE NAVIGATOR

Merchandising Operations

STUDY OBJECTIVE 1

Identify the differences between a service enterprise and a merchandiser.

Measuring net income for a merchandiser is conceptually the same as for a service enterprise. That is, net income (or loss) results from the matching of expenses with revenues. For a merchandiser, the primary source of revenues is the sale of merchandise. This revenue source is often referred to as **sales revenue** or **sales**. Unlike expenses for a service company, expenses for a merchandiser are divided into two categories: (1) the cost of goods sold and (2) operating expenses.

The **cost of goods sold** is the total cost of merchandise sold during the period. This expense is directly related to the revenue recognized from the sale of the goods. Sales revenue less cost of goods sold is called **gross profit** on sales. For example, when a calculator costing $15 is sold for $25, the gross profit is $10. Merchandisers report gross profit on sales in the income statement.

After gross profit is calculated, operating expenses are deducted to determine net income (or net loss). **Operating expenses** are expenses incurred in the process of earning sales revenue. Examples of operating expenses are sales salaries, advertising expense, and insurance expense. The operating expenses of a merchandiser include many of the expenses found in a service company.

The income measurement process for a merchandiser is diagrammed in Illustration 5-1. The items in the three blue boxes are peculiar to a merchandiser. They are not used by a service company.

Illustration 5-1
Income measurement process for a merchandiser

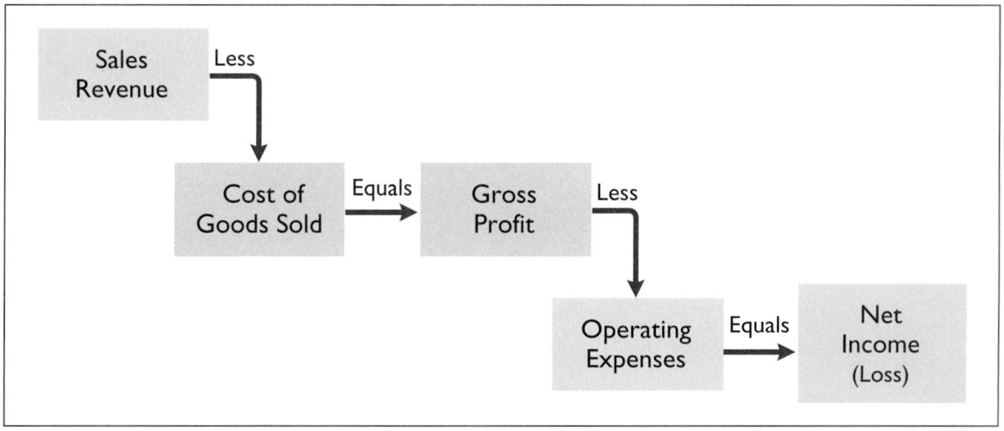

Operating Cycles

The operating cycle of a merchandiser differs from that of a service company, as shown in Illustration 5-2. The operating cycle of a merchandiser ordinarily is longer than that of a service company. The purchase of merchandise inventory and its

Illustration 5-2
Operating cycles for a service company and a merchandiser

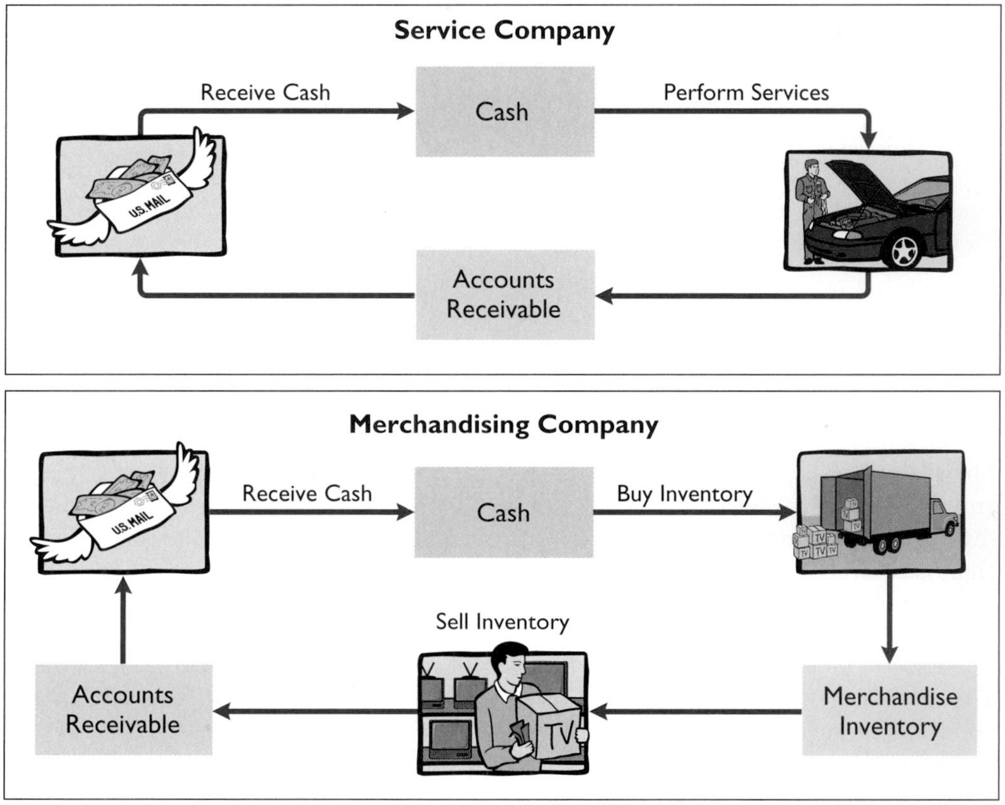

eventual sale lengthen the cycle. Note that the added asset account for a merchandising company is an **inventory** account. It is usually entitled Merchandise Inventory. Merchandise inventory is reported as a current asset on the balance sheet.

Inventory Systems

A merchandiser keeps track of its inventory to determine what is available for sale and what has been sold. One of two systems is used to account for inventory: a **perpetual inventory system** or a **periodic inventory system**.

Perpetual System

In a **perpetual inventory system**, detailed records of the cost of each inventory purchase and sale are maintained. This system continuously—perpetually—shows the inventory that should be on hand for every item. For example, a **Ford** dealership has separate inventory records for each automobile, truck, and van on its lot. With the use of bar codes and optical scanners, a grocery store can keep a daily running record of every box of cereal and every jar of jelly that it buys and sells. Under a perpetual inventory system, the cost of goods sold is **determined each time a sale occurs**.

HELPFUL HINT

For control purposes a physical inventory count is taken under the perpetual system, even though it is not needed to determine cost of goods sold.

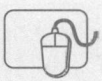

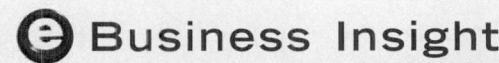

ACCOUNTING MATTERS! e Business Insight

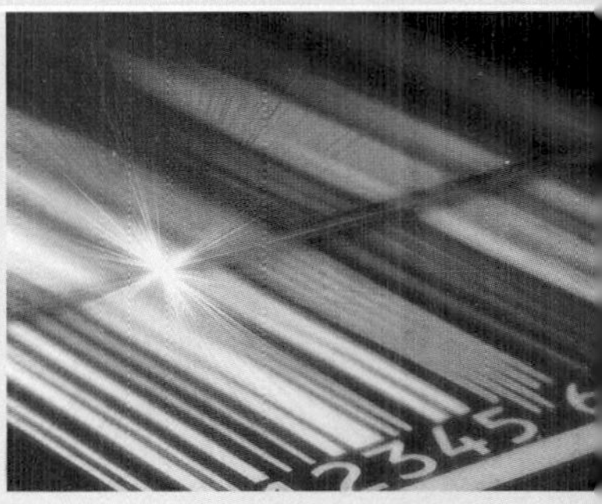

What's in a bar code? First, the bar code usually doesn't contain descriptive data (just as your Social Security number or car's license plate number doesn't have anything about your name or where you live). For example, the bar codes found on food items at grocery stores don't contain the price or description of the food item. Instead, the bar code has a 12-digit "product number" in it. When read by a bar code reader and transmitted to the computer, the computer finds the disk file item record(s) associated with that item number. In the disk file is the price, vendor name, quantity on-hand, description, and so on. The computer does a "price lookup" by reading the bar code, and then it creates a register of the items and adds the price to the subtotal of the groceries sold. It also subtracts the quantity from the "on-hand" total.

? How is a grocery store's accounting equation changed by the computer's bar-code actions?

Periodic System

In a **periodic inventory system**, detailed inventory records of the goods on hand are not kept throughout the period. The cost of goods sold is **determined only at the end of the accounting period**—that is, periodically. At that time, a physical inventory count is taken to determine the cost of goods on hand (Merchandise Inventory). To determine the cost of goods sold under a periodic inventory system, you must (1) determine the cost of goods on hand at the beginning of the accounting period, (2) add to it the cost of goods purchased, and (3) subtract the cost of goods on hand at the end of the accounting period.

Illustration 5-3 graphically compares the sequence of activities and the timing of the cost of goods sold computation under the two inventory systems.

Illustration 5-3
Comparing perpetual and periodic inventory systems

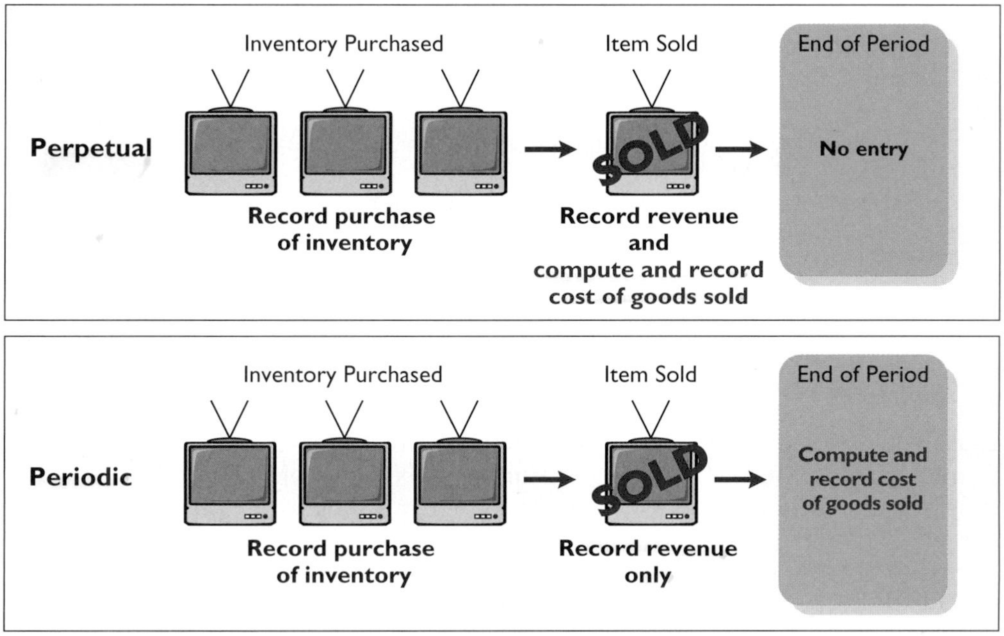

Additional Considerations

Perpetual systems have traditionally been used by companies that sell merchandise with high unit values. Examples are automobiles, furniture, and major home appliances. The widespread use of computers and electronic scanners now enables many more companies to install perpetual inventory systems. The perpetual inventory system is so named because the accounting records continuously—perpetually—show the quantity and cost of the inventory that should be on hand at any time.

A perpetual inventory system provides better control over inventories than a periodic system. The inventory records show the quantities that should be on hand. So, the goods can be counted at any time to see whether the amount of goods actually on hand agrees with the inventory records. Any shortages uncovered can be investigated immediately. A perpetual inventory system does require additional clerical work and additional cost to maintain the subsidiary records. But a computerized system can minimize this cost. Much of **Wal-Mart**'s success is attributed to its sophisticated perpetual inventory system. When snowboard maker **Morrow Snowboards Inc.** issued shares of stock to the public for the first time, some investors expressed reluctance to invest in Morrow. They were concerned about a number of accounting control problems. To reduce investor concerns, Morrow implemented a perpetual inventory system to improve its control over inventory.

Because the perpetual inventory system is growing in popularity and use, we illustrate it in this chapter. The periodic system, still widely used, is described in an appendix to this chapter.

Recording Purchases and Sales of Merchandise

Purchases

STUDY OBJECTIVE 2

Explain the entries for purchases under a perpetual inventory system.

Purchases of inventory may be made for cash or on account (credit). Purchases are normally recorded when the goods are received from the seller. Every purchase should be supported by business documents that provide written evidence of the transaction. Each cash purchase should be supported by a canceled check or a cash register receipt indicating the items purchased and amounts paid. Cash purchases are recorded by an increase in Merchandise Inventory and a decrease in Cash.

Each credit purchase should be supported by a **purchase invoice**. This document indicates the total purchase price and other relevant information. But the purchaser does not prepare a separate purchase invoice. Instead, the copy of the sales invoice sent by the seller is used by the buyer as a purchase invoice. In Illustration 5-4, for example, the sales invoice prepared by Sellers Electronix (the seller) is used as a purchase invoice by Beyer Video (the buyer).

Illustration 5-4
Sales invoice used as purchase invoice by Beyer Video

INVOICE NO. 731

SELLERS ELECTRONIX
27 CIRCLE DRIVE
HARDING, MICHIGAN 48281

SOLD TO
Firm Name: Beyer Video
Attention of: James Hoover, Purchasing Agent
Address: 125 Main Street
City: Chelsea State: Illinois Zip: 60915

Date 5/4/06	Salesperson Malone	Terms 2/10, n/30	Freight Paid by Buyer	
Catalog No.	**Description**	**Quantity**	**Price**	**Amount**
X572Y9820	Printed Circuit Board-prototype	1	2,300	$2,300
A2547Z45	Production Model Circuits	5	300	1,500

IMPORTANT: ALL RETURNS MUST BE MADE WITHIN 10 DAYS **TOTAL** $3,800

HELPFUL HINT

To better understand the contents of this invoice, identify these items:

1. Seller
2. Invoice date
3. Purchaser
4. Salesperson
5. Credit terms
6. Freight terms
7. Goods sold: catalog number, description, quantity, price per unit
8. Total invoice amount

The associated entry for Beyer Video for the invoice from Sellers Electronix is:

May 4	Merchandise Inventory	3,800	
	Accounts Payable		3,800
	(To record goods purchased on account from Sellers Electronix)		

A	=	L	+	SE
+3,800		+3,800		

Cash Flows
no effect

Under the perpetual inventory system, purchases of merchandise for sale are recorded in the Merchandise Inventory account. Thus, a retailer of general merchandise such as **Wal-Mart** would debit Merchandise Inventory for clothing, sporting goods, and anything else purchased for resale to customers.

Not all purchases are debited to Merchandise Inventory, however. Purchases of assets acquired for use and not for resale (such as supplies, equipment, and similar items) are recorded as increases to specific asset accounts rather than to Merchandise Inventory. Wal-Mart would increase Supplies to record the purchase of materials used to make shelf signs or for cash register receipt paper.

Freight Costs

The sales agreement should indicate whether the seller or the buyer is to pay the cost of transporting the goods to the buyer's place of business. When a common carrier such as a railroad, trucking company, or airline is used, the transportation company prepares a freight bill in accordance with the sales agreement. Freight terms are expressed as either **FOB shipping point** or **FOB destination**. The letters FOB mean **free on board**. Thus, **FOB shipping point** means that goods are placed free on board the carrier by the seller, and the buyer pays the freight costs. Conversely, **FOB destination** means that the goods are placed free on board to the buyer's place of business, and the seller pays the freight. For example, the sales invoice in Illustration 5-4 on page 195 indicates that the buyer (Beyer Video) pays the freight charges.

When the purchaser directly incurs the freight costs, the account Merchandise Inventory is debited. For example, if upon delivery of the goods on May 6, Beyer Video pays Acme Freight Company $150 for freight charges, the entry on Beyer Video's books is:

A	=	L	+	SE
+150				
−150				

Cash Flows
−150

May 6	Merchandise Inventory	150	
	Cash		150
	(To record payment of freight on goods purchased)		

In contrast, **freight costs incurred by the seller on outgoing merchandise are an operating expense to the seller**. These costs increase an expense account titled Freight-out or Delivery Expense. If the freight terms on the invoice in Illustration 5-4 had required that Sellers Electronix pay the $150 freight charges, the entry by Sellers Electronix would have been:

A	=	L	+	SE
−150				−150 Exp

Cash Flows
−150

May 4	Freight-out (or Delivery Expense)	150	
	Cash		150
	(To record payment of freight on goods sold)		

When the freight charges are paid by the seller, the seller will usually establish a higher invoice price for the goods to cover the expense of shipping.

Purchase Returns and Allowances

A purchaser may be dissatisfied with the merchandise received. The goods may be damaged or defective, of inferior quality, or perhaps they do not meet the purchaser's specifications. In such cases, the purchaser may return the goods to the seller. The purchaser is granted credit if the sale was made on credit, or a cash refund if the purchase was for cash. This transaction is known as a **purchase return**. Or the purchaser may choose to keep the merchandise if the seller is willing to grant an allowance (deduction) from the purchase price. This transaction is known as a **purchase allowance**.

Assume that Beyer Video returned goods costing $300 to Sellers Electronix on May 8. The entry by Beyer Video for the returned merchandise is:

A	=	L	+	SE
−300		−300		

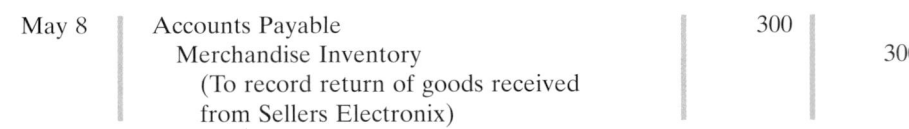

Cash Flows
no effect

May 8	Accounts Payable	300	
	Merchandise Inventory		300
	(To record return of goods received from Sellers Electronix)		

Beyer Video increased Merchandise Inventory when the goods were received. So, Beyer Video decreases Merchandise Inventory when it returns the goods or when it is granted an allowance.

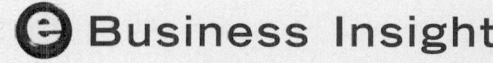

ACCOUNTING MATTERS! **Business Insight**

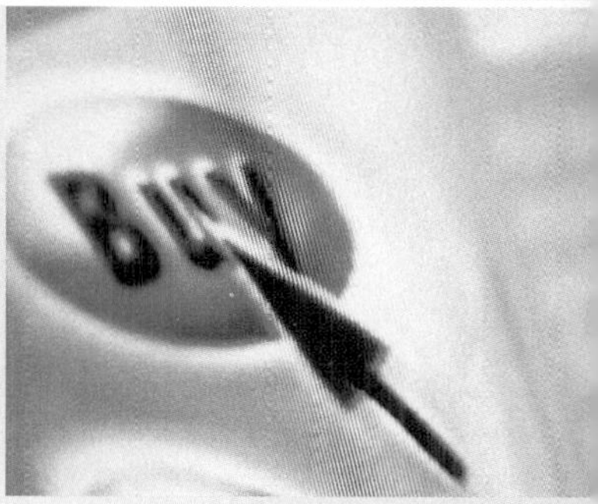

It can cost a lot to convert from traditional business to e-commerce. For example, when **Borders**, the second largest seller of books, went online, it had to build an entirely new $15 million distribution center. The reason? It previously shipped large orders of books to its stores. Instead, it now has to distribute tiny orders to individual customers. The distribution costs of online sales can be surprisingly high—as much as 15 percent of sales.

? The *distribution costs* of online sales can be greater than for traditional in-store sales. What costs may be less for online sales?

Purchase Discounts

The credit terms of a purchase on account may permit the buyer to claim a cash discount for prompt payment. The buyer calls this cash discount a **purchase discount**. This incentive offers advantages to both parties: The purchaser saves money, and the seller is able to shorten the operating cycle by converting the accounts receivable into cash earlier.

The **credit terms** specify the amount of the cash discount and time period during which it is offered. They also indicate the length of time in which the purchaser is expected to pay the full invoice price. In the sales invoice in Illustration 5-4, credit terms are 2/10, n/30. This is read "two-ten, net thirty." It means that a 2 percent cash discount may be taken on the invoice price, less any returns or allowances, if payment is made within 10 days of the invoice date (the **discount period**). If payment is not made in that time, the invoice price, less any returns or allowances, is due 30 days from the invoice date. Or, the discount period may extend to a specified number of days after the month in which the sale occurs. For example, 1/10 EOM (end of month) means that a 1 percent discount is available if the invoice is paid within the first 10 days of the next month.

HELPFUL HINT

The term *net* in "net 30" means the remaining amount due after subtracting any sales returns and allowances and partial payments.

The seller may elect not to offer a cash discount for prompt payment. In that case, credit terms will specify only the maximum time period for paying the balance due. For example, the time period may be stated as n/30, n/60, or n/10 EOM. These mean, respectively, that the net amount must be paid in 30 days, 60 days, or within the first 10 days of the next month.

When an invoice is paid within the discount period, the amount of the discount decreases Merchandise Inventory. Inventory is recorded at its cost and, by paying within the discount period, the merchandiser has reduced its cost. To illustrate, assume Beyer Video pays the balance due of $3,500 (gross invoice price of $3,800 less purchase returns and allowances of $300) on May 14, the last day of the discount period. The cash discount is $70 ($3,500 × 2%), and the amount of cash paid by Beyer Video is $3,430 ($3,500 − $70). The entry to record the May 14 payment by Beyer Video is:

May 14	Accounts Payable	3,500	
	Cash		3,430
	Merchandise Inventory		70
	(To record payment within discount period)		

A	=	L	+	SE
−3,430		−3,500		
−70				

Cash Flows
−3,430

If Beyer Video failed to take the discount and instead made full payment on June 3, Beyer Video's entry would be:

June 3	Accounts Payable	3,500	
	Cash		3,500
	(To record payment with no discount taken)		

A	=	L	+	SE
−3,500		−3,500		

Cash Flows
−3,500

A merchandiser usually should take all available discounts. Passing up the discount may be viewed as **paying interest** for use of the money. For example, if Beyer Video passed up the discount, it would be like paying an interest rate of 2 percent for the use of $3,500 for 20 days (30 days minus 10 days). This is the equivalent of an annual interest rate of approximately 36.5 percent (2% × 365/20). Obviously, it would be better for Beyer Video to borrow at prevailing bank interest rates of 8 percent to 12 percent than to lose the discount.

Sales

STUDY OBJECTIVE 3

Explain the entries for sales revenues under a perpetual inventory system.

Sales revenues, like service revenues, are recorded when earned. This is done in accord with the revenue recognition principle. Typically, sales revenues are earned when the goods are transferred from the seller to the buyer. At this point the sales transaction is completed, and the sales price has been established.

Sales may be made on credit or for cash. Every sales transaction should be supported by a **business document** that provides written evidence of the sale. **Cash register tapes** provide evidence of cash sales. A **sales invoice**, like the one that was shown in Illustration 5-4 (page 195), provides support for a credit sale. The original copy of the invoice goes to the customer. A copy is kept by the seller for use in recording the sale. The invoice shows the date of sale, customer name, total sales price, and other relevant information.

Two entries are made for each sale. The first entry records the sale: Cash (or Accounts Receivable, if a credit sale) is increased by a debit, and Sales is increased by a credit at the selling (invoice) price of the goods. The second entry records the cost of the merchandise sold: Cost of Goods Sold is increased by a debit, and Merchandise Inventory is decreased by a credit for the cost of those goods. As a result, the Merchandise Inventory account will show at all times the amount of inventory that should be on hand.

To illustrate a credit sales transaction, Sellers Electronix's sale of $3,800 on May 4 to Beyer Video (see Illustration 5-4, page 195) is recorded as follows. (Assume the merchandise cost Sellers Electronix $2,400.)

A	= L	+ SE
+3,800		+3,800 Rev

Cash Flows
no effect

May 4	Accounts Receivable	3,800	
	Sales		3,800
	(To record credit sale to Beyer Video per invoice #731)		
4	Cost of Goods Sold	2,400	
	Merchandise Inventory		2,400
	(To record cost of merchandise sold on invoice #731 to Beyer Video)		

A	= L	+ SE
−2,400		−2,400 Exp

Cash Flows
no effect

For internal decision-making purposes, merchandisers may use more than one sales account. For example, Sellers Electronix may keep separate sales accounts for its TV sets, DVD players, and microwave ovens. By using separate sales accounts for major product lines, company management can monitor sales trends more closely and respond more strategically to changes in sales patterns. For example, if TV sales are increasing while microwave oven sales are decreasing, the company could reevaluate its advertising and pricing policies on each of these items.

HELPFUL HINT

The Sales account is credited only for sales of goods held for resale. Sales of assets not held for resale (such as equipment or land) are credited directly to the asset account.

However, on its income statement presented to outside investors, a merchandiser would normally provide only a single sales figure—the sum of all of its individual sales accounts. This is done for two reasons. First, providing detail on individual sales accounts would add length to the income statement. Second, companies do not want their competitors to know the details of their operating results.

Sales Returns and Allowances

We now look at the "flipside" of purchase returns and allowances, which are **sales returns and allowances** recorded on the books of the seller. Sellers Electronix's entries to record credit for returned goods involve two entries: (1) The first is an increase in Sales Returns and Allowances and a decrease in Accounts Receivable at the $300 selling price. (2) The second is an increase in Merchandise Inventory (assume a $140 cost) and a decrease in Cost of Goods Sold. The entries are as follows.

May 8	Sales Returns and Allowances	300	
	Accounts Receivable		300
	(To record credit granted to Beyer Video for returned goods)		
8	Merchandise Inventory	140	
	Cost of Goods Sold		140
	(To record cost of goods returned)		

A	=	L	+	SE
−300				−300 Rev

Cash Flows
no effect

A	=	L	+	SE
+140				+140 Exp

Cash Flows
no effect

If goods are returned because they are damaged or defective, then the entry to Merchandise Inventory and Cost of Goods Sold should be for the estimated value of the returned goods, rather than their cost. For example, if the goods returned to Sellers Electronix were defective and had a scrap value of $50, Merchandise Inventory would be debited for $50, and Cost of Goods Sold would be credited for $50.

Sales Returns and Allowances is a **contra revenue account** to Sales. The normal balance of Sales Returns and Allowances is a debit. A contra account is used, instead of debiting Sales, to disclose in the accounts the amount of sales returns and allowances. This information is important to management. Excessive returns and allowances suggest inferior merchandise, inefficiencies in filling orders, errors in billing customers, and mistakes in delivery or shipment of goods. Also, a debit recorded directly to Sales could distort comparisons between total sales in different accounting periods.

HELPFUL HINT

Remember that the increases, decreases, and normal balances of contra accounts are the opposite of the accounts to which they correspond.

ACCOUNTING MATTERS! Ethics Insight

How high is too high? Returns can become so high that it is questionable whether sales revenue should have been recognized in the first place. An example of high returns is **Florafax International Inc.**, a floral supply company, which was alleged to have shipped its product without customer authorization on ten holiday occasions, including 8,562 shipments of flowers to customers for Mother's Day and 6,575 for Secretary's Day. The return rate on these shipments went as high as 69% of sales. As one employee noted: "Products went out the front door and came in the back door."

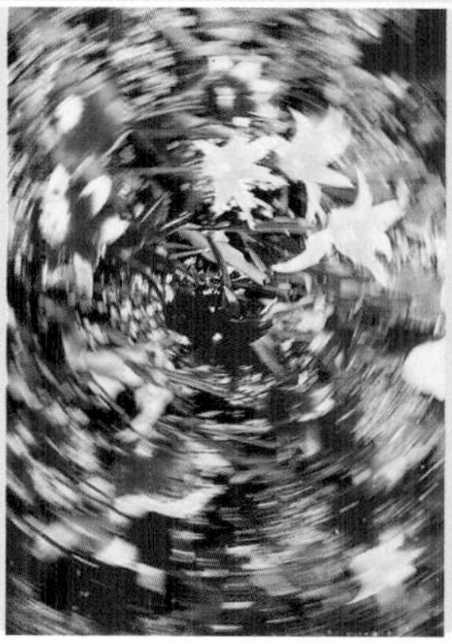

? How does management know the amount of sales returns? Would returns for a floral supply company have a greater negative impact on earnings than returns for a department store?

Sales Discounts

As mentioned in our discussion of purchase transactions, the seller may offer the customer a cash discount for the prompt payment of the balance due. From the seller's point of view, this is called a **sales discount**. Like a purchase discount, a sales discount is based on the invoice price less returns and allowances, if any. The Sales Discounts account is debited for discounts that are taken. The entry by Sellers Electronix to record the cash receipt on May 14 from Beyer Video within the discount period is:

May 14	Cash	3,430	
	Sales Discounts	70	
	Accounts Receivable		3,500
	(To record collection within 2/10, n/30 discount period from Beyer Video)		

A	=	L	+	SE
+3,430				−70 Rev
−3,500				

Cash Flows
+3,430

Like Sales Returns and Allowances, Sales Discounts is a **contra revenue account** to Sales. Its normal balance is a debit. This account is used, instead of debiting Sales, to disclose cash discounts taken by customers. If the discount is not taken, Sellers Electronix debits Cash for $3,500 and credits Accounts Receivable for the same amount at the date of collection.

BEFORE YOU GO ON...

Review It

1. How does the measurement of net income in a merchandising company differ from that in a service enterprise?
2. In what ways is a perpetual inventory system different from a periodic system?
3. Under the perpetual inventory system, what entries are made to record purchases, purchase returns and allowances, purchase discounts, and freight costs?
4. Under a perpetual inventory system, what are the two entries that must be recorded at the time of each sale?
5. Why is it important to use the Sales Returns and Allowances account, rather than simply reducing the Sales account, when goods are returned?

Do It

On September 5, NewIdea Company buys merchandise on account from Janet Diaz Company. The selling price of the goods is $1,500, and the cost to Diaz Company was $800. On September 8 defective goods with a selling price of $200 and a scrap value of $80 are returned. Record the transactions on the books of both companies.

ACTION PLAN

- Purchaser: Record purchases of inventory at its cost and directly reduce the Merchandise Inventory account for returned goods.
- Seller: Record both the sale and the cost of goods sold at the time of the sale. Record returns in a contra account, Sales Returns and Allowances.

SOLUTION

NewIdea Company

Sept. 5	Merchandise Inventory	1,500	
	Accounts Payable		1,500
	(To record goods purchased on account)		
8	Accounts Payable	200	
	Merchandise Inventory		200
	(To record return of defective goods)		

Janet Diaz Company

Sept. 5	Accounts Receivable	1,500	
	Sales		1,500
	(To record credit sale)		
5	Cost of Goods Sold	800	
	Merchandise Inventory		800
	(To record cost of goods sold on account)		
8	Sales Returns and Allowances	200	
	Accounts Receivable		200
	(To record credit granted for receipt of returned goods)		
8	Merchandise Inventory	80	
	Cost of Goods Sold		80
	(To record scrap value of goods returned)		

Related exercise material: *BE5-1, BE5-2, BE5-3, BE5-4, E5-1, E5-2, E5-3, and E5-4.*

THE NAVIGATOR

Completing the Accounting Cycle

Up to this point, we have illustrated the basic entries in recording transactions relating to purchases and sales in a perpetual inventory system. Now we consider the remaining steps in the accounting cycle for a merchandiser. Each of the required steps described in Chapter 4 for a service company applies to a merchandising company. Use of a worksheet by a merchandiser (an optional step) is shown in Appendix 5B at the end of this chapter.

STUDY OBJECTIVE 4

Explain the steps in the accounting cycle for a merchandiser.

Adjusting Entries

A merchandiser generally has the same types of adjusting entries as a service company. But a merchandiser using a perpetual system will require one additional adjustment to make the records agree with the actual inventory on hand. Here's why: At the end of each period, a merchandiser using a perpetual system will take a physical count of its goods on hand for control purposes. A company's unadjusted balance in Merchandise Inventory will usually not agree with the actual amount of inventory on hand at year-end. The perpetual inventory records may be incorrect due to a variety of causes such as recording errors, theft, or waste. As a result, the perpetual records need adjustment to ensure that the recorded inventory amount agrees with the actual inventory on hand. **This involves adjusting Merchandise Inventory and Cost of Goods Sold.**

HELPFUL HINT

The steps required to determine the actual inventory on hand are discussed in Chapter 6.

For example, suppose that the records of Sellers Electronix report an unadjusted balance in Merchandise Inventory of $40,500. Through a physical count, the company determines that its actual merchandise inventory on hand at year-end is $40,000. The adjusting entry would be to debit Cost of Goods Sold for $500 and to credit Merchandise Inventory for $500.

Closing Entries

For a merchandiser, like a service enterprise, all accounts that affect the determination of net income are closed to Income Summary. In journalizing, all temporary accounts with debit balances are credited, and all temporary accounts with credit balances are debited, as shown below for Sellers Electronix. Note that cost of goods sold must be closed to Income Summary.

Dec. 31	Sales	480,000	
	Income Summary		480,000
	(To close income statement accounts with credit balances)		
31	Income Summary	450,000	
	Sales Returns and Allowances		12,000
	Sales Discounts		8,000
	Cost of Goods Sold		316,000
	Store Salaries Expense		45,000
	Administrative Salaries Expense		19,000
	Freight-out		7,000
	Advertising Expense		16,000
	Utilities Expense		17,000
	Depreciation Expense		8,000
	Insurance Expense		2,000
	(To close income statement accounts with debit balances)		
31	Income Summary	30,000	
	Retained Earnings		30,000
	(To close net income to retained earnings)		

HELPFUL HINT

The easiest way to prepare the first two closing entries is to identify the temporary accounts by their balances and then prepare one entry for the credits and one for the debits.

(*continued from p. 201*)

31	Retained Earnings	15,000	
	Dividends		15,000
	(To close dividends to retained earnings)		

After the closing entries are posted, all temporary accounts have zero balances. In addition, Retained Earnings has a credit balance of $48,000: beginning balance + net income − dividends ($33,000 + $30,000 − $15,000).

Summary of Merchandising Entries

The entries for the merchandising accounts using a perpetual inventory system are summarized in Illustration 5-5.

Illustration 5-5
Daily recurring and adjusting and closing entries

	Transactions	Daily Recurring Entries	Dr.	Cr.
Sales Transactions	Selling merchandise to customers.	Cash or Accounts Receivable	XX	
		Sales		XX
		Cost of Goods Sold	XX	
		Merchandise Inventory		XX
	Granting sales returns or allowances to customers.	Sales Returns and Allowances	XX	
		Cash or Accounts Receivable		XX
		Merchandise Inventory	XX	
		Cost of Goods Sold		XX
	Paying freight costs on sales; FOB destination.	Freight-out	XX	
		Cash		XX
	Receiving payment from customers within discount period.	Cash	XX	
		Sales Discounts	XX	
		Accounts Receivable		XX
Purchase Transactions	Purchasing merchandise for resale.	Merchandise Inventory	XX	
		Cash or Accounts Payable		XX
	Paying freight costs on merchandise purchased; FOB shipping point.	Merchandise Inventory	XX	
		Cash		XX
	Receiving purchase returns or allowances from suppliers.	Cash or Accounts Payable	XX	
		Merchandise Inventory		XX
	Paying suppliers within discount period.	Accounts Payable	XX	
		Merchandise Inventory		XX
		Cash		XX
	Events	**Adjusting and Closing Entries**		
	Adjust because book amount is higher than the inventory amount determined to be on hand.	Cost of Goods Sold	XX	
		Merchandise Inventory		XX
	Closing temporary accounts with credit balances.	Sales	XX	
		Income Summary		XX
	Closing temporary accounts with debit balances.	Income Summary	XX	
		Sales Returns and Allowances		XX
		Sales Discounts		XX
		Cost of Goods Sold		XX
		Freight-out		XX
		Expenses		XX

BEFORE YOU GO ON...

Review It

1. Why is an adjustment to the Merchandise Inventory account usually needed?
2. What merchandising account(s) will appear in the post-closing trial balance?

Do It

The trial balance of Celine's Sports Wear Shop at December 31 shows Merchandise Inventory $25,000, Sales $162,400, Sales Returns and Allowances $4,800, Sales Discounts $3,600, Cost of Goods Sold $110,000, Rental Revenue $6,000, Freight-out $1,800, Rent Expense $8,800, and Salaries and Wages Expense $22,000. Prepare the closing entries for the above accounts.

ACTION PLAN

- Close all temporary accounts with credit balances to Income Summary by debiting these accounts.
- Close all temporary accounts with debit balances to Income Summary by crediting these accounts.

SOLUTION The two closing entries are:

Dec. 31	Sales	162,400	
	Rental Revenue	6,000	
	Income Summary		168,400
	(To close accounts with credit balances)		
Dec. 31	Income Summary	151,000	
	Cost of Goods Sold		110,000
	Sales Returns and Allowances		4,800
	Sales Discounts		3,600
	Freight-out		1,800
	Rent Expense		8,800
	Salaries and Wages Expense		22,000
	(To close accounts with debit balances)		

Related exercise material: *BE5-7, E5-5, and E5-6.*

THE NAVIGATOR

Forms of Financial Statements

STUDY OBJECTIVE 5

Distinguish between a multiple-step and a single-step income statement.

Two forms of the income statement are widely used by merchandisers. Also, merchandisers use the classified balance sheet, introduced in Chapter 4. The use of these financial statements by merchandisers is explained below.

Multiple-Step Income Statement

The **multiple-step income statement** is so named because it shows the steps in determining net income (or net loss). It shows two main steps: (1) Cost of goods sold is subtracted from net sales, to determine gross profit. (2) Operating expenses are deducted from gross profit, to determine net income. These steps relate to the company's principal operating activities. A multiple-step statement also distinguishes between **operating** and **non-operating activities**. This distinction provides users with more information about a company's income performance. The statement also highlights intermediate components of income and shows subgroupings of expenses.

Income Statement Presentation of Sales

The multiple-step income statement begins by presenting sales revenue. As contra revenue accounts, sales returns and allowances, and sales discounts are deducted from sales to arrive at **net sales**. The sales revenues section for Sellers Electronix, using assumed data, is as follows.

Illustration 5-6
Computation of net sales

SELLERS ELECTRONIX
Income Statement (partial)

Sales revenues		
Sales		$480,000
Less: Sales returns and allowances	$12,000	
Sales discounts	8,000	20,000
Net sales		**$460,000**

This presentation discloses the key aspects of the company's principal revenue-producing activities.

Gross Profit

STUDY OBJECTIVE 6

Explain the computation and importance of gross profit.

From Illustration 5-1, you learned that cost of goods sold is deducted from sales revenue to determine **gross profit**. Sales revenue used for this computation is **net sales**. On the basis of the sales data presented in Illustration 5-6 (net sales of $460,000) and the cost of goods sold under the perpetual inventory system (assume $316,000), the gross profit for Sellers Electronix is $144,000, computed as follows.

Illustration 5-7
Computation of gross profit

Net sales	$460,000
Cost of goods sold	316,000
Gross profit	**$144,000**

A company's gross profit may also be expressed as a percentage. This is done by dividing the amount of gross profit by net sales. For Sellers Electronix the **gross profit rate** is 31.3 percent, computed as follows.

Illustration 5-8
Gross profit rate formula and computation

Gross Profit	÷	Net Sales	=	Gross Profit Rate
$144,000	÷	$460,000	=	**31.3%**

The gross profit rate is generally considered to be more useful than the gross profit amount. The rate expresses a more meaningful (qualitative) relationship between net sales and gross profit. For example, a gross profit of $1,000,000 may be impressive. But, if it is the result of a gross profit rate of only 7 percent, it is not so impressive. The gross profit rate tells how many cents of each sales dollar go to gross profit.

Gross profit represents the **merchandising profit** of a company. It is not a measure of the overall profitability, because operating expenses have not been deducted. But the amount and trend of gross profit is closely watched by management and other interested parties. They compare current gross profit with amounts reported in past periods. They also compare the company's gross profit rate with rates of competitors and with industry averages. Such comparisons provide information about the effectiveness of a company's purchasing function and the soundness of its pricing policies.

Operating Expenses and Net Income

Operating expenses are the third component in measuring net income for a merchandiser. As indicated earlier, these expenses are similar in merchandising and service enterprises. At Sellers Electronix, operating expenses were $114,000. The firm's net income is determined by subtracting operating expenses from gross profit. Thus, net income is $30,000, as shown below.

Gross profit	$144,000
Operating expenses	**114,000**
Net income	$ 30,000

Illustration 5-9
Operating expenses in computing net income

The net income amount is the "bottom line" of a company's income statement.

Nonoperating Activities

Nonoperating activities consist of (1) revenues and expenses from auxiliary operations and (2) gains and losses that are unrelated to the company's operations. The results of nonoperating activities are shown in two sections: "**Other revenues and gains**" and "**Other expenses and losses**." For a merchandiser, these sections will typically include the following items.

Illustration 5-10
Items reported in nonoperating sections

Nonoperating Activities

Other revenues and gains	Other expenses and losses
Interest revenue from notes receivable and marketable securities	Interest expense on notes and loans payable
Dividend revenue from investments in capital stock	Casualty losses from recurring causes such as vandalism and accidents
Rent revenue from subleasing a portion of the store	Loss from the sale or abandonment of property, plant, and equipment
Gain from the sale of property, plant, and equipment	Loss from strikes by employees and suppliers

ACCOUNTING MATTERS! Ethics Insight

After **Enron**, many companies were forced by increased investor criticism and regulator scrutiny to improve the clarity of their financial disclosures. For example, **IBM** announced that it would begin providing more detail regarding its "Other gains and losses." It had previously included these items in its selling, general, and administrative expenses, with little disclosure.

Disclosing other gains and losses in a separate line item on the income statement won't have any effect on bottom-line income. However, analysts complained that burying these details in the selling, general, and administrative expense line reduced their ability to fully understand how well IBM was performing. For example, previously if IBM sold off one of its buildings at a gain, it would include this gain in the selling, general, and administrative expense line item, thus reducing that expense. This made it appear that the company had done a better job of controlling operating expenses than it actually had. Other companies recently announcing changes to increase the informativeness of their income statements included **PepsiCo**, **Krispy Kreme Doughnuts**, and **General Electric**.

? Why have investors and analysts demanded more accuracy in isolating "Other gains and losses" from operating items?

The nonoperating activities are reported in the income statement immediately after the company's primary operating activities. These sections are shown in Illustration 5-11, using assumed data for Sellers Electronix.

Illustration 5-11
Multiple-step income statement—nonoperating sections and subgroupings of operating expenses

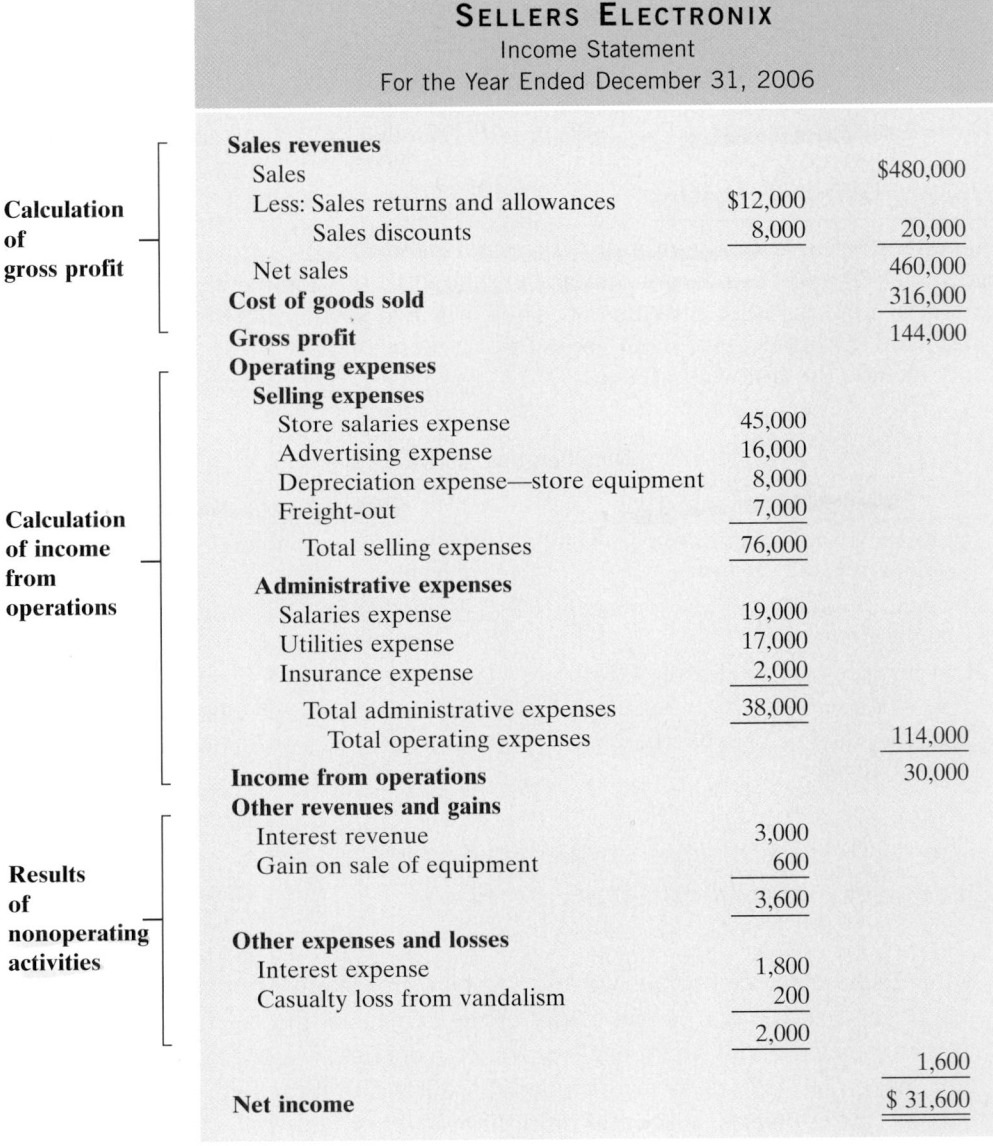

SELLERS ELECTRONIX
Income Statement
For the Year Ended December 31, 2006

Calculation of gross profit	**Sales revenues**		
	Sales		$480,000
	Less: Sales returns and allowances	$12,000	
	Sales discounts	8,000	20,000
	Net sales		460,000
	Cost of goods sold		316,000
	Gross profit		144,000
Calculation of income from operations	**Operating expenses**		
	Selling expenses		
	Store salaries expense	45,000	
	Advertising expense	16,000	
	Depreciation expense—store equipment	8,000	
	Freight-out	7,000	
	Total selling expenses	76,000	
	Administrative expenses		
	Salaries expense	19,000	
	Utilities expense	17,000	
	Insurance expense	2,000	
	Total administrative expenses	38,000	
	Total operating expenses		114,000
	Income from operations		30,000
Results of nonoperating activities	**Other revenues and gains**		
	Interest revenue	3,000	
	Gain on sale of equipment	600	
		3,600	
	Other expenses and losses		
	Interest expense	1,800	
	Casualty loss from vandalism	200	
		2,000	
			1,600
	Net income		$ 31,600

When the two nonoperating sections are included, the label "**Income from operations**" (or Operating income) precedes them. It clearly identifies the results of the company's normal operations. Income from operations is determined by subtracting cost of goods sold and operating expenses from net sales.

In the nonoperating activities sections, items are generally reported at the net amount. Thus, if a company received a $2,500 insurance settlement on vandalism losses of $2,700, the loss is reported at $200. Note, too, that the results of the two nonoperating sections are netted. The difference is added to or subtracted from income from operations to determine net income. It is not uncommon for companies to combine these two nonoperating sections into a single "Other revenues and expenses" section.

Subgrouping of Operating Expenses

In larger companies, operating expenses are often subdivided into selling expenses and administrative expenses, as illustrated in Illustration 5-11. **Selling expenses** are those associated with making sales. They include expenses for sales promotion as well as expenses of completing the sale, such as delivery and shipping. **Administrative expenses** (sometimes called general expenses) relate to general operating activities such as personnel management, accounting, and store security.

When subgroupings are made, some expenses may have to be prorated (e.g., 70% to selling and 30% to administrative expenses). For example, if a store building is used for both selling and general functions, building expenses such as depreciation, utilities, and property taxes will need to be allocated.

Any reasonable classification of expenses that serves to inform those who use the statement is satisfactory. The present tendency in statements prepared for management's internal use is to present in considerable detail expense data grouped along lines of responsibility.

Single-Step Income Statement

Another income statement format is the **single-step income statement.** The statement is so named because only one step, subtracting total expenses from total revenues, is required in determining net income (or net loss).

In a single-step statement, all data are classified under two categories: (1) revenues and (2) expenses. The **revenues** category includes both operating revenues and other revenues and gains. The **expenses** category includes cost of goods sold, operating expenses, and other expenses and losses. A condensed single-step statement for Sellers Electronix is shown in Illustration 5-12.

Illustration 5-12
Single-step income statement

SELLERS ELECTRONIX
Income Statement
For the Year Ended December 31, 2006

Revenues		
Net sales		$460,000
Interest revenue		3,000
Gain on sale of equipment		600
Total revenues		463,600
Expenses		
Cost of goods sold	$316,000	
Selling expenses	76,000	
Administrative expenses	38,000	
Interest expense	1,800	
Casualty loss from vandalism	200	
Total expenses		432,000
Net income		$ 31,600

There are two primary reasons for using the single-step format: (1) A company does not realize any type of profit or income until total revenues exceed total expenses, so it makes sense to divide the statement into these two categories. (2) The format is simpler and easier to read than the multiple-step format. But for homework problems, the single-step format should be used only when it is specifically requested.

Classified Balance Sheet

In the balance sheet, merchandise inventory is reported as a current asset immediately below accounts receivable. Recall from Chapter 4 that items are listed under current assets in their order of liquidity. Merchandise inventory is less liquid than accounts receivable because the goods must first be sold and then collection must be made from the customer. Illustration 5-13 presents the assets section of a classified balance sheet for Sellers Electronix.

Illustration 5-13
Assets section of a classified balance sheet (partial)

HELPFUL HINT

The $40,000 is the cost of the inventory on hand, not its expected selling price.

SELLERS ELECTRONIX
Balance Sheet (Partial)
December 31, 2006

Assets		
Current assets		
Cash		$ 9,500
Accounts receivable		16,100
Merchandise inventory		**40,000**
Prepaid insurance		1,800
Total current assets		67,400
Property, plant, and equipment		
Store equipment	$80,000	
Less: Accumulated depreciation—store equipment	24,000	56,000
Total assets		$123,400

BEFORE YOU GO ON...

Review It

1. Determine **PepsiCo**'s gross profit rate for 2003 and 2002. Indicate whether it increased or decreased from 2002 to 2003. The answer to this question is provided on page 237.
2. What are nonoperating activities, and how are they reported in the income statement?
3. How does a single-step income statement differ from a multiple-step income statement?

THE NAVIGATOR

Determining Cost of Goods Sold Under a Periodic System

STUDY OBJECTIVE 7

Determine cost of goods sold under a periodic system.

The determination of cost of goods sold is different under the periodic system than under the perpetual system. When a company uses a perpetual inventory system, all transactions affecting inventory (such as freight costs, returns, and discounts) are recorded directly to the Merchandise Inventory account. In addition, at the time of each sale the perpetual system requires a reduction in Merchandise Inventory and an increase in Cost of Goods Sold. But under a periodic system separate accounts are used to record freight costs, returns, and discounts. In addition, a running account of changes in inventory is not maintained. Instead, the balance in ending inventory, as well as the cost of goods sold for the period, is calculated at the end of the period. The determination of cost of goods sold for Sellers Electronix, using a periodic inventory system, is shown in Illustration 5-14.

Illustration 5-14
Cost of goods sold for a merchandiser using a periodic inventory system

SELLERS ELECTRONIX
Cost of Goods Sold
For the Year Ended December 31, 2006

Cost of goods sold				
Inventory, January 1			**$36,000**	
Purchases		$325,000		
Less: Purchase returns and allowances	$10,400			
Purchase discounts	6,800	17,200		
Net purchases		307,800		
Add: Freight-in		12,200		
Cost of goods purchased			**320,000**	
Cost of goods available for sale			356,000	
Inventory, December 31			**40,000**	
Cost of goods sold				**316,000**

HELPFUL HINT

The second column from the right identifies the primary items that make up cost of goods sold of $316,000. The third column explains cost of goods purchased of $320,000. The fourth column reports contra purchase items of $17,200.

The use of the periodic inventory system does not affect the content of the balance sheet. As under the perpetual system, merchandise inventory is reported at the same amount in the current assets section.

Further detail on the use of the periodic system is provided in the appendix to this chapter.

BEFORE YOU GO ON...

Review It

1. Name two basic systems of accounting for inventory.
2. What accounts are used in determining the cost of goods purchased?
3. What is included in cost of goods available for sale?

Do It

Aerosmith Company's accounting records show the following at year-end: Purchase Discounts $3,400; Freight-in $6,100; Sales $240,000; Purchases $162,500; Beginning Inventory $18,000; Ending Inventory $20,000; Sales Discounts $10,000; Purchase Returns $5,200; and Operating Expenses $57,000. Compute the following amounts for Aerosmith Company: net sales, cost of goods purchased, cost of goods sold, gross profit, and net income.

ACTION PLAN

- Understand the relationships of the cost components in measuring net income for a merchandising company.
- Compute net sales.
- Compute cost of goods purchased.
- Compute cost of goods sold.
- Compute gross profit.
- Compute net income.

SOLUTION

Net sales:

Sales − Sales discounts = Net sales
$240,000 − $10,000 = $230,000

Cost of goods purchased:

Purchases − Purchase returns − Purchase discounts + Freight-in = Cost of goods purchased
$162,500 − $5,200 − $3,400 + $6,100 = $160,000

Cost of goods sold:

Beginning inventory + Cost of goods purchased − Ending inventory = Cost of goods sold
$18,000 + $160,000 − $20,000 = $158,000

Gross profit:

Net sales − Cost of goods sold = Gross profit
$230,000 − $158,000 = $72,000

Net income:

Gross profit − Operating expenses = Net income
$72,000 − $57,000 = $15,000

Related exercise material: *BE5-10, BE5-11, E5-10, and E5-11.*

THE NAVIGATOR

DEMONSTRATION PROBLEM

The adjusted trial balance columns of the work sheet for the year ended December 31, 2006, for Falcetto Company are as follows.

Debit		Credit	
Cash	14,500	Accumulated Depreciation	18,000
Accounts Receivable	11,100	Notes Payable	25,000
Merchandise Inventory	29,000	Accounts Payable	10,600
Prepaid Insurance	2,500	Common Stock	50,000
Store Equipment	95,000	Retained Earnings	31,000
Dividends	12,000	Sales	536,800
Sales Returns and Allowances	6,700	Interest Revenue	2,500
Sales Discounts	5,000		673,900
Cost of Goods Sold	363,400		
Freight-out	7,600		
Advertising Expense	12,000		
Store Salaries Expense	56,000		
Utilities Expense	18,000		
Rent Expense	24,000		
Depreciation Expense	9,000		
Insurance Expense	4,500		
Interest Expense	3,600		
	673,900		

Instructions

Prepare an income statement assuming Falcetto Company does not use subgroupings for operating expenses.

SOLUTION TO DEMONSTRATION PROBLEM

FALCETTO COMPANY
Income Statement
For the Year Ended December 31, 2006

Sales revenues		
Sales		$536,800
Less: Sales returns and allowances	$6,700	
Sales discounts	5,000	11,700
Net sales		525,100
Cost of goods sold		363,400
Gross profit		161,700
Operating expenses		
Store salaries expense	56,000	
Rent expense	24,000	
Utilities expense	18,000	
Advertising expense	12,000	
Depreciation expense	9,000	
Freight-out	7,600	
Insurance expense	4,500	
Total operating expenses		131,100
Income from operations		30,600
Other revenues and gains		
Interest revenue	2,500	
Other expenses and losses		
Interest expense	3,600	1,100
Net income		$ 29,500

THE NAVIGATOR

ACTION PLAN

- Remember that the key components of the income statement are net sales, cost of goods sold, gross profit, total operating expenses, and net income (loss). Report these components in the right-hand column of the income statement.
- Put nonoperating items after income from operations.

SUMMARY OF STUDY OBJECTIVES

1. **Identify the differences between a service enterprise and a merchandiser.** Because of inventory, a merchandiser has sales revenue, cost of goods sold, and gross profit. To account for inventory, a merchandiser must choose between a perpetual inventory system and a periodic inventory system.
2. **Explain the entries for purchases under a perpetual inventory system.** The Merchandise Inventory account is debited for all purchases of merchandise, freight-in, and other costs, and it is credited for purchase discounts and purchase returns and allowances.
3. **Explain the entries for sales revenues under a perpetual inventory system.** When inventory is sold, Accounts Receivable (or Cash) is debited, and Sales is credited for the **selling price** of the merchandise. At the same time, Cost of Goods Sold is debited, and Merchandise Inventory is credited for the **cost** of the inventory items sold.
4. **Explain the steps in the accounting cycle for a merchandiser.** Each of the required steps in the accounting cycle for a service enterprise applies to a merchandiser. A work sheet is again an optional step. Under a perpetual inventory system, the Merchandise Inventory account must be adjusted to agree with the physical count.
5. **Distinguish between a multiple-step and a single-step income statement.** A multiple-step income statement shows numerous steps in determining net income, including nonoperating activities sections. In a single-step income statement all data are classified under two categories, revenues or expenses, and net income is determined by one step.
6. **Explain the computation and importance of gross profit.** Gross profit is computed by subtracting cost of goods sold from net sales. Gross profit represents the merchandising profit of a company. The amount and trend of gross profit are closely watched by management and other interested parties.
7. **Determine cost of goods sold under a periodic inventory system.** The steps in determining cost of goods sold are (a) record the purchases of merchandise, (b) determine the cost of goods purchased, and (c) determine the cost of goods on hand at the beginning and end of the accounting period.

THE NAVIGATOR

GLOSSARY

Administrative expenses Expenses relating to general operating activities such as personnel management, accounting, and store security. (p. 207).

Contra revenue account An account that is offset against a revenue account on the income statement. (p. 199).

Cost of goods sold The total cost of merchandise sold during the period. (p. 191).

FOB destination Freight terms indicating that the goods will be placed free on board at the buyer's place of business, and the seller pays the freight costs. (p. 196).

FOB shipping point Freight terms indicating that goods are placed free on board the carrier by the seller, and the buyer pays the freight costs. (p. 196).

Gross profit The excess of net sales over the cost of goods sold. (p. 191).

Income from operations Income from a company's principal operating activity; determined by subtracting cost of goods sold and operating expenses from net sales. (p. 206).

Multiple-step income statement An income statement that shows numerous steps in determining net income (or net loss). (p. 203).

Net sales Sales less sales returns and allowances and sales discounts. (p. 204).

Operating expenses Expenses incurred in the process of earning sales revenues that are deducted from gross profit in the income statement. (p. 192).

Other expenses and losses A nonoperating activities section of the income statement that shows expenses from auxiliary operations and losses unrelated to the company's operations. (p. 205).

Other revenues and gains A nonoperating activities section of the income statement that shows revenues from auxiliary operations and gains unrelated to the company's operations. (p. 205).

Periodic inventory system An inventory system in which detailed records are not maintained throughout the accounting period and the cost of goods sold is determined only at the end of an accounting period. (p. 193).

Perpetual inventory system An inventory system in which the cost of each inventory item is maintained throughout the accounting period and detailed records continuously show the inventory that should be on hand. (p. 193).

Purchase discount A cash discount claimed by a buyer for prompt payment of a balance due. (p. 197).

Purchase invoice A document that supports each credit purchase. (p. 195).

Sales discount A reduction given by a seller for prompt payment of a credit sale. (p. 199).

Sales invoice A document that supports each credit sale. (p. 198).

Sales revenue (sales) Primary source of revenue in a merchandising company. (p. 191).

Selling expenses Expenses associated with making sales. (p. 207).

Single-step income statement An income statement that shows only one step in determining net income (or net loss). (p. 207).

APPENDIX 5A PERIODIC INVENTORY SYSTEM

STUDY OBJECTIVE 8

Prepare the entries for purchases and sales of inventory under a periodic inventory system.

In a **periodic inventory system**, revenues from the sale of merchandise are recorded when sales are made, in the same way as in a perpetual system. But, no attempt is made on the date of sale to record the cost of the merchandise sold. Instead, a physical inventory count is taken at the end of the period. This count determines (1) the cost of the merchandise on hand and (2) the cost of the goods sold during the period. There is another key difference: Under a periodic system, purchases of merchandise are recorded in a Purchases account rather than a Merchandise Inventory account. Also, under a periodic system, it is customary to record the following in separate accounts: purchase returns and allowances, purchase discounts, and freight-in on purchases. That way, accumulated amounts for each are known.

Recording Transactions Under a Periodic Inventory System

To illustrate the recording of merchandise transactions under a periodic inventory system, we will use the purchase/sale transactions between Sellers Electronix and Beyer Video discussed in this chapter.

Recording Purchases of Merchandise

On the basis of the sales invoice (Illustration 5-4 shown on page 195) and receipt of the merchandise ordered from Sellers Electronix, Beyer Video records the $3,800 purchase as follows.

May 4	Purchases	3,800	
	Accounts Payable		3,800
	(To record goods purchased on account, terms 2/10, n/30)		

HELPFUL HINT

Be careful not to fall into the trap of debiting purchases of equipment or supplies to Purchases.

A	=	L	+	SE
		+3,800		−3,800 Exp

Cash Flows
no effect

Purchases is a temporary account whose normal balance is a debit.

Freight Costs

When the purchaser directly incurs the freight costs, the account Freight-in is debited. For example, upon delivery of the goods on May 6, Beyer pays Acme Freight Company $150 for freight charges on its purchase from Sellers Electronix. The entry on Beyer's books is:

May 6	Freight-in	150	
	Cash		150
	(To record payment of freight, terms FOB shipping point)		

A	=	L	+	SE
−150				−150 Exp

Cash Flows
−150

Like Purchases, Freight-in is a temporary account whose normal balance is a debit. **Freight-in is part of cost of goods purchased.** In accordance with the cost principle, cost of goods purchased should include any freight charges necessary to bring the goods to the purchaser. Freight costs are not subject to a purchase discount. Purchase discounts apply only on the invoice cost of the merchandise.

ALTERNATIVE TERMINOLOGY

Freight-in is frequently called *transportation-in.*

Purchase Returns and Allowances

Some of the merchandise received from Sellers Electronix is defective. Beyer Video returns $300 worth of the goods and prepares the following entry to recognize the purchase return.

May 8	Accounts Payable	300	
	Purchase Returns and Allowances		300
	(To record return of defective goods purchased from Sellers Electronix)		

A	=	L	+	SE
		−300		+300 Exp

Cash Flows
no effect

Purchase Returns and Allowances is a temporary account whose normal balance is a credit.

Purchase Discounts

On May 14 Beyer Video pays the balance due on account to Sellers Electronix. Beyer takes the 2% cash discount allowed by Sellers for payment within 10 days. The payment and discount are recorded by Beyer Video as follows.

May 14	Accounts Payable	3,500	
	Purchase Discounts		70
	Cash		3,430
	(To record payment to Sellers Electronix within the discount period)		

A	=	L	+	SE
−3,430		−3,500		+70 Exp

Cash Flows
−3,430

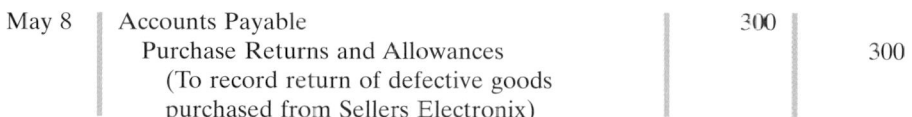

Purchase Discounts is a temporary account whose normal balance is a credit.

Recording Sales of Merchandise

The sale of $3,800 of merchandise to Beyer Video on May 4 (sales invoice No. 731, Illustration 5-4 on page 195) is recorded by Sellers Electronix as follows.

A	=	L	+	SE
+3,800				+3,800 Rev

Cash Flows
no effect

May 4	Accounts Receivable	3,800	
	Sales		3,800
	(To record credit sales per invoice #731 to Beyer Video)		

Sales Returns and Allowances

Based on the receipt of returned goods from Beyer Video on May 8, Sellers Electronix records the $300 sales return as follows.

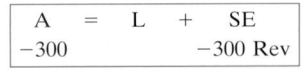

A	=	L	+	SE
−300				−300 Rev

Cash Flows
no effect

May 8	Sales Returns and Allowances	300	
	Accounts Receivable		300
	(To record return of goods from Beyer Video)		

Sales Discounts

On May 15, Sellers Electronix receives payment of $3,430 on account from Beyer Video. Sellers honors the 2% cash discount and records the payment of Beyer's account receivable in full as follows.

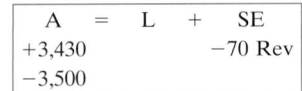

A	=	L	+	SE
+3,430				−70 Rev
−3,500				

Cash Flows
+3,430

May 15	Cash	3,430	
	Sales Discounts	70	
	Accounts Receivable		3,500
	(To record collection from Beyer Video within 2/10, n/30 discount period)		

Comparison of Entries—Perpetual vs. Periodic

The periodic inventory system entries shown in this appendix are reproduced in the righthand column of Illustration 5A-1. (They are printed in red.) In the middle column (printed in blue) are the entries from Chapter 5 (pages 195–197) for the perpetual inventory system for both Sellers Electronix and Beyer Video. Having these entries side-by-side should help you compare the differences. The entries that are different in the two inventory systems are highlighted.

Illustration 5A-1
Comparison of journal entries under perpetual and periodic inventory systems

ENTRIES ON BEYER VIDEO'S BOOKS

Transaction		Perpetual Inventory System			Periodic Inventory System		
May 4	Purchase of merchandise on credit.	**Merchandise Inventory**	3,800		**Purchases**	3,800	
		Accounts Payable		3,800	Accounts Payable		3,800
May 6	Freight costs on purchase.	**Merchandise Inventory**	150		**Freight-in**	150	
		Cash		150	Cash		150
May 8	Purchase returns and allowances.	**Merchandise Inventory**	300		Accounts Payable	300	
		Accounts Payable		300	**Purchase Returns and Allowances**		300
May 14	Payment on account with a discount.	Accounts Payable	3,500		Accounts Payable	3,500	
		Cash		3,430	Cash		3,430
		Merchandise Inventory		70	**Purchase Discounts**		70

Illustration 5A-1
(*continued from p. 214*)

Entries on Sellers Electronix's Books

Transaction		Perpetual Inventory System			Periodic Inventory System		
May 4	Sale of merchandise on credit.	Accounts Receivable	3,800		Accounts Receivable	3,800	
		Sales		3,800	Sales		3,800
		Cost of Goods Sold	2,400		**No entry for cost of goods sold**		
		Merchandise Inventory		2,400			
May 8	Return of merchandise sold.	Sales Returns and Allowances	300		Sales Returns and Allowances	300	
		Accounts Receivable		300	Accounts Receivable		300
		Merchandise Inventory	140		**No entry**		
		Cost of Goods Sold		140			
May 15	Cash received on account with a discount.	Cash	3,430		Cash	3,430	
		Sales Discounts	70		Sales Discounts	70	
		Accounts Receivable		3,500	Accounts Receivable		3,500

SUMMARY OF STUDY OBJECTIVE FOR APPENDIX 5A

8. **Prepare the entries for purchases and sales of inventory under a periodic inventory system.** In recording purchases, entries are required for (a) cash and credit purchases, (b) purchase returns and allowances, (c) purchase discounts, and (d) freight costs. In recording sales, entries are required for (a) cash and credit sales, (b) sales returns and allowances, and (c) sales discounts.

Appendix 5B Work Sheet for a Merchandiser

Using a Work Sheet

STUDY OBJECTIVE 9

Prepare a work sheet for a merchandiser.

As indicated in Chapter 4, a work sheet enables financial statements to be prepared before the adjusting entries are journalized and posted. The steps in preparing a work sheet for a merchandiser are the same as they are for a service enterprise (see page 142). The work sheet for Sellers Electronix is shown in Illustration 5B-1 (on page 216). The unique accounts for a merchandiser using a perpetual inventory system are shown in capital letters in red.

Trial Balance Columns

Data for the trial balance are obtained from the ledger balances of Sellers Electronix at December 31. The amount shown for Merchandise Inventory, $40,500, is the year-end inventory amount from the perpetual inventory system.

Illustration 5B-1
Work sheet for merchandiser

SELLERS ELECTRONIX
Work Sheet
For the Year Ended December 31, 2006

	Trial Balance		Adjustments		Adjusted Trial Balance		Income Statement		Balance Sheet	
	Dr.	Cr.	Dr.	Cr.	Dr.	Cr.	Dr.	Cr.	Dr.	Cr.
Cash	9,500				9,500				9,500	
Accounts Receivable	16,100				16,100				16,100	
MERCHANDISE INVENTORY	**40,500**			(a) 500	**40,000**				**40,000**	
Prepaid Insurance	3,800			(b) 2,000	1,800				1,800	
Store Equipment	80,000				80,000				80,000	
Accumulated Depreciation		16,000		(c) 8,000		24,000				24,000
Accounts Payable		20,400				20,400				20,400
Common Stock		50,000				50,000				50,000
Retained Earnings		33,000				33,000				33,000
Dividends	15,000				15,000				15,000	
SALES		**480,000**				**480,000**		**480,000**		
SALES RETURNS AND ALLOWANCES	**12,000**				**12,000**		**12,000**			
SALES DISCOUNTS	**8,000**				**8,000**		**8,000**			
COST OF GOODS SOLD	**315,500**		(a) 500		**316,000**		**316,000**			
Freight-out	7,000				7,000		7,000			
Advertising Expense	16,000				16,000		16,000			
Admin. Sal. Exp.	19,000				19,000		19,000			
Store Salaries Expense	40,000		(d) 5,000		45,000		45,000			
Utilities Expense	17,000				17,000		17,000			
Totals	599,400	599,400								
Insurance Expense			(b) 2,000		2,000		2,000			
Depreciation Expense			(c) 8,000		8,000		8,000			
Salaries Payable				(d) 5,000		5,000				5,000
Totals			15,500	15,500	612,400	612,400	450,000	480,000	162,400	132,400
Net Income							30,000			30,000
Totals							480,000	480,000	162,400	162,400

Key: (a) Adjustment to inventory on hand, (b) Insurance expired, (c) Depreciation expense, (d) Salaries accrued.

Adjustments Columns

A merchandiser generally has the same types of adjustments as a service company. As you see in the work sheet, adjustments (b), (c), and (d) are for insurance, depreciation, and salaries. These adjustments were also required for Pioneer Advertising Agency Inc., as illustrated in Chapters 3 and 4. Adjustment (a) was required to adjust the perpetual inventory carrying amount to the actual count.

After all adjustments data are entered on the work sheet, the equality of the adjustments column totals is established. The balances in all accounts are then extended to the adjusted trial balance columns.

Adjusted Trial Balance

The adjusted trial balance shows the balance of all accounts after adjustment at the end of the accounting period.

Income Statement Columns

The accounts and balances that affect the income statement are transferred from the adjusted trial balance columns to the income statement columns. For Sellers Electronix, Sales of $480,000 is shown in the credit column. The contra revenue accounts Sales Returns and Allowances $12,000 and Sales Discounts $8,000 are shown in the debit column. The difference of $460,000 is the net sales shown on the income statement (Illustration 5-11).

Finally, all the credits in the income statement column should be totaled and compared to the total of the debits in the income statement column. If the credits exceed the debits, the company has net income. In Sellers Electronix's case there was net income of $30,000. If the debits exceed the credits, the company would report a net loss.

Balance Sheet Columns

The major difference between the balance sheets of a service company and a merchandiser is inventory. For Sellers Electronix, the ending inventory amount of $40,000 is shown in the balance sheet debit column. The information to prepare the retained earnings statement is also found in these columns. That is, the retained earnings account beginning balance is $33,000. The dividends are $15,000. Net income results when the total of the debit column exceeds the total of the credit column in the balance sheet columns. A net loss results when the total of the credits exceeds the total of the debit balances.

SUMMARY OF STUDY OBJECTIVE FOR APPENDIX 5B

9. **Prepare a work sheet for a merchandiser.** The steps in preparing a work sheet for a merchandiser are the same as they are for a service company. The unique accounts for a merchandiser are Merchandise Inventory, Sales, Sales Returns and Allowances, Sales Discounts, and Cost of Goods Sold.

***Note**: All **asterisked** Questions, Exercises, and Problems relate to material in the appendixes to the chapter.

SELF-STUDY QUESTIONS

Self-Study/Self-Test

www.wiley.com/college/weygandt

Answers are at the end of the chapter.

(SO 1) 1. Gross profit will result if:
   a. operating expenses are less than net income.
   b. sales revenues are greater than operating expenses.
   c. sales revenues are greater than cost of goods sold.
   d. operating expenses are greater than cost of goods sold.

(SO 2) 2. Under a perpetual inventory system, when goods are purchased for resale by a company:
   a. purchases on account are debited to Merchandise Inventory.
   b. purchases on account are debited to Purchases.
   c. purchase returns are debited to Purchase Returns and Allowances.
   d. freight costs are debited to Freight-out.

(SO 3) 3. The sales accounts that normally have a debit balance are:
   a. Sales Discounts.
   b. Sales Returns and Allowances.
   c. both (a) and (b).
   d. neither (a) nor (b).

4. A credit sale of $750 is made on June 13, terms 2/10, net/30. A return of $50 is granted on June 16. The amount received as payment in full on June 23 is: (SO 3)
   a. $700.
   b. $686.
   c. $685.
   d. $650.

5. Which of the following accounts will normally appear in the ledger of a merchandising company that uses a perpetual inventory system? (SO 2)
   a. Purchases.
   b. Freight-in.
   c. Cost of Goods Sold.
   d. Purchase Discounts.

(SO 5) **6.** The multiple-step income statement for a merchandiser shows each of the following features *except*:
a. gross profit.
b. cost of goods sold.
c. a sales revenue section.
d. investing activities section.

(SO 6) **7.** If sales revenues are $400,000, cost of goods sold is $310,000, and operating expenses are $60,000, the gross profit is:
a. $30,000.
b. $90,000.
c. $340,000.
d. $400,000.

(SO 5) **8.** In a single-step income statement:
a. gross profit is reported.
b. cost of goods sold is not reported.
c. sales revenues and "other revenues and gains" are reported in the revenues section of the income statement.
d. operating income is separately reported.

(SO 5) **9.** Which of the following appears on both a single-step and a multiple-step income statement?
a. merchandise inventory.
b. gross profit.
c. income from operations.
d. cost of goods sold.

(SO 7) **10.** In determining cost of goods sold:
a. purchase discounts are deducted from net purchases.
b. freight-out is added to net purchases.
c. purchase returns and allowances are deducted from net purchases.
d. freight-in is added to net purchases.

11. If beginning inventory is $60,000, cost of goods purchased is $380,000, and ending inventory is $50,000, cost of goods sold is: (SO 7)
a. $390,000.
b. $370,000.
c. $330,000.
d. $420,000.

***12.** When goods are purchased for resale by a company using a periodic inventory system: (SO 8)
a. purchases on account are debited to Merchandise Inventory.
b. purchases on account are debited to Purchases.
c. purchase returns are debited to Purchase Returns and Allowances.
d. freight costs are debited to Purchases.

***13.** In a work sheet, Merchandise Inventory is shown in the following columns: (SO 9)
a. Adjusted trial balance debit and balance sheet debit.
b. Income statement debit and balance sheet debit.
c. Income statement credit and balance sheet debit.
d. Income statement credit and adjusted trial balance debit.

THE NAVIGATOR

QUESTIONS

1. (a)"The steps in the accounting cycle for a merchandising company are different from the accounting cycle for a service enterprise." Do you agree or disagree? (b) Is the measurement of net income for a merchandiser conceptually the same as for a service enterprise? Explain.

2. Why is the normal operating cycle for a merchandiser likely to be longer than for a service company?

3. (a) How do the components of revenues and expenses differ between a merchandiser and a service enterprise? (b) Explain the income measurement process in a merchandising company.

4. How does income measurement differ between a merchandiser and a service company?

5. When is cost of goods sold determined in a perpetual inventory system?

6. Distinguish between FOB shipping point and FOB destination. Identify the freight terms that will result in a debit to Merchandise Inventory by the purchaser and a debit to Freight-out by the seller.

7. Explain the meaning of the credit terms 2/10, n/30.

8. Goods costing $2,500 are purchased on account on July 15 with credit terms of 2/10, n/30. On July 18 a $200 credit memo is received from the supplier for damaged goods. Give the journal entry on July 24 to record payment of the balance due within the discount period using a perpetual inventory system.

9. Karen Lloyd believes revenues from credit sales may be earned before they are collected in cash. Do you agree? Explain.

10. (a) What is the primary source document for recording (1) cash sales, (2) credit sales, and (3) sales returns and allowances? (b) Using XXs for amounts, give the journal entry for each of the transactions in part (a).

11. A credit sale is made on July 10 for $700, terms 2/10, n/30. On July 12, $100 of goods are returned for credit. Give the journal entry on July 19 to record the receipt of the balance due within the discount period.

12. Explain why the Merchandise Inventory account will usually require adjustment at year-end.

13. Prepare the closing entries for the Sales account, assuming a balance of $200,000 and the Cost of Goods Sold account with a $145,000 balance.

14. What merchandising account(s) will appear in the post-closing trial balance?

15. Regis Co. has sales revenue of $109,000, cost of goods sold of $70,000, and operating expenses of $20,000. What is its gross profit?

16. Kathy Ho Company reports net sales of $800,000, gross profit of $570,000, and net income of $240,000. What are its operating expenses?
17. Identify the distinguishing features of an income statement for a merchandiser.
18. Identify the sections of a multiple-step income statement that relate to (a) operating activities, and (b) nonoperating activities.
19. Distinguish between the types of functional groupings of operating expenses. What problem is created by these groupings?
20. How does the single-step form of income statement differ from the multiple-step form?
21. Identify the accounts that are added to or deducted from Purchases to determine the cost of goods purchased. For each account, indicate whether it is added or deducted.

*22. Goods costing $2,000 are purchased on account on July 15 with credit terms of 2/10, n/30. On July 18 a $200 credit memo is received from the supplier for damaged goods. Give the journal entry on July 24 to record payment of the balance due within the discount period, assuming a periodic inventory system.

*23. Indicate the columns of the work sheet in which (a) merchandise inventory and (b) cost of goods sold will be shown.

BRIEF EXERCISES

Compute missing amounts in determining net income.
(SO 1)

BE5-1 Presented below are the components in Clearwater Company's income statement. Determine the missing amounts.

	Sales	Cost of Goods Sold	Gross Profit	Operating Expenses	Net Income
(a)	$75,000	?	$28,600	?	$10,800
(b)	$108,000	$70,000	?	?	$29,500
(c)	?	$71,900	$99,600	$39,500	?

Journalize perpetual inventory entries.
(SO 2, 3)

BE5-2 Giovanni Company buys merchandise on account from Gordon Company. The selling price of the goods is $780, and the cost of the goods is $560. Both companies use perpetual inventory systems. Journalize the transaction on the books of both companies.

Journalize sales transactions.
(SO 3)

BE5-3 Prepare the journal entries to record the following transactions on Benson Company's books using a perpetual inventory system.

(a) On March 2, Benson Company sold $800,000 of merchandise to Edgebrook Company, terms 2/10, n/30. The cost of the merchandise sold was $620,000.
(b) On March 6, Edgebrook Company returned $120,000 of the merchandise purchased on March 2 because it was defective. The cost of the returned merchandise was $90,000.
(c) On March 12, Benson Company received the balance due from Edgebrook Company.

Journalize purchase transactions.
(SO 2)

BE5-4 From the information in BE5-3, prepare the journal entries to record these transactions on Edgebrook Company's books under a perpetual inventory system.

Prepare sales revenues section of income statement.
(SO 3)

BE5-5 Piccola Company provides the following information for the month ended October 31, 2006: Sales on credit $280,000, cash sales $100,000 sales discounts $13,000, sales returns and allowances $21,000. Prepare the sales revenues section of the income statement based on this information.

Prepare adjusting entry for merchandise inventory.
(SO 4)

BE5-6 At year-end the perpetual inventory records of Salsa Company showed merchandise inventory of $98,000. The company determined, however, that its actual inventory on hand was $96,800. Record the necessary adjusting entry.

Prepare closing entries for merchandise accounts.
(SO 4)

BE5-7 Orlaida Company has the following merchandise account balances: Sales $192,000, Sales Discounts $2,000, Cost of Goods Sold $105,000, and Merchandise Inventory $40,000. Prepare the entries to record the closing of these items to Income Summary.

Contrast presentation in multiple-step and single-step income statements.
(SO 5)

BE5-8 Explain where each of the following items would appear on (1) a multiple-step income statement, and on (2) a single-step income statement: **(a)** gain on sale of equipment, **(b)** casualty loss from vandalism, and **(c)** cost of goods sold.

Compute net sales, gross profit, and income from operations.
(SO 3, 5, 6)

BE5-9 Assume Jose Company has the following account balances: Sales $506,000, Sales Returns and Allowances $15,000, Cost of Goods Sold $350,000, Selling Expenses $70,000, and Administrative Expenses $40,000. Compute the following: **(a)** net sales, **(b)** gross profit, and **(c)** income from operations.

Compute net purchases and cost of goods purchased.
(SO 7)

BE5-10 Assume that E. Guard Company uses a periodic inventory system and has these account balances: Purchases $400,000; Purchase Returns and Allowances $11,000; Purchase Discounts $8,000; and Freight-in $16,000. Determine net purchases and cost of goods purchased.

Compute cost of goods sold and gross profit.
(SO 7)

BE5-11 Assume the same information as in BE5-10 and also that E. Guard Company has beginning inventory of $60,000, ending inventory of $90,000, and net sales of $630,000. Determine the amounts to be reported for cost of goods sold and gross profit.

Journalize purchase transactions.
(SO, 8)

***BE5-12** Prepare the journal entries to record these transactions on H. Hunt Company's books using a periodic inventory system.

(a) On March 2, H. Hunt Company purchased $900,000 of merchandise from B. Streisand Company, terms 2/10, n/30.
(b) On March 6, H. Hunt Company returned $130,000 of the merchandise purchased on March 2 because it was defective.
(c) On March 12, H. Hunt Company paid the balance due to B. Streisand Company.

Identify work sheet columns for selected accounts.
(SO 7)

***BE5-13** Presented below is the format of the work sheet presented in the chapter.

Trial Balance		Adjustments		Adjusted Trial Balance		Income Statement		Balance Sheet	
Dr.	Cr.	Dr.	Cr.	Dr.	Cr.	Dr.	Cr.	Dr.	Cr.

Indicate where the following items will appear on the work sheet: **(a)** Cash, **(b)** Merchandise Inventory, **(c)** Sales, **(d)** Cost of goods sold.

Example:
Cash: Trial balance debit column; Adjusted trial balance debit column; and Balance sheet debit column.

EXERCISES

Journalize purchases transactions.
(SO 2)

E5-1 Information related to Gilberto Co. is presented below.

1. On April 5, purchased merchandise from Allman Company for $20,000 terms 2/10, net/30, FOB shipping point.
2. On April 6, paid freight costs of $900 on merchandise purchased from Allman.
3. On April 7, purchased equipment on account for $26,000.
4. On April 8, returned damaged merchandise to Allman Company and was granted a $4,000 allowance for returned merchandise.
5. On April 15, paid the amount due to Allman Company in full.

Instructions

(a) Prepare the journal entries to record these transactions on the books of Gilberto Co. under a perpetual inventory system.
(b) Assume that Gilberto Co. paid the balance due to Allman Company on May 4 instead of April 15. Prepare the journal entry to record this payment.

Journalize perpetual inventory entries.
(SO 2, 3)

E5-2 On September 1, Eden Office Supply had an inventory of 30 pocket calculators at a cost of $18 each. The company uses a perpetual inventory system. During September, the following transactions occurred.

Sept. 6 Purchased 80 calculators at $17 each from Mozart Co. for cash.
9 Paid freight of $80 on calculators purchased from Mozart Co.
10 Returned 2 calculators to Mozart Co. for $36 credit (including freight) because they did not meet specifications.
12 Sold 26 calculators costing $18 (including freight) for $31 each to Mega Book Store, terms n/30.
14 Granted credit of $31 to Mega Book Store for the return of one calculator that was not ordered.
20 Sold 30 calculators costing $18 for $31 each to Barbara's Card Shop, terms n/30.

Instructions
Journalize the September transactions.

E5-3 On June 10, Lippizan Company purchased $6,000 of merchandise from Bristol Company FOB shipping point, terms 2/10, n/30. Lippizan pays the freight costs of $400 on June 11. Damaged goods totaling $300 are returned to Bristol for credit on June 12. The scrap value of these goods is $150. On June 19, Lippizan pays Bristol Company in full, less the purchase discount. Both companies use a perpetual inventory system.

Prepare purchase and sale entries.

(SO 2, 3)

Instructions

(a) Prepare separate entries for each transaction on the books of Lippizan Company.

(b) Prepare separate entries for each transaction for Bristol Company. The merchandise purchased by Lippizan on June 10 had cost Bristol $3,000.

E5-4 Presented below are transactions related to Rebecca Company.

Journalize sales transactions.

(SO 3)

1. On December 3, Rebecca Company sold $480,000 of merchandise to Simonis Co., terms 2/10, n/30, FOB shipping point. The cost of the merchandise sold was $350,000.
2. On December 8, Simonis Co. was granted an allowance of $27,000 for merchandise purchased on December 3.
3. On December 13, Rebecca Company received the balance due from Simonis Co.

Instructions

(a) Prepare the journal entries to record these transactions on the books of Rebecca Company using a perpetual inventory system.

(b) Assume that Rebecca Company received the balance due from Simonis Co. on January 2 of the following year instead of December 13. Prepare the journal entry to record the receipt of payment on January 2.

E5-5 The adjusted trial balance of Schinzer Company shows the following data pertaining to sales at the end of its fiscal year October 31, 2006: Sales $800,000, Freight-out $16,000, Sales Returns and Allowances $20,000, and Sales Discounts $15,000.

Prepare sales revenues section and closing entries.

(SO 3, 4)

Instructions

(a) Prepare the sales revenues section of the income statement.

(b) Prepare separate closing entries for (1) sales, and (2) the contra accounts to sales.

E5-6 Presented is information related to Taylor Co. for the month of January 2006.

Prepare adjusting and closing entries.

(SO 4)

Ending inventory per perpetual records	$ 21,600	Salary expense	$ 61,000
Ending inventory actually on hand	21,000	Sales discounts	10,000
Cost of goods sold	208,000	Sales returns and allowances	13,000
Freight-out	7,000	Sales	350,000
Insurance expense	12,000		
Rent expense	20,000		

Instructions

(a) Prepare the necessary adjusting entry for inventory.

(b) Prepare the necessary closing entries.

E5-7 In its income statement for the year ended December 31, 2006, Bach Company reported the following condensed data.

Prepare multiple-step and single-step income statements.

(SO 5)

Administrative expenses	$ 435,000	Selling expenses	$ 490,000
Cost of goods sold	1,289,000	Loss on sale of equipment	10,000
Interest expense	70,000	Net sales	2,342,000
Interest revenue	28,000		

Instructions

(a) Prepare a multiple-step income statement.

(b) Prepare a single-step income statement.

E5-8 An inexperienced accountant for Gulliver Company made the following errors in recording merchandising transactions.

Prepare correcting entries for sales and purchases.

(SO 2, 3)

1. A $175 refund to a customer for faulty merchandise was debited to Sales $175 and credited to Cash $175.
2. A $160 credit purchase of supplies was debited to Merchandise Inventory $160 and credited to Cash $160.

3. A $110 sales discount was debited to Sales.
4. A cash payment of $30 for freight on merchandise purchases was debited to Freight-out $300 and credited to Cash $300.

Instructions

Prepare separate correcting entries for each error, assuming that the incorrect entry is not reversed. (Omit explanations.)

Compute missing amounts. (SO 5, 6)

E5-9 Presented below is financial information for two different companies.

	Lee Company	Chan Company
Sales	$90,000	(d)
Sales returns	(a)	$ 5,000
Net sales	81,000	95,000
Cost of goods sold	56,000	(e)
Gross profit	(b)	41,500
Operating expenses	15,000	(f)
Net income	(c)	15,000

Instructions

Determine the missing amounts.

Prepare cost of goods sold section. (SO 7)

E5-10 The trial balance of J. Harlow Company at the end of its fiscal year, August 31, 2006, includes these accounts: Merchandise Inventory $17,200; Purchases $144,000; Sales $190,000; Freight-in $4,000; Sales Returns and Allowances $3,000; Freight-out $1,000; and Purchase Returns and Allowances $2,000. The ending merchandise inventory is $25,000.

Instructions

Prepare a cost of goods sold section for the year ending August 31 (periodic inventory).

Complete the cost of goods sold sections. (SO 7)

E5-11 Below is a series of cost of goods sold sections for companies X, F, L, and S.

	X	F	L	S
Beginning inventory	$ 250	$ 120	$1,000	$ (j)
Purchases	1,500	1,080	(g)	43,590
Purchase returns and allowances	40	(d)	290	(k)
Net purchases	(a)	1,030	7,210	42,090
Freight-in	110	(e)	(h)	2,240
Cost of goods purchased	(b)	1,230	7,940	(l)
Cost of goods available for sale	1,820	1,350	(i)	49,530
Ending inventory	310	(f)	1,450	6,230
Cost of goods sold	(c)	1,230	7,490	43,300

Instructions

Fill in the lettered blanks to complete the cost of goods sold sections.

Journalize purchase transactions. (SO 8)

***E5-12** This information relates to Hans Olaf Co.

1. On April 5 purchased merchandise from D. DeVito Company for $18,000, terms 2/10, net/30, FOB shipping point.
2. On April 6 paid freight costs of $900 on merchandise purchased from D. DeVito Company.
3. On April 7 purchased equipment on account for $26,000.
4. On April 8 returned some of April 5 merchandise to D. DeVito Company which cost $2,800.
5. On April 15 paid the amount due to D. DeVito Company in full.

Instructions

(a) Prepare the journal entries to record these transactions on the books of Hans Olaf Co. using a periodic inventory system.

(b) Assume that Hans Olaf Co. paid the balance due to D. DeVito Company on May 4 instead of April 15. Prepare the journal entry to record this payment.

Journalize purchase transactions. (SO 8)

***E5-13** Presented below is the following information related to Argentina Co.

1. On April 5, purchased merchandise from Chile Company for $18,000, terms 2/10, net/30, FOB shipping point.

2. On April 6, paid freight costs of $800 on merchandise purchased from Chile.
3. On April 7, purchased equipment on account from Wayne Higley Mfg. Co. for $26,000.
4. On April 8, returned damaged merchandise to Chile Company and was granted a $4,000 allowance.
5. On April 15, paid the amount due to Chile Company in full.

Instructions

(a) Prepare the journal entries to record these transactions on the books of Argentina Co. using a periodic inventory system.

(b) Assume that Argentina Co. paid the balance due to Chile Company on May 4 instead of April 15. Prepare the journal entry to record this payment.

***E5-14** Presented below are selected accounts for Streisand Company as reported in the work sheet at the end of May 2006.

Complete work sheet.
(SO 9)

Accounts	Adjusted Trial Balance		Income Statement		Balance Sheet	
	Dr.	Cr.	Dr.	Cr.	Dr.	Cr.
Cash	9,000					
Merchandise Inventory	76,000					
Sales		450,000				
Sales Returns and Allowances	10,000					
Sales Discounts	9,000					
Cost of Goods Sold	250,000					

Instructions

Complete the work sheet by extending amounts reported in the adjusted trial balance to the appropriate columns in the work sheet. Do not total individual columns.

PROBLEMS: SET A

P5-1A Phantom Book Warehouse distributes hardback books to retail stores and extends credit terms of 2/10, n/30 to all of its customers. At the end of May, Phantom's inventory consisted of 240 books purchased at $1,200. During the month of June the following merchandising transactions occurred.

Journalize purchase and sales transactions under a perpetual inventory system.
(SO 2, 3)

Peachtree

June 1 Purchased 160 books on account for $5 each from Ex Libris Publishers, FOB destination, terms 2/10, n/30. The appropriate party also made a cash payment of $50 for the freight on this date.
3 Sold 120 books on account to Readers-R-Us for $10 each.
6 Received $50 credit for 10 books returned to Ex Libris Publishers.
9 Paid Ex Libris Publishers in full, less discount.
15 Received payment in full from Readers-R-Us.
17 Sold 120 books on account to Bargain Books for $10 each.
20 Purchased 110 books on account for $5 each from Bookem Publishers, FOB destination, terms 2/15, n/30. The appropriate party also made a cash payment of $50 for the freight on this date.
24 Received payment in full from Bargain Books.
26 Paid Bookem Publishers in full, less discount.
28 Sold 110 books on account to Read-n-Weep Bookstore for $10 each.
30 Granted Read-n-Weep Bookstore $150 credit for 15 books returned costing $75.

Phantom Book Warehouse's chart of accounts includes the following: No. 101 Cash, No. 112 Accounts Receivable, No. 120 Merchandise Inventory, No. 201 Accounts Payable, No. 401 Sales, No. 412 Sales Returns and Allowances, No. 414 Sales Discounts, No. 505 Cost of Goods Sold.

Instructions

Journalize the transactions for the month of June for Phantom Book Warehouse using a perpetual inventory system.

Journalize, post, and prepare a partial income statement.

(SO 2, 3, 5, 6)

P5-2A Copple Hardware Store completed the following merchandising transactions in the month of May. At the beginning of May, the ledger of Copple showed Cash of $5,000 and Common Stock of $5,000.

May 1 Purchased merchandise on account from Nute Wholesale Supply $6,000, terms 2/10, n/30.

2 Sold merchandise on account $5,000, terms 1/10, n/30. The cost of the merchandise sold was $3,100.

5 Received credit from Nute Wholesale Supply for merchandise returned $600.

9 Received collections in full, less discounts, from customers billed on sales of $5,000 on May 2.

10 Paid Nute Wholesale Supply in full, less discount.

11 Purchased supplies for cash $900.

12 Purchased merchandise for cash $2,700.

15 Received refund for poor quality merchandise from supplier on cash purchase $230.

17 Purchased merchandise from Sherrick Distributors $1,900, FOB shipping point, terms 2/10, n/30.

19 Paid freight on May 17 purchase $250.

24 Sold merchandise for cash $6,200. The merchandise sold had a cost of $4,600.

25 Purchased merchandise from Duffy Inc. $1,000, FOB destination, terms 2/10, n/30.

27 Paid Sherrick Distributors in full, less discount.

29 Made refunds to cash customers for defective merchandise $100. The returned merchandise had a scrap value of $20.

31 Sold merchandise on account $1,600, terms n/30. The cost of the merchandise sold was $1,120.

Copple Hardware's chart of accounts includes the following: No. 101 Cash, No. 112 Accounts Receivable, No. 120 Merchandise Inventory, No. 126 Supplies, No. 201 Accounts Payable, No. 311 Common Stock, No. 401 Sales, No. 412 Sales Returns and Allowances, No. 414 Sales Discounts, No. 505 Cost of Goods Sold.

Instructions

(a) Journalize the transactions using a perpetual inventory system.

(b) Enter the beginning cash and common stock balances and post the transactions. (Use J1 for the journal reference.)

(c) Gross profit $3,850

(c) Prepare an income statement through gross profit for the month of May 2006.

Prepare financial statements and adjusting and closing entries.

(SO 4, 5)

P5-3A Moulton Department Store is located in midtown Metropolis. During the past several years, net income has been declining because of suburban shopping centers. At the end of the company's fiscal year on November 30, 2006, the following accounts appeared in two of its trial balances.

	Unadjusted	Adjusted		Unadjusted	Adjusted
Accounts Payable	$ 47,310	$ 47,310	Interest Revenue	$ 5,000	$ 5,000
Accounts Receivable	11,770	11,770	Merchandise Inventory	36,200	36,200
Accumulated Depr.—Delivery Equip.	15,680	18,816	Notes Payable	46,000	46,000
Accumulated Depr.—Store Equip.	32,300	41,800	Prepaid Insurance	13,500	3,000
Cash	8,000	8,000	Property Tax Expense		3,500
Common Stock	60,000	60,000	Property Taxes Payable		3,500
Cost of Goods Sold	633,220	633,220	Rent Expense	19,000	19,000
Delivery Expense	8,200	8,200	Retained Earnings	24,200	24,200
Delivery Equipment	57,000	57,000	Salaries Expense	120,000	120,000
Depr. Expense—Delivery Equip.		3,136	Sales	850,000	850,000
Depr. Expense—Store Equip.		9,500	Sales Commissions Expense	8,000	10,500
Dividends	12,000	12,000	Sales Commissions Payable		2,500
Insurance Expense		10,500	Sales Returns and Allowances	10,000	10,000
Interest Expense	8,000	8,000	Store Equip.	125,000	125,000
			Utilities Expense	10,600	10,600

Analysis reveals the following additional data.

1. Salaries expense is 75% selling and 25% administrative.

2. Insurance expense is 50% selling and 50% administrative.

3. Rent expense, utilities expense, and property tax expense are administrative expenses.
4. Notes payable are due in 2009.

Instructions

(a) Prepare a multiple-step income statement, a retained earnings statement, and a classified balance sheet.
(b) Journalize the adjusting entries that were made.
(c) Journalize the closing entries that are necessary.

(a) Net income $8,844
Retained earnings $21,044
Total assets $180,354

Journalize, post, and prepare a trial balance.
(SO 2, 3, 4)

P5-4A Bill Kokott, a former professional golf star, operates Bill's Pro Shop at Bay Golf Course. At the beginning of the current season on April 1, the ledger of Bill's Pro Shop showed Cash $2,500, Merchandise Inventory $3,500, and Common Stock $6,000. The following transactions were completed during April.

Apr. 5 Purchased golf bags, clubs, and balls on account from Ellis Co. $1,800, FOB shipping point, terms 2/10, n/60.
7 Paid freight on Ellis purchase $80.
9 Received credit from Ellis Co. for merchandise returned $100.
10 Sold merchandise on account to members $1,200, terms n/30. The merchandise sold had a cost of $810.
12 Purchased golf shoes, sweaters, and other accessories on account from Penguin Sportswear $660, terms 1/10, n/30.
14 Paid Ellis Co. in full, less discount.
17 Received credit from Penguin Sportswear for merchandise returned $60.
20 Made sales on account to members $700, terms n/30. The cost of the merchandise sold was $490.
21 Paid Penguin Sportswear in full, less discount.
27 Granted an allowance to members for clothing that did not fit properly $40.
30 Received payments on account from members $1,000.

The chart of accounts for the pro shop includes the following: No. 101 Cash, No. 112 Accounts Receivable, No. 120 Merchandise Inventory, No. 201 Accounts Payable, No. 311 Common Stock, No. 401 Sales, No. 412 Sales Returns and Allowances, No. 505 Cost of Goods Sold.

Instructions

(a) Journalize the April transactions using a perpetual inventory system.
(b) Enter the beginning balances in the ledger accounts and post the April transactions. (Use J1 for the journal reference.)
(c) Prepare a trial balance on April 30, 2006.

(c) Total debits $7,900

Determine cost of goods sold and gross profit under periodic approach.
(SO 6, 7)

P5-5A At the end of Stampfer Department Store's fiscal year on November 30, 2006, these accounts appeared in its adjusted trial balance.

Freight-in	$ 5,060
Merchandise Inventory	44,360
Purchases	630,000
Purchase Discounts	7,000
Purchase Returns and Allowances	3,000
Sales	910,000
Sales Returns and Allowances	20,000

Additional facts:

1. Merchandise inventory on November 30, 2006, is $36,200.
2. Note that Stampfer Department Store uses a periodic system.

Instructions

Prepare an income statement through gross profit for the year ended November 30, 2006.

Gross profit $256,780

Calculate missing amounts and assess profitability.
(SO 6, 7)

P5-6A Psang Inc. operates a retail operation that purchases and sells snowmobiles, amongst other outdoor products. The company purchases all merchandise inventory on credit and uses a perpetual inventory system. The accounts payable account is used for recording inventory purchases only; all other current liabilities are accrued in separate accounts. You are provided with the following selected information for the fiscal years 2004 through 2007, inclusive.

	2004	2005	2006	2007
Income Statement Data				
Sales		$96,850	$ (e)	$82,220
Cost of goods sold		(a)	27,140	26,550
Gross profit		69,260	61,540	(i)
Operating expenses		63,500	(f)	52,060
Net income		$ (b)	$ 4,570	$ (j)
Balance Sheet Data				
Merchandise inventory	$13,000	$ (c)	$14,700	$ (k)
Accounts payable	5,000	6,500	4,600	(l)
Additional Information				
Purchases of merchandise inventory on account		$25,890	$ (g)	$24,050
Cash payments to suppliers		(d)	(h)	24,650

Instructions

(c) $11,300
(g) $30,540
(l) $ 4,000

(a) Calculate the missing amounts.
(b) Sales declined over the 3-year fiscal period, 2005–2007. Does that mean that profitability necessarily also declined? Explain, computing the gross profit rate and the profit margin ratio for each fiscal year to help support your answer.

Journalize, post, and prepare trial balance and partial income statement using periodic approach.
(SO 7, 8)

***P5-7A** At the beginning of the current season on April 1, the ledger of Tri-State Pro Shop showed Cash $2,500; Merchandise Inventory $3,500; and Common Stock $6,000. These transactions occured during April 2006.

Apr. 5 Purchased golf bags, clubs, and balls on account from Balata Co. $1,700, FOB shipping point, terms 2/10, n/60.
7 Paid freight on Balata Co. purchases $80.
9 Received credit from Balata Co. for merchandise returned $200.
10 Sold merchandise on account to members $950, terms n/30.
12 Purchased golf shoes, sweaters, and other accessories on account from Arrow Sportswear $660, terms 1/10, n/30.
14 Paid Balata Co. in full.
17 Received credit from Arrow Sportswear for merchandise returned $60.
20 Made sales on account to members $700, terms n/30.
21 Paid Arrow Sportswear in full.
27 Granted credit to members for clothing that did not fit properly $75.
30 Received payments on account from members $1,100.

The chart of accounts for the pro shop includes Cash; Accounts Receivable; Merchandise Inventory; Accounts Payable; Common Stock; Sales; Sales Returns and Allowances; Purchases; Purchase Returns and Allowances; Purchase Discounts, and Freight-in.

Instructions

(a) Journalize the April transactions using a periodic inventory system.
(b) Using T accounts, enter the beginning balances in the ledger accounts and post the April transactions.
(c) Prepare a trial balance on April 30, 2006.
(d) Prepare an income statement through gross profit, assuming merchandise inventory on hand at April 30 is $4,524.

(c) Tot. trial balance $7,946
Gross profit $ 455

***P5-8A** The trial balance of Loren Foelske Wholesale Company contained the following accounts at December 31, the end of the company's fiscal year.

Complete accounting cycle beginning with a work sheet.

(SO 4, 5, 6, 9)

LOREN FOELSKE WHOLESALE COMPANY
Trial Balance
December 31, 2006

	Debit	Credit
Cash	$ 25,400	
Accounts Receivable	37,600	
Merchandise Inventory	90,000	
Land	92,000	
Buildings	197,000	
Accumulated Depreciation—Buildings		$ 54,000
Equipment	83,500	
Accumulated Depreciation—Equipment		42,400
Notes Payable		50,000
Accounts Payable		39,000
Common Stock		200,000
Retained Earnings		67,800
Dividends	10,000	
Sales		904,100
Sales Discounts	6,100	
Cost of Goods Sold	709,900	
Salaries Expense	69,800	
Utilities Expense	19,400	
Repair Expense	5,900	
Gas and Oil Expense	7,200	
Insurance Expense	3,500	
Totals	$1,357,300	$1,357,300

Adjustment data:

1. Depreciation is $10,000 on buildings and $9,000 on equipment. (Both are administrative expenses.)
2. Interest of $5,000 is due and unpaid on notes payable at December 31.
3. Merchandise inventory actually on hand is $88,900.

Other data:

1. Salaries are 80% selling and 20% administrative.
2. Utilities expense, repair expense, and insurance expense are 100% administrative.
3. $10,000 of the notes payable are payable next year.
4. Gas and oil expense is a selling expense.

Instructions

(a) Enter the trial balance on a work sheet, and complete the work sheet.
(b) Prepare a multiple-step income statement and a retained earnings statement for the year, and a classified balance sheet at December 31, 2006.
(c) Journalize the adjusting entries.
(d) Journalize the closing entries.
(e) Prepare a post-closing trial balance.

(a) Adj. trial balance total $1,381,300
Net income $57,200
(b) Gross profit $187,000
Total assets $409,000
(e) Total debits $524,400

PROBLEMS: SET B

P5-1B Ready-Set-Go distributes suitcases to retail stores and extends credit terms of 1/10, n/30 to all of its customers. At the end of July, R-S-G's inventory consisted of 40 suitcases purchased at $30 each. During the month of July the following merchandising transactions occurred.

Journalize purchase and sales transactions under a perpetual inventory system.

(SO 2, 3)

July 1 Purchased 50 suitcases on account for $30 each from Trunk Manufacturers, FOB destination, terms 2/10, n/30. The appropriate party also made a cash payment of $100 for freight on this date.

3 Sold 40 suitcases on account to Satchel World for $55 each.

9 Paid Trunk Manufacturers in full.
12 Received payment in full from Satchel World.
17 Sold 30 suitcases on account to The Going Concern for $55 each.
18 Purchased 60 suitcases on account for $1,700 from Holiday Manufacturers, FOB shipping point, terms 1/10, n/30. The appropriate party also made a cash payment of $100 for freight on this date.
20 Received $300 credit (including freight) for 10 suitcases returned to Holiday Manufacturers.
21 Received payment in full from The Going Concern.
22 Sold 45 suitcases on account to Fly-By-Night for $55 each.
30 Paid Holiday Manufacturers in full.
31 Granted Fly-By-Night $220 credit for 4 suitcases returned costing $120.

Ready-Set-Go's chart of accounts includes the following: No. 101 Cash, No. 112 Accounts Receivable, No. 120 Merchandise Inventory, No. 201 Accounts Payable, No. 401 Sales, No. 412 Sales Returns and Allowances, No. 414 Sales Discounts, No. 505 Cost of Goods Sold.

Instructions

Journalize the transactions for the month of July for Ready-Set-Go using a perpetual inventory system.

Journalize, post, and prepare a partial income statement.
(SO 2, 3, 5, 6)

P5-2B Shmi Distributing Company completed the following merchandising transactions in the month of April. At the beginning of April, the ledger of Shmi showed Cash of $9,000 and Common Stock of $9,000.

Apr. 2 Purchased merchandise on account from Wookie Supply Co. $5,900, terms 1/10, n/30.
4 Sold merchandise on account $5,200, FOB destination, terms 1/10, n/30. The cost of the merchandise sold was $4,100.
5 Paid $240 freight on April 4 sale.
6 Received credit from Wookie Supply Co. for merchandise returned $500.
11 Paid Wookie Supply Co. in full, less discount.
13 Received collections in full, less discounts, from customers billed on April 4.
14 Purchased merchandise for cash $3,800.
16 Received refund from supplier for returned goods on cash purchase of April 14, $500.
18 Purchased merchandise from Skywalker Distributors $4,200, FOB shipping point, terms 2/10, n/30.
20 Paid freight on April 18 purchase $100.
23 Sold merchandise for cash $6,400. The merchandise sold had a cost of $5,120.
26 Purchased merchandise for cash $2,300.
27 Paid Skywalker Distributors in full, less discount.
29 Made refunds to cash customers for defective merchandise $90. The returned merchandise had a scrap value of $30.
30 Sold merchandise on account $3,700, terms n/30. The cost of the merchandise sold was $2,800.

Shmi Company's chart of accounts includes the following: No. 101 Cash, No. 112 Accounts Receivable, No. 120 Merchandise Inventory, No. 201 Accounts Payable, No. 311 Common Stock, No. 401 Sales, No. 412 Sales Returns and Allowances, No. 414 Sales Discounts, No. 505 Cost of Goods Sold, and No. 644 Freight-out.

Instructions

(a) Journalize the transactions using a perpetual inventory system.
(b) Enter the beginning cash and capital balances, and post the transactions. (Use J1 for the journal reference.)
(c) Prepare the income statement through gross profit for the month of April 2006.

(c) Gross profit $3,168

Prepare financial statements and adjusting and closing entries.
(SO 4, 5)

P5-3B Starz Department Store is located near the Village Shopping Mall. At the end of the company's fiscal year on December 31, 2006, the following accounts appeared in two of its trial balances.

	Unadjusted	Adjusted		Unadjusted	Adjusted
Accounts Payable	$ 78,700	$ 78,700	Interest Payable		$ 5,000
Accounts Receivable	50,300	50,300	Interest Revenue	$ 4,000	4,000
Accumulated Depr.—Building	42,100	52,500	Merchandise Inventory	75,000	75,000
Accumulated Depr.—Equipment	30,200	42,900	Mortgage Payable	80,000	80,000
Building	190,000	190,000	Office Salaries Expense	32,000	32,000
Cash	20,800	20,800	Prepaid Insurance	9,600	2,400
Common Stock	110,000	110,000	Property Taxes Expense		4,800
Cost of Goods Sold	412,700	412,700	Property Taxes Payable		4,800
Depr. Expense—Building		10,400	Retained Earnings	66,600	66,600
Depr. Expense—Equipment		12,700	Sales Salaries Expense	76,000	76,000
Dividends	28,000	28,000	Sales	628,000	628,000
Equipment	110,000	110,000	Sales Commissions Expense	10,200	15,500
Insurance Expense		7,200	Sales Commissions Payable		5,300
Interest Expense	6,000	11,000	Sales Returns and Allowances	8,000	8,000
			Utilities Expense	11,000	12,000
			Utilities Expense Payable		1,000

Analysis reveals the following additional data.

1. Insurance expense and utilities expense are 60% selling and 40% administrative.
2. $20,000 of the mortgage payable is due for payment next year.
3. Depreciation on the building and property tax expense are administrative expenses; depreciation on the equipment is a selling expense.

Instructions

(a) Net income $29,700
Retained earnings $68,300
Total assets $353,100

(a) Prepare a multiple-step income statement, a retained earnings statement, and a classified balance sheet.
(b) Journalize the adjusting entries that were made.
(c) Journalize the closing entries that are necessary.

Journalize, post, and prepare a trial balance.
(SO 2, 3, 4)

P5-4B J. Ackbar, a former professional tennis star, operates Ackbar's Tennis Shop at the Miller Lake Resort. At the beginning of the current season, the ledger of Ackbar's Tennis Shop showed Cash $2,500, Merchandise Inventory $1,700, and Common Stock $4,200. The following transactions were completed during April.

Apr. 4 Purchased racquets and balls from Jay-Mac Co. $640, FOB shipping point, terms 2/10, n/30.
6 Paid freight on purchase from Jay-Mac Co. $40.
8 Sold merchandise to members $1,150, terms n/30. The merchandise sold had a cost of $790.
10 Received credit of $40 from Jay-Mac Co. for a damaged racquet that was returned.
11 Purchased tennis shoes from Venus Sports for cash, $420.
13 Paid Jay-Mac Co. in full.
14 Purchased tennis shirts and shorts from Serena's Sportswear $700, FOB shipping point, terms 3/10, n/60.
15 Received cash refund of $50 from Venus Sports for damaged merchandise that was returned.
17 Paid freight on Serena's Sportswear purchase $30.
18 Sold merchandise to members $760, terms n/30. The cost of the merchandise sold was $530.
20 Received $500 in cash from members in settlement of their accounts.
21 Paid Serena's Sportswear in full.
27 Granted an allowance of $30 to members for tennis clothing that did not fit properly.
30 Received cash payments on account from members, $660.

The chart of accounts for the tennis shop includes the following: No. 101 Cash, No. 112 Accounts Receivable, No. 120 Merchandise Inventory, No. 201 Accounts Payable, No. 311 Common Stock, No. 401 Sales, No. 412 Sales Returns and Allowances, No. 505 Cost of Goods Sold.

Instructions

(a) Journalize the April transactions using a perpetual inventory system.
(b) Enter the beginning balances in the ledger accounts and post the April transactions. (Use J1 for the journal reference.)
(c) Prepare a trial balance on April 30, 2006.

(c) Total debits $5,110

Determine cost of goods sold and gross profit under periodic approach.
(SO 6, 7)

P5-5B At the end of High-Point Department Store's fiscal year on December 31, 2006, these accounts appeared in its adjusted trial balance.

Freight-in	$5,600
Merchandise Inventory	40,500
Purchases	442,000
Purchase Discounts	12,000
Purchase Returns and Allowances	6,400
Sales	718,000
Sales Returns and Allowances	8,000

Additional facts:

1. Merchandise inventory on December 31, 2006, is $75,000.
2. Note that High-Point Department Store uses a periodic system.

Instructions

Gross profit $315,300

Prepare an income statement through gross profit for the year ended December 31, 2006.

Calculate missing amounts and assess profitability.
(SO 6, 7)

P5-6B Danielle MacLean operates a retail clothing operation. She purchases all merchandise inventory on credit and uses a perpetual inventory system. The accounts payable account is used for recording inventory purchases only; all other current liabilities are accrued in separate accounts. You are provided with the following selected information for the fiscal years 2004, 2005, 2006, and 2007.

	2004	2005	2006	2007
Inventory (ending)	$ 13,000	$ 11,300	$ 14,700	$ 12,200
Accounts payable (ending)	20,000			
Sales		225,700	227,600	219,500
Purchases of merchandise inventory on account		141,000	150,000	132,000
Cash payments to suppliers		135,000	161,000	127,000

Instructions

(a) 2006 $146,600

(c) 2006 Ending accts payable $15,000

(a) Calculate cost of goods sold for each of the 2005, 2006, and 2007 fiscal years.
(b) Calculate the gross profit for each of the 2005, 2006, and 2007 fiscal years.
(c) Calculate the ending balance of accounts payable for each of the 2005, 2006, and 2007 fiscal years.
(d) Sales declined in fiscal 2007. Does that mean that profitability, as measured by the gross profit rate, necessarily also declined? Explain, calculating the gross profit rate for each fiscal year to help support your answer.

Journalize, post, and prepare trial balance and partial income statement using periodic approach.
(SO 7, 8)

***P5-7B** At the beginning of the current season, the ledger of Village Tennis Shop showed Cash $2,500; Merchandise Inventory $1,700; and Common Stock $4,200. The following transactions were completed during April.

Apr.	4	Purchased racquets and balls from Robert Co. $840, terms 3/10, n/30.
	6	Paid freight on Robert Co. purchase $60.
	8	Sold merchandise to members $900, terms n/30.
	10	Received credit of $40 from Robert Co. for a damaged racquet that was returned.
	11	Purchased tennis shoes from Newbee Sports for cash $300.
	13	Paid Robert Co. in full.
	14	Purchased tennis shirts and shorts from Venus's Sportswear $500, terms 2/10, n/60.
	15	Received cash refund of $50 from Newbee Sports for damaged merchandise that was returned.
	17	Paid freight on Venus's Sportswear purchase $30.
	18	Sold merchandise to members $800, terms n/30.
	20	Received $500 in cash from members in settlement of their accounts.
	21	Paid Venus's Sportswear in full.
	27	Granted an allowance of $30 to members for tennis clothing that did not fit properly.
	30	Received cash payments on account from members $500.

The chart of accounts for the tennis shop includes Cash; Accounts Receivable; Merchandise Inventory; Accounts Payable; Common Stock; Sales; Sales Returns and Allowances; Purchases; Purchase Returns and Allowances; Purchase Discounts; and Freight-in.

Instructions

(a) Journalize the April transactions using a periodic inventory system.
(b) Using T accounts, enter the beginning balances in the ledger accounts and post the April transactions.
(c) Prepare a trial balance on April 30, 2006.
(d) Prepare an income statement through gross profit, assuming merchandise inventory on hand at April 30 is $2,296.

(c) Tot. trial balance $6,024
(d) Gross profit $ 560

***P5-8B** The trial balance of Kevin Poorten Fashion Center contained the following accounts at November 30, the end of the company's fiscal year.

Complete accounting cycle beginning with a work sheet.

(SO 4, 5, 6, 9)

KEVIN POORTEN FASHION CENTER
Trial Balance
November 30, 2006

	Debit	Credit
Cash	$ 26,700	
Accounts Receivable	30,700	
Merchandise Inventory	44,700	
Store Supplies	6,200	
Store Equipment	85,000	
Accumulated Depreciation—Store Equipment		$ 18,000
Delivery Equipment	48,000	
Accumulated Depreciation—Delivery Equipment		6,000
Notes Payable		51,000
Accounts Payable		48,500
Common Stock		80,000
Retained Earnings		30,000
Dividends	12,000	
Sales		759,200
Sales Returns and Allowances	8,800	
Cost of Goods Sold	497,400	
Salaries Expense	140,000	
Advertising Expense	26,400	
Utilities Expense	14,000	
Repair Expense	12,100	
Delivery Expense	16,700	
Rent Expense	24,000	
Totals	$992,700	$992,700

Adjustment data:

1. Store supplies on hand totaled $3,500.
2. Depreciation is $9,000 on the store equipment and $6,000 on the delivery equipment.
3. Interest of $4,080 is accrued on notes payable at November 30.
4. Merchandise inventory actually on hand is $44,400.

Other data:

1. Salaries expense is 70% selling and 30% administrative.
2. Rent expense and utilities expense are 80% selling and 20% administrative.
3. $30,000 of notes payable are due for payment next year.
4. Repair expense is 100% administrative.

Instructions

(a) Enter the trial balance on a work sheet, and complete the work sheet.
(b) Prepare a multiple-step income statement and a retained earnings statement for the year, and a classified balance sheet as of November 30, 2006.
(c) Journalize the adjusting entries.
(d) Journalize the closing entries.
(e) Prepare a post-closing trial balance.

(a) Adj. trial balance $1,011,780
Net loss $2,280
(b) Gross profit $252,700
Total assets $199,300

BROADENING YOUR PERSPECTIVE

Financial Reporting and Analysis

■ FINANCIAL REPORTING PROBLEM: PepsiCo, Inc.

BYP5-1 The financial statements of **PepsiCo, Inc.** are presented in Appendix A at the end of this textbook.

Instructions

Answer the following questions using the Consolidated Statement of Income.

(a) What was the percentage change in (1) sales and in (2) net income from 2001 to 2002 and from 2002 to 2003?

(b) What was the company's gross profit rate in 2001, 2002, and 2003?

(c) What was the company's percentage of net income to net sales in 2001, 2002, and 2003? Comment on any trend in this percentage.

■ COMPARATIVE ANALYSIS PROBLEM: PepsiCo vs. Coca-Cola

BYP5-2 **PepsiCo**'s financial statements are presented in Appendix A. **The Coca-Cola Company**'s financial statements are presented in Appendix B.

Instructions

(a) Based on the information contained in these financial statements, determine each of the following for each company.

(1) Gross profit for 2003.

(2) Gross profit rate for 2003.

(3) Operating income for 2003.

(4) Percent change in operating income from 2002 to 2003.

(b) What conclusions concerning the relative profitability of the two companies can be drawn from these data?

■ RESEARCH CASE

BYP5-3 The January 25, 2001, issue of the *Wall Street Journal* includes an article by Nick Wingfield titled "**Webvan** Seeks to Refine Customers in Hopes of Surviving Cash Crunch."

Instructions

Read the article and answer the following questions.

(a) Describe in a few sentences Webvan's business plan.

(b) What was the biggest challenge to Webvan's survival?

(c) What was Webvan's gross profit rate (also called gross margin)? On the average $100 sale of goods, what was its gross profit? How did Webvan's gross profit rate compare to that of a traditional grocer?

(d) What operating expenses did Webvan have that a traditional grocer wouldn't have?

(e) According to the article, what were some things that Webvan could try to do to improve its profitability?

■ INTERPRETING FINANCIAL STATEMENTS

BYP5-4 **Zany Brainy, Inc.** was a specialty retailer of toys, games, books, and multimedia products for kids. As of the end of the fiscal year 2000, the company operated 188 stores in 34 states. On May 15, 2001, the company filed voluntary Chapter 11 bankruptcy. It went out of business in 2003. Provided below is financial information for the 2 years prior to the company's decision to file for bankruptcy, as well as information for a large competitor, **Toys R Us**.

ZANY BRAINY, INC.
(in millions of dollars, except number of shares)

	2/03/2001	1/29/2000
Current assets	$131.5	$142.5
Total assets	199.2	217.6
Current liabilities	117.8	57.3
Total liabilities	129.6	69.2
Average number of shares outstanding	31.3 million	25.2 million
Sales revenue	$400.5	$376.2
Cost of goods sold	312.5	267.8
Net income (loss)	(80.7)	17.1
Preferred stock dividends	0	0

At February 2, 2001, Toys R Us had the following ratio values.

Earnings per share	$ 0.34	Current ratio	1.32:1
Gross profit rate	31.0%	Debt to total assets ratio	58%
Profit margin ratio	3.6%		

Instructions

Use the information above to answer the following questions.

(a) Calculate the company's earnings per share, gross profit rate, and profit margin ratio for both years. Discuss the change in the company's profitability and its profitability relative to Toys R Us.

(b) Calculate the current ratio for both years. Discuss the change in the company's liquidity and its liquidity relative to Toys R Us. The company's current liabilities at January 30, 1999, were $28.0 million.

(c) Calculate the debt to total assets ratio for both years. Discuss the change in the company's solvency and its solvency relative to Toys R Us. The company's total liabilities at January 30, 1999, were $33.9 million.

(d) Discuss whether your findings would have been useful in predicting whether the company was going to have to file for bankruptcy. That is, based on this analysis, should investors have been surprised by the company's bankruptcy filing?

■ A GLOBAL FOCUS

BYP5-5 Recently it was announced that two giant French retailers, **Carrefour SA** and **Promodes SA**, would merge. A headline in the *Wall Street Journal* blared, "French Retailers Create New Wal-Mart Rival." While **Wal-Mart**'s total sales would still exceed those of the combined company, Wal-Mart's international sales are far less than those of the combined company. This is a serious concern for Wal-Mart, since its primary opportunity for future growth lies outside of the United States.

Below are basic financial data for the combined corporation (in French francs) and Wal-Mart (in U.S. dollars). Even though their results are presented in different currencies, by employing ratios we can make some basic comparisons.

	Carrefour/ Promodes (in billions)	Wal-Mart (in billions)
Sales	Fr 298.0	$137.6
Cost of goods sold	274.0	108.7
Operating expenses	9.6	22.4
Net income	5.5	4.4
Total assets	155.0	50.0
Average total assets	140.4	47.7
Current assets	63.5	21.1
Current liabilities	85.8	16.8
Total liabilities	114.2	28.9

Instructions

Compare the two companies by answering the following.

(a) Calculate the gross profit rate for each of the companies, and discuss their relative abilities to control cost of goods sold.

(b) Calculate the operating expense to sales ratio (operating expenses ÷ sales), and discuss the companies' relative abilities to control operating expenses.

(c) What concerns might you have in relying on this comparison?

■ EXPLORING THE WEB

BYP5-6 No financial decision maker should ever rely solely on the financial information reported in the annual report to make decisions. It is important to keep abreast of financial news. This activity demonstrates how to search for financial news on the Web.

Address: biz.yahoo.com/i, or go to www.wiley.com/college/weygandt

Steps:

1. Type in either PepsiCo or Coca-Cola.
2. Choose **News**.
3. Select an article that sounds interesting to you.

Instructions

(a) What was the source of the article? (For example, Reuters, Businesswire, PR Newswire.)

(b) Pretend that you are a personal financial planner and that one of your clients owns stock in the company. Write a brief memo to your client, summarizing the article and explaining the implications of the article for their investment.

Critical Thinking

■ GROUP DECISION CASE

BYP5-7 Three years ago, Debbie Sells and her brother-in-law Mike Mooney opened FedCo Department Store. For the first two years, business was good, but the following condensed income results for 2005 were disappointing.

FEDCO DEPARTMENT STORE
Income Statement
For the Year Ended December 31, 2005

Net sales		$700,000
Cost of goods sold		560,000
Gross profit		140,000
Operating expenses		
Selling expenses	$100,000	
Administrative expenses	20,000	120,000
Net income		$ 20,000

Debbie believes the problem lies in the relatively low gross profit rate of 20%. Mike believes the problem is that operating expenses are too high.

Debbie thinks the gross profit rate can be improved by making both of the following changes:

1. Increase average selling prices by 17%. This increase is expected to lower sales volume so that total sales will increase only 8%.
2. Buy merchandise in larger quantities and take all purchase discounts. These changes are expected to increase the gross profit rate to 23%.

Debbie does not anticipate that these changes will have any effect on operating expenses.

Mike thinks expenses can be cut by making both of the following changes.

1. Cut 2005 sales salaries of $60,000 in half and give sales personnel a commission of 2% of net sales.

2. Reduce store deliveries to one day per week rather than twice a week; this change will reduce 2005 delivery expenses of $40,000 by 40%.

Mike feels that these changes will not have any effect on net sales.

Debbie and Mike come to you for help in deciding the best way to improve net income.

Instructions

With the class divided into groups, answer the following.

(a) Prepare a condensed income statement for 2006 assuming (1) Debbie's changes are implemented and (2) Mike's ideas are adopted.
(b) What is your recommendation to Debbie and Mike?
(c) Prepare a condensed income statement for 2006 assuming both sets of proposed changes are made.

■ COMMUNICATION ACTIVITY

BYP5-8 The following situation is in chronological order.

1. Dexter decides to buy a surfboard.
2. He calls Surfing USA Co. to inquire about their surfboards.
3. Two days later he requests Surfing USA Co. to make him a surfboard.
4. Three days later, Surfing USA Co. sends him a purchase order to fill out.
5. He sends back the purchase order.
6. Surfing USA Co. receives the completed purchase order.
7. Surfing USA Co. completes the surfboard.
8. Dexter picks up the surfboard.
9. Surfing USA Co. bills Dexter.
10. Surfing USA Co. receives payment from Dexter.

Instructions

In a memo to the president of Surfing USA Co., answer the following.

(a) When should Surfing USA Co. record the sale?
(b) Suppose that with his purchase order, Dexter is required to make a down payment. Would that change your answer?

■ ETHICS CASE

Accounting Matters!

BYP5-9 Anita Zurbrugg was just hired as the assistant treasurer of Dorchester Stores. The company is a specialty chain store with nine retail stores concentrated in one metropolitan area. Among other things, the payment of all invoices is centralized in one of the departments Anita will manage. Her primary responsibility is to maintain the company's high credit rating by paying all bills when due and to take advantage of all cash discounts.

Chris Dadian, the former assistant treasurer who has been promoted to treasurer, is training Anita in her new duties. He instructs Anita that she is to continue the practice of preparing all checks "net of discount" and dating the checks the last day of the discount period. "But," Chris continues, "we always hold the checks at least 4 days beyond the discount period before mailing them. That way we get another 4 days of interest on our money. Most of our creditors need our business and don't complain. And, if they scream about our missing the discount period, we blame it on the mail room or the post office. We've only lost one discount out of every hundred we take that way. I think everybody does it. By the way, welcome to our team!"

Instructions

(a) What are the ethical considerations in this case?
(b) Who are the stakeholders that are harmed or benefitted in this situation?
(c) Should Anita continue the practice started by Chris? Does she have any choice?

■ CONTINUING COOKIE CHRONICLE

Accounting Matters!

(Note: The Continuing Cookie Chronicle was started in Chapter 1 and continued in Chapters 2 through 4. From the information gathered through Chapter 4, follow the instructions below, using the general ledger accounts you have already prepared.)

BYP5-10 Because Natalie has had such a successful first few months, she is considering other opportunities to develop her business. One opportunity is the sale of fine European mixers. The owner of Mixer Deluxe has approached Natalie to become the exclusive distributor of these fine mixers. The current cost of a mixer is approximately $525, and Natalie would sell each one for $1,050. Natalie comes to you for advice on how to account for these mixers. Each appliance has a serial number and can be easily identified.

Natalie asks you the following questions:

1. "Would you consider these mixers to be inventory? Or, should they be classified as supplies or equipment?"
2. "I've learned a little about keeping track of inventory using both the perpetual and the periodic systems of accounting for inventory. Which system do you think is better? Which one would you recommend for the type of inventory that I want to sell?"
3. "How often do I need to count inventory if I maintain it using the perpetual system? Do I need to count inventory at all?"

In the end, Natalie decides to use the perpetual method of accounting for inventory, and the following transactions happen during the month of January.

Jan.	4	She buys five deluxe mixers on account from Kzinski Supply Co. for $2,625, FOB shipping point, terms n/30.
	6	She pays $100 freight on the January 4 purchase.
	7	Natalie returns one of the mixers to Kzinski because it was damaged during shipping. Kzinski issues Cookie Creations credit for the cost of the mixer plus $20 for the cost of freight that was paid on January 6 for one mixer.
	8	She collects the amount due from the neighborhood community center that was accrued at the end of December, 2005.
	12	She sells three deluxe mixers on account for $3,150, FOB destination, terms n/30.
	13	Natalie pays her cell phone bill previously accrued in the December adjusting journal entries.
	14	She pays $75 of delivery charges for the three mixers that were sold on January 12.
	14	She buys four deluxe mixers on account from Kzinski Supply Co. for $2,100, FOB shipping point, terms n/30.
	17	Natalie is concerned that there is not enough cash available to pay for all of the mixers purchased. She issues additional common stock for $1,000.
	18	She pays $80 freight on the January 14 purchase.
	20	She sells two deluxe mixers for $2,100 cash.
	28	Natalie issues a check to her assistant. Her assistant worked 20 hours in January and is also paid for amounts owing at December 31, 2005. Recall that Natalie's assistant earns $8 an hour.
	28	Natalie collects amounts due from customers in the January 12 transaction.
	31	She pays Kzinski all amounts due.
	31	Cash dividends of $750 are paid.

As of January 31, the following adjusting entry data is available.

1. A count of brochures and posters reveals that none were used in January.
2. A count of baking supplies reveals that none were used in January.
3. Another month's worth of depreciation needs to be recorded on the baking equipment bought in November. (Recall that the baking equipment has a useful life of 5 years or 60 months.)
4. One month's worth of amortization (write-off) needs to be recorded on the Web site. (Recall that the Web site has a useful life of 2 years or 24 months.)
5. An additional month's worth of interest on her grandmother's loan needs to be accrued. (The interest rate is 6%.)
6. One month's worth of insurance has expired.
7. Natalie receives her cell phone bill, $75. The bill is for services provided in January and is due February 15. (Recall that the cell phone is used only for business purposes.)
8. An analysis of the unearned revenue account reveals that Natalie has not had time to teach any of these lessons this month because she has been so busy selling mixers. As a result there is no change to the unearned revenue account. Natalie hopes to book the outstanding lessons in February.
9. An inventory count of mixers at the end of January reveals that Natalie has three mixers remaining.

Instructions

Using the information that you have gathered through Chapter 4, and the new information on page 236, do the following.

(a) Answer Natalie's questions.
(b) Prepare and post the January 2006 transactions.
(c) Prepare a trial balance.
(d) Prepare and post the adjusting journal entries required.
(e) Prepare an adjusted trial balance.
(f) Prepare a multiple-step income statement and retained earnings statement for the month ended January 31, 2006.
(g) Prepare a classified balance sheet as of January 31, 2006.

Answers to Accounting Matters! Questions

Accounting Matters!

p. 193

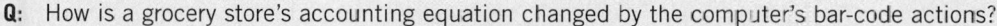

Q: How is a grocery store's accounting equation changed by the computer's bar-code actions?
A: Cash and Sales Revenue would increase; Inventory would decrease; and Cost of Goods Sold would increase.

p. 197

Q: The *distribution costs* of online sales can be greater than for traditional in-store sales. What costs may be less for online sales?
A: The costs of a sales force, store rent or depreciation, utilities, and other store operating expenses may decrease for online sales.

p. 199

Q: How does management know the amount of sales returns?
A: The activity in the contra sales account, Sales Returns and Allowances, communicates to management excessive returns.
Q: Would returns for a floral supply company have a greater negative impact on earnings than returns for a department store?
A: The negative impact of returned sales is probably greater for a floral supply company than for a department store because of the perishable nature of the inventory and the higher labor cost to prepare shipments.

p. 205

Q: Why have investors and analysts demanded more accuracy in isolating "Other gains and losses" from operating items?
A: Greater accuracy in the classification of operating versus nonoperating ("Other gains and losses") items permits investors and analysts to judge the real operating margin, the results of continuing operations, and management's ability to control operating expenses.

Answer to PepsiCo Review It Question 1, p. 208

For **PepsiCo**, the 2003 gross profit rate is 54.1% ($14,592 ÷ $26,971). The 2002 gross profit rate was 54.2% ($13,615 ÷ $25,112). The rate therefore decreased by 0.1% from 2002 to 2003.

Answers to Self-Study Questions

1. c **2.** a **3.** c **4.** b **5.** c **6.** d **7.** b **8.** c **9.** d **10.** d **11.** a ***12.** b ***13.** a

REMEMBER to go back to the Navigator box on the chapter-opening page and check off your completed work.

Chapter 6

Inventories

THE NAVIGATOR ✓

- Understand **Concepts for Review** ❑
- Read **Feature Story** ❑
- Scan **Study Objectives** ❑
- Read **Preview** ❑
- Read text and answer **Before You Go On** p. 245 ❑ p. 253 ❑ p. 258 ❑
- Work **Demonstration Problems** ❑
- Review **Summary of Study Objectives** ❑
- Answer **Self-Study Questions** ❑
- Complete **Assignments** ❑

CONCEPTS FOR REVIEW

Before studying this chapter, you should know or, if necessary, review:

- The cost principle (Ch. 1, p. 10) and matching principle of accounting. (Ch. 3, p. 95)
- How to record purchases, sales, and cost of goods sold under a perpetual inventory system. (Ch. 5, pp. 194–199)
- How to prepare financial statements for a merchandiser. (Ch. 5, pp. 203–208)

☑ THE NAVIGATOR

ACCOUNTING MATTERS! FEATURE STORY

Taking Stock—from Backpacks to Bicycles

Backpacks and jackets sporting the jagged peaks of the **Mountain Equipment Co-op** (MEC) logo are a familiar sight on hiking trails and campuses. Sales of these popular items help the Vancouver-based co-op to finance its primary goal: to provide members with products and services for wilderness recreational activities at a reasonable cost.

MEC has five retail stores across Canada and a huge market in catalog and online sales around the world. It ships everything from climbing ropes, kayaks, and bike helmets to destinations as far away as Japan and South America.

Keeping financial track of the flow of these items is a responsibility of Fara Jumani, a member of the inventory costing group at MEC and a part-time college student. "We have tens of thousands of items in inventory, and we are adding new ones all the time," says Ms. Jumani. "Because we make a lot of our own clothing goods, we also have a lot of in-house inventory—fabric and supplies that will be used to make products."

MEC tracks the cost of its inventory using the average cost of the various items in inventory, weighted by the number purchased at each different unit cost. (This procedure is called the weighted-average cost method.) "Because costs tend to fluctuate," explains Ms. Jumani, "that method best captures our overall costs."

Unlike most retail operations, MEC is not out to make a profit. As a co-op, it exists to serve its members. "But we have to stay fiscally healthy to do that," points out Ms. Jumani. "If we go bankrupt, we won't be serving anyone." Accounting for inventory—from backpacks to bicycles—is an important part of MEC's fiscal fitness routine.

THE NAVIGATOR

STUDY OBJECTIVES

After studying this chapter, you should be able to:

1. Describe the steps in determining inventory quantities.
2. Explain the basis of accounting for inventories, and describe the inventory cost flow methods.
3. Explain the financial statement and tax effects of each of the inventory cost flow methods.
4. Explain the lower of cost or market basis of accounting for inventories.
5. Indicate the effects of inventory errors on the financial statements.
6. Compute and interpret inventory turnover.

THE NAVIGATOR

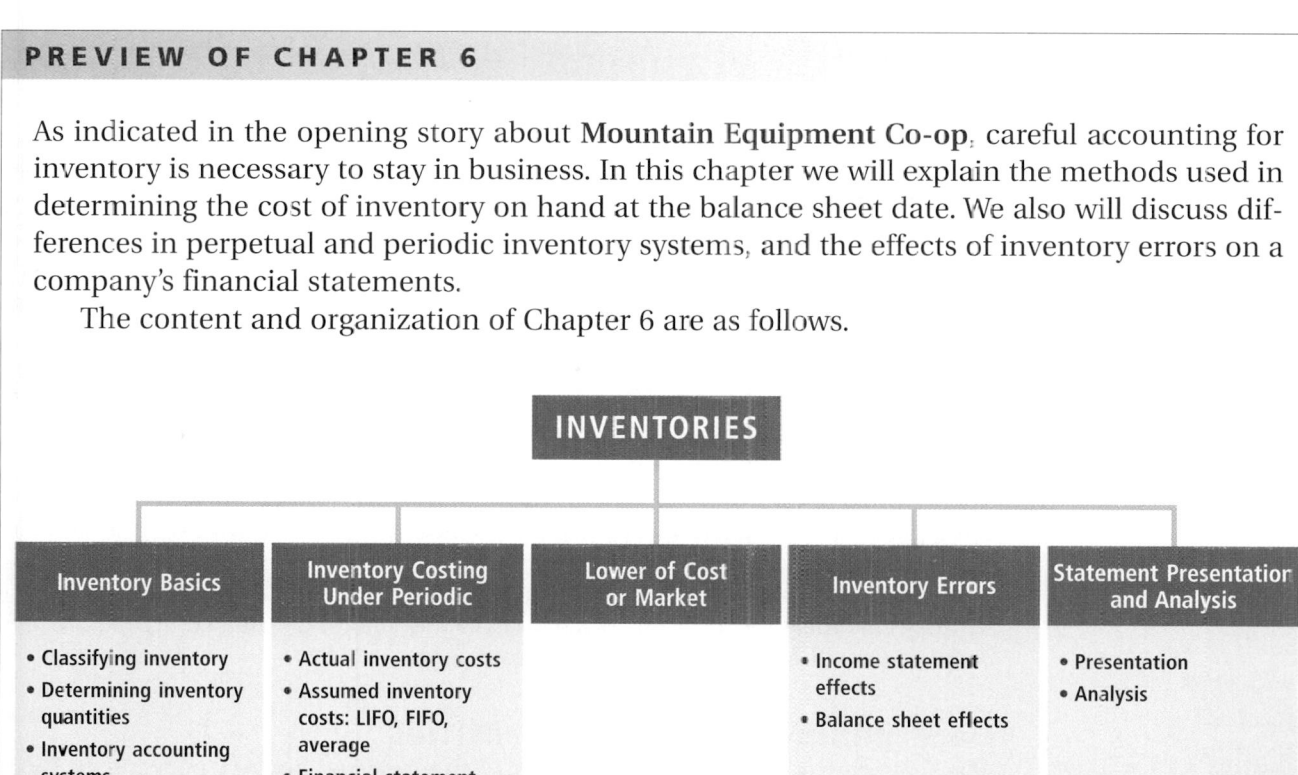

PREVIEW OF CHAPTER 6

As indicated in the opening story about **Mountain Equipment Co-op**, careful accounting for inventory is necessary to stay in business. In this chapter we will explain the methods used in determining the cost of inventory on hand at the balance sheet date. We also will discuss differences in perpetual and periodic inventory systems, and the effects of inventory errors on a company's financial statements.

The content and organization of Chapter 6 are as follows.

INVENTORIES

- **Inventory Basics**
  - Classifying inventory
  - Determining inventory quantities
  - Inventory accounting systems
- **Inventory Costing Under Periodic**
  - Actual inventory costs
  - Assumed inventory costs: LIFO, FIFO, average
  - Financial statement effects
  - Consistent use
- **Lower of Cost or Market**
- **Inventory Errors**
  - Income statement effects
  - Balance sheet effects
- **Statement Presentation and Analysis**
  - Presentation
  - Analysis

THE NAVIGATOR

Inventory Basics

In our economy, inventories are an important barometer of business activity. The U.S. Commerce Department publishes monthly inventory data for retailers, wholesalers, and manufacturers. The amount of inventories and the time required to sell the goods on hand are two closely watched indicators. During downturns in the economy, there is an initial buildup of inventories, as it takes longer to sell existing quantities. Inventories generally decrease with an upturn in business activity. A delicate balance must be maintained between too little inventory and too much. A company with too little inventory to meet demand will have dissatisfied customers and sales personnel. One with too much inventory will be burdened with unnecessary carrying costs.

Inventories affect both the balance sheet and the income statement. In the **balance sheet** of merchandising companies, inventory is frequently the most significant current asset. Of course, its amount and relative importance can vary, even for companies in the same industry. For example, **Wal-Mart** reported inventory of $23 billion, representing 80% of total current assets. For the same period, **J.C. Penney Company** reported $5 billion of inventory, representing 57% of total current assets. In the **income statement**, inventory is vital in determining the results of operations for a particular period. The income statement for a merchandiser, as shown in Chapter 5, contains three features not found in the income statement of a service enterprise. These features are: (1) a sales revenue section, (2) cost of goods sold, and (3) gross profit. Gross profit (net sales less cost of goods sold) is closely watched by management, owners, and other interested parties.

Classifying Inventory

How a company classifies its inventory depends on whether the firm is a merchandiser or a manufacturer. A **merchandiser's** inventory consists of many different items. For example, in a grocery store, canned goods, dairy products, meats, and produce are just a few of the inventory items on hand. These items have two common characteristics: (1) They are owned by the company, and (2) they are in a form ready for sale in the ordinary course of business. Only one inventory classification, **merchandise inventory**, is needed to describe the many different items in inventory.

A **manufacturer's** inventories are also owned by the company, but some goods may not yet be ready for sale. As a result, inventory is usually classified into three categories: finished goods, work in process, and raw materials. For example, **General Motors** classifies vehicles completed and ready for sale as **finished goods**. The vehicles in various stages of production are classified as **work in process**. The steel, glass, upholstery, and other components that are on hand waiting to be used in production are **raw materials**.

The accounting principles and concepts discussed in this chapter apply to inventory classifications of both merchandising and manufacturing companies. In this chapter we will focus on merchandise inventory.

Determining Inventory Quantities

STUDY OBJECTIVE 1

Describe the steps in determining inventory quantities.

Many businesses take a physical inventory count on the last day of the year. Businesses using the periodic inventory system **must** make such a count to determine the inventory on hand at the balance sheet date and to compute cost of goods sold. Even businesses using a perpetual inventory system must take a physical inventory at some time during the year.

Determining inventory quantities consists of two steps: (1) taking a physical inventory of goods on hand, and (2) determining the ownership of goods.

Taking a Physical Inventory

Taking a physical inventory involves actually counting, weighing, or measuring each kind of inventory on hand. In many companies, taking an inventory is a formidable task, even with the current widespread use of bar codes and scanning equipment. Retailers such as **Kmart**, **The Home Depot**, or your favorite music store have thousands of different inventory items. An inventory count is generally more accurate when goods are not being sold or received during the counting. So, companies often "take inventory" when the business is closed or when business is slow. Many retailers, for example, close early on a chosen day in January—after the holiday sales and returns—to count inventory.

To minimize errors in taking the inventory, a company should adhere to **internal control** principles and practices that safeguard inventory:

1. The counting should be done by employees who do not have custodial responsibility for the inventory.
2. Each counter should establish the authenticity of each inventory item. For example, does each box contain a 25-inch television set? Does each storage tank contain gasoline?
3. There should be a second count by another employee.
4. Prenumbered inventory tags (or scanning equipment) should be used. All inventory tags should be accounted for.
5. At the end of the count, a supervisor should check that all inventory items are tagged or scanned and that no items have been doubled-counted.

After the physical inventory is taken, the quantity of each kind of inventory is listed on **inventory summary sheets**. To ensure accuracy, the listing should be verified by a second employee. Later, unit costs will be applied to the quantities in order to determine a total cost of the inventory—which is the topic of later sections.[1]

ACCOUNTING MATTERS! Business Insight

Failure to observe the foregoing internal control procedures contributed to the Great Salad Oil Swindle. In this case, management intentionally overstated its salad oil inventory, which was stored in large holding tanks. Three procedures contributed to overstating the oil inventory: (1) Water added to the bottom of the holding tanks caused the oil to float to the top. Inventory-taking crews who viewed the holding tanks from the top observed only salad oil. In fact, as much as 37 out of 40 feet of many of the holding tanks contained water. (2) The company's inventory records listed more holding tanks than it actually had. The company repainted numbers on the tanks after inventory crews examined them, so the crews counted the same tanks twice. (3) Underground pipes pumped oil from one holding tank to another during the inventory taking. Therefore, the same salad oil was counted more than once. Although the salad oil swindle was unusual, it demonstrates the complexities involved in assuring that inventory is properly counted.

? What effect does an overstatement of inventory have on a company's financial statements?

Determining Ownership of Goods

Before we can begin to calculate the cost of inventory, we need to consider the ownership of goods. Specifically, we need to be sure that we have not included in the inventory any goods that do not belong to the company.

GOODS IN TRANSIT. Goods are considered **in transit** when they are in the hands of a public carrier (such as a railroad, trucking, or airline company) at the statement date. Goods in transit should be included in the inventory of the party that has legal title to the goods. Legal title is determined by the terms of sale, as shown in Illustration 6-1 and described on the next page.

Illustration 6-1
Terms of sale

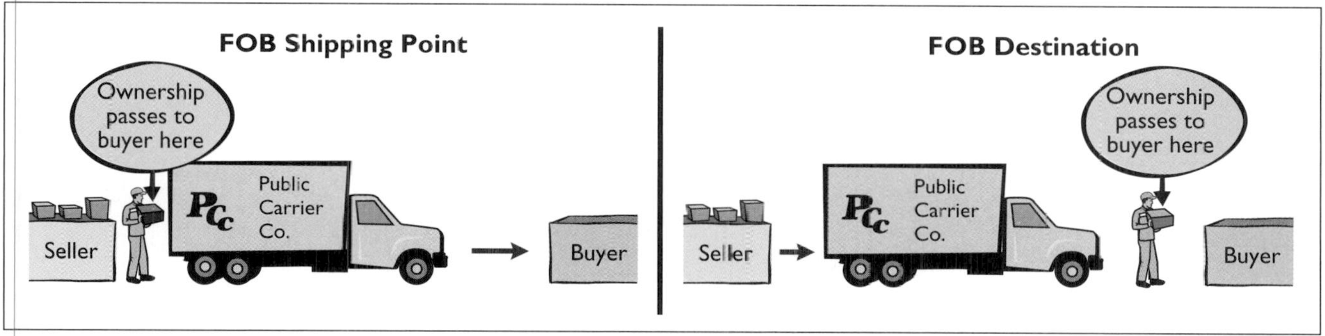

[1] To estimate the cost of inventory when a physical inventory cannot be taken (the inventory is destroyed) or when it is inconvenient (during interim periods), estimating methods are applied. These methods (gross profit method and retail inventory method) are discussed in Appendix 6B.

1. **FOB (free on board) shipping point:** Ownership of the goods passes to the buyer when the public carrier accepts the goods from the seller.
2. **FOB destination:** Legal title to the goods remains with the seller until the goods reach the buyer.

Inventory quantities may be seriously miscounted if goods in transit at the statement date are ignored. Assume that Hargrove Company has 20,000 units of inventory on hand on December 31. It also has the following goods in transit: (1) **sales** of 1,500 units shipped December 31 FOB destination, and (2) **purchases** of 2,500 units shipped FOB shipping point by the seller on December 31. Hargrove has legal title to both the units sold and the units purchased. If units in transit are ignored, inventory quantities would be understated by 4,000 units (1,500 + 2,500). As we will see later in the chapter, inaccurate inventory counts affect not only the inventory amount shown on the balance sheet but also the cost of goods sold calculation on the income statement.

ACCOUNTING MATTERS! **Business Insight**

Many companies have invested large amounts of time and money in automated inventory systems. One of the most sophisticated is **Federal Express**'s Digitally Assisted Dispatch System (DADS). It uses hand-held "SuperTrackers" to transmit data about the packages and documents to the firm's computer system. Based on bar codes, the system allows the firm to know where any package is at any time to prevent losses and to fulfill the firm's delivery commitments. More recently, FedEx's software enables customers to track shipments on their own PCs.

? Are the packages that are being tracked part of FedEx's "inventory"?

CONSIGNED GOODS. In some lines of business, it is customary to acquire merchandise on consignment. Under such an arrangement, the holder of the goods (the *consignee*) does not own the goods. Ownership remains with the shipper of the goods (the *consignor*) until the goods are actually sold to a customer. Because **consigned goods** are not owned by the consignee, they should not be included in the consignee's physical inventory count. But, the consignor should include merchandise held by the consignee as part of its inventory.

Inventory Accounting Systems

One of two basic systems of accounting for inventories may be used: **(1) the perpetual inventory system,** or **(2) the periodic inventory system**. Chapter 5 and Appendix 5A discussed and illustrated both systems. This chapter discusses and illustrates inventory cost flow methods under the periodic inventory system. Appendix 6A discusses and illustrates the same inventory cost flow methods under the perpetual inventory system.

Some businesses find it either unnecessary or uneconomical to invest in a computerized perpetual inventory system. As illustrated in Chapter 5, a perpetual inventory system keeps track of inventory in number of units **and** in dollar costs per unit. Many small merchandising business managers still feel that a perpetual inventory system costs more than it is worth. These managers can control merchandise and manage day-to-day operations either without detailed inventory records or with a perpetual **units only** inventory system.

BEFORE YOU GO ON...

Review It

1. What steps are involved in determining inventory quantities?
2. How is ownership determined for goods in transit at the balance sheet date?
3. Who has title to consigned goods?

Do It

Hasbeen Company completed its inventory count. It arrived at a total inventory value of $200,000. You have been informed of the information listed below. Discuss how this information affects the reported cost of inventory.

1. Goods held on consignment for Falls Co., costing $15,000, were included in the inventory.
2. Purchased goods of $10,000 which were in transit (terms: FOB shipping point) were not included in the count.
3. Sold inventory with a cost of $12,000 which was in transit (terms: FOB shipping point) was not included in the count.

ACTION PLAN

- Apply the rules of ownership to goods held on consignment.
- Apply the rules of ownership to goods in transit FOB shipping point.

SOLUTION The goods of $15,000 held on consignment should be deducted from the inventory count. The goods of $10,000 purchased FOB shipping point should be added to the inventory count. Sold goods of $12,000 which were in transit FOB shipping point should not be included in the ending inventory. Thus, inventory should be carried at $195,000.

Related exercise material: *BE6-1, E6-1, and E6-2.*

THE NAVIGATOR

Inventory Costing Under a Periodic Inventory System

STUDY OBJECTIVE 2

Explain the basis of accounting for inventories, and describe the inventory cost flow methods.

All expenditures needed to acquire goods and to make them ready for sale are included as inventoriable costs. **Inventoriable costs** may be regarded as a pool of costs that consists of two elements: (1) the cost of the beginning inventory and (2) the cost of goods purchased during the year. The sum of these two equals the cost of goods available for sale.

Conceptually, the costs of the purchasing, receiving, and warehousing departments (whose efforts make the goods available for sale) should also be included in inventoriable costs. But, there are practical difficulties in allocating these costs to inventory. So these costs are generally accounted for as **operating expenses** in the period in which they are incurred.

Inventoriable costs are allocated either to ending inventory or to cost of goods sold. Under a **periodic inventory system**, the allocation is made at the end of the accounting period. First, the costs for the ending inventory are determined. Next, the cost of the ending inventory is subtracted from the cost of goods available for sale, to determine the cost of goods sold.

To illustrate, assume that General Suppliers has a cost of goods available for sale of $120,000. This amount is based on a beginning inventory of $20,000 and cost of goods purchased of $100,000. The physical inventory indicates that 5,000 units are on hand. The costs applicable to the units are $3.00 per unit. The allocation of the pool of costs is shown in Illustration 6-2. As shown, the $120,000 of goods available for sale are allocated $15,000 to ending inventory (5,000 × $3.00) and $105,000 to cost of goods sold.

Illustration 6-2
Allocation (matching) of pool of costs

Pool of Costs
Cost of Goods Available for Sale

Beginning inventory	$ 20,000
Cost of goods purchased	100,000
Cost of goods available for sale	**$120,000**

Step 1			**Step 2**	
Ending Inventory			**Cost of Goods Sold**	
Units	**Unit Cost**	**Total Cost**		
5,000	$3.00	**$15,000**	Cost of goods available for sale	$120,000
			Less: Ending inventory	15,000
			Cost of goods sold	**$105,000**

Using Actual Physical Flow Costing—Specific Identification

Costing of the inventory is complicated because specific items of inventory on hand may have been purchased at different prices. For example, a company may experience several increases in the cost of identical goods within a given year. Or, unit costs may decline. Under such circumstances, how should different unit costs be allocated between the ending inventory and cost of goods sold?

One answer is to use **specific identification** of the units purchased. This method tracks the **actual physical flow** of the goods. **Each item of inventory is marked, tagged, or coded with its "specific" unit cost.** At the end of the year the specific costs of items still in inventory make up the total cost of the ending inventory. Assume, for example, that Southland Music Company purchases three 46-inch television sets at costs of $700, $750, and $800, respectively. During the year, two sets are sold at $1,200 each. At December 31, the $750 set is still on hand. The ending inventory is $750, and the cost of goods sold is $1,500 ($700 + $800). This is shown graphically in Illustration 6-3.

Illustration 6-3
Specific identification method

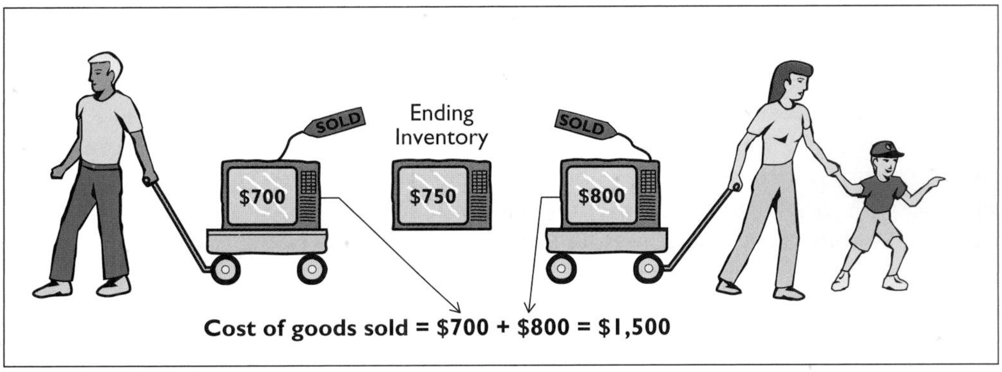

Specific identification is possible when a company sells a limited variety of high-unit-cost items that can be clearly identified from purchase through sale. Examples are automobile dealerships (cars, trucks, and vans), music stores (pianos and organs), and antique shops (tables and cabinets).

But what if we cannot specifically identify particular inventory items? For example, drug, grocery, and hardware stores sell thousands of relatively low-unit-cost items of inventory. These are often indistinguishable from one another. It may be impossible or impractical to track each item's cost. In that case (as the next section will show), we must make assumptions about which units were sold.

The general rule is this: When feasible, specific identification is the ideal method of allocating cost of goods available for sale. It reports ending inventory at actual cost and matches the actual cost of goods sold against sales revenue.

However, specific identification may enable management to manipulate net income. To see how, assume that a music store has three identical Steinway grand pianos, purchased at different costs. When selling one piano, management could maximize net income by selecting the piano with the lowest cost to match against revenues. Or, it could minimize net income (and lower its taxes) by selecting the highest-cost piano.

HELPFUL HINT

A major disadvantage of the specific identification method is that management may be able to manipulate net income through specific identification of items sold.

Using Assumed Cost Flow Methods—FIFO, LIFO, and Average Cost

Because specific identification is often impractical, other cost flow methods are allowed. These assume flows of costs that may be unrelated to the physical flow of goods. For this reason we call them **assumed cost flow methods** or **cost flow assumptions**. They are:

1. First-in, first-out (FIFO).
2. Last-in, first-out (LIFO).
3. Average cost.

To illustrate these three inventory cost flow methods, we will assume that Bow Valley Electronics uses a **periodic inventory system**.[2] The information shown in Illustration 6-4 relates to its Z202 Astro Condenser.

Illustration 6-4
Inventoriable units and costs for Bow Valley Electronics

BOW VALLEY ELECTRONICS
Z202 Astro Condensers

Date	Explanation	Units	Unit Cost	Total Cost
1/1	Beginning inventory	100	$10	$ 1,000
4/15	Purchase	200	11	2,200
8/24	Purchase	300	12	3,600
11/27	Purchase	400	13	5,200
	Total	1,000		$12,000

During the year, 550 units were sold, and 450 units are on hand at 12/31.

There is no accounting requirement that the cost flow assumption be consistent with the physical movement of the goods. Management selects the appropriate cost

[2] We have chosen to use the periodic approach for a number of reasons. First, many companies that use a perpetual inventory system use it to keep track of units on hand, but then determine cost of goods sold at the end of the period using one of the three cost flow approaches applied under essentially a periodic approach. Second, because of the complexity, few companies use average cost on a perpetual basis. Third, most companies that use perpetual LIFO employ dollar-value LIFO, which is presented in more advanced texts. Fourth, FIFO gives the same results under either perpetual or periodic. And finally, it is easier to demonstrate the cost flow assumptions under the periodic system, which makes it more pedagogically appropriate.

flow method. Even in the same industry, different companies may reach different conclusions as to the most appropriate method.

First-in, First-out (FIFO)

The **FIFO method** assumes that the **earliest goods** purchased are the first to be sold. FIFO often parallels the actual physical flow of merchandise because it generally is good business practice to sell the earliest units first. Under the FIFO method, the **costs** of the earliest goods purchased are the first to be recognized as cost of goods sold. (Note that this does not necessarily mean that the earliest units *are* sold first, but that the costs of the earliest units are recognized first. In a bin of picture hangers at the hardware store, for example, no one really knows, nor would it matter, which hangers are sold first.) The allocation of the cost of goods available for sale at Bow Valley Electronics under FIFO is shown in Illustrations 6-5 and 6-6.

Illustration 6-5
Allocation of costs—FIFO method

Pool of Costs
Cost of Goods Available for Sale

Date	Explanation	Units	Unit Cost	Total Cost
1/1	Beginning inventory	100	$10	$ 1,000
4/15	Purchase	200	11	2,200
8/24	Purchase	300	12	3,600
11/27	Purchase	400	13	5,200
	Total	1,000		**$12,000**

Step 1
Ending Inventory

Date	Units	Unit Cost	Total Cost
11/27	400	$13	$5,200
8/24	50	12	600
Total	450		**$5,800**

Step 2
Cost of Goods Sold

Cost of goods available for sale	$12,000
Less: Ending inventory	5,800
Cost of goods sold	**$ 6,200**

HELPFUL HINT

Note the sequencing of the allocation: (1) Compute ending inventory. (2) Determine cost of goods sold.

Illustration 6-6
FIFO—First costs in are first costs out in computing cost of goods sold

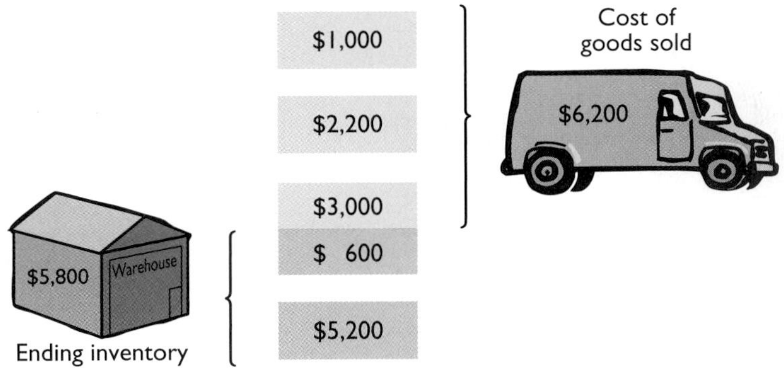

Note that the ending inventory is based on the latest units purchased. That is, **under FIFO, the cost of the ending inventory is found by taking the unit cost of the most recent purchase and working backward until all units of inventory are costed.**

We can verify the accuracy of the cost of goods sold by recognizing that the **first units acquired are the first units sold**. The computations for the 550 units sold are shown in Illustration 6-7.

Illustration 6-7
Proof of cost of goods sold

Date	Units		Unit Cost		Total Cost
1/1	100	×	$10	=	$1,000
4/15	200	×	11	=	2,200
8/24	250	×	12	=	3,000
Total	550				**$6,200**

Last-in, First-out (LIFO)

The **LIFO method** assumes that the **latest goods** purchased are the first to be sold. LIFO seldom coincides with the actual physical flow of inventory. Only for goods in piles, such as hay, coal, or produce at the grocery store would LIFO match the physical flow of inventory. Under the LIFO method, the **costs** of the latest goods purchased are the first to be assigned to cost of goods sold. The allocation of the cost of goods available for sale at Bow Valley Electronics under LIFO is shown in Illustration 6-8.

Illustration 6-8
Allocation of costs—LIFO method

Pool of Costs
Cost of Goods Available for Sale

Date	Explanation	Units	Unit Cost	Total Cost
1/1	Beginning inventory	100	$10	$ 1,000
4/15	Purchase	200	11	2,200
8/24	Purchase	300	12	3,600
11/27	Purchase	400	13	5,200
	Total	1,000		**$12,000**

Step 1
Ending Inventory

Date	Units	Unit Cost	Total Cost
1/1	100	$10	$1,000
4/15	200	11	2,200
8/24	150	12	1,800
Total	450		**$5,000**

Step 2
Cost of Goods Sold

Cost of goods available for sale	$12,000
Less: Ending inventory	5,000
Cost of goods sold	**$ 7,000**

HELPFUL HINT

The costs allocated to ending inventory ($5,000) plus the costs allocated to CGS ($7,000) must equal CGAS ($12,000).

Illustration 6-9 (page 250) graphically displays the LIFO cost flow.

Under the LIFO method, **the cost of the ending inventory is found by taking the unit cost of the oldest goods and working forward until all units of inventory are costed**. As a result, the first costs assigned to ending inventory are the costs of the beginning inventory. Proof of the costs allocated to cost of goods sold is shown in Illustration 6-10 (page 250).

Under a periodic inventory system, **all goods purchased during the period are assumed to be available for the first sale, regardless of the date of purchase.**

Illustration 6-9
LIFO—Last costs in are first costs out in computing cost of goods sold

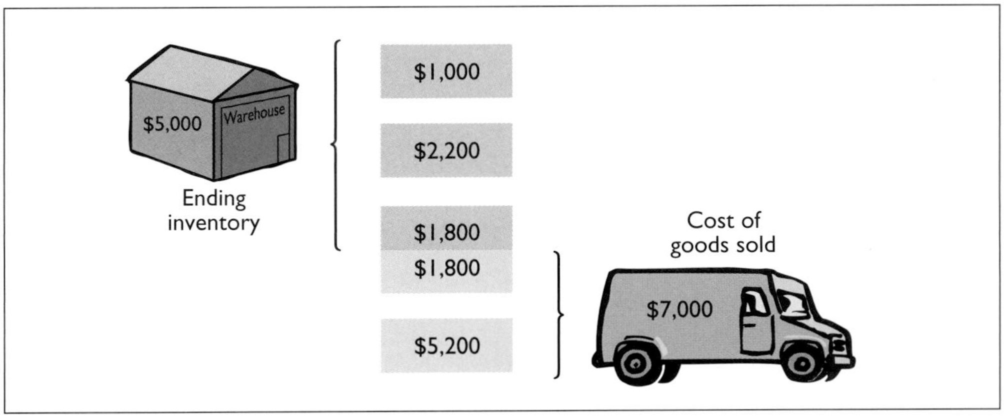

Illustration 6-10
Proof of cost of goods sold

Date	Units		Unit Cost		Total Cost
11/27	400	×	$13	=	$5,200
8/24	150	×	12	=	1,800
Total	550				**$7,000**

Average Cost

The **average cost method** assumes that the goods available for sale have the same (average) cost per unit. Generally such goods are identical. Under this method, the cost of goods available for sale is allocated on the basis of the **weighted-average unit cost**. The formula and a sample computation of the weighted-average unit cost are as follows.

Illustration 6-11
Formula for weighted-average unit cost

Cost of Goods Available for Sale	÷	Total Units Available for Sale	=	Weighted-Average Unit Cost
$12,000	÷	1,000	=	**$12.00**

The weighted-average unit cost is then applied to the units on hand. This computation determines the cost of the ending inventory. The allocation of the cost of goods available for sale at Bow Valley Electronics using average cost is shown in Illustrations 6-12 and 6-13 (below and on the next page).

To verify the cost of goods sold data in Illustration 6-12, multiply the units sold by the weighted-average unit cost (550 × $12 = $6,600). Note that this method does not use the average of the **unit costs**. That average is $11.50 ($10 + $11 + $12 + $13 = $46; $46 ÷ 4). Instead, the average cost method uses the average **weighted** by the quantities purchased at each unit cost.

Illustration 6-12
Allocation of costs—average cost method

Pool of Costs
Cost of Goods Available for Sale

Date	Explanation	Units	Unit Cost	Total Cost
1/1	Beginning inventory	100	$10	$ 1,000
4/15	Purchase	200	11	2,200
8/24	Purchase	300	12	3,600
11/27	Purchase	400	13	5,200
	Total	1,000		**$12,000**

Illustration 6-12
(continued from p. 250)

Step 1 Ending Inventory						**Step 2 Cost of Goods Sold**	
$12,000	÷	1,000	=	$12.00		Cost of goods available for sale	$12,000
		Unit		**Total**		Less: Ending inventory	5,400
Units		**Cost**		**Cost**		Cost of goods sold	**$ 6,600**
450	×	$12.00	=	**$5,400**			

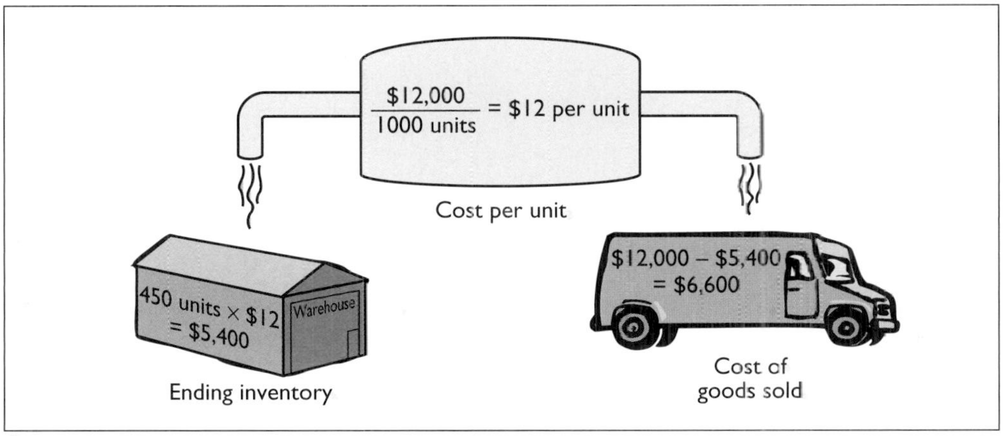

Illustration 6-13
Average cost—the average unit cost of the goods available for sale during the period is the cost used to compute cost of goods sold

Financial Statement Effects of Cost Flow Methods

Each of the three cost flow methods is acceptable. For example, **Black and Decker Manufacturing Company** and **Wendy's International** currently use the FIFO method. **Campbell Soup Company**, **Kroger Co.**, and **Walgreen Drugs** use LIFO. **Bristol-Myers-Squibb Co.** and **Motorola, Inc.** use the average cost method. A company may also use more than one cost flow method at the same time. **Del Monte Corporation** uses LIFO for domestic inventories and FIFO for foreign inventories. Illustration 6-14 shows the use of the three methods in the 600 largest U.S. companies. Companies adopt different inventory cost flow methods for various reasons. Usually, one of the following factors is involved:

1. Income statement effects.
2. Balance sheet effects.
3. Tax effects.

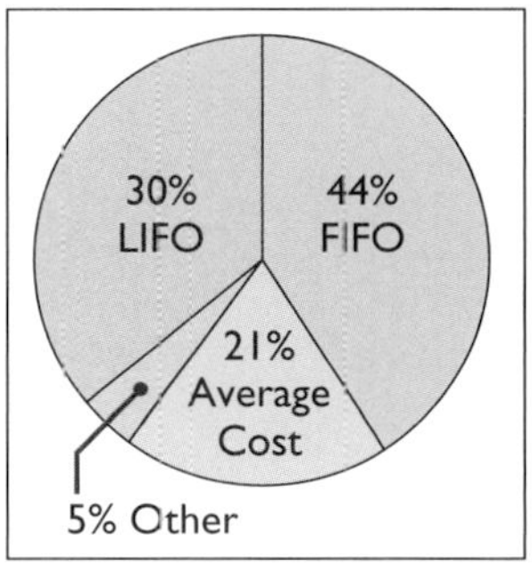

Illustration 6-14
Use of cost flow methods in major U.S. companies

Income Statement Effects

STUDY OBJECTIVE 3

Explain the financial statement and tax effects of each of the inventory cost flow methods.

To understand why a company might choose a particular cost flow method, let's compare the effects on the financial statements of Bow Valley Electronics. The condensed income statements in Illustration 6-15 (page 252) assume that Bow Valley sold its 550 units for $11,500, and its operating expenses were $2,000. Its income tax rate is 30%.

The cost of goods available for sale ($12,000) is the same under each of the three inventory cost flow methods. But the ending inventory is different in each method, and this difference affects cost of goods sold. Each dollar of difference in ending inventory therefore results in a corresponding dollar difference in income before income taxes. For Bow Valley, there is an $800 difference between FIFO and LIFO.

In a period of rising prices, FIFO produces higher net income. This happens because the expenses matched against revenues are the lower unit costs of the first units purchased. In a period of rising prices (as is the case here), FIFO reports the

Illustration 6-15
Comparative effects of cost flow methods

BOW VALLEY ELECTRONICS
Condensed Income Statements

	FIFO	LIFO	Average Cost
Sales	$11,500	$11,500	$11,500
Beginning inventory	1,000	1,000	1,000
Purchases	11,000	11,000	11,000
Cost of goods available for sale	12,000	12,000	12,000
Ending inventory	**5,800**	**5,000**	**5,400**
Cost of goods sold	6,200	7,000	6,600
Gross profit	5,300	4,500	4,900
Operating expenses	2,000	2,000	2,000
Income before income taxes[3]	3,300	2,500	2,900
Income tax expense (30%)	990	750	870
Net income	**$ 2,310**	**$ 1,750**	**$ 2,030**

HELPFUL HINT

If prices are falling, the results from the use of FIFO and LIFO are reversed: FIFO will report the lowest net income and LIFO the highest.

highest net income ($2,310) and LIFO the lowest ($1,750); average cost falls in the middle ($2,030). To management, higher net income is an advantage: It causes external users to view the company more favorably. Also, if management bonuses are based on net income, FIFO will provide the basis for higher bonuses.

Some argue that the use of LIFO in a period of rising prices enables the company to avoid reporting **paper or phantom profit** as economic gain. To illustrate, assume that Kralik Company buys 200 XR492s at $20 per unit on January 10. It buys 200 more on December 31 at $24 each. During the year, it sells 200 units at $30 each. The results under FIFO and LIFO are shown in Illustration 6-16.

Illustration 6-16
Income statement effects compared

	FIFO	LIFO
Sales (200 × $30)	$6,000	$6,000
Cost of goods sold	**4,000 (200 × $20)**	**4,800 (200 × $24)**
Gross profit	$2,000	$1,200

Under LIFO, the company has expensed the current replacement cost ($4,800) of the units sold. The gross profit in economic terms under LIFO is real. Under FIFO, the company has expensed only the January 10 cost ($4,000). To replace the units sold, it must reinvest $800 (200 × $4) of the gross profit. Thus, $800 of the gross profit under FIFO is phantom, or illusory. As a result, reported net income under FIFO is also overstated in real terms.

Balance Sheet Effects

A major advantage of FIFO is that in a period of rising prices, the costs allocated to ending inventory will be close to their current cost. For Bow Valley, for example, 400 of the 450 units in the ending inventory are costed at the November 27 unit cost of $13.

A major shortcoming of LIFO is that in a period of rising prices, the costs allocated to ending inventory may be understated in terms of current cost. This is true

[3] It is assumed that Bow Valley is a corporation, and corporations are required to pay income taxes.

for Bow Valley: The cost of the ending inventory includes the $10 unit cost of the beginning inventory. The understatement becomes even greater if the inventory includes goods purchased in one or more prior accounting periods.

Tax Effects

We have seen that both inventory on the balance sheet and net income on the income statement are higher when FIFO is used in a period of rising prices. Why, then, would a company use LIFO? The reason is that LIFO results in the lowest income taxes during times of rising prices. The lower net income reported by LIFO translates to a lower tax liability. For example, at Bow Valley Electronics, income taxes are $750 under LIFO, compared to $990 under FIFO. The tax saving of $240 makes more cash available for use in the business.

Using Inventory Cost Flow Methods Consistently

Whatever cost flow method a company chooses, it should be used consistently from one period to another. Consistent application makes financial statements more comparable over successive time periods. In contrast, using FIFO in one year and LIFO in the next would make it difficult to compare the net incomes of the two years.

Although consistent application is preferred, a company may change its method of inventory costing. Such a change and its effects on net income should be disclosed in the financial statements. A typical disclosure is shown in Illustration 6-17, using information from recent financial statements of **Quaker Oats Company**.

Illustration 6-17
Disclosure of change in cost flow method

QUAKER OATS COMPANY
Notes to the Financial Statements

Note 1 Effective July 1, the Company adopted the LIFO cost flow assumption for valuing the majority of U.S. Grocery Products inventories. The Company believes that the use of the LIFO method better matches current costs with current revenues. The effect of this change on the current year was to decrease net income by $16.0 million.

BEFORE YOU GO ON...

Review It

1. How do the cost and matching principles apply to inventoriable costs?
2. How are the three assumed cost flow methods applied in allocating inventoriable costs?
3. What factors should be considered by management in selecting an inventory cost flow method?
4. Which inventory cost flow method produces (a) the highest net income in a period of rising prices, and (b) the lowest income taxes?
5. What amount is reported by **PepsiCo, Inc.** in its 2003 Annual Report as inventories at December 27, 2003? Which inventory cost flow method does PepsiCo use? (See Note 14.) The answer to this question is provided on p. 288.

(*continued from p. 253*)

Do It

The accounting records of Wayne E. Weather Company show the following data.

Beginning inventory	4,000 units at $3
Purchases	6,000 units at $4
Sales	5,000 units at $8

Determine the cost of goods sold during the period under a periodic inventory system using (a) the FIFO method, (b) the LIFO method, and (c) the average cost method.

ACTION PLAN

- Understand the periodic inventory system.
- Compute the cost of goods sold under the periodic inventory system using the FIFO cost flow method.
- Compute the cost of goods sold under the periodic inventory system using the LIFO cost flow method.
- Compute the cost of goods sold under the periodic inventory system using the average cost method.

SOLUTION

(a) FIFO: (4,000 @ $3) + (1,000 @ $4) = $12,000 + $4,000 = $16,000.
(b) LIFO: 5,000 @ $4 = $20,000.
(c) Average cost: [(4,000 @ $3) + (6,000 @ $4)] ÷ 10,000 = ($12,000 + $24,000) ÷ 10,000 = $3.60 per unit; 5,000 @ $3.60 = $18,000.

Related exercise material: *BE6-3, BE6-4, BE6-5, BE6-6, E6-3, E6-4, E6-5, E6-6, and E6-7.*

THE NAVIGATOR

Valuing Inventory at the Lower of Cost or Market (LCM)

STUDY OBJECTIVE 4

Explain the lower of cost or market basis of accounting for inventories.

Inventory values sometimes fall due to changes in technology or in fashion. When the value of inventory is lower than its cost, the inventory is written down to its market value. This is done by valuing the inventory at the **lower of cost or market (LCM)** and recognizing the loss in the period in which the decline occurs. LCM is an example of the **conservatism** constraint: When choosing among alternatives, the best choice is the method that is least likely to overstate assets and net income.

Under the LCM basis, "market" is defined as **current replacement cost**, not selling price. For a merchandiser, "market" is the cost of purchasing the same goods at the present time from the usual suppliers in the usual quantities.

Assume that Ken Tuckie TV has the following lines of merchandise with costs and market values as indicated. LCM produces the following result.

Illustration 6-18
Computation of lower of cost or market

	Cost	Market	Lower of Cost or Market
Television sets			
Consoles	$ 60,000	$ 55,000	$ 55,000
Portables	45,000	52,000	45,000
Total	105,000	107,000	
Video equipment			
Recorders	48,000	45,000	45,000
Movies	15,000	14,000	14,000
Total	63,000	59,000	
Total inventory	$168,000	$166,000	**$159,000**

The amount entered in the final column is the lower of the cost or market amount for **each item**. The LCM method is applied to the items in inventory after one of the costing methods (specific identification, FIFO, LIFO, or average cost) has been applied to determine cost.

ACCOUNTING MATTERS! Business Insight

In January 2002 **Ford Motor Co.** shocked its investors with an announcement that it was going take a $1 billion lower of cost or market charge on the value of its inventory of palladium, a precious metal used in vehicle emission devices. Fearing a shortage of the metal, Ford managers bought a huge amount of it, just before prices plummeted. Investors were angry both because Ford clearly should have taken steps to insulate itself from the effects of such price swings and because they felt the company had not adequately disclosed its risk of losses due to changes in the value of this metal. In fact, one group of investors filed a suit against the company because of the losses they sustained.

? Why would investors sustain losses? What would the effect on future income have been if Ford had not taken the lower-of-cost-or-market charge in 2002?

Inventory Errors

STUDY OBJECTIVE 5

Indicate the effects of inventory errors on the financial statements.

Unfortunately, errors occasionally occur in taking or costing inventory. Some errors are caused by counting or pricing the inventory incorrectly. Others occur because of improper recognition of the transfer of legal title to goods in transit. When errors occur, they affect both the income statement and the balance sheet.

Income Statement Effects

Remember that both the beginning and ending inventories are used to determine cost of goods sold in a periodic system. The ending inventory of one period automatically becomes the beginning inventory of the next period. Inventory errors thus affect the determination of cost of goods sold and net income for two periods.

The effects on cost of goods sold can be determined by using the following formula. First enter the incorrect data in the formula. Then substitute the correct data, and find the difference between the two cost of goods sold amounts.

Illustration 6-19
Formula for cost of goods sold

Beginning Inventory	+	Cost of Goods Purchased	−	Ending Inventory	=	Cost of Goods Sold

If beginning inventory is understated, cost of goods sold will be understated. If ending inventory is understated, cost of goods sold will be overstated. The effects of inventory errors on the current year's income statement are shown in Illustration 6-20.

Illustration 6-20
Effects of inventory errors on current year's income statement

Inventory Error	Cost of Goods Sold	Net Income
Beginning inventory understated	Understated	Overstated
Beginning inventory overstated	Overstated	Understated
Ending inventory understated	Overstated	Understated
Ending inventory overstated	Understated	Overstated

ETHICS NOTE

Inventory fraud includes costing inventory at amounts in excess of actual value, or claiming to have inventory when no inventory exists. Inventory fraud is usually done to overstate ending inventory, which understates cost of goods sold and creates higher income.

An error in ending inventory in the current period will have a **reverse effect on net income of the next period**. This is shown in Illustration 6-21 below. Note that understating ending inventory in 2006 understates beginning inventory in 2007 and overstates net income in 2007.

Over the two years, total net income is correct. The errors offset one another. Notice that for 2006 and 2007 total income using incorrect data is $35,000 ($22,000 + $13,000). This is the same as the total income of $35,000 ($25,000 + $10,000) using correct data. Also note in this example that an error in the beginning inventory does not result in a corresponding error in the ending inventory. The correctness of the ending inventory depends entirely on the accuracy of taking and costing the inventory at the balance sheet date.

Illustration 6-21
Effects of inventory errors on two years' income statements

Condensed Income Statement

	2006				2007			
	Incorrect		Correct		Incorrect		Correct	
Sales		$80,000		$80,000		$90,000		$90,000
Beginning inventory	$20,000		$20,000		**$12,000**		**$15,000**	
Cost of goods purchased	40,000		40,000		68,000		68,000	
Cost of goods available for sale	60,000		60,000		80,000		83,000	
Ending inventory	**12,000**		**15,000**		23,000		23,000	
Cost of goods sold		48,000		45,000		57,000		60,000
Gross profit		32,000		35,000		33,000		30,000
Operating expenses		10,000		10,000		20,000		20,000
Net income		$22,000		$25,000		$13,000		$10,000

($3,000) Net income understated — **$3,000** Net income overstated

The total combined income for the 2 years is correct.

Balance Sheet Effects

The effect of ending-inventory errors on the balance sheet can be determined by the basic accounting equation: Assets = Liabilities + Stockholders' Equity. Errors in the ending inventory have the following effects on these components.

Illustration 6-22
Ending inventory error—balance sheet effects

Ending Inventory Error	Assets	Liabilities	Stockholders' Equity
Overstated	Overstated	None	Overstated
Understated	Understated	None	Understated

The effect of an error in ending inventory on the next period was shown in Illustration 6-21. If the error is not corrected, total net income for the two periods will be correct. Thus, total stockholders' equity reported on the balance sheet at the end of the next period will also be correct.

STATEMENT PRESENTATION AND ANALYSIS

Presentation

As indicated in Chapter 5, inventory is classified as a current asset after receivables in the balance sheet. In a multiple-step income statement, cost of goods sold is subtracted from sales. There also should be disclosure of (1) the major inventory classifications, (2) the basis of accounting (cost, or lower of cost or market), and (3) the costing method (FIFO, LIFO, or average).

Wal-Mart, for example, in its January 31, 2004, balance sheet reported inventories of $26,612 million as current assets. The accompanying notes to the financial statements, as shown in Illustration 6-23, disclosed the following information.

Illustration 6-23
Inventory disclosures by **Wal-Mart**

WAL*MART

WAL-MART STORES, INC.
Notes to the Financial Statements

Note 1. Summary of accounting policies

Inventories

The Company uses the retail last-in, first-out (LIFO) method for the Wal-Mart Stores segment, cost LIFO for the SAM'S CLUB segment, and other cost methods, including the retail first-in, first-out (FIFO) and average cost methods, for the International segment. Inventories are not recorded in excess of market value.

As indicated in this note, Wal-Mart values its inventories at the lower of cost or market using all three inventory costing methods—LIFO, FIFO, and average cost.

Analysis

The amount of inventory carried by a company has significant economic consequences. Inventory management is a double-edged sword that requires constant attention. On the one hand, management wants to have a great variety and quantity on hand so that customers have a wide selection and items are always in stock. But such a policy may incur high carrying costs (e.g., investment, storage, insurance, obsolescence, and damage). On the other hand, low inventory levels lead to stockouts and lost sales.

Common ratios used to manage and evaluate inventory levels are inventory turnover and a related measure, average days to sell the inventory.

STUDY OBJECTIVE 6
Compute and interpret inventory turnover.

Inventory turnover measures the number of times on average the inventory is sold during the period. Its purpose is to measure the liquidity of the inventory. The inventory turnover is computed by dividing cost of goods sold by the average inventory during the period. Unless seasonal factors are significant, average inventory can be computed from the beginning and ending inventory balances. For example, **Wal-Mart** reported in its 2004 Annual Report a beginning inventory of $24,401 million, an ending inventory of $26,612 million, and cost of goods sold for the year ended January 31, 2004, of $198,747 million. The inventory turnover formula and computation for Wal-Mart are shown below.

Illustration 6-24
Inventory turnover formula and computation for **Wal-Mart**

Cost of Goods Sold	÷	Average Inventory	=	Inventory Turnover
$198,747	÷	$\frac{\$24,401 + \$26,612}{2}$	=	**7.79 times**

A variant of the inventory turnover ratio is the **average days to sell inventory**. For example, the inventory turnover for Wal-Mart of 7.8 times divided into 365 is approximately 47 days. This is the approximate age of the inventory.

There are typical levels of inventory in every industry. Companies that are able to keep their inventory at lower levels with higher turnovers and still satisfy customer needs are the most successful.

BEFORE YOU GO ON...

Review It

1. Why is it appropriate to report inventories at the lower of cost or market?
2. How do inventory errors affect financial statements?
3. What does inventory turnover reveal?

THE NAVIGATOR

DEMONSTRATION PROBLEM 1

Gerald D. Englehart Company has the following inventory, purchases, and sales data for the month of March.

Inventory:	March 1	200 units @ $4.00	$ 800
Purchases:			
	March 10	500 units @ $4.50	2,250
	March 20	400 units @ $4.75	1,900
	March 30	300 units @ $5.00	1,500
Sales:			
	March 15	500 units	
	March 25	400 units	

The physical inventory count on March 31 shows 500 units on hand.

Instructions

Under a **periodic inventory system**, determine the cost of inventory on hand at March 31 and the cost of goods sold for March under the (a) first-in, first-out (FIFO) method, (b) last-in, first-out (LIFO) method, and (c) average cost method.

ACTION PLAN

- Compute the cost of inventory under the periodic FIFO method by allocating to the units on hand the **latest costs**.
- Compute the cost of inventory under the periodic LIFO method by allocating to the units on hand the **earliest costs**.
- Compute the cost of inventory under the periodic average cost method by allocating to the units on hand a **weighted-average cost**.

SOLUTION TO DEMONSTRATION PROBLEM 1

The cost of goods available for sale is $6,450, as follows.

Inventory:		200 units @ $4.00	$ 800
Purchases:			
	March 10	500 units @ $4.50	2,250
	March 20	400 units @ $4.75	1,900
	March 30	300 units @ $5.00	1,500
Total cost of goods available for sale			$6,450

Under a **periodic inventory system**, the cost of goods sold under each cost flow method is as follows.

FIFO Method

Ending inventory:

Date	Units	Unit Cost	Total Cost	
March 30	300	$5.00	$1,500	
March 20	200	4.75	950	$2,450

Cost of goods sold: $6,450 − $2,450 = $4,000

LIFO Method

Ending inventory:

Date	Units	Unit Cost	Total Cost	
March 1	200	$4.00	$ 800	
March 10	300	4.50	1,350	$2,150

Cost of goods sold: $6,450 − $2,150 = $4,300

Average Cost Method

Average unit cost: $6,450 ÷ 1,400 = $4.607
Ending inventory: 500 × $4.607 = $2,303.50

Cost of goods sold: $6,450 − $2,303.50 = $4,146.50

THE NAVIGATOR

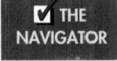

SUMMARY OF STUDY OBJECTIVES

1. **Describe the steps in determining inventory quantities.** The steps in determining inventory quantities are (1) taking a physical inventory of goods on hand and (2) determining the ownership of goods in transit.

2. **Explain the basis of accounting for inventories, and describe the inventory cost flow methods.** The primary basis of accounting for inventories is cost. Cost includes all expenditures necessary to acquire goods and to make them ready for sale. Inventoriable costs include (1) the cost of beginning inventory and (2) the cost of goods purchased. The inventory cost flow methods are: specific identification, FIFO, LIFO, and average cost.

3. **Explain the financial statement and tax effects of each of the inventory cost flow methods.** The cost of goods available for sale may be allocated to cost of goods sold and ending inventory by specific identification or by a method based on an assumed cost flow. These methods have different effects on financial statements during periods of changing prices. When prices are rising, FIFO results in lower cost of goods sold and higher net income than the average cost and the LIFO methods. LIFO results in the lowest income taxes (because of lower taxable income). In the balance sheet, FIFO results in an ending inventory that is closest to current value. The inventory under LIFO is the farthest from current value.

4. **Explain the lower of cost or market basis of accounting for inventories.** The lower of cost or market (LCM) basis is used when the current replacement cost (market) is less than cost. Under LCM, the loss is recognized in the period in which the price decline occurs.

5. **Indicate the effects of inventory errors on the financial statements.** In the income statement of the current year: (a) An error in beginning inventory will have a reverse effect on net income (overstatement of inventory results in understatement of net income); and (b) an error in ending inventory will have a similar effect on net income (overstatement of inventory results in overstatement of net income). If ending inventory errors are not corrected in the next period, their effect on net income for that period is reversed, and total net income for the two years will be correct. In the balance sheet, ending inventory errors will have the same effect on total assets and total stockholders' equity and no effect on liabilities.

6. **Compute and interpret inventory turnover.** Inventory turnover is calculated as cost of goods sold divided by average inventory. It can be converted to average days in inventory by dividing 365 days by the inventory turnover ratio. A higher turnover or lower average days in inventory suggests that management is trying to keep inventory levels low relative to sales.

THE NAVIGATOR

GLOSSARY

Average cost method Inventory costing method that assumes that the goods available for sale have the same (average) cost per unit; generally the goods are identical. (p. 250).

Consigned goods Goods shipped by a consignor, who retains ownership, to another party called the consignee. (p. 244).

Current replacement cost The amount that would be paid at the present time to acquire an identical item. (p. 254).

First-in, first-out (FIFO) method Inventory costing method that assumes that the costs of the earliest goods acquired are the first to be recognized as cost of goods sold. (p. 248).

Inventoriable costs The pool of costs that consists of two elements: (1) the cost of the beginning inventory and (2) the cost of goods purchased during the period. (p. 245).

Inventory turnover A measure of the number of times on average the inventory is sold during the period; computed by dividing cost of goods sold by the average inventory during the period. (p. 257).

Last-in, first-out (LIFO) method Inventory costing method that assumes that the costs of the latest units purchased are the first to be allocated to cost of goods sold. (p. 249).

Lower of cost or market (LCM) basis Method of valuing inventory that recognizes the decline in the value when the current purchase price (market) is less than cost. (p. 254).

Periodic inventory system An inventory system in which inventoriable costs are allocated to ending inventory and cost of goods sold at the end of the period. Cost of goods sold is computed at the end of the period by subtracting the ending inventory (costs are assigned based on a physical count of items on hand) from the cost of goods available for sale. (p. 245).

Specific identification method An actual, physical flow inventory costing method in which items still in inventory are specifically costed to arrive at the total cost of the ending inventory. (p. 246).

APPENDIX 6A INVENTORY COST FLOW METHODS IN PERPETUAL INVENTORY SYSTEMS

Each of the inventory cost flow methods described in the chapter for a periodic inventory system can be used in a perpetual inventory system. To illustrate the application of the three assumed cost flow methods (FIFO, LIFO, and average cost), we will use the data shown below and in this chapter for Bow Valley Electronics' product Z202 Astro Condenser.

STUDY OBJECTIVE 7

Apply the inventory cost flow methods to perpetual inventory records.

Illustration 6A-1
Inventoriable units and costs

BOW VALLEY ELECTRONICS
Z202 Astro Condensers

Date	Explanation	Units	Unit Cost	Total Cost	Balance in Units
1/1	Beginning inventory	100	$10	$ 1,000	100
4/15	Purchase	200	11	2,200	300
8/24	Purchase	300	12	3,600	600
9/10	Sales	550			50
11/27	Purchase	400	13	5,200	450
				$12,000	

First-In, First-Out (FIFO)

Under FIFO, the cost of the earliest goods on hand prior to each sale is charged to cost of goods sold. The cost of goods sold on September 10 consists of the units on hand January 1 and the units purchased April 15 and August 24. The inventory on a FIFO method perpetual system is shown in Illustration 6A-2.

Illustration 6A-2
Perpetual system—FIFO

Date	Purchases		Sales	Balance	
January 1				(100 @ $10)	$1,000
April 15	(200 @ $11)	$2,200		(100 @ $10) (200 @ $11)	$3,200
August 24	(300 @ $12)	$3,600		(100 @ $10) (200 @ $11) (300 @ $12)	$6,800
September 10			(100 @ $10) (200 @ $11) (250 @ $12) **$6,200**	(50 @ $12)	$ 600
November 27	(400 @ $13)	$5,200		(50 @ $12) (400 @ $13)	**$5,800**

The ending inventory in this situation is $5,800. The cost of goods sold is $6,200 [(100 @ $10) + (200 @ $11) + (250 @ $12)].

The results under FIFO in a perpetual system are the **same as in a periodic system**. See Illustration 6-5 on page 248. There, similarly, the ending inventory is $5,800 and cost of goods sold is $6,200. Regardless of the system, the first costs in are the costs assigned to cost of goods sold.

Last-In, First-Out (LIFO)

Under the LIFO method using a perpetual system, the cost of the most recent purchase prior to sale is allocated to the units sold. The cost of the goods sold on September 10 consists of all the units from the August 24 and April 15 purchases and 50 of the units in beginning inventory. The ending inventory on a LIFO method is computed in Illustration 6A-3.

Illustration 6A-3
Perpetual system—LIFO

Date	Purchases		Sales	Balance	
January 1				(100 @ $10)	$1,000
April 15	(200 @ $11)	$2,200		(100 @ $10) (200 @ $11)	$3,200
August 24	(300 @ $12)	$3,600		(100 @ $10) (200 @ $11) (300 @ $12)	$6,800
September 10			(300 @ $12) (200 @ $11) (50 @ $10) **$6,300**	(50 @ $10)	$ 500
November 27	(400 @ $13)	$5,200		(50 @ $10) (400 @ $13)	**$5,700**

The use of LIFO in a perpetual system will usually produce cost allocations that differ from using LIFO in a periodic system. In a perpetual system, the latest units incurred **prior to each sale** are allocated to cost of goods sold. In contrast, in a periodic system, the latest units incurred **during the period** are allocated to cost of goods sold. Thus, when a purchase is made after the last sale, the LIFO periodic system will apply this purchase to the previous sale. See Illustration 6-10 on page 250. There, the proof shows the 400 units @ $13 purchased on November 27 applied to the sale of 550 units on September 10. As shown above under the LIFO perpetual system, the 400 units @ $13 purchased on November 27 are all applied to the ending inventory.

The ending inventory in this LIFO perpetual example is $5,700 and cost of goods sold is $6,300. Compare these amounts to the LIFO periodic illustration (see Illustration 6-8 on page 249) where the ending inventory is $5,000 and cost of goods sold is $7,000.

Average Cost

The average cost method in a perpetual inventory system is called the **moving-average method**. Under this method a new average is computed **after each purchase**. The average cost is computed by dividing the cost of goods available for sale by the units on hand. The average cost is then applied to: (1) the units sold, to determine the cost of goods sold, and (2) the remaining units on hand, to determine the ending inventory amount. The application of the average cost method by Bow Valley Electronics is shown in Illustration 6A-4.

Illustration 6A-4
Perpetual system—average cost method

Date	Purchases		Sales	Balance	
January 1				(100 @ $10)	$1,000
April 15	(200 @ $11)	$2,200		(300 @ $10.667)	$3,200
August 24	(300 @ $12)	$3,600		(600 @ $11.333)	$6,800
September 10			(550 @ $11.333) **($6,233)**	(50 @ $11.333)	$ 567
November 27	(400 @ $13)	$5,200		(450 @ $12.816)	**$5,767**

As indicated above, **a new average is computed each time a purchase is made.** On April 15, after 200 units are purchased for $2,200, a total of 300 units costing $3,200 ($1,000 + $2,200) are on hand. The average unit cost is $10.667 ($3,200 ÷ 300). On August 24, after 300 units are purchased for $3,600, a total of 600 units costing $6,800 ($1,000 + $2,200 + $3,600) are on hand at an average cost per unit of $11.333 ($6,800 ÷ 600). This unit cost of $11.333 is used in costing sales until another purchase is made, when a new unit cost is computed. Thus, the unit cost of the 550 units sold on September 10 is $11.333, and the total cost of goods sold is $6,233. On November 27, following the purchase of 400 units for $5,200, there are 450 units on hand costing $5,767 ($567 + $5,200), with a new average cost of $12.816 ($5,767 ÷ 450).

Compare this moving-average cost under the perpetual inventory system to Illustration 6-12 on pages 250–251 showing the average cost method under a periodic inventory system.

DEMONSTRATION PROBLEM 2

Demonstration Problem 1 on pages 258–259 showed cost of goods sold computations under a periodic inventory system. Now let's assume that Gerald D. Englehart Company uses a perpetual inventory system. The company has the same inventory, purchases, and sales data for the month of March as shown earlier.

Inventory:	March 1	200 units @ \$4.00	\$ 800
Purchases:	March 10	500 units @ \$4.50	2,250
	March 20	400 units @ \$4.75	1,900
	March 30	300 units @ \$5.00	1,500
Sales:	March 15	500 units	
	March 25	400 units	

The physical inventory count on March 31 shows 500 units on hand.

Instructions

Under a **perpetual inventory system**, determine the cost of inventory on hand at March 31 and the cost of goods sold for March under the (a) first-in, first-out (FIFO) method, (b) last-in, first-out (LIFO) method, and (c) average cost method.

SOLUTION TO DEMONSTRATION PROBLEM 2

The cost of goods available for sale is \$6,450, as follows.

Inventory:		200 units @ \$4.00	\$ 800
Purchases:	March 10	500 units @ \$4.50	2,250
	March 20	400 units @ \$4.75	1,900
	March 30	300 units @ \$5.00	1,500
Total cost of goods available for sale			\$6,450

Under a **perpetual inventory system**, the cost of goods sold under each cost flow method is as follows.

FIFO Method

Date	Purchases	Sales	Balance
March 1			(200 @ \$4.00) \$ 800
March 10	(500 @ \$4.50) \$2,250		(200 @ \$4.00) (500 @ \$4.50) } \$3,050
March 15		(200 @ \$4.00) (300 @ \$4.50) \$2,150	(200 @ \$4.50) \$ 900
March 20	(400 @ \$4.75) \$1,900		(200 @ \$4.50) (400 @ \$4.75) } \$2,800
March 25		(200 @ \$4.50) (200 @ \$4.75) \$1,850	(200 @ \$4.75) \$ 950
March 30	(300 @ \$5.00) \$1,500		(200 @ \$4.75) (300 @ \$5.00) } \$2,450

Ending inventory, \$2,450 Cost of goods sold: \$6,450 − \$2,450 = \$4,000

ACTION PLAN

- Compute the cost of goods sold under the perpetual FIFO method by allocating to the goods sold the **earliest** cost of goods purchased.
- Compute the cost of goods sold under the perpetual LIFO method by allocating to the goods sold the **latest** cost of goods purchased.
- Compute the cost of goods sold under the perpetual average cost method by allocating to the goods sold a **moving-average** cost.

LIFO Method

Date	Purchases		Sales		Balance	
March 1					(200 @ $4.00)	$ 800
March 10	(500 @ $4.50)	$2,250			(200 @ $4.00) (500 @ $4.50)	$3,050
March 15			(500 @ $4.50)	$2,250	(200 @ $4.00)	$ 800
March 20	(400 @ $4.75)	$1,900			(200 @ $4.00) (400 @ $4.75)	$2,700
March 25			(400 @ $4.75)	$1,900	(200 @ $4.00)	$ 800
March 30	(300 @ $5.00)	$1,500			(200 @ $4.00) (300 @ $5.00)	$2,300

Ending inventory, $2,300 Cost of goods sold: $6,450 − $2,300 = $4,150

Moving-Average Cost Method

Date	Purchases		Sales		Balance	
March 1					(200 @ $ 4.00)	$ 800
March 10	(500 @ $4.50)	$2,250			(700 @ $4.357)	$3,050
March 15			(500 @ $4.357)	$2,179	(200 @ $4.357)	$ 871
March 20	(400 @ $4.75)	$1,900			(600 @ $4.618)	$2,771
March 25			(400 @ $4.618)	$1,847	(200 @ $4.618)	$ 924
March 30	(300 @ $5.00)	$1,500			(500 @ $4.848)	$2,424

Ending inventory, $2,424 Cost of goods sold: $6,450 − $2,424 = $4,026

THE NAVIGATOR

SUMMARY OF STUDY OBJECTIVE FOR APPENDIX 6A

7. **Apply the inventory cost flow methods to perpetual inventory records.** Under FIFO, the cost of the earliest goods on hand prior to each sale is charged to cost of goods sold. Under LIFO, the cost of the most recent purchase prior to sale is charged to cost of goods sold. Under the average cost method, a new average cost is computed after each purchase.

APPENDIX 6B ESTIMATING INVENTORIES

STUDY OBJECTIVE 8

Describe the two methods of estimating inventories.

We assumed in the chapter that a company would be able to physically count its inventory. But what if it cannot? What if the inventory were destroyed by fire, for example? In that case, we would use an estimate.

Two circumstances explain why inventories are sometimes estimated. First, management may want monthly or quarterly financial statements, but a physical inventory is taken only annually. Second, a casualty such as fire, flood, or earthquake may make it impossible to take a physical inventory. The need for estimating inventories is associated primarily with a periodic inventory system because of the absence of detailed inventory records.

There are two widely used methods of estimating inventories: (1) the gross profit method and (2) the retail inventory method.

Gross Profit Method

The **gross profit method** estimates the cost of ending inventory by applying a gross profit rate to net sales. It is used in preparing monthly financial statements under a periodic system. This method is relatively simple but effective. It will detect large errors. Accountants, auditors, and managers frequently use the gross profit method to test the reasonableness of the ending inventory amount.

To use this method, a company needs to know its net sales, cost of goods available for sale, and gross profit rate. With the gross profit rate, the company can estimate its gross profit for the period. The formulas for using the gross profit method are given in Illustration 6B-1.

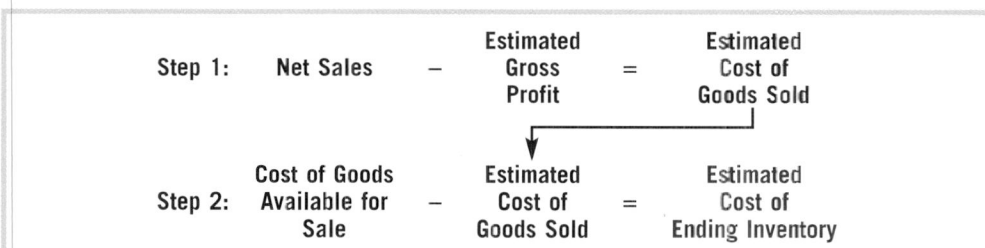

Illustration 6B-1
Gross profit method formulas

Step 1:	**Net Sales**	−	**Estimated Gross Profit**	=	**Estimated Cost of Goods Sold**
Step 2:	**Cost of Goods Available for Sale**	−	**Estimated Cost of Goods Sold**	=	**Estimated Cost of Ending Inventory**

To illustrate, assume that Kishwaukee Company wishes to prepare an income statement for the month of January. Its records show net sales $200,000, beginning inventory $40,000, and cost of goods purchased $120,000. In the preceding year, the company realized a 30% gross profit rate. It expects to earn the same rate this year. Given these facts and assumptions, the estimated cost of the ending inventory at January 31 can be computed under the gross profit method as follows.

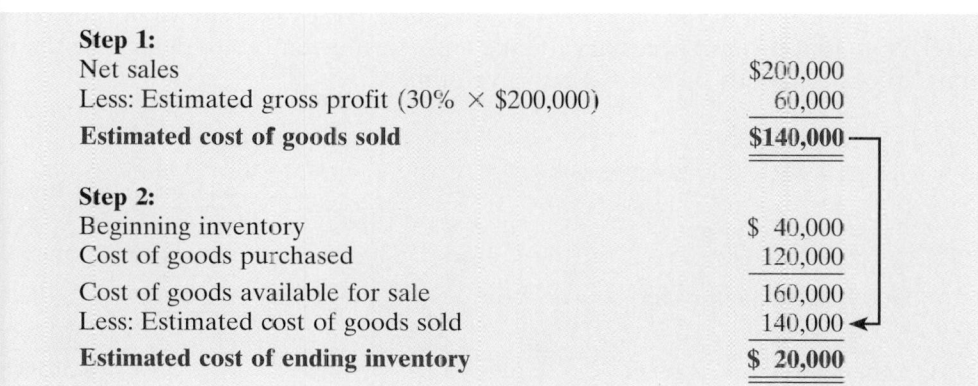

Illustration 6B-2
Example of gross profit method

Step 1:	
Net sales	$200,000
Less: Estimated gross profit (30% × $200,000)	60,000
Estimated cost of goods sold	**$140,000**
Step 2:	
Beginning inventory	$ 40,000
Cost of goods purchased	120,000
Cost of goods available for sale	160,000
Less: Estimated cost of goods sold	140,000
Estimated cost of ending inventory	**$ 20,000**

The gross profit method is based on the assumption that the gross profit rate will remain constant. But it may not remain constant, because of a change in merchandising policies or in market conditions. In such cases, the rate should be adjusted to reflect current operating conditions. In some cases, a more accurate estimate can be obtained by applying this method on a department or product-line basis.

The gross profit method should not be used in preparing a company's financial statements at the end of the year. These statements should be based on a physical inventory count.

Retail Inventory Method

A retail store such as **Kmart**, **Ace Hardware**, or **Wal-Mart** has thousands of different types of merchandise at low unit costs. In such cases it is difficult and time-consuming to apply unit costs to inventory quantities. An alternative is to use the **retail inventory method** to estimate the cost of inventory. In most retail concerns, a relationship between cost and sales price can be established. The cost-to-retail percentage is then applied to the ending inventory at retail prices to determine inventory at cost.

To use the retail inventory method, a company's records must show both the cost and retail value of the goods available for sale. The formulas for using the retail inventory method are presented in Illustration 6B-3.

Illustration 6B-3
Retail inventory method formulas

Step 1:	**Goods Available for Sale at Retail**	−	**Net Sales**	=	**Ending Inventory at Retail**
Step 2:	**Goods Available for Sale at Cost**	÷	**Goods Available for Sale at Retail**	=	**Cost-to-Retail Ratio**
Step 3:	**Ending Inventory at Retail**	×	**Cost-to-Retail Ratio**	=	**Estimated Cost of Ending Inventory**

The logic of the retail method can be demonstrated by using unit-cost data. Assume that 10 units purchased at $7 each are marked to sell for $10 per unit. Thus, the cost-to-retail ratio is 70% ($70 ÷ $100). If 4 units remain unsold, their retail value is $40 (4 × $10), and their cost is $28 ($40 × 70%). This amount agrees with the total cost of goods on hand on a per unit basis (4 × $7).

The application of the retail method for Valley West Co. is shown in Illustration 6B-4. Note that it is not necessary to take a physical inventory to determine the estimated cost of goods on hand at any given time.

Illustration 6B-4
Example of retail inventory method

	At Cost	At Retail
Beginning inventory	$14,000	$ 21,500
Goods purchased	61,000	78,500
Goods available for sale	$75,000	100,000
Net sales		70,000
(1) Ending inventory at retail		**$ 30,000**
(2) Cost-to-retail ratio = ($75,000 ÷ $100,000) = 75%		
(3) Estimated cost of ending inventory = ($30,000 × 75%)	**$22,500**	

HELPFUL HINT

In determining inventory at retail, selling prices of the units are used. Tracing actual unit costs to invoices is unnecessary.

The retail inventory method also facilitates taking a physical inventory at the end of the year. The goods on hand can be valued at the prices marked on the merchandise. The cost-to-retail ratio is then applied to the goods on hand at retail to determine the ending inventory at cost.

The major disadvantage of the retail method is that it is an averaging technique. It may produce an incorrect inventory valuation if the mix of the ending inventory is not representative of the mix in the goods available for sale. Assume, for example, that the cost-to-retail ratio of 75% for Valley West Co. consists of equal proportions of inventory items that have cost-to-retail ratios of 70%, 75%, and 80%. If the ending inventory contains only items with a 70% ratio, an incorrect inventory cost will result. This problem can be minimized by applying the retail method on a department or product-line basis.

SUMMARY OF STUDY OBJECTIVE FOR APPENDIX 6B

8. **Describe the two methods of estimating inventories.** The two methods of estimating inventories are the gross profit method and the retail inventory method. Under the gross profit method, a gross profit rate is applied to net sales to determine estimated cost of goods sold. Estimated cost of goods sold is then subtracted from cost of goods available for sale to determine the estimated cost of the ending inventory.

Under the retail inventory method, a cost-to-retail ratio is computed by dividing the cost of goods available for sale by the retail value of the goods available for sale. This ratio is then applied to the ending inventory at retail to determine the estimated cost of the ending inventory.

GLOSSARY FOR APPENDIX 6B

Gross profit method A method for estimating the cost of the ending inventory by applying a gross profit rate to net sales. (p. 264).

Retail inventory method A method used to estimate the cost of the ending inventory by applying a cost-to-retail ratio to the ending inventory at retail. (p. 266).

*__Note:__ All **asterisked** Questions, Exercises, and Problems relate to material in the appendixes to the chapter.

SELF-STUDY QUESTIONS

Self-Study/Self-Test

Answers are at the end of the chapter.

(SO 1) 1. Which of the following should *not* be included in the physical inventory of a company?
   a. Goods held on consignment from another company.
   b. Goods shipped on consignment to another company.
   c. Goods in transit from another company shipped FOB shipping point.
   d. None of the above.

(SO 2) 2. Inventoriable costs consist of two elements: beginning inventory and
   a. ending inventory.
   b. cost of goods purchased.
   c. cost of goods sold.
   d. cost of goods available for sale.

(SO 2) 3. Tinker Bell Company has the following:

	Units	Unit Cost
Inventory, Jan. 1	8,000	$11
Purchase, June 19	13,000	12
Purchase, Nov. 8	5,000	13

   If 9,000 units are on hand at December 31, the cost of the ending inventory under FIFO is:
   a. $99,000. **c.** $113,000.
   b. $108,000. **d.** $117,000.

(SO 2) 4. Using the data in (3) above, the cost of the ending inventory under LIFO is:
   a. $113,000. **c.** $99,000.
   b. $108,000. **d.** $100,000.

(SO 3) 5. In periods of rising prices, LIFO will produce:
   a. higher net income than FIFO.
   b. the same net income as FIFO.
   c. lower net income than FIFO.
   d. higher net income than average costing.

6. Factors that affect the selection of an inventory costing method do *not* include: (SO 3)
   a. tax effects.
   b. balance sheet effects.
   c. income statement effects.
   d. perpetual vs. periodic inventory system.

7. Rickety Company purchased 1,000 widgets and has 200 widgets in its ending inventory at a cost of $91 each and a current replacement cost of $80 each. The ending inventory under lower of cost or market is: (SO 4)
   a. $91,000.
   b. $80,000.
   c. $18,200.
   d. $16,000.

8. Atlantis Company's ending inventory is understated $4,000. The effects of this error on the current year's cost of goods sold and net income, respectively, are: (SO 5)
   a. understated, overstated.
   b. overstated, understated.
   c. overstated, overstated.
   d. understated, understated.

9. Which of these would cause the inventory turnover ratio to increase the most? (SO 6)
   a. Increasing the amount of inventory on hand.
   b. Keeping the amount of inventory on hand constant but increasing sales.
   c. Keeping the amount of inventory on hand constant but decreasing sales.
   d. Decreasing the amount of inventory on hand and increasing sales.

(SO 8) *10. Songbird Company has sales of $150,000 and cost of goods available for sale of $135,000. If the gross profit rate is 30%, the estimated cost of the ending inventory under the gross profit method is:
- **a.** $15,000.
- **b.** $30,000.
- **c.** $45,000.
- **d.** $75,000.

*11. In a perpetual inventory system, (SO 7)
- **a.** LIFO cost of goods sold will be the same as in a periodic inventory system.
- **b.** average costs are based entirely on unit cost averages.
- **c.** a new average is computed under the average cost method after each sale.
- **d.** FIFO cost of goods sold will be the same as in a periodic inventory system.

THE NAVIGATOR

QUESTIONS

1. "The key to successful business operations is effective inventory management." Do you agree? Explain.

2. An item must possess two characteristics to be classified as inventory by a merchandiser. What are these two characteristics?

3. Your friend Art Mega has been hired to help take the physical inventory in Hawkeye Hardware Store. Explain to Art Mega what this job will entail.

4. (a) Hansen Company ships merchandise to Fox Company on December 30. The merchandise reaches the buyer on January 6. Indicate the terms of sale that will result in the goods being included in (1) Hansen's December 31 inventory, and (2) Fox's December 31 inventory.
(b) Under what circumstances should Hansen Company include consigned goods in its inventory?

5. Topp Hat Shop received a shipment of hats for which it paid the wholesaler $2,970. The price of the hats was $3,000 but Topp was given a $30 cash discount and required to pay freight charges of $80. In addition, Topp paid $130 to cover the travel expenses of an employee who negotiated the purchase of the hats. What amount will Topp record for inventory? Why?

6. What is the primary basis of accounting for inventories? What is the major objective in accounting for inventories? What accounting principles are involved here?

7. Identify the distinguishing features of an income statement for a merchandiser.

8. Jason Bradley believes that the allocation of inventoriable costs should be based on the actual physical flow of the goods. Explain to Jason why this may be both impractical and inappropriate.

9. What is a major advantage and a major disadvantage of the specific identification method of inventory costing?

10. "The selection of an inventory cost flow method is a decision made by accountants." Do you agree? Explain. Once a method has been selected, what accounting requirement applies?

11. Which assumed inventory cost flow method:
(a) usually parallels the actual physical flow of merchandise?
(b) assumes that goods available for sale during an accounting period are identical?
(c) assumes that the latest units purchased are the first to be sold?

12. In a period of rising prices, the inventory reported in Barto Company's balance sheet is close to the current cost of the inventory. Cecil Company's inventory is considerably below its current cost. Identify the inventory cost flow method being used by each company. Which company has probably been reporting the higher gross profit?

13. Olsen Company has been using the FIFO cost flow method during a prolonged period of rising prices. During the same time period, Olsen has been paying out all of its net income as dividends. What adverse effects may result from this policy?

14. Steve Kerns is studying for the accounting mid-term examination. What should Steve know about (a) departing from the cost basis of accounting for inventories and (b) the meaning of "market" in the lower of cost or market method?

15. Steering Music Center has 5 CD players on hand at the balance sheet date. Each cost $400. The current replacement cost is $360 per unit. Under the lower of cost or market basis of accounting for inventories, what value should be reported for the CD players on the balance sheet? Why?

16. Maggie Stores has 20 toasters on hand at the balance sheet date. Each cost $28. The current replacement cost is $30 per unit. Under the lower of cost or market basis of accounting for inventories, what value should be reported for the toasters on the balance sheet? Why?

17. Cohen Company discovers in 2006 that its ending inventory at December 31, 2005, was $7,000 understated. What effect will this error have on (a) 2005 net income, (b) 2006 net income, and (c) the combined net income for the 2 years?

18. Yin & Yang Company's balance sheet shows Inventories $162,800. What additional disclosures should be made?

19. Under what circumstances might inventory turnover be too high? That is, what possible negative consequences might occur?

*__20.__ "When perpetual inventory records are kept, the results under the FIFO and LIFO methods are the same as they would be in a periodic inventory system." Do you agree? Explain.

*21. How does the average cost method of inventory costing differ between a perpetual inventory system and a periodic inventory system?

*22. When is it necessary to estimate inventories?

*23. Both the gross profit method and the retail inventory method are based on averages. For each method, indicate the average used, how it is determined, and how it is applied.

*24. Edmonds Company has net sales of $400,000 and cost of goods available for sale of $300,000. If the gross profit rate is 40%, what is the estimated cost of the ending inventory? Show computations.

*25. Park Shoe Shop had goods available for sale in 2006 with a retail price of $120,000. The cost of these goods was $84,000. If sales during the period were $90,000, what is the ending inventory at cost using the retail inventory method?

BRIEF EXERCISES

Identify items to be included in taking a physical inventory.
(SO 1)

BE6-1 Dayne Company identifies the following items for possible inclusion in the taking of a physical inventory. Indicate whether each item should be included or excluded from the inventory taking.

(a) Goods shipped on consignment by Dayne to another company.
(b) Goods in transit from a supplier shipped FOB destination.
(c) Goods sold but being held for customer pickup.
(d) Goods held on consignment from another company.

Identify the components of inventoriable costs.
(SO 2)

BE6-2 The ledger of Perez Company includes the following items: **(a)** Freight-in, **(b)** Purchase Returns and Allowances, **(c)** Purchases, **(d)** Sales Discounts, **(e)** Purchase Discounts. Identify which items are included in inventoriable costs.

Compute ending inventory using FIFO and LIFO.
(SO 2)

BE6-3 In its first month of operations, Rusch Company made three purchases of merchandise in the following sequence: (1) 300 units at $6, (2) 400 units at $7, and (3) 200 units at $8. Assuming there are 450 units on hand, compute the cost of the ending inventory under the **(a)** FIFO method and **(b)** LIFO method. Rusch uses a periodic inventory system.

Compute the ending inventory using average cost.
(SO 2)

BE6-4 Data for Rusch Company are presented in BE6-3. Compute the cost of the ending inventory under the average cost method, assuming there are 450 units on hand.

Explain the financial statement effect of inventory cost flow assumptions.
(SO 3)

BE6-5 The management of Muni Corp. is considering the effects of various inventory-costing methods on its financial statements and its income tax expense. Assuming that the price the company pays for inventory is increasing, which method will:

(a) provide the highest net income?
(b) provide the highest ending inventory?
(c) result in the lowest income tax expense?
(d) result in the most stable earnings over a number of years?

Explain the financial statement effect of inventory cost flow assumptions.
(SO 3)

BE6-6 In its first month of operation, Marquette Company purchased 100 units of inventory for $6, then 200 units for $7, and finally 150 units for $8. At the end of the month, 200 units remained. Compute the amount of phantom profit that would result if the company used FIFO rather than LIFO. Explain why this amount is referred to as phantom profit. The company uses the periodic method.

Determine the LCM valuation using inventory categories.
(SO 4)

BE6-7 Pena Appliance Center accumulates the following cost and market data at December 31.

Inventory Categories	Cost Data	Market Data
Cameras	$12,000	$12,100
Camcorders	9,000	9,700
VCRs	14,000	12,800

Compute the lower of cost or market valuation for the company's total inventory.

Determine correct income statement amounts.
(SO 5)

BE6-8 Farr Company reports net income of $90,000 in 2006. However, ending inventory was understated $5,000. What is the correct net income for 2006? What effect, if any, will this error have on total assets as reported in the balance sheet at December 31, 2006?

Compute inventory turnover and days in inventory.
(SO 6)

BE6-9 At December 31, 2006, the following information was available for J. Simon Company: ending inventory $40,000, beginning inventory $60,000, cost of goods sold $300,000, and sales revenue $380,000. Calculate inventory turnover and days in inventory for J. Simon Company.

Apply cost flow methods to perpetual inventory records.
(SO 7)

***BE6-10** Abbott's Department Store uses a perpetual inventory system. Data for product E2-D2 include the following purchases.

Date	Number of Units	Unit Price
May 7	50	$10
July 28	30	13

On June 1 Abbott's sold 30 units, and on August 27, 35 more units. Prepare the perpetual inventory calculations for the above transactions using (1) FIFO, (2) LIFO, and (3) average cost.

Apply the gross profit method.
(SO 8)

***BE6-11** At May 31, Stuart Company has net sales of $330,000 and cost of goods available for sale of $230,000. Compute the estimated cost of the ending inventory, assuming the gross profit rate is 40%.

Apply the retail inventory method.
(SO 8)

***BE6-12** On June 30, Dusto Fabrics has the following data pertaining to the retail inventory method: Goods available for sale: at cost $35,000, at retail $50,000; net sales $42,000, and ending inventory at retail $8,000. Compute the estimated cost of the ending inventory using the retail inventory method.

EXERCISES

Determine the correct inventory amount.
(SO 1)

E6-1 Premier Bank and Trust is considering giving Alou Company a loan. Before doing so, they decide that further discussions with Alou's accountant may be desirable. One area of particular concern is the inventory account, which has a year-end balance of $297,000. Discussions with the accountant reveal the following.

1. Alou sold goods costing $38,000 to Comerica Company, FOB shipping point, on December 28. The goods are not expected to arrive at Comerica until January 12. The goods were not included in the physical inventory because they were not in the warehouse.
2. The physical count of the inventory did not include goods costing $95,000 that were shipped to Alou FOB destination on December 27 and were still in transit at year-end.
3. Alou received goods costing $17,000 on January 2. The goods were shipped FOB shipping point on December 26 by Galant Co. The goods were not included in the physical count.
4. Alou sold goods costing $35,000 to Emerick Co., FOB destination, on December 30. The goods were received at Emerick on January 8. They were not included in Alou's physical inventory.
5. Alou received goods costing $44,000 on January 2 that were shipped FOB destination on December 29. The shipment was a rush order that was supposed to arrive December 31. This purchase was included in the ending inventory of $297,000.

Instructions
Determine the correct inventory amount on December 31.

Determine the correct inventory amount.
(SO 1)

E6-2 Kale Thompson, an auditor with Sneed CPAs, is performing a review of Platinum Company's inventory account. Platinum did not have a good year and top management is under pressure to boost reported income. According to its records, the inventory balance at year-end was $740,000. However, the following information was not considered when determining that amount.

1. Included in the company's count were goods with a cost of $250,000 that the company is holding on consignment. The goods belong to Superior Corporation.
2. The physical count did not include goods purchased by Platinum with a cost of $40,000 that were shipped FOB destination on December 28 and did not arrive at Platinum's warehouse until January 3.
3. Included in the inventory account was $17,000 of office supplies that were stored in the warehouse and were to be used by the company's supervisors and managers during the coming year.
4. The company received an order on December 29 that was boxed and was sitting on the loading dock awaiting pick-up on December 31. The shipper picked up the goods on January 1

and delivered them on January 6. The shipping terms were FOB shipping point. The goods had a selling price of $40,000 and a cost of $30,000. The goods were not included in the count because they were sitting on the dock.

5. On December 29 Platinum shipped goods with a selling price of $80,000 and a cost of $60,000 to District Sales Corporation FOB shipping point. The goods arrived on January 3. District Sales had only ordered goods with a selling price of $10,000 and a cost of $8,000. However, a sales manager at Platinum had authorized the shipment and said that if District wanted to ship the goods back next week, it could.
6. Included in the count was $50,000 of goods that were parts for a machine that the company no longer made. Given the high-tech nature of Platinum's products, it was unlikely that these obsolete parts had any other use. However, management would prefer to keep them on the books at cost, "since that is what we paid for them, after all."

Instructions

Prepare a schedule to determine the correct inventory amount. Provide explanations for each item above, saying why you did or did not make an adjustment for each item.

Calculate cost of goods sold using specific identification and FIFO.

(SO 2, 3)

E6-3 On December 1, Discount Electronics Ltd. has three DVD players left in stock. All are identical, all are priced to sell at $750. One of the three DVD players left in stock, with serial #1012, was purchased on June 1 at a cost of $500. Another, with serial #1045, was purchased on November 1 for $450. The last player, serial #1056, was purchased on November 30 for $400.

Instructions

(a) Calculate the cost of goods sold using the FIFO periodic inventory method assuming that two of the three players were sold by the end of December, Discount Electronic's year-end.

(b) If Discount Electronics used the specific identification method instead of the FIFO method, how might it alter its earnings by "selectively choosing" which particular players to sell to the two customers? What would Discount's cost of goods sold be if the company wished to minimize earnings? Maximize earnings?

(c) Which inventory method do you recommend that Discount use? Explain why.

Compute inventory and cost of goods sold using FIFO and LIFO.

(SO 2)

E6-4 Sherpers sells a snowboard, Xpert, that is popular with snowboard enthusiasts. Below is information relating to Sherpers's purchases of Xpert snowboards during September. During the same month, 124 Xpert snowboards were sold. Sherpers uses a periodic inventory system.

Date	Explanation	Units	Unit Cost	Total Cost
Sept. 1	Inventory	26	$ 97	$ 2,522
Sept. 12	Purchases	45	102	4,590
Sept. 19	Purchases	20	104	2,080
Sept. 26	Purchases	50	105	5,250
	Totals	141		$14,442

Instructions

(a) Compute the ending inventory at September 30 using the FIFO and LIFO methods. Prove the amount allocated to cost of goods sold under each method.

(b) For both FIFO and LIFO, calculate the sum of ending inventory and cost of goods sold. What do you notice about the answers you found for each method?

Compute inventory and cost of goods sold using FIFO and LIFO.

(SO 2)

Peachtree

E6-5 Zambia Co. uses a periodic inventory system. Its records show the following for the month of May, in which 70 units were sold.

		Units	Unit Cost	Total Cost
May 1	Inventory	30	$ 8	$240
15	Purchases	25	11	275
24	Purchases	35	12	420
	Totals	90		$935

Instructions

Compute the ending inventory at May 31 using the FIFO and LIFO methods. Prove the amount allocated to cost of goods sold under each method.

Compute inventory and cost of goods sold using FIFO and LIFO.
(SO 2, 3)

E6-6 Zambia Company reports the following for the month of June.

		Units	Unit Cost	Total Cost
June 1	Inventory	200	$5	$1,000
12	Purchase	300	6	1,800
23	Purchase	500	7	3,500
30	Inventory	160		

Instructions

(a) Compute the cost of the ending inventory and the cost of goods sold under (1) FIFO and (2) LIFO.
(b) Which costing method gives the higher ending inventory? Why?
(c) Which method results in the higher cost of goods sold? Why?

Compute inventory and cost of goods sold using average cost.
(SO 2, 3)

E6-7 Inventory data for Zambia Company are presented in E6-6.

Instructions

(a) Compute the cost of the ending inventory and the cost of goods sold using the average cost method.
(b) Will the results in (a) be higher or lower than the results under (1) FIFO and (2) LIFO?
(c) Why is the average unit cost not $6?

Determine ending inventory under lower of cost or market inventory method.
(SO 4)

E6-8 Kinshasa Camera Shop uses the lower of cost or market basis for its inventory. The following data are available at December 31.

Item	Units	Unit Cost	Market
Cameras:			
Minolta	5	$170	$156
Canon	6	150	152
Light Meters:			
Vivitar	12	125	110
Kodak	14	115	135

Instructions

Determine the amount of the ending inventory by applying the lower of cost or market basis.

Determine effects of inventory errors.
(SO 5)

E6-9 Delhi Hardware reported cost of goods sold as follows.

	2006	2007
Beginning inventory	$ 20,000	$ 30,000
Cost of goods purchased	150,000	175,000
Cost of goods available for sale	170,000	205,000
Ending inventory	30,000	35,000
Cost of goods sold	$140,000	$170,000

Delhi made two errors: (1) 2006 ending inventory was overstated $2,000, and (2) 2007 ending inventory was understated $6,000.

Instructions

Compute the correct cost of goods sold for each year.

Prepare correct income statements.
(SO 5)

E6-10 Horner Watch Company reported the following income statement data for a 2-year period.

	2006	2007
Sales	$210,000	$250,000
Cost of goods sold		
Beginning inventory	32,000	44,000
Cost of goods purchased	173,000	202,000
Cost of goods available for sale	205,000	246,000
Ending inventory	44,000	52,000
Cost of goods sold	161,000	194,000
Gross profit	$ 49,000	$ 56,000

Horner uses a periodic inventory system. The inventories at January 1, 2006, and December 31, 2007, are correct. However, the ending inventory at December 31, 2006, was overstated $3,000.

Instructions

(a) Prepare correct income statement data for the 2 years.
(b) What is the cumulative effect of the inventory error on total gross profit for the 2 years?
(c) Explain in a letter to the president of Horner Company what has happened—i.e., the nature of the error and its effect on the financial statements.

E6-11 This information is available for Tella's Photo Corporation for 2004, 2005, and 2006.

Compute inventory turnover, days in inventory, and gross profit rate.
(SO 6, 8)

	2004	2005	2006
Beginning inventory	$ 100,000	$ 300,000	$ 400,000
Ending inventory	300,000	400,000	480,000
Cost of goods sold	850,000	1,120,000	1,200,000
Sales	1,200,000	1,600,000	1,900,000

Instructions

Calculate inventory turnover, days in inventory, and gross profit rate (from Chapter 5) for Tella's Photo Corporation for 2004, 2005, 2006. Comment on any trends.

***E6-12** Simpson Appliance uses a perpetual inventory system. For its flat-screen television sets, the January 1 inventory was 3 sets at $600 each. On January 10, Alpine purchased 6 units at $660 each. The company sold 2 units on January 8 and 5 units on January 15.

Apply cost flow methods to perpetual records.
(SO 7)

Instructions

Compute the ending inventory under (1) FIFO, (2) LIFO, and (3) average cost.

***E6-13** Newport Company reports the following for the month of June.

Calculate inventory and cost of goods sold using three cost flow methods in a perpetual inventory system.
(SO 7)

Date	Explanation	Units	Unit Cost	Total Cost
June 1	Inventory	200	$5	$1,000
12	Purchase	300	6	1,800
23	Purchase	500	7	3,500
30	Inventory	160		

Instructions

(a) Calculate the cost of the ending inventory and the cost of goods sold for each cost flow assumption, using a perpetual inventory system. Assume a sale of 400 units occurred on June 15 for a selling price of $8 and a sale of 440 units on June 27 for $9.
(b) How do the results differ from E6-6 and E6-7?
(c) Why is the average unit cost not $6 [($5 + $6 + $7) ÷ 3 = $6]?

***E6-14** Information about Sherpers is presented in E6-4. Additional data regarding Sherpers's sales of Xpert snowboards are provided below. Assume that Sherpers uses a perpetual inventory system.

Apply cost flow methods to perpetual records.
(SO 7)

Date		Units	Unit Price	Total Cost
Sept. 5	Sale	12	$199	$ 2,388
Sept. 16	Sale	50	199	9,950
Sept. 29	Sale	62	209	12,958
	Totals	124		$25,296

Instructions

(a) Compute ending inventory at September 30 using FIFO, LIFO, and average cost.
(b) Compare ending inventory using a perpetual inventory system to ending inventory using a periodic inventory system (from E6-4).
(c) Which inventory cost flow method (FIFO, LIFO) gives the same ending inventory value under both periodic and perpetual? Which method gives different ending inventory values?

Determine merchandise lost using the gross profit method of estimating inventory.
(SO 8)

***E6-15** The inventory of Lemon Company was destroyed by fire on March 1. From an examination of the accounting records, the following data for the first 2 months of the year are obtained: Sales $51,000, Sales Returns and Allowances $1,000, Purchases $31,200, Freight-in $1,200, and Purchase Returns and Allowances $1,400.

Instructions

Determine the merchandise lost by fire, assuming:

(a) A beginning inventory of $20,000 and a gross profit rate of 30% on net sales.

(b) A beginning inventory of $30,000 and a gross profit rate of 25% on net sales.

Determine ending inventory at cost using retail method.
(SO 8)

***E6-16** Peacock Shoe Store uses the retail inventory method for its two departments, Women's Shoes and Men's Shoes. The following information for each department is obtained.

Item	Women's Department	Men's Department
Beginning inventory at cost	$ 32,000	$ 45,000
Cost of goods purchased at cost	148,000	137,300
Net sales	177,000	185,000
Beginning inventory at retail	45,000	60,000
Cost of goods purchased at retail	179,000	185,000

Instructions

Compute the estimated cost of the ending inventory for each department under the retail inventory method.

PROBLEMS: SET A

Determine items and amounts to be recorded in inventory.
(SO 1)

P6-1A Kananaskis Country Limited is trying to determine the value of its ending inventory as of February 28, 2005, the company's year-end. The following transactions occurred, and the accountant asked your help in determining whether they should be recorded or not.

(a) On February 26, Kananaskis shipped goods costing $800 to a customer and charged the customer $1,000. The goods were shipped with terms FOB destination and the receiving report indicates that the customer received the goods on March 2.

(b) On February 26, Seller Inc. shipped goods to Kananaskis under terms FOB shipping point. The invoice price was $350 plus $25 for freight. The receiving report indicates that the goods were received by Kananaskis on March 2.

(c) Kananaskis had $500 of inventory isolated in the warehouse. The inventory is designated for a customer who has requested that the goods be shipped on March 10.

(d) Also included in Kananaskis' warehouse is $400 of inventory that Craft Producers shipped to Kananaskis on consignment.

(e) On February 26, Kananaskis issued a purchase order to acquire goods costing $750. The goods were shipped with terms FOB destination on February 27. Kananaskis received the goods on March 2.

(f) On February 26, Kananaskis shipped goods to a customer under terms FOB shipping point. The invoice price was $350 plus $25 for freight; the cost of the items was $280. The receiving report indicates that the goods were received by the customer on March 2.

Instructions

For each of the above transactions, specify whether the item in question should be included in ending inventory, and if so, at what amount.

Determine cost of goods sold and ending inventory using FIFO, LIFO, and average cost with analysis.
(SO 2, 3)

P6-2A Breathless Distribution markets CDs of the performing artist Christina Spears. At the beginning of October, Breathless had in beginning inventory 1,000 Spears CDs with a unit cost of $5. During October Breathless made the following purchases of Spears CDs.

Oct. 3	3,500 @ $6	Oct. 19	2,000 @ $8
Oct. 9	4,000 @ $7	Oct. 25	2,000 @ $9

During October 10,000 units were sold. Breathless uses a periodic inventory system.

Instructions

(a) Determine the cost of goods available for sale.

(b) Determine (1) the ending inventory and (2) the cost of goods sold under each of the assumed cost flow methods (FIFO, LIFO, and average cost). Prove the accuracy of the cost of goods sold under the FIFO and LIFO methods.

(c) Which cost flow method results in (1) the highest inventory amount for the balance sheet and (2) the highest cost of goods sold for the income statement?

(b)(2) Cost of goods sold:
FIFO $66,000
LIFO $74,000
Average $70,400

P6-3A Milokimball Company had a beginning inventory on January 1 of 100 units of Product WD-44 at a cost of $21 per unit. During the year, the following purchases were made.

Determine cost of goods sold and ending inventory, using FIFO, LIFO, and average cost with analysis.

(SO 2, 3)

Mar. 15	300 units at $24	Sept. 4	300 units at $28
July 20	200 units at $25	Dec. 2	100 units at $30

700 units were sold. Milokimball Company uses a periodic inventory system.

Instructions

(a) Determine the cost of goods available for sale.

(b) Determine (1) the ending inventory, and (2) the cost of goods sold under each of the assumed cost flow methods (FIFO, LIFO, and average cost). Prove the accuracy of the cost of goods sold under the FIFO and LIFO methods.

(c) Which cost flow method results in (1) the highest inventory amount for the balance sheet, and (2) the highest cost of goods sold for the income statement?

(b)(2) Cost of goods sold:
FIFO $17,100
LIFO $18,800
Average $17,990

P6-4A The management of Red Robin Inc. is reevaluating the appropriateness of using its present inventory cost flow method, which is average cost. The company requests your help in determining the results of operations for 2006 if either the FIFO or the LIFO method had been used. For 2006 the accounting records show these data:

Compute ending inventory, prepare income statements, and answer questions using FIFO and LIFO.

(SO 2, 3)

Inventories		Purchases and Sales	
Beginning (10,000 units)	$22,800	Total net sales (225,000 units)	$865,000
Ending (15,000 units)		Total cost of goods purchased (230,000 units)	578,500

Purchases were made quarterly as follows.

Quarter	Units	Unit Cost	Total Cost
1	60,000	$2.30	$138,000
2	50,000	2.50	125,000
3	50,000	2.60	130,000
4	70,000	2.65	185,500
	230,000		$578,500

Operating expenses were $147,000, and the company's income tax rate is 32%.

Instructions

(a) Prepare comparative condensed income statements for 2006 under FIFO and LIFO. (Show computations of ending inventory.)

(a) Gross profit:
FIFO $303,450
LIFO $298,000

(b) Answer the following questions for management in business-letter form.

(1) Which cost flow method (FIFO or LIFO) produces the more meaningful inventory amount for the balance sheet? Why?

(2) Which cost flow method (FIFO or LIFO) produces the more meaningful net income? Why?

(3) Which cost flow method (FIFO or LIFO) is more likely to approximate the actual physical flow of goods? Why?

(4) How much more cash will be available for management under LIFO than under FIFO? Why?

(5) Will gross profit under the average cost method be higher or lower than FIFO? Than LIFO? (*Note*: It is not necessary to quantify your answer.)

Calculate ending inventory, cost of goods sold, gross profit, and gross profit rate under periodic method; compare results.

(SO 2, 3)

P6-5A You are provided with the following information for Danielle Inc. for the month ended June 30, 2006. Danielle uses the periodic method for inventory.

Date	Description	Quantity	Unit Cost or Selling Price
June 1	Beginning inventory	25	$60
June 4	Purchase	85	64
June 10	Sale	70	90
June 11	Sale return	10	90
June 18	Purchase	35	68
June 18	Purchase return	5	68
June 25	Sale	50	95
June 28	Purchase	20	72

Instructions

(a)(iii) Gross profit:
LIFO $2,830
FIFO $3,210
Average $2,986

(a) Calculate (i) ending inventory, (ii) cost of goods sold, (iii) gross profit, and (iv) gross profit rate under each of the following methods.
(1) LIFO. **(2)** FIFO. **(3)** Average cost.

(b) Compare results for the three cost flow assumptions.

Compare specific identification, FIFO, and LIFO under periodic method; use cost flow assumption to justify price increase.

(SO 2, 3)

P6-6A You are provided with the following information for Gas Guzzlers. Gas Guzzlers uses the periodic method of accounting for its inventory transactions.

March 1	Beginning inventory 1,500 litres at a cost of 40¢ per litre.
March 3	Purchased 2,000 litres at a cost of 45¢ per litre.
March 5	Sold 1,800 litres for 60¢ per litre.
March 10	Purchased 3,500 litres at a cost of 49¢ per litre.
March 20	Purchased 2,000 litres at a cost of 55¢ per litre.
March 30	Sold 5,000 litres for 70¢ per litre.

Instructions

(a) Prepare partial income statements through gross profit, and calculate the value of ending inventory that would be reported on the balance sheet, under each of the following cost flow assumptions.

(a)(1) Gross profit:
Specific identification
$1,331

(1) Specific identification method assuming:
(i) the March 5 sale consisted of 900 litres from the March 1 beginning inventory and 900 litres from the March 3 purchase; and
(ii) the March 30 sale consisted of the following number of units sold from each purchase: 400 litres from March 1; 500 litres from March 3; 2,600 litres from March 10; 1,500 litres from March 20.

(2) FIFO $1,463
(3) LIFO $1,180

(2) FIFO.
(3) LIFO.

(b) How can companies use a cost flow method to justify price increases? Which cost flow method would best support an argument to increase prices?

Compute ending inventory, prepare income statements, and answer questions using FIFO and LIFO.

(SO 2, 3)

P6-7A The management of Creek Co. asks your help in determining the comparative effects of the FIFO and LIFO inventory cost flow methods. For 2006, the accounting records show the following data.

Inventory, January 1 (10,000 units)	$ 37,000
Cost of 110,000 units purchased	479,000
Selling price of 95,000 units sold	665,000
Operating expenses	120,000

Units purchased consisted of 40,000 units at $4.20 on May 10; 50,000 units at $4.40 on August 15; and 20,000 units at $4.55 on November 20. Income taxes are 30%.

Instructions

(a) Net income
FIFO $99,400
LIFO $90,300

(a) Prepare comparative condensed income statements for 2006 under FIFO and LIFO. (Show computations of ending inventory.)

(b) Answer the following questions for management in the form of a business letter.
(1) Which inventory cost flow method produces the most meaningful inventory amount for the balance sheet? Why?

(2) Which inventory cost flow method produces the most meaningful net income? Why?
(3) Which inventory cost flow method is most likely to approximate actual physical flow of the goods? Why?
(4) How much additional cash will be available for management under LIFO than under FIFO? Why?
(5) How much of the gross profit under FIFO is illusory in comparison with the gross profit under LIFO?

***P6-8A** Matthew Inc. is a retailer operating in Dartmouth, Nova Scotia. Matthew uses the perpetual inventory method. All sales returns from customers result in the goods being returned to inventory; the inventory is not damaged. Assume that there are no credit transactions; all amounts are settled in cash. You are provided with the following information for Matthew Inc. for the month of January 2006.

Calculate cost of goods sold and ending inventory under LIFO, FIFO, and average cost under the perpetual system; compare gross profit under each assumption.

(SO 3, 7)

Date	Description	Quantity	Unit Cost or Selling Price
January 1	Beginning inventory	50	$12
January 5	Purchase	100	14
January 8	Sale	80	25
January 10	Sale return	10	25
January 15	Purchase	30	18
January 16	Purchase return	5	18
January 20	Sale	90	25
January 25	Purchase	10	20

Instructions

(a) For each of the following cost flow assumptions, calculate (i) cost of goods sold, (ii) ending inventory, and (iii) gross profit.
(1) LIFO. **(2)** FIFO. **(3)** Moving average cost.
(b) Compare results for the three cost flow assumptions.

Gross profit:
LIFO $1,730
FIFO $1,820
Average $1,767

***P6-9A** Ramos Co. began operations on July 1. It uses a perpetual inventory system. During July the company had the following purchases and sales.

Determine ending inventory under a perpetual inventory system.

(SO 7)

	Purchases		
Date	Units	Unit Cost	Sales Units
July 1	4	$ 90	
July 6			3
July 11	5	$ 99	
July 14			2
July 21	3	$106	
July 27			3

Instructions

(a) Determine the ending inventory under a perpetual inventory system using (1) FIFO, (2) average cost, and (3) LIFO.
(b) Which costing method produces the highest ending inventory valuation?

(a) Ending inventory
FIFO $417
Avg. $405
LIFO $387

***P6-10A** Virginia Company lost all of its inventory in a fire on December 26, 2006. The accounting records showed the following gross profit data for November and December.

Compute gross profit rate and inventory loss using gross profit method.

(SO 8)

	November	December (to 12/26)
Net sales	$500,000	$400,000
Beginning inventory	34,100	31,100
Purchases	319,975	236,000
Purchase returns and allowances	11,800	5,000
Purchase discounts	7,577	6,000
Freight-in	6,402	3,700
Ending inventory	31,100	?

Virginia is fully insured for fire losses but must prepare a report for the insurance company.

Instructions

(a) Compute the gross profit rate for November.

(b) Using the gross profit rate for November, determine the estimated cost of the inventory lost in the fire.

Compute ending inventory using retail method.
(SO 8)

***P6-11A** Hooked on Books uses the retail inventory method to estimate its monthly ending inventories. The following information is available for two of its departments at October 31, 2006.

	Hardcovers		Paperbacks	
	Cost	**Retail**	**Cost**	**Retail**
Beginning inventory	$ 256,000	$ 400,000	$ 65,000	$ 90,000
Purchases	1,180,000	1,825,000	266,000	380,000
Freight-in	4,000		2,000	
Purchase discounts	16,000		4,000	
Net sales		1,820,000		368,000

At December 31, Hooked on Books takes a physical inventory at retail. The actual retail values of the inventories in each department are Hardcovers $400,000 and Paperbacks $88,000.

Instructions

(a) Determine the estimated cost of the ending inventory for each department at **October 31**, 2006, using the retail inventory method.

(b) Compute the ending inventory at cost for each department at **December 31**, assuming the cost-to-retail ratios for the year are 65% for hardcovers and 70% for paperbacks.

PROBLEMS: SET B

Determine items and amounts to be recorded in inventory.
(SO 1)

P6-1B Banff Limited is trying to determine the value of its ending inventory at February 28, 2006, the company's year end. The accountant counted everything that was in the warehouse as of February 28, which resulted in an ending inventory valuation of $48,000. However, she didn't know how to treat the following transactions so she didn't record them.

(a) On February 26, Banff shipped to a customer goods costing $800. The goods were shipped FOB shipping point, and the receiving report indicates that the customer received the goods on March 2.

(b) On February 26, Seller Inc. shipped goods to Banff FOB destination. The invoice price was $350. The receiving report indicates that the goods were received by Banff on March 2.

(c) Banff had $500 of inventory at a customer's warehouse "on approval." The customer was going to let Banff know whether it wanted the merchandise by the end of the week, March 4.

(d) Banff also had $400 of inventory at a Jasper craft shop, on consignment from Banff.

(e) On February 26, Banff ordered goods costing $750. The goods were shipped FOB shipping point on February 27. Banff received the goods on March 1.

(f) On February 28, Banff packaged goods and had them ready for shipping to a customer FOB destination. The invoice price was $350; the cost of the items was $280. The receiving report indicates that the goods were received by the customer on March 2.

(g) Banff had damaged goods set aside in the warehouse because they are no longer saleable. These goods originally cost $400 and, originally, Banff expected to sell these items for $600.

Instructions

For each of the above transactions, specify whether the item in question should be included in ending inventory, and if so, at what amount. For each item that is not included in ending inventory, indicate who owns it and what account, if any, it should have been recorded in.

Determine cost of goods sold and ending inventory using FIFO, LIFO, and average cost with analysis.
(SO 2, 3)

P6-2B Doom's Day Distribution markets CDs of the performing artist Harrilyn Hannson. At the beginning of March, Doom's Day had in beginning inventory 1,500 Hannson CDs with a unit cost of $7. During March Doom's Day made the following purchases of Hannson CDs.

March 5	3,000 @ $8	March 21	4,000 @ $10
March 13	5,500 @ $9	March 26	2,000 @ $11

During March 13,500 units were sold. Doom's Day uses a periodic inventory system.

Instructions

(a) Determine the cost of goods available for sale.

(b) Determine (1) the ending inventory and (2) the cost of goods sold under each of the assumed cost flow methods (FIFO, LIFO, and average cost). Prove the accuracy of the cost of goods sold under the FIFO and LIFO methods.

(c) Which cost flow method results in (1) the highest inventory amount for the balance sheet and (2) the highest cost of goods sold for the income statement?

(b)(2) Cost of goods sold:
FIFO $119,000
LIFO $127,500
Average $123,187

P6-3B Collins Company had a beginning inventory of 400 units of Product E2-D2 at a cost of $8.00 per unit. During the year, purchases were:

Determine cost of goods sold and ending inventory, using FIFO, LIFO, and average cost with analysis.

(SO 2, 3)

Feb. 20	600 units at $9	Aug. 12	300 units at $11
May 5	500 units at $10	Dec. 8	200 units at $12

Collins Company uses a periodic inventory system. Sales totaled 1,400 units.

Instructions

(a) Determine the cost of goods available for sale.

(b) Determine (1) the ending inventory, and (2) the cost of goods sold under each of the assumed cost flow methods (FIFO, LIFO, and average cost). Prove the accuracy of the cost of goods sold under the FIFO and LIFO methods.

(c) Which cost flow method results in (1) the lowest inventory amount for the balance sheet, and (2) the lowest cost of goods sold for the income statement?

(b) Cost of goods sold:
FIFO $12,600
LIFO $14,300
Average $13,510

P6-4B The management of Gilbert Co. is reevaluating the appropriateness of using its present inventory cost flow method, which is average cost. They request your help in determining the results of operations for 2006 if either the FIFO method or the LIFO method had been used. For 2006, the accounting records show the following data.

Compute ending inventory, prepare income statements, and answer questions using FIFO and LIFO.

(SO 2, 3)

Inventories		**Purchases and Sales**	
Beginning (15,000 units)	$32,000	Total net sales (225,000 units)	$865,000
Ending (20,000 units)		Total cost of goods purchased (230,000 units)	595,000

Purchases were made quarterly as follows.

Quarter	Units	Unit Cost	Total Cost
1	60,000	$2.40	$144,000
2	50,000	2.50	125,000
3	50,000	2.60	130,000
4	70,000	2.80	196,000
	230,000		$595,000

Operating expenses were $147,000, and the company's income tax rate is 34%.

Instructions

(a) Prepare comparative condensed income statements for 2006 under FIFO and LIFO. (Show computations of ending inventory.)

(b) Answer the following questions for management in the form of a business letter.

(1) Which cost flow method (FIFO or LIFO) produces the more meaningful inventory amount for the balance sheet? Why?

(2) Which cost flow method (FIFO or LIFO) produces the more meaningful net income? Why?

(3) Which cost flow method (FIFO or LIFO) is more likely to approximate actual physical flow of the goods? Why?

(4) How much additional cash will be available for management under LIFO than under FIFO? Why?

(5) Will gross profit under the average cost method be higher or lower than (a) FIFO and (b) LIFO? (*Note*: It is not necessary to quantify your answer.)

(a) Net income
FIFO $97,020
LIFO $89,100
(b) (4) $ 4,080

Calculate ending inventory, cost of goods sold, gross profit, and gross profit rate under periodic method; compare results.
(SO 2, 3)

P6-5B You are provided with the following information for Lahti Inc. for the month ended October 31, 2006. Lahti uses a periodic method for inventory.

Date	Description	Units	Unit Cost or Selling Price
October 1	Beginning inventory	60	$25
October 9	Purchase	120	26
October 11	Sale	100	35
October 17	Purchase	70	27
October 22	Sale	60	40
October 25	Purchase	80	28
October 29	Sale	150	40

Instructions

(a)(iii) Gross profit:
LIFO $3,650
FIFO $3,710
Average $3,680

(a) Calculate (i) ending inventory, (ii) cost of goods sold, (iii) gross profit, and (iv) gross profit rate under each of the following methods.
(1) LIFO.
(2) FIFO.
(3) Average cost.
(b) Compare results for the three cost flow assumptions.

Compare specific identification, FIFO, and LIFO under periodic method; use cost flow assumption to influence earnings.
(SO 2, 3)

P6-6B You have the following information for Discount Diamonds. Discount Diamonds uses the periodic method of accounting for its inventory transactions. Discount only carries one brand and size of diamonds—all are identical. Each batch of diamonds purchased is carefully coded and marked with its purchase cost.

March 1	Beginning inventory 150 diamonds at a cost of $300 per diamond.
March 3	Purchased 200 diamonds at a cost of $350 each.
March 5	Sold 180 diamonds for $600 each.
March 10	Purchased 350 diamonds at a cost of $375 each.
March 25	Sold 500 diamonds for $650 each.

Instructions

(a) Gross profit:
(1) Maximum $194,250
(2) Minimum $192,750

(a) Assume that Discount Diamonds uses the specific identification cost flow method.
(1) Demonstrate how Discount Diamonds could maximize its gross profit for the month by specifically selecting which diamonds to sell on March 5 and March 25.
(2) Demonstrate how Discount Diamonds could minimize its gross profit for the month by selecting which diamonds to sell on March 5 and March 25.
(b) Assume that Discount Diamonds uses the FIFO cost flow assumption. Calculate cost of goods sold. How much gross profit would Discount Diamonds report under this cost flow assumption?
(c) Assume that Discount Diamonds uses the LIFO cost flow assumption. Calculate cost of goods sold. How much gross profit would the company report under this cost flow assumption?
(d) Which cost flow method should Discount Diamonds select? Explain.

Compute ending inventory, prepare income statements, and answer questions using FIFO and LIFO.
(SO 2, 3)

P6-7B The management of Zwick Inc. asks your help in determining the comparative effects of the FIFO and LIFO inventory cost flow methods. For 2006 the accounting records show these data.

Inventory, January 1 (10,000 units)	$ 35,000
Cost of 120,000 units purchased	504,500
Selling price of 95,000 units sold	665,000
Operating expenses	120,000

Units purchased consisted of 35,000 units at $4.00 on May 10; 60,000 units at $4.20 on August 15; and 25,000 units at $4.50 on November 20. Income taxes are 28%.

Instructions

Gross profit:
FIFO $280,000
LIFO $260,500

(a) Prepare comparative condensed income statements for 2006 under FIFO and LIFO. (Show computations of ending inventory.)
(b) Answer the following questions for management in the form of a business letter.
(1) Which inventory cost flow method produces the most meaningful inventory amount for the balance sheet? Why?

(2) Which inventory cost flow method produces the most meaningful net income? Why?
(3) Which inventory cost flow method is most likely to approximate the actual physical flow of the goods? Why?
(4) How much more cash will be available for management under LIFO than under FIFO? Why?
(5) How much of the gross profit under FIFO is illusory in comparison with the gross profit under LIFO?

***P6-8B** Yuan Li Ltd. is a retailer operating in Edmonton, Alberta. Yuan Li uses the perpetual inventory method. All sales returns from customers result in the goods being returned to inventory; the inventory is not damaged. Assume that there are no credit transactions; all amounts are settled in cash. You are provided with the following information for Yuan Li Ltd. for the month of January 2006.

Calculate cost of goods sold and ending inventory for FIFO, average cost, and LIFO under the perpetual system; compare gross profit under each assumption.

(SO 3, 7)

Date	Description	Quantity	Unit Cost or Selling Price
December 31	Ending inventory	150	$17
January 2	Purchase	100	21
January 6	Sale	150	40
January 9	Sale return	10	40
January 9	Purchase	75	24
January 10	Purchase return	15	24
January 10	Sale	50	45
January 23	Purchase	100	28
January 30	Sale	160	50

Instructions

(a) For each of the following cost flow assumptions, calculate (i) cost of goods sold, (ii) ending inventory, and (iii) gross profit.
(1) LIFO. (2) FIFO. (3) Moving average cost.
(b) Compare results for the three cost flow assumptions.

Gross profit:
LIFO $7,980
FIFO $8,640
Average $8,395

***P6-9B** Lemansky Appliance Mart began operations on May 1. It uses a perpetual inventory system. During May the company had the following purchases and sales for its Model 25 Sureshot camera.

Determine ending inventory under a perpetual inventory system.

(SO 7)

	Purchases		
Date	Units	Unit Cost	Sales Units
May 1	7	$150	
4			4
8	8	$170	
12			5
15	6	$185	
20			3
25			5

Instructions

(a) Determine the ending inventory under a perpetual inventory system using (1) FIFO, (2) average cost, and (3) LIFO.
(b) Which costing method produces (1) the highest ending inventory valuation and (2) the lowest ending inventory valuation?

(a) FIFO $740
Average $699
LIFO $620

***P6-10B** Levi Johnson Company lost 70% of its inventory in a fire on March 25, 2006. The accounting records showed the following gross profit data for February and March.

Estimate inventory loss using gross profit method.

(SO 8)

	February	March (to 3/25)
Net sales	$300,000	$260,000
Net purchases	197,800	191,000
Freight-in	2,900	4,000
Beginning inventory	4,500	25,200
Ending inventory	25,200	?

Levi Johnson Company is fully insured for fire losses but must prepare a report for the insurance company.

Instructions

(a) Compute the gross profit rate for the month of February.

(b) Using the gross profit rate for February, determine both the estimated total inventory and inventory lost in the fire in March.

Compute ending inventory and cost of inventory lost using retail method.

(SO 8)

***P6-11B** Thai Department Store uses the retail inventory method to estimate its monthly ending inventories. The following information is available for two of its departments at August 31, 2006.

	Sporting Goods		Jewelry and Cosmetics	
	Cost	**Retail**	**Cost**	**Retail**
Net sales		$1,010,000		$1,150,000
Purchases	$675,000	1,066,000	$741,000	1,158,000
Purchase returns	(26,000)	(40,000)	(12,000)	(20,000)
Purchase discounts	(12,360)	—	(2,440)	—
Freight-in	9,000	—	14,000	—
Beginning inventory	47,360	74,000	39,440	62,000

At December 31, Thai Department Store takes a physical inventory at retail. The actual retail values of the inventories in each department are Sporting Goods $85,000, and Jewelry and Cosmetics $54,000.

Instructions

(a) Determine the estimated cost of the ending inventory for each department on **August 31**, 2006, using the retail inventory method.

(b) Compute the ending inventory at cost for each department at **December 31**, assuming the cost-to-retail ratios are 60% for Sporting Goods and 64% for Jewelry and Cosmetics.

BROADENING YOUR PERSPECTIVE

Financial Reporting and Analysis

■ FINANCIAL REPORTING PROBLEM: PepsiCo

PEPSI.

BYP6-1 The notes that accompany a company's financial statements provide informative details that would clutter the amounts and descriptions presented in the statements. Refer to the financial statements of **PepsiCo, Inc.** and the Notes to Consolidated Financial Statements in Appendix A.

Instructions

Answer the following questions. Complete the requirements in millions of dollars, as shown in PepsiCo's annual report.

(a) What did PepsiCo report for the amount of inventories in its Consolidated Balance Sheet at December 27, 2003? At December 28, 2002?

(b) Compute the dollar amount of change and the percentage change in inventories between 2002 and 2003. Compute inventory as a percentage of current assets at December, 27, 2003.

(c) How does PepsiCo value its inventories? Which inventory cost flow method does PepsiCo use? (See Notes to the Financial Statements.)

(d) What is the cost of sales (cost of goods sold) reported by PepsiCo for 2003, 2002, and 2001? Compute the percentage of cost of sales to net sales in 2003.

■ COMPARATIVE ANALYSIS PROBLEM: PepsiCo vs. Coca-Cola

PEPSI.

BYP6-2 **PepsiCo**'s financial statements are presented in Appendix A. **Coca-Cola**'s financial statements are presented in Appendix B.

Instructions

(a) Based on the information contained in these financial statements, compute the following 2003 ratios for each company.

(1) Inventory turnover ratio

(2) Average days to sell inventory

(b) What conclusions concerning the management of the inventory can be drawn from these data?

■ RESEARCH CASE

BYP6-3 The April 27, 2001, issue of the *Wall Street Journal* contains an article by Scott Thurm and Jonathan Weil titled "Tech Companies Charge Now, May Profit Later."

Instructions

Read the article and answer the following questions.

(a) What is the amount of the write-off taken by **Cisco**?

(b) What reason does Cisco give for this write-off? How did Cisco end up with such a large balance of excess inventory?

(c) Why do some people suggest that Cisco intentionally took a larger than necessary write-off?

(d) What evidence is there that Cisco may, in fact, sell these parts in the future, even though the company has written them down to a zero value now?

(e) What are "pro forma" financial results?

■ INTERPRETING FINANCIAL STATEMENTS

BYP6-4 The following information was taken from the 2003 annual report of **Cooper Tire and Rubber Company** (all dollars in thousands).

	December 31	
	2003	**2002**
Inventories		
Finished goods	$ 158,416	$ 181,219
Work in process	35,485	33,457
Raw materials and supplies	88,451	65,965
	$ 282,352	$ 280,641
Cost of goods sold	$3,078,761	$2,839,757
Current assets	$1,024,409	
Current liabilities	$ 476,727	

From the company's notes: Inventories are valued at cost, which is not in excess of market. Inventory costs have been determined by the last-in, first-out (LIFO) method for substantially all domestic inventories. Costs of other inventories have been determined principally by the first-in, first-out (FIFO) method.

Under the LIFO method, inventories have been reduced by approximately $52,336 and $66,594 at December 31, 2002 and 2003, respectively, from current cost which would be reported under the first-in, first-out method.

Instructions

(a) Define each of the following: finished goods, work-in-process, and raw materials.

(b) The company experienced a decrease in finished goods inventory and an increase in raw materials. Discuss the likely cause of this.

(c) What might be a possible explanation for why the company uses FIFO for its nondomestic inventories?

(d) Calculate the company's inventory turnover ratio and days in inventory for 2002 and 2003. (2001 inventory was $306 million.) Discuss the implications of any change in the ratios.

(e) What percentage of total inventory does the 2003 LIFO reserve represent? If the company used FIFO in 2003, what would be the value of its inventory? Do you consider this difference a "material" amount from the perspective of an analyst? Which value accurately represents the value of the company's inventory?

(f) Calculate the company's 2003 current ratio with the numbers as reported, then recalculate after adjusting for the LIFO reserve.

■ A GLOBAL FOCUS

BYP6-5 **Fuji Photo Film Co., Ltd.** is a Japanese manufacturer of photographic products. Its U.S. counterpart, and arch rival, is **Eastman Kodak Company**. Together the two dominate the global market for film. The information below and on the next page was extracted from the financial statements of the two companies.

FUJI PHOTO FILM CO., LTD.
Notes to the Financial Statements

Summary of significant accounting policies
The Company and its domestic subsidiaries maintain their records and prepare their financial statements in accordance with accounting practices generally accepted in Japan. Certain reclassifications and adjustments have been incorporated in the consolidated financial statements to conform them to accounting principles generally accepted in the United States of America.

Inventories
Inventories are valued at the lower of cost or market with cost being determined principally by the moving-average method.

Note 6. Inventories
Inventories at March 31, 2002 and 2001, consisted of the following:

	(millions of yen)		(thousands of U.S. dollars)
	2002	**2001**	**2002**
Finished goods	¥222,523	¥218,507	$1,673,105
Work in process	65,714	67,399	494,090
Raw materials and supplies	70,266	68,415	528,316
	¥358,503	¥354,321	$2,695,511

EASTMAN KODAK COMPANY
Notes to the Financial Statements

Note: Significant accounting policies

Inventories

Inventories are stated at the lower of cost or market. The cost of most inventories in the U.S. is determined by the "last-in, first-out" (LIFO) method.

The cost of all of the Company's remaining inventories in and outside the U.S. is determined by the first-in, first-out (FIFO) or average cost method, which approximates current cost.

Note 3. Inventories

	(in millions)	
	2002	**2001**
At FIFO or average cost (approximates current cost)		
Finished goods	$ 831	$ 851
Work in process	322	318
Raw materials and supplies	301	346
	1,454	1,515
LIFO reserve	(392)	(444)
Total at LIFO	$1,062	$1,071

Inventories valued on the LIFO method are approximately 47% and 48% of total inventories in 2002 and 2001, respectively.

Additional information:

	Fuji Photo Film (yen)	**Eastman Kodak (dollars)**
2002 Cost of goods sold (millions)	1,268,521	8,225

Instructions

Answer each of the following questions.

(a) Why do you suppose that Fuji makes adjustments to its accounts so that they conform with U.S. accounting principles when it reports its results?

(b) What are the 2002 inventory turnover ratios and average days in inventory of the two companies (use inventory at FIFO, that is, before the LIFO reserve).

(c) What are the 2002 inventory turnover and average days in inventory of the two companies, adjusting for the LIFO reserve, if given? Do you encounter any problems when making this comparison?

(d) Calculate as a percentage of total inventory the portion that each of the components of 2002 inventory (raw materials, work in process, and finished goods) represents. Comment on your findings. (Use FIFO for Kodak.)

■ EXPLORING THE WEB

BYP6-6 A company's annual report usually will identify the inventory method used. Knowing that, you can analyze the effects of the inventory method on the income statement and balance sheet.

Address: www.cisco.com, or go to www.wiley.com/college/weygandt

Instructions

Answer the following questions based on the current year's Annual Report on Cisco's Web site.

(a) At Cisco's fiscal year-end, what was the net inventory on the balance sheet?
(b) How has this changed from the previous fiscal year-end?
(c) How much of the inventory was finished goods?
(d) What inventory method does Cisco use?

Critical Thinking

■ GROUP DECISION CASE

BYP6-7 On April 10, 2005, fire damaged the office and warehouse of Ehlert Company. Most of the accounting records were destroyed, but the following account balances were determined as of March 31, 2005: Merchandise Inventory, January 1, 2005, $80,000; Sales (January 1–March 31, 2005), $180,000; Purchases (January 1–March 31, 2005) $94,000.

The company's fiscal year ends on December 31. It uses a periodic inventory system.

From an analysis of the April bank statement, you discover cancelled checks of $4,200 for cash purchases during the period April 1–10. Deposits during the same period totaled $18,500. Of that amount, 60% were collections on accounts receivable, and the balance was cash sales.

Correspondence with the company's principal suppliers revealed $12,400 of purchases on account from April 1 to April 10. Of that amount, $1,600 was for merchandise in transit on April 10 that was shipped FOB destination.

Correspondence with the company's principal customers produced acknowledgments of credit sales totaling $28,000 from April 1 to April 10. It was estimated that $5,100 of credit sales will never be acknowledged or recovered from customers.

Ehlert Company reached an agreement with the insurance company that its fire-loss claim should be based on the average of the gross profit rates for the preceding 2 years. The financial statements for 2003 and 2004 showed the following data.

	2004	2003
Net sales	$600,000	$480,000
Cost of goods purchased	416,000	356,000
Beginning inventory	60,000	40,000
Ending inventory	80,000	60,000

Inventory with a cost of $17,000 was salvaged from the fire.

Instructions

With the class divided into groups, answer the following.

(a) Determine the balances in (1) Sales and (2) Purchases at April 10.
***(b)** Determine the average profit rate for the years 2003 and 2004. (*Hint*: Find the gross profit rate for each year and divide the sum by 2.)
***(c)** Determine the inventory loss as a result of the fire, using the gross profit method.

■ COMMUNICATION ACTIVITY

BYP6-8 You are the controller of Small Toys Inc. Denise Rode, the president, recently mentioned to you that she found an error in the 2005 financial statements which she believes has corrected itself. She determined, in discussions with the Purchasing Department, that 2005 ending inventory was overstated by $1 million. Denise says that the 2006 ending inventory is correct. Thus she assumes that 2006 income is correct. Denise says to you, "What happened has happened—there's no point in worrying about it anymore."

Instructions

You conclude that Denise is incorrect. Write a brief, tactful memo to Denise, clarifying the situation.

Accounting Matters!

■ ETHICS CASE

BYP6-9 S. R. Marsh Wholesale Corp. uses the LIFO method of inventory costing. In the current year, profit at S. R. Marsh is running unusually high. The corporate tax rate is also high this year, but it is scheduled to decline significantly next year. In an effort to lower the current year's net income and to take advantage of the changing income tax rate, the president of S. R. Marsh Wholesale instructs the plant accountant to recommend to the purchasing department a large purchase of inventory for delivery 3 days before the end of the year. The price of the inventory to be purchased has doubled during the year, and the purchase will represent a major portion of the ending inventory value.

Instructions

(a) What is the effect of this transaction on this year's and next year's income statement and income tax expense? Why?

(b) If S. R. Marsh Wholesale had been using the FIFO method of inventory costing, would the president give the same directive?

(c) Should the plant accountant order the inventory purchase to lower income? What are the ethical implications of this order?

■ CONTINUING COOKIE CHRONICLE

Accounting Matters!

(*Note*: This is a continuation of the Cookie Chronicle from Chapters 1 through 5.)

BYP6-10 Natalie is busy establishing both divisions of her business (cookie classes and mixer sales) and completing her business degree. Her goals for the next 11 months are to sell one mixer per month and to give two to three classes per week.

The cost of the fine European mixers is expected to increase. Natalie has just negotiated new terms with Kzinski that include shipping costs in the negotiated purchase price (mixers will be shipped FOB destination), but the supplier cannot guarantee the invoice price. Natalie has decided to use a periodic inventory system and now must choose a cost flow assumption for her mixer inventory.

The following transactions occur in February to May, 2006.

Feb.	2	Natalie buys two deluxe mixers on account from Kzinski Supply Co. for $1,100 ($550 each), FOB destination, terms n/30.
	16	She sells one deluxe mixer for $1,050 cash.
	25	She pays the amount owed to Kzinski.
Mar.	2	She buys one deluxe mixer on account from Kzinski Supply Co. for $567, FOB destination, terms n/30.
	30	Natalie sells two deluxe mixers for a total of $2,100 cash.
	31	She pays the amount owed to Kzinski.
Apr.	1	She buys two deluxe mixers on account from Kzinski Supply Co. for $1,122 ($561 each), FOB destination, terms n/30.
	13	She sells three deluxe mixers for a total of $3,150 cash.
	30	Natalie pays the amounts owed to Kzinski.
May	4	She buys three deluxe mixers on account from Kzinski Supply Co. for $1,720 ($573.33 each), FOB destination, terms n/30.
	27	She sells one deluxe mixer for $1,050 cash.

Instructions

(a) Prepare journal entries for each of the transactions.

(b) Determine the cost of goods available for sale. Recall from Chapter 5 that at the end of January, Cookie Creations had three mixers on hand at a cost of $545 each.

(c) Calculate (i) ending inventory, (ii) cost of goods sold, (iii) gross profit, and (iv) gross profit rate under each of the following methods: LIFO, FIFO, and average cost.

(d) Natalie is thinking of getting a bank loan. If this is the only factor Natalie has to consider in choosing an inventory cost flow assumption, which cost flow assumption would you recommend that Natalie use? Why?

Answers to Accounting Matters! Questions

Accounting Matters!

p. 243

Q: What effect does an overstatement of inventory have on a company's financial statements?

A: The balance sheet looks stronger because inventory and retained earnings are overstated. The income statement looks better because cost of goods sold is understated and income is overstated.

p. 244

Q: Are the packages that are being tracked part of FedEx's "inventory"?

A: No, FedEx does not own the packages; as a common carrier, the company merely transports them. The packages belong to the buyer or seller based on FOB specifications.

p. 255

Q: Why would investors sustain losses?

A: The "charge on the value of palladium" resulted in the recognition of a loss on Ford's income statement, which caused the price of Ford stock to drop.

Q: What would the effect on future income have been if Ford had not taken the lower-of-cost-or-market charge in 2002?

A: Ford would have continued to use the higher cost of palladium in its computation of cost of goods sold, and it would consequently have shown lower gross profits in subsequent reporting periods.

Answer to PepsiCo Review It Question 5, p. 253

PepsiCo reported inventories of $1,412 million in its balance sheet of December 27, 2003. On page 77 in its Note 14 to the financial statements, PepsiCo reported a breakdown of this total as follows: Raw materials, $618 million; Work in process, $160 million; and Finished goods, $634 million. Note 14 contains the following note revealing the inventory cost flow methods used by PepsiCo:

> **(c)** Inventories are valued at the lower of cost or market. Cost is determined using the average, first-in, first-out (FIFO) or last-in, first-out (LIFO) methods. Approximately 10% in 2003 and 19% in 2002 of the inventory cost was computed using the LIFO method. The differences between LIFO and FIFO methods of valuing these inventories are not material.

Answers to Self-Study Questions

1. a **2.** b **3.** c **4.** d **5.** c **6.** d **7.** d **8.** b **9.** d ***10.** b ***11.** d

REMEMBER to go back to the Navigator box on the chapter-opening page and check off your completed work.

Chapter 7

Accounting Principles

THE NAVIGATOR ✓

- Understand **Concepts for Review** ❑
- Read **Feature Story** ❑
- Scan **Study Objectives** ❑
- Read **Preview** ❑
- Read text and answer **Before You Go On** p. 295 ❑ p. 302 ❑ p. 310 ❑
- Work **Demonstration Problems** ❑
- Review **Summary of Study Objectives** ❑
- Answer **Self-Study Questions** ❑
- Complete **Assignments** ❑

CONCEPTS FOR REVIEW

Before studying this chapter, you should know or, if necessary, review:

- The two organizations primarily responsible for setting accounting standards. (Ch. 1, p. 10)
- The monetary unit assumption, the economic entity assumption, and the time period assumption. (Ch. 1, pp. 10–11 and Ch. 3, p. 94)
- The cost principle, the revenue recognition principle, and the matching principle. (Ch. 1, p. 10 and Ch. 3, pp. 95–96)
- The presentation of classified balance sheets (Ch. 4, pp. 158–163) and classified (multiple-step) income statements. (Ch. 5, p. 206)

✓ THE NAVIGATOR

ACCOUNTING MATTERS! FEATURE STORY

Certainly Worth Investigating!

It is often difficult to determine in what period some revenues and expenses should be reported. There are rules that give guidance, but occasionally these rules are overlooked, misinterpreted, or even intentionally ignored. Consider the following examples.

- **Policy Management Systems**, which makes insurance software, said that it reported some sales before contracts were signed or products delivered.
- **Sunbeam Corporation**, while under the control of the (in)famous "Chainsaw" Al Dunlap, prematurely booked revenues and recorded overly large restructuring charges. Ultimately the company was forced to restate its net income figures, and Mr. Dunlap lost his job.

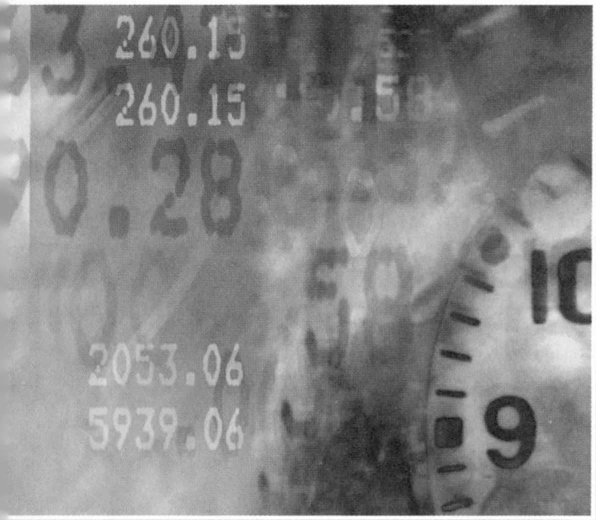

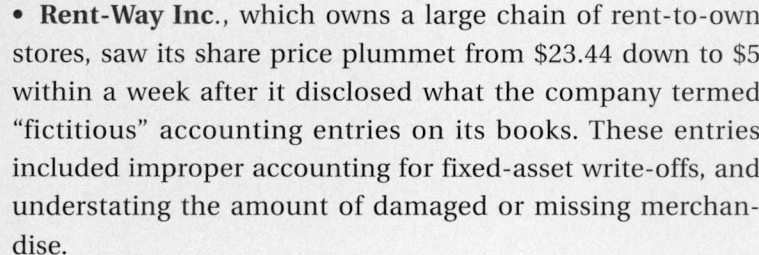

- **Rent-Way Inc.**, which owns a large chain of rent-to-own stores, saw its share price plummet from $23.44 down to $5 within a week after it disclosed what the company termed "fictitious" accounting entries on its books. These entries included improper accounting for fixed-asset write-offs, and understating the amount of damaged or missing merchandise.

Often in cases such as these, the company's stockholders sue the company because of the decline in the stock price due to the disclosure of the misinformation. In light of this eventuality, why might management want to report revenues or expenses in the wrong period? Company managers are under intense pressure to report higher earnings every year. If actual performance falls short of expectations, management might be tempted to bend the rules.

One analyst suggests that investors and auditors should be suspicious of sharp increases in monthly sales at the end of each quarter or big jumps in fourth-quarter sales. Such events don't always mean management is cheating, but they are certainly worth investigating.

☑ THE NAVIGATOR

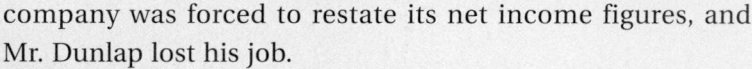

STUDY OBJECTIVES

After studying this chapter, you should be able to:

1. Explain the meaning of generally accepted accounting principles and identify the key items of the conceptual framework.
2. Describe the basic objectives of financial reporting.
3. Discuss the qualitative characteristics of accounting information and elements of financial statements.
4. Identify the basic assumptions used by accountants.
5. Identify the basic principles of accounting.
6. Identify the two constraints in accounting.
7. Understand and analyze classified financial statements.
8. Explain the accounting principles used in international operations.

☑ THE NAVIGATOR

PREVIEW OF CHAPTER 7

As indicated in the Feature Story, it is important that general guidelines be available to resolve accounting issues. Without these basic guidelines, each enterprise would have to develop its own set of accounting practices. If this happened, we would have to become familiar with every company's peculiar accounting and reporting rules in order to understand their financial statements. It would be difficult, if not impossible, to compare the financial statements of different companies. This chapter explores the basic accounting principles that are followed in developing specific accounting guidelines.

The content and organization of Chapter 7 are as follows.

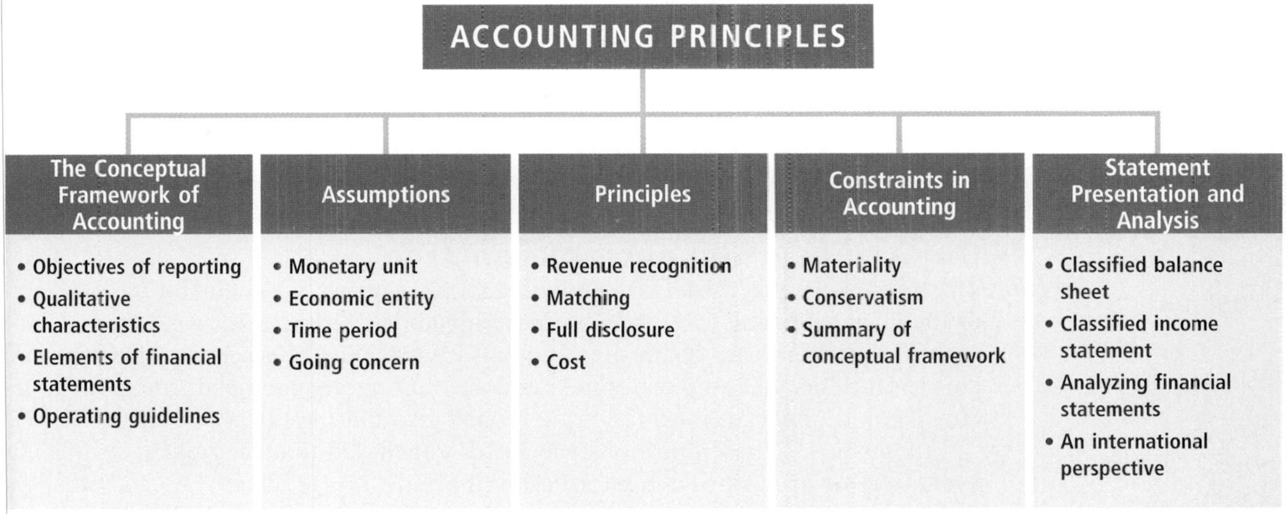

THE NAVIGATOR

The Conceptual Framework of Accounting

STUDY OBJECTIVE 1

Explain the meaning of generally accepted accounting principles and identify the key items of the conceptual framework.

What you have learned up to this point in the book is a process that leads to the preparation of financial reports about a company. These are the company's financial statements. This area of accounting is called **financial accounting**. The accounting profession has established a set of standards and rules that are recognized as a general guide for financial reporting. This recognized set of standards is called **generally accepted accounting principles (GAAP)**. "Generally accepted" means that these principles must have "substantial authoritative support." Such support usually comes from two standard-setting bodies: the Financial Accounting Standards Board (FASB) and the Securities and Exchange Commission (SEC).[1]

Since the early 1970s the business and governmental communities have given the FASB the responsibility for developing accounting principles in this country. This is an ongoing process; accounting principles change to reflect changes in the business environment and in the needs of users of accounting information.

[1]The SEC is an agency of the U.S. government that was established in 1933 to administer laws and regulations relating to the exchange of securities and the publication of financial information by U.S. businesses. The agency has the authority to mandate generally accepted accounting principles for companies under its jurisdiction. However, throughout its history, the SEC has been willing to accept the principles set forth by the FASB and similar bodies.

HELPFUL HINT

Accounting principles are affected by economic and political conditions which change over time. As a result, accounting principles are not cut into stone like the periodic table in chemistry or a formula in math.

Prior to the establishment of the FASB, accounting principles were developed on a problem-by-problem basis. Rule-making bodies developed accounting rules and methods to solve specific problems. Critics charged that the problem-by-problem approach led over time to inconsistent rules and practices. No clearly developed conceptual framework of accounting existed to refer to in solving new problems.

In response to these criticisms, the FASB developed a **conceptual framework**. It serves as the basis for resolving accounting and reporting problems. The FASB spent considerable time and effort on this project. The Board views its conceptual framework as ". . . a constitution, a coherent system of interrelated objectives and fundamentals."[2]

The FASB's conceptual framework consists of the following four items:

1. Objectives of financial reporting.
2. Qualitative characteristics of accounting information.
3. Elements of financial statements.
4. Operating guidelines (assumptions, principles, and constraints).

We will discuss these items on the following pages.

Objectives of Financial Reporting

STUDY OBJECTIVE 2

Describe the basic objectives of financial reporting.

The FASB began to work on the conceptual framework by looking at the objectives of financial reporting. Determining these objectives required answers to such basic questions as: Who uses financial statements? Why? What information do they need? How knowledgeable about business and accounting are financial statement users? How should financial information be reported so that it is best understood?

In answering these questions, the FASB concluded that the objectives of financial reporting are to provide information that:

1. Is useful to those making investment and credit decisions.
2. Is helpful in assessing future cash flows.
3. Identifies the economic resources (assets), the claims to those resources (liabilities), and the changes in those resources and claims.

The FASB then undertook to describe the characteristics that make accounting information useful.

Qualitative Characteristics of Accounting Information

STUDY OBJECTIVE 3

Discuss the qualitative characteristics of accounting information and elements of financial statements.

How does a company like **Microsoft** decide on the amount of financial information to disclose? In what format should its financial information be presented? How should assets, liabilities, revenues, and expenses be measured? The FASB concluded that the overriding criterion for such accounting choices is **decision usefulness**. The accounting practice selected should be the one that generates the most useful financial information for making a decision. To be useful, information should possess the following qualitative characteristics: relevance, reliability, comparability, and consistency.

Relevance

Accounting information has **relevance** if it makes a difference in a decision. Relevant information has either predictive or feedback value or both. **Predictive value**

[2]"Conceptual Framework for Financial Accounting and Reporting: Elements of Financial Statements and Their Measurement," *FASB Discussion Memorandum* (Stamford, Conn.: 1976), p. 1.

helps users forecast future events. For example, when **ExxonMobil** issues financial statements, the information in them is considered relevant because it provides a basis for predicting future earnings. **Feedback value** confirms or corrects prior expectations. When ExxonMobil issues financial statements, it confirms or corrects prior expectations about the financial health of the company.

In addition, accounting information has relevance if it is **timely**. It must be available to decision makers before it loses its capacity to influence decisions. If ExxonMobil reported its financial information only every five years, the information would be of limited use in decision-making.

HELPFUL HINT

What makes accounting information relevant? Answer: Relevant accounting information provides feedback, serves as a basis for predictions, and is timely (current).

Reliability

Reliability of information means that the information is free of error and bias. In short, it can be depended on. To be reliable, accounting information must be **verifiable**: We must be able to prove that it is free of error and bias. It also must be a **faithful representation** of what it purports to be: It must be factual. If **Sears, Roebuck**'s income statement reports sales of $100 billion when it had sales of $51 billion, then the statement is not a faithful representation. Finally, accounting information must be **neutral**: It cannot be selected, prepared, or presented to favor one set of interested users over another. To ensure reliability, certified public accountants audit financial statements.

HELPFUL HINT

What makes accounting information reliable? Answer: Reliable accounting information is free of error and bias, is factual, verifiable, and neutral.

Comparability

Accounting information about an enterprise is most useful when it can be compared with accounting information about other enterprises. **Comparability** results when different companies use the same accounting principles. For example, **Sears**, **L. L. Bean**, and **The Limited** all use the cost principle in reporting plant assets on the balance sheet. Also, each company uses the revenue recognition and matching principles in determining its net income.

Conceptually, comparability should also extend to the methods used by companies in complying with an accounting principle. Accounting methods include the FIFO and LIFO methods of inventory costing, and various depreciation methods. At this point, comparability of methods is not required, even for companies in the same industry. Thus, **Ford**, **General Motors**, and **DaimlerChrysler** may use different inventory costing and depreciation methods in their financial statements. The only accounting requirement is that each company **must disclose** the accounting methods used. From the disclosures, the external user can determine whether the financial information is comparable.

Consistency

Consistency means that a company uses the same accounting principles and methods from year to year. If a company selects FIFO as the inventory costing method in the first year of operations, it is expected to use FIFO in succeeding years. When financial information has been reported on a consistent basis, the financial statements permit meaningful analysis of trends within a company.

A company *can* change to a new method of accounting. To do so, management must justify that the new method results in more meaningful financial information. In the year in which the change occurs, the change must be disclosed in the notes to the financial statements. Such disclosure makes users of the financial statements aware of the lack of consistency.

The characteristics that make accounting information useful are summarized in Illustration 7-1 (on page 294).

Illustration 7-1
Characteristics of useful information

Relevance
1. Provides a basis for forecasts
2. Confirms or corrects prior expectations
3. Is timely

Reliability
1. Is verifiable
2. Is a faithful representation
3. Is neutral

Comparability
Different companies use similar accounting principles

Consistency
Company uses same accounting methods from year to year

Elements of Financial Statements

An important part of the accounting conceptual framework is a set of definitions that describe the basic terms used in accounting. The FASB refers to this set of definitions as the **elements of financial statements**. They include such terms as assets, liabilities, equity, revenues, and expenses.

Because these elements are so important, it is crucial that they be precisely defined and universally applied. Finding the appropriate definition for many of these elements is not easy. For example, should the value of a company's employees be reported as an asset on a balance sheet? Should the death of the company's president be reported as a loss? A good set of definitions should provide answers to these types of questions. Because you have already encountered most of these definitions in earlier chapters, they are not repeated here.

Operating Guidelines

The objectives of financial reporting, the qualitative characteristics of accounting information, and the elements of financial statements are very broad. Because practicing accountants must solve practical problems, more detailed guidelines are needed. In its conceptual framework, the FASB recognized the need for operating guidelines. We classify these guidelines as assumptions, principles, and constraints. These guidelines are well-established and accepted in accounting.

Assumptions provide a foundation for the accounting process. **Principles** are specific rules that indicate how economic events should be reported in the accounting process. **Constraints** on the accounting process allow for a relaxation of the principles under certain circumstances. Illustration 7-2 provides a road-map of the operating guidelines of accounting. These guidelines (some of which you know from earlier chapters) are discussed in more detail in the following sections.

Illustration 7-2
The operating guidelines of accounting

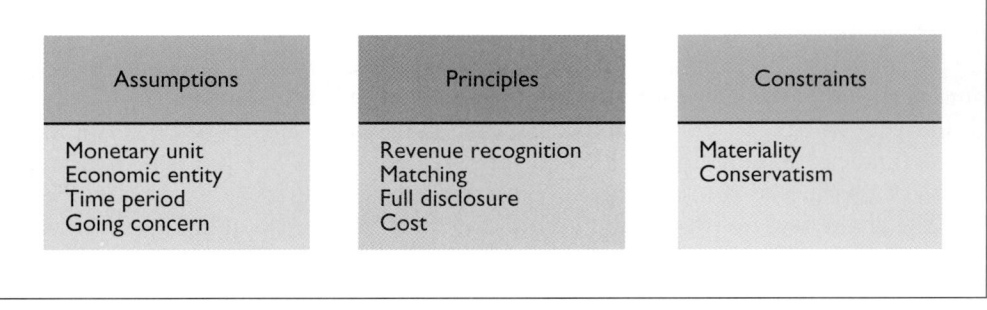

Assumptions	Principles	Constraints
Monetary unit Economic entity Time period Going concern	Revenue recognition Matching Full disclosure Cost	Materiality Conservatism

BEFORE YOU GO ON...

Review It

1. What are generally accepted accounting principles?
2. What is stated about generally accepted accounting principles in the Independent Auditors' Report for **PepsiCo**? The answer to this question appears on page 332.
3. What are the basic objectives of financial information?
4. What are the qualitative characteristics that make accounting information useful? Identify two elements of the financial statements.

THE NAVIGATOR

Assumptions

As noted above, assumptions provide a foundation for the accounting process. You already know three of the major assumptions—the monetary unit, economic entity, and time period assumptions. The fourth is the going concern assumption.

STUDY OBJECTIVE 4

Identify the basic assumptions used by accountants.

Monetary Unit Assumption

The **monetary unit assumption** states that only transaction data that can be expressed in terms of money be included in the accounting records. For example, the value of a company president is not reported in a company's financial records because it cannot be expressed easily in dollars.

An important corollary to the monetary unit assumption is the assumption that the unit of measure remains relatively constant over time. This point will be discussed in more detail later in this chapter.

ETHICS NOTE

In an action that sent shock waves through the French business community, the CEO of Alcatel-Alsthom was taken into custody for an apparent violation of the economic entity assumption. Allegedly, the executive improperly used company funds to install an expensive security system in his home.

Economic Entity Assumption

The **economic entity assumption** states that the activities of the entity be kept separate and distinct from the activities of the owner and of all other economic entities. For example, it is assumed that the activities of **IBM** can be distinguished from those of other computer companies such as **Apple**, **Dell**, and **Hewlett-Packard**.

Time Period Assumption

The **time period assumption** states that the economic life of a business can be divided into artificial time periods. Thus, it is assumed that the activities of business enterprises such as **General Electric**, **Time Warner**, **ExxonMobil**, or any enterprise can be subdivided into months, quarters, or a year for meaningful financial reporting purposes.

Going Concern Assumption

The **going concern assumption** assumes that the enterprise will continue in operation long enough to carry out its existing objectives. In spite of numerous business failures, companies have a fairly high continuance rate. It has proved useful to adopt a going concern assumption for accounting purposes.

The accounting implications of this assumption are critical. If a going concern assumption is not used, then plant assets should be stated at their liquidation value (selling price less cost of disposal)—not at their cost. In that case, depreciation of these assets would not be needed. Each period, these assets would simply be reported at their liquidation value. Also, without this assumption, the current–noncurrent classification of assets and liabilities would not matter. Labeling anything as long-term would be difficult to justify.

Acceptance of the going concern assumption gives credibility to the cost principle. Only when liquidation appears imminent is the going concern assumption inapplicable. In that case, assets would be better stated at liquidation value than at cost.

These basic accounting assumptions are illustrated graphically in Illustration 7-3 below.

Illustration 7-3
Assumptions used in accounting

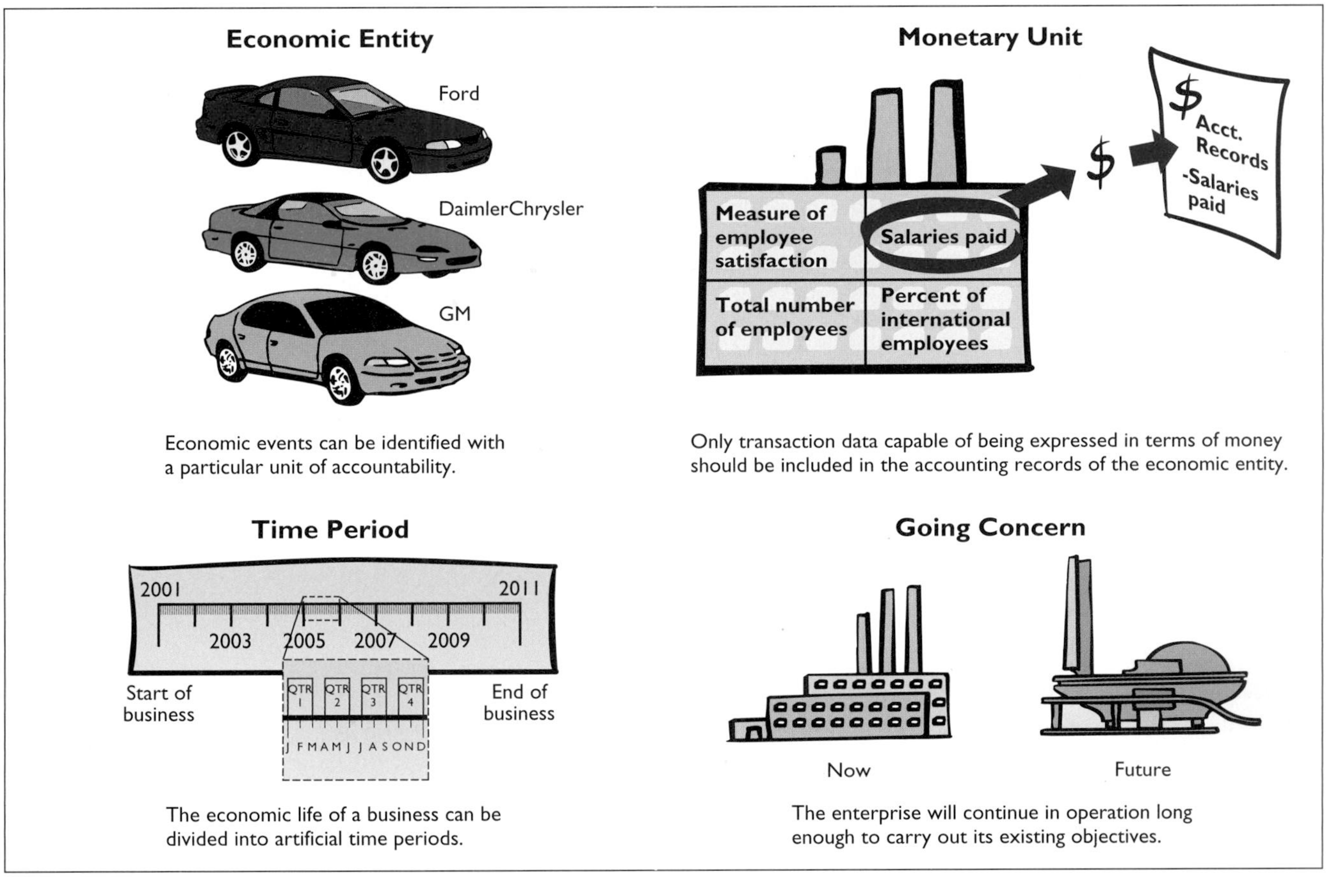
Economic Entity
Ford
DaimlerChrysler
GM
Economic events can be identified with a particular unit of accountability.
Monetary Unit
Measure of employee satisfaction
Salaries paid
Total number of employees
Percent of international employees
$
$
Acct. Records
-Salaries paid
Only transaction data capable of being expressed in terms of money should be included in the accounting records of the economic entity.
Time Period
2001
2011
2003
2005
2007
2009
Start of business
End of business
QTR 1
QTR 2
QTR 3
QTR 4
J F M A M J J A S O N D
The economic life of a business can be divided into artificial time periods.
Going Concern
Now
Future
The enterprise will continue in operation long enough to carry out its existing objectives.

Principles

STUDY OBJECTIVE 5

Identify the basic principles of accounting.

On the basis of the fundamental assumptions of accounting, the accounting profession has developed principles that dictate how economic events should be recorded and reported. In earlier chapters we discussed the cost principle (Chapter 1) and the revenue recognition and matching principles (Chapter 3). Here we now examine a number of reporting issues related to these principles. In addition, we introduce another principle, the full disclosure principle.

Revenue Recognition Principle

The **revenue recognition principle** dictates that revenue should be recognized in the accounting period in which it is earned. But applying this general principle in practice can be difficult. For example, some companies improperly recognize revenue on goods that have not been shipped to customers. Similarly, until recently, financial institutions immediately recorded a large portion of their fees for granting a loan as revenue rather than spreading those fees over the life of the loan.

When a sale is involved, revenue is recognized at the point of sale. This **sales basis** involves an exchange transaction between the seller and buyer. The sales price is an objective measure of the amount of revenue realized. However, there are two exceptions to the sales basis for revenue recognition that have become generally accepted. These methods are left for more advanced courses.

HELPFUL HINT

Revenue should be recognized in the accounting period in which it is earned. This may not be the period in which the related cash is received.

Matching Principle (Expense Recognition)

Expense recognition is traditionally tied to revenue recognition: "Let the expense follow the revenue." As you learned in Chapter 3, this practice is referred to as the **matching principle**. It dictates that expenses be matched with revenues in the period in which efforts are made to generate revenues. Expenses are not recognized when cash is paid, or when the work is performed, or when the product is produced. Rather, they are recognized when the labor (service) or the product actually makes its contribution to revenue.

But, it is sometimes difficult to determine the accounting period in which the expense contributed to revenues. Several approaches have therefore been devised for matching expenses and revenues on the income statement.

To understand these approaches, you need to understand the nature of expenses. Costs are the source of expenses. Costs that will generate revenues only in the current accounting period are expensed immediately. They are reported as **operating expenses** in the income statement. Examples include costs for advertising, sales salaries, and repairs. These expenses are often called **expired costs**.

HELPFUL HINT

Costs become expenses when they are charged against revenue.

ETHICS NOTE

Many appear to do it, but few like to discuss it: It's earnings management, and it's a clear violation of the revenue recognition and matching principles. Banks sometimes time the sale of investments or the expensing of bad debts to accomplish earnings objectives. Prominent companies have been accused of matching one-time gains with one-time charge-offs so that current-period earnings are not so high that they can't be surpassed next period.

Costs that will generate revenues in future accounting periods are recognized as assets. Examples include merchandise inventory, prepaid expenses, and plant assets. These costs represent **unexpired costs**. Unexpired costs become expenses in two ways:

1. **Cost of goods sold.** Costs carried as merchandise inventory become expenses when the inventory is sold. They are expensed as cost of goods sold in the period when the sale occurs. Thus, there is a direct matching of expenses with revenues.
2. **Operating expenses.** Other unexpired costs become operating expenses through use or consumption (as in the case of store supplies) or through the passage of time (as in the case of prepaid insurance). The costs of plant assets and other long-lived resources are expensed through rational and systematic allocation methods—periodic depreciation. Operating expenses contribute to the revenues for the period, but their association with revenues is less direct than for cost of goods sold.

These points about expense recognition are illustrated in Illustration 7-4.

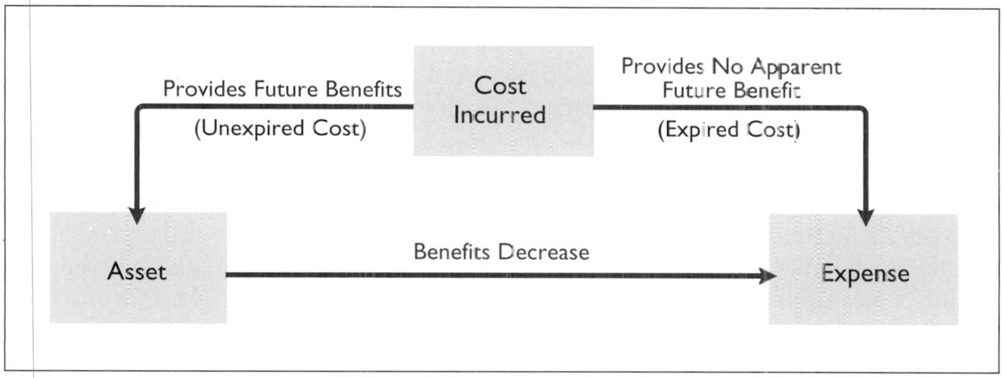

Illustration 7-4
Expense recognition pattern

ACCOUNTING MATTERS! Business Insight

Implementing expense recognition guidelines can be difficult. Consider, for example, **Harold's Club** (a gambling casino) in Reno, Nevada. How should it report expenses related to the payoff of its progressive slot machines? Progressive slot machines, which generally have no ceiling on their jackpots, provide a lucky winner with all the money that many losers had previously put in. Payoffs tend to be huge, but infrequent. At Harold's, the progressive slots pay off on average every 4½ months.

The basic accounting question is: Can Harold's deduct the millions of dollars sitting in its progressive slot machines from the revenue recognized at the end of the accounting period? One might argue that no, you cannot deduct the money until the "winning handle pull." However, a winning handle pull might not occur for many months or even years. Although an estimate would have to be used, the better answer is to match these costs with the revenue recognized, assuming that an average 4½ months' payout is well documented.

? What accounting principles are applicable to the Harold's Club progressive slot machines? If Harold's fails to use an estimate for expenses, what effect will this have on financial statements in a period when no payouts occur?

Full Disclosure Principle

Accounting Matters!

The **full disclosure principle** requires that circumstances and events that make a difference to financial statement users be disclosed. For example, investors who lost money in **Enron**, **WorldCom**, and **Global Crossing** have complained that the lack of full disclosure regarding some of the companies' transactions caused the financial statements to be misleading. Investors want to be made aware of events that can affect the financial health of a company.

Compliance with the full disclosure principle occurs through the data in the financial statements and the information in the notes that accompany the statements. The first note in most cases is a **summary of significant accounting policies**. It includes, among others, the methods used for inventory costing and depreciation of plant assets.

Deciding how much disclosure is enough can be difficult. Accountants could disclose every financial event that occurs and every contingency that exists. But the benefits of providing additional information in some cases may be less than the costs of doing so. Many companies complain of an accounting standards overload. They also object to requirements that force them to disclose confidential information. Determining where to draw the line on disclosure is not easy.

One thing is certain: financial statements were much simpler years ago. In 1930, **General Electric** had no notes to its financial statements. Today it has over 30 pages of notes! Why this change? A major reason is that the objectives of financial statements have changed. In the past, information was generally presented on what the business had done. Today, the objectives of financial reporting are more future-oriented. The goal is to provide information that makes it possible to predict the amounts, timing, and uncertainty of future cash flows.

ACCOUNTING MATTERS! **Business Insight**

Some accountants are reconsidering the current means of financial reporting. They propose a database concept of financial reporting. In such a system, all the information from transactions would be stored in a computerized database to be instantly accessed by various user groups. The main benefit of such a system is the ability to tailor the information requested to the needs of each user on a real-time basis.

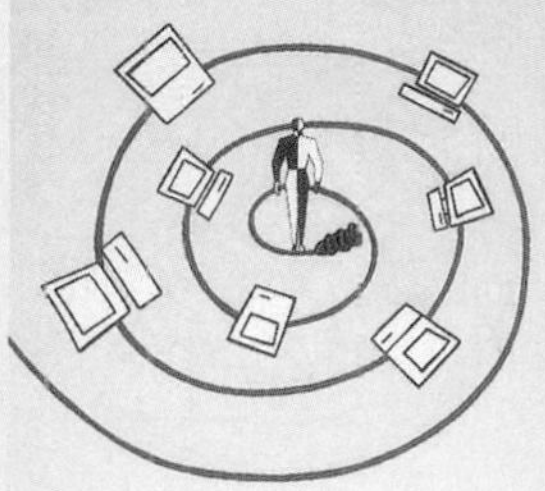

What makes this idea controversial? Discussion currently revolves around access and aggregation issues. Questions abound: "Who should be allowed to make inquiries of the system?" "What is the lowest/smallest level of information to be provided?" "Will such a system necessarily improve on the current means of disclosure?" Such questions must be answered before database financial accounting can be implemented on a large scale.

? Would instant access to financial information provide more relevant information? Do you think such an approach would do away with the need for annual reports?

Cost Principle

As you know, the **cost principle** dictates that assets be recorded at their cost. Cost is used because it is both relevant and reliable. Cost is **relevant** because it represents the price paid, the assets sacrificed, or the commitment made at date of acquisition. Cost is **reliable** because it is objectively measurable, factual, and verifiable. It is the result of an exchange transaction. Cost is the basis used in preparing financial statements.

The cost principle, however, has come under criticism. Some criticize it as irrelevant. After acquisition, the argument goes, the cost of an asset is not equivalent to market value or current value. Also, as the purchasing power of the dollar changes, so does the meaning associated with the dollar used as the basis of measurement. Consider the classic story about the individual who went to sleep and woke up 10 years later. Hurrying to a telephone, he called his broker and asked what his formerly modest stock portfolio was worth. He was told that he was a multi-millionaire. His **General Motors** stock was worth $5 million, and his **Microsoft** stock was up to $10 million. Elated, he was about to inquire about his other holdings, when the telephone operator cut in with "Your time is up. Please deposit $100,000 for the next three minutes."[3]

HELPFUL HINT

Are you a winner or loser when you hold cash in a period of inflation? Answer: A loser, because the value of the cash declines as inflation climbs.

Despite the inevitability of changing prices due to inflation, the accounting profession still follows the stable monetary unit assumption in preparing the primary financial statements. While admitting that some changes in prices do occur, the profession believes the unit of measure—the dollar—has remained sufficiently constant over time to provide meaningful financial information. Sometimes, the **disclosure of price-level adjusted data is in the form of supplemental information** that accompanies the financial statements.

The basic principles of accounting are summarized in Illustration 7-5.

[3] Adapted from *Barron's*, January 28, 1980, p. 27.

Illustration 7-5
Basic principles used in accounting

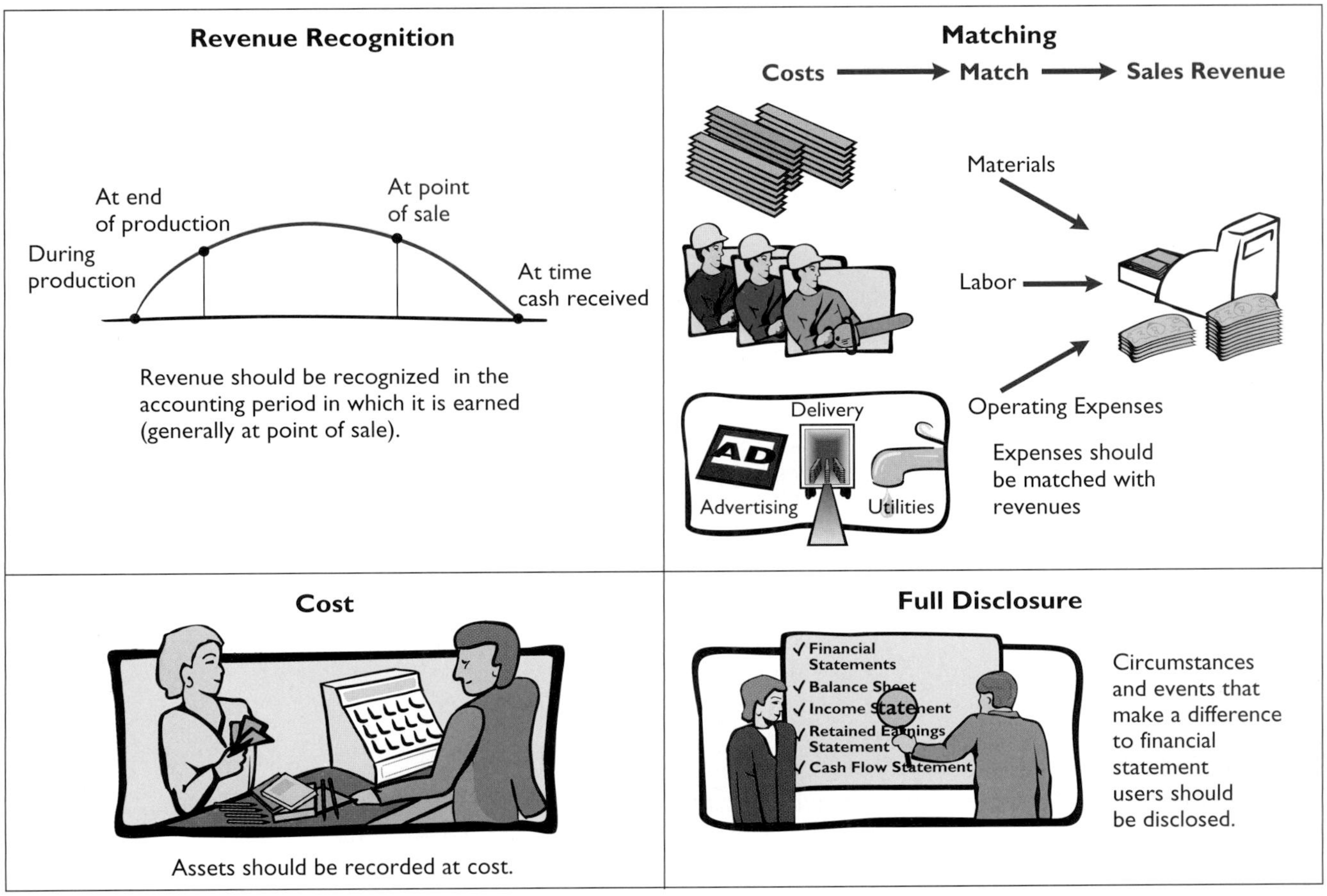

Constraints in Accounting

STUDY OBJECTIVE 6

Identify the two constraints in accounting.

Constraints permit a company to modify generally accepted accounting principles without reducing the usefulness of the reported information. The constraints are materiality and conservatism.

Materiality

Materiality relates to an item's impact on a firm's overall financial condition and operations. An item is **material** when it is likely to influence the decision of a reasonably prudent investor or creditor. It is immaterial if its inclusion or omission has no impact on a decision maker. In short, if the item does not make a difference in decision making, GAAP does not have to be followed. To determine the materiality of an amount, the accountant usually compares it with such items as total assets, total liabilities, and net income.

To illustrate how the materiality constraint is applied, assume that Rodriguez Co. purchases a number of low-cost plant assets, such as wastepaper baskets. Although the proper accounting would appear to be to depreciate these wastepaper baskets over their useful life, they are usually expensed immediately. This practice is justified because these costs are considered immaterial. Establishing depreciation schedules for these assets is costly and time-consuming and will not make a material difference on total assets and net income. Another application of the materiality constraint would be the expensing of small tools. Some companies expense any plant assets under a specified dollar amount.

Conservatism

The **conservatism** constraint dictates that when in doubt, choose the method that will be least likely to overstate assets and income. It does **not** mean **understating** assets or income. Conservatism provides a reasonable guide in difficult situations: Do not overstate assets and income.

A common application of the conservatism constraint is the use of the lower of cost or market method for inventories. As indicated in Chapter 6, inventories are reported at market value if market value is below cost. This practice results in a higher cost of goods sold and lower net income. In addition, inventory on the balance sheet is stated at a lower amount.

Other examples of conservatism in accounting are the use of the LIFO method for inventory valuation when prices are rising and the use of accelerated depreciation methods for plant assets (faster write-off in earlier years). Both these methods result in lower asset carrying values and lower net income than alternative methods.

The two constraints in accounting are graphically depicted in Illustration 7-6.

> **HELPFUL HINT**
>
> In other words, if two methods are otherwise equally appropriate, choose the one that will least likely overstate assets and income.

Illustration 7-6
Constraints in accounting

Materiality | **Conservatism**

For small amounts, GAAP does not have to be followed.

When in doubt, choose the solution that will be least likely to overstate assets and income.

Summary of Conceptual Framework

As we have seen, the conceptual framework for developing sound reporting practices starts with a set of objectives for financial reporting. It follows with the description of qualities that make information useful. In addition, elements of financial statements are defined. More detailed operating guidelines are then provided. These guidelines take the form of assumptions and principles. The conceptual framework also recognizes that constraints exist on the reporting environment. The conceptual framework is illustrated graphically in Illustration 7-7.

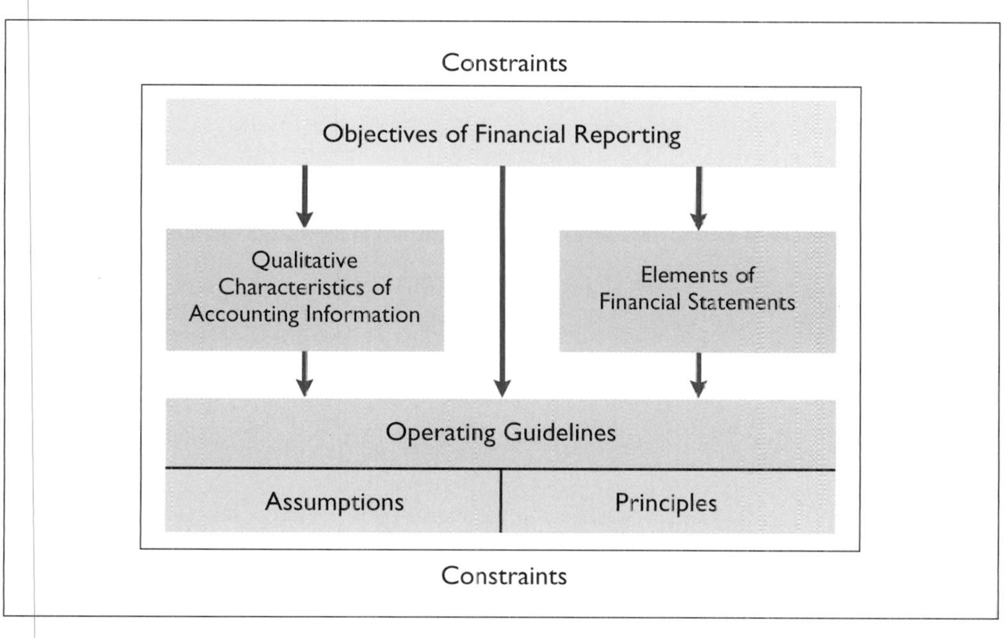

Illustration 7-7
Conceptual framework

BEFORE YOU GO ON...

Review It

1. What are the monetary unit assumption, the economic entity assumption, the time period assumption, and the going concern assumption?
2. What are the revenue recognition principle, the matching principle, the full disclosure principle, and the cost principle?
3. What are the materiality constraint and the conservatism constraint?

THE NAVIGATOR

Statement Presentation and Analysis

STUDY OBJECTIVE 7

Understand and analyze classified financial statements.

Financial statements play an important role in attempting to meet the objectives of financial reporting. "Bottom line" information such as total assets and net income are useful to investors, but these single numbers lack sufficient detail for serious analysis. Investors and creditors generally find the parts of a financial statement more useful than the whole. Proper classification within the financial statements is therefore extremely important.

Classified Balance Sheet

The balance sheet is composed of three major elements: assets, liabilities, and stockholders' equity. Additional segregation within these groups, however, is considered useful to financial statement readers. As indicated in Chapter 4, the following classification is generally found.

Illustration 7-8
Standard classification of balance sheet

Assets	Liabilities and Stockholders' Equity
Current assets	Current liabilities
Long-term investments	Long-term liabilities
Property, plant, and equipment	Stockholders' equity
Intangible assets	

If the form of organization is a proprietorship, the term "Owner's equity" instead of "Stockholders' equity" is used to describe that section of the balance sheet. An account called Capital is reported in the owner's equity section of the balance sheet for a proprietorship. **Capital** is the owner's investment in the business.

To illustrate, assume that Sally Field invests $90,000 on July 10, 2006, to start up Med/Waste Company. The company's balance sheet immediately after the investment is as follows.

Illustration 7-9
Proprietorship balance sheet

MED/WASTE COMPANY
Balance Sheet
July 10, 2006

Cash	$90,000	Sally Field, Capital	$90,000

Because Sally Field owns the business and has chosen not to incorporate, common stock is not issued and net income (net loss) belongs to her. Therefore, common stock and retained earnings accounts are not needed. Instead, her capital account is increased by investments and by net income. It is decreased by withdrawals of assets for personal use and by net losses. The capital account represents Sally Field's claim to the net assets (assets less liabilities) of the company.

If the form of organization is a partnership, each partner has a separate capital account, and the owners' equity section shows the capital accounts of all the partners. For example, assume that A. Roy and B. Siegfried form a partnership on December 11, 2006, at which time Roy and Siegfried each invest $60,000. The balance sheet immediately after their investments is as follows.

HELPFUL HINT

Note "Owners' equity" instead of "Owner's equity" is used for a partnership to indicate multiple owners.

Illustration 7-10
Partnership balance sheet

ROY AND SIEGFRIED
Balance Sheet
December 11, 2006

Cash	$120,000	A. Roy, Capital	$ 60,000
		B. Siegfried, Capital	60,000
			$120,000

Classified Income Statement

Chapter 5 presented a multiple-step income statement for Sellers Electronix. The multiple-step income statement included the following.

Sales revenue section—Presents the sales, discounts, allowances, and other related information to arrive at the net amount of sales revenue.

Cost of goods sold—Indicates the cost of goods sold to produce sales.

Operating expenses—Provides information on both selling and administrative expenses.

Other revenues and gains—Indicates revenues earned or gains resulting from nonoperating transactions.

Other expenses and losses—Indicates expenses or losses incurred from nonoperating transactions.

Two additional items are income tax expense and earnings per share.

Income Tax Expense

Income taxes must be paid and therefore reported for a corporation because a corporation is a legal entity separate and distinct from its owners. Proprietorships and partnerships are not separate legal entities; owners are therefore taxed directly on their business income. Stockholders are taxed only on the dividends they receive.

Corporate **income taxes (or income tax expense)** are reported in a separate section of the income statement, before net income. The condensed income statement for Leads Inc. in Illustration 7-11 (on page 304) shows a typical presentation. Note that "Income before income taxes" is reported before "Income tax expense."

Income tax expense and the related liability for income taxes payable are recorded as part of the adjusting process, preceding financial statement preparation. Using the data above for Leads Inc., the adjusting entry for income tax expense at December 31, 2006, would be as follows.

Income Tax Expense	46,800	
Income Taxes Payable		46,800
(To record income taxes for 2006)		

A	=	L	+	SE
		+46,800		−46,800

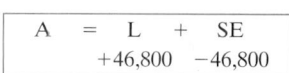

Cash Flows
no effect

Illustration 7-11
Income statement with income taxes

LEADS INC.
Income Statement
For the Year Ended December 31, 2006

Sales	$800,000
Cost of goods sold	600,000
Gross profit	200,000
Operating expenses	50,000
Income from operations	150,000
Other revenues and gains	10,000
Other expenses and losses	4,000
Income before income taxes	**156,000**
Income tax expense	**46,800**
Net income	$109,200

HELPFUL HINT

Corporations may also use the single-step form of income statements discussed in Chapter 5.

Other examples of income tax presentation appear in the Demonstration Problem income statement of Chapter 15 and the income statement of **PepsiCo** in Appendix A.

Earnings Per Share

Earnings per share data are frequently reported in the financial press and are widely used by stockholders and potential investors in evaluating the profitability of a company. Investors, especially, attempt to link earnings per share to the market price per share.[4] **Earnings per share (EPS)** indicates the net income earned by each share of outstanding common stock. Thus, **earnings per share is reported only for common stock.** The formula for computing earnings per share when there has been no change in outstanding shares during the year is as follows.

Illustration 7-12
Earnings per share formula—no change in outstanding shares

Net Income ÷ **Number of Common Shares Outstanding** = **Earnings per Share**

For example, Leads Inc. (Illustration 7-11) has net income of $109,200. Assuming that it has 54,600 shares of common stock outstanding for the year, earnings per share is $2 ($109,200 ÷ 54,600).[5]

Because of the importance of earnings per share, most companies are required to report it on the face of the income statement. Generally this amount is simply reported below net income on the statement. For Leads Inc. the presentation would be as follows.

[4] The ratio of the market price per share to the earnings per share is referred to as the *price-earnings (P-E) ratio*. This ratio is reported in the *Wall Street Journal* and other newspapers for common stocks listed on major stock exchanges.

[5] Whenever the number of outstanding shares changes during the year, the calculation of EPS becomes more complicated. These computations are covered in Chapter 15.

Illustration 7-13
Basic earnings per share disclosure

LEADS INC.
Income Statement (partial)
For the Year Ended December 31, 2006

Net income	$109,200
Earnings per share	**$2.00**

Analyzing Financial Statements

The financial statements should provide financial information that is useful for helping make sound investment and credit decisions. Presented below are the condensed balance sheet and income statement of Genlyte Inc. for 2006.

Illustration 7-14
Financial statements—Genlyte Inc.

GENLYTE INC.
Balance Sheet
December 31, 2006

Assets		Liabilities and Stockholders' Equity	
Current assets	$156,000	Current liabilities	$ 70,000
Plant and equipment (net)	74,000	Long-term liabilities	114,000
Intangible assets	14,000	Stockholders' equity	60,000
Total assets	$244,000	Total liabilities and stockholders' equity	$244,000

GENLYTE INC.
Income Statement
For the Year Ended December 31, 2006

Net sales	$430,000
Cost of sales	295,000
Gross profit	135,000
Selling and administrative expenses	109,000
Income from operations	26,000
Other expenses and losses	5,000
Income before income taxes	21,000
Income tax expense	7,000
Net income	$ 14,000
Earnings per share	$0.35

In analyzing and interpreting financial statement information, three major characteristics are generally evaluated: **liquidity**, **profitability**, and **solvency**. A **short-term debt holder**, for example, is primarily interested in the ability of a borrower to pay obligations when they become due. The liquidity of the borrower in such a case is extremely important in assessing the safety of a loan. A **long-term debt holder**, however, looks to indicators such as profitability and solvency that point to the firm's ability to survive over a long period of time. Long-term debt holders analyze earnings per share, the relationship of income to total assets invested, and the amount of debt in relation to total assets to determine whether money should be lent and at what interest rate. Similarly, **stockholders** are interested in the profitability and solvency of a company when assessing the likelihood of dividends and the growth potential of the common stock.

Liquidity

What is Genlyte's ability to pay its maturing obligations and meet unexpected needs for cash? The relationship between current assets and current liabilities is critical to helping answer this question. These relationships are expressed as a ratio, called the **current ratio**, and as a dollar amount, called **working capital**.

CURRENT RATIO. The **current ratio** is current assets divided by current liabilities. For Genlyte Inc., the ratio is 2.23:1, computed as follows.

Illustration 7-15
Current ratio formula and computation

Current Assets	÷	Current Liabilities	=	Current Ratio
$156,000	÷	$70,000	=	**2.23:1**

This ratio means that current assets are more than two times greater than current liabilities. Bankers, other creditors, and agencies such as **Dun & Bradstreet** use this ratio to determine whether the company is a good credit risk. Traditionally, a ratio of 2:1 is considered to be the standard for a good credit rating. Today, however, many sound companies have current ratios of less than 2:1. With its 2.23:1 ratio, Genlyte's short-term debt-paying ability appears to be very favorable.

From the foregoing, you might at first assume that the higher the current ratio, the better. This is not necessarily true. A very high current ratio may indicate that the company is holding more current assets than it currently needs in the business. It is possible, therefore, that the excess resources might be directed to more profitable investment opportunities.

WORKING CAPITAL. The excess of current assets over current liabilities is called **working capital**. For Genlyte Inc., working capital is $86,000, as shown below.

Illustration 7-16
Working capital formula and computation

Current Assets	–	Current Liabilities	=	Working Capital
$156,000	–	$70,000	=	**$86,000**

The amount of working capital provides some indication of the company's ability to meet its existing current obligations. A large amount of working capital generally means a company can meet its current liabilities as they fall due and, if desired, pay dividends. Although no set standards exist for the level of working capital a company should maintain, the general adequacy of a company's working capital is often determined by comparing data from prior periods and from similar companies of comparable size. Genlyte's working capital appears adequate.

Profitability

Profitability ratios measure the income or operating success of an enterprise for a given period of time. Income, or the lack of it, affects the company's ability to obtain debt or equity financing and the company's ability to grow.

PROFIT MARGIN PERCENTAGE. One important ratio used to measure profitability is the **profit margin percentage** (or rate of return on sales). It measures the percentage of each dollar of sales that results in net income. It is calculated by dividing net income by net sales for the period. Genlyte Inc.'s profit margin percentage is 3.3 percent, computed as follows.

Net Income	÷	Net Sales	=	Profit Margin Percentage
$14,000	÷	$430,000	=	**3.3%**

Illustration 7-17
Profit margin formula and computation

This ratio seems low. Much, however, depends on the type of industry. High-volume retailers, such as grocery stores (**Safeway** or **Kroger**) or discount stores (**Wal-Mart** or **Kmart**), generally have a low profit margin. They make a small profit on each sale but have many sales.

ACCOUNTING MATTERS! Business Insight

The type of industry can make a difference in the profit margin percentage investors and creditors expect. Profit margins among service companies—from airlines and banks to telecommunications companies and utilities—have traditionally been lower than those among manufacturers. **MCI**, for example, showed a profit margin percentage of 4.9 percent which is high for a telecommunications company. **Sprint**'s profit margin percentage was only 0.5 percent, and **AT&T** posted a loss. By contrast, the top three pharmaceutical firms—**Johnson & Johnson**, **Bristol-Meyers Squibb**, and **Merck**—had a profit margin percentage of 12.6 percent, 17.2 percent, and 20.6 percent, respectively. Before using a ratio like the profit margin percentage to evaluate company performance, you need to know what is reasonable performance for the industry.

? If service companies have a profit margin much lower than manufacturers (a third as large), why would anyone invest in a service company over a manufacturer?

RETURN ON ASSETS. In making an investment, an investor wants to know what rate of return to expect and what risks are associated with that rate of return. The greater the risk, the higher the rate of return the investor will demand on the investment.

One overall measure of profitability of a company is its rate of **return on assets**. It is calculated by dividing net income by total assets.[6] Genlyte Inc.'s rate of return is 5.7 percent, computed as follows.

[6] For simplicity, the rate of return calculations are based on end-of-year total amounts. The more conceptually correct *average* total assets and *average* common stockholders' equity are used in later chapters.

Illustration 7-18
Return on assets formula and computation

Net Income	÷	Total Assets	=	Return on Assets
$14,000	÷	$244,000	=	**5.7%**

The rate of return on assets is relatively low, which suggests that Genlyte may not be using its assets effectively.

RETURN ON COMMON STOCKHOLDERS' EQUITY. Another widely used rate that measures profitability from the common stockholders' viewpoint is **return on common stockholders' equity**. This rate shows the percentage of net income earned for each dollar of owners' investment. It is calculated by dividing net income by common stockholders' equity. In Genlyte Inc.'s case, the rate of return is 23.3 percent (or 23.3 cents per dollar), computed as follows.

Illustration 7-19
Return on common stockholders' equity formula and computation

Net Income	÷	Common Equity	=	Return on Common Stockholders' Equity
$14,000	÷	$60,000	=	**23.3%**

Genlyte's return on common stockholders' equity is quite good. The reason for this high rate of return is that Genlyte's assets are earning a return higher than the borrowing costs the company incurs.

Solvency

Solvency measures the ability of an enterprise to survive over a long period of time. Long-term debt holders and stockholders are interested in a company's ability to pay periodic interest and to repay the face value of the debt at maturity.

DEBT TO TOTAL ASSETS. One useful measure of solvency is the **debt to total assets ratio**. It measures the percentage of total assets that creditors, as opposed to stockholders, provide. It is calculated by dividing total debt (liabilities) by total assets, normally expressed as a percentage. Genlyte Inc.'s debt to total assets ratio is 75.4 percent, computed as follows.

Illustration 7-20
Debt to total assets formula and computation

Total Debt	÷	Total Assets	=	Debt to Total Assets Ratio
$184,000	÷	$244,000	=	**75.4%**

Debt to total assets of 75.4 percent means that Genlyte's creditors have provided approximately three-quarters of its total assets. The higher the percentage of debt to total assets, the greater the risk that the company may be unable to meet its maturing obligations. The lower the percentage, the greater the "buffer" available to creditors should the company become insolvent. In Genlyte Inc.'s case, unless earnings are positive and very stable, the company may have too much debt.

These percentage and ratio relationships are often used in comparison with (1) expected results, (2) prior year results, and (3) published results of other companies in the same line of business. Conclusions based on a single year's results are hazardous at best. Chapter 15 provides more detailed consideration of the analysis of financial statements.

Financial Statement Presentation—An International Perspective

STUDY OBJECTIVE 8

Explain the accounting principles used in international operations.

World markets are becoming increasingly intertwined. Foreigners use American computers, eat American breakfast cereals, read American magazines, listen to American rock music, watch American movies and TV shows, and drink American soda. Americans drive Japanese cars, wear Italian shoes and Scottish woolens, drink Brazilian coffee and Indian tea, eat Swiss chocolate bars, sit on Danish furniture, and use Arabian oil. The variety and volume of exported and imported goods indicates the extensive involvement of U.S. business in international trade. Many U.S. companies consider the world their market.

Firms that conduct operations in more than one country through subsidiaries, divisions, or branches in foreign countries are referred to as **multinational corporations (MNCs)**. The accounting for such corporations is complicated because foreign currencies are involved. These international transactions must be translated into U.S. dollars.

Differences in Standards

In the new global economy many investment and credit decisions require the analysis of foreign financial statements. Unfortunately, accounting standards are not uniform from country to country. This lack of uniformity results from differences in legal systems, in processes for developing accounting standards, in governmental requirements, and in economic environments.

ACCOUNTING MATTERS! International Insight

Research and development costs are an example of different international accounting standards. Compare how four countries account for research and development (R&D):

Country	Accounting Treatment
United States	Expenditures are expensed.
United Kingdom	Certain expenditures may be capitalized.
Germany	Expenditures are expensed.
Japan	Expenditures may be capitalized and written off over 5 years.

Thus, an R&D expenditure of $100 million is charged totally to expense in the current period in the United States and Germany. This same expense could range from zero to $100 million in the United Kingdom and from $20 million to $100 million in Japan!

? What would be the advantage of similar accounting standards for all countries? How can the financial and operating performance of international companies be compared?

Uniformity in Standards

Recently, the **International Accounting Standards Board (IASB)** has been formed. The board is working toward the development of a single set of high-quality global accounting standards. Its purpose is to formulate international accounting standards and to promote their acceptance worldwide.

At present these standards are not universally applied. However, more international companies are now considering adopting international standards. The foundation has therefore been laid for progress toward greater uniformity in international accounting.

BEFORE YOU GO ON...

Review It

1. What is the major difference in the equity section of the balance sheet between a corporation and proprietorship?
2. Where are income tax expense and earnings per share reported on the income statement? How is earnings per share computed?
3. How are the current ratio, working capital, profit margin percentage, return on assets, return on common stockholders' equity, and debt to total assets computed?
4. Explain how these ratios are useful in financial statement analysis.
5. What is the purpose of the International Accounting Standards Board?

THE NAVIGATOR

www.wiley.com/college/weygandt

DEMONSTRATION PROBLEM 1

Presented below are a number of operational guidelines and practices that have developed over time.

Instructions

Identify the accounting assumption, accounting principle, or reporting constraint that most appropriately justifies these procedures and practices. Use only one item per description.

(a) The first note, "Summary of Significant Accounting Policies," presents information on the subclassification of plant assets and discusses the company's depreciation methods.

(b) The local hamburger restaurant expenses all spatulas, french fry baskets, and other cooking utensils when purchased.

(c) Retailers recognize revenue at the point of sale.

(d) Green-Grow Lawn Mowers, Inc. includes an estimate of warranty expense in the year in which it sells its lawn mowers, which carry a 2-year warranty.

(e) Companies present sufficient financial information so that creditors and reasonably prudent investors will not be misled.

(f) Companies listed on U.S. stock exchanges report audited financial information annually and report unaudited information quarterly.

(g) Beach Resorts, Inc. does not record the 2006 value of $1.5 million for a piece of beachfront property it purchased in 1993 for $500,000.

ACTION PLAN

Remember that:

- The four principles are cost, revenue recognition, matching, and full disclosure.
- The two constraints are materiality and conservatism.
- Full disclosure relates generally to the item; materiality to the amount.

(h) Office Systems, Inc. takes a $32,000 loss on a number of older microcomputers in its inventory; it paid the manufacturer $107,000 for them but can sell them for only $75,000.

(i) **Frito Lay** is a wholly owned subsidiary of **PepsiCo, Inc.**, and Frito Lay's operating results and financial condition are included in the consolidated financial statements of PepsiCo. (Do not use full disclosure.)

SOLUTION TO DEMONSTRATION PROBLEM 1

(a) Full disclosure principle
(b) Materiality constraint
(c) Revenue recognition principle
(d) Matching principle
(e) Full disclosure principle
(f) Time period assumption
(g) Cost principle
(h) Conservatism constraint
(i) Economic entity assumption

THE NAVIGATOR

DEMONSTRATION PROBLEM 2

Presented below is financial information related to Notting Hill Corporation for the year 2006. All balances are ending balances unless stated otherwise.

Accounts payable	$ 868,000
Accounts receivable	700,000
Accumulated depreciation—equipment	100,000
Administrative expenses	280,000
Bonds payable	1,600,000
Cash	800,000
Common stock	500,000
Cost of goods sold	1,600,000
Dividends	60,000
Equipment	1,100,000
Income tax expense	83,000
Interest expense	60,000
Interest revenue	120,000
Inventories	500,000
Loss on the sale of equipment	35,000
Marketable (trading) securities	400,000
Net sales	2,400,000
Notes payable (short-term)	800,000
Other long-term debt	387,000
Patents and other intangibles	900,000
Prepaid expenses	200,000
Retained earnings (January 1, 2006)	80,000
Selling expenses	220,000
Taxes payable	83,000

Notting Hill Corporation had 88,000 shares of common stock outstanding for the entire year.

Instructions

(a) Prepare a multiple-step income statement.
(b) Prepare a single-step income statement.
(c) Prepare a retained earnings statement.
(d) Prepare a classified balance sheet.

ACTION PLAN

- Review the format in Chapter 5, page 206, for a multiple-step income statement. Note the multiple-step income statement reports gross profit and income from operations. A single-step income statement does not report these items.
- Remember that income tax expense is reported immediately after "Income before income taxes" for both a multiple-step and single-step income statement.
- Report earnings per share on both a multiple-step and a single-step income statement.
- Disclose net income and dividends on a retained earnings statement.
- Refer to Chapter 4, pp. 162–163, for examples of a classified balance sheet.

(*continued from p. 311*)

(e) Compute the following balance sheet relationships.
(1) Current ratio.
(2) The amount of working capital.
(3) Debt to total assets ratio.
What insights do these relationships provide to the reader of the financial statements?

(f) Compute three measures of profitability from the income statement and balance sheet information. What insights do these relationships provide to the reader of the financial statements?

SOLUTION TO DEMONSTRATION PROBLEM 2

(a) Multiple-step income statement

NOTTING HILL CORPORATION
Income Statement
For the Year Ended December 31, 2006

Net sales		$2,400,000
Cost of goods sold		1,600,000
Gross profit		800,000
Selling expenses	$220,000	
Administrative expenses	280,000	500,000
Income from operations		300,000
Other revenues and gains		
Interest revenue		120,000
Other expenses and losses		
Loss on sale of equipment	35,000	
Interest expense	60,000	95,000
Income before income taxes		325,000
Income tax expense		83,000
Net income		$ 242,000
Earnings per share		$2.75

(b) Single-step income statement

NOTTING HILL CORPORATION
Income Statement
For the Year Ended December 31, 2006

Revenues		
Net sales		$2,400,000
Interest revenue		120,000
Total revenues		2,520,000
Expenses		
Cost of goods sold	$1,600,000	
Selling expenses	220,000	
Administrative expenses	280,000	
Interest expense	60,000	
Loss on the sale of equipment	35,000	2,195,000
Income before income taxes		325,000
Income tax expense		83,000
Net income		$ 242,000
Earnings per share		$2.75

(c) Retained earnings statement

NOTTING HILL CORPORATION
Retained Earnings Statement
For the Year Ended December 31, 2006

Retained earnings, January 1	$ 80,000
Add: Net income	242,000
	322,000
Less: Dividends	60,000
Retained earnings, December 31	$262,000

(d) Classified balance sheet

NOTTING HILL CORPORATION
Balance Sheet
December 31, 2006

Current assets		
Cash		$ 800,000
Marketable (trading) securities		400,000
Accounts receivable		700,000
Inventories		500,000
Prepaid expenses		200,000
Total current assets		2,600,000
Property, plant, and equipment		
Equipment	$1,100,000	
Less: Accumulated depreciation	100,000	1,000,000
Intangible assets		
Patents and other intangible assets		900,000
Total assets		$4,500,000
Current liabilities		
Notes payable		$ 800,000
Accounts payable		868,000
Taxes payable		83,000
Total current liabilities		1,751,000
Long-term liabilities		
Bonds payable	$1,600,000	
Other long-term debt	387,000	1,987,000
Total liabilities		3,738,000
Stockholders' equity		
Common stock	500,000	
Retained earnings	262,000	762,000
Total liabilities and stockholders' equity		$4,500,000

(e) Balance sheet relationships

(1) $\text{Current ratio} = \dfrac{\text{Current assets}}{\text{Current liabilities}} = \dfrac{\$2,600,000}{\$1,751,000} = 1.48:1$

(2) Working capital = Current assets − Current liabilities

Current assets	$2,600,000
Current liabilities	1,751,000
Working capital	$ 849,000

(3) $\text{Debt to total assets} = \dfrac{\text{Debt}}{\text{Total assets}} = \dfrac{\$3,738,000}{\$4,500,000} = 83.07\%$

(continued from p. 313)

Notting Hill's liquidity and solvency are of mixed quality. The current ratio is satisfactory with its working capital healthy, i.e., current assets well in excess of current liabilities. However, its debt to total assets, at well over 80%, is too high. Given the company's relatively low profitability (see below), its creditors might be concerned.

(f) Profitability relationships

$$\text{Profit margin percentage} = \frac{\text{Net income}}{\text{Net sales}} = \frac{\$242{,}000}{\$2{,}400{,}000} = 10.08\%$$

$$\text{Return on assets} = \frac{\text{Net income}}{\text{Total assets}} = \frac{\$242{,}000}{\$4{,}500{,}000} = 5.38\%$$

$$\frac{\text{Return on common}}{\text{stockholders' equity}} = \frac{\text{Net income}}{\text{Common stockholders' equity}} = \frac{\$242{,}000}{\$762{,}000} = 31.76\%$$

The profit margin percentage (return on sales) for Notting Hill seems adequate. Given the company's large asset base, however, it should probably generate a higher profit. The company's overall financial picture, then, could be better.

THE NAVIGATOR

SUMMARY OF STUDY OBJECTIVES

1. **Explain the meaning of generally accepted accounting principles and identify the key items of the conceptual framework.** Generally accepted accounting principles are a set of rules and practices that are recognized as a general guide for financial reporting purposes. Generally accepted means that these principles must have "substantial authoritative support." The key items of the conceptual framework are: (1) objectives of financial reporting; (2) qualitative characteristics of accounting information; (3) elements of financial statements; and (4) operating guidelines (assumptions, principles, and constraints).
2. **Describe the basic objectives of financial reporting.** The basic objectives of financial reporting are to provide information that is (1) useful to those making investment and credit decisions; (2) helpful in assessing future cash flows; and (3) helpful in identifying economic resources (assets), the claims to those resources (liabilities), and the changes in those resources and claims.
3. **Discuss the qualitative characteristics of accounting information and elements of financial statements.** To be judged useful, information should possess the following qualitative characteristics: relevance, reliability, comparability, and consistency. The elements of financial statements are a set of definitions that can be used to describe the basic terms used in accounting.
4. **Identify the basic assumptions used by accountants.** The major assumptions are: monetary unit, economic entity, time period, and going concern.
5. **Identify the basic principles of accounting.** The major principles are revenue recognition, matching, full disclosure, and cost.
6. **Identify the two constraints in accounting.** The major constraints are materiality and conservatism.
7. **Understand and analyze classified financial statements.** We presented classified balance sheets and classified (multiple-step) income statements in Chapters 4 and 5, respectively. Two new items added to the classified income statement in this chapter are income taxes and earnings per share. Three items used to analyze the balance sheet are the current ratio, working capital, and debt to total assets. Earnings per share, profit margin percentage (return on sales), return on assets, and return on common stockholders' equity are used to analyze profitability.
8. **Explain the accounting principles used in international operations.** There are few recognized worldwide accounting standards. The International Accounting Standards Board (IASB), of which the United States is a member, is working to obtain conformity in international accounting practices.

THE NAVIGATOR

GLOSSARY

www.wiley.com/college/weygandt

Comparability Ability to compare accounting information of different companies because they use the same accounting principles. (p. 293).

Conceptual framework A coherent system of interrelated objectives and fundamentals that can lead to consistent standards. (p. 292).

Conservatism The approach of choosing an accounting method when in doubt that will least likely overstate assets and net income. (p. 301).

Consistency Use of the same accounting principles and methods from year to year within a company. (p. 293).

Cost principle Accounting principle that assets should be recorded at their historical cost. (p. 299).

Current ratio A measure that expresses the relationship of current assets to current liabilities by dividing current assets by current liabilities. (p. 306).

Debt to total assets ratio Solvency measure that indicates the percentage of total assets provided by creditors; calculated as total debt divided by total assets. (p. 308).

Earnings per share (EPS) The net income earned by each share of outstanding common stock. (p. 304).

Economic entity assumption Accounting assumption that economic events can be identified with a particular unit of accountability. (p. 295).

Elements of financial statements Definitions of basic terms used in accounting. (p. 294).

Full disclosure principle Accounting principle that circumstances and events that make a difference to financial statement users should be disclosed. (p. 298).

Generally accepted accounting principles (GAAP) A set of rules and practices, having substantial authoritative support, that are recognized as a general guide for financial reporting purposes. (p. 291).

Going concern assumption The assumption that the enterprise will continue in operation long enough to carry out its existing objectives and commitments. (p. 295).

International Accounting Standards Board (IASB) An accounting organization whose purpose is to formulate and publish international accounting standards and to promote their acceptance worldwide. (p. 310).

Matching principle Accounting principle that expenses should be matched with revenues in the period when efforts are expended to generate revenues. (p. 297).

Materiality The constraint of determining if an item is important enough to likely influence the decision of a reasonably prudent investor or creditor. (p. 300).

Monetary unit assumption Accounting assumption that only transaction data capable of being expressed in monetary terms should be included in accounting records. (p. 295).

Profit margin percentage Profitability measure that indicates the percentage of each dollar of sales that results in net income; calculated as net income divided by net sales. Also called *rate of return on sales.* (p. 307).

Relevance The quality of information that indicates the information makes a difference in a decision. (p. 292).

Reliability The quality of information that gives assurance that it is free of error and bias. (p. 293).

Return on assets An overall measure of a company's profitability; calculated as net income divided by total assets. (p. 307).

Return on common stockholders' equity Profitability measure that shows the rate of net income earned for each dollar of owners' investment; calculated as net income divided by common stockholders' equity. (p. 308).

Revenue recognition principle Accounting principle that revenue should be recognized in the accounting period in which it is earned (generally at the point of sale). (p. 296).

Time period assumption Accounting assumption that the economic life of a business can be divided into artificial time periods. (p. 295).

Working capital The excess of current assets over current liabilities. (p. 306).

SELF-STUDY QUESTIONS

Self-Study/Self-Test www.wiley.com/college/weygandt

Answers are at the end of the chapter.

(SO 1) **1.** Generally accepted accounting principles are:
- **a.** a set of standards and rules that are recognized as a general guide for financial reporting.
- **b.** usually established by the Internal Revenue Service.
- **c.** the guidelines used to resolve ethical dilemmas.
- **d.** fundamental truths that can be derived from the laws of nature.

(SO 2) **2.** Which of the following is *not* an objective of financial reporting?
- **a.** Provide information that is useful in investment and credit decisions.
- **b.** Provide information about economic resources, claims to those resources, and changes in them.
- **c.** Provide information that is useful in assessing future cash flows.
- **d.** Provide information on the liquidation value of a business.

3. The primary criterion by which accounting information can be judged is: (SO 3)
- **a.** consistency.
- **b.** predictive value.
- **c.** decision-usefulness.
- **d.** comparability.

4. Verifiable is an ingredient of: (SO 3)

	Reliability	Relevance
a.	Yes	Yes
b.	No	No
c.	Yes	No
d.	No	Yes

5. Valuing assets at their liquidation value rather than their cost is *inconsistent* with the: (SO 4, 5, 6)
- **a.** time period assumption.
- **b.** matching principle.
- **c.** going concern assumption.
- **d.** materiality constraint.

(SO 4, 5, 6) **6.** The accounting constraint that says that when in doubt the accountant should choose the method that will be least likely to overstate assets and income is called:
a. matching principle.
b. materiality.
c. conservatism.
d. monetary unit assumption.

(SO 7) **7.** Erika Pechacek Inc. has current assets of $90,000 and current liabilities of $30,000. Its current ratio and working capital are:
a. .33:1; $60,000.
b. 3:1; $60,000.
c. .33:1; $90,000.
d. 3:1; $90,000.

(SO 7) **8.** Suster Company has a retained earnings balance of $170,000 at the beginning of the period. At the end of the period, the retained earnings balance was $222,000. Assuming a dividend of $25,000 was declared and paid during the period, the net income for the period was:
a. $27,000.
b. $52,000.
c. $77,000.
d. $197,000.

9. The basic formula for computing earnings per share is net income divided by: (SO 7)
a. common shares authorized.
b. common shares issued.
c. common shares outstanding.
d. common stock purchased.

10. Phish Corp. has total liabilities of $1,200,000, total stockholders' equity of $1,800,000, current assets of $800,000, and current liabilities of $400,000. Phish's debt to total assets ratio is: (SO 7)
a. 50%. **c.** 33.3%.
b. 40%. **d.** 26.6%.

THE NAVIGATOR

QUESTIONS

1. (a) What are generally accepted accounting principles (GAAP)? (b) What bodies provide authoritative support for GAAP?

2. What elements comprise the FASB's conceptual framework?

3. (a) What are the objectives of financial reporting? (b) Identify the qualitative characteristics of accounting information.

4. Kirk Douglas, the president of Spartan Company, is pleased. Spartan substantially increased its net income in 2006 while keeping the number of **units** in its inventory relatively the same. Toni Curtis, chief accountant, cautions Douglas, however. Curtis says that since Spartan changed its method of inventory **valuation**, there is a consistency problem and it would be difficult to determine if Spartan is better off. Is Curtis correct? Why?

5. What is the distinction between comparability and consistency?

6. Why is it necessary for accountants to assume that an economic entity will remain a going concern?

7. When should revenue be recognized? Why has the date of sale been chosen as the point at which to recognize the revenue resulting from the entire producing and selling process?

8. Distinguish between expired costs and unexpired costs.

9. (a) Where does the accountant disclose information about an entity's financial position, operations, and cash flows? (b) The full disclosure principle recognizes that the nature and amount of information included in financial reports reflects a series of judgmental trade-offs. What are the objectives of these trade-offs?

10. Betsy McCall is the president of Brew News. She has no accounting background. McCall cannot understand why current cost is not used as the basis for accounting measurement and reporting. Explain what basis is used and why.

11. Describe the two constraints inherent in the presentation of accounting information.

12. In February 2006, Matt Osterhaus invested an additional $5,000 in his business, Osterhaus Pharmacy, which is organized as a corporation. Osterhaus' accountant, Kate Mulgrew, recorded this receipt as an increase in cash and revenues. Is this treatment appropriate? Why or why not?

13. Identify three financial relationships that are useful in analyzing the profitability of a company. Why might we want more than one measure of profitability?

14. Natasha Company has current assets of $60,000 and current liabilities of $20,000. What is its (a) working capital and (b) current ratio?

15. If current assets are less than current liabilities, will working capital be positive or negative? Will the current ratio be greater than or less than 1:1?

16. Bozeman Inc.'s debt to total asset ratio stands at 62 percent. If you were a banker, would you be comfortable about extending additional credit to Bozeman? Why or why not?

17. Your roommate believes that international accounting standards are uniform throughout the world. Is your roommate correct? Explain.

18. What organization establishes international accounting standards?

BRIEF EXERCISES

BE7-1 Indicate whether each of the following statements is true or false.

Identify generally accepted accounting principles.
(SO 1)

(a) ____ "*Generally accepted*" means that these principles must have "substantial authoritative support."
(b) ____ Substantial authoritative support for GAAP usually comes from two standard-setting bodies: the FASB and the IRS.
(c) ____ GAAP is a set of rules and practices established by the accounting profession to serve as a general guide for financial reporting purposes.

BE7-2 Indicate which of the following items is(are) included in the FASB's conceptual framework. (Use "Yes" or "No" to answer this question.)

Identify items included in conceptual framework.
(SO 1)

(a) ____ Analysis of financial statement ratios.
(b) ____ Objectives of financial reporting.
(c) ____ Qualitative characteristics of accounting information.

BE7-3 According to the FASB's conceptual framework, which of the following are objectives of financial reporting? (Use "Yes" or "No" to answer this question.)

Identify objectives of financial reporting.
(SO 2)

(a) ____ Provide information that is helpful in assessing past cash flows and stock prices.
(b) ____ Provide information that is useful to those making investment and credit decisions.
(c) ____ Provide information that identifies the economic resources (assets), the claims to those resources (liabilities), and the changes in those resources and claims.

BE7-4 Presented below is a chart of the qualitative characteristics of accounting information. Fill in the blanks from (a) to (e).

Identify qualitative characteristics.
(SO 3)

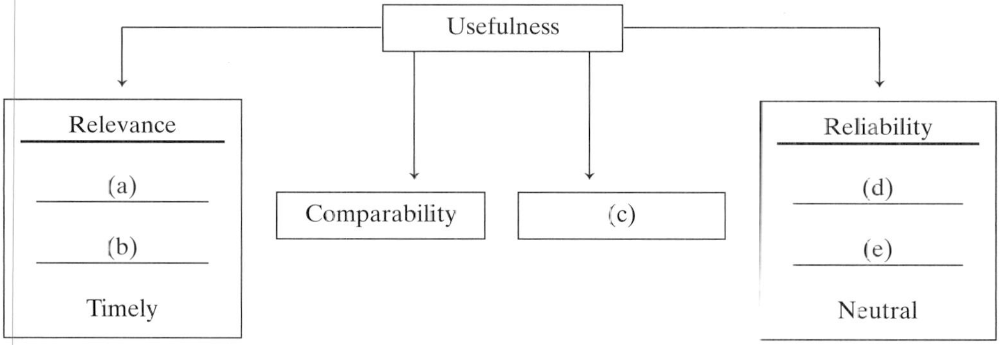

BE7-5 Given the *qualitative characteristics* of accounting established by the FASB's conceptual framework, complete each of the following statements:

Identify qualitative characteristics.
(SO 3)

(a) For information to be ____, it should have predictive or feedback value, and it must be presented on a timely basis.
(b) ____ is the quality of information that gives assurance that it is free of error and bias; it can be depended on.
(c) ____ means using the same accounting principles and methods from year to year within a company.

BE7-6 Presented below is a set of qualitative characteristics of accounting information.

Identify qualitative characteristics.
(SO 3)

1. Predictive value
2. Neutral
3. Verifiable
4. Timely

Match these qualitative characteristics to the following statements, using numbers 1 through 4.

(a) ____ Accounting information should help users make predictions about the outcome of past, present, and future events.
(b) ____ Accounting information cannot be selected, prepared, or presented to favor one set of interested users over another.
(c) ____ Accounting information must be proved to be free of error and bias.
(d) ____ Accounting information must be available to decision makers before it loses its capacity to influence their decisions.

Identify operating guidelines.
(SO 4, 5, 6)

BE7-7 Presented below are four concepts discussed in this chapter.

1. Time period assumption
2. Cost principle
3. Full disclosure principle
4. Conservatism

Match these concepts to the following accounting practices. Each number can be used only once.

(a) ____ Recording inventory at its purchase price.
(b) ____ Using notes and supplementary schedules in the financial statements.
(c) ____ Preparing financial statements on an annual basis.
(d) ____ Using the lower of cost or market method for inventory valuation.

Identify the constraints that have been violated.
(SO 6)

BE7-8 Fast Forward Company uses the following accounting practices.

(a) Inventory is reported at cost when market value is lower.
(b) The alternative accounting methods are selected in order to avoid reporting a higher net income.
(c) Small tools are recorded as plant assets and depreciated.
(d) The income statement shows paper clips expense of $10.

Indicate the accounting constraint, if any, that has been violated by each practice.

Perform balance sheet analysis.
(SO 7)

BE7-9 The following data are taken from the balance sheet of **Nike, Inc.** The data are arranged in alphabetical order (in millions).

Accounts payable	$ 584,600	Other current liabilities	$ 608,500
Accounts receivable	1,674,400	Retained earnings	3,043,400
Cash	110,600	Income taxes payable	25,900

Compute Nike's (a) current ratio and (b) working capital.

Compute income statement relationships.
(SO 7)

BE7-10 The following information, presented in alphabetical order, is taken from the financial statements of **Palpatine Inc.**

Gross profit	$907,000	Other revenues and gains	$ 36,000
Income before income taxes	276,000	Net income	179,400
Income from operations	240,000	Net sales	1,652,000

Compute Palpatine's (a) operating expenses and (b) income tax expense for the period.

Compute earnings per share.
(SO 7)

BE7-11 Additional information for **Palpatine Inc.** (BE7-10) is as follows.

Common shares outstanding for the entire year	46,000	Dividends on common stock paid during the year	$34,500

Given the information above and in BE7-10, compute Palpatine's earnings per share.

EXERCISES

Identify the assumption, principle, or constraint that has been violated.
(SO 4, 5, 6)

E7-1 A number of accounting reporting situations are described below.

1. Church Company recognizes revenue at the end of the production cycle, but before sale. The price of the product, as well as the amount that can be sold, is not certain.
2. In preparing its financial statements, Leask Company omitted information concerning its method of accounting for inventories.
3. Zareena Corp. charges the entire premium on a 2-year insurance policy to the first year.
4. Whitney Hospital Supply Corporation reports only current assets and current liabilities on its balance sheet. Property, plant, and equipment and bonds payable are reported as current assets and current liabilities, respectively. Liquidation of the company is unlikely.
5. Dean Inc. is carrying inventory at its current market value of $100,000. Inventory had an original cost of $110,000.
6. Hot Shot Company is in its fifth year of operation and has yet to issue financial statements. (Do not use full disclosure principle.)

7. Silas Rupe Co. has inventory on hand that cost $400,000. Rupe Co. reports inventory on its balance sheet at its current market value of $425,000.
8. Charlotte Webb, president of the Always Music Company, bought a computer for her personal use. She paid for the computer by using company funds and debited the "Computers" account.

Instructions

For each of the above, list the assumption, principle, or constraint that has been violated, if any. List only one term for each case.

Identify the assumption, principle, or constraint that has been violated and prepare correct entries.

(SO 4, 5, 6)

E7-2 Presented below are some business transactions that occurred during 2006 for Vicki Prowitz Company.

(a) Merchandise inventory with a cost of $208,000 is reported at its market value of $260,000. The following entry was made.

Merchandise Inventory	52,000	
Gain		52,000

(b) Equipment worth $62,000 was acquired at a cost of $41,000 from a company that had water damage in a flood. The following entry was made.

Equipment	62,000	
Cash		41,000
Gain		21,000

(c) The president of Vicki Prowitz Company, Mark Nabke, purchased a truck for personal use and charged it to his expense account. The following entry was made.

Travel Expense	18,000	
Cash		18,000

(d) An electric pencil sharpener costing $50 is being depreciated over 5 years. The following entry was made.

Depreciation Expense—Pencil Sharpener	10	
Accumulated Depreciation—Pencil Sharpener		10

Instructions

In each of the situations above, identify the assumption, principle, or constraint that has been violated, if any. Discuss the appropriateness of the journal entries, and give the correct journal entry, if necessary.

Identify accounting assumptions, principles, and constraints.

(SO 4, 5, 6)

E7-3 Presented below are the assumptions, principles, and constraints discussed in this chapter.

1. Economic entity assumption
2. Going concern assumption
3. Monetary unit assumption
4. Time period assumption
5. Cost principle
6. Matching principle
7. Full disclosure principle
8. Revenue recognition principle
9. Materiality
10. Conservatism

Instructions

Identify by number the accounting assumption, principle, or constraint that describes each situation below. Do not use a number more than once.

(a) Is the rationale for why plant assets are not reported at liquidation value. (Do not use historical cost principle.)
(b) Indicates that personal and business record-keeping should be separately maintained.
(c) Ensures that all relevant financial information is reported.
(d) Assumes that the dollar is the "measuring stick" used to report on financial performance.
(e) Requires that the operational guidelines be followed for all significant items.
(f) Separates financial information into time periods for reporting purpose.
(g) Requires recognition of expenses in the same period as related revenues.
(h) Indicates that market value changes subsequent to purchase are not recorded in the accounts.

Determine the amount of revenue to be recognized.
(SO 5)

E7-4 Consider the following transactions of Parolini Company for 2006.

1. Sold a 6-month insurance policy to Orosco Corporation for $9,000 on March 1.
2. Leased office space to Easley Supplies for a 1-year period beginning September 1. The rent of $30,000 was paid in advance.
3. A sales order for merchandise costing $9,000 that had a sales price of $14,000 was received on December 28 from Guiterrez Company. The goods were shipped FOB shipping point on December 31 and Guiterrez received them on January 3, 2007.
4. Merchandise inventory on hand at year-end amounted to $160,000. Parolini expects to sell the inventory in 2007 for $180,000.

Instructions

For each item above, indicate the amount of revenue Parolini should recognize in calendar year 2006. Explain.

Compute earnings per share.
(SO 7)

E7-5 The ledger of Jean Sartre Corporation at December 31, 2006, contains the following summary information.

Administrative expenses	$116,000	Other expenses and losses	$34,700
Cost of goods sold	409,200	Other revenues and gains	17,500
Net sales	696,000	Selling expenses	98,600

The income tax rate for all items is 30%. Sartre Corp. had 10,000 shares of common stock outstanding throughout the year, and the company paid $15,000 in dividends during 2006.

Instructions

Compute earnings per share for 2006.

Prepare an income statement and calculate related information.
(SO 7)

E7-6 Presented below, in alphabetical order, is information related to Wilkinson Corporation for the year 2006.

Cost of goods sold	$1,499,900
Dividends on common stock	140,000
Gain on the sale of equipment	80,000
Income tax expense	150,000
Interest expense	90,000
Interest revenue	300,000
Net sales	2,156,900
Selling and administrative expenses	340,750

Wilkinson had 35,500 shares outstanding for the entire year.

Instructions

(a) Prepare in good form a single-step income statement for Wilkinson Corporation for 2006.
(b) Assuming a multiple-step income statement was prepared instead, compute:
  (1) Gross profit.
  (2) Income from operations.
  (3) Net income.
(c) Calculate Wilkinson Corporation's profit margin percentage (return on sales).

Calculate and analyze profitability and solvency relationships.
(SO 7)

E7-7 Net sales, net income, total assets, and total common stockholders' equity information for the year 2003 is available for the following three companies.

Company	Net Sales (in millions)	Net Income (in millions)	Total Assets (in millions)	Total Common Equity (in millions)
Intel Corporation	$30,141	$5,641	$47,143	$37,846
Johnson & Johnson	$41,862	$7,197	$48,263	$26,869
Motorola, Inc.	$27,058	$ 893	$32,098	$12,689

Instructions

(a) Compute the following relationships for each company.
  (1) Debt to total assets ratio.
  (2) Return on sales (profit margin percentage).

(3) Return on assets.
(4) Return on common stockholders' equity.

(b) What reasons might there be for the differing relationships among these three companies? In your answer, consider the different kinds of industries these companies represent. Do any similarities or differences in the type of business help account for the differences you see?

Calculate and analyze profitability and solvency relationships.
(SO 7)

E7-8 Net sales, net income, total assets, and total common stockholders' equity information for the year 2003 is available for the following three companies.

Company	Net Sales (in millions)	Net Income (in millions)	Total Assets (in millions)	Total Common Equity (in millions)
Southern Company	$11,251	$1,474	$35,045	$ 9,648
Toys "R" Us, Inc.	$11,305	$ 229	$10,218	$ 4,222
Intel Corp.	$30,141	$5,641	$47,143	$37,846

Instructions

(a) Compute the following relationships for each company.
(1) Debt to total assets ratio.
(2) Return on sales (profit margin percentage).
(3) Return on assets.
(4) Return on common stockholders' equity.

(b) What reasons might there be for the differing relationships among these three companies? In your answer, consider the different kinds of industries these companies represent. Do any similarities or differences in the type of business help account for the differences you see?

Use balance sheet relationships to prepare a balance sheet.
(SO 7)

E7-9 As of December 31, 2006, Aruba Corporation has a current ratio of 2.6:1 and working capital of $800,000. Aruba's total debt is 60% of its total assets. All of Aruba's long-term assets, which are exactly half of total assets, are properly categorized as property, plant, and equipment.

Instructions

Prepare a summary classified balance sheet for Aruba Corporation at year-end 2006. (*Hint:* First calculate Aruba's current asset and current liability amounts.)

Restate foreign financial statements.
(SO 8)

E7-10 Presented below is partial balance sheet information related to **Batten Ltd.**, a United Kingdom company. All financial information has been translated from pounds to dollars.

BATTEN LTD.
Balance Sheet (partial)
December 31, 2003
(in thousands)

Fixed assets		
Tangible assets		$ 900,000
Current assets		
Stocks (inventory)	$300,000	
Debtors	121,000	
Investments	53,000	
Cash	62,000	
	536,000	
Creditors		
Amount falling due within one year	100,000	
Net current assets		436,000
Total assets less current liabilities		1,336,000
Creditors		
Amounts falling due after one year		240,000
Total net assets		$1,096,000

Instructions

(a) Restate the asset side of the balance sheet in accordance with generally accepted accounting principles in the United States.

(b) What is the amount of total stockholders' equity?

PROBLEMS: SET A

Analyze transactions to identify accounting principle or assumption violated, and prepare correct entries.

(SO 4, 5)

P7-1A Scott and Quick are accountants for Millenium Computers. They disagree over the following transactions that occurred during the calendar year 2006.

1. Scott suggests that equipment should be reported on the balance sheet at its liquidation value, which is $15,000 less than its cost.
2. Millenium bought a custom-made piece of equipment for $36,000. This equipment has a useful life of 6 years. Millenium depreciates equipment using the straight-line method. "Since the equipment is custom-made, it will have no resale value. Therefore, it shouldn't be depreciated but instead should be expensed immediately," argues Scott. "Besides, it provides for lower net income."
3. Depreciation for the year was $18,000. Since net income is expected to be lower this year, Scott suggests deferring depreciation to a year when there is more net income.
4. Land costing $60,000 was appraised at $90,000. Scott suggests the following journal entry.

Land	30,000	
Gain on Appreciation of Land		30,000

5. Millenium purchased equipment for $35,000 at a going-out-of-business sale. The equipment was worth $45,000. Scott believes that the following entry should be made.

Equipment	45,000	
Cash		35,000
Gain on Purchase of Equipment		10,000

Quick disagrees with Scott on each of the above situations.

Instructions

For each transaction, indicate why Quick disagrees. Identify the accounting principle or assumption that Scott would be violating if his suggestions were used. Prepare the correct journal entry for each transaction, if any.

Determine the appropriateness of journal entries in terms of generally accepted accounting principles or assumptions.

(SO 4, 5)

P7-2A Presented below are a number of business transactions that occurred during the current year for Yerkes, Inc.

1. Because the general level of prices increased during the current year, Yerkes, Inc. determined that there was a $10,000 understatement of depreciation expense on its equipment and decided to record it in its accounts. The following entry was made.

Depreciation Expense	10,000	
Accumulated Depreciation		10,000

2. Because of a "flood sale," equipment obviously worth $250,000 was acquired at a cost of $200,000. The following entry was made.

Equipment	250,000	
Cash		200,000
Gain on Purchase of Equipment		50,000

3. The president of Yerkes, Inc. used his expense account to purchase a new Saab 9000 solely for personal use. The following entry was made.

Miscellaneous Expense	34,000	
Cash		34,000

4. An order for $30,000 has been received from a customer for products on hand. This order is to be shipped on January 9 next year. The following entry was made.

Accounts Receivable	30,000	
Sales		30,000

5. Materials were purchased on March 31 for $65,000. This amount was entered in the Inventory account. On December 31, the materials would have cost $80,000, so the following entry was made.

Inventory	15,000	
Gain on Inventories		15,000

Instructions

In each situation, discuss the appropriateness of the journal entries in terms of generally accepted accounting principles.

Identify accounting assumptions, principles, and constraints.

(SO 4, 5, 6)

P7-3A Presented below are the assumptions, principles, and constraints used in this chapter.

1. Economic entity assumption	**6.** Revenue recognition principle
2. Going concern assumption	**7.** Matching principle
3. Monetary unit assumption	**8.** Cost principle
4. Time period assumption	**9.** Materiality
5. Full disclosure principle	**10.** Conservatism

Identify by number the accounting assumption, principle, or constraint that matches each description below. Do not use a number more than once.

(a) Assets are not stated at their liquidation value. (Do not use cost principle.)
(b) The death of the president is not recorded in the accounts.
(c) Pencil sharpeners are expensed when purchased.
(d) Depreciation is recorded in the accounts over the life of an asset. (Do not use the going concern assumption.)
(e) Each entity is kept as a unit distinct from its owner or owners.
(f) Reporting must be done at defined intervals.
(g) Revenue is recorded at the point of sale.
(h) When in doubt, it is better to understate rather than overstate net income.
(i) All important information related to inventories is presented in the footnotes or in the financial statements.

Prepare a classified balance sheet and analyze financial position.

(SO 7)

P7-4A The adjusted trial balance of Quad Cities Tours Inc. as of October 31, 2006 (its year-end) contains the following information.

Accounts payable	$170,000
Accounts receivable	15,000
Accumulated depreciation—Buildings	144,000
Accumulated depreciation—Equipment	715,000
Bonds payable	600,000
Buildings—Offices and cabins	660,000
Cash	36,000
Common stock	300,000
Equipment	840,000
Income taxes payable	56,250
Interest payable	30,000
Inventories	485,000
Investment in Iowa Trading Post, Inc. (trading—short-term)	140,000
Land	653,000
Mortgage payable (on fishing cabins—long-term)	247,750
Notes payable (short-term)	164,000
Prepaid advertising	17,000
Prepaid insurance	9,000
Retained earnings (October 31, 2006)	440,000
Supplies	12,000

(a) Total current liabilities $420,250

Instructions

(a) Prepare in good form a classified balance sheet for Quad Cities Tours Inc.
(b) Calculate the following balance sheet relationships: current ratio, debt to total assets ratio, and working capital.
(c) Assume that Quad Cities has come to you, as the senior loan officer of Big Woods Credit Union, seeking a $500,000 loan to help defray the costs of replacing much of its rental camping gear and canoes. Would you be willing to approve the loan? Is there any additional information you would like to have before making your decision?

Prepare a multiple-step income statement and analyze profitability.
(SO 7)

P7-5A The ledgers of Mid City Galleries Inc. contain the following balances as of December 31, 2006.

Advertising expense	$ 123,000
Commissions expense on art sales	1,200,000
Depreciation expense (administrative)	98,000
Dividend revenue	50,000
Insurance expense	600,000
Interest expense	98,000
Inventory, January 1	1,650,000
Inventory, December 31	1,424,000
Loss on the sale of office equipment	21,300
Miscellaneous administrative expenses	53,200
Miscellaneous selling expenses	39,000
Net purchases	3,200,000
Net sales	9,275,000
Rent expense	808,000
Freight-in	232,000
Freight-out	82,500
Utilities expense	117,000
Wages and salaries	1,264,000

Income taxes are calculated at 30 percent of income. The galleries had 90,000 shares of common stock outstanding for the entire year. Total assets amounted to $7,509,000, and common stockholder's equity was $3,975,400.

(a) Net income $814,100

Instructions

(a) Prepare in good form a multiple-step income statement for Mid City Galleries.
(b) Calculate three measures of profitability and one ratio of solvency.
(c) Assume that you are considering supplying Mid City Galleries with a line of miniature replicas of fine arts sculptures for sale in its gift shops. Is this a company for which you would like to be a supplier? What additional information would you like to have before deciding to become a major supplier for Mid City Galleries?

PROBLEMS: SET B

Analyze transactions to identify accounting principle or assumption violated, and prepare correct entries.
(SO 4, 5)

P7-1B Mary Kate and Ashley are accountants for Olsen Printers. They disagree over the following transactions that occurred during the year.

1. Land costing $41,000 was appraised at $49,000. Mary Kate suggests the following journal entry.

Land	8,000	
Gain on Appreciation of Land		8,000

2. Olsen bought equipment for $60,000, including installation costs. The equipment has a useful life of 5 years. Olsen depreciates equipment using the straight-line method. "Since the equipment as installed into our system cannot be removed without considerable damage, it

will have no resale value. Therefore, it should not be depreciated, but instead should be expensed immediately," argues Mary Kate. "Besides, it lowers net income."

3. Depreciation for the year was $26,000. Since net income is expected to be lower this year, Mary Kate suggests deferring depreciation to a year when there is more net income.
4. Olsen purchased equipment at a fire sale for $18,000. The equipment was worth $26,000. Mary Kate believes that the following entry should be made.

Equipment	26,000	
Cash		18,000
Gain on Purchase of Equipment		8,000

5. Mary Kate suggests that Olsen should carry equipment on the balance sheet at its liquidation value, which is $20,000 less than its cost.
6. Olsen rented office space for 1 year starting October 1, 2006. The total amount of $24,000 was paid in advance. Mary Kate believes that the following entry should be made on October 1.

Rent Expense	24,000	
Cash		24,000

Ashley disagrees with Mary Kate on each of the situations above.

Instructions

For each transaction, indicate why Ashley disagrees. Identify the accounting principle or assumption that Mary Kate would be violating if her suggestions were used. Prepare the correct journal entry for each transaction, if any.

Determine the appropriateness of journal entries in terms of generally accepted accounting principles or assumptions.

(SO 4, 5)

P7-2B Presented below are a number of business transactions that occurred during the current year for Renteria, Inc.

1. Because the general level of prices increased during the current year, Renteria, Inc. determined that there was a $40,000 understatement of depreciation expense on its equipment and decided to record it in its accounts. The following entry was made.

Depreciation Expense	40,000	
Accumulated Depreciation		40,000

2. Because of a "flood sale," equipment obviously worth $300,000 was acquired at a cost of $225,000. The following entry was made.

Equipment	300,000	
Cash		225,000
Gain on Purchase of Equipment		75,000

3. An order for $60,000 has been received from a customer for products on hand. This order is to be shipped on January 9 next year. The following entry was made.

Accounts Receivable	60,000	
Sales		60,000

4. Land was purchased on April 30 for $200,000. This amount was entered in the Land account. On December 31, the land would have cost $240,000, so the following entry was made.

Land	40,000	
Gain on Land		40,000

5. The president of Renteria, Inc. used his expense account to purchase a pre-owned Mercedes-Benz E420 solely for personal use. The following entry was made.

Miscellaneous Expense	54,000	
Cash		54,000

Instructions

In each situation, discuss the appropriateness of the journal entries in terms of generally accepted accounting principles.

Identify accounting assumptions, principles, and constraints.
(SO 4, 5, 6)

P7-3B Presented below are the assumptions, principles, and constraints used in this chapter.

1. Economic entity assumption	**6.** Revenue recognition principle
2. Going concern assumption	**7.** Matching principle
3. Monetary unit assumption	**8.** Cost principle
4. Time period assumption	**9.** Materiality
5. Full disclosure principle	**10.** Conservatism

Identify by number the accounting assumption, principle, or constraint that matches each description below. Do not use a number more than once.

(a) Repair tools are expensed when purchased. (Do not use conservatism.)
(b) Allocates expenses to revenues in proper period.
(c) Assumes that the dollar is the measuring stick used to report financial information.
(d) Separates financial information into time periods for reporting purposes.
(e) Market value changes subsequent to purchase are not recorded in the accounts. (Do not use revenue recognition principle.)
(f) Indicates that personal and business record keeping should be separately maintained.
(g) Ensures that all relevant financial information is reported.
(h) Lower of cost or market is used to value inventories.

Prepare a classified balance sheet and analyze financial position.
(SO 7)

P7-4B The adjusted trial balance of Gabelli Equipment, Inc., as of June 30, 2006 (its year-end) contains the following information.

Accounts payable	$ 486,000
Accounts receivable	420,000
Accumulated depreciation—Buildings	180,000
Accumulated depreciation—Equipment	577,500
Bonds payable	1,750,000
Buildings—Manufacturing plant and offices	680,000
Cash	87,000
Common stock	500,000
Equipment	1,650,000
Income taxes payable	47,000
Interest payable	70,000
Interest receivable	21,000
Inventories	845,000
Investment in Spartan, Inc. bonds (held-to-maturity—long-term)	600,000
Land	212,000
Mortgage payable (on manufacturing plant—long-term)	310,000
Notes payable (short-term)	210,000
Prepaid advertising	9,500
Prepaid insurance	21,000
Retained earnings (June 30, 2006)	447,000
Supplies	32,000

Instructions

(a) Total current assets $1,435,500

(a) Prepare in good form a classified balance sheet for Gabelli Equipment.
(b) Calculate the following balance sheet relationships: current ratio, debt to total assets ratio, and working capital.
(c) Assume that Gabelli has come to you, as vice president of Illinois National Bank, seeking a $450,000 loan to help defray the costs of upgrading some of its machinery. Would you be willing to approve the loan? Is there any additional information you would like to have before making your decision?

Prepare a multiple-step income statement and analyze profitability.
(SO 7)

P7-5B The ledgers of Campo Leathers Inc. contain the following balances as of January 31, 2006 (its year-end).

Advertising expense	$ 130,000
Depreciation expense (administrative)	53,000
Freight-in	27,900
Freight-out	6,800
Gain on the sale of equipment	8,500
Insurance expense	57,000
Interest expense	13,600
Interest revenue	7,000
Inventory, February 1, 2005	296,400
Inventory, January 31, 2006	303,400
Managerial salaries	129,800
Miscellaneous administrative expenses	22,200
Miscellaneous selling expenses	39,000
Net purchases	1,697,000
Net sales	2,660,000
Rent expense	81,000
Sales staff wages	155,000
Utilities expense	30,300

Income taxes are calculated at 30 percent of income. Campo had 84,000 shares of common stock outstanding for the entire year. Total assets amounted to $5,460,000, and common stockholders' equity was $1,966,200 at year end.

Instructions

(a) Prepare in good form a multiple-step income statement for Campo Leathers Inc.

(a) Net income $157,930

(b) Calculate three measures of profitability and one ratio of solvency.

(c) Assume that you are considering supplying Campo Leathers with a line of wallets, key holders, and other small leather goods for sale in its two stores. Is this a company for which you would like to be a supplier? What additional information would you like to have before deciding to become a supplier for Campo Leathers?

COMPREHENSIVE PROBLEM: CHAPTERS 2 TO 7

Presented below is financial information related to Nu Wood Corporation for the year 2006. Unless otherwise stated, all balances are ending balances.

Accounts payable	$ 874,200
Accounts receivable	1,000,800
Accumulated depreciation—Equipment	1,560,000
Administrative expenses	420,000
Bonds payable	3,300,000
Cash	165,000
Common stock	2,200,000
Cost of goods sold	2,285,000
Dividends	250,000
Equipment	5,894,000
Gain on the sale of land	87,000
Interest expense	108,000
Interest revenue	99,000
Inventories	984,000
Marketable securities (short-term)	1,175,000
Net sales	3,590,000
Notes payable (short-term)	1,136,500
Other long-term debt	401,300
Patents and other intangibles	1,150,100
Prepaid expenses	356,100
Retained earnings (January 1, 2006)	877,200
Selling expenses	361,000
Taxes payable	234,500

Nu Wood Corporation had 80,000 shares of common stock outstanding for the entire year. Its effective income tax rate for state and federal income taxes combined is 35 percent.

Instructions

(a) Net income $391,300

(c) Retained earnings, Dec. 31 $1,018,500

(a) Prepare a multiple-step income statement.
(b) Prepare a single-step income statement.
(c) Prepare a retained earnings statement.
(d) Prepare a classified balance sheet.
(e) Compute the following balance sheet relationships:
  (1) current ratio.
  (2) the amount of working capital.
  (3) debt to total assets ratio.
  What insights do these relationships provide to the reader of the financial statements?
(f) Compute three measures of profitability. What insights do these relationships provide to the reader of the financial statements?
(g) Compare the results for Nu Wood Corporation, calculated here, and the results for Notting Hill Corporation in Demonstration Problem 2. As an investor, which corporation seems more attractive to you? Why?

BROADENING YOUR PERSPECTIVE

Financial Reporting and Analysis

■ FINANCIAL REPORTING PROBLEM

BYP7-1 Marcey Leuck successfully completed her first accounting course during the spring semester. She is now working as a management trainee for Midwest Bank, N.A. during the summer. One of her fellow management trainees, Reed LaDue, is taking the same accounting course this summer and has been having a "lot of trouble." On the second exam, for example, Reed became confused about inventory valuation methods. He completely missed all the points on a problem involving LIFO and FIFO.

Reed's instructor recently indicated that the third exam will probably have a number of essay questions dealing with accounting principles issues. Reed is quite concerned about the third exam for two reasons. First, he has never taken an accounting exam in which essay answers were required. Second, Reed feels he must do well on this exam to get an acceptable grade in the course.

Reed has asked Marcey to help him prepare for the next exam. She agrees, and suggests that Reed develop a set of possible questions on the accounting principles material that they might discuss.

Instructions

Answer the following questions that were developed by Reed.

(a) What is a conceptual framework?
(b) Why is there a need for a conceptual framework?
(c) What are the objectives of financial reporting?
(d) If you had to explain generally accepted accounting principles to a nonaccountant, what essential characteristics would you include in your explanation?
(e) What are the qualitative characteristics of accounting? Explain each one.
(f) Identify the basic assumptions used in accounting.
(g) What are two major constraints involved in financial reporting? Explain both of them.

■ COMPARATIVE ANALYSIS PROBLEM: PepsiCo vs. Coca-Cola

BYP7-2 **PepsiCo**'s financial statements are presented in Appendix A. **Coca-Cola**'s financial statements are presented in Appendix B.

Instructions

(a) Based on the information contained in these financial statements, compute the following 2003 ratios for each company.

(1) Current ratio.
(2) Working capital.
(3) Profit margin percentage.
(4) Return on assets.
(5) Return on common stockholders' equity.
(6) Debt to total assets ratio.

(b) Compare and evaluate the liquidity, profitability, and solvency of the two companies.

■ RESEARCH CASE

BYP7-3 During the years 1978–85, the Financial Accounting Standards Board (FASB) issued six *Statements of Financial Accounting Concepts* (SFACs). From the library, obtain copies of SFAC No. 2 (*Qualitative Characteristics of Accounting Information*) and SFAC No. 3 (*Elements of Financial Statements of Business Enterprises*).

Instructions

Use these statements to answer the following questions.

(a) Your textbook indicates that "an item is material when it is likely to influence the decision of a reasonably prudent investor or creditor." SFAC No. 2 identifies a number of examples in which specific quantitative guidelines are provided to accountants and auditors. Identify two of these examples. Do you think that materiality guidelines should be quantified? Why or why not?

(b) SFAC No. 3 discusses the concept of "articulation" between financial statement elements. Briefly summarize the meaning of this term and how it relates to an entity's financial statements.

■ INTERPRETING FINANCIAL STATEMENTS

BYP7-4 **Weyerhaeuser Company** is one of the world's largest growers and producers of forest and lumber products, with assets of $14 billion and annual sales of over $12 billion. Weyerhaeuser employs over 38,000 workers and has as its most significant assets its many acres of prime timberland.

Presented below is a statement that appeared about Weyerhaeuser Company in a financial magazine.

> The land and timber holdings are now carried on the company's books at a mere $422 million. The value of the timber alone is variously estimated at $3 billion to $7 billion and is rising all the time. "The understatement of the company is pretty severe," conceded Charles W. Bingham, a senior vice-president. Adds Robert L. Schuyler, another senior vice-president: "We have a whole stream of profit nobody sees and there is no way to show it on our books."

Instructions

Answer the following questions.

(a) What does Schuyler mean when he says that "we have a whole stream of profit nobody sees and there is no way to show it on our books"?

(b) If the understatement of the company's assets is severe, why doesn't accounting report this information?

■ A GLOBAL FOCUS

BYP7-5 The results of **RJR Nabisco** and **Philip Morris Companies, Inc.** are frequently compared since the two are fierce international competitors. RJR Nabisco makes Winston, Camel, and Salem cigarettes, while Philip Morris makes Marlboro and L&M cigarettes. Both companies also have significant operations in other product lines—RJR Nabisco makes Oreo cookies, Ritz crackers, and Planters nuts, while Philip Morris makes Post cereals, Maxwell House coffee, and Miller beer. The following information is provided in order to compare the profitability of these two companies.

(all amounts in millions)	RJR Nabisco	Philip Morris
Net sales	$17,037	$74,391
Net income	(516)	5,372
Total assets	15,545	59,920
Common stockholders' equity	9,886	16,197

Instructions
Use the above information to answer the following.

(a) Compare the profitability of these two companies using each of the following measures. In each case describe what the ratio is intended to measure.
  (1) Profit margin percentage.
  (2) Return on assets.
  (3) Return on common stockholders' equity.

(b) Comment on any problems or challenges incurred by comparing the two companies in this fashion.

■ EXPLORING THE WEB

BYP7-6 The **Financial Accounting Standards Board (FASB)** is a private organization established to improve accounting standards and financial reporting. The FASB conducts extensive research before issuing a "Statement of Financial Accounting Standards," which represents an authoritative expression of generally accepted accounting principles.

Address: www.rutgers.edu/accounting, or go to www.wiley.com/college/weygandt

Steps

1. Choose **FASB**.
2. Choose **FASB Facts**.

Instructions
Answer the following questions.

(a) What is the mission of the FASB?
(b) How are topics added to the FASB technical agenda?
(c) What characteristics make the FASB's procedures an "open" decision-making process?

Critical Thinking

■ GROUP DECISION CASE

BYP7-7 Presented below are key figures and relationships from the financial statements of a prominent company in each of three different industries for two recent fiscal years.

	Manufacturing		Mining/Oil		Merchandising	
	2003	**2004**	**2003**	**2004**	**2003**	**2004**
From the balance sheets:						
Total assets (millions)	$11,079	$11,083	$33,884	$35,089	$8,524	$9,485
Current ratio	1.72	1.73	1.14	1.12	1.51	1.56
Working capital (millions)	$2,390	$2,349	$1,037	$1,072	$1,236	$1,452
Debt to total assets ratio	0.45	0.43	0.59	0.58	0.72	0.72
Profitability:						
Total sales (millions)	$13,021	$13,340	$31,916	$41,540	$14,739	$16,115
Profit margin percentage	10.0%	8.7%	0.8%	5.2%	2.8%	1.9%
Return on assets	11.8%	10.4%	0.7%	6.1%	4.8%	3.2%
Return on common equity	21.4%	18.3%	1.8%	15.0%	20.1%	13.5%
Earnings per common share	$5.91	$5.26	$0.73	$6.10	$5.20	$3.72
From the annual reports:						
End-of-year stock price	$67.75	$72.63	$85.75	$95.25	$56.50	$62.00

Instructions
With the class divided into groups, answer the following.

(a) The benchmark for the current ratio is generally 2:1. None of these companies has a ratio that high, yet all three are well regarded firms. Why might a current ratio less than 2:1 *not* signal a problem?

(b) The merchandising company acquired a chain of well-known department stores just prior to 2003. Apart from such major acquisitions, what else might contribute to differing debt to total assets ratios? Consider industry-specific as well as company-specific considerations.

(c) For all three companies, the ratio of debt to total assets changed little from 2003 to 2004, yet for two of the three companies return on common stockholders' equity decreased. What might cause this pattern?

(d) The profitability relationships and earnings per share for both the manufacturing and the merchandising companies decreased from 2003 to 2004, yet the price per share of stock for each company increased. Why might investors have been willing to pay more for these companies in 2004?

COMMUNICATION ACTIVITY

BYP7-8 If you go on to advanced accounting courses, you'll study the differences between accounting in the business world and university accounting. You'll find that there's one major similarity: both depend heavily on the matching principle.

At Long Beach City College, a two-year community college with 30,000 students, most of the revenues come from the state of California and the federal government. As a condition of receiving these grants, "we must match expenses against revenues in the right fiscal year," says the school's accounting manager.

For example, the college receives federal funding under the Job Training Partnership Act. "We receive funding from the federal government, which allows us to offer classes to students for job preparation. The government specifies the grant periods, for instance, from July 1 to June 30. We therefore have to ensure that all transactions for that project are completed within that fiscal year." Another project is the amnesty program, the federal government's legalization of foreign nationals. Expenses to offset the grant money are mostly teaching salaries and instructional materials.

By year-end, the goal is to break even. Excess funds, if any, have to be returned. But program managers do not want a deficit, either, because these projects are accountable to the college administration and any overspending will come from the college's general fund.

Instructions

Write a letter to your instructor covering the following points.

1. Why is the matching principle important in accounting for government grants?
2. Give some examples of grant or special programs to which the matching principle might be applied at your college or university.
3. What are some examples of costs that Long Beach Community College might properly charge to its grant or special programs?

ETHICS CASE

Accounting Matters!

BYP7-9 When the Financial Accounting Standards Board issues new standards, the required implementation date is usually 12 months or more from the date of issuance, with early implementation encouraged. Michael Peeples, accountant at Bruno Corporation, discusses with his financial vice president the need for early implementation of a recently issued standard that would result in a much fairer presentation of the company's financial condition and earnings. When the financial vice president determines that early implementation of the standard will adversely affect reported net income for the year, he strongly discourages Michael from implementing the standard until it is required.

Instructions

(a) Who are the stakeholders in this situation?

(b) What, if any, are the ethical considerations in this situation?

(c) What does Michael have to gain by advocating early implementation? Who might be affected by the decision against early implementation?

CONTINUING COOKIE CHRONICLE

Accounting Matters!

(Note: This is a continuation of the Cookie Chronicle from Chapters 1 through 6.)

BYP7-10 Natalie's biggest competitor is Trial Appliances. Trial Appliances sells a fine European mixer similar to the one that customers are able to buy from Cookie Creations. Natalie estimates that Trial Appliances sells twice as many mixers as she does. Trial Appliances also sells microwaves, dishwashers, washing machines, and refrigerators. Natalie believes that one of the major reasons Trial Appliances sells the number of mixers that it does is because it sells all of its appliances on an extended payment plan.

Natalie knows that Trial Appliances sells its mixers for $1,100. She also knows that under the extended payment plan approximately $275 (25%) is collected in the year the mixer is sold,

$550 (50%) is collected the year after the appliance is sold, and the remaining $275 (25%) is collected in the third year. Trial Appliances sells approximately 65 mixers a year and tries to keep a gross profit margin of approximately 50%.

Natalie comes to you to ask about the accounting for revenues when mixers are sold on an extended payment plan. She would really like to generate more sales revenues and cash flow. Based on her discussions with the sales manager at Trial Appliances, she believes that she could sell more mixers if she offered her customers the option of paying over an extended period of time.

Natalie asks you the following questions.

1. I currently sell 32 mixers a year at $1,025 apiece. My cost of goods sold averages $566 per mixer. What is my gross profit margin?
2. I've heard that sometimes revenue cannot be recorded until the cash is collected. What are the guidelines that determine when revenue should be recorded? How will these guidelines affect me if I start selling mixers on an extended payment plan?
3. What are some of the advantages and disadvantages of giving my customers the option of paying through an extended payment plan?

Instructions

(a) Answer Natalie's questions.

(b) Do you think Natalie should offer her customers the option of paying through an extended payment plan? Why or why not?

Accounting Matters!

Answers to Accounting Matters! Questions

p. 298

Q: What accounting principles are applicable to the Harold's Club progressive slot machines?

A: The revenue recognition and the matching principles are applicable.

Q: If Harold's fails to use an estimate for expenses, what effect will this have on financial statements in a period when no payouts occur?

A: In periods without a payout, revenues will be very high, expenses will be too low, and income will be overstated. In a subsequent period, when a payout occurs, expenses will be very high and net income very low.

p. 299

Q: Would instant access to financial information provide more relevant information?

A: Such access should be more relevant since it would be more timely.

Q: Do you think such an approach would do away with the need for annual reports?

A: No. To ensure compliance with GAAP and various regulatory agencies, it will still be necessary to have audited financial statements and regulatory filings. Reports based upon a consistent time period will be necessary to allow for comparison with prior years and with other companies.

p. 307

Q: If service companies have a profit margin much lower than manufacturers (a third as large), why would anyone invest in a service company over a manufacturer?

A: The profit margin is only a percentage, not an absolute amount. A service company may have a profit margin only a third that of a manufacturer but have a greater amount of net profit in total dollars and per-share amount.

p. 309

Q: What would be the advantage of similar accounting standards for all countries?

A: Similar accounting standards would make comparable the financial statements of companies from all countries.

Q: How can the financial and operating performance of international companies be compared?

A: Adjustments must be made to the reported financial data to make analysis and ratios comparable.

Answer to PepsiCo Review It Question 2, p. 295

PEPSI

The Report of Independent Auditors indicates that **PepsiCo**'s financial statements (balance sheet and statements of income, cash flows, and common shareholders' equity) are presented fairly, in conformity with accounting principles generally accepted in the U.S.A.

Answers to Self-Study Questions

1. a **2.** d **3.** c **4.** c **5.** c **6.** c **7.** b **8.** c **9.** c **10.** b

✓ **REMEMBER** to go back to the Navigator box on the chapter-opening page and check off your completed work.

Chapter 8

Internal Control and Cash

THE NAVIGATOR ✓

- Understand **Concepts for Review** ❑
- Read **Feature Story** ❑
- Scan **Study Objectives** ❑
- Read **Preview** ❑
- Read text and answer **Before You Go On** p. 341 ❑ p. 349 ❑ p. 357 ❑ p. 358 ❑
- Work **Demonstration Problem** ❑
- Review **Summary of Study Objectives** ❑
- Answer **Self-Study Questions** ❑
- Complete **Assignments** ❑

CONCEPTS FOR REVIEW

Before studying this chapter, you should know or, if necessary, review:

- How cash transactions are recorded. (Ch. 2, pp. 53–66)
- How cash is classified on a balance sheet. (Ch. 4, pp. 158–159)
- The role ethics plays in proper financial reporting. (Ch. 1, p. 9)

THE NAVIGATOR

ACCOUNTING MATTERS! FEATURE STORY

Minding the Money in Moose Jaw

If you're ever looking for a cappuccino in Moose Jaw, Saskatchewan, stop by **Stephanie's Gourmet Coffee and More**, located on Main Street. Staff there serve, on average, 646 cups of coffee a day—including both regular and specialty coffees—not to mention soups, Italian sandwiches, and a wide assortment of gourmet cheesecakes.

"We've got high school students who come here, and students from the community college," says owner/manager Stephanie Mintenko, who has run the place since opening it in 1995. "We have customers who are retired, and others who are working people and have only 30 minutes for lunch. We have to be pretty quick."

That means that the cashiers have to be efficient. Like most businesses where purchases are low-cost and high-volume, cash control has to be simple.

"We have an electronic cash register, but it's not the fancy new kind where you just punch in the item," explains Ms. Mintenko. "You have to punch in the prices." The machine does keep track of sales in several categories, however. Cashiers punch a button to indicate whether each item is a beverage, a meal, or a charge for the cafe's Internet connections. All transactions are recorded on an internal tape in the machine; the customer receives a receipt only upon request.

There is only one cash register. "Up to three of us might operate it on any given shift, including myself," says Ms. Mintenko.

She and her staff do two "cashouts" each day—one with the shift change at 5:00, and one when the shop closes at 10:00. The cash in the register drawer is counted. That amount, minus the cash change carried forward (the float), should match the shift total on the register tape. If there's a discrepancy, they do another count. Then, if necessary, "we go through the whole tape to find the mistake," she explains. "It usually turns out to be someone who punched in $18 instead of $1.80, or something like that."

Ms. Mintenko sends all the cash tapes and float totals to a bookkeeper, who double checks everything and provides regular reports. "We try to keep the accounting simple, so we can concentrate on making great coffee and food."

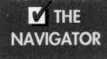

☑ THE NAVIGATOR

STUDY OBJECTIVES

After studying this chapter, you should be able to:

1. Define internal control.
2. Identify the principles of internal control.
3. Explain the applications of internal control principles to cash receipts.
4. Explain the applications of internal control principles to cash disbursements.
5. Describe the operation of a petty cash fund.
6. Indicate the control features of a bank account.
7. Prepare a bank reconciliation.
8. Explain the reporting of cash.

☑ THE NAVIGATOR

PREVIEW OF CHAPTER 8

As the story about recording cash sales at **Stephanie's Gourmet Coffee and More** indicates, control of cash is important. Controls are also needed to safeguard other types of assets. For example, Stephanie's undoubtedly has controls to prevent the theft of food and supplies, and controls to prevent the theft of silverware and dishes from its kitchen.

In this chapter, we explain the essential features of an internal control system and then describe how those controls apply to cash. The applications include some controls with which you may be already familiar. Toward the end of the chapter, we describe the use of a bank and explain how cash is reported on the balance sheet.

The content and organization of Chapter 8 are as follows.

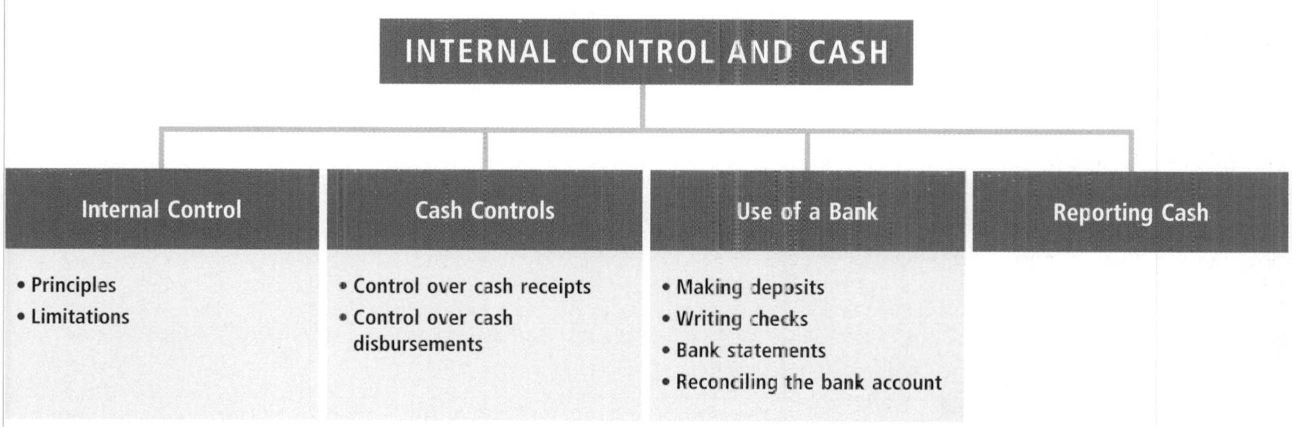

THE NAVIGATOR

Internal Control

STUDY OBJECTIVE 1

Define internal control.

Could there be dishonest employees where you work? Unfortunately, the answer sometimes is Yes. For example, in addition to the highly publicized frauds at **Enron**, **WorldCom**, **Tyco**, and **Global Crossing**, the financial press recently reported the following.

A bookkeeper in a small company diverted $750,000 of bill payments to a personal bank account over a 3-year period.

A shipping clerk with 28 years of service shipped $125,000 of merchandise to himself.

A computer operator embezzled $21 million from **Wells Fargo Bank** over a 2-year period.

A church treasurer "borrowed" $150,000 of church funds to finance a friend's business dealings.

Accounting Matters!

These situations emphasize the need for a good system of internal control.

Internal control consists of the plan of organization and all the related methods and measures adopted within a business to:

1. **Safeguard its assets** from employee theft, robbery, and unauthorized use.
2. **Enhance the accuracy and reliability of its accounting records.** This is done by reducing the risk of **errors** (unintentional mistakes) and **irregularities** (intentional mistakes and misrepresentations) in the accounting process.

The Foreign Corrupt Practices Act of 1977 and more recently, the Sarbanes-Oxley Act of 2002 require all major U.S. corporations to maintain an adequate system of internal control. Companies that fail to comply are subject to fines, and company officers may be imprisoned. Also, the National Commission on Fraudulent Financial Reporting concluded that all companies whose stock is publicly traded should maintain internal controls that can provide reasonable assurance that fraudulent financial reporting will be prevented or subject to early detection.

ACCOUNTING MATTERS! Ethics Insight

Fraud takes many forms. Here are two of the dumbest: (1) In Wichita, Kansas, police arrested a 22-year-old male who tried to pass two counterfeit $16 bills at an airport hotel. (2) And in Newport, Pennsylvania, a new-accounts bank clerk accepted for deposit a fake $1 million bill, which was 10 times the value of the largest bill ever printed by the government (a $100,000 bill existed for three weeks in the 1930s) and 10,000 times larger than the $100 bill, which is the largest bill now in circulation. While the bank clerk learned a hard lesson, the fake bill passer learned about "hard time."

Source: Joseph R. Wells, "The World's Dumbest Fraudsters," *Journal of Accountancy* (May 2003), p. 55.

? What could the Pennsylvania bank mentioned above have done to prevent such an error?

STUDY OBJECTIVE 2

Identify the principles of internal control.

Principles of Internal Control

To safeguard its assets and enhance the accuracy and reliability of its accounting records, a company follows specific control principles. Of course, internal control measures vary with the size and nature of the business and with management's control philosophy. The six principles listed in Illustration 8-1 apply to most enterprises. Each principle is explained in the following sections.

Illustration 8-1
Principles of internal control

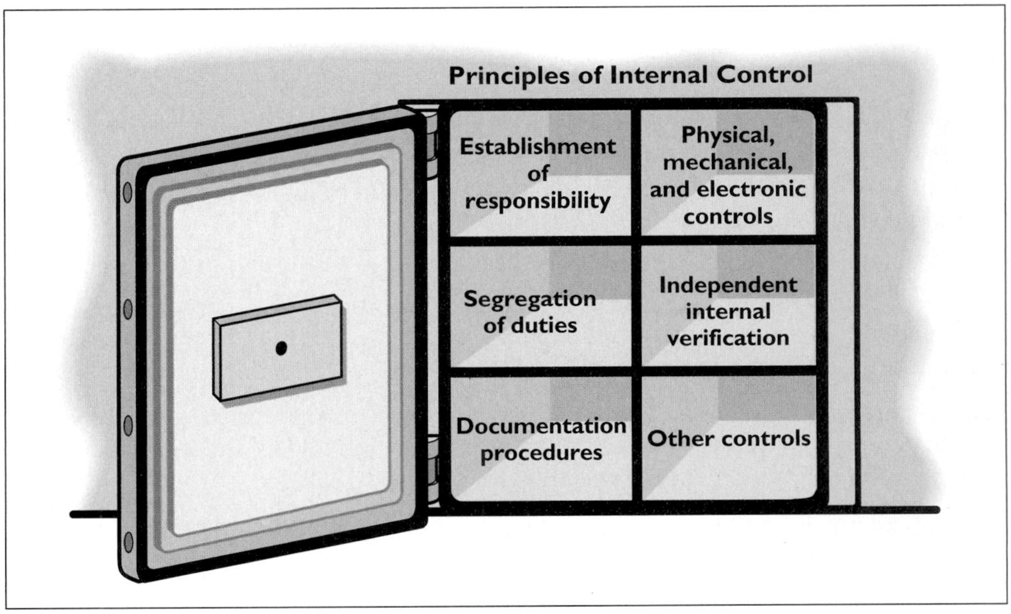

Establishment of Responsibility

An essential characteristic of internal control is the assignment of responsibility to specific employees. **Control is most effective when only one person is responsible for a given task.** To illustrate, assume that the cash on hand at the end of the day in a **Safeway** supermarket is $10 short of the cash rung up on the cash register. If only one person has operated the register, responsibility for the shortage can be assessed quickly. If two or more individuals have worked the register, it may be impossible to determine who is responsible for the error unless each person is assigned a separate cash drawer and register key. The principle of establishing responsibility does not appear to be strictly applied by **Stephanie's** (in the Feature Story) since three people operate the cash register on any given shift. To identify any shortages quickly at Stephanie's, two cashouts are performed each day.

Establishing responsibility includes the authorization and approval of transactions. For example, the vice president of sales should have the authority to establish policies for making credit sales. The policies ordinarily will require written credit department approval of credit sales.

It's your shift now. I'm turning in my cash drawer and heading home.

Transfer of cash drawers

Segregation of Duties

Segregation of duties (also called separation of functions or division of work) is indispensable in a system of internal control. There are two common applications of this principle:

1. Related activities should be assigned to different individuals.
2. Establishing the accountability (keeping the records) for an asset should be separate from the physical custody of that asset.

The rationale for segregation of duties is this: **The work of one employee should, without a duplication of effort, provide a reliable basis for evaluating the work of another employee.**

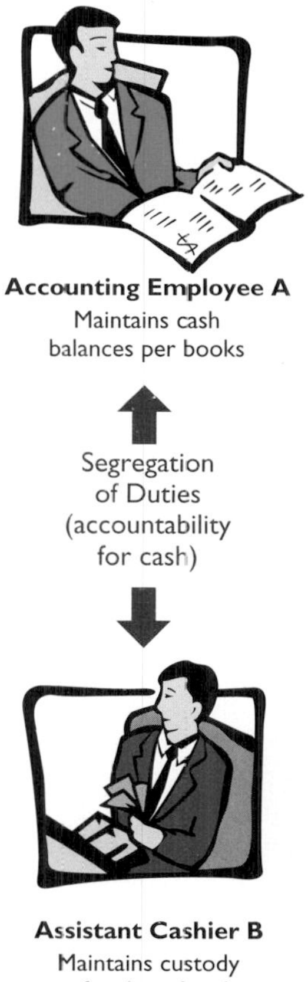

RELATED ACTIVITIES. Related activities that should be assigned to different individuals arise in both purchasing and selling. **When one individual is responsible for all of the related activities, the potential for errors and irregularities is increased.** Related purchasing activities include ordering merchandise, receiving the goods, and paying (or authorizing payment) for the merchandise. In purchasing, for example, orders could be placed with friends or with suppliers who give kickbacks. Or, only a cursory count and inspection could be made upon receiving the goods, which could lead to errors and poor-quality merchandise. Payment might be authorized without a careful review of the invoice. Even worse, fictitious invoices might be approved for payment. When the ordering, receiving, and paying are assigned to different individuals, the risk of such abuses is minimized.

Similarly, related sales activities should be assigned to different individuals. Related selling activities include making a sale, shipping (or delivering) the goods to the customer, billing the customer, and receiving payment. When one person handles related sales transactions, a salesperson could make sales at unauthorized prices to increase sales commissions; a shipping clerk could ship goods to himself; a billing clerk could understate the amount billed for sales made to friends and relatives. These abuses are reduced by dividing the sales tasks: the salespersons make the sale; the shipping department ships the goods on the basis of the sales order; and the billing department prepares the sales invoice after comparing the sales order with the report of goods shipped.

ACCOUNTABILITY FOR ASSETS. To provide a valid basis of accountability for an asset, the accountant should have neither physical custody of the asset nor access to it. Likewise, the custodian of the asset should not maintain or have access to the accounting records. **When one employee maintains the record of the asset that should be on hand, and a different employee has physical custody of the asset, the custodian of the asset is not likely to convert the asset to personal use.** The separation of accounting responsibility from the custody of assets is especially important for cash and inventories because these assets are very vulnerable to unauthorized use or misappropriation.

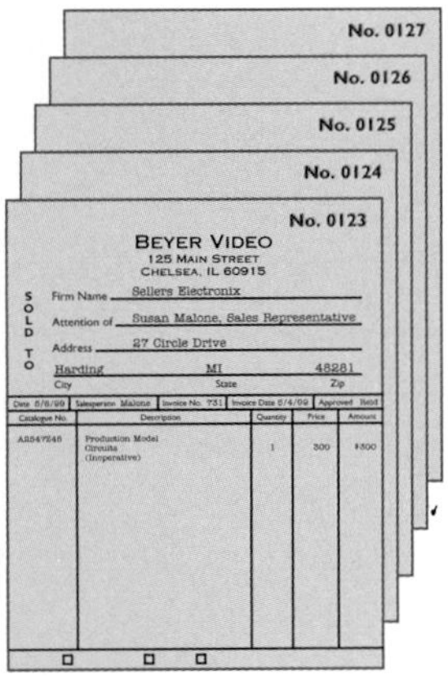

Prenumbered invoices

Documentation Procedures

Documents provide evidence that transactions and events have occurred. At **Stephanie's Gourmet Coffee and More**, the cash register tape was the restaurant's documentation for the sale and the amount of cash received. Similarly, the shipping document indicates that the goods have been shipped, and the sales invoice indicates that the customer has been billed for the goods. By adding signatures (or initials) to the documents, the individual(s) responsible for the transaction or event can be identified. Documentation of transactions should be made when the transaction occurs. Documentation of events, such as those leading to adjusting entries, is generally developed when the adjustments are made.

Several procedures should be established for documents. First, whenever possible, **documents should be prenumbered, and all documents should be accounted for.** Prenumbering helps to prevent a transaction from being recorded more than once. It also helps to prevent the transactions from not being recorded. Second, documents that are **source documents for accounting entries should be promptly forwarded to the accounting department. This control measure helps to ensure timely recording of the transaction** and contributes directly to the accuracy and reliability of the accounting records.

Physical, Mechanical, and Electronic Controls

Use of physical, mechanical, and electronic controls is essential. Physical controls relate primarily to the safeguarding of assets. Mechanical and electronic controls also safeguard assets; some enhance the accuracy and reliability of the accounting records. Examples of these controls are shown in Illustration 8-2 on page 339.

Independent Internal Verification

Most internal control systems provide for **independent internal verification**. This principle involves the review, comparison, and reconciliation of data prepared by other employees. To obtain maximum benefit from independent internal verification:

1. The verification should be made periodically or on a surprise basis.
2. The verification should be done by someone who is independent of the employee responsible for the information.
3. Discrepancies and exceptions should be reported to a management level that can take appropriate corrective action.

Independent internal verification is especially useful in comparing recorded accountability with existing assets. The reconciliation of the cash register tape with the cash in the register at **Stephanie's Gourmet Coffee and More** is an example of this internal control principle. Another common example is the reconciliation by an independent person of the cash balance per books with the cash balance per bank. The relationship between this principle and the segregation of duties principle is shown graphically in Illustration 8-3 on page 339.

Illustration 8-2
Physical, mechanical, and electronic controls

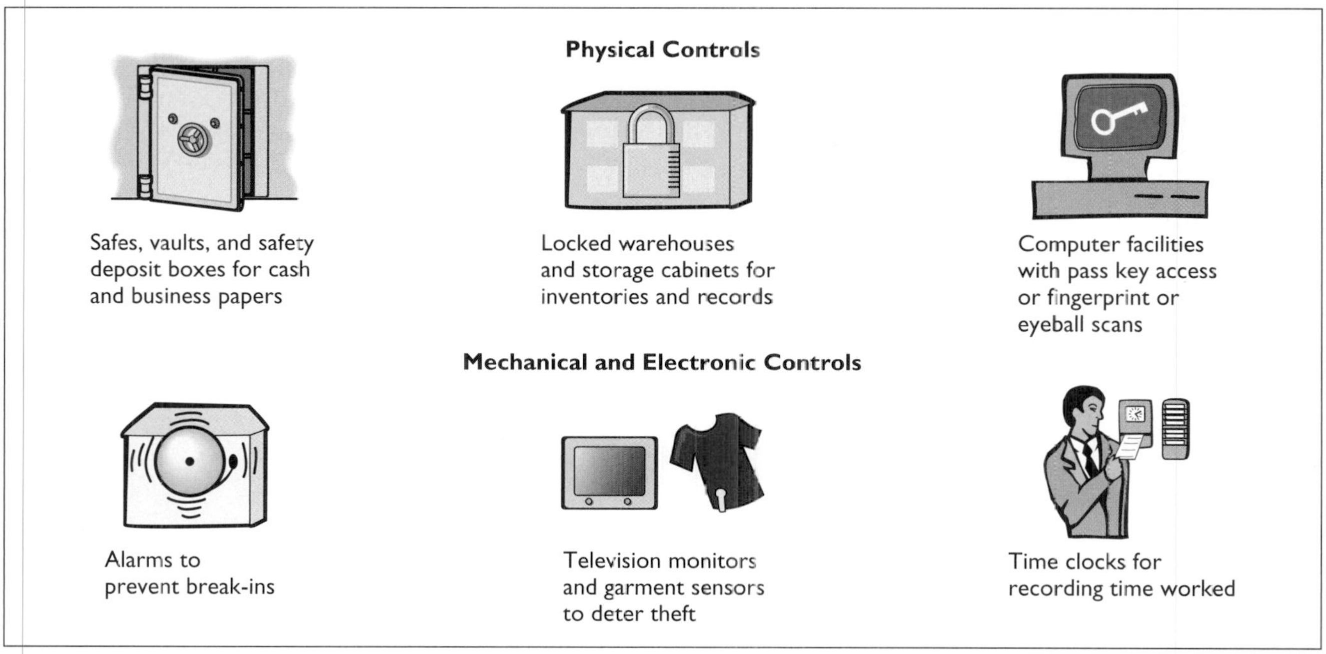

Illustration 8-3
Comparison of segregation of duties principle with independent internal verification principle

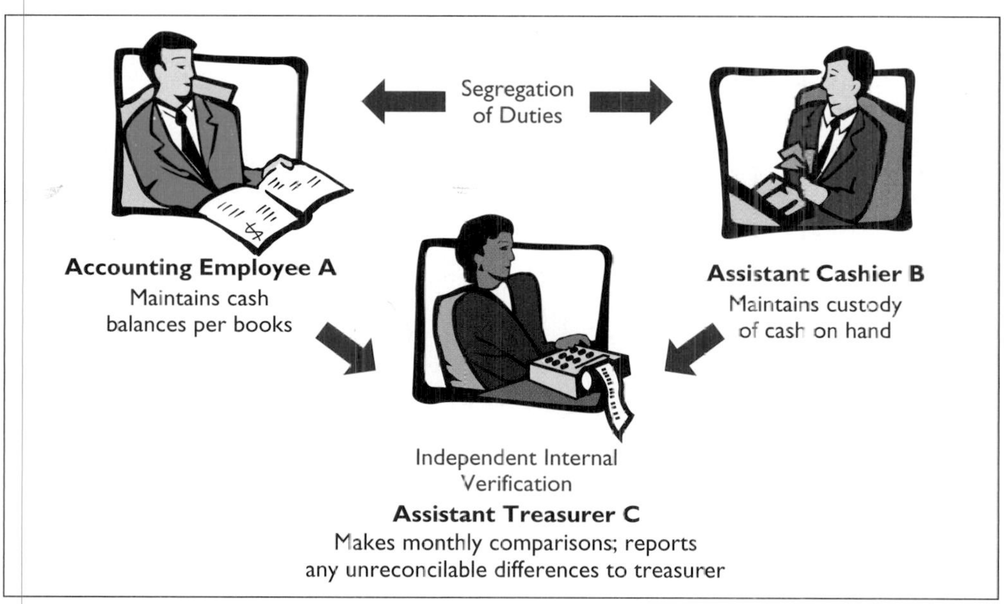

In large companies, independent internal verification is often assigned to internal auditors. **Internal auditors** are company employees who evaluate on a continuous basis the effectiveness of the company's system of internal control. They periodically review the activities of departments and individuals to determine whether prescribed internal controls are being followed. They also recommend improvements when needed. The importance of this function is illustrated by the fact that most fraud is discovered by the company through internal mechanisms, such as existing internal controls and internal audits. The recent alleged fraud at **WorldCom** involving billions of dollars, for example, was uncovered by an internal auditor.

Accounting Matters!

Other Controls

Other control measures include the following.

1. **Bonding of employees who handle cash.** Bonding involves obtaining insurance protection against misappropriation of assets by dishonest employees. This measure contributes to the safeguarding of cash in two ways: First, the insurance company carefully screens all individuals before adding them to the policy and may reject risky applicants. Second, bonded employees know that the insurance company will vigorously prosecute all offenders.
2. **Rotating employees' duties and requiring employees to take vacations.** These measures are designed to deter employees from attempting any thefts since they will not be able to permanently conceal their improper actions. Many bank embezzlements, for example, have been discovered when the perpetrator was on vacation or assigned to a new position.

ACCOUNTING MATTERS! International Insight

It's said that accountants' predecessors were the scribes of ancient Egypt, who kept the pharaohs' books. They inventoried grain, gold, and other assets. Unfortunately, some fell victim to temptation and stole from their leader, as did other employees of the king. The solution was to have two scribes independently record each transaction (the first internal control). As long as the scribes' totals agreed exactly, there was no problem. But if the totals were materially different, both scribes would be put to death. That proved to be a great incentive for them to carefully check all the numbers and make sure the help wasn't stealing. In fact, fraud prevention and detection became the royal accountants' main duty.

Source: Joseph T. Wells, "So That's Why It's Called a Pyramid Scheme," *Journal of Accountancy* (October 2000), p. 91. Copyright © 2000 from the *Journal of Accountancy by the American Institute of Certified Public Accountants, Inc.* Opinions of the authors are their own and do not necessarily reflect policies of the AICPA. Reprinted with permission.

? Which principle of internal control was implemented in ancient Egypt? Who do you think investors today expect to detect and prevent fraud?

Limitations of Internal Control

HELPFUL HINT

Controls may vary with the risk level of the activity. For example, management may consider cash to be high risk and maintaining inventories in the stock room as low risk. Thus management would have stricter controls for cash.

A company's system of internal control is generally designed to provide **reasonable assurance** that assets are properly safeguarded and that the accounting records are reliable. **The concept of reasonable assurance rests on the premise that the costs of establishing control procedures should not exceed their expected benefit.** To illustrate, consider shoplifting losses in retail stores. Such losses could be eliminated by having a security guard stop and search customers as they leave the store. But, store managers have concluded that the negative effects of adopting such a procedure cannot be justified. Instead, stores have attempted to "control" shoplifting losses by less costly procedures such as: (1) posting signs saying, "We reserve the right to inspect all packages," and "All shoplifters will be prosecuted," (2) using hidden TV cameras and store detectives to monitor customer activity, and (3) using sensoring equipment at exits.

The **human element** is an important factor in every system of internal control. A good system can become ineffective as a result of employee fatigue, carelessness, or indifference. For example, a receiving clerk may not bother to count goods received or may just "fudge" the counts. Occasionally, two or more individuals may work together to get around prescribed controls. Such **collusion** can significantly impair the effectiveness of a system, eliminating the protection offered by segregation of duties. If a supervisor and a cashier collaborate to understate cash receipts, the system of internal control may be negated. No system of internal control is perfect.

The size of the business also may impose limitations on internal control. In a small company, for example, it may be difficult to segregate duties or to provide for independent internal verification.

ACCOUNTING MATTERS! **e Business Insight**

Unfortunately, computer-related frauds have become a major concern. The average computer fraud loss is $650,000, compared with an average loss of only $19,000 resulting from other types of white-collar crime.

Computer fraud can be perpetrated almost invisibly and done with electronic speed. Psychologically, stealing with impersonal computer tools can seem far less criminal to some people. Therefore, the moral threshold to commit computer fraud is lower than fraud involving person-to-person contact.

Preventing and detecting computer fraud represents a major challenge. One of the best ways for a company to minimize the likelihood of computer fraud is to have a good system of internal control that allows the benefits of computerization to be gained without opening the possibility for rampant fraud.

? Is a computer capable of committing fraud? Discuss.

BEFORE YOU GO ON...

Review It

1. What are the two primary objectives of internal control?
2. Identify and describe the principles of internal control.
3. What are the limitations of internal control?

Do It

Li Song owns a small retail store. Li wants to establish good internal control procedures but is confused about the difference between segregation of duties and independent internal verification. Explain the differences to Li.

ACTION PLAN

- Understand and explain the differences between (1) segregation of duties and (2) independent internal verification.

SOLUTION Segregation of duties involves assigning responsibility so that the work of one employee evaluates the work of another employee. Segregation of duties occurs daily in executing and recording transactions. In contrast, independent internal verification involves reviewing, comparing, and reconciling data prepared by one or several employees. Independent internal verification occurs after the fact, as in the case of reconciling cash register totals at the end of the day with cash on hand.

Related exercise material: *BE8-1, BE8-2, and E8-1.*

THE NAVIGATOR

Cash Controls

Just as cash is the beginning of a company's operating cycle, it is also usually the starting point for a company's system of internal control. Cash is the one asset that is readily convertible into any other type of asset. It is easily concealed and transported, and it is highly desired. Because of these characteristics, **cash is the asset most susceptible to improper diversion and use**. Moreover, because of the large volume of cash transactions, numerous errors may occur in executing and recording them. To safeguard cash and to ensure the accuracy of the accounting records for cash, effective internal control over cash is imperative.

Cash consists of coins, currency (paper money), checks, money orders, and money on hand or on deposit in a bank or similar depository. The general rule is that if the bank will accept it for deposit, it is cash. Items such as postage stamps and postdated checks (checks payable in the future) are not cash. Stamps are a prepaid expense; the postdated checks are accounts receivable. In the following sections we explain the application of internal control principles to cash receipts and cash disbursements.

Internal Control over Cash Receipts

STUDY OBJECTIVE 3

Explain the applications of internal control principles to cash receipts.

Cash receipts come from a variety of sources: cash sales; collections on account from customers; the receipt of interest, rent, and dividends; investments by owners; bank loans; and proceeds from the sale of noncurrent assets. Illustration 8-4 (page 343) shows how the internal control principles explained earlier apply to cash receipts transactions.

As might be expected, companies vary considerably in how they apply these principles. To illustrate internal control over cash receipts, we will examine control measures for a retail store with both over-the-counter and mail receipts.

Over-the-Counter Receipts

Control of over-the-counter receipts in retail businesses is centered on cash registers that are visible to customers. In supermarkets and in variety stores such as **Kmart**, cash registers are placed in check-out lines near the exit. In stores such as **Sears, Roebuck & Co.** and **J. C. Penney**, each department has its own cash register. A cash sale is "rung up" on a cash register **with the amount clearly visible to the customer**. This measure prevents the cashier from ringing up a lower amount and pocketing the difference. The customer receives an itemized cash register receipt slip and is expected to count the change received. A cash register tape is locked into the register until removed by a supervisor or manager. This tape accumulates the daily transactions and totals. When the tape is removed, the supervisor compares the total with the amount of cash in the register. The tape should show all registered receipts accounted for. The supervisor's findings are reported on a cash count sheet which is signed by both the cashier and supervisor. The cash count sheet used by Alrite Food Mart is shown in Illustration 8-5 (page 343).

The count sheets, register tapes, and cash are then given to the head cashier. This individual prepares a daily cash summary showing the total cash received and the amount from each source, such as cash sales and collections on account. The head cashier sends one copy of the summary to the accounting department for entry into the cash receipts journal. The other copy goes to the treasurer's office for later comparison with the daily bank deposit (see daily cash summary in Illustration 8-6, page 344).

Next, the head cashier prepares a deposit slip (see Illustration 8-9 on page 350) and makes the bank deposit. The total amount deposited should be equal to the total receipts on the daily cash summary. This will ensure that all receipts have been placed in the custody of the bank. In accepting the bank deposit, the bank stamps (authenticates) the duplicate deposit slip and sends it to the company treasurer, who makes the comparison with the daily cash summary.

Illustration 8-4
Application of internal control principles to cash receipts

Internal Control over Cash Receipts

Establishment of Responsibility

Only designated personnel are authorized to handle cash receipts (cashiers)

Physical, Mechanical, and Electronic Controls

Store cash in safes and bank vaults; limit access to storage areas; use cash registers

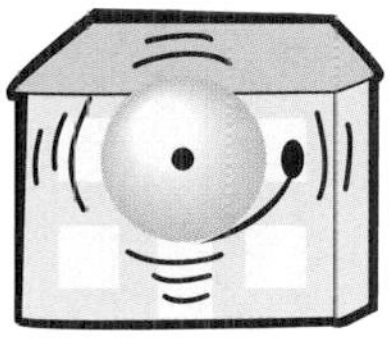

Segregation of Duties

Different individuals receive cash, record cash receipts, and hold the cash

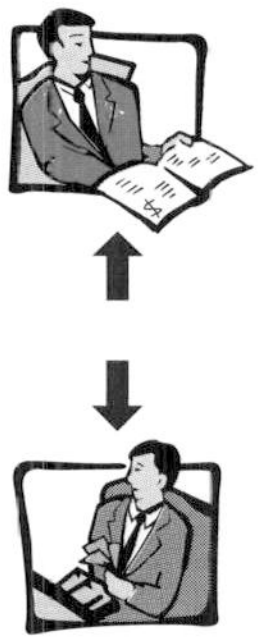

Independent Internal Verification

Supervisors count cash receipts daily; treasurer compares total receipts to bank deposits daily

Documentation Procedures

Use remittance advice (mail receipts), cash register tapes, and deposit slips

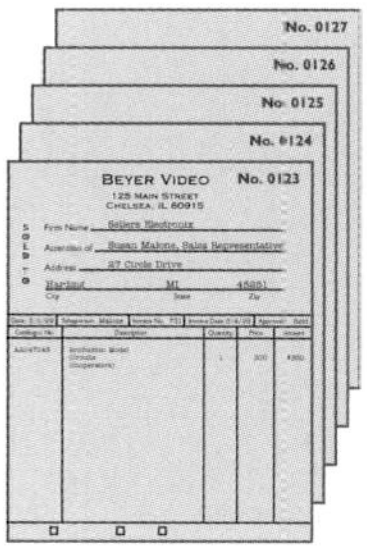

Other Controls

Bond personnel who handle cash; require employees to take vacations; deposit all cash in bank daily

Illustration 8-5
Cash count sheet

Store No. 8 | Date March 8, 2006

1. Opening cash balance	$ 50.00
2. Cash sales per tape (attached)	6,956.20
3. Total cash to be accounted for	7,006.20
4. Less: Cash on hand (see list)	6,996.10
5. Cash (short) or over	$ (10.10)
6. Ending cash balance	$ 50.00
7. Cash for deposit (Line 4 – Line 6)	$6,946.10

Cashier J. Cruse   Supervisor M. Braun

These measures for cash sales are graphically presented in Illustration 8-6. The activities of the sales department are shown separately from those of the cashier's department to indicate the segregation of duties in handling cash.

Illustration 8-6
Executing over-the-counter cash sales

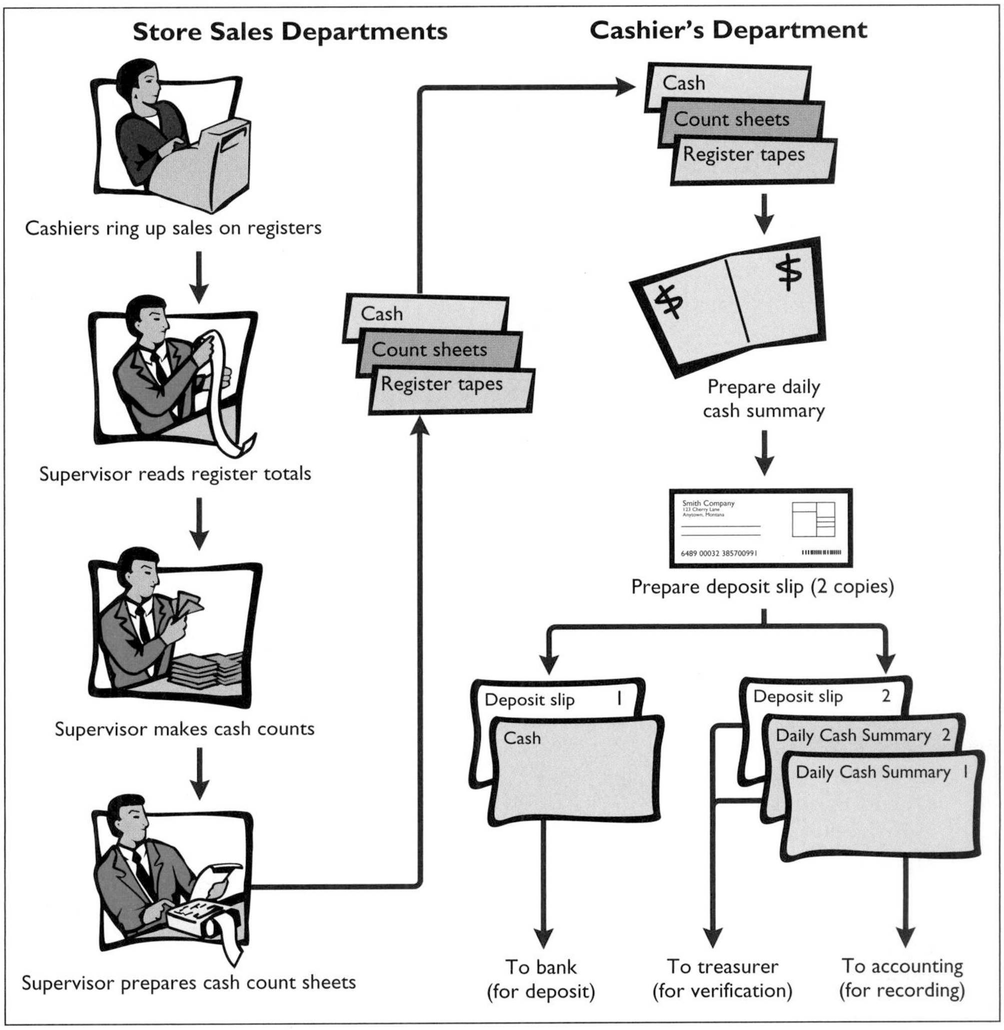

HELPFUL HINT

Flowcharts such as this one enhance the understanding of the flow of documents, the processing steps, and the internal control procedures.

Mail Receipts

As an individual customer, you may be more familiar with over-the-counter receipts than with mail receipts. However, mail receipts resulting from billings and credit sales are by far the most common way cash is received by businesses. Think, for example, of the number of checks received through the mail daily by a national retailer such as **J. Crew** or **Abercrombie & Fitch**.

All mail receipts should be opened in the presence of two mail clerks. These receipts are generally in the form of checks or money orders. They frequently are accompanied by a remittance advice stating the purpose of the check (sometimes attached to the check, but often a part of the bill that the customer tears off and returns). Each check should be promptly endorsed "For Deposit Only" by use of a company stamp. This **restrictive endorsement** reduces the likelihood that the check will be diverted to personal use. Banks will not give an individual any cash under this type of endorsement.

A list of the checks received each day should be prepared in duplicate. This list shows the name of the issuer of the check, the purpose of the payment, and the amount of the check. Each mail clerk should sign the list to establish responsibility for the data. The original copy of the list, along with the checks and remittance advices, are then sent to the cashier's department. There they are added to over-the-counter receipts (if any) in preparing the daily cash summary and in making the daily bank deposit. Also, a copy of the list is sent to the treasurer's office for comparison with the total mail receipts shown on the daily cash summary. This copy ensures that all mail receipts have been included.

Internal Control over Cash Disbursements

STUDY OBJECTIVE 4

Explain the applications of internal control principles to cash disbursements.

Cash may be disbursed for a variety of reasons, such as to pay expenses and liabilities, or to purchase assets. **Generally, internal control over cash disbursements is more effective when payments are made by check, rather than by cash.** One exception is **for incidental amounts that are paid out of petty cash.**[1] Payment by check generally occurs only after specified control procedures have been followed. In addition, the "paid" check provides proof of payment. Illustration 8-7 shows how principles of internal control apply to cash disbursements.

Illustration 8-7
Application of internal control principles to cash disbursements

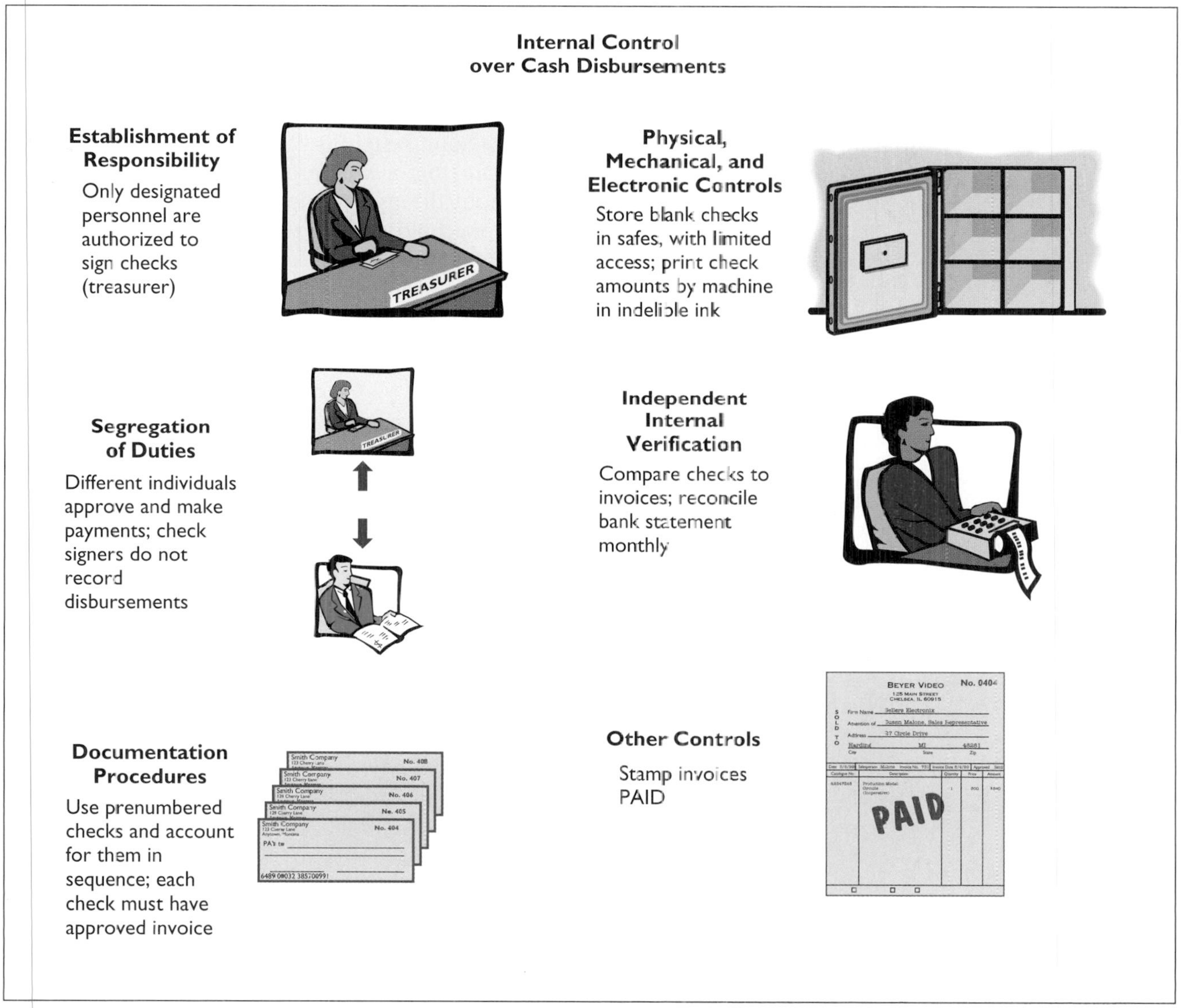
Internal Control over Cash Disbursements
Establishment of Responsibility
Only designated personnel are authorized to sign checks (treasurer)
TREASURER
Physical, Mechanical, and Electronic Controls
Store blank checks in safes, with limited access; print check amounts by machine in indelible ink
Segregation of Duties
Different individuals approve and make payments; check signers do not record disbursements
Independent Internal Verification
Compare checks to invoices; reconcile bank statement monthly
Documentation Procedures
Use prenumbered checks and account for them in sequence; each check must have approved invoice
Other Controls
Stamp invoices PAID
BEYER VIDEO
PAID

[1]The operation of a petty cash fund is explained on pages 346–349.

Voucher System

Most medium and large companies use vouchers as part of their internal control over cash disbursements. A **voucher system** is a network of approvals by authorized individuals acting independently to ensure that all disbursements by check are proper.

The system begins with the authorization to incur a cost or expense. It ends with the issuance of a check for the liability incurred. A **voucher** is an authorization form prepared for each expenditure. Vouchers are required for all types of cash disbursements except those from petty cash. The voucher generally is prepared in the accounts payable department.

The starting point in preparing a voucher is to fill in the appropriate information about the liability on the face of the voucher. The vendor's invoice provides most of the needed information. Then, the voucher must be recorded (in a journal called a **voucher register**) and filed according to the date on which it is to be paid. A check is sent on that date, the voucher is stamped "paid," and the paid voucher is sent to the accounting department for recording (in a journal called the **check register**). A voucher system involves two journal entries, one to issue the voucher and a second to pay the voucher.

Electronic Funds Transfer (EFT) System

Accounting for and controlling cash is an expensive and time-consuming process. The cost to process a check through a bank system is about $1.00 per check and is increasing. It is not surprising, therefore, that new approaches are being developed to transfer funds among parties without the use of paper (deposit tickets, checks, etc.). Such procedures, called **electronic funds transfers (EFT)**, are disbursement systems that use wire, telephone, or computers to transfer cash from one location to another. Use of EFT is quite common. For example, many employees receive no formal payroll checks from their employers, which instead send electronic depository information to the appropriate banks. Regular payments such as those for house, car, and utilities are frequently made by EFT.

ACCOUNTING MATTERS! Business Insight

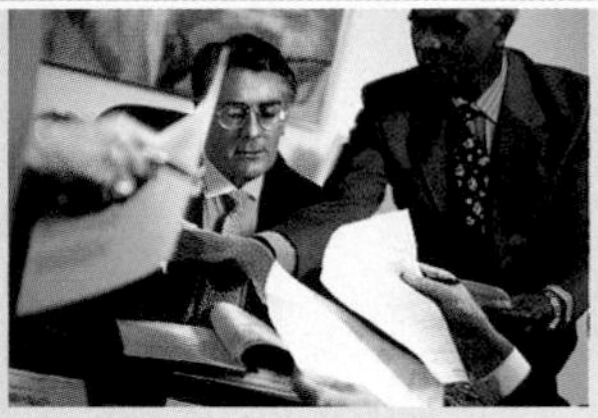

A study by the Association of Certified Fraud Examiners indicates that businesses with fewer than 100 employees are most at risk for employee theft. Also, the average loss per incident for small companies—$127,500—was actually higher than the average loss for larger companies. The high degree of trust often found in small companies makes them more vulnerable to dishonest employees. For example, in one small company the employee responsible for paying bills would intentionally ask the owner to sign checks only when the owner was extremely busy. The employee would slip in one check that was made out to himself, and the owner didn't notice because he was too busy to carefully review each check.

Source: Joseph T. Wells, "Occupational Fraud: The Audit as Deterrent," *Journal of Accountancy* (April 2002), pp. 24–28.

? Which principles of internal control should have prevented such fraud?

Petty Cash Fund

As you learned earlier in the chapter, better internal control over cash disbursements is possible when payments are made by check. However, using checks to pay small amounts is both impractical and a nuisance. For instance, a company would not want to write checks to pay for postage due, employee lunches, or taxi fares. A common way of handling such payments, while maintaining satisfactory control, is to use a petty cash fund. A **petty cash fund** is a cash fund used to pay relatively small amounts but still maintain satisfactory control. The operation of a petty cash fund, often called an **imprest system**, involves three steps: (1) establishing the fund, (2) making payments from the fund, and (3) replenishing the fund.[2]

STUDY OBJECTIVE 5

Describe the operation of a petty cash fund.

ESTABLISHING THE FUND. Two essential steps in establishing a petty cash fund are (1) appointing a petty cash custodian who will be responsible for the fund and (2) determining the size of the fund. Ordinarily, the amount is expected to cover anticipated disbursements for a 3- to 4-week period. To establish the fund, a check payable to the petty cash custodian is issued for the stipulated amount. If the Laird Company decides to establish a $100 fund on March 1, the entry in general journal form is:

Mar. 1	Petty Cash	100	
	Cash		100
	(To establish a petty cash fund)		

A	=	L	+	SE
+100				
−100				

Cash Flows
no effect

The custodian cashes the check and places the proceeds in a locked petty cash box or drawer. Most petty cash funds are established on a fixed-amount basis. No additional entries will be made to the Petty Cash account unless management changes the stipulated amount of the fund. For example, if Laird Company decides on July 1 to increase the size of the fund to $250, it would debit Petty Cash $150 and credit Cash $150.

MAKING PAYMENTS FROM THE FUND. The custodian of the petty cash fund has the authority to make payments from the fund that conform to prescribed management policies. Usually, management limits the size of expenditures that may be made. Likewise, it may not permit use of the fund for certain types of transactions (such as making short-term loans to employees). Each payment from the fund must be documented on a prenumbered petty cash receipt (or petty cash voucher), as shown in Illustration 8-8. Note that the signatures of both the custodian and the person receiving payment are required on the receipt. If other supporting documents such as a freight bill or invoice are available, they should be attached to the petty cash receipt.

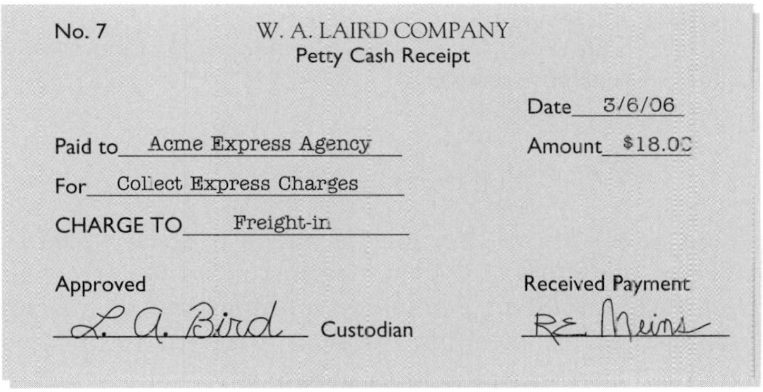
No. 7
W. A. LAIRD COMPANY
Petty Cash Receipt

Date 3/6/06

Paid to Acme Express Agency

Amount $18.00

For Collect Express Charges

CHARGE TO Freight-in

Approved

L. A. Bird Custodian

Received Payment

R. E. Meins

Illustration 8-8
Petty cash receipt

[2]The term "imprest" means an advance of money for a designated purpose.

The receipts are kept in the petty cash box until the fund runs low and needs to be replenished. The sum of the petty cash receipts and money in the fund should equal the established total at all times. Surprise counts can be made at any time by an independent person, such as an internal auditor, to determine whether the fund is being maintained intact.

No accounting entry is made to record a payment at the time it is made from petty cash. It is considered unnecessary to do so. Instead, the accounting effects of each payment are recognized when the fund is replenished.

REPLENISHING THE FUND. When the money in the petty cash fund reaches a minimum level, the fund is replenished. The request for reimbursement is initiated by the petty cash custodian. This individual prepares a schedule (or summary) of the payments that have been made and sends the schedule, supported by petty cash receipts and other documentation, to the treasurer's office. The receipts and supporting documents are examined in the treasurer's office to verify that they were proper payments from the fund. The treasurer then approves the request and a check is prepared to restore the fund to its established amount. At the same time, all supporting documentation (vouchers and/or receipts) is stamped "paid" so that it cannot be submitted again for payment.

A	=	L	+	SE
−87				−44 Exp
				−38 Exp
				−5 Exp

Cash Flows
−87

To illustrate, assume that on March 15 the petty cash custodian requests a check for $87. The fund contains $13 cash and petty cash receipts for postage $44, freight-out $38, and miscellaneous expenses $5. The general journal entry to record the check is:

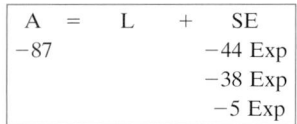

Mar. 15	Postage Expense	44	
	Freight-out	38	
	Miscellaneous Expense	5	
	Cash		87
	(To replenish petty cash fund)		

HELPFUL HINT

Cash over and short situations result from mathematical errors or from failure to keep accurate records.

Note that the Petty Cash account is not affected by the reimbursement entry. Replenishment changes the composition of the fund by replacing the petty cash receipts with cash. It does not change the balance in the fund.

It may be necessary in replenishing a petty cash fund to recognize a cash shortage or overage. This results when the cash plus receipts in the petty cash box do not equal the established amount of the petty cash fund. To illustrate, assume in the example above that the custodian had only $12 in cash in the fund plus the receipts as listed. The request for reimbursement would, therefore, have been for $88. The following entry would be made:

A	=	L	+	SE
−88				−44 Exp
				−38 Exp
				−5 Exp
				−1 Exp

Cash Flows
−88

Mar. 15	Postage Expense	44	
	Freight-out	38	
	Miscellaneous Expense	5	
	Cash Over and Short	1	
	Cash		88
	(To replenish petty cash fund)		

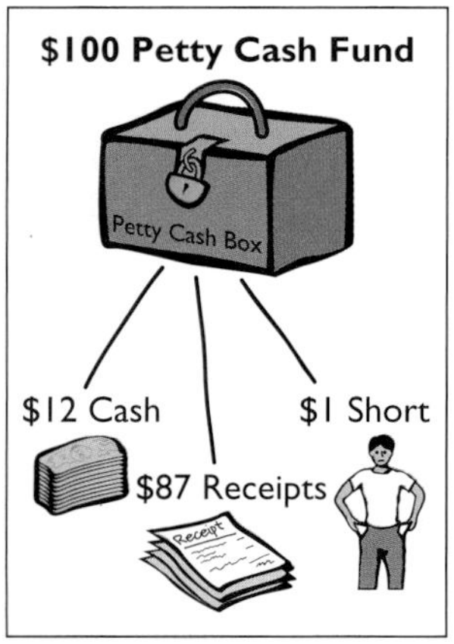

If the custodian had $14 in cash, the reimbursement request would have been for $86 and Cash Over and Short would have been credited for $1 (overage). A debit balance in Cash Over and Short is reported in the income statement as miscellaneous expense. A credit balance in the account is reported as miscellaneous revenue. Cash Over and Short is closed to Income Summary at the end of the period.

A petty cash fund should be replenished at the end of the accounting period regardless of the cash in the fund. Replenishment at this time is necessary in order to recognize the effects of the petty cash payments on the financial statements.

Internal control over a petty cash fund is strengthened by (1) having a supervisor make surprise counts of the fund to ascertain whether the paid vouchers and fund cash equal the imprest amount and (2) canceling or mutilating the paid vouchers or receipts so they cannot be resubmitted for reimbursement.

BEFORE YOU GO ON...

Review It

1. How do the principles of internal control apply to cash receipts?
2. How do the principles of internal control apply to cash disbursements?
3. When are entries required in a petty cash system?

Do It

L. R. Cortez is concerned about the control over cash receipts in his fast-food restaurant, Big Cheese. The restaurant has two cash registers. At no time do more than two employees take customer orders and ring up sales. Work shifts for employees range from 4 to 8 hours. Cortez asks your help in installing a good system of internal control over cash receipts.

ACTION PLAN

- Differentiate among the internal control principles of (1) establishing responsibility, (2) using electronic controls, and (3) independent internal verification.
- Design an effective system of internal control over cash receipts.

SOLUTION Cortez should assign a cash register to each employee at the start of each work shift, with register totals set at zero. Each employee should be instructed to use only the assigned register and to ring up all sales. At the end of each work shift, Cortez or a supervisor/manager should total the register and make a cash count to see whether all cash is accounted for.

Related exercise material: *BE8-3, BE8-4, BE8-5, E8-2, E8-3, E8-4, and E8-5.*

THE NAVIGATOR

Use of a Bank

STUDY OBJECTIVE 6

Indicate the control features of a bank account.

The use of a bank contributes significantly to good internal control over cash. A company can safeguard its cash by using a bank as a depository and as a clearing house for checks received and checks written. Use of a bank minimizes the amount of currency that must be kept on hand. Also, the use of a bank facilitates the control of cash because it creates a double record of all bank transactions—one by the business and the other by the bank. The asset account Cash maintained by the depositor is the reciprocal of the bank's liability account for each depositor. It should be possible to **reconcile these accounts** (make them agree) at any time.

Opening a bank checking account is a relatively simple procedure. Typically, the bank makes a credit check on the new customer and the depositor is required to sign a **signature card**. The card contains the signatures of each person authorized to sign checks on the account. The signature card is used by bank employees to validate signatures on the checks.

Soon after an account is opened, the bank provides the depositor with serially numbered checks and deposit slips imprinted with the depositor's name and address. Each check and deposit slip is imprinted with both a bank and a depositor identification number. This number, printed in magnetic ink, permits computer processing of transactions.

Many companies have more than one bank account. For efficiency of operations and better control, national retailers like **Wal-Mart** and **Kmart** may have regional bank accounts. A company such as **Intel** with more than 70,000 employees may have a payroll bank account, as well as one or more general bank accounts. Also, a company may maintain several bank accounts in order to have more than one source for short-term loans when needed.

Making Bank Deposits

Bank deposits should be made by an authorized employee, such as the head cashier. Each deposit must be documented by a deposit slip (ticket), as shown in Illustration 8-9.

Illustration 8-9
Deposit slip

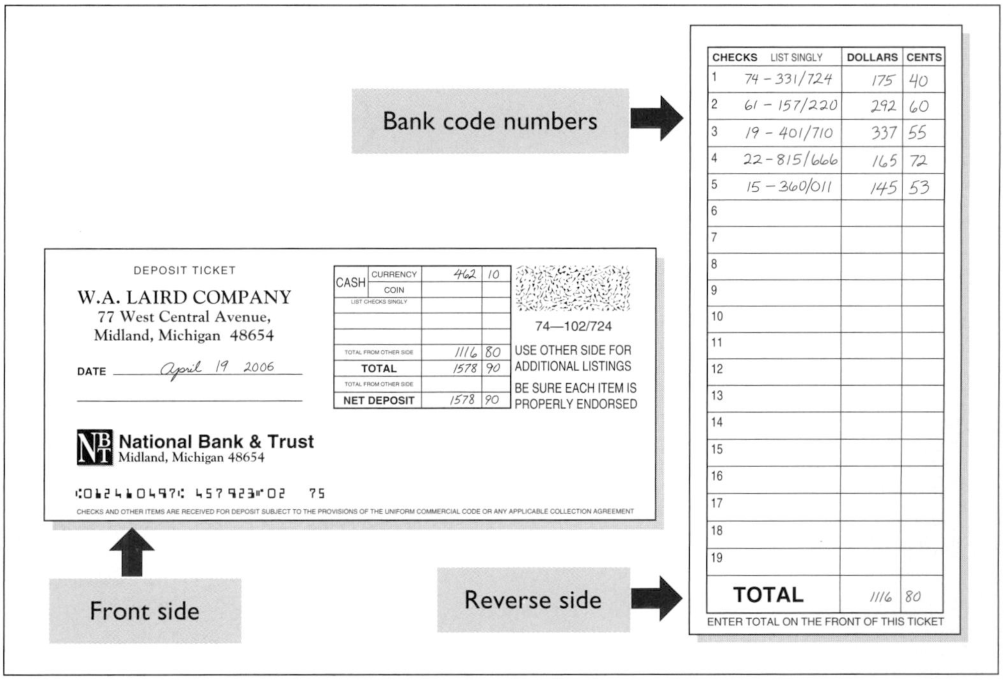

Deposit slips are prepared in duplicate (see Illustration 8-6 on page 344). The original is retained by the bank; the duplicate, machine-stamped by the bank to establish its authenticity, is retained by the depositor.

Writing Checks

A **check** is a written order signed by the depositor directing the bank to pay a specified sum of money to a designated recipient. There are three parties to a check: (1) the **maker** (or drawer) who issues the check; (2) the **bank** (or payer) on which the check is drawn; and (3) the **payee** to whom the check is payable. A check is a **negotiable instrument** that can be transferred to another party by endorsement. Each check should be accompanied by an explanation of its purposes. In many businesses, this is done by a remittance advice attached to the check, as shown in Illustration 8-10 (page 351).

It is important to know the balance in the checking account at all times. To keep the balance current, each deposit and check should be entered on running balance memorandum forms provided by the bank or on the check stubs contained in the checkbook.

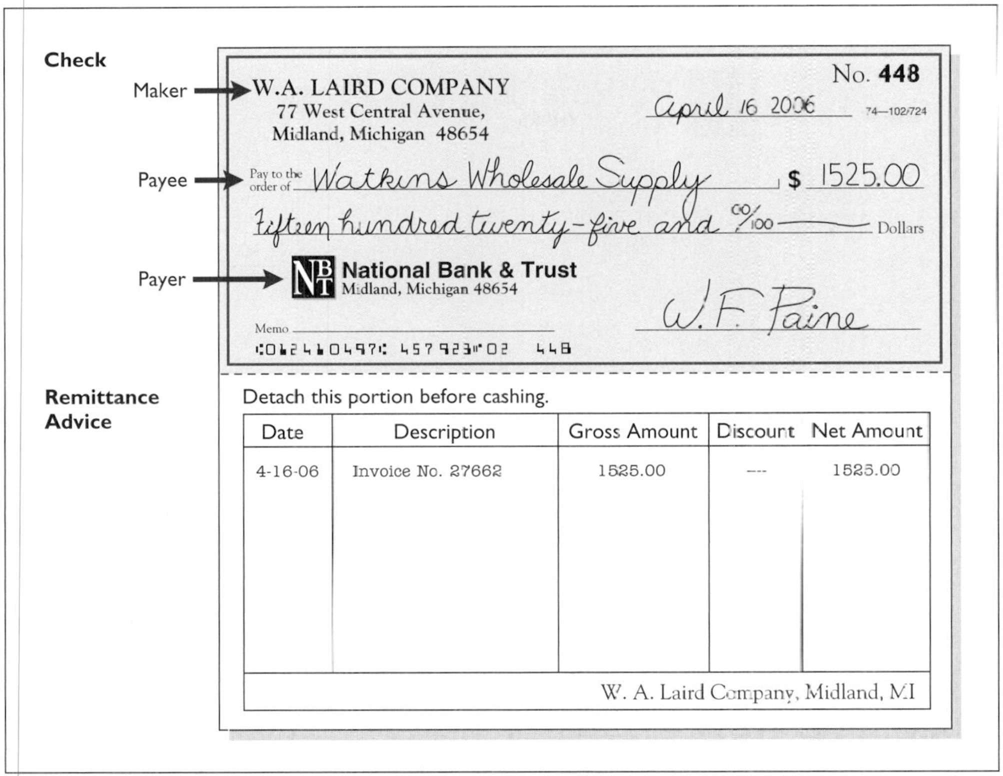
Check

Maker → W.A. LAIRD COMPANY
77 West Central Avenue,
Midland, Michigan 48654

No. 448

April 16 2006 74—102/724

Payee → Pay to the order of Watkins Wholesale Supply $ 1525.00

Fifteen hundred twenty-five and 00/100 Dollars

Payer → National Bank & Trust
Midland, Michigan 48654

Memo

W. F. Paine

⑆0162410497⑆ 457923⑈02 448

Remittance Advice

Detach this portion before cashing.

Date	Description	Gross Amount	Discount	Net Amount
4-16-06	Invoice No. 27662	1525.00	---	1525.00

W. A. Laird Company, Midland, MI

Illustration 8-10
Check with remittance advice

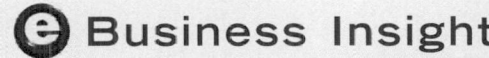

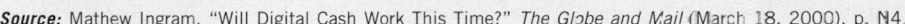

ACCOUNTING MATTERS! **Business Insight**

Cash is virtually obsolete. Today, many people use debit cards and credit cards to pay for most of their purchases. But debit cards are usable only at specified locations, and credit cards are cumbersome for small transactions. They are no good for transferring cash between individuals or to small companies that do not want to pay credit card fees. Digital cash is the next online wave.

There are many digital-cash companies. One of the most flexible appears to be **PayPal** (*www.paypal.com*). PayPal became popular with users of the auction site **eBay**, because it allows them to transfer funds to each other as easily as sending e-mail. (PayPal is now owned by eBay, though it is operated as an independent site.)

Source: Mathew Ingram, "Will Digital Cash Work This Time?" *The Globe and Mail* (March 18, 2000), p. N4.

? Will "cash" be obsolete in terms of financial statement reporting?

Bank Statements

Each month, the depositor receives a bank statement from the bank. A **bank statement** shows the depositor's bank transactions and balances.[3] A typical statement is presented in Illustration 8-11 (page 352). It shows (1) checks paid and other debits that reduce the balance in the depositor's account, (2) deposits and other credits that increase the balance in the depositor's account, and (3) the account balance after each day's transactions.

HELPFUL HINT

Essentially, the bank statement is a copy of the bank's records sent to the customer for periodic review.

[3]Our presentation assumes that all adjustments are made at the end of the month. In practice, a company may also make journal entries during the month as it receives information from the bank regarding its account.

Illustration 8-11
Bank statement

National Bank & Trust
Midland, Michigan 48654 Member FDIC

ACCOUNT STATEMENT

LAIRD COMPANY
77 WEST CENTRAL AVENUE
MIDLAND, MICHIGAN 48654

Statement Date/Credit Line Closing Date	ACCOUNT NUMBER
April 30, 2006	457923

Balance Last Statement	Deposits and Credits No.	Deposits and Credits Total Amount	Checks and Debits No.	Checks and Debits Total Amount	Balance This Statement
13,256.90	20	34,805.10	26	32,154.55	15,907.45

CHECKS AND DEBITS Date	No.	Amount	DEPOSITS AND CREDITS Date	Amount	DAILY BALANCE Date	Amount
4-2	435	644.95	4-2	4,276.85	4-2	16,888.80
4-5	436	3,260.00	4-3	2,137.50	4-3	18,249.65
4-4	437	1,185.79	4-5	1,350.47	4-4	17,063.86
4-3	438	776.65	4-7	982.46	4-5	15,154.33
4-8	439	1,781.70	4-8	1,320.28	4-7	14,648.89
4-7	440	1,487.90	4-9 CM	1,035.00	4-8	11,767.47
4-8	441	2,420.00	4-11	2,720.00	4-9	12,802.47
4-11	442	1,585.60	4-12	757.41	4-11	13,936.87
4-12	443	1,226.00	4-13	1,218.56	4-12	13,468.28
4-29	NSF	425.60	4-27	1,545.57	4-27	13,005.45
4-29	459	1,080.30	4-29	2,929.45	4-29	14,429.00
4-30	DM	30.00	4-30	2,128.60	4-30	15,907.45
4-30	461	620.15				

Symbols: **CM** Credit Memo **EC** Error Correction **NSF** Not Sufficient Funds
DM Debit Memo **INT** Interest Earned **SC** Service Charge

Reconcile Your Account Promptly

HELPFUL HINT

Every deposit received by the bank is *credited* to the customer's account. The reverse occurs when the bank "pays" a check issued by a company on its checking account balance. Payment reduces the bank's liability. Thus it is *debited* to the customer's account with the bank.

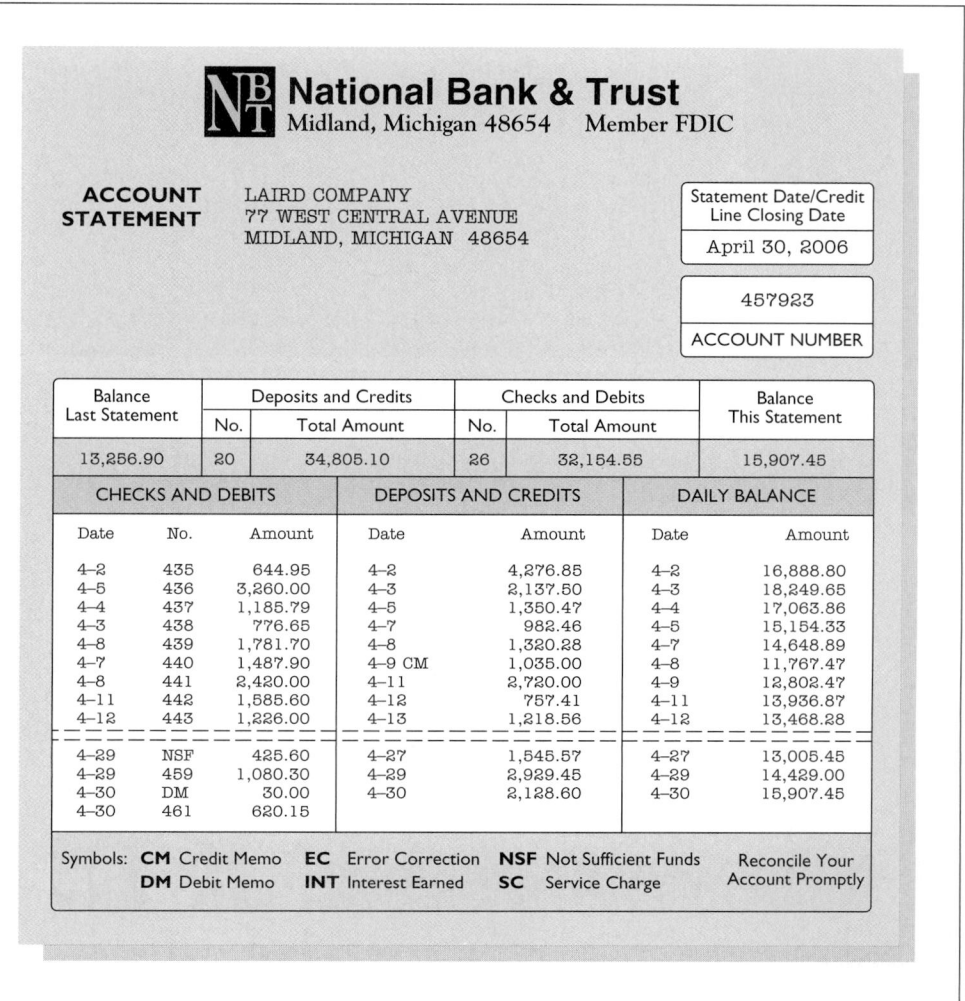

All "paid" checks are listed in numerical sequence on the bank statement along with the date the check was paid and its amount. Upon paying a check, the bank stamps the check "paid"; a paid check is sometimes referred to as a **canceled** check. Some banks offer depositors the option of receiving "paid" checks with their bank statements. For those who decline, the bank keeps a record of each check on microfilm.

The bank also includes on the bank statement memoranda explaining other debits and credits made by the bank to the depositor's account.

Debit Memorandum

Banks charge a monthly fee for their services. Often the fee is charged only when the average monthly balance in a checking account falls below a specified amount. The fee, called a **bank service charge**, is identified on the bank statement by a code symbol such as SC. A debit memorandum explaining the charge is included with the bank statement and noted on the statement. Separate debit memoranda may also be issued for other bank services such as the cost of printing checks, issuing traveler's checks, and wiring funds to other locations. The symbol DM is often used for such charges.

A debit memorandum is also used by the bank when a deposited check from a customer "bounces" because of insufficient funds. In such a case, the check is marked

NSF (not sufficient funds) by the customer's bank and is returned to the depositor's bank. The bank then debits the depositor's account, as shown by the symbol NSF on the bank statement in Illustration 8-11 (on page 352). The bank sends the NSF check and debit memorandum to the depositor as notification of the charge. Notice of an NSF check creates an account receivable (from the bad check writer) for the depositor and reduces cash in the bank account.

Credit Memorandum

A depositor may ask the bank to collect its notes receivable. In such a case, the bank will credit the depositor's account for the cash proceeds of the note. This is illustrated on the W. A. Laird Company bank statement by the symbol CM. The bank will issue a credit memorandum which is sent with the statement to explain the entry. Many banks also offer interest on checking accounts. The interest earned may be indicated on the bank statement by the symbol CM or INT.

Reconciling the Bank Account

STUDY OBJECTIVE 7

Prepare a bank reconciliation.

The bank and the depositor maintain independent records of the depositor's checking account. If you've never had a checking account, you might assume that the respective balances will always agree. In fact, the two balances are seldom the same at any given time. It is therefore necessary to make the balance per books agree with the balance per bank—a process called **reconciling the bank account**. The lack of agreement between the two balances is due to:

1. **Time lags** that prevent one of the parties from recording the transaction in the same period.
2. **Errors** by either party in recording transactions.

Time lags occur frequently. For example, several days may elapse between the time a check is mailed to a payee and the date the check is paid by the bank. Similarly, when the depositor uses the bank's night depository to make its deposits, there will be a difference of at least one day between the time the receipts are recorded by the depositor and the time they are recorded by the bank. A time lag also occurs whenever the bank mails a debit or credit memorandum to the depositor.

Also, errors sometimes occur. The incidence of errors depends on the effectiveness of the internal controls of the depositor and the bank. Bank errors are infrequent. However, either party could accidentally record a $450 check as $45 or $540. In addition, the bank might mistakenly charge a check drawn by C. D. Berg to the account of C. D. Burg.

Reconciliation Procedure

Accounting Matters!

To obtain maximum benefit from a bank reconciliation, the reconciliation should be prepared by an employee who has no other responsibilities pertaining to cash. When the internal control principle of independent internal verification is not followed in preparing the reconciliation, cash embezzlements may go unnoticed. For example, a cashier who prepares the reconciliation can embezzle cash and conceal the embezzlement by misstating the reconciliation. Thus, the bank accounts would reconcile, and the embezzlement would not be detected.

In reconciling the bank account, it is customary to reconcile the balance per books and balance per bank to their adjusted (correct or true) cash balances. The reconciliation schedule is divided into two sections. The starting point in preparing the reconciliation is to enter the balance per bank statement and balance per books on the schedule. Adjustments are then made to each section, as shown in

Illustration 8-12. The steps listed below and on the next page should reveal all the reconciling items that cause the difference between the two balances.

Illustration 8-12
Bank reconciliation procedures

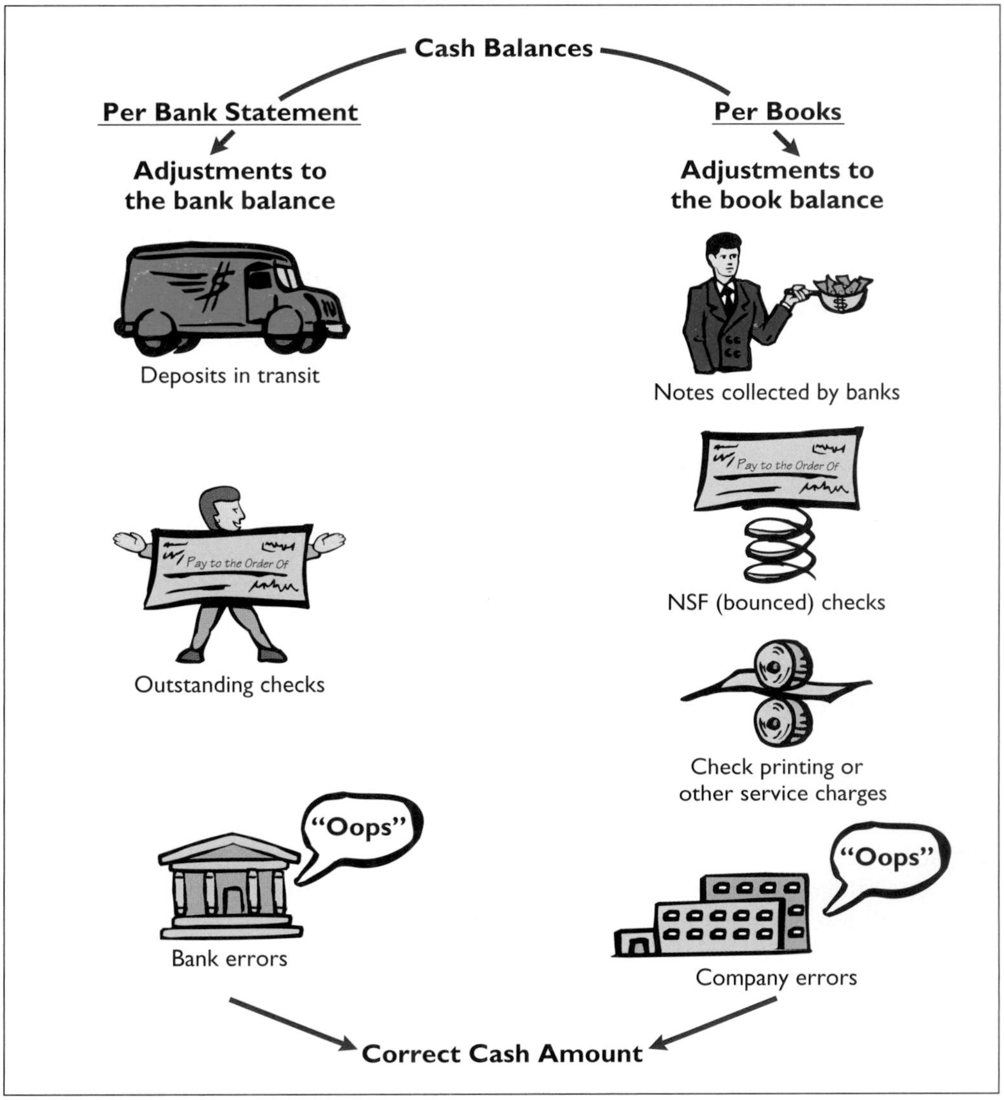

Steps in the Reconciliation Procedure

1. **Deposits in transit.** Compare the individual deposits on the bank statement with deposits in transit from the preceding bank reconciliation and with the deposits per company records or duplicate deposit slips. Deposits recorded by the depositor that have not been recorded by the bank represent **deposits in transit**. They are added to the balance per bank.

HELPFUL HINT

Deposits in transit and outstanding checks are reconciling items because of time lags.

2. **Outstanding checks.** Compare the paid checks shown on the bank statement or the paid checks returned with the bank statement with (a) checks outstanding from the preceding bank reconciliation, and (b) checks issued by the company as recorded in a special cash payments journal. Issued checks recorded by the company that have not been paid by the bank represent **outstanding checks**. They are deducted from the balance per the bank.
3. **Errors.** Note any **errors** discovered in the foregoing steps. List them in the appropriate section of the reconciliation schedule. For example, if a paid check correctly written by the company for $195 was mistakenly recorded by the com-

pany for $159, the error of $36 is deducted from the balance per books. All errors made by the depositor are reconciling items in determining the adjusted cash balance per books. In contrast, all errors made by the bank are reconciling items in determining the adjusted cash balance per the bank.

4. **Bank memoranda.** Trace **bank memoranda** to the depositor's records. Any unrecorded memoranda should be listed in the appropriate section of the reconciliation schedule. For example, a $5 debit memorandum for bank service charges is deducted from the balance per books, and $32 of interest earned is added to the balance per books.

Bank Reconciliation Illustrated

The bank statement for Laird Company was shown in Illustration 8-11 (page 352). It shows a balance per bank of $15,907.45 on April 30, 2006. On this date the balance of cash per books is $11,589.45. From the foregoing steps, the following reconciling items are determined.

1. **Deposits in transit:** April 30 deposit (received by bank on May 1).	$2,201.40
2. **Outstanding checks:** No. 453, $3,000.00; no. 457, $1,401.30; no. 460, $1,502.70.	5,904.00
3. **Errors:** Check no. 443 was correctly written by Laird for $1,226.00 and was correctly paid by the bank. However, it was recorded for $1,262.00 by Laird Company.	36.00
4. **Bank memoranda:**	
a. Debit—NSF check from J. R. Baron for $425.60	425.60
b. Debit—Printing company checks charge $30.00	30.00
c. Credit—Collection of note receivable for $1,000 plus interest earned $50, less bank collection fee $15.00	1,035.00

The bank reconciliation is shown in Illustration 8-13.

HELPFUL HINT

Note in the bank statement that checks no. 459 and 461 have been paid but check no. 460 is not listed. Thus, this check is outstanding. If a complete bank statement were provided, checks no. 453 and 457 would also not be listed. The amounts for these three checks are obtained from the company's cash payments records.

Illustration 8-13
Bank reconciliation

W. A. LAIRD COMPANY
Bank Reconciliation
April 30, 2006

Cash balance per bank statement		$15,907.45
Add: Deposits in transit		2,201.40
		18,108.85
Less: Outstanding checks		
No. 453	$3,000.00	
No. 457	1,401.30	
No. 460	1,502.70	5,904.00
Adjusted cash balance per bank		**$12,204.85**
Cash balance per books		$11,589.45
Add: Collection of note receivable $1,000, plus interest earned $50, less collection fee $15	$1,035.00	
Error in recording check no. 443	36.00	1,071.00
		12,660.45
Less: NSF check	425.60	
Bank service charge	30.00	455.60
Adjusted cash balance per books		**$12,204.85**

ALTERNATIVE TERMINOLOGY

The terms *adjusted balance, true cash balance,* and *correct cash balance* may be used interchangeably.

Entries from Bank Reconciliation

HELPFUL HINT

The entries that follow are adjusting entries. In prior chapters, Cash was an account that did not require adjustment. That was a simplifying assumption for learning purposes, because a bank reconciliation had not been explained.

Each reconciling item in determining the **adjusted cash balance per books** should be recorded by the depositor. **If these items are not journalized and posted, the Cash account will not show the correct balance.** The entries for W. A. Laird Company on April 30 are as follows.

COLLECTION OF NOTE RECEIVABLE. This entry involves four accounts. Assuming that the interest of $50 has not been accrued and the collection fee is charged to Miscellaneous Expense, the entry is:

A	=	L	+	SE
+1,035				−15 Exp
−1,000				+50 Rev

Cash Flows
+1,035

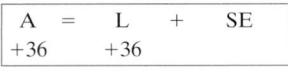

Apr. 30	Cash	1,035.00	
	Miscellaneous Expense	15.00	
	Notes Receivable		1,000.00
	Interest Revenue		50.00
	(To record collection of note receivable by bank)		

BOOK ERROR. A cash disbursements journal shows that check no. 443 was a payment on account to Andrea Company, a supplier. The correcting entry is:

A	=	L	+	SE
+36		+36		

Cash Flows
+36

Apr. 30	Cash	36.00	
	Accounts Payable—Andrea Company		36.00
	(To correct error in recording check no. 443)		

NSF CHECK. As indicated earlier, an NSF check becomes an account receivable to the depositor. The entry is:

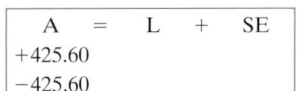

A	=	L	+	SE
+425.60				
−425.60				

Cash Flows
−425.60

Apr. 30	Accounts Receivable—J. R. Baron	425.60	
	Cash		425.60
	(To record NSF check)		

BANK SERVICE CHARGES. Check printing charges (DM) and other bank service charges (SC) are debited to Miscellaneous Expense. They are usually nominal in amount. The entry is:

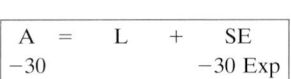

A	=	L	+	SE
−30				−30 Exp

Cash Flows
−30

Apr. 30	Miscellaneous Expense	30.00	
	Cash		30.00
	(To record charge for printing company checks)		

The foregoing four entries could also be combined into one compound entry.

After the entries are posted, the cash account will show the following.

Illustration 8-14
Adjusted balance in cash account

Cash

Apr. 30 Bal.	11,589.45	Apr. 30	425.60
30	1,035.00	30	30.00
30	36.00		
Apr. 30 Bal.	**12,204.85**		

The adjusted cash balance in the ledger should agree with the adjusted cash balance per books in the bank reconciliation in Illustration 8-13.

What entries does the bank make? If any bank errors are discovered in preparing the reconciliation, the bank should be notified. It then can make the necessary corrections on its records. The bank does not make any entries for deposits in transit or outstanding checks. Only when these items reach the bank will the bank record these items.

BEFORE YOU GO ON...

Review It

1. Why is it necessary to reconcile a bank account?
2. What steps are involved in the reconciliation procedure?
3. What information is included in a bank reconciliation?

Do It

Sally Kist owns Linen Kist Fabrics. Sally asks you to explain how the following reconciling items should be treated in reconciling the bank account: (1) a debit memorandum for an NSF check, (2) a credit memorandum for a note collected by the bank, (3) outstanding checks, and (4) a deposit in transit.

ACTION PLAN

- Understand the purpose of a bank reconciliation.
- Identify time lags and explain how they cause reconciling items.

SOLUTION In reconciling the bank account, the reconciling items are treated as follows.

NSF check: Deducted from balance per books.
Collection of note: Added to balance per books.
Outstanding checks: Deducted from balance per bank.
Deposit in transit: Added to balance per bank.

Related exercise material: *BE8-6, BE8-7, BE8-8, BE8-9, BE8-10, E8-6, E8-7, E8-8, E8-9, and E8-10.*

THE NAVIGATOR

Reporting Cash

Cash on hand, cash in banks, and petty cash are often combined and reported simply as **Cash**. Because it is the most liquid asset owned by a company, cash is listed first in the current assets section of the balance sheet. Some companies use the term "Cash and cash equivalents" in reporting cash, as illustrated by the following.

STUDY OBJECTIVE 8

Explain the reporting of cash.

Illustration 8-15
Presentation of cash and cash equivalents

EASTMAN KODAK COMPANY
Balance Sheets (partial)

	2003	2002
Current assets (in millions)		
Cash and cash equivalents	$1,250	$569

Cash equivalents are highly liquid investments that can be converted into a specific amount of cash. They typically have maturities of three months or less when purchased. They include money market funds, money market savings certificates, bank certificates of deposit, and U.S. Treasury bills and notes.

A company may have cash that is restricted for a special purpose. An example is a payroll bank account for paying salaries and wages. Another would be a plant expansion cash fund for financing new construction. If the restricted cash is expected to be used **within the next year**, the amount should be reported as a current asset. When the restricted funds will not be used in that time, they should be reported as a noncurrent asset. Since a payroll bank account will be used as early as the next payday, it is reported as a current asset. In contrast, unless the new construction will begin within the next year, plant expansion fund cash is classified as a noncurrent asset (long-term investment).

In making loans to depositors, banks commonly require borrowers to maintain minimum cash balances. These minimum balances, called **compensating balances**, provide the bank with support for the loans. They are a restriction on the use of cash that may affect a company's liquidity. Thus, compensating balances should be disclosed in the financial statements.

BEFORE YOU GO ON...

Review It

1. What is generally reported as cash on a company's balance sheet?
2. What is meant by cash equivalents and compensating balances?
3. At what amount does **PepsiCo** report cash and cash equivalents in its 2003 consolidated balance sheet? The answer to this question is provided on page 378.

THE NAVIGATOR

DEMONSTRATION PROBLEM

Kevin Poorten Company's bank statement for May 2006 shows the following data.

Balance 5/1	$12,650	Balance 5/31	$14,280
Debit memorandum:		Credit memorandum:	
NSF check	$175	Collection of note receivable	$505

The cash balance per books at May 31 is $13,319. Your review of the data reveals the following.

1. The NSF check was from Brad Copple Co., a customer.
2. The note collected by the bank was a $500, 3-month, 12% note. The bank charged a $10 collection fee. No interest has been accrued.
3. Outstanding checks at May 31 total $2,410.
4. Deposits in transit at May 31 total $1,752.
5. A Kevin Poorten Company check for $352 dated May 10 cleared the bank on May 25. This check, which was a payment on account, was journalized for $325.

Instructions

(a) Prepare a bank reconciliation at May 31.
(b) Journalize the entries required by the reconciliation.

SOLUTION TO DEMONSTRATION PROBLEM

(a)

KEVIN POORTEN COMPANY
Bank Reconciliation
May 31, 2006

Cash balance per bank statement		$14,280
Add: Deposits in transit		1,752
		16,032
Less: Outstanding checks		2,410
Adjusted cash balance per bank		$13,622
Cash balance per books		$13,319
Add: Collection of note receivable $500, plus $15 interest, less collection fee $10		505
		13,824
Less: NSF check	$175	
Error in recording check	27	202
Adjusted cash balance per books		$13,622

(b)

May 31	Cash	505	
	Miscellaneous Expense	10	
	Notes Receivable		500
	Interest Revenue		15
	(To record collection of note by bank)		
31	Accounts Receivable—Brad Copple Co.	175	
	Cash		175
	(To record NSF check from Brad Copple Co.)		
31	Accounts Payable	27	
	Cash		27
	(To correct error in recording check)		

THE NAVIGATOR

ACTION PLAN

- Follow the four steps in the reconciliation procedure. (pp. 354–355).
- Work carefully to minimize mathematical errors in the reconciliation.
- Prepare adjusting entries from reconciling items per books.
- Make sure the cash ledger balance after posting the reconciling entries agrees with the adjusted cash balance per books.

SUMMARY OF STUDY OBJECTIVES

1. **Define internal control.** Internal control is the plan of organization and related methods and procedures adopted within a business to safeguard its assets and to enhance the accuracy and reliability of its accounting records.
2. **Identify the principles of internal control.** The principles of internal control are: establishment of responsibility; segregation of duties; documentation procedures; physical, mechanical, and electronic controls; independent internal verification; and other controls.
3. **Explain the applications of internal control principles to cash receipts.** Internal controls over cash receipts include: (a) designating only personnel such as cashiers to handle cash; (b) assigning the duties of receiving cash, recording cash, and custody of cash to different individuals; (c) preparing remittance advices for mail receipts, cash register tapes for over-the-counter receipts, and deposit slips for bank deposits; (d) using company safes and bank vaults to store cash with access limited to authorized personnel, and using cash registers in executing over-the-counter receipts; (e) making independent daily counts of register receipts and daily comparisons of total receipts with total deposits; and (f) bonding personnel that handle cash and requiring them to take vacations.
4. **Explain the applications of internal control principles to cash disbursements.** Internal controls over cash disbursements include: (a) having only specified individuals such as the treasurer authorized to sign checks; (b) assigning the duties of approving items for payment, paying the items, and recording the payment to different individuals; (c) using prenumbered checks and accounting for all checks, with each check supported by an approved invoice; (d) storing blank checks in a safe or vault with access restricted to authorized personnel, and using a machine to imprint amounts on checks; (e) comparing each check with the

approved invoice before issuing the check, and making monthly reconciliations of bank and book balances; and (f) after payment, stamping each approved invoice "paid."

5. **Describe the operation of a petty cash fund.** In operating a petty cash fund, it is necessary to establish the fund, make payments from the fund, and replenish the fund.

6. **Indicate the control features of a bank account.** A bank account contributes to good internal control by providing physical controls for the storage of cash. It minimizes the amount of currency that must be kept on hand, and it creates a double record of a depositor's bank transactions.

7. **Prepare a bank reconciliation.** It is customary to reconcile the balance per books and balance per bank to their adjusted balances. The steps in determining the reconciling items are to ascertain deposits in transit, outstanding checks, errors by the depositor or the bank, and unrecorded bank memoranda.

8. **Explain the reporting of cash.** Cash is listed first in the current assets section of the balance sheet. In some cases, cash is reported together with cash equivalents. Cash restricted for a special purpose is reported separately as a current asset or as a noncurrent asset, depending on when the cash is expected to be used.

☑ THE NAVIGATOR

GLOSSARY

www.wiley.com/college/weygandt

Bank service charge A fee charged by a bank for the use of its services. (p. 352).

Bank statement A statement received monthly from the bank that shows the depositor's bank transactions and balances. (p. 351).

Cash Resources that consist of coins, currency, checks, money orders, and money on hand or on deposit in a bank or similar depository. (p. 342).

Cash equivalents Highly liquid investments, with maturities of three months or less when purchased, that can be converted to a specific amount of cash. (p. 357).

Check A written order signed by the depositor directing the bank to pay a specified sum of money to a designated recipient. (p. 350).

Compensating balances Minimum cash balances required by a bank in support of bank loans. (p. 358).

Deposits in transit Deposits recorded by the depositor that have not been recorded by the bank. (p. 354).

Electronic funds transfer (EFT) A disbursement system that uses wire, telephone, or computers to transfer cash from one location to another. (p. 346).

Internal auditors Company employees who evaluate on a continuous basis the effectiveness of the company's system of internal control. (p. 339).

Internal control The plan of organization and all the related methods and measures adopted within a business to safeguard its assets and enhance the accuracy and reliability of its accounting records. (p. 335).

NSF check A check that is not paid by a bank because of insufficient funds in a customer's bank account. (p. 353).

Outstanding checks Checks issued and recorded by a company that have not been paid by the bank. (p. 354).

Petty cash fund A cash fund used to pay relatively small amounts. (p. 347).

Voucher An authorization form prepared for each payment by check in a voucher system. (p. 346).

Voucher system A network of approvals by authorized individuals acting independently to ensure that all disbursements by check are proper. (p. 346).

SELF-STUDY QUESTIONS

Self-Study/Self-Test

www.wiley.com/college/weygandt

Answers are at the end of the chapter.

(SO 1) 1. Internal control is used in a business to enhance the accuracy and reliability of its accounting records and to:
   a. safeguard its assets.
   b. prevent fraud.
   c. produce correct financial statements.
   d. deter employee dishonesty.

(SO 2) 2. The principles of internal control do **not** include:
   a. establishment of responsibility.
   b. documentation procedures.
   c. management responsibility.
   d. independent internal verification.

3. Physical controls do *not* include: (SO 2)
   a. safes and vaults to store cash.
   b. independent bank reconciliations.
   c. locked warehouses for inventories.
   d. bank safety deposit boxes for important papers.

4. Which of the following items in a cash drawer at November 30 is *not* cash? (SO 3)
   a. Money orders.
   b. Coins and currency.
   c. A customer check dated December 1.
   d. A customer check dated November 28.

(SO 3) **5.** Permitting only designated personnel to handle cash receipts is an application of the principle of:
a. segregation of duties.
b. establishment of responsibility.
c. independent check.
d. other controls.

(SO 4) **6.** The use of prenumbered checks in disbursing cash is an application of the principle of:
a. establishment of responsibility.
b. segregation of duties.
c. physical, mechanical, and electronic controls.
d. documentation procedures.

(SO 5) **7.** A check is written to replenish a $100 petty cash fund when the fund contains receipts of $94 and $3 in cash. In recording the check,
a. Cash Over and Short should be debited for $3.
b. Petty Cash should be debited for $94.
c. Cash should be credited for $94.
d. Petty Cash should be credited for $3.

(SO 6) **8.** The control features of a bank account do *not* include:
a. having bank auditors verify the correctness of the bank balance per books.
b. minimizing the amount of cash that must be kept on hand.
c. providing a double record of all bank transactions.
d. safeguarding cash by using a bank as a depository.

9. In a bank reconciliation, deposits in transit are: (SO 7)
a. deducted from the book balance.
b. added to the book balance.
c. added to the bank balance.
d. deducted from the bank balance.

10. The reconciling item in a bank reconciliation that will result in an adjusting entry by the depositor is: (SO 7)
a. outstanding checks.
b. deposit in transit.
c. a bank error.
d. bank service charges.

11. The statement that correctly describes the reporting of cash is: (SO 8)
a. Cash cannot be combined with cash equivalents.
b. Restricted cash funds may be combined with Cash.
c. Cash is listed first in the current assets section.
d. Restricted cash funds cannot be reported as a current asset.

THE NAVIGATOR

QUESTIONS

1. "Internal control is concerned only with enhancing the accuracy of the accounting records." Do you agree? Explain.

2. What principles of internal control apply to most business enterprises?

3. At the corner grocery store, all sales clerks make change out of one cash register drawer. Is this a violation of internal control? Why?

4. Pam Duffy is reviewing the principle of segregation of duties. What are the two common applications of this principle?

5. How do documentation procedures contribute to good internal control?

6. What internal control objectives are met by physical, mechanical, and electronic controls?

7. (a) Explain the control principle of independent internal verification. (b) What practices are important in applying this principle?

8. The management of Yaeger Company asks you, as the company accountant, to explain (a) the concept of reasonable assurance in internal control and (b) the importance of the human factor in internal control.

9. Yorkville Fertilizer Co. owns the following assets at the balance sheet date.

Cash in bank savings account	$ 6,000
Cash on hand	850
Cash refund due from the IRS	1,000
Checking account balance	12,000
Postdated checks	500

What amount should be reported as cash in the balance sheet?

10. What principle(s) of internal control is (are) involved in making daily cash counts of over-the-counter receipts?

11. Aurora Department Stores has just installed new electronic cash registers in its stores. How do cash registers improve internal control over cash receipts?

12. At Oswego Wholesale Company, two mail clerks open all mail receipts. How does this strengthen internal control?

13. "To have maximum effective internal control over cash disbursements, all payments should be made by check." Is this true? Explain.

14. Ted Rampolla Company's internal controls over cash disbursements provide for the treasurer to sign checks imprinted by a checkwriter after comparing the check with the approved invoice. Identify the internal control principles that are present in these controls.

15. How do the principles of (a) physical, mechanical, and electronic controls and (b) other controls apply to cash disbursements?

16. (a) What is a voucher system? (b) What principles of internal control apply to a voucher system?

17. What is the essential feature of an electronic funds transfer (EFT) procedure?

18. (a) Identify the three activities that pertain to a petty cash fund, and indicate an internal control principle that is applicable to each activity. (b) When are journal entries required in the operation of a petty cash fund?

19. "The use of a bank contributes significantly to good internal control over cash." Is this true? Why or why not?

20. Faye Uhlik is confused about the lack of agreement between the cash balance per books and the balance per the bank. Explain the causes for the lack of agreement to Faye, and give an example of each cause.

21. What are the four steps involved in finding differences between the balance per books and balance per bank?

22. Pauline Duch asks your help concerning an NSF check. Explain to Pauline (a) what an NSF check is, (b) how it is treated in a bank reconciliation, and (c) whether it will require an adjusting entry.

23. (a) "Cash equivalents are the same as cash." Do you agree? Explain. (b) How should restricted cash funds be reported on the balance sheet?

BRIEF EXERCISES

Explain the importance of internal control.
(SO 1)

BE8-1 Pam Duffy is the new owner of Duffy Parking. She has heard about internal control but is not clear about its importance for her business. Explain to Pam the two purposes of internal control and give her one application of each purpose for Duffy Parking.

Identify internal control principles.
(SO 2)

BE8-2 The internal control procedures in Naperville Company provide that:

(a) Employees who have physical custody of assets do not have access to the accounting records.
(b) Each month the assets on hand are compared to the accounting records by an internal auditor.
(c) A prenumbered shipping document is prepared for each shipment of goods to customers.

Identify the principles of internal control that are being followed.

Identify the internal control principles applicable to cash receipts.
(SO 3)

BE8-3 Sycamore Company has the following internal control procedures over cash receipts. Identify the internal control principle that is applicable to each procedure.

1. All over-the-counter receipts are registered on cash registers.
2. All cashiers are bonded.
3. Daily cash counts are made by cashier department supervisors.
4. The duties of receiving cash, recording cash, and custody of cash are assigned to different individuals.
5. Only cashiers may operate cash registers.

Identify the internal control principles applicable to cash disbursements.
(SO 4)

BE8-4 Helen Hunt Company has the following internal control procedures over cash disbursements. Identify the internal control principle that is applicable to each procedure.

1. Company checks are prenumbered.
2. The bank statement is reconciled monthly by an internal auditor.
3. Blank checks are stored in a safe in the treasurer's office.
4. Only the treasurer or assistant treasurer may sign checks.
5. Check signers are not allowed to record cash disbursement transactions.

Prepare entry to replenish a petty cash fund.
(SO 5)

BE8-5 On March 20, Batavia's petty cash fund of \$100 is replenished when the fund contains \$9 in cash and receipts for postage \$52, freight-out \$26, and travel expense \$10. Prepare the journal entry to record the replenishment of the petty cash fund.

Identify the control features of a bank account.
(SO 6)

BE8-6 Louis St. Pierre is uncertain about the control features of a bank account. Explain the control benefits of **(a)** a signature card, **(b)** a check, and **(c)** a bank statement.

Indicate location of reconciling items in a bank reconciliation.
(SO 7)

BE8-7 The following reconciling items are applicable to the bank reconciliation for Hinckley Company: (1) outstanding checks, (2) bank debit memorandum for service charge, (3) bank credit memorandum for collecting a note for the depositor, (4) deposits in transit. Indicate how each item should be shown on a bank reconciliation.

Identify reconciling items that require adjusting entries.
(SO 7)

BE8-8 Using the data in BE8-7, indicate **(a)** the items that will result in an adjustment to the depositor's records and **(b)** why the other items do not require adjustment.

Prepare partial bank reconciliation.
(SO 7)

BE8-9 At July 31, Shabbona Company has the following bank information: cash balance per bank \$7,420, outstanding checks \$762, deposits in transit \$1,620, and a bank service charge \$20. Determine the adjusted cash balance per bank at July 31.

BE8-10 At August 31, DeKalb Company has a cash balance per books of $8,900 and the following additional data from the bank statement: charge for printing DeKalb Company checks $35, interest earned on checking account balance $40, and outstanding checks $800. Determine the adjusted cash balance per books at August 31.

Prepare partial bank reconciliation.

(SO 7)

BE8-11 Plano Company has the following cash balances: Cash in Bank $15,742, Payroll Bank Account $6,000, and Plant Expansion Fund Cash $25,000. Explain how each balance should be reported on the balance sheet.

Explain the statement presentation of cash balances.

(SO 8)

EXERCISES

E8-1 Sue Ernesto is the owner of Ernesto's Pizza. Ernesto's is operated strictly on a carryout basis. Customers pick up their orders at a counter where a clerk exchanges the pizza for cash. While at the counter, the customer can see other employees making the pizzas and the large ovens in which the pizzas are baked.

Identify the principles of internal control.

(SO 2)

Instructions

Identify the six principles of internal control and give an example of each principle that you might observe when picking up your pizza. (*Note*: It may not be possible to observe all the principles.)

E8-2 The following control procedures are used at Sandwich Company for over-the-counter cash receipts.

Identify internal control weaknesses over cash receipts and suggest improvements.

(SO 2, 3)

1. To minimize the risk of robbery, cash in excess of $100 is stored in an unlocked attaché case in the stock room until it is deposited in the bank.
2. All over-the-counter receipts are registered by three clerks who use a cash register with a single cash drawer.
3. The company accountant makes the bank deposit and then records the day's receipts.
4. At the end of each day, the total receipts are counted by the cashier on duty and reconciled to the cash register total.
5. Cashiers are experienced; they are not bonded.

Instructions

(a) For each procedure, explain the weakness in internal control, and identify the control principle that is violated.

(b) For each weakness, suggest a change in procedure that will result in good internal control.

E8-3 The following control procedures are used in Morgan's Boutique Shoppe for cash disbursements.

Identify internal control weaknesses over cash disbursements and suggest improvements.

(SO 2, 4)

1. The company accountant prepares the bank reconciliation and reports any discrepancies to the owner.
2. The store manager personally approves all payments before signing and issuing checks.
3. Each week, Morgan leaves 100 company checks in an unmarked envelope on a shelf behind the cash register.
4. After payment, bills are filed in a paid invoice folder.
5. The company checks are unnumbered.

Instructions

(a) For each procedure, explain the weakness in internal control, and identify the internal control principle that is violated.

(b) For each weakness, suggest a change in the procedure that will result in good internal control.

E8-4 At Teresa Speck Company, checks are not prenumbered because both the purchasing agent and the treasurer are authorized to issue checks. Each signer has access to unissued checks kept in an unlocked file cabinet. The purchasing agent pays all bills pertaining to goods purchased for resale. Prior to payment, the purchasing agent determines that the goods have been received and verifies the mathematical accuracy of the vendor's invoice. After payment, the invoice is filed by vendor, and the purchasing agent records the payment in the cash disbursements journal. The treasurer pays all other bills following approval by authorized employees. After payment, the treasurer stamps all bills PAID, files them by payment date, and

Identify internal control weaknesses for cash disbursements and suggest improvements.

(SO 4)

records the checks in the cash disbursements journal. Teresa Speck Company maintains one checking account that is reconciled by the treasurer.

Instructions

(a) List the weaknesses in internal control over cash disbursements.

(b) Write a memo to the company treasurer indicating your recommendations for improvement.

Prepare journal entries for a petty cash fund.

(SO 5)

Peachtree

E8-5 LaSalle-Peru Company uses an imprest petty cash system. The fund was established on March 1 with a balance of $100. During March the following petty cash receipts were found in the petty cash box.

Date	Receipt No.	For	Amount
3/5	1	Stamp Inventory	$39
7	2	Freight-out	19
9	3	Miscellaneous Expense	6
11	4	Travel Expense	24
14	5	Miscellaneous Expense	5

The fund was replenished on March 15 when the fund contained $4 in cash. On March 20, the amount in the fund was increased to $150.

Instructions

Journalize the entries in March that pertain to the operation of the petty cash fund.

Prepare bank reconciliation and adjusting entries.

(SO 7)

E8-6 Lisa Ceja is unable to reconcile the bank balance at January 31. Lisa's reconciliation is as follows.

Cash balance per bank	$3,660.20
Add: NSF check	590.00
Less: Bank service charge	25.00
Adjusted balance per bank	$4,225.20
Cash balance per books	$3,875.20
Less: Deposits in transit	530.00
Add: Outstanding checks	930.00
Adjusted balance per books	$4,275.20

Instructions

(a) Prepare a correct bank reconciliation.

(b) Journalize the entries required by the reconciliation.

Determine outstanding checks.

(SO 7)

E8-7 On April 30, the bank reconciliation of Ottawa Company shows three outstanding checks: no. 254, $650, no. 255, $720, and no. 257, $410. The May bank statement and the May cash payments journal show the following.

Bank Statement — Checks Paid

Date	Check No.	Amount
5/4	254	650
5/2	257	410
5/17	258	159
5/12	259	275
5/20	261	500
5/29	263	480
5/30	262	750

Cash Payments Journal — Checks Issued

Date	Check No.	Amount
5/2	258	159
5/5	259	275
5/10	260	790
5/15	261	500
5/22	262	750
5/24	263	480
5/29	264	560

Instructions

Using step 2 in the reconciliation procedure, list the outstanding checks at May 31.

Prepare bank reconciliation and adjusting entries.

(SO 7)

E8-8 The following information pertains to Worthy Video Company.

1. Cash balance per bank, July 31, $7,263.
2. July bank service charge not recorded by the depositor $28.
3. Cash balance per books, July 31, $7,284.
4. Deposits in transit, July 31, $1,500.
5. Bank collected $800 note for Worthy in July, plus interest $36, less collection fee $20. The collection has not been recorded by Worthy, and no interest has been accrued.
6. Outstanding checks, July 31, $691.

Instructions

(a) Prepare a bank reconciliation at July 31.
(b) Journalize the adjusting entries at July 31 on the books of Worthy Video Company.

Prepare bank reconciliation and adjusting entries.

(SO 7)

Peachtree

E8-9 The information below relates to the Cash account in the ledger of Dick Wasson Company.

Balance September 1—$17,150; Cash deposited—$64,000.
Balance September 30—$17,404; Checks written—$63,746.

The September bank statement shows a balance of $16,422 on September 30 and the following memoranda.

Credits		**Debits**	
Collection of $1,500 note plus interest $30	$1,530	NSF check: J. E. Hoover	$725
Interest earned on checking account	$45	Safety deposit box rent	$65

At September 30, deposits in transit were $4,150, and outstanding checks totaled $2,383.

Instructions

(a) Prepare the bank reconciliation at September 30.
(b) Prepare the adjusting entries at September 30, assuming (1) the NSF check was from a customer on account, and (2) no interest had been accrued on the note.

Compute deposits in transit and outstanding checks for two bank reconciliations.

(SO 7)

E8-10 The cash records of Satter Company show the following four situations.

1. The June 30 bank reconciliation indicated that deposits in transit total $920. During July the general ledger account Cash shows deposits of $15,750, but the bank statement indicates that only $15,600 in deposits were received during the month.
2. The June 30 bank reconciliation also reported outstanding checks of $880. During the month of July, Satter Company books show that $17,200 of checks were issued. The bank statement showed that $16,400 of checks cleared the bank in July.
3. In September, deposits per the bank statement totaled $26,700, deposits per books were $25,400, and deposits in transit at September 30 were $2,600.
4. In September, cash disbursements per books were $23,700, checks clearing the bank were $24,000, and outstanding checks at September 30 were $2,100.

There were no bank debit or credit memoranda. No errors were made by either the bank or Satter Company.

Instructions

Answer the following questions.

(a) In situation (1), what were the deposits in transit at July 31?
(b) In situation (2), what were the outstanding checks at July 31?
(c) In situation (3), what were the deposits in transit at August 31?
(d) In situation (4), what were the outstanding checks at August 31?

PROBLEMS: SET A

Identify internal control weaknesses over cash receipts.

(SO 2, 3)

P8-1A Anita Theater is located in the Zurbrugg Mall. A cashier's booth is located near the entrance to the theater. Two cashiers are employed. One works from 1–5 P.M., the other from 5–9 P.M. Each cashier is bonded. The cashiers receive cash from customers and operate a machine that ejects serially numbered tickets. The rolls of tickets are inserted and locked into the machine by the theater manager at the beginning of each cashier's shift.

After purchasing a ticket, the customer takes the ticket to an usher stationed at the entrance of the theater lobby some 60 feet from the cashier's booth. The usher tears the ticket in half, admits the customer, and returns the ticket stub to the customer. The other half of the ticket is dropped into a locked box by the usher.

At the end of each cashier's shift, the theater manager removes the ticket rolls from the machine and makes a cash count. The cash count sheet is initialed by the cashier. At the end of the day, the manager deposits the receipts in total in a bank night deposit vault located in the mall. The manager also sends copies of the deposit slip and the initialed cash count sheets to the theater company treasurer for verification and to the company's accounting department. Receipts from the first shift are stored in a safe located in the manager's office.

Instructions

(a) Identify the internal control principles and their application to the cash receipts transactions of the Anita Theater.

(b) If the usher and cashier decide to collaborate to misappropriate cash, what actions might they take?

Journalize and post petty cash fund transactions.

(SO 5)

P8-2A M.L. McArtor Company maintains a petty cash fund for small expenditures. The following transactions occurred over a 2-month period.

July 1 Established petty cash fund by writing a check on Landmark Bank for $200.

15 Replenished the petty cash fund by writing a check for $196.30. On this date the fund consisted of $3.70 in cash and the following petty cash receipts: freight-out $94.00, postage expense $42.40, entertainment expense $45.90, and miscellaneous expense $10.70.

31 Replenished the petty cash fund by writing a check for $192.00. At this date, the fund consisted of $8.00 in cash and the following petty cash receipts: freight-out $82.10, charitable contributions expense $30.00, postage expense $47.80, and miscellaneous expense $32.10.

Aug. 15 Replenished the petty cash fund by writing a check for $188.00. On this date, the fund consisted of $12.00 in cash and the following petty cash receipts: freight-out $74.40, entertainment expense $41.50, postage expense $33.00, and miscellaneous expense $38.00.

16 Increased the amount of the petty cash fund to $300 by writing a check for $100.

31 Replenished petty cash fund by writing a check for $283.00. On this date, the fund consisted of $17 in cash and the following petty cash receipts: postage expense $145.00, entertainment expense $90.60, and freight-out $46.00.

Instructions

(a) July 15 Cash short $3.30
(b) Aug. 31 balance $300

(a) Journalize the petty cash transactions.

(b) Post to the Petty Cash account.

(c) What internal control features exist in a petty cash fund?

Prepare a bank reconciliation and adjusting entries.

(SO 7)

P8-3A Agricultural Genetics Company of Lawrence, Kansas, spreads herbicides and applies liquid fertilizer for local farmers. On May 31, 2006, the company's cash account per its general ledger showed the following balance.

CASH **No. 101**

Date	Explanation	Ref.	Debit	Credit	Balance
May 31	Balance				6,781.50

The bank statement from Lawrence State Bank on that date showed the following balance.

LAWRENCE STATE BANK

Checks and Debits	Deposits and Credits	Daily Balance
XXX	XXX	5/31 6,804.60

A comparison of the details on the bank statement with the details in the cash account revealed the following facts.

1. The statement included a debit memo of $40 for the printing of additional company checks.
2. Cash sales of $836.15 on May 12 were deposited in the bank. The cash receipts journal entry and the deposit slip were incorrectly made for $846.15. The bank credited Agricultural Genetics Company for the correct amount.

3. Outstanding checks at May 31 totaled $315.25, and deposits in transit were $936.15.
4. On May 18, the company issued check no. 1181 for $685 to M. Datz, on account. The check, which cleared the bank in May, was incorrectly journalized and posted by Agricultural Genetics Company for $658.
5. A $2,000 note receivable was collected by the bank for Agricultural Genetics Company on May 31 plus $80 interest. The bank charged a collection fee of $25. No interest has been accrued on the note.
6. Included with the cancelled checks was a check issued by Bohr Company to Fred Mertz for $600 that was incorrectly charged to Agricultural Genetics Company by the bank.
7. On May 31, the bank statement showed an NSF charge of $734 for a check issued by Tyler Gricius, a customer, to Agricultural Genetics Company on account.

Instructions

(a) Prepare the bank reconciliation at May 31, 2006.

(a) Adj. cash bal. $8,025.50

(b) Prepare the necessary adjusting entries for Agricultural Genetics Company at May 31, 2006.

P8-4A The bank portion of the bank reconciliation for Michael Mooney Company at October 31, 2006 was as follows.

Prepare a bank reconciliation and adjusting entries from detailed data.

(SO 7)

Peachtree

MICHAEL MOONEY COMPANY
Bank Reconciliation
October 31, 2006

Cash balance per bank			$12,444.70
Add: Deposits in transit			1,530.20
			13,974.90
Less: Outstanding checks			
	Check Number	Check Amount	
	2451	$1,260.40	
	2470	720.10	
	2471	844.50	
	2472	503.60	
	2474	1,050.00	4,378.60
Adjusted cash balance per bank			$ 9,596.30

The adjusted cash balance per bank agreed with the cash balance per books at October 31. The November bank statement showed the following checks and deposits:

Bank Statement

Checks			Deposits	
Date	**Number**	**Amount**	**Date**	**Amount**
11-1	2470	$ 720.10	11-1	$ 1,530.20
11-2	2471	844.50	11-4	1,211.60
11-5	2474	1,050.00	11-8	990.10
11-4	2475	1,640.70	11-13	2,575.00
11-8	2476	2,830.00	11-18	1,472.70
11-10	2477	600.00	11-21	2,945.00
11-15	2479	1,750.00	11-25	2,567.30
11-18	2480	1,330.00	11-28	1,650.00
11-27	2481	695.40	11-30	1,186.00
11-30	2483	575.50	Total	$16,127.90
11-29	2486	900.00		
	Total	$12,936.20		

The cash records per books for November showed the following.

Cash Payments Journal

Date	Number	Amount	Date	Number	Amount
11-1	2475	$1,640.70	11-20	2483	$ 575.50
11-2	2476	2,830.00	11-22	2484	829.50
11-2	2477	600.00	11-23	2485	974.80
11-4	2478	538.20	11-24	2486	900.00
11-8	2479	1,570.00	11-29	2487	398.00
11-10	2480	1,330.00	11-30	2488	1,200.00
11-15	2481	695.40	Total		$14,694.10
11-18	2482	612.00			

Cash Receipts Journal

Date	Amount
11-3	$ 1,211.60
11-7	990.10
11-12	2,575.00
11-17	1,472.70
11-20	2,954.00
11-24	2,567.30
11-27	1,650.00
11-29	1,186.00
11-30	1,338.00
Total	$15,944.70

The bank statement contained two bank memoranda:

1. A credit of $1,505 for the collection of a $1,400 note for Mooney Company plus interest of $120 and less a collection fee of $15. Mooney Company has not accrued any interest on the note.
2. A debit for the printing of additional company checks $72.

At November 30, the cash balance per books was $10,846.90, and the cash balance per the bank statement was $17,069.40. The bank did not make any errors, but two errors were made by Mooney Company.

Instructions

(a) Adjusted cash balance per bank $12,090.90

(a) Using the four steps in the reconciliation procedure described on pages 354–355, prepare a bank reconciliation at November 30.

(b) Prepare the adjusting entries based on the reconciliation. (*Hint*: The correction of any errors pertaining to recording checks should be made to Accounts Payable. The correction of any errors relating to recording cash receipts should be made to Accounts Receivable).

Prepare a bank reconciliation and adjusting entries.
(SO 7)

P8-5A Mario Tizani Company's bank statement from Last National Bank at August 31, 2006, shows the following information.

Balance, August 1	$17,400	Bank credit memoranda:	
August deposits	73,110	Collection of note receivable plus $90 interest	$5,090
Checks cleared in August	69,660	Interest earned	32
Balance, August 31	25,932	Bank debit memorandum:	
		Safety deposit box rent	40

A summary of the Cash account in the ledger for August shows: Balance, August 1, $16,900; receipts $77,000; disbursements $73,570; and balance, August 31, $20,330. Analysis reveals that the only reconciling items on the July 31 bank reconciliation were a deposit in transit for $4,000 and outstanding checks of $4,500. The deposit in transit was the first deposit recorded by the bank in August. In addition, you determine that there were two errors involving company checks drawn in August: (1) A check for $400 to a creditor on account that cleared the bank in August was journalized and posted for $420. (2) A salary check to an employee for $275 was recorded by the bank for $278.

Instructions

(a) Adjusted balance per books $25,432

(a) Prepare a bank reconciliation at August 31.

(b) Journalize the adjusting entries to be made by Mario Tizani Company at August 31. Assume the interest on the note has been accrued by the company.

Prepare comprehensive bank reconciliation with theft and internal control deficiencies.
(SO 2, 3, 4, 7)

P8-6A Stupendous Company is a very profitable small business. It has not, however, given much consideration to internal control. For example, in an attempt to keep clerical and office expenses to a minimum, the company has combined the jobs of cashier and bookkeeper. As a result, Jake Stickyfingers handles all cash receipts, keeps the accounting records, and prepares the monthly bank reconciliations.

The balance per the bank statement on October 31, 2006, was $18,280. Outstanding checks were: no. 62 for $326.75, no. 183 for $150, no. 284 for $253.25, no. 862 for $190.71, no. 863 for $226.80, and no. 864 for $165.28. Included with the statement was a credit memorandum of $300 indicating the collection of a note receivable for Stupendous Company by the bank on October 25. This memorandum has not been recorded by Stupendous Company.

The company's ledger showed one cash account with a balance of $21,892.72. The balance included undeposited cash on hand. Because of the lack of internal controls, Stickyfingers took for personal use all of the undeposited receipts in excess of $3,795.51. He then prepared the following bank reconciliation in an effort to conceal his theft of cash.

Bank Reconciliation

Cash balance per books, October 31		$21,892.72
Add: Outstanding checks		
No. 862	$190.71	
No. 863	226.80	
No. 864	165.28	482.79
		22,375.51
Less: Undeposited receipts		3,795.51
Unadjusted balance per bank, October 31		18,580.00
Less: Bank credit memorandum		300.00
Cash balance per bank statement, October 31		$18,280.00

Instructions

(a) Prepare a correct bank reconciliation. (*Hint*: Deduct the amount of the theft from the adjusted balance per books.)

(a) Adjusted balance per books $20,762.72

(b) Indicate the three ways that Stickyfingers attempted to conceal the theft and the dollar amount pertaining to each method.

(c) What principles of internal control were violated in this case?

PROBLEMS: SET B

Identify internal control principles over cash disbursements.

(SO 2, 4)

P8-1B Gore Office Supply Company recently changed its system of internal control over cash disbursements. The system includes the following features.

Instead of being unnumbered and manually prepared, all checks must now be prenumbered and written by using the new checkwriter purchased by the company. Before a check can be issued, each invoice must have the approval of Sally Morgan, the purchasing agent, and John Countryman, the receiving department supervisor. Checks must be signed by either Ann Lynn, the treasurer, or Bob Skabo, the assistant treasurer. Before signing a check, the signer is expected to compare the amount of the check with the amount on the invoice.

After signing a check, the signer stamps the invoice PAID and inserts within the stamp, the date, check number, and amount of the check. The "paid" invoice is then sent to the accounting department for recording.

Blank checks are stored in a safe in the treasurer's office. The combination to the safe is known only by the treasurer and assistant treasurer. Each month, the bank statement is reconciled with the bank balance per books by the assistant chief accountant.

Instructions

Identify the internal control principles and their application to cash disbursements of Gore Office Supply Company.

Journalize and post petty cash fund transactions.

(SO 5)

P8-2B Sammy Sosa Company maintains a petty cash fund for small expenditures. The following transactions occurred over a 2-month period.

July 1 Established petty cash fund by writing a check on Cubs Bank for $200.

15 Replenished the petty cash fund by writing a check for $198.00. On this date the fund consisted of $2.00 in cash and the following petty cash receipts: freight-out $94.00, postage expense $42.40, entertainment expense $46.60, and miscellaneous expense $11.20.

31 Replenished the petty cash fund by writing a check for $192.00. At this date, the fund consisted of $8.00 in cash and the following petty cash receipts: freight-out $82.10, charitable contributions expense $45.00, postage expense $25.50, and miscellaneous expense $39.40.

Aug. 15 Replenished the petty cash fund by writing a check for $187.00. On this date, the fund consisted of $13.00 in cash and the following petty cash receipts: freight-out $74.60, entertainment expense $43.00, postage expense $33.00, and miscellaneous expense $37.00.

16 Increased the amount of the petty cash fund to $300 by writing a check for $100.

31 Replenished petty cash fund by writing a check for $284.00. On this date, the fund consisted of $16 in cash and the following petty cash receipts: postage expense $140.00, travel expense $95.60, and freight-out $47.10.

Instructions

(a) July 15, Cash short $3.80
(b) Aug. 31 balance $300

(a) Journalize the petty cash transactions.
(b) Post to the Petty Cash account.
(c) What internal control features exist in a petty cash fund?

Prepare a bank reconciliation and adjusting entries.
(SO 7)

P8-3B On May 31, 2006, Terry Duffy Company had a cash balance per books of $6,781.50. The bank statement from Farmers State Bank on that date showed a balance of $6,804.60. A comparison of the statement with the cash account revealed the following facts.

1. The statement included a debit memo of $40 for the printing of additional company checks.
2. Cash sales of $836.15 on May 12 were deposited in the bank. The cash receipts journal entry and the deposit slip were incorrectly made for $886.15. The bank credited Duffy Company for the correct amount.
3. Outstanding checks at May 31 totaled $276.25. Deposits in transit were $1,916.15.
4. On May 18, the company issued check No. 1181 for $685 to Barry Trest, on account. The check, which cleared the bank in May, was incorrectly journalized and posted by Duffy Company for $658.
5. A $3,000 note receivable was collected by the bank for Duffy Company on May 31 plus $80 interest. The bank charged a collection fee of $20. No interest has been accrued on the note.
6. Included with the cancelled checks was a check issued by Bridgetown Company to Tom Lujak for $600 that was incorrectly charged to Duffy Company by the bank.
7. On May 31, the bank statement showed an NSF charge of $680 for a check issued by Sandy Grifton, a customer, to Duffy Company on account.

Instructions

(a) Adjusted cash balance per bank $9,044.50

(a) Prepare the bank reconciliation at May 31, 2006.
(b) Prepare the necessary adjusting entries for Duffy Company at May 31, 2006.

Prepare a bank reconciliation and adjusting entries from detailed data.
(SO 7)

P8-4B The bank portion of the bank reconciliation for Heinisch Company at November 30, 2006, was as follows.

HEINISCH COMPANY
Bank Reconciliation
November 30, 2006

Cash balance per bank		$14,367.90
Add: Deposits in transit		2,530.20
		16,898.10
Less: Outstanding checks		
Check Number	Check Amount	
3451	$2,260.40	
3470	720.10	
3471	844.50	
3472	1,426.80	
3474	1,050.00	6,301.80
Adjusted cash balance per bank		$10,596.30

The adjusted cash balance per bank agreed with the cash balance per books at November 30.

The December bank statement showed the following checks and deposits.

Bank Statement

Checks			Deposits	
Date	**Number**	**Amount**	**Date**	**Amount**
12-1	3451	$ 2,260.40	12-1	$ 2,530.20
12-2	3471	844.50	12-4	1,211.60
12-7	3472	1,426.80	12-8	2,365.10
12-4	3475	1,640.70	12-16	2,672.70
12-8	3476	1,300.00	12-21	2,945.00
12-10	3477	2,130.00	12-26	2,567.30
12-15	3479	3,080.00	12-29	2,836.00
12-27	3480	600.00	12-30	1,025.00
12-30	3482	475.50	Total	$18,152.90
12-29	3483	1,140.00		
12-31	3485	540.80		
	Total	$15,438.70		

The cash records per books for December showed the following.

Cash Payments Journal

Date	Number	Amount	Date	Number	Amount
12-1	3475	$1,640.70	12-20	3482	$ 475.50
12-2	3476	1,300.00	12-22	3483	1,140.00
12-2	3477	2,130.00	12-23	3484	798.00
12-4	3478	621.30	12-24	3485	450.80
12-8	3479	3,080.00	12-30	3486	1,889.50
12-10	3480	600.00	Total		$14,933.20
12-17	3481	807.40			

Cash Receipts Journal

Date	Amount
12-3	$ 1,211.60
12-7	2,365.10
12-15	2,672.70
12-20	2,954.00
12-25	2,567.30
12-28	2,836.00
12-30	1,025.00
12-31	1,190.40
Total	$16,822.10

The bank statement contained two memoranda:

1. A credit of $3,645 for the collection of a $3,500 note for Heinisch Company plus interest of $160 and less a collection fee of $15. Heinisch Company has not accrued any interest on the note.
2. A debit of $572.80 for an NSF check written by D. Chagnon, a customer. At December 31, the check had not been redeposited in the bank.

At December 31 the cash balance per books was $12,485.20, and the cash balance per the bank statement was $20,154.30. The bank did not make any errors, but two errors were made by Heinisch Company.

Instructions

(a) Using the four steps in the reconciliation procedure, prepare a bank reconciliation at December 31.

(a) Adjusted balance per books $15,458.40

(b) Prepare the adjusting entries based on the reconciliation. (*Hint*: The correction of any errors pertaining to recording checks should be made to Accounts Payable. The correction of any errors relating to recording cash receipts should be made to Accounts Receivable.)

Prepare a bank reconciliation and adjusting entries.

(SO 7)

P8-5B Cell Ten Company maintains a checking account at the Commerce Bank. At July 31, selected data from the ledger balance and the bank statement are as follows.

	Cash in Bank	
	Per Books	Per Bank
Balance, July 1	$17,600	$18,800
July receipts	81,400	
July credits		80,470
July disbursements	77,150	
July debits		74,756
Balance, July 31	$21,850	$24,514

Analysis of the bank data reveals that the credits consist of $79,000 of July deposits and a credit memorandum of $1,470 for the collection of a $1,400 note plus interest revenue of $70. The July debits per bank consist of checks cleared $74,700 and a debit memorandum of $56 for printing additional company checks.

You also discover the following errors involving July checks: (1) A check for $230 to a creditor on account that cleared the bank in July was journalized and posted as $320. (2) A salary check to an employee for $255 was recorded by the bank for $155.

The June 30 bank reconciliation contained only two reconciling items: deposits in transit $5,000 and outstanding checks of $6,200.

Instructions

(a) Adjusted balance per books $23,354

(a) Prepare a bank reconciliation at July 31.

(b) Journalize the adjusting entries to be made by Cell Ten Company at July 31, 2006. Assume that the interest on the note has been accrued.

Identify internal control weaknesses in cash receipts and cash disbursements.

(SO 2, 3, 4)

P8-6B Anamosa Middle School wants to raise money for a new sound system for its auditorium. The primary fund-raising event is a dance at which the famous disc jockey Obnoxious Al will play classic and not-so-classic dance tunes. Rob Drexler, the music and theater instructor, has been given the responsibility for coordinating the fund-raising efforts. This is Rob's first experience with fund-raising. He decides to put the eighth-grade choir in charge of the event; he will be a relatively passive observer.

Rob had 500 unnumbered tickets printed for the dance. He left the tickets in a box on his desk and told the choir students to take as many tickets as they thought they could sell for $5 each. In order to ensure that no extra tickets would be floating around, he told them to dispose of any unsold tickets. When the students received payment for the tickets, they were to bring the cash back to Rob, and he would put it in a locked box in his desk drawer.

Some of the students were responsible for decorating the gymnasium for the dance. Rob gave each of them a key to the money box and told them that if they took money out to purchase materials, they should put a note in the box saying how much they took and what it was used for. After 2 weeks the money box appeared to be getting full, so Rob asked Erik Radley to count the money, prepare a deposit slip, and deposit the money in a bank account Rob had opened.

The day of the dance, Rob wrote a check from the account to pay the DJ. Obnoxious Al, however, said that he accepted only cash and did not give receipts. So Rob took $200 out of the cash box and gave it to Al. At the dance Rob had Mel Harris working at the entrance to the gymnasium, collecting tickets from students and selling tickets to those who had not prepurchased them. Rob estimated that 400 students attended the dance.

The following day Rob closed out the bank account, which had $250 in it, and gave that amount plus the $180 in the cash box to Principal Foran. Principal Foran seemed surprised that, after generating roughly $2,000 in sales, the dance netted only $430 in cash. Rob did not know how to respond.

Instructions

Identify as many internal control weaknesses as you can in this scenario, and suggest how each could be addressed.

BROADENING YOUR PERSPECTIVE

Financial Reporting and Analysis

■ FINANCIAL REPORTING PROBLEM: PepsiCo

BYP8-1 The financial statements of **PepsiCo, Inc.** are presented in Appendix A at the end of this textbook.

Instructions

(a) What comments, if any, are made about cash in the report of the independent auditors?

(b) What data about cash and cash equivalents are shown in the consolidated balance sheet?

(c) In its notes to Consolidated Financial Statements, how does PepsiCo, Inc. define cash equivalents?

(d) In management's letter that assumes "Responsibility for Financial Statements," what does PepsiCo's management say about internal control? (See page 78 of its 2003 Annual Report or page A7 of Appendix A in this book.)

■ COMPARATIVE ANALYSIS PROBLEM: PepsiCo vs. Coca-Cola

BYP8-2 **PepsiCo**'s financial statements are presented in Appendix A. **Coca-Cola Company**'s financial statements are presented in Appendix B.

Instructions

(a) Based on the information contained in these financial statements, determine each of the following for each company:

(1) Cash and cash equivalents balance at December 27, 2003, for PepsiCo and at December 31, 2003, for Coca-Cola.

(2) Increase (decrease) in cash and cash equivalents from 2002 to 2003.

(3) Cash provided by operating activities during the year ended December 2003 (from Statement of Cash Flows).

(b) What conclusions concerning the management of cash can be drawn from these data?

■ RESEARCH CASE

BYP8-3 The September 6, 2001, issue of the *Wall Street Journal* includes an article by Shirley Leung titled "Checks, Balances Were Needed to Avert Alleged Game Scam by Simon Worldwide."

Instructions

Read the article and answer the following questions.

(a) Describe the nature of the theft that is described in the article.

(b) What were the internal control weaknesses that allowed this theft to occur?

(c) What methods do other companies in this industry use to avoid a similar type of theft?

(d) What was one "clue" that the company managers overlooked that should have alerted them that there was a problem?

■ INTERPRETING FINANCIAL STATEMENTS

BYP8-4 **Microsoft** is the leading developer of software in the world. To continue to be successful Microsoft must generate new products, and generating new products requires significant amounts of cash. Shown on page 374 is the current assets and current liabilities information from Microsoft's June 30, 2003, balance sheet (in millions). Following the Microsoft data is the current assets and current liabilities information for **Oracle** (in millions), another major software developer.

MICROSOFT, INC.
Balance Sheets (partial)
As of June 30
(in millions)

	2003	2002
Current assets		
Cash and equivalents	$ 6,438	$ 3,016
Short-term investments	42,610	35,636
Accounts receivable	5,196	5,129
Other	4,729	4,795
Total current assets	$58,973	$48,576
Total current liabilities	$13,974	$12,744

ORACLE®

ORACLE
Balance Sheets (partial)
As of May 31
(in millions)

	2003	2002
Current assets		
Cash and cash equivalents	$4,737	$3,095
Short-term investments	1,782	2,746
Receivables	1,920	2,036
Other current assets	788	851
Total current assets	$9,227	$8,728
Current liabilities	$4,158	$3,960

Instructions

(a) What is the definition of a cash equivalent? Give some examples of cash equivalents. How do cash equivalents differ from other types of short-term investments?

(b) Calculate (1) the current ratio and (2) working capital for each company for 2003 and discuss your results.

(c) Is it possible to have too many liquid assets?

■ A GLOBAL FOCUS

BYP8-5 The international accounting firm **KPMG** performed a global survey on e-fraud. Included in its virtual library, at its Web site, is a March 29, 2001, article titled "E-fraud: Is Technology Running Unchecked?" that summarizes the findings of that global survey.

Address: www.kpmg.com/about/press.asp?cid=469, or go to www.wiley.com/college/weygandt

Instructions

Read the article at the Web site, and answer the following questions.

(a) What do most senior managers in corporations believe to be the most likely perpetrator of a breach of their network systems, and in fact, what is the actual greatest threat?

(b) What percentage of firms perform security audits of their e-commerce systems?

(c) What is the problem with fixing a security breach immediately upon learning that a breach of the system has occurred?

(d) What percentage of the companies had experienced a security breach in the last year? In these instances, what percentage did not take legal action against the perpetrator of the breach?

(e) How did the findings of the survey vary across countries and across other geographic distinctions?

■ EXPLORING THE WEB

BYP8-6 All organizations should have systems of internal control. Universities are no exception. This site discusses the basics of internal control in a university setting.

Address: www.bc.edu/offices/audit/controls/, or go to www.wiley.com/college/weygandt

Steps: Go the site shown above.

Instructions

The front page of this site provides links to pages that answer six critical questions. Use these links to answer the following questions.

(a) In a university setting who has responsibility for evaluating the adequacy of the system of internal control?
(b) What do reconciliations ensure in the university setting? Who should review the reconciliation?
(c) What are some examples of physical controls?
(d) What are two ways to accomplish inventory counts?

Critical Thinking

■ GROUP DECISION CASE

BYP8-7 The board of trustees of a local church is concerned about the internal accounting controls for the offering collections made at weekly services. The trustees ask you to serve on a three-person audit team with the internal auditor of a local college and a CPA who has just joined the church.

At a meeting of the audit team and the board of trustees you learn the following.

1. The church's board of trustees has delegated responsibility for the financial management and audit of the financial records to the finance committee. This group prepares the annual budget and approves major disbursements. It is not involved in collections or record keeping. No audit has been made in recent years because the same trusted employee has kept church records and served as financial secretary for 15 years. The church does not carry any fidelity insurance.
2. The collection at the weekly service is taken by a team of ushers who volunteer to serve one month. The ushers take the collection plates to a basement office at the rear of the church. They hand their plates to the head usher and return to the church service. After all plates have been turned in, the head usher counts the cash received. The head usher then places the cash in the church safe along with a notation of the amount counted. The head usher volunteers to serve for 3 months.
3. The next morning the financial secretary opens the safe and recounts the collection. The secretary withholds \$150–\$200 in cash, depending on the cash expenditures expected for the week, and deposits the remainder of the collections in the bank. To facilitate the deposit, church members who contribute by check are asked to make their checks payable to "Cash."
4. Each month, the financial secretary reconciles the bank statement and submits a copy of the reconciliation to the board of trustees. The reconciliations have rarely contained any bank errors and have never shown any errors per books.

Instructions

With the class divided into groups, answer the following.

(a) Indicate the weaknesses in internal accounting control over the handling of collections.
(b) List the improvements in internal control procedures that you plan to make at the next meeting of the audit team for (1) the ushers, (2) the head usher, (3) the financial secretary, and (4) the finance committee.
(c) What church policies should be changed to improve internal control?

■ COMMUNICATION ACTIVITY

BYP8-8 As a new auditor for the CPA firm of Croix, Marais, and Kale, you have been assigned to review the internal controls over mail cash receipts of Stillwater Company. Your review reveals the following: Checks are promptly endorsed "For Deposit Only," but no list of the checks is prepared by the person opening the mail. The mail is opened either by the cashier or by the employee who maintains the accounts receivable records. Mail receipts are deposited in the bank weekly by the cashier.

Instructions
Write a letter to Peter A. Bridgman, owner of the Stillwater Company, explaining the weaknesses in internal control and your recommendations for improving the system.

Accounting Matters!

■ ETHICS CASES

BYP8-9 You are the assistant controller in charge of general ledger accounting at Springtime Bottling Company. Your company has a large loan from an insurance company. The loan agreement requires that the company's cash account balance be maintained at $200,000 or more, as reported monthly.

At June 30 the cash balance is $80,000, which you report to Anne Shirley, the financial vice president. Anne excitedly instructs you to keep the cash receipts book open for one additional day for purposes of the June 30 report to the insurance company. Anne says, "If we don't get that cash balance over $200,000, we'll default on our loan agreement. They could close us down, put us all out of our jobs!" Anne continues, "I talked to Oconto Distributors (one of Springtime's largest customers) this morning. They said they sent us a check for $150,000 yesterday. We should receive it tomorrow. If we include just that one check in our cash balance, we'll be in the clear. It's in the mail!"

Instructions
(a) Who will suffer negative effects if you do not comply with Anne Shirley's instructions? Who will suffer if you do comply?
(b) What are the ethical considerations in this case?
(c) What alternatives do you have?

www.wiley.com/college/weygandt

BYP8-10 **Fraud Bureau** is a free service, established to alert consumers and investors about prior complaints relating to online vendors, including sellers at online auctions, and to provide consumers, investors, and users with information and news. One of the services it provides is a collection of online educational articles related to fraud.

Address: www.fraudbureau.com/articles/, or go to www.wiley.com/college/weygandt

Instructions
Go to this site and choose an article of interest to you. Write a short summary of your findings.

Accounting Matters!

■ CONTINUING COOKIE CHRONICLE

(Note: This is a continuation of the Cookie Chronicle from Chapters 1 through 7.)

BYP8-11

Part 1 Natalie is struggling to keep up with the recording of her accounting transactions. She is spending a lot of time marketing and selling mixers and giving her cookie classes. Her friend John is an accounting student who runs his own accounting service. He has asked Natalie if she would like to have him do her accounting.

John and Natalie meet and discuss her business. John suggests that he do the following for Natalie.

1. Hold onto cash until there is enough to be deposited. (He would keep the cash locked up in his vehicle). He would also take all of the deposits to the bank at least twice a month.
2. Write and sign all of the checks.
3. Record all of the deposits in the accounting records.
4. Record all of the checks in the accounting records.
5. Prepare the monthly bank reconciliation.
6. Transfer all of Natalie's manual accounting records to his computer accounting program. John maintains all of the accounting information that he keeps for his clients on his laptop computer.
7. Prepare monthly financial statements for Natalie to review.
8. Write himself a check every month for the work he has done for Natalie.

Instructions
Identify the weaknesses in internal control that you see in the system that John is recommending. (Consider the principles of internal control identified in the chapter.) Can you suggest any improvements if John is hired to do Natalie's accounting?

Part 2 Natalie decides that she cannot afford to hire John to do her accounting. One way that she can ensure that her cash account does not have any errors and is accurate and up-to-date is to prepare a bank reconciliation at the end of each month.

Natalie would like you to help her. She asks you to prepare a bank reconciliation for June 2006 using the following information.

GENERAL LEDGER—COOKIE CREATIONS

Cash

Date	Explanation	Ref.	Debit	Credit	Balance
2006					
June 1	Balance				2,657
1			750		3,407
3	Check #600			625	2,782
3	Check #601			95	2,687
8	Check #602			56	2,631
9			1,050		3,681
13	Check #603			425	3,256
20			155		3,411
28	Check #604			247	3,164
28			110		3,274

PREMIER BANK

Statement of Account—Cookie Creations
June 30, 2006

Date	Explanation	Checks and Other Debits	Deposits	Balance
May 31	Balance			3,256
June 1	Deposit		750	4,006
6	Check #600	625		3,381
6	Check #601	95		3,286
8	Check #602	56		3,230
9	Deposit		1,050	4,280
10	NSF check	100		4,180
10	NSF–fee	35		4,145
14	Check #603	452		3,693
20	Deposit		125	3,818
23	EFT–Telus	85		3,733
28	Check #599	361		3,372
30	Bank charges	13		3,359

Additional information:

1. On May 31, there were two outstanding checks: #595 for $238 and #599 for $361.
2. Premier Bank made a posting error to the bank statement: check #603 was issued for $425, not $452.
3. The deposit made on June 20 was for $125 that Natalie received for teaching a class. Natalie made an error in recording this transaction.
4. The electronic funds transfer (EFT) was for Natalie's cell phone use. Remember that she uses this phone only for business.
5. The NSF check was from Ron Black. Natalie received this check for teaching a class to Ron's children. Natalie contacted Ron and he assured her that she will receive a check in the mail for the outstanding amount of the invoice and the NSF bank charge.

Instructions

(a) Prepare Cookie Creations' bank reconciliation for June 2006.

(b) Prepare any necessary general journal entries.

(c) If a balance sheet is prepared for Cookie Creations at June 30, 2006, what balance will be reported as cash in the current assets section?

Accounting Matters!

Answers to Accounting Matters! Questions

p. 336

Q: What could the Pennsylvania bank mentioned above have done to prevent such an error?

A: It could have educated its tellers with regard to money currently in circulation; it could have required a supervisor to approve all transactions in excess of a predetermined limit, such as $50,000; or it could have had mechanical controls that notified supervisors when a transaction exceeded a certain maximum amount.

p. 338

Q: Which principle of internal control was implemented in ancient Egypt?

A: The principle of *independent internal verification* was implemented in ancient Egypt.

Q: Who do you think investors today expect to detect and prevent fraud?

A: Today, investors probably expect independent auditors to detect and prevent fraud. In reality, management is assigned this important responsibility. Auditors attest to compliance with GAAP and specifically state that financial statements and the system of internal control are the responsibility of management.

p. 341

Q: Is a computer capable of committing fraud? Discuss.

A: People commit fraud by misdirecting or programming the computer to misstate numbers or misappropriate assets. Computers do not commit fraud—people do. (Does that make the computer an accomplice?)

p. 346

Q: Which principles of internal control should have prevented such fraud?

A: Three principles could have been used: (1) *segregation of duties*, with one employee requesting payment, another preparing the checks, and a third signing the checks; (2) *documentation procedures*, which require that each check have an approved, pre-numbered voucher; or (3) *independent internal verification*.

p. 351

Q: Will "cash" be obsolete in terms of financial statement reporting?

A: Cash, as the most liquid asset, will continue to be reported on balance sheets, and cash flows will still be reported on the statement of cash flows. Coins and currency may be less popular, but cash in the form of virtual cash (balances or deposits in accounts) will exist in a big way and will continue to appear in financial statements.

Answer to PepsiCo Review It Question 3, p. 358

PepsiCo reports cash and cash equivalents on its balance sheet for 2003 of $820 million.

Answers to Self-Study Questions

1. a **2.** c **3.** b **4.** c **5.** b **6.** d **7.** a **8.** a **9.** c **10.** d **11.** c

REMEMBER to go back to the Navigator box on the chapter-opening page and check off your completed work.

Chapter 9

Accounting for Receivables

THE NAVIGATOR ✓

- Understand **Concepts for Review** ❑
- Read **Feature Story** ❑
- Scan **Study Objectives** ❑
- Read **Preview** ❑
- Read text and answer **Before You Go On** p. 389 ❑ p. 392 ❑ p. 397 ❑ p. 399 ❑
- Work **Demonstration Problem** ❑
- Review **Summary of Study Objectives** ❑
- Answer **Self-Study Questions** ❑
- Complete **Assignments** ❑

CONCEPTS FOR REVIEW

Before studying this chapter, you should know or, if necessary, review:

- How to record sales transactions. (Ch. 5, pp. 198–199)
- Why adjusting entries are made. (Ch. 3, p. 96)
- How to compute interest. (Ch. 3, pp. 105–106)

☑ THE NAVIGATOR

ACCOUNTING MATTERS! **FEATURE STORY**

How Do You Spell Relief?

Fred Tarter believes that in every problem lies an opportunity—and sometimes that opportunity can mean a big profit. For example, today fewer people pay cash for their prescriptions. Instead, pharmacies bill a customer's health plan for some or all of the prescription's cost. As a result, pharmacies must spend a lot of time and energy collecting cash from these health plans. This procedure is a headache for pharmacies because there are 4,500 different health plans in the United States. Also, it often leaves pharmacies with too many receivables and not enough cash. Their suppliers want to be paid within 15 days, but their receivables are outstanding for 30 and often 60 days.

Enter Fred Tarter. Having recently sold his advertising agency, Fred had some spare time and money on his hands. While reading a pharmacy trade journal, he learned of the pharmacies' headache. To Fred this problem spelled opportunity.

Fred found out that 56,000 pharmacies are connected by computer to a claims-processing business. Fred's idea was this: Using this network, he would purchase pharmacy receivables, charging a fee of 1.4–2 percent. Pharmacies would be willing to pay this fee because they would get their cash sooner and would be spared the headache of having to collect the accounts. Fred would then use the receivables as backing to raise new money so he could buy more receivables.

Based on this idea, Fred started a company called the **Pharmacy Fund**. Over 500 small pharmacies sell their receivables to his company. By means of a computer link with each pharmacy, the Pharmacy Fund buys the receivables at the end of each day and credits the pharmacy's account immediately. Rather than having to wait weeks to receive its cash from insurance companies, the pharmacy gets its cash the same day as the sale. The Pharmacy Fund's customers say that this has solved their cash-flow problems. It also has reduced their overhead costs and allowed them to automate their billing and record-keeping.

Fred Tarter has already identified his next opportunity—a target some would say is a "natural" for him: dentistry receivables. (Get it? Tarter—dentistry. We'll stick to accounting jokes from now on!)

☑ THE NAVIGATOR

STUDY OBJECTIVES

After studying this chapter, you should be able to:

1. Identify the different types of receivables.
2. Explain how accounts receivable are recognized in the accounts.
3. Distinguish between the methods and bases used to value accounts receivable.
4. Describe the entries to record the disposition of accounts receivable.
5. Compute the maturity date of and interest on notes receivable.
6. Explain how notes receivable are recognized in the accounts.
7. Describe how notes receivable are valued.
8. Describe the entries to record the disposition of notes receivable.
9. Explain the statement presentation and analysis of receivables.

☑ THE NAVIGATOR

PREVIEW OF CHAPTER 9

As indicated in the Feature Story, receivables are a significant asset on the books of many pharmacies. Receivables are significant to companies in other industries as well, because a significant portion of sales are done on credit in the United States. As a consequence, companies must pay close attention to their receivables and manage them carefully. In this chapter you will learn what journal entries companies make when products are sold, when cash is collected from those sales, and when accounts that cannot be collected are written off.

The content and organization of the chapter are as follows.

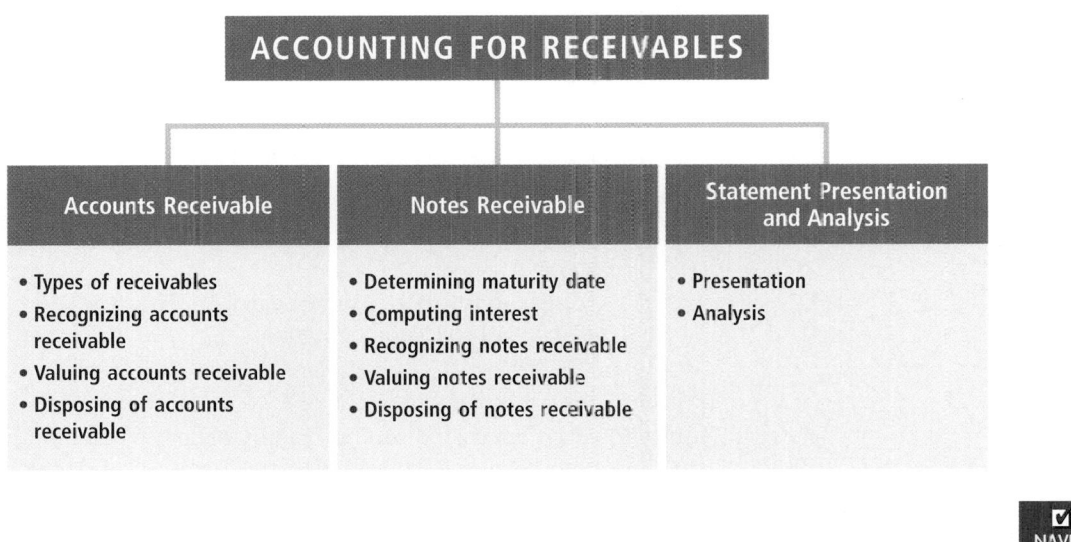

ACCOUNTING FOR RECEIVABLES

Accounts Receivable
- Types of receivables
- Recognizing accounts receivable
- Valuing accounts receivable
- Disposing of accounts receivable

Notes Receivable
- Determining maturity date
- Computing interest
- Recognizing notes receivable
- Valuing notes receivable
- Disposing of notes receivable

Statement Presentation and Analysis
- Presentation
- Analysis

THE NAVIGATOR

Accounts Receivable

Types of Receivables

STUDY OBJECTIVE 1

Identify the different types of receivables.

The term "receivables" refers to amounts due from individuals and other companies. They are claims that are expected to be collected in cash. Receivables are frequently classified as (1) accounts, (2) notes, and (3) other.

Accounts receivable are amounts owed by customers on account. They result from the sale of goods and services. These receivables generally are expected to be collected within 30 to 60 days. They are the most significant type of claim held by a company.

Notes receivable are claims for which formal instruments of credit are issued as proof of the debt. A note receivable normally extends for time periods of 60–90 days or longer and requires the debtor to pay interest. Notes and accounts receivable that result from sales transactions are often called **trade receivables**.

Other receivables include nontrade receivables. Examples are interest receivable, loans to company officers, advances to employees, and income taxes refundable. These do not generally result from the operations of the business. Therefore they are generally classified and reported as separate items in the balance sheet.

ETHICS NOTE

Receivables from employees and officers of a company are reported separately in the financial statements. The reason: Sometimes those assets are valued inappropriately or are not based on an "arm's length" transaction.

Three primary accounting issues are associated with accounts receivable.

1. **Recognizing** accounts receivable.
2. **Valuing** accounts receivable.
3. **Disposing of** accounts receivable.

Recognizing Accounts Receivable

STUDY OBJECTIVE 2

Explain how accounts receivable are recognized in the accounts.

Recognizing accounts receivable is relatively straightforward. In Chapter 5 we saw how accounts receivable are affected by the sale of merchandise. To illustrate, assume that Jordache Co. on July 1, 2006, sells merchandise on account to Polo Company for $1,000 terms 2/10, n/30. On July 5, Polo returns merchandise worth $100 to Jordache Co. On July 11, Jordache receives payment from Polo Company for the balance due. The journal entries to record these transactions on the books of Jordache Co. are as follows.

A	=	L	+	SE
+1,000				+1,000 Rev

Cash Flows
no effect

A	=	L	+	SE
−100				−100 Rev

Cash Flows
no effect

A	=	L	+	SE
+882				−18 Rev
−900				

Cash Flows
+882

July 1	Accounts Receivable—Polo Company	1,000	
	Sales		1,000
	(To record sales on account)		
July 5	Sales Returns and Allowances	100	
	Accounts Receivable—Polo Company		100
	(To record merchandise returned)		
July 11	Cash ($900 − $18)	882	
	Sales Discounts ($900 × .02)	18	
	Accounts Receivable—Polo Company		900
	(To record collection of accounts receivable)		

The opportunity to receive a cash discount usually occurs when a manufacturer sells to a wholesaler or a wholesaler sells to a retailer. A discount is given in these situations either to encourage prompt payment or for competitive reasons.

Retailers rarely grant cash discounts to customers. We would be surprised if you ever received a cash discount in purchasing goods from any well-known retailer, such as **Sears**, **Target**, or **Wal-Mart**. In fact, when you use a retailer's credit card (Sears, for example), instead of giving a discount, the retailer charges interest on the balance due if not paid within a specified period (usually 25–30 days).

HELPFUL HINT

The preceding entries are the same as those described in Chapter 5. For simplicity, inventory and cost of goods sold are omitted from this set of journal entries and from end-of-chapter material.

To illustrate, assume that you use your **JCPenney Co.** credit card to purchase an outfit with a sales price of $300. JCPenney will make the following entry at the date of sale.

A	=	L	+	SE
+300				+300 Rev

Cash Flows
no effect

Accounts Receivable	300	
Sales		300
(To record sale of merchandise)		

JCPenney will send you a monthly statement of this transaction and any others that have occurred during the month. If you do not pay in full within 30 days, JCPenney adds an interest (financing) charge to the balance due. Although interest rates vary by region and over time, a common rate for retailers is 18% per year (1.5% per month).

When financing charges are added, the seller recognizes interest revenue. Assuming that you owe $300 at the end of the month, and JCPenney charges 1.5% per month on the balance due, the adjusting entry to record interest revenue of $4.50 ($300 × 1.5%) is as follows.

A	=	L	+	SE
+4.50				+4.50 Rev

Cash Flows
no effect

Accounts Receivable	4.50	
Interest Revenue		4.50
(To record interest on amount due)		

Interest revenue is often substantial for many retailers.

ACCOUNTING MATTERS! **Business Insight**

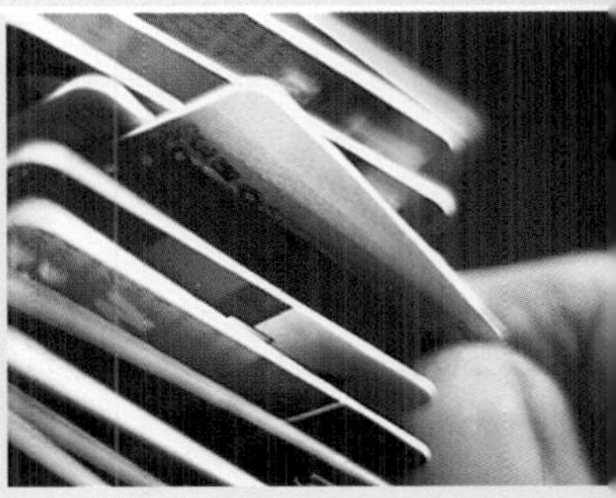

Interest rates on most credit cards are quite high, sometimes 18 percent or higher. As a result, consumers often look for companies that charge lower rates. Be careful—some companies offer lower interest rates but have eliminated the standard 25-day grace period before finance charges are incurred. Other companies encourage consumers to get more in debt by advertising that only a $1 minimum payment is due on a $1,000 account balance. One bank markets a credit card that allows cardholders to skip a payment twice a year. However, the outstanding balance continues to incur interest. Other credit card companies calculate finance charges initially on two-month, rather than one-month, averages. Be sure to read the fine print.

? Why are credit card companies willing to offer such relaxed repayment options?

Valuing Accounts Receivable

STUDY OBJECTIVE 3

Distinguish between the methods and bases used to value accounts receivable.

Once receivables are recorded in the accounts, the next question is: How should receivables be reported in the financial statements? They are reported on the balance sheet as an asset. But determining the **amount** to report is sometimes difficult because some receivables will become uncollectible.

Each customer must satisfy the credit requirements of the seller before the credit sale is approved. Inevitably, though, some accounts receivable become uncollectible. For example, one of your customers may not be able to pay because of a decline in sales due to a downturn in the economy. Similarly, individuals may be laid off from their jobs or be faced with unexpected hospital bills. Credit losses are recorded as debits to **Bad Debts Expense** (or Uncollectible Accounts Expense). Such losses are considered a normal and necessary risk of doing business on a credit basis.

Two methods are used in accounting for uncollectible accounts: (1) the direct write-off method and (2) the allowance method. These methods are explained in the following sections.

Direct Write-off Method for Uncollectible Accounts

Under the **direct write-off method**, when a particular account is determined to be uncollectible, the loss is charged to Bad Debts Expense. Assume, for example, that Warden Co. writes off M. E. Doran's $200 balance as uncollectible on December 12. The entry is:

Dec. 12	Bad Debts Expense	200	
	Accounts Receivable—M. E. Doran		200
	(To record write-off of M. E. Doran account)		

A	=	L	+	SE
−200				−200 Exp

Cash Flows
no effect

When this method is used, bad debts expense will show only **actual losses** from uncollectibles. Accounts receivable will be reported at its gross amount.

Although this method is simple, its use can reduce the usefulness of both the income statement and balance sheet. Consider the following example. Assume that in 2006, Quick Buck Computer Company decided it could increase its revenues by offering computers to college students without requiring any money down and with no credit-approval process. On campuses across the country it distributed 1,000,000 computers with a selling price of $800 each. This increased Quick Buck's revenues and receivables by $800,000,000. The promotion was a huge success! The 2006 balance sheet and income statement looked great. Unfortunately, during 2007, nearly 40 percent of the college student customers defaulted on their loans. This made the 2007 income statement and balance sheet look terrible. Illustration 9-1 shows the effect of these events on the financial statements if the direct write-off method is used.

Illustration 9-1
Effects of direct write-off method

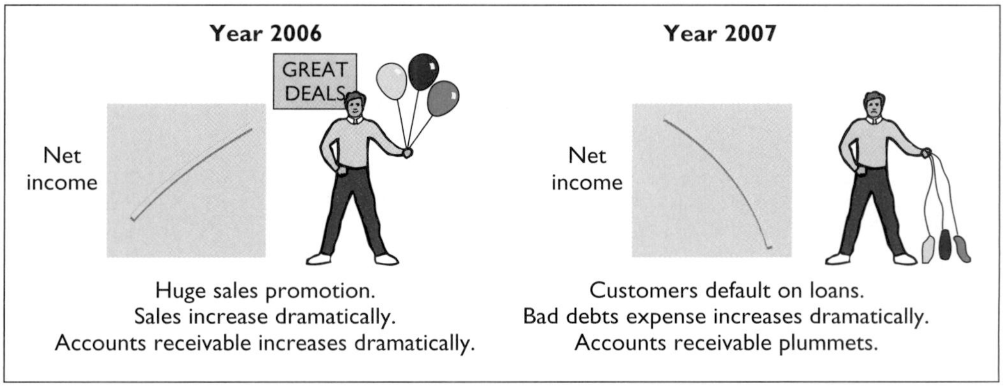

Under the direct write-off method, bad debts expense is often recorded in a period different from the period in which the revenue was recorded. No attempt is made to match bad debts expense to sales revenues in the income statement. Nor does the direct write-off method show accounts receivable in the balance sheet at the amount actually expected to be received. **Consequently, unless bad debts losses are insignificant, the direct write-off method is not acceptable for financial reporting purposes.**

Allowance Method for Uncollectible Accounts

The **allowance method** of accounting for bad debts involves estimating uncollectible accounts at the end of each period. This provides better matching on the income statement and ensures that receivables are stated at their cash (net) realizable value on the balance sheet. **Cash (net) realizable value** is the net amount expected to be received in cash. It excludes amounts that the company estimates it will not collect. Receivables are therefore reduced by estimated uncollectible receivables in the balance sheet through use of this method.

The allowance method is required for financial reporting purposes when bad debts are material in amount. It has three essential features:

HELPFUL HINT
In this context, *material* means significant or important to financial statement users.

1. Uncollectible accounts receivable are **estimated**. This estimate is treated as an expense and is **matched against revenues** in the same accounting period in which the revenues are recorded.
2. Estimated uncollectibles are debited to Bad Debts Expense and are credited to Allowance for Doubtful Accounts (a contra asset account) through an adjusting entry at the end of each period.
3. When a specific account is written off, actual uncollectibles are debited to Allowance for Doubtful Accounts and credited to Accounts Receivable.

RECORDING ESTIMATED UNCOLLECTIBLES. To illustrate the allowance method, assume that Hampson Furniture has credit sales of $1,200,000 in 2006. Of this amount, $200,000 remains uncollected at December 31. The credit manager estimates that $12,000 of these sales will be uncollectible. The adjusting entry to record the estimated uncollectibles is:

Dec. 31	Bad Debts Expense	12,000	
	Allowance for Doubtful Accounts		12,000
	(To record estimate of uncollectible accounts)		

A	=	L	+	SE
−12,000				−12,000 Exp

Cash Flows
no effect

Bad Debts Expense is reported in the income statement as an operating expense (usually as a selling expense). Thus, the estimated uncollectibles are matched with sales in 2006. The expense is recorded in the same year the sales are made.

Allowance for Doubtful Accounts shows the estimated amount of claims on customers that are expected to become uncollectible in the future. This contra account is used instead of a direct credit to Accounts Receivable because we do not know which customers will not pay. The credit balance in the allowance account will absorb the specific write-offs when they occur. It is deducted from accounts receivable in the current assets section of the balance sheet as shown in Illustration 9-2.

Illustration 9-2
Presentation of allowance for doubtful accounts

HAMPSON FURNITURE
Balance Sheet (partial)

Current assets		
Cash		$ 14,800
Accounts receivable	**$200,000**	
Less: Allowance for doubtful accounts	**12,000**	**188,000**
Merchandise inventory		310,000
Prepaid expense		25,000
Total current assets		$537,800

The amount of $188,000 in Illustration 9-2 represents the expected **cash realizable value** of the accounts receivable at the statement date. **Allowance for Doubtful Accounts is not closed at the end of the fiscal year.**

RECORDING THE WRITE-OFF OF AN UNCOLLECTIBLE ACCOUNT. Companies use various methods of collecting past-due accounts, such as letters, calls, and legal action. When all means of collecting a past-due account have been exhausted and collection appears impossible, the account should be written off. In the credit card industry, for example, it is standard practice to write off accounts that are 210 days past due. To prevent premature or unauthorized write-offs, each write-off should be formally approved in writing by management. To maintain good internal control, authorization to write off accounts should not be given to someone who also has daily responsibilities related to cash or receivables.

To illustrate a receivables write-off, assume that the vice-president of finance of Hampson Furniture authorizes a write-off of the $500 balance owed by R. A. Ware on March 1, 2007. The entry to record the write-off is:

Mar. 1	Allowance for Doubtful Accounts	500	
	Accounts Receivable—R. A. Ware		500
	(Write-off of R. A. Ware account)		

A	=	L	+	SE
+500				
−500				

Cash Flows
no effect

Bad Debts Expense is not increased when the write-off occurs. **Under the allowance method, every bad debt write-off is debited to the allowance account rather than to**

Bad Debts Expense. A debit to Bad Debts Expense would be incorrect because the expense has already been recognized when the adjusting entry was made for estimated bad debts. Instead, the entry to record the write-off of an uncollectible account reduces both Accounts Receivable and the Allowance for Doubtful Accounts. After posting, the general ledger accounts will appear as in Illustration 9-3.

Illustration 9-3
General ledger balances after write-off

Accounts Receivable		Allowance for Doubtful Accounts	
Jan. 1 Bal. 200,000	Mar. 1 **500**	Mar. 1 **500**	Jan. 1 Bal. 12,000
Mar. 1 Bal. 199,500			Mar. 1 Bal. 11,500

A write-off affects only balance sheet accounts—not income statement accounts. The write-off of the account reduces both Accounts Receivable and Allowance for Doubtful Accounts. Cash realizable value in the balance sheet, therefore, remains the same, as shown in Illustration 9-4.

Illustration 9-4
Cash realizable value comparison

	Before Write-off	**After Write-off**
Accounts receivable	$200,000	$199,500
Allowance for doubtful accounts	12,000	11,500
Cash realizable value	**$188,000**	**$188,000**

RECOVERY OF AN UNCOLLECTIBLE ACCOUNT. Occasionally, a company collects from a customer after the account has been written off. Two entries are required to record the recovery of a bad debt: (1) The entry made in writing off the account is reversed to reinstate the customer's account. (2) The collection is journalized in the usual manner.

To illustrate, assume that on July 1, R. A. Ware pays the $500 amount that had been written off on March 1. These are the entries:

A	=	L	+	SE
+500				
−500				

Cash Flows
no effect

(1)

July 1	Accounts Receivable—R. A. Ware	500	
	Allowance for Doubtful Accounts		500
	(To reverse write-off of R. A. Ware account)		

A	=	L	+	SE
+500				
−500				

Cash Flows
+500

(2)

July 1	Cash	500	
	Accounts Receivable—R. A. Ware		500
	(To record collection from R. A. Ware)		

Note that the recovery of a bad debt, like the write-off of a bad debt, affects only balance sheet accounts. The net effect of the two entries above is a debit to Cash and a credit to Allowance for Doubtful Accounts for $500. Accounts Receivable is debited and the Allowance for Doubtful Accounts is credited in entry (1) for two reasons: First, the company made an error in judgment when it wrote off the account receivable. Second, after R. A. Ware did pay, Accounts Receivable in the general ledger and Ware's account in the subsidiary ledger should show the collection for possible future credit purposes.

BASES USED FOR ALLOWANCE METHOD. To simplify the preceding explanation, we assumed we knew the amount of the expected uncollectibles. In "real life," companies must estimate that amount if they use the allowance method. Two bases are used to determine this amount: **(1) percentage of sales,** and **(2) percentage of receivables.** Both bases are generally accepted. The choice is a management decision. It depends on the relative emphasis that management wishes to give to expenses and revenues on the one hand or to cash realizable value of the accounts receivable on the other. The choice is whether to emphasize income statement or balance sheet relationships. Illustration 9-5 compares the two bases.

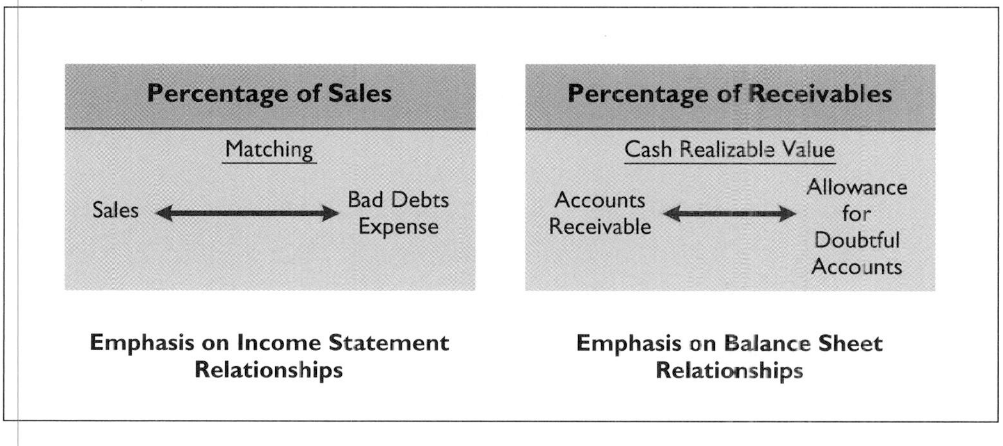

Illustration 9-5
Comparison of bases for estimating uncollectibles

The percentage of sales basis results in a better matching of expenses with revenues—an income statement viewpoint. The percentage of receivables basis produces the better estimate of cash realizable value—a balance sheet viewpoint. Under both bases, it is necessary to determine the company's past experience with bad debt losses.

Percentage of Sales. In the **percentage of sales basis**, management estimates what percentage of credit sales will be uncollectible. This percentage is based on past experience and anticipated credit policy.

The percentage is applied to either total credit sales or net credit sales of the current year. To illustrate, assume that Gonzalez Company elects to use the percentage of sales basis. It concludes that 1 percent of net credit sales will become uncollectible. If net credit sales for 2006 are $800,000, the estimated bad debts expense is $8,000 (1% × $800,000). The adjusting entry is:

Dec. 31	Bad Debts Expense	8,000	
	Allowance for Doubtful Accounts		8,000
	(To record estimated bad debts for year)		

A	=	L	+	SE
−8,000				−8,000 Exp

Cash Flows
no effect

After the adjusting entry is posted, assuming the allowance account already has a credit balance of $1,723, the accounts of Gonzalez Company will show:

Illustration 9-6
Bad debts accounts after posting

Bad Debts Expense		Allowance for Doubtful Accounts	
Dec. 31 Adj. **8,000**			Jan. 1 Bal. 1,723
			Dec. 31 Adj. **8,000**
			Dec. 31 Bal. 9,723

This basis of estimating uncollectibles emphasizes the matching of expenses with revenues. As a result, Bad Debts Expense will show a direct percentage relationship to the sales base on which it is computed. **When the adjusting entry is made, the existing balance in Allowance for Doubtful Accounts is disregarded.** The adjusted balance in this account should be a reasonable approximation of the realizable value of the receivables. If actual write-offs differ significantly from the amount estimated, the percentage for future years should be modified.

Percentage of Receivables. Under the **percentage of receivables basis**, management estimates what percentage of receivables will result in losses from uncollectible accounts. An **aging schedule** is prepared, in which customer balances are classified by the length of time they have been unpaid. Because of its emphasis on time, the analysis is often called **aging the accounts receivable**.

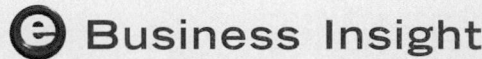

ACCOUNTING MATTERS! Business Insight

Companies that provide services and bill on a per hour basis often must spend considerable time preparing detailed bills that specify the billable activities performed. **Open Air** has an online product that reduces the amount of time it takes to prepare a bill, while increasing the information provided to the customer. To use the service, you create an electronic record that lists the type of project, customer name, project dates, and billing rate. By clicking on the "timer" function, you can automatically track time spent on a particular project as the work is being performed. Open Air's software will either mail or e-mail invoices to customers, and keep track of collections, including providing an aging schedule.

? Why is timely billing important to a business?

After the accounts are aged, the expected bad debt losses are determined. This is done by applying percentages based on past experience to the totals in each category. The longer a receivable is past due, the less likely it is to be collected. So, the estimated percentage of uncollectible debts increases as the number of days past due increases. An aging schedule for Dart Company is shown in Illustration 9-7. Note the increasing percentages from 2 to 40 percent.

Illustration 9-7
Aging schedule

			Number of Days Past Due			
Customer	**Total**	**Not Yet Due**	**1–30**	**31–60**	**61–90**	**Over 90**
T. E. Adert	$ 600		$ 300		$ 200	$ 100
R. C. Bortz	300	$ 300				
B. A. Carl	450		200	$ 250		
O. L. Diker	700	500			200	
T. O. Ebbet	600			300		300
Others	36,950	26,200	5,200	2,450	1,600	1,500
	$39,600	$27,000	$5,700	$3,000	$2,000	$1,900
Estimated Percentage Uncollectible		2%	4%	10%	20%	40%
Total Estimated Bad Debts	**$ 2,228**	$ 540	$ 228	$ 300	$ 400	$ 760

HELPFUL HINT

The higher percentages are used for the older categories because the longer an account is past due, the less likely it is to be collected.

Total estimated bad debts for Dart Company ($2,228) represent the amount of existing customer claims expected to become uncollectible in the future. This amount represents the **required balance** in Allowance for Doubtful Accounts at the balance sheet date. **The amount of the bad debt adjusting entry is the difference between the required balance and the existing balance in the allowance account.** If the trial balance shows Allowance for Doubtful Accounts with a credit balance of $528, an adjusting entry for $1,700 ($2,228 − $528) is necessary, as shown on page 389.

Dec. 31	Bad Debts Expense	1,700	
	Allowance for Doubtful Accounts		1,700
	(To adjust allowance account to total estimated uncollectibles)		

A	=	L	+	SE
−1,700				−1,700 Exp

Cash Flows
no effect

After the adjusting entry is posted, the accounts of the Dart Company will show:

Illustration 9-8
Bad debts accounts after posting

Bad Debts Expense		Allowance for Doubtful Accounts	
Dec. 31 Adj. **1,700**			Bal. 528
			Dec. 31 Adj. **1,700**
			Bal. 2,228

Occasionally the allowance account will have a **debit balance** prior to adjustment. This occurs when write-offs during the year have exceeded previous provisions for bad debts. In such a case **the debit balance is added to the required balance** when the adjusting entry is made. Thus, if there had been a $500 debit balance in the allowance account before adjustment, the adjusting entry would have been for $2,728 ($2,228 + $500) to arrive at a credit balance of $2,228.

The percentage of receivables method will normally result in the better approximation of cash realizable value. But it will not result in the better matching of expenses with revenues if some customers' accounts are more than one year past due. In such a case, bad debts expense for the current period would include amounts related to the sales of a prior year.

BEFORE YOU GO ON...

Review It

1. What is the primary criticism of the direct write-off method?
2. Explain the difference between the percentage of sales and the percentage of receivables methods.
3. What percentage does **PepsiCo**'s allowance for doubtful accounts represent as a percent of its gross receivables? (*Hint:* See PepsiCo's Note 14.) The answer to this question is provided on page 418.

Do It

Brule Co. has been in business 5 years. The ledger at the end of the current year shows: Accounts Receivable $30,000, Sales $180,000, and Allowance for Doubtful Accounts with a debit balance of $2,000. Bad debts are estimated to be 10% of receivables. Prepare the entry to adjust the Allowance for Doubtful Accounts.

ACTION PLAN

- Report receivables at their cash (net) realizable value.
- Estimate the amount the company does not expect to collect.
- Consider the existing balance in the allowance account when using the percentage of receivables basis.

SOLUTION The following entry should be made to bring the balance in the Allowance for Doubtful Accounts up to a balance of $3,000 (0.1 × $30,000):

Bad Debts Expense	5,000	
Allowance for Doubtful Accounts		5,000
(To record estimate of uncollectible accounts)		

Related exercise material: *BE9-3, BE9-4, BE9-5, BE9-6, BE9-7, E9-2, E9-3, and E9-4.*

THE NAVIGATOR

Disposing of Accounts Receivable

STUDY OBJECTIVE 4

Describe the entries to record the disposition of accounts receivable.

In the normal course of events, accounts receivable are collected in cash and removed from the books. However, as credit sales and receivables have grown in significance, their "normal course of events" has changed. As indicated in our Feature Story, companies now frequently sell their receivables to another company for cash, thereby shortening the cash-to-cash operating cycle.

Receivables are sold for two major reasons. First, **receivables may be sold because they may be the only reasonable source of cash**. When money is tight, companies may not be able to borrow money in the usual credit markets. Or, if money is available, the cost of borrowing may be prohibitive.

A second reason for selling receivables is that **billing and collection are often time consuming and costly**. It is often easier for a retailer to sell the receivables to another party with expertise in billing and collection matters. Credit card companies such as **MasterCard**, **VISA**, **American Express**, and **Diners Club** specialize in billing and collecting accounts receivable.

Sale of Receivables

A common sale of receivables is a sale to a factor. A **factor** is a finance company or bank that buys receivables from businesses and then collects the payments directly from the customers. Factoring is a multibillion dollar business. For example, **Sears, Roebuck and Co.** recently sold $14.8 billion of customer accounts receivable to a factor.

Factoring arrangements vary widely. Typically the factor charges a commission to the company that is selling the receivables. This fee ranges from 1–3 percent of the amount of receivables purchased. To illustrate, assume that Henderson Furniture factors $600,000 of receivables to Federal Factors. Federal Factors assesses a service charge of 2 percent of the amount of receivables sold. The journal entry to record the sale by Henderson Furniture is as follows.

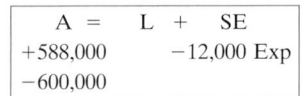

A	=	L	+	SE
+588,000				−12,000 Exp
−600,000				

Cash Flows
+588,000

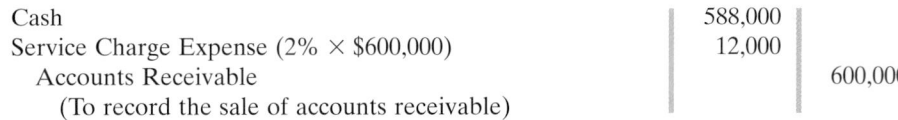

Cash	588,000	
Service Charge Expense (2% × $600,000)	12,000	
Accounts Receivable		600,000
(To record the sale of accounts receivable)		

If the company often sells its receivables, the service charge expense (such as that incurred by Henderson) is recorded as selling expense. If receivables are sold infrequently, this amount may be reported in the "other expenses and losses" section of the income statement.

Credit Card Sales

One billion credit cards were estimated to be in use recently—more than three credit cards for every man, woman, and child in this country. Companies such as **VISA**, **MasterCard**, **Discover**, **American Express**, and **Diners Club** offer national credit cards. Three parties are involved when national credit cards are used in making retail sales: (1) the credit card issuer, who is independent of the retailer, (2) the retailer, and (3) the customer. A retailer's acceptance of a national credit card is another form of selling (factoring) the receivable.

The major advantages of these national credit cards to the retailer are shown in Illustration 9-9 on page 391. In exchange for these advantages, the retailer pays the credit card issuer a fee of 2–6 percent of the invoice price for its services.

CASH SALES: VISA AND MASTERCARD. Sales resulting from the use of **VISA** and **MasterCard** are considered cash sales by the retailer. These cards are is-

Illustration 9-9
Advantages of credit cards to the retailer

sued by banks. Upon receipt of credit card sales slips from a retailer, the bank immediately adds the amount to the seller's bank balance, deducting a fee of 2–4 percent of the credit card sales slips for this service. These credit card sales slips are recorded in the same manner as checks deposited from a cash sale.

To illustrate, Barbara Hardy purchases $1,000 of compact discs for her restaurant from Ty Parker Music Co., using her VISA First Bank Card. The service fee that First Bank charges is 3 percent. The entry to record this transaction by Ty Parker Music is as follows.

Cash	970	
Service Charge Expense	30	
Sales		1,000
(To record VISA credit card sales)		

A	=	L	+	SE
+970				−30 Exp
				+1,000 Rev

Cash Flows
+970

CREDIT SALES: AMERICAN EXPRESS AND DINERS CLUB. Sales using **American Express** and **Diners Club** cards are reported as credit sales, not cash sales. Conversion into cash does not occur until these companies remit the net amount to the seller. To illustrate, assume that Four Seasons restaurant accepts an American Express card for a $300 bill. The entry for the sale by Four Seasons, assuming a 5 percent service fee, is:

Accounts Receivable—American Express	285	
Service Charge Expense	15	
Sales		300
(To record American Express credit card sales)		

A	=	L	+	SE
+285				−15 Exp
				+300 Rev

Cash Flows
no effect

American Express will subsequently pay the restaurant $285. The restaurant will record this payment as follows.

A	=	L	+	SE
+285				
−285				

Cash Flows
+285

Cash	285	
Accounts Receivable—American Express		285
(To record redemption of credit card billings)		

Service Charge Expense is reported by the restaurant as a selling expense in the income statement.

ACCOUNTING MATTERS! Business Insight

It used to be that cash was king. Over the past five decades, though, "plastic" has taken over the top spot. Since 1995 the amount that American consumers buy in stores using credit cards has increased 430 percent, according to a Dove Consulting study on consumer preferences. In 2003, for the first time, Americans bought more using cards than they did using cash.

Total in-store purchases by type

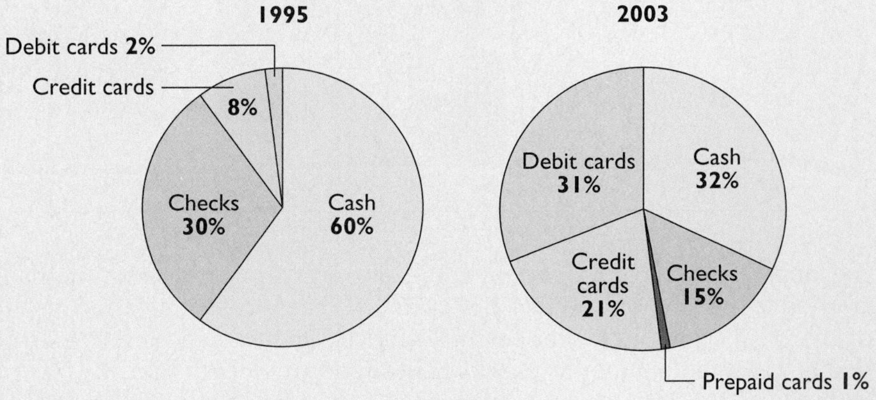

Source: *Fortune* (February 23, 2004), p. 132.

? How will this trend affect the amount and mix of retail businesses' expenses?

BEFORE YOU GO ON...

Review It

1. Why do companies sell their receivables?
2. What is the journal entry when a company sells its receivables to a factor?
3. How are sales using a VISA or MasterCard reported? Is a sale using an American Express card recorded differently? Explain.

Do It

Peter M. Dell Wholesalers Co. has been expanding faster than it can raise capital. According to its local banker, the company has reached its debt ceiling. Dell's customers are slow in paying (60–90 days), but its suppliers (creditors) are demanding 30-day payment. Dell has a cash flow problem.

Dell needs $120,000 in cash to safely cover next Friday's employee payroll. Its balance of outstanding receivables totals $750,000. What might Dell do to alleviate this cash crunch? Record the entry that Dell would make when it raises the needed cash.

ACTION PLAN

- To speed up the collection of cash, sell receivables to a factor.
- Calculate service charge expense as a percentage of the factored receivables.

SOLUTION Assuming that Dell Co. factors $125,000 of its accounts receivable at a 1% service charge, the following entry would be made.

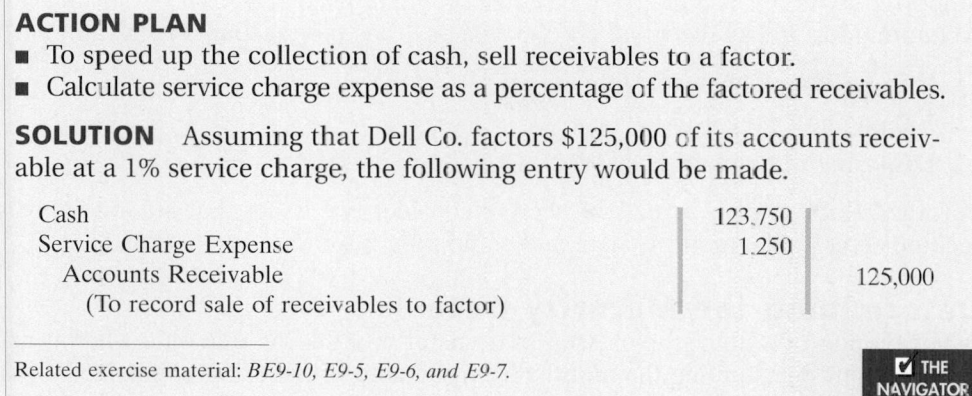

Cash	123,750	
Service Charge Expense	1,250	
Accounts Receivable		125,000
(To record sale of receivables to factor)		

Related exercise material: *BE9-10, E9-5, E9-6, and E9-7.*

THE NAVIGATOR

Notes Receivable

Credit may also be granted in exchange for a promissory note. A **promissory note** is a written promise to pay a specified amount of money on demand or at a definite time. Promissory notes may be used (1) when individuals and companies lend or borrow money; (2) when the amount of the transaction and the credit period exceed normal limits; or (3) in settlement of accounts receivable.

In a promissory note, the party making the promise to pay is called the **maker**. The party to whom payment is to be made is called the **payee**. The payee may be specifically identified by name or may be designated simply as the bearer of the note. In the note shown in Illustration 9-10, Brent Company is the maker, Wilma Company is the payee. To Wilma Company, the promissory note is a note receivable; to Brent Company, it is a note payable.

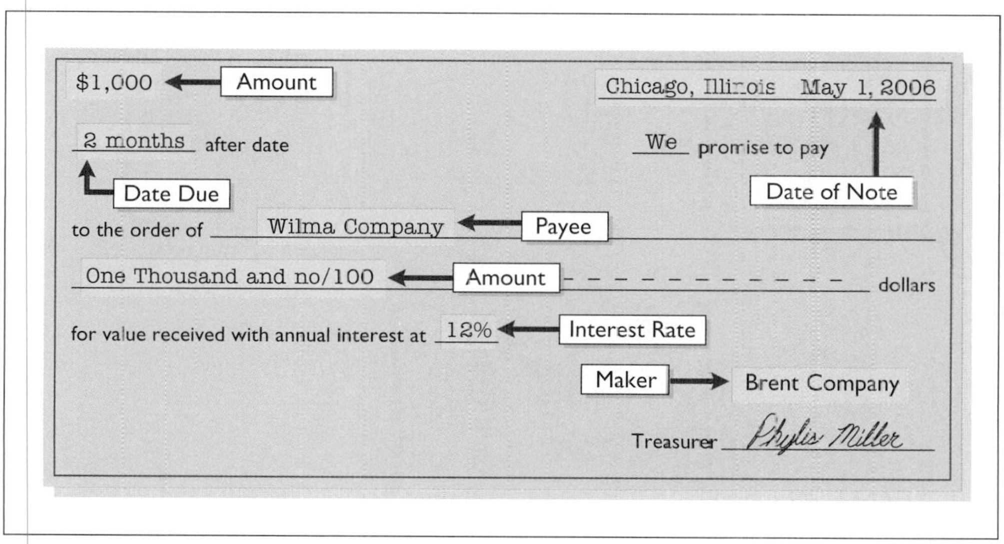

Illustration 9-10
Promissory note

HELPFUL HINT

Who are the two key parties to a note, and what entry does each party make when the note is issued?

Answer:

1. The maker, Brent Company, credits Notes Payable.
2. The payee, Wilma Company, debits Notes Receivable.

Notes receivable give the payee a stronger legal claim to assets than accounts receivable. Like accounts receivable, notes receivable can be readily sold to another party. Promissory notes are negotiable instruments (as are checks), which means that they can be transferred to another party by endorsement.

Notes receivable are frequently accepted from customers who need to extend the payment of an account receivable. They are often required from high-risk customers. In some industries (such as the pleasure boat industry), all credit sales are supported by notes. The majority of notes originate from loans. The basic issues in accounting for notes receivable are the same as those for accounts receivable:

1. **Recognizing** notes receivable.
2. **Valuing** notes receivable.
3. **Disposing of** notes receivable.

Before we look at these issues, we need to consider two issues that did not apply to accounts receivable: maturity date and computing interest.

Determining the Maturity Date

STUDY OBJECTIVE 5

Compute the maturity date of and interest on notes receivable.

When the life of a note is expressed in terms of months, the due date when it matures is found by counting the months from the date of issue. For example, the maturity date of a three-month note dated May 1 is August 1. A note drawn on the last day of a month matures on the last day of a subsequent month. That is, a July 31 note due in two months matures on September 30. When the due date is stated in terms of days, you need to count the exact number of days to determine the maturity date. In counting, **the date the note is issued is omitted but the due date is included**. For example, the maturity date of a 60-day note dated July 17 is September 15, computed as follows.

Illustration 9-11
Computation of maturity date

Term of note		60 days
July (31−17)	14	
August	31	45
Maturity date: September		**15**

The due date (maturity date) of a promissory note may be stated in one of three ways, as shown in Illustration 9-12.

Illustration 9-12
Maturity date of different notes

Computing Interest

As indicated in Chapter 3, the basic formula for computing interest on an interest-bearing note is:

Illustration 9-13
Formula for computing interest

$$\text{Face Value of Note} \times \text{Annual Interest Rate} \times \text{Time in Terms of One Year} = \text{Interest}$$

The interest rate specified in a note is an **annual** rate of interest. The time factor in the formula in Illustration 9-13 expresses the fraction of a year that the note is outstanding. When the maturity date is stated in days, the time factor is often the number of days divided by 360. When the due date is stated in months, the time factor is the number of months divided by 12. Computation of interest for various time periods is shown in Illustration 9-14.

HELPFUL HINT

The interest rate specified is the *annual* rate.

Illustration 9-14
Computation of interest

Terms of Note	Interest Computation
	Face × Rate × Time = Interest
$ 730, 18%, 120 days	$ 730 × 18% × 120/360 = $ 43.80
$1,000, 15%, 6 months	$1,000 × 15% × 6/12 = $ 75.00
$2,000, 12%, 1 year	$2,000 × 12% × 1/1 = $240.00

There are many different ways to calculate interest. The computation above assumed 360 days for the length of the year. Financial instruments actually use 365 days. In order to simplify calculations in our illustrations, we have assumed 360 days. For homework problems, assume 360 days.

Recognizing Notes Receivable

STUDY OBJECTIVE 6

Explain how notes receivable are recognized in the accounts.

To illustrate the basic entry for notes receivable, we will use the $1,000, 2-month, 12% promissory note on page 393. Assuming that the note was written to settle an open account, the entry for the receipt of the note by Wilma Company is:

May 1	Notes Receivable	1,000	
	Accounts Receivable—Brent Company		1,000
	(To record acceptance of Brent Company note)		

A	=	L	+	SE
+1,000				
−1,000				

Cash Flows
no effect

Observe that the note receivable is recorded at its **face value**, the value shown on the face of the note. No interest revenue is reported when the note is accepted because the revenue recognition principle does not recognize revenue until earned. Interest is earned (accrued) as time passes.

If a note is exchanged for cash, the entry is a debit to Notes Receivable and a credit to Cash in the amount of the loan.

Valuing Notes Receivable

STUDY OBJECTIVE 7

Describe how notes receivable are valued.

Valuing short-term notes receivable is the same as valuing accounts receivable. Like accounts receivable, short-term notes receivable are reported at their **cash (net) realizable value**. The notes receivable allowance account is Allowance for Doubtful Accounts. The estimations involved in determining cash realizable value and in recording bad debts expense and related allowance are similar.

Disposing of Notes Receivable

STUDY OBJECTIVE 8

Describe the entries to record the disposition of notes receivable.

Notes may be held to their maturity date, at which time the face value plus accrued interest is due. Sometimes the maker of the note defaults and an adjustment to the accounts must be made. At other times the holder of the note speeds up the conversion to cash by selling the note. The entries for honoring and dishonoring notes are illustrated below.

Honor of Notes Receivable

A note is **honored** when it is paid in full at its maturity date. For an interest-bearing note, the amount due at maturity is the face value of the note plus interest for the length of time specified on the note.

To illustrate, assume that Betty Co. lends Wayne Higley Inc. \$10,000 on June 1, accepting a 5-month, 9% interest note. Interest will be \$375 (\$10,000 × 9% × 5/12). The amount due, the maturity value, will be \$10,375. To obtain payment, Betty Co. (the payee) must present the note either to Wayne Higley Inc. (the maker) or to the maker's duly appointed agent, such as a bank. Assuming that Betty Co. presents the note to Wayne Higley Inc. on the maturity date, the entry by Betty Co. to record the collection is:

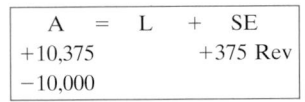

A	=	L	+	SE
+10,375				+375 Rev
−10,000				

Cash Flows
+10,375

Nov. 1	Cash	10,375	
	Notes Receivable		10,000
	Interest Revenue		375
	(To record collection of Higley Inc. note)		

If Betty Co. prepares financial statements as of September 30, it would be necessary to accrue interest. In this case, the adjusting entry by Betty Co. would be to record 4 months' interest (\$300), as shown below.

A	=	L	+	SE
+300				+300 Rev

Cash Flows
no effect

Sept. 30	Interest Receivable (\$10,000 × 9% × 4/12)	300	
	Interest Revenue		300
	(To accrue 4 months' interest)		

When interest has been accrued, at maturity it is necessary to credit Interest Receivable. In addition, since an additional month has passed, one month of interest revenue is recorded. The entry by Betty Co. to record the honoring of the Wayne Higley Inc. note on November 1 is:

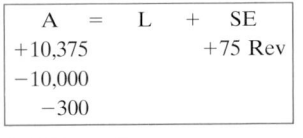

A	=	L	+	SE
+10,375				+75 Rev
−10,000				
−300				

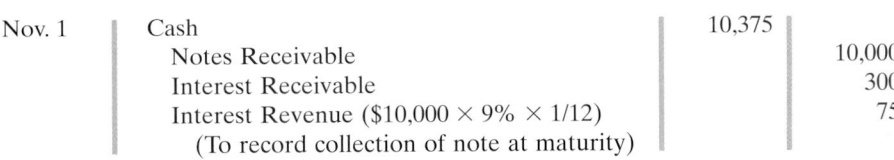

Cash Flows
+10,375

Nov. 1	Cash	10,375	
	Notes Receivable		10,000
	Interest Receivable		300
	Interest Revenue (\$10,000 × 9% × 1/12)		75
	(To record collection of note at maturity)		

In this case, Interest Receivable is credited because the receivable was established in the adjusting entry.

Dishonor of Notes Receivable

A **dishonored note** is a note that is not paid in full at maturity. A dishonored note receivable is no longer negotiable. However, the payee still has a claim against the maker of the note. Therefore the Notes Receivable account is usually transferred to an Account Receivable.

To illustrate, assume that Wayne Higley Inc. on November 1 indicates that it cannot pay at the present time. The entry to record the dishonor of the note depends on whether eventual collection is expected. If Betty Co. expects eventual collection, the amount due (face value and interest) on the note is debited to Accounts Receivable. Betty Co. would make the following entry at the time the note is dishonored (assuming no previous accrual of interest).

A	=	L	+	SE
+10,375				+375 Rev
−10,000				

Cash Flows
no effect

Nov. 1	Accounts Receivable—Wayne Higley Inc.	10,375	
	Notes Receivable		10,000
	Interest Revenue		375
	(To record the dishonor of Higley Inc. note)		

If there is no hope of collection, the face value of the note would be written off by debiting the Allowance for Doubtful Accounts. No interest revenue would be recorded because collection will not occur.

ACCOUNTING MATTERS! Business Insight

In the weeks prior to **Kmart**'s decision in early 2002 to file for Chapter 11 bankruptcy protection, many of its suppliers were taking concrete steps to protect themselves. For example, the garden supply company **The Scotts Company**, which in the previous year sold Kmart $175 million in goods, decided to quit shipping to Kmart until its survival plans were more clear. This was a big decision for Scotts, since Kmart represented 10% of its sales in the previous year. One consultant said that in an informal survey of Kmart suppliers, one-third weren't shipping to Kmart, one-third were holding back shipments until they learned more, and one-third were doing business as usual. All of this meant that Kmart had a lot of empty shelves, at a time when it was hard-pressed for cash.

Source: Amy Merrick, "Kmart Suppliers Limit Risk in Case of Chapter 11 Filing," *Wall Street Journal Online* (January 21, 2002).

? Rather than refusing to ship to Kmart, what could suppliers have done to protect their interests?

Sale of Notes Receivable

The accounting for the sale of notes receivable is recorded similarly to the sale of accounts receivable. The accounting entries for the sale of notes receivable are left for a more advanced course.

BEFORE YOU GO ON...

Review It

1. What is the basic formula for computing interest?
2. At what value are notes receivable reported on the balance sheet?
3. Explain the difference between honoring and dishonoring a note receivable.

Do It

Gambit Stores accepts from Leonard Co. a $3,400, 90-day, 12% note dated May 10 in settlement of Leonard's overdue account. What is the maturity date of the note? What is the entry made by Gambit at the maturity date, assuming Leonard pays the note and interest in full at that time?

ACTION PLAN

- Count the exact number of days to determine the maturity date. Omit the date the note is issued, but include the due date.
- Determine whether interest was accrued. The entry here assumes that no interest has been previously accrued on this note.

SOLUTION The maturity date is August 8, computed as follows.

Term of note:		90 days
May (31−10)	21	
June	30	
July	31	82
Maturity date: August		8

The interest payable at maturity date is $102, computed as follows.

Face	× Rate ×	Time	= Interest
$3,400 ×	12% ×	90/360 =	$102

(continued from p. 397)

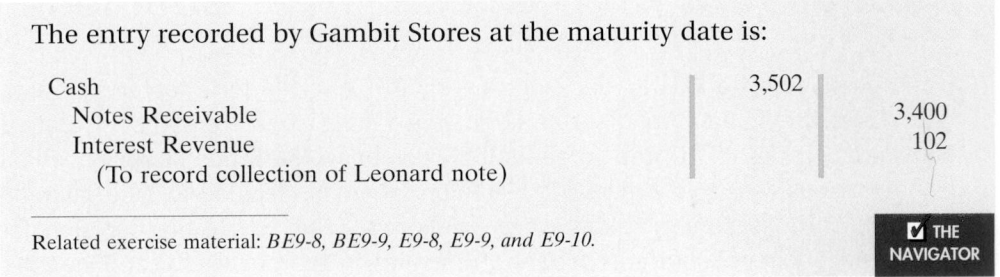

The entry recorded by Gambit Stores at the maturity date is:

Cash	3,502	
Notes Receivable		3,400
Interest Revenue		102
(To record collection of Leonard note)		

Related exercise material: *BE9-8, BE9-9, E9-8, E9-9, and E9-10.*

THE NAVIGATOR

STATEMENT PRESENTATION AND ANALYSIS

Presentation

STUDY OBJECTIVE 9

Explain the statement presentation and analysis of receivables.

Each of the major types of receivables should be identified in the balance sheet or in the notes to the financial statements. Short-term receivables are reported in the current assets section of the balance sheet, below short-term investments. Short-term investments appear before receivables, because short-term investments are more liquid (nearer to cash). Both the gross amount of receivables and the allowance for doubtful accounts should be reported.

In a multiple-step income statement, bad debts expense and service charge expense are reported as selling expenses in the operating expenses section. Interest revenue is shown under "other revenues and gains" in the nonoperating activities section of the income statement.

Analysis

Financial ratios are frequently computed to evaluate the liquidity of a company's accounts receivable. The **accounts receivable turnover ratio** is used to assess the liquidity of the receivables. This ratio measures the number of times, on average, accounts receivable are collected during the period. It is computed by dividing net credit sales (net sales less cash sales) by the average net accounts receivable during the year. Unless seasonal factors are significant, average net accounts receivable outstanding can be computed from the beginning and ending balances of net accounts receivable.

For example, in 2003, **Cisco Systems** had net sales of $18,878 million for the year. It had a beginning accounts receivable (net) balance of $1,351 million and an ending accounts receivable (net) balance of $1,105 million. Assuming that Cisco's sales were all on credit, its accounts receivable turnover ratio is computed as follows.

Illustration 9-15
Accounts receivable turnover ratio and computation

Net Credit Sales	÷	Average Net Accounts Receivable	=	Accounts Receivable Turnover
$18,878	÷	$\frac{\$1,105 + \$1,351}{2}$	=	**15.4 times**

The result indicates an accounts receivable turnover ratio of 15.4 times per year. The higher the turnover ratio the more liquid the company's receivables.

A variant of the accounts receivable turnover ratio that makes the liquidity even more evident is the conversion of it into an **average collection period** in terms of days. This is done by dividing the turnover ratio into 365 days. For example, Cisco's turnover of 15.4 times is divided into 365 days, as shown in Illustration 9-16, to obtain approximately 23.7 days.

Days in Year	÷	Accounts Receivable Turnover	=	Average Collection Period in Days
365 days	÷	15.4 times	=	**23.7 days**

Illustration 9-16
Average collection period for receivables formula and computation

This means that it takes Cisco about 24 days to collect its accounts receivable.

The average collection period is frequently used to assess the effectiveness of a company's credit and collection policies. The general rule is that the collection period should not greatly exceed the credit term period (i.e., the time allowed for payment).

BEFORE YOU GO ON...

Review It

1. Explain where accounts and notes receivable are reported on the balance sheet.
2. Where are bad debts expense, service charge expense, and interest revenue reported on the multiple-step income statement?

THE NAVIGATOR

DEMONSTRATION PROBLEM

The following selected transactions relate to J. Child Company.

Mar. 1 Sold $20,000 of merchandise to Potter Company, terms 2/10, n/30.
11 Received payment in full from Potter Company for balance due.
12 Accepted Juno Company's $20,000, 6-month, 12% note for balance due.
13 Made J. Child Company credit card sales for $13,200.
15 Made American Express credit sales totaling $6,700. A 5% service fee is charged by American Express.
30 Received payment in full from American Express Company.
Apr. 11 Sold accounts receivable of $8,000 to Harcot Factor. Harcot Factor assesses a service charge of 2% of the amount of receivables sold.
13 Received collections of $8,200 on J. Child Company credit card sales and added finance charges of 1.5% to the remaining balances.
May 10 Wrote off as uncollectible $16,000 of accounts receivable. J. Child uses the percentage of sales basis to estimate bad debts.
June 30 Credit sales for the first 6 months total $2,000,000. The bad debt percentage is 1% of credit sales. At June 30, the balance in the allowance account is $3,500.
July 16 One of the accounts receivable written off in May was from J. Simon, who pays the amount due, $4,000, in full.

Instructions

Prepare the journal entries for the transactions.

ACTION PLAN

- Generally, record accounts receivable at invoice price.
- Recognize that sales returns and allowances and cash discounts reduce the amount received on accounts receivable.
- Record a service charge expense on the seller's books when accounts receivable are sold.
- Prepare an adjusting entry for bad debts expense.
- Ignore any balance in the allowance account under the percentage of sales basis. Recognize the balance in the allowance account under the percentage of receivables basis.
- Record write-offs of accounts receivable only in balance sheet accounts.

SOLUTION TO DEMONSTRATION PROBLEM

Mar. 1	Accounts Receivable–Potter	20,000	
	Sales		20,000
	(To record sales on account)		
Mar. 11	Cash	19,600	
	Sales Discounts (2% × $20,000)	400	
	Accounts Receivable—Potter		20,000
	(To record collection of accounts receivable)		
Mar. 12	Notes Receivable	20,000	
	Accounts Receivable—Juno		20,000
	(To record acceptance of Juno Company note)		
Mar. 13	Accounts Receivable	13,200	
	Sales		13,200
	(To record company credit card sales)		
Mar. 15	Accounts Receivable—American Express	6,365	
	Service Charge Expense (5% × $6,700)	335	
	Sales		6,700
	(To record credit card sales)		
Mar. 30	Cash	6,365	
	Accounts Receivable—American Express		6,365
	(To record redemption of credit card billings)		
Apr. 11	Cash	7,840	
	Service Charge Expense (2% × $8,000)	160	
	Accounts Receivable		8,000
	(To record sale of receivables to factor)		
Apr. 13	Cash	8,200	
	Accounts Receivable		8,200
	(To record collection of accounts receivable)		
Apr. 13	Accounts Receivable [($13,200 − $8,200) × 1.5%]	75	
	Interest Revenue		75
	(To record interest on amount due)		
May 10	Allowance for Doubtful Accounts	16,000	
	Accounts Receivable		16,000
	(To record write-off of accounts receivable)		
June 30	Bad Debts Expense ($2,000,000 × 1%)	20,000	
	Allowance for Doubtful Accounts		20,000
	(To record estimate of uncollectible accounts)		
July 16	Accounts Receivable—J. Simon	4,000	
	Allowance for Doubtful Accounts		4,000
	(To reverse write-off of accounts receivable)		
	Cash	4,000	
	Accounts Receivable—J. Simon		4,000
	(To record collection of accounts receivable)		

THE NAVIGATOR

SUMMARY OF STUDY OBJECTIVES

1. **Identify the different types of receivables.** Receivables are frequently classified as (1) accounts, (2) notes, and (3) other. Accounts receivable are amounts owed by customers on account. Notes receivable are claims for which formal instruments of credit are issued as proof of the debt. Other receivables include nontrade receivables such as interest receivable, loans to company officers, advances to employees, and income taxes refundable.
2. **Explain how accounts receivable are recognized in the accounts.** Accounts receivable are recorded at invoice price. They are reduced by Sales Returns and Allowances. Cash discounts reduce the amount received on accounts receivable. When interest is charged on a past due receivable, this interest is added to the accounts receivable balance and is recognized as interest revenue.
3. **Distinguish between the methods and bases used to value accounts receivable.** There are two methods of accounting for uncollectible accounts: (1) the allowance method and (2) the direct write-off method. Either the percentage of sales or the percentage of receivables basis may be used to estimate uncollectible accounts using the allowance method. The percentage of sales basis emphasizes the matching principle. The percentage of receivables basis emphasizes the cash realizable value of the accounts receivable. An aging schedule is often used with this basis.
4. **Describe the entries to record the disposition of accounts receivable.** When an account receivable is collected, Accounts Receivable is credited. When an account receivable is sold, a service charge expense is charged which reduces the amount collected.
5. **Compute the maturity date of and interest on notes receivable.** The maturity date of a note must be computed unless the due date is specified or the note is payable on demand. For a note stated in months, the maturity date is found by counting the months from the date of issue. For a note stated in days, the number of days is counted, omitting the issue date and counting the due date. The formula for computing interest is face value × interest rate × time.
6. **Explain how notes receivable are recognized in the accounts.** Notes receivable are recorded at face value. In some cases, it is necessary to accrue interest prior to maturity. In this case, Interest Receivable is debited and Interest Revenue is credited.
7. **Describe how notes receivable are valued.** Like accounts receivable, notes receivable are reported at their cash (net) realizable value. The notes receivable allowance account is the Allowance for Doubtful Accounts. The computation and estimations involved in valuing notes receivable at cash realizable value, and in recording the proper amount of bad debts expense and related allowance are similar to those for accounts receivable.
8. **Describe the entries to record the disposition of notes receivable.** Notes can be held to maturity. At that time the face value plus accrued interest is due, and the note is removed from the accounts. In many cases, the holder of the note speeds up the conversion by selling the receivable to another party. In some situations, the maker of the note dishonors the note (defaults), and the note is written off.
9. **Explain the statement presentation and analysis of receivables.** Each major type of receivable should be identified in the balance sheet or in the notes to the financial statements. Short-term receivables are considered current assets. The gross amount of receivables and the allowance for doubtful accounts should be reported. Bad debts and service charge expenses are reported in the multiple-step income statement as operating (selling) expenses; interest revenue is shown as other revenues and gains in the nonoperating activities section of the statement. Accounts receivable may be evaluated for liquidity by computing a turnover ratio and an average collection period.

THE NAVIGATOR

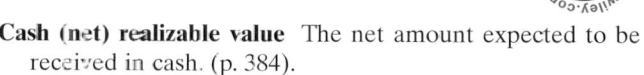

GLOSSARY

Accounts receivable turnover ratio A measure of the liquidity of accounts receivable; computed by dividing net credit sales by average net accounts receivable. (p. 398).

Aging the accounts receivable The analysis of customer balances by the length of time they have been unpaid. (p. 388).

Allowance method A method of accounting for bad debts that involves estimating uncollectible accounts at the end of each period. (p. 384).

Average collection period The average amount of time that a receivable is outstanding; calculated by dividing 365 days by the receivables turnover ratio. (p. 398).

Bad Debts Expense An expense account to record uncollectible receivables. (p. 383).

Cash (net) realizable value The net amount expected to be received in cash. (p. 384).

Direct write-off method A method of accounting for bad debts that involves expensing accounts at the time they are determined to be uncollectible. (p. 383).

Dishonored note A note that is not paid in full at maturity. (p. 396).

Factor A finance company or bank that buys receivables from businesses and then collects the payments directly from the customers. (p. 390).

Maker The party in a promissory note who is making the promise to pay. (p. 393).

Payee The party to whom payment of a promissory note is to be made. (p. 393).

Percentage of receivables basis Management establishes a percentage relationship between the amount of receivables and the expected losses from uncollectible accounts. (p. 388).

Percentage of sales basis Management establishes a percentage relationship between the amount of credit sales and expected losses from uncollectible accounts. (p. 387).

Promissory note A written promise to pay a specified amount of money on demand or at a definite time. (p. 393).

Trade receivables Notes and accounts receivable that result from sales transactions. (p. 381).

SELF-STUDY QUESTIONS

Self-Study/Self-Test www.wiley.com/college/weygandt

Answers are at the end of the chapter.

(SO 2) **1.** Buehler Company on June 15 sells merchandise on account to Chaz Co. for $1,000, terms 2/10, n/30. On June 20, Chaz Co. returns merchandise worth $300 to Buehler Company. On June 24, payment is received from Chaz Co. for the balance due. What is the amount of cash received?
- **a.** $700.
- **b.** $680.
- **c.** $686.
- **d.** None of the above.

(SO 3) **2.** Which of the following approaches for bad debts is best described as a balance sheet method?
- **a.** Percentage of receivables basis.
- **b.** Direct write-off method.
- **c.** Percentage of sales basis.
- **d.** Both a and b.

(SO 3) **3.** Net sales for the month are $800,000, and bad debts are expected to be 1.5% of net sales. The company uses the percentage of sales basis. If the Allowance for Doubtful Accounts has a credit balance of $15,000 before adjustment, what is the balance after adjustment?
- **a.** $15,000.
- **b.** $27,000.
- **c.** $23,000.
- **d.** $31,000.

(SO 3) **4.** In 2006, Roso Carlson Company had net credit sales of $750,000. On January 1, 2006, Allowance for Doubtful Accounts had a credit balance of $18,000. During 2006, $30,000 of uncollectible accounts receivable were written off. Past experience indicates that 3% of net credit sales become uncollectible. What should be the adjusted balance of Allowance for Doubtful Accounts at December 31, 2006?
- **a.** $10,050.
- **b.** $10,500.
- **c.** $22,500.
- **d.** $40,500.

(SO 3) **5.** An analysis and aging of the accounts receivable of Prince Company at December 31 reveals the following data.

Accounts receivable	$800,000
Allowance for doubtful accounts per books before adjustment	50,000
Amounts expected to become uncollectible	65,000

The cash realizable value of the accounts receivable at December 31, after adjustment, is:
- **a.** $685,000.
- **b.** $750,000.
- **c.** $800,000.
- **d.** $735,000.

6. One of the following statements about promissory notes is incorrect. The *incorrect* statement is: (SO 6)
- **a.** The party making the promise to pay is called the maker.
- **b.** The party to whom payment is to be made is called the payee.
- **c.** A promissory note is not a negotiable instrument.
- **d.** A promissory note is more liquid than an account receivable.

7. Which of the following statements about VISA credit card sales is *incorrect*? (SO 4)
- **a.** The credit card issuer makes the credit investigation of the customer.
- **b.** The retailer is not involved in the collection process.
- **c.** Two parties are involved.
- **d.** The retailer receives cash more quickly than it would from individual customers on account.

8. Blinka Retailers accepted $50,000 of Citibank VISA credit card charges for merchandise sold on July 1. Citibank charges 4% for its credit card use. The entry to record this transaction by Blinka Retailers will include a credit to Sales of $50,000 and a debit(s) to: (SO 4)

a. Cash	$48,000
and Service Charge Expense	2,000
b. Accounts Receivable	$48,000
and Service Charge Expense	$2,000
c. Cash	$50,000
d. Accounts Receivable	$50,000

9. Foti Co. accepts a $1,000, 3-month, 12% promissory note in settlement of an account with Bartelt Co. The entry to record this transaction is as follows. (SO 6)

a. Notes Receivable	1,030	
Accounts Receivable		1,030
b. Notes Receivable	1,000	
Accounts Receivable		1,000
c. Notes Receivable	1,000	
Sales		1,000
d. Notes Receivable	1,020	
Accounts Receivable		1,020

(SO 8) **10.** Ginter Co. holds Kolar Inc.'s $10,000, 120-day, 9% note. The entry made by Ginter Co. when the note is collected, assuming no interest has been previously accrued, is:

a. Cash	10,300	
Notes Receivable		10,300
b. Cash	10,000	
Notes Receivable		10,000
c. Accounts Receivable	10,300	
Notes Receivable		10,000
Interest Revenue		300
d. Cash	10,300	
Notes Receivable		10,000
Interest Revenue		300

THE NAVIGATOR

QUESTIONS

1. What is the difference between an account receivable and a note receivable?

2. What are some common types of receivables other than accounts receivable and notes receivable?

3. Texaco Oil Company issues its own credit cards. Assume that Texaco charges you $40 on an unpaid balance. Prepare the journal entry that Texaco makes to record this revenue.

4. What are the essential features of the allowance method of accounting for bad debts?

5. Michael Sondgeroth cannot understand why cash realizable value does not decrease when an uncollectible account is written off under the allowance method. Clarify this point for Michael Sondgeroth.

6. Distinguish between the two bases that may be used in estimating uncollectible accounts.

7. Borke Company has a credit balance of $3,200 in Allowance for Doubtful Accounts. The estimated bad debts expense under the percentage of sales basis is $4,100. The total estimated uncollectibles under the percentage of receivables basis is $5,800. Prepare the adjusting entry under each basis.

8. How are bad debts accounted for under the direct write-off method? What are the disadvantages of this method?

9. Freida Company accepts both its own credit cards and national credit cards. What are the advantages of accepting both types of cards?

10. An article recently appeared in the *Wall Street Journal* indicating that companies are selling their receivables at a record rate. Why are companies selling their receivables?

11. WestSide Textiles decides to sell $800,000 of its accounts receivable to First Factors Inc. First Factors assesses a service charge of 3% of the amount of receivables sold. Prepare the journal entry that WestSide Textiles makes to record this sale.

12. Your roommate is uncertain about the advantages of a promissory note. Compare the advantages of a note receivable with those of an account receivable.

13. How may the maturity date of a promissory note be stated?

14. Indicate the maturity date of each of the following promissory notes:

Date of Note	Terms
(a) March 13	one year after date of note
(b) May 4	3 months after date
(c) June 20	30 days after date
(d) July 1	60 days after date

15. Compute the missing amounts for each of the following notes.

	Face Value	Annual Interest Rate	Time	Total Interest
(a)	?	9%	120 days	$ 450
(b)	$30,000	10%	3 years	?
(c)	$60,000	?	5 months	$3,000
(d)	$45,000	8%	?	$1,200

16. In determining interest revenue, some financial institutions use 365 days per year and others use 360 days. Why might a financial institution use 360 days?

17. Jana Company dishonors a note at maturity. What actions by Jana may occur with the dishonoring of the note?

18. **General Motors Corporation** has accounts receivable and notes receivable. How should the receivables be reported on the balance sheet?

19. The accounts receivable turnover ratio is 8.14, and average net receivables during the period are $300,000. What is the amount of net credit sales for the period?

BRIEF EXERCISES

Identify different types of receivables.

(SO 1)

BE9-1 Presented below are three receivables transactions. Indicate whether these receivables are reported as accounts receivable, notes receivable, or other receivables on a balance sheet.

(a) Sold merchandise on account for $64,000 to a customer.
(b) Received a promissory note of $57,000 for services performed.
(c) Advanced $10,000 to an employee.

Record basic accounts receivable transactions.
(SO 2)

BE9-2 Record the following transactions on the books of Galaxy Co.

(a) On July 1, Galaxy Co. sold merchandise on account to Kingston Inc. for $17,200, terms 2/10, n/30.
(b) On July 8, Kingston Inc. returned merchandise worth $3,800 to Galaxy Co.
(c) On July 11, Kingston Inc. paid for the merchandise.

Prepare entry for allowance method and partial balance sheet.
(SO 3, 9)

BE9-3 During its first year of operations, Energy Company had credit sales of $3,000,000; $600,000 remained uncollected at year-end. The credit manager estimates that $32,000 of these receivables will become uncollectible.

(a) Prepare the journal entry to record the estimated uncollectibles.
(b) Prepare the current assets section of the balance sheet for Energy Company. Assume that in addition to the receivables it has cash of $90,000, merchandise inventory of $130,000, and prepaid expenses of $7,500.

Prepare entry for write-off; determine cash realizable value.
(SO 3)

BE9-4 At the end of 2006, Endrun Co. has accounts receivable of $700,000 and an allowance for doubtful accounts of $54,000. On January 24, 2007, the company learns that its receivable from Oswego Inc. is not collectible, and management authorizes a write-off of $6,400.

(a) Prepare the journal entry to record the write-off.
(b) What is the cash realizable value of the accounts receivable (1) before the write-off and (2) after the write-off?

Prepare entries for collection of bad debts write-off.
(SO 3)

BE9-5 Assume the same information as BE9-4. On March 4, 2007, Endrun Co. receives payment of $6,400 in full from Oswego Inc. Prepare the journal entries to record this transaction.

Prepare entry using percentage of sales method.
(SO 3)

BE9-6 Elgin Co. elects to use the percentage of sales basis in 2006 to record bad debts expense. It estimates that 2% of net credit sales will become uncollectible. Sales are $800,000 for 2006, sales returns and allowances are $37,000, and the allowance for doubtful accounts has a credit balance of $9,000. Prepare the adjusting entry to record bad debts expense in 2006.

Prepare entry using percentage of receivables method.
(SO 3)

BE9-7 Gleason Co. uses the percentage of accounts receivable basis to record bad debts expense. It estimates that 1% of accounts receivable will become uncollectible. Accounts receivable are $400,000 at the end of the year, and the allowance for doubtful accounts has a credit balance of $1,500.

(a) Prepare the adjusting journal entry to record bad debts expense for the year.
(b) If the allowance for doubtful accounts had a debit balance of $800 instead of a credit balance of $1,500, determine the amount to be reported for bad debts expense.

Compute interest and determine maturity dates on notes.
(SO 5)

BE9-8 Compute interest and find the maturity date for the following notes.

	Date of Note	Face Value	Interest Rate (%)	Terms
(a)	June 10	$100,000	6%	60 days
(b)	July 14	$ 50,000	$7\frac{1}{2}$%	90 days
(c)	April 27	$ 12,000	8%	75 days

Determine maturity dates and compute interest and rates on notes.
(SO 5)

BE9-9 Presented below are data on three promissory notes. Determine the missing amounts.

	Date of Note	Terms	Maturity Date	Face Value	Annual Interest Rate	Total Interest
(a)	April 1	60 days	?	$900,000	9%	?
(b)	July 2	30 days	?	90,000	?	$600
(c)	March 7	6 months	?	120,000	11%	?

Prepare entries to dispose of accounts receivable.
(SO 4)

BE9-10 Presented below are two independent transactions.

(a) St. Charles Restaurant accepted a VISA card in payment of a $200 lunch bill. The bank charges a 4% fee. What entry should St. Charles make?
(b) Marge Company sold its accounts receivable of $80,000. What entry should Marge make, given a service charge of 3% on the amount of receivables sold?

Prepare entry for note receivable exchanged for account receivable.
(SO 6)

BE9-11 On January 10, 2006, Batavia Co. sold merchandise on account to Dustin Eola for $11,600, n/30. On February 9, Dustin Eola gave Batavia Co. a 10% promissory note in settlement of this account. Prepare the journal entry to record the sale and the settlement of the account receivable.

BE9-12 The financial statements of **Minnesota Mining and Manufacturing Company (3M)** report net sales of $15.0 billion. Accounts receivable (net) are $2.5 billion at the beginning of the year and $2.8 billion at the end of the year. Compute 3M's receivables turnover ratio. Compute 3M's average collection period for accounts receivable in days.

Compute ratios to analyze receivables.

(SO 9)

EXERCISES

E9-1 Presented below are two independent situations.

Journalize entries for recognizing accounts receivable.

(SO 2)

(a) On January 6, Bennett Co. sells merchandise on account to Jackie, Inc. for $7,000, terms 2/10, n/30. On January 16, Jackie Inc. pays the amount due. Prepare the entries on Bennett's books to record the sale and related collection.

(b) On January 10, Erin Bybee uses her Sheridan Co. credit card to purchase merchandise from Sheridan Co. for $9,000. On February 10, Bybee is billed for the amount due of $9,000. On February 12, Bybee pays $6,000 on the balance due. On March 10, Bybee is billed for the amount due, including interest at 2% per month on the unpaid balance as of February 12. Prepare the entries on Sheridan Co.'s books related to the transactions that occurred on January 10, February 12, and March 10.

E9-2 The ledger of Elburn Company at the end of the current year shows Accounts Receivable $110,000, Sales $840,000, and Sales Returns and Allowances $28,000.

Journalize entries to record allowance for doubtful accounts using two different bases.

(SO 3)

Instructions

(a) If Elburn uses the direct write-off method to account for uncollectible accounts, journalize the adjusting entry at December 31, assuming Elburn determines that Copp's $1,400 balance is uncollectible.

(b) If Allowance for Doubtful Accounts has a credit balance of $2,100 in the trial balance, journalize the adjusting entry at December 31, assuming bad debts are expected to be (1) 1% of net sales, and (2) 10% of accounts receivable.

(c) If Allowance for Doubtful Accounts has a debit balance of $200 in the trial balance, journalize the adjusting entry at December 31, assuming bad debts are expected to be (1) 0.75% of net sales and (2) 6% of accounts receivable.

E9-3 Leland Company has accounts receivable of $98,100 at March 31. An analysis of the accounts shows the following.

Determine bad debts expense; prepare the adjusting entry for bad debts expense.

(SO 3)

Month of Sale	Balance, March 31
March	$65,000
February	17,600
January	8,500
Prior to January	7,000
	$98,100

Credit terms are 2/10, n/30. At March 31, Allowance for Doubtful Accounts has a credit balance of $1,200 prior to adjustment. The company uses the percentage of receivables basis for estimating uncollectible accounts. The company's estimate of bad debts is as follows.

Age of Accounts	Estimated Percentage Uncollectible
1–30 days	2.0%
30–60 days	5.0%
60–90 days	30.0%
Over 90 days	50.0%

Instructions

(a) Determine the total estimated uncollectibles.

(b) Prepare the adjusting entry at March 31 to record bad debts expense.

E9-4 On December 31, 2006, Crawford Co. estimated that 1.5% of its net sales of $400,000 will become uncollectible. The company recorded this amount as an addition to Allowance for Doubtful Accounts. On May 11, 2007, Crawford Co. determined that Kevin Hayes' account was uncollectible and wrote off $1,100. On June 12, 2007, Hayes' paid the amount previously written off.

Journalize percentage of sales basis, write-off, recovery.

(SO 3)

Instructions

Prepare the journal entries on December 31, 2006, May 11, 2007, and June 12, 2007.

Journalize entries for the sale of accounts receivable.
(SO 4)

E9-5 Presented below are two independent situations.

(a) On March 3, Hinckley Appliances sells $580,000 of its receivables to Marsh Factors Inc. Marsh Factors assesses a finance charge of 3% of the amount of receivables sold. Prepare the entry on Hinckley Appliances' books to record the sale of the receivables.

(b) On May 10, Cody Company sold merchandise for $3,800 and accepted the customer's Allstar Bank MasterCard. At the end of the day, the Allstar Bank MasterCard receipts were deposited in the company's bank account. Allstar Bank charges a 4% service charge for credit card sales. Prepare the entry on Cody Company's books to record the sale of merchandise.

Journalize entries for credit card sales.
(SO 4)

E9-6 Presented below are two independent situations.

(a) On April 2, Julie Keiser uses her JCPenney Company credit card to purchase merchandise from a JCPenney store for $1,800. On May 1, Keiser is billed for the $1,800 amount due. Keiser pays $700 on the balance due on May 3. On June 1, Keiser receives a bill for the amount due, including interest at 1% per month on the unpaid balance as of May 3. Prepare the entries on JCPenney Co.'s books related to the transactions that occurred on April 2, May 3, and June 1.

(b) On July 4, Newark's Restaurant accepts an American Express card for a $350 dinner bill. American Express charges a 4% service fee. On July 10, American Express pays Newark $336. Prepare the entries on Newark's books related to the transactions.

Journalize credit card sales, and indicate the statement presentation of financing charges and service charge expense.
(SO 4)

E9-7 Ottawa Stores accepts both its own and national credit cards. During the year the following selected summary transactions occurred.

Jan.	15	Made Ottawa credit card sales totaling $18,000. (There were no balances prior to January 15.)
	20	Made American Express credit card sales (service charge fee 5%) totaling $4,100.
	30	Received payment in full from American Express less the 5% service charge.
Feb.	10	Collected $12,000 on Ottawa credit card sales.
	15	Added finance charges of 1% to Ottawa credit card balance.

Instructions

(a) Journalize the transactions for Ottawa Stores.

(b) Indicate the statement presentation of the financing charges and the credit card service charge expense for Ottawa Stores.

Journalize entries for notes receivable transactions.
(SO 5, 6)

E9-8 Mexico Supply Co. has the following transactions related to notes receivable during the last 2 months of 2006.

Nov.	1	Loaned $18,000 cash to Norma Hanson on a 1-year, 10% note.
Dec.	11	Sold goods to John Countryman, Inc., receiving a $6,750, 90-day, 8% note.
	16	Received a $4,000, 6-month, 9% note in exchange for Bob Shabo's outstanding accounts receivable.
	31	Accrued interest revenue on all notes receivable.

Instructions

(a) Journalize the transactions for Mexico Supply Co.

(b) Record the collection of the Hanson note at its maturity in 2007.

Journalize entries for notes receivable.
(SO 5, 6)

E9-9 Record the following transactions for Sandwich Co. in the general journal.

<u>2006</u>

May	1	Received an $8,700, 1-year, 10% note in exchange for Linda Anderson's outstanding accounts receivable.
Dec.	31	Accrued interest on the Anderson note.
Dec.	31	Closed the interest revenue account.

<u>2007</u>

May	1	Received principal plus interest on the Anderson note. (No interest has been accrued in 2007.)

Journalize entries for dishonor of notes receivable.
(SO 5, 8)

E9-10 On May 2, Maple Park Company lends $6,600 to Cortland, Inc., issuing a 6-month, 9% note. At the maturity date, November 2, Cortland indicates that it cannot pay.

Instructions

(a) Prepare the entry to record the issuance of the note.

(b) Prepare the entry to record the dishonor of the note, assuming that Maple Park Company expects collection will occur.

(c) Prepare the entry to record the dishonor of the note, assuming that Maple Park Company does not expect collection in the future.

Determine missing amounts related to sales and accounts receivable.

(SO 2, 4, 9)

E9-11 The following information pertains to Sosa Merchandising Company.

Merchandise inventory at end of year	$33,000
Accounts receivable at beginning of year	24,000
Cash sales made during the year	18,000
Gross profit on sales	25,000
Accounts receivable written off during the year	1,000
Purchases made during the year	60,000
Accounts receivable collected during the year	78,000
Merchandise inventory at beginning of year	36,000

Instructions

(a) Calculate the amount of credit sales made during the year. (*Hint*: You will need to use income statement relationships—introduced in Chapter 5—in order to determine this.)

(b) Calculate the balance of accounts receivable at the end of the year.

PROBLEMS: SET A

Prepare journal entries related to bad debts expense.

(SO 2, 3, 9)

Peachtree

P9-1A At December 31, 2006, Sycamore Imports reported the following information on its balance sheet.

Accounts receivable	$1,020,000
Less: Allowance for doubtful accounts	60,000

During 2007, the company had the following transactions related to receivables.

1. Sales on account	$2,670,000
2. Sales returns and allowances	40,000
3. Collections of accounts receivable	2,300,000
4. Write-offs of accounts receivable deemed uncollectible	65,000
5. Recovery of bad debts previously written off as uncollectible	20,000

Instructions

(a) Prepare the journal entries to record each of these five transactions. Assume that no cash discounts were taken on the collections of accounts receivable.

(b) Enter the January 1, 2007, balances in Accounts Receivable and Allowance for Doubtful Accounts. Post the entries to the two accounts (use T accounts), and determine the balances.

(c) Prepare the journal entry to record bad debts expense for 2007, assuming that an aging of accounts receivable indicates that estimated bad debts are $95,000.

(d) Compute the accounts receivable turnover ratio for the year 2007.

(b) Accounts receivable $1,285,000
ADA $15,000

(c) Bad debts expense $80,000

Compute bad debts amounts.

(SO 3)

P9-2A Information related to DeKalb Company for 2006 is summarized below.

Total credit sales	$1,640,000
Accounts receivable at December 31	620,000
Bad debts written off	26,000

Instructions

(a) What amount of bad debts expense will DeKalb Company report if it uses the direct write-off method of accounting for bad debts?

(b) Assume that DeKalb Company decides to estimate its bad debts expense to be 2% of credit sales. What amount of bad debts expense will DeKalb record if Allowance for Doubtful Accounts has a credit balance of $3,000?

(c) Assume that DeKalb Company decides to estimate its bad debts expense based on 5% of accounts receivable. What amount of bad debts expense will DeKalb Company record if Allowance for Doubtful Accounts has a credit balance of $4,000?

(d) Assume the same facts as in (c), except that there is a $2,000 debit balance in Allowance for Doubtful Accounts. What amount of bad debts expense will DeKalb record?

(e) What is the weakness of the direct write-off method of reporting bad debts expense?

Journalize entries to record transactions related to bad debts.

(SO 2, 3)

P9-3A Presented below is an aging schedule for Emporia Company.

			Number of Days Past Due			
Customer	**Total**	**Not Yet Due**	**1–30**	**31–60**	**61–90**	**Over 90**
Anders	$ 20,000		$ 9,000	$11,000		
Baietto	30,000	$ 30,000				
Cyrs	50,000	15,000	5,000		$30,000	
DeJong	38,000					$38,000
Others	126,000	92,000	15,000	13,000		6,000
	$264,000	$137,000	$29,000	$24,000	$30,000	$44,000
Estimated Percentage Uncollectible		2%	5%	10%	24%	50%
Total Estimated Bad Debts	$ 35,790	$ 2,740	$ 1,450	$ 2,400	$ 7,200	$22,000

At December 31, 2006, the unadjusted balance in Allowance for Doubtful Accounts is a credit of $8,000.

Instructions

(a) Bad debts expense $27,790

(a) Journalize and post the adjusting entry for bad debts at December 31, 2006.

(b) Journalize and post to the allowance account the following events and transactions in the year 2007.

(1) March 1, an $1,100 customer balance originating in 2006 is judged uncollectible.

(2) May 1, a check for $1,100 is received from the customer whose account was written off as uncollectible on March 1.

(c) Bad debts expense $32,500

(c) Journalize the adjusting entry for bad debts on December 31, 2007. Assume that the unadjusted balance in Allowance for Doubtful Accounts is a debit of $1,200, and the aging schedule indicates that total estimated bad debts will be $31,300.

Journalize transactions related to bad debts.

(SO 2, 3)

P9-4A The following represents selected information taken from a company's aging schedule to estimate uncollectible accounts receivable at year end.

		Number of Days Outstanding				
	Total	**0–30**	**31–60**	**61–90**	**91–120**	**Over 120**
Accounts receivable	$260,000	$100,000	$60,000	$50,000	$30,000	$20,000
% uncollectible		1%	5%	7.5%	10%	12%
Estimated bad debts						

Instructions

(a) Total estimated bad debts $13,150

(a) Calculate the total estimated bad debts based on the above information.

(b) Prepare the year-end adjusting journal entry to record the bad debts using the allowance method and the aged uncollectible accounts receivable determined in (a). Assume the opening balance in the Allowance for Doubtful Accounts account is a $10,000 credit.

(c) Of the above accounts, $2,000 is determined to be specifically uncollectible. Prepare the journal entry to write off the uncollectible accounts.

(d) The company subsequently collects $1,000 on a specific account that had previously been determined to be uncollectible in (c). Prepare the journal entry(ies) necessary to restore the account and record the cash collection.

(e) Explain how establishing an allowance account satisfies the matching principle.

P9-5A At December 31, 2006, the trial balance of Larry Falcetto Company contained the following amounts before adjustment.

Journalize entries to record transactions related to bad debts.

(SO 3)

	Debits	Credits
Accounts Receivable	$350,000	
Allowance for Doubtful Accounts		$ 1,300
Sales		880,000

Instructions

(a) Prepare the adjusting entry at December 31, 2006, to record bad debts expense under each of the following independent assumptions.

(1) An aging schedule indicates that $17,550 of accounts receivable will be uncollectible.

(2) The company estimates that 2% of sales will be uncollectible.

(a) (2) $17,600

(b) Repeat part (a) assuming that instead of a credit balance, there is a $1,300 debit balance in Allowance for Doubtful Accounts.

(c) During the next month, January 2007, a $4,500 account receivable is written off as uncollectible. Prepare the journal entry to record the write-off.

(d) Repeat part (c) assuming that Larry Falcetto Company uses the direct write-off method instead of the allowance method in accounting for uncollectible accounts receivable.

(e) What are the advantages of using the allowance method in accounting for uncollectible accounts as compared to the direct write-off method?

P9-6A Rochelle Graves Co. closes its books monthly. On June 30, selected ledger account balances are:

Prepare entries for various notes receivable transactions.

(SO 2, 4, 5, 8, 9)

Peachtree

Notes Receivable	$30,000
Interest Receivable	$ 240

Notes Receivable include the following.

Date	Maker	Face	Term	Interest
May 16	Alexis Inc.	$ 6,000	60 days	10%
May 25	Domino Co.	15,000	60 days	11%
June 30	ERV Corp.	9,000	6 months	8%

During July, the following transactions were completed.

July 5 Made sales of $6,200 on Rochelle Graves Co. credit cards.
14 Made sales of $700 on VISA credit cards. The credit card service charge is 4%.
14 Added $440 to Rochelle Graves Co. credit card customer balances for finance charges on unpaid balances.
15 Received payment in full from Alexis Inc. on the amount due.
25 Received notice that the Domino Co. note has been dishonored. (Assume that Domino Co. is expected to pay in the future.)

Instructions

(a) Journalize the July transactions and the July 31 adjusting entry for accrued interest receivable. (Interest is computed using 360 days.)

(b) Enter the balances at July 1 in the receivable accounts. Post the entries to all of the receivable accounts.

(b) Accounts receivable $21,915

(c) Show the balance sheet presentation of the receivable accounts at July 31.

(c) Total receivables $30,975

P9-7A On January 1, 2006, Bettendorf Company had Accounts Receivable $56,900 and Allowance for Doubtful Accounts $4,700. Bettendorf Company prepares financial statements annually. During the year the following selected transactions occurred.

Prepare entries for various receivables transactions.

(SO 2, 4, 5, 6, 7, 8)

Jan. 5 Sold $6,900 of merchandise to John Yockey Company, terms n/30.
Feb. 2 Accepted a $6,900, 4-month, 10% promissory note from John Yockey Company for the balance due.
12 Sold $7,800 of merchandise to Skosey Company and accepted Skosey's $7,800, 2-month, 10% note for the balance due.
26 Sold $3,000 of merchandise to Platz Co., terms n/10.
Apr. 5 Accepted a $3,000, 3-month, 8% note from Platz Co. for the balance due.
12 Collected the Skosey Company note in full.
June 2 Collected the John Yockey Company note in full.

July 5	Platz Co. dishonors its note of April 5. It is expected that Platz will eventually pay the amount owed.
15	Sold $7,000 of merchandise to King Co. and accepted King's $7,000, 3-month, 12% note for the amount due.
Oct. 15	King Co.'s note was dishonored. King Co. is bankrupt, and there is no hope of future settlement.

Instructions

Journalize the transactions.

PROBLEMS: SET B

Prepare journal entries related to bad debts expense.

(SO 2, 3, 9)

P9-1B At December 31, 2006, Hilo Co. reported the following information on its balance sheet.

Accounts receivable	$960,000
Less: Allowance for doubtful accounts	70,000

During 2007, the company had the following transactions related to receivables.

1. Sales on account	$3,315,000
2. Sales returns and allowances	50,000
3. Collections of accounts receivable	2,810,000
4. Write-offs of accounts receivable deemed uncollectible	90,000
5. Recovery of bad debts previously written off as uncollectible	29,000

Instructions

(a) Prepare the journal entries to record each of these five transactions. Assume that no cash discounts were taken on the collections of accounts receivable.

(b) Accounts receivable $1,325,000 ADA $9,000

(b) Enter the January 1, 2007, balances in Accounts Receivable and Allowance for Doubtful Accounts, post the entries to the two accounts (use T accounts), and determine the balances.

(c) Bad debts expense $116,000

(c) Prepare the journal entry to record bad debts expense for 2007, assuming that an aging of accounts receivable indicates that expected bad debts are $125,000.

(d) Compute the accounts receivable turnover ratio for 2007.

Compute bad debts amounts.

(SO 3)

P9-2B Information related to Kap Shin Company for 2006 is summarized below.

Total credit sales	$2,100,000
Accounts receivable at December 31	837,000
Bad debts written off	33,000

Instructions

(a) What amount of bad debts expense will Kap Shin Company report if it uses the direct write-off method of accounting for bad debts?

(b) Assume that Kap Shin Company estimates its bad debts expense to be 2% of credit sales. What amount of bad debts expense will Kap Shin record if it has an Allowance for Doubtful Accounts credit balance of $4,000?

(c) Assume that Kap Shin Company estimates its bad debts expense based on 6% of accounts receivable. What amount of bad debts expense will Kap Shin record if it has an Allowance for Doubtful Accounts credit balance of $3,000?

(d) Assume the same facts as in (c), except that there is a $3,000 debit balance in Allowance for Doubtful Accounts. What amount of bad debts expense will Kap Shin record?

(e) What is the weakness of the direct write-off method of reporting bad debts expense?

P9-3B Presented below is an aging schedule for Yee Chow Company.

Journalize entries to record transactions related to bad debts.

(SO 2, 3)

Customer	Total	Not Yet Due	Number of Days Past Due 1–30	31–60	61–90	Over 90
Arndt	$ 22,000		$10,000	$12,000		
Blair	40,000	$ 40,000				
Chase	57,000	16,000	6,000		$35,000	
Drea	34,000					$34,000
Others	132,000	96,000	16,000	14,000		6,000
	$285,000	$152,000	$32,000	$26,000	$35,000	$40,000
Estimated Percentage Uncollectible		3%	6%	13%	25%	60%
Total Estimated Bad Debts	$ 42,610	$ 4,560	$ 1,920	$ 3,380	$ 8,750	$24,000

At December 31, 2006, the unadjusted balance in Allowance for Doubtful Accounts is a credit of $9,000.

Instructions

(a) Journalize and post the adjusting entry for bad debts at December 31, 2006.

(b) Journalize and post to the allowance account the following events and transactions in the year 2007.

(1) On March 31, a $1,000 customer balance originating in 2006 is judged uncollectible.

(2) On May 31, a check for $1,000 is received from the customer whose account was written off as uncollectible on March 31.

(c) Journalize the adjusting entry for bad debts on December 31, 2007, assuming that the unadjusted balance in Allowance for Doubtful Accounts is a debit of $800 and the aging schedule indicates that total estimated bad debts will be $31,600.

(a) Bad debts expense $33,610

(c) Bad debts expense $32,400

P9-4B Image.com uses the allowance method to estimate uncollectible accounts receivable. The company produced the following aging of the accounts receivable at year end.

Journalize transactions related to bad debts.

(SO 2, 3)

	Total	Number of Days Outstanding 0–30	31–60	61–90	91–120	Over 120
Accounts receivable	$375,000	$220,000	$90,000	$40,000	$10,000	$15,000
% uncollectible		1%	4%	5%	6%	10%
Estimated bad debts						

Instructions

(a) Calculate the total estimated bad debts based on the above information.

(b) Prepare the year-end adjusting journal entry to record the bad debts using the aged uncollectible accounts receivable determined in (a). Assume the opening balance in Allowance for Doubtful Accounts is a $10,000 debit.

(c) Of the above accounts, $5,000 is determined to be specifically uncollectible. Prepare the journal entry to write off the uncollectible account.

(d) The company collects $5,000 subsequently on a specific account that had previously been determined to be uncollectible in (c). Prepare the journal entry(ies) necessary to restore the account and record the cash collection.

(e) Comment on how your answers to (a)–(d) would change if Image.com used 3% of *total* accounts receivable, rather than aging the accounts receivable. What are the advantages to the company of aging the accounts receivable rather than applying a percentage to total accounts receivable?

(a) Total estimated bad debts $9,900

Journalize entries to record transactions related to bad debts.

(SO 3)

P9-5B At December 31, 2006, the trial balance of Videosoft Company contained the following amounts before adjustment.

	Debits	Credits
Accounts Receivable	$385,000	
Allowance for Doubtful Accounts		$ 800
Sales		918,000

Instructions

(a) Based on the information given, which method of accounting for bad debts is Videosoft Company using—the direct write-off method or the allowance method? How can you tell?

(b) (2) $9,180

(b) Prepare the adjusting entry at December 31, 2006, for bad debts expense under each of the following independent assumptions.

(1) An aging schedule indicates that $11,750 of accounts receivable will be uncollectible.

(2) The company estimates that 1% of sales will be uncollectible.

(c) Repeat part (b) assuming that instead of a credit balance there is an $800 debit balance in Allowance for Doubtful Accounts.

(d) During the next month, January 2007, a $3,000 account receivable is written off as uncollectible. Prepare the journal entry to record the write-off.

(e) Repeat part (d) assuming that Videosoft uses the direct write-off method instead of the allowance method in accounting for uncollectible accounts receivable.

(f) What type of account is Allowance for Doubtful Accounts? How does it affect how accounts receivable is reported on the balance sheet at the end of the accounting period?

Prepare entries for various notes receivable transactions.

(SO 2, 4, 5, 8, 9)

P9-6B Derek Lu Company closes its books monthly. On September 30, selected ledger account balances are:

Notes Receivable	$29,000
Interest Receivable	$ 210

Notes Receivable include the following.

Date	Maker	Face	Term	Interest
Aug. 16	Demaster Inc.	$ 8,000	60 days	12%
Aug. 25	Almer Co.	9,000	60 days	10%
Sept. 30	Skinner Corp.	12,000	6 months	9%

Interest is computed using a 360-day year. During October, the following transactions were completed.

Oct. 7 Made sales of $6,900 on Derek Lu credit cards.
12 Made sales of $800 on MasterCard credit cards. The credit card service charge is 3%.
15 Added $460 to Derek Lu customer balance for finance charges on unpaid balances.
15 Received payment in full from Demaster Inc. on the amount due.
24 Received notice that the Almer note has been dishonored. (Assume that Almer is expected to pay in the future.)

Instructions

(a) Journalize the October transactions and the October 31 adjusting entry for accrued interest receivable.

(b) Accounts receivable $16,510

(b) Enter the balances at October 1 in the receivable accounts. Post the entries to all of the receivable accounts.

(c) Total receivables $28,600

(c) Show the balance sheet presentation of the receivable accounts at October 31.

Prepare entries for various receivable transactions.

(SO 2, 4, 5, 6, 7, 8)

P9-7B On January 1, 2006, Cedar Grove Company had Accounts Receivable $139,000, Notes Receivable $15,000, and Allowance for Doubtful Accounts $13,200. The note receivable is from Sara Rogers Company. It is a 4-month, 12% note dated December 31, 2005. Cedar Grove Company prepares financial statements annually. During the year the following selected transactions occurred.

Jan. 5 Sold $16,000 of merchandise to Billings Company, terms n/15.
20 Accepted Billings Company's $16,000, 3-month, 9% note for the balance due.
Feb. 18 Sold $8,000 of merchandise to Grania Company and accepted Grania's $8,000, 6-month, 9% note for the amount due.

Apr. 20 Collected the Billings Company note in full.
30 Received payment in full from Sara Rogers Company on the amount due.
May 25 Accepted Fiona Inc.'s $6,000, 3-month, 7% note in settlement of a past-due balance on account.
Aug. 18 Received payment in full from Grania Company on the note due.
25 The Fiona Inc. note was dishonored. Fiona Inc. is not bankrupt; future payment is anticipated.
Sept. 1 Sold $12,000 of merchandise to Lena Torme Company and accepted a $12,000, 6-month, 10% note for the amount due.

Instructions
Journalize the transactions.

BROADENING YOUR PERSPECTIVE

Financial Reporting and Analysis

FINANCIAL REPORTING PROBLEM: CAF Company

BYP9-1 CAF Company sells office equipment and supplies to many organizations in the city and surrounding area on contract terms of 2/10, n/30. In the past, over 75% of the credit customers have taken advantage of the discount by paying within 10 days of the invoice date.

The number of customers taking the full 30 days to pay has increased within the last year. Current indications are that less than 60% of the customers are now taking the discount. Bad debts as a percentage of gross credit sales have risen from the 2.5% provided in past years to about 4.5% in the current year.

The company's Finance Committee has requested more information on the collections of accounts receivable. The controller responded to this request with the report reproduced below.

CAF COMPANY
Accounts Receivable Collections
May 31, 2006

The fact that some credit accounts will prove uncollectible is normal. Annual bad debts write-offs have been 2.5% of gross credit sales over the past 5 years. During the last fiscal year, this percentage increased to slightly less than 4.5%. The current Accounts Receivable balance is $1,400,000. The condition of this balance in terms of age and probability of collection is as follows.

Proportion of Total	Age Categories	Probability of Collection
60%	not yet due	98%
22%	less than 30 days past due	96%
9%	30 to 60 days past due	94%
5%	61 to 120 days past due	91%
2½%	121 to 180 days past due	75%
1½%	over 180 days past due	30%

The Allowance for Doubtful Accounts had a credit balance of $29,500 on June 1, 2005. CAF has provided for a monthly bad debts expense accrual during the current fiscal year based on the assumption that 4.5% of gross credit sales will be uncollectible. Total gross credit sales for the 2005–06 fiscal year amounted to $2,800,000. Write-offs of uncollectible accounts during the year totaled $102,000.

Instructions

(a) Prepare an accounts receivable aging schedule for CAF Company using the age categories identified in the controller's report to the Finance Committee showing the following.

(1) The amount of accounts receivable outstanding for each age category and in total.

(2) The estimated amount that is uncollectible for each category and in total.

(b) Compute the amount of the year-end adjustment necessary to bring Allowance for Doubtful Accounts to the balance indicated by the aging analysis. Then prepare the necessary journal entry to adjust the accounting records.

(c) In a recessionary environment with tight credit and high interest rates:

(1) Identify steps CAF Company might consider to improve the accounts receivable situation.

(2) Then evaluate each step identified in terms of the risks and costs involved.

■ COMPARATIVE ANALYSIS PROBLEM: PepsiCo vs. Coca-Cola

BYP9-2 **PepsiCo**'s financial statements are presented in Appendix A. **Coca-Cola**'s financial statements are presented in Appendix B.

Instructions

(a) Based on the information contained in these financial statements, compute the following 2003 ratios for each company. (Assume all sales are credit sales. See PepsiCo's Note 14 for some additional information.)

(1) Accounts receivable turnover ratio.

(2) Average collection period for receivables.

(b) What conclusions concerning the management of accounts receivable can be drawn from these data?

■ RESEARCH CASE

BYP9-3 The May 13, 2002, issue of the *Wall Street Journal* includes an article by Paul Beckett titled "Is **Citigroup** Set for a Rainy Day? Reserves Make Investors Uneasy."

Instructions

Read the article and answer the following questions.

(a) How do Citigroup's "reserve" accounts (such as allowance for bad debts) compare to those of other large financial institutions?

(b) What reasons are given for expecting that Citigroup should actually have larger reserves than its peer institutions, rather than smaller reserves?

(c) How does the article suggest that a bank's expectations about the future economy affect the amount of reserves that the bank sets up? What does this suggest about Citigroup's expectations about the future economy?

(d) What are some reasons given for not being alarmed about the adequacy of Citigroup's reserves?

■ INTERPRETING FINANCIAL STATEMENTS

BYP9-4 The following information was taken from the 2003 financial statements and accompanying notes of **The Scotts Company**, a major manufacturer of lawn-care products.

(in millions)	2003	2002
Accounts receivable (gross)	$ 304.7	$ 283.1
Allowance for uncollectible accounts	20.0	33.2
Sales	1,910.1	1,748.7
Total current assets	810.2	730.1

THE SCOTTS COMPANY
Notes to the Financial Statements

Note 17. Concentrations of Credit Risk
Financial instruments which potentially subject the Company to concentration of credit risk consist principally of trade accounts receivable. The Company sells its consumer products to a wide variety of retailers, including mass merchandisers, home centers, independent hardware stores, nurseries, garden outlets, warehouse clubs and local and regional chains. Professional products are sold to commercial nurseries, greenhouses, landscape services, and growers of specialty agriculture crops.

At September 30, 2003, 68% of the Company's accounts receivable was due in North America, with 7% related to ongoing litigation documented in Note 16 to the Consolidated Financial Statements. Approximately 75% of the North American receivables were generated from the Company's North American Consumer segment. The most significant concentration of receivables within this segment was from our top 3 customers, which accounted for 79% of the total.

The remaining 25% of North American accounts receivable was generated from customers of the Scotts Lawn Service® and Global Professional segments located in North America. Nearly all of the Global Professional segment's North American accounts receivable at September 30, 2003 was due from distributors.

The 32% of accounts receivable generated outside of North America was due from retailers, distributors, nurseries and growers. No concentrations of customers or individual customers within this group account for more than 10% of the Company's accounts receivable balance at September 30, 2003.

At September 30, 2003, the Company's concentrations of credit risk were similar to those existing at September 30, 2002.

The Company's two largest customers accounted for the following percentage of net sales in each respective period:

	Largest Customer	2nd Largest Customer
2003	24.8%	13.9%
2002	25.8%	13.2%
2001	24.3%	12.5%

Sales to the Company's two largest customers are reported within Scotts' North American Consumer segment. No other customers accounted for more than 10% of fiscal 2003, 2002 or 2001 net sales.

Instructions
Answer each of the following questions.

(a) Calculate the receivables turnover ratio and average collection period for 2003 for the company.
(b) Is accounts receivable a material component of the company's total current assets?
(c) Scotts sells seasonal products. How might this affect the accuracy of your answer to part (a)?
(d) Evaluate the credit risk of Scotts' concentrated receivables.
(e) Comment on the informational value of Scotts' Note 17 on concentrations of credit risk.

■ A GLOBAL FOCUS

BYP9-5 **Art World Industries, Inc.** was incorporated in 1986 in Delaware, and is located in Los Angeles. The company prints, publishes, and sells limited-edition graphics and reproduction prints in the wholesale market.

The company's balance sheet at the end of a recent year showed an allowance for doubtful accounts of $175,477. The allowance was set up against certain Japanese accounts receivable that average more than one year in age. The Japanese acknowledge the amount due, but with the slow economy in Japan lack the resources to pay at this time.

Instructions

(a) Which method of accounting for uncollectible accounts does Art World Industries use?

(b) Explain the difference between the direct write-off and percentage of receivables methods. Based on Art World's disclosure above, what important factor would you have to consider in arriving at appropriate percentages to apply for the percentage of receivables method?

(c) What are the implications for a company's receivables management of selling its products internationally?

■ EXPLORING THE WEB

BYP9-6 Purpose: To learn more about factoring from the Web site of a company that provides factoring services.

Address: www.invoicefinancial.com, or go to www.wiley.com/college/weygandt

Steps: Go to the Web site.

Instructions

Answer the following questions.

(a) What are some of the benefits of factoring?

(b) What is the range of the percentages of the typical discount rate?

(c) If a company factors its receivables, what percentage of the value of the receivables can it expect to receive from the factor in the form of cash, and how quickly will it receive the cash?

Critical Thinking

■ GROUP DECISION CASE

BYP9-7 Hilda and Jan Piwek own Campus Fashions. From its inception Campus Fashions has sold merchandise on either a cash or credit basis, but no credit cards have been accepted. During the past several months, the Piweks have begun to question their sales policies. First, they have lost some sales because of refusing to accept credit cards. Second, representatives of two metropolitan banks have been persuasive in almost convincing them to accept their national credit cards. One bank, City National Bank, has stated that its credit card fee is 4%.

The Piweks decide that they should determine the cost of carrying their own credit sales. From the accounting records of the past 3 years they accumulate the following data.

	2006	2005	2004
Net credit sales	$530,000	$650,000	$400,000
Collection agency fees for slow-paying customers	2,450	2,500	2,400
Salary of part-time accounts receivable clerk	4,100	4,100	4,100

Credit and collection expenses as a percentage of net credit sales are: uncollectible accounts 1.6%, billing and mailing costs 0.5%, and credit investigation fee on new customers 0.15%.

Hilda and Jan also determine that the average accounts receivable balance outstanding during the year is 5% of net credit sales. The Piweks estimate that they could earn an average of 8% annually on cash invested in other business opportunities.

Instructions

With the class divided into groups, answer the following.

(a) Prepare a table showing, for each year, total credit and collection expenses in dollars and as a percentage of net credit sales.

(b) Determine the net credit and collection expense in dollars and as a percentage of sales after considering the revenue not earned from other investment opportunities.

(c) Discuss both the financial and nonfinancial factors that are relevant to the decision.

■ COMMUNICATION ACTIVITY

BYP9-8 Lily Pao, a friend of yours, overheard a discussion at work about changes her employer wants to make in accounting for uncollectible accounts. Lily knows little about accounting, and she asks you to help make sense of what she heard. Specifically, she asks you to explain the differences between the percentage of sales, percentage of receivables, and the direct write-off methods for uncollectible accounts.

Instructions
In a letter of one page (or less), explain to Lily the three methods of accounting for uncollectibles. Be sure to discuss differences among these methods.

■ ETHICS CASE

Accounting Matters!

BYP9-9 The controller of Vest Co. believes that the yearly allowance for doubtful accounts for Shirt Co. should be 2% of net credit sales. The president of Vest Co., nervous that the stockholders might expect the company to sustain its 10% growth rate, suggests that the controller increase the allowance for doubtful accounts to 4%. The president thinks that the lower net income, which reflects a 6% growth rate, will be a more sustainable rate for Vest Co.

Instructions
(a) Who are the stakeholders in this case?
(b) Does the president's request pose an ethical dilemma for the controller?
(c) Should the controller be concerned with Vest Co.'s growth rate in estimating the allowance? Explain your answer.

■ CONTINUING COOKIE CHRONICLE

Accounting Matters!

(Note: This is a continuation of the Cookie Chronicle from Chapters 1 through 8.)

BYP9-10 Natalie has been approached by one of her friends, Curtis Lesperance. Curtis runs a coffee shop where he sells specialty coffees, and prepares and sells muffins and cookies. He is eager to buy one of Natalie's fine European mixers because he would then be able to prepare larger batches of muffins and cookies. However, Curtis cannot afford to pay for the mixer for at least 30 days. He has asked Natalie if she would be willing to sell him the mixer on credit.

Natalie comes to you for advice and asks the following questions.

1. Curtis has provided me with a set of his most recent financial statements. What calculations should I do with the data from these statements, and what questions should I ask him after I have analyzed the statements? How will this information help me decide if I should extend credit to Curtis?
2. Is there an alternative other than extending credit to Curtis for 30 days?
3. I am thinking seriously about being able to have my customers use credit cards. What are some of the advantages and disadvantages of letting my customers pay by credit card?

The following transactions occurred in June through August.

June 1 After much thought, Natalie sells a mixer to Curtis on credit, terms n/30, for $1,025 (cost of mixer $566).

2 Natalie meets with the bank manager and arranges to get access to a credit card account. The terms of credit card transactions are 3% of the sales transaction and a monthly equipment rental charge of $75.

30 Natalie teaches 12 classes in June. Seven classes were paid for in cash, $875; the other five classes were paid for by credit card, $750.

30 Natalie receives and reconciles her bank statement. She makes sure that the monthly $75 charge for the rental of the credit card equipment and the 3% fee on the credit card transactions have been correctly processed by the bank.

30 Curtis calls Natalie. He is unable to pay the amount outstanding for another month, so he signs a one-month, 8.25% note receivable.

July 15 Natalie sells a mixer to a friend of Curtis's. The friend pays $1,025 for the mixer by credit card (cost of mixer $566).

30 Natalie teaches 15 classes in July. Eight classes are paid for in cash, $1,000; and seven classes are paid for by credit card, $1,050.

31 Natalie reconciles her bank statement and makes sure the bank has recorded the correct amounts for the rental of the credit card equipment and the credit card sales.

31 Curtis calls Natalie. He cannot pay today but hopes to have a check for her at the end of the week. Natalie prepares the appropriate journal entry.

Aug. 10 Curtis calls again and promises to pay at the end of August, including interest for 2 months.

31 Natalie receives a check from Curtis in payment of his balance plus interest outstanding.

Instructions

(a) Answer Natalie's questions.

(b) Prepare journal entries for the transactions that occurred in June, July, and August.

Accounting Matters!

Answers to Accounting Matters! Questions

p. 383

Q: Why are credit card companies willing to offer such relaxed repayment options?

A: Credit card companies generate their income primarily from interest charges on cardholders' balances. The larger the outstanding balances, the greater the interest income.

p. 388

Q: Why is timely billing important to a business?

A: The sooner a business receives cash, the sooner it can use the cash to pay its bills (and avoid interest charges on unpaid balances) or invest in income-generating opportunities.

p. 392

Q: How will this trend affect the amount and mix of retail businesses' expenses?

A: Retail business will have lower collection expenses (fewer bad debts and fewer NSF checks) but higher credit card charges. There probably is little long-term effect on net income.

p. 397

Q: Rather than refusing to ship to Kmart, what could suppliers have done to protect their interests?

A: Suppliers could have demanded cash payment upon delivery, no longer offering Kmart the option of purchasing on credit.

PEPSI.

Answer to PepsiCo Review It Question 3, p. 389

According to Note 14, **PepsiCo**'s gross receivables were $2,935 million. Its allowance for doubtful accounts was $105 million. Therefore, the allowance is 3.6% of the gross receivables balance.

Answers to Self-Study Questions

1. c **2.** a **3.** b **4.** b **5.** d **6.** c **7.** c **8.** a **9.** b **10.** d

REMEMBER to go back to the Navigator box on the chapter-opening page and check off your completed work.

Chapter 10

Plant Assets, Natural Resources, and Intangible Assets

THE NAVIGATOR ✓

- Understand **Concepts for Review** ❑
- Read **Feature Story** ❑
- Scan **Study Objectives** ❑
- Read **Preview** ❑
- Read text and answer **Before You Go On** p. 424 ❑ p. 432 ❑ p. 436 ❑ p. 443 ❑
- Work **Demonstration Problems** ❑
- Review **Summary of Study Objectives** ❑
- Answer **Self-Study Questions** ❑
- Complete **Assignments** ❑

CONCEPTS FOR REVIEW

Before studying this chapter, you should know or, if necessary, review:

- The time period assumption. (Ch. 3, p. 94)
- The cost principle (Ch. 1, p. 10) and the matching principle. (Ch. 3, p. 95)
- What is depreciation? (Ch. 3, p. 100)
- How to make adjustments for depreciation. (Ch. 3, pp. 100–101)

☑ THE NAVIGATOR

ACCOUNTING MATTERS! **FEATURE STORY**

How Much for a Ride to the Beach?

It's spring break. Your plane has landed, you've finally found your bags, and you're dying to hit the beach—but first you need a "vehicular unit" to get you there. As you turn away from baggage claim you see a long row of rental agency booths. Many are names you are familiar with—Hertz, Avis, and Budget. But a booth at the far end catches your eye—**Rent-A-Wreck**. Now there's a company making a clear statement!

Any company that relies on equipment to generate revenues must make decisions about what kind of equipment to buy, how long to keep it, and how vigorously to maintain it. Rent-A-Wreck has decided to rent used rather than new cars and trucks. It rents these vehicles across the United States, Europe, and Asia. While the big-name agencies push vehicles with that "new car smell," Rent-A-Wreck competes on price. The message is simple: Rent a used car and save some cash. It's not a message that appeals to everyone. If you're a marketing executive wanting to impress a big client, you probably don't want to pull up in a Rent-A-Wreck car. But if you want to get from point A to point B for the minimum cash per mile, then they are playing your tune. The company's message seems to be getting across to the right clientele. Revenues have increased from $29.9 million in 1996 to $51.7 million in 2000.

When you rent a car from Rent-A-Wreck, you are renting from an independent business person who has paid a "franchise fee" for the right to use the Rent-A-Wreck name. In order to gain a franchise, he or she must meet financial and other criteria, and must agree to run the rental agency according to rules prescribed by Rent-A-Wreck. Some of these rules require that each franchise maintain its cars in a reasonable fashion. This ensures that, though you won't be cruising down Daytona Beach's Atlantic Avenue in a Mercedes convertible, you can be reasonably assured that you won't be calling a towtruck.

www.rent-a-wreck.com

☑ THE NAVIGATOR

STUDY OBJECTIVES

After studying this chapter, you should be able to:

1. Describe how the cost principle applies to plant assets.
2. Explain the concept of depreciation.
3. Compute periodic depreciation using different methods.
4. Describe the procedure for revising periodic depreciation.
5. Distinguish between revenue and capital expenditures, and explain the entries for these expenditures.
6. Explain how to account for the disposal of a plant asset.
7. Compute periodic depletion of natural resources.
8. Explain the basic issues related to accounting for intangible assets.
9. Indicate how plant assets, natural resources, and intangible assets are reported and analyzed.

☑ THE NAVIGATOR

PREVIEW OF CHAPTER 10

The accounting for long-term assets has important implications for a company's reported results. In this chapter, we explain the application of the cost principle of accounting to property, plant, and equipment, such as **Rent-A-Wreck** vehicles, as well as to natural resources and intangible assets such as the "Rent-A-Wreck" trademark. We also describe the methods that may be used to allocate an asset's cost over its useful life. In addition, the accounting for expenditures incurred during the useful life of assets, such as the cost of replacing tires and brake pads on rental cars, is discussed.

The content and organization of Chapter 10 are as follows.

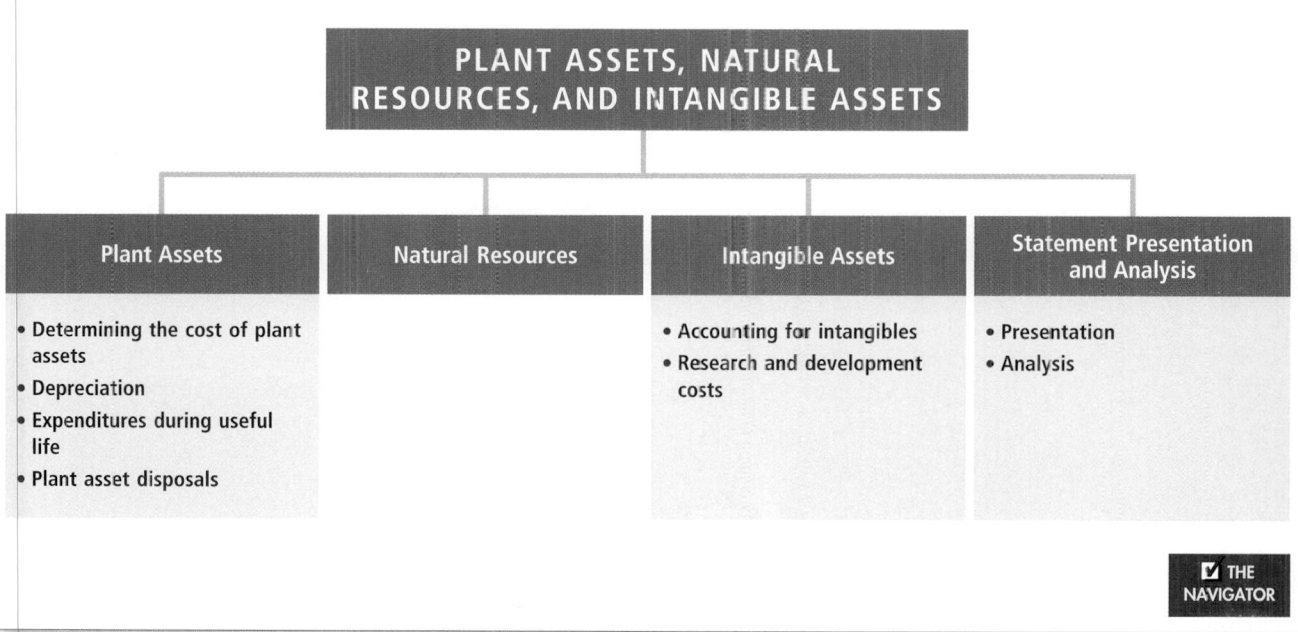

PLANT ASSETS, NATURAL RESOURCES, AND INTANGIBLE ASSETS

Plant Assets
- Determining the cost of plant assets
- Depreciation
- Expenditures during useful life
- Plant asset disposals

Natural Resources

Intangible Assets
- Accounting for intangibles
- Research and development costs

Statement Presentation and Analysis
- Presentation
- Analysis

THE NAVIGATOR

SECTION 1 PLANT ASSETS

Plant assets are resources that have three characteristics: they have a physical substance (a definite size and shape), are used in the operations of a business, and are not intended for sale to customers. They are also called **property, plant, and equipment**; **plant and equipment**; or **fixed assets**. These assets are expected to provide services to the company for a number of years. Except for land, plant assets decline in service potential over their useful lives.

It is important for a business to keep plant assets in good operating condition, replace worn-out or outdated plant assets, and expand its productive resources as needed. The decline of rail travel in the United States can be traced in part to the failure of railroad companies to meet the first two conditions. The growth of U.S. air travel is due in part to airlines having generally met these conditions.

Many companies have substantial investments in plant assets. Illustration 10-1 shows the percentages of plant assets in relation to total assets of companies in a number of industries.

Illustration 10-1
Percentages of plant assets in relation to total assets

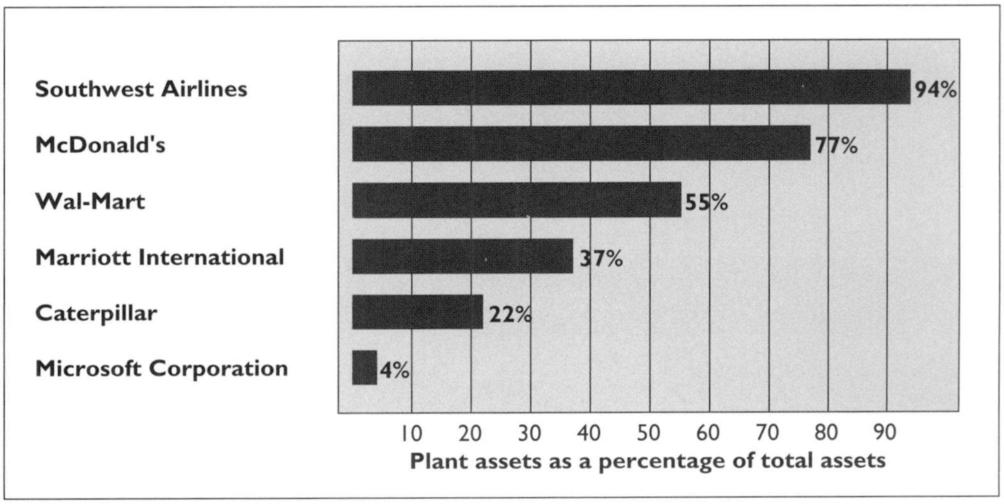

Determining the Cost of Plant Assets

STUDY OBJECTIVE 1

Describe how the cost principle applies to plant assets.

The cost principle requires that plant assets be recorded at cost. Thus the vehicles at **Rent-A-Wreck** are recorded at cost. Cost consists of **all expenditures necessary to acquire the asset and make it ready for its intended use**. For example, the cost of factory machinery includes the purchase price, freight costs paid by the purchaser, and installation costs. Once cost is established, it becomes the basis of accounting for the plant asset over its useful life. Current market or replacement values are not used after acquisition.

The application of the cost principle to each of the major classes of plant assets is explained in the following sections.

Land

Land is often used as a building site for a manufacturing plant or office building. The cost of land includes (1) the cash purchase price, (2) closing costs such as title and attorney's fees, (3) real estate brokers' commissions, and (4) accrued property taxes and other liens on the land assumed by the purchaser. For example, if the cash price is $50,000 and the purchaser agrees to pay accrued taxes of $5,000, the cost of the land is $55,000.

HELPFUL HINT

Management's intended use is important in applying the cost principle.

All necessary costs incurred to make land **ready for its intended use** are debited to the Land account. When vacant land is acquired, these costs include expenditures for clearing, draining, filling, and grading. Sometimes the land has a building on it that must be removed before construction of a new building. In this case, all demolition and removal costs, less any proceeds from salvaged materials, are debited to the Land account.

To illustrate, assume that Hayes Manufacturing Company acquires real estate at a cash cost of $100,000. The property contains an old warehouse that is razed at a net cost of $6,000 ($7,500 in costs less $1,500 proceeds from salvaged materials). Additional expenditures are the attorney's fee, $1,000, and the real estate broker's commission, $8,000. The cost of the land is $115,000, computed as follows.

Illustration 10-2
Computation of cost of land

Land	
Cash price of property	$100,000
Net removal cost of warehouse	6,000
Attorney's fee	1,000
Real estate broker's commission	8,000
Cost of land	**$115,000**

When the acquisition is recorded, Land is debited for $115,000 and Cash is credited for $115,000.

Land Improvements

Land improvements are structural additions made to land, such as driveways, parking lots, fences, landscaping, and underground sprinklers. The cost of land improvements includes all expenditures necessary to make the improvements ready for their intended use. For example, the cost of a new company parking lot includes the amount paid for paving, fencing, and lighting; thus the total of all of these costs would be debited to Land Improvements. Land improvements have limited useful lives, and their maintenance and replacement are the responsibility of the company. Because of their limited useful life, the cost of land improvements are expensed (depreciated) over their useful life.

Buildings

Buildings are facilities used in operations, such as stores, offices, factories, warehouses, and airplane hangars. All necessary expenditures related to the purchase or construction of a building are debited to the Buildings account. When a building is **purchased**, such costs include the purchase price, closing costs (attorney's fees, title insurance, etc.) and real estate broker's commission. Costs to make the building ready for its intended use include expenditures for remodeling and replacing or repairing the roof, floors, electrical wiring, and plumbing.

When a new building is **constructed**, cost consists of the contract price plus payments for architects' fees, building permits, and excavation costs. In addition, interest costs incurred to finance the project are included when a significant period of time is required to get the building ready for use. In these circumstances, interest costs are considered as necessary as materials and labor. However, the inclusion of interest costs in the cost of a constructed building is **limited to the construction period**. When construction has been completed, subsequent interest payments on funds borrowed to finance the construction are debited to Interest Expense.

Equipment

Equipment includes assets used in operations, such as store check-out counters, office furniture, factory machinery, delivery trucks, and airplanes. The cost of equipment, such as **Rent-A-Wreck** vehicles, consists of the **cash purchase price, sales taxes, freight charges, and insurance during transit paid by the purchaser**. It also includes expenditures required in assembling, installing, and testing the unit. However, motor vehicle licenses and accident insurance on company trucks and cars are not included in the cost of equipment. They are treated as expenses as they are incurred. They represent annual recurring expenditures and do not benefit future periods.

To illustrate, assume Merten Company purchases factory machinery at a cash price of $50,000. Related expenditures are for sales taxes $3,000, insurance during shipping $500, and installation and testing $1,000. The cost of the factory machinery is $54,500, computed as follows.

Illustration 10-3
Computation of cost of factory machinery

Factory Machinery	
Cash price	$50,000
Sales taxes	3,000
Insurance during shipping	500
Installation and testing	1,000
Cost of factory machinery	**$54,500**

The summary entry to record the purchase and related expenditures is:

A	=	L	+	SE
+54,500				
−54,500				

Cash Flows
−54,500

Factory Machinery	54,500	
Cash		54,500
(To record purchase of factory machine)		

For another example, assume that Lenard Company purchases a delivery truck at a cash price of $22,000. Related expenditures consist of sales taxes $1,320, painting and lettering $500, motor vehicle license $80, and a 3-year accident insurance policy $1,600. The cost of the delivery truck is $23,820, computed as follows.

Illustration 10-4
Computation of cost of delivery truck

Delivery Truck	
Cash price	$22,000
Sales taxes	1,320
Painting and lettering	500
Cost of delivery truck	**$23,820**

The cost of the motor vehicle license is treated as an expense, and the cost of the insurance policy is considered a prepaid asset. Thus, the entry to record the purchase of the truck and related expenditures is:

A	=	L	+	SE
+23,820				−80 Exp
+1,600				
−25,500				

Cash Flows
−25,500

Delivery Truck	23,820	
License Expense	80	
Prepaid Insurance	1,600	
Cash		25,500
(To record purchase of delivery truck and related expenditures)		

BEFORE YOU GO ON...

Review It

1. What are plant assets? What are the major classes of plant assets? How is the cost principle applied to accounting for plant assets?
2. What classifications and amounts are shown in **PepsiCo**'s Note 4 to explain its total property, plant, and equipment (net) of $7,828,000,000? The answer to this question is provided on p. 466.

Do It

Assume that a delivery truck is purchased for $15,000 cash, plus sales taxes of $900 and delivery costs of $500. The buyer also pays $200 for painting and lettering, $600 for an annual insurance policy, and $80 for a motor vehicle license. Explain how each of these costs would be accounted for.

ACTION PLAN

- Identify expenditures made in order to get delivery equipment ready for its intended use.
- Treat operating costs as expenses.

SOLUTION The first four payments ($15,000, $900, $500, and $200) are considered to be expenditures necessary to make the truck ready for its intended use. Thus, the cost of the truck is $16,600. The payments for insurance and the license are considered to be operating costs and therefore are expensed.

Related exercise material: *BE10-1, BE10-2, E10-1, and E10-2.*

THE NAVIGATOR

Depreciation

STUDY OBJECTIVE 2

Explain the concept of depreciation.

As explained in Chapter 3, **depreciation is the allocation of the cost of a plant asset to expense over its useful (service) life in a rational and systematic manner**. Cost allocation provides for the proper matching of expenses with revenues in accordance with the matching principle (see Illustration 10-5).

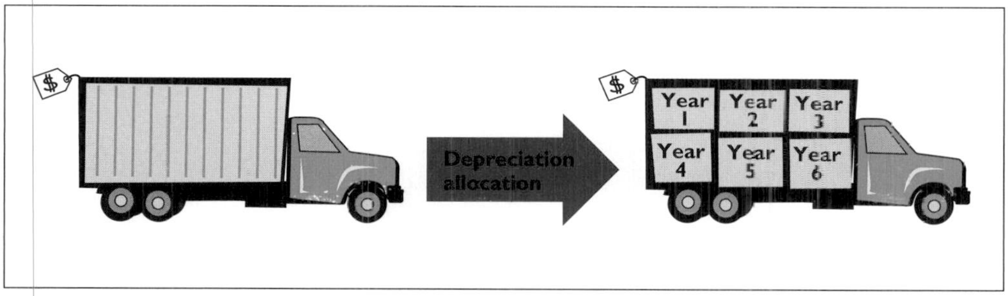

Illustration 10-5
Depreciation as an allocation concept

HELPFUL HINT

Remember that depreciation is the allocation of cost over the useful life of an asset. It is not a measure of value.

Depreciation is a process of cost allocation, not a process of asset valuation. The change in an asset's market value is not measured during ownership because plant assets are not held for resale. So, the **book value** (cost less accumulated depreciation) of a plant asset may be quite different from its market value.

Depreciation applies to three classes of plant assets: land improvements, buildings, and equipment. Each asset in these classes is considered to be a **depreciable asset**. Why? Because the usefulness to the company and revenue-producing ability of each asset will decline over the asset's useful life. Depreciation does not apply to land because its usefulness and revenue-producing ability generally remain intact over time. In fact, in many cases, the usefulness of land is greater over time because of the scarcity of good land sites. Thus, **land is not a depreciable asset**.

During a depreciable asset's useful life its revenue-producing ability will decline because of **wear and tear**. A delivery truck that has been driven 100,000 miles will be less useful to a company than one driven only 800 miles. Trucks and planes exposed to snow and salt will deteriorate faster than equipment that is not exposed to these elements.

Revenue-producing ability may also decline because of **obsolescence**. Obsolescence is the process of becoming out of date before the asset physically wears out. Major airlines were re-routed from Chicago's Midway Airport to Chicago-O'Hare International Airport because Midway's runways were too short for jumbo jets, for example.

It is important to understand that **recognizing depreciation on an asset does not result in an accumulation of cash for replacement of the asset**. The balance in Accumulated Depreciation represents the total cost that has been charged to expense. It is not a cash fund.

Factors in Computing Depreciation

Three factors affect the computation of depreciation:

1. **Cost.** Issues affecting the cost of a depreciable asset were explained earlier in this chapter. Recall that plant assets are recorded at cost, in accordance with the cost principle.
2. **Useful life.** Useful life is an estimate of the expected productive life, also called service life, of the asset. Useful life may be expressed in terms of time, units of activity (such as machine hours), or units of output. Useful life is an estimate. In making the estimate, management considers such factors as the intended use of the asset, its expected repair and maintenance, and its vulnerability to obsolescence. Past experience with similar assets is often helpful in deciding on expected useful life. We might reasonably expect the estimated useful life used by **Rent-A-Wreck** to differ from that used by **Avis**.
3. **Salvage value.** Salvage value is an estimate of the asset's value at the end of its useful life. This value may be based on the asset's worth as scrap or on its expected trade-in value. Like useful life, salvage value is an estimate. In making the estimate, management considers how it plans to dispose of the asset and its experience with similar assets.

ALTERNATIVE TERMINOLOGY

Another term sometimes used for salvage value is *residual value*.

Illustration 10-6 summarizes the three factors used in computing depreciation.

Illustration 10-6
Three factors in computing depreciation

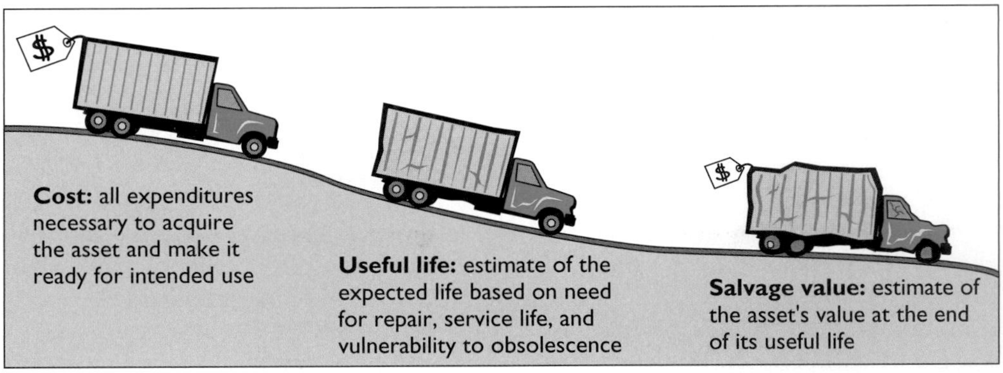

$
$
Cost: all expenditures necessary to acquire the asset and make it ready for intended use
Useful life: estimate of the expected life based on need for repair, service life, and vulnerability to obsolescence
Salvage value: estimate of the asset's value at the end of its useful life

HELPFUL HINT

Depreciation expense is reported on the income statement, and accumulated depreciation is reported as a deduction from plant assets on the balance sheet.

ACCOUNTING MATTERS! Business Insight

Willamette Industries, Inc., of Portland, Oregon, recently changed its accounting estimates relating to depreciation of certain assets. The vertically integrated forest products company said the changes were due to advances in technology that have increased the service life on its equipment an extra five years. Willamette expected the accounting changes to increase its full-year earnings by about $57 million, or $0.52 a share. Its prior-year earnings were $89 million, or $0.80 a share. Imagine a 65 percent improvement in earnings per share from a mere change in the estimated life of equipment!

? The effect on the income statement is discussed above. What effect does the change in the estimated life of equipment have on the balance sheet?

Depreciation Methods

STUDY OBJECTIVE 3

Compute periodic depreciation using different methods.

Depreciation is generally computed using one of the following methods:

1. Straight-line
2. Units-of-activity
3. Declining-balance

Each method is acceptable under generally accepted accounting principles. Management selects the method(s) it believes to be appropriate. The objective is to select the method that best measures an asset's contribution to revenue over its useful life. Once a method is chosen, it should be applied consistently over the useful life of the asset. Consistency enhances the comparability of financial statements.

We will compare the three depreciation methods using the following data for a small delivery truck purchased by Barb's Florists on January 1, 2006.

Illustration 10-7
Delivery truck data

Cost	$ 13,000
Expected salvage value	$ 1,000
Estimated useful life in years	5
Estimated useful life in miles	100,000

Depreciation affects the balance sheet through accumulated depreciation and the income statement through depreciation expense. Illustration 10-8 (in the margin) shows the use of the different depreciation methods in 600 of the largest companies in the United States.

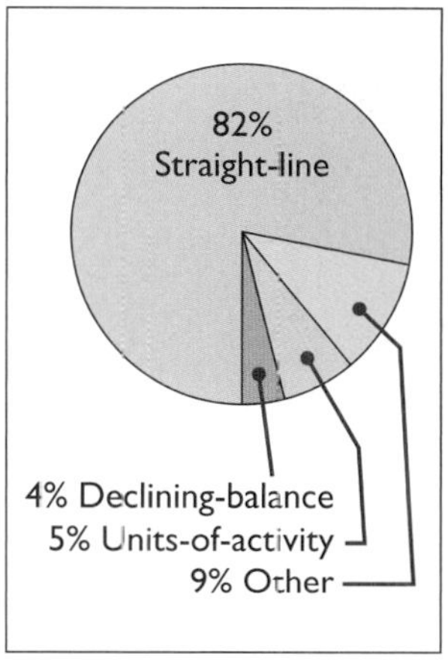

Illustration 10-8
Use of depreciation methods in 600 large U.S. companies

Straight-Line

Under the **straight-line method**, depreciation is the same for each year of the asset's useful life. It is measured solely by the passage of time.

In order to compute depreciation expense under the straight-line method, it is necessary to determine depreciable cost. **Depreciable cost** is the cost of the asset less its salvage value. It represents the total amount subject to depreciation. Under the straight-line method, depreciable cost is divided by the asset's useful life to determine annual depreciation expense. The computation of depreciation expense in the first year for Barb's Florists is shown in Illustration 10-9 (on page 428).

Illustration 10-9
Formula for straight-line method

Cost	−	Salvage Value	=	Depreciable Cost
$13,000	−	$1,000	=	$12,000

Depreciable Cost	÷	Useful Life (in years)	=	Annual Depreciation Expense
$12,000	÷	5	=	**$2,400**

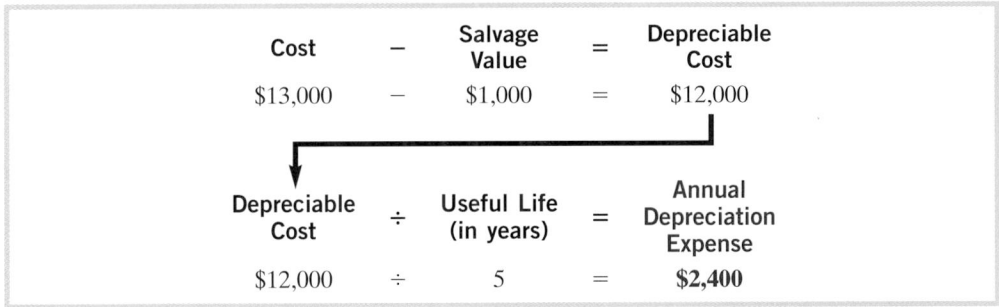

Alternatively, we also can compute an **annual rate of depreciation**. In this case, the rate is 20% (100% ÷ 5 years). When an annual straight-line rate is used, the percentage rate is applied to the depreciable cost of the asset. The use of an annual rate is shown in the following **depreciation schedule**.

Illustration 10-10
Straight-line depreciation schedule

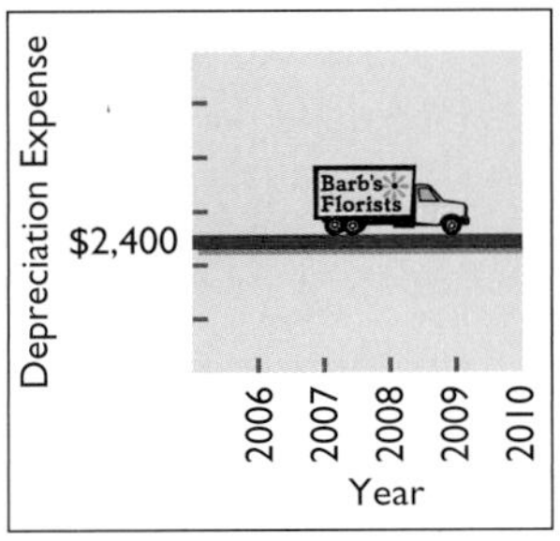

BARB'S FLORISTS

	Computation					End of Year	
Year	Depreciable Cost	×	Depreciation Rate	=	Annual Depreciation Expense	Accumulated Depreciation	Book Value
2006	$12,000		20%		**$2,400**	$ 2,400	$10,600*
2007	12,000		20		**2,400**	4,800	8,200
2008	12,000		20		**2,400**	7,200	5,800
2009	12,000		20		**2,400**	9,600	3,400
2010	12,000		20		**2,400**	12,000	**1,000**

*($13,000 − $2,400).

Note that the depreciation expense of $2,400 is the same each year. The book value at the end of the useful life is equal to the estimated $1,000 salvage value.

What happens when an asset is purchased **during** the year, rather than on January 1, as in our example? In that case, it is necessary to **prorate the annual depreciation** on a time basis. If Barb's Florists had purchased the delivery truck on April 1, 2006, the depreciation for 2006 would be $1,800 ($12,000 × 20% × 9/12 of a year).

The straight-line method predominates in practice. Such large companies as **Campbell Soup**, **Marriott Corporation**, and **General Mills** use the straight-line method. It is simple to apply, and it matches expenses with revenues when the use of the asset is reasonably uniform throughout the service life. In the Feature Story, for simplicity **Rent-A-Wreck** is probably using the straight-line method of depreciation for its vehicles.

Units-of-Activity

ALTERNATIVE TERMINOLOGY

Another term often used is the *units-of-production method.*

Under the **units-of-activity method**, useful life is expressed in terms of the total units of production or use expected from the asset, rather than as a time period. The units-of-activity method is ideally suited to factory machinery. Production can be measured in units of output or in machine hours. This method can also be used for such assets as delivery equipment (miles driven) and airplanes (hours in use). The units-of-activity method is generally not suitable for buildings or furniture, because depreciation for these assets is more a function of time than of use.

To use this method, the total units of activity for the entire useful life are estimated, and these units are divided into depreciable cost. The resulting number represents the depreciation cost per unit. The depreciation cost per unit is then applied to the units of activity during the year to determine the annual depreciation expense.

To illustrate, assume that Barb's Florists' delivery truck is driven 15,000 miles in the first year. The computation of depreciation expense in the first year is:

HELPFUL HINT

Under any method, depreciation stops when the asset's book value equals expected salvage value.

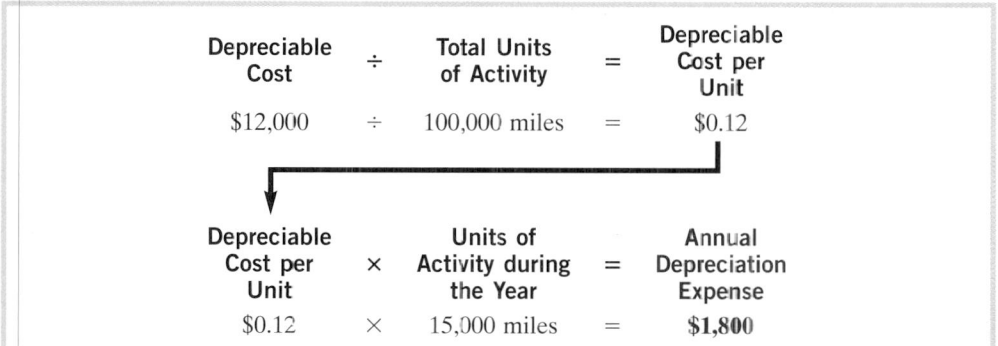

Depreciable Cost	÷	Total Units of Activity	=	Depreciable Cost per Unit
$12,000	÷	100,000 miles	=	$0.12

Depreciable Cost per Unit	×	Units of Activity during the Year	=	Annual Depreciation Expense
$0.12	×	15,000 miles	=	**$1,800**

Illustration 10-11
Formula for units-of-activity method

The units-of-activity depreciation schedule, using assumed mileage, is as follows.

Illustration 10-12
Units-of-activity depreciation schedule

BARB'S FLORISTS

	Computation					End of Year	
Year	**Units of Activity**	×	**Depreciation Cost/Unit**	=	**Annual Depreciation Expense**	**Accumulated Depreciation**	**Book Value**
2006	15,000		$0.12		**$1,800**	$ 1,800	$11,200*
2007	30,000		0.12		**3,600**	5,400	7,600
2008	20,000		0.12		**2,400**	7,800	5,200
2009	25,000		0.12		**3,000**	10,800	2,200
2010	10,000		0.12		**1,200**	12,000	**1,000**

*($13,000 − $1,800).

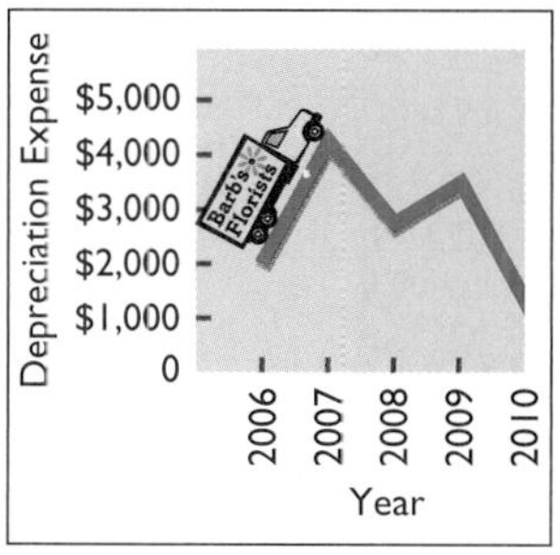

This method is easy to apply when assets are purchased mid-year. In such a case, the productivity of the asset for the partial year is used in computing the depreciation.

The units-of-activity method is not nearly as popular as the straight-line method (see Illustration 10-8), primarily because it is often difficult to make a reasonable estimate of total activity. However, this method is used by some very large companies, such as **Chevron Oil** and **Boise Cascade Corporation** (a forestry company). When the productivity of an asset varies significantly from one period to another, the units-of-activity method results in the best matching of expenses with revenues.

Declining-Balance

The **declining-balance method** produces a decreasing annual depreciation expense over the asset's useful life. The method is so named because the periodic depreciation is based on a **declining book value** (cost less accumulated depreciation) of the asset. Annual depreciation expense is computed by multiplying the book value at the beginning of the year by the declining-balance depreciation rate. **The depreciation rate remains constant from year to year, but the book value to which the rate is applied declines each year.**

Book value at the beginning of the first year is the cost of the asset. This is so because the balance in accumulated depreciation at the beginning of the asset's useful life is zero. In subsequent years, book value is the difference between cost and accumulated depreciation to date. Unlike the other depreciation methods, the declining-balance method does not use depreciable cost. That is, **salvage value is ignored in determining the amount to which the declining-balance rate is applied**. Salvage value, however, does limit the total depreciation that can be taken. Depreciation stops when the asset's book value equals expected salvage value.

A common declining-balance rate is double the straight-line rate. As a result, the method is often referred to as the **double-declining-balance method**. If Barb's Florists uses the double-declining-balance method, the depreciation rate is 40% (2 × the straight-line rate of 20%). The computation of depreciation for the first year on the delivery truck is:

Illustration 10-13
Formula for declining-balance method

Book Value at Beginning of Year	×	Declining-Balance Rate	=	Annual Depreciation Expense
$13,000	×	40%	=	**$5,200**

The depreciation schedule under this method is as follows.

Illustration 10-14
Double-declining-balance depreciation schedule

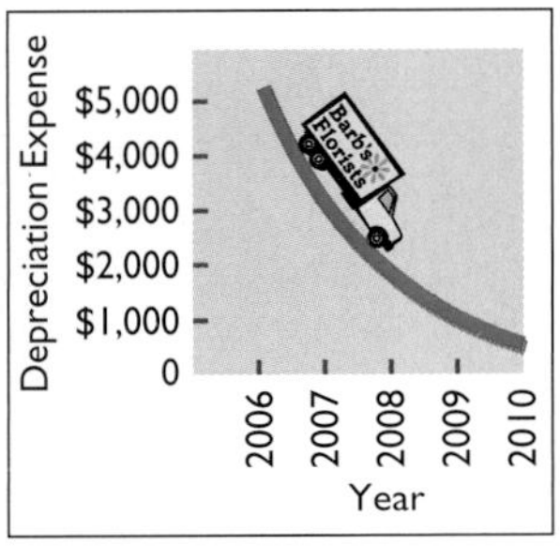

BARB'S FLORISTS

	Computation				Annual	End of Year	
Year	**Book Value Beginning of Year**	×	**Depreciation Rate**	=	**Depreciation Expense**	**Accumulated Depreciation**	**Book Value**
2006	$13,000		40%		**$5,200**	$ 5,200	$7,800
2007	7,800		40		**3,120**	8,320	4,680
2008	4,680		40		**1,872**	10,192	2,808
2009	2,808		40		**1,123**	11,315	1,685
2010	1,685		40		**685***	12,000	**1,000**

*Computation of $674 ($1,685 × 40%) is adjusted to $685 in order for book value to equal salvage value.

HELPFUL HINT

The method recommended for an asset that is expected to be more productive in the first half of its useful life is the declining-balance method.

You can see that the delivery equipment is 69% depreciated ($8,320 ÷ $12,000) at the end of the second year. Under the straight-line method it would be depreciated 40% ($4,800 ÷ $12,000) at that time. Because the declining-balance method produces higher depreciation expense in the early years than in the later years, it is considered an **accelerated-depreciation method**.

The declining-balance method is compatible with the matching principle. The higher depreciation expense in early years is matched with the higher benefits received in these years. On the other hand, lower depreciation expense is recognized in later years when the asset's contribution to revenue is less. Also, some assets lose usefulness rapidly because of obsolescence. In these cases, the declining-balance method provides a more appropriate depreciation amount.

When an asset is purchased during the year, the first year's declining-balance depreciation must be prorated on a time basis. For example, if Barb's Florists had purchased the truck on April 1, 2006, depreciation for 2006 would become $3,900 ($13,000 × 40% × 9/12). The book value at the beginning of 2007 is then $9,100 ($13,000 − $3,900), and the 2007 depreciation is $3,640 ($9,100 × 40%). Subsequent computations would follow from those amounts.

Comparison of Methods

A comparison of annual and total depreciation expense under each of the three methods is shown for Barb's Florists in Illustration 10-15.

Illustration 10-15
Comparison of depreciation methods

Year	Straight-Line	Units-of-Activity	Declining-Balance
2006	$ 2,400	$ 1,800	$ 5,200
2007	2,400	3,600	3,120
2008	2,400	2,400	1,872
2009	2,400	3,000	1,123
2010	2,400	1,200	685
	$12,000	**$12,000**	**$12,000**

Observe that annual depreciation varies considerably among the methods. But total depreciation is the same for the 5-year period under all three methods. Each method is acceptable in accounting, because each recognizes the decline in service potential of the asset in a rational and systematic manner. The depreciation expense pattern under each method is presented graphically in Illustration 10-16.

Illustration 10-16
Patterns of depreciation

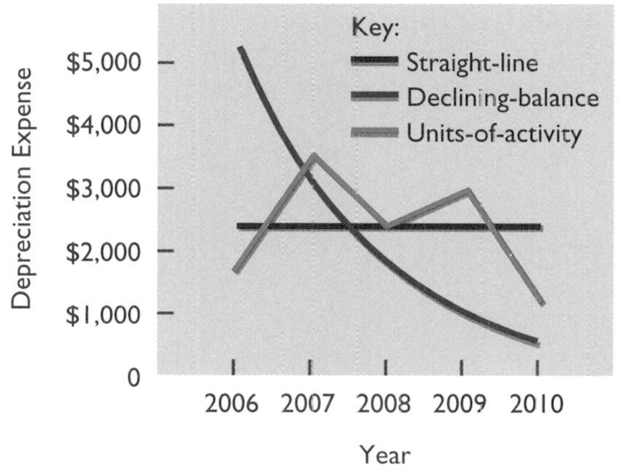

Depreciation and Income Taxes

The Internal Revenue Service (IRS) allows corporate taxpayers to deduct depreciation expense when they compute taxable income. However, the IRS does not require the taxpayer to use the same depreciation method on the tax return that is used in preparing financial statements. Many corporations use straight-line in their financial statements to maximize net income. At the same time, they use a special accelerated-depreciation method on their tax returns to minimize their income taxes. Taxpayers must use on their tax returns either the straight-line method or a special accelerated-depreciation method called the **Modified Accelerated Cost Recovery System** (MACRS).

Revising Periodic Depreciation

STUDY OBJECTIVE 4
Describe the procedure for revising periodic depreciation.

Depreciation is one example of the use of estimation in the accounting process. Annual depreciation expense should be reviewed periodically by management. If wear and tear or obsolescence indicate that annual depreciation estimates are inadequate or excessive, a change should be made.

When a change in an estimate is required, the change is made in **current and future years**. It is not made retroactively **to prior periods**. Thus, there is no correction of previously recorded depreciation expense. Instead, depreciation expense for current and future years is revised. The rationale is that continual restatement of prior periods would adversely affect confidence in financial statements.

To determine the new annual depreciation expense, we first compute the asset's depreciable cost at the time of the revision. We then allocate the revised depreciable cost to the remaining useful life. To illustrate, assume that Barb's Florists decides on January 1, 2009, to extend the useful life of the truck one year because of its excellent condition. The company has used the straight-line method to depreciate the asset to date, and book value is $5,800 ($13,000 − $7,200). The new annual depreciation is $1,600, computed as follows.

Illustration 10-17
Revised depreciation computation

Book value, 1/1/09	$5,800	
Less: Salvage value	1,000	
Depreciable cost	$4,800	
Remaining useful life	3 years	(2009–2011)
Revised annual depreciation ($4,800 ÷ 3)	**$1,600**	

HELPFUL HINT

Use a step-by-step approach: (1) determine new depreciable cost; (2) divide by remaining useful life.

Barb's Florists makes no entry for the change in estimate. On December 31, 2009, during the preparation of adjusting entries, it would record depreciation expense of $1,600. Significant changes in estimates must be described in the financial statements.

BEFORE YOU GO ON...

Review It

1. What is the relationship, if any, of depreciation to (a) cost allocation, (b) asset valuation, and (c) cash accumulation?
2. Explain the factors that affect the computation of depreciation.
3. What are the formulas for computing annual depreciation under each of the depreciation methods?
4. How do the methods differ in terms of their effects on annual depreciation over the useful life of the asset?
5. Are revisions of periodic depreciation made to prior periods? Explain.

Do It

On January 1, 2006, Iron Mountain Ski Corporation purchased a new snow-grooming machine for $50,000. The machine is estimated to have a 10-year life with a $2,000 salvage value. What journal entry would Iron Mountain Ski Corporation make at December 31, 2006, if it uses the straight-line method of depreciation?

ACTION PLAN

- Calculate depreciable cost (Cost − Salvage value).
- Divide the depreciable cost by the estimated useful life.

SOLUTION

$$\text{Depreciation expense} = \frac{\text{Cost} - \text{Salvage value}}{\text{Useful life}} = \frac{\$50{,}000 - \$2{,}000}{10} = \$4{,}800$$

The entry to record the first year's depreciation would be:

Dec. 31	Depreciation Expense	4,800	
	Accumulated Depreciation		4,800
	(To record annual depreciation on snow-grooming machine)		

Related exercise material: *BE10-3, BE10-4, BE10-5, BE10-6, BE10-7, E10-3, E10-4, and E10-5.*

THE NAVIGATOR

Expenditures During Useful Life

STUDY OBJECTIVE 5

Distinguish between revenue and capital expenditures, and explain the entries for these expenditures.

During the useful life of a plant asset a company may incur costs for ordinary repairs, additions, or improvements. **Ordinary repairs** are expenditures to maintain the operating efficiency and productive life of the unit. They usually are fairly small amounts that occur frequently. Motor tune-ups and oil changes, the painting of buildings, and the replacing of worn-out gears on machinery are examples. Such repairs are debited to Repair (or Maintenance) Expense as they are incurred. Because they are immediately charged as an expense against revenues, these costs are often referred to as **revenue expenditures**.

Additions and improvements are costs incurred to increase the operating efficiency, productive capacity, or useful life of a plant asset. They are usually material in amount and occur infrequently. Additions and improvements increase the company's investment in productive facilities and are generally debited to the plant asset affected. They are often referred to as **capital expenditures**. Most major U.S. corporations disclose annual capital expenditures. In a recent year, both **IBM** and **General Motors** reported capital expenditures slightly in excess of $6 billion.

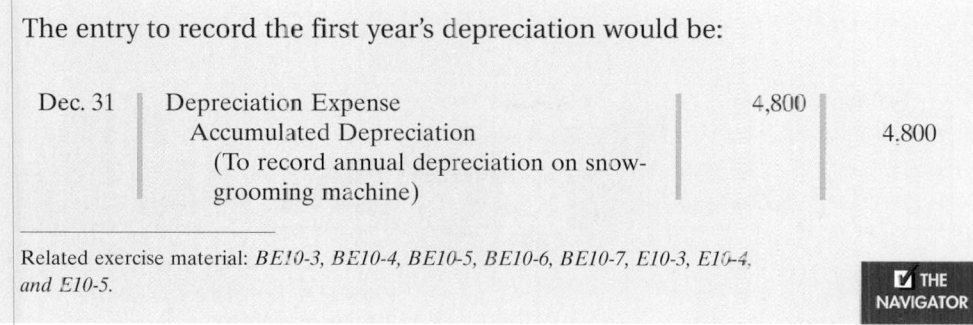

ACCOUNTING MATTERS! Ethics Insight

In what could become one of the largest accounting frauds in history, **WorldCom** announced the discovery of $7 billion in expenses improperly booked as capital expenditures, a gimmick that boosted profit over a recent five-quarter period. If these expenses had been recorded properly, WorldCom, one of the biggest stock market stars of the 1990s, would have reported a net loss for 2001, as well as for the first quarter of 2002. Instead, WorldCom reported a profit of $1.4 billion for 2001 and $130 million for the first quarter of 2002. As a result of these problems, WorldCom declared bankruptcy, to the dismay of its investors and creditors.

? What erroneous accounting entries (accounts debited and credited) were made by WorldCom? What is the correcting entry that should be recorded, and what is its effect on WorldCom's financial statements?

Plant Asset Disposals

STUDY OBJECTIVE 6

Explain how to account for the disposal of a plant asset.

Plant assets may be disposed of in three ways—retirement, sale, or exchange—as shown in Illustration 10-18 (on page 434). Whatever the method, at the time of disposal it is necessary to determine the book value of the plant asset. As noted earlier, book value is the difference between the cost of a plant asset and the accumulated depreciation to date.

Illustration 10-18
Methods of plant asset disposal

At the time of disposal, depreciation for the fraction of the year to the date of disposal must be recorded. The book value is then eliminated by debiting (decreasing) Accumulated Depreciation for the total depreciation to date and crediting (decreasing) the asset account for the cost of the asset. In this chapter we will examine the accounting for the retirement and sale of plant assets. In the appendix to this chapter we will examine and demonstrate the method of accounting for exchanges of plant assets.

Retirement of Plant Assets

To illustrate the retirement of plant assets, assume that Hobart Enterprises retires its computer printers, which cost $32,000. The accumulated depreciation on these printers is $32,000. The equipment, therefore, is fully depreciated (zero book value). The entry to record this retirement is as follows.

A	=	L	+	SE
+32,000				
−32,000				

Cash Flows
no effect

Accumulated Depreciation—Printing Equipment	32,000	
Printing Equipment		32,000
(To record retirement of fully depreciated equipment)		

HELPFUL HINT

When a plant asset is disposed of, all amounts related to the asset must be removed from the accounts. This includes the original cost in the asset account and the total depreciation to date in the accumulated depreciation account.

What happens if a fully depreciated plant asset is still useful to the company? In this case, the asset and its accumulated depreciation continue to be reported on the balance sheet without further depreciation adjustment until the asset is retired. Reporting the asset and related accumulated depreciation on the balance sheet informs the financial statement reader that the asset is still in use. However, once an asset is fully depreciated, even if it is still being used, no additional depreciation should be taken. In no situation can the accumulated depreciation on a plant asset exceed its cost.

If a plant asset is retired before it is fully depreciated, and no cash is received for scrap or salvage value, a loss on disposal occurs. For example, assume that Sunset Company discards delivery equipment that cost $18,000 and has accumulated depreciation of $14,000. The entry is as follows.

A	=	L	+	SE
+14,000				−4,000 Exp
−18,000				

Cash Flows
no effect

Accumulated Depreciation—Delivery Equipment	14,000	
Loss on Disposal	4,000	
Delivery Equipment		18,000
(To record retirement of delivery equipment at a loss)		

The loss on disposal is reported in the "Other expenses and losses" section of the income statement.

Sale of Plant Assets

In a disposal by sale, the book value of the asset is compared with the proceeds received from the sale. **If the proceeds of the sale exceed the book value of the plant asset, a gain on disposal occurs. If the proceeds of the sale are less than the book value of the plant asset sold, a loss on disposal occurs.**

Only by coincidence will the book value and the fair market value of the asset be the same when the asset is sold. Gains and losses on sales of plant assets are therefore quite common. For example, **Delta Airlines** reported a $94,343,000 gain on the sale of five **Boeing** B727-200 aircraft and five **Lockheed** L-1011-1 aircraft.

Gain on Disposal

To illustrate a gain, assume that on July 1, 2006, Wright Company sells office furniture for $16,000 cash. The office furniture originally cost $60,000. As of January 1, 2006, it had accumulated depreciation of $41,000. Depreciation for the first 6 months of 2006 is $8,000. The entry to record depreciation expense and update accumulated depreciation to July 1 is as follows.

July 1	Depreciation Expense	8,000	
	Accumulated Depreciation—Office Furniture		8,000
	(To record depreciation expense for the first 6 months of 2006)		

A	=	L	+	SE
−8,000				−8,000 Exp

Cash Flows
no effect

After the accumulated depreciation balance is updated, a gain on disposal of $5,000 is computed:

Illustration 10-19
Computation of gain on disposal

Cost of office furniture	$60,000
Less: Accumulated depreciation ($41,000 + $8,000)	49,000
Book value at date of disposal	11,000
Proceeds from sale	16,000
Gain on disposal	**$ 5,000**

The entry to record the sale and the gain on disposal is as follows.

July 1	Cash	16,000	
	Accumulated Depreciation—Office Furniture	49,000	
	Office Furniture		60,000
	Gain on Disposal		5,000
	(To record sale of office furniture at a gain)		

A	=	L	+	SE
+16,000				+5,000 Rev
+49,000				
−60,000				

Cash Flows
+16,000 

The gain on disposal is reported in the "Other revenues and gains" section of the income statement.

Loss on Disposal

Assume that instead of selling the office furniture for $16,000, Wright sells it for $9,000. In this case, a loss of $2,000 is computed:

Illustration 10-20
Computation of loss on disposal

Cost of office furniture	$60,000
Less: Accumulated depreciation	49,000
Book value at date of disposal	11,000
Proceeds from sale	9,000
Loss on disposal	**$ 2,000**

The entry to record the sale and the loss on disposal is as follows.

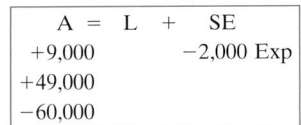

A	=	L	+	SE
+9,000				−2,000 Exp
+49,000				
−60,000				

Cash Flows
+9,000

July 1	Cash	9,000	
	Accumulated Depreciation—Office Furniture	49,000	
	Loss on Disposal	2,000	
	Office Furniture		60,000
	(To record sale of office furniture at a loss)		

The loss on disposal is reported in the "Other expenses and losses" section of the income statement.

BEFORE YOU GO ON...

Review It

1. How does a capital expenditure differ from a revenue expenditure?
2. What is the proper accounting for the retirement and sale of plant assets?

Do It

Overland Trucking has an old truck that cost $30,000. The truck has accumulated depreciation of $16,000 and a fair value of $17,000. Overland has decided to sell the truck for $17,000 cash. What is the entry that Overland Trucking would make to record the sale of the truck? What is the entry that Overland trucking would make to record the sale of the truck, assuming it sold for $10,000 cash?

ACTION PLAN

- At the time of disposal, determine the book value of the asset.
- Compare the asset's book value with the proceeds received to determine whether a gain or loss has occurred.

SOLUTION

Sale of truck for cash at a gain:

Cash	17,000	
Accumulated Depreciation—Truck	16,000	
Truck		30,000
Gain on Disposal [$17,000 − ($30,000 − $16,000)]		3,000
(To record sale of truck at a gain)		

Sale of truck for cash at a loss:

Cash	10,000	
Loss on Disposal [$10,000 − ($30,000 − $16,000)]	4,000	
Accumulated Depreciation—Truck	16,000	
Truck		30,000
(To record sale of truck at a loss)		

Related exercise material: *BE10-8, BE10-9, and E10-6.*

THE NAVIGATOR

SECTION 2 NATURAL RESOURCES

Natural resources consist of standing timber and underground deposits of oil, gas, and minerals. These long-lived productive assets have two distinguishing characteristics: (1) They are physically extracted in operations (such as mining, cutting, or pumping), and (2) they are replaceable only by an act of nature. The acquisition cost of a natural resource is the price needed to acquire the resource and prepare it for its intended use. For an already discovered resource, such as an existing coal mine, cost is the price paid for the property.

The allocation of the cost of natural resources to expense in a rational and systematic manner over the resource's useful life is called **depletion**. **The units-of-activity method** (learned earlier in the chapter) **is generally used to compute depletion**. The reason it is used is that **depletion generally is a function of the units extracted during the year**.

Under the units-of-activity method, the total cost of the natural resource minus salvage value is divided by the number of units estimated to be in the resource. The result is a depletion cost per unit of product. The depletion cost per unit is then multiplied by the number of units extracted and sold. The result is the annual depletion expense. The formula is as follows.

HELPFUL HINT

On a balance sheet, natural resources may be described more specifically as timberlands, mineral deposits, oil reserves, and so on.

STUDY OBJECTIVE 7

Compute periodic depletion of natural resources.

Total Cost minus Salvage Value	÷	Total Estimated Units	=	Depletion Cost per Unit
Depletion Cost per Unit	×	Number of Units Extracted and Sold	=	Annual Depletion Expense

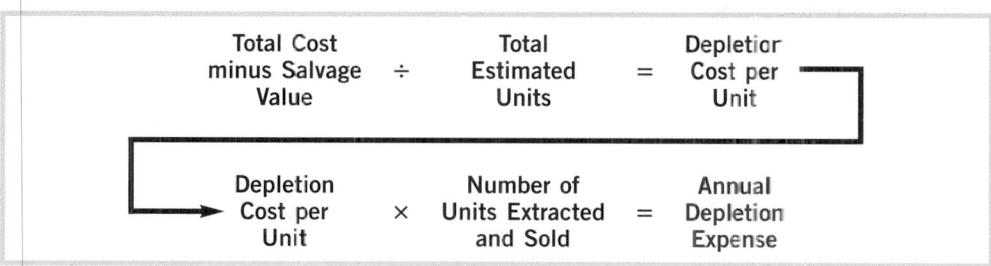

Illustration 10-21
Formula to compute depletion expense

To illustrate, assume that Lane Coal Company invests $5 million in a mine estimated to have 10 million tons of coal and no salvage value. In the first year, 800,000 tons of coal are extracted and sold. Using the formulas above, the computations are as follows:

$$\$5{,}000{,}000 \div 10{,}000{,}000 = \$0.50 \text{ depletion cost per ton}$$

$$\$0.50 \times 800{,}000 = \$400{,}000 \text{ annual depletion expense}$$

The entry to record depletion expense for the first year of operation is as follows.

Dec. 31	Depletion Expense	400,000	
	Accumulated Depletion		400,000
	(To record depletion expense on coal deposits)		

A	=	L	+	SE
−400,000				−400,000 Exp

Cash Flows
no effect

The account Depletion Expense is reported as a part of the cost of producing the product. Accumulated Depletion is a contra asset account similar to accumulated depreciation. It is deducted from the cost of the natural resource in the balance sheet, as shown in Illustration 10-22.

LANE COAL COMPANY
Balance Sheet (partial)

Coal mine	$5,000,000	
Less: Accumulated depletion	**400,000**	$4,600,000

Illustration 10-22
Statement presentation of accumulated depletion

However, in many companies an Accumulated Depletion account is not used. In such cases, the amount of depletion is credited directly to the natural resources account.

Sometimes, natural resources extracted in one accounting period will not be sold until a later period. In this case, depletion is not expensed until the resource is sold. The amount not sold is reported in the current assets section as inventory.

SECTION 3 INTANGIBLE ASSETS

Intangible assets are rights, privileges, and competitive advantages that result from the ownership of long-lived assets that do not possess physical substance. Evidence of intangibles may exist in the form of contracts or licenses. Intangibles may arise from:

1. Government grants, such as patents, copyrights, and trademarks.
2. Acquisition of another business, in which the purchase price includes a payment for the company's favorable attributes (called goodwill).
3. Private monopolistic arrangements arising from contractual agreements, such as franchises and leases.

Some widely known intangibles are the patents of **Intel**, the franchises of **McDonald's**, the trade name of Col. Sander's **Kentucky Fried Chicken**, and the trademark **Rent-A-Wreck** in the Feature Story.

Accounting for Intangible Assets

STUDY OBJECTIVE 8

Explain the basic issues related to accounting for intangible assets.

Intangible assets are recorded at cost. The cost of an intangible asset should be allocated over its useful life, assuming the useful life is limited. If the life of the intangible is indefinite, the cost of the intangible should not be allocated. **Indefinite** means that no legal, regulatory, contractual, competitive, economic, or other factors limit the intangible's useful life. At disposal, the book value of the intangible asset is eliminated, and a gain or loss, if any, is recorded.

There are several differences between accounting for intangible assets and accounting for plant assets. First, assuming an intangible has a limited life, the term used to describe the allocation of the cost of an intangible asset to expense is **amortization**, rather than depreciation. Also, to record amortization of an intangible, an amortization expense is debited and the specific intangible asset is credited (rather than crediting a contra account). An alternative is to credit an Accumulated Amortization account, similar to Accumulated Depreciation.

There is also a difference in determining cost. For plant assets, cost includes both the purchase price of the asset and the costs incurred in designing and constructing the asset. In contrast, cost for an intangible asset includes only the purchase price. Any costs incurred in developing an intangible asset are expensed as incurred.

The method of amortizing an intangible asset with a limited life should reflect the pattern in which the asset's economic benefits are used. If such a pattern cannot be reliably determined, a straight-line method of amortization should be used. For homework purposes, use the straight-line method, unless otherwise indicated.

An indefinite-life intangible asset should not be amortized until its life is determined to be limited. At that time, the intangible asset should be amortized.

Patents

A **patent** is an exclusive right issued by the U.S. Patent Office that enables the recipient to manufacture, sell, or otherwise control an invention for a period of 20 years from the date of the grant. A patent is nonrenewable. But the legal life of a patent may be extended by obtaining new patents for improvements or other changes in the basic design.

The initial cost of a patent is the cash or cash equivalent price paid to acquire the patent. The saying, "A patent is only as good as the money you're prepared to spend defending it" is very true. Many patents are subject to some type of litigation. For example, in 2003 **Intel** won a patent infringement suit against **Broadcom** in protecting its patent, receiving $60 million in cash. Legal costs an owner incurs in successfully defending a patent in an infringement suit are considered necessary to establish the validity of the patent. **They are added to the Patent account and amortized over the remaining life of the patent.**

The cost of a patent should be amortized over its 20-year legal life or its useful life, whichever is shorter. Obsolescence and inadequacy should be considered in determining useful life. These factors may cause a patent to become economically ineffective before the end of its legal life.

To illustrate the computation of patent expense, assume that National Labs purchases a patent at a cost of $60,000. If the useful life of the patent is 8 years, the annual amortization expense is $7,500 ($60,000 ÷ 8). The entry to record the annual amortization is:

Dec. 31	Amortization Expense—Patents	7,500	
	Patents		7,500
	(To record patent amortization)		

A	=	L	+	SE
−7,500				−7,500 Exp

Cash Flows
no effect

Amortization Expense—Patents is classified as an **operating expense** in the income statement.

Copyrights

Copyrights are grants from the federal government, giving the owner the exclusive right to reproduce and sell an artistic or published work. Copyrights extend for the life of the creator plus 70 years. The cost of a copyright is the **cost of acquiring and defending it**. The cost may be only the small fee paid to the U.S. Copyright Office. Or it may amount to a great deal more if a copyright infringement suit is involved.

The useful life of a copyright generally is significantly shorter than its legal life. Therefore, copyrights usually are amortized over a relatively short period of time.

Trademarks and Trade Names

A **trademark** or **trade name** is a word, phrase, jingle, or symbol that identifies a particular enterprise or product. Trade names like Wheaties, Game Boy, Sunkist, Kleenex, Windows, Coca-Cola, Big Mac, and Jeep create immediate product identification. They also generally enhance the sale of the product. The creator or original user may obtain exclusive legal right to the trademark or trade name by registering it with the U.S. Patent Office. Such registration provides 20 years' protection. The registration may be renewed indefinitely as long as the trademark or trade name is in use.

If the trademark or trade name is **purchased** by the company that will sell the product, its cost is the purchase price. If the trademark or trade name is **developed** by the company itself, the cost includes attorney's fees, registration fees, successful legal defense costs, and other expenditures directly related to securing it.

Because trademarks and trade names have indefinite lives, they are not amortized.

ACCOUNTING MATTERS! **Business Insight**

Domain names are a good example of a trade name. Buying domain names is a hot market these days. While the cost of registration is negligible, if a company has to purchase its name from a cybersquatter—people who register names in the hopes of reselling them for a profit—the cost can rise quickly.

When **eBay Inc.**, the world's largest online auction house, recently tried to register www.ebay.ca in Canada, it discovered that the name had been registered previously by an entrepreneur. eBay then had two options to consider. Since eBay is a registered trademark around the world, the company could take legal action, or it could negotiate to buy the name from the current registrant. In the meantime, eBay is using the domain name www.ebaycanada.ca, which had also been registered previously by a self-described "Internet entrepreneur." This entrepreneur said he hoped to make some quick money when he registered www.ebaycanada.ca last year. He eventually gave up the name without a fight rather than go to court and face huge legal bills.

? How should eBay Inc. account for the purchase of an additional domain name? How would it account for a domain name developed by its own employees?

Franchises and Licenses

When you drive down the street in your RAV4 purchased from a **Toyota** dealer, fill up your tank at the corner **Shell** station, eat lunch at **Taco Bell**, or rent a car from **Rent-A-Wreck**, you are dealing with franchises. A **franchise** is a contractual arrangement under which the franchisor grants the franchisee the right to sell certain products, provide specific services, or use certain trademarks or trade names. The franchise is usually restricted to a designated geographical area.

Another type of franchise is that entered into between a governmental body (commonly municipalities) and a business enterprise. This franchise permits the enterprise to use public property in performing its services. Examples are the use of city streets for a bus line or taxi service, use of public land for telephone and electric lines, and the use of airwaves for radio or TV broadcasting. Such operating rights are referred to as **licenses**.

When costs can be identified with the acquisition of a franchise or license, an intangible asset should be recognized. Franchises and licenses may be granted for a period of time, limited or indefinite. The cost of a limited-life franchise (or license) should be amortized over the useful life. If the life is indefinite, the cost is not amortized. Annual payments made under a franchise agreement are recorded as **operating expenses** in the period in which they are incurred.

Goodwill

Usually, the largest intangible asset that appears on a company's balance sheet is goodwill. **Goodwill** is the value of all favorable attributes that relate to a business enterprise. These include exceptional management, desirable location, good customer relations, skilled employees, high-quality products, and harmonious relations with labor unions. Some view goodwill as expected earnings in excess of normal earnings. Goodwill is therefore unusual: Unlike other assets such as investments and plant assets, which can be sold individually in the marketplace, goodwill can be identified only with the business as a whole.

If goodwill can be identified only with the business as a whole, how can it be determined? One could try to put a dollar value on the factors listed above (exceptional management, desirable location, and so on), but the results would be very subjective. Such subjective valuations would not contribute to the reliability of financial statements. **Therefore, goodwill is recorded only when there is a transaction that involves the purchase of an entire business. In that case, goodwill is the excess of cost over the fair market value of the net assets (assets less liabilities) acquired.**

In recording the purchase of a business, the net assets are debited at their fair market values, cash is credited for the purchase price, and goodwill is debited for the difference. **Goodwill is not amortized** (because it is considered to have an indefinite life), **but it must be written down if its value is determined to have declined** (been permanently impaired). Goodwill is reported in the balance sheet under intangible assets.

HELPFUL HINT

Goodwill is recorded only when it has been purchased along with tangible and identifiable intangible assets of a business.

Research and Development Costs

Research and development costs are expenditures that may lead to patents, copyrights, new processes, and new products. Many companies spend considerable sums of money on research and development (R&D). For example, in a recent year **IBM** spent over $5.2 billion on R&D.

Research and development costs present accounting problems. For one thing, it is sometimes difficult to assign the costs to specific projects. Also, there are uncertainties in identifying the extent and timing of future benefits. As a result, R&D costs are **usually recorded as an expense when incurred**, whether the research and development is successful or not.

To illustrate, assume that Laser Scanner Company spent $3 million on research and development. This expenditure resulted in the development of two highly successful patents obtained with $20,000 in lawyers' fees. The lawyers' fees would be added to the patent account. The R&D costs, however, cannot be included in the cost of the patent. Rather, they are recorded as an expense when incurred.

Many disagree with this accounting approach. They argue that expensing R&D costs leads to understated assets and net income. Others, however, argue that capitalizing these costs will lead to highly speculative assets on the balance sheet. It is difficult to determine who is right. The controversy illustrates how difficult it is to establish proper guidelines for financial reporting.

HELPFUL HINT

Research and development (R&D) costs are not intangible assets. But because they may lead to patents and copyrights, we discuss them in this section.

STATEMENT PRESENTATION AND ANALYSIS

Presentation

STUDY OBJECTIVE 9

Indicate how plant assets, natural resources, and intangible assets are reported and analyzed.

Usually plant assets and natural resources are combined under "Property, plant, and equipment" in the balance sheet. Intangibles are shown separately. The balances of the major classes of assets, such as land, buildings, and equipment, and accumulated depreciation by major classes or in total should be disclosed in the balance sheet or notes. In addition, the depreciation and amortization methods that were used should be described. Finally, the amount of depreciation and amortization expense for the period should be disclosed.

The financial statement presentation of property, plant, and equipment and intangibles by **The Procter & Gamble Company (P&G)** in its 2003 balance sheet is shown in Illustration 10-23 (on page 442).

Illustration 10-23
P&G's presentation of property, plant, and equipment, and intangible assets

THE PROCTER & GAMBLE COMPANY
Balance Sheet (partial)
(in millions)

	June 30 2003	June 30 2002
Property, plant, and equipment		
Buildings	$ 4,729	$ 4,532
Machinery and equipment	18,222	17,963
Land	591	575
	23,542	23,070
Accumulated depreciation	(10,438)	(9,721)
Net property, plant, and equipment	13,104	13,349
Goodwill and other intangible assets		
Goodwill	11,132	10,966
Trademarks and other intangible assets, net	2,375	2,464
Net goodwill and other intangible assets	13,507	13,430

The notes to P&G's financial statements present greater details about the accounting for its long-term tangible and intangible assets.

Another comprehensive presentation of property, plant, and equipment, excerpted from the balance sheet of **Owens-Illinois**, is shown in Illustration 10-24.

Illustration 10-24
Owens-Illinois' presentation of property, plant, and equipment, and intangible assets

OWENS-ILLINOIS, INC.
Balance Sheet (partial)
(in millions)

Property, plant, and equipment			
Timberlands, at cost, less accumulated depletion		$ 95.4	
Buildings and equipment, at cost	$2,207.1		
Less: Accumulated depreciation	1,229.0	978.1	
Total property, plant, and equipment			$1,073.5
Intangibles			
Patents			410.0
Total			$1,483.5

The notes to the financial statements of Owens-Illinois identify the major classes of property, plant, and equipment. They also indicate that depreciation is by the straight-line method, depletion is by the units-of-activity method, and amortization is by the straight-line method.

Analysis

We can analyze how efficiently a company uses its assets to generate sales. The **asset turnover ratio** analyzes the productivity of a company's assets. It is computed by dividing net sales by average total assets for the period, as shown in the formula in Illustration 10-25 (on page 443). The computation is for **Proctor & Gamble Company**. Its net sales for 2003 were $43,377 million. Its total ending assets were $43,706 million, and beginning assets were $40,776 million.

Net Sales	÷	Average Total Assets	=	Asset Turnover Ratio
\$43,377	÷	$\frac{\$43,706 + \$40,776}{2}$	=	**1.03 times**

Illustration 10-25
Asset turnover formula and computation

This ratio shows the dollars of sales produced for each dollar invested in average total assets. Each dollar invested in assets produced \$1.03 in sales for P&G. If a company is using its assets efficiently, each dollar of assets will create a high amount of sales. This ratio varies greatly among different industries—from those that are asset intensive (utilities) to those that are not (services).

BEFORE YOU GO ON...

Review It

1. How is depletion expense computed?
2. What are the main differences between accounting for intangible assets and for plant assets?
3. Identify the major types of intangibles and the proper accounting for them.
4. Explain the accounting for research and development costs.
5. What ratio may be computed to analyze property, plant, and equipment?

THE NAVIGATOR

DEMONSTRATION PROBLEM 1

DuPage Company purchases a factory machine at a cost of \$18,000 on January 1, 2006. The machine is expected to have a salvage value of \$2,000 at the end of its 4-year useful life.

During its useful life, the machine is expected to be used 160,000 hours. Actual annual hourly use was: 2006, 40,000; 2007, 60,000; 2008, 35,000; and 2009, 25,000.

Instructions

Prepare depreciation schedules for the following methods: (a) the straight-line, (b) units-of-activity, and (c) declining-balance using double the straight-line rate.

SOLUTION TO DEMONSTRATION PROBLEM 1

(a)

Straight-Line Method

	Computation					End of Year	
Year	Depreciable Cost	×	Depreciation Rate	=	Annual Depreciation Expense	Accumulated Depreciation	Book Value
2006	\$16,000		25%		\$4,000	\$ 4,000	\$14,000*
2007	16,000		25%		4,000	8,000	10,000
2008	16,000		25%		4,000	12,000	6,000
2009	16,000		25%		4,000	16,000	2,000

*\$18,000 − \$4,000.

ACTION PLAN

- Under the straight-line method, apply the depreciation rate to depreciable cost.
- Under the units-of-activity method, compute the depreciation cost per unit by dividing depreciable cost by total units of activity.
- Under the declining-balance method, apply the depreciation rate to **book value** at the beginning of the year.

(b)

Units-of-Activity Method

	Computation					End of Year	
Year	**Units of Activity**	×	**Depreciation Cost/Unit**	=	**Annual Depreciation Expense**	**Accumulated Depreciation**	**Book Value**
2006	40,000		$0.10		$4,000	$ 4,000	$14,000
2007	60,000		0.10		6,000	10,000	8,000
2008	35,000		0.10		3,500	13,500	4,500
2009	25,000		0.10		2,500	16,000	2,000

(c)

Declining-Balance Method

	Computation					End of Year	
Year	**Book Value Beginning of Year**	×	**Depreciation Rate**	=	**Annual Depreciation Expense**	**Accumulated Depreciation**	**Book Value**
2006	$18,000		50%		$9,000	$ 9,000	$9,000
2007	9,000		50%		4,500	13,500	4,500
2008	4,500		50%		2,250	15,750	2,250
2009	2,250		50%		250*	16,000	2,000

*Adjusted to $250 because ending book value should not be less than expected salvage value.

THE NAVIGATOR

DEMONSTRATION PROBLEM 2

On January 1, 2004, Skyline Limousine Co. purchased a limo at an acquisition cost of $28,000. The vehicle has been depreciated by the straight-line method using a 4-year service life and a $4,000 salvage value. The company's fiscal year ends on December 31.

Instructions

Prepare the journal entry or entries to record the disposal of the limousine assuming that it was:

(a) Retired and scrapped with no salvage value on January 1, 2008.
(b) Sold for $5,000 on July 1, 2007.

SOLUTION TO DEMONSTRATION PROBLEM 2

(a)	1/1/08	Accumulated Depreciation—Limousine	24,000	
		Loss on Disposal	4,000	
		Limousine		28,000
		(To record retirement of limousine)		
(b)	7/1/07	Depreciation Expense	3,000	
		Accumulated Depreciation—Limousine		3,000
		(To record depreciation to date of disposal)		
		Cash	5,000	
		Accumulated Depreciation—Limousine	21,000	
		Loss on Disposal	2,000	
		Limousine		28,000
		(To record sale of limousine)		

THE NAVIGATOR

ACTION PLAN

- At the time of disposal, determine the book value of the asset.
- Recognize any gain or loss from disposal of the asset.
- Remove the book value of the asset from the records by debiting Accumulated Depreciation for the total depreciation to date of disposal and crediting the asset account for the cost of the asset.

SUMMARY OF STUDY OBJECTIVES

1. **Describe how the cost principle applies to plant assets.** The cost of plant assets includes all expenditures necessary to acquire the asset and make it ready for its intended use. Cost is measured by the cash or cash equivalent price paid.

2. **Explain the concept of depreciation.** Depreciation is the allocation of the cost of a plant asset to expense over its useful (service) life in a rational and systematic manner. Depreciation is not a process of valuation, nor is it a process that results in an accumulation of cash.

3. **Compute periodic depreciation using different methods.** Three popular depreciation methods are:

Method	Effect on Annual Depreciation	Formula
Straight-line	Constant amount	Depreciable cost ÷ Useful life (in years)
Units-of-activity	Varying amount	Depreciation cost per unit × Units of activity during the year
Declining-balance	Decreasing amount	Book value at beginning of year × Declining-balance rate

4. **Describe the procedure for revising periodic depreciation.** Revisions of periodic depreciation are made in present and future periods, not retroactively. The new annual depreciation is found by dividing the depreciable cost at the time of the revision by the remaining useful life.

5. **Distinguish between revenue and capital expenditures, and explain the entries for these expenditures.** Revenue expenditures are incurred to maintain the operating efficiency and expected productive life of the asset. These expenditures are debited to Repair Expense as incurred. Capital expenditures increase the operating efficiency, productive capacity, or expected useful life of the asset. These expenditures are generally debited to the plant asset affected.

6. **Explain how to account for the disposal of a plant asset.** The accounting for disposal of a plant asset through retirement or sale is as follows:
   (a) Eliminate the book value of the plant asset at the date of disposal.
   (b) Record cash proceeds, if any.
   (c) Account for the difference between the book value and the cash proceeds as a gain or loss on disposal.

7. **Compute periodic depletion of natural resources.** Compute depletion cost per unit by dividing the total cost of the natural resource minus salvage value by the number of units estimated to be in the resource. Then multiply the depletion cost per unit by the number of units extracted and sold.

8. **Explain the basic issues related to accounting for intangible assets.** The accounting for intangible assets and plant assets is much the same. One difference is that the term used to describe the write-off of an intangible asset is amortization, rather than depreciation. The straight-line method is normally used for amortizing intangible assets.

9. **Indicate how plant assets, natural resources, and intangible assets are reported and analyzed.** Usually plant assets and natural resources are combined under property, plant, and equipment; intangibles are shown separately under intangible assets. Either within the balance sheet or in the notes, the balances of the major classes of assets, such as land, buildings, and equipment, and accumulated depreciation by major classes or in total, should be disclosed. Also, the depreciation and amortization methods used should be described, and the amount of depreciation and amortization expense for the period should be disclosed. The asset turnover ratio measures the productivity of a company's assets in generating sales.

THE NAVIGATOR

GLOSSARY

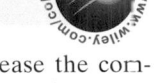

Accelerated-depreciation method Depreciation method that produces higher depreciation expense in the early years than in the later years. (p. 430).

Additions and improvements Costs incurred to increase the operating efficiency, productive capacity, or useful life of a plant asset. (p. 433).

Amortization The allocation of the cost of an intangible asset to expense over its useful life in a systematic and rational manner. (p. 438).

Asset turnover ratio A measure of how efficiently a company uses its assets to generate sales; calculated as net sales divided by average total assets. (p. 442).

Capital expenditures Expenditures that increase the company's investment in productive facilities. (p. 433).

Copyright Exclusive grant from the federal government that allows the owner to reproduce and sell an artistic or published work. (p. 439).

Declining-balance method Depreciation method that applies a constant rate to the declining book value of the asset and produces a decreasing annual depreciation expense over the useful life of the asset. (p. 429).

Depletion The allocation of the cost of a natural resource to expense in a rational and systematic manner over the resource's useful life. (p. 437).

Depreciable cost The cost of a plant asset less its salvage value. (p. 427).

Franchise (license) A contractual arrangement under which the franchisor grants the franchisee the right to sell certain products, provide specific services, or use certain trademarks or trade names, usually within a designated geographical area. (p. 440).

Goodwill The value of all favorable attributes that relate to a business enterprise. (p. 440).

Intangible assets Rights, privileges, and competitive advantages that result from the ownership of long-lived assets that do not possess physical substance. (p. 438).

Licenses Operating rights to use public property, granted to a business enterprise by a governmental agency. (p. 440).

Natural resources Assets that consist of standing timber and underground deposits of oil, gas, or minerals. (p. 436).

Ordinary repairs Expenditures to maintain the operating efficiency and productive life of the unit. (p. 433).

Patent An exclusive right issued by the U.S. Patent Office that enables the recipient to manufacture, sell, or otherwise control an invention for a period of 20 years from the date of the grant. (p. 439).

Plant assets Tangible resources that are used in the operations of the business and are not intended for sale to customers. (p. 421).

Research and development (R&D) costs Expenditures that may lead to patents, copyrights, new processes, or new products. (p. 441).

Revenue expenditures Expenditures that are immediately charged against revenues as an expense. (p. 433).

Salvage value An estimate of an asset's value at the end of its useful life. (p. 426).

Straight-line method Depreciation method in which periodic depreciation is the same for each year of the asset's useful life. (p. 427).

Trademark (trade name) A word, phrase, jingle, or symbol that identifies a particular enterprise or product. (p. 439).

Units-of-activity method Depreciation method in which useful life is expressed in terms of the total units of production or use expected from an asset. (p. 428).

Useful life An estimate of the expected productive life, also called service life, of an asset. (p. 426).

APPENDIX EXCHANGE OF PLANT ASSETS

STUDY OBJECTIVE 10

Explain how to account for the exchange of plant assets.

Plant assets may also be disposed of through exchange. Exchanges can be for either similar or dissimilar assets. Because exchanges of similar assets are more common, they are discussed here. An exchange of similar assets occurs, for example, when old office furniture is exchanged for new office furniture. In an exchange of similar assets, the new asset performs the **same function** as the old asset.

In exchanges of similar plant assets, it is necessary to determine two things: (1) the cost of the asset acquired, and (2) the gain or loss on the asset given up. Because a noncash asset is given up in the exchange, cost is the **cash equivalent price** paid. That is, cost is the fair market value of the asset given up plus the cash paid. The gain or loss on disposal is the **difference between the fair market value and the book value of the asset given up**. These determinations are explained and illustrated below.

Loss Treatment

A loss on the exchange of similar assets is recognized immediately. To illustrate, assume that Roland Company exchanged old office equipment for new office equipment. The book value of the old equipment is $26,000 (cost $70,000 less accumulated depreciation $44,000). Its fair market value is $10,000, and cash of $81,000 is paid. The cost of the new office equipment, $91,000, is computed as follows.

Illustration 10A-1
Computation of cost of new office equipment

Fair market value of old office equipment	$10,000
Cash	81,000
Cost of new office equipment	**$91,000**

A loss on disposal of $16,000 on this exchange is incurred. The reason is that the book value is greater than the fair market value of the asset given up. The computation is as follows.

Illustration 10A-2
Computation of loss on disposal

Book value of old office equipment ($70,000 – $44,000)	$26,000
Fair market value of old office equipment	10,000
Loss on disposal	**$16,000**

In recording an exchange at a loss, three steps are required: (1) Eliminate the book value of the asset given up, (2) record the cost of the asset acquired, and (3) recognize the loss on disposal. The entry for Roland Company is as follows.

Office Equipment (new)	91,000	
Accumulated Depreciation—Office Equipment (old)	44,000	
Loss on Disposal	16,000	
Office Equipment (old)		70,000
Cash		81,000
(To record exchange of old office equipment for similar new equipment)		

A	=	L	+	SE
+91,000				−16,000 Exp
+44,000				
−70,000				
−81,000				

Cash Flows
−81,000

Gain Treatment

A gain on the exchange of similar assets is not recognized immediately but, instead, is deferred. This is done by reducing the cost basis of the new asset. In determining the cost of the new asset, compute the **cost before deferral of the gain** and then the **cost after deferral of the gain**.

To illustrate, assume that Mark's Express Delivery decides to exchange its old delivery equipment plus cash of $3,000 for new delivery equipment. The book value of the old delivery equipment is $12,000 (cost $40,000 less accumulated depreciation $28,000). The fair market value of the old delivery equipment is $19,000.

The cost of the new asset (before deferral of the gain) is the **fair market value of the old asset exchanged plus any cash (or other consideration given up)**. The cost of the new delivery equipment (before deferral of the gain) is $22,000, computed as follows.

HELPFUL HINT

Why aren't gains on the exchange of similar assets recognized? Because the earnings process is not considered complete. To be conservative, however, losses are recognized.

Illustration 10A-3
Cost of new equipment (before deferral of gain)

Fair market value of old delivery equipment	$19,000
Cash	3,000
Cost of new delivery equipment (before deferral of gain)	**$22,000**

A gain results when the fair market value of the asset given up is greater than its book value. For Mark's Express, there is a gain of $7,000, computed as follows, on the disposal.

Illustration 10A-4
Computation of gain on disposal

Fair market value of old delivery equipment	$19,000
Book value of old delivery equipment ($40,000 – $28,000)	12,000
Gain on disposal	**$7,000**

The $7,000 gain on disposal is then offset against the $22,000 cost of the new delivery equipment. The result is a $15,000 cost of the new delivery equipment, after deferral of the gain, as shown in Illustration 10A-5.

Illustration 10A-5
Cost of new equipment (after deferral of gain)

Cost of new delivery equipment (before deferral of gain)	$22,000
Less: Gain on disposal	7,000
Cost of new delivery equipment (after deferral of gain)	**$15,000**

The entry to record the exchange is as follows.

A	=	L	+	SE
+15,000				
+28,000				
−40,000				
−3,000				

Cash Flows
−3,000

Delivery Equipment (new)	15,000	
Accumulated Depreciation—Delivery Equipment (old)	28,000	
Delivery Equipment (old)		40,000
Cash		3,000
(To record exchange of old delivery equipment for similar new delivery equipment)		

This entry does not eliminate the gain; it just postpones or defers it to future periods. The deferred gain of $7,000 reduces the $22,000 cost to $15,000. As a result, net income in future periods increases because depreciation expense on the newly acquired delivery equipment is less by $7,000.

Summarizing, the rules for accounting for exchanges of similar assets are as follows.

Illustration 10A-6
Accounting rules for plant asset exchanges

Type of Event	Recognition
Loss	Recognize immediately by debiting Loss on Disposal
Gain	Defer and reduce cost of new asset

SUMMARY OF STUDY OBJECTIVE FOR APPENDIX

10. Explain how to account for the exchange of plant assets. In accounting for exchanges of similar assets:
(a) Eliminate the book value of the old asset at the date of the exchange.
(b) Record the acquisition cost of the new asset.
(c) Account for the loss or gain, if any, on the old asset:
(1) If a loss, recognize it immediately.
(2) If a gain, defer and reduce the cost of the new asset.

*__Note:__ All **asterisked** Questions, Exercises, and Problems relate to material in the appendix to the chapter.

SELF-STUDY QUESTIONS

Self-Study/Self-Test

Answers are at the end of the chapter.

(SO 1) **1.** Erin Danielle Company purchased equipment and incurred the following costs.

Cash price	$24,000
Sales taxes	1,200
Insurance during transit	200
Installation and testing	400
Total costs	$25,800

What amount should be recorded as the cost of the equipment?
a. $24,000.
b. $25,200.
c. $25,400.
d. $25,800.

2. Depreciation is a process of: (SO 2)
a. valuation.
b. cost allocation.

c. cash accumulation.
d. appraisal.

(SO 3) **3.** Micah Bartlett Company purchased equipment on January 1, 2005, at a total invoice cost of $400,000. The equipment has an estimated salvage value of $10,000 and an estimated useful life of 5 years. The amount of accumulated depreciation at December 31, 2006, if the straight-line method of depreciation is used, is:
a. $80,000.
b. $160,000.
c. $78,000.
d. $156,000.

(SO 3) **4.** Ann Torbert purchased a truck for $11,000 on January 1, 2005. The truck will have an estimated salvage value of $1,000 at the end of 5 years. Using the units-of-activity method, the balance in accumulated depreciation at December 31, 2006, can be computed by the following formula:
a. ($11,000 ÷ Total estimated activity) × Units of activity for 2006.
b. ($10,000 ÷ Total estimated activity) × Units of activity for 2006.
c. ($11,000 ÷ Total estimated activity) × Units of activity for 2005 and 2006.
d. ($10,000 ÷ Total estimated activity) × Units of activity for 2005 and 2006.

(SO 4) **5.** When there is a change in estimated depreciation:
a. previous depreciation should be corrected.
b. current and future years' depreciation should be revised.
c. only future years' depreciation should be revised.
d. None of the above.

(SO 5) **6.** Additions to plant assets are:
a. revenue expenditures.
b. debited to a Repair Expense account.
c. debited to a Purchases account.
d. capital expenditures.

(SO 7) **7.** Maggie Sharrer Company expects to extract 20 million tons of coal from a mine that cost $12 million. If no salvage value is expected, and 2 million tons are mined and sold in the first year, the entry to record depletion will include a:
a. debit to Accumulated Depletion of $2,000,000.
b. credit to Depletion Expense of $1,200,000.
c. debit to Depletion Expense of $1,200,000.
d. credit to Accumulated Depletion of $2,000,000.

8. Martha Beyerlein Company incurred $150,000 of research and development costs in its laboratory to develop a patent granted on January 2, 2006. On July 31, 2006, Beyerlein paid $35,000 for legal fees in a successful defense of the patent. The total amount debited to Patents through July 31, 2006, should be: (SO 8, 9)
a. $150,000.
b. $35,000.
c. $185,000.
d. some other amount.

9. Indicate which of the following statements is *true*. (SO 9)
a. Since intangible assets lack physical substance, they need be disclosed only in the notes to the financial statements.
b. Goodwill should be reported as a contra-account in the owner's equity section.
c. Totals of major classes of assets can be shown in the balance sheet, with asset details disclosed in the notes to the financial statements.
d. Intangible assets are typically combined with plant assets and natural resources and shown in the property, plant, and equipment section.

***10.** Schopenhauer Company exchanged an old machine, with a book value of $39,000 and a fair market value of $35,000, and paid $10,000 cash for a similar new machine. At what amount should the machine acquired in the exchange be recorded on Schopenhauer's books? (SO 10)
a. $45,000. **c.** $49,000.
b. $46,000. **d.** $50,000.

***11.** In exchanges of similar assets: (SO 10)
a. neither gains nor losses are recognized immediately.
b. gains, but not losses, are recognized immediately.
c. losses, but not gains, are recognized immediately.
d. both gains and losses are recognized immediately.

THE NAVIGATOR

QUESTIONS

1. Rick Baden is uncertain about the applicability of the cost principle to plant assets. Explain the principle to Rick.
2. What are some examples of land improvements?
3. Hilo Company acquires the land and building owned by Corrs Company. What types of costs may be incurred to make the asset ready for its intended use if Hilo Company wants to use (a) only the land, and (b) both the land and the building?
4. In a recent newspaper release, the president of Wanzo Company asserted that something has to be done about depreciation. The president said, "Depreciation does not come close to accumulating the cash needed to replace the asset at the end of its useful life." What is your response to the president?
5. Jeremy is studying for the next accounting examination. He asks your help on two questions: (a) What is salvage value? (b) Is salvage value used in determining periodic depreciation under each depreciation method? Answer Jeremy's questions.
6. Contrast the straight-line method and the units-of-activity method as to (a) useful life, and (b) the pattern of periodic depreciation over useful life.

7. Contrast the effects of the three depreciation methods on annual depreciation expense.

8. In the fourth year of an asset's 5-year useful life, the company decides that the asset will have a 6-year service life. How should the revision of depreciation be recorded? Why?

9. Distinguish between revenue expenditures and capital expenditures during useful life.

10. How is a gain or loss on the sale of a plant asset computed?

11. Garcia Corporation owns a machine that is fully depreciated but is still being used. How should Garcia account for this asset and report it in the financial statements?

12. What are natural resources, and what are their distinguishing characteristics?

13. Explain what depletion is and how it is computed.

14. What are the similarities and differences between the terms depreciation, depletion, and amortization?

15. Teresa Speck Company hires an accounting intern who says that intangible assets should always be amortized over their legal lives. Is the intern correct? Explain.

16. Goodwill has been defined as the value of all favorable attributes that relate to a business enterprise. What types of attributes could result in goodwill?

17. Jerry Sain, a business major, is working on a case problem for one of his classes. In the case problem, the company needs to raise cash to market a new product it developed. Sam Morris, an engineering major, takes one look at the company's balance sheet and says, "This company has an awful lot of goodwill. Why don't you recommend that they sell some of it to raise cash?" How should Jerry respond to Sam?

18. Under what conditions is goodwill recorded?

19. Often research and development costs provide companies with benefits that last a number of years. (For example, these costs can lead to the development of a patent that will increase the company's income for many years.) However, generally accepted accounting principles require that such costs be recorded as an expense when incurred. Why?

20. **Toys "R" Us, Inc.** in 2003 reported total average assets of $9.8 billion and net sales of $11.6 billion. What was the company's asset turnover ratio?

21. Wanzo Corporation and Cheng Corporation operate in the same industry. Wanzo uses the straight-line method to account for depreciation; Cheng uses an accelerated method. Explain what complications might arise in trying to compare the results of these two companies.

22. Shuey Corporation uses straight-line depreciation for financial reporting purposes but an accelerated method for tax purposes. Is it acceptable to use different methods for the two purposes? What is Shuey's motivation for doing this?

23. You are comparing two companies in the same industry. You have determined that Lam Corp. depreciates its plant assets over a 40-year life, whereas Hoi Corp. depreciates its plant assets over a 20-year life. Discuss the implications this has for comparing the results of the two companies.

24. Zito Company is doing significant work to revitalize its warehouses. It is not sure whether it should capitalize these costs or expense them. What are the implications for current-year net income and future net income of expensing versus capitalizing these costs?

***25.** When similar assets are exchanged, how is the gain or loss on disposal computed?

***26.** Alpha Refrigeration Company trades in an old machine on a new model when the fair market value of the old machine is greater than its book value. Should Alpha recognize a gain on disposal? If the fair market value of the old machine is less than its book value, should Alpha recognize a loss on disposal?

***27.** Riko Company experienced a gain on disposal when exchanging similar machines. In accordance with generally accepted accounting principles, the gain was not recognized. How will Riko's future financial statements be affected by not recognizing the gain?

BRIEF EXERCISES

Determine the cost of land. (SO 1)

BE10-1 The following expenditures were incurred by Rosenberg Company in purchasing land: cash price $50,000, accrued taxes $3,000, attorneys' fees $2,500, real estate broker's commission $2,000, and clearing and grading $3,500. What is the cost of the land?

Determine the cost of a truck. (SO 1)

BE10-2 Jawson Company incurs the following expenditures in purchasing a truck: cash price $25,000, accident insurance $2,000, sales taxes $1,500, motor vehicle license $100, and painting and lettering $400. What is the cost of the truck?

Compute straight-line depreciation. (SO 3)

BE10-3 Weller Company acquires a delivery truck at a cost of $40,000. The truck is expected to have a salvage value of $6,000 at the end of its 4-year useful life. Compute annual depreciation for the first and second years using the straight-line method.

Compute depreciation and evaluate treatment. (SO 3)

BE10-4 Pioneer Company purchased land and a building on January 1, 2005. Management's best estimate of the value of the land was $100,000 and of the building $200,000. Management told the accounting department to record the land at $180,000 and the building at $120,000. The building is being depreciated on a straight-line basis over 20 years with no salvage value. Why do you suppose management requested this accounting treatment? Is it ethical?

BE10-5 Depreciation information for Weller Company is given in BE10-3. Assuming the declining-balance depreciation rate is double the straight-line rate, compute annual depreciation for the first and second years under the declining-balance method.

Compute declining-balance depreciation.
(SO 3)

BE10-6 Yellow Taxi Service uses the units-of-activity method in computing depreciation on its taxicabs. Each cab is expected to be driven 150,000 miles. Taxi no. 10 cost $30,500 and is expected to have a salvage value of $500. Taxi no. 10 is driven 30,000 miles in year 1 and 20,000 miles in year 2. Compute the depreciation for each year.

Compute depreciation using the units-of-activity method.
(SO 3)

BE10-7 On January 1, 2006, the Vasquez Company ledger shows Equipment $32,000 and Accumulated Depreciation $9,000. The depreciation resulted from using the straight-line method with a useful life of 10 years and salvage value of $2,000. On this date, the company concludes that the equipment has a remaining useful life of only 4 years with the same salvage value. Compute the revised annual depreciation.

Compute revised depreciation.
(SO 4)

BE10-8 Prepare journal entries to record the following.

(a) Perez Company retires its delivery equipment, which cost $41,000. Accumulated depreciation is also $41,000 on this delivery equipment. No salvage value is received.
(b) Assume the same information as (a), except that accumulated depreciation for Perez Company is $37,000, instead of $41,000.

Prepare entries for disposal by retirement.
(SO 6)

BE10-9 Tong Company sells office equipment on September 30, 2006, for $20,000 cash. The office equipment originally cost $72,000 and as of January 1, 2006, had accumulated depreciation of $42,000. Depreciation for the first 9 months of 2006 is $4,500. Prepare the journal entries to **(a)** update depreciation to September 30, 2006, and **(b)** record the sale of the equipment.

Prepare entries for disposal by sale.
(SO 6)

BE10-10 Arma Mining Co. purchased for $7 million a mine that is estimated to have 28 million tons of ore and no salvage value. In the first year, 6 million tons of ore are extracted and sold.

(a) Prepare the journal entry to record depletion expense for the first year.
(b) Show how this mine is reported on the balance sheet at the end of the first year.

Prepare depletion expense entry and balance sheet presentation for natural resources.
(SO 7)

BE10-11 Felipe Company purchases a patent for $150,000 on January 2, 2006. Its estimated useful life is 10 years.

(a) Prepare the journal entry to record patent expense for the first year.
(b) Show how this patent is reported on the balance sheet at the end of the first year.

Prepare patent expense entry and balance sheet presentation for intangibles.
(SO 8)

BE10-12 Information related to plant assets, natural resources, and intangibles at the end of 2006 for Lumas Company is as follows: buildings $1,100,000; accumulated depreciation—buildings $650,000; goodwill $410,000; coal mine $300,000; accumulated depletion—coal mine $108,000. Prepare a partial balance sheet of Lumas Company for these items.

Classify long-lived assets on balance sheet.
(SO 9)

BE10-13 In its 2003 annual report **McDonald's Corporation** reported beginning total assets of $24.0 billion; ending total assets of $25.5 billion; property, plant, and equipment (at cost) of $31.4 billion; and net sales of $17.1 billion. Compute McDonald's asset turnover ratio.

Analyze long-lived assets.
(SO 9)

***BE10-14** Cordero Company exchanges old delivery equipment for similar new delivery equipment. The book value of the old delivery equipment is $31,000 (cost $61,000 less accumulated depreciation $30,000). Its fair market value is $19,000, and cash of $3,000 is paid. Prepare the entry to record the exchange.

Prepare entry for disposal by exchange.
(SO 10)

***BE10-15** Assume the same information as BE10-14, except that the fair market value of the old delivery equipment is $38,000. Prepare the entry to record the exchange.

Prepare entry for disposal by exchange.
(SO 10)

EXERCISES

E10-1 The following expenditures relating to plant assets were made by Devereaux Company during the first 2 months of 2006.

Determine cost of plant acquisitions.
(SO 1)

1. Paid $5,000 of accrued taxes at the time the plant site was acquired.
2. Paid $200 insurance to cover possible accident loss on new factory machinery while the machinery was in transit.

3. Paid $850 sales taxes on new delivery truck.
4. Paid $17,500 for parking lots and driveways on new plant site.
5. Paid $250 to have company name and advertising slogan painted on new delivery truck.
6. Paid $8,000 for installation of new factory machinery.
7. Paid $900 for one-year accident insurance policy on new delivery truck.
8. Paid $75 motor vehicle license fee on the new truck.

Instructions

(a) Explain the application of the cost principle in determining the acquisition cost of plant assets.

(b) List the numbers of the foregoing transactions, and opposite each indicate the account title to which each expenditure should be debited.

Determine acquisition costs on land.
(SO 1)

E10-2 On March 1, 2006, Tanger Company acquired real estate on which it planned to construct a small office building. The company paid $90,000 in cash. An old warehouse on the property was razed at a cost of $6,600; the salvaged materials were sold for $1,700. Additional expenditures before construction began included $1,100 attorney's fee for work concerning the land purchase, $5,000 real estate broker's fee, $7,800 architect's fee, and $14,000 to put in driveways and a parking lot.

Instructions

(a) Determine the amount to be reported as the cost of the land.

(b) For each cost not used in part (a), indicate the account to be debited.

Compute depreciation under units-of-activity method.
(SO 3)

E10-3 Wheeler Bus Lines uses the units-of-activity method in depreciating its buses. One bus was purchased on January 1, 2006, at a cost of $148,000. Over its 4-year useful life, the bus is expected to be driven 100,000 miles. Salvage value is expected to be $8,000.

Instructions

(a) Compute the depreciation cost per unit.

(b) Prepare a depreciation schedule assuming actual mileage was: 2006, 26,000; 2007, 32,000; 2008, 25,000; and 2009, 17,000.

Determine depreciation for partial periods.
(SO 3)

E10-4 Solo Company purchased a new machine on October 1, 2006, at a cost of $96,000. The company estimated that the machine will have a salvage value of $12,000. The machine is expected to be used for 10,000 working hours during its 5-year life.

Instructions

Compute the depreciation expense under the following methods for the year indicated.

(a) Straight-line for 2006.

(b) Units-of-activity for 2006, assuming machine usage was 1,700 hours.

(c) Declining-balance using double the straight-line rate for 2006 and 2007.

Compute revised annual depreciation.
(SO 4)

E10-5 Steve Grant, the new controller of Greenberg Company, has reviewed the expected useful lives and salvage values of selected depreciable assets at the beginning of 2006. His findings are as follows.

Type of Asset	Date Acquired	Cost	Accumulated Depreciation 1/1/06	Useful Life in Years		Salvage Value	
				Old	Proposed	Old	Proposed
Building	1/1/98	$800,000	$152,000	40	50	$40,000	$18,000
Warehouse	1/1/01	100,000	19,000	25	20	5,000	3,600

All assets are depreciated by the straight-line method. Greenberg Company uses a calendar year in preparing annual financial statements. After discussion, management has agreed to accept Steve's proposed changes.

Instructions

(a) Compute the revised annual depreciation on each asset in 2006. (Show computations.)

(b) Prepare the entry (or entries) to record depreciation on the building in 2006.

Journalize entries for disposal of plant assets.
(SO 6)
Peachtree

E10-6 Presented below are selected transactions at Thomas Company for 2006.

Jan. 1 Retired a piece of machinery that was purchased on January 1, 1996. The machine cost $62,000 on that date. It had a useful life of 10 years with no salvage value.

June 30 Sold a computer that was purchased on January 1, 2003. The computer cost $35,000. It had a useful life of 5 years with no salvage value. The computer was sold for $12,000.

Dec. 31 Discarded a delivery truck that was purchased on January 1, 2002. The truck cost $33,000. It was depreciated based on a 6-year useful life with a $3,000 salvage value.

Instructions

Journalize all entries required on the above dates, including entries to update depreciation, where applicable, on assets disposed of. Thomas Company uses straight-line depreciation. (Assume depreciation is up to date as of December 31, 2005.)

Journalize entries for natural resources depletion.

(SO 7)

E10-7 On July 1, 2006, Sutton Inc. invested $480,000 in a mine estimated to have 800,000 tons of ore of uniform grade. During the last 6 months of 2006, 100,000 tons of ore were mined and sold.

Instructions

(a) Prepare the journal entry to record depletion expense.

(b) Assume that the 100,000 tons of ore were mined, but only 80,000 units were sold. How are the costs applicable to the 20,000 unsold units reported?

Prepare adjusting entries for amortization.

(SO 8)

E10-8 The following are selected 2006 transactions of Yosuke Corporation.

Jan. 1 Purchased a small company and recorded goodwill of $150,000. Its useful life is indefinite.

May 1 Purchased for $60,000 a patent with an estimated useful life of 5 years and a legal life of 20 years.

Instructions

Prepare necessary adjusting entries at December 31 to record amortization required by the events above.

Prepare entries to set up appropriate accounts for different intangibles; amortize intangible assets.

(SO 8)

E10-9 Ziegler Company, organized in 2006, has the following transactions related to intangible assets.

1/2/06	Purchased patent (7-year life)	$420,000
4/1/06	Goodwill purchased (indefinite life)	360,000
7/1/06	10-year franchise; expiration date 7/1/2015	480,000
9/1/06	Research and development costs	185,000

Instructions

Prepare the necessary entries to record these intangibles. All costs incurred were for cash. Make the adjusting entries as of December 31, 2006, recording any necessary amortization and reflecting all balances accurately as of that date.

Calculate asset turnover ratio.

(SO 9)

E10-10 During 2006 Otaki Corporation reported net sales of $4,200,000 and net income of $1,500,000. Its balance sheet reported average total assets of $1,400,000.

Instructions

Calculate the asset turnover ratio.

Journalize entries for exchange of similar assets.

(SO 10)

***E10-11** Presented below are two independent transactions.

1. Global Co. exchanged old trucks (cost $64,000 less $22,000 accumulated depreciation) plus cash of $17,000 for new trucks. The old trucks had a fair market value of $38,000.
2. Rijo Inc. trades its used machine (cost $12,000 less $4,000 accumulated depreciation) for a new machine. In addition to exchanging the old machine (which had a fair market value of $9,000), Rijo also paid cash of $2,000.

Instructions

(a) Prepare the entry to record the exchange of similar assets by Global Co.

(b) Prepare the entry to record the exchange of similar assets by Rijo Inc.

Journalize entries for the exchange of similar plant assets.

(SO 10)

***E10-12** Astro Company exchanges similar equipment with Logan Company. Also Jay Company exchanges similar equipment with Moon Company. The following information pertains to these two exchanges.

	Astro Co.	Jay Co.
Equipment (cost)	$28,000	$22,000
Accumulated depreciation	21,000	5,000
Fair market value of equipment	12,000	15,000
Cash paid	3,000	-0-
Cash received		3,000

Instructions

Prepare the journal entries to record the exchange on the books of Astro Company and Jay Company.

Journalize entries for the exchange of similar plant assets.
(SO 10)

***E10-13** Brown's Delivery Company and Roether's Express Delivery exchanged similar delivery trucks on January 1, 2006. Brown's truck cost $22,000. It has accumulated depreciation of $13,000 and a fair market value of $4,000. Roether's truck cost $10,000. It has accumulated depreciation of $7,000 and a fair market value of $4,000.

Instructions

(a) Journalize the exchange for Brown's Delivery Company.
(b) Journalize the exchange for Roether's Express Delivery.

PROBLEMS: SET A

Determine acquisition costs of land and building.
(SO 1)

P10-1A Ripley Company was organized on January 1. During the first year of operations, the following plant asset expenditures and receipts were recorded in random order.

Debits

1. Accrued real estate taxes paid at time of purchase of real estate	$ 2,000
2. Real estate taxes on land paid for the current year	3,000
3. Full payment to building contractor	600,000
4. Excavation costs for new building	25,000
5. Cost of real estate purchased as a plant site (land $100,000 and building $25,000)	125,000
6. Cost of parking lots and driveways	15,000
7. Architect's fees on building plans	10,000
8. Installation cost of fences around property	4,000
9. Cost of demolishing building to make land suitable for construction of new building	21,000
	$805,000

Credit

10. Proceeds from salvage of demolished building	$ 2,500

Totals
Land $145,500
Building $635,000

Instructions

Analyze the foregoing transactions using the following column headings. Insert the number of each transaction in the Item space, and insert the amounts in the appropriate columns. For amounts entered in the Other Accounts column, also indicate the account title.

Item	Land	Building	Other Accounts

Compute depreciation under different methods.
(SO 3)

P10-2A In recent years, Hrubeck Company purchased three machines. Because of heavy turnover in the accounting department, a different accountant was in charge of selecting the depreciation method for each machine, and various methods were selected. Information concerning the machines is summarized below.

Machine	Acquired	Cost	Salvage Value	Useful Life in Years	Depreciation Method
1	1/1/03	$76,000	$ 6,000	10	Straight-line
2	1/1/04	80,000	10,000	8	Declining-balance
3	11/1/06	78,000	6,000	6	Units-of-activity

For the declining-balance method, the company uses the double-declining rate. For the units-of-activity method, total machine hours are expected to be 24,000. Actual hours of use in the first 3 years were: 2006, 1,000; 2007, 4,500; and 2008, 5,000.

Instructions

(a) Compute the amount of accumulated depreciation on each machine at December 31, 2006.
(b) If machine 2 had been purchased on April 1 instead of January 1, what would be the depreciation expense for this machine in (1) 2004 and (2) 2005?

P10-3A On January 1, 2006, Solomon Company purchased the following two machines for use in its production process.

Compute depreciation under different methods.

(SO 3)

Machine A: The cash price of this machine was $38,500. Related expenditures included: sales tax $2,200, shipping costs $175, insurance during shipping $75, installation and testing costs $50, and $90 of oil and lubricants to be used with the machinery during its first year of operation. Solomon estimates that the useful life of the machine is 4 years with a $5,000 salvage value remaining at the end of that time period.

Machine B: The recorded cost of this machine was $100,000. Solomon estimates that the useful life of the machine is 4 years with a $8,000 salvage value remaining at the end of that time period.

Instructions

(a) Prepare the following for Machine A.
- **(1)** The journal entry to record its purchase on January 1, 2006.
- **(2)** The journal entry to record annual depreciation at December 31, 2006, assuming the straight-line method of depreciation is used.

(a) (2) $9,000

(b) Calculate the amount of depreciation expense that Solomon should record for machine B each year of its useful life under the following assumption.
- **(1)** Solomon uses the straight-line method of depreciation.
- **(2)** Solomon uses the declining-balance method. The rate used is twice the straight-line rate.
- **(3)** Solomon uses the units-of-activity method and estimates the useful life of the machine is 25,000 units. Actual usage is as follows: 2006, 6,500 units; 2007, 7,500 units; 2008, 6,000 units; 2009, 5,000 units.

(c) Which method used to calculate depreciation on machine B reports the lowest amount of depreciation expense in year 1 (2006)? The lowest amount in year 4 (2009)? The lowest total amount over the 4-year period?

P10-4A At the beginning of 2004, Bellamy Company acquired equipment costing $60,000. It was estimated that this equipment would have a useful life of 6 years and a residual value of $6,000 at that time. The straight-line method of depreciation was considered the most appropriate to use with this type of equipment. Depreciation is to be recorded at the end of each year.

Calculate revisions to depreciation expense.

(SO 3, 4)

Peachtree

During 2006 (the third year of the equipment's life), the company's engineers reconsidered their expectations, and estimated that the equipment's useful life would probably be 7 years (in total) instead of 6 years. The estimated residual value was not changed at that time. However, during 2009 the estimated residual value was reduced to $3,000.

Instructions

Indicate how much depreciation expense should be recorded for this equipment each year by completing the following table.

Year	Depreciation Expense	Accumulated Depreciation
2004		
2005		
2006		
2007		
2008		
2009		
2010		

2010 depreciation expense, $8,700

P10-5A At December 31, 2006, Walton Company reported the following as plant assets.

Journalize a series of equipment transactions related to purchase, sale, retirement, and depreciation.

(SO 6, 9)

Land		$ 3,000,000
Buildings	$26,500,000	
Less: Accumulated depreciation—buildings	12,100,000	14,400,000
Equipment	40,000,000	
Less: Accumulated depreciation—equipment	5,000,000	35,000,000
Total plant assets		$52,400,000

During 2007, the following selected cash transactions occurred.

April 1 Purchased land for $2,200,000.

May 1 Sold equipment that cost $750,000 when purchased on January 1, 2003. The equipment was sold for $460,000.

June 1 Sold land purchased on June 1, 1997, for $1,800,000. The land cost $300,000.
July 1 Purchased equipment for $2,400,000.
Dec. 31 Retired equipment that cost $500,000 when purchased on December 31, 1997. No salvage value was received.

Instructions

(b) Depreciation expense—Building $530,000; Equipment $3,995,000
(c) Total plant assets $51,675,000

(a) Journalize the above transactions. Walton uses straight-line depreciation for buildings and equipment. The buildings are estimated to have a 50-year useful life and no salvage value. The equipment is estimated to have a 10-year useful life and no salvage value. Update depreciation on assets disposed of at the time of sale or retirement.
(b) Record adjusting entries for depreciation for 2007.
(c) Prepare the plant assets section of Walton's balance sheet at December 31, 2007.

Record disposals.
(SO 6)

P10-6A Yount Co. has delivery equipment that cost $50,000 and that has been depreciated $22,000. Record the disposal under the following assumptions.
(a) It was scrapped as having no value.
(b) It was sold for $31,000.
(c) It was sold for $18,000.

Prepare entries to record transactions related to acquisition and amortization of intangibles; prepare the intangible assets section.
(SO 8, 9)

Peachtree

P10-7A The intangible assets section of Glover Company at December 31, 2006, is presented below.

Patent ($60,000 cost less $6,000 amortization)	$54,000
Copyright ($36,000 cost less $14,400 amortization)	21,600
Total	$75,600

The patent was acquired in January 2006 and has a useful life of 10 years. The copyright was acquired in January 2003 and also has a useful life of 10 years. The following cash transactions may have affected intangible assets during 2007.

Jan. 2 Paid $36,000 legal costs to successfully defend the patent against infringement by another company.
Jan.–June Developed a new product, incurring $140,000 in research and development costs. A patent was granted for the product on July 1. Its useful life is equal to its legal life.
Sept. 1 Paid $75,000 to a quarterback to appear in commercials advertising the company's products. The commercials will air in September and October.
Oct. 1 Acquired a copyright for $80,000. The copyright has a useful life of 50 years.

Instructions

(b) Amortization Expense—Patents $10,000; Amortization Expense—Copyrights $4,000
(c) Total intangible assets, $177,600

(a) Prepare journal entries to record the transactions above.
(b) Prepare journal entries to record the 2007 amortization expense for intangible assets.
(c) Prepare the intangible assets section of the balance sheet at December 31, 2007.
(d) Prepare the note to the financials on Glover's intangibles as of December 31, 2007.

Prepare entries to correct errors made in recording and amortizing intangible assets.
(SO 8)

P10-8A Due to rapid turnover in the accounting department, a number of transactions involving intangible assets were improperly recorded by Buek Company in 2006.

1. Buek developed a new manufacturing process, incurring research and development costs of $95,000. The company also purchased a patent for $27,000. In early January, Buek capitalized $122,000 as the cost of the patents. Patent amortization expense of $6,100 was recorded based on a 20-year useful life.
2. On July 1, 2006, Buek purchased a small company and as a result acquired goodwill of $80,000. Buek recorded a half-year's amortization in 2006, based on a 50-year life ($800 amortization). The goodwill has an indefinite life.

Instructions

R&D Exp. $95,000

Prepare all journal entries necessary to correct any errors made during 2006. Assume the books have not yet been closed for 2006.

Calculate and comment on asset turnover ratio.
(SO 9)

P10-9A Dirks Corporation and Hewes Corporation, two corporations of roughly the same size, are both involved in the manufacture of canoes and sea kayaks. Each company depreciates its plant assets using the straight-line method. An investigation of their financial statements reveals the following information.

	Dirks Corp.	Hewes Corp.
Net income	$ 400,000	$ 450,000
Sales	1,200,000	1,140,000
Average total assets	2,000,000	1,500,000
Plant assets	1,500,000	800,000

Instructions

(a) For each company, calculate (1) the asset turnover ratio and (2) the return on assets ratio.

(a) (1) Dirks Corp. .60 times

(b) Based on your calculations in part (a), comment on the relative effectiveness of the two companies in using their assets to generate sales and produce net income.

PROBLEMS: SET B

P10-1B Foxx Company was organized on January 1. During the first year of operations, the following plant asset expenditures and receipts were recorded in random order.

Determine acquisition costs of land and building.

(SO 1)

Debits

1. Cost of filling and grading the land	$ 4,000
2. Full payment to building contractor	700,000
3. Real estate taxes on land paid for the current year	5,000
4. Cost of real estate purchased as a plant site (land $100,000 and building $45,000)	145,000
5. Excavation costs for new building	30,000
6. Architect's fees on building plans	10,000
7. Accrued real estate taxes paid at time of purchase of real estate	2,000
8. Cost of parking lots and driveways	14,000
9. Cost of demolishing building to make land suitable for construction of new building	20,000
	$930,000

Credit

10. Proceeds from salvage of demolished building	$ 3,500

Instructions

Analyze the foregoing transactions using the following column headings. Insert the number of each transaction in the Item space, and insert the amounts in the appropriate columns. For amounts entered in the Other Accounts column, also indicate the account titles.

Totals
Land $167,500
Building $740,000

Item	Land	Building	Other Accounts

P10-2B In recent years, Freeman Transportation purchased three used buses. Because of frequent turnover in the accounting department, a different accountant selected the depreciation method for each bus, and various methods were selected. Information concerning the buses is summarized below.

Compute depreciation under different methods.

(SO 3)

Bus	Acquired	Cost	Salvage Value	Useful Life in Years	Depreciation Method
1	1/1/04	$ 96,000	$ 6,000	5	Straight-line
2	1/1/04	140,000	10,000	4	Declining-balance
3	1/1/05	92,000	8,000	5	Units-of-activity

For the declining-balance method, the company uses the double-declining rate. For the units-of-activity method, total miles are expected to be 120,000. Actual miles of use in the first 3 years were: 2005, 24,000; 2006, 34,000; and 2007, 30,000.

Instructions

(a) Compute the amount of accumulated depreciation on each bus at December 31, 2006.

(b) If bus no. 2 was purchased on April 1 instead of January 1, what is the depreciation expense for this bus in (1) 2004 and (2) 2005?

Compute depreciation under different methods.

(SO 3)

P10-3B On January 1, 2006, Thao Company purchased the following two machines for use in its production process.

Machine A: The cash price of this machine was $35,000. Related expenditures included: sales tax $1,700, shipping costs $150, insurance during shipping $80, installation and testing costs $70, and $100 of oil and lubricants to be used with the machinery during its first year of operations. Thao estimates that the useful life of the machine is 5 years with a $5,000 salvage value remaining at the end of that time period. Assume that the straight-line method of depreciation is used.

Machine B: The recorded cost of this machine was $80,000. Thao estimates that the useful life of the machine is 4 years with a $5,000 salvage value remaining at the end of that time period.

Instructions

(a) Prepare the following for Machine A.
  (1) The journal entry to record its purchase on January 1, 2006.
  (2) The journal entry to record annual depreciation at December 31, 2006.

(b) (2) 2006 DDB depreciation $40,000

(b) Calculate the amount of depreciation expense that should record for machine B each year of its useful life under the following assumptions.
  (1) Thao uses the straight-line method of depreciation.
  (2) Thao uses the declining-balance method. The rate used is twice the straight-line rate.
  (3) Thao uses the units-of-activity method and estimates that the useful life of the machine is 125,000 units. Actual usage is as follows: 2006, 45,000 units; 2007, 35,000 units; 2008, 25,000 units; 2009, 20,000 units.

(c) Which method used to calculate depreciation on machine B reports the highest amount of depreciation expense in year 1 (2006)? The highest amount in year 4 (2009)? The highest total amount over the 4-year period?

Calculate revisions to depreciation expense.

(SO 3, 4)

P10-4B At the beginning of 2004, Murphy Company acquired equipment costing $80,000. It was estimated that this equipment would have a useful life of 6 years and a residual value of $8,000 at that time. The straight-line method of depreciation was considered the most appropriate to use with this type of equipment. Depreciation is to be recorded at the end of each year.

During 2006 (the third year of the equipment's life), the company's engineers reconsidered their expectations, and estimated that the equipment's useful life would probably be 7 years (in total) instead of 6 years. The estimated residual value was not changed at that time. However, during 2009 the estimated residual value was reduced to $4,400.

Instructions

Indicate how much depreciation expense should be recorded each year for this equipment, by completing the following table.

Year	Depreciation Expense	Accumulated Depreciation
2004		
2005		
2006		
2007		
2008		
2009		
2010		

2010 depreciation expense, $11,400

Journalize a series of equipment transactions related to purchase, sale, retirement, and depreciation.

(SO 6, 9)

P10-5B At December 31, 2006, Angelos Company reported the following as plant assets.

Land		$ 4,000,000
Buildings	$28,500,000	
Less: Accumulated depreciation—buildings	12,100,000	16,400,000
Equipment	48,000,000	
Less: Accumulated depreciation—equipment	5,000,000	43,000,000
Total plant assets		$63,400,000

During 2007, the following selected cash transactions occurred.

April 1	Purchased land for $2,130,000.
May 1	Sold equipment that cost $720,000 when purchased on January 1, 2003. The equipment was sold for $430,000.
June 1	Sold land purchased on June 1, 1997, for $1,500,000. The land cost $200,000.
July 1	Purchased equipment for $3,000,000.
Dec. 31	Retired equipment that cost $500,000 when purchased on December 31, 1997. No salvage value was received.

Instructions

(a) Journalize the above transactions. The company uses straight-line depreciation for buildings and equipment. The buildings are estimated to have a 50-year life and no salvage value. The equipment is estimated to have a 10-year useful life and no salvage value. Update depreciation on assets disposed of at the time of sale or retirement.
(b) Record adjusting entries for depreciation for 2007.
(c) Prepare the plant assets section of Angelos' balance sheet at December 31, 2007.

(b) Depreciation Expense—building $570,000; equipment $4,828,000
(c) Total plant assets $62,450,000

P10-6B Spencer Co. has office furniture that cost $80,000 and that has been depreciated $50,000. Record the disposal under the following assumptions.

Record disposals.

(SO 6)

(a) It was scrapped as having no value.
(b) It was sold for $21,000.
(c) It was sold for $61,000.

P10-7B The intangible assets section of Whitley Company at December 31, 2006, is presented below.

Prepare entries to record transactions related to acquisition and amortization of intangibles; prepare the intangible assets section.

(SO 8, 9)

Patent ($70,000 cost less $7,000 amortization)	$63,000
Franchise ($48,000 cost less $19,200 amortization)	28,800
Total	$91,800

The patent was acquired in January 2006 and has a useful life of 10 years. The franchise was acquired in January 2003 and also has a useful life of 10 years. The following cash transactions may have affected intangible assets during 2007.

Jan. 2	Paid $18,000 legal costs to successfully defend the patent against infringement by another company.
Jan.–June	Developed a new product, incurring $140,000 in research and development costs. A patent was granted for the product on July 1. Its useful life is equal to its legal life.
Sept. 1	Paid $50,000 to an extremely large defensive lineman to appear in commercials advertising the company's products. The commercials will air in September and October.
Oct. 1	Acquired a franchise for $80,000. The franchise has a useful life of 50 years.

Instructions

(a) Prepare journal entries to record the transactions above.
(b) Prepare journal entries to record the 2007 amortization expense.
(c) Prepare the intangible assets section of the balance sheet at December 31, 2007.

(b) Amortization Expense—Patents $9,000
Amortization Expense—Franchise $5,200
(c) Total intangible assets $175,600

P10-8B Due to rapid turnover in the accounting department, a number of transactions involving intangible assets were improperly recorded by the Goslin Company in 2006.

Prepare entries to correct errors made in recording and amortizing intangible assets.

(SO 8)

1. Goslin developed a new manufacturing process, incurring research and development costs of $136,000. The company also purchased a patent for $48,000. In early January, Goslin capitalized $184,000 as the cost of the patents. Patent amortization expense of $9,200 was recorded based on a 20-year useful life.
2. On July 1, 2006, Goslin purchased a small company and as a result acquired goodwill of $92,000. Goslin recorded a half-year's amortization in 2006, based on a 50-year life ($920 amortization). The goodwill has an indefinite life.

Instructions

Prepare all journal entries necessary to correct any errors made during 2006. Assume the books have not yet been closed for 2006.

1. R&D Exp. $136,000

Calculate and comment on asset turnover ratio.

(SO 9)

P10-9B Nina Company and Vernon Corporation, two corporations of roughly the same size, are both involved in the manufacture of in-line skates. Each company depreciates its plant assets using the straight-line method. An investigation of their financial statements reveals the following information.

	Nina Co.	Vernon Corp.
Net income	$ 750,000	$1,000,000
Sales	1,200,000	1,100,000
Average total assets	2,500,000	2,000,000
Plant assets	1,800,000	1,000,000

Instructions

(a) For each company, calculate (1) the asset turnover ratio and (2) the return on assets ratio.

(b) Based on your calculations in part (a), comment on the relative effectiveness of the two companies in using their assets to generate sales and produce net income.

COMPREHENSIVE PROBLEM: CHAPTERS 3 TO 10

Squarepants Corporation's trial balance at December 31, 2005, is presented below. All 2005 transactions have been recorded except for the items described on page 461.

	Debit	Credit
Cash	$ 28,000	
Accounts Receivable	36,800	
Notes Receivable	10,000	
Interest Receivable	–0–	
Merchandise Inventory	36,200	
Prepaid Insurance	3,600	
Land	20,000	
Building	150,000	
Equipment	60,000	
Patent	9,000	
Allowance for Doubtful Accounts		$ 500
Accumulated Depreciation—Building		50,000
Accumulated Depreciation—Equipment		24,000
Accounts Payable		27,300
Salaries Payable		–0–
Unearned Rent		6,000
Notes Payable (short-term)		11,000
Interest Payable		–0–
Notes Payable (long-term)		35,000
Common Stock		50,000
Retained Earnings		63,600
Dividends	12,000	
Sales		900,000
Interest Revenue		–0–
Rent Revenue		–0–
Gain on Disposal		–0–
Bad Debts Expense	–0–	
Cost of Goods Sold	630,000	
Depreciation Expense—Buildings	–0–	
Depreciation Expense—Equipment	–0–	
Insurance Expense	–0–	
Interest Expense	–0–	
Other Operating Expenses	61,800	
Amortization Expense—Patents	–0–	
Salaries Expense	110,000	
Total	$1,167,400	$1,167,400

Unrecorded transactions

1. On May 1, 2005, Squarepants purchased equipment for $12,000 plus sales taxes of $600 (all paid in cash).
2. On July 1, 2005, Squarepants sold for $3,500 equipment which originally cost $5,000. Accumulated depreciation on this equipment at January 1, 2005, was $1,800; 2005 depreciation prior to the sale of equipment was $450.
3. On December 31, 2005, Squarepants sold for $3,000 on account inventory that cost $2,100.
4. Squarepants estimates that uncollectible accounts receivable at year-end is $4,000.
5. The note receivable is a one-year, 12% note dated April 1, 2005. No interest has been recorded.
6. The balance in prepaid insurance represents payment of a $3,600 6-month premium on September 1, 2005.
7. The building is being depreciated using the straight-line method over 30 years. The salvage value is $30,000.
8. The equipment owned prior to this year is being depreciated using the straight-line method over 5 years. The salvage value is 10% of cost.
9. The equipment purchased on May 1, 2005, is being depreciated using the straight-line method over 5 years, with a salvage value of $1,800.
10. The patent was acquired on January 1, 2005, and has a useful life of 10 years from that date.
11. Unpaid salaries at December 31, 2005, total $2,200.
12. The unearned rent of $6,000 was received on December 1, 2005, for 3 months rent.
13. Both the short-term and long-term notes payable are dated January 1, 2005, and carry a 12% interest rate. All interest is payable in the next 12 months.

Instructions

(a) Prepare journal entries for the transactions listed above.

(b) Prepare an updated December 31, 2005, trial balance.

(b) Total $1,196,810

(c) Prepare a 2005 income statement and a 2005 retained earnings statement.

(d) Prepare a December 31, 2005, balance sheet.

(d) Total assets $259,060

BROADENING YOUR PERSPECTIVE

Financial Reporting and Analysis

■ FINANCIAL REPORTING PROBLEM: PepsiCo

BYP10-1 The financial statements and the Notes to Consolidated Financial Statements of **PepsiCo** are presented in Appendix A.

PEPSI

Instructions

Refer to PepsiCo's financial statements and answer the following questions.

(a) What was the total cost and book value of property, plant, and equipment at December 27, 2003?

(b) What method or methods of depreciation are used by the company for financial reporting purposes?

(c) What was the amount of depreciation and amortization expense for each of the three years 2001–2003?

(d) Using the statement of cash flows, what is the amount of capital spending in 2003 and 2002?

(e) Where does the company disclose its intangible assets, and what types of intangibles did it have at December 27, 2003?

■ COMPARATIVE ANALYSIS PROBLEM: PepsiCo vs. Coca-Cola

BYP10-2 **PepsiCo**'s financial statements are presented in Appendix A. **Coca-Cola**'s financial statements are presented in Appendix B.

PEPSI

Instructions

(a) Compute the asset turnover ratio for each company for 2003.

(b) What conclusions concerning the efficiency of assets can be drawn from these data?

■ RESEARCH CASE

BYP10-3 The June 26, 2002, issue of the *Wall Street Journal* includes an article by Jared Sandberg, Rebecca Blumenstein, and Shawn Young titled "**WorldCom** Internal Probe Uncovers Massive Fraud."

Instructions

Read this article and answer the following questions.

(a) What was the fraud that occurred at WorldCom, and what was its impact on net income in 2001 and 2002?
(b) How was the massive fraud discovered?
(c) As a result of this fraud, WorldCom eventually declared bankruptcy. Explain what factors probably led the company to declare bankruptcy.
(d) The article notes that the fraud helped WorldCom increase its cash flow from operations. Explain how the company's cash flow was increased.
(e) What happened to WorldCom's stock price as a result of this fraud?

■ INTERPRETING FINANCIAL STATEMENTS

BYP10-4 **Bob Evans Farms, Inc.** operates 495 restaurants in 22 states and produces fresh and fully cooked sausage products, fresh salads, and related products distributed to grocery stores in the Midwest, Southwest, and Southeast. For a recent 3-year period Bob Evans Farms reported the following selected income statement data (in millions of dollars).

	2002	2001	2000
Sales	$1,061.8	$1,007.5	$947.9
Cost of goods sold	300.4	292.9	274.4
Net income	67.7	50.8	52.9
Total assets	721.9	678.7	624.4

In his letter to stockholders, the chief executive officer (CEO) expressed great enthusiasm for the company's future. Here is an excerpt from that letter:

BOB EVANS FARMS, INC.
Letter to Stockholders (partial)

Fiscal 2002 was a record-breaking year for Bob Evans Farms. The company's financial performance on both sides of the business exceeded our expectations. Strategically, the Bob Evans brand is stronger than ever, and we see plenty of opportunities to leverage it and continue building stockholder value in the years ahead.

Instructions

(a) Compute the percentage change in sales and in net income from 2000 to 2002.
(b) What contribution, if any, did the company's gross profit rate make to the improved earnings?
(c) What was Bob Evans's profit margin ratio in each of the 3 years? Comment on any trend in this percentage.
(d) The CEO's letter also stated that the company's "same-store sales" have increased by 5% from the previous year. What effect would you expect this change to have on return on assets? Calculate the company's return on assets for 2001 and 2002 to see if it reflects the increase in same-store sales.
(e) Based on the trends in these ratios, does the CEO's optimism seem appropriate?

■ A GLOBAL FOCUS

BYP10-5 As you can imagine, the accounting for goodwill differs in countries around the world. The following discussion of a change in goodwill accounting practices was taken from the notes to the financial statements of **J Sainsbury Plc**, one of the world's leading retailers. Headquartered in the United Kingdom, it serves 15 million customers a week.

J SAINSBURY PLC
Notes to the Financial Statements

Accounting Policies

Goodwill arising in connection with the acquisition of shares in subsidiaries and associated undertakings is calculated as the excess of the purchase price over the fair value of the net tangible assets acquired. In prior years goodwill has been deducted from reserves in the period of acquisition. FRS 10 is applicable in the current financial year, and in accordance with the standard acquired goodwill is now shown as an asset on the Group's Balance Sheet. As permitted by FRS 10, goodwill written off to reserves in prior periods has not been restated as an asset.

Goodwill is treated as having an indefinite economic life where it is considered that the acquired business has strong customer loyalty built up over a long period of time, based on advantageous store locations and a commitment to maintain the marketing advantage of the retail brand. The carrying value of the goodwill will be reviewed annually for impairment and adjusted to its recoverable amount if required. Where goodwill is considered to have a finite life, amortisation will be applied over that period.

For amounts stated as goodwill which are considered to have indefinite life, no amortisation is charged to the Profit and Loss Account.

Instructions

(a) How does the initial determination and recording of goodwill compare with that in the United States? That is, is goodwill initially recorded in the same circumstances, and is the calculation of the initial amount the same in both the United Kingdom and the United States?

(b) Prior to adoption of the new accounting standard (FRS 10), how did the company account for goodwill? What were the implications for the income statement?

(c) Under the new accounting standard, how does the company account for its goodwill? Is it possible, under the new standard, for a company to avoid charging goodwill amortization to net income?

(d) In what ways is the new standard similar to U.S. standards?

■ EXPLORING THE WEB

BYP10-6 A company's annual report identifies the amount of its plant assets and the depreciation method used.

Address: www.reportgallery.com, or go to www.wiley.com/college/weygandt

Steps

1. From Report Gallery Homepage, choose a letter (a–z).
2. Select a particular company.
3. Choose the most recent Annual Report.
4. Follow instructions below.

Instructions

(a) What is the name of the company?

(b) At fiscal year-end, what is the net amount of its plant assets?

(c) What is the accumulated depreciation?

(d) Which method of depreciation does the company use?

Critical Thinking

■ GROUP DECISION CASE

BYP10-7 Givens Company and Runge Company are two companies that are similar in many respects. One difference is that Givens Company uses the straight-line method and Runge

Company uses the declining-balance method at double the straight-line rate. On January 2, 2004, both companies acquired the following depreciable assets.

Asset	Cost	Salvage Value	Useful Life
Building	$320,000	$20,000	40 years
Equipment	125,000	10,000	10 years

Including the appropriate depreciation charges, annual net income for the companies in the years 2004, 2005, and 2006 and total income for the 3 years were as follows.

	2004	2005	2006	Total
Givens Company	$84,000	$88,400	$100,000	$272,400
Runge Company	68,000	76,000	85,000	229,000

At December 31, 2006, the balance sheets of the two companies are similar except that Runge Company has more cash than Givens Company.

Linda Yanik is interested in buying one of the companies. She comes to you for advice.

Instructions

With the class divided into groups, answer the following.

(a) Determine the annual and total depreciation recorded by each company during the 3 years.

(b) Assuming that Runge Company also uses the straight-line method of depreciation instead of the declining-balance method as in (a), prepare comparative income data for the 3 years.

(c) Which company should Linda Yanik buy? Why?

■ COMMUNICATION ACTIVITY

BYP10-8 The following was published with the financial statements to **American Exploration Company**.

AMERICAN EXPLORATION COMPANY
Notes to the Financial Statements

Property, Plant, and Equipment—The Company accounts for its oil and gas exploration and production activities using the successful efforts method of accounting. Under this method, acquisition costs for proved and unproved properties are capitalized when incurred.... The costs of drilling exploratory wells are capitalized pending determination of whether each well has discovered proved reserves. If proved reserves are not discovered, such drilling costs are charged to expense.... Depletion of the cost of producing oil and gas properties is computed on the units-of-activity method.

Instructions

Write a brief memo to your instructor discussing American Exploration Company's note regarding property, plant, and equipment. Your memo should address what is meant by the "successful efforts method" and "units-of-activity method."

■ ETHICS CASE

Accounting Matters!

BYP10-9 Dieker Container Company is suffering declining sales of its principal product, non-biodegradeable plastic cartons. The president, Edward Mohling, instructs his controller, Betty Fetters, to lengthen asset lives to reduce depreciation expense. A processing line of automated plastic extruding equipment, purchased for $3.5 million in January 2006, was originally estimated to have a useful life of 8 years and a salvage value of $300,000. Depreciation has been recorded for 2 years on that basis. Edward wants the estimated life changed to 12 years total, and the straight-line method continued. Betty is hesitant to make the change, believing it is unethical to increase net income in this manner. Edward says, "Hey, the life is only an estimate, and I've heard that our competition uses a 12-year life on their production equipment."

Instructions

(a) Who are the stakeholders in this situation?

(b) Is the change in asset life unethical, or is it simply a good business practice by an astute president?

(c) What is the effect of Edward Mohling's proposed change on income before taxes in the year of change?

■ CONTINUING COOKIE CHRONICLE

Accounting Matters!

(Note: This is a continuation of the Cookie Chronicle from Chapters 1 through 9.)

BYP10-10

Part 1 Now that she is selling mixers and her customers can use credit cards to pay for them, Natalie is thinking of upgrading her Web site to include the online sale of mixers and payment by credit card. This would enable her to sell these mixers to a wider range of customers using the Internet.

Natalie contacts her brother who originally prepared the Web site for her. He agrees to upgrade the site so it can handle credit card security issues as well as direct order entry. The estimated cost of the upgrade is $1,800. This cost would be incurred and paid for during the month of August 2006, and the upgrade would be operational September 1, 2006. Recall that Natalie's Web site had an original cost of $600 and is being amortized using the straight-line method over 24 months, starting December 1, 2005, with zero residual value. Additional costs for Web site maintenance and insurance are estimated to be $1,200 per year.

If Natalie decides to upgrade the Web site, its useful life will not change and there will be no change in residual value.

Instructions

(a) Prepare the journal entry to record the upgrade.

(b) Calculate the monthly amortization expense before the upgrade and the accumulated amortization and book value on August 31, 2006.

(c) Calculate the revised monthly amortization expense as of September 1, 2006.

(d) Calculate the accumulated amortization and book value on December 31, 2006.

(e) Explain to Natalie the difference in accounting for the Web site upgrade costs and accounting for the costs incurred for Web site maintenance and insurance. In your explanation, comment on the generally accepted accounting principles that affect the accounting for these transactions.

Part 2 Natalie is also thinking of buying a van that will be used only for business. The cost of the van is estimated at $32,500. Natalie would spend an additional $2,500 to have the van painted. In addition, she wants the back seat of the van removed so that she will have lots of room to transport her mixer inventory as well as her baking supplies. The cost of taking out the back seat and installing shelving units is estimated at $1,500. She expects the van to last her about 5 years, and she expects to drive it for 100,000 miles. The annual cost of vehicle insurance will be $2,400. Natalie estimates that at the end of the 5-year useful life the van will sell for $6,500. Assume that she will buy the van on August 15, 2006, and it will be ready for use on September 1, 2006.

Natalie is concerned about the impact of the van's cost on her income statement and balance sheet. She has come to you for advice on calculating the van's depreciation.

Instructions

(a) Determine the cost of the van.

(b) Prepare three depreciation tables: one for straight-line depreciation (similar to the one in Illustration 10-10), one for double-declining-balance depreciation (Illustration 10-14), and one for units-of-activity depreciation (Illustration 10-12). For units-of-activity, Natalie estimates she will drive the van as follows: 7,500 miles in 2006; 22,500 miles in 2007; 25,000 miles in 2008; 22,500 miles in 2009; 17,500 miles in 2010; and 5,000 miles in 2011. Recall that Cookie Creations has a December 31 fiscal year end.

(c) What impact will the three methods of depreciation have on Natalie's balance sheet at December 31, 2006? What impact will the three methods have on Natalie's income statement in 2006?

(d) What impact will the three methods of depreciation have on Natalie's income statement over the van's total 5-year useful life?

(e) What impact will the three methods of depreciation have on her cash flow over the van's total 5-year useful life?

(f) Which method of depreciation would you recommend Natalie use?

Accounting Matters!

Answers to Accounting Matters! Questions

p. 427

Q: The effect on the income statement is discussed in the boxed story. What effect does the change in the estimated life of equipment have on the balance sheet?

A: Accumulated depreciation (the contra asset account) grows at a smaller amount each year as a result of the longer asset life; therefore, the book value of plant assets is larger. Because earnings are greater, retained earnings per the balance sheet are greater.

p. 433

Q: What erroneous accounting entries (accounts debited and credited) were made by WorldCom?

A: WorldCom erroneously debited Assets and credited Cash/Accounts Payable.

Q: What is the correcting entry that should be recorded, and what is its effect on WorldCom's financial statements?

A: The correcting entry would be a debit to Expenses and a credit to Assets. This correction would decrease reported income and assets and increase expenses.

p. 440

Q: How should eBay Inc. account for the purchase of an additional domain name?

A: The purchase price would be recorded (debited) as an Intangible Asset.

Q: How would it account for a domain name developed by its own employees?

A: The costs associated with "in-house" development of a domain name would be expensed.

Answer to PepsiCo Review It Question 2, p. 424

In Note 4, **PepsiCo** reports the following categories and amounts under the heading "Property, plant and equipment (net)": Land and improvements $557,000,000; Buildings and improvements $3,449,000,000; Machinery and equipment, including fleet $10,170,000,000; and Construction in progress $579,000,000. In addition, accumulated depreciation of $6,927,000,000 was deducted.

Answers to Self-Study Questions

1. d **2.** b **3.** d **4.** d **5.** b **6.** d **7.** c **8.** b **9.** c ***10.** a ***11.** c

REMEMBER to go back to the Navigator box on the chapter-opening page and check off your completed work.

Chapter 11

Liabilities

THE NAVIGATOR ✓

- Understand **Concepts for Review** ❑
- Read **Feature Story** ❑
- Scan **Study Objectives** ❑
- Read **Preview** ❑
- Read text and answer **Before You Go On** p. 476 ❑ p. 481 ❑ p. 485 ❑ p. 486 ❑ p. 489 ❑
- Work **Demonstration Problems** ❑
- Review **Summary of Study Objectives** ❑
- Answer **Self-Study Questions** ❑
- Complete **Assignments** ❑

CONCEPTS FOR REVIEW

Before studying this chapter, you should know or, if necessary, review:

- What is a current liability? a long-term liability? (Ch. 4, pp. 160–161)
- The importance of liquidity in evaluating the financial position of a company. (Ch. 4, p. 161)
- How to make adjusting entries related to unearned revenue (Ch. 3, pp. 101–102) and accrued expenses. (Ch. 3, pp. 105–107)
- How to record adjusting entries for interest expense and interest payable. (Ch. 3, pp. 105–106)

THE NAVIGATOR

ACCOUNTING MATTERS! **FEATURE STORY**

Financing His Dreams

What would you do if you had a great idea for a new product, but couldn't come up with the cash to get the business off the ground? Small businesses often can't attract investors, nor can they obtain traditional debt financing through bank loans or bond issuances. Instead, they often resort to unusual, and costly, forms of nontraditional financing.

Such was the case for Wilbert Murdock. Murdock grew up in a New York housing project, and always had great ambitions. This ambitious spirit led him into some business ventures that failed: a medical diagnostic tool, a device to eliminate carpal-tunnel syndrome, custom sneakers, and a device to keep people from falling asleep while driving.

His latest idea was computerized golf clubs that analyze a golfer's swing and provide immediate feedback. Murdock saw great potential in the idea: Many golfers are willing to shell out considerable sums of money for devices that might improve their game. But Murdock had no cash to develop his product, and banks and other lenders had shied away. Rather than give up, Murdock resorted to credit cards—in a big way. He quickly owed $25,000 to credit card companies.

While funding a business with credit cards might sound unusual, it isn't. A recent study found that one-third of businesses with fewer than 20 employees financed at least part of their operations with credit cards. As Murdock explained, credit cards are an appealing way to finance a start-up because "credit-card companies don't care how the money is spent." But they do care how they are paid. And so Murdock faced high interest charges and a barrage of credit card collection letters.

Murdock's debt forced him to sacrifice nearly everything in order to keep his business afloat. His car stopped running, he barely had enough money to buy food, and he lived and worked out of a dimly lit apartment in his mother's basement. Through it all he tried to maintain a positive spirit, joking that, if he becomes successful, he might some day get to appear in an American Express commercial.

Source: Rodney Ho, "Banking on Plastic: To Finance a Dream, Many Entrepreneurs Binge on Credit Cards," *Wall Street Journal* (March 9, 1998), p. A1.

☑ THE NAVIGATOR

STUDY OBJECTIVES

After studying this chapter, you should be able to:

1. Explain a current liability, and identify the major types of current liabilities.
2. Describe the accounting for notes payable.
3. Explain the accounting for other current liabilities.
4. Explain why bonds are issued, and identify the types of bonds.
5. Prepare the entries for the issuance of bonds and interest expense.
6. Describe the entries when bonds are redeemed or converted.
7. Describe the accounting for long-term notes payable.
8. Identify the methods for the presentation and analysis of long-term liabilities.

☑ THE NAVIGATOR

PREVIEW OF CHAPTER 11

Inventor-entrepreneur Wilbert Murdock, as you can tell from the Feature Story, has had to use multiple credit cards to finance his business ventures. Murdock's credit card debts would be classified as *current liabilities* because they are due every month. Yet by making minimal payments and paying high interest each month, Murdock uses this credit source long-term. Some credit card balances remain outstanding for years as they accumulate interest.

In Chapter 4, we defined liabilities as creditors' claims on total assets and as existing debts and obligations. These claims, debts, and obligations must be settled or paid at some time **in the future** by the transfer of assets or services. The future date on which they are due or payable (maturity date) is a significant feature of liabilities. This "future date" feature gives rise to two basic classifications of liabilities: (1) current liabilities and (2) long-term liabilities. Thus, our discussion of liabilities in this chapter is divided into these two classifications.

The content and organization of Chapter 11 are as follows.

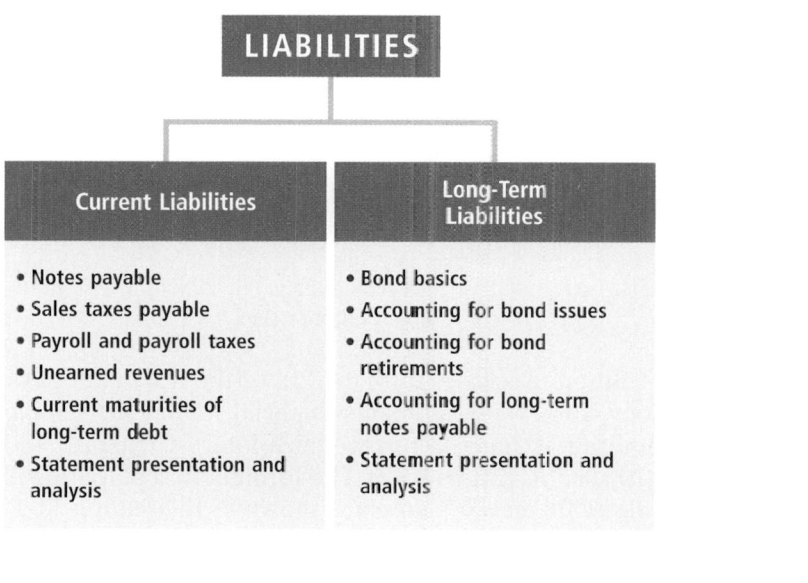

LIABILITIES

Current Liabilities	Long-Term Liabilities
• Notes payable • Sales taxes payable • Payroll and payroll taxes • Unearned revenues • Current maturities of long-term debt • Statement presentation and analysis	• Bond basics • Accounting for bond issues • Accounting for bond retirements • Accounting for long-term notes payable • Statement presentation and analysis

THE NAVIGATOR

SECTION 1 CURRENT LIABILITIES

What Is a Current Liability?

STUDY OBJECTIVE 1

Explain a current liability, and identify the major types of current liabilities.

As explained in Chapter 4, a **current liability** is a debt with two key features: (1) It can reasonably be expected to be paid from existing current assets or through the creation of other current liabilities. And (2) it will be paid within one year or the operating cycle, whichever is longer. Debts that do not meet **both criteria** are classified as long-term liabilities. Most companies pay current liabilities within one year out of current assets, rather than by creating other liabilities.

Companies must carefully monitor the relationship of current liabilities to current assets. This relationship is critical in evaluating a company's short-term debt-paying ability. A company that has more current liabilities than current assets is usually the subject of some concern because the company may not be able to meet its current obligations when they become due.

Current liabilities include notes payable, accounts payable, and unearned revenues. They also include accrued liabilities such as taxes, salaries and wages, and interest payable. The entries for accounts payable and adjusting entries for some current liabilities have been explained in previous chapters. Other types of current liabilities that are often encountered are discussed in the following sections.

Notes Payable

STUDY OBJECTIVE 2

Describe the accounting for notes payable.

Obligations in the form of written promissory notes are recorded as **notes payable**. Notes payable are often used instead of accounts payable. Doing so gives the lender formal proof of the obligation in case legal remedies are needed to collect the debt. Notes payable usually require the borrower to pay interest and frequently are issued to meet short-term financing needs.

Notes are issued for varying periods. **Those due for payment within one year of the balance sheet date are usually classified as current liabilities.** Most notes are interest bearing.

To illustrate the accounting for notes payable, assume that First National Bank agrees to lend $100,000 on March 1, 2006, if Cole Williams Co. signs a $100,000, 12%, 4-month note. With an interest-bearing promissory note, the amount of assets received upon issuance of the note generally equals the note's face value. Cole Williams Co. therefore will receive $100,000 cash and will make the following journal entry.

A	=	L	+	SE
+100,000		+100,000		

Cash Flows
+100,000

Mar. 1	Cash	100,000	
	Notes Payable		100,000
	(To record issuance of 12%, 4-month note to First National Bank)		

Interest accrues over the life of the note and must be recorded periodically. If Cole Williams Co. prepares financial statements semiannually, an adjusting entry is required at June 30 to recognize interest expense and interest payable of $4,000 ($100,000 × 12% × 4/12). The formula for computing interest and its application to Cole Williams Co.'s note are shown in Illustration 11-1.

Illustration 11-1
Formula for computing interest

Face Value of Note	×	Annual Interest Rate	×	Time in Terms of One Year	=	Interest
$100,000	×	12%	×	4/12	=	**$4,000**

The adjusting entry is:

A	=	L	+	SE
		+4,000		−4,000 Exp

Cash Flows
no effect

June 30	Interest Expense	4,000	
	Interest Payable		4,000
	(To accrue interest for 4 months on First National Bank note)		

In the June 30 financial statements, the current liabilities section of the balance sheet will show notes payable $100,000 and interest payable $4,000. In addition, interest expense of $4,000 will be reported under "Other expenses and losses" in the income statement. If Cole Williams Co. prepared financial statements monthly, the adjusting entry at the end of each month would have been $1,000 ($100,000 × 12% × 1/12).

At maturity (July 1, 2006), Cole Williams Co. must pay the face value of the note ($100,000) plus $4,000 interest ($100,000 × 12% × 4/12). The entry to record payment of the note and accrued interest is as follows.

July 1	Notes Payable	100,000	
	Interest Payable	4,000	
	Cash		104,000
	(To record payment of First National Bank interest-bearing note and accrued interest at maturity)		

A	=	L	+	SE
−104,000		−100,000		
		−4,000		

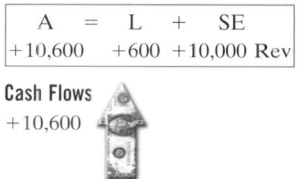

Cash Flows
−104,000

Sales Taxes Payable

STUDY OBJECTIVE 3

Explain the accounting for other current liabilities.

As a consumer, you know that many of the products you purchase at retail stores are subject to sales taxes. The tax is expressed as a stated percentage of the sales price. The retailer collects the tax from the customer when the sale occurs. Periodically (usually monthly), the retailer remits the collections to the state's department of revenue.

Under most state sales tax laws, the amount of the sale and the amount of the sales tax collected must be rung up separately on the cash register. (Gasoline sales are a major exception.) The cash register readings are then used to credit Sales and Sales Taxes Payable. For example, if the March 25 cash register reading for Cooley Grocery shows sales of $10,000 and sales taxes of $600 (sales tax rate of 6%), the entry is:

Mar. 25	Cash	10,600	
	Sales		10,000
	Sales Taxes Payable		600
	(To record daily sales and sales taxes)		

A	=	L	+	SE
+10,600		+600		+10,000 Rev

Cash Flows
+10,600

When the taxes are remitted to the taxing agency, Sales Taxes Payable is debited and Cash is credited. The company does not report sales taxes as an expense. It simply forwards to the government the amount paid by the customers. Thus, Cooley Grocery serves only as a **collection agent** for the taxing authority.

When sales taxes are not rung up separately on the cash register, they must be extracted from the total receipts. To determine the amount of sales in such cases, divide total receipts by 100% plus the sales tax percentage. To illustrate, assume that in the above example Cooley Grocery rings up total receipts, which are $10,600. The receipts from the sales are equal to the sales price (100%) plus the tax percentage (6% of sales), or 1.06 times the sales total. We can compute the sales amount as follows.

$$\$10,600 \div 1.06 = \$10,000$$

Thus, Cooley Grocery could find the sales tax amount it must remit to the state by subtracting sales from total receipts ($10,600 − $10,000).

HELPFUL HINT

Alternatively, Cooley could find the tax by multiplying sales by the sales tax rate ($10,000 × .06).

ACCOUNTING MATTERS! e Business Insight

If you buy a book at a bookstore, you pay sales tax. If you buy the same book over the Internet, you don't pay sales tax (in most cases). This is one reason why e-commerce, as it has come to be called, has been growing exponentially and why Web sites like **Amazon.com** have become so popular. A recent study suggested that Internet sales would fall by 30 percent if sales tax were applied. In December 2001 Congress passed and President Bush signed into law a two-year extension to the ban on sales taxes on Internet purchases. While Internet retailers were pleased, the American Booksellers Association protested the ban, saying it gives online booksellers such as Amazon.com an unfair advantage over brick-and-mortar bookstores.

Source: Edward Nawotka, "Bush Extends Internet Tax Ban," *Publishers Weekly* (December 3, 2001), p. 18.

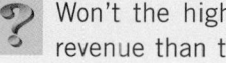

? Won't the higher payment received at the bookstore result in higher sales revenue than that recorded by the online seller?

Payroll and Payroll Taxes Payable

Every employer incurs liabilities relating to employees' salaries and wages. One is the amount of wages and salaries owed to employees—**wages and salaries payable**. Another is the amount required by law to be withheld from employees' gross pay. Until these **withholding taxes** (federal and state income taxes, and Social Security taxes) are remitted to the governmental taxing authorities, they are credited to appropriate liability accounts. For example, if a corporation withholds taxes from its employees' wages and salaries, accrual and payment of a $100,000 payroll would be recorded as follows.

A =	L	+ SE
	+7,650	−100,000
	+21,864	
	+2,922	
	+67,564	

Cash Flows
no effect

Date	Account	Debit	Credit
March 7	Salaries and Wages Expense	100,000	
	FICA Taxes Payable[1]		7,650
	Federal Income Taxes Payable		21,864
	State Income Taxes Payable		2,922
	Salaries and Wages Payable		67,564
	(To record payroll and withholding taxes for the week ending March 7)		
March 11	Salaries and Wages Payable	67,564	
	Cash		67,564
	(To record payment of the March 7 payroll)		

A	= L	+ SE
−67,564	−67,564	

Cash Flows
−67,564

Illustration 11-2 summarizes the types of payroll deductions.

Illustration 11-2
Payroll deductions

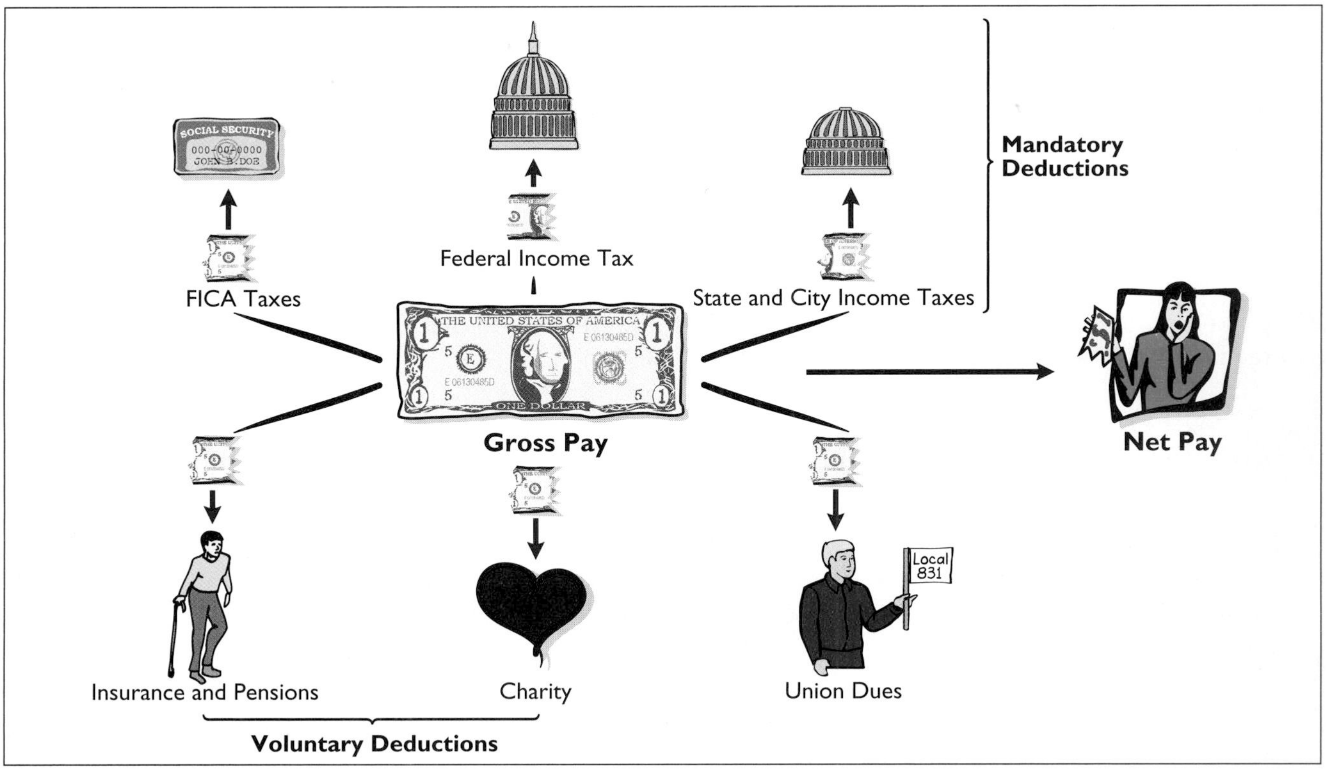

[1]Social Security taxes are commonly referred to as **FICA taxes**. In 1937, Congress enacted the Federal Insurance Contribution Act (FICA). This act and other payroll issues are discussed in greater detail in Appendix D.

Also, with every payroll, the employer incurs liabilities to pay various **payroll taxes** levied upon the employer. These payroll taxes include the employer's share of Social Security taxes and the state and federal unemployment taxes. Based on the $100,000 payroll in the previous example, the following entry would be made to record the employer's expense and liability for these payroll taxes.

March 7	Payroll Tax Expense	13,850	
	FICA Taxes Payable		7,650
	Federal Unemployment Taxes Payable		800
	State Unemployment Taxes Payable		5,400
	(To record employer's payroll taxes on March 7 payroll)		

A	=	L	+	SE
		+7,650		−13,850
		+800		
		+5,400		

Cash Flows
no effect

Illustration 11-3 shows the types of taxes levied on employers.

Illustration 11-3
Employer payroll taxes

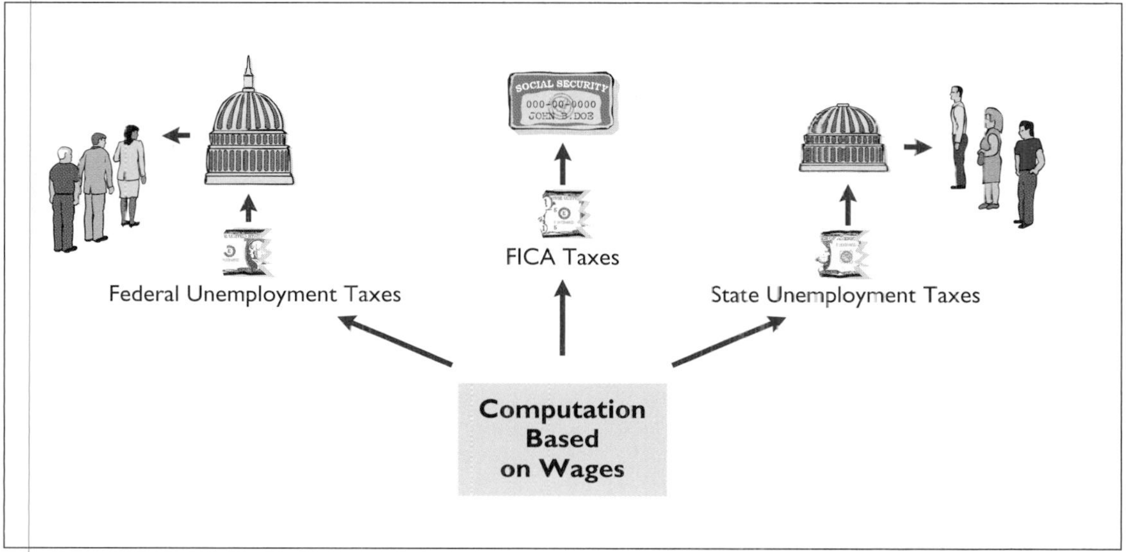

The payroll and payroll tax liability accounts are classified as current liabilities because they must be paid to employees or remitted to taxing authorities in the near term. Taxing authorities impose substantial fines and penalties on employers if the withholding and payroll taxes are not computed correctly and paid on time.

Unearned Revenues

A magazine publisher, such as **Sports Illustrated**, receives a customer's check when magazines are ordered. An airline company, such as **American Airlines**, receives cash when it sells tickets for future flights. Through these transactions, both companies have incurred unearned revenues—revenues that are received before goods are delivered or services are rendered. How do companies account for unearned revenues?

1. When the advance payment is received, Cash is debited, and a current liability account identifying the source of the unearned revenue is credited.
2. When the revenue is earned, the Unearned Revenue account is debited, and an earned revenue account is credited.

To illustrate, assume that Superior University sells 10,000 season football tickets at $50 each for its five-game home schedule. The entry for the sale of season tickets is:

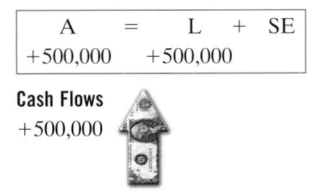

A	=	L	+	SE
+500,000		+500,000		

Cash Flows
+500,000

Aug. 6	Cash	500,000	
	Unearned Football Ticket Revenue		500,000
	(To record sale of 10,000 season tickets)		

As each of the five home games is completed, one-fifth of the revenue is earned. The following entry is made:

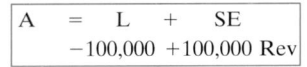

A	=	L	+	SE
		−100,000		+100,000 Rev

Cash Flows
no effect

Sept. 7	Unearned Football Ticket Revenue	100,000	
	Football Ticket Revenue		100,000
	(To record football ticket revenue earned)		

Any balance in an unearned revenue account (in Unearned Football Ticket Revenue, for example) is reported as a current liability in the balance sheet. As revenue is earned, a transfer from unearned revenue to earned revenue occurs. Unearned revenue is material for some companies: In the airline industry, for example, tickets sold for future flights represent almost 50% of total current liabilities. At **United Air Lines**, unearned ticket revenue is the largest current liability, recently amounting to over $1 billion.

Illustration 11-4 shows specific unearned and earned revenue accounts used in selected types of businesses.

Illustration 11-4
Unearned and earned revenue accounts

Type of Business	Account Title	
	Unearned Revenue	**Earned Revenue**
Airline	Unearned Passenger Ticket Revenue	Passenger Revenue
Magazine publisher	Unearned Subscription Revenue	Subscription Revenue
Hotel	Unearned Rental Revenue	Rental Revenue
Insurance company	Unearned Premium Revenue	Premium Revenue

Current Maturities of Long-Term Debt

Companies often have a portion of long-term debt that comes due in the current year. That amount would be considered a current liability. For example, assume that Wendy Construction issues a 5-year interest-bearing $25,000 note on January 1, 2006. Each January 1, starting January 1, 2007, $5,000 of the note is due to be paid. When financial statements are prepared on December 31, 2006, $5,000 should be reported as a current liability. The remaining $20,000 on the note would be reported as a long-term liability. Current maturities of long-term debt are often termed **long-term debt due within one year**.

It is not necessary to prepare an adjusting entry to recognize the current maturity of long-term debt. The proper statement classification of each balance sheet account is recognized when the balance sheet is prepared.

STATEMENT PRESENTATION AND ANALYSIS

Presentation

As indicated in Chapter 4, current liabilities are the first category under liabilities on the balance sheet. Each of the principal types of current liabilities is listed separately. In addition, the terms of notes payable and other key information about the individual items are disclosed in the notes to the financial statements.

Current liabilities are seldom listed in the order of maturity. The reason is that varying maturity dates may exist for specific obligations such as notes payable. A more common method of presenting current liabilities is to list them by **order of magnitude**, with the largest ones first. Or, many companies, as a matter of custom, show notes payable and accounts payable first, regardless of amount. The following adapted excerpt from the balance sheet of **Caterpillar Inc.** illustrates its order of presentation.

CATERPILLAR®

Illustration 11-5
Balance sheet presentation of current liabilities

CATERPILLAR INC.
Balance Sheet
December 31, 2003
(in millions)

Assets	
Current assets	$16,791
Property, plant and equipment (net)	7,290
Other long-term assets	12,384
Total assets	$36,465
Liabilities and Stockholders' Equity	
Current liabilities	
Short-term borrowings	**$ 2,757**
Accounts payable	**3,100**
Accrued expenses	**1,638**
Accrued wages, salaries, and employee benefits	**1,802**
Dividends payable	**127**
Deferred and current income taxes payable	**216**
Long-term debt due within one year	**2,981**
Total current liabilities	**12,621**
Noncurrent liabilities	17,766
Total liabilities	30,387
Stockholders' equity	6,078
Total liabilities and stockholders' equity	$36,465

HELPFUL HINT

For other examples of current liabilities sections, refer to the **PepsiCo** and **Coca-Cola** balance sheets in Appendixes A and B.

Analysis

Use of current and noncurrent classifications makes it possible to analyze a company's liquidity. **Liquidity** refers to the ability to pay maturing obligations and meet unexpected needs for cash. The relationship of current assets to current liabilities is critical in analyzing liquidity. This relationship can be expressed as a dollar amount (called working capital) and as a ratio (called the current ratio).

The excess of current assets over current liabilities is **working capital**. The formula for the computation of Caterpillar's working capital is shown in Illustration 11-6 on page 476 (dollar amounts in millions).

Illustration 11-6
Working capital formula and computation

Current Assets	−	Current Liabilities	=	Working Capital
$16,791	−	$12,621	=	**$4,170**

As an absolute dollar amount, working capital is limited in its informational value. For example, $1 million of working capital may be far more than needed for a small company but be inadequate for a large corporation. And, $1 million of working capital may be adequate for a company at one time but be inadequate at another time.

The **current ratio** permits us to compare the liquidity of different sized companies and of a single company at different times. The current ratio is current assets divided by current liabilities. The formula for this ratio is illustrated below, along with its computation using Caterpillar's current asset and current liability data (dollar amounts in millions).

Illustration 11-7
Current ratio formula and computation

Current Assets	÷	Current Liabilities	=	Current Ratio
$16,791	÷	$12,621	=	**1.33:1**

Historically, a ratio of 2:1 was considered to be the standard for a good credit rating. In recent years, however, many healthy companies have maintained ratios well below 2:1 by improving management of their current assets and liabilities. Caterpillar's ratio of 1.33:1 is adequate but certainly below the standard of 2:1.

BEFORE YOU GO ON...

Review It

1. What are the two criteria for classifying a debt as a current liability?
2. Identify three liabilities classified as current by **PepsiCo**. The answer to this question is provided on page 523.
3. What entries are made for an interest-bearing note payable?
4. How are sales taxes recorded by a retailer? Identify three unearned revenues.
5. What are the three taxes generally withheld from employees' wages or salaries?
6. How may the liquidity of a company be analyzed?

Do It

You and several classmates are studying for the next accounting examination. They ask you to answer the following questions: (1) How is the sales tax amount determined when the cash register total includes sales taxes? (2) What are the taxes to be withheld from an employee's payroll check?

ACTION PLAN

- Remove the sales taxes from the total combined amount.
- Determine the applicable federal and state taxes that apply to employees' earnings. (The current tax rates and the related computations are presented in Appendix D at the back of this book.)

SOLUTION

(1) First, divide the total proceeds by 100% plus the sales tax percentage to find the sales amount; second, subtract the sales amount from the total proceeds to determine the sales taxes.

(2) Employees' earnings are subject to FICA tax, and to federal and state income taxes.

Related exercise material: *BE11-1, BE11-2, BE11-3, BE11-4, BE11-5, BE11-6, E11-1, E11-2, and E11-3.*

THE NAVIGATOR

SECTION 2 LONG-TERM LIABILITIES

Long-term liabilities are obligations that are expected to be paid after one year. In this section we will explain the accounting for the principal types of obligations reported in the long-term liability section of the balance sheet. These obligations often are in the form of bonds or long-term notes.

Bond Basics

Bonds are a form of interest-bearing notes payable. They are issued by corporations, universities, and governmental agencies. Bonds, like common stock, are sold in small denominations (usually a thousand dollars or thousand-dollar multiples). As a result, bonds attract many investors.

Why Issue Bonds?

STUDY OBJECTIVE 4

Explain why bonds are issued, and identify the types of bonds.

A corporation may use long-term financing other than bonds, such as notes payable and leasing. These other forms of financing involve finding an individual, a company, or a financial institution willing to supply the needed funds. Notes payable and leasing are therefore seldom sufficient to furnish the funds needed for plant expansion and major projects like new buildings. To obtain **large amounts of long-term capital**, corporate management usually must decide whether to issue common stock (equity financing) or bonds.

From the standpoint of the corporation seeking long-term financing, bonds offer the following advantages over common stock:

Illustration 11-8
Advantages of bond financing over common stock

Bond Financing	Advantages
	1. **Stockholder control is not affected.** Bondholders do not have voting rights, so current owners (stockholders) retain full control of the company.
	2. **Tax savings result.** Bond interest is deductible for tax purposes; dividends on stock are not.
	3. **Earnings per share may be higher.** Although bond interest expense reduces net income, earnings per share on common stock often is higher under bond financing because no additional shares of common stock are issued.

To illustrate the potential effect on earnings per share, assume that Microsystems, Inc. is considering two plans for financing the construction of a new $5 million plant. Plan A involves issuance of 200,000 shares of common stock at the current market price of $25 per share. Plan B involves issuance of $5 million, 8% bonds at face value. Income before interest and taxes on the new plant will be $1.5 million. Income taxes are expected to be 30%. Microsystems currently has 100,000 shares of common stock outstanding. The alternative effects on earnings per share are shown in Illustration 11-9.

Illustration 11-9
Effects on earnings per share—stocks vs. bonds

	Plan A Issue Stock	Plan B Issue Bonds
Income before interest and taxes	$1,500,000	$1,500,000
Interest (8% × $5,000,000)	—	400,000
Income before income taxes	1,500,000	1,100,000
Income tax expense (30%)	450,000	330,000
Net income	$1,050,000	$ 770,000
Outstanding shares	300,000	100,000
Earnings per share	**$3.50**	**$7.70**

Note that net income is $280,000 less ($1,050,000 − $770,000) with long-term debt financing (bonds). However, earnings per share is higher because there are 200,000 fewer shares of common stock outstanding.

The major disadvantages resulting from the use of bonds are that interest must be paid on a periodic basis and the principal (face value) of the bonds must be paid at maturity. A company with fluctuating earnings and a relatively weak cash position may have great difficulty making interest payments when earnings are low.

Types of Bonds

Bonds may have many different features. Types of bonds commonly issued are described on the next page.

ACCOUNTING MATTERS! Business Insight

Although bonds are generally secured by solid, substantial assets like land, buildings, and equipment, exceptions occur. **Trans World Airlines Inc.** (TWA) at one time decided to issue $300 million of high-yielding 5-year bonds. TWA's bonds would be secured by a grab bag of assets, including some durable spare parts, but also a lot of disposable items that TWA had in its warehouses, such as light bulbs and gaskets. Some called the planned TWA bonds "light-bulb bonds." As one financial expert noted, "You've got to admit that some security is better than none." Another noted, "They're digging pretty far down in the barrel."

? Why would investors have been cautious about buying TWA's "light-bulb bonds"?

Secured and Unsecured Bonds

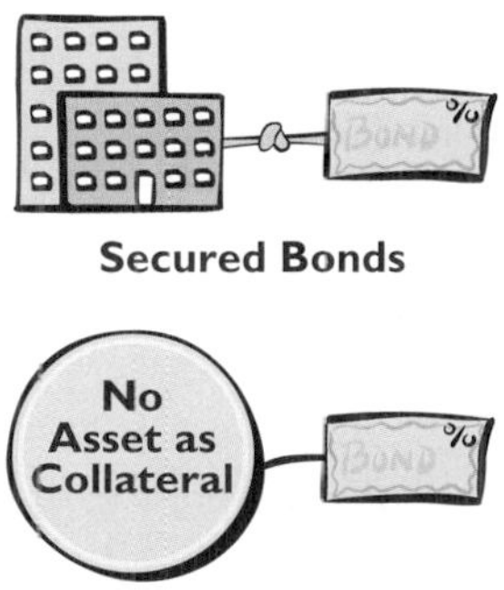

Secured bonds have specific assets of the issuer pledged as collateral for the bonds. A bond secured by real estate, for example, is called a **mortgage bond**. A bond secured by specific assets set aside to retire the bonds is called a **sinking fund bond**. **Unsecured bonds** are issued against the general credit of the borrower. These bonds, called **debenture bonds**, are used extensively by large corporations with good credit ratings. For example, in a recent annual report, **DuPont** reported over $2 billion of debenture bonds outstanding.

Term and Serial Bonds

Bonds that mature (are due for payment) at a single specified future date are called **term bonds**. In contrast, bonds that mature in installments are called **serial bonds**. For example, **Caterpillar Inc.** debentures due in 2007 are term bonds. Caterpillar's debentures due between 2004 and 2007 are serial bonds (maturing annually).

Registered and Bearer Bonds

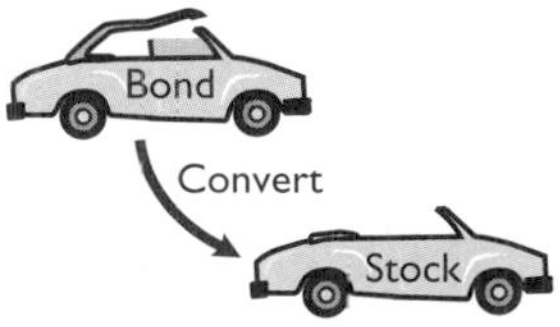

Bonds issued in the name of the owner are called **registered bonds**. Interest payments on registered bonds are made by check to bondholders of record. Bonds not registered are called **bearer** (or **coupon**) **bonds**. Holders of bearer bonds must send in coupons to receive interest payments. Coupon bonds may be transferred directly to another party. In contrast, the transfer of registered bonds requires cancellation of the bonds by the corporation and the issuance of new bonds. Most bonds issued today are registered bonds.

Convertible and Callable Bonds

Bonds that can be converted into common stock at the bondholder's option are called **convertible bonds**. The conversion feature generally is attractive to bond buyers. Bonds subject to retirement at a stated dollar amount prior to maturity at the option of the issuer are known as **callable bonds**. A call feature is included in nearly all corporate bond issues.

Issuing Procedures

State laws grant corporations the power to issue bonds. Within the corporation, approval by both the board of directors and stockholders is usually required. **In authorizing the bond issue, the board of directors must stipulate the number of bonds to be authorized, total face value, and contractual interest rate.** The total bond authorization often exceeds the number of bonds originally issued. This gives the corporation the flexibility it needs to meet future cash requirements.

The **face value** is the amount of principal the issuer must pay at the maturity date. The **contractual interest rate**, often referred to as the **stated rate**, is the rate used to determine the amount of cash interest the borrower pays and the investor receives. Usually the contractual rate is stated as an annual rate. Interest is generally paid semiannually.

The terms of the bond issue are set forth in a legal document called a **bond indenture**. In addition to the terms, the indenture summarizes the rights of the bondholders and their trustees, as well as the obligations of the issuing company. The **trustee** (usually a financial institution) keeps records of each bondholder, maintains custody of unissued bonds, and holds conditional title to pledged property.

After the bond indenture is prepared, **bond certificates** are printed. The indenture and the certificate are separate documents. As shown in Illustration 11-10 (next page), a bond certificate provides information such as the following: name of the issuer, face value, contractual interest rate, and maturity date. Bonds are generally sold through an investment company that specializes in selling securities.

Illustration 11-10
Bond certificate

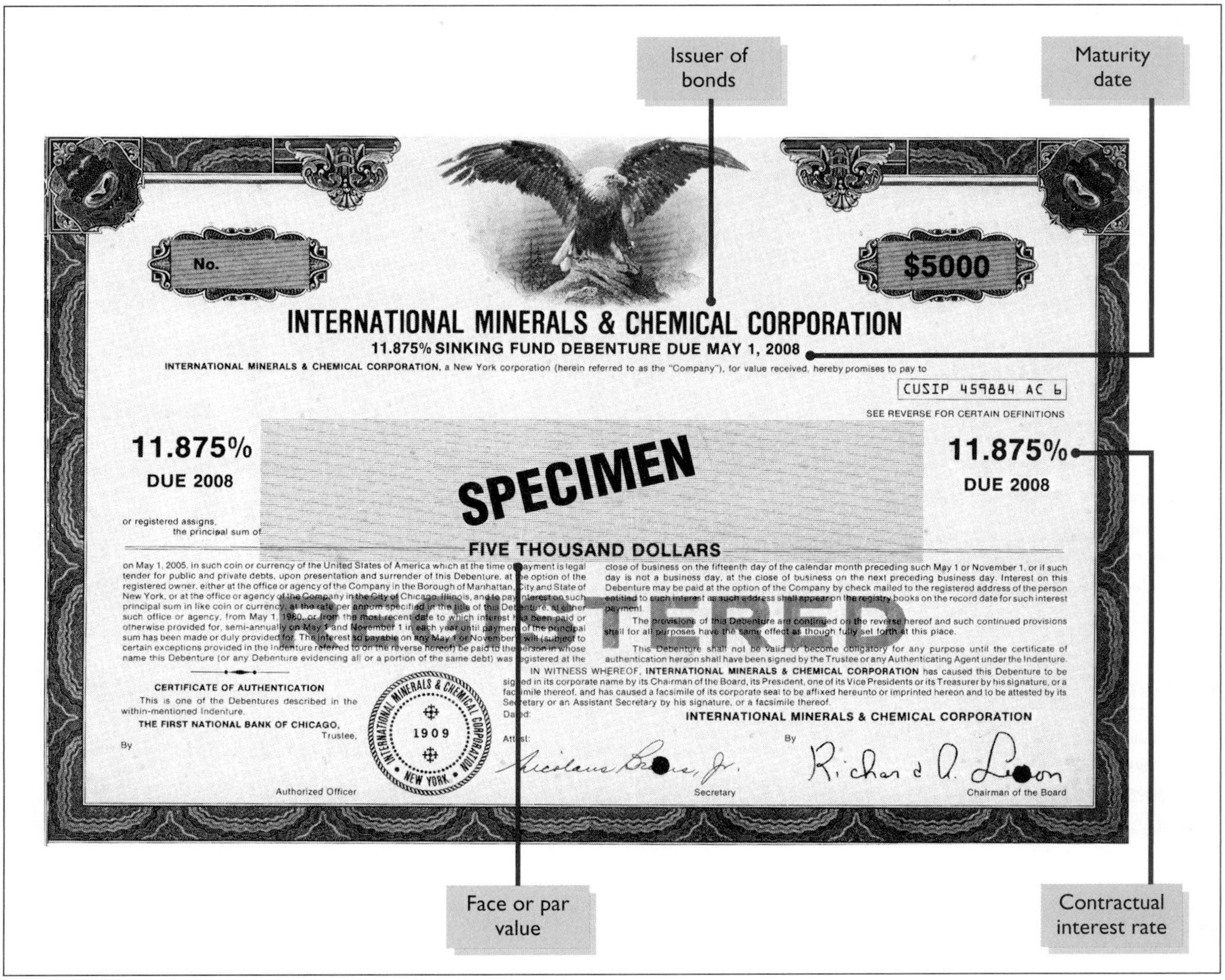

Bond Trading

Corporate bonds, like capital stock, are traded on national securities exchanges. Thus, bondholders have the opportunity to convert their holdings into cash at any time by selling the bonds at the current market price.

Bond prices are quoted as a percentage of the face value of the bond, which is usually $1,000. A $1,000 bond with a quoted price of 97 means that the selling price of the bond is 97% of face value, or $970. Bond prices and trading activity are published daily in newspapers and the financial press, as illustrated by the following.

Illustration 11-11
Market information for bonds

Bonds	Maturity	Close	Yield	Est. Volume (000)
General Motors 7.2	Jan. 15, 2011	101.110	7.007	62,427

This bond listing indicates that **General Motors** has outstanding 7.2%, $1,000 bonds that mature in 2011. They currently yield a 7.007% return. On this day, $62,427,000 of these bonds were traded. At the close of trading, the price was 101.110% of face value, or $1,011.10.

Transactions between a bondholder and other investors **are not journalized by the issuing corporation**. If Tom Smith sells bonds to Faith Jones, the issuing corporation does not journalize the transaction. (The issuer or its trustee does keep records of the names of bondholders in the case of registered bonds.) A corporation makes journal entries **only when it issues or buys back bonds**, and when bondholders convert bonds into common stock.

HELPFUL HINT

(1) What is the price of a $1,000 bond trading at 95¼?

(2) What is the price of a $1,000 bond trading at 101⅞?

Answers: (1) $952.50.
(2) $1,018.75.

Determining the Market Value of Bonds

If you were an investor wanting to purchase a bond, how would you determine how much to pay? To be more specific, assume that Coronet, Inc. issues a zero-interest bond (pays no interest) with a face value of $1,000,000 due in 20 years. For this bond, the only cash you receive is a million dollars at the end of 20 years. Would you pay a million dollars for this bond? We hope not! A million dollars received 20 years from now is not the same as a million dollars received today.

Same dollars at different times are not equal.

The reason you should not pay a million dollars for Coronet's bond relates to what is called the **time value of money**. If you had a million dollars today, you would invest it. From that investment, you would earn interest such that at the end of 20 years, you would have much more than a million dollars. If someone is going to pay you a million dollars 20 years from now, you would want to find its equivalent today. In other words, you would want to determine how much must be invested today at current interest rates to have a million dollars in 20 years. That amount, that must be invested today at a given rate of interest over a specified time, is called **present value**.

The present value of a bond is the value at which it should sell in the marketplace. Market value therefore is a function of the three factors that determine present value: (1) the dollar amounts to be received, (2) the length of time until the amounts are received, and (3) the market rate of interest. The **market interest rate** is the rate investors demand for loaning funds. The process of finding the present value for bonds is discussed in Appendix 11A. Additional material for time value of money computations is also provided in Appendix C near the end of the book.

BEFORE YOU GO ON...

Review It

1. What are the advantages of bond versus stock financing?
2. What are secured versus unsecured bonds, term versus serial bonds, registered versus bearer bonds, and callable versus convertible bonds?
3. Explain the terms face value, contractual interest rate, and bond indenture.
4. Explain why you would prefer to receive $1 million today rather than 5 years from now.

THE NAVIGATOR

Accounting for Bond Issues

Bonds may be issued at face value, below face value (at a discount), or above face value (at a premium).

STUDY OBJECTIVE 5

Prepare the entries for the issuance of bonds and interest expense.

Issuing Bonds at Face Value

To illustrate the accounting for bonds, assume that on January 1, 2006, Devor Corporation issues 1,000, 10-year, 9%, $1,000 bonds at 100 (100% of face value). The entry to record the sale is:

Jan. 1	Cash	1,000,000	
	Bonds Payable		1,000,000
	(To record sale of bonds at face value)		

A	=	L	+	SE
+1,000,000		+1,000,000		

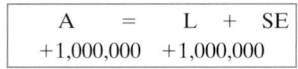

Cash Flows
+1,000,000

Bonds payable are reported in the long-term liabilities section of the balance sheet because the maturity date is more than one year away.

Over the term (life) of the bonds, entries are required for bond interest. Interest on bonds payable is computed in the same manner as interest on notes payable, as explained on page 470. Assume that interest is payable semiannually on January 1 and July 1 on the bonds described above. In that case, interest of $45,000 ($1,000,000 × 9% × 6/12) must be paid on July 1, 2006. The entry for the payment, assuming no previous accrual of interest, is:

July 1	Bond Interest Expense	45,000	
	Cash		45,000
	(To record payment of bond interest)		

A	=	L	+	SE
−45,000				−45,000 Exp

Cash Flows
−45,000

At December 31, an adjusting entry is required to recognize the $45,000 of interest expense incurred since July 1. The entry is:

Dec. 31	Bond Interest Expense	45,000	
	Bond Interest Payable		45,000
	(To accrue bond interest)		

A	=	L	+	SE
		+45,000		−45,000 Exp

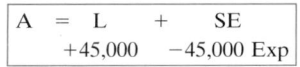

Cash Flows
no effect

Bond interest payable is classified as a current liability, because it is scheduled for payment within the next year. When the interest is paid on January 1, 2007, Bond Interest Payable is debited and Cash is credited for $45,000.

Discount or Premium on Bonds

In the previous illustrations, we assumed that the contractual (stated) interest rate paid on bonds and the market (effective) interest rate were the same. The contractual interest rate is the rate applied to the face (par) value to arrive at the interest paid in a year. The **market interest rate** is the rate investors demand for loaning funds to the corporation. When the contractual interest rate and the market interest rate are the same, bonds sell at face value, as shown above.

However, market interest rates change daily. They are influenced by the type of bond issued, the state of the economy, current industry conditions, and the company's performance. The contractual and market interest rates often differ. As a result, bonds sell below or above face value.

To illustrate, suppose that investors have one of two options: (1) purchase bonds that have a contractual interest rate of 10%, or (2) purchase bonds that have a contractual interest rate of 8%. If the bonds are of equal risk, investors will select the 10% investment. To make the investments equal, investors will demand a rate of interest higher than the 8% contractual interest rate. But investors cannot change the contractual interest rate. What they can do is to pay less than the face value for the bonds. By paying less for the bonds, investors can obtain the market rate of interest. In these cases, **bonds sell at a discount**.

On the other hand, the market interest rate may be **lower** than the contractual interest rate. In that case investors will have to pay more than face value for the bonds. That is, if the market interest rate is 8% and the contractual interest rate is

9%, the issuer will require more funds from the investor. In these cases, **bonds sell at a premium**. These relationships are shown graphically in Illustration 11-12.

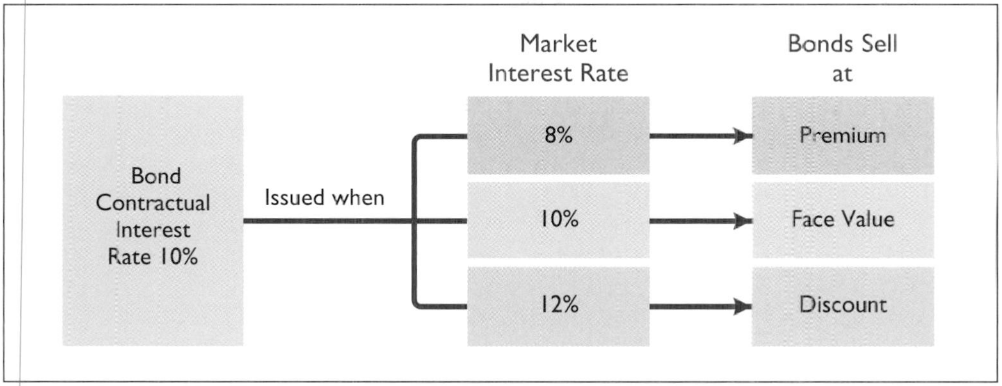

Illustration 11-12
Interest rates and bond prices

Issuing bonds at an amount different from face value is quite common. By the time a company prints the bond certificates and markets the bonds, it will be a coincidence if the market rate and the contractual rate are the same. Thus, the sale of bonds at a discount does not mean that the issuer's financial strength is suspect. Nor does the sale of bonds at a premium indicate exceptional financial strength.

HELPFUL HINT

Discount on Bonds Payable	
Increase Debit ↓ Normal Balance	Decrease Credit

Issuing Bonds at a Discount

To illustrate issuance of bonds at a discount, assume that on January 1, 2006, Candlestick, Inc. sells $100,000, 5-year, 10% bonds for $92,639 (92.639% of face value). Interest is payable on July 1 and January 1. The entry to record the issuance is:

Jan. 1	Cash	92,639	
	Discount on Bonds Payable	7,361	
	Bonds Payable		100,000
	(To record sale of bonds at a discount)		

A	=	L	+	SE
+92,639		−7,361		
		+100,000		

Cash Flows
+92,639

Although Discount on Bonds Payable has a debit balance, **it is not an asset**. Rather, it is a **contra account**. This account is **deducted from bonds payable** on the balance sheet, as illustrated below.

Illustration 11-13
Statement presentation of discount on bonds payable

CANDLESTICK, INC.
Balance Sheet (partial)

Long-term liabilities		
Bonds payable	$100,000	
Less: Discount on bonds payable	**7,361**	$92,639

The $92,639 represents the **carrying (or book) value** of the bonds. On the date of issue this amount equals the market price of the bonds.

The issuance of bonds below face value, at a discount, causes the total cost of borrowing to differ from the bond interest paid. That is, the issuing corporation must pay not only the contractual interest rate over the term of the bonds, but also the face value (rather than the issuance price) at maturity. Therefore, the difference between the issuance price and face value of the bonds—the discount—is an **additional cost of borrowing. This additional cost should be recorded as bond interest**

HELPFUL HINT

Carrying value (book value) of bonds issued at a discount is determined by subtracting the balance of the discount account from the balance of the Bonds Payable account.

expense over the life of the bonds. The procedures for recording this additional cost are shown in Appendixes 11B and 11C.

The total cost of borrowing $92,639 for Candlestick, Inc. is $57,361, computed as follows.

Illustration 11-14
Total cost of borrowing—bonds issued at a discount

Bonds Issued at a Discount	
Semiannual interest payments	
($100,000 × 10% × ½ = $5,000; $5,000 × 10)	$50,000
Add: Bond discount ($100,000 − $92,639)	7,361
Total cost of borrowing	**$57,361**

Alternatively, the total cost of borrowing can be computed as follows.

Illustration 11-15
Alternative computation of total cost of borrowing—bonds issued at a discount

Bonds Issued at a Discount	
Principal at maturity	$100,000
Semiannual interest payments ($5,000 × 10)	50,000
Cash to be paid to bondholders	150,000
Cash received from bondholders	92,639
Total cost of borrowing	**$ 57,361**

Issuing Bonds at a Premium

To illustrate the issuance of bonds at a premium, we now assume the Candlestick, Inc. bonds described above are sold for $108,111 (108.111% of face value) rather than for $92,639.

The entry to record the sale is:

A	=	L	+	SE
+108,111		+100,000		
		+8,111		

Cash Flows
+108,111

Jan. 1	Cash	108,111	
	Bonds Payable		100,000
	Premium on Bonds Payable		8,111
	(To record sale of bonds at a premium)		

Premium on bonds payable is **added to bonds payable** on the balance sheet, as shown below.

Illustration 11-16
Statement presentation of bond premium

CANDLESTICK, INC. Balance Sheet (partial)		
Long-term liabilities		
Bonds payable	$100,000	
Add: Premium on bonds payable	**8,111**	$108,111

HELPFUL HINT

Premium on Bonds Payable	
Decrease Debit	Increase Credit ↓ Normal Balance

The sale of bonds above face value causes the total cost of borrowing to be **less than the bond interest paid**. The bond premium is considered to be **a reduction in the cost of borrowing**. It should be credited to Bond Interest Expense over the life of the bonds. The procedures for recording this reduction in the cost of borrowing are shown in Appendixes 11B and 11C. The total cost of borrowing $108,111 for Candlestick, Inc. is computed as shown in Illustration 11-17 on the next page.

Bonds Issued at a Premium	
Semiannual interest payments	
($100,000 × 10% × ½ = $5,000; $5,000 × 10)	$50,000
Less: Bond premium ($108,111 − $100,000)	8,111
Total cost of borrowing	**$41,889**

Illustration 11-17
Total cost of borrowing—bonds issued at a premium

Alternatively, the cost of borrowing can be computed as follows.

Bonds Issued at a Premium	
Principal at maturity	$100,000
Semiannual interest payments ($5,000 × 10)	50,000
Cash to be paid to bondholders	150,000
Cash received from bondholders	108,111
Total cost of borrowing	**$ 41,889**

Illustration 11-18
Alternative computation of total cost of borrowing—bonds issued at a premium

BEFORE YOU GO ON...

Review It

1. What entry is made to record the issuance of bonds payable of $1 million at 100? At 96? At 102?
2. Why do bonds sell at a discount? At a premium? At face value?

Related exercise material: *BE11-7, BE11-8, BE11-9, BE11-10, E11-4, E11-5, and E11-6.*

THE NAVIGATOR

Accounting for Bond Retirements

STUDY OBJECTIVE 6

Describe the entries when bonds are redeemed or converted.

Bonds may be retired either when they are redeemed by the issuing corporation or when they are converted into common stock by bondholders. The appropriate entries for these transactions are explained in the following sections.

Redeeming Bonds at Maturity

Regardless of the issue price of bonds, the book value of the bonds at maturity will equal their face value. Assuming that the interest for the last interest period is paid and recorded separately, the entry to record the redemption of the Candlestick bonds at maturity is:

A	=	L	+	SE
−100,000		−100,000		

Cash Flows
−100,000

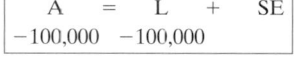

Bonds Payable	100,000	
Cash		100,000
(To record redemption of bonds at maturity)		

Redeeming Bonds before Maturity

Bonds may be redeemed before maturity. A company may decide to retire bonds before maturity to reduce interest cost and remove debt from its balance sheet. A company should retire debt early only if it has sufficient cash resources.

When bonds are retired before maturity, it is necessary to: (1) Eliminate the carrying value of the bonds at the redemption date. (2) Record the cash paid. (3) Recognize the gain or loss on redemption. The carrying value of the bonds is the face

HELPFUL HINT

Question: A bond is redeemed prior to its maturity date. Its carrying value exceeds its redemption price. Will the retirement result in a gain or a loss on redemption?
Answer: Gain.

value of the bonds less unamortized bond discount or plus unamortized bond premium at the redemption date.

To illustrate, assume that Candlestick, Inc. has sold its bonds at a premium. At the end of the eighth period Candlestick retires these bonds at 103 after paying the semiannual interest. Assume also that the carrying value of the bonds at the redemption date is $101,623. The entry to record the redemption at the end of the eighth interest period (January 1, 2010) is:

A	=	L	+	SE
−103,000		−100,000		−1,377 Exp
		−1,623		

Cash Flows
−103,000

Jan. 1	Bonds Payable	100,000	
	Premium on Bonds Payable	1,623	
	Loss on Bond Redemption	1,377	
	Cash		103,000
	(To record redemption of bonds at 103)		

Note that the loss of $1,377 is the difference between the cash paid of $103,000 and the carrying value of the bonds of $101,623.

Converting Bonds into Common Stock

Convertible bonds have features that are attractive both to bondholders and to the issuer. The conversion often gives bondholders an opportunity to benefit if the market price of the common stock increases substantially. Until conversion, though, the bondholder receives interest on the bond. For the issuer, the bonds sell at a higher price and pay a lower rate of interest than comparable debt securities without the conversion option. Many corporations, such as **USAir**, **USX Corp.**, and **DaimlerChrysler Corporation**, have convertible bonds outstanding.

When bonds are converted into common stock and the conversion is recorded, the current market prices of the bonds and the stock are ignored. Instead, the **carrying value** of the bonds is transferred to paid-in capital accounts. **No gain or loss is recognized.** To illustrate, assume that on July 1 Saunders Associates converts $100,000 bonds sold at face value into 2,000 shares of $10 par value common stock. Both the bonds and the common stock have a market value of $130,000. The entry to record the conversion is:

A	=	L	+	SE
		−100,000		+20,000 CS
				+80,000 CS

Cash Flows
no effect

July 1	Bonds Payable	100,000	
	Common Stock		20,000
	Paid-in Capital in Excess of Par Value		80,000
	(To record bond conversion)		

Note that the current market price of the bonds and stock ($130,000) is not considered in making the entry. This method of recording the bond conversion is often referred to as the **carrying (or book) value method**.

BEFORE YOU GO ON...

Review It

1. Explain the accounting for redemption of bonds at maturity, before maturity by payment in cash, and by conversion into common stock.
2. Did **PepsiCo** redeem any of its debt during the fiscal year ended December 27, 2003? (*Hint:* To find information related to this question, examine PepsiCo's statement of cash flows.) The answer to this question is provided on page 523.

Do It

R & B Inc. issued $500,000, 10-year bonds at a premium. Prior to maturity, when the carrying value of the bonds is $508,000, the company retires the bonds at 102. Prepare the entry to record the redemption of the bonds.

ACTION PLAN

- Determine and eliminate the carrying value of the bonds.
- Record the cash paid.
- Compute and record the gain or loss (which is the difference between the first two items).

SOLUTION There is a loss on redemption: The cash paid, $510,000 ($500,000 × 102%), is greater than the carrying value of $508,000. The entry is:

Bonds Payable	500,000	
Premium on Bonds Payable	8,000	
Loss on Bond Redemption	2,000	
Cash		510,000
(To record redemption of bonds at 102)		

Related exercise material: *BE11-11, E11-6, and E11-7.*

THE NAVIGATOR

Accounting for Long-Term Notes Payable

STUDY OBJECTIVE 7

Describe the accounting for long-term notes payable.

The use of notes payable in long-term debt financing is quite common. Long-term notes payable are similar to short-term interest-bearing notes payable except that the terms of the notes exceed one year. In periods of unstable interest rates, the interest rate on long-term notes may be tied to changes in the market rate. Examples are the 8.03% adjustable-rate notes issued by **General Motors** and the floating-rate notes issued by **American Express Company**.

A long-term note may be secured by a **mortgage** that pledges title to specific assets as security for a loan. **Mortgage notes payable** are widely used by individuals to purchase homes and by many small and some large companies to acquire plant assets. Approximately 18 percent of **McDonald's** long-term debt relates to mortgage notes on land, buildings, and improvements. Mortgage loan terms may stipulate either a fixed or an adjustable interest rate. Typically, the terms require the borrower to make installment payments over the term of the loan. Each payment consists of (1) interest on the unpaid balance of the loan and (2) a reduction of loan principal. The interest decreases each period, while the portion applied to the loan principal increases.

Mortgage notes payable are recorded initially at face value. Subsequent entries are required for each installment payment. To illustrate, assume that Porter Technology Inc. issues a $500,000, 12%, 20-year mortgage note on December 31, 2006, to obtain needed financing for a new research laboratory. The terms provide for semiannual installment payments of $33,231 (not including real estate taxes and insurance). The installment payment schedule for the first 2 years is as follows.

Illustration 11-19
Mortgage installment payment schedule

Semiannual Interest Period	(A) Cash Payment	(B) Interest Expense (D) × 6%	(C) Reduction of Principal (A) − (B)	(D) Principal Balance (D) − (C)
Issue date				$500,000
1	$33,231	$30,000	$3,231	496,769
2	33,231	29,806	3,425	493,344
3	33,231	29,601	3,630	489,714
4	33,231	29,383	3,848	485,866

The entries to record the mortgage loan and first installment payment are as follows.

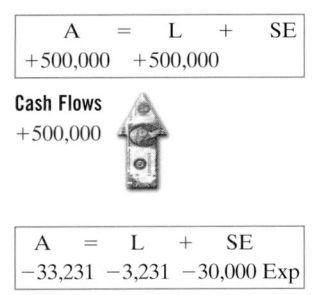

A	=	L	+	SE
+500,000		+500,000		

Cash Flows
+500,000

Dec. 31	Cash	500,000	
	Mortgage Notes Payable		500,000
	(To record mortgage loan)		
June 30	Interest Expense	30,000	
	Mortgage Notes Payable	3,231	
	Cash		33,231
	(To record semiannual payment on mortgage)		

A	=	L	+	SE
−33,231		−3,231		−30,000 Exp

Cash Flows
−33,231

In the balance sheet, the reduction in principal for the next year is reported as a current liability. The remaining unpaid principal balance is classified as a long-term liability. At December 31, 2007, the total liability is $493,344. Of that amount, $7,478 ($3,630 + $3,848) is current, and $485,866 ($493,344 − $7,478) is long-term.

ACCOUNTING MATTERS! Business Insight

Mortgage.com, a pioneer in one of the Web's more promising ideas, exited the online home-lending business and laid off most of its 618 employees. A study of Internet consumers showed that only 4 percent of them have applied online for a mortgage, and fewer than 1 percent have closed a loan. "The fact is, there is still a lot about getting a mortgage that can't be done online," says Dianne Glossman, an analyst with UBS Marburg. Although a recent change in federal law allows people to send their signatures electronically, "in most cases, you still need to sign paper documents, someone to visit the property and appraise it, and these loans still usually need to be closed in person."

Source: Excerpts from Aaron Elstein, "Mortgage.com Plans to Cease Its Lending and Pare Its Staff," *Wall Street Journal* (November 1, 2000). Reprinted by permission of the Wall Street Journal. © 2000 Dow Jones & Co, Inc. All Rights Reserved Worldwide.

? What differentiates "notes payable" from "mortgage notes payable"?

STATEMENT PRESENTATION AND ANALYSIS

STUDY OBJECTIVE 8

Identify the methods for the presentation and analysis of long-term liabilities.

Presentation

Long-term liabilities are reported in a separate section of the balance sheet immediately following current liabilities, as shown in Illustration 11-20 on the next page.

Alternatively, summary data may be presented in the balance sheet with detailed data (interest rates, maturity dates, conversion privileges, and assets pledged as collateral) shown in a supporting schedule. The current maturities of long-term debt should be reported under current liabilities if they are to be paid from current assets.

LAX CORPORATION
Balance Sheet (partial)

Long-term liabilities		
Bonds payable, 10%, due in 2012	$1,000,000	
Less: Discount on bonds payable	80,000	$ 920,000
Mortgage notes payable, 11%, due in 2018 and secured by plant assets		500,000
Lease liability		540,000
Total long-term liabilities		$1,960,000

Illustration 11-20
Balance sheet presentation of long-term liabilities

Analysis

Long-term creditors and stockholders are interested in a company's long-run solvency. Of particular interest is the company's ability to pay interest as it comes due and to repay the face value of the debt at maturity. Debt to total assets and times interest earned are two ratios that provide information about debt-paying ability and long-run solvency.

The **debt to total assets ratio** measures the percentage of the total assets provided by creditors. It is computed, as shown in the formula below, by dividing total debt (both current and long-term liabilities) by total assets. The higher the percentage of debt to total assets, the greater the risk that the company may be unable to meet its maturing obligations.

The **times interest earned ratio** indicates the company's ability to meet interest payments as they come due. It is computed by dividing income before income taxes and interest expense by interest expense.

To illustrate these ratios, we will use data from **Johnson & Johnson**'s 2003 annual report. The company had total liabilities of $21,394 million, total assets of $48,263 million, interest expense of $207 million, income taxes of $3,111 million, and net income of $7,197 million. Johnson & Johnson's debt to total assets ratio and times interest earned ratio are shown below, along with their computations.

Total Debt	÷	**Total Assets**	=	**Debt to Total Assets**
$21,394	÷	$48,263	=	**44.3%**
Income before Income Taxes and Interest Expense	÷	**Interest Expense**	=	**Times Interest Earned**
$7,197 + $3,111 + $207	÷	$207	=	**50.8 times**

Illustration 11-21
Debt to total assets and times interest earned ratios, with computations

Johnson & Johnson has a relatively low debt to total assets percentage of 44.3%. Its interest coverage of 50.8 times appears extremely safe.

BEFORE YOU GO ON...

Review It

1. Explain the accounting for long-term mortgage notes payable.
2. Where are current maturities of long-term debt reported in the financial statements?
3. What ratios may be computed to analyze a company's long-run solvency?

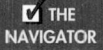

THE NAVIGATOR

DEMONSTRATION PROBLEM

Snyder Software Inc. has successfully developed a new spreadsheet program. To produce and market the program, the company needed $2.0 million of additional financing. On December 31, 2006, Snyder borrowed money as follows.

1. Snyder issued $500,000, 11%, 10-year convertible bonds. The bonds sold at face value and pay semiannual interest on January 1 and July 1. Each $1,000 bond is convertible into 30 shares of Snyder's $20 par value common stock.
2. Snyder issued $1.0 million, 10%, 10-year bonds at face value. Interest is payable semiannually on January 1 and July 1.
3. Snyder also issued a $500,000, 12%, 15-year mortgage note payable. The terms provide for semiannual installment payments of $36,324 on June 30 and December 31.

Instructions

1. For the convertible bonds, prepare journal entries for:
   - **(a)** The issuance of the bonds on January 1, 2007.
   - **(b)** Interest expense on July 1 and December 31, 2007.
   - **(c)** The payment of interest on January 1, 2008.
   - **(d)** The conversion of all bonds into common stock on January 1, 2008, when the market value of the common stock was $67 per share.
2. For the 10-year, 10% bonds:
   - **(a)** Journalize the issuance of the bonds on January 1, 2007.
   - **(b)** Prepare the journal entries for interest expense in 2007. Assume no accrual of interest on July 1.
   - **(c)** Prepare the entry for the redemption of the bonds at 101 on January 1, 2010, after paying the interest due on this date.
3. For the mortgage note payable:
   - **(a)** Prepare the entry for the issuance of the note on December 31, 2006.
   - **(b)** Prepare a payment schedule for the first four installment payments.
   - **(c)** Indicate the current and noncurrent amounts for the mortgage note payable at December 31, 2007.

SOLUTION TO DEMONSTRATION PROBLEM

ACTION PLAN

- Compute interest semiannually (6 months).
- Record the accrual and payment of interest on appropriate dates.
- Record the conversion of the bonds into common stock by removing the book (carrying) value of the bonds from the liability account.

1. (a)

2007			
Jan. 1	Cash	500,000	
	Bonds Payable		500,000
	(To record issue of 11%, 10-year convertible bonds at face value)		

(b)

2007			
July 1	Bond Interest Expense	27,500	
	Cash ($500,000 × 0.055)		27,500
	(To record payment of semiannual interest)		
Dec. 31	Bond Interest Expense	27,500	
	Bond Interest Payable		27,500
	(To record accrual of semiannual bond interest)		

(c) 2008			
Jan. 1	Bond Interest Payable	27,500	
	Cash		27,500
	(To record payment of accrued interest)		
(d) Jan. 1	Bonds Payable	500,000	
	Common Stock		300,000*
	Paid-in Capital in Excess of Par Value		200,000
	(To record conversion of bonds into common stock)		
	*($500,000 ÷ $1,000 = 500 bonds; 500 × 30 = 15,000 shares; 15,000 × $20 = $300,000)		

2. (a) 2007			
Jan. 1	Cash	1,000,000	
	Bonds Payable		1,000,000
	(To record issuance of bonds)		
(b) 2007			
July 1	Bond Interest Expense	50,000	
	Cash		50,000
	(To record payment of semiannual interest)		
Dec. 31	Bond Interest Expense	50,000	
	Bond Interest Payable		50,000
	(To record accrual of semiannual interest)		
(c) 2010			
Jan. 1	Bonds Payable	1,000,000	
	Loss on Bond Redemption	10,000*	
	Cash		1,010,000
	(To record redemption of bonds at 101)		
	*($1,010,000 − $1,000,000)		

ACTION PLAN

- Record the issuance of the bonds
- Compute interest expense for each period.
- Compute the loss on bond redemption as the excess of the cash paid over the carrying value of the redeemed bonds.

3. (a) 2006			
Dec. 31	Cash	500,000	
	Mortgage Notes Payable		500,000
	(To record issuance of mortgage note payable)		

(b) Semiannual

Interest Period	Cash Payment	Interest Expense	Reduction of Principal	Principal Balance
Issue date				$500,000
1	$36,324	$30,000	$6,324	493,676
2	36,324	29,621	6,703	486,973
3	36,324	29,218	7,106	479,867
4	36,324	28,792	7,532	472,335

(c) Current liability $14,638 ($7,106 + $7,532)
Long-term liability $472,335

THE NAVIGATOR

ACTION PLAN

- Compute periodic interest expense on a mortgage note, recognizing that as the principal amount decreases, so does the interest expense.
- Record mortgage payments, recognizing that each payment consists of (1) interest on the unpaid loan balance and (2) a reduction of the loan principal.

SUMMARY OF STUDY OBJECTIVES

1. **Explain a current liability, and identify the major types of current liabilities.** A current liability is a debt that can reasonably be expected to be paid (1) from existing current assets or through the creation of other current liabilities, and (2) within one year or the operating cycle, whichever is longer. The major types of current liabilities are notes payable, accounts payable, sales taxes payable, unearned revenues, and accrued liabilities such as taxes, salaries and wages, and interest payable.
2. **Describe the accounting for notes payable.** When a promissory note is interest-bearing, the amount of assets received upon the issuance of the note is generally equal to the face value of the note. Interest expense is accrued over the life of the note. At maturity, the amount paid is equal to the face value of the note plus accrued interest.
3. **Explain the accounting for other current liabilities.** Sales taxes payable are recorded at the time the related sales occur. The company serves as a collection agent for the taxing authority. Sales taxes are not an expense to the company. Until employee withholding taxes are remitted to governmental taxing authorities, they are credited to appropriate liability accounts. Unearned revenues are initially recorded in an unearned revenue account. As the revenue is earned, a transfer from unearned revenue to earned revenue occurs. The current maturities of long-term debt should be reported as a current liability in the balance sheet.
4. **Explain why bonds are issued, and identify the types of bonds.** Bonds may be sold to many investors, and they offer the following advantages over common stock: (a) stockholder control is not affected, (b) tax savings result, and (c) earnings per share of common stock may be higher. The following different types of bonds may be issued: secured and unsecured bonds, term and serial bonds, registered and bearer bonds, convertible and callable bonds.
5. **Prepare the entries for the issuance of bonds and interest expense.** When bonds are issued, Cash is debited for the cash proceeds, and Bonds Payable is credited for the face value of the bonds. The account Premium on Bonds Payable is used to show a bond premium; Discount on Bonds Payable is used to show a bond discount.
6. **Describe the entries when bonds are redeemed or converted.** When bonds are redeemed at maturity, Cash is credited and Bonds Payable is debited for the face value of the bonds. When bonds are redeemed before maturity, it is necessary to (a) eliminate the carrying value of the bonds at the redemption date, (b) record the cash paid, and (c) recognize the gain or loss on redemption. When bonds are converted to common stock, the carrying (or book) value of the bonds is transferred to appropriate paid-in capital accounts; no gain or loss is recognized.
7. **Describe the accounting for long-term notes payable.** Each payment consists of (1) interest on the unpaid balance of the loan and (2) a reduction of loan principal. The interest decreases each period, while the portion applied to the loan principal increases.
8. **Identify the methods for the presentation and analysis of long-term liabilities.** The nature and amount of each long-term debt should be reported in the balance sheet or in the notes accompanying the financial statements. Stockholders and long-term creditors are interested in a company's long-run solvency. Debt to total assets and times interest earned are two ratios that provide information about debt-paying ability and long-run solvency.

THE NAVIGATOR

GLOSSARY

www.wiley.com/college/weygandt

Bearer (coupon) bonds Bonds not registered. (p. 479).

Bond certificate A legal document that indicates the name of the issuer, the face value of the bonds, and such other data as the contractual interest rate and maturity date of the bonds. (p. 479).

Bond discount The amount by which a bond sells at less than its face value. (p. 482).

Bond indenture A legal document that sets forth the terms of the bond issue. (p. 479).

Bond premium The amount by which a bond sells above its face value. (p. 483).

Bonds A form of interest-bearing notes payable issued by corporations, universities, and governmental entities. (p. 477).

Callable bonds Bonds that are subject to retirement at a stated dollar amount prior to maturity at the option of the issuer. (p. 479).

Contractual interest rate Rate used to determine the amount of interest the borrower pays and the investor receives. (p. 479).

Convertible bonds Bonds that permit bondholders to convert them into common stock at their option. (p. 479).

Current ratio A measure of a company's liquidity; computed as current assets divided by current liabilities. (p. 476).

Debenture bonds Bonds issued against the general credit of the borrower. Also called unsecured bonds. (p. 479).

Debt to total assets ratio A solvency measure that indicates the percentage of total assets provided by creditors; computed as total debt divided by total assets. (p. 489).

Face value Amount of principal the issuer must pay at the maturity date of the bond. (p. 479).

Long-term liabilities Obligations expected to be paid after one year. (p. 477).

Market interest rate The rate investors demand for loaning funds to the corporation. (p. 481).

Mortgage bond A bond secured by real estate. (p. 479).

Mortgage note payable A long-term note secured by a mortgage that pledges title to specific assets as security for a loan. (p. 487).

Notes payable Obligations in the form of written promissory notes. (p. 470).

Registered bonds Bonds issued in the name of the owner. (p. 479).

Secured bonds Bonds that have specific assets of the issuer pledged as collateral. (p. 479).

Serial bonds Bonds that mature in installments. (p. 479).

Sinking fund bonds Bonds secured by specific assets set aside to retire them. (p. 479).

Term bonds Bonds that mature at a single specified future date. (p. 479).

Times interest earned ratio A solvency measure that indicates a company's ability to meet interest payments; computed by dividing income before income taxes and interest expense by interest expense. (p. 489).

Unsecured bonds Bonds issued against the general credit of the borrower. Also called debenture bonds. (p. 479).

Working capital A measure of a company's liquidity; computed as current assets minus current liabilities. (p. 475).

Appendix 11A Present Value Concepts Related to Bond Pricing

Congratulations! You have a winning lottery ticket and the state has provided you with three possible options for payment. They are:

1. Receive $10,000,000 in 3 years.
2. Receive $7,000,000 immediately.
3. Receive $3,500,000 at the end of each year for 3 years.

Which of these options would you select? The answer is not easy to determine at a glance. To make a dollar-maximizing choice, you must perform present value computations. A present value computation is based on the concept of time value of money. Time value of money concepts are useful for the lottery situation and for pricing other amounts to be received in the future. This appendix discusses how present value concepts are used to price bonds. It also will tell you how to determine what option you should take as a lottery winner.

Present Value of Face Value

STUDY OBJECTIVE 9

Compute the market price of a bond.

To illustrate present value concepts, assume that you are willing to invest a sum of money that will yield $1,000 at the end of one year. In other words, what amount would you need to invest today to have $1,000 one year from now? If you want to earn 10%, the investment or present value is $909.09 ($1,000 ÷ 1.10). The computation of this amount is shown in Illustration 11A-1.

Present value	×	(1 + Interest rate)	=	Future amount
Present value	×	(1 + 10%)	=	$1,000
Present value			=	$1,000 ÷ 1.10
Present value			=	**$909.09**

Illustration 11A-1
Present value computation—$1,000 discounted at 10% for 1 year

The future amount ($1,000), the interest rate (10%), and the number of periods (1) are known. The variables in this situation can be depicted in the time diagram in Illustration 11A-2 on the next page.

Illustration 11A-2
Finding present value if discounted for one period

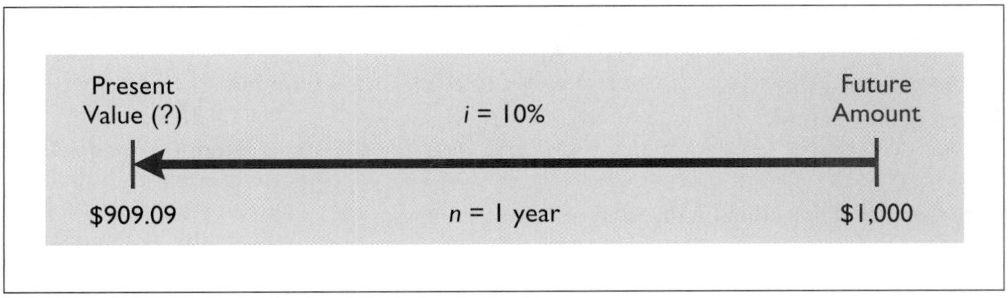

If the single future amount of $1,000 is to be received **in 2 years** and discounted at 10%, its present value is $826.45 [($1,000 ÷ 1.10) ÷ 1.10], depicted as follows.

Illustration 11A-3
Finding present value if discounted for two periods

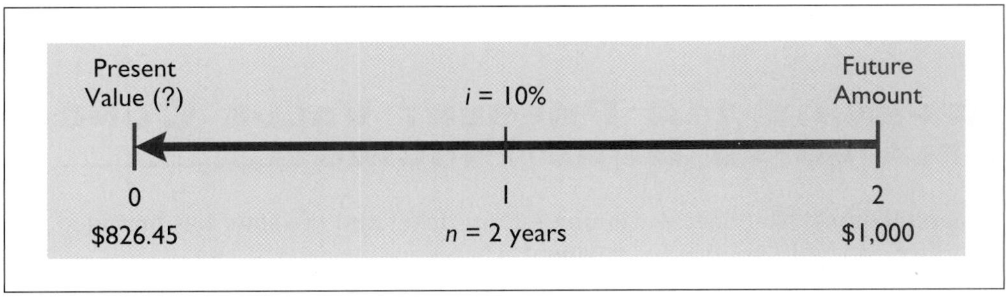

The present value of 1 may also be determined through tables that show the present value of 1 for *n* periods. In Table 11A-1 below, *n* is the number of discounting periods involved. The percentages are the periodic interest rates, and the 5-digit decimal numbers in the respective columns are the factors for the present value of 1.

When Table 11A-1 is used, the future amount is multiplied by the present value factor specified at the intersection of the number of periods and the interest rate. For example, the present value factor for 1 period at an interest rate of 10% is .90909, which equals the $909.09 ($1,000 × .90909) computed in Illustration 11A-1.

TABLE 11A-1
Present Value of 1

(*n*) Periods	4%	5%	6%	8%	9%	10%	11%	12%	15%
1	.96154	.95238	.94340	.92593	.91743	.90909	.90090	.89286	.86957
2	.92456	.90703	.89000	.85734	.84168	.82645	.81162	.79719	.75614
3	.88900	.86384	.83962	.79383	.77218	.75132	.73119	.71178	.65752
4	.85480	.82270	.79209	.73503	.70843	.68301	.65873	.63552	.57175
5	.82193	.78353	.74726	.68058	.64993	.62092	.59345	.56743	.49718
6	.79031	.74622	.70496	.63017	.59627	.56447	.53464	.50663	.43233
7	.75992	.71068	.66506	.58349	.54703	.51316	.48166	.45235	.37594
8	.73069	.67684	.62741	.54027	.50187	.46651	.43393	.40388	.32690
9	.70259	.64461	.59190	.50025	.46043	.42410	.39092	.36061	.28426
10	.67556	.61391	.55839	.46319	.42241	.38554	.35218	.32197	.24719

For 2 periods at an interest rate of 10%, the present value factor is .82645, which equals the $826.45 ($1,000 × .82645) computed previously.

Let's go back to our lottery example now. Given the present value concepts just learned, we can determine whether receiving $10,000,000 in 3 years is better than receiving $7,000,000 today, assuming the appropriate discount rate is 9%. The computation is as follows.

$10,000,000 × PV of 1 due in 3 years at 9% =	
$10,000,000 × .77218 (Table 11A-1)	$7,721,800
Amount to be received from state immediately	7,000,000
Difference	**$ 721,800**

Illustration 11A-4
Present value of $10,000,000 to be received in 3 years

What this computation shows you is that you would be better off receiving the $10,000,000 at the end of 3 years rather than taking $7,000,000 immediately.

Present Value of Interest Payments (Annuities)

In addition to receiving the face value of a bond at maturity, an investor also receives periodic interest payments over the life of the bonds. These periodic payments are called **annuities**.

In order to compute the present value of an annuity, it is necessary to know (1) the interest rate, (2) the number of interest periods, and (3) the amount of the periodic receipts or payments. To illustrate the computation of the present value of an annuity, assume that you will receive $1,000 cash annually for 3 years and the interest rate is 10%. This situation is depicted in the following time diagram.

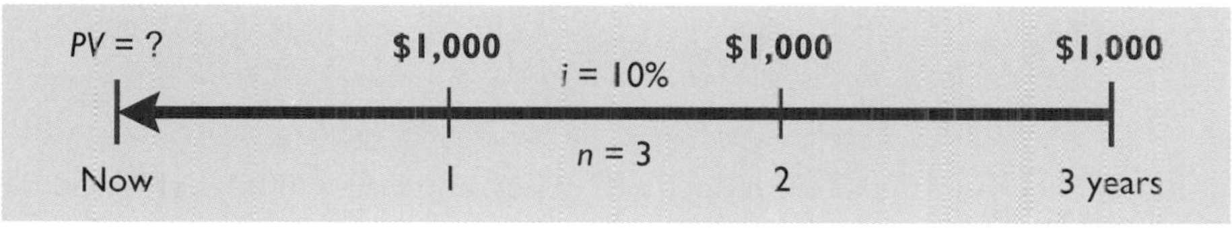

Illustration 11A-5
Time diagram for a 3-year annuity

The present value in this situation may be computed as follows.

Future Amount	×	Present Value of 1 Factor at 10%	=	Present Value
$1,000 (1 year away)		.90909		$ 909.09
1,000 (2 years away)		.82645		826.45
1,000 (3 years away)		.75132		751.32
		2.48686		**$2,486.86**

Illustration 11A-6
Present value of a series of future amounts computation

Annuity tables may also be used to value annuities. As illustrated in Table 11A-2 on following page, these tables show the present value of 1 to be received periodically for a given number of periods.

TABLE 11A-2
Present Value of an Annuity of 1

(*n*) Periods	4%	5%	6%	8%	9%	10%	11%	12%	15%
1	.96154	.95238	.94340	.92593	.91743	.90909	.90090	.89286	.86957
2	1.88609	1.85941	1.83339	1.78326	1.75911	1.73554	1.71252	1.69005	1.62571
3	2.77509	2.72325	2.67301	2.57710	2.53130	2.48685	2.44371	2.40183	2.28323
4	3.62990	3.54595	3.46511	3.31213	3.23972	3.16986	3.10245	3.03735	2.85498
5	4.45182	4.32948	4.21236	3.99271	3.88965	3.79079	3.69590	3.60478	3.35216
6	5.24214	5.07569	4.91732	4.62288	4.48592	4.35526	4.23054	4.11141	3.78448
7	6.00205	5.78637	5.58238	5.20637	5.03295	4.86842	4.71220	4.56376	4.16042
8	6.73274	6.46321	6.20979	5.74664	5.53482	5.33493	5.14612	4.96764	4.48732
9	7.43533	7.10782	6.80169	6.24689	5.99525	5.75902	5.53705	5.32825	4.77158
10	8.11090	7.72173	7.36009	6.71008	6.41766	6.14457	5.88923	5.65022	5.01877

From Table 11A-2 you can see that the present value factor of an annuity of 1 for 3 periods at 10% is 2.48685.[2] This present value factor is the total of the three individual present value factors as shown in Illustration 11A-6. Applying this amount to the annual cash flow of $1,000 produces a present value of $2,486.85.

Let's now go back to our lottery example. We determined that you would get more money if you wait and take the $10,000,000 in 3 years rather than take $7,000,000 immediately. But there is still another option—to receive $3,500,000 at the end of **each year** for 3 years (an annuity). The computation to evaluate this option (again assuming a 9% discount rate) is as follows.

Illustration 11A-7
Present value of lottery payments to be received over three years

$3,500,000 × PV of 1 due yearly for 3 years at 9% =	
$3,500,000 × 2.53130 (Table 11A-2)	$8,859,550
Present value of $10,000,000 to be received in 3 years	7,721,800
Difference	**$1,137,750**

Take the annuity of $3,500,000 for each of 3 years, and you will be $1,137,750 richer as a result.

Time Periods and Discounting

We have used an annual interest rate to determine present value. Present value computations may also be done over shorter periods of time, such as monthly, quarterly, or semiannually. When the time frame is less than one year, it is necessary to convert the annual interest rate to the shorter time frame. Assume, for example, that the investor in Illustration 11A-6 received $500 **semiannually** for 3 years instead of $1,000 annually. In this case, the number of periods becomes 6 (3 × 2), the interest rate is 5% (10% ÷ 2), the present value factor from Table 11A-2 is 5.07569, and the present value of the future cash flows is $2,537.85 (5.07569 × $500). This amount is slightly higher than the $2,486.86 computed in Illustration 11A-6 because interest is computed twice during the same year. That is, interest is earned on the first half year's interest.

[2]The difference of .00001 between 2.48686 and 2.48685 is due to rounding.

Computing the Present Value of a Bond

The present value (or market price) of a bond is a function of three variables: (1) the payment amounts, (2) the length of time until the amounts are paid, and (3) the interest (discount) rate.

The first variable (dollars to be paid) is made up of two elements: (1) a series of interest payments (an annuity) and (2) the principal amount (a single sum). To compute the present value of the bond, both the interest payments and the principal amount must be discounted.

When the investor's interest (discount) rate is equal to the bond's contractual interest rate, the present value of the bonds will equal the face value of the bonds. To illustrate, assume a bond issue of 10%, 5-year bonds with a face value of $100,000 with interest payable **semiannually** on January 1 and July 1. If the discount rate is the same as the contractual rate, the bonds will sell **at face value**. In this case, the investor will receive (1) $100,000 at maturity and (2) a series of ten $5,000 interest payments [($100,000 × 10%) ÷ 2] over the term of the bonds. The length of time is expressed in terms of interest periods (in this case, 10) and the discount rate per interest period (5%). The following time diagram (Illustration 11A-8) depicts the variables involved in this discounting situation.

Illustration 11A-8
Time diagram for the present value of a 10%, 5-year bond paying interest semiannually

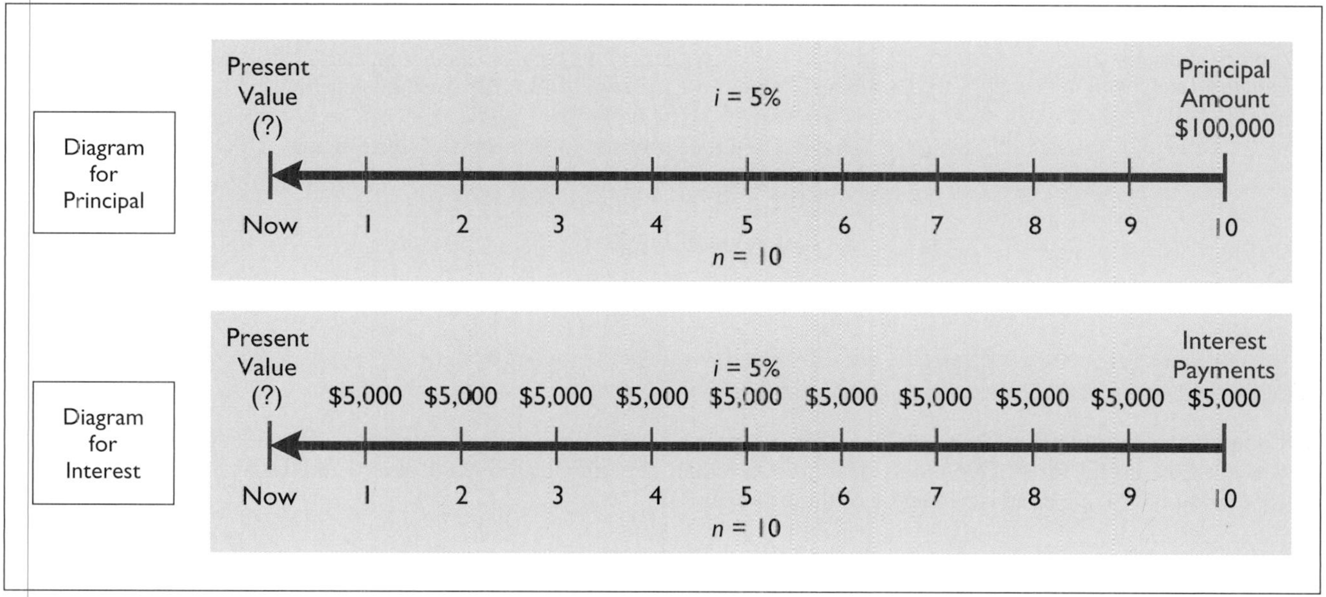

The computation of the present value of Candlestick's bonds, had they been issued at face value (pages 482–483), is shown below.

Illustration 11A-9
Present value of principal and interest (face value)

10% Contractual Rate—10% Discount Rate	
Present value of principal to be received at maturity	
$100,000 × PV of 1 due in 10 periods at 5%	
$100,000 × .61391 (Table 11A-1)	$61,391
Present value of interest to be received periodically over the term of the bonds	
$5,000 × PV of 1 due periodically for 10 periods at 5%	
$5,000 × 7.72173 (Table 11A-2)	38,609*
Present value of bonds	**$100,000**

*(Rounded).

Now assume that the investor's required rate of return is 12%, not 10%. The future amounts are again $100,000 and $5,000, respectively. But now a discount rate of 6% (12% ÷ 2) must be used. The present value of Candlestick's bonds issued at a discount (page 483) is $92,639 as computed below.

Illustration 11A-10
Present value of principal and interest (discount)

10% Contractual Rate—12% Discount Rate	
Present value of principal to be received at maturity	
$100,000 × .55839 (Table 11A-1)	$55,839
Present value of interest to be received periodically over the term of the bonds	
$5,000 × 7.36009 (Table 11A-2)	36,800
Present value of bonds	**$92,639**

If the discount rate is 8% and the contractual rate is 10%, the present value of Candlestick's bonds issued at a premium (pages 483–484) is $108,111, computed as follows.

Illustration 11A-11
Present value of principal and interest (premium)

10% Contractual Rate—8% Discount Rate	
Present value of principal to be received at maturity	
$100,000 × .67556 (Table 11A-1)	$67,556
Present value of interest to be received periodically over the term of the bonds	
$5,000 × 8.11090 (Table 11A-2)	40.555
Present value of bonds	**$108,111**

SUMMARY OF STUDY OBJECTIVE FOR APPENDIX 11A

9. **Compute the market price of a bond.** Time value of money concepts are useful for pricing bonds. The present value (or market price) of a bond is a function of three variables: (1) the payment amounts, (2) the length of time until the amounts are paid, and (3) the interest rate.

APPENDIX 11B EFFECTIVE-INTEREST AMORTIZATION

STUDY OBJECTIVE 10

Apply the effective-interest method of amortizing bond discount and bond premium.

Under the **effective-interest method**, the amortization of bond discount or bond premium results in periodic interest expense equal to a constant percentage of the carrying value of the bonds. The effective-interest method results in varying amounts of amortization and interest expense per period but **a constant percentage rate**.

The following steps are required under the effective-interest method.

1. Compute the **bond interest expense**. To do so, multiply the carrying value of the bonds at the beginning of the interest period by the effective-interest rate.
2. Compute the **bond interest paid** (or accrued). To do so, multiply the face value of the bonds by the contractual interest rate.
3. Compute the **amortization amount**. To do so, determine the difference between the amounts computed in steps (1) and (2).

These steps are depicted in Illustration 11B-1 on the next page.

Illustration 11B-1
Computation of amortization—effective-interest method

(1) Bond Interest Expense		(2) Bond Interest Paid		(3)
(Carrying Value of Bonds at Beginning of Period × Effective Interest Rate)	−	(Face Amount of Bonds × Contractual Interest Rate)	=	Amortization Amount

When the difference between the straight-line method of amortization (Appendix 11C) and the effective-interest method is material, the use of the effective-interest method is required under generally accepted accounting principles.

Amortizing Bond Discount

To illustrate the effective-interest method of bond discount amortization, assume that Candlestick, Inc. (as per this chapter pages 483–484) issues $100,000 of 10%, 5-year bonds on January 1, 2006, with interest payable each July 1 and January 1. The bonds sell for $92,639 (92.639% of face value). This sales price results in bond discount of $7,361 ($100,000 − $92,639) and an effective-interest rate of 12%. A bond discount amortization schedule as shown in Illustration 11B-2 facilitates the recording of interest expense and the discount amortization. Note that interest expense as a percentage of carrying value remains constant at 6%.

Illustration 11B-2
Bond discount amortization schedule

CANDLESTICK, INC.
Bond Discount Amortization
Effective-Interest Method—Semiannual Interest Payments
10% Bonds Issued at 12%

Semiannual Interest Periods	(A) Interest to Be Paid (5% × $100,000)	(B) Interest Expense to Be Recorded (6% × Preceding Bond Carrying Value)	(C) Discount Amortization (B) − (A)	(D) Unamortized Discount (D) − (C)	(E) Bond Carrying Value ($100,000 − D)
Issue date				$7,361	$ 92,639
1	**$ 5,000**	**$5,558 (6% × $92,639)**	**$ 558**	**6,803**	**93,197**
2	5,000	5,592 (6% × $93,197)	592	6,211	93,789
3	5,000	5,627 (6% × $93,789)	627	5,584	94,416
4	5,000	5,665 (6% × $94,416)	665	4,919	95,081
5	5,000	5,705 (6% × $95,081)	705	4,214	95,786
6	5,000	5,747 (6% × $95,786)	747	3,467	96,533
7	5,000	5,792 (6% × $96,533)	792	2,675	97,325
8	5,000	5,840 (6% × $97,325)	840	1,835	98,165
9	5,000	5,890 (6% × $98,165)	890	945	99,055
10	5,000	5,945* (6% × $99,055)	945	-0-	100,000
	$50,000	$57,361	$7,361		

Column **(A)** remains constant because the face value of the bonds ($100,000) is multiplied by the semiannual contractual interest rate (5%) each period.
Column **(B)** is computed as the preceding bond carrying value times the semiannual effective-interest rate (6%).
Column **(C)** indicates the discount amortization each period.
Column **(D)** decreases each period until it reaches zero at maturity.
Column **(E)** increases each period until it equals face value at maturity.

*$2 difference due to rounding.

We have highlighted columns (A), (B), and (C) in the amortization schedule to emphasize their importance. These three columns provide the numbers for each period's journal entries. They are the primary reason for preparing the schedule.

For the first interest period, the computations of bond interest expense and the bond discount amortization are:

Illustration 11B-3
Computation of bond discount amortization

Bond interest expense ($92,639 × 6%)	$5,558
Contractual interest ($100,000 × 5%)	5,000
Bond discount amortization	**$ 558**

The entry to record the payment of interest and amortization of bond discount by Candlestick, Inc. on July 1, 2006, is:

A	=	L	+	SE
−5,000		+558		−5,558 Exp

Cash Flows
−5,000

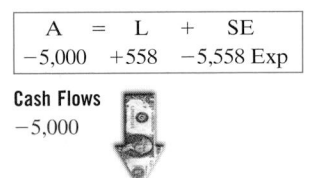

July 1	Bond Interest Expense	5,558	
	Discount on Bonds Payable		558
	Cash		5,000
	(To record payment of bond interest and amortization of bond discount)		

For the second interest period, bond interest expense will be $5,592 ($93,197 × 6%), and the discount amortization will be $592. At December 31, the following adjusting entry is made.

A	=	L	+	SE
		+592		−5,592 Exp
		+5,000		

Cash Flows
no effect

Dec. 31	Bond Interest Expense	5,592	
	Discount on Bonds Payable		592
	Bond Interest Payable		5,000
	(To record accrued interest and amortization of bond discount)		

Total bond interest expense for 2006 is $11,150 ($5,558 + $5,592). On January 1, payment of the interest is recorded by a debit to Bond Interest Payable and a credit to Cash.

Amortizing Bond Premium

HELPFUL HINT

When a bond sells for $108,111, it is quoted as 108.111% of face value. Note that $108,111 can be proven as shown in Appendix 11A.

The amortization of bond premium by the effective-interest method is similar to the procedures described for bond discount. For example, assume that Candlestick, Inc. issues $100,000, 10%, 5-year bonds on January 1, 2006, with interest payable on July 1 and January 1. In this case, the bonds sell for $108,111. This sales price results in bond premium of $8,111 and an effective-interest rate of 8%. The bond premium amortization schedule is shown in Illustration 11B-4 on the next page.

Illustration 11B-4
Bond premium amortization schedule

CANDLESTICK, INC.
Bond Premium Amortization
Effective-Interest Method—Semiannual Interest Payments
10% Bonds Issued at 8%

Semiannual Interest Periods	(A) Interest to Be Paid (5% × $100,000)	(B) Interest Expense to Be Recorded (4% × Preceding Bond Carrying Value)	(C) Premium Amortization (A) − (B)	(D) Unamortized Premium (D) − (C)	(E) Bond Carrying Value ($100,000 + D)
Issue date				$8,111	$108,111
1	**$ 5,000**	**$ 4,324 (4% × $108,111)**	**$ 676**	**7,435**	**107,435**
2	5,000	4,297 (4% × $107,435)	703	6,732	106,732
3	5,000	4,269 (4% × $106,732)	731	6,001	106,001
4	5,000	4,240 (4% × $106,001)	760	5,241	105,241
5	5,000	4,210 (4% × $105,241)	790	4,451	104,451
6	5,000	4,178 (4% × $104,451)	822	3,629	103,629
7	5,000	4,145 (4% × $103,629)	855	2,774	102,774
8	5,000	4,111 (4% × $102,774)	889	1,885	101,885
9	5,000	4,075 (4% × $101,885)	925	960	100,960
10	5,000	4,040* (4% × $100,960)	960	-0-	100,000
	$50,000	$41,889	$8,111		

Column **(A)** remains constant because the face value of the bonds ($100,000) is multiplied by the semiannual contractual interest rate (5%) each period.
Column **(B)** is computed as the carrying value of the bonds times the semiannual effective-interest rate (4%).
Column **(C)** indicates the premium amortization each period.
Column **(D)** decreases each period until it reaches zero at maturity.
Column **(E)** decreases each period until it equals face value at maturity.

*$2 difference due to rounding.

For the first interest period, the computations of bond interest expense and the bond premium amortization are:

Illustration 11B-5
Computation of bond premium amortization

Bond interest expense ($108,111 × 4%)	$4,324
Contractual interest ($100,000 × 5%)	5,000
Bond premium amortization	**$ 676**

The entry on the first interest date is:

July 1	Bond Interest Expense	4,324	
	Premium on Bonds Payable	676	
	Cash		5,000
	(To record payment of bond interest and amortization of bond premium)		

A	=	L	+	SE
−5,000		−676		−4,324 Exp

Cash Flows
−5,000

For the second interest period, interest expense will be $4,297, and the premium amortization will be $703. Total bond interest expense for 2006 is $8,621 ($4,324 + $4,297).

DEMONSTRATION PROBLEM FOR APPENDIX 11B

Gardner Corporation issues $1,750,000, 10-year, 12% bonds on January 1, 2006, at $1,820,000 to yield 10%. The bonds pay semiannual interest July 1 and January 1. Gardner uses the effective-interest method of amortization.

Instructions

(a) Prepare the journal entry to record the issuance of the bonds.
(b) Prepare the journal entry to record the payment of interest on July 1, 2006.

ACTION PLAN

- Compute interest expense by multiplying bond carrying value at the beginning of the period by the effective-interest rate.
- Compute credit to cash (or bond interest payable) by multiplying the face value of the bonds by the contractual interest rate.
- Compute bond premium or discount amortization, which is the difference between (1) and (2).
- Interest expense increases when the effective-interest method is used for bonds issued at a discount. The reason is that a constant percentage is applied to an increasing book value to compute interest expense.

SOLUTION TO DEMONSTRATION PROBLEM

(a) 2006

Jan. 1	Cash	1,820,000	
	Bonds Payable		1,750,000
	Premium on Bonds Payable		70,000
	(To record issuance of bonds at a premium)		

(b) 2006

July 1	Bond Interest Expense	91,000*	
	Premium on Bonds Payable	14,000**	
	Cash		105,000
	(To record payment of semiannual interest and amortization of bond premium)		
	*($1,820,000 × 5%)		
	**($105,000 − $91,000)		

THE NAVIGATOR

SUMMARY OF STUDY OBJECTIVE FOR APPENDIX 11B

10. **Apply the effective-interest method of amortizing bond discount and bond premium.** The effective-interest method results in varying amounts of amortization and interest expense per period but a constant percentage rate of interest. When the difference between the straight-line and effective-interest method is material, the use of the effective-interest method is required under GAAP.

GLOSSARY FOR APPENDIX 11B

Effective-interest method of amortization A method of amortizing bond discount or bond premium that results in periodic interest expense equal to a constant percentage of the carrying value of the bonds. (p. 498).

APPENDIX 11C STRAIGHT-LINE AMORTIZATION

Amortizing Bond Discount

STUDY OBJECTIVE 11

Apply the straight-line method of amortizing bond discount and bond premium.

To follow the matching principle, bond discount should be allocated systematically to each period in which the bonds are outstanding. The **straight-line method of amortization** allocates the same amount to interest expense in each interest period. The amount is determined using the formula in Illustration 11C-1.

Illustration 11C-1
Formula for straight-line method of bond discount amortization

$$\text{Bond Discount} \div \text{Number of Interest Periods} = \text{Bond Discount Amortization}$$

In the Candlestick, Inc. example (page 483), the company sold $100,000, 5-year, 10% bonds on January 1, 2006, for $92,639. This price resulted in a $7,361 bond discount ($100,000 − $92,639). Interest is payable on July 1 and January 1. The bond discount amortization for each interest period is $736 ($7,361 ÷ 10). The entry to record the payment of bond interest and the amortization of bond discount on the first interest date (July 1, 2006) is:

July 1	Bond Interest Expense	5,736	
	Discount on Bonds Payable		736
	Cash		5,000
	(To record payment of bond interest and amortization of bond discount)		

A	=	L	+	SE
−5,000		+736		−5,736 Exp

Cash Flows
−5,000

At December 31, the adjusting entry is:

Dec. 31	Bond Interest Expense	5,736	
	Discount on Bonds Payable		736
	Bond Interest Payable		5,000
	(To record accrued bond interest and amortization of bond discount)		

A	=	L	+	SE
		+736		−5,736 Exp
		+5,000		

Cash Flows
no effect

ALTERNATIVE TERMINOLOGY

The amount in the Discount on Bonds Payable account is often referred to as *Unamortized Discount on Bonds Payable.*

Over the term of the bonds, the balance in Discount on Bonds Payable will decrease annually by the same amount until it has a zero balance at the maturity date of the bonds. Thus, the carrying value of the bonds at maturity will be equal to the face value.

Preparing a bond discount amortization schedule as shown in Illustration 11C-2 is useful. The schedule shows interest expense, discount amortization, and the carrying value of the bond for each interest period. As indicated, the interest expense recorded each period for the Candlestick bond is $5,736. Also note that the carrying value of the bond increases $736 each period until it reaches its face value $100,000 at the end of period 10.

Illustration 11C-2
Bond discount amortization schedule

CANDLESTICK, INC.
Bond Discount Amortization
Straight-Line Method—Semiannual Interest Payments

Semiannual Interest Periods	(A) Interest to Be Paid (5% × $100,000)	(B) Interest Expense to Be Recorded (A) + (C)	(C) Discount Amortization ($7,361 ÷ 10)	(D) Unamortized Discount (D) − (C)	(E) Bond Carrying Value ($100,000 − D)
Issue date				$7,361	$92,639
1	$ 5,000	$ 5,736	$ 736	6,625	93,375
2	5,000	5,736	736	5,889	94,111
3	5,000	5,736	736	5,153	94,847
4	5,000	5,736	736	4,417	95,583
5	5,000	5,736	736	3,681	96,319
6	5,000	5,736	736	2,945	97,055
7	5,000	5,736	736	2,209	97,791
8	5,000	5,736	736	1,473	98,527
9	5,000	5,736	736	737	99,263
10	5,000	5,737*	737*	-0-	100,000
	$50,000	$57,361	$7,361		

Column **(A)** remains constant because the face value of the bonds ($100,000) is multiplied by the semiannual contractual interest rate (5%) each period.
Column **(B)** is computed as the interest paid (Column A) plus the discount amortization (Column C).
Column **(C)** indicates the discount amortization each period.
Column **(D)** decreases each period by the same amount until it reaches zero at maturity.
Column **(E)** increases each period by the amount of discount amortization until it equals the face value at maturity.

*One dollar difference due to rounding.

We have highlighted columns (A), (B), and (C) in the amortization schedule to emphasize their importance. These three columns provide the numbers for each period's journal entries. They are the primary reason for preparing the schedule. Column (A) provides the amount of the credit to Cash. Column (B) shows the debit to Bond Interest Expense. And column (C) is the credit to Discount on Bonds Payable.

Amortizing Bond Premium

The amortization of bond premium parallels that of bond discount. The formula for determining bond premium amortization under the straight-line method is presented in Illustration 11C-3.

Illustration 11C-3
Formula for straight-line method of bond premium amortization

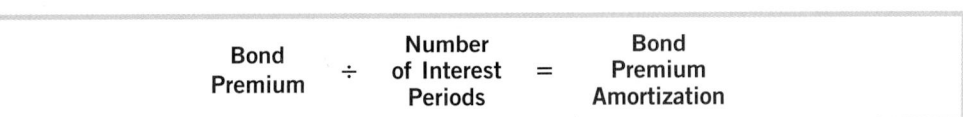

Bond Premium ÷ **Number of Interest Periods** = **Bond Premium Amortization**

Continuing our example of Candlestick, Inc., assume the bonds described above are sold for \$108,111, rather than \$92,639. This sale price results in a bond premium of \$8,111 (\$108,111 − \$100,000). The bond premium amortization for each interest period is \$811 (\$8,111 ÷ 10). The entry to record the first payment of interest on July 1 is:

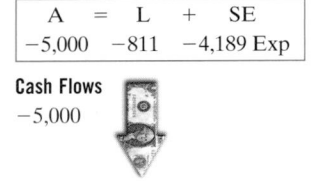

A	=	L	+	SE
−5,000		−811		−4,189 Exp

Cash Flows
−5,000

July 1	Bond Interest Expense	4,189	
	Premium on Bonds Payable	811	
	Cash		5,000
	(To record payment of bond interest and amortization of bond premium)		

At December 31, the adjusting entry is:

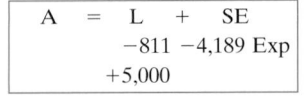

A	=	L	+	SE
		−811		−4,189 Exp
		+5,000		

Cash Flows
no effect

Dec. 31	Bond Interest Expense	4,189	
	Premium on Bonds Payable	811	
	Bond Interest Payable		5,000
	(To record accrued bond interest and amortization of bond premium)		

Over the term of the bonds, the balance in Premium on Bonds Payable will decrease annually by the same amount until it has a zero balance at maturity.

Preparing a bond premium amortization schedule as shown in Illustration 11C-4 (next page) is useful. It shows interest expense, premium amortization, and the carrying value of the bond. The interest expense recorded each period for the Candlestick bond is \$4,189. Also note that the carrying value of the bond decreases \$811 each period until it reaches its face value \$100,000 at the end of period 10.

Illustration 11C-4
Bond premium amortization schedule

CANDLESTICK, INC.
Bond Premium Amortization
Straight-Line Method—Semiannual Interest Payments

Semiannual Interest Periods	(A) Interest to Be Paid (5% × $100,000)	(B) Interest Expense to Be Recorded (A) − (C)	(C) Premium Amortization ($8,111 ÷ 10)	(D) Unamortized Premium (D) − (C)	(E) Bond Carrying Value ($100,000 + D)
Issue date				$8,111	$108,111
1	$ 5,000	$ 4,189	$ 811	7,300	107,300
2	5,000	4,189	811	6,489	106,489
3	5,000	4,189	811	5,678	105,678
4	5,000	4,189	811	4,867	104,867
5	5,000	4,189	811	4,056	104,056
6	5,000	4,189	811	3,245	103,245
7	5,000	4,189	811	2,434	102,434
8	5,000	4,189	811	1,623	101,623
9	5,000	4,189	811	812	100,812
10	5,000	4,188*	812*	-0-	100,000
	$50,000	$41,889	$8,111		

Column **(A)** remains constant because the face value of the bonds ($100,000) is multiplied by the semiannual contractual interest rate (5%) each period.
Column **(B)** is computed as the interest paid (Column A) less the premium amortization (Column C).
Column **(C)** indicates the premium amortization each period.
Column **(D)** decreases each period by the same amount until it reaches zero at maturity.
Column **(E)** decreases each period by the amount of premium amortization until it equals the face value at maturity.

*One dollar difference due to rounding.

DEMONSTRATION PROBLEM FOR APPENDIX 11C

Glenda Corporation issues $1,750,000, 10-year, 12% bonds on January 1, 2006, for $1,820,000 to yield 10%. The bonds pay semiannual interest July 1 and January 1. Glenda uses the straight-line method of amortization.

Instructions

(a) Prepare the journal entry to record the issuance of the bonds.
(b) Prepare the journal entry to record the payment of interest on July 1, 2006.

ACTION PLAN

- Compute credit to cash (or bond interest payable) by multiplying the face value of the bonds by the contractual interest rate.
- Compute bond premium or discount amortization by dividing bond premium or discount by the total number of periods.
- Understand that interest expense is decreased when bonds are issued at a premium. The reason is that the amortization of premium reduces the total cost of borrowing.

SOLUTION TO DEMONSTRATION PROBLEM

(a) 2006

Jan. 1	Cash	1,820,000	
	Bonds Payable		1,750,000
	Premium on Bonds Payable		70,000

(b) 2006

July 1	Bond Interest Expense	101,500**	
	Premium on Bonds Payable	3,500*	
	Cash		105,000
	*$70,000 ÷ 20		
	**$105,000 − $3,500		

THE NAVIGATOR

SUMMARY OF STUDY OBJECTIVE FOR APPENDIX 11C

11. **Apply the straight-line method of amortizing bond discount and bond premium.** The straight-line method of amortization results in a constant amount of amortization and interest expense per period.

GLOSSARY FOR APPENDIX 11C

Straight-line method of amortization. A method of amortizing bond discount or bond premium that results in allocating the same amount to interest expense in each interest period. (p. 502)

*__Note__: All asterisked Questions, Exercises, and Problems relate to material in the appendixes to the chapter.

SELF-STUDY QUESTIONS

Self-Study/Self-Test

Answers are at the end of the chapter.

(SO 1) **1.** The time period for classifying a liability as current is one year or the operating cycle, whichever is:
a. longer.
b. shorter.
c. probable.
d. possible.

(SO 1) **2.** To be classified as a current liability, a debt must be expected to be paid:
a. out of existing current assets.
b. by creating other current liabilities.
c. within 2 years.
d. both (a) and (b).

(SO 2) **3.** Shari Uecker Company borrows $88,500 on September 1, 2006, from Egg Harbor State Bank by signing an $88,500, 12%, one-year note. What is the accrued interest at December 31, 2006?
a. $2,655.
b. $3,540.
c. $4,425.
d. $10,620.

(SO 3) **4.** Becky Sherrick Company has total proceeds from sales of $4,515. If the proceeds include sales taxes of 5%, the amount to be credited to Sales is:
a. $4,000.
b. $4,300.
c. $4,289.25.
d. No correct answer given.

(SO 4) **5.** The term used for bonds that are unsecured is:
a. callable bonds.
b. indenture bonds.
c. debenture bonds.
d. bearer bonds.

(SO 5) **6.** Karson Inc. issues 10-year bonds with a maturity value of $200,000. If the bonds are issued at a premium, this indicates that:
a. the contractual interest rate exceeds the market interest rate.
b. the market interest rate exceeds the contractual interest rate.
c. the contractual interest rate and the market interest rate are the same.
d. no relationship exists between the two rates.

7. Gester Corporation retires its $100,000 face value bonds at 105 on January 1, following the payment of semiannual interest. The carrying value of the bonds at the redemption date is $103,745. The entry to record the redemption will include a: (SO 6)
a. credit of $3,745 to Loss on Bond Redemption.
b. debit of $3,745 to Premium on Bonds Payable.
c. credit of $1,255 to Gain on Bond Redemption.
d. debit of $5,000 to Premium on Bonds Payable.

8. Colson Inc. converts $600,000 of bonds sold at face value into 10,000 shares of common stock, par value $1. Both the bonds and the stock have a market value of $760,000. What amount should be credited to Paid-in Capital in Excess of Par as a result of the conversion? (SO 6)
a. $10,000.
b. $160,000.
c. $600,000.
d. $590,000.

9. Andrews Inc. issues a $497,000, 10% 3-year mortgage note on January 1. The note will be paid in three annual installments of $200,000, each payable at the end of the year. What is the amount of interest expense that should be recognized by Andrews Inc. in the second year? (SO 7)
a. $16,567.
b. $49,740.
c. $34,670.
d. $346,700.

***10.** On January 1, Besalius Inc. issued $1,000,000, 9% bonds for $939,000. The market rate of interest for these bonds is 10%. Interest is payable annually on December 31. (SO 10)

Besalius uses the effective-interest method of amortizing bond discount. At the end of the first year, Besalius should report unamortized bond discount of:

a. $54,900.
b. $57,100.
c. $51,610.
d. $51,000.

(SO 10) *11. On January 1, Dias Corporation issued $1,000,000, 14%, 5-year bonds with interest payable on July 1 and January 1. The bonds sold for $1,098,540. The market rate of interest for these bonds was 12%. On the first interest date, using the effective-interest method, the debit entry to Bond Interest Expense is for:

a. $60,000.
b. $76,898.
c. $65,912.
d. $131,825.

*12. On January 1, Hurley Corporation issues $500,000, 5-year, 12% bonds at 96 with interest payable on July 1 and January 1. The entry on July 1 to record payment of bond interest and the amortization of bond discount using the straight-line method will include a: (SO 11)

a. debit to Interest Expense $30,000.
b. debit to Interest Expense $60,000.
c. credit to Discount on Bonds Payable $4,000.
d. credit to Discount on Bonds Payable $2,000.

*13. For the bonds issued in question 12, above, what is the carrying value of the bonds at the end of the third interest period? (SO 11)

a. $486,000.
b. $488,000.
c. $472,000.
d. $464,000.

THE NAVIGATOR

QUESTIONS

1. Brad Goebel believes a current liability is a debt that can be expected to be paid in one year. Is Brad correct? Explain.
2. Mark McGwire Company obtains $30,000 in cash by signing a 9%, 6-month, $30,000 note payable to First Bank on July 1. Mark McGwire's fiscal year ends on September 30. What information should be reported for the note payable in the annual financial statements?
3. (a) Your roommate says, "Sales taxes are reported as an expense in the income statement." Do you agree? Explain.
   (b) Planet Hollywood has cash proceeds from sales of $8,400. This amount includes $400 of sales taxes. Give the entry to record the proceeds.
4. Ottawa University sold 10,000 season football tickets at $90 each for its five-game home schedule. What entries should be made (a) when the tickets were sold, and (b) after each game?
5. Identify three taxes commonly withheld by the employer from an employee's gross pay.
6. (a) Identify the three types of employer payroll taxes.
   (b) How are tax liability accounts and payroll tax expense accounts classified in the financial statements?
7. (a) What are long-term liabilities? Give two examples.
   (b) What is a bond?
8. (a) As a source of long-term financing, what are the major advantages of bonds over common stock? (b) What are the major disadvantages in using bonds for long-term financing?
9. Contrast the following types of bonds: (a) secured and unsecured, (b) term and serial, (c) registered and bearer, and (d) convertible and callable.
10. The following terms are important in issuing bonds: (a) face value, (b) contractual interest rate, (c) bond indenture, and (d) bond certificate. Explain each of these terms.
11. Describe the two major obligations incurred by a company when bonds are issued.
12. Assume that Bedazzled Inc. sold bonds with a par value of $100,000 for $104,000. Was the market interest rate equal to, less than, or greater than the bonds' contractual interest rate? Explain.
13. If a 9%, 10-year, $800,000 bond is issued at par and interest is paid semiannually, what is the amount of the interest payment at the end of the first semiannual period?
14. If the Bonds Payable account has a balance of $900,000 and the Discount on Bonds Payable account has a balance of $60,000, what is the carrying value of the bonds?
15. Which accounts are debited and which are credited if a bond issue originally sold at a premium is redeemed before maturity at 97 immediately following the payment of interest?
16. Karistad Corporation is considering issuing a convertible bond. What is a convertible bond? Discuss the advantages of a convertible bond from the standpoint of (a) the bondholders and (b) the issuing corporation.
17. Roy Brown, a friend of yours, has recently purchased a home for $125,000, paying $25,000 down and the remainder financed by a 10.5%, 20-year mortgage, payable at $998.38 per month. At the end of the first month, Roy receives a statement from the bank indicating that only $123.38 of principal was paid during the month. At this rate, he calculates that it will take over 67 years to pay off the mortgage. Is he right? Discuss.
18. In general, what are the requirements for the financial statement presentation of long-term liabilities?

*19. Ginny Innis is discussing the advantages of the effective-interest method of bond amortization with her accounting staff. What do you think Ginny is saying?

*20. Redbone Corporation issues $500,000 of 9%, 5-year bonds on January 1, 2006, at 104. If Redbone uses the effective-interest method in amortizing the premium, will the annual interest expense increase or decrease over the life of the bonds? Explain.

*21. Vera Cruz and Swen Varberg are discussing how the market price of a bond is determined. Vera believes that the market price of a bond is solely a function of the amount of the principal payment at the end of the term of a bond. Is she right? Discuss.

*22. Explain the straight-line method of amortizing a discount or premium on bonds payable.

*23. Fleming Corporation issues $300,000 of 8%, 5-year bonds on January 1, 2006, at 105. Assuming that the straight-line method is used to amortize the premium, what is the total amount of interest expense for 2006?

BRIEF EXERCISES

Identify whether obligations are current liabilities.
(SO 1)

BE11-1 Cardinal Company has the following obligations at December 31: (a) a note payable for $100,000 due in 2 years, (b) a 10-year mortgage payable of $300,000 payable in ten $30,000 annual payments, (c) interest payable of $15,000 on the mortgage, and (d) accounts payable of $60,000. For each obligation, indicate whether it should be classified as a current liability. (Assume an operating cycle of less than one year.)

Prepare entries for an interest-bearing note payable.
(SO 2)

BE11-2 Becky Company borrows $60,000 on July 1 from the bank by signing a $60,000, 10%, one-year note payable.

(a) Prepare the journal entry to record the proceeds of the note.
(b) Prepare the journal entry to record accrued interest at December 31, assuming adjusting entries are made only at the end of the year.

Compute and record sales taxes payable.
(SO 3)

BE11-3 Goodwin Auto Supply does not segregate sales and sales taxes at the time of sale. The register total for March 16 is $13,440. All sales are subject to a 5% sales tax. Compute sales taxes payable, and make the entry to record sales taxes payable and sales.

Compute gross earnings and net pay.
(SO 3)

BE11-4 Sandy Teter's regular hourly wage rate is $16, and she receives an hourly rate of $24 for work in excess of 40 hours. During a January pay period, Sandy works 45 hours. Sandy's federal income tax withholding is $95, and she has no voluntary deductions. Compute Sandy Teter's gross earnings and net pay for the pay period. (Assume a FICA tax rate of 8%.)

Record a payroll and the payment of wages.
(SO 3)

BE11-5 Data for Sandy Teter are presented in BE11-4. Prepare the journal entries to record (a) Sandy's pay for the period and (b) the payment of Sandy's wages. Use January 15 for the end of the pay period and the payment date.

Prepare entries for unearned revenues.
(SO 3)

BE11-6 Wichita State University sells 4,000 season basketball tickets at $120 each for its 12-game home schedule. Give the entry to record (a) the sale of the season tickets and (b) the revenue earned by playing the first home game.

Compare bond versus stock financing.
(SO 4)

BE11-7 Shaffer Inc. is considering two alternatives to finance its construction of a new $2 million plant.

(a) Issuance of 200,000 shares of common stock at the market price of $10 per share.
(b) Issuance of $2 million, 8% bonds at par.

Complete the following table, and indicate which alternative is preferable.

	Issue Stock	Issue Bonds
Income before interest and taxes	$900,000	$900,000
Interest expense from bonds		
Income before income taxes	$	$
Income tax expense (30%)		
Net income	$	$
Outstanding shares		500,000
Earnings per share		

Prepare entries for bonds issued at face value.
(SO 5)

BE11-8 Quincy Corporation issued 4,000, 8%, 5-year, $1,000 bonds dated January 1, 2006, at 100.

(a) Prepare the journal entry to record the sale of these bonds on January 1, 2006.
(b) Prepare the journal entry to record the first interest payment on July 1, 2006 (interest payable semiannually), assuming no previous accrual of interest.
(c) Prepare the adjusting journal entry on December 31, 2006, to record interest expense.

BE11-9 Sandstone Company issues $1 million, 10-year, 8% bonds at 97, with interest payable on July 1 and January 1.

Prepare entries for bonds sold at a discount and a premium. (SO 5)

(a) Prepare the journal entry to record the sale of these bonds on January 1, 2006.
(b) Assuming instead that the above bonds sold for 104, prepare the journal entry to record the sale of these bonds on January 1, 2006.

BE11-10 Carrolla Company has issued three different bonds during 2006. Interest is payable semiannually on each of these bonds.

Prepare entries for bonds issued. (SO 5)

1. On January 1, 2006, 1,000, 8%, 5-year, $1,000 bonds dated January 1, 2006, were issued at face value.
2. On July 1, $500,000, 9%, 5-year bonds dated July 1, 2006, were issued at 102.
3. On September 1, $200,000, 7%, 5-year bonds dated September 1, 2006, were issued at 99.

Prepare the journal entry to record each bond transaction at the date of issuance.

BE11-11 The balance sheet for Jones Company reports the following information on July 1, 2006.

Prepare entry for redemption of bonds. (SO 6)

Long-term liabilities		
Bonds payable	$1,000,000	
Less: Discount on bonds payable	60,000	$940,000

Jones decides to redeem these bonds at 103 after paying semiannual interest. Prepare the journal entry to record the redemption on July 1, 2006.

BE11-12 McEntire Inc. issues a $400,000, 10%, 10-year mortgage note on December 31, 2006, to obtain financing for a new building. The terms provide for semiannual installment payments of $32,097. Prepare the entry to record the mortgage loan on December 31, 2006, and the first installment payment.

Prepare entries for long-term notes payable. (SO 7)

BE11-13 Presented below are long-term liability items for Saurez Company at December 31, 2006. Prepare the long-term liabilities section of the balance sheet for Saurez Company.

Prepare statement presentation of long-term liabilities. (SO 8)

Bonds payable, due 2008	$500,000
Mortgage payable	50,000
Notes payable, due 2011	80,000
Discount on bonds payable	45,000

***BE11-14** (a) What is the present value of $10,000 due 8 periods from now, discounted at 10%?
(b) What is the present value of $10,000 to be received at the end of each of 6 periods, discounted at 8%?

Determine present value. (SO 9)

***BE11-15** Presented below is the partial bond discount amortization schedule for Cardosa Corp. Cardosa uses the effective-interest method of amortization.

Use effective-interest method of bond amortization. (SO 10)

Semiannual Interest Periods	Interest to Be Paid	Interest Expense to Be Recorded	Discount Amortization	Unamortized Discount	Bond Carrying Value
Issue date				$62,311	$937,689
1	$45,000	$46,884	$1,884	60,427	939,573
2	45,000	46,979	1,979	58,448	941,552

Instructions

(a) Prepare the journal entry to record the payment of interest and the discount amortization at the end of period 1.
(b) Explain why interest expense is greater than interest paid.
(c) Explain why interest expense will increase each period.

Prepare entries for bonds issued at a discount. (SO 11)

***BE11-16** Bowie Company issues $3 million, 10-year, 9% bonds at 96, with interest payable on July 1 and January 1. The straight-line method is used to amortize bond discount.

(a) Prepare the journal entry to record the sale of these bonds on January 1, 2006.
(b) Prepare the journal entry to record interest expense and bond discount amortization on July 1, 2006, assuming no previous accrual of interest.

Prepare entries for bonds issued at a premium. (SO 11)

***BE11-17** Allman Inc. issues $2 million, 5-year, 10% bonds at 102, with interest payable on July 1 and January 1. The straight-line method is used to amortize bond premium.

(a) Prepare the journal entry to record the sale of these bonds on January 1, 2006.
(b) Prepare the journal entry to record interest expense and bond premium amortization on July 1, 2006, assuming no previous accrual of interest.

EXERCISES

Prepare entries for interest-bearing notes. (SO 2)

E11-1 On June 1, Padillio Company borrows $70,000 from First Bank on a 6-month, $70,000, 12% note.

Instructions

(a) Prepare the entry on June 1.
(b) Prepare the adjusting entry on June 30.
(c) Prepare the entry at maturity (December 1), assuming monthly adjusting entries have been made through November 30.
(d) What was the total financing cost (interest expense)?

Journalize sales and related taxes. (SO 3)

E11-2 In providing accounting services to small businesses, you encounter the following situations pertaining to cash sales.

1. Sue Jackson Company rings up sales and sales taxes separately on its cash register. On April 10, the register totals are sales $25,000 and sales taxes $1,500.
2. Person Company does not segregate sales and sales taxes. Its register total for April 15 is $20,330, which includes a 7% sales tax.

Instructions

Prepare the entry to record the sales transactions and related taxes for each client.

Journalize unearned subscription revenue. (SO 3)

E11-3 Nevin Company publishes a monthly sports magazine, *Fishing Preview*. Subscriptions to the magazine cost $20 per year. During November 2006, Nevin sells 9,000 subscriptions beginning with the December issue. Nevin prepares financial statements quarterly and recognizes subscription revenue earned at the end of the quarter. The company uses the accounts Unearned Subscriptions and Subscription Revenue.

Instructions

(a) Prepare the entry in November for the receipt of the subscriptions.
(b) Prepare the adjusting entry at December 31, 2006, to record subscription revenue earned in December 2006.
(c) Prepare the adjusting entry at March 31, 2007, to record subscription revenue earned in the first quarter of 2007.

Compare two alternatives of financing—issuance of common stock vs. issuance of bonds. (SO 4)

E11-4 Southeast Airlines is considering two alternatives for the financing of a purchase of a fleet of airplanes. These two alternatives are:

1. Issue 60,000 shares of common stock at $45 per share. (Cash dividends have not been paid nor is the payment of any contemplated).
2. Issue 10%, 10-year bonds at par for $2,700,000.

It is estimated that the company will earn $600,000 before interest and taxes as a result of this purchase. The company has an estimated tax rate of 30% and has 90,000 shares of common stock outstanding prior to the new financing.

Instructions

Determine the effect on net income and earnings per share for these two methods of financing.

Prepare entries for issuance of bonds, and payment and accrual of bond interest. (SO 5)

E11-5 On January 1, Payne Company issued $200,000, 10%, 10-year bonds at par. Interest is payable semiannually on July 1 and January 1.

Instructions

Present journal entries to record the following.

(a) The issuance of the bonds.
(b) The payment of interest on July 1, assuming that interest was not accrued on June 30.
(c) The accrual of interest on December 31.

Prepare entries for bond interest and redemption.
(SO 5, 6)

E11-6 The following section is taken from Disch Corp.'s balance sheet at December 31, 2005.

Current liabilities	
Bond interest payable	$ 72,000
Long-term liabilities	
Bonds payable, 9%, due January 1, 2010	1,600,000

Interest is payable semiannually on January 1 and July 1. The bonds are callable on any interest date.

Instructions

(a) Journalize the payment of the bond interest on January 1, 2006.
(b) Assume that on January 1, 2006, after paying interest, Disch calls bonds having a face value of $400,000. The call price is 104. Record the redemption of the bonds.
(c) Prepare the entry to record the payment of interest on July 1, 2006, assuming no previous accrual of interest on the remaining bonds.

Prepare entries for redemption of bonds and conversion of bonds into common stock.
(SO 6)

E11-7 Presented below are three independent situations.

1. Voris Corporation retired $130,000 face value, 12% bonds on June 30, 2006, at 102. The carrying value of the bonds at the redemption date was $107,500. The bonds pay semiannual interest, and the interest payment due on June 30, 2006, has been made and recorded.
2. Lamp Inc. retired $150,000 face value, 12.5% bonds on June 30, 2006, at 98. The carrying value of the bonds at the redemption date was $151,000. The bonds pay semiannual interest, and the interest payment due on June 30, 2006, has been made and recorded.
3. Keho Company has $80,000, 8%, 12-year convertible bonds outstanding. These bonds were sold at face value and pay semiannual interest on June 30 and December 31 of each year. The bonds are convertible into 30 shares of Keho $5 par value common stock for each $1,000 worth of bonds. On December 31, 2006, after the bond interest has been paid, $40,000 face value bonds were converted. The market value of Keho common stock was $44 per share on December 31, 2006.

Instructions

For each independent situation above, prepare the appropriate journal entry for the redemption or conversion of the bonds.

Prepare entries to record mortgage note and installment payments.
(SO 7)

E11-8 Tucki Co. receives $240,000 when it issues a $240,000, 10%, mortgage note payable to finance the construction of a building at December 31, 2006. The terms provide for semiannual installment payments of $16,000 on June 30 and December 31.

Instructions

Prepare the journal entries to record the mortgage loan and the first two installment payments.

Prepare long-term liabilities section.
(SO 8)

E11-9 The adjusted trial balance for Matthews Corporation at the end of the current year contained the following accounts.

Bond Interest Payable	$ 9,000
Notes Payable, due 2010	59,500
Bonds Payable, due 2014	180,000
Premium on Bonds Payable	32,000

Instructions

Prepare the long-term liabilities section of the balance sheet.

Prepare entries for issuance of bonds, payment of interest, and amortization of discount using effective-interest method
(SO 5, 10)

***E11-10** Neagle Corporation issued $500,000, 9%, 10-year bonds on January 1, 2006, for $468,844. This price resulted in an effective-interest rate of 10% on the bonds. Interest is payable semiannually on July 1 and January 1. Neagle uses the effective-interest method to amortize bond premium or discount.

Instructions

Prepare the journal entries to record the following. (Round to the nearest dollar.)

(a) The issuance of the bonds.
(b) The payment of interest and the discount amortization on July 1, 2006, assuming that interest was not accrued on June 30.
(c) The accrual of interest and the discount amortization on December 31, 2006.

Prepare entries for issuance of bonds, payment of interest, and amortization of premium using effective-interest method.
(SO 5, 10)

***E11-11** Hurley Company issued $400,000, 11%, 10-year bonds on January 1, 2006, for $424,925. This price resulted in an effective-interest rate of 10% on the bonds. Interest is payable semiannually on July 1 and January 1. Hurley uses the effective-interest method to amortize bond premium or discount.

Instructions

Prepare the journal entries to record the following. (Round to the nearest dollar).

(a) The issuance of the bonds.
(b) The payment of interest and the premium amortization on July 1, 2006, assuming that interest was not accrued on June 30.
(c) The accrual of interest and the premium amortization on December 31, 2006.

Prepare entries to record issuance of bonds, payment of interest, amortization of premium, and redemption at maturity.
(SO 5, 11)

***E11-12** Manilow Company issued $600,000, 9%, 20-year bonds on January 1, 2006, at 103. Interest is payable semiannually on July 1 and January 1. Manilow uses straight-line amortization for bond premium or discount.

Instructions

Prepare the journal entries to record the following.

(a) The issuance of the bonds.
(b) The payment of interest and the premium amortization on July 1, 2006, assuming that interest was not accrued on June 30.
(c) The accrual of interest and the premium amortization on December 31, 2006.
(d) The redemption of the bonds at maturity, assuming interest for the last interest period has been paid and recorded.

Prepare entries to record issuance of bonds, payment of interest, amortization of discount, and redemption at maturity.
(SO 5, 11)

***E11-13** Newton Company issued $600,000, 11%, 10-year bonds on December 31, 2005, for $550,000. Interest is payable semiannually on June 30 and December 31. Newton Company uses the straight-line method to amortize bond premium or discount.

Instructions

Prepare the journal entries to record the following.

(a) The issuance of the bonds.
(b) The payment of interest and the discount amortization on June 30, 2006.
(c) The payment of interest and the discount amortization on December 31, 2006.
(d) The redemption of the bonds at maturity, assuming interest for the last interest period has been paid and recorded.

PROBLEMS: SET A

Prepare current liability entries, adjusting entries, and current liabilities section.
(SO 1, 2, 3)

Peachtree

P11-1A On January 1, 2006, the ledger of Shumway Software Company contains the following liability accounts.

Accounts Payable	$42,500
Sales Taxes Payable	5,800
Unearned Service Revenue	15,000

During January the following selected transactions occurred.

Jan. 1 Borrowed $15,000 in cash from Amsterdam Bank on a 4-month, 8%, $15,000 note.
5 Sold merchandise for cash totaling $10,400, which includes 4% sales taxes.
12 Provided services for customers who had made advance payments of $9,000. (Credit Service Revenue.)
14 Paid state treasurer's department for sales taxes collected in December 2005, $5,800.
20 Sold 700 units of a new product on credit at $52 per unit, plus 4% sales tax.
25 Sold merchandise for cash totaling $12,480, which includes 4% sales taxes.

Instructions

(a) Journalize the January transactions.

(b) Journalize the adjusting entry at January 31 for the outstanding notes payable.

(c) Prepare the current liabilities section of the balance sheet at January 31, 2006. Assume no change in accounts payable.

(c) Current liability total $65,936

P11-2A The following are selected transactions of Talley Company. Talley prepares financial statements quarterly.

Journalize and post note transactions; show balance sheet presentation.

(SO 2)

Jan. 2	Purchased merchandise on account from Jones Company, $20,000, terms 2/10, n/30.
Feb. 1	Issued a 9%, 2-month, $20,000 note to Jones in payment of account.
Mar. 31	Accrued interest for 2 months on Jones note.
Apr. 1	Paid face value and interest on Jones note.
July 1	Purchased equipment from Seguin Equipment paying $11,000 in cash and signing a 10%, 3-month, $30,000 note.
Sept. 30	Accrued interest for 3 months on Seguin note.
Oct. 1	Paid face value and interest on Seguin note.
Dec. 1	Borrowed $15,000 from the Otago Bank by issuing a 3-month, 8% interest-bearing note with a face value of $15,000.
Dec. 31	Recognized interest expense for 1 month on Otago Bank note.

Instructions

(a) Prepare journal entries for the above transactions and events.

(b) Post to the accounts Notes Payable, Interest Payable, and Interest Expense.

(c) Show the balance sheet presentation of notes payable at December 31.

(d) What is total interest expense for the year?

(d) $1,150

P11-3A On June 1, 2006, Hopkins Corp. issued $1,000,000, 8%, 5-year bonds at face value. The bonds were dated June 1, 2006, and pay interest semiannually on June 1 and December 1. Financial statements are prepared annually on December 31.

Prepare entries to record issuance of bonds, interest accrual, and bond redemption.

(SO 5, 6, 8)

Instructions

(a) Prepare the journal entry to record the issuance of the bonds.

(b) Prepare the adjusting entry to record the accrual of interest on December 31, 2006.

(c) Show the balance sheet presentation on December 31, 2006.

(d) Prepare the journal entry to record payment of interest on June 1, 2007, assuming no accrual of interest from January 1, 2007, to June 1, 2007.

(d) Int. exp. $33,333

(e) Prepare the journal entry to record payment of interest on December 1, 2007.

(f) Assume that on December 1, 2007, Hopkins calls the bonds at 101. Record the redemption of the bonds.

(f) Loss $10,000

P11-4A Formosa Co. sold $400,000, 9%, 10-year bonds on January 1, 2006. The bonds were dated January 1, and interest is paid on January 1 and July 1. The bonds were sold at 105.

Prepare entries to record issuance of bonds, interest accrual, and bond redemption.

(SO 5, 6, 8)

Instructions

(a) Prepare the journal entry to record the issuance of the bonds on January 1, 2006.

(b) At December 31, 2006, the balance in the Premium on Bonds Payable account is $18,000. Show the balance sheet presentation of accrued interest and the bond liability at December 31, 2006.

(c) On January 1, 2008, when the carrying value of the bonds was $416,000, the company redeemed the bonds at 105. Record the redemption of the bonds assuming that interest for the period has already been paid.

(c) Loss $4,000

P11-5A Otto Electronics issues an $800,000, 8%, 10-year mortgage note on December 31, 2006, to help finance a plant expansion program. The terms provide for semiannual installment payments, not including real estate taxes and insurance, of $58,865. Payments are due June 30 and December 31.

Prepare installment payments schedule and journal entries for a mortgage note payable.

(SO 7)

Instructions

(a) Prepare an installment payments schedule for the first 2 years.

(b) Prepare the entries for (1) the mortgage loan and (2) the first two installment payments.

(c) Show how the total mortgage liability should be reported on the balance sheet at December 31, 2007.

(b) June 30 Mortgage Notes Payable $26,865

(c) Current liability—2007: $59,276

Prepare entries to record issuance of bonds, payment of interest, and amortization of bond discount using effective-interest method.
(SO 5, 10)

***P11-6A** On July 1, 2006, Kingston Satellites issued $3,600,000 face value, 9%, 10-year bonds at $3,375,680. This price resulted in an effective-interest rate of 10% on the bonds. Kingston uses the effective-interest method to amortize bond premium or discount. The bonds pay semiannual interest July 1 and January 1.

Instructions

(Round all computations to the nearest dollar.)

(a) Prepare the journal entry to record the issuance of the bonds on July 1, 2006.

(b) Amortization $6,784

(b) Prepare the journal entry to record the accrual of interest and the amortization of the discount on December 31, 2006.

(c) Amortization $7,123

(c) Prepare the journal entry to record the payment of interest and the amortization of the discount on July 1, 2007, assuming that interest was not accrued on June 30.

(d) Amortization $7,479

(d) Prepare the journal entry to record the accrual of interest and the amortization of the discount on December 31, 2007.

(e) Prepare an amortization table through December 31, 2007 (3 interest periods) for this bond issue.

Prepare entries to record issuance of bonds, payment of interest, and amortization of premium using effective-interest method. In addition, answer questions.
(SO 5, 10)

***P11-7A** On July 1, 2006, S. Strigel Chemical Company issued $5,000,000 face value, 10%, 10-year bonds at $5,679,533. This price resulted in an 8% effective-interest rate on the bonds. Strigel uses the effective-interest method to amortize bond premium or discount. The bonds pay semiannual interest on each July 1 and January 1.

Instructions

(Round all computations to the nearest dollar.)

(a) Prepare the journal entries to record the following transactions.
   (1) The issuance of the bonds on July 1, 2006.

(a) (2) Amortization $22,819

   (2) The accrual of interest and the amortization of the premium on December 31, 2006.

(a) (3) Amortization $23,731

   (3) The payment of interest and the amortization of the premium on July 1, 2007, assuming no accrual of interest on June 30.

(a) (4) Amortization $24,681

   (4) The accrual of interest and the amortization of the premium on December 31, 2007.

(b) $5,608,302

(b) Show the proper balance sheet presentation for the liability for bonds payable on the December 31, 2007, balance sheet.

(c) Provide the answers to the following questions in letter form.
   (1) What amount of interest expense is reported for 2007?
   (2) Would the bond interest expense reported in 2007 be the same as, greater than, or less than the amount that would be reported if the straight-line method of amortization were used?
   (3) Determine the total cost of borrowing over the life of the bond.
   (4) Would the total bond interest expense be greater than, the same as, or less than the total interest expense if the straight-line method of amortization were used?

Prepare entries to record issuance of bonds, interest accrual, and amortization for 2 years.
(SO 5, 11)

Peachtree

***P11-8A** Travis Company sold $2,000,000, 9%, 20-year bonds on January 1, 2006. The bonds were dated January 1, 2006, and pay interest on January 1 and July 1. Travis Company uses the straight-line method to amortize bond premium or discount. The bonds were sold at 96. Assume no interest is accrued on June 30.

Instructions

(a) Prepare the journal entry to record the issuance of the bonds on January 1, 2006.

(b) Amortization $2,000

(b) Prepare a bond discount amortization schedule for the first 4 interest periods.

(d) Discount on bonds payable $72,000

(c) Prepare the journal entries for interest and the amortization of the discount in 2006 and 2007.

(d) Show the balance sheet presentation of the bond liability at December 31, 2007.

Prepare entries to record issuance of bonds, interest, and amortization of bond premium and discount.
(SO 5, 11)

***P11-9A** Guehler Corporation sold $3,000,000, 8%, 10-year bonds on January 1, 2006. The bonds were dated January 1, 2006, and pay interest on July 1 and January 1. Guehler Corporation uses the straight-line method to amortize bond premium or discount. Assume no interest is accrued on June 30.

(a) Amortization $4,500
(b) Amortization $6,000
(c) Premium on bonds payable $81,000
Discount on bonds payable $108,000

Instructions

(a) Prepare all the necessary journal entries to record the issuance of the bonds and bond interest expense for 2006, assuming that the bonds sold at 103.

(b) Prepare journal entries as in part (a) assuming that the bonds sold at 96.

(c) Show the balance sheet presentation for each bond issue at December 31, 2006.

***P11-10A** The following is taken from the Jaggar Corp. balance sheet.

Prepare entries to record interest payments, discount amortization, and redemption of bonds.

(SO 6, 11)

JAGGAR CORPORATION
Balance Sheet (partial)
December 31, 2006

Current liabilities		
Bond interest payable (for 6 months from July 1 to December 31)		$ 96,000
Long-term liabilities		
Bonds payable, 8%, due January 1, 2017	$2,400,000	
Less: Discount on bonds payable	90,000	$2,310,000

Interest is payable semiannually on January 1 and July 1. The bonds are callable on any semiannual interest date. Jaggar uses straight-line amortization for any bond premium or discount. From December 31, 2006, the bonds will be outstanding for an additional 10 years (120 months).

Instructions

(Round all computations to the nearest dollar).

(a) Journalize the payment of bond interest on January 1, 2007.

(b) Prepare the entry to amortize bond discount and to pay the interest due on July 1, 2007, assuming that interest was not accrued on June 30. (b) Amortization $4,500

(c) Assume that on July 1, 2007, after paying interest, Jaggar Corp. calls bonds having a face value of $800,000. The call price is 102. Record the redemption of the bonds. (c) Loss $44,500

(d) Prepare the adjusting entry at December 31, 2007, to amortize bond discount and to accrue interest on the remaining bonds. (d) Amortization $3,000

PROBLEMS: SET B

P11-1B On January 1, 2006, the ledger of Zaur Company contains the following liability accounts.

Prepare current liability entries, adjusting entries, and current liabilities section.

(SO 1, 2, 3)

Accounts Payable	$52,000
Sales Taxes Payable	7,700
Unearned Service Revenue	16,000

During January the following selected transactions occurred.

Jan. 5 Sold merchandise for cash totaling $17,280, which includes 8% sales taxes.
12 Provided services for customers who had made advance payments of $10,000. (Credit Service Revenue.)
14 Paid state revenue department for sales taxes collected in December 2005 ($7,700).
20 Sold 600 units of a new product on credit at $50 per unit, plus 8% sales tax.
21 Borrowed $18,000 from UCLA Bank on a 3-month, 9%, $18,000 note.
25 Sold merchandise for cash totaling $12,420, which includes 8% sales taxes.

Instructions

(a) Journalize the January transactions.

(b) Journalize the adjusting entry at January 31 for the outstanding notes payable. (*Hint:* Use one-third of a month for the UCLA Bank note.)

(c) Prepare the current liabilities section of the balance sheet at January 31, 2006. Assume no change in accounts payable. (c) Current liability total $80,645

P11-2B On May 1, 2006, Sator Corp. issued $800,000, 9%, 5-year bonds at face value. The bonds were dated May 1, 2006, and pay interest semiannually on May 1 and November 1. Financial statements are prepared annually on December 31.

Prepare entries to record issuance of bonds, interest accrual, and bond redemption.

(SO 5, 6, 8)

Instructions

(a) Prepare the journal entry to record the issuance of the bonds.

(b) Prepare the adjusting entry to record the accrual of interest on December 31, 2006.

(c) Show the balance sheet presentation on December 31, 2006.

(d) Int. exp. $24,000

(d) Prepare the journal entry to record payment of interest on May 1, 2007, assuming no accrual of interest from January 1, 2007, to May 1, 2007.

(e) Prepare the journal entry to record payment of interest on November 1, 2007.

(f) Loss $8,000

(f) Assume that on November 1, 2007, Sator calls the bonds at 101. Record the redemption of the bonds.

Prepare entries to record issuance of bonds, interest accrual, and bond redemption.

(SO 5, 6, 8)

P11-3B Hornung Electric sold $300,000, 10%, 10-year bonds on January 1, 2006. The bonds were dated January 1 and paid interest on January 1 and July 1. The bonds were sold at 104.

Instructions

(a) Prepare the journal entry to record the issuance of the bonds on January 1, 2006.

(b) At December 31, 2006, the balance in the Premium on Bonds Payable account is $10,800. Show the balance sheet presentation of accrued interest and the bond liability at December 31, 2006.

(c) Loss $5,400

(c) On January 1, 2008, when the carrying value of the bonds was $309,600, the company redeemed the bonds at 105. Record the redemption of the bonds assuming that interest for the period has already been paid.

Prepare installment payments schedule and journal entries for a mortgage note payable.

(SO 7)

P11-4B Hamilton Electronics issues a $600,000, 8%, 10-year mortgage note on December 31, 2005. The proceeds from the note are to be used in financing a new research laboratory. The terms of the note provide for semiannual installment payments, exclusive of real estate taxes and insurance, of $44,149. Payments are due June 30 and December 31.

Instructions

(a) Prepare an installment payments schedule for the first 2 years.

(b) June 30 Mortgage Notes Payable $20,149

(b) Prepare the entries for (1) the loan and (2) the first two installment payments.

(c) Current liability—2006: $44,458

(c) Show how the total mortgage liability should be reported on the balance sheet at December 31, 2006.

Prepare entries to record issuance of bonds, payment of interest, and amortization of bond premium using effective-interest method.

(SO 5, 10)

***P11-5B** On July 1, 2006, Clintin Corporation issued $4,000,000 face value, 10%, 10-year bonds at $4,543,626. This price resulted in an effective-interest rate of 8% on the bonds. Clintin uses the effective-interest method to amortize bond premium or discount. The bonds pay semiannual interest July 1 and January 1.

Instructions

(Round all computations to the nearest dollar.)

(a) Prepare the journal entry to record the issuance of the bonds on July 1, 2006.

(b) Amortization $18,255

(b) Prepare the journal entry to record the accrual of interest and the amortization of the premium on December 31, 2006.

(c) Amortization $18,985

(c) Prepare the journal entry to record the payment of interest and the amortization of the premium on July 1, 2007, assuming no accrual of interest on June 30.

(d) Amortization $19,745

(d) Prepare the journal entry to record the accrual of interest and the amortization of the premium on December 31, 2007.

(e) Prepare an amortization table through December 31, 2007 (3 interest periods) for this bond issue.

Prepare entries to record issuance of bonds, payment of interest, and amortization of discount using effective-interest method. In addition, answer questions.

(SO 5, 10)

***P11-6B** On July 1, 2006, Wilkowski Company issued $2,000,000 face value, 8%, 10-year bonds at $1,750,757. This price resulted in an effective-interest rate of 10% on the bonds. Wilkowski uses the effective-interest method to amortize bond premium or discount. The bonds pay semiannual interest July 1 and January 1.

Instructions

(Round all computations to the nearest dollar.)

(a) Prepare the journal entries to record the following transactions.

(1) The issuance of the bonds on July 1, 2006.

(2) The accrual of interest and the amortization of the discount on December 31, 2006.

(3) The payment of interest and the amortization of the discount on July 1, 2007, assuming no accrual of interest on June 30.

(a) (3) Amortization $7,915

(4) The accrual of interest and the amortization of the discount on December 31, 2007.

(a) (4) Amortization $8,311

(b) Show the proper balance sheet presentation for the liability for bonds payable on the December 31, 2007, balance sheet.

(b) $1,774,521

(c) Provide the answers to the following questions in letter form.
(1) What amount of interest expense is reported for 2007?
(2) Would the bond interest expense reported in 2007 be the same as, greater than, or less than the amount that would be reported if the straight-line method of amortization were used?
(3) Determine the total cost of borrowing over the life of the bond.
(4) Would the total bond interest expense be greater than, the same as, or less than the total interest expense that would be reported if the straight-line method of amortization were used?

***P11-7B** Toshiba Electric sold $5,000,000, 10%, 10-year bonds on January 1, 2006. The bonds were dated January 1 and pay interest July 1 and January 1. Toshiba Electric uses the straight-line method to amortize bond premium or discount. The bonds were sold at 104. Assume no interest is accrued on June 30.

Prepare entries to record issuance of bonds, interest accrual, and amortization for 2 years.

(SO 5, 11)

Instructions

(a) Prepare the journal entry to record the issuance of the bonds on January 1, 2006.
(b) Prepare a bond premium amortization schedule for the first 4 interest periods.

(b) Amortization $10,000

(c) Prepare the journal entries for interest and the amortization of the premium in 2006 and 2007.
(d) Show the balance sheet presentation of the bond liability at December 31, 2007.

(d) Premium on bonds payable $160,000

***P11-8B** McLain Company sold $2,000,000, 8%, 10-year bonds on July 1, 2006. The bonds were dated July 1, 2006, and pay interest July 1 and January 1. McLain Company uses the straight-line method to amortize bond premium or discount. Assume no interest is accrued on June 30.

Prepare entries to record issuance of bonds, interest, and amortization of bond premium and discount.

(SO 5, 11)

Instructions

(a) Prepare all the necessary journal entries to record the issuance of the bonds and bond interest expense for 2006, assuming that the bonds sold at 104.
(b) Prepare journal entries as in part (a) assuming that the bonds sold at 98.
(c) Show the balance sheet presentation for each bond issue at December 31, 2006.

(a) Amortization $4,000
(b) Amortization $2,000
(c) Premium on bonds payable $76,000
Discount on bonds payable $38,000

***P11-9B** The following is taken from the McGovern Company balance sheet.

Prepare entries to record interest payments, premium amortization, and redemption of bonds.

(SO 6, 11)

MCGOVERN COMPANY
Balance Sheet (partial)
December 31, 2006

Current liabilities		
Bond interest payable (for 6 months from July 1 to December 31)		$ 120,000
Long-term liabilities		
Bonds payable, 8% due January 1, 2017	$3,000,000	
Add: Premium on bonds payable	200,000	$3,200,000

Interest is payable semiannually on January 1 and July 1. The bonds are callable on any semiannual interest date. McGovern uses straight-line amortization for any bond premium or discount. From December 31, 2006, the bonds will be outstanding for an additional 10 years (120 months).

Instructions

(a) Journalize the payment of bond interest on January 1, 2007
(b) Prepare the entry to amortize bond premium and to pay the interest due on July 1, 2007, assuming no accrual of interest on June 30.

(b) Amortization $10,000

(c) Assume that on July 1, 2007, after paying interest, McGovern Company calls bonds having a face value of $1,800,000. The call price is 101. Record the redemption of the bonds.

(c) Gain $96,000

(d) Prepare the adjusting entry at December 31, 2007, to amortize bond premium and to accrue interest on the remaining bonds.

(d) Amortization $4,000

COMPREHENSIVE PROBLEM: CHAPTERS 6 TO 11

Paris Company and Troyer Company are competing businesses. Both began operations 6 years ago and are quite similar in most respects. The current balance sheet data for the two companies are as follows.

	Paris Company	Troyer Company
Cash	$ 70,300	$ 48,400
Accounts receivable	309,700	312,500
Allowance for doubtful accounts	(13,600)	–0–
Merchandise inventory	463,900	520,200
Plant and equipment	255,300	257,300
Accumulated depreciation, plant and equipment	(112,650)	(189,850)
Total assets	972,950	$948,550
Current liabilities	$440,200	$436,500
Long-term liabilities	78,000	80,000
Total liabilities	518,200	516,500
Stockholders' equity	454,750	432,050
Total liabilities and stockholders' equity	$972,950	$948,550

You have been engaged as a consultant to conduct a review of the two companies. Your goal is to determine which of them is in the stronger financial position.

Your review of their financial statements quickly reveals that the two companies have not followed the same accounting practices. The differences and your conclusions regarding them are summarized below.

1. Paris Company has used the allowance method of accounting for bad debts. A review shows that the amount of its write-offs each year has been quite close to the allowances that have been provided. It therefore seems reasonable to have confidence in its current estimate of bad debts.

   Troyer Company has used the direct write-off method for bad debts, and it has been somewhat slow to write off its uncollectible accounts. Based upon an aging analysis and review of its accounts receivable, it is estimated that $20,000 of its existing accounts will probably prove to be uncollectible.
2. Paris Company has determined the cost of its merchandise inventory on a LIFO basis. The result is that its inventory appears on the balance sheet at an amount that is below its current replacement cost. Based upon a detailed physical examination of its merchandise on hand, the current replacement cost of its inventory is estimated at $517,000.

   Troyer Company has used the FIFO method of valuing its merchandise inventory. Its ending inventory appears on the balance sheet at an amount that quite closely approximates its current replacement cost.
3. Paris Company estimated a useful life of 12 years and a salvage value of $30,000 for its plant and equipment. It has been depreciating them on a straight-line basis.

   Troyer Company has the same type of plant and equipment. However, it estimated a useful life of 10 years and a salvage value of $10,000. It has been depreciating its plant and equipment using the double-declining-balance method.

   Based upon engineering studies of these types of plant and equipment, you conclude that Troyer's estimates and method for calculating depreciation are the more appropriate.
4. Among its current liabilities, Paris has included the portions of long-term liabilities that become due within the next year. Troyer has not done so.

   You find that $16,000 of Troyer's $80,000 of long-term liabilities are due to be repaid in the current year.

Instructions

(a) Total assets:
Paris $950,325
Troyer $928,550

(a) Revise the balance sheets presented above so that the data are comparable and reflect the current financial position for each of the two companies.

(b) Prepare a brief report to your client stating your conclusions.

BROADENING YOUR PERSPECTIVE

Financial Reporting and Analysis

■ FINANCIAL REPORTING PROBLEM: PepsiCo

BYP11-1 The financial statements of **PepsiCo** and the Notes to Consolidated Financial Statements appear in Appendix A.

Instructions

Refer to PepsiCo's financial statements and answer the following questions about current and long-term liabilities.

(a) What were PepsiCo's total current liabilities at December 27, 2003? What was the increase/decrease in PepsiCo's total current liabilities from the prior year?

(b) In PepsiCo's Note 2 ("Our Significant Accounting Policies"), the company explains the nature of its contingencies. Under what conditions does PepsiCo recognize (record and report) liabilities for contingencies?

(c) What were the components of total current liabilities on December 27, 2003?

(d) What was PepsiCo's total long-term debt (excluding deferred income taxes) at December 27, 2003? What was the increase/decrease in total long-term debt (excluding deferred income taxes) from the prior year? What does Note 9 to the financial statements indicate about the composition of PepsiCo's long-term debt obligation?

(e) What are the total long-term contractual commitments that PepsiCo reports as of December 27, 2003? (See Note 9.)

■ COMPARATIVE ANALYSIS PROBLEM: PepsiCo vs. Coca-Cola

BYP11-2 **PepsiCo**'s financial statements are presented in Appendix A. **Coca-Cola**'s financial statements are presented in Appendix B.

Instructions

(a) At December 27, 2003, what was PepsiCo's largest current liability account? What were its total current liabilities? At December 31, 2003, what was Coca-Cola's largest current liability account? What were its total current liabilities?

(b) Based on information contained in those financial statements, compute the following 2003 values for each company.
  (1) Working capital.
  (2) Current ratio.

(c) What conclusions concerning the relative liquidity of these companies can be drawn from these data?

(d) Based on the information contained in these financial statements, compute the following 2003 ratios for each company.
  (1) Debt (excluding "deferred income taxes") to total assets.
  (2) Times interest earned.

(e) What conclusions concerning the companies' long-run solvency can be drawn from these ratios?

■ RESEARCH CASE

BYP11-3 Rapidly declining stock prices sometimes "trigger" other problems for a company. The May 3, 2002, edition of the *Wall Street Journal* contains an article by John Carreyrou titled "**Vivendi** Reveals Another Liability from Off-Balance-Sheet Accounting. The July 10, 2002, edition of the *Wall Street Journal* contains an article, also by John Carreyrou, titled "Vivendi Headquarters Raided in Disclosures-Related Probe," which summarizes the culmination of the liquidity problems brought on by the earlier events.

Instructions

Read the articles and answer the following questions.

(a) What is a put option? What is the total cost that Vivendi incurred in one week due to put options triggered by the drop in its stock price?
(b) In order to pay its obligation related to these options, the company will have to borrow money. What will be the likely outcome of having to borrow more money? What implications does this have for the company's profitability?
(c) Why did French stock market regulators raid Vivendi's headquarters?
(d) Why does the timing of the company's announcement about its liquidity problems matter to investors?
(e) In what significant way does the power of French stock market regulators differ from that of the U.S. Securities and Exchange Commission?

■ INTERPRETING FINANCIAL STATEMENTS

BYP11-4 **Lufkin Industries** and **CNH Global N.V.** are two manufacturers of construction and agricultural machinery.

Here are recent financial data for both companies (in millions).

	Lufkin Industries	CNH Global N.V.
Total current assets	$ 97.6	$ 7,431
Beginning total assets	233.6	17,577
Ending total assets	246.1	17,212
Beginning current liabilities	40.4	9,210
Ending current liabilities	37.0	7,353
Beginning total liabilities	80.9	15,063
Ending total liabilities	75.1	15,303
Interest expense	0.9	726
Income tax expense (refund)	12.7	(105)
Cash provided (used) by operations	34.8	(182)
Net income (loss)	19.5	(332)
Net sales	278.9	9,030

Instructions

Using the data, perform the following analysis.

(a) Calculate working capital and the current ratio for each company. Discuss their relative liquidity.
(b) Calculate the debt to total assets ratio and times interest earned for each company. Discuss their relative solvency.
(c) Calculate the return on assets ratio and profit margin ratio for each company. Comment on their relative profitability.

■ A GLOBAL FOCUS

BYP11-5 Many multinational companies find it beneficial to have their shares listed on stock exchanges in foreign countries. In order to do this, they must comply with the securities laws of those countries. Some of these laws relate to the form of financial disclosure the company must provide, including disclosures related to contingent liabilities. This exercise investigates the **Tokyo Stock Exchange**, the largest stock exchange in Japan.

Address: www.tse.or.jp/english/index.shtml, or go to www.wiley.com/college/weygandt

Steps

1. Choose **About TSE** and then **History**. Answer questions (a) and (b).
2. Choose **Listed Companies**.
3. Choose **Disclosure**. Answer questions (c) and (d).

Instructions

Answer the following questions.

(a) When was the first stock exchange opened in Japan? How many exchanges does Japan have today?
(b) What event caused trading to stop for a period of time in Japan?
(c) What are four examples of decisions by corporations that must be disclosed at the time of their occurrence?
(d) What are four examples of "occurrence of material fact" that must be disclosed at the time of their occurrence?

BYP11-6 **Apache Corporation** is an international, independent energy enterprise engaged in the exploration, development, production, gathering, processing, and marketing of natural gas and crude oil. Its corporate headquarters are located in Houston, Texas, and it has operations in North America, Australia, Egypt, Poland and the People's Republic of China.

The 1994 annual report of Apache Corporation disclosed the following information in its management discussion section.

APACHE CORPORATION
Management Discussion

In May 1994, Apache issued 9.25% bonds due 2002 in the principal amount of $100 million. The proceeds of $99 million from the offering were used to reduce bank debt, to pay off the 9.5% convertible debentures due 1996, and for general corporate purposes. In December 1994, the company privately placed 3.93% convertible notes due 1997 in the principal amount of $75 million. The notes are not redeemable before maturity and are convertible into Apache common stock at the option of the holders at any time prior to maturity, at a conversion price of $27 per share. Proceeds from the sale of the notes were used for the repayment of bank debt.

Instructions

(a) Identify the face amount, contractual interest rate, and selling price of the newly issued bonds due in 2002. Explain whether the bonds sold at a premium or a discount.

(b) For what purposes has Apache Corporation been incurring more debt?

■ EXPLORING THE WEB

BYP11-7 Bond or debt securities pay a stated rate of interest. This rate of interest is dependent on the risk associated with the investment. **Moody's Investment Service** provides ratings for companies that issue debt securities.

Address: www.moodys.com, or go to www.wiley.com/college/weygandt [Use of the Moody's address requires registration for parts (b) and (c).]

Steps: From Moody's homepage, choose **About Moody's** and **Moody's History**.

Instructions

(a) What year did Moody's introduce the first bond rating?

(b) List three basic principles Moody's uses in rating bonds.

(c) What is the definition of Moody's Aaa rating on long-term taxable debt?

Critical Thinking

■ GROUP DECISION CASE

***BYP11-8** On January 1, 2004, Bailey Corporation issued $6,000,000 of 5-year, 8% bonds at 96; the bonds pay interest semiannually on July 1 and January 1. By January 1, 2006, the market rate of interest for bonds of risk similar to those of Bailey Corporation had risen. As a result the market value of these bonds was $5,000,000 on January 1, 2006—below their carrying value. Debbie Bailey, president of the company, suggests repurchasing all of these bonds in the open market at the $5,000,000 price. To do so the company will have to issue $5,000,000 (face value) of new 10-year, 11% bonds at par. The president asks you, as controller, "What is the feasibility of my proposed repurchase plan?"

Instructions

With the class divided into groups, answer the following.

(a) What is the carrying value of the outstanding Bailey Corporation 5-year bonds on January 1, 2006? (Assume straight-line amortization.)
(b) Prepare the journal entry to retire the 5-year bonds on January 1, 2006. Prepare the journal entry to issue the new 10-year bonds.
(c) Prepare a short memo to the president in response to her request for advice. List the economic factors that you believe should be considered for her repurchase proposal.

■ COMMUNICATION ACTIVITY

BYP11-9 Ken Robson, president of the Robson Corporation, is considering the issuance of bonds to finance an expansion of his business. He has asked you to (1) discuss the advantages of bonds over common stock financing, (2) indicate the type of bonds he might issue, and (3) explain the issuing procedures used in bond transactions.

Instructions
Write a memo to the president, answering his request.

Accounting Matters!

■ ETHICS CASE

BYP11-10 Mel Horn is the president, founder, and majority owner of Wesley Medical Corporation, an emerging medical technology products company. Wesley is in dire need of additional capital to keep operating and to bring several promising products to final development, testing, and production. Mel, as owner of 51% of the outstanding stock, manages the company's operations. He places heavy emphasis on research and development and on long-term growth. The other principal stockholder is Mary Sommers who, as a nonemployee investor, owns 40% of the stock. Mary would like to deemphasize the R&D functions and emphasize the marketing function, to maximize short-run sales and profits from existing products. She believes this strategy would raise the market price of Wesley's stock.

All of Mel's personal capital and borrowing power is tied up in his 51% stock ownership. He knows that any offering of additional shares of stock will dilute his controlling interest because he won't be able to participate in such an issuance. But, Mary has money and would likely buy enough shares to gain control of Wesley. She then would dictate the company's future direction, even if it meant replacing Mel as president and CEO.

The company already has considerable debt. Raising additional debt will be costly, will adversely affect Wesley's credit rating, and will increase the company's reported losses due to the growth in interest expense. Mary and the other minority stockholders express opposition to the assumption of additional debt, fearing the company will be pushed to the brink of bankruptcy. Wanting to maintain his control and to preserve the direction of "his" company, Mel is doing everything to avoid a stock issuance. He is contemplating a large issuance of bonds, even if it means the bonds are issued with a high effective-interest rate.

Instructions
(a) Who are the stakeholders in this situation?
(b) What are the ethical issues in this case?
(c) What would you do if you were Mel?

Accounting Matters!

■ CONTINUING COOKIE CHRONICLE

(Note: This is a continuation of the Cookie Chronicle from Chapters 1 through 10.)

BYP11-11 Natalie is thinking of repaying all amounts outstanding to her grandmother. Recall that Cookie Creations borrowed $2,000 on November 16, 2005, from Natalie's grandmother. Interest on the note is 6% per year, and the note plus interest was to be repaid in 24 months. Recall that a monthly adjusting journal entry was prepared for the months of November 2005 (1/2 month), December 2005, and January 2006.

Instructions
(a) Calculate the interest payable that was accrued and recorded to January 31, 2006.
(b) Calculate the total interest expense and interest payable to August 31, 2006. Prepare the journal entry at August 31, 2006, to bring the accounting records up to date.

(c) Natalie repays her grandmother on September 15, 2006—10 months after her grandmother extended the loan to Cookie Creations. Prepare the journal entry for the loan repayment.

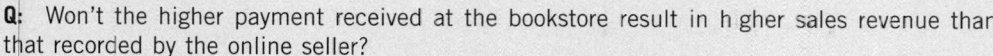

Answers to Accounting Matters! Questions

Accounting Matters!

p. 471

Q: Won't the higher payment received at the bookstore result in higher sales revenue than that recorded by the online seller?

A: No. The bookstore must collect sales tax at the time of a sale, but this collection is recorded as a liability rather than as revenue.

p. 478

Q: Why would investors have been cautious about buying TWA's "light-bulb bonds"?

A: The assets securing these bonds may not have had a ready market, nor may these assets have held their value as well as more traditional collateral. In addition, the fact that TWA was required to offer high yield (i.e., pay high interest rates) indicates higher risk for investors.

p. 488

Q: What differentiates "notes payable" from "mortgage notes payable"?

A: Plain "notes payable" has no specific collateral, whereas "mortgage notes payable" is secured by a mortgage that pledges title to specific assets, generally real estate. (A "chattel mortgage" is secured by personal property, such as a piece of furniture or an automobile.)

Answers to PepsiCo Review It Questions

Question 2, p. 476

PepsiCo reports three current liabilities: short-term obligations, accounts payable and other current liabilities, and income taxes payable.

Question 2, p. 486

An examination of **PepsiCo**'s statement of cash flows indicates the following reductions of debt: payments of long-term debt, $641 million, and payments of short-term borrowings of more than 3 months, $115 million.

Answers to Self-Study Questions

1. a **2.** d **3.** b **4.** b **5.** c **6.** a **7.** b **8.** d **9.** c ***10.** b ***11.** c ***12.** d ***13.** a

REMEMBER to go back to the Navigator box on the chapter-opening page and check off your completed work.

Chapter 12

Corporations: Organization, Stock Transactions, Dividends, and Retained Earnings

THE NAVIGATOR ✓

- Understand **Concepts for Review** ❑
- Read **Feature Story** ❑
- Scan **Study Objectives** ❑
- Read **Preview** ❑
- Read text and answer **Before You Go On**
  p. 533 ❑ p. 535 ❑ p. 538 ❑ p. 542 ❑
  p. 545 ❑ p. 552 ❑ p. 556 ❑ p. 559 ❑
- Work **Demonstration Problem** ❑
- Review **Summary of Study Objectives** ❑
- Answer **Self-Study Questions** ❑
- Complete **Assignments** ❑

CONCEPTS FOR REVIEW

Before studying this chapter, you should know or, if necessary, review:

- The content of the stockholders' equity section of a balance sheet. (Ch. 4, pp. 161–162)
- How to prepare closing entries for a corporation. (Ch. 4, pp. 148–151)
- What is the difference between paid-in capital and retained earnings. (Ch. 1, p. 13)

THE NAVIGATOR

ACCOUNTING MATTERS! FEATURE STORY

"Have You Driven a Ford Lately?"

A company that has produced such renowned successes as the Model T and the Mustang, and such a dismal failure as the Edsel, would have some interesting tales to tell. Henry Ford was a defiant visionary from the day **Ford Motor Company** was formed in 1903. His goal from day one was to design a car he could mass-produce and sell at a price that was affordable to the masses. In short order he accomplished this goal. By 1920, 60 percent of all vehicles on U.S. roads were Fords.

Henry Ford was intolerant of anything that stood between him and success. In the early years Ford had issued shares to the public in order to finance the company's exponential growth. In 1916 he decided not to pay a dividend in order to increase the funds available to expand the company.

The shareholders sued. Henry Ford's reaction was swift and direct: If the shareholders didn't see things his way, he would get rid of them. In 1919 the Ford family purchased 100 percent of the outstanding shares of Ford, eliminating any outside "interference." It was over 35 years before shares were again issued to the public.

Ford Motor Company has continued to evolve and grow over the years into one of the largest international corporations. Today there are nearly a billion shares of publicly traded Ford stock outstanding. But some aspects of the company have changed very little. The chairman and chief executive of the company is a member of the Ford family. Also, the Ford family still retains a significant stake in Ford Motor Company. In a move Henry Ford might have supported, top management recently decided to centralize decision making—that is, to have more key decisions made by top management, rather than by division managers. And, reminiscent of Henry Ford's most famous car, the company is attempting to make a "global car"—a mass-produced car that can be sold around the world with only minor changes.

www.ford.com

THE NAVIGATOR

STUDY OBJECTIVES

After studying this chapter, you should be able to:

1. Identify the major characteristics of a corporation.
2. Record the issuance of common stock.
3. Explain the accounting for treasury stock.
4. Differentiate preferred stock from common stock.
5. Prepare the entries for cash dividends and stock dividends.
6. Identify the items that are reported in a retained earnings statement.
7. Prepare and analyze a comprehensive stockholders' equity section.

THE NAVIGATOR

PREVIEW OF CHAPTER 12

Corporations like **Ford Motor Company** have substantial resources. In fact, the corporation is the dominant form of business organization in the United States in terms of dollar volume of sales and earnings, and number of employees. All of the 500 largest companies in the United States are corporations. In this chapter we will explain the essential features of a corporation and the accounting for a corporation's capital stock transactions, dividends, and retained earnings.

The content and organization of Chapter 12 are as follows.

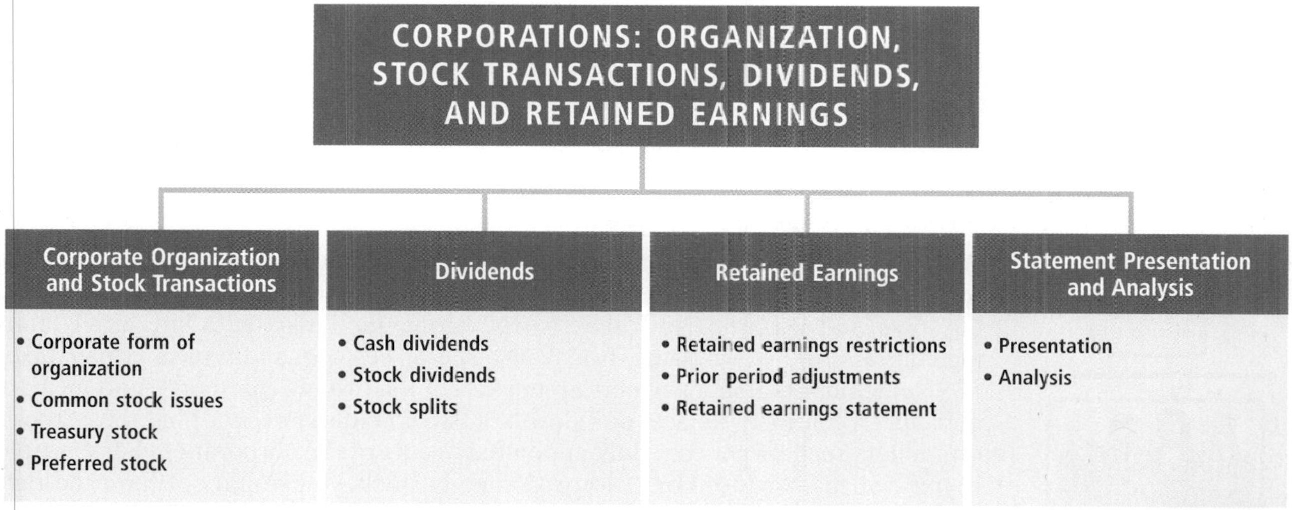

THE NAVIGATOR

SECTION 1 THE CORPORATE FORM OF ORGANIZATION AND STOCK TRANSACTIONS

The Corporate Form of Organization

In 1819, Chief Justice John Marshall defined a corporation as "an artificial being, invisible, intangible, and existing only in contemplation of law." This definition is the foundation for the prevailing legal interpretation that a **corporation** is an **entity separate and distinct from its owners**.

A corporation is created by law, and its continued existence depends upon the statutes of the state in which it is incorporated. As a legal entity, a corporation has most of the rights and privileges of a person. The major exceptions relate to privileges that only a living person can exercise, such as the right to vote or to hold public office. A corporation is subject to the same duties and responsibilities as a person. For example, it must abide by the laws and it must pay taxes.

Corporations may be classified in a variety of ways. Two common bases are by purpose and by ownership. A corporation may be organized for the purpose of making a **profit**, or it may be **nonprofit**. Corporations for profit include such well-known companies as **McDonald's**, **Ford Motor Company**, **PepsiCo**, and **Apple Computer**. Nonprofit corporations are organized for charitable, medical, or educational purposes. Examples are the **Salvation Army**, the **American Cancer Society**, and the **Ford Foundation**.

Classification by **ownership** distinguishes between publicly held and privately held corporations. A **publicly held corporation** may have thousands of stockholders.

Its stock is regularly traded on a national securities exchange such as the New York Stock Exchange. Most of the largest U.S. corporations are publicly held. Examples of publicly held corporations are **Intel**, **IBM**, **Caterpillar Inc.**, and **General Electric**. In contrast, a **privately held corporation**, often referred to as a closely held corporation, usually has only a few stockholders, and does not offer its stock for sale to the general public. Privately held companies are generally much smaller than publicly held companies, although some notable exceptions exist. **Cargill Inc.**, a private corporation that trades in grain and other commodities, is one of the largest companies in the United States.

STUDY OBJECTIVE 1

Identify the major characteristics of a corporation.

Characteristics of a Corporation

A number of characteristics distinguish a corporation from proprietorships and partnerships. The most important of these characteristics are explained below.

Separate Legal Existence

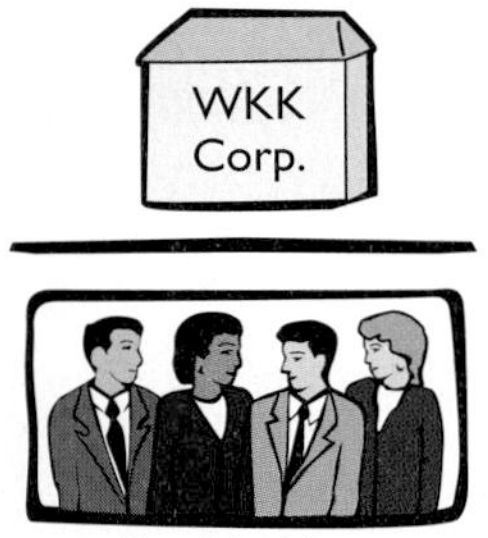

Legal existence separate from owners

As an entity separate and distinct from its owners, the corporation acts under its own name rather than in the name of its stockholders. **Ford Motor Company** may buy, own, and sell property. It may borrow money, and may enter into legally binding contracts in its own name. It may also sue or be sued, and it pays its own taxes.

Remember that in a partnership the acts of the owners (partners) bind the partnership. In contrast, the acts of its owners (stockholders) do not bind the corporation unless such owners are duly appointed agents of the corporation. For example, if you owned shares of Ford Motor Company stock, you would not have the right to purchase automobile parts for the company unless you were appointed as an agent of the corporation.

Limited Liability of Stockholders

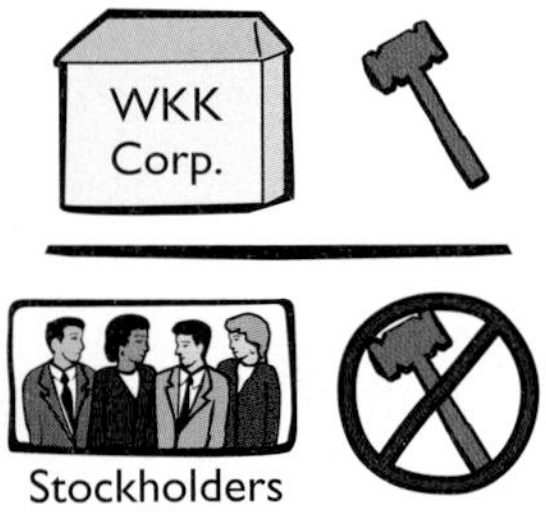

Limited liability of stockholders

Since a corporation is a separate legal entity, creditors have recourse only to corporate assets to satisfy their claims. The liability of stockholders is normally limited to their investment in the corporation. Creditors have no legal claim on the personal assets of the owners unless fraud has occurred. Even in the event of bankruptcy, stockholders' losses are generally limited to their capital investment in the corporation.

Transferable Ownership Rights

Transferable ownership rights

Ownership of a corporation is held in shares of capital stock. These are transferable units. Stockholders may dispose of part or all of their interest in a corporation simply by selling their stock. The transfer of an ownership interest in a partnership requires the consent of each owner. In contrast, the transfer of stock is entirely at the discretion of the stockholder. It does not require the approval of either the corporation or other stockholders.

The transfer of ownership rights between stockholders normally has no effect on the operating activities of the corporation. Nor does it affect the corporation's assets, liabilities, and total ownership equity. The transfer of these ownership rights is a transaction between individual owners. The enterprise does not participate in such transfers after it issues the capital stock.

Ability to Acquire Capital

Ability to acquire capital

It is relatively easy for a corporation to obtain capital through the issuance of stock. Buying stock in a corporation is often attractive to an investor because a stockholder has limited liability and shares of stock are readily transferable. Also, numerous individuals can become stockholders by investing small amounts of money. In sum, the ability of a successful corporation to obtain capital is virtually unlimited.

Continuous Life

The life of a corporation is stated in its charter. The life may be perpetual or it may be limited to a specific number of years. If it is limited, the life can be extended through renewal of the charter. Since a corporation is a separate legal entity, its continuance as a going concern is not affected by the withdrawal, death, or incapacity of a stockholder, employee, or officer. As a result, a successful enterprise can have a continuous and perpetual life.

Continuous life

Corporation Management

As in **Ford Motor Company**, stockholders legally own the corporation. But they manage the corporation indirectly through a board of directors they elect. The board, in turn, formulates the ethical and operating policies for the company, and it assumes an oversight responsibility on behalf of the stockholders and other third parties. The board also selects officers, such as a president and one or more vice presidents, to execute policy and to perform daily management functions.

A typical organization chart showing the delegation of responsibility is presented in Illustration 12-1.

Illustration 12-1 Corporation organization chart

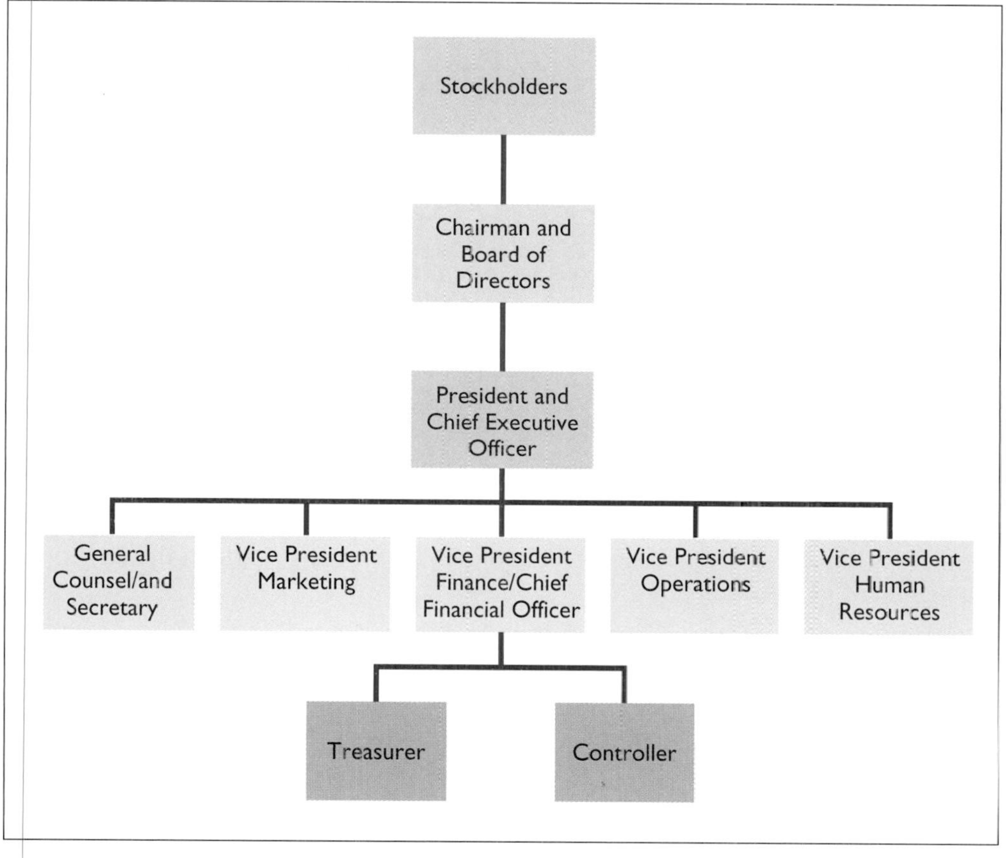

ETHICS NOTE

Managers who are not owners are often compensated based upon the performance of the firm. They thus may be tempted to exaggerate firm performance by inflating income figures.

The chief executive officer (CEO) has overall responsibility for managing the business. As the organization chart shows, the CEO delegates responsibility to other officers. The chief accounting officer is the **controller**. The controller's responsibilities include (1) maintaining the accounting records, (2) maintaining an adequate system of internal control, and (3) preparing financial statements, tax returns, and internal reports. The **treasurer** has custody of the corporation's funds and is responsible for maintaining the company's cash position.

The organizational structure of a corporation enables a company to hire professional managers to run the business. On the other hand, the separation of ownership and management prevents owners from having an active role in managing the company, which some owners like to have.

ACCOUNTING MATTERS! Ethics Perspective

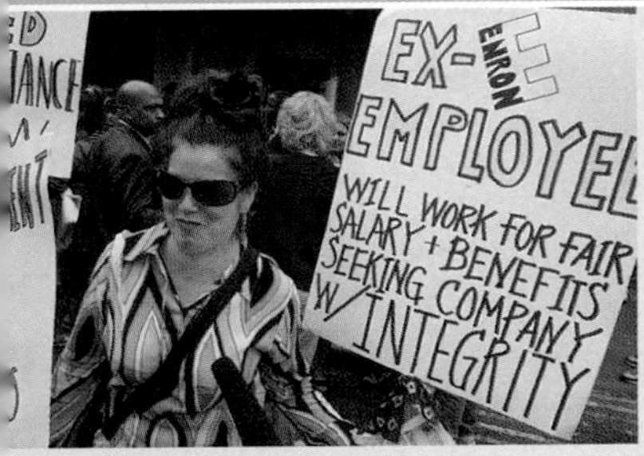

In the wake of **Enron**'s collapse, the members of Enron's board of directors have been questioned and scrutinized to determine what they knew, and when they knew it. A *Wall Street Journal* story reported that Enron's board contends it was "kept in the dark" by management and by Arthur Andersen—Enron's longtime auditors—and didn't learn about the company's troublesome accounting until October 2001. But, the *Wall Street Journal* reported that according to outside attorneys, "directors on at least two occasions waived Enron's ethical code of conduct to approve partnerships between Enron and its chief financial officer. Those partnerships kept significant debt off of Enron's books and masked actual company finances."

Source: Carol Hymowitz, "Serving on a Board Now Means Less Talk, More Accountability," *Wall Street Journal Online* (January 29, 2002).

? Was Enron's board of directors fulfilling its role in a corporate organization when it waived Enron's ethical code on two occasions?

Government Regulations

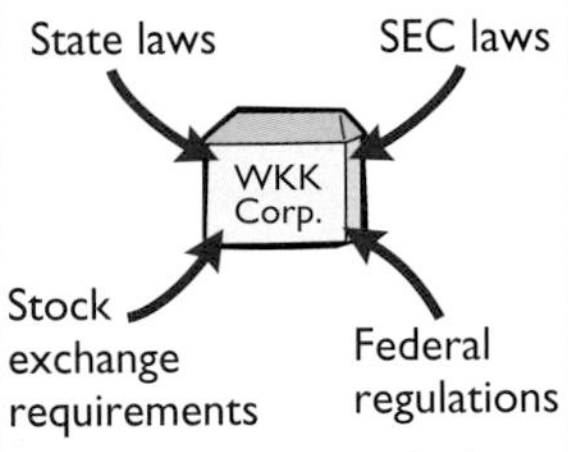

Government regulations

A corporation is subject to numerous state and federal regulations. State laws usually prescribe the requirements for issuing stock, the distributions of earnings permitted to stockholders, and the effects of retiring stock. Federal securities laws govern the sale of capital stock to the general public. Also, most publicly held corporations are required to make extensive disclosure of their financial affairs to the Securities and Exchange Commission through quarterly and annual reports. In addition, when a corporate stock is traded on organized securities exchanges, the corporation must comply with the reporting requirements of these exchanges. Government regulations are designed to protect the owners of the corporation. Such protection is needed because most stockholders do not participate in the day-to-day management of the company.

Additional Taxes

Additional taxes

Neither proprietorships nor partnerships pay income taxes. The owner's share of earnings from these organizations is reported on his or her personal income tax return. Taxes are then paid by the individual on this amount. Corporations, on the other hand, must pay federal and state income taxes as a separate legal entity. These taxes are substantial: They can amount to more than 40 percent of taxable income.

In addition, stockholders are required to pay taxes on cash dividends (pro rata distributions of net income). Thus, many argue that corporate income is **taxed twice (double taxation)**, once at the corporate level, and again at the individual level.

From the foregoing, we can identify the following advantages and disadvantages of a corporation compared to a proprietorship and partnership.

Illustration 12-2
Advantages and disadvantages of a corporation

Advantages	Disadvantages
Separate legal existence	Corporation management—separation of ownership and management
Limited liability of stockholders	Government regulations
Transferable ownership rights	Additional taxes
Ability to acquire capital	
Continuous life	
Corporation management—professional managers	

Forming a Corporation

The initial step in forming a corporation is to file an application with the Secretary of State in the state in which incorporation is desired. The application contains such information as: (1) the name and purpose of the proposed corporation; (2) amounts, kinds, and number of shares of capital stock to be authorized; (3) the names of the incorporators; and (4) the shares of stock to which each has subscribed.

After the application is approved, a **charter** is granted. The charter may be an approved copy of the application form or it may be a separate document containing the same basic data. The issuance of the charter creates the corporation. Upon receipt of the charter, the corporation develops its by-laws. The **by-laws** establish the internal rules and procedures for conducting the affairs of the corporation. They also indicate the powers of the stockholders, directors, and officers of the enterprise.[1]

ALTERNATIVE TERMINOLOGY

The charter is often referred to as the *articles of incorporation.*

Regardless of the number of states in which a corporation has operating divisions, it is incorporated in only one state. It is to the company's advantage to incorporate in a state whose laws are favorable to the corporate form of business organization. **General Motors**, for example, is incorporated in Delaware, whereas **QUALCOMM** is a New Jersey corporation. Many corporations choose to incorporate in states with rules favorable to existing management. For example, **Gulf Oil** at one time changed its state of incorporation to Delaware to thwart possible unfriendly takeovers. There, certain defensive tactics against takeovers can be approved by the board of directors alone, without a vote by shareholders.

Corporations engaged in interstate commerce must also obtain a license from each state in which they do business. The license subjects the corporation's operating activities to the corporation laws of the state.

Costs incurred in the formation of a corporation are called **organization costs**. These costs include legal and state fees, and promotional expenditures involved in the organization of the business. **Organization costs are expensed as incurred.** To determine the amount and timing of future benefits is so difficult that a conservative approach of expensing these costs immediately is followed.

Corporate Capital

Owners' equity in a corporation is identified as **stockholders' equity**, **shareholders' equity**, or **corporate capital**. The stockholders' equity section of a corporation's balance sheet consists of: (1) paid-in (contributed) capital and (2) retained earnings (earned capital). The distinction between paid-in capital and retained earnings is important from both a legal and a financial point of view. Legally, distributions of earnings (dividends) can be declared out of retained earnings in all states, but in many states they cannot be declared out of paid-in capital. Financially, management, stockholders, and others look to earnings for the continued existence and growth of the corporation.

[1] Following approval by two-thirds of the stockholders, the by-laws become binding upon all stockholders, directors, and officers. Legally, a corporation is regulated first by the laws of the state, second by its charter, and third by its by-laws. Care must be exercised to ensure that the provisions of the by-laws are not in conflict with either state laws or the charter.

Ownership Rights of Stockholders

When chartered, the corporation may begin selling ownership rights in the form of shares of stock. When a corporation has only one class of stock, it is identified as **common stock**. Each share of common stock gives the stockholder the ownership rights pictured in Illustration 12-3. The ownership rights of a share of stock are stated in the articles of incorporation or in the by-laws.

Illustration 12-3
Ownership rights of stockholders

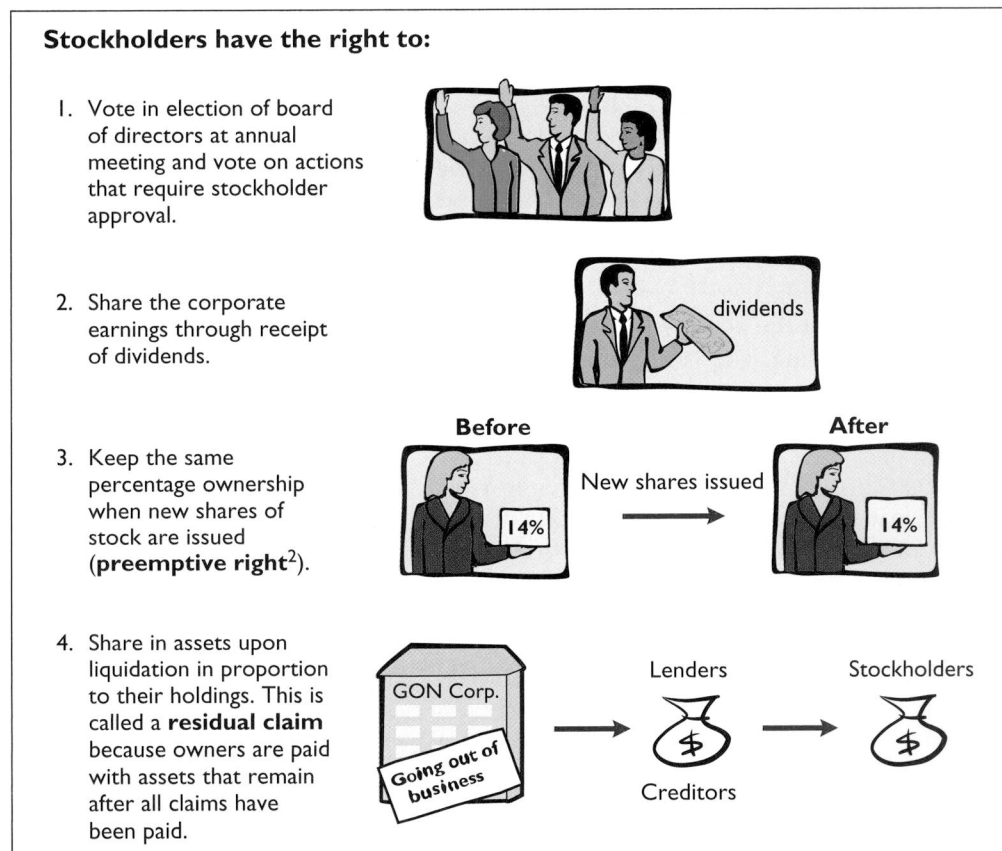

Stockholders have the right to:

1. Vote in election of board of directors at annual meeting and vote on actions that require stockholder approval.

2. Share the corporate earnings through receipt of dividends.

3. Keep the same percentage ownership when new shares of stock are issued (**preemptive right**[2]).

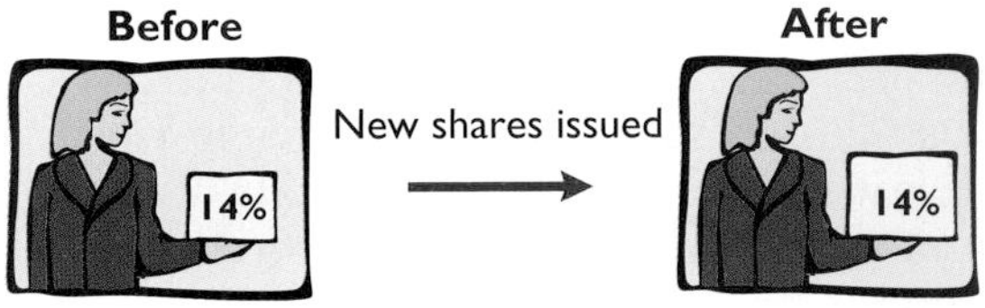

4. Share in assets upon liquidation in proportion to their holdings. This is called a **residual claim** because owners are paid with assets that remain after all claims have been paid.

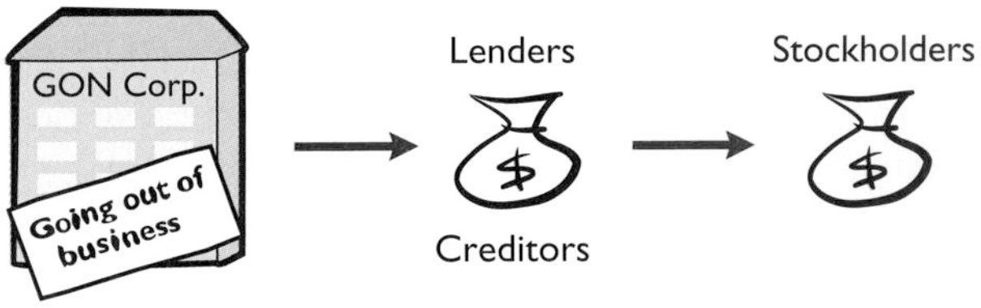

ACCOUNTING MATTERS! International Insight

In Japan, stockholders are considered to be far less important to a corporation than employees, customers, and suppliers. There, stockholders are rarely asked to vote on an issue, and the notion of changing corporate policy to favor stockholders borders on the heretical. This attitude toward stockholders appears to be slowly changing, however, as influential Japanese are advocating listening to investors, raising the extremely low dividends paid by Japanese corporations, and improving disclosure of financial information.

? In contrast to Japanese stockholders, what are the ownership rights of stockholders in U.S. corporations?

[2] A number of companies have eliminated the preemptive right, because they believe it makes an unnecessary and cumbersome demand on management. For example, by stockholder approval, **IBM** has dropped its preemptive right for stockholders.

Proof of stock ownership is evidenced by a form known as a **stock certificate**. As shown in Illustration 12-4 below, the face of the certificate shows the name of the corporation, the stockholder's name, the class and special features of the stock, the number of shares owned, and the signatures of duly authorized corporate officials. Certificates are prenumbered to facilitate accountability. They may be issued for any quantity of shares.

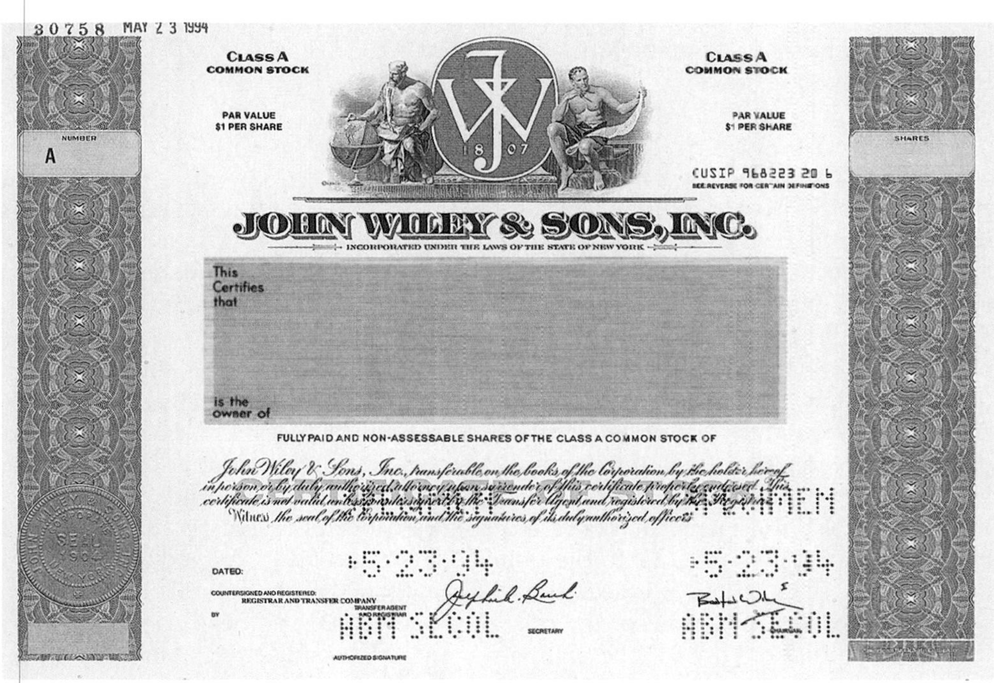

Illustration 12-4
A stock certificate

BEFORE YOU GO ON...

Review It

1. What are the advantages and disadvantages of a corporation compared to a proprietorship and a partnership?
2. Identify the principal steps in forming a corporation.
3. What are the two types of corporate capital shown on a balance sheet? Which form of capital typically may be used for payment of dividends?
4. What rights are inherent in owning a share of stock in a corporation?

THE NAVIGATOR

Stock Issue Considerations

In considering the issuance of stock, a corporation must resolve a number of basic questions: How many shares should be authorized for sale? How should the stock be issued? At what price should the shares be issued? What value should be assigned to the stock? These questions are answered in the following sections.

Authorized Stock

The amount of stock that a corporation is **authorized** to sell is indicated in its charter. The total amount of **authorized stock** at the time of incorporation normally anticipates both initial and subsequent capital needs. As a result, the number of shares authorized generally exceeds the number initially sold. If all authorized stock is sold, a corporation must obtain consent of the state to amend its charter before it can issue additional shares.

The authorization of capital stock does not result in a formal accounting entry. This event has no immediate effect on either corporate assets or stockholders' equity. But, disclosure of the number of authorized shares is often reported in the stockholders' equity section. It is then simple to determine the number of unissued shares that can be issued without amending the charter: subtract the total shares issued from the total authorized. For example, if Advanced Micro was authorized to sell 100,000 shares of common stock and issued 80,000 shares, 20,000 shares would remain unissued.

Indirect Issuance

Issuance of Stock

A corporation can issue common stock **directly** to investors. Or it can issue the stock **indirectly** through an investment banking firm (brokerage house) that specializes in bringing securities to the attention of prospective investors. Direct issue is typical in closely held companies. Indirect issue is customary for a publicly held corporation.

In an indirect issue, the investment banking firm may agree to **underwrite** the entire stock issue. In this arrangement, the investment banker buys the stock from the corporation at a stipulated price and resells the shares to investors. The corporation thus avoids any risk of being unable to sell the shares. Also, it obtains immediate use of the cash received from the underwriter. The investment banking firm, in turn, assumes the risk of reselling the shares in return for an underwriting fee.[3] For example, **Kolff Medical**, maker of the Jarvik artificial heart, used an underwriter to help it issue common stock to the public. The underwriter charged a 6.6 percent underwriting fee on Kolff Medical's approximately $20 million public offering.

How does a corporation set the price for a new issue of stock? Among the factors to be considered are (1) the company's anticipated future earnings, (2) its expected dividend rate per share, (3) its current financial position, (4) the current state of the economy, and (5) the current state of the securities market. The calculation can be complex and is properly the subject of a finance course.

Market Value of Stock

The stock of publicly held companies is traded on organized exchanges. The dollar prices per share are established by the interaction between buyers and sellers. In general, the prices set by the marketplace tend to follow the trend of a company's earnings and dividends. But, factors beyond a company's control, such as an oil embargo, changes in interest rates, and the outcome of a presidential election, may cause day-to-day fluctuations in market prices. (For more, see the box at the top of page 535.)

The trading of capital stock on securities exchanges involves the transfer of **already issued shares** from an existing stockholder to another investor. These transactions have no impact on a corporation's stockholders' equity.

Par and No-Par Value Stocks

Par value stock is capital stock that has been assigned a value per share in the corporate charter. Years ago, par value was used to determine the **legal capital** per share that must be retained in the business for the protection of corporate creditors.

[3] Alternatively, the investment banking firm may agree only to enter into a **best efforts** contract with the corporation. In such cases, the banker agrees to sell as many shares as possible at a specified price. The corporation bears the risk of unsold stock. Under a best efforts arrangement, the banking firm is paid a fee or commission for its services.

ACCOUNTING MATTERS! Business Insight

The volume of trading on national and international exchanges is heavy. Shares in excess of a billion are often traded daily on the New York Stock Exchange alone. For each listed stock, the *Wall Street Journal Online* reports the total volume of stock traded for a given day, the high and low price for the day (now in decimals), the closing market price, and the net change for the day. A recent listing for **PepsiCo** is shown below.

Stock	Volume	High	Low	Close	Net Change
PepsiCo	2,942,400	48.88	47.31	47.50	−0.10

These numbers indicate that PepsiCo's trading volume was 2,942,400 shares. The high, low, and closing prices for that date were $48.88, $47.31, and $47.50, respectively. The net change for the day was a decrease of $0.10 per share.

? For stocks traded on organized stock exchanges, how are the dollar prices per share established? What factors might influence the price of shares in the marketplace?

That amount is not available for withdrawal by stockholders. Thus, in the past, most states required the corporation to sell its shares at par or above.

However, the usefulness of par value as a protective device to creditors was questionable because par value was often immaterial relative to the value of the company's stock—even at the time of issue. For example, **Reebok**'s par value is $0.01 per share, yet a new issue in 2003 would have sold at a **market value** in the $33 per share range. Thus, par has no relationship with market value and in the vast majority of cases is an immaterial amount. As a consequence, today many states do not require a par value. Instead, other means are used to determine legal capital to protect creditors.

No-par value stock is capital stock that has not been assigned a value in the corporate charter. No-par value stock is quite common today. For example, **Nike**, **Procter & Gamble**, and **North American Van Lines** all have no-par stock. In many states the board of directors is permitted to assign a **stated value** to the no-par shares.

BEFORE YOU GO ON...

Review It

1. Of what significance to a corporation is the amount of authorized stock?
2. What alternative approaches may a corporation use in issuing stock?
3. Distinguish between par value and fair market value.

Do It

At the end of its first year of operation, Doral Corporation has $750,000 of common stock and net income of $122,000. Prepare (a) the closing entry for net income (as shown in Illustration 4-7, page 150), and (b) the stockholders' equity section at year-end (as shown in Illustration 4-24, page 162).

ACTION PLAN

- Record net income in Retained Earnings by a closing entry in which Income Summary is debited and Retained Earnings is credited.
- In the stockholders' equity section, show (1) paid-in capital and (2) retained earnings.

SOLUTION

(a) Income Summary	122,000	
Retained Earnings		122,000
(To close Income Summary and transfer net income to retained earnings)		

(b) Stockholders' equity		
Paid-in capital		
Common stock	$750,000	
Retained earnings	122,000	
Total stockholders' equity		$872,000

Related exercise material: *BE12-12, E12-5, and E12-6.*

☑ THE NAVIGATOR

Accounting for Common Stock Issues

STUDY OBJECTIVE 2

Record the issuance of common stock.

Let's now look at how to account for issues of common stock. The primary objectives in accounting for the issuance of common stock are: (1) to identify the specific sources of paid-in capital and (2) to maintain the distinction between paid-in capital and retained earnings. **The issuance of common stock affects only paid-in capital accounts.**

Issuing Par Value Common Stock for Cash

As discussed earlier, par value does not indicate a stock's market value. Therefore, the cash proceeds from issuing par value stock may be equal to, greater than, or less than par value. When the issuance of common stock for cash is recorded, the par value of the shares is credited to Common Stock. The portion of the proceeds that is above or below par value is recorded in a separate paid-in capital account.

To illustrate, assume that Hydro-Slide, Inc. issues 1,000 shares of $1 par value common stock at par for cash. The entry to record this transaction is:

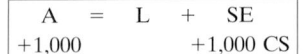

A	=	L	+	SE
+1,000				+1,000 CS

Cash Flows
+1,000

Cash	1,000	
Common Stock		1,000
(To record issuance of 1,000 shares of $1 par common stock at par)		

ALTERNATIVE TERMINOLOGY

Paid-in Capital in Excess of Par is also called *Premium on Stock.*

If Hydro-Slide issues an additional 1,000 shares of the $1 par value common stock for cash at $5 per share, the entry is:

A	=	L	+	SE
+5,000				+1,000 CS
				+4,000 CS

Cash Flows
+5,000

Cash	5,000	
Common Stock		1,000
Paid-in Capital in Excess of Par Value		4,000
(To record issuance of 1,000 shares of common stock in excess of par)		

The total paid-in capital from these two transactions is $6,000, and the legal capital is $2,000. If Hydro-Slide, Inc. has retained earnings of $27,000, the stockholders' equity section is as shown in Illustration 12-5 (page 537).

Illustration 12-5
Stockholders' equity—paid-in capital in excess of par value

HYDRO-SLIDE, INC.
Balance Sheet (partial)

Stockholders' equity	
Paid-in-capital	
Common stock	$ 2,000
Paid-in capital in excess of par value	**4,000**
Total paid-in capital	6,000
Retained earnings	27,000
Total stockholders' equity	$33,000

When stock is issued for less than par value, the account Paid-in Capital in Excess of Par Value is debited, if a credit balance exists in this account. If a credit balance does not exist, then the amount less than par is debited to Retained Earnings. This situation occurs only rarely: The sale of common stock below par value is not permitted in most states, because stockholders may be held personally liable for the difference between the price paid upon original sale and par value.

Issuing No-Par Common Stock for Cash

When no-par common stock has a stated value, the entries are similar to those illustrated for par value stock. The stated value it is credited to Common Stock. Also, when the selling price of no-par stock exceeds stated value, the excess is credited to Paid-in Capital in Excess of Stated Value. For example, assume that instead of $1 par value stock, Hydro-Slide, Inc. has $5 stated value no-par stock and the company issues 5,000 shares at $8 per share for cash. The entry is:

Cash	40,000	
Common Stock		25,000
Paid-in Capital in Excess of Stated Value		15,000
(To record issue of 5,000 shares of $5 stated value no-par stock)		

A	=	L	+	SE
+40,000				+25,000 CS
				+15,000 CS

Cash Flows
+40,000

Paid-in Capital in Excess of Stated Value is reported as part of paid-in capital in the stockholders' equity section.

What happens when no-par stock does not have a stated value? In that case, the entire proceeds are credited to Common Stock. Thus, if Hydro-Slide does not assign a stated value to its no-par stock, the issuance of the 5,000 shares at $8 per share for cash is recorded as follows.

Cash	40,000	
Common Stock		40,000
(To record issue of 5,000 shares of no-par stock)		

A	=	L	+	SE
+40,000				+40,000 CS

Cash Flows
+40,000

Issuing Common Stock for Services or Noncash Assets

Stock may also be issued for services (compensation to attorneys or consultants) or for noncash assets (land, buildings, or equipment). In such cases, what cost should be recognized in the exchange transaction? To comply with the **cost principle**, in a noncash transaction **cost is the cash equivalent price.** Thus, **cost is either the fair market value of the consideration given up, or the fair market value of the consideration received**, whichever is more clearly determinable.

To illustrate, assume that attorneys have helped Jordan Company incorporate. They have billed the company $5,000 for their services. They agree to accept 4,000

shares of $1 par value common stock in payment of their bill. At the time of the exchange, there is no established market price for the stock. In this case, the market value of the consideration received, $5,000, is more clearly evident. Accordingly, the entry is:

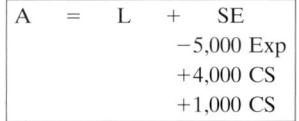

A	=	L	+	SE
				−5,000 Exp
				+4,000 CS
				+1,000 CS

Cash Flows
no effect

Organization Expense	5,000	
Common Stock		4,000
Paid-in Capital in Excess of Par Value		1,000
(To record issuance of 4,000 shares of $1 par value stock to attorneys)		

As explained on page 531, organization costs are expensed as incurred.

In contrast, assume that Athletic Research Inc. is an existing publicly held corporation. Its $5 par value stock is actively traded at $8 per share. The company issues 10,000 shares of stock to acquire land recently advertised for sale at $90,000. The most clearly evident value in this noncash transaction is the market price of the consideration given, $80,000. The transaction is recorded as follows.

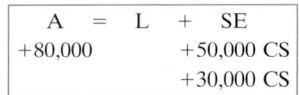

A	=	L	+	SE
+80,000				+50,000 CS
				+30,000 CS

Cash Flows
no effect

Land	80,000	
Common Stock		50,000
Paid-in Capital in Excess of Par Value		30,000
(To record issuance of 10,000 shares of $5 par value stock for land)		

As illustrated in these examples, **the par value of the stock is never a factor in determining the cost of the assets received**. This is also true of the stated value of no-par stock.

BEFORE YOU GO ON...

Review It

1. Explain the accounting for par and no-par common stock issued for cash.
2. Explain the accounting for the issuance of stock for services or noncash assets.
3. What is the par or stated value per share of **PepsiCo**'s common stock? How many shares has PepsiCo issued at December 27, 2003? The answers to these questions are provided on page 583.

Do It

Cayman Corporation begins operations on March 1 by issuing 100,000 shares of $10 par value common stock for cash at $12 per share. On March 15 it issues 5,000 shares of common stock to attorneys in settlement of their bill of $50,000 for organization costs. Journalize the issuance of the shares, assuming the stock is not publicly traded.

ACTION PLAN

- In issuing shares for cash, credit Common Stock for par value per share.
- Credit any additional proceeds in excess of par value to a separate paid-in capital account.
- When stock is issued for services, use the cash equivalent price.
- For the cash equivalent price use either the fair market value of what is given up or the fair market value of what is received, whichever is more clearly determinable.

SOLUTION

		Debit	Credit
Mar. 1	Cash	1,200,000	
	Common Stock		1,000,000
	Paid-in Capital in Excess of Par Value		200,000
	(To record issuance of 100,000 shares at $12 per share)		
Mar. 15	Organization Expense	50,000	
	Common Stock		50,000
	(To record issuance of 5,000 shares for attorneys' fees)		

Related exercise material: *BE12-2, BE12-4, E12-1, E12-3, and E12-6.*

THE NAVIGATOR

Accounting for Treasury Stock

STUDY OBJECTIVE 3

Explain the accounting for treasury stock.

Treasury stock is a corporation's own stock that has been issued, fully paid for, and reacquired by the corporation but not retired (still authorized but no longer outstanding). A corporation may acquire treasury stock for various reasons:

1. To reissue the shares to officers and employees under bonus and stock compensation plans.
2. To increase trading of the company's stock in the securities market in the hopes of enhancing its market value.
3. To have additional shares available for use in the acquisition of other companies.
4. To reduce the number of shares outstanding and thereby increase earnings per share.
5. To rid the company of disgruntled investors, perhaps to avoid a takeover, as illustrated in the **Ford Motor Company** Feature Story.

HELPFUL HINT

Treasury shares do not have dividend rights or voting rights.

Many corporations have treasury stock. One survey of 600 companies in the United States found that 66 percent have treasury stock.[4] Specifically, **The Gillette Company** recently reported 326 million treasury shares, **The Coca-Cola Company** 1,053 million shares, and **United Airlines** 16.1 million shares.

Purchase of Treasury Stock

Treasury stock is generally accounted for by the **cost method**. This method uses the cost of the shares purchased to value the treasury stock. Under the cost method, **Treasury Stock is debited for the price paid to reacquire the shares.**

The same amount is credited to Treasury Stock when the shares are disposed of. To illustrate, assume that on January 1, 2006, the stockholders' equity section of Mead, Inc. has 100,000 shares of $5 par value common stock outstanding (all issued at par value) and Retained Earnings of $200,000. The stockholders' equity section before purchase of treasury stock is shown on page 540.

[4] *Accounting Trends & Techniques 2003* (New York: American Institute of Certified Public Accountants).

Illustration 12-6
Stockholders' equity with no treasury stock

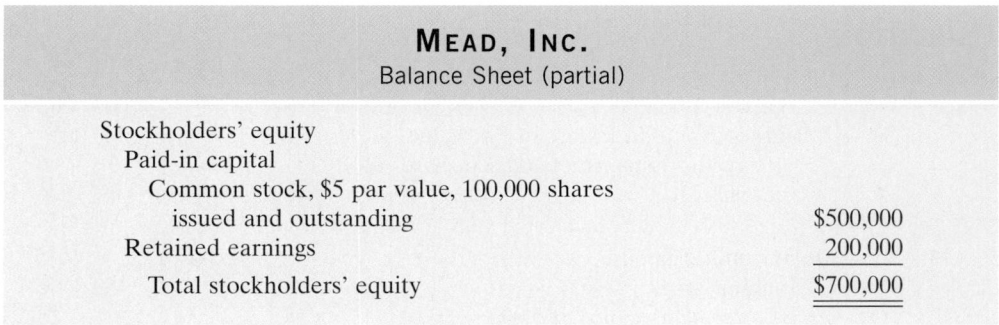

MEAD, INC.
Balance Sheet (partial)

Stockholders' equity	
Paid-in capital	
Common stock, $5 par value, 100,000 shares issued and outstanding	$500,000
Retained earnings	200,000
Total stockholders' equity	$700,000

On February 1, 2006, Mead acquires 4,000 shares of its stock at $8 per share. The entry is:

A	=	L	+	SE
−32,000				−32,000 TS

Cash Flows
−32,000

Feb. 1	Treasury Stock	32,000	
	Cash		32,000
	(To record purchase of 4,000 shares of treasury stock at $8 per share)		

Note that Treasury Stock is debited for the cost of the shares purchased. Is the original paid-in capital account, Common Stock, affected? No, because the number of issued shares does not change. In the stockholders' equity section of the balance sheet, treasury stock is deducted from total paid-in capital and retained earnings. Treasury Stock is a contra stockholders' equity account.

The stockholders' equity section of Mead, Inc. after purchase of treasury stock is as follows.

Illustration 12-7
Stockholders' equity with treasury stock

MEAD, INC.
Balance Sheet (partial)

Stockholders' equity	
Paid-in capital	
Common stock, $5 par value, 100,000 shares issued and 96,000 shares outstanding	$500,000
Retained earnings	200,000
Total paid-in capital and retained earnings	700,000
Less: Treasury stock (4,000 shares)	**32,000**
Total stockholders' equity	$668,000

Thus, the acquisition of treasury stock reduces stockholders' equity.

In the balance sheet, both the number of shares issued (100,000) and the number in the treasury (4,000) are disclosed. The difference between these two amounts is the number of shares of stock outstanding (96,000). The term **outstanding stock** means the number of shares of issued stock that are being held by stockholders.

Some maintain that treasury stock should be reported as an asset because it can be sold for cash. Under this reasoning, unissued stock should also be shown as an asset, clearly an erroneous conclusion. Rather than being an asset, treasury stock reduces stockholder claims on corporate assets. This effect is correctly shown by reporting treasury stock as a deduction from total paid-in capital and retained earnings.

ACCOUNTING MATTERS! **Business Insight**

In a bold (and some would say risky) move **Reebok** at one time bought back nearly a *third* of its shares. This repurchase of shares dramatically reduced Reebok's available cash. In fact, the company borrowed significant funds to accomplish the repurchase. In a press release, management stated that it was repurchasing the shares because it believed its stock was severely underpriced. The repurchase of so many shares was meant to signal management's belief in good future earnings.

Skeptics, however, suggested that Reebok's management was repurchasing shares to make it less likely that the company would be acquired by another company (in which case Reebok's top managers would likely lose their jobs). By depleting its cash, Reebok became a less likely acquisition target. Acquiring companies prefer to purchase companies with large cash reserves so they can pay off debt used in the acquisition.

? When a corporation acquires treasury stock, what is the effect upon the price of its shares of stock?

Disposal of Treasury Stock

Treasury stock is usually sold or retired. The accounting for its sale is different when treasury stock is sold above cost than when it is sold below cost.

Sale of Treasury Stock Above Cost

If the selling price of the treasury shares is equal to cost, the sale of the shares is recorded by a debit to Cash and a credit to Treasury Stock. When the selling price of the shares is greater than cost, the difference is credited to Paid-in Capital from Treasury Stock.

To illustrate, assume that 1,000 shares of treasury stock of Mead, Inc., previously acquired at $8 per share, are sold at $10 per share on July 1. The entry is as follows.

July 1	Cash	10,000	
	Treasury Stock		8,000
	Paid-in Capital from Treasury Stock		2,000
	(To record sale of 1,000 shares of treasury stock above cost)		

HELPFUL HINT

Treasury stock transactions are classified as capital stock transactions. As in the case when stock is issued, the income statement is not involved.

A	=	L	+	SE
+10,000				+8,000 TS
				+2,000 CS

Cash Flows
+10,000

The $2,000 credit in the entry would not be considered a gain on sale of treasury stock for two reasons: (1) Gains on sales occur when **assets** are sold, and treasury stock is not an asset. (2) A corporation does not realize a gain or suffer a loss from stock transactions with its own stockholders. Thus, paid-in capital arising from the sale of treasury stock should not be included in the measurement of net income. Paid-in Capital from Treasury Stock is listed separately on the balance sheet as a part of paid-in capital.

Sale of Treasury Stock Below Cost

When treasury stock is sold below its cost, the excess of cost over selling price is usually debited to Paid-in Capital from Treasury Stock. Thus, if Mead, Inc. sells an additional 800 shares of treasury stock on October 1 at $7 per share, the entry is as follows.

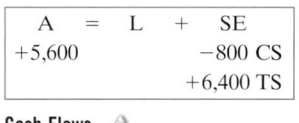

A	=	L	+	SE
+5,600				−800 CS
				+6,400 TS

Cash Flows
+5,600

Oct. 1	Cash	5,600	
	Paid-in Capital from Treasury Stock	800	
	Treasury Stock		6,400
	(To record sale of 800 shares of treasury stock below cost)		

Observe the following from the two sales entries: (1) Treasury Stock is credited at cost in each entry. (2) Paid-in Capital from Treasury Stock is used for the difference between cost and the resale price of the shares. And (3) the original paid-in capital account, Common Stock, is not affected. **The sale of treasury stock increases both total assets and total stockholders' equity.**

After posting the foregoing entries, the treasury stock accounts will show the following balances on October 1.

Illustration 12-8
Treasury stock accounts

Treasury Stock			
Feb. 1	32,000	July 1	8,000
		Oct. 1	6,400
Oct. 1 Bal.	17,600		

Paid-in Capital from Treasury Stock			
Oct. 1	800	July 1	2,000
		Oct. 1 Bal.	1,200

When the credit balance in Paid-in Capital from Treasury Stock is depleted, any additional excess of cost over selling price is debited to Retained Earnings. To illustrate, assume that Mead, Inc. sells its remaining 2,200 shares at $7 per share on December 1. The excess of cost over selling price is $2,200 [2,200 × ($8 − $7)]. In this case, $1,200 of the excess is debited to Paid-in Capital from Treasury Stock. The remainder is debited to Retained Earnings. The entry is:

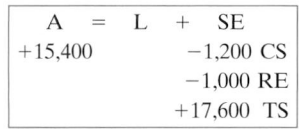

A	=	L	+	SE
+15,400				−1,200 CS
				−1,000 RE
				+17,600 TS

Cash Flows
+15,400

Dec. 1	Cash	15,400	
	Paid-in Capital from Treasury Stock	1,200	
	Retained Earnings	1,000	
	Treasury Stock		17,600
	(To record sale of 2,200 shares of treasury stock at $7 per share)		

BEFORE YOU GO ON...

Review It

1. What is treasury stock, and why do companies acquire it?
2. How is treasury stock recorded?
3. Where is treasury stock reported in the financial statements? Does a company record gains and losses on treasury stock transactions? Explain.
4. How many shares of treasury stock did **PepsiCo** have at December 27, 2003 and at December 28, 2002? The answer to this question is provided on page 583.

Do It

Santa Anita Inc. purchases 3,000 shares of its $50 par value common stock for $180,000 cash on July 1. The shares are to be held in the treasury until resold. On November 1, the corporation sells 1,000 shares of treasury stock for cash at $70 per share. Journalize the treasury stock transactions.

ACTION PLAN

- Record the purchase of treasury stock at cost.
- When treasury stock is sold above its cost, credit the excess of the selling price over cost to Paid-in Capital from Treasury Stock.
- When treasury stock is sold below its cost, debit the excess of cost over selling price to Paid-in Capital from Treasury Stock.

SOLUTION

July 1	Treasury Stock	180,000	
	Cash		180,000
	(To record the purchase of 3,000 shares at $60 per share)		
Nov. 1	Cash	70,000	
	Treasury Stock		60,000
	Paid-in Capital from Treasury Stock		10,000
	(To record the sale of 1,000 shares at $70 per share)		

Related exercise material: *BE12-5, E12-2, and E12-4.*

THE NAVIGATOR

Preferred Stock

STUDY OBJECTIVE 4

Differentiate preferred stock from common stock.

To appeal to more potential investors, a corporation may issue an additional class of stock, called preferred stock. **Preferred stock** has contractual provisions that give it a preference or priority over common stock in certain areas. Typically, preferred stockholders have a priority as to (1) distributions of earnings (dividends) and (2) assets in the event of liquidation. However, they generally do not have voting rights.

Like common stock, preferred stock may be issued for cash or for noncash assets. The entries for these transactions are similar to the entries for common stock. When a corporation has more than one class of stock, each paid-in capital account title should identify the stock to which it relates. For example, a company might have the following accounts: Preferred Stock, Common Stock, Paid-in Capital in Excess of Par Value—Preferred Stock, and Paid-in Capital in Excess of Par Value—Common Stock. Assume that Stine Corporation issues 10,000 shares of $10 par value preferred stock for $12 cash per share. The entry to record the issuance is:

Cash	120,000	
Preferred Stock		100,000
Paid-in Capital in Excess of Par Value–Preferred Stock		20,000
(To record the issuance of 10,000 shares of $10 par value preferred stock)		

A	=	L	+	SE
+120,000				+100,000 PS
				+20,000 PS

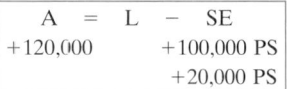

Cash Flows
+120,000

Preferred stock may have either a par value or no-par value. In the stockholders' equity section of the balance sheet, preferred stock is shown first because of its dividend and liquidation preferences over common stock. A **callable** feature grants the issuing corporation the right to purchase preferred stock from stockholders at specified future dates and prices. Various features associated with the issuance of preferred stock are discussed on the following pages.

I hope there is some money left when it's my turn.
Preferred stockholders
Common stockholders

Dividend Preference

Dividend Preferences

As noted earlier, **preferred stockholders have the right to share in the distribution of corporate income before common stockholders**. For example, if the dividend rate on preferred stock is \$5 per share, common shareholders will not receive any dividends in the current year until preferred stockholders have received \$5 per share. The first claim to dividends does not, however, guarantee the payment of dividends. Dividends depend on many factors, such as adequate retained earnings and availability of cash.

The per share dividend amount is stated as a percentage of the preferred stock's par value or as a specified amount. For example, at one time **Crane Company** specified a $3\frac{3}{4}$ percent dividend on its \$100 par value preferred (\$100 × $3\frac{3}{4}$% = \$3.75 per share). **PepsiCo** has a \$5.46 series of no-par preferred stock.

Cumulative Dividend

Preferred stock often contains a **cumulative dividend** feature. This means that preferred stockholders must be paid both current-year dividends and any unpaid prior-year dividends before common stockholders receive dividends. When preferred stock is cumulative, preferred dividends not declared in a given period are called **dividends in arrears**.

To illustrate, assume that Scientific-Leasing has 5,000 shares of 7 percent, \$100 par value, cumulative preferred stock outstanding. The annual dividend is \$35,000 (5,000 × \$7 per share), but dividends are two years in arrears. In this case preferred stockholders are entitled to receive the following dividends in the current year.

Illustration 12-9
Computation of total dividends to preferred stock

Dividends in arrears (\$35,000 × 2)	\$ 70,000
Current-year dividends	35,000
Total preferred dividends	**\$105,000**

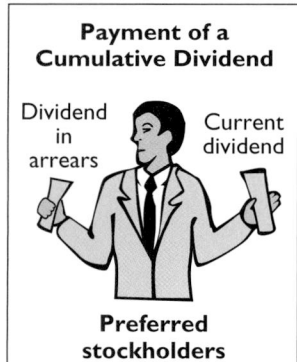

Payment of a Cumulative Dividend

No distribution can be made to common stockholders until this entire preferred dividend is paid. In other words, dividends cannot be paid to common stockholders while any preferred stock is in arrears.

Dividends in arrears are not considered a liability. No payment obligation exists until a dividend is declared by the board of directors. However, the amount of dividends in arrears should be disclosed in the notes to the financial statements. Doing so enables investors to assess the potential impact of this commitment on the corporation's financial position.

Companies that are unable to meet their dividend obligations are not looked upon favorably by the investment community. As a financial officer noted in discussing one company's failure to pay its cumulative preferred dividend for a period of time, "Not meeting your obligations on something like that is a major black mark on your record." The accounting entries for preferred stock dividends are explained later in this chapter.

Liquidation Preference

Most preferred stocks also have a preference on corporate assets if the corporation fails. This feature provides security for the preferred stockholder. The preference to assets may be for the par value of the shares or for a specified liquidating value. **EarthLink**'s preferred stock entitles the holders to receive \$20.83 per share, plus accrued and unpaid dividends, in the event of involuntary liquidation. The liquidation preference establishes the respective claims of creditors and preferred stockholders.

BEFORE YOU GO ON...

Review It

1. Preferred stock has what preferences over common stock?
2. Why are dividends in arrears on preferred stock not considered a liability?
3. Of what value is the preference in liquidation to preferred stockholders?

THE NAVIGATOR

SECTION 2 DIVIDENDS

STUDY OBJECTIVE 5

Prepare the entries for cash dividends and stock dividends.

A dividend **is a distribution by a corporation to its stockholders on a pro rata (proportional) basis.** Potential buyers and sellers of stock are very interested in a company's dividend policies and practices. Dividends can take four forms: cash, property, scrip (a promissory note to pay cash), or stock. Cash dividends predominate in practice. Also, stock dividends are declared with some frequency. These two forms of dividends will be the focus of discussion in this chapter.

Dividends may be expressed in two ways: (1) as a percentage of the par or stated value of the stock, or (2) as a dollar amount per share. In the financial press, **dividends are generally reported quarterly as a dollar amount per share**. For example, **Boeing Company**'s quarterly dividend rate is 17 cents a share, **Hershey Foods Corp.**'s is 31.5 cents, and **Nike**'s is 12 cents.

Cash Dividends

A cash dividend is a pro rata distribution of cash to stockholders. For a corporation to pay a cash dividend, it must have:

1. **Retained earnings.** The legality of a cash dividend depends on the laws of the state in which the company is incorporated. Payment of cash dividends from retained earnings is legal in all states. In general, cash dividend distributions based only on the balance in Common Stock (legal capital) are illegal. Statutes vary considerably with respect to cash dividends based on paid-in capital in excess of par or stated value. Many states permit such dividends. A dividend declared out of paid-in capital is termed a liquidating dividend. The amount originally paid in by stockholders is being reduced or "liquidated" by such a dividend.
2. **Adequate cash.** The legality of a dividend and the ability to pay a dividend are two different things. For example, **Nike**, with retained earnings of over $3 billion, could legally declare a dividend of at least $3 billion. But Nike's cash balance is only $198 million. In order to pay a $3 billion dividend, Nike would need to raise additional cash through the sale of other assets or through additional financing.

   Before declaring a cash dividend, a company's board of directors must carefully consider both current and future demands on the company's cash resources. In some cases, current liabilities may make a cash dividend inappropriate. In other cases, a major plant expansion program may warrant only a relatively small dividend.
3. **A declaration of dividends.** A company does not pay dividends unless its board of directors decides to do so, at which point the board "declares" the dividend. The board of directors has full authority to determine the amount of income to be distributed in the form of a dividend and the amount to be retained in the business. Dividends do not accrue like interest on a note payable, and they are not a liability until declared.

The amount and timing of a dividend are important issues. The payment of a large cash dividend could lead to liquidity problems for the enterprise. On the other hand, a small dividend or a missed dividend may cause unhappiness among stockholders. Many of them expect to receive a reasonable cash payment from the company on a periodic basis. Many companies declare and pay cash dividends quarterly.

ACCOUNTING MATTERS! **Business Insight**

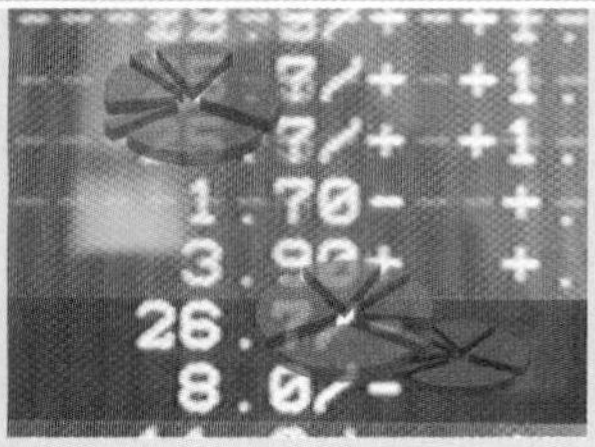

To pay, or not to pay, that seems to be the question. As stock prices fall and the market becomes more volatile, investors become more interested in dividends. And what they found recently was not too pleasing. One article noted that "According to Standard and Poor's, only 72% of companies in its S&P 500 index paid a dividend last year [2001], down from 94% in 1980." However, as a result of new tax regulations reducing the tax on dividends to only 15 percent, many corporate boards increased their dividend in 2003.

Source: "Dividends' End: Should Technology Companies Pay Dividends?" *The Economist* (January 12, 2002), p. 68.

? What factors must a board of directors consider before declaring a cash dividend?

Entries for Cash Dividends

Three dates are important in connection with dividends: (1) the declaration date, (2) the record date, and (3) the payment date. Normally, there are two to four weeks between each date. Accounting entries are required on two of the dates—the declaration date and the payment date.

On the **declaration date**, the board of directors formally declares (authorizes) the cash dividend and announces it to stockholders. Declaration of a cash dividend **commits the corporation to a legal obligation**. The obligation is binding and cannot be rescinded. An entry is required to recognize the decrease in retained earnings and the increase in the liability Dividends Payable. To illustrate, assume that on December 1, 2006, the directors of Media General declare a 50¢ per share cash dividend on 100,000 shares of $10 par value common stock. The dividend is $50,000 (100,000 × 50¢). The entry to record the declaration is:

A	=	L	+	SE
		+50,000		−50,000 Div

Cash Flows
no effect

Declaration Date

Dec. 1	Retained Earnings	50,000	
	Dividends Payable		50,000
	(To record declaration of cash dividend)		

Dividends Payable is a current liability: it will normally be paid within the next several months.

Instead of debiting Retained Earnings, the account Dividends may be debited. This account provides additional information in the ledger. Also, a company may have separate dividend accounts for each class of stock. When a dividend account is used, its balance is transferred to Retained Earnings at the end of the year by a closing entry. Whichever account is used for the dividend declaration, the effect is the same: retained earnings is decreased and a current liability is increased. For homework problems, you should use the Retained Earnings account for recording dividend declarations.

At the **record date**, ownership of the outstanding shares is determined for dividend purposes. The records maintained by the corporation supply this information. In the interval between the declaration date and the record date, the corporation updates its stock ownership records. For Media General, the record date is December 30. No entry is required on this date because the corporation's liability recognized on the declaration date is unchanged.

HELPFUL HINT

Between the declaration date and record date, the number of shares outstanding should remain the same. The purpose of the record date is to identify the persons or entities that will receive the dividend, not to determine the amount of the dividend liability.

Record Date

Dec. 30	No entry necessary		

On the **payment date**, dividend checks are mailed to the stockholders and the payment of the dividend is recorded. Assuming that the payment date is January 23 for Media General, the entry on that date is:

Payment Date

Jan. 23	Dividends Payable	50,000	
	Cash		50,000
	(To record payment of cash dividend)		

A	=	L	+	SE
−50,000		−50,000		

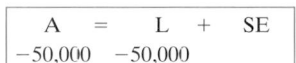

Cash Flows

−50,000

Note that payment of the dividend reduces both current assets and current liabilities. It has no effect on stockholders' equity. The **cumulative effect** of the **declaration and payment** of a cash dividend is to **decrease both stockholders' equity and total assets**. Illustration 12-10 summarizes the three important dates associated with dividends.

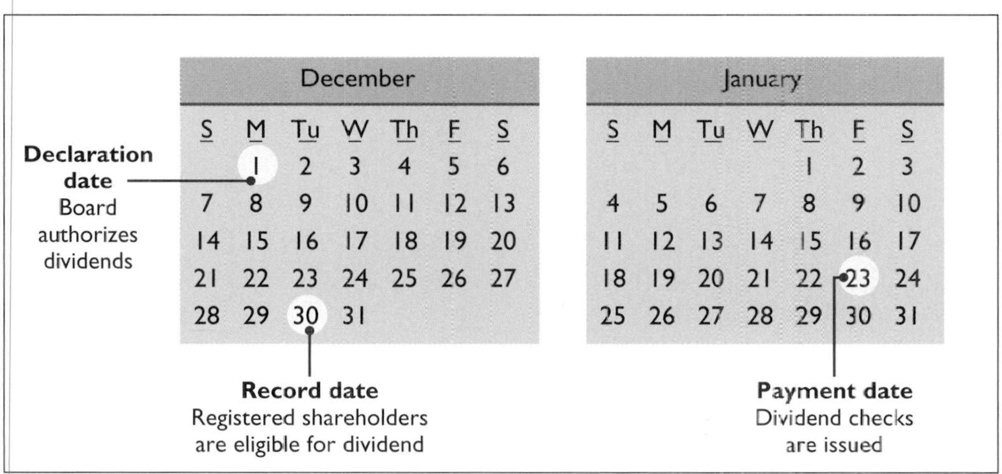

Illustration 12-10
Key dividend dates

Allocating Cash Dividends between Preferred and Common Stock

As explained earlier in this chapter, preferred stock has priority over common stock in regard to dividends. Holders of cumulative preferred stock must be paid any unpaid prior-year dividends before common stockholders receive dividends.

To illustrate, assume that at December 31, 2006, IBR Inc. has 1,000 shares of 8%, $100 par value cumulative preferred stock. It also has 50,000 shares of $10 par value common stock outstanding. The dividend per share for preferred stock is $8

($100 par value × 8%). The required annual dividend for preferred stock is therefore $8,000 (1,000 × $8). At December 31, 2006, the directors declare a $6,000 cash dividend. In this case, the entire dividend amount goes to preferred stockholders because of their dividend preference. The entry to record the declaration of the dividend is:

A	=	L	+	SE
		+6,000		−6,000 Div

Cash Flows
no effect

Dec. 31	Retained Earnings	6,000	
	Dividends Payable		6,000
	(To record $6 per share cash dividend to preferred stockholders)		

Because of the cumulative feature, dividends of $2 per share are in arrears on preferred stock for 2006. These dividends must be paid to preferred stockholders before any future dividends can be paid to common stockholders. Dividends in arrears should be disclosed in the financial statements.

At December 31, 2007, IBR declares a $50,000 cash dividend. The allocation of the dividend to the two classes of stock is as follows.

Illustration 12-11
Allocating dividends to preferred and common stock

Total dividend		$50,000
Allocated to preferred stock		
Dividends in arrears, 2006 (1,000 × $2)	**$2,000**	
2007 dividend (1,000 × $8)	**8,000**	10,000
Remainder allocated to common stock		$40,000

The entry to record the declaration of the dividend is:

A	=	L	+	SE
		+50,000		−50,000 Div

Cash Flows
no effect

Dec. 31	Retained Earnings	50,000	
	Dividends Payable		50,000
	(To record declaration of cash dividends of $10,000 to preferred stock and $40,000 to common stock)		

What if IBR's preferred stock were not cumulative? In that case preferred stockholders would have received only $8,000 in dividends in 2007. Common stockholders would have received $42,000.

Stock Dividends

A **stock dividend** is a pro rata distribution to stockholders of the corporation's own stock. Whereas a cash dividend is paid in cash, a stock dividend is paid in stock. **A stock dividend results in a decrease in retained earnings and an increase in paid-in capital.** Unlike a cash dividend, a stock dividend does not decrease total stockholders' equity or total assets.

To illustrate, assume that you have a 2% ownership interest in Cetus Inc.; you own 20 of its 1,000 shares of common stock. If Cetus declares a 10% stock dividend, it would issue 100 shares (1,000 × 10%) of stock. You would receive 2 shares (2% × 100). Would your ownership interest change? No, it would remain at 2% (22 ÷ 1,100). **You now own more shares of stock, but your ownership interest has not changed.** Illustration 12-12 shows the effect of a stock dividend for stockholders.

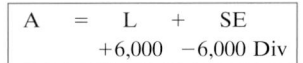

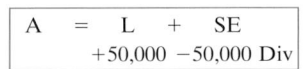

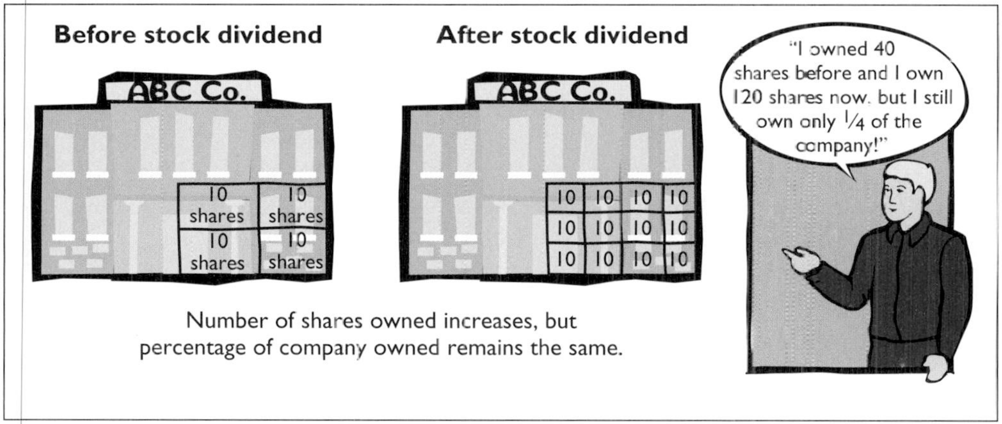

Illustration 12-12
Effect of stock dividend for stockholders

From the company's point of view, no cash has been disbursed, and no liabilities have been assumed by the corporation. What are the purposes and benefits of a stock dividend? Corporations issue stock dividends generally for one or more of the following reasons.

1. To satisfy stockholders' dividend expectations without spending cash.
2. To increase the marketability of the corporation's stock. When the number of shares outstanding increases, the market price per share decreases. Decreasing the market price of the stock makes it easier for smaller investors to purchase the shares.
3. To emphasize that a portion of stockholders' equity has been permanently reinvested in the business (and is unavailable for cash dividends).

The size of the stock dividend and the value to be assigned to each dividend share are determined by the board of directors when the dividend is declared. The per share amount must be at least equal to the par or stated value in order to meet legal requirements.

The accounting profession distinguishes between a **small stock dividend** (less than 20–25% of the corporation's issued stock) and a **large stock dividend** (greater than 20–25%). For small stock dividends, it recommends that the directors assign the **fair market value per share**. This treatment is based on the assumption that a small stock dividend will have little effect on the market price of the outstanding shares. Many stockholders consider small stock dividends to be distributions of earnings equal to the fair market value of the shares distributed. The amount to be assigned for a large stock dividend is not specified by the accounting profession. **Par or stated value per share** is normally assigned. Small stock dividends predominate in practice. Thus, we will illustrate only the entries for small stock dividends.

Entries for Stock Dividends

To illustrate the accounting for small stock dividends, assume that Medland Corporation has a balance of $300,000 in retained earnings. It declares a 10% stock dividend on its 50,000 shares of $10 par value common stock. The current fair market value of its stock is $15 per share. The number of shares to be issued is 5,000 (10% × 50,000). Therefore the total amount to be debited to Retained Earnings is $75,000 (5,000 × $15). The entry to record the declaration of the stock dividend is as follows.

Retained Earnings	75,000	
Common Stock Dividends Distributable		50,000
Paid-in Capital in Excess of Par Value		25,000
(To record declaration of 10% stock dividend)		

A	=	L	+	SE
				−75,000 Div
				+50,000 CS
				+25,000 CS

Cash Flows
no effect

Note that Retained Earnings is debited for the fair market value of the stock issued ($15 × 5,000). Common Stock Dividends Distributable is credited for the par value of the dividend shares ($10 × 5,000), and the excess over par ($5 × 5,000) is credited to Paid-in Capital in Excess of Par Value.

Common Stock Dividends Distributable is a **stockholders' equity account**. It is not a liability because assets will not be used to pay the dividend. If a balance sheet is prepared before the dividend shares are issued, the distributable account is reported under Paid-in capital, as an addition to common stock issued:

Illustration 12-13
Statement presentation of common stock dividends distributable

Paid-in capital		
Common stock	$500,000	
Common stock dividends distributable	**50,000**	$550,000

When the dividend shares are issued, Common Stock Dividends Distributable is debited, and Common Stock is credited as follows.

A	=	L	+	SE
				−50,000 CS
				+50,000 CS

Cash Flows
no effect

Common Stock Dividends Distributable	50,000	
Common Stock		50,000
(To record issuance of 5,000 shares in a stock dividend)		

Effects of Stock Dividends

How do stock dividends affect stockholders' equity? They **change the composition of stockholders' equity**, because a portion of retained earnings is transferred to paid-in capital. However, **total stockholders' equity remains the same**. Stock dividends also have no effect on the par or stated value per share. But the number of shares outstanding increases. These effects are shown for Medland Corporation in Illustration 12-14.

Illustration 12-14
Stock dividend effects

	Before Dividend	After Dividend
Stockholders' equity		
Paid-in capital		
Common stock, $10 par	$500,000	$550,000
Paid-in capital in excess of par value	—	25,000
Total paid-in capital	500,000	575,000
Retained earnings	300,000	225,000
Total stockholders' equity	**$800,000**	**$800,000**
Outstanding shares	**50,000**	**55,000**

In this example, total paid-in capital is increased by $75,000, and retained earnings is decreased by the same amount. Note also that total stockholders' equity remains unchanged at $800,000.

Stock Splits

A **stock split**, like a stock dividend, involves the issuance of additional shares to stockholders according to their percentage ownership. **A stock split results in a reduction in the par or stated value per share.** The purpose of a stock split is to increase the marketability of the stock by lowering its market value per share. A lower market value also makes it easier for the corporation to issue additional stock.

The effect of a split on market value is generally inversely proportional to the size of the split. For example, after a recent 2-for-1 stock split, the market value of **Nike**'s stock fell from $111 to approximately $55. The lower market value stimulated market activity, and within one year the stock was trading above $100 again.

In a stock split, the number of shares is increased in the same proportion that par or stated value per share is decreased. For example, in a 2-for-1 split, one share of $10 par value stock is exchanged for two shares of $5 par value stock. **A stock split does not have any effect on total paid-in capital, retained earnings, or total stockholders' equity.** But the number of shares outstanding increases. This effect is shown in Illustration 12-15 for Medland Corporation, assuming that it splits its 50,000 shares of common stock on a 2-for-1 basis.

HELPFUL HINT

A stock split changes the par value per share but does not affect any balances in stockholders' equity.

Illustration 12-15
Stock split effects

	Before Stock Split	After Stock Split
Stockholders' equity		
Paid-in capital		
Common stock	$500,000	$500,000
Paid-in capital in excess of par value	-0-	-0-
Total paid-in capital	500,000	500,000
Retained earnings	300,000	300,000
Total stockholders' equity	**$800,000**	**$800,000**
Outstanding shares	**50,000**	**100,000**

A stock split does not affect the balances in any stockholders' equity accounts. Therefore **it is not necessary to journalize a stock split.**

The significant differences between stock splits and stock dividends are shown in Illustration 12-16.

Illustration 12-16
Differences between the effects of stock splits and stock dividends

Item	Stock Split	Stock Dividend
Total paid-in capital	No change	Increase
Total retained earnings	No change	Decrease
Total par value (common stock)	No change	Increase
Par value per share	Decrease	No change

ACCOUNTING MATTERS! **Business Insight**

A handful of U.S. companies have no intention of keeping their stock trading in a range accessible to mere mortals. These companies never split their stock, no matter how high their stock price gets. The king is investment company **Berkshire Hathaway**'s Class A stock, which sells for a pricey $85,200—per share! The company's Class B stock is a relative bargain at roughly $2,831 per share.

? How does the effect on share price of a stock split compare to the effect on share price of treasury shares acquired?

BEFORE YOU GO ON...

Review It

1. What entries are made for cash dividends on (a) the declaration date, (b) the record date, and (c) the payment date?
2. Distinguish between a small and large stock dividend, and indicate the basis for valuing each kind of dividend.
3. Contrast the effects of a small stock dividend and a 2-for-1 stock split on (a) stockholders' equity and (b) outstanding shares.
4. What were the amounts of the dividends declared per share of common stock by **PepsiCo** during the years 1999 to 2003? Is the trend in dividends consistent with the company's net income trend during that period? The answers to these questions are provided on page 583.

PEPSI

Do It

Sing CD Company has had 5 years of record earnings. Due to this success, the market price of its 500,000 shares of $2 par value common stock has tripled from $15 per share to $45. During this period, paid-in capital remained the same at $2,000,000. Retained earnings increased from $1,500,000 to $10,000,000. President Joan Elbert is considering either (1) a 10% stock dividend or (2) a 2-for-1 stock split. She asks you to show the before-and-after effects of each option on (a) retained earnings and (b) shares outstanding.

ACTION PLAN

- Calculate the stock dividend's effect on retained earnings by multiplying the number of new shares times the market price of the stock (or par value for a large stock dividend).
- Recall that a stock dividend increases the number of shares without affecting total equity, thus decreasing the book value per share.
- Recall that a stock split only increases the number of shares outstanding and decreases the par value per share.

SOLUTION

(a) **(1)** The stock dividend amount is $2,250,000 [(500,000 × 10%) × $45]. The new balance in retained earnings is $7,750,000 ($10,000,000 − $2,250,000).

(2) The retained earnings balance after the stock split would be the same as it was before the split: $10,000,000.

(b) The effects on total stockholders' equity and total shares outstanding are:

	Original Balances	After Dividend	After Split
Paid-in capital	$ 2,000,000	$ 4,250,000	$ 2,000,000
Retained earnings	10,000,000	7,750,000	10,000,000
Total stockholders' equity	$12,000,000	$12,000,000	$12,000,000
Shares outstanding	500,000	550,000	1,000,000

Related exercise material: *BE12-8, BE12-9, E12-9, E12-10, and E12-11.*

THE NAVIGATOR

SECTION 3 RETAINED EARNINGS

STUDY OBJECTIVE 6

Identify the items that are reported in a retained earnings statement.

Retained earnings is net income that is retained in the business. The balance in retained earnings is part of the stockholders' claim on the total assets of the corporation. It does not, though, represent a claim on any specific asset. Nor can the amount of retained earnings be associated with the balance of any asset account. For example, a $100,000 balance in retained earnings does not mean that there should be $100,000 in cash. The reason is that the cash resulting from the excess of revenues over expenses may have been used to purchase buildings, equipment, and other assets. To illustrate that retained earnings and cash may be quite different, Illustration 12-17 shows recent amounts of retained earnings and cash in selected companies.

Company	Retained Earnings (in millions)	Cash (in millions)
Walt Disney Co.	$12,979	$1,239
Intel Corp.	27,847	7,404
Kellogg Co.	1,873	100.6
Amazon.com	(2,861)	540

Illustration 12-17
Retained earnings and cash balances

Remember that when a company has net profit, the net income that is retained in the business is recorded in retained earnings by means of a closing entry. This entry debits Income Summary and credits Retained Earnings.

However, when expenses exceed revenues, a **net loss** results. A net loss is debited to Retained Earnings in a closing entry. This is done even if it results in a debit balance in Retained Earnings. **Net losses are not debited to paid-in capital accounts.** To do so would destroy the distinction between paid-in and earned capital. A debit balance in Retained Earnings is identified as a **deficit**. It is reported as a deduction in the stockholders' equity section, as shown below.

HELPFUL HINT

Remember that Retained Earnings is a stockholders' equity account, whose normal balance is a credit.

Balance Sheet (partial)

Stockholders' equity	
Paid-in capital	
Common stock	$800,000
Retained earnings (deficit)	**(50,000)**
Total stockholders' equity	$750,000

Illustration 12-18
Stockholders' equity with deficit

Retained Earnings Restrictions

The balance in retained earnings is generally available for dividend declarations. Some companies state this fact. For example, in the notes to financial statements in a recent year, **Lockheed Martin Corporation** stated:

LOCKHEED MARTIN CORPORATION
Notes to the Financial Statements

At December 31, retained earnings were unrestricted and available for dividend payments.

Illustration 12-19
Disclosure of unrestricted retained earnings

In some cases, there may be **retained earnings restrictions**. These make a portion of the retained earnings balance currently unavailable for dividends. Restrictions result from one or more of the following causes: legal, contractual, or voluntary.

1. **Legal restrictions.** Many states require a corporation to restrict retained earnings for the cost of treasury stock purchased. The restriction keeps intact the corporation's legal capital that is being temporarily held as treasury stock. When the treasury stock is sold, the restriction is lifted.
2. **Contractual restrictions.** Long-term debt contracts may restrict retained earnings as a condition for the loan. The restriction limits the use of corporate assets for payment of dividends. Thus, it increases the likelihood that the corporation will be able to meet required loan payments.
3. **Voluntary restrictions.** The board of directors may voluntarily create retained earnings restrictions for specific purposes. For example, the board may authorize a restriction for future plant expansion. By reducing the amount of retained earnings available for dividends, more cash may be available for the planned expansion.

Retained earnings restrictions are generally disclosed in the notes to the financial statements. For example, **Tektronix Inc.**, a manufacturer of electronic measurement devices, had total retained earnings of $774 million, but the unrestricted portion was only $223.8 million.

Illustration 12-20
Disclosure of restriction

Tektronix®

TEKTRONIX INC.
Notes to the Financial Statements

Certain of the Company's debt agreements require compliance with debt covenants. Management believes that the Company is in compliance with such requirements for the fiscal year ended May 26, 2001. The Company had unrestricted retained earnings of $223.8 million after meeting those requirements.

Prior Period Adjustments

Suppose that a corporation's books have been closed and the financial statements have been issued. The corporation then discovers that a material error has been made in reporting net income of a prior year. How should this situation be recorded in the accounts and reported in the financial statements?

The correction of an error in previously issued financial statements is known as a **prior period adjustment**. The correction is made directly to Retained Earnings because the effect of the error is now in this account: The net income for the prior period has been recorded in retained earnings through the journalizing and posting of closing entries.

To illustrate, assume that General Microwave discovers in 2006 that it understated depreciation expense in 2005 by $300,000 due to computational errors. These errors overstated both net income for 2005 and the current balance in retained earnings. The entry for the prior period adjustment, assuming all tax effects are ignored, is shown on page 555.

Retained Earnings	300,000		
Accumulated Depreciation		300,000	
(To adjust for understatement of depreciation in a prior period)			

A	=	L	+	SE
−300,000				−300,000 RE

Cash Flows
no effect

A debit to an income statement account in 2006 would be incorrect because the error pertains to a prior year.

Prior period adjustments are reported in the retained earnings statement.[5] They are added (or deducted, as the case may be) from the beginning retained earnings balance. This results in an adjusted beginning balance. Assuming General Microwave has a beginning balance of $800,000 in retained earnings, the prior period adjustment is reported as follows.

Illustration 12-21
Statement presentation of prior period adjustments

GENERAL MICROWAVE
Retained Earnings Statement (partial)

Balance, January 1, as reported	$ 800,000
Correction for overstatement of net income in prior period (depreciation error)	**(300,000)**
Balance, January 1, as adjusted	$ 500,000

Again, reporting the correction in the current year's income statement would be incorrect because it applies to a prior year's income statement.

Retained Earnings Statement

The **retained earnings statement** shows the changes in retained earnings during the year. The statement is prepared from the Retained Earnings account. Transactions and events that affect retained earnings are tabulated in account form as shown in Illustration 12-22.

Illustration 12-22
Debits and credits to retained earnings

Retained Earnings

1. Net loss	1. Net income
2. Prior period adjustments for overstatement of net income	2. Prior period adjustments for understatement of net income
3. Cash dividends and stock dividends	
4. Some disposals of treasury stock	

As indicated, net income increases retained earnings, and a net loss decreases retained earnings. Prior period adjustments may either increase or decrease retained earnings. Both cash dividends and stock dividends decrease retained earnings. The circumstances under which treasury stock transactions decrease retained earnings were explained earlier on page 542.

A complete retained earnings statement for Graber Inc., based on assumed data, is shown on page 556.

[5] A complete retained earnings statement is shown in Illustration 12-23 on the next page.

Illustration 12-23
Retained earnings statement

GRABER INC.
Retained Earnings Statement
For the Year Ended December 31, 2006

Balance, January 1, as reported		$ 1,050,000
Correction for understatement of net income in prior period (inventory error)		50,000
Balance, January 1, as adjusted		1,100,000
Add: Net income		360,000
		1,460,000
Less: Cash dividends	$ 100,000	
Stock dividends	200,000	300,000
Balance, December 31		$1,160,000

BEFORE YOU GO ON...

Review It

1. How are retained earnings restrictions generally reported?
2. What is a prior period adjustment, and how is it reported?
3. What are the principal sources of debits and credits to Retained Earnings?

Do It

Vega Corporation has retained earnings of $5,130,000 on January 1, 2006. During the year, Vega earns $2,000,000 of net income. It declares and pays a $250,000 cash dividend. In 2006, Vega records an adjustment of $180,000 due to the understatement of 2005 depreciation expense from a mathematical error. Prepare a retained earnings statement for 2006.

ACTION PLAN

- Recall that a retained earnings statement begins with retained earnings, as reported at the end of the previous year.
- Add or subtract any prior period adjustments to arrive at the adjusted beginning figure.
- Add net income and subtract dividends declared to arrive at the ending balance in retained earnings.

SOLUTION

VEGA CORPORATION
Retained Earnings Statement
For the Year Ended December 31, 2006

Balance, January 1, as reported	$5,130,000
Correction for overstatement of net income in prior period (depreciation error)	(180,000)
Balance, January 1, as adjusted	4,950,000
Add: Net income	2,000,000
	6,950,000
Less: Cash dividends	250,000
Balance, December 31	$6,700,000

Related exercise material: *BE12-10, BE12-11, and E12-12.*

THE NAVIGATOR

Statement Presentation and Analysis

STUDY OBJECTIVE 7

Prepare and analyze a comprehensive stockholders' equity section.

In the stockholders' equity section of the balance sheet, paid-in capital and retained earnings are reported. The specific sources of paid-in capital are identified. Within paid-in capital, two classifications are recognized:

1. **Capital stock.** This category consists of preferred and common stock. Preferred stock is shown before common stock because of its preferential rights. Par value, shares authorized, shares issued, and shares outstanding are reported for each class of stock.
2. **Additional paid-in capital.** This includes the excess of amounts paid over par or stated value and paid-in capital from treasury stock.

Presentation

The stockholders' equity section of Graber Inc.'s balance sheet is presented in Illustration 12-24. Note the following: (1) "Common stock dividends distributable" is shown under "Capital stock," in "Paid-in capital." (2) A retained earnings restriction is disclosed in the notes.

Illustration 12-24
Comprehensive stockholders' equity section

GRABER INC.
Balance Sheet (partial)

Stockholders' equity		
Paid-in capital		
Capital stock		
9% Preferred stock, $100 par value, cumulative, callable at $120, 10,000 shares authorized, 6,000 shares issued and outstanding		$ 600,000
Common stock, no par, $5 stated value, 500,000 shares authorized, 400,000 shares issued and 390,000 outstanding	$2,000,000	
Common stock dividends distributable	**50,000**	2,050,000
Total capital stock		2,650,000
Additional paid-in capital		
In excess of par value—preferred stock	30,000	
In excess of stated value—common stock	1,050,000	
Total additional paid-in capital		1,080,000
Total paid-in capital		3,730,000
Retained earnings **(see Note R)**		1,160,000
Total paid-in capital and retained earnings		4,890,000
Less: Treasury stock—common (10,000 shares)		80,000
Total stockholders' equity		$4,810,000

Note R: Retained earnings is restricted for the cost of treasury stock, $80,000.

The stockholders' equity section of Graber Inc. in Illustration 12-24 includes most of the accounts discussed in this chapter. The disclosures pertaining to Graber's common stock indicate that: 400,000 shares are issued; 100,000 shares are unissued (500,000 authorized less 400,000 issued); and 390,000 shares are outstanding (400,000 issued less 10,000 shares in treasury).

In published annual reports, the individual sources of additional paid-in capital are often combined and reported as a single amount, as shown in Illustration 12-25. In addition, authorized shares are sometimes not reported.

Illustration 12-25
Published stockholders' equity section

Kellogg's®

KELLOGG COMPANY
Balance Sheet (partial)
($ in millions)

Stockholders' equity	
Common stock, $0.25 par value, 1,000,000,000 shares authorized	
Issued: 415,451,198 shares	$ 103.8
Capital in excess of par value	49.9
Retained earnings	1,873.0
Treasury stock, at cost	
7,598,923 shares	(278.2)
Accumulated other comprehensive income	(853.4)
Total stockholders' equity	$ 895.1

In practice, the term "capital surplus" is sometimes used in place of additional paid-in capital and "earned surplus" in place of retained earnings. The use of the term "surplus" suggests that an excess amount of funds is available. Such is not necessarily the case. Therefore, **the term "surplus" should not be employed in accounting**. Unfortunately, a number of financial statements still do use it.

Instead of presenting a detailed stockholders' equity section in the balance sheet and a retained earnings statement, many companies prepare a **stockholders' equity statement**. This statement shows the changes in each stockholders' equity account and in total that have occurred during the year. An example of a stockholders' equity statement is illustrated in **PepsiCo**'s financial statements in Appendix A and in an appendix to this chapter (Illustration 12-A1).

Analysis

Profitability from the viewpoint of the common stockholder can be measured by the **return on common stockholders' equity**. This ratio shows how many dollars of net income were earned for each dollar invested by the stockholders. It is computed by dividing net income available to common stockholders (which is net income minus preferred stock dividends) by average common stockholders' equity. To illustrate, **Kellogg Company**'s beginning-of-the-year and end-of-the-year common stockholders' equity were $871.5 and $895.1 million respectively. Its net income was $720.9 million, and no preferred stock was outstanding. The return on common stockholders' equity ratio is computed as follows.

Illustration 12-26
Return on common stockholders' equity ratio and computation

Net Income minus Preferred Dividends	÷	Average Common Stockholders' Equity	=	Return on Common Stockholders' Equity
($720.9 − $0)	÷	$\frac{(\$871.5 + \$895.1)}{2}$	=	**81.6%**

As shown above, if a company has preferred stock, the amount of **preferred dividends** is deducted from net income to compute income available to common stockholders. Also, the par value of preferred stock is deducted from total average stockholders' equity to arrive at the amount of common stockholders' equity.

BEFORE YOU GO ON...

Review It

1. Identify the classifications within the paid-in capital section and the totals that are stated in the stockholders' equity section of a balance sheet.
2. Explain the return on common stockholders' equity ratio.

THE NAVIGATOR

DEMONSTRATION PROBLEM

www.wiley.com/college/weygandt

Peachtree

The Rolman Corporation is authorized to issue 1,000,000 shares of $5 par value common stock. In its first year, the company has the following stock transactions.

Jan. 10	Issued 400,000 shares of stock at $8 per share.
July 1	Issued 100,000 shares of stock for land. The land had an asking price of $900,000. The stock is currently selling on a national exchange at $8.25 per share.
Sept. 1	Purchased 10,000 shares of common stock for the treasury at $9 per share.
Dec. 1	Sold 4,000 shares of the treasury stock at $10 per share.

Instructions

(a) Journalize the transactions.

(b) Prepare the stockholders' equity section assuming the company had retained earnings of $200,000 at December 31.

SOLUTION TO DEMONSTRATION PROBLEM

(a) Jan. 10	Cash	3,200,000	
	Common Stock		2,000,000
	Paid-in Capital in Excess of Par Value		1,200,000
	(To record issuance of 400,000 shares of $5 par value stock)		
July 1	Land	825,000	
	Common Stock		500,000
	Paid-in Capital in Excess of Par Value		325,000
	(To record issuance of 100,000 shares of $5 par value stock for land)		
Sept. 1	Treasury Stock	90,000	
	Cash		90,000
	(To record purchase of 10,000 shares of treasury stock at cost)		
Dec. 1	Cash	40,000	
	Treasury Stock		36,000
	Paid-in Capital from Treasury Stock		4,000
	(To record sale of 4,000 shares of treasury stock above cost)		

ACTION PLAN

- When common stock has a par value, credit Common Stock for par value.
- Use fair market value in a noncash transaction.
- Debit and credit the Treasury Stock account at cost.
- Record differences between the cost and selling price of treasury stock in stockholders' equity accounts, not as gains or losses.

(b)

ROLMAN CORPORATION
Balance Sheet (partial)

Stockholders' equity		
Paid-in capital		
Capital stock		
Common stock, $5 par value, 1,000,000 shares authorized, 500,000 shares issued, 494,000 shares outstanding		$2,500,000
Additional paid-in capital		
In excess of par value	$1,525,000	
From treasury stock	4,000	
Total additional paid-in capital		1,529,000
Total paid-in capital		4,029,000
Retained earnings		200,000
Total paid-in capital and retained earnings		4,229,000
Less: Treasury stock (6,000 shares)		(54,000)
Total stockholders' equity		$4,175,000

THE NAVIGATOR

SUMMARY OF STUDY OBJECTIVES

1. **Identify the major characteristics of a corporation.** The major characteristics of a corporation are separate legal existence, limited liability of stockholders, transferable ownership rights, ability to acquire capital, continuous life, corporation management, government regulations, and additional taxes.

2. **Record the issuance of common stock.** When the issuance of common stock for cash is recorded, the par value of the shares is credited to Common Stock. The portion of the proceeds that is above or below par value is recorded in a separate paid-in capital account. When no-par common stock has a stated value, the entries are similar to those for par value stock. When no-par stock does not have a stated value, the entire proceeds are credited to Common Stock.

3. **Explain the accounting for treasury stock.** The cost method is generally used in accounting for treasury stock. Under this approach, Treasury Stock is debited at the price paid to reacquire the shares. The same amount is credited to Treasury Stock when the shares are sold. The difference between the sales price and cost is recorded in stockholders' equity accounts, not in income statement accounts.

4. **Differentiate preferred stock from common stock.** Preferred stock has contractual provisions that give it priority over common stock in certain areas. Typically, preferred stockholders have a preference to (1) dividends and (2) assets in liquidation. They usually do not have voting rights.

5. **Prepare the entries for cash dividends and stock dividends.** Entries for both cash and stock dividends are required on the declaration date and the payment date. At the declaration date the entries are: cash dividend—debit Retained Earnings, and credit Dividends Payable; small stock dividend—debit Retained Earnings, credit Paid-in Capital in Excess of Par (or Stated) Value, and credit Common Stock Dividends Distributable. On the payment date, the entries for cash and stock dividends are: cash dividend—debit Dividends Payable and credit Cash; small stock dividend—debit Common Stock Dividends Distributable and credit Common Stock.

6. **Identify the items that are reported in a retained earnings statement.** Each of the individual debits and credits to retained earnings should be reported in the retained earnings statement. Additions consist of net income and prior period adjustments to correct understatements of prior years' net income. Deductions consist of net loss, adjustments to correct overstatements of prior years' net income, cash and stock dividends, and some disposals of treasury stock.

7. **Prepare and analyze a comprehensive stockholders' equity section.** In the stockholders' equity section, paid-in capital and retained earnings are reported and specific sources of paid-in capital are identified. Within paid-in capital, two classifications are shown: capital stock and additional paid-in capital. If a corporation has treasury stock, the cost of treasury stock is deducted from total paid-in capital and retained earnings to obtain total stockholders' equity. One measure of profitability is the return on common stockholders' equity. It is calculated by dividing net income minus preferred stock dividends by average common stockholders' equity.

THE NAVIGATOR

GLOSSARY

Authorized stock The amount of stock that a corporation is authorized to sell as indicated in its charter. (p. 533).

By-laws The internal rules and procedures for conducting the affairs of a corporation. (p. 531).

Cash dividend A pro rata distribution of cash to stockholders. (p. 545).

Charter A document that creates a corporation. (p. 531).

Corporation A business organized as a legal entity separate and distinct from its owners under state corporation law. (p. 527).

Corporate capital The owners' equity in a corporation. Also called *stockholders' equity* or *shareholders' equity*. (p. 531).

Cumulative dividend A feature of preferred stock entitling the stockholder to receive current and unpaid prior-year dividends before common stockholders receive any dividends. (p. 544).

Declaration date The date the board of directors formally declares the dividend and announces it to stockholders. (p. 546).

Deficit A debit balance in retained earnings. (p. 553).

Dividend A distribution by a corporation to its stockholders on a pro rata (proportional) basis. (p. 545).

Legal capital The amount per share of stock that must be retained in the business for the protection of corporate creditors. (p. 534).

Liquidating dividend A dividend declared out of paid-in capital. (p. 545).

No-par value stock Capital stock that has not been assigned a value in the corporate charter. (p. 535).

Organization costs Costs incurred in the formation of a corporation. (p. 531).

Outstanding stock Capital stock that has been issued and is being held by stockholders. (p. 540).

Par value stock Capital stock that has been assigned a value per share in the corporate charter. (p. 534).

Payment date The date dividend checks are mailed to stockholders. (p. 547).

Preferred stock Capital stock that has contractual preferences over common stock in certain areas. (p. 543).

Prior period adjustment The correction of an error in previously issued financial statements. (p. 554).

Privately held corporation A corporation that has only a few stockholders and whose stock is not available for sale to the general public. (p. 528).

Publicly held corporation A corporation that may have thousands of stockholders and whose stock is regularly traded on a national securities exchange. (p. 527).

Record date The date when ownership of outstanding shares is determined for dividend purposes. (p. 547).

Retained earnings Net income that is retained in the business. (p. 553).

Retained earnings restrictions Circumstances that make a portion of retained earnings currently unavailable for dividends. (p. 554).

Retained earnings statement A financial statement that shows the changes in retained earnings during the year. (p. 555).

Return on common stockholders' equity ratio A ratio that measures profitability from the stockholders' point of view. It is computed by dividing net income available to common stockholders by average common stockholders' equity. (p. 558).

Stated value The amount per share assigned by the board of directors to no-par stock that becomes legal capital per share. (p. 535).

Stock dividend A pro rata distribution of the corporation's own stock to stockholders. (p. 548).

Stock split The issuance of additional shares of stock to stockholders accompanied by a reduction in the par or stated value per share. (p. 550).

Stockholders' equity statement A statement that shows the changes in each stockholders' equity account and in total stockholders' equity during the year. (p. 558).

Treasury stock A corporation's own stock that has been issued, fully paid for, and reacquired by the corporation but not retired. (p. 539).

APPENDIX 12A STOCKHOLDERS' EQUITY STATEMENT

STUDY OBJECTIVE 8

Describe the use and content of the stockholders' equity statement.

When balance sheets and income statements are presented by a corporation, changes in the separate accounts comprising stockholders' equity should also be disclosed. Disclosure of such changes is necessary to make the financial statements sufficiently informative for users. The disclosures may be made in an additional statement or in the notes to the financial statements.

Many corporations make the disclosures in a **stockholders' equity statement**. The statement shows the changes in **each** stockholders' equity account and in **total** stockholders' equity during the year. As shown in Illustration 12A-1 the stockholders' equity statement is prepared in columnar form. It contains columns for each account and for total stockholders' equity. The transactions are then identified and their effects are shown in the appropriate columns.

Illustration 12A-1
Stockholders' equity statement

HAMPTON CORPORATION
Stockholders' Equity Statement
For the Year Ended December 31, 2006

	Common Stock ($5 Par)	Paid-in Capital in Excess of Par	Retained Earnings	Treasury Stock	Total
Balance January 1	$300,000	$200,000	$650,000	$(34,000)	$1,116,000
Issued 5,000 shares of common stock at $15	25,000	50,000			75,000
Declared a $40,000 cash dividend			(40,000)		(40,000)
Purchased 2,000 shares for treasury at $16				(32,000)	(32,000)
Net income for year			240,000		240,000
Balance December 31	$325,000	$250,000	$850,000	$(66,000)	$1,359,000

In practice, additional columns are usually provided to show the number of shares of issued stock and treasury stock. The stockholders' equity statement for **PepsiCo**, for a three-year period, is shown in Appendix A. **When a stockholders' equity statement is presented, a retained earnings statement is not necessary** because the retained earnings column explains the changes in this account.

SUMMARY OF STUDY OBJECTIVE FOR APPENDIX 12A

8. Describe the use and content of the stockholders' equity statement. Corporations must disclose changes in stockholders' equity accounts and may choose to do so by issuing a separate stockholders' equity statement. This statement, prepared in columnar form, shows changes in each stockholders' equity account and in total stockholders' equity during the accounting period. When this statement is presented, a retained earnings statement is not necessary.

APPENDIX 12B BOOK VALUE—ANOTHER PER-SHARE AMOUNT

Book Value Per Share

STUDY OBJECTIVE 9

Compute book value per share.

You have learned about a number of per share amounts in this chapter. Another per-share amount of some importance is **book value per share**. It represents **the equity a common stockholder has in the net assets of the corporation** from owning one share of stock. Remember that the net assets (total assets minus total liabilities) of a corporation must be equal to total stockholders' equity. Therefore, the formula for computing book value per share when a company has only one class of stock outstanding is:

Total Stockholders' Equity	÷	Number of Common Shares Outstanding	=	Book Value per Share

Illustration 12B-1
Book value per share formula

Thus, if Marlo Corporation has total stockholders' equity of $1,500,000 (common stock $1,000,000 and retained earnings $500,000) and 50,000 shares of common stock outstanding, book value per share is $30 ($1,500,000 ÷ 50,000).

When a company has both preferred and common stock, the computation of book value is more complex. Since preferred stockholders have a prior claim on net assets over common stockholders, their equity must be deducted from total stockholders' equity. Then we can determine the stockholders' equity that applies to the common stock. The computation of book value per share involves the following steps.

1. **Compute the preferred stock equity.** This equity is equal to the sum of the call price of preferred stock plus any cumulative dividends in arrears. If the preferred stock does not have a call price, the par value of the stock is used.
2. **Determine the common stock equity.** Subtract the preferred stock equity from total stockholders' equity.
3. **Determine book value per share.** Divide common stock equity by shares of common stock outstanding.

Illustration

We will use the stockholders' equity section of Graber Inc. shown in Illustration 12-24. Graber's preferred stock is callable at $120 per share and is cumulative. Assume that dividends on Graber's preferred stock were in arrears for one year, $54,000 (6,000 × $9). The computation of preferred stock equity (Step 1 in the preceding list) is:

Call price (6,000 shares × $120)	$720,000
Dividends in arrears (6,000 shares × $9)	54,000
Preferred stock equity	**$774,000**

Illustration 12B-2
Computation of preferred stock equity—Step 1

The computation of book value (Steps 2 and 3) is as follows.

Total stockholders' equity	$4,810,000
Less: **Preferred stock equity**	**774,000**
Common stock equity	**$4,036,000**
Shares of common stock outstanding	**390,000**
Book value per share ($4,036,000 ÷ 390,000)	**$10.35**

Illustration 12B-3
Computation of book value per share with preferred stock—Steps 2 and 3

Note that we used the call price of $120 instead of the par value of $100. Note also that the paid-in capital in excess of par value of preferred stock, $30,000, **is not assigned to the preferred stock equity**. Preferred stockholders ordinarily do not have a right to amounts paid-in in excess of par value. Therefore, such amounts are assigned to the common stock equity in computing book value.

Book Value versus Market Value

Be sure you understand that **book value per share may not equal market value per share**. Book value generally is based on recorded costs. Market value reflects the subjective judgments of thousands of stockholders and prospective investors about a company's potential for future earnings and dividends. Market value per share may exceed book value per share, but that fact does not necessarily mean that the stock is overpriced. The correlation between book value and the annual range of a company's market value per share is often remote, as indicated by the following recent data.

Illustration 12B-4
Book and market values compared

Company	Book Value (year-end)	Market Value Range (for year 2002)
The Limited, Inc.	$8.25	$22.34–$12.53
H. J. Heinz Company	$5.25	$43.48–$29.60
Cisco Systems	$3.92	$21.84–$12.24
Wal-Mart Stores	$9.10	$63.90–$43.70

Book value per share **is useful** in determining the trend of a stockholder's per share equity in a corporation. It is also significant in many contracts and in court cases where the rights of individual parties are based on cost information.

SUMMARY OF STUDY OBJECTIVE FOR APPENDIX 12B

9. **Compute book value per share.** Book value per share represents the equity a common stockholder has in the net assets of a corporation from owning one share of stock. When there is only common stock outstanding, the formula for computing book value is: Total stockholders' equity ÷ Number of common shares outstanding = Book value per share.

GLOSSARY FOR APPENDIX 12B

Book value per share The equity a common stockholder has in the net assets of the corporation from owning one share of stock. (p. 562).

*__Note:__ All asterisked Questions, Exercises, and Problems relate to material in the appendixes to the chapter.

SELF-STUDY QUESTIONS

Self-Study/Self-Test

Answers are at the end of the chapter.

(SO 1) 1. Which of the following is *not* a major advantage of a corporation?
   a. Separate legal existence.
   b. Continuous life.
   c. Government regulations.
   d. Transferable ownership rights.

(SO 1) 2. A major disadvantage of a corporation is:
   a. limited liability of stockholders.
   b. additional taxes.
   c. transferable ownership rights.
   d. none of the above.

3. Which of the following statements is *false*? (SO 2)
   a. Ownership of common stock gives the owner a voting right.
   b. The stockholders' equity section begins with paid-in capital.
   c. The authorization of capital stock does not result in a formal accounting entry.
   d. The par value of a share of stock is equal to its market value.

(SO 2) 4. ABC Corporation issues 1,000 shares of $10 par value common stock at $12 per share. In recording the transaction, credits are made to:
   a. Common Stock $10,000 and Paid-in Capital in Excess of Stated Value $2,000.
   b. Common Stock $12,000.
   c. Common Stock $10,000 and Paid-in Capital in Excess of Par Value $2,000.
   d. Common Stock $10,000 and Retained Earnings $2,000.

(SO 3) 5. XYZ, Inc. sells 100 shares of $5 par value treasury stock at $13 per share. If the cost of acquiring the shares was $10 per share, the entry for the sale should include credits to:
   a. Treasury Stock $1,000 and Paid-in Capital from Treasury Stock $300.
   b. Treasury Stock $500 and Paid-in Capital from Treasury Stock $800.
   c. Treasury Stock $1,000 and Retained Earnings $300.
   d. Treasury Stock $500 and Paid-in Capital in Excess of Par Value $800.

(SO 3) 6. In the stockholders' equity section, the cost of treasury stock is deducted from:
   a. total paid-in capital and retained earnings.
   b. retained earnings.
   c. total stockholders' equity.
   d. common stock in paid-in capital.

(SO 4) 7. Preferred stock may have priority over common stock *except* in:
   a. dividends.
   b. assets in the event of liquidation.
   c. cumulative dividend features.
   d. voting.

(SO 5) 8. Entries for cash dividends are required on the:
   a. declaration date and the payment date.
   b. record date and the payment date.
   c. declaration date, record date, and payment date.
   d. declaration date and the record date.

(SO 5) 9. Which of the following statements about small stock dividends is true?
   a. A debit to Retained Earnings for the par value of the shares issued should be made.
   b. A small stock dividend decreases total stockholders' equity.
   c. Market value per share should be assigned to the dividend shares.
   d. A small stock dividend ordinarily will have no effect on book value per share of stock.

10. All *but one* of the following is reported in a retained earnings statement. The exception is: (SO 6)
   a. cash and stock dividends.
   b. net income and net loss.
   c. some disposals of treasury stock below cost.
   d. sales of treasury stock above cost.

11. A prior period adjustment is: (SO 6)
   a. reported in the income statement as a nontypical item.
   b. a correction of an error that is made directly to retained earnings.
   c. reported directly in the stockholders' equity section.
   d. reported in the retained earnings statement as an adjustment of the ending balance of retained earnings.

*12. When a stockholders' equity statement is presented, it is not necessary to prepare a(an): (SO 8)
   a. retained earnings statement.
   b. balance sheet.
   c. income statement.
   d. None of the above.

*13. The ledger of JFK, Inc. shows common stock, common treasury stock, and no preferred stock. For this company, the formula for computing book value per share is: (SO 9)
   a. Total paid-in capital and retained earnings divided by the number of shares of common stock issued.
   b. Common stock divided by the number of shares of common stock issued.
   c. Total stockholders' equity divided by the number of shares of common stock outstanding.
   d. Total stockholders' equity divided by the number of shares of common stock issued.

☑ THE NAVIGATOR

QUESTIONS

1. Mike Horn, a student, asks your help in understanding the following characteristics of a corporation: (a) separate legal existence, (b) limited liability of stockholders, and (c) transferable ownership rights. Explain these characteristics to Mike.

2. (a) Your friend Veena Gall cannot understand how the characteristic of corporation management is both an advantage and a disadvantage. Clarify this problem for Veena.
   (b) Identify and explain two other disadvantages of a corporation.

3. Kari Jonas believes a corporation must be incorporated in the state in which its headquarters office is located. Is Kari correct? Explain.

4. What are the basic ownership rights of common stockholders in the absence of restrictive provisions?

5. A corporation has been defined as an entity separate and distinct from its owners. In what ways is a corporation a separate legal entity?

6. (a) What are the two principal components of stockholders' equity?
   (b) What is paid-in capital? Give three examples.

7. The corporate charter of Sokol Corporation allows the issuance of a maximum of 100,000 shares of common stock. During its first two years of operations, Sokol sold 80,000 shares to stockholders and reacquired 7,000 of these shares. After these transactions, how many shares are authorized, issued, and outstanding?

8. Which is the better investment—common stock with a par value of $5 per share, or common stock with a par value of $20 per share? Why?

9. What factors help determine the market value of stock?

10. Why is common stock usually not issued at a price that is less than par value?

11. Land appraised at $80,000 is purchased by issuing 1,000 shares of $20 par value common stock. The market price of the shares at the time of the exchange, based on active trading in the securities market, is $90 per share. Should the land be recorded at $20,000, $80,000, or $90,000? Explain.

12. For what reasons might a company like **IBM** repurchase some of its stock (treasury stock)?

13. Chen, Inc. purchases 1,000 shares of its own previously issued $5 par common stock for $12,000. Assuming the shares are held in the treasury, what effect does this transaction have on (a) net income, (b) total assets, (c) total paid-in capital, and (d) total stockholders' equity?

14. The treasury stock purchased in question 13 is resold by Chen, Inc. for $15,000. What effect does this transaction have on (a) net income, (b) total assets, (c) total paid-in capital, and (d) total stockholders' equity?

15. (a) What are the principal differences between common stock and preferred stock?
    (b) Preferred stock may be cumulative. Discuss this feature.
    (c) How are dividends in arrears presented in the financial statements?

16. Identify the events that result in credits and debits to retained earnings.

17. Indicate how each of the following accounts should be classified in the stockholders' equity section.
    (a) Common Stock.
    (b) Paid-in Capital in Excess of Par Value.
    (c) Retained Earnings.
    (d) Treasury Stock.
    (e) Paid-in Capital from Treasury Stock.
    (f) Paid-in Capital in Excess of Stated Value.
    (g) Preferred Stock.

18. What three conditions must exist before a cash dividend is paid?

19. Three dates associated with Naperville Company's cash dividend are May 1, May 15, and May 31. Discuss the significance of each date and give the entry at each date.

20. Contrast the effects of a cash dividend and a stock dividend on a corporation's balance sheet.

21. Mark Federia asks, "Since stock dividends don't change anything, why declare them?" What is your answer to Mark?

22. Fields Corporation has 20,000 shares of $10 par value common stock outstanding when it announces a 2-for-1 stock split. Before the split, the stock had a market price of $120 per share. After the split, how many shares of stock will be outstanding? What will be the approximate market price per share?

23. The board of directors is considering either a stock split or a stock dividend. They understand that total stockholders' equity will remain the same under either action. However, they are not sure of the different effects of the two types of actions on other aspects of stockholders' equity. Explain the differences to the directors.

24. What is a prior period adjustment, and how is it reported in the financial statements?

25. What is the purpose of a retained earnings restriction? Identify the possible causes of retained earnings restrictions.

*26. What is the formula for computing book value per share when a corporation has only common stock?

*27. Alou Inc.'s common stock has a par value of $1, a book value of $29, and a current market value of $15. Explain why these amounts are all different.

BRIEF EXERCISES

List the advantages and disadvantages of a corporation.
(SO 1)

BE12-1 Ron Child is studying for his accounting midterm examination. Identify for Ron the advantages and disadvantages of the corporate form of business organization.

Prepare entry for issuance of par value common stock.
(SO 2)

BE12-2 On May 10, Romano Corporation issues 1,000 shares of $10 par value common stock for cash at $18 per share. Journalize the issuance of the stock.

Prepare entry for issuance of no-par value common stock.
(SO 2)

BE12-3 On June 1, Herrera Inc. issues 3,000 shares of no-par common stock at a cash price of $7 per share. Journalize the issuance of the shares assuming the stock has a stated value of $1 per share.

Prepare entry for issuance of stock in a noncash transaction.
(SO 2)

BE12-4 Tara Inc.'s $10 par value common stock is actively traded at a market value of $16 per share. Tara issues 5,000 shares to purchase land advertised for sale at $85,000. Journalize the issuance of the stock in acquiring the land.

BE12-5 On July 1, Fritz Corporation purchases 500 shares of its $5 par value common stock for the treasury at a cash price of $9 per share. On September 1, it sells 300 shares of the treasury stock for cash at $11 per share. Journalize the two treasury stock transactions.

Prepare entries for treasury stock transactions.
(SO 3)

BE12-6 Ervay Inc. issues 5,000 shares of $100 par value preferred stock for cash at $120 per share. Journalize the issuance of the preferred stock.

Prepare entry for issuance of preferred stock.
(SO 4)

BE12-7 Chavez Corporation has 50,000 shares of common stock outstanding. It declares a $1 per share cash dividend on November 1 to stockholders of record on December 1. The dividend is paid on December 31. Prepare the entries on the appropriate dates to record the declaration and payment of the cash dividend.

Prepare entries for a cash dividend.
(SO 5)

BE12-8 Walters Corporation has 60,000 shares of $10 par value common stock outstanding. It declares a 10% stock dividend on December 1 when the market value per share is $16. The dividend shares are issued on December 31. Prepare the entries for the declaration and payment of the stock dividend.

Prepare entries for a stock dividend.
(SO 5)

BE12-9 The stockholders' equity section of Martin Corporation consists of common stock ($10 par) $2,000,000 and retained earnings $300,000. A 10% stock dividend (20,000 shares) is declared when the market value per share is $14. Show the before and after effects of the dividend on the following.
(a) The components of stockholders' equity.
(b) Shares outstanding.

Show before and after effects of a stock dividend.
(SO 5)

BE12-10 For the year ending December 31, 2006, Mount Inc. reports net income $120,000 and dividends $85,000. Prepare the retained earnings statement for the year assuming the balance in retained earnings on January 1, 2006, was $220,000.

Prepare a retained earnings statement.
(SO 6)

BE12-11 The balance in retained earnings on January 1, 2006, for Ola Smith Inc, was $800,000. During the year, the corporation paid cash dividends of $90,000 and distributed a stock dividend of $8,000. In addition, the company determined that it had understated its depreciation expense in prior years by $50,000. Net income for 2006 was $150,000. Prepare the retained earnings statement for 2006.

Prepare a retained earnings statement.
(SO 6)

BE12-12 Ingram Corporation has the following accounts at December 31: Common Stock, $10 par, 5,000 shares issued, $50,000; Paid-in Capital in Excess of Par Value $10,000; Retained Earnings $45,000; and Treasury Stock—Common, 500 shares, $11,000. Prepare the stockholders' equity section of the balance sheet.

Prepare stockholders' equity section.
(SO 7)

***BE12-13** The balance sheet for Jimenez Inc. shows the following: total paid-in capital and retained earnings $870,000, total stockholders' equity $810,000, common stock issued 44,000 shares, and common stock outstanding 40,000 shares. Compute the book value per share.

Compute book value per share.
(SO 9)

EXERCISES

E12-1 During its first year of operations, Klumpe Corporation had the following transactions pertaining to its common stock.

Journalize issuance of common stock.
(SO 2)

Jan.	10	Issued 70,000 shares for cash at $5 per share.
July	1	Issued 40,000 shares for cash at $8 per share.

Instructions
(a) Journalize the transactions, assuming that the common stock has a par value of $5 per share.
(b) Journalize the transactions, assuming that the common stock is no-par with a stated value of $1 per share.

E12-2 Garza Co. had the following transactions during the current period.

Journalize issuance of common and preferred stock and purchase of treasury stock.
(SO 2, 3, 4)

Mar.	2	Issued 5,000 shares of $1 par value common stock to attorneys in payment of a bill for $30,000 for services provided in helping the company to incorporate.
June	12	Issued 60,000 shares of $1 par value common stock for cash of $375,000.
July	11	Issued 1,000 shares of $100 par value preferred stock for cash at $110 per share.
Nov.	28	Purchased 2,000 shares of treasury stock for $80,000.

Instructions

Journalize the transactions.

Journalize noncash common stock transactions.

(SO 2)

E12-3 As an auditor for the CPA firm of Agler and Carl, you encounter the following situations in auditing different clients.

1. Desi Corporation is a closely held corporation whose stock is not publicly traded. On December 5, the corporation acquired land by issuing 5,000 shares of its $20 par value common stock. The owners' asking price for the land was $120,000, and the fair market value of the land was $110,000.
2. Lucille Corporation is a publicly held corporation whose common stock is traded on the securities markets. On June 1, it acquired land by issuing 20,000 shares of its $10 par value stock. At the time of the exchange, the land was advertised for sale at $250,000. The stock was selling at $11 per share.

Instructions

Prepare the journal entries for each of the situations above.

Journalize treasury stock transactions.

(SO 3)

E12-4 On January 1, 2006, the stockholders' equity section of Rowen Corporation shows: Common stock ($5 par value) $1,500,000; paid-in capital in excess of par value $1,000,000; and retained earnings $1,200,000. During the year, the following treasury stock transactions occurred.

Mar. 1 Purchased 50,000 shares for cash at $16 per share.
July 1 Sold 10,000 treasury shares for cash at $17 per share.
Sept. 1 Sold 8,000 treasury shares for cash at $15 per share.

Instructions

(a) Journalize the treasury stock transactions.
(b) Restate the entry for September 1, assuming the treasury shares were sold at $13 per share.

Journalize preferred stock transactions and indicate statement presentation.

(SO 4, 7)

Peachtree

E12-5 Tinker Corporation is authorized to issue both preferred and common stock. The par value of the preferred is $50. During the first year of operations, the company had the following events and transactions pertaining to its preferred stock.

Feb. 1 Issued 20,000 shares for cash at $51 per share.
July 1 Issued 10,000 shares for cash at $57 per share.

Instructions

(a) Journalize the transactions.
(b) Post to the stockholders' equity accounts.
(c) Indicate the financial statement presentation of the related accounts.

Answer questions about stockholders' equity section.

(SO 2, 3, 4, 7)

E12-6 The stockholders' equity section of Lumley Corporation at December 31 is as follows.

LUMLEY CORPORATION
Balance Sheet (partial)

Paid-in capital	
Preferred stock, cumulative, 10,000 shares authorized, 6,000 shares issued and outstanding	$ 600,000
Common stock, no par, 750,000 shares authorized, 600,000 shares issued	1,200,000
Total paid-in capital	1,800,000
Retained earnings	1,858,000
Total paid-in capital and retained earnings	3,658,000
Less: Treasury stock (12,000 common shares)	(64,000)
Total stockholders' equity	$3,594,000

Instructions

From a review of the stockholders' equity section, as chief accountant, write a memo to the president of the company answering the following questions.

(a) How many shares of common stock are outstanding?
(b) Assuming there is a stated value, what is the stated value of the common stock?
(c) What is the par value of the preferred stock?

(d) If the annual dividend on preferred stock is $30,000, what is the dividend rate on preferred stock?

(e) If dividends of $60,000 were in arrears on preferred stock, what would be the balance in Retained Earnings?

Prepare correct entries for capital stock transactions.
(SO 2, 3, 4)

E12-7 Flores Corporation recently hired a new accountant with extensive experience in accounting for partnerships. Because of the pressure of the new job, the accountant was unable to review his textbooks on the topic of corporation accounting. During the first month, the accountant made the following entries for the corporation's capital stock.

May 2	Cash	120,000	
	Capital Stock		120,000
	(Issued 10,000 shares of $10 par value common stock at $12 per share)		
10	Cash	600,000	
	Capital Stock		600,000
	(Issued 10,000 shares of $50 par value preferred stock at $60 per share)		
15	Capital Stock	14,000	
	Cash		14,000
	(Purchased 1,000 shares of common stock for the treasury at $14 per share)		
31	Cash	8,000	
	Capital Stock		5,000
	Gain on Sale of Stock		3,000
	(Sold 500 shares of treasury stock at $16 per share)		

Instructions

On the basis of the explanation for each entry, prepare the entry that should have been made for the capital stock transactions.

Journalize cash dividends; indicate statement presentation.
(SO 5)

E12-8 On January 1, Armada Corporation had 95,000 shares of no-par common stock issued and outstanding. The stock has a stated value of $5 per share. During the year, the following occurred.

Apr. 1 Issued 15,000 additional shares of common stock for $17 per share.
June 15 Declared a cash dividend of $1 per share to stockholders of record on June 30.
July 10 Paid the $1 cash dividend.
Dec. 1 Issued 2,000 additional shares of common stock for $19 per share.
15 Declared a cash dividend on outstanding shares of $1.20 per share to stockholders of record on December 31.

Instructions

(a) Prepare the entries, if any, on each of the three dividend dates.

(b) How are dividends and dividends payable reported in the financial statements prepared at December 31?

Journalize stock dividends.
(SO 5)

E12-9 On January 1, 2006, Abdella Corporation had $1,000,000 of common stock outstanding that was issued at par. It also had retained earnings of $750,000. The company issued 60,000 shares of common stock at par on July 1 and earned net income of $400,000 for the year.

Instructions

Journalize the declaration of a 15% stock dividend on December 10, 2006, for the following independent assumptions.

1. Par value is $10, and market value is $18.
2. Par value is $5, and market value is $20.

Compare effects of a stock dividend and a stock split.
(SO 5)

E12-10 On October 31, the stockholders' equity section of Omar Company consists of common stock $600,000 and retained earnings $900,000. Omar is considering the following two courses of action: (1) declaring a 5% stock dividend on the 60,000, $10 par value shares outstanding, or (2) effecting a 2-for-1 stock split that will reduce par value to $5 per share. The current market price is $14 per share.

Instructions

Prepare a tabular summary of the effects of the alternative actions on the components of stockholders' equity, outstanding shares, and book value per share. Use the following column headings: Before Action, After Stock Dividend, and After Stock Split.

Prepare correcting entries for dividends and a stock split.
(SO 5)

E12-11 Before preparing financial statements for the current year, the chief accountant for Springer Company discovered the following errors in the accounts.

1. The declaration and payment of $50,000 cash dividend was recorded as a debit to Interest Expense $50,000 and a credit to Cash $50,000.
2. A 10% stock dividend (1,000 shares) was declared on the $10 par value stock when the market value per share was $16. The only entry made was: Retained Earnings (Dr.) $10,000 and Dividends Payable (Cr.) $10,000. The shares have not been issued.
3. A 4-for-1 stock split involving the issue of 400,000 shares of $5 par value common stock for 100,000 shares of $20 par value common stock was recorded as a debit to Retained Earnings $2,000,000 and a credit to Common Stock $2,000,000.

Instructions

Prepare the correcting entries at December 31.

Prepare a retained earnings statement.
(SO 6)

E12-12 On January 1, 2006, Castle Corporation had retained earnings of $550,000. During the year, Castle had the following selected transactions.

1. Declared cash dividends of $120,000.
2. Corrected overstatement of 2005 net income because of depreciation error $30,000.
3. Earned net income of $350,000.
4. Declared stock dividends of $80,000.

Instructions

Prepare a retained earnings statement for the year.

Classify stockholders' equity accounts.
(SO 7)

E12-13 The ledger of O'Dell Corporation contains the following accounts: Common Stock, Preferred Stock, Treasury Stock—Common, Paid-in Capital in Excess of Par Value—Preferred Stock, Paid-in Capital in Excess of Stated Value—Common Stock, Paid-in Capital from Treasury Stock, and Retained Earnings.

Instructions

Classify each account using the following table headings.

	Paid-in Capital			
Account	**Capital Stock**	**Additional**	**Retained Earnings**	**Other**

Prepare a stockholders' equity section.
(SO 7)

E12-14 The following accounts appear in the ledger of Tiger Inc. after the books are closed at December 31.

Common Stock, no par, $1 stated value, 400,000 shares authorized; 300,000 shares issued	$ 300,000
Common Stock Dividends Distributable	60,000
Paid-in Capital in Excess of Stated Value—Common Stock	1,200,000
Preferred Stock, $5 par value, 8%, 40,000 shares authorized; 30,000 shares issued	150,000
Retained Earnings	700,000
Treasury Stock (10,000 common shares)	74,000
Paid-in Capital in Excess of Par Value—Preferred Stock	344,000

Instructions

Prepare the stockholders' equity section at December 31, assuming retained earnings is restricted for plant expansion in the amount of $100,000.

Prepare a stockholders' equity section.
(SO 7, 9)

***E12-15** In a recent year, the stockholders' equity section of **Aluminum Company of America (Alcoa)** showed the following (in alphabetical order): additional paid-in capital $6,101, common stock $925, preferred stock $56, retained earnings $7,428, and treasury stock $2,828. All dollar data are in millions.

The preferred stock has 557,740 shares authorized, with a par value of $100 and an annual $3.75 per share cumulative dividend preference. At December 31, 557,649 shares of preferred are issued and 546,024 shares are outstanding. There are 1.8 billion shares of $1 par value common stock authorized, of which 924.6 million are issued and 844.8 million are outstanding at December 31.

Instructions

(a) Prepare the stockholders' equity section, including disclosure of all relevant data.

(b) Compute the book value per share of common stock, assuming there are no preferred dividends in arrears. (Round to two decimals.)

Compute book value per share with preferred stock.

(SO 4, 9)

***E12-16** At December 31, Missouri Corporation has total stockholders' equity of $3,000,000. Included in this total are preferred stock $500,000 and paid-in capital in excess of par value—preferred stock $50,000. There are 10,000 shares of $50 par value 10% cumulative preferred stock outstanding. At year-end, 200,000 shares of common stock are outstanding.

Instructions

Compute the book value per share of common stock, under each of the following assumptions.

(a) There are no preferred dividends in arrears, and the preferred stock does not have a call price.

(b) Preferred dividends are one year in arrears, and the preferred stock has a call price of $60 per share.

Compute book value per share; indicate account balances after a stock dividend.

(SO 5, 7, 9)

*** E12-17** On October 1, Chile Corporation's stockholders' equity is as follows.

Common stock, $5 par value	$200,000
Paid-in capital in excess of par value	25,000
Retained earnings	75,000
Total stockholders' equity	$300,000

On October 1, Chile declares and distributes a 10% stock dividend when the market value of the stock is $15 per share.

Instructions

(a) Compute the book value per share (1) before the stock dividend and (2) after the stock dividend. (Round to two decimals.)

(b) Indicate the balances in the three stockholders' equity accounts after the stock dividend shares have been distributed.

PROBLEMS: SET A

Journalize stock transactions, post, and prepare paid-in capital section.

(SO 2, 4, 7)

P12-1A Hayslett Corporation was organized on January 1, 2006. It is authorized to issue 20,000 shares of 6%, $50 par value preferred stock, and 500,000 shares of no-par common stock with a stated value of $2 per share. The following stock transactions were completed during the first year.

Jan. 10	Issued 100,000 shares of common stock for cash at $3 per share.
Mar. 1	Issued 10,000 shares of preferred stock for cash at $55 per share.
Apr. 1	Issued 25,000 shares of common stock for land. The asking price of the land was $90,000. The company's estimate of the fair market value of the land was $85,000.
May 1	Issued 75,000 shares of common stock for cash at $4 per share.
Aug. 1	Issued 10,000 shares of common stock to attorneys in payment of their bill for $50,000 for services provided in helping the company organize.
Sept. 1	Issued 5,000 shares of common stock for cash at $6 per share.
Nov. 1	Issued 2,000 shares of preferred stock for cash at $58 per share.

Instructions

(a) Journalize the transactions.

(b) Post to the stockholders' equity accounts. (Use J1 as the posting reference.)

(c) Prepare the paid-in capital section of stockholders' equity at December 31, 2006.

(c) Total paid-in capital $1,431,000

Journalize and post treasury stock transactions, and prepare stockholders' equity section.
(SO 3, 7)

P12-2A Greeve Corporation had the following stockholders' equity accounts on January 1, 2006: Common Stock ($1 par) $400,000, Paid-in Capital in Excess of Par Value $500,000, and Retained Earnings $100,000. In 2006, the company had the following treasury stock transactions.

Mar.	1	Purchased 5,000 shares at $7 per share.
June	1	Sold 1,000 shares at $10 per share.
Sept.	1	Sold 2,000 shares at $9 per share.
Dec.	1	Sold 1,000 shares at $5 per share.

Greeve Corporation uses the cost method of accounting for treasury stock. In 2006, the company reported net income of $60,000.

Instructions

(a) Journalize the treasury stock transactions, and prepare the closing entry at December 31, 2006, for net income.

(b) Treasury Stock $7,000
(c) Total stockholders' equity $1,058,000

(b) Open accounts for (1) Paid-in Capital from Treasury Stock, (2) Treasury Stock, and (3) Retained Earnings. Post to these accounts using J12 as the posting reference.

(c) Prepare the stockholders' equity section for Greeve Corporation at December 31, 2006.

Journalize and post transactions, prepare stockholders' equity section.
(SO 2, 3, 4, 7, 9)

P12-3A The stockholders' equity accounts of Jajoo Corporation on January 1, 2006, were as follows.

Preferred Stock (10%, $100 par noncumulative, 5,000 shares authorized)	$ 300,000
Common Stock ($5 stated value, 300,000 shares authorized)	1,000,000
Paid-in Capital in Excess of Par Value—Preferred Stock	20,000
Paid-in Capital in Excess of Stated Value—Common Stock	425,000
Retained Earnings	488,000
Treasury Stock—Common (5,000 shares)	40,000

During 2006, the corporation had the following transactions and events pertaining to its stockholders' equity.

Feb. 1	Issued 3,000 shares of common stock for $25,000.
Mar. 20	Purchased 1,500 additional shares of common treasury stock at $8 per share.
June 14	Sold 4,000 shares of treasury stock—common for $36,000.
Sept. 3	Issued 2,000 shares of common stock for a patent valued at $17,000.
Dec. 31	Determined that net income for the year was $340,000.

Instructions

(a) Journalize the transactions and the closing entry for net income.

(b) Enter the beginning balances in the accounts and post the journal entries to the stockholders' equity accounts. (Use J1 as the posting reference.)

(c) Total stockholders' equity $2,599,000

(c) Prepare a stockholders' equity section at December 31, 2006.

* **(d)** Compute the book value per share of common stock at December 31, 2006. (Round to two decimals.)

Prepare dividend entries and stockholders' equity section.
(SO 5, 7)

Peachtree

P12-4A On January 1, 2006, Galactica Corporation had the following stockholders' equity accounts.

Common Stock ($20 par value, 60,000 shares issued and outstanding)	$1,200,000
Paid-in Capital in Excess of Par Value	200,000
Retained Earnings	500,000

During the year, the following transactions occurred.

Feb.	1	Declared a $1 cash dividend per share to stockholders of record on February 15, payable March 1.
Mar.	1	Paid the dividend declared in February.
Apr.	1	Announced a 5-for-1 stock split. Prior to the split, the market price per share was $35.
July	1	Declared a 5% stock dividend to stockholders of record on July 15, distributable July 31. On July 1, the market price of the stock was $7 per share.
July	31	Issued the shares for the stock dividend.
Dec.	1	Declared a $0.50 per share dividend to stockholders of record on December 15, payable January 5, 2007.
	31	Determined that net income for the year was $380,000.

Instructions

(a) Journalize the transactions and closing entries.

(b) Enter the beginning balances and post the entries to the stockholders' equity accounts. (*Note:* Open additional stockholders' equity accounts as needed.)

(c) Prepare a stockholders' equity section at December 31.

(c) Total stockholders' equity $2,062,500

Prepare retained earnings statement and stockholders' equity section, and compute earnings per share.

(SO 5, 6, 7)

P12-5A The ledger of Nakona Corporation at December 31, 2006, after the books have been closed, contains the following stockholders' equity accounts.

Preferred Stock (10,000 shares issued)	$1,000,000
Common Stock (400,000 shares issued)	2,000,000
Paid-in Capital in Excess of Par Value—Preferred	200,000
Paid-in Capital in Excess of Stated Value—Common	1,100,000
Common Stock Dividends Distributable	200,000
Retained Earnings	2,365,000

A review of the accounting records reveals the following.

1. No errors have been made in recording 2006 transactions or in preparing the closing entry for net income.
2. Preferred stock is 8%, $100 par value, noncumulative, and callable at $125. Since January 1, 2005, 10,000 shares have been outstanding; 20,000 shares are authorized.
3. Common stock is no-par with a stated value of $5 per share; 600,000 shares are authorized.
4. The January 1 balance in Retained Earnings was $2,450,000.
5. On October 1, 100,000 shares of common stock were sold for cash at $8 per share.
6. A cash dividend of $600,000 was declared and properly allocated to preferred and common stock on November 1. No dividends were paid to preferred stockholders in 2005.
7. On December 31, a 10% common stock dividend was declared out of retained earnings on common stock when the market price per share was $7.
8. Net income for the year was $795,000.
9. On December 31, 2006, the directors authorized disclosure of a $100,000 restriction of retained earnings for plant expansion. (Use Note A.)

Instructions

(a) Reproduce the Retained Earnings account (T-account) for the year.

(b) Prepare a retained earnings statement for the year.

(c) Prepare a stockholders' equity section at December 31.

(d) Compute the earnings per share of common stock using 325,000 as the weighted average shares outstanding for the year.

(e) Compute the allocation of the cash dividend to preferred and common stock.

(b) Retained earnings $2,365,000
(c) Total stockholders' equity $6,865,000

Prepare entries for stock transactions and stockholders' equity section.

(SO 2, 3, 4, 7)

P12-6A Arnold Corporation has been authorized to issue 40,000 shares of $100 par value, 8%, noncumulative preferred stock and 2,000,000 shares of no-par common stock. The corporation assigned a $5 stated value to the common stock. At December 31, 2006, the ledger contained the following balances pertaining to stockholders' equity.

Preferred Stock	$ 240,000
Paid-in Capital in Excess of Par Value—Preferred	56,000
Common Stock	2,000,000
Paid-in Capital in Excess of Stated Value—Common	5,700,000
Treasury Stock—Common (1,000 shares)	22,000
Paid-in Capital from Treasury Stock	3,000
Retained Earnings	560,000

The preferred stock was issued for land having a fair market value of $296,000. All common stock issued was for cash. In November, 1,500 shares of common stock were purchased for the treasury at a per share cost of $22. In December, 500 shares of treasury stock were sold for $28 per share. No dividends were declared in 2006.

Instructions

(a) Prepare the journal entries for the:

(1) Issuance of preferred stock for land.

(2) Issuance of common stock for cash.

(3) Purchase of common treasury stock for cash.

(4) Sale of treasury stock for cash.

(b) Prepare the stockholders' equity section at December 31, 2006.

(b) Total stockholders' equity $8,537,000

Prepare dividend entries and stockholders' equity section.
(SO 5, 7)

P12-7A On January 1, 2006, Snider Corporation had the following stockholders' equity accounts.

Common Stock ($10 par value, 90,000 shares issued and outstanding)	$900,000
Paid-in Capital in Excess of Par Value	200,000
Retained Earnings	540,000

During the year, the following transactions occurred.

Jan. 15	Declared a $1 cash dividend per share to stockholders of record on January 31, payable February 15.
Feb. 15	Paid the dividend declared in January.
Apr. 15	Declared a 10% stock dividend to stockholders of record on April 30, distributable May 15. On April 15, the market price of the stock was $15 per share.
May 15	Issued the shares for the stock dividend.
July 1	Announced a 2-for-1 stock split. The market price per share prior to the announcement was $17. (The new par value is $5.)
Dec. 1	Declared a $0.50 per share cash dividend to stockholders of record on December 15, payable January 10, 2007.
31	Determined that net income for the year was $250,000.

Instructions

(a) Journalize the transactions and the closing entry for net income.

(b) Enter the beginning balances, and post the entries to the stockholders' equity accounts. (*Note*: Open additional stockholders' equity accounts as needed.)

(c) Prepare a stockholders' equity section at December 31.

(c) Total stockholders' equity $1,701,000

Prepare stockholders' equity section; compute book value per share.
(SO 7, 9)

***P12-8A** The following stockholders' equity accounts arranged alphabetically are in the ledger of McGrath Corporation at December 31, 2006.

Common Stock ($10 stated value)	$1,500,000
Paid-in Capital from Treasury Stock	6,000
Paid-in Capital in Excess of Stated Value—Common Stock	690,000
Paid-in Capital in Excess of Par Value—Preferred Stock	288,400
Preferred Stock (8%, $100 par, noncumulative)	400,000
Retained Earnings	776,000
Treasury Stock—Common (8,000 shares)	88,000

Instructions

(a) Prepare a stockholders' equity section at December 31, 2006.

(b) Compute the book value per share of the common stock, assuming the preferred stock has a call price of $110 per share.

Total stockholders' equity $3,572,400

Prepare stockholders' equity statement.
(SO 8)

***P12-9A** On January 1, 2006, Hamblin Inc. had the following stockholders' equity balances.

Common Stock (500,000 shares issued)	$1,000,000
Paid-in Capital in Excess of Par Value	500,000
Common Stock Dividends Distributable	100,000
Retained Earnings	600,000

During 2006, the following transactions and events occurred.

1. Issued 50,000 shares of $2 par value common stock as a result of 10% stock dividend declared on December 15, 2005.
2. Issued 30,000 shares of common stock for cash at $5 per share.
3. Purchased 25,000 shares of common stock for the treasury at $6 per share.
4. Declared and paid a cash dividend of $111,000.
5. Sold 8,000 shares of treasury stock for cash at $6 per share.
6. Earned net income of $360,000.

Instructions

Prepare a stockholders' equity statement for the year.

Total stockholders' equity $2,497,000

PROBLEMS: SET B

Journalize stock transactions, post, and prepare paid-in capital section.

(SO 2, 4, 7)

P12-1B Keeler Corporation was organized on January 1, 2006. It is authorized to issue 10,000 shares of 8%, $100 par value preferred stock, and 500,000 shares of no-par common stock with a stated value of $3 per share. The following stock transactions were completed during the first year.

Jan.	10	Issued 80,000 shares of common stock for cash at $4 per share.
Mar.	1	Issued 5,000 shares of preferred stock for cash at $105 per share.
Apr.	1	Issued 24,000 shares of common stock for land. The asking price of the land was $90,000. The fair market value of the land was $85,000.
May	1	Issued 80,000 shares of common stock for cash at $4.50 per share.
Aug.	1	Issued 10,000 shares of common stock to attorneys in payment of their bill of $40,000 for services provided in helping the company organize.
Sept.	1	Issued 10,000 shares of common stock for cash at $5 per share.
Nov.	1	Issued 1,000 shares of preferred stock for cash at $109 per share.

Instructions

(a) Journalize the transactions.

(b) Post to the stockholders' equity accounts. (Use J5 as the posting reference.)

(c) Prepare the paid-in capital section of stockholders' equity at December 31, 2006.

(c) Total paid-in capital $1,489,000

Journalize and post treasury stock transactions, and prepare stockholders' equity section.

(SO 3, 7)

P12-2B Goldberg Corporation had the following stockholders' equity accounts on January 1, 2006: Common Stock ($5 par) $500,000, Paid-in Capital in Excess of Par Value $200,000, and Retained Earnings $100,000. In 2006, the company had the following treasury stock transactions.

Mar.	1	Purchased 5,000 shares at $8 per share.
June	1	Sold 1,000 shares at $12 per share.
Sept.	1	Sold 2,000 shares at $10 per share.
Dec.	1	Sold 1,000 shares at $6 per share.

Goldberg Corporation uses the cost method of accounting for treasury stock. In 2006, the company reported net income of $40,000.

Instructions

(a) Journalize the treasury stock transactions, and prepare the closing entry at December 31, 2006, for net income.

(b) Open accounts for (1) Paid-in Capital from Treasury Stock, (2) Treasury Stock, and (3) Retained Earnings. Post to these accounts using J10 as the posting reference.

(c) Prepare the stockholders' equity section for Goldberg Corporation at December 31, 2006.

(b) Treasury Stock $8,000
(c) Total stockholders' equity $838,000

Journalize and post transactions, prepare stockholders' equity section.

(SO 2, 3, 4, 7, 9)

P12-3B The stockholders' equity accounts of Port Corporation on January 1, 2006, were as follows.

Preferred Stock (8%, $50 par cumulative, 10,000 shares authorized)	$ 400,000
Common Stock ($1 stated value, 2,000,000 shares authorized)	1,000,000
Paid-in Capital in Excess of Par Value—Preferred Stock	100,000
Paid-in Capital in Excess of Stated Value—Common Stock	1,450,000
Retained Earnings	1,816,000
Treasury Stock—Common (10,000 shares)	40,000

During 2006, the corporation had the following transactions and events pertaining to its stockholders' equity.

Feb.	1	Issued 25,000 shares of common stock for $100,000.
Apr.	14	Sold 6,000 shares of treasury stock—common for $33,000.
Sept.	3	Issued 5,000 shares of common stock for a patent valued at $30,000.
Nov.	10	Purchased 1,000 shares of common stock for the treasury at a cost of $6,000.
Dec.	31	Determined that net income for the year was $452,000.

No dividends were declared during the year.

Instructions

(a) Journalize the transactions and the closing entry for net income.

(b) Enter the beginning balances in the accounts, and post the journal entries to the stockholders' equity accounts. (Use J5 for the posting reference.)

(c) Total stockholders' equity $5,335,000

(c) Prepare a stockholders' equity section at December 31, 2006, including the disclosure of the preferred dividends in arrears.

***(d)** Compute the book value per share of common stock at December 31, 2006, assuming the preferred stock does not have a call price.

Prepare dividend entries and stockholders' equity section.

(SO 5, 7)

P12-4B On January 1, 2006, Argentina Corporation had the following stockholders' equity accounts.

Common Stock ($20 par value, 75,000 shares issued and outstanding)	$1,500,000
Paid-in Capital in Excess of Par Value	200,000
Retained Earnings	600,000

During the year, the following transactions occurred.

Feb. 1	Declared a $1 cash dividend per share to stockholders of record on February 15, payable March 1.
Mar. 1	Paid the dividend declared in February.
Apr. 1	Announced a 2-for-1 stock split. Prior to the split, the market price per share was $36.
July 1	Declared a 10% stock dividend to stockholders of record on July 15, distributable July 31. On July 1, the market price of the stock was $13 per share.
31	Issued the shares for the stock dividend.
Dec. 1	Declared a $0.50 per share dividend to stockholders of record on December 15, payable January 5, 2007.
31	Determined that net income for the year was $350,000.

Instructions

(a) Journalize the transactions and the closing entry for net income.

(b) Enter the beginning balances, and post the entries to the stockholders' equity accounts. (*Note*: Open additional stockholders' equity accounts as needed.)

(c) Total stockholders' equity $2,492,500

(c) Prepare a stockholders' equity section at December 31.

Prepare retained earnings statement and stockholders' equity section.

(SO 6, 7)

P12-5B On December 31, 2005, Bradstrom Company had 1,500,000 shares of $10 par common stock issued and outstanding. The stockholders' equity accounts at December 31, 2005, had the following balances.

Common Stock	$15,000,000
Additional Paid-in Capital	1,500,000
Retained Earnings	900,000

Transactions during 2006 and other information related to stockholders' equity accounts were as follows.

1. On January 10, 2006, Bradstrom issued at $105 per share 100,000 shares of $100 par value, 7% cumulative preferred stock.
2. On February 8, 2006, Bradstrom reacquired 15,000 shares of its common stock for $16 per share.
3. On June 8, 2006, Bradstrom declared a cash dividend of $1 per share on the common stock outstanding, payable on July 10, 2006, to stockholders of record on July 1, 2006.
4. On December 15, 2006, Bradstrom declared the yearly cash dividend on preferred stock, payable January 10, 2007, to stockholders of record on December 15, 2006.
5. Net income for the year is $3,600,000.
6. It was discovered that depreciation expense had been overstated in 2005 by $80,000.

Instructions

(a) Prepare a retained earnings statement for the year ended December 31, 2006.

(b) Total stockholders' equity $29,155,000

(b) Prepare the stockholders' equity section of Bradstrom's balance sheet at December 31, 2006.

Prepare retained earnings statement and stockholders' equity section, and compute earnings per share.

(SO 5, 6, 7)

P12-6B The post-closing trial balance of Chen Corporation at December 31, 2006, contains the following stockholders' equity accounts.

Preferred Stock (15,000 shares issued)	$ 750,000
Common Stock (250,000 shares issued)	2,500,000
Paid-in Capital in Excess of Par Value—Preferred	250,000
Paid-in Capital in Excess of Par Value—Common	400,000
Common Stock Dividends Distributable	250,000
Retained Earnings	902,000

A review of the accounting records reveals the following.

1. No errors have been made in recording 2006 transactions or in preparing the closing entry for net income.
2. Preferred stock is $50 par, 8%, and cumulative; 15,000 shares have been outstanding since January 1, 2005.
3. Authorized stock is 20,000 shares of preferred, 500,000 shares of common with a $10 par value.
4. The January 1 balance in Retained Earnings was $1,170,000.
5. On July 1, 20,000 shares of common stock were sold for cash at $16 per share.
6. On September 1, the company discovered an understatement error of $90,000 in computing depreciation in 2005. The net of tax effect of $63,000 was properly debited directly to Retained Earnings.
7. A cash dividend of $250,000 was declared and properly allocated to preferred and common stock on October 1. No dividends were paid to preferred stockholders in 2005.
8. On December 31, a 10% common stock dividend was declared out of retained earnings on common stock when the market price per share was $18.
9. Net income for the year was $495,000.
10. On December 31, 2006, the directors authorized disclosure of a $200,000 restriction of retained earnings for plant expansion. (Use Note X.)

Instructions

(a) Reproduce the Retained Earnings account for the year.
(b) Prepare a retained earnings statement for the year.
(c) Prepare a stockholders' equity section at December 31.
(d) Compute the earnings per share of common stock using 240,000 as the weighted average shares outstanding for the year.
(e) Compute the allocation of the cash dividend to preferred and common stock.

(b) Retained earnings $902,000
(c) Total stockholders' equity $5,052,000

***P12-7B** The following stockholders' equity accounts arranged alphabetically are in the ledger of Rizzo Corporation at December 31, 2005.

Prepare stockholders' equity section; compute book value per share.

(SO 7, 9)

Common Stock ($5 stated value)	$2,500,000
Paid-in Capital from Treasury Stock	10,000
Paid-in Capital in Excess of Stated Value—Common Stock	1,600,000
Paid-in Capital in Excess of Par Value—Preferred Stock	679,000
Preferred Stock (8%, $50 par, noncumulative)	800,000
Retained Earnings	1,448,000
Treasury Stock—Common (10,000 shares)	130,000

Instructions

(a) Prepare a stockholders' equity section at December 31, 2006.
(b) Compute the book value per share of the common stock, assuming the preferred stock has a call price of $60 per share.

Total stockholders' equity $6,907,000

BROADENING YOUR PERSPECTIVE

Financial Reporting and Analysis

FINANCIAL REPORTING PROBLEM: PepsiCo

BYP12-1 The stockholders' equity section for **PepsiCo, Inc.** is shown in Appendix A. You will also find data relative to this problem on other pages of the appendix.

Instructions

(a) What is the par or stated value per share of PepsiCo's common stock?
(b) What percentage of PepsiCo's authorized common stock was issued at December 27, 2003?
(c) How many shares of common stock were outstanding at December 27, 2003, and at December 28, 2002?
***(d)** What was the book value per share at December 27, 2003, and at December 28, 2002?

(e) What were the high and low market price per share in the fourth quarter of fiscal 2003, as reported under Selected Financial Data?

■ COMPARATIVE ANALYSIS PROBLEM: PepsiCo vs. Coca-Cola

PEPSI

BYP12-2 **PepsiCo**'s financial statements are presented in Appendix A. **Coca-Cola**'s financial statements are presented in Appendix B.

Instructions

(a) Based on the information contained in these financial statements, compute the 2003 book value per share for each company. (*Hint:* Use the value reported for "common shareholders' equity" as the numerator for PepsiCo.)

(b) Compare the market value per share for each company to the book value per share at year-end 2003. Assume that the market value of Coca-Cola's stock was $50.90 at year-end 2003.

(c) Why are book value and market value per share different?

(d) Compute earnings per share and return on common stockholders' equity for both companies for the year ending in January 2003. Assume PepsiCo's weighted average shares were 1,718 million and Coca-Cola's weighted average shares were 2,462 million. Can these measures be used to compare the profitability of the two companies? Why or why not?

(e) What was the total amount of dividends paid by each company in 2003?

■ RESEARCH CASE

BYP12-3 The March 28, 2001, edition of the *Wall Street Journal* contains an article by Cassell Bryan-Low titled "A Growing Number of Firms Pull Back on Stock Buybacks."

Instructions

Read the article and answer the following questions.

(a) In what way does the article say that the current trend in treasury stock repurchases is "a reversal of the traditional logic"?

(b) What are the reasons given in the article for why companies are buying back fewer shares?

(c) How much did **International Business Machines (IBM)** spend on treasury stock purchases between 1995 and the end of 2000?

(d) What is given as a possible explanation for the timing of **Yahoo**'s first-ever treasury stock repurchase?

■ INTERPRETING FINANCIAL STATEMENTS

BYP12-4 **Marriott Corporation** split into two companies: **Host Marriott Corporation** and **Marriott International**. Host Marriott retained ownership of the corporation's vast hotel and other properties, while Marriott International, rather than owning hotels, managed them. The purpose of this split was to free Marriott International from the "baggage" associated with Host Marriott, thus allowing it to be more aggressive in its pursuit of growth. The following information (in millions) is provided for each corporation for their first full year operating as independent companies.

	Host Marriott	Marriott International
Sales	$1,501	$8,415
Net income	(25)	200
Total assets	3,822	3,207
Total liabilities	3,112	2,440
Stockholders' equity	710	767

Instructions

(a) The two companies were split by the issuance of shares of Marriott International to all shareholders of the previous combined company. Discuss the nature of this transaction.

(b) Calculate the debt to total assets ratio for each company.

(c) Calculate the return on assets and return on common stockholders' equity ratios for each company.
(d) The company's debtholders were fiercely opposed to the original plan to split the two companies because the original plan had Host Marriott absorbing the majority of the company's debt. They relented only when Marriott International agreed to absorb a larger share of the debt. Discuss the possible reasons the debtholders were opposed to the plan to split the company.

A GLOBAL FOCUS

BYP12-5 American depositary receipts (ADRs) represent a way for U.S. investors to invest in foreign corporations without directly purchasing actual foreign shares of stock. Instead, a U.S. bank purchases the shares in a foreign company and then issues to investors securities (the ADRs) which pass through the risks and rewards of the underlying stock. For example, when the underlying stock pays a dividend the U.S. bank pays a dividend to the holder of the ADR. The March 1, 2001, issue of the *Wall Street Journal* contains an article by Craig Karmin titled "ADR Holders Find They Retain Unequal Rights" that discusses one potential drawback of this system.

Instructions
Read the article and answer the following questions.

(a) What is the nature of the shareholder resolution that the holders of the **BP Amoco** ADRs are trying to pass?
(b) What do these investors hope to accomplish by getting their resolution on the ballot?
(c) Are ADRs common?
(d) What are some of the advantages of ADRs to U.S. investors as compared to owning local shares?

EXPLORING THE WEB

BYP12-6 SEC filings of publicly traded companies are available to view online.

Address: http//biz.yahoo.com/i, or go to www.wiley.com/college/weygandt

Steps

1. Pick a company and type in the company's name.
2. Choose **Quote**.

Instructions
Answer the following questions.

(a) What company did you select?
(b) What is its stock symbol?
(c) What was the stock's trading range today?
(d) What was the stock's trading range for the year?

Critical Thinking

GROUP DECISION CASE

BYP12-7 The stockholders' meeting for Harris Corporation has been in progress for some time. The chief financial officer for Harris is presently reviewing the company's financial statements and is explaining the items that comprise the stockholders' equity section of the balance sheet for the current year. The stockholders' equity section of Harris Corporation at December 31, 2006, is shown on page 580.

HARRIS CORPORATION
Balance Sheet (partial)
December 31, 2006

Paid in capital		
Capital stock		
Preferred stock, authorized 1,000,000 shares cumulative, $100 par value, $8 per share, 6,000 shares issued and outstanding		$ 600,000
Common stock, authorized 5,000,000 shares, $1 par value, 3,000,000 shares issued, and 2,700,000 outstanding		3,000,000
Total capital stock		3,600,000
Additional paid-in capital		
In excess of par value—preferred stock	$ 50,000	
In excess of par value—common stock	25,000,000	
Total additional paid-in capital		25,050,000
Total paid-in capital		28,650,000
Retained earnings		900,000
Total paid-in capital and retained earnings		29,550,000
Less: Common treasury stock (300,000 shares)		9,300,000
Total stockholders' equity		$20,250,000

At the meeting, stockholders have raised a number of questions regarding the stockholders' equity section.

Instructions

With the class divided into groups, answer the following questions as if you were the chief financial officer for Harris Corporation.

(a) "What does the cumulative provision related to the preferred stock mean?"

(b) "I thought the common stock was presently selling at $29.75, but the company has the stock stated at $1 per share. How can that be?"

(c) "Why is the company buying back its common stock? Furthermore, the treasury stock has a debit balance because it is subtracted from stockholders' equity. Why is treasury stock not reported as an asset if it has a debit balance?"

(d) "Why is it necessary to show additional paid-in capital? Why not just show common stock at the total amount paid in?"

■ COMMUNICATION ACTIVITY

BYP12-8 Sal Greco, your uncle, is an inventor who has decided to incorporate. Uncle Sal knows that you are an accounting major at U.N.O. In a recent letter to you, he ends with the question, "I'm filling out a state incorporation application. Can you tell me the difference in the following terms: (1) authorized stock, (2) issued stock, (3) outstanding stock, (4) preferred stock?"

Instructions

In a brief note, differentiate for Uncle Sal among the four different stock terms. Write the letter to be friendly, yet professional.

Accounting Matters!

■ ETHICS CASE

BYP12-9 The R&D division of Healy Chemical Corp. has just developed a chemical for sterilizing the vicious Brazilian "killer bees" which are invading Mexico and the southern states of the United States. The president of Healy is anxious to get the chemical on the market to boost Healy's profits. He believes his job is in jeopardy because of decreasing sales and profits. Healy has an opportunity to sell this chemical in Central American countries, where the laws are much more relaxed than in the United States.

The director of Healy's R&D division strongly recommends further testing in the laboratory for side-effects of this chemical on other insects, birds, animals, plants, and even humans.

He cautions the president, "We could be sued from all sides if the chemical has tragic side-effects that we didn't even test for in the labs." The president answers, "We can't wait an additional year for your lab tests. We can avoid losses from such lawsuits by establishing a separate wholly owned corporation to shield Healy Corp. from such lawsuits. We can't lose any more than our investment in the new corporation, and we'll invest just the patent covering this chemical. We'll reap the benefits if the chemical works and is safe, and avoid the losses from lawsuits if it's a disaster." The following week Healy creates a new wholly owned corporation called Dryden Inc., sells the chemical patent to it for $10, and watches the spraying begin.

Instructions

(a) Who are the stakeholders in this situation?
(b) Are the president's motives and actions ethical?
(c) Can Healy shield itself against losses of Dryden Inc.?

■ CONTINUING COOKIE CHRONICLE

Accounting Matters!

(Note: This is a continuation of the Cookie Chronicle from Chapters 1 through 11.)

BYP12-10

Part 1 Because Natalie has been so successful with Cookie Creations and Curtis has been just as successful with his coffee shop, they both conclude that they could benefit from each other's business expertise. Curtis and Natalie next evaluate the different types of business organization, and because of the advantage of limited personal liability, decide to form a new corporation.

Curtis has operated his coffee shop for 2 years. He buys coffee, muffins, and cookies from a local supplier. Natalie's business consists of giving cookie-making classes and selling fine European mixers. The plan is for Natalie to use the premises Curtis currently rents to give her cookie-making classes and demonstrations of the mixers that she sells. Natalie will also hire, train, and supervise staff hired to bake cookies and muffins sold in the coffee shop. By offering her classes on the premises, Natalie will save on travel, and the coffee shop will provide one central location for selling the mixers. Combining forces will also allow Natalie and Curtis to pool their resources and buy a few more assets to run their new business venture.

The current market values of the assets of both businesses are as follows.

Description	Curtis' Coffee	Cookie Creations
Cash	$7,500	$10,000
Accounts receivable	100	500
Merchandise inventory	450	1,130
Equipment	2,500	1,000

Curtis and Natalie meet with a lawyer and form their corporation, called Cookie & Coffee Creations Inc., on November 1, 2006. The new corporation is authorized to issue 50,000 shares of $1 par common stock and 10,000 shares of no par, $6 cumulative preferred stock.

The assets held by each business will be transferred into the corporation at current market value. Curtis will receive 10,550 common shares and Natalie will receive 12,630 common shares in the corporation.

Natalie and Curtis are very excited about this new business venture. They come to you with the following questions:

1. Curtis' Dad and Natalie's grandmother are interested in investing $5,000 each in the business venture. Curtis and Natalie are considering issuing them preferred shares. What would be the advantage of issuing them preferred stock instead of common?
2. What would be the advantages and disadvantages of issuing cumulative preferred?
3. "Our lawyer has sent us a bill for $750. When we talked the bill over with her, she said that she would be willing to receive common stock in our new corporation instead of cash. We would be happy to issue her stock, but we're a bit worried about accounting for this transaction. Can we do this? If so, how do we determine how many shares to give to her?"

Instructions

(a) Answer Natalie and Curtis' questions.
(b) Prepare the journal entries required on November 1, 2006, the date when Natalie and Curtis transfer the assets of their respective businesses into Cookie & Coffee Creations Inc.

(c) Assume that Cookie & Coffee Creations Inc. issues 1,000 $6 cumulative preferred shares to Curtis' Dad and the same number to Natalie's grandmother, in both cases for $5,000. Also assume that Cookie & Coffee Creations Inc. issues 750 common shares to its lawyer. Prepare the journal entries required for each of these transactions that also occurred on November 1.

(d) Prepare the opening balance sheet for Cookie & Coffee Creations Inc. as of November 1, 2006, including the journal entries in (b) and (c) above.

Part 2 After establishing their company's fiscal year end to be October 31, Natalie and Curtis began operating Cookie & Coffee Creations Inc. on November 1, 2006. The company had the following selected transactions during its first year of operations, 2007.

Jan. 1	Issued an additional 500 preferred shares to Natalie's brother for $2,500 cash.
June 30	Repurchased 750 shares issued to the lawyer, for $500 cash. The lawyer had decided to retire and wanted to liquidate all of her assets.
Oct. 15	The company had a very successful first year of operations and as a result declared dividends of $25,000, payable November 15, 2007. (Indicate the amounts payable to the preferred stockholders and to the common stockholders.)
Oct. 31	The company earned revenues of $462,500 and incurred expenses of $406,500 (including the $750 legal expense from Nov. 1 but excluding income tax). Record income tax expense, assuming the company has a 20% income tax rate.

Instructions

(a) Prepare the journal entries to record each of the above transactions.
(b) Prepare all of the closing entries required on October 31, 2007.
(c) Prepare the retained earnings statement for the year ended October 31, 2007.
(d) Prepare the stockholders' equity section of the balance sheet as of October 31, 2007.

Accounting Matters!

Answers to Accounting Matters! Questions

p. 530

Q: Was Enron's board of directors fulfilling its role in a corporate organization when it waived Enron's ethical code on two occasions?

A: The board of directors is elected by the owners (stockholders) of the corporation to manage the corporation. One of its roles is to formulate the ethical and operating policies for the company and to assume an oversight responsibility on behalf of the stockholders and other third parties. It was the responsibility of the board of directors to enforce the corporation's ethical code, not to waive it.

p. 532

Q: In contrast to Japanese stockholders, what are the ownership rights of stockholders in U.S. corporations?

A: Stockholders in U.S. corporations are given various voting and financial rights, stated in the corporate charter. Stockholders vote to elect directors and to decide other actions that require stockholder approval. They share in the corporate earnings through the receipt of dividends, and U.S. laws for publicly traded firms ensure financial disclosure. The stockholders also have the right to keep the same percentage ownership when additional shares are issued and to share in assets upon liquidation in proportion to their holdings.

p. 535

Q: For stocks traded on organized stock exchanges, how are the dollar prices per share established?

A: The dollar prices per share are established by the interaction between buyers and sellers of the shares.

Q: What factors might influence the price of shares in the marketplace?

A: The prices of shares are influenced by a company's earnings and dividends as well as by factors beyond a company's control, such as changes in interest rates, labor strikes, scarcity of supplies or resources, and politics. The number of willing buyers and sellers (demand and supply) also plays a part in the price of shares.

p. 541

Q: When a corporation acquires treasury stock, what is the effect upon the price of its shares of stock?

A: When treasury shares are acquired, the number of shares outstanding decreases. This change increases earnings per share, making the stock more attractive and thus higher-priced. (The higher stock price also makes it somewhat more difficult for "suitors" who would like to acquire a company to propose a higher offering price to stockholders.)

p. 546

Q: What factors must a board of directors consider before declaring a cash dividend?

A: Before declaring a cash dividend, a board of directors must consider: (1) the legality of the cash dividend (generally, the existence of retained earnings), (2) the adequacy of cash, and (3) the past dividend-paying practice of the company.

p. 551

Q: How does the effect on share price of a stock split compare to the effect on share price of treasury shares acquired?

A: A stock split and the acquisition of treasury shares have the opposite effects on share price: A stock split *decreases* the share price, whereas the acquisition of treasury shares *increases* the share price. Accounting does matter!

Answer to PepsiCo Review It Questions

Question 3, p. 538

The par value of **PepsiCo**'s common stock is $0.0167 per share. On December 27, 2003, PepsiCo had issued 1,782 million shares.

Question 4, p. 542

Treasury shares held by **PepsiCo** on December 27, 2003, were 77 million, and on December 28, 2002, were 60 million.

Question 4, p. 552

Dividends declared per share of common stock by **PepsiCo** during 1999 were 53.5 cents; in 2000, 55.5 cents; in 2001, 57.5 cents; in 2002, 59.5 cents, and in 2003, 63.0 cents. The increase in dividends per share was 17.8% since 1999, compared to a 42.4% increase in net income during that period.

Answers to Self-Study Questions

1. c **2.** b **3.** d **4.** c **5.** a **6.** a **7.** d **8.** a **9.** c **10.** d **11.** b ***12.** a ***13.** c

✓ **REMEMBER** to go back to the Navigator box on the chapter-opening page and check off your completed work.

Chapter 13

Investments

THE NAVIGATOR ✓

- Understand **Concepts for Review** ❑
- Read **Feature Story** ❑
- Scan **Study Objectives** ❑
- Read **Preview** ❑
- Read text and answer **Before You Go On** p. 590 ❑ p. 596 ❑ p. 601 ❑
- Work **Demonstration Problem** ❑
- Review **Summary of Study Objectives** ❑
- Answer **Self-Study Questions** ❑
- Complete **Assignments** ❑

CONCEPTS FOR REVIEW

Before studying this chapter, you should know or, if necessary, review:

- How to record the issuance of bonds. (Ch. 11, pp. 482–484)
- How to compute and record interest. (Ch. 3, pp. 105–106, Ch. 9, pp. 394–396, and Ch. 11, pp. 482–485, 487–488)
- How to record amortization of bond discount and bond premium using the effective-interest method (Ch. 11, pp. 498–502) or the straight-line method. (Ch. 11, pp. 502–505)
- Where short-term and long-term investments are classified on a balance sheet. (Ch. 4, pp. 160–162)

☑ THE NAVIGATOR

ACCOUNTING MATTERS! **FEATURE STORY**

Is There Anything Else We Can Buy?

In a rapidly changing world you must change rapidly or suffer the consequences. In business, change requires investment.

A case in point is found in the entertainment industry. Technology is bringing about innovations so quickly that it is nearly impossible to guess which technologies will last and which will soon fade away. For example, will both satellite TV and cable TV survive, or will just one succeed, or will both be replaced by something else? Or consider the publishing industry. Will paper newspapers and magazines be replaced by online news via the World Wide Web? If you are a publisher, you have to make your best guess about what the future holds and invest accordingly.

Time Warner, Inc. lives at the center of this arena. It is not an environment for the timid, and Time Warner's philosophy is anything but timid. It might be characterized as, "If we can't beat you, we will buy you." Its mantra is "invest, invest, invest." A list of Time Warner's holdings gives an idea of its reach. Magazines: *People, Time, Sports Illustrated, Fortune, In Style*. Book publishers: Time-Life Books, Book-of-the-Month Club, Little, Brown & Co, Sunset Books. Music: Warner Bros. Records, Reprise, Atlantic, Rhino, Elektra, and Asylum, representing such artists as Tori Amos, Eric Clapton, R. E. M., Red Hot Chili Peppers, Brandy, and Madonna. Television and movies: Warner Bros. ("Cold Case," "The O.C.," "Two and a Half Men," the WB Network), HBO ("The Sopranos"), and movies like *The Lord of the Rings*, the Harry Potter movies, and *The Polar Express*. Broadcasting: TNT, CNN news, and Turner's library of thousands of classic movies. Internet: America Online and AOL Anywhere. Time Warner owns more information and entertainment copyrights and brands than any other company in the world.

So what has Time Warner's aggressive acquisition spree meant for the bottom line? It has left the company with huge debt and massive interest costs. Also, some of the acquisitions have not come cheap, resulting in large amounts of reported goodwill and goodwill amortization. The merger of America Online (AOL) with Time Warner was billed as a merger of equals. But, it was AOL's phenomenal growth and astronomical stock price that made this merger possible. Unfortunately, investors involved in this merger have faired poorly. From a high of $95.80, Time Warner's stock price recently fell to $8.70 per share.

www.timewarner.com

THE NAVIGATOR

STUDY OBJECTIVES

After studying this chapter, you should be able to:

1. Discuss why corporations invest in debt and stock securities.
2. Explain the accounting for debt investments.
3. Explain the accounting for stock investments.
4. Describe the use of consolidated financial statements.
5. Indicate how debt and stock investments are valued and reported on the financial statements.
6. Distinguish between short-term and long-term investments.

THE NAVIGATOR

PREVIEW OF CHAPTER 13

Time Warner's management believed in aggressive growth through investing in the stock of existing companies. Besides purchasing stock, companies also purchase other securities such as bonds issued by corporations or by governments. Investments can be purchased for a short or long period of time, as a passive investment, or with the intent to control another company. As you will see in this chapter, the way in which a company accounts for its investments is determined by a number of factors.

The content and organization of Chapter 13 are as follows.

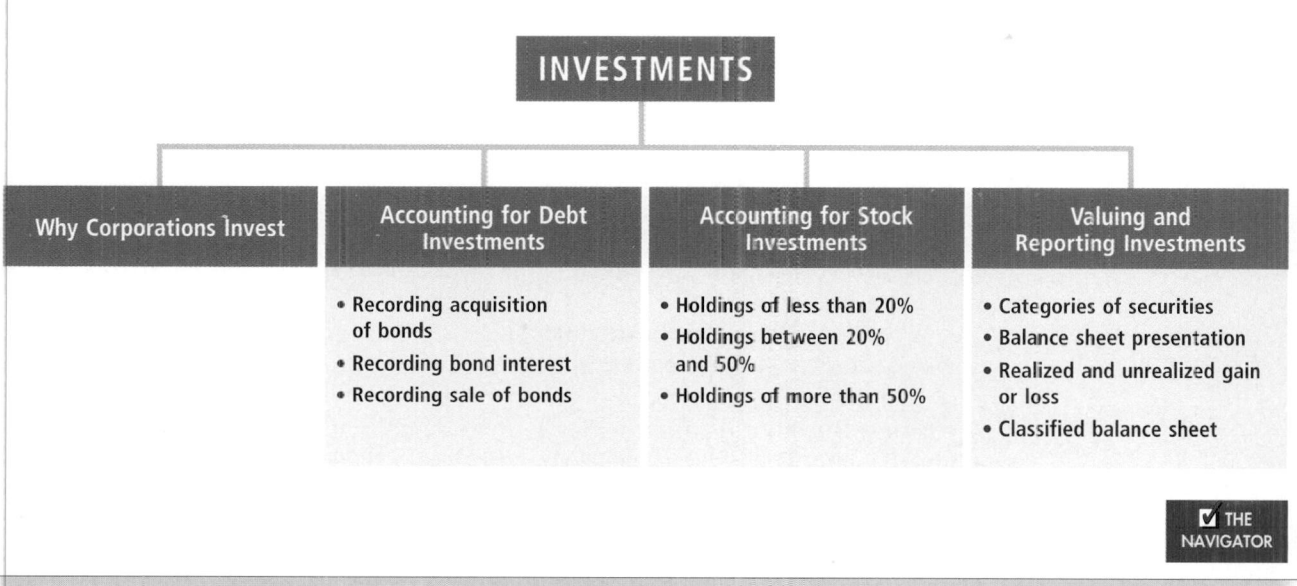

INVESTMENTS

Why Corporations Invest	Accounting for Debt Investments	Accounting for Stock Investments	Valuing and Reporting Investments
	• Recording acquisition of bonds • Recording bond interest • Recording sale of bonds	• Holdings of less than 20% • Holdings between 20% and 50% • Holdings of more than 50%	• Categories of securities • Balance sheet presentation • Realized and unrealized gain or loss • Classified balance sheet

THE NAVIGATOR

Why Corporations Invest

STUDY OBJECTIVE 1

Discuss why corporations invest in debt and stock securities.

Corporations purchase investments in debt or stock securities generally for one of three reasons. First, a corporation may **have excess cash** that it does not need for the immediate purchase of operating assets. For example, many companies experience seasonal fluctuations in sales. A Cape Cod marina has more sales in the spring and summer than in the fall and winter. The reverse is true for an Aspen ski shop. At the end of an operating cycle, many companies have cash on hand that is temporarily idle until the start of another operating cycle. These companies may invest the excess funds to earn a greater return than they would get by just holding the funds in the bank. The role that such temporary investments play in the operating cycle is depicted in Illustration 13-1 (page 588).

Excess cash may also result from economic cycles. For example, when the economy is booming, **General Motors** generates considerable excess cash. It uses some of this cash to purchase new plant and equipment and pays out some of the cash in dividends. But it may also invest excess cash in liquid assets in anticipation of a future downturn in the economy. It can then liquidate these investments during a recession, when sales slow down and cash is scarce.

When investing excess cash for short periods of time, corporations invest in low-risk, highly liquid securities—most often short-term government securities. It is generally not wise to invest short-term excess cash in shares of common stock

Illustration 13-1
Temporary investments and the operating cycle

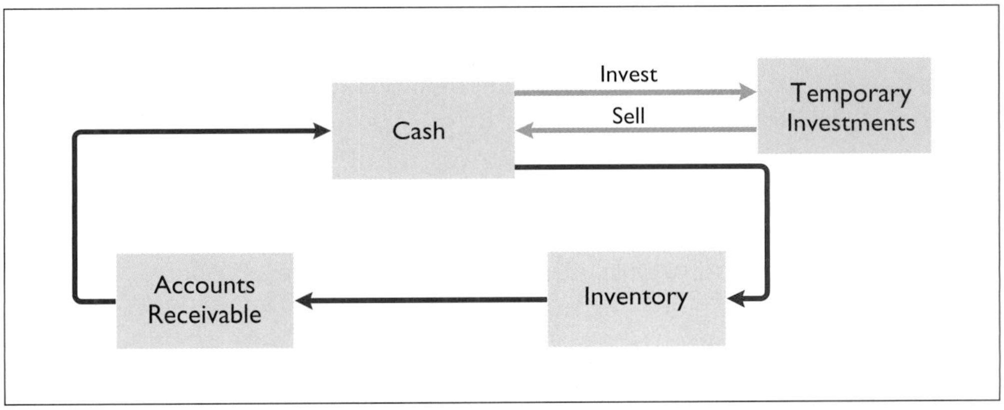

because stock investments can experience rapid price changes. If you did invest your short-term excess cash in stock and the price of the stock declined significantly just before you needed cash again, you would be forced to sell your stock investment at a loss.

A second reason some companies such as banks purchase investments is to generate **earnings from investment income**. Although banks make most of their earnings by lending money, they also generate earnings by investing in debt and equity securities. But loan demand varies both seasonally and with changes in the economic climate. Thus, when loan demand is low, a bank must find other uses for its cash. Bank regulators severely limit the ability of banks to invest in common stock because of the risk involved. Therefore, most investments held by banks are debt securities.

Pension funds and mutual funds are corporations that also regularly invest to generate earnings. However, they do so for **speculative reasons**. They are speculating that the investment will increase in value and thus result in positive returns. Therefore, they invest primarily in the common stock of other corporations. These investments are passive in nature. The pension fund or mutual fund does not usually take an active role in controlling the affairs of the companies in which they invest.

Companies also invest for **strategic reasons**. A company may purchase a noncontrolling interest in another company in a related industry in which it wishes to establish a presence. For example, **Time Warner** initially purchased an interest of less than 20 percent in **Turner Broadcasting** to have a stake in Turner's expanding business opportunities. At a later date **Time Warner** acquired the remaining 80 percent. Subsequently, Time Warner was merged into **AOL** and named **AOL Time Warner, Inc.** (Not even a huge corporation like Time Warner is at the top of the corporate "food-chain.") But, it is again just **Time Warner, Inc.**, having dropped the "AOL" from its name in late 2003. Or, a company can exercise some influence over a customer or supplier by purchasing a significant, but not controlling, interest in that company.

A corporation may also choose to purchase a controlling interest in another company. This might be done to enter a new industry without incurring the tremendous costs and risks associated with starting from scratch. Or a company might purchase another company in its same industry. The purchase of a company that is in your industry, but involved in a different activity, is called a **vertical acquisition**. For example, **Nike** might purchase a chain of athletic shoe stores, such as **The Athlete's Foot**. In a **horizontal acquisition** you purchase a company that does the same activity as your company. For example, Nike might purchase **Reebok**.

In summary, businesses invest in other companies for the reasons shown in Illustration 13-2 on page 589.

Illustration 13-2
Why corporations invest

Reason	Typical Investment
To house excess cash until needed 	Low-risk, high-liquidity, short-term securities such as government-issued securities
To generate earnings 	Debt securities (banks and other financial institutions); and stock securities (mutual funds and pension funds)
To meet strategic goals 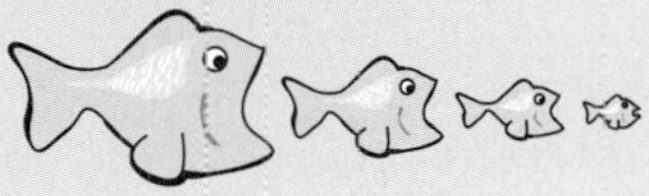	Stocks of companies in a related industry or in an unrelated industry that the company wishes to enter

Accounting for Debt Investments

STUDY OBJECTIVE 2

Explain the accounting for debt investments.

Debt investments are investments in government and corporation bonds. In accounting for debt investments, entries are required to record (1) the acquisition, (2) the interest revenue, and (3) the sale.

Recording Acquisition of Bonds

At acquisition, the cost principle applies. Cost includes all expenditures necessary to acquire these investments, such as the price paid plus brokerage fees (commissions), if any. Assume, for example, that Kuhl Corporation acquires 50 Doan Inc. 8%, 10-year, $1,000 bonds on January 1, 2006, for $54,000, including brokerage fees of $1,000. The entry to record the investment is:

Jan. 1	Debt Investments	54,000	
	Cash		54,000
	(To record purchase of 50 Doan Inc. bonds)		

A	=	L	+	SE
+54,000				
−54,000				

Cash Flows
−54,000

Recording Bond Interest

The bonds pay interest of $2,000 semiannually on July 1 and January 1 ($50,000 × 8% × ½). The entry for the receipt of interest on July 1 is:

July 1	Cash	2,000	
	Interest Revenue		2,000
	(To record receipt of interest on Doan Inc. bonds)		

A	=	L	+	SE
+2,000				+2,000 Rev

Cash Flows
+2,000

If Kuhl Corporation's fiscal year ends on December 31, it is necessary to accrue the interest of $2,000 earned since July 1. The adjusting entry is:

Dec. 31	Interest Receivable	2,000	
	Interest Revenue		2,000
	(To accrue interest on Doan Inc. bonds)		

A	=	L	+	SE
+2,000				+2,000 Rev

Cash Flows
no effect

Interest Receivable is reported as a current asset in the balance sheet; Interest Revenue is reported under "Other revenues and gains" in the income statement.

When the interest is received on January 1, the entry is:

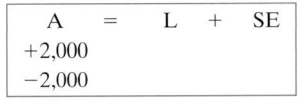

A	=	L	+	SE
+2,000				
−2,000				

Cash Flows
+2,000

Jan. 1	Cash	2,000	
	Interest Receivable		2,000
	(To record receipt of accrued interest)		

A credit to Interest Revenue at this time would be incorrect. Why? Because the interest revenue was earned and accrued in the preceding accounting period.

Recording Sale of Bonds

When the bonds are sold, it is necessary to credit the investment account for the cost of the bonds. Any difference between the net proceeds from the sale (sales price less brokerage fees) and the cost of the bonds is recorded as a gain or loss.

Assume, for example, that Kuhl Corporation receives net proceeds of $58,000 on the sale of the Doan Inc. bonds on January 1, 2007, after receiving the interest due. Since the securities cost $54,000, a gain of $4,000 has been realized. The entry to record the sale is:

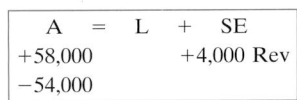

A	=	L	+	SE
+58,000				+4,000 Rev
−54,000				

Cash Flows
+54,000

Jan. 1	Cash	58,000	
	Debt Investments		54,000
	Gain on Sale of Debt Investments		4,000
	(To record sale of Doan Inc. bonds)		

The gain on sale of debt investments is reported under "Other revenues and gains" in the income statement.

BEFORE YOU GO ON...

Review It

1. Why might a company make investments in debt or stock securities?
2. What entries are required in accounting for debt investments?
3. How are gains and losses from the sale of bonds reported in the income statement?

Do It

Waldo Corporation had the following transactions pertaining to debt investments.

Jan. 1 Purchased 30 10%, $1,000 Hillary Co. bonds for $30,000, plus brokerage fees of $900. Interest is payable semiannually on July 1 and January 1.

July 1 Received semiannual interest on Hillary Co. bonds.

July 1 Sold 15 Hillary Co. bonds for $15,000, less $400 brokerage fees.

(a) Journalize the transactions, and **(b)** prepare the adjusting entry for the accrual of interest on December 31.

ACTION PLAN

- Record bond investments at cost.
- Record interest when received and/or accrued.
- When bonds are sold, credit the investment account for the cost of the bonds.

- Record any difference between the cost and the net proceeds as a gain or loss.

SOLUTION

(a) Jan. 1	Debt Investments	30,900	
	Cash		30,900
	(To record purchase of 30 Hillary Co. bonds)		
July 1	Cash	1,500	
	Interest Revenue ($30,000 × .10 × 6/12)		1,500
	(To record receipt of interest on Hillary Co. bonds)		
July 1	Cash	14,600	
	Loss on Sale of Debt Investments	850	
	Debt Investments ($30,900 × 15/30)		15,450
	(To record sale of 15 Hillary Co. bonds)		
(b) Dec. 31	Interest Receivable	750	
	Interest Revenue ($15,000 × .10 × 6/12)		750
	(To accrue interest on Hillary Co. bonds)		

Related exercise material: *BE13-1 and E13-1.*

THE NAVIGATOR

Accounting for Stock Investments

STUDY OBJECTIVE 3

Explain the accounting for stock investments.

Stock investments are investments in the capital stock of corporations. When a company holds stock (and/or debt) of several different corporations, the group of securities is identified as an **investment portfolio.**

The accounting for investments in common stock is based on the extent of the investor's influence over the operating and financial affairs of the issuing corporation (commonly called the **investee**). Illustration 13-3 shows the guidelines for three levels of influence.

Illustration 13-3
Accounting guidelines for stock investments

Investor's Ownership Interest in Investee's Common Stock	Presumed Influence on Investee	Accounting Guidelines
 Less than 20%	Insignificant	Cost method
 Between 20% and 50%	Significant	Equity method
 More than 50%	Controlling	Consolidated financial statements

The presumed influence may be negated by extenuating circumstances. For example, a company that acquires a 25% interest in another company in a "hostile" takeover may not have significant influence over the investee. Companies are required to use judgment instead of blindly following the guidelines.[1] On the following pages we will explain the application of each guideline.

Holdings of Less Than 20%

In accounting for stock investments of less than 20%, the cost method is used. Under the **cost method**, the investment is recorded at cost, and revenue is recognized only when cash dividends are received.

Recording Acquisition of Stock Investments

At acquisition, the cost principle applies. Cost includes all expenditures necessary to acquire these investments such as the price paid plus any brokerage fees (commissions). Assume, for example, that on July 1, 2006, Sanchez Corporation acquires 1,000 shares (10% ownership) of Beal Corporation common stock. Sanchez pays $40 per share plus brokerage fees of $500. The entry for the purchase is:

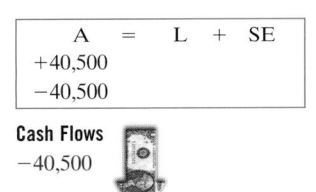

A	=	L	+	SE
+40,500				
−40,500				

Cash Flows
−40,500

July 1	Stock Investments	40,500	
	Cash		40,500
	(To record purchase of 1,000 shares of Beal Corporation common stock)		

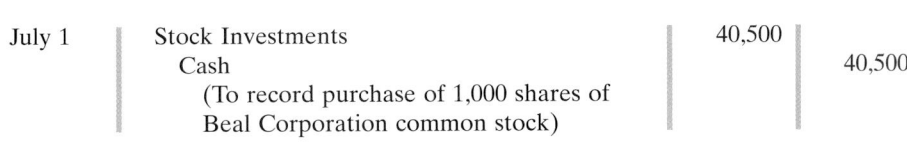

ACCOUNTING MATTERS! **Business Insight**

Amazon.com's Web site receives many "hits" each day. Because of this Amazon earns significant revenue by allowing other companies to advertise there. Many of them pay with stock in their company (since dot-coms often have very little cash). When Amazon receives the stock, it debits Investment in XYZ Company and credits Unearned Revenue for the market value of the shares on the day they are received. It then recognizes revenue over the life of the advertising agreement. In the future, Amazon hopes to do more cash deals and fewer stock deals.

? What does Amazon.com do with the balance in Unearned Revenue if it sells, within days, the shares of stock it received in payment for a long-term advertising agreement?

Recording Dividends

During the time the stock is held, entries are required for any cash dividends received. If a $2.00 per share dividend is received by Sanchez Corporation on December 31, the entry is:

[1] Among the questions that are considered in determining an investor's influence are these: (1) Does the investor have representation on the investee's board? (2) Does the investor participate in the investee's policy-making process? (3) Are there material transactions between the investor and investee? (4) Is the common stock held by other stockholders concentrated or dispersed?

Dec. 31	Cash (1,000 × $2)	2,000	
	Dividend Revenue		2,000
	(To record receipt of a cash dividend)		

A	=	L	+	SE
+2,000				+2,000 Rev

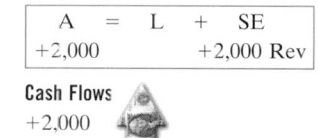

Cash Flows
+2,000

Dividend Revenue is reported under "Other revenues and gains" in the income statement. Unlike interest on notes and bonds, dividends do not accrue. Therefore, adjusting entries are not made to accrue dividends.

Recording Sale of Stock

When stock is sold, the difference between the net proceeds from the sale (sales price less brokerage fees) and the cost of the stock is recognized as a gain or a loss. Assume that Sanchez Corporation receives net proceeds of $39,500 on the sale of its Beal stock on February 10, 2007. Because the stock cost $40,500, a loss of $1,000 has been incurred. The entry to record the sale is:

Feb. 10	Cash	39,500	
	Loss on Sale of Stock Investments	1,000	
	Stock Investments		40,500
	(To record sale of Beal common stock)		

A	=	L	+	SE
+39,500				−1,000 Exp
−40,500				

Cash Flows
+39,500

The loss account is reported under "Other expenses and losses" in the income statement. A gain on sale is shown under "Other revenues and gains."

Holdings Between 20% and 50%

When an investor company owns only a small portion of the shares of stock of another company, the investor cannot exercise control over the investee. But, when an investor owns between 20% and 50% of the common stock of a corporation, it is presumed that the investor has significant influence over the financial and operating activities of the investee. The investor probably has a representative on the investee's board of directors. Through that representative, the investor begins to exercise some control over the investee. The investee company in some sense becomes part of the investor company. For example, even prior to purchasing all of Turner Broadcasting, **Time Warner** owned 20% of Turner and could exercise significant control over major decisions made by Turner.

HELPFUL HINT

The entries for investments in common stock also apply to investments in preferred stock.

Companies with stock holdings between 20% and 50% in an investee use an approach called the equity method. Under the **equity method**, **the investor records its share of the net income of the investee in the year when it is earned**. An alternative might be to delay recognizing the investor's share of net income until a cash dividend is declared. But that approach would ignore the fact that the investor and investee are, in some sense, one company, making the investor better off by the investee's earned income.

Under the equity method, the investment in common stock is initially recorded at cost. After that, the investment account is **adjusted annually** to show the investor's equity in the investee. Each year, the investor does the following: (1) It increases (debits) the investment account and increases (credits) revenue for its share of the investee's net income.[2] (2) The investor also decreases (credits) the investment account for the amount of dividends received. The investment account is reduced for dividends received because the net assets of the investee are decreased when a dividend is paid.

HELPFUL HINT

Under the equity method revenue is recognized on the accrual basis—i.e., when it is earned by the investee.

[2] Or, the investor increases (debits) a loss account and decreases (credits) the investment account for its share of the investee's net loss.

Recording Acquisition of Stock Investments

Assume that Milar Corporation acquires 30% of the common stock of Beck Company for $120,000 on January 1, 2006. The entry to record this transaction is:

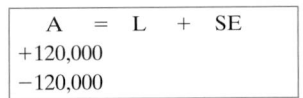

A	=	L	+	SE
+120,000				
−120,000				

Cash Flows
−120,000

Jan. 1	Stock Investments	120,000	
	Cash		120,000
	(To record purchase of Beck common stock)		

Recording Revenue and Dividends

For 2006, Beck reports net income of $100,000. It declares and pays a $40,000 cash dividend. Milar is required to record (1) its share of Beck's income, $30,000 (30% × $100,000) and (2) the reduction in the investment account for the dividends received, $12,000 ($40,000 × 30%). The entries are:

A	=	L	+	SE
+30,000				+30,000 Rev

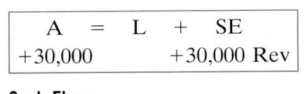

Cash Flows
no effect

(1)

Dec. 31	Stock Investments	30,000	
	Revenue from Investment in Beck Company		30,000
	(To record 30% equity in Beck's 2006 net income)		

A	=	L	+	SE
+12,000				
−12,000				

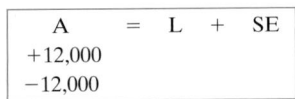

Cash Flows
+12,000

(2)

Dec. 31	Cash	12,000	
	Stock Investments		12,000
	(To record dividends received)		

After posting the transactions for the year, the investment and revenue accounts will show the following.

Illustration 13-4
Investment and revenue accounts after posting

Stock Investments

Jan. 1	120,000	Dec. 31	**12,000**
Dec. 31	**30,000**		
Dec. 31 Bal.	138,000		

Revenue from Investment in Beck Company

		Dec. 31	**30,000**

During the year, the investment account has increased by $18,000. This $18,000 is Milar's 30% equity in the $60,000 increase in Beck's retained earnings ($100,000 − $40,000). In addition, Milar will report $30,000 of revenue from its investment, which is 30% of Beck's net income of $100,000. Note that the difference between reported revenue under the cost method and reported revenue under the equity method can be significant. For example, Milar would report only $12,000 of dividend revenue (30% × $40,000) if the cost method were used.

Holdings of More than 50%

STUDY OBJECTIVE 4

Describe the use of consolidated financial statements.

A company that owns more than 50% of the common stock of another entity is known as the **parent company**. The entity whose stock is owned by the parent company is called the **subsidiary (affiliated) company**. Because of its stock ownership, the parent company has a **controlling interest** in the subsidiary.

When a company owns more than 50% of the common stock of another company, **consolidated financial statements** are usually prepared. Consolidated financial statements present the total assets and liabilities controlled by the parent company.

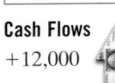

They also present the total revenues and expenses of the subsidiary companies. Consolidated statements are prepared **in addition to** the financial statements for the parent and individual subsidiary companies. When Time Warner had a 20% investment in Turner, this investment was reported in a single line item—Other Investments—in Time Warner's balance sheet. After the merger, Time Warner instead consolidated Turner's results with its own. Under this approach, the individual assets and liabilities of Turner are included with those of Time Warner: its plant and equipment are added to Time Warner's plant and equipment, its receivables are added to Time Warner's receivables, and so on.

HELPFUL HINT

If parent (A) has three wholly owned subsidiaries (B, C, & D), there are four separate legal entities. But, from the viewpoint of the parent company, there is only one economic entity.

ACCOUNTING MATTERS! Business Insight

Time Warner, Inc. owns 100% of the common stock of **Home Box Office (HBO) Corporation**. The common stockholders of Time Warner elect the board of directors of the company, who, in turn, select the officers and managers of the company. Time Warner's board of directors controls the property owned by the corporation, which includes the common stock of HBO. Thus, they are in a position to elect the board of directors of HBO and, in effect, control its operations. These relationships are graphically illustrated here.

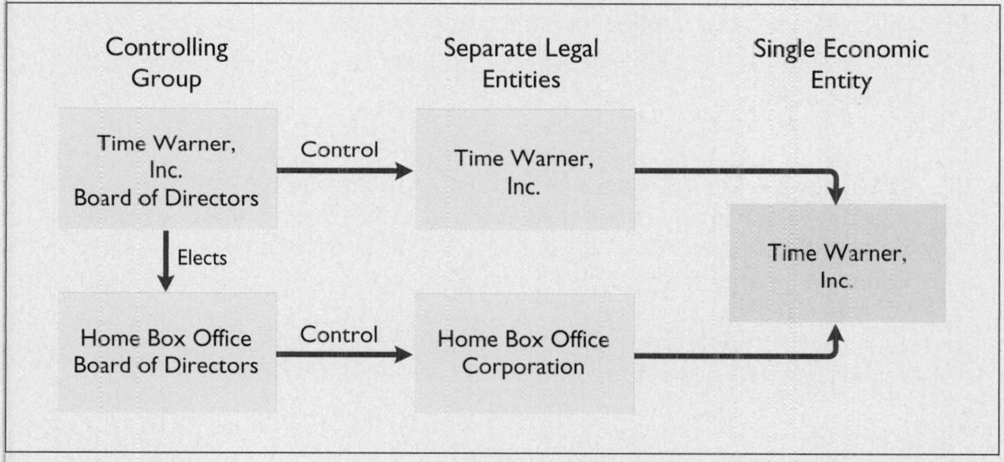

? Where in Time Warner's balance sheet will you find its investment in Home Box Office (HBO) Corporation?

Consolidated statements are useful because they indicate the magnitude and scope of operations of the companies under common control. For example, regulators and the courts undoubtedly used the consolidated statements of **AT&T** to determine whether a breakup of AT&T was in the public interest. Listed below are three companies that prepare consolidated statements and some of the companies they have owned. Note that one, **Walt Disney**, is Time Warner's arch rival.

Toys "R" Us, Inc.	Cendant	The Walt Disney Company
Kids "R" Us	Howard Johnson	Capital Cities/ABC, Inc.
Babies "R" Us	Ramada Inn	Disneyland, Disney World
Imaginarium	Century 21	Mighty Ducks
Toysrus.com	Coldwell Banker	Anaheim Angels
	Avis	ESPN

BEFORE YOU GO ON...

Review It

1. What are the accounting entries for stock investments of less than 20%?
2. What entries are made under the equity method when (a) the investor receives a cash dividend from the investee and (b) the investee reports net income for the year?
3. What is the purpose of consolidated financial statements?
4. What does **PepsiCo** state regarding its accounting policy involving consolidated financial statements? The answer to this question is provided on page 626.

Do It

Presented below are two independent situations.

1. Rho Jean Inc. acquired 5% of the 400,000 shares of common stock of Stillwater Corp. at a total cost of $6 per share on May 18, 2006. On August 30, Stillwater declared and paid a $75,000 dividend. On December 31, Stillwater reported net income of $244,000 for the year.
2. Debbie, Inc. obtained significant influence over North Sails by buying 40% of North Sails' 60,000 outstanding shares of common stock at a cost of $12 per share on January 1, 2006. On April 15, North Sails declared and paid a cash dividend of $45,000. On December 31, North Sails reported net income of $120,000 for the year.

Prepare all necessary journal entries for 2006 for (1) Rho Jean Inc. and (2) Debbie, Inc.

ACTION PLAN

- Presume that the investor has relatively little influence over the investee when an investor owns less than 20% of the common stock of another corporation. In this case, net income earned by the investee is not considered a proper basis for recognizing income from the investment by the investor.
- Presume significant influence for investments of 20%–50%. Therefore, record the investor's share of the net income of the investee.

SOLUTION

(1) May 18	Stock Investments (20,000 × $6)	120,000	
	Cash		120,000
	(To record purchase of 20,000 shares of Stillwater Co. stock)		
Aug. 30	Cash	3,750	
	Dividend Revenue ($75,000 × 5%)		3,750
	(To record receipt of cash dividend)		
(2) Jan. 1	Stock Investments (60,000 × 40% × $12)	288,000	
	Cash		288,000
	(To record purchase of 24,000 shares of North Sails' stock)		
Apr. 15	Cash	18,000	
	Stock Investments ($45,000 × 40%)		18,000
	(To record receipt of cash dividend)		

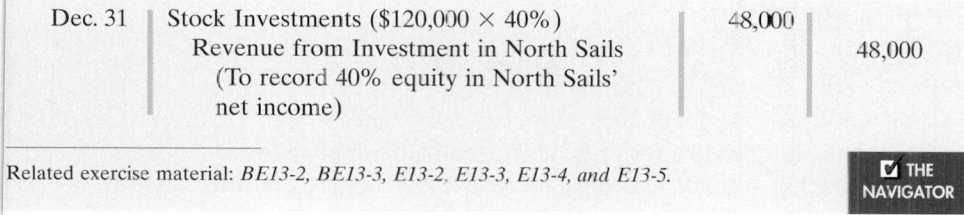

Dec. 31	Stock Investments ($120,000 × 40%)	48,000	
	Revenue from Investment in North Sails		48,000
	(To record 40% equity in North Sails' net income)		

Related exercise material: *BE13-2, BE13-3, E13-2, E13-3, E13-4, and E13-5.*

THE NAVIGATOR

Valuing and Reporting Investments

STUDY OBJECTIVE 5

Indicate how debt and stock investments are valued and reported on the financial statements.

The value of debt and stock investments may fluctuate greatly during the time they are held. For example, in one 12-month period, the stock price of **Dell Computer Corp.** hit a high of $59.70 and a low of $16. In light of such price fluctuations, how should investments be valued at the balance sheet date? Valuation could be at cost, at fair value (market value), or at the lower of cost or market value. Many people argue that fair value offers the best approach because it represents the expected cash realizable value of securities. **Fair value** is the amount for which a security could be sold in a normal market. Others counter that, unless a security is going to be sold soon, the fair value is not relevant because the price of the security will likely change again.

Categories of Securities

For purposes of valuation and reporting at a financial statement date, debt and stock investments are classified into three categories of securities:

1. **Trading securities** are securities bought and held primarily for sale in the near term to generate income on short-term price differences.
2. **Available-for-sale securities** are securities that are held with the intent of selling them sometime in the future.
3. **Held-to-maturity securities** are debt securities that the investor has the intent and ability to hold to maturity.[3]

The valuation guidelines for these securities are shown in Illustration 13-5. **These guidelines apply to all debt securities and all stock investments in which the holdings are less than 20%.**

Illustration 13-5
Valuation guidelines

[3]This category is provided for completeness. The accounting and valuation issues related to held-to-maturity securities are discussed in more advanced accounting courses.

Trading Securities

Trading securities are held with the intention of selling them in a short period (generally less than a month). Trading means frequent buying and selling. Trading securities are reported at fair value, and changes from cost are reported as part of net income. The changes are reported as **unrealized gains or losses** because the securities have not been sold. The unrealized gain or loss is the difference between the **total cost** of trading securities and their **total fair value**.

Illustration 13-6 shows the cost and fair values for investments classified as trading securities for Pace Corporation on December 31, 2006. Pace has an unrealized gain of $7,000 because total fair value ($147,000) is $7,000 greater than total cost ($140,000).

Illustration 13-6
Valuation of trading securities

Trading Securities, December 31, 2006

Investments	Cost	Fair Value	Unrealized Gain (Loss)
Yorkville Company bonds	$ 50,000	$ 48,000	$ (2,000)
Kodak Company stock	90,000	99,000	9,000
Total	$140,000	$147,000	**$ 7,000**

HELPFUL HINT

The fact that trading securities are short-term investments increases the likelihood that they will be sold at fair value (the company may not be able to time their sale) and the likelihood that there will be realized gains or losses.

Fair value and unrealized gain or loss are recorded through an adjusting entry at the time financial statements are prepared. In the entry, a valuation allowance account, Market Adjustment—Trading, is used to record the difference between the total cost and the total fair value of the securities. The adjusting entry for Pace Corporation is:

A	=	L	+	SE
+7,000				+7,000 Rev

Cash Flows
no effect

Dec. 31	Market Adjustment—Trading	7,000	
	Unrealized Gain—Income		7,000
	(To record unrealized gain on trading securities)		

The use of a Market Adjustment—Trading account enables the company to maintain a record of the investment cost. Actual cost is needed to determine the gain or loss realized when the securities are sold. The Market Adjustment—Trading balance is added to the cost of the investments to arrive at a fair value for the trading securities.

The fair value of the securities is the amount reported on the balance sheet. The unrealized gain is reported in the income statement in the "Other revenues and gains" section. The term "Income" is used in the account title to indicate that the gain affects net income.

When the total cost of the trading securities is greater than total fair value, an unrealized loss has occurred. In such a case, the adjusting entry is a debit to Unrealized Loss—Income and a credit to Market Adjustment—Trading. The unrealized loss is reported under "Other expenses and losses" in the income statement.

The market adjustment account is carried forward into future accounting periods. No entries are made to this account during the period. At the end of each reporting period, the balance in the account is adjusted to the difference between cost and fair value. For trading securities, the Unrealized Gain (Loss)—Income account is closed at the end of the reporting period.

Available-for-Sale Securities

As indicated earlier, available-for-sale securities are held with the intent of selling them sometime in the future. If the intent is to sell the securities within the next year or operating cycle, the securities are classified as current assets in the balance sheet. Otherwise, they are classified as long-term assets in the investments section of the balance sheet.

Available-for-sale securities are also reported at fair value. The procedure for determining fair value and the unrealized gain or loss for these securities is the same as for trading securities. To illustrate, assume that Ingrao Corporation has two securities that are classified as available-for-sale. Illustration 13-7 provides information on their valuation. There is an unrealized loss of $9,537 because total cost ($293,537) is $9,537 more than total fair value ($284,000).

ETHICS NOTE

Some managers appear to hold their available-for-sale securities that have experienced losses, while selling those that have gains, thus increasing income. Do you think this is ethical?

Available-for-Sale Securities, December 31, 2006

Investments	Cost	Fair Value	Unrealized Gain (Loss)
Campbell Soup Corporation			
8% bonds	$ 93,537	$103,600	$10,063
Hershey Corporation stock	200,000	180,400	(19,600)
Total	$293,537	$284,000	**$(9,537)**

Illustration 13-7
Valuation of available-for-sale securities

Both the adjusting entry and the reporting of the unrealized gain or loss for available-for-sale securities differ from those illustrated for trading securities. The differences result because these securities are not expected to be sold in the near term. Thus, prior to actual sale it is more likely that changes in fair value may change either unrealized gains or losses. Therefore, an unrealized gain or loss is not reported in the income statement. Instead, it is reported as a **separate component of stockholders' equity**.

In the adjusting entry, the market adjustment account is identified with available-for-sale securities; the unrealized gain or loss account is identified with stockholders' equity. The adjusting entry to record the unrealized loss of $9,537 for Ingrao Corporation is as follows:

Dec. 31	Unrealized Gain or Loss—Equity	9,537	
	Market Adjustment—Available-for-Sale		9,537
	(To record unrealized loss on available-for-sale securities)		

A	=	L	+	SE
−9,537				−9,537 Exp

Cash Flows
no effect

If total fair value exceeds total cost, the adjusting entry would have a debit to the market adjustment account and a credit to an unrealized gain or loss account.

For available-for-sale securities, the unrealized gain or loss account is carried forward to future periods. At each future balance sheet date, it is adjusted with the market adjustment account to show the difference between cost and fair value at that time.

Balance Sheet Presentation

In the balance sheet, investments are classified as either short-term or long-term.

Short-Term Investments

STUDY OBJECTIVE 6

Distinguish between short-term and long-term investments.

Short-term investments are securities held by a company that are (1) **readily marketable** and (2) **intended to be converted into cash** within the next year or operating cycle, whichever is longer. Investments that do not meet **both criteria** are classified as **long-term investments**.

HELPFUL HINT

Trading securities are always classified as short-term. Available-for-sale securities can be either short-term or long-term.

READILY MARKETABLE. **An investment is readily marketable when it can be sold easily whenever the need for cash arises.** Short-term paper[4] meets this criterion. It can be readily sold to other investors. Stocks and bonds traded on organized securities exchanges, such as the New York Stock Exchange, are readily marketable. They can be bought and sold daily. In contrast, there may be only a limited market for the securities issued by small corporations, and no market for the securities of a privately held company.

INTENT TO CONVERT. **Intent to convert means that management intends to sell the investment within the next year or operating cycle, whichever is longer.** Generally, this criterion is satisfied when the investment is considered a resource that will be used whenever the need for cash arises. For example, a ski resort may invest idle cash during the summer months with the intent to sell the securities to buy supplies and equipment shortly before the next winter season. This investment is considered short-term even if lack of snow cancels the next ski season and eliminates the need to convert the securities into cash as intended.

Because of their high liquidity, short-term investments are listed immediately below cash in the current assets section of the balance sheet. They are reported at fair value. For example, Pace Corporation would report its trading securities as shown in Illustration 13-8.

Illustration 13-8
Presentation of short-term investments

PACE CORPORATION
Balance Sheet (partial)

Current assets	
Cash	$ 21,000
Short-term investments, at fair value	147,000

HELPFUL HINT

In a recent survey of 600 large U.S. companies, over 400 reported short-term investments.

Long-Term Investments

Long-term investments are generally reported in a separate section of the balance sheet immediately below current assets, as shown later in Illustration 13-11 (page 602). Long-term investments in available-for-sale securities are reported at fair value. Investments in common stock accounted for under the equity method are reported at their equity value.

Presentation of Realized and Unrealized Gain or Loss

Gains and losses on investments, whether realized or unrealized, must be presented in the financial statements. In the income statement, gains and losses are reported in the nonoperating activities section under the categories listed in Illustration 13-9. Interest and dividend revenue are also reported in that section.

Illustration 13-9
Nonoperating items related to investments

Other Revenue and Gains	Other Expenses and Losses
Interest Revenue	Loss on Sale of Investments
Dividend Revenue	Unrealized Loss—Income
Gain on Sale of Investments	
Unrealized Gain—Income	

[4]Short-term paper includes (1) certificates of deposit (CDs) issued by banks, (2) money market certificates issued by banks and savings and loan associations, (3) Treasury bills issued by the U.S. government, and (4) commercial paper (notes) issued by corporations with good credit ratings.

As indicated earlier, an unrealized gain or loss on available-for-sale securities is reported as a separate component of stockholders' equity. To illustrate, assume that Dawson Inc. has common stock of $3,000,000, retained earnings of $1,500,000, and an unrealized loss on available-for-sale securities of $100,000. The statement presentation of the unrealized loss is shown in Illustration 13-10.

Illustration 13-10
Unrealized loss in stockholders' equity section

DAWSON INC.
Balance Sheet (partial)

Stockholders' equity	
Common stock	$3,000,000
Retained earnings	1,500,000
Total paid-in capital and retained earnings	4,500,000
Less: **Unrealized loss on available-for-sale securities**	**(100,000)**
Total stockholders' equity	$4,400,000

Note that the loss decreases stockholders' equity. The cost of treasury stock is presented in the same way. An unrealized gain would be added to stockholders' equity. Reporting the unrealized gain or loss in the stockholders' equity section serves two important purposes: (1) It reduces the volatility of net income due to fluctuations in fair value. (2) It informs the financial statement user of the gain or loss that would occur if the securities were sold at fair value.

Accounting standards require that items such as this, which affect stockholders' equity but are not included in the calculation of net income, must be reported as part of a more inclusive measure called *comprehensive income*. Comprehensive income is discussed in more advanced courses.

Classified Balance Sheet

Many sections of classified balance sheets have been presented in this and preceding chapters. The classified balance sheet in Illustration 13-11 on page 602 includes, in one place, key topics from previous chapters: the issuance of par value common stock, restrictions of retained earnings, and issuance of long-term bonds. From this chapter, the statement includes (highlighted in red) short-term and long-term investments. The investments in short-term securities are considered trading securities. The long-term investments in stock of less than 20% owned companies are considered available-for-sale securities. Illustration 13-11 also includes a long-term investment reported at equity and descriptive notations within the statement, such as the basis for valuing merchandise and one note to the statement.

BEFORE YOU GO ON...

Review It

1. What is the proper valuation and reporting of trading and available-for-sale securities on a balance sheet?
2. Explain how the unrealized gain or loss for both trading and available-for-sale securities is reported.
3. Explain where short-term and long-term investments are reported on a balance sheet.

THE NAVIGATOR

Illustration 13-11
Classified balance sheet

PACE CORPORATION
Balance Sheet
December 31, 2006

Assets			
Current assets			
Cash			$ 21,000
Short-term investments, at fair value			**147,000**
Accounts receivable		$ 84,000	
Less: Allowance for doubtful accounts		4,000	80,000
Merchandise inventory, at FIFO cost			43,000
Prepaid insurance			23,000
Total current assets			314,000
Investments			
Investments in stock of less than 20% owned companies, at fair value		**50,000**	
Investment in stock of 20–50% owned company, at equity		**150,000**	
Total investments			200,000
Property, plant, and equipment			
Land		200,000	
Buildings	$800,000		
Less: Accumulated depreciation	200,000	600,000	
Equipment	180,000		
Less: Accumulated depreciation	54,000	126,000	
Total property, plant, and equipment			926,000
Intangible assets			
Goodwill			270,000
Total assets			$1,710,000
Liabilities and Stockholders' Equity			
Current liabilities			
Accounts payable			$185,000
Federal income taxes payable			60,000
Bond interest payable			10,000
Total current liabilities			255,000
Long-term liabilities			
Bonds payable, 10%, due 2017		$ 300,000	
Less: Discount on bonds		10,000	
Total long-term liabilities			290,000
Total liabilities			545,000
Stockholders' equity			
Paid-in capital			
Common stock, $10 par value, 200,000 shares authorized, 80,000 shares issued and outstanding		800,000	
Paid-in capital in excess of par value		100,000	
Total paid-in capital		900,000	
Retained earnings (Note 1)		255,000	
Total paid-in capital and retained earnings		1,155,000	
Add: **Unrealized gain on available-for-sale securities**		**10,000**	
Total stockholders' equity			1,165,000
Total liabilities and stockholders' equity			$1,710,000

Note 1. Retained earnings of $100,000 is restricted for plant expansion.

DEMONSTRATION PROBLEM

In its first year of operations, DeMarco Company had the following selected transactions in stock investments that are considered trading securities.

June 1 Purchased for cash 600 shares of Sanburg common stock at $24 per share, plus $300 brokerage fees.
July 1 Purchased for cash 800 shares of Cey common stock at $33 per share, plus $600 brokerage fees.
Sept. 1 Received a $1 per share cash dividend from Cey Corporation.
Nov. 1 Sold 200 shares of Sanburg common stock for cash at $27 per share, less $150 brokerage fees.
Dec. 15 Received a $0.50 per share cash dividend on Sanburg common stock.

At December 31, the fair values per share were: Sanburg $25 and Cey $30.

Instructions

(a) Journalize the transactions.
(b) Prepare the adjusting entry at December 31 to report the securities at fair value.

SOLUTION TO DEMONSTRATION PROBLEM

(a) June 1	Stock Investments	14,700	
	Cash		14,700
	(To record purchase of 600 shares of Sanburg common stock)		
July 1	Stock Investments	27,000	
	Cash		27,000
	(To record purchase of 800 shares of Cey common stock)		
Sept. 1	Cash	800	
	Dividend Revenue		800
	(To record receipt of $1 per share cash dividend from Cey Corporation)		
Nov. 1	Cash	5,250	
	Stock Investments		4,900
	Gain on Sale of Stock Investments		350
	(To record sale of 200 shares of Sanburg common stock)		
Dec. 15	Cash	200	
	Dividend Revenue		200
	(To record receipt of $0.50 per share dividend from Sanburg Corporation)		
(b) Dec. 31	Unrealized Loss—Income	2,800	
	Market Adjustment—Trading		2,800
	(To record unrealized loss on trading securities)		

Investment	Cost	Fair Value	Unrealized Gain (Loss)
Sanburg common stock	$ 9,800	$10,000	$ 200
Cey common stock	27,000	24,000	(3,000)
Totals	$36,800	$34,000	$(2,800)

THE NAVIGATOR

ACTION PLAN

- Include the price paid plus brokerage fees in the cost of the investment.
- Compute the gain or loss on sales as the difference between net selling price and the cost of the securities.
- Base the adjustment to fair value on the total difference between the cost and the fair value of the securities.

SUMMARY OF STUDY OBJECTIVES

1. **Discuss why corporations invest in debt and stock securities.** Corporations invest for three primary reasons: (a) They have excess cash. (b) They view investments as a significant revenue source. (c) They have strategic goals such as gaining control of a competitor or moving into a new line of business.
2. **Explain the accounting for debt investments.** Entries for investments in debt securities are required when the bonds are purchased, interest is received or accrued, and the bonds are sold. Gains or losses on the sale of bonds are reported in the "Other revenues and gains" or "Other expenses and losses" sections of the income statement.
3. **Explain the accounting for stock investments.** Entries for investments in common stock are required when the stock is purchased, dividends are received, and stock is sold. When ownership is less than 20%, the cost method is used. When ownership is between 20% and 50%, the equity method should be used. When ownership is more than 50%, consolidated financial statements should be prepared.
4. **Describe the use of consolidated financial statements.** When a company owns more than 50% of the common stock of another company, consolidated financial statements are usually prepared. These statements are useful because they indicate the magnitude and scope of operations of the companies under common control.
5. **Indicate how debt and stock investments are valued and reported on the financial statements.** Investments in debt and stock securities are classified as trading, available-for-sale, or held-to-maturity securities for valuation and reporting purposes. Trading securities are reported in current assets at fair value, with changes from cost reported in net income. Available-for-sale securities are also reported at fair value, with the changes from cost reported in stockholders' equity. Available-for-sale securities are classified as short-term or long-term depending on their expected realization.
6. **Distinguish between short-term and long-term investments.** Short-term investments are securities, held by a company, that are (a) readily marketable and (b) intended to be converted to cash within the next year or operating cycle, whichever is longer. Investments that do not meet both criteria are classified as long-term investments.

THE NAVIGATOR

www.wiley.com/college/weygandt

GLOSSARY

Available-for-sale securities Securities that are held with the intent of selling them sometime in the future. (p. 597).

Consolidated financial statements Financial statements that present the assets and liabilities controlled by the parent company and the aggregate profitability of the affiliated companies. (p. 594).

Controlling interest Ownership of more than 50% of the common stock of another entity. (p. 594).

Cost method An accounting method in which the investment in common stock is recorded at cost, and revenue is recognized only when cash dividends are received. (p. 592).

Debt investments Investments in government and corporation bonds. (p. 589).

Equity method An accounting method in which the investment in common stock is initially recorded at cost, and the investment account is then adjusted annually to show the investor's equity in the investee. (p. 593).

Fair value Amount for which a security could be sold in a normal market. (p. 597).

Held-to-maturity securities Debt securities that the investor has the intent and ability to hold to their maturity date. (p. 597).

Investment portfolio A group of stocks in different corporations held for investment purposes. (p. 591).

Long-term investments Investments that are not readily marketable or that management does not intend to convert into cash within the next year or operating cycle, whichever is longer. (p. 599).

Parent company A company that owns more than 50% of the common stock of another entity. (p. 594).

Short-term investments Investments that are readily marketable and intended to be converted into cash within the next year or operating cycle, whichever is longer. (p. 599).

Stock investments Investments in the capital stock of corporations. (p. 591).

Subsidiary (affiliated) company A company in which more than 50% of its stock is owned by another company. (p. 594).

Trading securities Securities bought and held primarily for sale in the near term to generate income on short-term price differences. (p. 597).

Appendix Preparing Consolidated Financial Statements

Most of the large U.S. corporations are holding companies that own other corporations. They therefore prepare consolidated financial statements that combine the separate companies.

Consolidated Balance Sheet

Consolidated balance sheets are prepared from the individual balance sheets of the affiliated companies. They are not prepared from ledger accounts kept by the consolidated entity because only the separate legal entities maintain accounting records.

All items in the individual balance sheets are included in the consolidated balance sheet except amounts that pertain to transactions between the affiliated companies. Transactions between the affiliated companies are identified as **intercompany transactions**. The process of excluding these transactions in preparing consolidated statements is referred to as **intercompany eliminations**. These eliminations are necessary to avoid overstating assets, liabilities, and stockholders' equity in the consolidated balance sheet. For example, amounts owed by a subsidiary to a parent company and the related receivable reported by the parent company would be eliminated. The objective in a consolidated balance sheet is to show only obligations to and receivables from parties who are not part of the affiliated group of companies.

To illustrate, assume that on January 1, 2006, Powers Construction Company pays $150,000 in cash for 100% of Serto Brick Company's common stock. Powers Company records the investment at cost, as required by the cost principle. The separate balance sheets of the two companies immediately after the purchase, together with combined and consolidated data, are presented in Illustration 13A-1.[5] The balances in the "combined" column are obtained by adding the items in the separate balance sheets of the affiliated companies. The combined totals do not represent a consolidated balance sheet, because there has been a double counting of assets and owners' equity in the amount of $150,000.

HELPFUL HINT

Eliminations are aptly named because they eliminate duplicate data. They are not adjustments.

Illustration 13A-1
Combined and consolidated data

POWERS COMPANY AND SERTO COMPANY
Balance Sheet
January 1, 2006

Assets	Powers Company	Serto Company	Combined Data	Consolidated Data
Current assets	$ 50,000	$ 80,000	$130,000	**$130,000**
Investment in Serto Company common stock	150,000		150,000	**-0-**
Plant and equipment (net)	325,000	145,000	470,000	**470,000**
Total assets	$525,000	$225,000	$750,000	**$600,000**
Liabilities and Stockholders' Equity				
Current liabilities	$ 50,000	$ 75,000	$125,000	**$125,000**
Common stock	300,000	100,000	400,000	**300,000**
Retained earnings	175,000	50,000	225,000	**175,000**
Total liabilities and stockholders' equity	$525,000	$225,000	$750,000	**$600,000**

[5] Condensed data will be used throughout this material to keep details at a minimum.

The Investment in Serto Company common stock that appears on the balance sheet of Powers Company represents an interest in the net assets of Serto. As a result, there has been a double counting of assets. Similarly, there has been a double counting in stockholders' equity, because the common stock of Serto Company is completely owned by the stockholders of Powers Company.

The balances in the consolidated data column are the amounts that should appear in the consolidated balance sheet. The double counting has been eliminated by showing Investment in Serto Company at zero and by reporting only the common stock and retained earnings of Powers Company as stockholders' equity.

STUDY OBJECTIVE 7

Describe the content of a work sheet for a consolidated balance sheet.

Use of a Work Sheet—Cost Equal to Book Value

The preparation of consolidated balance sheets is usually facilitated by the use of a work sheet. As shown in Illustration 13A-2, the work sheet for a consolidated balance sheet contains columns for (1) the balance sheet data for the separate legal entities, (2) intercompany eliminations, and (3) consolidated data. All data in the work sheet relate to the preceding example in which Powers Company acquires 100% ownership of Serto Company for $150,000. In this case, the cost of the investment, $150,000, is equal to the book value $150,000 ($225,000 − $75,000) of the subsidiary's net assets. The intercompany elimination results in a credit to the Investment account maintained by Powers Company for its balance, $150,000, and debits to the Common Stock and Retained Earnings accounts of Serto Company for their respective balances, $100,000 and $50,000.

Illustration 13A-2
Work sheet—Cost equal to book value

POWERS COMPANY AND SUBSIDIARY
Work Sheet—Consolidated Balance Sheet
January 1, 2006 (Acquisition Date)

	Powers	Serto	Eliminations		Consolidated
Assets	**Company**	**Company**	**Dr.**	**Cr.**	**Data**
Current assets	50,000	80,000			130,000
Investment in Serto Company common stock	150,000			**150,000**	-0-
Plant and equipment (net)	325,000	145,000			470,000
Totals	525,000	225,000			600,000
Liabilities and Stockholders' Equity					
Current liabilities	50,000	75,000			125,000
Common stock—Powers Company	300,000				300,000
Common stock—Serto Company		100,000	**100,000**		-0-
Retained earnings—Powers Company	175,000				175,000
Retained earnings—Serto Company		50,000	**50,000**		-0-
Totals	525,000	225,000	150,000	150,000	600,000

HELPFUL HINT

As in the case of the work sheets explained earlier in this textbook, consolidated work sheets are also optional.

It is important to recognize that intercompany eliminations are made solely on the work sheet to present correct consolidated data. They are not journalized or posted by either of the affiliated companies. Therefore, they do not affect the ledger accounts. Powers Company's investment account and Serto Company's common stock and retained earnings accounts are reported by the separate entities in preparing their own financial statements.

Use of a Work Sheet—Cost Above Book Value

The cost of acquiring the common stock of another company may be above or below its book value. The management of the parent company may pay more than book value for the stock. Why? Because it believes the fair market values of identifiable assets such as land, buildings, and equipment are higher than their recorded book values. Or it may believe the subsidiary's future earnings prospects warrant a payment for goodwill.

To illustrate, assume the same data used above, except that Powers Company pays $165,000 in cash for 100% of Serto's common stock. The excess of cost over book value is $15,000 ($165,000 – $150,000). This amount is separately recognized in eliminating the parent company's investment account, as shown in Illustration 13A-3.

Total assets and total liabilities and stockholders' equity are the same as in the preceding example ($600,000). However, in this case, total assets include $15,000 of Excess of Cost Over Book Value of Subsidiary. The disposition of the excess is explained in the next section.

HELPFUL HINT

The consolidated work sheet is another good spreadsheet application. This is a good work sheet to attempt since the required instructions are very straightforward.

Illustration 13A-3
Work sheet—Cost above book value

POWERS COMPANY AND SUBSIDIARY
Work Sheet—Consolidated Balance Sheet
January 1, 2006 (Acquisition Date)

Assets	Powers Company	Serto Company	Eliminations Dr.	Eliminations Cr.	Consolidated Data
Current assets	35,000	80,000			115,000
Investment in Serto Company common stock	165,000			**165,000**	-0-
Plant and equipment (net)	325,000	145,000			470,000
Excess of cost over book value of subsidiary			**15,000**		**15,000**
Totals	525,000	225,000			600,000
Liabilities and Stockholders' Equity					
Current liabilities	50,000	75,000			125,000
Common stock—Powers Company	300,000				300,000
Common stock—Serto Company		100,000	**100,000**		-0-
Retained earnings—Powers Company	175,000				175,000
Retained earnings—Serto Company		50,000	**50,000**		-0-
Totals	525,000	225,000	165,000	165,000	600,000

Note that a separate line is added to the work sheet for the excess of cost over book value of subsidiary.

Content of a Consolidated Balance Sheet

STUDY OBJECTIVE 8

Explain the form and content of consolidated financial statements.

To illustrate a consolidated balance sheet, we will use the work sheet shown in Illustration 13A-3. This work sheet shows an excess of cost over book value of $15,000. In the consolidated balance sheet, this amount is first allocated to specific assets, such as inventory and plant equipment, if their fair market values on the acquisition date exceed their book values. Any remainder is considered to be goodwill. For Serto Company, assume that the fair market value of property and equipment is $155,000. Thus, $10,000 of the excess of cost over book value is allocated to property and equipment, and the remainder, $5,000, is allocated to goodwill. The condensed consolidated balance sheet of Powers Company is shown in Illustration 13A-4 on page 608.

Illustration 13A-4
Consolidated balance sheet

POWERS COMPANY
Consolidated Balance Sheet
January 1, 2006

Assets		
Current assets		$115,000
Plant and equipment (net)		480,000
Goodwill		5,000
Total assets		$600,000
Liabilities and Stockholders' Equity		
Current liabilities		$125,000
Stockholders' equity		
Common stock	$300,000	
Retained earnings	175,000	475,000
Total liabilities and stockholders' equity		$600,000

Accounting Matters!

Through innovative financial restructuring, the **Coca-Cola Company** at one time eliminated a substantial amount of non-intercompany debt. It sold to the public 51% of two bottling companies. The "49% solution," as insiders call the strategy, enabled Coca-Cola to keep effective control over the businesses, and it swept $3 billion of debt from its consolidated balance sheet. (It no longer consolidated the two bottling companies.) At the same time the new companies obtained independent access to equity markets to satisfy their own voracious appetites for capital.

Consolidated Income Statement

A consolidated income statement is also prepared for affiliated companies. This statement shows the results of operations of affiliated companies as though they are one economic unit. This means that the statement shows only revenue and expense transactions between the consolidated entity and companies and individuals who are outside the affiliated group. Consequently, all intercompany revenue and expense transactions must be eliminated. Intercompany transactions such as sales between affiliates and interest on loans charged by one affiliate to another must be eliminated. A work sheet facilitates the preparation of consolidated income statements in the same manner as it does for the balance sheet.

SUMMARY OF STUDY OBJECTIVES FOR APPENDIX

7. **Describe the content of a work sheet for a consolidated balance sheet.** The work sheet for a consolidated balance sheet contains columns for (a) the balance sheet data for the separate entities, (b) intercompany eliminations, and (c) consolidated data.

8. **Explain the form and content of consolidated financial statements.** Consolidated financial statements are similar in form and content to the financial statements of an individual corporation. A consolidated balance sheet shows the assets and liabilities controlled by the parent company. A consolidated income statement shows the results of operations of affiliated companies as though they are one economic unit.

GLOSSARY FOR APPENDIX

Intercompany eliminations Eliminations made to exclude the effects of intercompany transactions in preparing consolidated statements. (p. 605).

Intercompany transactions Transactions between affiliated companies. (p. 605).

*__Note:__ All asterisked Questions, Exercises, and Problems relate to material in the appendix to the chapter.

SELF-STUDY QUESTIONS

Self-Study/Self-Test

www.wiley.com/college/weygandt

Answers are at the end of the chapter.

(SO 2) 1. Debt investments are initially recorded at:
- **a.** cost.
- **b.** cost plus accrued interest.
- **c.** fair value.
- **d.** None of the above.

(SO 2) 2. Hanes Company sells debt investments costing $26,000 for $28,000, plus accrued interest that has been recorded. In journalizing the sale, credits are to:
- **a.** Debt Investments and Loss on Sale of Debt Investments.
- **b.** Debt Investments, Gain on Sale of Debt Investments, and Bond Interest Receivable.
- **c.** Stock Investments and Bond Interest Receivable.
- **d.** No correct answer given.

(SO 3) 3. Pryor Company receives net proceeds of $42,000 on the sale of stock investments that cost $39,500. This transaction will result in reporting in the income statement a:
- **a.** loss of $2,500 under "Other expenses and losses."
- **b.** loss of $2,500 under "Operating expenses."
- **c.** gain of $2,500 under "Other revenues and gains."
- **d.** gain of $2,500 under "Operating revenues."

(SO 3) 4. The equity method of accounting for long-term investments in stock should be used when the investor has significant influence over an investee and owns:
- **a.** between 20% and 50% of the investee's common stock.
- **b.** 20% or more of the investee's common stock.
- **c.** more than 50% of the investee's common stock.
- **d.** less than 20% of the investee's common stock.

(SO 4) 5. Which of the following statements is *not true*? Consolidated financial statements are useful to:
- **a.** determine the profitability of specific subsidiaries.
- **b.** determine the total profitability of enterprises under common control.
- **c.** determine the breadth of a parent company's operations.
- **d.** determine the full extent of total obligations of enterprises under common control.

(SO 5) 6. At the end of the first year of operations, the total cost of the trading securities portfolio is $120,000. Total fair value is $115,000. The financial statements should show:
- **a.** a reduction of an asset of $5,000 and a realized loss of $5,000.
- **b.** a reduction of an asset of $5,000 and an unrealized loss of $5,000 in the stockholders' equity section.
- **c.** a reduction of an asset of $5,000 in the current assets section and an unrealized loss of $5,000 in "Other expenses and losses."
- **d.** a reduction of an asset of $5,000 in the current assets section and a realized loss of $5,000 in "Other expenses and losses."

7. In the balance sheet, a debit balance in Unrealized Gain or Loss—Equity is reported as a: (SO 5)
- **a.** contra asset account.
- **b.** contra stockholders' equity account.
- **c.** loss in the income statement.
- **d.** loss in the retained earnings statement.

8. Short-term debt investments must be readily marketable and be expected to be sold within: (SO 6)
- **a.** 3 months from the date of purchase.
- **b.** the next year or operating cycle, whichever is shorter.
- **c.** the next year or operating cycle, whichever is longer.
- **d.** the operating cycle.

*9. Pate Company pays $175,000 for 100% of Sinko's common stock when Sinko's stockholders' equity consists of Common Stock $100,000 and Retained Earnings $60,000. In the work sheet for the consolidated balance sheet, the eliminations will include a: (SO 7)
- **a.** credit to Investment in Sinko Common Stock $160,000.
- **b.** credit to Excess of Book Value over Cost of Subsidiary $15,000.
- **c.** debit to Retained Earnings $75,000.
- **d.** debit to Excess of Cost over Book Value of Subsidiary $15,000.

*10. Which of the following statements about intercompany eliminations is *true*? (SO 7)
- **a.** They are not journalized or posted by any of the subsidiaries.
- **b.** They do not affect the ledger accounts of any of the subsidiaries.
- **c.** Intercompany eliminations are made solely on the work sheet to arrive at correct consolidated data.
- **d.** All of these statements are true.

*11. Which one of the following statements about consolidated income statements is *false*? (SO 8)
- **a.** A work sheet facilitates the preparation of the statement.
- **b.** The consolidated income statement shows the results of operations of affiliated companies as a single economic unit.
- **c.** All revenue and expense transactions between parent and subsidiary companies are eliminated.
- **d.** When a subsidiary is wholly owned, the form and content of the statement will differ from the income statement of an individual corporation.

☑ THE NAVIGATOR

QUESTIONS

1. What are the reasons that corporations invest in securities?
2. (a) What is the cost of an investment in bonds?
(b) When is interest on bonds recorded?
3. Jose Gonzalez is confused about losses and gains on the sale of debt investments. Explain to Jose (a) how the gain or loss is computed, and (b) the statement presentation of the gains and losses.
4. Sablow Company sells Gish's bonds costing $40,000 for $45,000, including $1,000 of accrued interest. In recording the sale, Sablow books a $5,000 gain. Is this correct? Explain.
5. What is the cost of an investment in stock?
6. To acquire Jackson Corporation stock, R. Toni pays $62,000 in cash, plus $1,500 broker's fees. What entry should be made for this investment, assuming the stock is readily marketable?
7. (a) When should a long-term investment in common stock be accounted for by the equity method? (b) When is revenue recognized under this method?
8. Diaz Corporation uses the equity method to account for its ownership of 25% of the common stock of Victor Packing. During 2006 Victor reported a net income of $80,000 and declares and pays cash dividends of $10,000. What recognition should Diaz Corporation give to these events?
9. What constitutes "significant influence" when an investor's financial interest is below the 50% level?
10. Distinguish between the cost and equity methods of accounting for investments in stocks.
11. What are consolidated financial statements?
12. What are the valuation guidelines for investments at a balance sheet date?
13. Jane Clemens is the controller of Nakoma Inc. At December 31, the company's investments in trading securities cost $74,000. They have a fair value of $72,000. Indicate how Jane would report these data in the financial statements prepared on December 31.
14. Using the data in question 13, how would Jane report the data if the investment were long-term and the securities were classified as available-for-sale?
15. Sajjad Company's investments in available-for-sale securities at December 31 show total cost of $195,000 and total fair value of $210,000. Prepare the adjusting entry.
16. Using the data in question 15, prepare the adjusting entry assuming the securities are classified as trading securities.
17. What is the proper statement presentation of the account Unrealized Loss—Equity?
18. What purposes are served by reporting Unrealized Gains (Losses)—Equity in the stockholders' equity section?
19. Jamaica Wholesale Supply owns stock in Ivy Corporation. Jamaica intends to hold the stock indefinitely because of some negative tax consequences if sold. Should the investment in Ivy be classified as a short-term investment? Why or why not?

*20. (a) What asset and stockholders' equity balances are eliminated in preparing a consolidated balance sheet for a parent and a wholly owned subsidiary? (b) Why are they eliminated?

*21. Bohanon Company pays $318,000 to purchase all the outstanding common stock of Erin Corporation. At the date of purchase the net assets of Erin have a book value of $290,000. Bohanon's management allocates $20,000 of the excess cost to undervalued land on the books of Erin. What should be done with the rest of the excess?

BRIEF EXERCISES

Journalize entries for debt investments.
(SO 2)

BE13-1 Buslik Corporation purchased debt investments for $46,800 on January 1, 2006. On July 1, 2006, Buslik received cash interest of $2,340. Journalize the purchase and the receipt of interest. Assume that no interest has been accrued.

Journalize entries for stock investments.
(SO 3)

BE13-2 On August 1, Hyun Company buys 1,000 shares of Morgan common stock for $35,000 cash, plus brokerage fees of $600. On December 1, Hyun sells the stock investments for $40,000 in cash. Journalize the purchase and sale of the common stock.

Record transactions under the equity method of accounting.
(SO 3)

BE13-3 Iguana Company owns 30% of Hyde Company. For the current year Hyde reports net income of $180,000 and declares and pays a $50,000 cash dividend. Record Iguana's equity in Hyde's net income and the receipt of dividends from Hyde.

Prepare adjusting entry using fair value.
(SO 5)

BE13-4 The cost of the trading securities of Homura Company at December 31, 2006, is $64,000. At December 31, 2006, the fair value of the securities is $59,000. Prepare the adjusting entry to record the securities at fair value.

Indicate statement presentation using fair value.
(SO 5, 6)

BE13-5 For the data presented in BE13-4, show the financial statement presentation of the trading securities and related accounts.

BE13-6 Karpman Corporation holds as a long-term investment available-for-sale stock securities costing $72,000. At December 31, 2006, the fair value of the securities is $68,000. Prepare the adjusting entry to record the securities at fair value.

Prepare adjusting entry using fair value.
(SO 5)

BE13-7 For the data presented in BE13-6, show the financial statement presentation of the available-for-sale securities and related accounts. Assume the available-for-sale securities are noncurrent.

Indicate statement presentation using fair value.
(SO 5, 6)

BE13-8 Cobbs Corporation has the following long-term investments: (1) Common stock of Kubek Co (10% ownership) held as available-for-sale securities, cost $108,000, fair value $115,000. (2) Common stock of Ely Inc. (30% ownership), cost $210,000, equity $250,000. Prepare the investments section of the balance sheet.

Prepare investments section of balance sheet.
(SO 5, 6)

***BE13-9** Paula Company acquires 100% of the common stock of Shannon Company for $190,000 cash. On the acquisition date, Shannon's ledger shows Common Stock $120,000 and Retained Earnings $70,000. Complete the work sheet for the following accounts: Paula—Investment in Shannon Common Stock, Shannon—Common Stock, and Shannon—Retained Earnings.

Prepare partial consolidated work sheet when cost equals book value.
(SO 7)

***BE13-10** Data for the Paula and Shannon companies are given in BE13-9. Instead of paying $190,000, assume that Paula pays $200,000 to acquire the 100% interest in Shannon Company. Complete the work sheet for the accounts identified in BE13-9 and for the excess of cost over book value.

Prepare partial consolidated work sheet when cost exceeds book value.
(SO 7)

EXERCISES

E13-1 Issel Corporation had the following transactions pertaining to debt investments.

Journalize debt investment transactions and accrue interest.
(SO 2)

Jan. 1	Purchased 60 8%, $1,000 Hollis Co. bonds for $60,000 cash plus brokerage fees of $900. Interest is payable semiannually on July 1 and January 1.
July 1	Received semiannual interest on Hollis Co. bonds.
July 1	Sold 30 Hollis Co. bonds for $34,000 less $500 brokerage fees.

Instructions

(a) Journalize the transactions.
(b) Prepare the adjusting entry for the accrual of interest at December 31.

E13-2 Batazar Company had the following transactions pertaining to stock investments.

Journalize stock investment transactions.
(SO 3)

Feb. 1	Purchased 800 shares of Hippo common stock (2%) for $8,000 cash, plus brokerage fees of $200.
July 1	Received cash dividends of $1 per share on Hippo common stock.
Sept. 1	Sold 300 shares of Hippo common stock for $4,400 less brokerage fees of $100.
Dec. 1	Received cash dividends of $1 per share on Hippo common stock.

Instructions

(a) Journalize the transactions.
(b) Explain how dividend revenue and the gain (loss) on sale should be reported in the income statement.

E13-3 Hermes Inc. had the following transactions pertaining to investments in common stock.

Journalize transactions for investments in stocks.
(SO 3)

Jan. 1	Purchased 2,000 shares of Lanier Corporation common stock (5%) for $140,000 cash plus $2,100 broker's commission.
July 1	Received a cash dividend of $3 per share.
Dec. 1	Sold 500 shares of Lanier Corporation common stock for $37,000 cash, less $800 broker's commission.
Dec. 31	Received a cash dividend of $3 per share.

Instructions

Journalize the transactions.

Journalize transactions, and report results using equity method.
(SO 3)

E13-4 On January 1 Jazz Corporation purchased a 30% equity in Snapper Corporation for $180,000. At December 31 Snapper declared and paid a $60,000 cash dividend and reported net income of $200,000.

Instructions
(a) Journalize the transactions.
(b) Determine the amount to be reported as an investment in Snapper stock at December 31.

Journalize entries under cost and equity methods.
(SO 3)

E13-5 Presented below are two independent situations.

1. Galex Cosmetics acquired 10% of the 200,000 shares of common stock of Yen Fashion at a total cost of $13 per share on March 18, 2006. On June 30, Yen declared and paid a $60,000 dividend. On December 31, Yen reported net income of $122,000 for the year. At December 31, the market price of Yen Fashion was $15 per share. The stock is classified as available-for-sale.
2. Smart, Inc., obtained significant influence over Gamma Corporation by buying 25% of Gamma's 30,000 outstanding shares of common stock at a total cost of $9 per share on January 1, 2006. On June 15, Gamma declared and paid a cash dividend of $30,000. On December 31, Gamma reported a net income of $80,000 for the year.

Instructions
Prepare all the necessary journal entries for 2006 for (a) Galex Cosmetics and (b) Smart, Inc.

Prepare adjusting entry to record fair value, and indicate statement presentation.
(SO 5, 6)

E13-6 At December 31, 2006, the trading securities for Jeng, Inc. are as follows.

Security	Cost	Fair Value
A	$17,500	$16,000
B	12,500	14,000
C	23,000	17,000
	$53,000	$47,000

Instructions
(a) Prepare the adjusting entry at December 31, 2006, to report the securities at fair value.
(b) Show the balance sheet and income statement presentation at December 31, 2006, after adjustment to fair value.

Prepare adjusting entry to record fair value, and indicate statement presentation.
(SO 5, 6)

E13-7 Data for investments in stock classified as trading securities are presented in E13-6. Assume instead that the investments are classified as available-for-sale securities. They have the same cost and fair value. The securities are considered to be a long-term investment.

Instructions
(a) Prepare the adjusting entry at December 31, 2006, to report the securities at fair value.
(b) Show the statement presentation at December 31, 2006, after adjustment to fair value.
(c) M. Istanbel, a member of the board of directors, does not understand the reporting of the unrealized gains or losses. Write a letter to Mr. Istanbel explaining the reporting and the purposes that it serves.

Prepare adjusting entries for fair value, and indicate statement presentation for two classes of securities.
(SO 5, 6)

E13-8 Kanjo Company has the following data at December 31, 2006.

Securities	Cost	Fair Value
Trading	$120,000	$123,000
Available-for-sale	100,000	92,000

The available-for-sale securities are held as a long-term investment.

Instructions
(a) Prepare the adjusting entries to report each class of securities at fair value.
(b) Indicate the statement presentation of each class of securities and the related unrealized gain (loss) accounts.

Prepare consolidated work sheet when cost equals book value.
(SO 7, 8)

***E13-9** On January 1, 2006, Lennon Corporation acquires 100% of Ono Inc. for $220,000 in cash. The condensed balance sheets of the two corporations immediately following the acquisition are as follows.

	Lennon Corporation	Ono Inc.
Current assets	$ 60,000	$ 50,000
Investment in Ono Inc. common stock	220,000	
Plant and equipment (net)	300,000	220,000
	$580,000	$270,000
Current liabilities	$180,000	$ 50,000
Common stock	230,000	80,000
Retained earnings	170,000	140,000
	$580,000	$270,000

Instructions

Prepare a work sheet for a consolidated balance sheet.

Prepare consolidated work sheet when cost exceeds book value.

(SO 7, 8)

***E13-10** Data for the Lennon and Ono corporations are presented in E13-9. Assume that instead of paying $220,000 in cash for Ono Inc., Lennon Corporation pays $225,000 in cash. Thus, at the acquisition date, the assets of Lennon Corporation are: Current assets $55,000, Investment in Ono Inc. common stock $225,000, and Plant and equipment (net) $300,000.

Instructions

Prepare a work sheet for a consolidated balance sheet.

PROBLEMS: SET A

Journalize debt investment transactions and show financial statement presentation.

(SO 2, 5, 6)

P13-1A Strawder Farms is a grower of hybrid seed corn for DeKalb Genetics Corporation. It has had two exceptionally good years and has elected to invest its excess funds in bonds. The following selected transactions relate to bonds acquired as an investment by Strawder Farms, whose fiscal year ends on December 31.

2006

Jan. 1 Purchased at par $800,000 of Lesley Corporation 10-year, 9% bonds dated January 1, 2006, directly from the issuing corporation.
July 1 Received the semiannual interest on the Lesley bonds.
Dec. 31 Accrued interest at year-end on the Lesley bonds.

(Assume that all intervening transactions and adjustments have been properly recorded and the number of bonds owned has not changed from December 31, 2006, to December 31, 2008.)

2009

Jan. 1 Received the semiannual interest on the Lesley bonds.
Jan. 1 Sold $400,000 of Lesley bonds at 114. The broker deducted $7,000 for commissions and fees on the sale.
July 1 Received the semiannual interest on the Lesley bonds.
Dec. 31 Accrued interest at year-end on the Lesley bonds.

Instructions

(a) Journalize the listed transactions for the years 2006 and 2009.

(b) Assume that the fair value of the bonds at December 31, 2006, was $770,000. These bonds are classified as available-for-sale securities. Prepare the adjusting entry to record these bonds at fair value.

(a) Gain on sale of debt investments $49,000

(c) Based on your analysis in part (b) show the balance sheet presentation of the bonds and interest receivable at December 31, 2006. Assume the investments are considered long-term. Indicate where any unrealized gain or loss is reported in the financial statements.

Journalize investment transactions, prepare adjusting entry, and show statement presentation.

(SO 2, 3, 5, 6)

P13-2A In January 2006, the management of Ralley Company concludes that it has sufficient cash to purchase some short-term investments in debt and stock securities. During the year, the following transactions occurred.

Feb. 1 Purchased 600 shares of IBT common stock for $40,000, plus brokerage fees of $800.
Mar. 1 Purchased 500 shares of IMA common stock for $15,000, plus brokerage fees of $300.

Apr. 1 Purchased 60 $1,000, 12% CRE bonds for $60,000, plus $1,200 brokerage fees. Interest is payable semiannually on April 1 and October 1.
July 1 Received a cash dividend of $0.60 per share on the IBT common stock.
Aug. 1 Sold 300 shares of IBT common stock at $70 per share, less brokerage fees of $350.
Sept. 1 Received a $1 per share cash dividend on the IMA common stock.
Oct. 1 Received the semiannual interest on the CRE bonds.
Oct. 1 Sold the CRE bonds for $65,000, less $1,000 brokerage fees.

At December 31, the fair value of the IBT common stock was $66 per share. The fair value of the IMA common stock was $30 per share.

Instructions

(a) Journalize the transactions and post to the accounts Debt Investments and Stock Investments. (Use the T-account form.)

(b) Unrealized loss $900

(b) Prepare the adjusting entry at December 31, 2006, to report the investments at fair value. All securities are considered to be trading securities.

(c) Show the balance sheet presentation of investment securities at December 31, 2006.

(d) Identify the income statement accounts and give the statement classification of each account.

Journalize transactions and adjusting entry for stock investments.

(SO 3, 5, 6)

Peachtree

P13-3A On December 31, 2006, Carlin Associates owned the following securities, held as long-term investments.

Common Stock	Shares	Cost
Ace Co.	2,000	$50,000
Burns Co.	6,000	36,000
Cruz Co.	1,200	24,000

On this date, the total fair value of the securities was equal to its cost. The securities are not held for influence or control over the investees. In 2007, the following transactions occurred.

July 1 Received $1 per share semiannual cash dividend on Burns Co. common stock.
Aug. 1 Received $0.50 per share cash dividend on Ace Co. common stock.
Sept. 1 Sold 2,000 shares of Burns Co. common stock for cash at $7 per share, less brokerage fees of $300.
Oct. 1 Sold 600 shares of Ace Co. common stock for cash at $28 per share, less brokerage fees of $600.
Nov. 1 Received $1 per share cash dividend on Cruz Co. common stock.
Dec. 15 Received $0.50 per share cash dividend on Ace Co. common stock.
31 Received $1 per share semiannual cash dividend on Burns Co. common stock.

At December 31, the fair values per share of the common stocks were: Ace Co. $24, Burns Co. $6, and Cruz Co. $19.

Instructions

(a) Gain on sale, $1,700 and $1,200

(a) Journalize the 2007 transactions and post to the account Stock Investments. (Use the T-account form.)

(b) Prepare the adjusting entry at December 31, 2007, to show the securities at fair value. The stock should be classified as available-for-sale securities.

(c) Show the balance sheet presentation of the investments at December 31, 2007. At this date, Carlin Associates has common stock of $2,000,000 and retained earnings of $1,200,000.

Prepare entries under the cost and equity methods, and tabulate differences.

(SO 3)

P13-4A Penny's Concrete acquired 25% of the outstanding common stock of Cardinal, Inc. on January 1, 2006, by paying $1,200,000 for 50,000 shares. Cardinal declared and paid a $0.50 per share cash dividend on June 30 and again on December 31, 2006. Cardinal reported net income of $600,000 for the year. At December 31, 2006, the market price of Cardinal's common stock was $30 per share.

Instructions

(a) Total dividend revenue $50,000

(a) Prepare the journal entries for Penny's Concrete for 2006 assuming Penny's cannot exercise significant influence over Cardinal. (Use the cost method and assume Cardinal common stock should be classified as available-for-sale.)

(b) Revenue from investments $150,000

(b) Prepare the journal entries for Penny's Concrete for 2006, assuming Penny's can exercise significant influence over Cardinal. (Use the equity method.)

(c) In tabular form, indicate the investment and income account balances at December 31, 2006, under each method of accounting.

P13-5A The following are in Sanders Company's portfolio of long-term available-for-sale securities at December 31, 2006.

Journalize stock investment transactions and show statement presentation.

(SO 3, 5, 6)

	Cost
500 shares of Bonds Corporation common stock	$26,000
700 shares of Ruth Corporation common stock	42,000
600 shares of Edmonds Corporation preferred stock	16,800

On December 31, the total cost of the portfolio equaled total fair value. Sanders Company had the following transactions related to the securities during 2007.

Jan.	7	Sold 500 shares of Bonds Corporation common stock at $58 per share, less brokerage fees of $700.
	10	Purchased 200 shares of the $70 par value common stock of Schilling Corporation at $78 per share, plus brokerage fees of $240.
	26	Received a cash dividend of $1.15 per share on Ruth Corporation common stock.
Feb.	2	Received cash dividends of $0.40 per share on Edmonds Corporation preferred stock.
	10	Sold all 600 shares of Edmonds Corporation preferred stock at $25 per share less brokerage fees of $180.
July	1	Received a cash dividend of $1.00 per share on Ruth Corporation common stock.
Sept.	1	Purchased an additional 800 shares of the $70 par value common stock of Schilling Corporation at $75 per share, plus brokerage fees of $900.
Dec.	15	Received a cash dividend of $1.50 per share on Schilling Corporation common stock.

At December 31, 2007, the fair values of the securities were:

Ruth Corporation common stock	$63 per share
Schilling Corporation common stock	$72 per share

Sanders uses separate account titles for each investment, such as Investment in Ruth Corporation Common Stock.

Instructions

(a) Prepare journal entries to record the transactions.

(b) Post to the investment accounts. (Use T accounts.)

(c) Prepare the adjusting entry at December 31, 2007, to report the portfolio at fair value.

(d) Show the balance sheet presentation at December 31, 2007.

(a) Loss on sale $1,980

(c) Unrealized loss $2,640

P13-6A The following data, presented in alphabetical order, are taken from the records of Allison Corporation.

Prepare a balance sheet.

(SO 5, 6)

Accounts payable	$ 280,000
Accounts receivable	90,000
Accumulated depreciation—building	180,000
Accumulated depreciation—equipment	52,000
Allowance for doubtful accounts	6,000
Bonds payable (10%, due 2019)	400,000
Buildings	900,000
Cash	142,000
Common stock ($5 par value; 500,000 shares authorized, 300,000 shares issued)	1,500,000
Discount on bonds payable	20,000
Dividends payable	50,000
Equipment	275,000
Goodwill	200,000
Income taxes payable	120,000
Investment in Saratoga Inc. stock (30% ownership), at equity	600,000
Land	570,000
Merchandise inventory	170,000
Notes payable (due 2007)	70,000
Paid-in capital in excess of par value	200,000
Prepaid insurance	16,000
Retained earnings	310,000
Short-term stock investment, at fair value (and cost)	185,000

Total assets $2,910,000

Instructions

Prepare a balance sheet at December 31, 2006.

Prepare consolidated work sheet and balance sheet when cost exceeds book value.

(SO 7, 8)

***P13-7A** Robinson Corporation purchased all the outstanding common stock of Hoffman Plastics, Inc. on December 31, 2006. Just before the purchase, the condensed balance sheets of the two companies appeared as follows.

	Robinson Corporation	Hoffman Plastics, Inc.
Current assets	$1,480,000	$ 435,500
Plant and equipment (net)	2,100,000	676,000
	$3,580,000	$1,111,500
Current liabilities	$ 578,000	$ 92,500
Common stock	1,950,000	525,000
Retained earnings	1,052,000	494,000
	$3,580,000	$1,111,500

Robinson used current assets of $1,225,000 to acquire the stock of Hoffman Plastics. The excess of this purchase price over the book value of Hoffman Plastics' net assets is determined to be attributable $86,000 to Hoffman Plastics' plant and equipment and the remainder to goodwill.

Excess cost over book value $120,000

Instructions

(a) Prepare the entry for Robinson's acquisition of Hoffman Plastics, Inc. stock.

(b) Prepare a consolidated work sheet at December 31, 2006.

(c) Prepare a consolidated balance sheet at December 31, 2006.

PROBLEMS: SET B

Journalize debt investment transactions and show financial statement presentation.

(SO 2, 5, 6)

P13-1B Chelsea Carecenters Inc. provides financing and capital to the health-care industry, with a particular focus on nursing homes for the elderly. The following selected transactions relate to bonds acquired as an investment by Chelsea, whose fiscal year ends on December 31.

2006

Jan. 1	Purchased at par $3,000,000 of Caring Nursing Centers, Inc., 10-year, 8% bonds dated January 1, 2006, directly from Caring.
July 1	Received the semiannual interest on the Caring bonds.
Dec. 31	Accrued interest at year-end on the Caring bonds.

(Assume that all intervening transactions and adjustments have been properly recorded and that the number of bonds owned has not changed from December 31, 2006, to December 31, 2008.)

2009

Jan. 1	Received the semiannual interest on the Caring bonds.
Jan. 1	Sold $1,500,000 Caring bonds at 106. The broker deducted $6,000 for commissions and fees on the sale.
July 1	Received the semiannual interest on the Caring bonds.
Dec. 31	Accrued interest at year-end on the Caring bonds.

(a) Gain on sale of debt investment $84,000

Instructions

(a) Journalize the listed transactions for the years 2006 and 2009.

(b) Assume that the fair value of the bonds at December 31, 2006, was $3,300,000. These bonds are classified as available-for-sale securities. Prepare the adjusting entry to record these bonds at fair value.

(c) Based on your analysis in part (b), show the balance sheet presentation of the bonds and interest receivable at December 31, 2006. Assume the investments are considered long-term. Indicate where any unrealized gain or loss is reported in the financial statements.

Journalize investment transactions, prepare adjusting entry, and show statement presentation.

(SO 2, 3, 5, 6)

Peachtree

P13-2B In January 2006, the management of Match Company concludes that it has sufficient cash to permit some short-term investments in debt and stock securities. During the year, the following transactions occurred.

Feb. 1	Purchased 600 shares of Loder common stock for $31,800, plus brokerage fees of $600.
Mar. 1	Purchased 800 shares of Greer common stock for $20,000, plus brokerage fees of $400.
Apr. 1	Purchased 50 $1,000, 8% Roy bonds for $50,000, plus $1,000 brokerage fees. Interest is payable semiannually on April 1 and October 1.
July 1	Received a cash dividend of $0.60 per share on the Loder common stock.
Aug. 1	Sold 200 shares of Loder common stock at $57 per share less brokerage fees of $200.
Sept. 1	Received a $1 per share cash dividend on the Greer common stock.
Oct. 1	Received the semiannual interest on the Roy bonds.
Oct. 1	Sold the Roy bonds for $49,000 less $1,000 brokerage fees.

At December 31, the fair value of the Loder common stock was $55 per share. The fair value of the Greer common stock was $23 per share.

Instructions

(a) Journalize the transactions and post to the accounts Debt Investments and Stock Investments. (Use the T-account form.)

(a) Gain on stock sale $400

(b) Prepare the adjusting entry at December 31, 2006, to report the investment securities at fair value. All securities are considered to be trading securities.

(c) Show the balance sheet presentation of investment securities at December 31, 2006.

(d) Identify the income statement accounts and give the statement classification of each account.

Journalize transactions and adjusting entry for stock investments.

(SO 3, 5, 6)

P13-3B On December 31, 2006, Mauro Associates owned the following securities, held as a long-term investment. The securities are not held for influence or control of the investee.

Common Stock	Shares	Cost
Kline Co.	3,000	$90,000
Mann Co.	5,000	45,000
Scott Co.	1,500	30,000

On this date, the total fair value of the securities was equal to its cost. In 2007, the following transactions occurred.

July 1	Received $1 per share semiannual cash dividend on Mann Co. common stock.
Aug. 1	Received $0.50 per share cash dividend on Kline Co. common stock.
Sept. 1	Sold 1,500 shares of Mann Co. common stock for cash at $8 per share, less brokerage fees of $300.
Oct. 1	Sold 800 shares of Kline Co. common stock for cash at $31 per share, less brokerage fees of $500.
Nov. 1	Received $1 per share cash dividend on Scott Co. common stock.
Dec. 15	Received $0.50 per share cash dividend on Kline Co. common stock.
31	Received $1 per share semiannual cash dividend on Mann Co. common stock.

At December 31, the fair values per share of the common stocks were: Kline Co. $32, Mann Co. $8, and Scott Co. $18.

Instructions

(a) Journalize the 2007 transactions and post to the account Stock Investments. (Use the T-account form.)

(b) Prepare the adjusting entry at December 31, 2007, to show the securities at fair value. The stock should be classified as available-for-sale securities.

(b) Unrealized loss $2,100

(c) Show the balance sheet presentation of the investments at December 31, 2007. At this date, Mauro Associates has common stock $1,500,000 and retained earnings $1,000,000.

Prepare entries under the cost and equity methods, and tabulate differences.

(SO 3)

P13-4B Marley Services acquired 25% of the outstanding common stock of Stevens Company on January 1, 2006, by paying $800,000 for the 40,000 shares. Stevens declared and paid $0.30 per share cash dividends on March 15, June 15, September 15, and December 15, 2006. Stevens reported net income of $320,000 for the year. At December 31, 2006, the market price of Stevens common stock was $24 per share.

(a) Total dividend revenue $48,000

(b) Revenue from investments $80,000

Instructions

(a) Prepare the journal entries for Marley Services for 2006 assuming Marley cannot exercise significant influence over Stevens. (Use the cost method and assume that Stevens' common stock should be classified as a trading security.)

(b) Prepare the journal entries for Marley Services for 2006, assuming Marley can exercise significant influence over Stevens. Use the equity method.

(c) In tabular form, indicate the investment and income statement account balances at December 31, 2006, under each method of accounting.

Journalize stock investment transactions and show statement presentation.

(SO 3, 5, 6)

P13-5B The following securities are in Morales Company's portfolio of long-term available-for-sale securities at December 31, 2006.

	Cost
1,000 shares of Abel Corporation common stock	$52,000
1,400 shares of HAL Corporation common stock	84,000
1,200 shares of Reese Corporation preferred stock	33,600

On December 31, 2006, the total cost of the portfolio equaled total fair value. Morales had the following transactions related to the securities during 2007.

Jan.	20	Sold 1,000 shares of Abel Corporation common stock at $54 per share less brokerage fees of $600.
	28	Purchased 400 shares of $70 par value common stock of Nolan Corporation at $78 per share, plus brokerage fees of $480.
	30	Received a cash dividend of $1.15 per share on HAL Corp. common stock.
Feb.	8	Received cash dividends of $0.40 per share on Reese Corp. preferred stock.
	18	Sold all 1,200 shares of Reese Corp. preferred stock at $26 per share less brokerage fees of $360.
July	30	Received a cash dividend of $1.00 per share on HAL Corp. common stock.
Sept.	6	Purchased an additional 600 shares of $10 par value common stock of Nolan Corporation at $82 per share, plus brokerage fees of $800.
Dec.	1	Received a cash dividend of $1.50 per share on Nolan Corporation common stock.

At December 31, 2007, the fair values of the securities were:

HAL Corporation common stock	$64 per share
Nolan Corporation common stock	$72 per share

Morales Company uses separate account titles for each investment, such as "Investment in HAL Corporation Common Stock."

(a) Loss on sale of preferred stock $2,760

(c) Unrealized loss $4,080

Instructions

(a) Prepare journal entries to record the transactions.

(b) Post to the investment accounts. (Use T accounts.)

(c) Prepare the adjusting entry at December 31, 2007 to report the portfolio at fair value.

(d) Show the balance sheet presentation at December 31, 2007.

Prepare a balance sheet.

(SO 5, 6)

P13-6B The following data, presented in alphabetical order, are taken from the records of Lefever Corporation.

Accounts payable	$ 210,000
Accounts receivable	140,000
Accumulated depreciation—building	180,000
Accumulated depreciation—equipment	52,000
Allowance for doubtful accounts	6,000
Bonds payable (10%, due 2017)	500,000
Buildings	950,000
Cash	42,000
Common stock ($10 par value; 500,000 shares authorized, 150,000 shares issued)	1,500,000
Dividends payable	80,000
Equipment	275,000
Goodwill	200,000
Income taxes payable	120,000
Investment in Dodge common stock (10% ownership), at cost	278,000
Investment in Portico common stock (30% ownership), at equity	380,000

Land	430,000
Market adjustment—available-for-sale securities (Dr)	8,000
Merchandise inventory	170,000
Notes payable (due 2007)	70,000
Paid-in capital in excess of par value	200,000
Premium on bonds payable	40,000
Prepaid insurance	16,000
Retained earnings	103,000
Short-term stock investment, at fair value (and cost)	180,000
Unrealized gain—available-for-sale securities	8,000

The investment in Dodge common stock is considered to be a long-term available-for-sale security.

Instructions

Prepare a balance sheet at December 31, 2006.

Total assets $2,831,000

***P13-7B** Patel Company purchased all the outstanding common stock of Singh Company on December 31, 2006. Just before the purchase, the condensed balance sheets of the two companies were as follows.

Prepare consolidated work sheet and balance sheet when cost exceeds book value.

(SO 7, 8)

	Patel Company	Singh Company
Current assets	$1,478,000	$379,000
Plant and equipment (net)	1,882,000	351,000
	$3,360,000	$730,000
Current liabilities	$ 870,000	$ 90,000
Common stock	1,947,000	360,000
Retained earnings	543,000	280,000
	$3,360,000	$730,000

Patel used current assets of $710,000 to acquire the stock of Singh. The excess of this purchase price over the book value of Patel's net assets is determined to be attributable $20,000 to Singh's plant and equipment and the remainder to goodwill.

Instructions

(a) Prepare the entry for Patel Company's acquisition of Singh Company stock.
(b) Prepare a consolidated work sheet at December 31, 2006.
(c) Prepare a consolidated balance sheet at December 31, 2006.

Excess of cost over book value $50,000

COMPREHENSIVE PROBLEM: CHAPTERS 11 TO 13

Part I

Megan Bergeron and her two colleagues, Jesse Ortiz and Tara Sheley, are personal trainers at an upscale health spa/resort in Tampa, Florida. They want to start a health club that specializes in health plans for people in the 50+ age range. The growing population in this age range and strong consumer interest in the health benefits of physical activity have convinced them they can profitably operate their own club. In addition to many other decisions, they need to determine what type of business organization they want. Jesse believes there are more advantages to the corporate form than a partnership, but he hasn't yet convinced Megan and Tara. They have come to you, a small business consulting specialist, seeking information and advice regarding the choice of starting a partnership versus a corporation.

Instructions

(a) Prepare a memo (dated May 26, 2005) that describes the advantages and disadvantages of both partnerships and corporations. Advise Megan, Jesse, and Tara regarding which organizational form you believe would better serve their purposes. Make sure to include reasons supporting your advice.

Part II

After deciding to incorporate, each of the three investors receives 20,000 shares of $2 par common stock on June 12, 2005, in exchange for their co-owned building ($200,000 market value) and $100,000 total cash they contributed to the business. The next decision that Megan, Jesse, and Tara need to make is how to obtain financing for renovation and equipment. They understand the difference between equity securities and debt securities, but do not understand the tax, net income, and earnings per share consequences of equity versus debt financing on the future of their business.

Instructions

(b) Prepare notes for a discussion with the three entrepreneurs in which you will compare the consequences of using equity versus debt financing. As part of your notes, show the differences in interest and tax expense assuming $1,400,000 is financed with common stock, and then alternatively with debt. Assume that when common stock is used, 140,000 shares will be issued. When debt is used, assume the interest rate on debt is 9%, the tax rate is 32%, and income before interest and taxes is $200,000. (You may want to use an electronic spreadsheet.)

Part III

During the discussion about financing, Tara mentions that one of her clients, Antonio Cepeda, has approached her about buying a significant interest in the new club. Having an interested investor sways the three to issue equity securities to provide the financing they need. On July 21, 2005, Mr. Cepeda buys 140,000 shares at a price of $10 per share.

The club, LifePath Fitness, opens on January 12, 2006, and after a slow start, begins to produce the revenue desired by the owners. The owners decide to pay themselves a stock dividend, since cash has been less than abundant since they opened their doors. The 5% stock dividend is declared by the owners on July 27, 2006. The market value of the stock is $3 on the declaration date. The date of record is July 31, 2006 (there have been no changes in stock ownership since the initial issuance), and the issue date is August 15, 2006. By the middle of the fourth quarter of 2006, the cash flow of LifePath Fitness has improved to the point that the owners feel ready to pay themselves a cash dividend. They declare a $0.05 cash dividend on December 4, 2005. The record date is December 14, 2006, and the payment date is December 24, 2006.

Instructions

(c) **(1)** Record all of the transactions related to the common stock of LifePath Fitness during the years 2005 and 2006. **(2)** Indicate how many shares are issued and outstanding after the stock dividend is issued.

Part IV

Since the club opened, a major concern has been the pool facilities. Although the existing pool is adequate, Megan, Jesse, and Tara all desire to make LifePath a cutting-edge facility. Until the end of 2006, financing concerns prevented this improvement. However, because there has been steady growth in clientele, revenue, and income since the fourth quarter of 2006, the owners have explored possible financing options. They are hesitant to issue stock and change the ownership mix because they have been able to work together as a team with great effectiveness. They have formulated a plan to issue secured term bonds to raise the needed $500,000 for the pool facilities. By the end of April 2007 everything was in place for the bond issue to go ahead. On June 1, 2007, the bonds were issued for $456,000. The bonds pay semiannual interest of 3% (6% annual) on December 1 and June 1 of each year. The bonds mature in 10 years, and amortization is computed using the straight-line method.

Instructions

(d) Record **(1)** the issuance of the secured bonds, **(2)** the interest payment made on December 1, 2007, **(3)** the adjusting entry required at December 31, 2007, and **(4)** the interest payment made on June 1, 2008.

Part V

Mr. Cepeda's purchase of LifePath Fitness was done through his business. The investment has always been accounted for using the cost method on his firm's books. However, early in 2008 he decided to take his company public. He is preparing an IPO (initial public offering), and he needs to have the firm's financial statements audited. One of the issues to be resolved is to restate the investment in LifePath Fitness using the equity method, since Mr. Cepeda's ownership percentage is greater than 20%.

Instructions

(e) **(1)** Give the entries that would have been made on Cepeda's books if the equity method of accounting for investments had been used since the initial investment. Assume the following data for LifePath.

	2005	2006	2007
Net income	$30,000	$70,000	$105,000
Total cash dividends	$ 2,100	$20,000	$ 50,000

(2) Compute the balance in the LifePath Investment account at the end of 2007.

BROADENING YOUR PERSPECTIVE

Financial Reporting and Analysis

■ FINANCIAL REPORTING PROBLEM: PepsiCo

BYP13-1 The annual report of **PepsiCo. Inc.** is presented in Appendix A.

Instructions

(a) See Note 1 to the financial statements and indicate what the consolidated financial statements include.

(b) Using **PepsiCo**'s consolidated statement of cash flows, determine how much was spent for capital acquisitions during the current year.

■ COMPARATIVE ANALYSIS PROBLEM: PepsiCo vs. Coca-Cola

BYP13-2 **PepsiCo**'s financial statements are presented in Appendix A. **Coca-Cola**'s financial statements are presented in Appendix B.

Instructions

(a) Based on the information contained in these financial statements, determine each of the following for each company.

(1) Net cash used for investing (investment) activities for the current year (from the statement of cash flows).

(2) Cash used for capital expenditures during the current year.

(b) Each of PepsiCo's financial statements is labeled "consolidated." What has been consolidated? That is, from the contents of PepsiCo's annual report, identify by name the corporations that have been consolidated (parent and subsidiaries).

■ RESEARCH CASE

BYP13-3 The January 9, 1999, issue of *The Economist* includes an article titled "How to Make Mergers Work."

Instructions

Read the article and answer the following questions.

(a) What percentage of mergers actually added value to the combined company? Which investors tend to gain from the merger, and which tend to lose?

(b) The article suggests that mergers in the past tended to be undertaken to create diversified conglomerates, but that mergers of today tend to be defensive in nature. Give examples of motivations for defensive mergers and industries where they have taken place.

(c) What are some reasons why mergers often fail?

(d) What are some methods for increasing the likelihood of success?

INTERPRETING FINANCIAL STATEMENTS

BYP13-4 **Delta Air Lines, Inc.**, is based in Atlanta, Georgia, and is one of the world's largest air carriers. Besides carrying passengers, Delta also provides freight and mail transportation services.

Here is the assets section of a recent Delta balance sheet (excluding dollar amounts):

DELTA AIR LINES
Balance Sheet (partial)

Current assets
- Cash and cash equivalents
- Short-term investments
- Accounts receivable, net of allowance for uncollectible accounts
- Maintenance and operating supplies, at average cost
- Deferred income taxes
- Prepaid expenses and other

Property and equipment
- Flight equipment, less accumulated depreciation
- Flight equipment under capital leases, less accumulated amortization
- Ground property and equipment, less accumulated depreciation
- Advance payments for equipment

Other assets
- Investments in stock of less than 20% owned companies
- Deferred income taxes
- Investments in associated companies
- Cost in excess of net assets acquired, net of accumulated amortization
- Leasehold and operating rights, net of accumulated amortization
- Other

Delta also reported the following information concerning certain of its investments:

1. Investments in **TransQuest Information Solutions** (TransQuest), an information technology joint venture, are accounted for under the equity method.
2. Investments with an original maturity of 3 months or less are stated at cost, which approximates fair value.
3. Cost in excess of net assets acquired (goodwill), which is being amortized over 40 years, is related to the company's acquisition of **Western Air Lines, Inc.**, on December 18, 1986.
4. The company's investments in **Singapore Air Lines Limited** are accounted for under the cost method and are classified as available-for-sale and carried at aggregate market value.
5. Cash in excess of operating requirements is invested in short-term, highly liquid investments. These investments are classified as available-for-sale and are stated at fair value.

Instructions

(a) For each item 1–5 above, determine where it should be shown on Delta's balance sheet, using the account titles listed earlier.

(b) Assume that item 2 includes an investment in **IBM Corporation** bonds consisting of ten bonds of $10,000 each. What accounting treatment is required for the following?

- **(1)** Singapore Air Lines Limited announces net income for the year of $3.15 per share. Assume that Delta holds 3,500 shares.
- **(2)** Western Air Lines announces a net loss of $18,000,000, or $0.63 per share for the quarter.
- **(3)** IBM Corporation declares and pays a $0.25 dividend per share.

A GLOBAL FOCUS

BYP13-5 **Xerox Corporation** has a 50% investment interest in a joint venture with the Japanese corporation Fuji, called **Fuji Xerox**. Xerox accounts for this investment using the equity method. The following additional information regarding this investment was taken from a recent Xerox annual report (in millions).

Investment in Fuji Xerox per balance sheet	$ 1,354
Fuji Xerox net income	108
Xerox total assets	30,024
Xerox total liabilities	25,167
Fuji Xerox total assets	6,279
Fuji Xerox total liabilities	3,757

Instructions

(a) What alternative approaches are available for accounting for long-term investments in stock? Discuss whether Xerox is correct in using the equity method to account for this investment.

(b) Under the equity method, how does Xerox report its investment in Fuji Xerox? If Xerox owned a majority of Fuji Xerox, it then would have to consolidate Fuji Xerox instead of using the equity method. Discuss how this would change Xerox's financial statements. That is, in what way and by how much would assets and liabilities change?

(c) The use of 50% joint ventures is becoming a fairly common practice. Why might companies like Xerox prefer to participate in a joint venture rather than own a majority share?

EXPLORING THE WEB

BYP13-6 The **American Association of Individual Investors (AAII)** provides considerable useful information and services for people interested in investing.

Address: www.aaii.org/invbas/, or go to www.wiley.com/college/weygandt

Steps

1. Go to the site shown above.
2. Choose **Glossary**.

Instructions

Find the definition of the following terms.

(a) Ask price.
(b) Margin.
(c) Prospectus.
(d) Yield.

BYP13-7 Most publicly traded companies are analyzed by numerous analysts. These analysts often don't agree about a company's future prospects. In this exercise you will find analysts' ratings about companies and make comparisons over time and across companies in the same industry. You will also see to what extent the analysts experienced "earnings surprises." Earnings surprises can cause changes in stock prices.

Address: biz.yahoo.com/i, or go to www.wiley.com/college/weygandt

Steps

1. Choose a company.
2. Use the index to find the company's name.
3. Choose **Research**.

Instructions

(a) How many brokers rated the company?
(b) What percentage rated it a strong buy?
(c) What was the average rating for the week?
(d) Did the average rating improve or decline relative to the previous week?
(e) How do the brokers rank this company among all the companies in its industry?
(f) What was the amount of the earnings surprise during the last quarter?

Critical Thinking

■ GROUP DECISION CASE

BYP13-8 At the beginning of the question and answer portion of the annual stockholders' meeting of Reiley Corporation, stockholder Matt Finley asks, "Why did management sell the holdings in SRI Company at a loss when this company has been very profitable during the period its stock was held by Reiley?"

Since president Tony Garcia has just concluded his speech on the recent success and bright future of Reiley, he is taken aback by this question and responds, "I remember we paid $1,100,000 for that stock some years ago, and I am sure we sold that stock at a much higher price. You must be mistaken."

Finley retorts, "Well, right here in footnote number 7 to the annual report it shows that 240,000 shares, a 25% interest in SRI, were sold on the last day of the year. Also, it states that SRI earned $520,000 this year and paid out $160,000 in cash dividends. Further, a summary statement indicates that in past years, while Reiley held SRI stock, SRI earned $1,240,000 and paid out $440,000 in dividends. Finally, the income statement for this year shows a loss on the sale of SRI stock of $180,000. So, I doubt that I am mistaken."

Red-faced, president Garcia turns to you.

Instructions

With the class divided into groups, answer the following.

(a) What dollar amount did Reiley receive upon the sale of the SRI stock?
(b) Explain why both stockholder Finley and president Garcia are correct.

■ COMMUNICATION ACTIVITY

BYP13-9 Fargo Corporation has purchased two securities for its portfolio. The first is a stock investment in Tierney Corporation, one of its suppliers. Fargo purchased 10% of Tierney with the intention of holding it for a number of years, but has no intention of purchasing more shares. The second investment was a purchase of debt securities. Fargo purchased the debt securities because its analysts believe that changes in market interest rates will cause these securities to increase in value in a short period of time. Fargo intends to sell the securities as soon as they have increased in value.

Instructions

Write a memo to Dipak Ghosh, the chief financial officer, explaining how to account for each of these investments. Explain what the implications for reported income are from this accounting treatment.

Accounting Matters!

■ ETHICS CASE

BYP13-10 Kreider Financial Services Company holds a large portfolio of debt and stock securities as an investment. The total fair value of the portfolio at December 31, 2006, is greater than total cost. Some securities have increased in value and others have decreased. Ann Lemke, the financial vice president, and Sue Greene, the controller, are in the process of classifying for the first time the securities in the portfolio.

Lemke suggests classifying the securities that have increased in value as trading securities in order to increase net income for the year. She wants to classify the securities that have decreased in value as long-term available-for-sale securities, so that the decreases in value will not affect 2006 net income.

Greene disagrees. She recommends classifying the securities that have decreased in value as trading securities and those that have increased in value as long-term available-for-sale securities. Greene argues that the company is having a good earnings year and that recognizing the losses now will help to smooth income for this year. Moreover, for future years, when the company may not be as profitable, the company will have built-in gains.

Instructions

(a) Will classifying the securities as Lemke and Greene suggest actually affect earnings as each says it will?
(b) Is there anything unethical in what Lemke and Greene propose? Who are the stakeholders affected by their proposals?

(c) Assume that Lemke and Greene properly classify the portfolio. Assume, at year-end, that Lemke proposes to sell the securities that will increase 2006 net income, and that Greene proposes to sell the securities that will decrease 2006 net income. Is this unethical?

■ CONTINUING COOKIE CHRONICLE

Accounting Matters!

(Note: This is a continuation of the Cookie Chronicle from Chapters 1 through 12.)

BYP13-11 Natalie has been approached by Ken Thornton, a stockholder of The Beanery Coffee Inc. Ken wants to retire and would like to sell his 1,000 shares in The Beanery Coffee, which represents 20% of all shares issued. The Beanery is currently operated by Ken's twin daughters, who each own 40% of the common shares. The Beanery not only operates a coffee shop but also roasts and sells beans to retailers, under the name "Rocky Mountain Beanery."

The business has been operating for approximately 5 years, and in the last 2 years Ken has lost interest and left the day-to-day operations to his daughters. Both daughters at times find the work at the coffee shop overwhelming. They would like to have a third stockholder involved to take over some of the responsibilities of running a small business. Both feel that Natalie and Curtis are entrepreneurial in spirit and that their expertise would be a welcome addition to the business operation. The twins have also said that they plan to operate this business for another 10 years and then retire.

Ken has met with Curtis and Natalie to discuss the business operation. All have concluded that there would be many advantages for Cookie & Coffee Creations Inc. to acquire an interest in The Beanery Coffee. One of the major advantages would be volume discounts for purchases of coffee bean inventory.

Despite the apparent advantages, Natalie and Curtis are still not convinced that they should participate in this business venture. They come to you with the following questions.

1. "We are a little concerned about how much influence we would have in the decision-making process for The Beanery Coffee. Would the amount of influence we have affect how we would account for this investment?"
2. Can you think of other advantages of going ahead with this investment?
3. Can you think of any disadvantages of going ahead with this investment?

Instructions

(a) Answer Natalie and Curtis' questions.
(b) Assume that Ken wants to sell his 1,000 shares of The Beanery Coffee for $12,500. Prepare the journal entry required if Cookie & Coffee Creations Inc. buys Ken's shares.
(c) Assume that Cookie & Coffee Creations Inc. buys the shares and in the following year The Beanery Coffee earns $50,000 net income and pays $40,000 in dividends. Prepare the journal entries required under both the cost method and the equity method of accounting for this investment.
(d) Identify where this investment would be classified on the balance sheet of Cookie & Coffee Creations Inc. and explain why. What amount would appear on the balance sheet under each of the methods of accounting for the investment?

Answers to Accounting Matters! Questions

Accounting Matters!

p. 592

Q: What does Amazon.com do with the balance in Unearned Revenue if it sells, within days, the shares of stock it received in payment for a long-term advertising agreement?

A: Amazon.com continues to recognize the revenue from the stock sale over the term of the advertising agreement, which is the period over which the advertising revenue is earned. The sale and disappearance of the shares of stock (now turned into cash) does not affect the revenue recognition principle.

p. 595

Q: Where in Time Warner's balance sheet will you find its investment in Home Box Office (HBO) Corporation?

A: Because ownership is 100%, HBO does not appear as an investment item in Time Warner's balance sheet. Rather, the assets and liabilities of HBO are included and commingled with the assets and liabilities of Time Warner.

Answer to PepsiCo Review It Question 4, page 596

In Note 1, the following statement is made regarding **PepsiCo**'s consolidation policy:

> "Our financial statements include the consolidated accounts of PepsiCo, Inc. and the affiliates that we control. In addition, we include our share of the results of certain other affiliates based on our ownership interest. We do not control these other affiliates, as our ownership in these other affiliates is generally less than fifty percent. Our share of the net income of noncontrolled bottling affiliates is reported in our income statement as bottling equity income. See Note 8 for additional information on our noncontrolled bottling affiliates. Our share of other noncontrolled affiliates is included in division operating profit. Intercompany balances and transactions are eliminated. . . .
>
> **SVE Consolidation**—As a result of changes in the operations of our European snack joint venture (SVE), we determined that effective in 2002, consolidation was required.

Answers to Self-Study Questions

1. a **2.** b **3.** c **4.** a **5.** a **6.** c **7.** b **8.** c ***9.** d ***10.** d ***11.** d

REMEMBER to go back to the Navigator box on the chapter-opening page and check off your completed work.

Chapter 14

The Statement of Cash Flows

THE NAVIGATOR ✓

- Understand **Concepts for Review** ❑
- Read **Feature Story** ❑
- Scan **Study Objectives** ❑
- Read **Preview** ❑
- Read text and answer **Before You Go On** p. 633 ❑ p. 635 ❑ p. 643 ❑ p. 652 ❑ p. 655 ❑
- Work **Demonstration Problem** ❑
- Review **Summary of Study Objectives** ❑
- Answer **Self-Study Questions** ❑
- Complete **Assignments** ❑

CONCEPTS FOR REVIEW

Before studying this chapter, you should know or, if necessary, review:

- The difference between the accrual basis and the cash basis of accounting. (Ch. 3, pp. 94–95)
- The major items included in a corporation's balance sheet. (Ch. 4, pp. 158–163)
- The major items included in a corporation's income statement. (Ch. 5, pp. 203–207)

☑ THE NAVIGATOR

ACCOUNTING MATTERS! **FEATURE STORY**

"Cash Is Cash, and Everything Else Is Accounting"

For Gerald Biby, vice president and chief financial officer of **Kilian Community College** in Sioux Falls, South Dakota, the statement of cash flows was the difference between being able to refinance a mortgage and being turned down by six local banks. "We recently wanted to refinance a $125,000 mortgage on a piece of property that we own," he says. "It was the statement of cash flows that finally showed our lender that we had the cash flow to service the debt."

As he explains, the traditional statement of cash flows for a not-for-profit, educational institution shows revenues and all expenditures, even the capital expenditures. According to this format, which the banks focused on initially, Kilian Community College was just breaking even. "In the business world, if we had spent $250,000 on a computer system, then we would have put that on a depreciation schedule. But in the non-profit arena, it's typical that the entire $250,000 is written off as an expense against the general fund." The statement of cash flows showed the bankers that one of the uses of funds was really the purchase of computer equipment that had several years of life.

The college's statement of cash flows has over 30 classifications including tuition, fees, and bookstore revenues. The school serves 250 students, charges $70 a credit hour (12 hours is a full-time schedule), and has five terms each year.

The bankers granted the refinancing when they saw that the college's sources of funds exceeded the loan repayments, including principal and interest, by a ratio of 3-to-1. Not only did the school get the loan, but it did so at a favorable rate. "We were able to cut the mortgage rate to prime plus 1 percent from prime plus 3 percent."

THE NAVIGATOR

STUDY OBJECTIVES

After studying this chapter, you should be able to:

1. Indicate the usefulness of the statement of cash flows.
2. Distinguish among operating, investing, and financing activities.
3. Prepare a statement of cash flows using the indirect method.
4. Prepare a statement of cash flows using the direct method.
5. Analyze the statement of cash flows.

THE NAVIGATOR

PREVIEW OF CHAPTER 14

As the story about Kilian Community College indicates, the balance sheet, income statement, and retained earnings statement do not always show the whole picture of the financial condition of a company or institution. In fact, looking at the financial statements of some well-known companies, a thoughtful investor might ask questions like these: How did **Eastman Kodak** finance cash dividends of $649 million in a year in which it earned only $17 million? How could **United Airlines** purchase new planes that cost $1.9 billion in a year in which it reported a net loss of over $2 billion? How did the companies that spent a combined fantastic $3.4 trillion on mergers and acquisitions in a recent year finance those deals? Answers to these and similar questions can be found in this chapter, which illustrates the statement of cash flows.

The content and organization of this chapter are as follows.

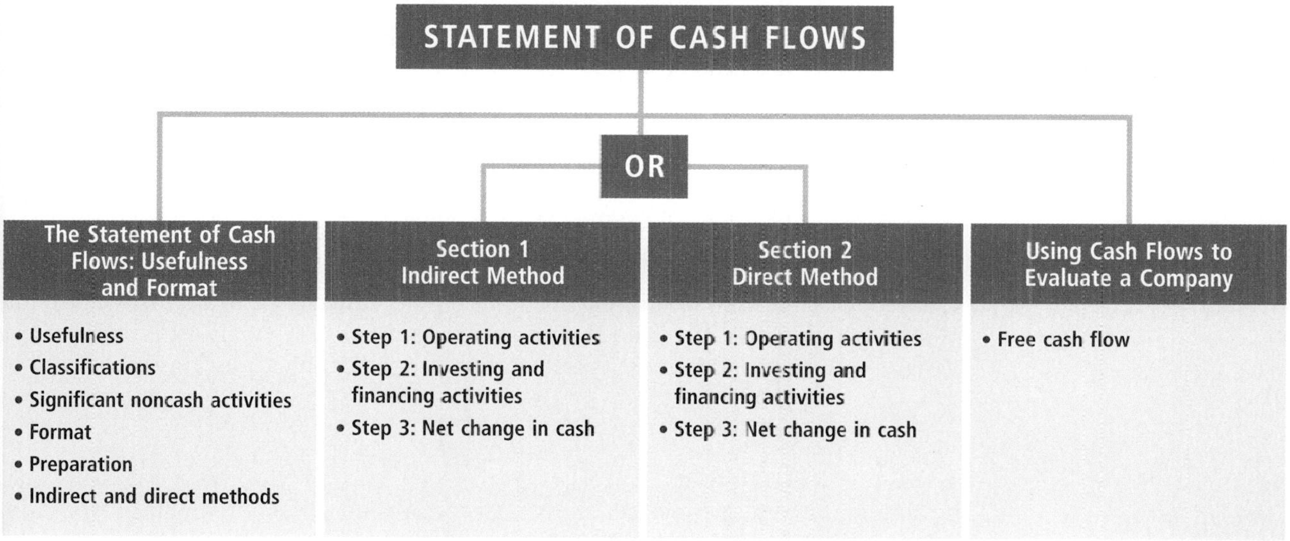

THE NAVIGATOR

The Statement of Cash Flows: Usefulness and Format

The basic financial statements we have presented so far provide only limited information about a company's cash flows (cash receipts and cash payments). For example, comparative balance sheets show the increase in property, plant, and equipment during the year. But they do not show how the additions were financed or paid for. The income statement shows net income. But it does not indicate the amount of cash generated by operating activities. The retained earnings statement shows cash dividends declared but not the cash dividends paid during the year. None of these statements presents a detailed summary of where cash came from and how it was used.

HELPFUL HINT

Recall that the retained earnings statement is often presented in the statement of stockholders' equity.

STUDY OBJECTIVE 1

Indicate the usefulness of the statement of cash flows.

Usefulness of the Statement of Cash Flows

The **statement of cash flows** reports the cash receipts, cash payments, and net change in cash resulting from operating, investing, and financing activities during a period. The information in a statement of cash flows should help investors, creditors, and others assess:

1. **The entity's ability to generate future cash flows.** By examining relationships between items in the statement of cash flows, investors and others can make predictions of the amounts, timing, and uncertainty of future cash flows better than they can from accrual basis data.
2. **The entity's ability to pay dividends and meet obligations.** If a company does not have adequate cash, it cannot pay employees, settle debts, or pay dividends. Employees, creditors, and stockholders should be particularly interested in this statement, because it alone shows the flows of cash in a business.
3. **The reasons for the difference between net income and net cash provided (used) by operating activities.** Net income provides information on the success or failure of a business enterprise. However, some are critical of accrual basis net income because it requires many estimates. As a result, the reliability of the number is often challenged. Such is not the case with cash. Many readers of the statement of cash flows want to know the reasons for the difference between net income and net cash provided by operating activities. Then they can assess for themselves the reliability of the income number.
4. **The cash investing and financing transactions during the period.** By examining a company's investing and financing transactions, a financial statement reader can better understand why assets and liabilities changed during the period.

ETHICS NOTE

Many believe that cash flow is less susceptible to management manipulation than traditional accounting measures such as net income. Though we would discourage reliance on cash flows to the exclusion of accrual accounting, comparing cash from operations to net income can reveal important information about the "quality" of reported net income. Such a comparison can reveal the extent to which net income provides a good measure of actual performance.

Classification of Cash Flows

STUDY OBJECTIVE 2

Distinguish among operating, investing, and financing activities.

The statement of cash flows classifies cash receipts and cash payments as operating, investing, and financing activities. Transactions and other events characteristic of each kind of activity are described in the list below.

1. **Operating activities** include the cash effects of transactions that create revenues and expenses. They thus enter into the determination of net income.
2. **Investing activities** include (a) acquiring and disposing of investments and property, plant, and equipment, and (b) lending money and collecting the loans.
3. **Financing activities** include (a) obtaining cash from issuing debt and repaying the amounts borrowed, and (b) obtaining cash from stockholders and providing them with a return on their investment.

The category of operating activities is the most important. As noted above, it shows the cash provided by company operations. This source of cash is generally considered to be the best measure of a company's ability to generate sufficient cash to continue as a going concern.

Illustration 14-1 on page 631 lists typical cash receipts and cash payments within each of the three classifications. **Study the list carefully.** It will prove very useful in solving homework exercises and problems.

Illustration 14-1
Typical receipts and payments classified by business activity and shown in the statement of cash flows

Types of Cash Inflows and Outflows

Operating activities—Income statement items
Cash inflows:
From sale of goods or services.
From returns on loans (interest received) and on equity securities (dividends received).
Cash outflows:
To suppliers for inventory.
To employees for services.
To government for taxes.
To lenders for interest.
To others for expenses.

Investing activities—Changes in investments and long-term assets
Cash inflows:
From sale of property, plant, and equipment.
From sale of debt or equity securities of other entities.
From collection of principal on loans to other entities.
Cash outflows:
To purchase property, plant, and equipment.
To purchase debt or equity securities of other entities.
To make loans to other entities.

Financing activities—Changes in long-term liabilities and stockholders' equity
Cash inflows:
From sale of common stock.
From issuance of debt (bonds and notes).
Cash outflows:
To stockholders as dividends.
To redeem long-term debt or reacquire capital stock.

Operating activities

Investing activities

Financing activities

Note the following general guidelines: (1) Operating activities involve income statement items. (2) Investing activities involve cash flows resulting from changes in investments and long-term asset items. (3) Financing activities involve cash flows resulting from changes in long-term liability and stockholders' equity items.

Some cash flows related to investing or financing activities are classified as operating activities. For example, receipts of investment revenue (interest and dividends) are classified as operating activities. So are payments of interest to lenders. Why are these considered operating activities? **Because these items are reported in the income statement, where results of operations are shown.**

Significant Noncash Activities

Not all of a company's significant activities involve cash. Examples of significant noncash activities are:

1. Issuance of common stock to purchase assets.
2. Conversion of bonds into common stock.
3. Issuance of debt to purchase assets.
4. Exchanges of plant assets.

Significant financing and investing activities that do not affect cash are not reported in the body of the statement of cash flows. However, these activities are reported in either a **separate schedule** at the bottom of the statement of cash flows or in a **separate note or supplementary schedule** to the financial statements.

HELPFUL HINT

Do not include **noncash** investing and financing activities in the body of the statement of cash flows. Report this information in a separate schedule.

The reporting of these noncash activities in a separate schedule satisfies the **full disclosure principle**. In solving homework assignments you should present significant noncash investing and financing activities in a separate schedule at the bottom of the statement of cash flows. (See lower section of Illustration 14-2, below, for an example.)

ACCOUNTING MATTERS! Business Insight

Net income is not the same as net cash provided by operations. The differences are illustrated by the following results from annual reports for 2003 ($ in millions). Note the wide disparity among these companies that all engaged in similar types of retail merchandising.

Company	Net Income	Net Cash Provided by Operations
Kmart Corporation	$ 248	$ 736
Wal-Mart Stores, Inc.	9,054	15,946
JCPenney Company, Inc.	(928)	812
Sears, Roebuck & Co.	3,397	2,524
Target Corporation	1,841	3,160

? For all but one of the companies listed above, the cash-basis amount "Net cash provided by operations," from the statement of cash flows, is much greater than the accrual-basis amount "Net income," from the income statement. What explanation can you give for this difference?

Format of the Statement of Cash Flows

The general format of the statement of cash flows presents the results of the three activities discussed previously—operating, investing, and financing—plus the significant noncash investing and financing activities. A widely used form of the statement of cash flows is shown in Illustration 14-2.

Illustration 14-2
Format of statement of cash flows

COMPANY NAME
Statement of Cash Flows
Period Covered

Cash flows from operating activities		
(List of individual items)	XX	
Net cash provided (used) by operating activities		XXX
Cash flows from investing activities		
(List of individual inflows and outflows)	XX	
Net cash provided (used) by investing activities		XXX
Cash flows from financing activities		
(List of individual inflows and outflows)	XX	
Net cash provided (used) by financing activities		XXX
Net increase (decrease) in cash		XXX
Cash at beginning of period		XXX
Cash at end of period		XXX
Noncash investing and financing activities		
(List of individual noncash transactions)		XXX

The cash flows from operating activities section always appears first. It is followed by the investing activities and the financing activities sections.

BEFORE YOU GO ON...

Review It

1. What is the primary purpose of a statement of cash flows?
2. Why is the statement of cash flows useful?
3. What are the major classifications of cash flows on the statement of cash flows?
4. In its 2003 statement of cash flows, what amounts are reported by **PepsiCo** for: (1) net cash provided by operating activities, (2) net cash used for investing activities, and (3) net cash used for financing activities? The answer to this question is provided on page 684.
5. What are some examples of significant noncash activities?
6. What is the general format of the statement of cash flows? In what sequence are the three types of business activities presented?

Do It

During its first week, Duffy & Stevenson Company had these transactions.

1. Issued 100,000 shares of $5 par value common stock for $800,000 cash.
2. Borrowed $200,000 from Castle Bank, signing a 5-year note bearing 8% interest.
3. Purchased two semi-trailer trucks for $170,000 cash.
4. Paid employees $12,000 for salaries and wages.
5. Collected $20,000 cash for services rendered.

Classify each of these transactions by type of cash flow activity.

ACTION PLAN

- Identify the three types of activities used to report all cash inflows and outflows.
- Report as operating activities the cash effects of transactions that create revenues and expenses and enter into the determination of net income.
- Report as investing activities transactions that (a) acquire and dispose of investments and productive long-lived assets and (b) lend money and collect loans.
- Report as financing activities transactions that (a) obtain cash from issuing debt and repay the amounts borrowed and (b) obtain cash from stockholders and pay them dividends.

SOLUTION

1. Financing activity
2. Financing activity
3. Investing activity
4. Operating activity
5. Operating activity

Related exercise material: *BE14-3, BE14-5, E14-1, and E14-6.*

THE NAVIGATOR

Preparing the Statement of Cash Flows

The statement of cash flows is prepared differently from the three other basic financial statements. First, it is not prepared from an adjusted trial balance. The statement requires detailed information concerning the changes in account balances that occurred between two points in time. An adjusted trial balance will not provide the necessary data. Second, the statement of cash flows deals with cash receipts and payments. As a result, the effects of the use of accrual accounting **must be adjusted to determine cash flows**.

The information to prepare this statement usually comes from three sources:

- **Comparative balance sheets.** Information in the comparative balance sheets indicates the amount of the changes in assets, liabilities, and stockholders' equities from the beginning to the end of the period.
- **Current income statement.** Information in this statement helps determine the amount of cash provided or used by operations during the period.
- **Additional information.** Such information includes transaction data that are needed to determine how cash was provided or used during the period.

Preparing the statement of cash flows from these data sources involves three major steps, explained in Illustration 14-3.

Illustration 14-3
Three major steps in preparing the statement of cash flows

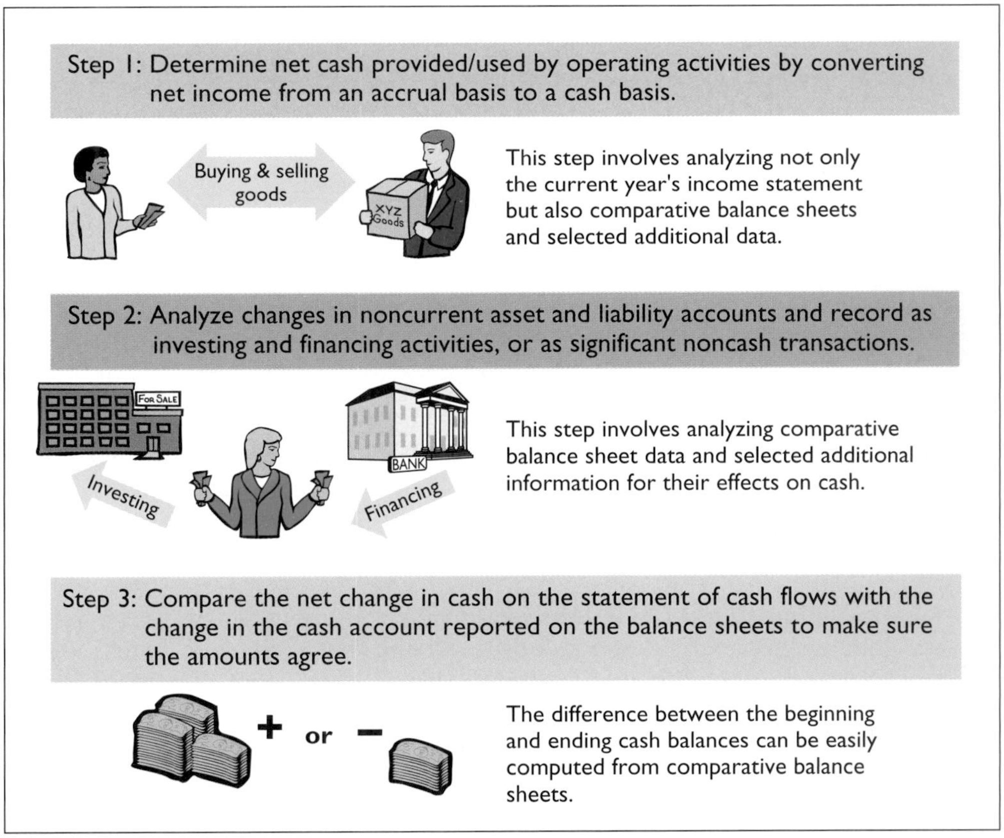

Step 1: Determine net cash provided/used by operating activities by converting net income from an accrual basis to a cash basis.
Buying & selling goods
XYZ Goods
This step involves analyzing not only the current year's income statement but also comparative balance sheets and selected additional data.
Step 2: Analyze changes in noncurrent asset and liability accounts and record as investing and financing activities, or as significant noncash transactions.
For Sale
Bank
Investing
Financing
This step involves analyzing comparative balance sheet data and selected additional information for their effects on cash.
Step 3: Compare the net change in cash on the statement of cash flows with the change in the cash account reported on the balance sheets to make sure the amounts agree.
+ or −
The difference between the beginning and ending cash balances can be easily computed from comparative balance sheets.

Indirect and Direct Methods

In order to perform step 1, **net income must be converted from an accrual basis to a cash basis**. This conversion may be done by either of two methods: (1) the indirect method or (2) the direct method. **Both methods arrive at the same total amount** for "Net cash provided by operating activities." They differ in **how** they arrive at the amount.

The indirect method is used extensively in practice, as shown in the nearby chart.[1] Companies (98.8%) favor the indirect method for two reasons: (1) It is easier and less costly to prepare, and (2) it focuses on the differences between net income and net cash flow from operating activities.

The direct method shows operating cash receipts and payments, making it more consistent with the objective of a statement of cash flows. The FASB has expressed a preference for the direct method, but allows the use of either method.

Usage of Methods

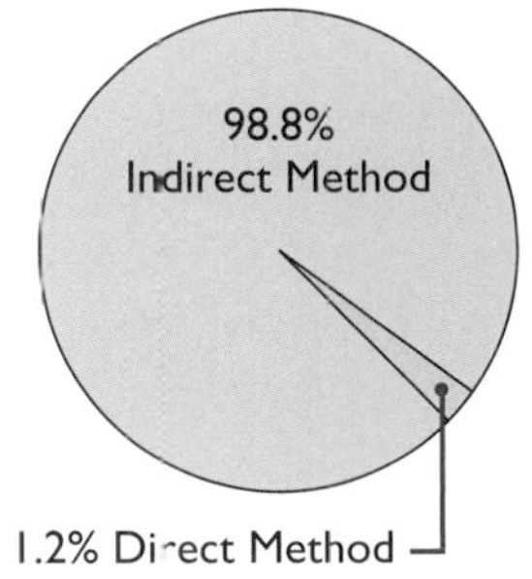

BEFORE YOU GO ON...

Review It

1. What is the primary difference between the indirect and direct approaches to the statement of cash flows? Which method is more commonly used in practice?
2. What are the three major steps in the preparation of a statement of cash flows?

THE NAVIGATOR

ACCOUNTING MATTERS! Ethics Insight

During the 1990s, analysts increasingly used cash-flow-based measures of income, such as cash flow provided by operations, instead of or in addition to net income. The reason for the change was that they were losing faith in accrual-accounting-based net income numbers. Sadly, these days even cash flow from operations isn't always what it seems to be. For example, in 2002 **WorldCom, Inc.** disclosed that it had improperly capitalized expenses: It moved $3.8 billion of cash outflows from the "Cash from operating activities" section of the cash flow statement to the "Investing activities" section, thereby greatly enhancing cash provided by operating activities. Similarly, in 2002 **Dynegy, Inc.** restated its cash flow statement for 2001 so that $300 million tied to its complex natural gas trading operation was removed from cash flow from operations and instead put into the financing section—a drop of 37% in cash flow from operations.

Source: Henny Sender, "Sadly, These Days Even Cash Flow Isn't Always What It Seems To Be," *Wall Street Journal Online* (May 8, 2002).

? Since these and numerous other financial accounting corrections and misstatements were reported in 2000, 2001, and 2002, what actions have been taken to curb such misdeeds?

On the following pages, in two separate sections, we describe the use of the two methods of preparation. Section 1 illustrates the indirect method. Section 2 illustrates the direct method. These sections are independent of each other. *Only one or the other* need be covered in order to understand and prepare the statement of cash flows. When you have finished the section assigned by your instructor, turn to "Using Cash Flows to Evaluate a Company" on page 654.

[1] *Accounting Trends and Techniques—2003* (New York: American Institute of Certified Public Accountants, 2003).

SECTION 1 STATEMENT OF CASH FLOWS—INDIRECT METHOD

STUDY OBJECTIVE 3

Prepare a statement of cash flows using the indirect method.

To explain how to prepare a statement of cash flows using the indirect method, we use financial information from Computer Services Company. Illustration 14-4 presents Computer Services' current and previous-year balance sheets, its current-year income statement, and related financial information.

Illustration 14-4
Comparative balance sheets, income statement, and additional information for Computer Services Company

COMPUTER SERVICES COMPANY
Comparative Balance Sheets
December 31

Assets	**2006**	**2005**	**Change in Account Balance Increase/Decrease**
Current assets			
Cash	$ 55,000	$ 33,000	$ 22,000 Increase
Accounts receivable	20,000	30,000	10,000 Decrease
Merchandise inventory	15,000	10,000	5,000 Increase
Prepaid expenses	5,000	1,000	4,000 Increase
Property, plant, and equipment			
Land	130,000	20,000	110,000 Increase
Building	160,000	40,000	120,000 Increase
Accumulated depreciation—building	(11,000)	(5,000)	6,000 Increase
Equipment	27,000	10,000	17,000 Increase
Accumulated depreciation—equipment	(3,000)	(1,000)	2,000 Increase
Total assets	$398,000	$138,000	
Liabilities and Stockholders' Equity			
Current liabilities			
Accounts payable	$ 28,000	$ 12,000	$ 16,000 Increase
Income tax payable	6,000	8,000	2,000 Decrease
Long-term liabilities			
Bonds payable	130,000	20,000	110,000 Increase
Stockholders' equity			
Common stock	70,000	50,000	20,000 Increase
Retained earnings	164,000	48,000	116,000 Increase
Total liabilities and stockholders' equity	$398,000	$138,000	

COMPUTER SERVICES COMPANY
Income Statement
For the Year Ended December 31, 2006

Revenues		$507,000
Cost of goods sold	$150,000	
Operating expenses (excluding depreciation)	111,000	
Depreciation	9,000	
Interest expense	42,000	
Loss on sale of equipment	3,000	315,000
Income before income taxes		192,000
Income tax expense		47,000
Net income		$145,000

Additional information for 2006:

1. The company declared and paid a $29,000 cash dividend.
2. Issued $110,000 of long-term bonds in exchange for land.
3. A building costing $120,000 was purchased for cash. Equipment costing $25,000 was also purchased for cash.
4. The company sold equipment with a book value of $7,000 (cost $8,000, less accumulated depreciation $1,000) for $4,000 cash.
5. Issued common stock for $20,000 cash.
6. Depreciation expense was comprised of $6,000 for building and $3,000 for equipment.

We will now apply the three steps to the information provided for Computer Services Company.

Step 1: Operating Activities

DETERMINE NET CASH PROVIDED/USED BY OPERATING ACTIVITIES BY CONVERTING NET INCOME FROM AN ACCRUAL BASIS TO A CASH BASIS

To determine net cash provided by operating activities under the **indirect method** (or reconciliation method), **net income is adjusted in numerous ways for items that did not affect cash**.

A useful starting point is to understand **why** net income must be converted to net cash provided by operating activities. Under generally accepted accounting principles, most companies use the accrual basis of accounting. As you have learned, this basis requires that revenue be recorded when earned and that expenses be recorded when incurred. Earned revenues may include credit sales that have not yet been collected in cash. Expenses incurred may include some items that have not been paid in cash. Thus, under the accrual basis of accounting, net income is not the same as net cash provided by operating activities. Therefore, under the indirect method, net income must be adjusted to convert certain items to the cash basis. Illustration 14-5 lists the three types of adjustments to net income.

Net Income	+/−	Adjustments	=	Net Cash Provided/Used by Operating Activities
		• Add back noncash expenses, such as depreciation expense, amortization, or depletion. • Deduct gains and add losses that resulted from investing and financing activities. • Analyze changes to noncash current asset and current liability accounts.		

Illustration 14-5
Three types of adjustments to convert net income to net cash provided by operating activities

The three types of adjustments are explained in the next three sections.

Depreciation Expense

Computer Services' income statement reports depreciation expense of $9,000. Although depreciation expense reduces net income, it does not reduce cash. In other words, depreciation expense is a noncash charge. It is added back to net income to

HELPFUL HINT

Depreciation is similar to any other expense in that it reduces net income. It differs in that it does not involve a current cash outflow; that is why it must be *added back* to net income to arrive at cash provided by operations.

arrive at net cash provided by operating activities. Depreciation expense is reported as follows in the statement of cash flows.

Illustration 14-6
Adjustment for depreciation

Cash flows from operating activities	
Net income	$145,000
Adjustments to reconcile net income to net cash provided by operating activities:	
Depreciation expense	**9,000**
Net cash provided by operating activities	$154,000

Depreciation and similar noncash charges such as amortization of intangible assets, and depletion expense are frequently listed in the statement of cash flows as the first adjustments to net income.

Loss on Sale of Equipment

Computer Services' income statement reports a $3,000 loss on the sale of equipment (book value $7,000, less cash received from sale of equipment $4,000). Illustration 14-1 states that cash received from the sale of plant assets should be reported in the investing activities section. Because of this, **all gains and losses must be eliminated from net income to arrive at cash from operating activities**. In our example, Computer Services Company's loss of $3,000 should not be included in the operating activities section of the statement of cash flows. Illustration 14-7 shows that the $3,000 loss is eliminated by adding $3,000 back to net income to arrive at net cash provided by operating activities.

Illustration 14-7
Adjustment for loss on sale of equipment

Cash flows from operating activities		
Net income		$145,000
Adjustments to reconcile net income to net cash provided by operating activities:		
Depreciation expense	$9,000	
Loss on sale of equipment	**3,000**	12,000
Net cash provided by operating activities		$157,000

If a gain on sale occurs, the gain is deducted from net income in order to determine net cash provided by operating activities. **In the case of either a gain or a loss, the actual amount of cash received from the sale is reported as a source of cash in the investing activities section of the statement of cash flows.**

Changes to Noncash Current Asset and Current Liability Accounts

A final adjustment in reconciling net income to net cash provided by operating activities involves examining all changes in current asset and current liability accounts. The accrual accounting process records revenues in the period earned and expenses in the period incurred. For example, Accounts Receivable is used to record amounts owed to the company for sales that have been made and cash collections that have not yet been received. The Prepaid Insurance account is used to reflect insurance that has been paid for, but which has not yet expired, and therefore has not been expensed. Similarly, the Salaries Payable account reflects salaries expense that has been incurred by the company but has not been paid. As a result, we need to adjust net income for these accruals and prepayments to determine net cash provided by operating activities. Thus we must analyze the change in each current asset and current liability account to determine its impact on net income and cash.

Changes in Noncash Current Assets

The adjustments required for changes in noncash current asset accounts are as follows: **Increases in current asset accounts are deducted from net income, and decreases in current asset accounts are added to net income, to arrive at net cash provided by operating activities.** We can observe these relationships by analyzing the accounts of Computer Services Company.

DECREASE IN ACCOUNTS RECEIVABLE. Computer Services Company's accounts receivable decreased by $10,000 (from $30,000 to $20,000) during the period. For Computer Services Company this means that cash receipts were $10,000 higher than revenues. Illustration 14-8 shows that Computer Services Company had $507,000 in revenues (as reported on the income statement), but it collected $517,000 in cash. As shown in Illustration 14-9 (on page 640), to adjust net income to net cash provided by operating activities, the decrease of $10,000 in accounts receivable is added to net income.

Illustration 14-8
Analysis of accounts receivable

Accounts Receivable				
1/1/06	Balance	30,000	**Receipts from customers**	**517,000**
	Revenues	**507,000**		
12/31/06	Balance	20,000		

When the Accounts Receivable balance increases, cash receipts are lower than revenue earned under the accrual basis. Therefore, the amount of the increase in accounts receivable is deducted from net income to arrive at net cash provided by operating activities.

INCREASE IN MERCHANDISE INVENTORY. Computer Services Company's Merchandise Inventory balance increased $5,000 (from $10,000 to $15,000) during the period. The Merchandise Inventory account reflects the difference between the amount of inventory that has been purchased and the amount which has been sold. For Computer Services this means that the cost of merchandise purchased exceeded the cost of goods sold by $5,000. As a result, cost of goods sold does not reflect $5,000 of cash payments made for merchandise. This inventory increase of $5,000 during the period is deducted from net income to arrive at net cash provided by operating activities (see Illustration 14-9, next page). If inventory decreases, the amount of the change is added to net income to arrive at net cash provided by operating activities.

INCREASE IN PREPAID EXPENSES. Prepaid expenses increased during the period by $4,000. This means that cash paid for expenses is higher than expenses reported on an accrual basis. Cash payments have been made in the current period, but expenses (as charges to the income statement) have been deferred to future periods. To adjust net income to net cash provided by operating activities, the $4,000 increase in prepaid expenses is deducted from net income (see Illustration 14-9).

If prepaid expenses decrease, reported expenses are higher than the expenses paid. Therefore, the decrease in prepaid expense is added to net income to arrive at net cash provided by operating activities.

Illustration 14-9
Adjustments for changes in current asset accounts

Cash flows from operating activities		
Net income		$145,000
Adjustments to reconcile net income to net cash provided by operating activities:		
Depreciation expense	$ 9,000	
Loss on sale of equipment	3,000	
Decrease in accounts receivable	**10,000**	
Increase in merchandise inventory	**(5,000)**	
Increase in prepaid expenses	**(4,000)**	13,000
Net cash provided by operating activities		$158,000

Changes in Current Liabilities

The adjustments required for changes in current liability accounts are as follows: **Increases in current liability accounts are added to net income, and decreases in current liability accounts are deducted from net income, to arrive at net cash provided by operating activities.**

INCREASE IN ACCOUNTS PAYABLE. For Computer Services Company, Accounts Payable increased by $16,000 during the period. That means the company received $16,000 more in goods than it actually paid for. As shown in Illustration 14-10, to adjust net income to determine net cash provided by operating activities, the $16,000 increase in Accounts Payable is added to net income.

DECREASE IN INCOME TAX PAYABLE. When a company incurs income tax expense but has not yet paid its taxes, it records income tax payable. A change in the Income Tax Payable account reflects the difference between income tax expense incurred and income tax actually paid. Computer Services' Income Tax Payable account decreased by $2,000. That means the $47,000 of income tax expense reported on the income statement was $2,000 less than the amount of taxes paid during the period of $49,000. As shown in Illustration 14-10, to adjust net income to a cash basis, net income must be reduced by $2,000.

Illustration 14-10
Adjustments for changes in current liability accounts

Cash flows from operating activities		
Net income		$145,000
Adjustments to reconcile net income to net cash provided by operating activities:		
Depreciation expense	$ 9,000	
Loss on sale of equipment	3,000	
Decrease in accounts receivable	10,000	
Increase in merchandise inventory	(5,000)	
Increase in prepaid expenses	(4,000)	
Increase in accounts payable	**16,000**	
Decrease in income tax payable	**(2,000)**	27,000
Net cash provided by operating activities		$172,000

Illustration 14-10 shows that, after starting with net income of $145,000, the sum of all of the adjustments to net income was $27,000. This resulted in net cash provided by operating activities of $172,000.

Summary of Conversion to Net Cash Provided by Operating Activities—Indirect Method

The statement of cash flows prepared by the indirect method starts with net income. It then adds or deducts items to arrive at net cash provided by operating activities. The required adjustments are of three types: (1) noncash charges such as depreciation, amortization, and depletion; (2) gains and losses resulting from investing and financing activities; and (3) changes in noncash current asset and current liability accounts. A summary of these changes is provided in Illustration 14-11.

		Adjustment Required to Convert Net Income to Net Cash Provided by Operating Activities
Noncash Charges	Depreciation expense	Add
	Patent amortization expense	Add
	Depletion expense	Add
Gains and Losses	Loss on sale of plant asset	Add
	Gain on sale of plant asset	Deduct
Changes in Current Assets and Current Liabilities	Increase in current asset account	Deduct
	Decrease in current asset account	Add
	Increase in current liability account	Add
	Decrease in current liability account	Deduct

Illustration 14-11
Adjustments required to convert net income to net cash provided by operating activities

Step 2: Investing and Financing Activities

ANALYZE CHANGES IN NONCURRENT ASSET AND LIABILITY ACCOUNTS AND RECORD AS INVESTING AND FINANCING ACTIVITIES, OR AS NONCASH INVESTING AND FINANCING ACTIVITIES

INCREASE IN LAND. As indicated from the change in the Land account and the additional information, land of $110,000 was purchased through the issuance of long-term bonds. The issuance of bonds payable for land has no effect on cash. But it is a significant noncash investing and financing activity that merits disclosure in a separate schedule.

HELPFUL HINT

The investing and financing activities are measured and reported in the same manner under both the direct and indirect methods.

INCREASE IN BUILDING. As the additional data indicate, a building was acquired for $120,000 cash. This is a cash outflow reported in the investing section.

INCREASE IN EQUIPMENT. The Equipment account increased $17,000. The additional information explains that this was a net increase that resulted from two transactions: (1) a purchase of equipment of $25,000 and (2) the sale for $4,000 of equipment costing $8,000. These transactions are classified as investing activities. Each transaction should be reported separately. Thus the purchase of equipment should be reported as an outflow of cash for $25,000. The sale should be reported as an inflow of cash for $4,000. The T account below shows the reasons for the change in this account during the year.

Equipment				
1/1/06	Balance	10,000	Cost of equipment sold	8,000
	Purchase of equipment	**25,000**		
12/31/06	Balance	27,000		

Illustration 14-12
Analysis of equipment

The following entry shows the details of the equipment sale transaction.

Cash	4,000	
Accumulated Depreciation	1,000	
Loss on Sale of Equipment	3,000	
Equipment		8,000

A	=	L	+	SE
+4,000				−3,000 Exp
+1,000				
−8,000				

Cash Flows
+4,000

HELPFUL HINT

When stocks or bonds are issued for cash, the actual proceeds will appear in the statement of cash flows as a financing inflow (rather than the par value of the stocks or face value of bonds).

INCREASE IN BONDS PAYABLE. The Bonds Payable account increased $110,000. As indicated in the additional information, land was acquired from the issuance of these bonds. This noncash transaction is reported in a separate schedule at the bottom of the statement.

INCREASE IN COMMON STOCK. The balance sheet reports an increase in Common Stock of $20,000. The additional information section notes that this increase resulted from the issuance of new shares of stock. This is a cash inflow reported in the financing section.

INCREASE IN RETAINED EARNINGS. Retained earnings increased $116,000 during the year. This increase can be explained by two factors: (1) Net income of $145,000 increased retained earnings. (2) Dividends of $29,000 decreased retained earnings. Net income is adjusted to net cash provided by operating activities in the operating activities section. Payment of the dividends is a **cash outflow that is reported as a financing activity**.

Statement of Cash Flows—2006

Using the previous information, we can now prepare a statement of cash flows for 2006 for Computer Services Company as shown in Illustration 14-13.

Illustration 14-13
Statement of cash flows, 2006—indirect method

COMPUTER SERVICES COMPANY
Statement of Cash Flows—Indirect Method
For the Year Ended December 31, 2006

Cash flows from operating activities		
Net income		$145,000
Adjustments to reconcile net income to net cash provided by operating activities:		
Depreciation expense	$ 9,000	
Loss on sale of equipment	3,000	
Decrease in accounts receivable	10,000	
Increase in merchandise inventory	(5,000)	
Increase in prepaid expenses	(4,000)	
Increase in accounts payable	16,000	
Decrease in income tax payable	(2,000)	27,000
Net cash provided by operating activities		172,000
Cash flows from investing activities		
Purchase of building	(120,000)	
Purchase of equipment	(25,000)	
Sale of equipment	4,000	
Net cash used by investing activities		(141,000)
Cash flows from financing activities		
Issuance of common stock	20,000	
Payment of cash dividends	(29,000)	
Net cash used by financing activities		(9,000)
Net increase in cash		22,000
Cash at beginning of period		33,000
Cash at end of period		$ 55,000
Noncash investing and financing activities		
Issuance of bonds payable to purchase land		$110,000

HELPFUL HINT

Note that in the investing and financing activities sections, positive numbers indicate cash inflows (receipts), and negative numbers indicate cash outflows (payments).

Step 3: Net Change in Cash

COMPARE THE NET CHANGE IN CASH ON THE STATEMENT OF CASH FLOWS WITH THE CHANGE IN THE CASH ACCOUNT REPORTED ON THE BALANCE SHEETS TO MAKE SURE THE AMOUNTS AGREE

Illustration 14-13 indicates that the net change in cash during the period was an increase of $22,000. This agrees with the change in the Cash account reported on the balance sheets in Illustration 14-4 (page 636).

BEFORE YOU GO ON...

Review It

1. What is the format of the operating activities section of the statement of cash flows using the indirect method?
2. Where is depreciation expense shown on a statement of cash flows using the indirect method?
3. Where are significant noncash investing and financing activities shown in a statement of cash flows? Give some examples.

Do It

Presented below is information related to Reynolds Company. Use it to prepare a statement of cash flows using the **indirect method**.

REYNOLDS COMPANY
Comparative Balance Sheets
December 31

Assets	**2005**	**2004**	**Change Increase/Decrease**
Cash	$ 54,000	$ 37,000	$ 17,000 Increase
Accounts receivable	68,000	26,000	42,000 Increase
Inventories	54,000	-0-	54,000 Increase
Prepaid expenses	4,000	6,000	2,000 Decrease
Land	45,000	70,000	25,000 Decrease
Buildings	200,000	200,000	-0-
Accumulated depreciation—buildings	(21,000)	(11,000)	10,000 Increase
Equipment	193,000	68,000	125,000 Increase
Accumulated depreciation—equipment	(28,000)	(10,000)	18,000 Increase
Totals	$569,000	$386,000	
Liabilities and Stockholders' Equity			
Accounts payable	$ 23,000	$ 40,000	$ 17,000 Decrease
Accrued expenses payable	10,000	-0-	10,000 Increase
Bonds payable	110,000	150,000	40,000 Decrease
Common stock ($1 par)	220,000	60,000	160,000 Increase
Retained earnings	206,000	136,000	70,000 Increase
Totals	$569,000	$386,000	

REYNOLDS COMPANY
Income Statement
For the Year Ended December 31, 2005

Revenues		$890,000
Cost of goods sold	$465,000	
Operating expenses	221,000	
Interest expense	12,000	
Loss on sale of equipment	2,000	700,000
Income before income taxes		190,000
Income tax expense		65,000
Net income		$125,000

Additional information

1. Operating expenses include depreciation expense of $33,000 and charges from prepaid expenses of $2,000.
2. Land was sold at its book value for cash.
3. Cash dividends of $55,000 were declared and paid in 2005.
4. Interest expense of $12,000 was paid in cash.
5. Equipment with a cost of $166,000 was purchased for cash. Equipment with a cost of $41,000 and a book value of $36,000 was sold for $34,000 cash.
6. Bonds of $10,000 were redeemed at their book value for cash. Bonds of $30,000 were converted into common stock.
7. Common stock ($1 par) of $130,000 was issued for cash.
8. Accounts payable pertain to merchandise suppliers.

ACTION PLAN

- Determine net cash provided/used by operating activities by converting net income from an accrual basis to a cash basis.
- Determine net cash provided/used by investing activities and financing activities.
- Determine the net increase/decrease in cash.

SOLUTION

REYNOLDS COMPANY
Statement of Cash Flows—Indirect Method
For the Year Ended December 31, 2005

Cash flows from operating activities		
Net income		$125,000
Adjustments to reconcile net income to net cash provided by operating activities:		
Depreciation expense	$ 33,000	
Loss on sale of equipment	2,000	
Increase in accounts receivable	(42,000)	
Increase in inventories	(54,000)	
Decrease in prepaid expenses	2,000	
Decrease in accounts payable	(17,000)	
Increase in accrued expenses payable	10,000	(66,000)
Net cash provided by operating activities		59,000
Cash flows from investing activities		
Sale of land	25,000	
Sale of equipment	34,000	
Purchase of equipment	(166,000)	
Net cash used by investing activities		(107,000)
Cash flows from financing activities		
Redemption of bonds	(10,000)	
Sale of common stock	130,000	
Payment of dividends	(55,000)	
Net cash provided by financing activities		65,000
Net increase in cash		17,000
Cash at beginning of period		37,000
Cash at end of period		$ 54,000
Noncash investing and financing activities		
Conversion of bonds into common stock		$ 30,000

Related exercise material: *BE14-1, BE14-2, BE14-4, E14-2, E14-3, E14-4, and E14-5.*

THE NAVIGATOR

HELPFUL HINT

1. Determine net cash provided/used by operating activities, recognizing that operating activities generally relate to changes in current assets and current liabilities.
2. Determine net cash provided/used by investing activities, recognizing that investing activities generally relate to changes in noncurrent assets.
3. Determine net cash provided/used by financing activities, recognizing that financing activities generally relate to changes in long-term liabilities and stockholders' equity accounts.

Note: This concludes Section 1 on preparation of the statement of cash flows using the indirect method. Unless your instructor assigns Section 2, turn to the concluding section of the chapter, "Using Cash Flows to Evaluate A Company," on p. 654.

SECTION 2 STATEMENT OF CASH FLOWS—DIRECT METHOD

To explain and illustrate the direct method, we will use the transactions of Juarez Company for 2006, to prepare an annual statement of cash flows. Illustration 14-14 presents information related to 2006 for Juarez Company.

STUDY OBJECTIVE 4

Prepare a statement of cash flows using the direct method.

Illustration 14-14
Comparative balance sheets, income statement, and additional information for Juarez Company

JUAREZ COMPANY
Comparative Balance Sheets
December 31

Assets	2006	2005	Change Increase/Decrease
Cash	$191,000	$159,000	$ 32,000 Increase
Accounts receivable	12,000	15,000	3,000 Decrease
Inventory	170,000	160,000	10,000 Increase
Prepaid expenses	6,000	8,000	2,000 Decrease
Land	140,000	80,000	60,000 Increase
Equipment	160,000	-0-	160,000 Increase
Accumulated depreciation—equipment	(16,000)	-0-	16,000 Increase
Total assets	$663,000	$422,000	
Liabilities and Stockholders' Equity			
Accounts payable	$ 52,000	$ 60,000	$ 8,000 Decrease
Accrued expenses payable	15,000	20,000	5,000 Decrease
Income taxes payable	12,000	-0-	12,000 Increase
Bonds payable	130,000	-0-	130,000 Increase
Common stock	360,000	300,000	60,000 Increase
Retained earnings	94,000	42,000	52,000 Increase
Total liabilities and stockholders' equity	$663,000	$422,000	

JUAREZ COMPANY
Income Statement
For the Year Ended December 31, 2006

Revenues		$975,000
Cost of goods sold	$660,000	
Operating expenses (excluding depreciation)	176,000	
Depreciation expense	18,000	
Loss on sale of store equipment	1,000	855,000
Income before income taxes		120,000
Income tax expense		36,000
Net income		$ 84,000

Additional information

1. In 2006, the company declared and paid a $32,000 cash dividend.
2. Bonds were issued at face value for $130,000 in cash.
3. Equipment costing $180,000 was purchased for cash.
4. Equipment costing $20,000 was sold for $17,000 cash when the book value of the equipment was $18,000.
5. Common stock of $60,000 was issued to acquire land.

To prepare a statement of cash flows under the direct approach, we will apply the three steps outlined in Illustration 14-3 (page 634).

Step 1: Operating Activities

DETERMINE NET CASH PROVIDED/USED BY OPERATING ACTIVITIES BY CONVERTING NET INCOME FROM AN ACCRUAL BASIS TO A CASH BASIS

Under the **direct method**, net cash provided by operating activities is computed by **adjusting each item in the income statement** from the accrual basis to the cash basis. To simplify and condense the operating activities section, **only major classes of operating cash receipts and cash payments are reported**. For these major classes, the difference between cash receipts and cash payments is the net cash provided by operating activities. These relationships are as shown in Illustration 14-15.

Illustration 14-15
Major classes of cash receipts and payments

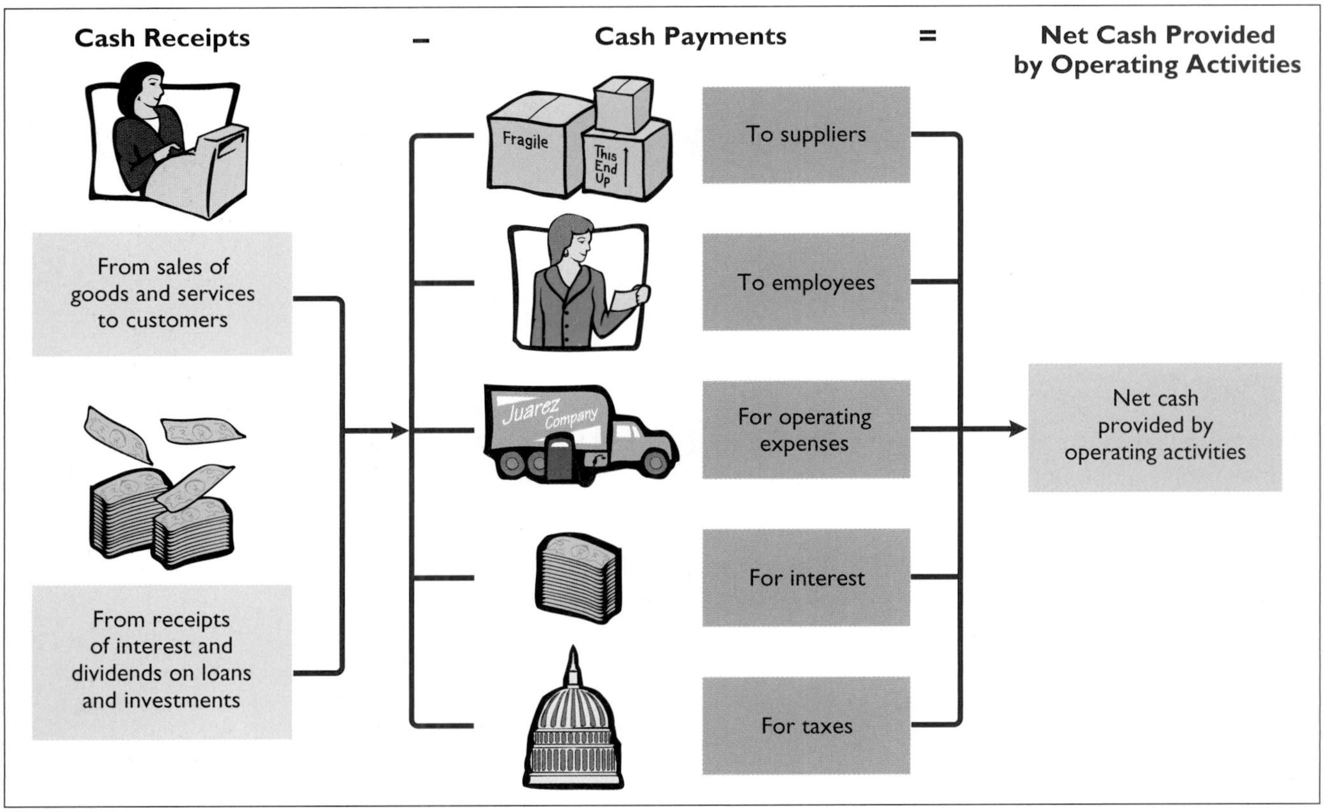

An efficient way to apply the direct method is to analyze the items reported in the income statement in the order in which they are listed. Cash receipts and cash payments related to these revenues and expenses are then determined. The direct method adjustments for Juarez Company in 2006 to determine net cash provided by operating activities are presented on the following pages.

CASH RECEIPTS FROM CUSTOMERS. The income statement for Juarez Company reported revenues from customers of $975,000. How much of that was cash receipts? To answer, it is necessary to consider the change in accounts receivable during the year. When accounts receivable increase during the year, revenues on an accrual basis are higher than cash receipts from customers. Operations led to revenues, but not all of these revenues resulted in cash receipts. To determine the amount of cash receipts, the increase in accounts receivable is deducted from sales revenues. On the other hand, there may be a decrease in accounts receivable. That would occur if cash receipts from customers exceeded sales revenues. In that case, the decrease in accounts receivable is added to sales revenues.

For Juarez Company, accounts receivable decreased S3,000. Thus, cash receipts from customers were $978,000, computed as follows.

Revenues from sales	$975,000
Add: Decrease in accounts receivable	3,000
Cash receipts from customers	**$978,000**

Illustration 14-16
Computation of cash receipts from customers

Cash receipts from customers may also be determined from an analysis of the Accounts Receivable account, as shown in Illustration 14-17.

Accounts Receivable				
1/1/06	Balance	15,000	**Receipts from customers**	**978,000**
	Revenues from sales	975,000		
12/31/06	Balance	12,000		

Illustration 14-17
Analysis of accounts receivable

HELPFUL HINT

The T account shows that revenue plus decrease in receivables equals cash receipts.

The relationships among cash receipts from customers, revenues from sales, and changes in accounts receivable are shown in Illustration 14-18.

$$\text{Cash Receipts from Customers} = \text{Revenues from Sales} \begin{cases} + \text{ Decrease in Accounts Receivable} \\ \text{or} \\ - \text{ Increase in Accounts Receivable} \end{cases}$$

Illustration 14-18
Formula to compute cash receipts from customers—direct method

CASH PAYMENTS TO SUPPLIERS. Juarez Company reported cost of goods sold of $660,000 on its income statement. How much of that was cash payments to suppliers? To answer, it is first necessary to find purchases for the year. To find purchases, cost of goods sold is adjusted for the change in inventory. When inventory increases during the year, purchases for the year have exceeded cost of goods sold. As a result, to determine the amount of purchases, the increase in inventory is added to cost of goods sold.

In 2006, Juarez Company's inventory increased $10,000. Purchases are computed as follows.

Cost of goods sold	$660,000
Add: Increase in inventory	10,000
Purchases	**$670,000**

Illustration 14-19
Computation of purchases

After purchases are computed, cash payments to suppliers can be determined. This is done by adjusting purchases for the change in accounts payable. When accounts payable increase during the year, purchases on an accrual basis are higher than they are on a cash basis. As a result, to determine cash payments to suppliers, an increase in accounts payable is deducted from purchases. On the other hand, there may be a decrease in accounts payable. That would occur if cash payments to suppliers exceed purchases. In that case, the decrease in accounts payable is added to purchases.

For Juarez Company, cash payments to suppliers were $468,000, computed as follows.

Illustration 14-20
Computation of cash payments to suppliers

Purchases	$670,000
Add: Decrease in accounts payable	8,000
Cash payments to suppliers	**$678,000**

Cash payments to suppliers may also be determined from an analysis of the Accounts Payable account as shown in Illustration 14-21.

Illustration 14-21
Analysis of accounts payable

Accounts Payable

Payments to suppliers	**678,000**	1/1/06	Balance	60,000
			Purchases	670,000
		12/31/06	Balance	52,000

HELPFUL HINT

The T account shows that purchases plus decrease in accounts payable equals payments to suppliers.

The relationships among cash payments to suppliers, cost of goods sold, changes in inventory, and changes in accounts payable are shown in the following formula.

Illustration 14-22
Formula to compute cash payments to suppliers—direct method

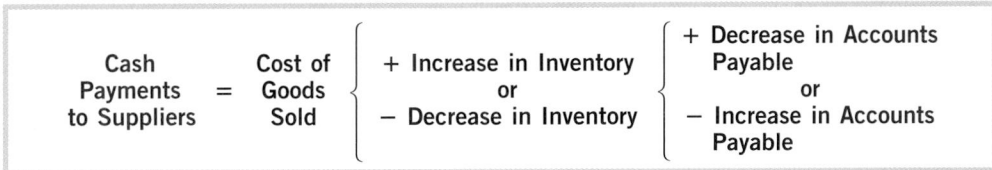

$$\text{Cash Payments to Suppliers} = \text{Cost of Goods Sold} \begin{Bmatrix} + \text{ Increase in Inventory} \\ \text{or} \\ - \text{ Decrease in Inventory} \end{Bmatrix} \begin{Bmatrix} + \text{ Decrease in Accounts Payable} \\ \text{or} \\ - \text{ Increase in Accounts Payable} \end{Bmatrix}$$

CASH PAYMENTS FOR OPERATING EXPENSES. Operating expenses of $176,000 were reported on Juarez's income statement. How much of that amount was cash paid for operating expenses? To answer, we need to adjust this amount for any changes in prepaid expenses and accrued expenses payable. For example, if prepaid expenses increased during the year, cash paid for operating expenses is higher than operating expenses reported on the income statement. To convert operating expenses to cash payments for operating expenses, the increase must be added to operating expenses. On the other hand, if prepaid expenses decrease during the year, the decrease must be deducted from operating expenses.

Operating expenses must also be adjusted for changes in accrued expenses payable. When accrued expenses payable increase during the year, operating expenses on an accrual basis are higher than they are on a cash basis. As a result, to determine cash payments for operating expenses, an increase in accrued expenses payable is deducted from operating expenses. On the other hand, a decrease in accrued expenses payable is added to operating expenses because cash payments exceed operating expenses.

Juarez Company's cash payments for operating expenses were $179,000, computed as follows.

Illustration 14-23
Computation of cash payments for operating expenses

Operating expenses	$176,000
Deduct: Decrease in prepaid expenses	(2,000)
Add: Decrease in accrued expenses payable	5,000
Cash payments for operating expenses	**$179,000**

The relationships among cash payments for operating expenses, changes in prepaid expenses, and changes in accrued expenses payable are shown in the following formula.

Illustration 14-24
Formula to compute cash payments for operating expenses—direct method

Cash Payments for Operating Expenses = Operating Expenses { + Increase in Prepaid Expenses or − Decrease in Prepaid Expenses } { + Decrease in Accrued Expenses Payable or − Increase in Accrued Expenses Payable }

DEPRECIATION EXPENSE AND LOSS ON SALE OF EQUIPMENT. Operating expenses are shown exclusive of depreciation. Depreciation expense in 2006 was $18,000. Depreciation expense is not shown on a statement of cash flows because it is a noncash charge. If the amount for operating expenses includes depreciation expense, operating expenses must be reduced by the amount of depreciation to determine cash payments for operating expenses.

The loss on sale of equipment of $1,000 is also a noncash charge. The loss on sale of equipment reduces net income, but it does not reduce cash. Thus, the loss on sale of equipment is not reported on a statement of cash flows.

Other charges to expense that do not require the use of cash, such as the amortization of intangible assets, depletion expense, and bad debt expense, are treated in the same manner as depreciation.

CASH PAYMENTS FOR INCOME TAXES. Income tax expense reported on the income statement was $36,000. Income taxes payable, however, increased $12,000. This increase means that $12,000 of the income taxes have not been paid. As a result, income taxes paid were less than income taxes reported in the income statement. Cash payments for income taxes were, therefore, $24,000 as shown below.

Illustration 14-25
Computation of cash payments for income taxes

Income tax expense	$36,000
Deduct: Increase in income taxes payable	12,000
Cash payments for income taxes	**$24,000**

The relationships among cash payments for income taxes, income tax expense, and changes in income taxes payable are shown in the following formula.

Illustration 14-26
Formula to compute cash payments for income taxes—direct method

Cash Payments for Income Taxes = Income Tax Expense { + Decrease in Income Taxes Payable or − Increase in Income Taxes Payable }

The results of the previous analysis are presented in the operating activities section of the statement of cash flows of Juarez Company in Illustration 14-27.

Illustration 14-27
Operating activities section of the statement of cash flows

Cash flows from operating activities		
Cash receipts from customers		$978,000
Cash payments:		
To suppliers	$678,000	
For operating expenses	179,000	
For income taxes	24,000	881,000
Net cash provided by operating activities		$ 97,000

When the direct method is used, the net cash flows from operating activities as computed under the indirect method must also be provided in a separate schedule (not shown here).

Step 2: Investing and Financing Activities

ANALYZE CHANGES IN NONCURRENT ASSET AND LIABILITY ACCOUNTS AND RECORD AS INVESTING AND FINANCING ACTIVITIES, OR AS SIGNIFICANT NONCASH TRANSACTIONS

INCREASE IN LAND. Land increased $60,000. The additional information section indicates that common stock was issued to purchase the land. The issuance of common stock for land has no effect on cash. But it is a **significant noncash investing and financing transaction**. This transaction requires disclosure in a separate schedule at the bottom of the statement of cash flows.

INCREASE IN EQUIPMENT. The comparative balance sheets show that equipment increased $160,000 in 2006. The additional information in Illustration 14-14 (page 645) indicates that the increase resulted from two investing transactions: (1) Equipment costing $180,000 was purchased for cash. And (2) equipment costing $20,000 was sold for $17,000 cash when its book value was $18,000. The relevant data for the statement of cash flows is the cash paid for the purchase and the cash proceeds from the sale. For Juarez Company, the investing activities section will show the following: The $180,000 purchase of equipment as an outflow of cash, and the $17,000 sale of equipment as an inflow of cash. The two amounts **should not be netted. Both individual outflows and inflows of cash should be shown.**

The analysis of the changes in equipment should include the related Accumulated Depreciation account. These two accounts for Juarez Company are shown in Illustration 14-28.

Illustration 14-28
Analysis of equipment and related accumulated depreciation

Equipment

1/1/06	Balance	–0–	Cost of equipment sold	20,000
	Cash purchase	**180,000**		
12/31/06	Balance	160,000		

Accumulated Depreciation—Equipment

Sale of equipment	2,000	1/1/06	Balance	–0–
			Depreciation expense	18,000
		12/31/06	Balance	16,000

INCREASE IN BONDS PAYABLE. Bonds Payable increased $130,000. The additional information in Illustration 14-14 indicated that bonds with a face value of $130,000 were issued for $130,000 cash. The issuance of bonds is a financing activity. For Juarez Company, there is an inflow of cash of $130,000 from the issuance of bonds.

INCREASE IN COMMON STOCK. The Common Stock account increased $60,000. The additional information indicated that land was acquired from the issuance of common stock. This transaction is a **significant noncash investing and financing transaction** that should be reported separately at the bottom of the statement.

INCREASE IN RETAINED EARNINGS. The $52,000 net increase in Retained Earnings resulted from net income of $84,000 and the declaration and payment of a cash dividend of $32,000. **Net income is not reported in the statement of cash flows under the direct method.** Cash dividends paid of $32,000 are reported in the financing activities section as an outflow of cash.

Statement of Cash Flows—2006

The statement of cash flows for Juarez Company is shown in Illustration 14-29.

Illustration 14-29
Statement of cash flows, 2006—direct method

JUAREZ COMPANY
Statement of Cash Flows—Direct Method
For the Year Ended December 31, 2006

Cash flows from operating activities		
Cash receipts from customers		$ 978,000
Cash payments:		
To suppliers	$ 678,000	
For operating expenses	179,000	
For income taxes	24,000	881,000
Net cash provided by operating activities		97,000
Cash flows from investing activities		
Purchase of equipment	(180,000)	
Sale of equipment	17,000	
Net cash used by investing activities		(163,000)
Cash flows from financing activities		
Issuance of bonds payable	130,000	
Payment of cash dividends	(32,000)	
Net cash provided by financing activities		98,000
Net increase in cash		32,000
Cash at beginning of period		159,000
Cash at end of period		$ 191,000
Noncash investing and financing activities		
Issuance of common stock to purchase land		$ 60,000

Step 3: Net Change in Cash

COMPARE THE NET CHANGE IN CASH ON THE STATEMENT OF CASH FLOWS WITH THE CHANGE IN THE CASH ACCOUNT REPORTED ON THE BALANCE SHEETS TO MAKE SURE THE AMOUNTS AGREE

Illustration 14-29 indicates that the net change in cash during the period was an increase of $32,000. This agrees with the change in balances in the cash account reported on the balance sheets in Illustration 14-14.

BEFORE YOU GO ON...

Review It

1. What is the format of the operating activities section of the statement of cash flows using the direct method?
2. Where is depreciation expense shown on a statement of cash flows using the direct method?
3. Where are significant noncash investing and financing activities shown on a statement of cash flows? Give some examples.

Do It

Presented below is information related to Reynolds Company. Use it to prepare a statement of cash flows using the **direct method**.

REYNOLDS COMPANY
Comparative Balance Sheets
December 31

Assets	2006	2005	Change Increase/Decrease
Cash	$ 54,000	$ 37,000	$ 17,000 Increase
Accounts receivable	68,000	26,000	42,000 Increase
Inventories	54,000	–0–	54,000 Increase
Prepaid expenses	4,000	6,000	2,000 Decrease
Land	45,000	70,000	25,000 Decrease
Buildings	200,000	200,000	–0–
Accumulated depreciation—buildings	(21,000)	(11,000)	10,000 Increase
Equipment	193,000	68,000	125,000 Increase
Accumulated depreciation—equipment	(28,000)	(10,000)	18,000 Increase
Totals	$569,000	$386,000	
Liabilities and Stockholders' Equity			
Accounts payable	$ 23,000	$ 40,000	$ 17,000 Decrease
Accrued expenses payable	10,000	–0–	10,000 Increase
Bonds payable	110,000	150,000	40,000 Decrease
Common stock ($1 par)	220,000	60,000	160,000 Increase
Retained earnings	206,000	136,000	70,000 Increase
Totals	$569,000	$386,000	

REYNOLDS COMPANY
Income Statement
For the Year Ended December 31, 2006

Revenues		$890,000
Cost of goods sold	$465,000	
Operating expenses	221,000	
Interest expense	12,000	
Loss on sale of equipment	2,000	700,000
Income before income taxes		190,000
Income tax expense		65,000
Net income		$125,000

Additional information:

1. Operating expenses include depreciation expense of $33,000 and charges from prepaid expenses of $2,000.

2. Land was sold at its book value for cash.
3. Cash dividends of $55,000 were declared and paid in 2006.
4. Interest expense of $12,000 was paid in cash.
5. Equipment with a cost of $166,000 was purchased for cash. Equipment with a cost of $41,000 and a book value of $36,000 was sold for $34,000 cash.
6. Bonds of $10,000 were redeemed at their book value for cash. Bonds of $30,000 were converted into common stock.
7. Common stock ($1 par) of $130,000 was issued for cash.
8. Accounts payable pertain to merchandise suppliers.

ACTION PLAN

- Determine net cash provided/used by operating activities by adjusting each item in the income statement from the accrual basis to the cash basis.
- Determine net cash provided/used by investing activities.
- Determine net cash provided/used by financing activities.
- Determine the net increase/decrease in cash.

SOLUTION

REYNOLDS COMPANY
Statement of Cash Flows—Direct Method
For the Year Ended December 31, 2006

Cash flows from operating activities		
Cash receipts from customers		$848,000[a]
Cash payments:		
To suppliers	$536,000[b]	
For operating expenses	176,000[c]	
For interest expense	12,000	
For income taxes	65,000	789,000
Net cash provided by operating activities		59,000
Cash flows from investing activities		
Sale of land	25,000	
Sale of equipment	34,000	
Purchase of equipment	(166,000)	
Net cash used by investing activities		(107,000)
Cash flows from financing activities		
Redemption of bonds	(10,000)	
Sale of common stock	130,000	
Payment of dividends	(55,000)	
Net cash provided by financing activities		65,000
Net increase in cash		17,000
Cash at beginning of period		37,000
Cash at end of period		$ 54,000
Noncash investing and financing activities		
Conversion of bonds into common stock		$ 30,000

Computations:
[a]$848,000 = $890,000 − $42,000
[b]$536,000 = $465,000 + $54,000 + $17,000
[c]$176,000 = $221,000 − $33,000 − $2,000 − $10,000

Technically, an additional schedule reconciling net income to net cash provided by operating activities should be presented as part of the statement of cash flows when using the direct method (not shown here).

Related exercise material: *BE14-6, BE14-7, BE14-8, E14-7, E14-8, E14-9, and E14-10.*

THE NAVIGATOR

HELPFUL HINT

1. Determine net cash provided/used by operating activities, recognizing that each item in the income statement must be adjusted to the cash basis.
2. Determine net cash provided/used by investing activities, recognizing that investing activities generally relate to changes in noncurrent assets.
3. Determine net cash provided/used by financing activities, recognizing that financing activities generally relate to changes in long-term liabilities and stockholders' equity accounts.

Note: This concludes Section 2 on preparation of the statement of cash flows using the direct method. You should now proceed to the concluding section of the chapter, "Using Cash Flows to Evaluate a Company."

Using Cash Flows to Evaluate a Company

STUDY OBJECTIVE 5

Analyze the statement of cash flows.

Traditionally, the ratios most commonly used by investors and creditors have been based on accrual accounting. In this section we introduce a cash-flow measure of analysis—free cash flow.

Free Cash Flow

In the statement of cash flows, cash provided by operating activities is intended to indicate the cash-generating capability of the company. Analysts have noted, however, that **cash provided by operating activities fails to take into account that a company must invest in new fixed assets** just to maintain its current level of operations. Companies also must at least **maintain dividends at current levels** to satisfy investors. A measurement to provide additional insight regarding a company's cash generating ability is free cash flow. **Free cash flow** describes the cash remaining from operations after adjustment for capital expenditures and dividends.

Consider the following example: Suppose that MPC produced and sold 10,000 personal computers this year. It reported $100,000 cash provided by operating activities. In order to maintain production at 10,000 computers, MPC invested $15,000 in equipment. It chose to pay $5,000 in dividends. Its free cash flow was $80,000 ($100,000 − $15,000 − $5,000). The company could use this $80,000 either to purchase new assets to expand the business or to pay an $80,000 dividend and continue to produce 10,000 computers. In practice, free cash flow is often calculated with the formula in Illustration 14-30. Alternative definitions also exist.

Illustration 14-30
Free cash flow

Free Cash Flow = **Cash Provided by Operations** − **Capital Expenditures** − **Cash Dividends**

Illustration 14-31 provides basic information excerpted from the 2002 statement of cash flows of **Microsoft Corporation**.

Illustration 14-31
Microsoft cash flow information ($ in millions)

MICROSOFT CORPORATION
Statement of Cash Flows (partial)
2002 (in millions)

Cash provided by operations		$11,426
Cash flows from investing activities		
Additions to property, plant, and equipment	$ (879)	
Purchases of investments	(42,290)	
Sales of investments	33,777	
Cash used by investing activities		(9,392)
Cash paid for dividends on preferred stock		(13)

Microsoft's free cash flow is calculated as shown in Illustration 14-32.

Illustration 14-32
Calculation of Microsoft's free cash flow ($ in millions)

Cash provided by operating activities	$11,426
Less: Expenditures on property, plant, and equipment	879
Dividends paid	13
Free cash flow	$10,534

This free cash flow of $10.534 billion is a tremendous amount of cash generated in a single year. It is available for the acquisition of new assets, the retirement of stock or debt, or the payment of dividends. It should also be noted that this amount far exceeds Microsoft's 2002 net income of $9,421 million. This lends additional credibility to Microsoft's income number as an indicator of potential future performance. If anything, Microsoft's net income might understate its actual performance.

Oracle Corporation is the world's largest seller of database software and information management services. Like Microsoft, its success depends on continuing to improve its existing products while developing new products to keep pace with rapid changes in technology. Oracle's free cash flow for 2002 was $2.965 billion. This is impressive, but significantly less than Microsoft's amazing ability to generate cash.

BEFORE YOU GO ON...

Review It

1. What is the difference between cash from operations and free cash flow?
2. What does it mean if a company has negative free cash flow?

☑ THE NAVIGATOR

DEMONSTRATION PROBLEM

The income statement for the year ended December 31, 2006, for John Kosinski Manufacturing Company contains the following condensed information.

JOHN KOSINSKI MANUFACTURING COMPANY
Income Statement

Revenues		$6,583,000
Operating expenses (excluding depreciation)	$4,920,000	
Depreciation expense	880,000	5,800,000
Income before income taxes		783,000
Income tax expense		353,000
Net income		$ 430,000

Included in operating expenses is a $24,000 loss resulting from the sale of machinery for $270,000 cash. Machinery was purchased at a cost of $750,000.

The following balances are reported on Kosinski's comparative balance sheets at December 31.

JOHN KOSINSKI MANUFACTURING COMPANY
Comparative Balance Sheets (partial)

	2006	2005
Cash	$672,000	$130,000
Accounts receivable	775,000	610,000
Inventories	834,000	867,000
Accounts payable	521,000	501,000

Income tax expense of $353,000 represents the amount paid in 2006. Dividends declared and paid in 2006 totaled $200,000.

Instructions

(a) Prepare the statement of cash flows using the indirect method.

OR

(b) Prepare the statement of cash flows using the direct method.

ACTION PLAN

- Apply the same data to the preparation of a statement of cash flows under both the indirect and direct methods.
- Note the similarities of the two methods: Both methods report the same information in the investing and financing sections.
- Note the differences between the two methods: The cash flows from operating activities sections report different information (but the amount of net cash provided by operating activities is the same for both methods).

SOLUTION TO DEMONSTRATION PROBLEM

(a)

JOHN KOSINSKI MANUFACTURING COMPANY
Statement of Cash Flows—**Indirect Method**
For the Year Ended December 31, 2006

Cash flows from operating activities		
Net income		$ 430,000
Adjustments to reconcile net income to net cash provided by operating activities:		
Depreciation expense	$ 880,000	
Loss on sale of machinery	24,000	
Increase in accounts receivable	(165,000)	
Decrease in inventories	33,000	
Increase in accounts payable	20,000	792,000
Net cash provided by operating activities		1,222,000
Cash flows from investing activities		
Sale of machinery	270,000	
Purchase of machinery	(750,000)	
Net cash used by investing activities		(480,000)
Cash flows from financing activities		
Payment of cash dividends		(200,000)
Net increase in cash		542,000
Cash at beginning of period		130,000
Cash at end of period		$ 672,000

(b)

JOHN KOSINSKI MANUFACTURING COMPANY
Statement of Cash Flows—**Direct Method**
For the Year Ended December 31, 2006

Cash flows from operating activities		
Cash receipts from customers		$6,418,000*
Cash payments:		
For operating expenses	$4,843,000**	
For income taxes	353,000	5,196,000
Net cash provided by operating activities		1,222,000
Cash flows from investing activities		
Sale of machinery	270,000	
Purchase of machinery	(750,000)	
Net cash used by investing activities		(480,000)
Cash flows from financing activities		
Payment of cash dividends		(200,000)
Net increase in cash		542,000
Cash at beginning of period		130,000
Cash at end of period		$ 672,000

Direct Method Computations:

* Computation of cash receipts from customers:	
Revenues per the income statement	$6,583,000
Less increase in accounts receivable	165,000
Cash receipts from customers	$6,418,000
** Computation of cash payments for operating expenses:	
Operating expenses per the income statement	$4,920,000
Deduct loss from sale of machinery	(24,000)
Deduct decrease in inventories	(33,000)
Deduct increase in accounts payable	(20,000)
Cash payments for operating expenses	$4,843,000

THE NAVIGATOR

SUMMARY OF STUDY OBJECTIVES

1. **Indicate the usefulness of the statement of cash flows.** The statement of cash flows provides information about the cash receipts and cash payments during a period. A secondary objective is to provide information about the operating, investing, and financing activities during the period.
2. **Distinguish among operating, investing, and financing activities.** Operating activities include the cash effects of transactions that enter into the determination of net income. Investing activities involve cash flows resulting from changes in investments and long-term asset items. Financing activities involve cash flows resulting from changes in long-term liability and stockholders' equity items.
3. **Prepare a statement of cash flows using the indirect method.** The preparation of a statement of cash flows involves three major steps: (1) Determine net cash provided/used by operating activities, by converting net income from an accrual basis to a cash basis. (2) Analyze changes in noncurrent asset and liability accounts and record as investing and financing activities or as significant noncash transactions. (3) Compare the net change in cash on the statement of cash flows with the change in the cash account reported on the balance sheets, to make sure the amounts agree.
4. **Prepare a statement of cash flows using the direct method.** The preparation of the statement of cash flows involves three major steps: (1) Determine net cash provided/used by operating activities, by converting net income from an accrual basis to a cash basis. (2) Analyze changes in noncurrent asset and liability accounts and record as investing and financing activities or as significant noncash transactions. (3) Compare the net change in cash on the statement of cash flows with the change in the cash account reported on the balance sheets, to make sure the amounts agree.
5. **Analyze the statement of cash flows.** The statement of cash flows can be used for cash-based ratio analysis. Free cash flow provides information about a company's cash-generating capabilities. It is calculated as cash from operations less capital expenditures and cash dividends.

THE NAVIGATOR

GLOSSARY

Direct method A method of determining the net cash provided by operating activities by adjusting each item in the income statement from the accrual basis to the cash basis. (p. 646).

Financing activities Cash flow activities that include (a) obtaining cash from issuing debt and repaying the amounts borrowed and (b) obtaining cash from stockholders and providing them with a return on their investment. (p. 630).

Free cash flow Cash provided by operating activities adjusted for capital expenditures and dividends paid. (p. 654).

Indirect method A method of preparing a statement of cash flows in which net income is adjusted for items that did not affect cash, to determine net cash provided by operating activities. (p. 637).

Investing activities Cash flow activities that include (a) acquiring and disposing of investments and productive long-lived assets and (b) lending money and collecting on the loans. (p. 630).

Operating activities Cash flow activities that include the cash effects of transactions that create revenues and expenses and thus enter into the determination of net income. (p. 630).

Statement of cash flows A financial statement that provides information about the cash receipts and cash payments of an entity during a period, classified as operating, investing, and financing activities, in a format that reconciles the beginning and ending cash balances. (p. 630).

APPENDIX USING A WORK SHEET TO PREPARE THE STATEMENT OF CASH FLOWS—INDIRECT METHOD

STUDY OBJECTIVE 6

Explain the guidelines and procedural steps in using a work sheet to prepare the statement of cash flows using the indirect method.

When preparing a statement of cash flows, numerous adjustments of net income may be necessary. In such cases, **a work sheet is often used to assemble and classify the data that will appear on the statement**. The work sheet is merely an aid in the preparation of the statement. Its use is optional. The skeleton format of the work sheet for preparation of the statement of cash flows is shown in Illustration 14A-1 on the next page.

Illustration 14A-1
Format of work sheet

XYZ COMPANY
Work Sheet
Statement of Cash Flows
For the Year Ended . . .

Balance Sheet Accounts	Beginning Balances	Reconciling Items Debits	Reconciling Items Credits	Ending Balances
Debit balance accounts	XX	XX	XX	XX
	XX	XX	XX	XX
Totals	XXX			XXX
Credit balance accounts	XX	XX	XX	XX
	XX	XX	XX	XX
Totals	XXX			XXX
Statement of Cash Flows Effects				
Operating activities				
Net income		XX		
Adjustments to net income		XX	XX	
Investing activities				
Receipts and payments		XX	XX	
Financing activities				
Receipts and payments		XX	XX	
Totals		XXX	XXX	
Increase (decrease) in cash		(XX)	XX	
Totals		XXX	XXX	

The following guidelines are important in using a work sheet.

1. In the balance sheet accounts section, **accounts with debit balances are listed separately from those with credit balances**. This means, for example, that Accumulated Depreciation is listed under credit balances and not as a contra account under debit balances. The beginning and ending balances of each account are entered in the appropriate columns. The transactions that caused the change in the account balance during the year are entered as reconciling items in the two middle columns.

   After all reconciling items have been entered, each line pertaining to a balance sheet account should "foot across." That is, the beginning balance plus or minus the reconciling item(s) must equal the ending balance. When this agreement exists for all balance sheet accounts, all changes in account balances have been reconciled.

2. The bottom portion of the work sheet consists of the operating, investing, and financing activities sections. It provides the information necessary to prepare the formal statement of cash flows. **Inflows of cash are entered as debits in the reconciling columns. Outflows of cash are entered as credits in the reconciling columns.** Thus, in this section, the sale of equipment for cash at book value is entered as a debit under investing activities. Similarly, the purchase of land for cash is entered as a credit under investing activities.

3. **The reconciling items shown in the work sheet are not entered in any journal or posted to any account.** They do not represent either adjustments or corrections of the balance sheet accounts. They are used only to facilitate the preparation of the statement of cash flows.

Preparing the Work Sheet

As in the case of work sheets illustrated in earlier chapters, the preparation of a work sheet involves a series of prescribed steps. The steps in this case are:

1. Enter in the balance sheet accounts section the balance sheet accounts and their beginning and ending balances.
2. Enter in the reconciling columns of the work sheet the data that explain the changes in the balance sheet accounts other than cash and their effects on the statement of cash flows.
3. Enter on the cash line and at the bottom of the work sheet the increase or decrease in cash. This entry should make the totals of the reconciling columns agree.

To illustrate the preparation of a work sheet, we will use the 2006 data for Computer Services Company. Your familiarity with these data should help you understand the use of a work sheet. For ease of reference, the comparative balance sheets, income statement, and selected data for 2006 are presented in Illustration 14A-2, below and on the next page.

Illustration 14A-2
Comparative balance sheets, income statement, and additional information for Computer Services Company

COMPUTER SERVICES COMPANY
Comparative Balance Sheets
December 31

Assets	**2006**	**2005**	**Change in Account Balance Increase/Decrease**
Current assets			
Cash	$ 55,000	$ 33,000	$ 22,000 Increase
Accounts receivable	20,000	30,000	10,000 Decrease
Merchandise inventory	15,000	10,000	5,000 Increase
Prepaid expenses	5,000	1,000	4,000 Increase
Property, plant, and equipment			
Land	130,000	20,000	110,000 Increase
Building	160,000	40,000	120,000 Increase
Accumulated depreciation—building	(11,000)	(5,000)	6,000 Increase
Equipment	27,000	10,000	17,000 Increase
Accumulated depreciation—equipment	(3,000)	(1,000)	2,000 Increase
Total assets	$398,000	$138,000	
Liabilities and Stockholders' Equity			
Current liabilities			
Accounts payable	$ 28,000	$ 12,000	$ 16,000 Increase
Income tax payable	6,000	8,000	2,000 Decrease
Long-term liabilities			
Bonds payable	130,000	20,000	110,000 Increase
Stockholders' equity			
Common stock	70,000	50,000	20,000 Increase
Retained earnings	164,000	48,000	116,000 Increase
Total liabilities and stockholders' equity	$398,000	$138,000	

Illustration 14A-2
(continued)

COMPUTER SERVICES COMPANY
Income Statement
For the Year Ended December 31, 2006

Revenues		$507,000
Cost of goods sold	$150,000	
Operating expenses (excluding depreciation)	111,000	
Depreciation expense	9,000	
Interest expense	42,000	
Loss on sale of equipment	3,000	315,000
Income before income taxes		192,000
Income tax expense		47,000
Net income		$145,000

Additional information for 2006:

1. The company declared and paid a $29,000 cash dividend.
2. Issued $110,000 of long-term bonds in exchange for land.
3. A building costing $120,000 was purchased for cash. Equipment costing $25,000 was also purchased for cash.
4. The company sold equipment with a book value of $7,000 (cost $8,000, less accumulated depreciation $1,000) for $4,000 cash.
5. Issued common stock for $20,000 cash.
6. Depreciation expense was comprised of $6,000 for building and $3,000 for equipment.

Determining the Reconciling Items

Several approaches may be used to determine the reconciling items. For example, the changes affecting net cash provided by operating activities can be completed first, and then the effects of financing and investing transactions can be determined. Or, the balance sheet accounts can be analyzed in the order in which they are listed on the work sheet. We will follow this latter approach for Computer Services, except for cash. As indicated above, **cash is handled last**.

Accounts Receivable

The decrease of $10,000 in accounts receivable means that cash collections from revenues are higher than the revenues reported in the income statement. To convert net income to net cash provided by operating activities, the decrease of $10,000 is added to net income. The entry in the reconciling columns of the work sheet is:

(a)	Operating—Decrease in Accounts Receivable	10,000	
	Accounts Receivable		10,000

Merchandise Inventory

Computer Services Company's Merchandise Inventory balance increases $5,000 during the period. The Merchandise Inventory account reflects the difference between the amount of inventory that has been purchased and the amount which has been sold. For Computer Services this means that the cost of merchandise purchased exceeds the cost of goods sold by $5,000. As a result, cost of goods sold does not reflect $5,000 of cash payments made for merchandise. This inventory increase of $5,000 during the period is deducted from net income to arrive at net cash provided by operating activities. The work sheet entry is:

(b)	Merchandise Inventory	5,000	
	Operating—Increase in Merchandise Inventory		5,000

Prepaid Expenses

An increase of $4,000 in prepaid expenses means that expenses deducted in determining net income are less than expenses that were paid in cash. The increase of $4,000 must be deducted from net income in determining net cash provided by operating activities. The work sheet entry is:

(c)	Prepaid Expenses	4,000	
	Operating—Increase in Prepaid Expenses		4,000

Land

The increase in land of $110,000 resulted from a purchase through the issuance of long-term bonds. This transaction should be reported as a significant noncash investing and financing activity. The work sheet entry is:

(d)	Land	110,000	
	Bonds Payable		110,000

HELPFUL HINT

These amounts are asterisked in the work sheet to indicate that they result from a significant noncash transaction.

Building

The cash purchase of a building for $120,000 is an investing activity cash outflow. The entry in the reconciling columns of the work sheet is:

(e)	Building	120,000	
	Investing—Purchase of Building		120,000

Equipment

The increase in equipment of $17,000 resulted from a cash purchase of $25,000 and the sale of equipment costing $8,000. The book value of the equipment was $7,000, the cash proceeds were $4,000, and a loss of $3,000 was recorded. The work sheet entries are:

(f)	Equipment	25,000	
	Investing—Purchase of Equipment		25,000
(g)	Investing—Sale of Equipment	4,000	
	Operating—Loss on Sale of Equipment	3,000	
	Accumulated Depreciation—Equipment	1,000	
	Equipment		8,000

Accounts Payable

The increase of $16,000 in accounts payable must be added to net income to determine net cash provided by operating activities. The following work sheet entry is made.

(h)	Operating—Increase in Accounts Payable	16,000	
	Accounts Payable		16,000

Income Tax Payable

When a company incurs income tax expense but has not yet paid its taxes, it records income tax payable. A change in the Income Tax Payable account reflects the difference between income tax expense incurred and income tax actually paid. Computer Services' Income Tax Payable account decreased by $2,000. That means the $47,000 of income tax expense reported on the income statement was $2,000 less than the amount of taxes paid during the period of $49,000. To adjust net income to a cash basis, net income must be reduced by $2,000. The work sheet entry is:

(i)	Income Taxes Payable	2,000	
	Operating—Decrease in Income Taxes Payable		2,000

Bonds Payable

The increase of $110,000 in this account resulted from the issuance of bonds for land. This is a significant noncash investing and financing activity. Work sheet entry (d) above is the only entry necessary.

Common Stock

The balance sheet reports an increase in Common Stock of $20,000. The additional information section notes that this increase resulted from the issuance of new shares of stock. This is a cash inflow reported in the financing section. The work sheet entry is:

(j)	Financing—Issuance of Common Stock	20,000	
	Common Stock		20,000

Accumulated Depreciation—Building, and Accumulated Depreciation—Equipment

Increases in these accounts of $6,000 and $3,000, respectively, resulted from depreciation expense. Depreciation expense is a **noncash charge that must be added to net income** to determine net cash provided by operating activities. The work sheet entries are:

(k)	Operating—Depreciation Expense—Building	6,000	
	Accumulated Depreciation—Building		6,000
(l)	Operating—Depreciation Expense—Equipment	3,000	
	Accumulated Depreciation—Equipment		3,000

Retained Earnings

The $116,000 increase in retained earnings resulted from net income of $145,000 and the declaration and payment of a $29,000 cash dividend. Net income is included in net cash provided by operating activities, and the dividends are a financing activity cash outflow. The entries in the reconciling columns of the work sheet are:

(m)	Operating—Net Income	145,000	
	Retained Earnings		145,000
(n)	Retained Earnings	29,000	
	Financing—Payment of Dividends		29,000

Disposition of Change in Cash

The firm's cash increased $22,000 in 2006. The final entry on the work sheet, therefore, is:

(o)	Cash	22,000	
	Increase in Cash		22,000

As shown in the work sheet, the increase in cash is entered in the reconciling credit column as a **balancing** amount. This entry should complete the reconciliation of the changes in the balance sheet accounts. Also, it should permit the totals of the reconciling columns to be in agreement. When all changes have been explained and the reconciling columns are in agreement, the reconciling columns are ruled to complete the work sheet. The completed work sheet for Computer Services Company is shown in Illustration 14A-3.

Illustration 14A-3
Completed work sheet—indirect method

COMPUTER SERVICES COMPANY
Work Sheet
Statement of Cash Flows
For the Year Ended December 31, 2006

Balance Sheet Accounts	Balance 12/31/05	Reconciling Items Debit	Reconciling Items Credit	Balance 12/31/06
Debits				
Cash	33,000	(o) 22,000		55,000
Accounts Receivable	30,000		(a) 10,000	20,000
Merchandise Inventory	10,000	(b) 5,000		15,000
Prepaid Expenses	1,000	(c) 4,000		5,000
Land	20,000	(d) 110,000*		130,000
Building	40,000	(e) 120,000		160,000
Equipment	10,000	(f) 25,000	(g) 8,000	27,000
Total	144,000			412,000
Credits				
Accounts Payable	12,000		(h) 16,000	28,000
Income Tax Payable	8,000	(i) 2,000		6,000
Bonds Payable	20,000		(d) 110,000*	130,000
Accumulated Depreciation—Building	5,000		(k) 6,000	11,000
Accumulated Depreciation—Equipment	1,000	(g) 1,000	(l) 3,000	3,000
Common Stock	50,000		(j) 20,000	70,000
Retained Earnings	48,000	(n) 29,000	(m) 145,000	164,000
Total	144,000			412,000
Statement of Cash Flows Effects				
Operating activities				
Net income		(m) 145,000		
Decrease in accounts receivable		(a) 10,000		
Increase in merchandise inventory			(b) 5,000	
Increase in prepaid expenses			(c) 4,000	
Increase in accounts payable		(h) 16,000		
Decrease in income tax payable			(i) 2,000	
Depreciation expense—building		(k) 6,000		
Depreciation expense—equipment		(l) 3,000		
Loss on sale of equipment		(g) 3,000		
Investing activities				
Purchase of building			(e) 120,000	
Purchase of equipment			(f) 25,000	
Sale of equipment		(g) 4,000		
Financing activities				
Issuance of common stock		(j) 20,000		
Payment of dividends			(n) 29,000	
Totals		525,000	503,000	
Increase in cash			(o) 22,000	
Totals		525,000	525,000	

*Significant noncash investing and financing activity.

Preparing the Statement

The statement of cash flows is prepared primarily from the data that appear in the work sheet under "Statement of Cash Flows Effects." The reconciling columns should also be scanned for any asterisked items that designate significant noncash activities. The formal statement was shown in Illustration 14-13 (page 642).

SUMMARY OF STUDY OBJECTIVE FOR APPENDIX

6. **Explain the guidelines and procedural steps in using a work sheet to prepare the statement of cash flows using the indirect method.** When there are numerous adjustments, a work sheet can be a helpful tool in preparing the statement of cash flows. Key guidelines for using a work sheet are: (1) List accounts with debit balances separately from those with credit balances. (2) In the reconciling columns in the bottom portion of the work sheet, show cash inflows as debits and cash outflows as credits. (3) Do not enter reconciling items in any journal or account, but use them only to help prepare the statement of cash flows.

   The steps in preparing the work sheet are: (1) Enter beginning and ending balances of balance sheet accounts. (2) Enter debits and credits in reconciling columns. (3) Enter the cash increase or decrease in Cash as a balancing amount.

*__Note:__ All **asterisked** Questions, Exercises, and Problems relate to material in the appendix to the chapter.

SELF-STUDY QUESTIONS

Self-Study/Self-Test

www.wiley.com/college/weygandt

Answers are at the end of the chapter.

(SO 1) 1. Which of the following is *incorrect* about the statement of cash flows?
- **a.** It is a fourth basic financial statement.
- **b.** It provides information about cash receipts and cash payments of an entity during a period.
- **c.** It reconciles the ending cash account balance to the balance per the bank statement.
- **d.** It provides information about the operating, investing, and financing activities of the business.

(SO 2) 2. The statement of cash flows classifies cash receipts and cash payments by the following activities:
- **a.** operating and nonoperating.
- **b.** investing, financing, and operating.
- **c.** financing, operating, and nonoperating.
- **d.** investing, financing, and nonoperating.

(SO 2) 3. An example of a cash flow from an operating activity is:
- **a.** payment of cash to lenders for interest.
- **b.** receipt of cash from the sale of capital stock.
- **c.** payment of cash dividends to the company's stockholders.
- **d.** None of the above.

(SO 2) 4. An example of a cash flow from an investing activity is:
- **a.** receipt of cash from the issuance of bonds payable.
- **b.** payment of cash to repurchase outstanding capital stock.
- **c.** receipt of cash from the sale of equipment.
- **d.** payment of cash to suppliers for inventory.

(SO 2) 5. Cash dividends paid to stockholders are classified on the statement of cash flows as:
- **a.** operating activities.
- **b.** investing activities.
- **c.** a combination of the above.
- **d.** financing activities.

6. An example of a cash flow from a financing activity is: (SO 2)
- **a.** receipt of cash from sale of land.
- **b.** issuance of debt for cash.
- **c.** purchase of equipment for cash.
- **d.** None of the above.

7. Which of the following about the statement of cash flows (SO 2)
is *incorrect?*
- **a.** The direct method may be used to report cash provided by operations.
- **b.** The statement shows the cash provided (used) for three categories of activity.
- **c.** The operating section is the last section of the statement.
- **d.** The indirect method may be used to report cash provided by operations.

Questions 8 and 9 apply only to the indirect method.

8. Net income is $132,000. During the year, accounts payable (SO 3)
increased $10,000, inventory decreased $6,000, and accounts receivable increased $12,000. Under the indirect method, net cash provided by operations is:
- **a.** $102,000.
- **b.** $112,000.
- **c.** $124,000.
- **d.** $136,000.

9. Noncash charges that are added back to net income in (SO 3)
determining cash provided by operations under the indirect method do *not* include:
- **a.** depreciation expense.
- **b.** an increase in inventory.
- **c.** amortization expense.
- **d.** loss on sale of equipment.

Questions 10 and 11 apply only to the direct method.

(SO 4) **10.** The beginning balance in accounts receivable is $44,000. The ending balance is $42,000. Sales during the period are $129,000. Cash receipts from customers are:
a. $127,000.
b. $129,000.
c. $131,000.
d. $141,000.

(SO 4) **11.** Which of the following items is reported on a cash flow statement prepared by the direct method?
a. Loss on sale of building.
b. Increase in accounts receivable.
c. Depreciation expense.
d. Cash payments to suppliers.

(SO 5) **12.** The formula for calculating free cash flow is:
a. Cash provided by operations minus interest expense and minus cash dividends.
b. Cash provided by operations minus purchases of investments and minus cash dividends.
c. Cash provided by operations minus capital expenditures and minus cash dividends.
d. Cash provided by operations minus capital expenditures and minus interest expenses.

13. The statement of cash flows should *not* be used to evaluate an entity's ability to: (SO 1)
a. earn net income.
b. generate future cash flows.
c. pay dividends.
d. meet obligations.

***14.** In a work sheet for the statement of cash flows, a decrease in accounts receivable is entered in the reconciling columns as a credit to Accounts Receivable and a debit in the: (SO 6)
a. investing activities section.
b. operating activities section.
c. financing activities section.
d. None of the above.

☑ THE NAVIGATOR

QUESTIONS

1. What is the statement of cash flows?
2. Omar Morena maintains that the statement of cash flows is an optional financial statement. Do you agree? Explain.
3. Why is the statement of cash flows useful?
4. Distinguish among the three types of activities reported in the statement of cash flows.
5. What are the major sources (inflows) of cash in a statement of cash flows? What are the major uses (outflows) of cash?
6. Why is it important to disclose certain noncash transactions? How should they be disclosed?
7. George Burns and Gracie Allen were discussing the presentation format of the statement of cash flows of Classic Comedy Co. At the bottom of Classic Comedy's statement of cash flows was a separate section entitled "Noncash investing and financing activities." Give three examples of significant noncash transactions that would be reported in this section.
8. Why is it necessary to use comparative balance sheets, a current income statement, and certain transaction data in preparing a statement of cash flows?
9. Contrast the advantages and disadvantages of the direct and indirect methods. Are both methods acceptable? Which method is preferred by the FASB? Which method is more popular?
10. When the total cash inflows exceed the total cash outflows in the statement of cash flows, how and where is this excess identified?
11. Describe the indirect method for determining net cash provided by operating activities.
12. Why is it necessary to convert accrual-based net income to cash-basis net income when preparing a statement of cash flows?
13. The president of Argot Company is puzzled. During the year, the company experienced a net loss of $800,000, yet its cash increased $300,000 during the same period. Explain to the president how this situation could occur.
14. Identify five items that are adjustments to reconcile net income to net cash provided by operating activities under the indirect method.
15. Why and how is depreciation expense reported in a statement of cash flows prepared using the indirect method?
16. Identify two noncash charges other than depreciation expense that are treated like depreciation expense in a statement of cash flows.
17. During 2006, Brett Favre Company converted $1,600,000 of its total $2,000,000 of bonds payable into common stock. Indicate how the transaction would be reported on a statement of cash flows, if at all.
18. Describe the direct method for determining net cash provided by operating activities.
19. Give the formulas under the direct method for computing (a) cash receipts from customers and (b) cash payments to suppliers.
20. George Bell Inc. reported sales of $2 million for 2006. Accounts receivable decreased $400,000 and accounts payable increased $325,000. Compute cash receipts from customers, assuming that the receivable and payable transactions related to operations.
21. Why is depreciation expense not reported in the direct-method cash flow from operating activities section?
22. What does free cash flow indicate, and how is it calculated?

*23. Why is it advantageous to use a work sheet when preparing a statement of cash flows? Is a work sheet required to prepare a statement of cash flows?

BRIEF EXERCISES

Compute cash provided by operating activities—indirect method.
(SO 3)

BE14-1 Blair Co. reported net income of $2.5 million in 2006. Depreciation for the year was $180,000, accounts receivable decreased $350,000, and accounts payable decreased $310,000. Compute net cash provided by operating activities using the indirect approach.

Compute cash provided by operating activities—indirect method.
(SO 3)

BE14-2 The net income for Karen Sepaniak Co. for 2006 was $280,000. For 2006, depreciation on plant assets was $60,000, and the company incurred a loss on sale of plant assets of $10,000. Compute net cash provided by operating activities under the indirect method.

Indicate statement presentation of selected transactions.
(SO 2)

BE14-3 Each of the following items must be considered in preparing a statement of cash flows for Catherine Janeway Co. for the year ended December 31, 2006. For each item, state how it should be shown in the statement of cash flows for 2006.

(a) Issued bonds for $300,000 cash.
(b) Purchased equipment for $140,000 cash.
(c) Sold land costing $20,000 for $20,000 cash.
(d) Declared and paid a $50,000 cash dividend.

Compute net cash provided by operating activities using indirect method.
(SO 3)

BE14-4 The comparative balance sheets for Mogilny Company show the following changes in noncash current asset accounts: accounts receivable decrease $75,000, prepaid expenses increase $16,000, and inventories increase $30,000. Compute net cash provided by operating activities using the indirect method, assuming that net income is $250,000.

Classify items by activities.
(SO 2)

BE14-5 Classify the following items as an operating, investing, or financing activity. Assume all items involve cash unless there is information to the contrary.

(a) Purchase of equipment.
(b) Sale of building.
(c) Redemption of bonds.
(d) Depreciation.
(e) Payment of dividends.
(f) Issuance of capital stock.

Compute receipts from customers using direct method.
(SO 4)

BE14-6 Beverly Crusher Co. has accounts receivable of $14,000 at January 1, 2006, and $21,000 at December 31, 2006. Sales revenues for 2006 were $470,000. What is the amount of cash receipts from customers in 2006?

Compute cash payments for income taxes using direct method.
(SO 4)

BE14-7 Pelican Company reported income taxes of $87,000 in its 2006 income statement and income taxes payable of $14,000 at December 31, 2005 and $9,000 at December 31, 2006. What amount of cash payments was made for income taxes during 2006?

Compute cash payments for operating expenses using direct method.
(SO 4)

BE14-8 Willis Company reports operating expenses of $100,000 excluding depreciation expense of $15,000 for 2006. During the year prepaid expenses decreased $6,600, and accrued expenses payable increased $2,900. Compute the cash payments for operating expenses in 2006.

Determine cash received in sale of equipment.
(SO 3, 4)

BE14-9 The T accounts for Equipment and the related Accumulated Depreciation for Wanda Landowski Company at the end of 2006 are as follows.

Equipment

Beg. bal.	80,000	Disposals	22,000
Acquisitions	41,600		
End. bal.	99,600		

Accumulated Depreciation

Disposals	5,500	Beg. bal.	44,500
		Depr.	12,000
		End. bal.	51,000

Wanda Landowski Company's income statement reported a loss on the sale of equipment of $4,100. What amount was reported on the statement of cash flows as "Cash flow from sale of equipment"?

BE14-10 The following T account is a summary of the cash account of Martinez Company.

Identify financing activity transactions.

(SO 2)

Cash (Summary Form)

Balance, 1/1/06	8,000		
Receipts from customers	364,000	Payments for goods	200,000
Dividends on stock investments	6,000	Payments for operating expenses	140,000
Proceeds from sale of equipment	36,000	Interest paid	10,000
Proceeds from issuance of bonds		Taxes paid	8,000
payable	200,000	Dividends paid	41,000
Balance, 12/31/06	215,000		

For Martinez Company what amount of net cash provided (used) by financing activities should be reported in the statement of cash flows?

BE14-11 Matt Damon Company reported cash from operations of $450,000, cash spent for capital assets of $110,000, and $40,000 of dividends paid. Calculate the free cash flow.

Calculate free cash flow.

(SO 5)

* **BE14-12** Using the data in BE14-8, indicate how the changes in prepaid expenses and accrued expenses payable should be entered in the reconciling columns of a work sheet. Assume that beginning balances were: prepaid expenses $18,600 and accrued expenses payable $8,700.

Indicate entries in work sheet.

(SO 6)

EXERCISES

E14-1 Antoine Watteau Corporation had the following transactions during 2006.

Classify transactions by type of activity.

(SO 2)

1. Issued $50,000 par value common stock for cash.
2. Collected $11,000 of accounts receivable.
3. Declared and paid a cash dividend of $25,000.
4. Sold a long-term investment with a cost of $15,000 for $15,000 cash.
5. Issued $200,000 par value common stock upon conversion of bonds having a face value of $200,000.
6. Paid $14,000 on accounts payable.
7. Purchased a machine for $30,000, giving a long-term note in exchange.

Instructions

Analyze the transactions above and indicate whether each transaction resulted in a cash flow from **(a)** operating activities, **(b)** investing activities, **(c)** financing activities, or **(d)** noncash investing and financing activities.

E14-2 Duggan Company reported net income of $195,000 for 2006. Duggan also reported depreciation expense of $25,000, and a loss of $5,000 on the sale of equipment. The comparative balance sheets show an increase in accounts receivable of $15,000 for the year, an $8,000 increase in accounts payable, and a decrease in prepaid expenses of $7,000.

Prepare the operating activities section—indirect method.

(SO 3)

Instructions

Prepare the operating activities section of the statement of cash flows for 2006 using the indirect method.

Prepare the operating activities section—indirect method.
(SO 3)

E14-3 The current sections of Blues Traveler Co. balance sheets at December 31, 2005 and 2006, are presented below.

BLUES TRAVELER CO.
Comparative Balance Sheets (partial)
December 31

	2006	2005
Current assets		
Cash	$105,000	$ 99,000
Accounts receivable	110,000	85,000
Inventory	171,000	186,000
Prepaid expenses	27,000	32,000
Total current assets	$413,000	$402,000
Current liabilities		
Accrued expenses payable	$ 15,000	$ 5,000
Accounts payable	$ 88,000	$ 92,000
Total current liabilities	$103,000	$ 97,000

Blues Traveler's net income for 2006 was $163,000. Depreciation expense was $30,000.

Instructions
Prepare the operating activities section of Blues Traveler's statement of cash flows for the year ended December 31, 2006, using the indirect method.

Prepare a partial statement of cash flows—indirect method.
(SO 3)

E14-4 Presented below are three accounts that appear in the general ledger of Karen Weller Co. during 2006.

Equipment

Date		Debit	Credit	Balance
Jan. 1	Balance			160,000
July 31	Purchase of equipment	70,000		230,000
Sept. 2	Cost of equipment constructed	53,000		283,000
Nov. 10	Cost of equipment sold		45,000	238,000

Accumulated Depreciation—Equipment

Date		Debit	Credit	Balance
Jan. 1	Balance			71,000
Nov. 10	Accumulated depreciation on equipment sold	35,000		36,000
Dec. 31	Depreciation for year		24,000	60,000

Retained Earnings

Date		Debit	Credit	Balance
Jan. 1	Balance			105,000
Aug. 23	Dividends (cash)	14,000		91,000
Dec. 31	Net income		61,000	152,000

Instructions
From the postings in the accounts above, indicate how the information is reported on a statement of cash flows by preparing a partial statement of cash flows using the indirect method. The loss on sale of equipment was $6,000.

E14-5 Comparative balance sheets for Will Smith Company are presented below.

Prepare a statement of cash flows—indirect method.

(SO 3, 5)

WILL SMITH COMPANY
Comparative Balance Sheets
December 31

Assets	2006	2005
Cash	$ 58,000	$ 22,000
Accounts receivable	85,000	76,000
Inventories	180,000	189,000
Land	80,000	100,000
Equipment	260,000	200,000
Accumulated depreciation	(66,000)	(42,000)
Total	$597,000	$545,000
Liabilities and Stockholders' Equity		
Accounts payable	$ 34,000	$ 47,000
Bonds payable	150,000	200,000
Common stock ($1 par)	194,000	164,000
Retained earnings	219,000	134,000
Total	$597,000	$545,000

Additional information:

1. Net income for 2006 was $125,000.
2. Cash dividends of $40,000 were declared and paid.
3. Bonds payable amounting to $50,000 were redeemed for cash $50,000.
4. Common stock was issued for $30,000 cash.
5. Depreciation expense was $24,000.
6. Sales for the year were $978,000.

Instructions

(a) Prepare a statement of cash flows for 2006 using the indirect method.
(b) Compute free cash flow.

E14-6 An analysis of comparative balance sheets, the current year's income statement, and the general ledger accounts of Homer Winslow Corp. uncovered the following items. Assume all items involve cash unless there is information to the contrary.

Classify transactions by type of activity.

(SO 2)

1. Issuance of capital stock.
2. Amortization of patent.
3. Issuance of bonds for land.
4. Payment of interest on notes payable.
5. Conversion of bonds into common stock.
6. Sale of land at a loss.
7. Receipt of dividends on investment in stock.
8. Purchase of land.
9. Payment of dividends.
10. Sale of building at book value.
11. Exchange of land for patent.
12. Depreciation.
13. Redemption of bonds.
14. Receipt of interest on notes receivable.

Instructions

Indicate how the above items should be classified in the statement of cash flows using the following four major classifications: operating activity (indirect method), investing activity, financing activity, and significant noncash investing and financing activity.

E14-7 R. L. Stein Company has just completed its first year of operations on December 31, 2006. Its initial income statement showed that R. L. Stein had revenues of $137,000 and operating expenses of $81,000. Accounts receivable at year-end were $42,000. Accounts payable at year-end were $37,000. Assume that accounts payable related to operating expenses. Ignore income taxes.

Compute cash provided by operating activities—direct method.

(SO 4)

Instructions

Compute net cash provided by operating activities using the direct method.

Compute cash payments—direct method.
(SO 4)

E14-8 The income statement for Alatorre Company shows cost of goods sold of $317,000 and operating expenses (exclusive of depreciation) of $250,000. The comparative balance sheets for the two years show that inventory increased $6,000, prepaid expenses decreased $6,000, accounts payable (merchandise suppliers) decreased $8,000, and accrued expenses payable increased $8,000.

Instructions
Using the direct method, compute (a) cash payments to suppliers and (b) cash payments for operating expenses.

Compute cash flow from operating activities—direct method.
(SO 2, 4)

E14-9 The 2006 accounting records of Eduardo Co. reveal the following transactions and events.

Payment of interest	$ 4,000	Collection of accounts receivable	$170,000
Cash sales	38,000	Payment of salaries and wages	65,000
Receipt of dividend revenue	14,000	Depreciation expense	24,000
Payment of income taxes	15,000	Proceeds from sale of aircraft	812,000
Net income	38,000	Purchase of equipment for cash	22,000
Payment of accounts payable for merchandise	90,000	Loss on sale of aircraft	3,000
		Payment of dividends	14,000
Payment for land	74,000	Payment of operating expenses	20,000

Instructions
Prepare the cash flows from operating activities section using the direct method. (Not all of the above items will be used.)

Calculate cash flows—direct method.
(SO 4)

E14-10 The following information is taken from the 2006 general ledger of Ed Bradley Company.

Rent	Rent expense	$ 33,000
	Prepaid rent, January 1	7,900
	Prepaid rent, December 31	3,000
Salaries	Salaries expense	$ 54,000
	Salaries payable, January 1	3,000
	Salaries payable, December 31	9,000
Sales	Revenue from sales	$180,000
	Accounts receivable, January 1	12,000
	Accounts receivable, December 31	7,000

Instructions
In each of the above cases, compute the amount that should be reported in the operating activities section of the statement of cash flows using the direct method.

Compare two companies by using cash-based ratios.
(SO 5)

E14-11 Presented here is information for two companies in the same industry: Pamela Corporation and Dean Corporation.

	Pamela Corporation	**Dean Corporation**
Cash provided by operations	$300,000	$300,000
Capital expenditures	50,000	150,000
Cash dividends	80,000	100,000
Net income	200,000	200,000
Sales	400,000	800,000

Instructions
Calculate the free cash flow for each company. Comment on each company's ability to generate cash.

Prepare a work sheet.
(SO 6)

***E14-12** Information for Will Smith Company is presented in E14-5.

Instructions
Use the data in E14-5 to prepare a work sheet for a statement of cash flows for 2006. Enter the reconciling items directly on the work sheet, presenting the entries alphabetically.

PROBLEMS: SET A

Prepare the operating activities section—indirect method.

(SO 3)

P14-1A The income statement of Noah's Ark is shown below.

NOAH'S ARK
Income Statement
For the Year Ended November 30, 2006

Sales		$6,800,000
Cost of goods sold		
Beginning inventory	$2,000,000	
Purchases	4,300,000	
Goods available for sale	6,300,000	
Ending inventory	1,400,000	
Cost of goods sold		4,900,000
Gross profit		1,900,000
Operating expenses		
Selling expenses	450,000	
Administrative expenses	600,000	1,050,000
Net income		$ 850,000

Additional information:

1. Accounts receivable decreased $230,000 during the year.
2. Prepaid expenses increased $150,000 during the year.
3. Accounts payable to suppliers of merchandise decreased $200,000 during the year.
4. Accrued expenses payable decreased $100,000 during the year.
5. Administrative expenses include depreciation expense of $90,000.

Instructions

Prepare the operating activities section of the statement of cash flows for the year ended November 30, 2006, for Noah's Ark using the indirect method.

Net cash provided $1,320,000

Prepare the operating activities section—direct method.

(SO 4)

P14-2A Data for Noah's Ark Company are presented in P14-1A.

Instructions

Prepare the operating activities section of the statement of cash flows using the direct method.

Net cash provided $1,320,000

Prepare the operating activities section—direct method.

(SO 4)

P14-3A Ana Alicia Company's income statement for the year ended December 31, 2006, contained the following condensed information.

Revenue from fees		$900,000
Operating expenses (excluding depreciation)	$624,000	
Depreciation expense	56,000	
Loss on sale of equipment	20,000	700,000
Income before income taxes		200,000
Income tax expense		60,000
Net income		$140,000

Alicia's balance sheet contained the following comparative data at December 31.

	2006	2005
Accounts receivable	$47,000	$57,000
Accounts payable	41,000	36,000
Income taxes payable	4,000	7,000

(Accounts payable pertains to operating expenses.)

Net cash provided $228,000

Instructions

Prepare the operating activities section of the statement of cash flows using the direct method.

Prepare the operating activities section—indirect method.

(SO 3)

Net cash provided $228,000

P14-4A Data for Ana Alicia Company are presented in P14-3A.

Instructions

Prepare the operating activities section of the statement of cash flows for Ana Alicia Company using the indirect method.

Prepare a statement of cash flows—indirect method, and perform analysis.

(SO 3, 5)

P14-5A The financial statements of Louis Zimmer Company appear below:

LOUIS ZIMMER COMPANY
Comparative Balance Sheets
December 31

Assets	2006	2005
Cash	$ 31,000	$ 13,000
Accounts receivable	28,000	14,000
Merchandise inventory	25,000	35,000
Property, plant, and equipment	60,000	78,000
Accumulated depreciation	(22,000)	(24,000)
Total	$122,000	$116,000
Liabilities and Stockholders' Equity		
Accounts payable	$ 27,000	$ 23,000
Income taxes payable	5,000	8,000
Bonds payable	27,000	35,000
Common stock	18,000	14,000
Retained earnings	45,000	36,000
Total	$122,000	$116,000

LOUIS ZIMMER COMPANY
Income Statement
For the Year Ended December 31, 2006

Sales		$220,000
Cost of goods sold		180,000
Gross profit		40,000
Selling expenses	$14,000	
Administrative expenses	8,000	22,000
Income from operations		18,000
Interest expense		1,000
Income before income taxes		17,000
Income tax expense		4,000
Net income		$ 13,000

Additional information:

1. Dividends declared and paid were $4,000.
2. During the year equipment was sold for $8,500 cash. This equipment cost $18,000 originally and had a book value of $8,500 at the time of sale.
3. All depreciation expense is in the selling expense category.
4. All sales and purchases are on account.

Instructions

(a) Net cash provided by operating activities $17,500

(a) Prepare a statement of cash flows using the indirect method.
(b) Compute free cash flow.

P14-6A Data for Louis Zimmer Company are presented in P14-5A. Further analysis reveals the following.

Prepare a statement of cash flows—direct method, and perform analysis.

(SO 4, 5)

1. Accounts payable pertain to merchandise suppliers.
2. All operating expenses except for depreciation were paid in cash.

Instructions

(a) Prepare a statement of cash flows for Louis Zimmer Company using the direct method.
(b) Compute free cash flow.

(a) Cash receipts from customers $206,000

P14-7A The financial statements of Ernest Banks Company appear below.

Prepare a statement of cash flows—indirect method.

(SO 3)

ERNEST BANKS COMPANY
Comparative Balance Sheets
December 31

Assets	2006	2005
Cash	$ 23,000	$ 13,000
Accounts receivable	24,000	33,000
Merchandise inventory	20,000	27,000
Prepaid expenses	20,000	13,000
Land	40,000	40,000
Property, plant, and equipment	200,000	225,000
Less: Accumulated depreciation	(50,000)	(67,500)
Total	$277,000	$283,500
Liabilities and Stockholders' Equity		
Accounts payable	$ 9,000	$ 18,500
Accrued expenses payable	9,500	7,500
Interest payable	1,000	1,500
Income taxes payable	3,000	2,000
Bonds payable	50,000	80,000
Common stock	123,000	105,000
Retained earnings	81,500	69,000
Total	$277,000	$283,500

ERNEST BANKS COMPANY
Income Statement
For the Year Ended December 31, 2006

Revenues		
Sales	$600,000	
Gain on sale of plant assets	2,500	$602,500
Less: Expenses		
Cost of goods sold	500,000	
Operating expenses (excluding depreciation)	60,000	
Depreciation expense	7,500	
Interest expense	5,000	
Income tax expense	9,000	581,500
Net income		$ 21,000

Additional information:

1. Plant assets were sold at a sales price of $62,500.
2. Additional equipment was purchased at a cost of $60,000.
3. Dividends of $8,500 were paid.
4. All sales and purchases were on account.
5. Bonds were redeemed at face value.
6. Additional shares of stock were issued for cash.

Net cash provided by operating activities $28,000
Investing activities provided $2,500

Instructions
Prepare a statement of cash flows for Ernest Banks Company for the year ended December 31, 2006, using the indirect method.

Prepare a statement of cash flows—direct method.
(SO 4)

P14-8A Data for Ernest Banks Company is presented in P14-7A. Further analysis reveals the following.

1. Accounts payable relates to merchandise creditors.
2. All operating expenses, except depreciation expense, were paid in cash.

Net cash provided by operating activities $28,000
Investing activities provided $2,500

Instructions
Prepare a statement of cash flows for Ernest Banks Company for the year ended December 31, 2006, using the direct method.

Prepare a statement of cash flows—indirect method, and perform analysis.
(SO 3, 5)

P14-9A Presented below are the comparative balance sheets for Creative Works Company as of December 31.

CREATIVE WORKS COMPANY
Comparative Balance Sheets
December 31

Assets	2006	2005
Cash	$ 38,000	$ 45,000
Accounts receivable	49,500	52,000
Inventory	153,450	142,000
Prepaid expenses	15,780	21,000
Land	100,000	130,000
Equipment	228,000	155,000
Accumulated depreciation—equipment	(45,000)	(35,000)
Building	200,000	200,000
Accumulated depreciation—building	(60,000)	(40,000)
	$679,730	$670,000
Liabilities and Stockholders' Equity		
Accounts payable	$ 35,730	$ 40,000
Bonds payable	250,000	300,000
Common stock, $1 par	200,000	150,000
Retained earnings	194,000	180,000
	$679,730	$670,000

Additional information:

1. Operating expenses include depreciation expense of $42,000.
2. Land was sold for cash at book value.
3. Cash dividends of $24,000 were paid.
4. Net income for 2006 was $38,000.
5. Equipment was purchased for $95,000 cash. In addition, equipment costing $22,000 with a book value of $10,000 was sold for $8,100 cash.
6. Bonds were converted at face value by issuing 50,000 shares of $1 par value common stock.
7. Net sales for 2006 totaled $420,000.

Instructions

(a) Net cash from operating activities $73,900

(a) Prepare a statement of cash flows for the year ended December 31, 2006, using the indirect method.
(b) Compute free cash flow for 2006.

Prepare a work sheet.
(SO 6)

***P14-10A** Data for Ernest Banks Company are presented in P14-7A.

Total reconciling items $278,500

Instructions
Prepare a work sheet for a statement of cash flows for 2006. Enter the reconciling entries directly on the work sheet, presenting the entries alphabetically.

PROBLEMS: SET B

Prepare the operating activities section—indirect method.

(SO 3)

P14-1B The income statement of Wayne Rogers Company is shown below.

WAYNE ROGERS COMPANY
Income Statement
For the Year Ended December 31, 2006

Sales		$7,200,000
Cost of goods sold		
Beginning inventory	$1,700,000	
Purchases	5,430,000	
Goods available for sale	7,130,000	
Ending inventory	1,920,000	
Cost of goods sold		5,210,000
Gross profit		1,990,000
Operating expenses		
Selling expenses	380,000	
Administrative expense	525,000	
Depreciation expense	95,000	
Amortization expense	30,000	1,030,000
Net income		$ 960,000

Additional information:

1. Accounts receivable increased $690,000 during the year.
2. Prepaid expenses increased $170,000 during the year.
3. Accounts payable to merchandise suppliers increased $35,000 during the year.
4. Accrued expenses payable decreased $190,000 during the year.

Instructions

Prepare the operating activities section of the statement of cash flows for the year ended December 31, 2006, for Wayne Rogers Company using the indirect method.

Net cash used $150,000

Prepare the operating activities section—direct method.

(SO 4)

P14-2B Data for Wayne Rogers Company are presented in P14-1B.

Instructions

Prepare the operating activities section of the statement of cash flows using the direct method.

Net cash used $150,000

Prepare the operating activities section—direct method.

(SO 4)

P14-3B The income statement of Jurassic Park Co. for the year ended December 31, 2006, reported the following condensed information.

Revenue from fees	$510,000
Operating expenses	280,000
Income from operations	230,000
Income tax expense	57,000
Net income	$173,000

Jurassic Park's balance sheet contained the following comparative data at December 31.

	2006	2005
Accounts receivable	$55,000	$60,000
Accounts payable	32,000	41,000
Income taxes payable	2,000	4,000

Jurassic Park has no depreciable assets. (Accounts payable pertains to operating expenses.)

Net cash provided $167,000

Instructions

Prepare the operating activities section of the statement of cash flows using the direct method.

Prepare the operating activities section—indirect method.

(SO 3)

Net cash provided $167,000

P14-4B Data for Jurassic Park Co. are presented in P14-3B.

Instructions

Prepare the operating activities section of the statement of cash flows using the indirect method.

Prepare a statement of cash flows—indirect method, and perform analysis.

(SO 3, 5)

P14-5B The financial statements of James Lyman Company appear below.

JAMES LYMAN COMPANY
Comparative Balance Sheets
December 31

Assets		**2006**		**2005**
Cash		$ 24,000		$ 16,000
Accounts receivable		20,000		11,000
Merchandise inventory		38,000		35,000
Property, plant, and equipment	$70,000		$78,000	
Less: Accumulated depreciation	(30,000)	40,000	(24,000)	54,000
Total		$122,000		$116,000
Liabilities and Stockholders' Equity				
Accounts payable		$ 23,000		$ 33,000
Income taxes payable		15,000		20,000
Bonds payable		20,000		10,000
Common stock		25,000		25,000
Retained earnings		39,000		28,000
Total		$122,000		$116,000

JAMES LYMAN COMPANY
Income Statement
For the Year Ended December 31, 2006

Sales		$240,000
Cost of goods sold		180,000
Gross profit		60,000
Selling expenses	$23,000	
Administrative expenses	10,000	33,000
Income from operations		27,000
Interest expense		2,000
Income before income taxes		25,000
Income tax expense		7,000
Net income		$ 18,000

Additional information:

1. Dividends of $7,000 were declared and paid.
2. During the year equipment was sold for $11,000 cash. This equipment cost $15,000 originally and had a book value of $11,000 at the time of sale.
3. All depreciation expense, $10,000, is in the selling expense category.
4. All sales and purchases are on account.
5. Additional equipment was purchased for $7,000 cash.

Instructions

(a) Net cash provided by operating activities $1,000

(a) Prepare a statement of cash flows using the indirect method.
(b) Compute free cash flow.

P14-6B Data for James Lyman Company are presented in P14-5B. Further analysis reveals the following.

Prepare a statement of cash flows—direct method, and perform analysis.
(SO 4, 5)

1. Accounts payable pertains to merchandise creditors.
2. All operating expenses except for depreciation are paid in cash.

Instructions

(a) Prepare a statement of cash flows using the direct method.
(b) Compute free cash flow.

(a) Net cash provided by operating activities $1,000

P14-7B Condensed financial data of Daniel Barenboim Company appear below.

Prepare a statement of cash flows—indirect method.
(SO 3)

DANIEL BARENBOIM COMPANY
Comparative Balance Sheets
December 31

Assets	2006	2005
Cash	$ 98,700	$ 47,250
Accounts receivable	87,800	56,000
Inventories	121,900	103,650
Investments	81,500	87,000
Plant assets	250,000	205,000
Accumulated depreciation	(49,500)	(40,000)
	$590,400	$458,900
Liabilities and Stockholders' Equity		
Accounts payable	$ 57,700	$ 48,280
Accrued expenses payable	12,100	18,830
Bonds payable	100,000	80,000
Common stock	250,000	200,000
Retained earnings	170,600	111,790
	$590,400	$458,900

DANIEL BARENBOIM COMPANY
Income Statement Data
For the Year Ended December 31, 2006

Sales		$312,500
Gain on sale of plant assets		8,750
		321,250
Less:		
Cost of goods sold	$99,460	
Operating expenses (excluding depreciation expense)	14,670	
Depreciation expense	49,700	
Income taxes	7,270	
Interest expense	2,940	174,040
Net income		$147,210

Additional information:

1. New plant assets costing $92,000 were purchased for cash during the year.
2. Investments were sold at cost.
3. Plant assets costing $47,000 were sold for $15,550, resulting in a gain of $8,750.
4. A cash dividend of $88,400 was declared and paid during the year.

Instructions

Prepare a statement of cash flows using the indirect method.

Net cash provided by operating activities $140,800
Investing activities used $70,950

Prepare a statement of cash flows—direct method.
(SO 4)

Cash receipts from customers $280,700
Investing activities used $70,950

P14-8B Data for Daniel Barenboim Company are presented in P14-7B. Further analysis reveals that accounts payable pertains to merchandise creditors.

Instructions

Prepare a statement of cash flows for Daniel Barenboim Company using the direct method.

Prepare a statement of cash flows—indirect method, and perform analysis.
(SO 3, 5)

P14-9B Presented below are the comparative balance sheets for Isao Aoki Company at December 31.

ISAO AOKI COMPANY
Comparative Balance Sheets
December 31

Assets	**2006**	**2005**
Cash	$ 45,000	$ 57,000
Accounts receivable	72,000	64,000
Inventory	132,000	147,000
Prepaid expenses	12,140	16,540
Land	125,000	150,000
Equipment	200,000	175,000
Accumulated depreciation—equipment	(60,000)	(49,000)
Building	250,000	250,000
Accumulated depreciation—building	(75,000)	(50,000)
	$701,140	$760,540
Liabilities and Stockholders' Equity		
Accounts payable	$ 44,000	$ 45,000
Bonds payable	235,000	265,000
Common stock, $1 par	280,000	250,000
Retained earnings	142,140	200,540
	$701,140	$760,540

Additional information:

1. Operating expenses include depreciation expense of $60,000 and charges from prepaid expenses of $4,400.
2. Land was sold for cash at cost.
3. Cash dividends of $105,290 were paid.
4. Net income for 2006 was $46,890.
5. Equipment was purchased for $65,000 cash. In addition, equipment costing $40,000 with a book value of $16,000 was sold for $14,000 cash.
6. Bonds were converted at face value by issuing 30,000 shares of $1 par value common stock.
7. Net sales in 2006 were $367,000.

Instructions

(a) Net cash provided by operating activities $119,290

(a) Prepare a statement of cash flows for 2006 using the indirect method.
(b) Compute free cash flow for 2006.

Prepare a work sheet
(SO 6)

Total reconciling columns $626,210

***P14-10B** Data for Daniel Barenboim Company are presented in P14-7B.

Instructions

Prepare a work sheet for a statement of cash flows. Enter the reconciling items directly in the work sheet columns, identifying the debit and credit amounts alphabetically.

BROADENING YOUR PERSPECTIVE

Financial Reporting and Analysis

FINANCIAL REPORTING PROBLEM: PepsiCo

BYP14-1 Refer to the financial statements of **PepsiCo Inc.** presented in Appendix A, and answer the following questions.

(a) What was the amount of net cash provided by operating activities for the year ended December 27, 2003? For the year ended December 28, 2002?
(b) What was the amount of increase or decrease in cash and cash equivalents for the year ended December 27, 2003? For the year ended December 28, 2002?
(c) Which method of computing net cash provided by operating activities does PepsiCo use?
(d) From your analysis of the 2003 statement of cash flows, did the change in accounts and notes receivable require or provide cash? Did the change in inventories require or provide cash? Did the change in accounts payable and other current liabilities require or provide cash?
(e) What was the net outflow or inflow of cash from investing activities for the year ended December 27, 2003?
(f) What was the amount of interest paid in the year ended December 27, 2003? What was the amount of income taxes paid in the year ended December 27, 2003? (See Note 14.)

COMPARATIVE ANALYSIS PROBLEM: PepsiCo vs. Coca-Cola

BYP14-2 **PepsiCo**'s financial statements are presented in Appendix A. **Coca-Cola**'s financial statements are presented in Appendix B.

Instructions

(a) Based on the information contained in these financial statements, compute free cash flow for each company.
(b) What conclusions concerning the management of cash can be drawn from these data?

RESEARCH CASE

BYP14-3 The March 5, 2002, issue of the *Wall Street Journal* contains an article by Mark Maremont titled "'Cash Flow,' a Highly Touted Measure of Strength, Is Open to Interpretation."

Instructions

Read the article and answer the following questions.

(a) What does the article say is the "conventional wisdom" regarding the measurement of cash flow versus that of net income?
(b) Describe the two methods by which **Tyco** acquires customer contracts.
(c) Explain briefly how it is that the method by which Tyco acquires customer contracts can have a dramatic effect on its reported cash flow.
(d) What measure does Tyco's chief financial officer want investors to focus on, rather than reported earnings?

INTERPRETING FINANCIAL STATEMENTS

BYP14-4 **Praxair** was founded in 1907 as Linde-Air Products Company and was a pioneer in separating oxygen from air. It was purchased and run as a division of Union Carbide. In 1992 Praxair became an independent public company. Today, the company is one of the three largest suppliers of industrial gases worldwide. Praxair has operations in all regions of the world, with half of its sales occurring outside of the United States.

The management discussion shown below was included in a recent annual report.

> **PRAXAIR INCORPORATED**
> Management Discussion and Analysis
>
> **Liquidity, Capital Resources and Other Financial Data:** This year, Praxair changed its presentation of the Statement of Cash Flows to the direct method to report major classes of cash receipts and payments from operations. Praxair believes the direct method more clearly presents its operating cash flows. Prior years' cash flow information has been reclassified to conform to the current year presentation.

Instructions

(a) What method has Praxair changed from?

(b) What will the newly prepared cash flow statement show that the former one did not?

(c) Will the cash flows from investing and financing appear any differently under the new method of preparation than they did under the old method?

■ A GLOBAL FOCUS

BYP14-5 The statement of cash flows has become a commonly provided financial statement by companies throughout the world. It is interesting to note, however, that its format does vary across countries. The statement of cash flows on page 681 is from the 2001 financial statements of Irish pharmaceutical company **Elan Corporation**.

Instructions

(a) What similarities to U.S. cash flow statements do you notice in terms of general format, as well as terminology?

(b) What differences do you notice in terms of general format, as well as terminology?

■ EXPLORING THE WEB

BYP14-6 Purpose: Learn about the SEC.

Address: www.sec.gov, or go to www.wiley.com/college/weygandt

From the SEC homepage, choose **About the SEC, What We Do**.

Instructions

Answer the following questions.

(a) How many enforcement actions does the SEC take each year against securities law violators? What are typical infractions?

(b) After the Depression, Congress passed the Securities Acts of 1933 and 1934 to improve investor confidence in the markets. What two "common sense" notions are these laws based on?

(c) Who was the President of the United States at the time of the creation of the SEC? Who was the first SEC Chairperson?

Critical Thinking

■ GROUP DECISION CASE

BYP14-7 Kirby Garok and Jana Kingston are examining the statement of cash flows for Poquito Trading Company for the year ended January 31, 2006, which is shown at the top of page 682.

Kirby claims that Poquito's statement of cash flows is an excellent example of a superb first year, with cash increasing $125,000. Jana replies that it was not a superb first year—but rather, that the year was an operating failure. She says that the statement was incorrectly presented and that $125,000 is not the actual increase in cash. The cash balance at the beginning of the year was $140,000.

ELAN CORPORATION
Consolidated Statement of Cash Flows

	Notes	Year Ended 31 December 2001 $m	2000 $m
Cash Flow from Operating Activities	28(a)	524.6	272.2
Returns on Investments and Servicing of Finance			
Interest received		80.3	111.8
Interest paid		(124.1)	(76.4)
Cash (outflow)/inflow from returns on investments and servicing of finance		(43.8)	35.4
Taxation		(6.5)	(3.6)
Capital Expenditure and Financial Investment			
Additions to property, plant and equipment		(120.8)	(64.4)
Receipts from disposal of property, plant and equipment		2.0	9.8
Payments to acquire intangible assets		(286.7)	(79.5)
Receipts from disposal of intangible assets		11.2	—
Payments to acquire financial current assets		(148.2)	(54.6)
Sale and maturity of financial current assets		143.3	100.1
Payments to acquire financial fixed assets		(624.3)	(411.9)
Receipts from disposal of financial fixed assets		76.2	6.7
Cash outflow from capital expenditure and financial investment		(947.3)	(493.8)
Acquisitions and Disposals			
Cash paid on acquisitions	28(d)	(9.5)	(8.0)
Receipts from part disposal of subsidiary		41.9	—
Cash inflow/(outflow) from acquisitions and disposals		32.4	(8.0)
Cash outflow before use of liquid resources and financing		(440.6)	(197.8)
Management of Liquid Resources	28(b)	106.8	399.1
Financing			
Proceeds from issue of share capital		304.8	76.9
Purchase of treasury shares		—	—
Issue of loan notes		1,185.7	444.1
Repayment of loans		(555.7)	(496.0)
Bank borrowing		342.8	200.0
Cash inflow from financing		1,277.6	225.0
Net increase in cash		943.8	426.3
Reconciliation of Net Cash Flow to Movement in Net Debt			
Increase in cash for the period		943.8	426.3
Cash inflow from movement in liquid resources		(106.8)	(399.1)
		837.0	27.2
Other borrowing		(347.4)	(200.0)
Repayment of loans		557.6	512.4
Issue of loan notes		(1,185.7)	(444.1)
Change in net debt resulting from cash flows		(138.5)	(104.5)
Liquid resources acquired with subsidiary undertaking		—	214.2
Loans acquired with subsidiary undertaking		(0.3)	(363.7)
Non-cash movement—translation differences		(1.4)	(1.1)
Non-cash movement—notes		255.3	(54.4)
Non-cash movement—other		1.1	(1.3)
Decrease/(increase) in net debt	28(c)	116.2	(310.8)

POQUITO TRADING COMPANY
Statement of Cash Flows
For the Year Ended January 31, 2006

Sources of cash	
From sales of merchandise	$390,000
From sale of capital stock	420,000
From sale of investment (purchased below)	80,000
From depreciation	55,000
From issuance of note for truck	25,000
From interest on investments	6,000
Total sources of cash	976,000
Uses of cash	
For purchase of fixtures and equipment	320,000
For merchandise purchased for resale (all sold)	258,000
For operating expenses (including depreciation)	160,000
For purchase of investment	75,000
For purchase of truck by issuance of note	25,000
For purchase of treasury stock	10,000
For interest on note payable	3,000
Total uses of cash	851,000
Net increase in cash	$125,000

Instructions
With the class divided into groups, answer the following.

(a) With whom do you agree, Kirby or Jana? Explain your position.

(b) Using the data provided, prepare a statement of cash flows in proper form using the indirect method. The only noncash items in the income statement are depreciation and the gain from the sale of the investment.

■ COMMUNICATION ACTIVITY

BYP14-8 Gary Geek, the owner of Computer Services Company, is unfamiliar with the statement of cash flows which you, as his accountant, prepared. He asks for further explanation.

Instructions
Write him a brief memo explaining the form and content of the statement of cash flows as shown in Illustration 14-13 on page 642.

Accounting Matters!

■ ETHICS CASE

BYP14-9 Tappit Corporation is a medium-sized wholesaler of automotive parts. It has ten stockholders, who have been paid a total of $1 million in cash dividends for eight consecutive years. The policy of the Board of Directors requires that in order for this dividend to be declared, net cash provided by operating activities as reported in Tappit's current year's statement of cash flows must be in excess of $1 million. President and CEO Ray Thomas's job is secure so long as he produces annual operating cash flows to support the usual dividend.

At the end of the current year, controller Jon Lawler presents president Thomas with some disappointing news: The net cash provided by operating activities is calculated, by the indirect method, to be only $970,000. The president says to Jon, "We must get that amount above $1 million. Isn't there some way to increase operating cash flow by another $30,000?" Jon answers, "These figures were prepared by my assistant. I'll go back to my office and see what I can do." The president replies, "I know you won't let me down, Jon."

Upon close scrutiny of the statement of cash flows, Jon concludes that he can get the operating cash flows above $1 million by reclassifying a $60,000, 2-year note payable listed in the financing activities section as "Proceeds from bank loan—$60,000." He will report the note instead as "Increase in payables—$60,000" and treat it as an adjustment of net income in the operating activities section. He returns to the president saying, "You can tell the Board to declare their usual dividend. Our net cash flow provided by operating activities is $1,030,000." "Good man, Jon! I knew I could count on you," exults the president.

Instructions

(a) Who are the stakeholders in this situation?

(b) Was there anything unethical about the president's actions? Was there anything unethical about the controller's actions?

(c) Are the Board members or anyone else likely to discover the misclassification?

■ CONTINUING COOKIE CHRONICLE

Accounting Matters!

(Note: This is a continuation of the Cookie Chronicle from Chapters 1 through 13.)

BYP14-10 Natalie is preparing the balance sheet and income statement of Cookie & Coffee Creations Inc. and would like you to prepare the cash flow statement. The comparative balance sheet of Cookie & Coffee Creations Inc. at October 31, 2008, for the years 2008 and 2007, and the income statement for the year ended October 31, 2008, are presented below and on page 684.

Additional information:

1. All of the computer equipment was disposed of at the beginning of the year for $500 cash. New computer equipment was then bought for $4,000 cash.
2. Additional kitchen equipment was bought for $14,000 on November 1, 2007. A $9,000 note payable was signed. The terms provide for equal semi-annual installment payments of $1,500 on May 1 and November 1 of each year, plus interest of 5% on the outstanding principal balance.
3. Additional furniture was bought for $7,500 cash.
4. Dividends were declared on the preferred and common stock on October 15, 2008, to be paid on November 15, 2008.
5. Accounts payable relate only to merchandise creditors.
6. Prepaid expenses relate only to other operating expenses.

COOKIE & COFFEE CREATIONS INC.
Balance Sheet
October 31, 2008

Assets	2008	2007
Cash	$ 34,324	$13,050
Accounts receivable	3,250	2,710
Inventory	7,897	7,450
Prepaid expenses	6,300	6,050
Furniture and fixtures	12,500	5,000
Accumulated depreciation—furniture and fixtures	(2,000)	(1,000)
Computer equipment	4,000	4,500
Accumulated depreciation—computer equipment	(600)	(1,500)
Kitchen equipment	80,000	66,000
Accumulated depreciation—kitchen equipment	(22,600)	(6,600)
Total assets	$123,071	$95,660
Liabilities and Stockholders' Equity		
Accounts payable	$ 3,650	$ 2,450
Income taxes payable	10,251	11,200
Dividends payable	28,000	25,000
Salaries payable	2,250	1,280
Interest payable	188	0
Note payable	7,500	0
Preferred stock, no par, $6 cumulative, 3,000 and 2,500 shares issued, respectively	15,000	12,500
Common stock, $1 par—23,180 shares issued and outstanding	23,180	23,180
Additional paid-in capital—Treasury stock	250	250
Retained earnings	32,802	19,800
Total liabilities and stockholders' equity	$123,071	$95,660

COOKIE & COFFEE CREATIONS INC.
Income Statement
Year Ended October 31, 2008

Sales		$485,625
Cost of goods sold		222,694
Gross profit		262,931
Operating expenses		
Depreciation expense	$ 17,600	
Salaries and wages expense	147,979	
Other operating expenses	43,186	208,765
Income from operations		54,166
Other expenses		
Interest expense	$ 413	
Loss on sale of computer equipment	2,500	2,913
Income before income tax		51,253
Income tax expense		10,251
Net income		$ 41,002

Instructions

(a) Prepare a statement of cash flows for Cookie & Coffee Creations Inc. for the year ended October 31, 2008, using the indirect method.

(b) Prepare a statement of cash flows for Cookie & Coffee Creations Inc. for the year ended October 31, 2008, using the direct method.

Accounting Matters!

Answers to Accounting Matters! Questions

p. 632

Q: For all but one of the companies listed above, the cash-basis amount "Net cash provided by operations," from the statement of cash flows, is much greater than the accrual-basis amount "Net income," from the income statement. What explanation can you give for this difference?

A: The differences can be explained by the reported amounts of revenues and expenses. The accrual-basis income statements for these companies evidently report lower revenues or greater expenses, or both, than a cash-basis statement of cash flows. A cash-basis statement would not report revenue that has been earned but for which the cash has not been received, nor would it match expenses with earned revenues. Because of these violations of, respectively, the revenue recognition and the matching principles, cash-basis income statements are prohibited under GAAP.

p. 635

Q: Since these and numerous other financial accounting corrections and misstatements were reported in 2000, 2001, and 2002, what actions have been taken to curb such misdeeds?

A: The federal government has passed legislation—the Sarbanes-Oxley Act—that (1) requires corporate boards to assume more responsibility for accurate and transparent financial reporting, and (2) levies stronger sanctions (jail terms) on abusers. The accounting profession has issued *Statements on Auditing Standard No. 99,* which requires independent auditors to include fraud detection procedures in their audits.

Answer to PepsiCo Review It Question 4, p. 633

In its 2003 statement of cash flows, **PepsiCo** reported:

(1) net cash provided by operating activities of $4.328 billion;
(2) net cash used for investing activities of $2.271 billion; and
(3) net cash used for financing activities of $2.902 billion.

Answers to Self-Study Questions

1. c **2.** b **3.** a **4.** c **5.** d **6.** b **7.** c **8.** d **9.** b **10.** c
11. d **12.** c **13.** a ***14.** b

REMEMBER to go back to the Navigator box on the chapter-opening page and check off your completed work.

Chapter 15

Financial Statement Analysis

THE NAVIGATOR ✓

- Understand **Concepts for Review** ❑
- Read **Feature Story** ❑
- Scan **Study Objectives** ❑
- Read **Preview** ❑
- Read text and answer **Before You Go On** p. 694 ❑ p. 705 ❑ p. 710 ❑ p. 712 ❑
- Work **Demonstration Problems** ❑
- Review **Summary of Study Objectives** ❑
- Answer **Self-Study Questions** ❑
- Complete **Assignments** ❑

CONCEPTS FOR REVIEW

Before studying this chapter, you should know or, if necessary, review:

- The contents and classification of a balance sheet. (Ch. 4, pp. 158–163)
- The contents and classification of an income statement. (Ch. 5, pp. 203–207)
- Who are the various users of financial statement information. (Ch. 1, pp. 5–6)
- How to compute earnings per share (EPS). (Ch. 7, p. 304)
- How the liquidity of a company is determined. (Ch. 4, p. 161)

☑ THE NAVIGATOR

ACCOUNTING MATTERS! FEATURE STORY

"Follow That Stock!"

If you thought cab drivers with cell phones were scary, how about a cab driver with a trading desk in the front seat?

When a stoplight turns red or traffic backs up, New York City cabby Carlos Rubino morphs into a day trader, scanning real-time quotes of his favorite stocks as they spew across a PalmPilot mounted next to the steering wheel. "It's kind of stressful," he says. "But I like it."

Itching to know how a particular stock is doing? Mr. Rubino is happy to look up quotes for passengers. **Yahoo!**, **Amazon.com**, and **America Online** are the most requested ones. He even lets customers use his **Hitachi** Traveler laptop to send urgent e-mails from the back seat. Aware of a new local law prohibiting cabbies from using cell phones while they're driving, Mr. Rubino extends that rule to his trading. "I stop the cab at the side of the road if I have to make a trade," he says. "Safety first."

Originally from São Paulo, Brazil, Mr. Rubino has been driving his cab since 1987, and started trading stocks a few years ago. His curiosity grew as he began to educate himself by reading business publications. The Wall Street brokers he picks up are usually impressed with his knowledge, he says. But the feeling generally isn't mutual. Some of them "don't know much," he says. "They buy what people tell them to buy—they're like a toll collector."

Mr. Rubino is an enigma to his fellow cab drivers. A lot of his colleagues say they want to trade too. "But cab drivers are a little cheap," he says. "The [real-time] quotes cost $100 a month. The wireless Internet access is $54 a month."

Will he give up his brokerage firm on wheels for a stationary job? Not likely. Though he claims a 70 percent return on his investments in some months, he says he makes $1,300 and up a week driving his cab—more than he does trading. Besides, he adds, "Why go somewhere and have a boss?"

Source: Excerpted from Barbara Boydston, "With this Cab, People Jump in and Shout, 'Follow that Stock!'," *Wall Street Journal* (August 18, 1999), p. C1. Reprinted by permission of the Wall Street Journal © 1999 Dow Jones & Company, Inc. All Rights Reserved Worldwide.

☑ THE NAVIGATOR

STUDY OBJECTIVES

After studying this chapter, you should be able to:

1. Discuss the need for comparative analysis.
2. Identify the tools of financial statement analysis.
3. Explain and apply horizontal analysis.
4. Describe and apply vertical analysis.
5. Identify and compute ratios, and describe their purpose and use in analyzing a firm's liquidity, profitability, and solvency.
6. Understand the concept of earning power, and indicate how material items not typical of regular operations are presented.
7. Recognize the limitations of financial statement analysis.

☑ THE NAVIGATOR

PREVIEW OF CHAPTER 15

An important lesson can be learned from the Feature Story: Experience is the best teacher. By now you have learned a significant amount about financial reporting by U.S. corporations. Using some of the basic decision tools presented in this book, you can perform a rudimentary analysis on any U.S. company and draw basic conclusions about its financial health. Although it would not be wise for you to bet your life savings on a company's stock relying solely on your current level of knowledge, we strongly encourage you to practice your new skills wherever possible. Only with practice will you improve your ability to interpret financial numbers.

Before unleashing you on the world of high finance, we will present a few more important concepts and techniques, as well as provide you with one more comprehensive review of corporate financial statements. We use all of the decision tools presented in this text to analyze a single company—**Sears, Roebuck and Co.**, one of the country's oldest and largest retail store chains.

The content and organization of Chapter 15 are as follows.

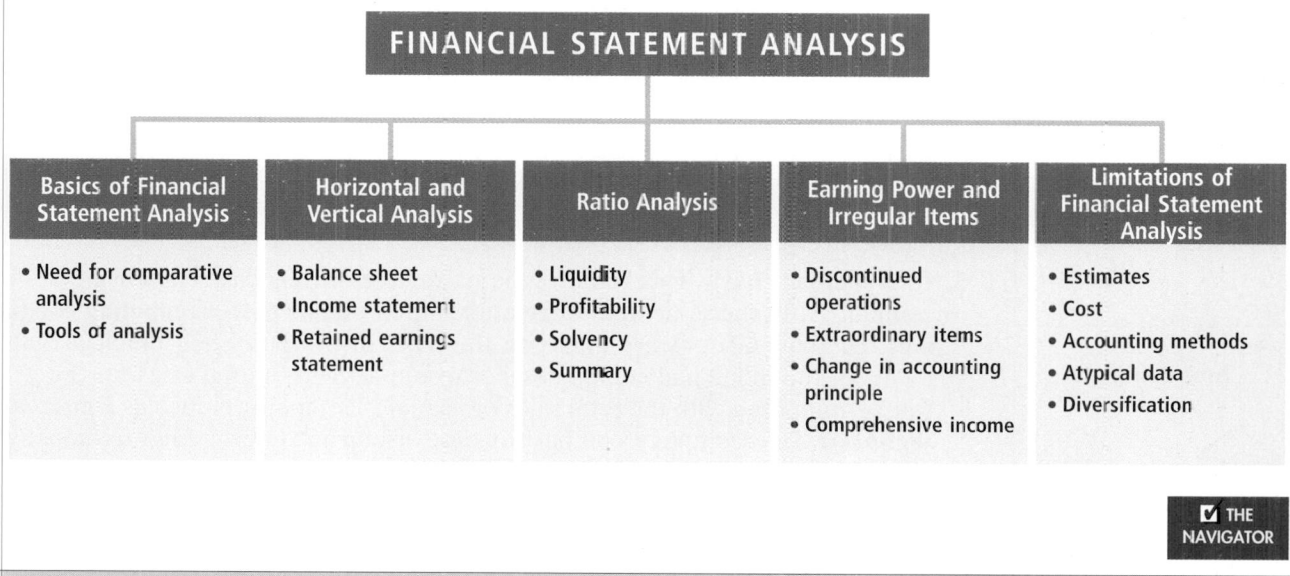

FINANCIAL STATEMENT ANALYSIS

Basics of Financial Statement Analysis
- Need for comparative analysis
- Tools of analysis

Horizontal and Vertical Analysis
- Balance sheet
- Income statement
- Retained earnings statement

Ratio Analysis
- Liquidity
- Profitability
- Solvency
- Summary

Earning Power and Irregular Items
- Discontinued operations
- Extraordinary items
- Change in accounting principle
- Comprehensive income

Limitations of Financial Statement Analysis
- Estimates
- Cost
- Accounting methods
- Atypical data
- Diversification

THE NAVIGATOR

Basics of Financial Statement Analysis

Analyzing financial statements involves evaluating three characteristics of a company: its liquidity, its profitability, and its solvency. A **short-term creditor**, such as a bank, is primarily interested in the ability of the borrower to pay obligations when they come due. The liquidity of the borrower is extremely important in evaluating the safety of a loan. A **long-term creditor**, such as a bondholder, however, looks to profitability and solvency measures that indicate the company's ability to survive over a long period of time. Long-term creditors consider such measures as the amount of debt in the company's capital structure and its ability to meet interest payments. Similarly, **stockholders** are interested in the profitability and solvency of the company. They want to assess the likelihood of dividends and the growth potential of the stock.

STUDY OBJECTIVE 1

Discuss the need for comparative analysis.

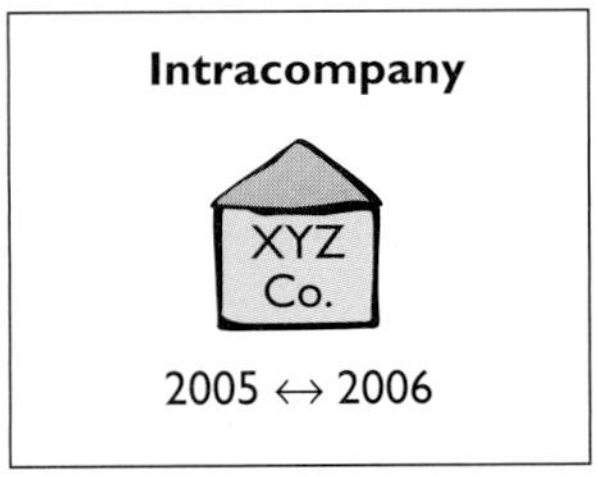

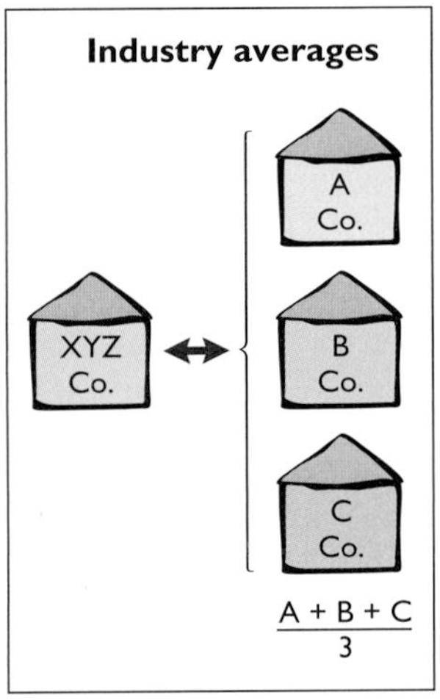

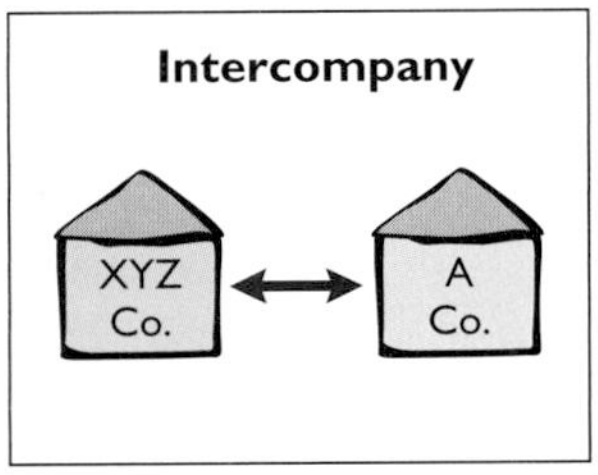

Need for Comparative Analysis

Every item reported in a financial statement has significance. When **Sears, Roebuck and Co.** reports cash of $9,057 million on its balance sheet, we know the company had that amount of cash on the balance sheet date. But, we do not know whether the amount represents an increase over prior years, or whether it is adequate in relation to the company's need for cash. To obtain such information, it is necessary to compare the amount of cash with other financial statement data.

Comparisons can be made on a number of different bases. Three are illustrated in this chapter.

1. **Intracompany basis.** This basis compares an item or financial relationship **within a company** in the current year with the same item or relationship in one or more prior years. For example, Sears, Roebuck and Co. can compare its cash balance at the end of the current year with last year's balance to find the amount of the increase or decrease. Likewise, Sears can compare the percentage of cash to current assets at the end of the current year with the percentage in one or more prior years. Intracompany comparisons are useful in detecting changes in financial relationships and significant trends.
2. **Industry averages.** This basis compares an item or financial relationship of a company with **industry averages** (or **norms**) published by financial ratings organizations such as **Dun & Bradstreet**, **Moody's**, and **Standard & Poor's**. For example, Sears's net income can be compared with the average net income of all companies in the retail chain-store industry. Comparisons with industry averages provide information as to a company's relative performance within the industry.
3. **Intercompany basis.** This basis compares an item or financial relationship of one company with the same item or relationship in **one or more competing companies**. The comparisons are made on the basis of the published financial statements of the individual companies. For example, Sears's total sales for the year can be compared with the total sales of its major competitors such as **Kmart** and **Wal-Mart**. Intercompany comparisons are useful in determining a company's competitive position.

STUDY OBJECTIVE 2

Identify the tools of financial statement analysis.

Tools of Financial Statement Analysis

Various tools are used to evaluate the significance of financial statement data. Three commonly used tools are these:

- **Horizontal analysis** evaluates a series of financial statement data over a period of time.
- **Vertical analysis** evaluates financial statement data by expressing each item in a financial statement as a percent of a base amount.
- **Ratio analysis** expresses the relationship among selected items of financial statement data.

Horizontal analysis is used primarily in intracompany comparisons. Two features in published financial statements facilitate this type of comparison: First, each of the basic financial statements is presented on a comparative basis for a minimum of two years. Second, a summary of selected financial data is presented for a series of five to ten years or more. Vertical analysis is used in both intra- and intercompany comparisons. Ratio analysis is used in all three types of comparisons. In the following sections, we will explain and illustrate each of the three types of analysis.

Horizontal Analysis

STUDY OBJECTIVE 3

Explain and apply horizontal analysis.

Horizontal analysis, also called **trend analysis**, is a technique for evaluating a series of financial statement data over a period of time. Its purpose is to determine the increase or decrease that has taken place. This change may be expressed as either an amount or a percentage. For example, the recent net sales figures of **Sears, Roebuck and Co.** are as follows.

Illustration 15-1 Sears, Roebuck and Co.'s net sales

SEARS

SEARS, ROEBUCK AND CO.
Net Sales (in millions)

2003	2002	2001
$41,124	$41,366	$40,990

If we assume that 2001 is the base year, we can measure all percentage increases or decreases from this base period amount as follows.

Illustration 15-2 Formula for horizontal analysis of changes since base period

$$\text{Change Since Base Period} = \frac{\text{Current Year Amount} - \text{Base Year Amount}}{\text{Base Year Amount}}$$

For example, we can determine that net sales for Sears increased from 2001 to 2002 approximately 0.9% [($41,366 – $40,990) ÷ $40,990]. Similarly, we can determine that net sales increased from 2001 to 2003 approximately 0.3% [($41,124 – $40,990) ÷ $40,990].

Alternatively, we can express current year sales as a percentage of the base period. This is done by dividing the current year amount by the base year amount, as shown below.

Illustration 15-3 Formula for horizontal analysis of current year in relation to base year

$$\text{Current Results in Relation to Base Period} = \frac{\text{Current Year Amount}}{\text{Base Year Amount}}$$

Illustration 15-4 presents this analysis for Sears for a three-year period using 2001 as the base period.

Illustration 15-4 Horizontal analysis of Sears, Roebuck and Co.'s net sales in relation to base period

SEARS

SEARS, ROEBUCK AND CO.
Net Sales (in millions)
in relation to base period 2001

2003	2002	2001
$41,124	$41,366	$40,990
100.3%	100.9%	100.0%

Balance Sheet

To further illustrate horizontal analysis, we will use the financial statements of Quality Department Store Inc. It is a downtown, full-line department store in a southeastern city of 55,000 people. A horizontal analysis of its two-year condensed balance sheets, showing dollar and percentage changes, is presented in Illustration 15-5.

Illustration 15-5
Horizontal analysis of balance sheets

QUALITY DEPARTMENT STORE INC.
Condensed Balance Sheets
December 31

			Increase or (Decrease) during 2003	
	2003	**2002**	**Amount**	**Percent**
Assets				
Current assets	$1,020,000	$ 945,000	**$ 75,000**	**7.9%**
Plant assets (net)	800,000	632,500	**167,500**	**26.5%**
Intangible assets	15,000	17,500	**(2,500)**	**(14.3%)**
Total assets	$1,835,000	$1,595,000	**$240,000**	**15.0%**
Liabilities				
Current liabilities	$ 344,500	$ 303,000	**$ 41,500**	**13.7%**
Long-term liabilities	487,500	497,000	**(9,500)**	**(1.9%)**
Total liabilities	832,000	800,000	**32,000**	**4.0%**
Stockholders' Equity				
Common stock, $1 par	275,400	270,000	**5,400**	**2.0%**
Retained earnings	727,600	525,000	**202,600**	**38.6%**
Total stockholders' equity	1,003,000	795,000	**208,000**	**26.2%**
Total liabilities and stockholders' equity	$1,835,000	$1,595,000	**$240,000**	**15.0%**

The comparative balance sheets in Illustration 15-5 show that a number of significant changes have occurred in Quality Department Store's financial structure from 2002 to 2003. In the assets section, plant assets (net) increased $167,500, or 26.5%. In the liabilities section, current liabilities increased $41,500, or 13.7%. In the stockholders' equity section, retained earnings increased $202,600, or 38.6%. This suggests that the company expanded its asset base during 2003 and **financed this expansion primarily by retaining income** rather than assuming additional long-term debt.

Income Statement

Illustration 15-6 (page 691) presents a horizontal analysis of the two-year condensed income statements of Quality Department Store Inc. for the years 2003 and 2002.

Horizontal analysis of the income statements shows the following changes:

1. Net sales increased $260,000, or 14.2% ($260,000 ÷ $1,837,000).
2. Cost of goods sold increased $141,000, or 12.4% ($141,000 ÷ $1,140,000).
3. Total operating expenses increased $37,000, or 11.6% ($37,000 ÷ $320,000).

Overall, gross profit and net income were up substantially. Gross profit increased 17.1%, and net income, 26.5%. Quality's profit trend appears favorable.

Illustration 15-6
Horizontal analysis of income statements

QUALITY DEPARTMENT STORE INC.
Condensed Income Statements
For the Years Ended December 31

			Increase or (Decrease) during 2003	
	2003	2002	Amount	Percent
Sales	$2,195,000	$1,960,000	$235,000	12.0%
Sales returns and allowances	98,000	123,000	(25,000)	(20.3%)
Net sales	2,097,000	1,837,000	260,000	14.2%
Cost of goods sold	1,281,000	1,140,000	141,000	12.4%
Gross profit	816,000	697,000	119,000	17.1%
Selling expenses	253,000	211,500	41,500	19.6%
Administrative expenses	104,000	108,500	(4,500)	(4.1%)
Total operating expenses	357,000	320,000	37,000	11.6%
Income from operations	459,000	377,000	82,000	21.8%
Other revenues and gains				
Interest and dividends	9,000	11,000	(2,000)	(18.2%)
Other expenses and losses				
Interest expense	36,000	40,500	(4,500)	(11.1%)
Income before income taxes	432,000	347,500	84,500	24.3%
Income tax expense	168,200	139,000	29,200	21.0%
Net income	$ 263,800	$ 208,500	$ 55,300	26.5%

HELPFUL HINT

Note that though the amount column is additive (the total is $55,300), the percentage column is not additive (26.5% is not the total). A separate percentage has been calculated for each item.

Retained Earnings Statement

A horizontal analysis of Quality Department Store's comparative retained earnings statements is presented in Illustration 15-7. Analyzed horizontally, net income increased $55,300, or 26.5%, whereas dividends on the common stock increased only $1,200, or 2%. We saw in the horizontal analysis of the balance sheet that ending retained earnings increased 38.6%. As indicated earlier, the company retained a significant portion of net income to finance additional plant facilities.

Illustration 15-7
Horizontal analysis of retained earnings statements

QUALITY DEPARTMENT STORE INC.
Retained Earnings Statements
For the Years Ended December 31

			Increase or (Decrease) during 2003	
	2003	2002	Amount	Percent
Retained earnings, Jan. 1	$525,000	$376,500	$148,500	39.4%
Add: Net income	263,800	208,500	55,300	26.5%
	788,800	585,000	203,800	
Deduct: Dividends	61,200	60,000	1,200	2.0%
Retained earnings, Dec. 31	$727,600	$525,000	$202,600	38.6%

Horizontal analysis of changes from period to period is relatively straightforward and is quite useful. But complications can occur in making the computations. If an item has no value in a base year or preceding year and a value in the next year, no percentage change can be computed. Similarly, if a negative amount appears in the base or preceding period and a positive amount exists the following year (or vice versa), no percentage change can be computed.

Vertical Analysis

STUDY OBJECTIVE 4

Describe and apply vertical analysis.

Vertical analysis, also called **common size analysis**, is a technique for evaluating financial statement data that expresses each item within a financial statement as a percent of a base amount. On a balance sheet we might say that current assets are 22% of total assets (total assets being the base amount). Or on an income statement, we might say that selling expenses are 16% of net sales (net sales being the base amount).

Balance Sheet

Presented in Illustration 15-8 is the vertical analysis of Quality Department Store Inc.'s comparative balance sheets. The base for the asset items is **total assets**. The base for the liability and stockholders' equity items is **total liabilities and stockholders' equity**.

Illustration 15-8
Vertical analysis of balance sheets

QUALITY DEPARTMENT STORE INC.
Condensed Balance Sheets
December 31

	2003		2002	
	Amount	**Percent**	**Amount**	**Percent**
Assets				
Current assets	$1,020,000	**55.6%**	$ 945,000	**59.2%**
Plant assets (net)	800,000	**43.6%**	632,500	**39.7%**
Intangible assets	15,000	**0.8%**	17,500	**1.1%**
Total assets	$1,835,000	**100.0%**	$1,595,000	**100.0%**
Liabilities				
Current liabilities	$ 344,500	**18.8%**	$ 303,000	**19.0%**
Long-term liabilities	487,500	**26.5%**	497,000	**31.2%**
Total liabilities	832,000	**45.3%**	800,000	**50.2%**
Stockholders' Equity				
Common stock, $1 par	275,400	**15.0%**	270,000	**16.9%**
Retained earnings	727,600	**39.7%**	525,000	**32.9%**
Total stockholders' equity	1,003,000	**54.7%**	795,000	**49.8%**
Total liabilities and stockholders' equity	$1,835,000	**100.0%**	$1,595,000	**100.0%**

HELPFUL HINT

The formula for calculating these balance sheet percentages is:

$$\frac{\text{Each item on B/S}}{\text{Total assets}} = \%$$

Vertical analysis shows the relative size of each category in the balance sheet. It also can show the **percentage change** in the individual asset, liability, and stockholders' equity items. For example, we can see that current assets decreased from 59.2% of total assets in 2002 to 55.6% in 2003 (even though the absolute dollar amount increased $75,000 in that time). Plant assets (net) have increased from 39.7% to 43.6% of total assets. Retained earnings have increased from 32.9% to 39.7% of total liabilities and stockholders' equity. These results reinforce the earlier observations that **Quality is choosing to finance its growth through retention of earnings rather than through issuing additional debt**.

Income Statement

Vertical analysis of Quality's income statements is shown in Illustration 15-9. We see that cost of goods sold as a percentage of net sales declined 1% (62.1% vs. 61.1%) and total operating expenses declined 0.4% (17.4% vs. 17.0%). As a result, it is not surprising to see net income as a percent of net sales increase from 11.4% to 12.6%. Quality appears to be a profitable enterprise that is becoming even more successful.

Illustration 15-9
Vertical analysis of income statements

QUALITY DEPARTMENT STORE INC.
Condensed Income Statements
For the Years Ended December 31

	2003		2002	
	Amount	**Percent**	**Amount**	**Percent**
Sales	$2,195,000	**104.7%**	$1,960,000	**106.7%**
Sales returns and allowances	98,000	**4.7%**	123,000	**6.7%**
Net sales	2,097,000	**100.0%**	1,837,000	**100.0%**
Cost of goods sold	1,281,000	**61.1%**	1,140,000	**62.1%**
Gross profit	816,000	**38.9%**	697,000	**37.9%**
Selling expenses	253,000	**12.0%**	211,500	**11.5%**
Administrative expenses	104,000	**5.0%**	108,500	**5.9%**
Total operating expenses	357,000	**17.0%**	320,000	**17.4%**
Income from operations	459,000	**21.9%**	377,000	**20.5%**
Other revenues and gains				
Interest and dividends	9,000	**0.4%**	11,000	**0.6%**
Other expenses and losses				
Interest expense	36,000	**1.7%**	40,500	**2.2%**
Income before income taxes	432,000	**20.6%**	347,500	**18.9%**
Income tax expense	168,200	**8.0%**	139,000	**7.5%**
Net income	$ 263,800	**12.6%**	$ 208,500	**11.4%**

HELPFUL HINT

The formula for calculating these income statement percentages is:

$$\frac{\text{Each item on I/S}}{\text{Net sales}} = \%$$

An associated benefit of vertical analysis is that it enables you to compare companies of different sizes. For example, Quality's main competitor is a Sears store in a nearby town. Using vertical analysis, the condensed income statements of the small local retail enterprise, Quality Department Store Inc., can be more meaningfully compared with the 2003 income statement of the giant international retailer, **Sears, Roebuck and Co.**, as shown in Illustration 15-10.

Illustration 15-10
Intercompany income statement comparison

CONDENSED INCOME STATEMENTS
(in thousands)

	Quality Department Store Inc.		Sears, Roebuck and Co.[1]	
	Dollars	**Percent**	**Dollars**	**Percent**
Net sales	$2,097	**100.0%**	$41,124,000	**100.0%**
Cost of goods sold	1,281	**61.1%**	26,231,000	**63.8%**
Gross profit	816	**38.9%**	14,893,000	**36.2%**
Selling and administrative expenses	357	**17.0%**	13,695,000	**33.3%**
Income from operations	459	**21.9%**	1,198,000	**2.9%**
Other expenses and revenues (including income taxes)	195	**9.3%**	2,199,000[2]	**5.4%**
Net income	$ 264	**12.6%**	$ 3,397,000	**8.3%**

[1] Sears, Roebuck and Co., *2003 Annual Report* (Hoffman Estates, Illinois).
[2] In 2003 Sears reported a $4.224 billion "gain on the sale of businesses" as part of its "Other expenses and revenues."

Sears's net sales are 19,611 times as great as the net sales of relatively tiny Quality Department Store. But vertical analysis eliminates this difference in size. The percentages show that Quality's and Sears's gross profit rates were comparable at 38.9% and 36.2%. However, the percentages related to income from operations were significantly different at 21.9% and 2.9%. This disparity can be attributed to Quality's selling and administrative expense percentage (17%) which is much lower than Sears's (33.3%). Although Sears earned net income more than 12,867 times as large as Quality's, Sears's net income as a **percent of each sales dollar** (8.3%) is only 66% of Quality's (12.6%).

BEFORE YOU GO ON...

Review It

1. What are the different tools that might be used to compare financial information?
2. What is horizontal analysis?
3. What is vertical analysis?
4. Identify the specific sections in **PepsiCo**'s 2003 Annual Report where horizontal and vertical analysis of financial data is presented. The answer to this question is provided on page 737.

Do It

Summary financial information for Rosepatch Company is as follows.

	December 31, 2006	December 31, 2005
Current assets	$234,000	$180,000
Plant assets (net)	756,000	420,000
Total assets	$990,000	$600,000

Compute the amount and percentage changes in 2006 using horizontal analysis, assuming 2005 is the base year.

ACTION PLAN

- Find the percentage change by dividing the amount of the increase by the 2005 amount (base year).

SOLUTION

	Increase in 2006	
	Amount	**Percent**
Current assets	$ 54,000	30% [($234,000 – $180,000) ÷ $180,000]
Plant assets (net)	336,000	80% [($756,000 – $420,000) ÷ $420,000]
Total assets	$390,000	65% [($990,000 – $600,000) ÷ $600,000]

Related exercise material: *BE15-1, BE15-3, BE15-4, BE15-6, E15-1, E15-3, and E15-4.*

THE NAVIGATOR

Ratio Analysis

Ratio analysis expresses the relationship among selected items of financial statement data. A **ratio** expresses the mathematical relationship between one quantity and another. The relationship is expressed in terms of either a percentage, a rate, or a simple proportion. To illustrate, in 2003 **Motorola, Inc.** had current assets of $17,907 million and current liabilities of $9,433 million. The relationship is determined by dividing current assets by current liabilities. The alternative means of expression are:

Percentage:	Current assets are 190% of current liabilities.
Rate:	Current assets are 1.9 times current liabilities.
Proportion:	The relationship of current assets to liabilities is 1.9 : 1.

STUDY OBJECTIVE 5

Identify and compute ratios, and describe their purpose and use in analyzing a firm's liquidity, profitability, and solvency.

For analysis of the primary financial statements, ratios can be used to evaluate liquidity, profitability, and solvency. These classifications are described and pictured in Illustration 15-11.

Illustration 15-11
Financial ratio classifications

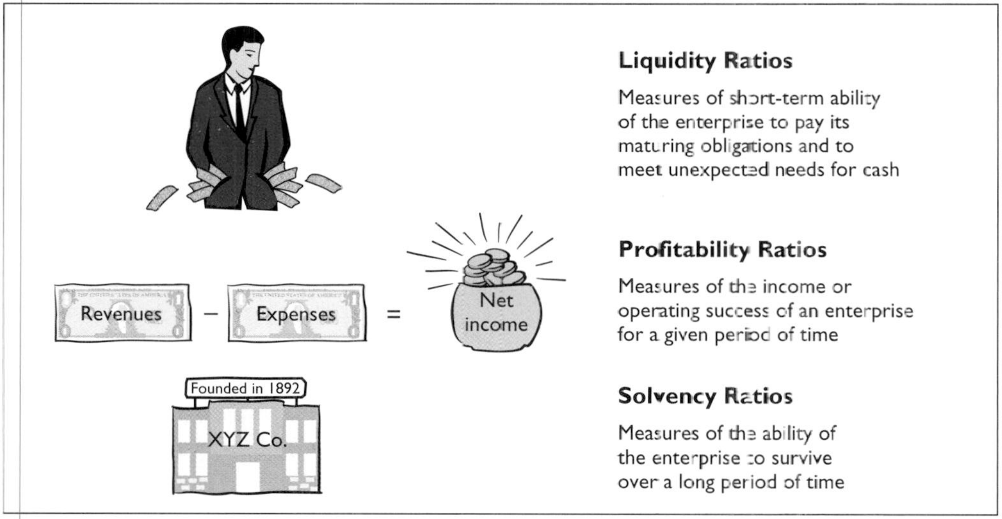
Liquidity Ratios
Measures of short-term ability of the enterprise to pay its maturing obligations and to meet unexpected needs for cash
Revenues
Expenses
Net income
Profitability Ratios
Measures of the income or operating success of an enterprise for a given period of time
Founded in 1892
XYZ Co.
Solvency Ratios
Measures of the ability of the enterprise to survive over a long period of time

Ratios can provide clues to underlying conditions that may not be apparent from individual financial statement components. However, a single ratio by itself is not very meaningful. Accordingly, in the discussion of ratios we will use the following types of comparisons.

1. **Intracompany comparisons** for two years for Quality Department Store.
2. **Industry average comparisons** based on median ratios for department stores.
3. **Intercompany comparisons** based on **Sears, Roebuck and Co.** as Quality Department Store's principal competitor.

Liquidity Ratios

Liquidity ratios measure the short-term ability of the enterprise to pay its maturing obligations and to meet unexpected needs for cash. Short-term creditors such as bankers and suppliers are particularly interested in assessing liquidity. The ratios that can be used to determine the enterprise's short-term debt-paying ability are the current ratio, the acid-test ratio, receivables turnover, and inventory turnover.

1. Current Ratio

The **current ratio** is a widely used measure for evaluating a company's liquidity and short-term debt-paying ability. The ratio is computed by dividing current assets by current liabilities.

The 2003 and 2002 current ratios for Quality Department Store and comparative data are shown in Illustration 15-12.

Illustration 15-12
Current ratio

$$\text{Current Ratio} = \frac{\text{Current Assets}}{\text{Current Liabilities}}$$

Quality Department Store

2003	2002
$\frac{\$1,020,000}{\$344,500} = 2.96:1$	$\frac{\$945,000}{\$303,000} = 3.12:1$
Industry average	Sears, Roebuck and Co.
1.28:1	1.32:1

HELPFUL HINT

Can any company operate successfully without working capital? Yes, if it has very predictable cash flows and solid earnings. A number of companies (e.g., **Whirlpool**, **American Standard**, and **Campbell's Soup**) are pursuing this goal. The rationale: Less money tied up in working capital means more money to invest in the business.

What does the ratio actually mean? The 2003 ratio of 2.96:1 means that for every dollar of current liabilities, Quality has $2.96 of current assets. Quality's current ratio has decreased in the current year. But, compared to the industry average of 1.28:1, and Sears's 1.32:1 current ratio, Quality appears to be reasonably liquid.

The current ratio is sometimes referred to as the **working capital ratio** because **working capital** is the excess of current assets over current liabilities. The current ratio is a more dependable indicator of liquidity than working capital. Two companies with the same amount of working capital may have significantly different current ratios.

The current ratio is only one measure of liquidity. It does not take into account the composition of the current assets. For example, a satisfactory current ratio does not disclose the fact that a portion of the current assets may be tied up in slow-moving inventory. A dollar of cash would be more readily available to pay the bills than a dollar of slow-moving inventory.

ACCOUNTING MATTERS! **Business Insight**

The apparent simplicity of the current ratio can have real-world limitations. An addition of equal amounts to both the numerator and the denominator causes the ratio to decrease. Assume, for example, that a company has $2,000,000 of current assets and $1,000,000 of current liabilities. Its current ratio is 2:1. If it purchases $1,000,000 of inventory on account, it will have $3,000,000 of current assets and $2,000,000 of current liabilities. Its current ratio will decrease to 1.5:1. If, instead, the company pays off $500,000 of its current liabilities, it will have $1,500,000 of current assets and $500,000 of current liabilities, and its current ratio will increase to 3:1. Any trend analysis should be done with care, since the ratio is susceptible to quick changes and is easily influenced by management.

? How might management influence the company's current ratio?

2. Acid-Test Ratio

ALTERNATIVE TERMINOLOGY

The acid-test ratio is also called the *quick ratio.*

The **acid-test (quick) ratio** is a measure of a company's immediate short-term liquidity. It is computed by dividing the sum of cash, short-term investments, and net receivables by current liabilities. Thus, it is an important complement to the current ratio. For example, assume that the current assets of Quality Department Store for 2003 and 2002 consist of the following items.

Illustration 15-13
Current assets of Quality Department Store

QUALITY DEPARTMENT STORE INC.
Balance Sheet (partial)

	2003	2002
Current assets		
Cash	**$ 100,000**	**$155,000**
Short-term investments	**20,000**	**70,000**
Receivables (net*)	**230,000**	**180,000**
Inventory	620,000	500,000
Prepaid expenses	50,000	40,000
Total current assets	$1,020,000	$945,000

*Allowance for doubtful accounts is $10,000 at the end of each year.

Cash, short-term investments, and receivables (net) are highly liquid compared to inventory and prepaid expenses. The inventory may not be readily saleable, and the prepaid expenses may not be transferable to others. Thus, the acid-test ratio measures **immediate** liquidity. The 2003 and 2002 acid-test ratios for Quality Department Store and comparative data are as follows.

Illustration 15-14
Acid-test ratio

$$\text{Acid-Test Ratio} = \frac{\text{Cash + Short-Term Investments + Receivables (Net)}}{\text{Current Liabilities}}$$

Quality Department Store

2003	2002
$\frac{\$100{,}000 + \$20{,}000 + \$230{,}000}{\$344{,}500} = 1.02:1$	$\frac{\$155{,}000 + \$70{,}000 + \$180{,}000}{\$303{,}000} = 1.34:1$
Industry average	Sears, Roebuck and Co.
0.33:1	0.85:1

The ratio has declined in 2003. Is an acid-test ratio of 1.02:1 adequate? When compared with the industry average of 0.33:1 and Sears's of 0.85:1, Quality's acid-test ratio seems adequate.

3. Receivables Turnover

Liquidity may be measured by how quickly certain assets can be converted to cash. How liquid, for example, are the receivables? The ratio used to assess the liquidity of the receivables is **receivables turnover**. It measures the number of times, on average, receivables are collected during the period. Receivables turnover is computed by dividing net credit sales (net sales less cash sales) by the average net receivables. Unless seasonal factors are significant, average net receivables can be computed from the beginning and ending balances of the net receivables.[3]

Assume that all sales are credit sales. The balance of net receivables at the beginning of 2002 is $200,000; at the end of 2002 it is $180,000, and at the end of 2003 it is $230,000. The receivables turnover for Quality Department Store and comparative

[3]If seasonal factors are significant, the average receivables balance might be determined by using monthly amounts.

data are shown in Illustration 15-15 below. Quality's receivables turnover improved in 2003. The turnover of 10.2 times compares quite favorably with Sears's 2.4 times and is similar to the department store industry's average of 10.8 times.

Illustration 15-15
Receivables turnover

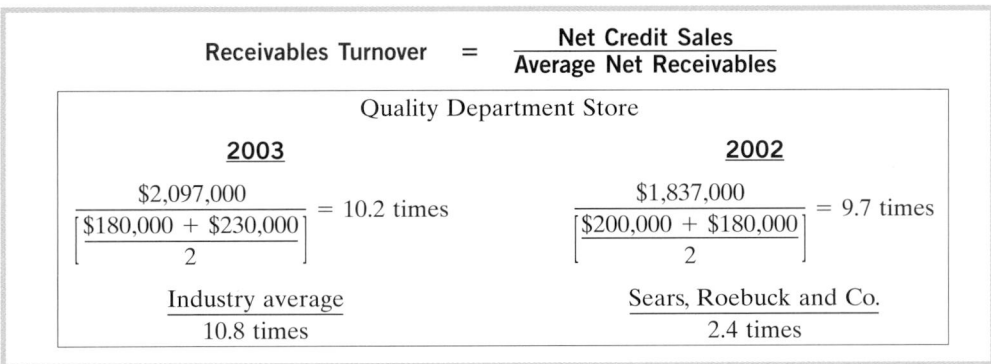

$$\text{Receivables Turnover} = \frac{\text{Net Credit Sales}}{\text{Average Net Receivables}}$$

Quality Department Store

2003	2002
$\dfrac{\$2{,}097{,}000}{\left[\dfrac{\$180{,}000 + \$230{,}000}{2}\right]} = 10.2 \text{ times}$	$\dfrac{\$1{,}837{,}000}{\left[\dfrac{\$200{,}000 + \$180{,}000}{2}\right]} = 9.7 \text{ times}$
Industry average	Sears, Roebuck and Co.
10.8 times	2.4 times

In some cases, receivables turnover may be misleading. Some companies, especially large retail chains, encourage credit and revolving charge sales. They may even slow collections in order to earn a healthy return on the outstanding receivables at interest rates of 18% to 22%. This may explain why **Sears**'s turnover is only 2.4 times. In general, however, the faster the turnover, the greater the reliance that can be placed on the current and acid-test ratios for assessing liquidity.

AVERAGE COLLECTION PERIOD. A popular variant of the receivables turnover ratio is to convert it to an **average collection period** in terms of days. This is done by dividing the receivables turnover ratio into 365 days. For example, the receivables turnover of 10.2 times is divided into 365 days to obtain approximately 36 days. This means that receivables are collected on average every 36 days, or about every 5 weeks. The average collection period is frequently used to assess the effectiveness of a company's credit and collection policies. The general rule is that the collection period should not greatly exceed the credit term period (the time allowed for payment).

4. Inventory Turnover

Inventory turnover measures the number of times on average the inventory is sold during the period. Its purpose is to measure the liquidity of the inventory. The inventory turnover is computed by dividing cost of goods sold by the average inventory. Unless seasonal factors are significant, average inventory can be computed from the beginning and ending inventory balances.

Assuming that the inventory balance for Quality Department Store at the beginning of 2002 was $450,000, its inventory turnover and comparative data are as shown in Illustration 15-16 (on page 699). Quality's inventory turnover declined slightly in 2003. The turnover of 2.3 times is relatively low compared with the industry average of 6.7 and Sears's 5.0. Generally, the faster the inventory turnover, the less cash that is tied up in inventory and the less the chance of inventory obsolescence. Inventory turnover ratios vary considerably among industries. For example, grocery store chains have a turnover of 10 times and an average selling period of 37 days. In contrast, jewelry stores have an average turnover of 1.3 times and an average selling period of 281 days.

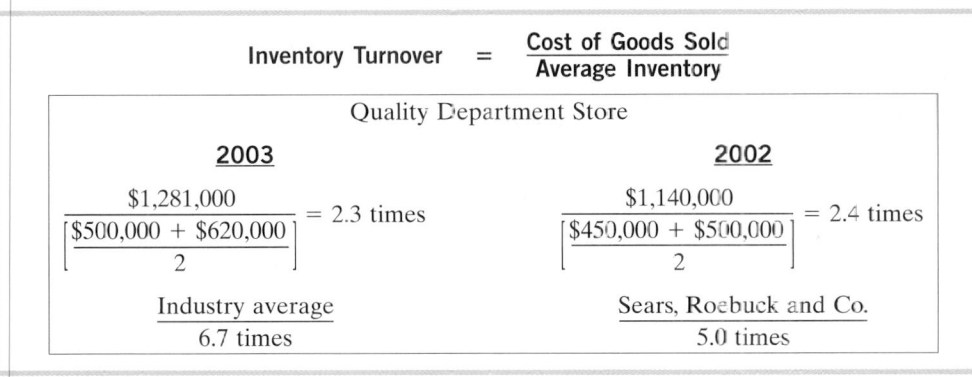

Illustration 15-16
Inventory turnover

$$\text{Inventory Turnover} = \frac{\text{Cost of Goods Sold}}{\text{Average Inventory}}$$

Quality Department Store

2003	2002
$\frac{\$1,281,000}{\left[\frac{\$500,000 + \$620,000}{2}\right]} = 2.3 \text{ times}$	$\frac{\$1,140,000}{\left[\frac{\$450,000 + \$500,000}{2}\right]} = 2.4 \text{ times}$
Industry average	Sears, Roebuck and Co.
6.7 times	5.0 times

AVERAGE DAYS TO SELL INVENTORY. A variant of inventory turnover is the **average days to sell the inventory**. It is calculated by dividing the inventory turnover into 365. For example, Quality's 2003 inventory turnover of 2.3 times divided into 365 is approximately 159 days. An average selling time of 159 days is also relatively high compared with the industry average of 54.5 days (365 ÷ 6.7) and Sears's 73 days (365 ÷ 5.0).

Profitability Ratios

Profitability ratios measure the income or operating success of an enterprise for a given period of time. Income, or the lack of it, affects the company's ability to obtain debt and equity financing. It also affects the company's liquidity position and the company's ability to grow. As a consequence, both creditors and investors are interested in evaluating earning power—profitability. Profitability is frequently used as the ultimate test of management's operating effectiveness.

5. Profit Margin

ALTERNATIVE TERMINOLOGY

Profit margin is also called the *rate of return on sales.*

Profit margin is a measure of the percentage of each dollar of sales that results in net income. It is computed by dividing net income by net sales. Quality Department Store's profit margin and comparative data are shown in Illustration 15-17.

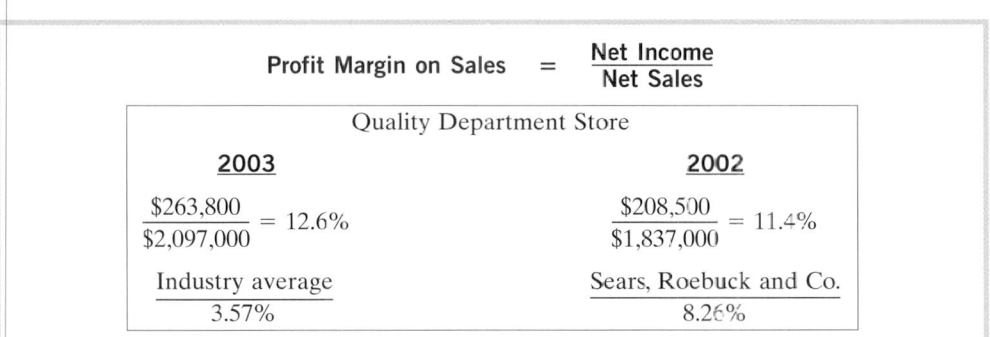

Illustration 15-17
Profit margin

$$\text{Profit Margin on Sales} = \frac{\text{Net Income}}{\text{Net Sales}}$$

Quality Department Store

2003	2002
$\frac{\$263,800}{\$2,097,000} = 12.6\%$	$\frac{\$208,500}{\$1,837,000} = 11.4\%$
Industry average	Sears, Roebuck and Co.
3.57%	8.26%

Quality experienced an increase in its profit margin from 2002 to 2003. Its profit margin is unusually high in comparison with the industry average of 3.57% and Sears's 8.26%.

High-volume (high inventory turnover) enterprises such as grocery stores (**Safeway** or **Kroger**) and discount stores (**Kmart** or **Wal-Mart**) generally experience low profit margins. In contrast, low-volume enterprises such as jewelry stores (**Tiffany & Co.**) or airplane manufacturers (**Boeing Co.**) have high profit margins.

6. Asset Turnover

Asset turnover measures how efficiently a company uses its assets to generate sales. It is determined by dividing net sales by average assets. The resulting number shows the dollars of sales produced by each dollar invested in assets. Unless seasonal factors are significant, average total assets can be computed from the beginning and ending balance of total assets. Assuming that total assets at the beginning of 2002 were $1,446,000, the 2003 and 2002 asset turnover for Quality Department Store and comparative data are as follows.

Illustration 15-18
Asset turnover

$$\text{Asset Turnover} = \frac{\text{Net Sales}}{\text{Average Assets}}$$

Quality Department Store

2003

$$\frac{\$2{,}097{,}000}{\left[\frac{\$1{,}595{,}000 + \$1{,}835{,}000}{2}\right]} = 1.22 \text{ times}$$

2002

$$\frac{\$1{,}837{,}000}{\left[\frac{\$1{,}446{,}000 + \$1{,}595{,}000}{2}\right]} = 1.21 \text{ times}$$

Industry average	Sears, Roebuck and Co.
2.37 times	1.05 times

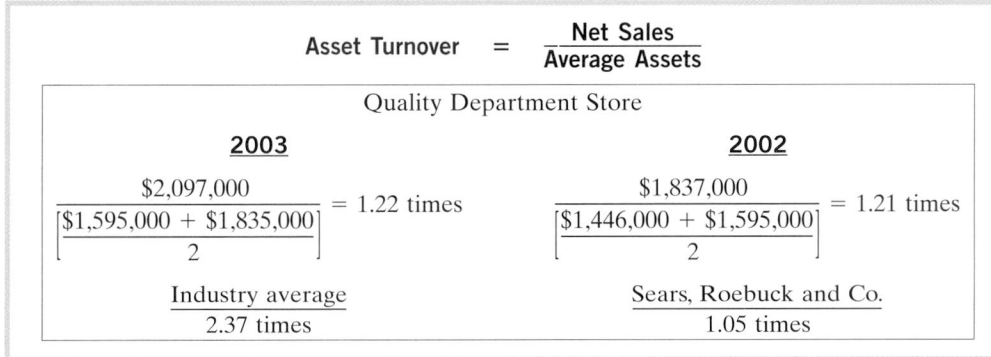

Asset turnover shows that in 2003 Quality generated sales of $1.22 for each dollar it had invested in assets. The ratio changed little from 2002 to 2003. Quality's asset turnover is below the industry average of 2.37 times but above Sears's ratio of 1.05 times.

Asset turnover ratios vary considerably among industries. For example, a large utility company like **Consolidated Edison** (New York) has a ratio of 0.49 times, and the large grocery chain **Kroger Stores** has a ratio of 4.34 times.

7. Return on Assets

An overall measure of profitability is **return on assets**. This ratio is computed by dividing net income by average assets. The 2003 and 2002 return on assets for Quality Department Store and comparative data are shown below.

Illustration 15-19
Return on assets

$$\text{Return on Assets} = \frac{\text{Net Income}}{\text{Average Assets}}$$

Quality Department Store

2003

$$\frac{\$263{,}800}{\left[\frac{\$1{,}595{,}000 + \$1{,}835{,}000}{2}\right]} = 15.4\%$$

2002

$$\frac{\$208{,}500}{\left[\frac{\$1{,}446{,}000 + \$1{,}595{,}000}{2}\right]} = 13.7\%$$

Industry average	Sears, Roebuck and Co.
8.29%	8.7%

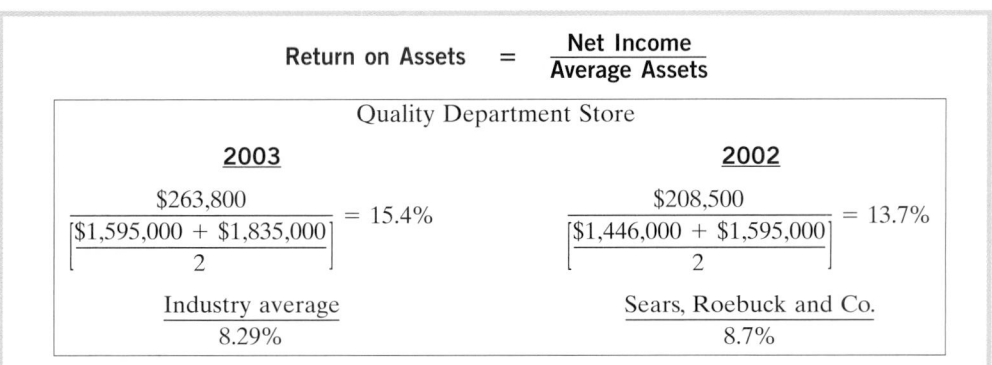

Quality's return on assets improved from 2002 to 2003. Its return of 15.4% is very high, compared with the department store industry average of 8.29% and Sears's 8.7%.

8. Return on Common Stockholders' Equity

Another widely used profitability ratio is **return on common stockholders' equity**. It measures profitability from the common stockholders' viewpoint. This ratio shows how many dollars of net income were earned for each dollar invested by the owners. It is computed by dividing net income by average common stockholders' equity. Assuming that common stockholders' equity at the beginning of 2002 was \$667,000, the 2003 and 2002 ratios for Quality Department Store and comparative data are shown in Illustration 15-20.

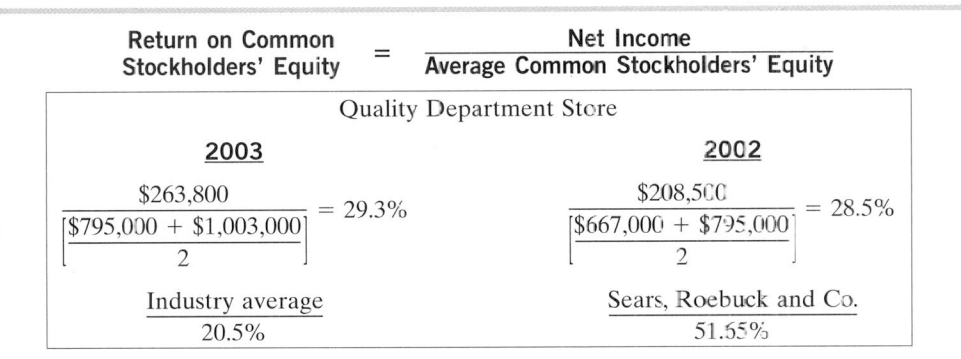

Illustration 15-20
Return on common stockholders' equity

$$\text{Return on Common Stockholders' Equity} = \frac{\text{Net Income}}{\text{Average Common Stockholders' Equity}}$$

Quality Department Store

2003	2002
$\frac{\$263{,}800}{\left[\frac{\$795{,}000 + \$1{,}003{,}000}{2}\right]} = 29.3\%$	$\frac{\$208{,}500}{\left[\frac{\$667{,}000 + \$795{,}000}{2}\right]} = 28.5\%$
Industry average	Sears, Roebuck and Co.
20.5%	51.65%

Quality's rate of return on common stockholders' equity is high at 29.3%, considering an industry average of 20.5% but low compared to 51.65% for Sears.

WITH PREFERRED STOCK. When preferred stock is present, **preferred dividend** requirements are deducted from net income to compute income available to common stockholders. Similarly, the par value of preferred stock (or call price, if applicable) must be deducted from total stockholders' equity to determine the amount of common stock equity used in this ratio. The ratio then appears as follows.

Illustration 15-21
Return on common stockholders' equity with preferred stock

$$\text{Return on Common Stockholders' Equity} = \frac{\text{Net Income} - \text{Preferred Dividends}}{\text{Average Common Stockholders' Equity}}$$

Note that Quality's rate of return on stockholders' equity (29.3%) is substantially higher than its rate of return on assets (15.4%). The reason is that Quality has made effective use of **leverage** or **trading on the equity** at a gain. Trading on the equity at a gain means that the company has borrowed money at a lower rate of interest than it is able to earn by using the borrowed money. Leverage enables Quality Department Store to use money supplied by nonowners to increase the return to the owners. A comparison of the rate of return on total assets with the rate of interest paid for borrowed money indicates the profitability of trading on the equity. Quality Department Store earns more on its borrowed funds than it has to pay in the form of interest. Thus the return to stockholders exceeds the return on the assets, benefiting from the positive leveraging.

ALTERNATIVE TERMINOLOGY

Trading on the equity is called *leveraging.*

9. Earnings per Share (EPS)

Earnings per share (EPS) is a measure of the net income earned on each share of common stock. It is computed by dividing net income by the number of weighted average common shares outstanding during the year. A measure of net income earned on a per share basis provides a useful perspective for determining profitability. Assuming that there is no change in the number of outstanding shares during 2002 and that the 2003 increase occurred midyear, the net income per share for Quality Department Store for 2003 and 2002 is computed as shown in Illustration 15-22 (page 702).

Illustration 15-22
Earnings per share

$$\text{Earnings per Share} = \frac{\text{Net Income}}{\text{Weighted Average Common Shares Outstanding}}$$

Quality Department Store

2003	2002
$\dfrac{\$263{,}800}{\left[\dfrac{270{,}000 + 275{,}400}{2}\right]} = \$0.97$	$\dfrac{\$208{,}500}{270{,}000} = \$0.77$

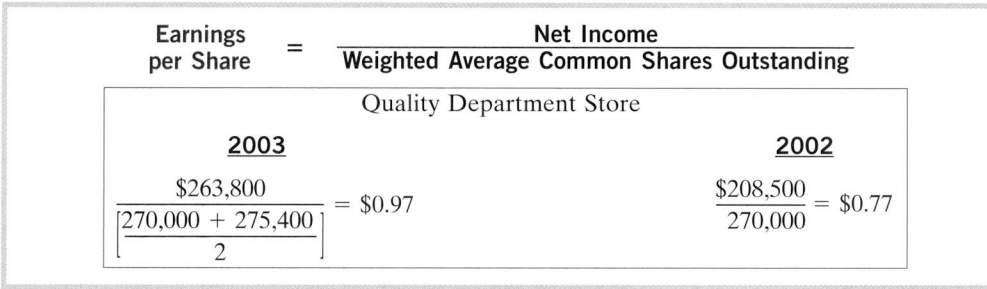

Note that no industry or Sears data are presented. Such comparisons are not meaningful because of the wide variations in the number of shares of outstanding stock among companies. The only meaningful EPS comparison is an intracompany trend comparison: Quality's earnings per share increased 20 cents per share in 2003. This represents a 26% increase over the 2002 earnings per share of 77 cents.

The terms "earnings per share" and "net income per share" refer to the amount of net income applicable to each share of **common stock**. Therefore, in computing EPS, if there are preferred dividends declared for the period, they must be deducted from net income to determine income available to the common stockholders.

10. Price-Earnings Ratio

The **price-earnings (P-E) ratio** is an oft-quoted measure of the ratio of the market price of each share of common stock to the earnings per share. The price-earnings (P-E) ratio reflects investors' assessments of a company's future earnings. It is computed by dividing the market price per share of the stock by earnings per share. Assuming that the market price of Quality Department Store Inc. stock is $8 in 2002 and $12 in 2003, the price-earnings ratio is computed as follows.

Illustration 15-23
Price-earnings ratio

$$\text{Price-Earnings Ratio} = \frac{\text{Market Price per Share of Stock}}{\text{Earnings per Share}}$$

Quality Department Store

2003	2002
$\dfrac{\$12.00}{\$0.97} = 12.4 \text{ times}$	$\dfrac{\$8.00}{\$0.77} = 10.4 \text{ times}$
Industry average	Sears, Roebuck and Co.
26 times	3.8 times

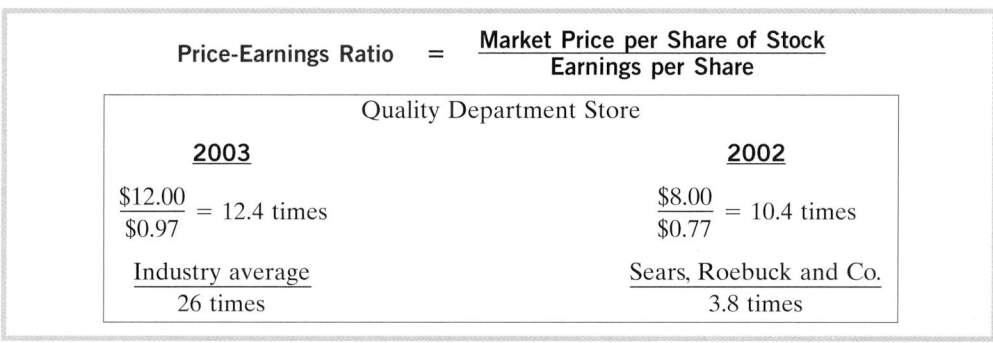

In 2003 each share of Quality's stock sold for 12.4 times the amount that was earned on each share. Quality's price-earnings ratio is lower than the industry average of 26 times, but it is higher than the ratio of 3.8 times for Sears. The average price-earnings ratio for the stocks that constitute the Standard and Poor's 500 Index (500 largest U.S. firms) in June 2003 was an unusually high 24 times.

11. Payout Ratio

The **payout ratio** measures the percentage of earnings distributed in the form of cash dividends. It is computed by dividing cash dividends by net income. Companies that have high growth rates generally have low payout ratios because they reinvest most of their net income into the business. The 2003 and 2002 payout ratios for Quality Department Store are computed as follows.

Illustration 15-24
Payout ratio

$$\text{Payout Ratio} = \frac{\text{Cash Dividends}}{\text{Net Income}}$$

Quality Department Store

2003	2002
$\frac{\$61,200}{\$263,800} = 23.2\%$	$\frac{\$60,000}{\$208,500} = 28.8\%$
Industry average	Sears, Roebuck and Co.
16.0%	9.6%

Quality's payout ratio is high when compared to Sears's payout ratio of 9.6%, but not as high when compared to other companies. As indicated earlier (page 690), Quality apparently has decided to fund its purchase of plant assets through retention of earnings.

ACCOUNTING MATTERS! Business Insight

Many companies with stable earnings have high payout ratios. For example, **Baltimore Gas and Electric** had an 84% payout ratio over a recent five-year period. **Omega Healthcare**'s dividends exceeded net income over the same period. Conversely, companies that are expanding rapidly, such as **Toys "R" Us** and **Tellabs Inc.** have never paid a cash dividend.

? Why would you purchase the stock of a company that has never paid a dividend?

Solvency Ratios

Solvency ratios measure the ability of the company to survive over a long period of time. Long-term creditors and stockholders are particularly interested in a company's ability to pay interest as it comes due and to repay the face value of debt at maturity. Debt to total assets and times interest earned are two ratios that provide information about debt-paying ability.

12. Debt to Total Assets Ratio

The **debt to total assets ratio** measures the percentage of the total assets provided by creditors. It is computed by dividing total debt (both current and long-term liabilities) by total assets. This ratio indicates the company's degree of leverage. It also can indicate the company's ability to withstand losses without impairing creditors' interests. The higher the percentage of debt to total assets, the greater the risk that the company may be unable to meet its maturing obligations. The 2003 and 2002 ratios for Quality Department Store and comparative data are as follows.

Illustration 15-25
Debt to total assets ratio

$$\text{Debt to Total Assets} = \frac{\text{Total Debt}}{\text{Total Assets}}$$

Quality Department Store

2003	2002
$\frac{\$832,000}{\$1,835,000} = 45.3\%$	$\frac{\$800,000}{\$1,595,000} = 50.2\%$
Industry average	Sears, Roebuck and Co.
40.1%	76.9%

A ratio of 45.3% means that creditors have provided 45.3% of Quality Department Store's total assets. Quality's 45.3% is above the industry average of 40.1%. But it is considerably below the high 76.9% ratio of Sears. The lower the ratio, the more equity "buffer" there is available to the creditors. Thus, from the creditors' point of view, a low ratio of debt to total assets is usually desirable.

The adequacy of this ratio is often judged in the light of the company's earnings. Generally, companies with relatively stable earnings (such as public utilities) have higher debt to total assets ratios than cyclical companies with widely fluctuating earnings (such as many high-tech companies).

13. Times Interest Earned

ALTERNATIVE TERMINOLOGY

Times interest earned is also called *interest coverage.*

Times interest earned provides an indication of the company's ability to meet interest payments as they come due. It is computed by dividing income before interest expense and income taxes by interest expense. The 2003 and 2002 ratios for Quality Department Store and comparative data are shown in Illustration 15-26. Note that times interest earned uses income before income taxes and interest expense. This represents the amount available to cover interest. For Quality Department Store the 2003 amount of $468,000 is computed by taking the income before income taxes of $432,000 and adding back the $36,000 of interest expense.

Illustration 15-26
Times interest earned

$$\text{Times Interest Earned} = \frac{\text{Income before Income Taxes and Interest Expense}}{\text{Interest Expense}}$$

Quality Department Store

2003	2002
$\frac{\$468,000}{\$36,000} = 13$ times	$\frac{\$388,000}{\$40,500} = 9.6$ times
Industry average	Sears, Roebuck and Co.
11.98 times	6.3 times

Quality's interest expense is well covered at 13 times, compared with the industry average of 11.98 times and Sears's 6.3 times.

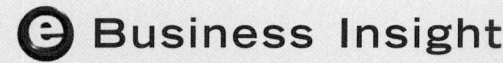

ACCOUNTING MATTERS! e Business Insight

Today, investors have access to information provided by corporate managers that used to be available only to professional analysts. Corporate managers have always made themselves available to security analysts for questions at the end of every quarter. Now, because of a combination of new corporate disclosure requirements by the Securities and Exchange Commission and technologies that make communication to large numbers of people possible at a very low price, the average investor can listen in on these discussions. For example, one individual investor, Matthew Johnson, a **Nortel Networks** local area network engineer in Belfast, Northern Ireland, "stayed up past midnight to listen to **Apple Computer**'s recent Internet conference call. Hearing the company's news 'from the dog's mouth,' he says 'gave me better information' than hunting through chat-rooms."

Source: Jeff D. Opdyke, "Individuals Pick Up on Conference Calls," *Wall Street Journal* (November 20, 2000).

If you want to keep current with the financial and operating developments of a company in which you own shares, what are some ways you can do so?

Summary of Ratios

A summary of the ratios discussed in the chapter is presented in Illustration 15-27. The summary includes the formula and purpose or use of each ratio.

Illustration 15-27
Summary of liquidity, profitability, and solvency ratios

Ratio	Formula	Purpose or Use
Liquidity Ratios		
1. Current ratio	$\frac{\text{Current assets}}{\text{Current liabilities}}$	Measures short-term debt-paying ability.
2. Acid-test (quick) ratio	$\frac{\text{Cash + Short-term investments + Receivables (net)}}{\text{Current liabilities}}$	Measures immediate short-term liquidity.
3. Receivables turnover	$\frac{\text{Net credit sales}}{\text{Average net receivables}}$	Measures liquidity of receivables.
4. Inventory turnover	$\frac{\text{Cost of goods sold}}{\text{Average inventory}}$	Measures liquidity of inventory.
Profitability Ratios		
5. Profit margin	$\frac{\text{Net income}}{\text{Net sales}}$	Measures net income generated by each dollar of sales.
6. Asset turnover	$\frac{\text{Net sales}}{\text{Average assets}}$	Measures how efficiently assets are used to generate sales.
7. Return on assets	$\frac{\text{Net income}}{\text{Average assets}}$	Measures overall profitability of assets.
8. Return on common stockholders' equity	$\frac{\text{Net income}}{\text{Average common stockholders' equity}}$	Measures profitability of owners' investment.
9. Earnings per share (EPS)	$\frac{\text{Net income}}{\text{Weighted average common shares outstanding}}$	Measures net income earned on each share of common stock.
10. Price-earnings (P-E) ratio	$\frac{\text{Market price per share of stock}}{\text{Earnings per share}}$	Measures the ratio of the market price per share to earnings per share.
11. Payout ratio	$\frac{\text{Cash dividends}}{\text{Net income}}$	Measures percentage of earnings distributed in the form of cash dividends.
Solvency Ratios		
12. Debt to total assets ratio	$\frac{\text{Total debt}}{\text{Total assets}}$	Measures the percentage of total assets provided by creditors.
13. Times interest earned	$\frac{\text{Income before income taxes and interest expense}}{\text{Interest expense}}$	Measures ability to meet interest payments as they come due.

BEFORE YOU GO ON...

Review It

1. What are liquidity ratios? Explain the current ratio, acid-test ratio, receivables turnover, and inventory turnover.
2. What are profitability ratios? Explain the profit margin, asset turnover ratio, return on assets, return on common stockholders' equity, earnings per share, price-earnings ratio, and payout ratio.
3. What are solvency ratios? Explain the debt to total assets ratio and times interest earned.

Do It

Selected financial data for Drummond Company at December 31, 2006, are as follows: cash $60,000; receivables (net) $80,000; inventory $70,000; current liabilities $140,000. Compute the current and acid-test ratios.

ACTION PLAN

- Use the formula for the current ratio: Current assets ÷ Current liabilities.
- Use the formula for the acid-test ratio: [Cash + Short-term investments + Receivables (net)] ÷ Current liabilities.

SOLUTION The current ratio is 1.5:1 ($210,000 ÷ $140,000). The acid-test ratio is 1:1 ($140,000 ÷ $140,000).

Related exercise material: *BE15-7, BE15-8, BE15-9, BE15-10, BE15-11, E15-5, E15-6, E15-7, E15-8, E15-9, and E15-10.*

THE NAVIGATOR

Earning Power and Irregular Items

STUDY OBJECTIVE 6

Understand the concept of earning power, and indicate how material items not typical of regular operations are presented.

Users of financial statements are interested in the concept of "earning power." Earning power means the normal level of income to be obtained in the future. Earning power differs from actual net income by the amount of irregular revenues, expenses, gains, and losses. Users are interested in earning power because it helps them derive an estimate of future earnings without the "noise" of irregular items.

For users of financial statements to determine "earning power" or regular income, the "irregular" items are separately identified on the income statement. Three types of "irregular" items are reported:

1. Discontinued operations.
2. Extraordinary items.
3. Changes in accounting principle.

All these "irregular" items are reported net of income taxes. That is, income tax is first calculated for the income before "irregular" items. Then it is calculated for each of the listed "irregular" items. The general concept is "let the tax follow income or loss."

Discontinued Operations

Discontinued operations refers to the disposal of a **significant segment** of a business. Examples are the cessation of an entire activity and the elimination of a major class of customers. **Kmart**'s decision to terminate its interest in four business activities, including **PACE Membership Warehouse** and **PayLess Drug Stores Northwest**, was reported as discontinued operations. On the other hand, the phasing out of a model such as the **GM** Chevette or part of a line of business is not considered to be a disposal of a segment.

Following the disposal of a significant segment, the income statement should report both income from continuing operations and income (or loss) from discontinued operations. **The income (loss) from discontinued operations consists of two parts: the income (loss) from operations and the gain (loss) on disposal of the segment.**

To illustrate, assume that during 2006 Acro Energy Inc. has income before income taxes of $800,000. During 2006 Acro discontinued and sold its unprofitable chemical division. The loss in 2006 from chemical operations (net of $60,000 taxes) was $140,000. The loss on disposal of the chemical division (net of $30,000 taxes) was $70,000. Assuming a 30% tax rate on income, the income statement presentation is shown below.

Illustration 15-28
Statement presentation of discontinued operations

ACRO ENERGY INC.
Income Statement (partial)
For the Year Ended December 31, 2006

Income before income taxes		$800,000
Income tax expense		240,000
Income from continuing operations		560,000
Discontinued operations		
Loss from operations of chemical division, net of $60,000 income tax saving	**$140,000**	
Loss from disposal of chemical division, net of $30,000 income tax saving	**70,000**	**210,000**
Net income		$350,000

HELPFUL HINT

Observe the dual disclosures: (1) The results of operations of the discontinued division must be eliminated from the results of continuing operations. (2) The disposal of the operation must also be reported.

Note that the caption "Income from continuing operations" is used and that a new section "Discontinued operations" is added. **Within the new section, both the operating loss and the loss on disposal are reported net of applicable income taxes.** This presentation clearly indicates the separate effects of continuing operations and discontinued operations on net income.

Extraordinary Items

Extraordinary items are events and transactions that meet two conditions: They are (1) **unusual in nature and** (2) **infrequent in occurrence**. To be "unusual," the item should be abnormal and only incidentally related to the company's customary activities. To be "infrequent," the item should not be reasonably expected to recur in the foreseeable future. Both criteria must be evaluated in terms of the company's operating environment. Thus, **Weyerhaeuser Co.** reported the $36 million in damages to its timberland caused by the volcanic eruption of Mount St. Helens as an extraordinary item. The eruption was both unusual and infrequent. In contrast, Florida Citrus Company does not report frost damage to its citrus crop as an extraordinary item. Frost damage is not viewed as infrequent. Illustration 15-29 (page 708) shows the classification of extraordinary and ordinary items.

ACCOUNTING MATTERS! Business Insight

In the recession of the early 1990s, many companies closed plants and reduced their work forces. The costs incurred in these activities are called plant restructuring costs. Such costs are reported as other expenses and losses in the income statement. They are not considered an extraordinary item because plant closings are neither unusual nor infrequent in many industries.

Plant restructuring costs often have a significant effect on net income. For example, **Union Pacific Corp.** had a $585 million after-tax charge, of which $492 million applied to the disposal of 7,100 miles of the Union Pacific Railroad.

? If a company takes a large restructuring charge, what is the effect on the company's current income statements versus its future ones?

Illustration 15-29
Examples of extraordinary and ordinary items

Extraordinary items

1. Effects of major casualties (acts of God), if rare in the area.

2. Expropriation (takeover) of property by a foreign government.

3. Effects of a newly enacted law or regulation, such as a condemnation action.

Ordinary items

1. Effects of major casualties (acts of God), not uncommon in the area.

2. Write-down of inventories or write-off of receivables.

3. Losses attributable to labor strikes.

4. Gains or losses from sales of property, plant, or equipment.

Extraordinary items are reported net of taxes in a separate section of the income statement immediately below discontinued operations. To illustrate, assume that in 2006 a foreign government expropriated property held as an investment by Acro Energy Inc. If the loss is $70,000 before applicable income taxes of $21,000, the income statement will report a deduction of $49,000 as shown in Illustration 15-30. When there is an extraordinary item to report, the caption "Income before extraordinary item" is added immediately before the section for the extraordinary item. This presentation clearly indicates the effect of the extraordinary item on net income.

Illustration 15-30
Statement presentation of extraordinary items

ACRO ENERGY INC.
Income Statement (partial)
For the Year Ended December 31, 2006

Income before income taxes		$800,000
Income tax expense		240,000
Income from continuing operations		560,000
Discontinued operations		
Loss from operations of chemical division, net of $60,000 income tax saving	$140,000	
Loss from disposal of chemical division, net of $30,000 income tax saving	70,000	210,000
Income before extraordinary item		350,000
Extraordinary item		
Expropriation of investment, net of $21,000 income tax saving		**49,000**
Net income		$301,000

HELPFUL HINT

If there are no discontinued operations, the third line of the income statement would be labeled "Income before extraordinary item."

What if a transaction or event meets one (but not both) of the criteria for an extraordinary item? In that case it is reported under either "Other revenues and gains" or "Other expenses and losses" at its gross amount (not net of tax). This is true, for example, of gains (losses) resulting from the sale of property, plant, and equipment, as explained in Chapter 10. It has become quite common for companies to use the label "Nonrecurring charges" for losses that do not meet the extraordinary item criteria.

Change in Accounting Principle

For ease of comparison, financial statements are expected to be prepared on a basis **consistent** with the preceding period. Where a choice of accounting principles is available, the principle initially chosen should be consistently applied from period to period. A **change in accounting principle** occurs when the principle used in the current year is different from the one used in the preceding year. Examples include a change in depreciation methods (declining-balance to straight-line) and a change in inventory costing methods (FIFO to average cost). When is a change in accounting principle permitted? When two conditions are met: (1) management can show that the new principle is preferable to the old principle, and (2) the effects of the change are clearly disclosed in the income statement.

When a change in accounting principle has occurred:

1. The new principle should be used in reporting the results of operations of the current year.
2. The cumulative effect of the change on all prior year income statements should be disclosed net of applicable taxes in a special section immediately preceding net income.

To illustrate, assume that at the beginning of 2006, Acro Energy Inc. changes from the straight-line method of depreciation to the declining-balance method for equipment purchased on January 1, 2003. The cumulative effect on prior year income statements (statements for 2003–2005) is to increase depreciation expense and decrease income before income taxes by $24,000. Assuming a 30 percent tax rate, the net-of-tax effect of the change is $16,800 ($24,000 × 70%). The income statement presentation for the change in accounting principle is shown in Illustration 15-31.

Illustration 15-31
Statement presentation of cumulative effect of change in accounting principle

ACRO ENERGY INC.
Income Statement (partial)
For the Year Ended December 31, 2006

Income before income taxes		$800,000
Income tax expense		240,000
Income from continuing operations		560,000
Discontinued operations		
Loss from operations of chemical division, net of $60,000 income tax saving	$140,000	
Loss from disposal of chemical division, net of $30,000 income tax saving	70,000	210,000
Income before extraordinary item and cumulative effect of change in accounting principle		350,000
Extraordinary item		
Expropriation of investment, net of $21,000 income tax saving		49,000
Cumulative effect of change in accounting principle		
Effect on prior years of change in depreciation method, net of $7,200 income tax saving		**16,800**
Net income		$284,200

HELPFUL HINT

If a company does not have either discontinued operations or extraordinary items, the label "Income before cumulative effect of change in accounting principle" is used in place of "Income from continuing operations."

ETHICS NOTE

Changes in accounting principle should result in financial statements that are more informative for statement users. They should not be used to artificially improve the reported performance or financial position of the corporation.

The income statement for Acro Energy will also show depreciation expense for the current year. The amount is based on the new depreciation method. The caption "Income before extraordinary item and cumulative effect of change in accounting principle" is inserted immediately following the effects of discontinued operations. This presentation clearly indicates the cumulative effect of the change on prior years' income.

A complete income statement showing all material items not typical of regular operations is illustrated in Demonstration Problem 2 (page 714).

Comprehensive Income

Most revenues, expenses, gains, and losses recognized during the period are included in income. However, over time, specific exceptions to this general practice have developed. Certain items now bypass income and are reported directly in stockholders' equity. For example, in Chapter 13 you learned that unrealized gains and losses on available-for-sale securities are not included in income but instead are reported in the balance sheet as adjustments to stockholders' equity.

Why are these gains and losses on available-for-sale securities excluded from net income? Because disclosing them separately (1) reduces the volatility of net income due to fluctuations in fair value, yet (2) informs the financial statement user of the gain or loss that would be incurred if the securities were sold at fair value.

Many analysts have expressed concern over the significant increase in the number of items that bypass the income statement. They feel that this has reduced the usefulness of the income statement. To address this concern, the FASB now requires that, in addition to reporting net income, a company must also report comprehensive income. **Comprehensive income** includes all changes in stockholders' equity during a period except those resulting from investments by stockholders and distributions to stockholders. A number of alternative formats for reporting comprehensive income are allowed. These formats are discussed in advanced accounting courses.

BEFORE YOU GO ON...

Review It

1. What are the similarities and differences in reporting material items not typical of regular operations?
2. What is included in comprehensive income?

Do It

In its proposed 2006 income statement, AIR Corporation reports income before income taxes $400,000, extraordinary loss $100,000, income taxes (30%) $120,000, and net income $210,000. Prepare a correct income statement, beginning with income before income taxes.

ACTION PLAN

- Recall that the loss is extraordinary because it meets the criteria of being both unusual and infrequent.
- Disclose the income tax effect of each component of income, beginning with income before any irregular items.
- Report irregular items net of any income tax effect.

SOLUTION

AIR CORPORATION
Income Statement (partial)

Income before income taxes	$400,000
Income tax expense (30%)	120,000
Income before extraordinary item	280,000
Extraordinary loss net of $30,000 income tax saving	70,000
Net income	$210,000

Related exercise material: *BE15-12, BE15-13, BE15-14, E15-11, and E15-12.*

THE NAVIGATOR

Limitations of Financial Statement Analysis

STUDY OBJECTIVE 7

Recognize the limitations of financial statement analysis.

Significant business decisions are frequently made using one or more of the analytical tools illustrated in this chapter. But, you should be aware of the limitations of these tools and of the financial statements on which they are based.

Estimates

Financial statements contain numerous estimates. Estimates are used in determining the allowance for uncollectible receivables, periodic depreciation, and contingent losses. To the extent that these estimates are inaccurate, the financial ratios and percentages are inaccurate.

Cost

Traditional financial statements are based on cost. They are not adjusted for price-level changes. Comparisons of unadjusted financial data from different periods may be rendered invalid by significant inflation or deflation. For example, a five-year comparison of Sears's revenues might show a growth of 36%. But this growth trend would be misleading if the general price level had increased significantly during the same period.

Alternative Accounting Methods

Companies vary in the generally accepted accounting principles they use. Such variations may hamper comparability. For example, one company may use the FIFO method of inventory costing; another company in the same industry may use LIFO. If inventory is a significant asset to both companies, it is unlikely that their current ratios are comparable. For example, if **General Motors Corporation** had used FIFO instead of LIFO in valuing its inventories, its inventories would have been 26% higher. This difference would significantly affect the current ratio (and other ratios as well). In addition to differences in inventory costing methods, differences also exist in reporting such items as depreciation, depletion, and amortization. These differences in accounting methods might be detectable from reading the notes to the financial statements. But, adjusting the financial data to compensate for the different methods is difficult, if not impossible in some cases.

ETHICS NOTE

When investigating diversified firms, investors are often most interested to learn about the results of particular divisions. Firms are required to disclose the results of distinct lines of business separately if they are a material part of operations. Unfortunately, shifting revenues and expenses across divisions to achieve desired results reduces the usefulness of this information for financial statement analysis.

Atypical Data

Fiscal year-end data may not be typical of the financial condition during the year. Firms frequently establish a fiscal year-end that coincides with the low point in operating activity or in inventory levels. Therefore, certain account balances (cash, receivables, payables, and inventories) may not be representative of the balances in the accounts during the year.

Diversification of Firms

Diversification within a global environment also limits the usefulness of financial analysis. Many firms today are so diversified that they cannot be classified by a single industry—they are true conglomerates. Others appear to be comparable but are not.

BEFORE YOU GO ON...

Review It

1. What are some limitations of financial statement analysis?
2. Give examples of alternative accounting methods that hamper comparability.
3. In what way does diversification limit the usefulness of financial statement analysis?

THE NAVIGATOR

DEMONSTRATION PROBLEM 1

The condensed financial statements of The Estée Lauder Companies, Inc., for the years ended June 30, 2002 and 2001, are presented below.

THE ESTÉE LAUDER COMPANIES, INC.
Balance Sheets
June 30

	(in millions) 2002	2001
Assets		
Current assets		
Cash and cash equivalents	$ 546.9	$ 346.7
Accounts receivable (net)	624.8	580.6
Inventories	544.5	630.3
Prepaid expenses and other current assets	211.4	181.3
Total current assets	1,927.6	1,738.9
Property, plant, and equipment (net)	580.7	528.7
Investments	30.3	41.0
Intangibles and other assets	877.9	910.2
Total assets	$3,416.5	$3,218.8
Liabilities and Stockholders' Equity		
Current liabilities	$ 959.6	$ 856.7
Long-term liabilities	635.0	650.0
Stockholders' equity—common	1,821.9	1,712.1
Total liabilities and stockholders' equity	$3,416.5	$3,218.8

The Estée Lauder Companies, Inc.
Income Statements
For the Year Ended June 30

	(in millions) 2002	2001
Revenues	$4,751.5	$4,682.1
Costs and expenses		
Cost of goods sold	1,273.4	1,226.4
Selling and administrative expenses	3,133.6	2,947.6
Interest expense	17.6	26.7
Total costs and expenses	4,424.6	4,200.7
Income before income taxes	326.9	481.4
Income tax expense	114.4	174.0
Net income	$ 212.5	$ 307.4

Instructions

Compute the following ratios for 2002 and 2001.

(a) Current ratio.
(b) Inventory turnover. (Inventory on 6/30/00 was $546.3.)
(c) Profit margin ratio.
(d) Return on assets. (Assets on 6/30/00 were $3,043.3.)
(e) Return on common stockholders' equity. (Equity on 6/30/00 was $1,520.3.)
(f) Debt to total assets ratio.
(g) Times interest earned.

SOLUTION TO DEMONSTRATION PROBLEM 1

	2002	2001
(a) Current ratio:		
$1,927.6 ÷ $959.6 =	2.0:1	
$1,738.9 ÷ $856.7 =		2.0:1
(b) Inventory turnover:		
$1,273.4 ÷ [($544.5 + $630.3) ÷ 2] =	2.2 times	
$1,226.4 ÷ [($630.3 + $546.3) ÷ 2] =		2.1 times
(c) Profit margin:		
$212.5 ÷ $4,751.5 =	4.5%	
$307.4 ÷ $4,682.1 =		6.6%
(d) Return on assets:		
$212.5 ÷ [($3,416.5 + $3,218.8) ÷ 2] =	6.4%	
$307.4 ÷ [($3,218.8 + $3,043.3) ÷ 2] =		9.8%
(e) Return on common stockholders' equity:		
$212.5 ÷ [($1,821.9 + $1,712.1) ÷ 2] =	12%	
$307.4 ÷ [($1,712.1 + $1,520.3) ÷ 2] =		19%
(f) Debt to total assets ratio:		
($959.6 + $635.0) ÷ $3,416.5 =	47%	
($856.7 + $650.0) ÷ $3,218.8 =		47%
(g) Times interest earned:		
($212.5 + $114.4 + $17.6) ÷ $17.6 =	19.6 times	
($307.4 + $174.0 + $26.7) ÷ $26.7 =		19.0 times

THE NAVIGATOR

ACTION PLAN

- Remember that the current ratio includes all current assets. The acid-test ratio uses only cash, short-term investments, and net receivables.
- Use average balances for turnover ratios like inventory, receivables, and assets.
- Remember that return on assets is less than or equal to return on common stockholders' equity depending on cost of debt.

DEMONSTRATION PROBLEM 2

The events and transactions of Dever Corporation for the year ending December 31, 2006, resulted in the following data.

Cost of goods sold	$2,600,000
Net sales	4,400,000
Other expenses and losses	9,600
Other revenues and gains	5,600
Selling and administrative expenses	1,100,000
Income from operations of plastics division	70,000
Gain from disposal of plastics division	500,000
Loss from tornado disaster (extraordinary loss)	600,000
Cumulative effect of changing from straight-line depreciation to double-declining-balance (increase in depreciation expense)	300,000

Analysis reveals that:

1. All items are before the applicable income tax rate of 30%.
2. The plastics division was sold on July 1.
3. All operating data for the plastics division have been segregated.

Instructions

Prepare an income statement for the year.

SOLUTION TO DEMONSTRATION PROBLEM 2

DEVER CORPORATION
Income Statement
For the Year Ended December 31, 2006

Net sales		$4,400,000
Cost of goods sold		2,600,000
Gross profit		1,800,000
Selling and administrative expenses		1,100,000
Income from operations		700,000
Other revenues and gains	$ 5,600	
Other expenses and losses	9,600	4,000
Income before income taxes		696,000
Income tax expense ($696,000 × 30%)		208,800
Income from continuing operations		487,200
Discontinued operations		
Income from operations of plastics division, net of $21,000 income taxes ($70,000 × 30%)	49,000	
Gain from disposal of plastics division, net of $150,000 income taxes ($500,000 × 30%)	350,000	399,000
Income before extraordinary item and cumulative effect of change in accounting principle		886,200
Extraordinary item		
Tornado loss, net of $180,000 income tax saving ($600,000 × 30%)		420,000
Cumulative effect of change in accounting principle		
Effect on prior years of change in depreciation method, net of $90,000 income tax saving ($300,000 × 30%)		210,000
Net income		$ 256,200

THE NAVIGATOR

ACTION PLAN

- Report material items not typical of operations in separate sections, net of taxes.
- Associate income taxes with the item that affects the taxes.
- Apply the corporate tax rate to income before income taxes to determine tax expense.
- Recall that all data presented in determining income before income taxes are the same as for unincorporated companies.

SUMMARY OF STUDY OBJECTIVES

1. **Discuss the need for comparative analysis.** There are three bases of comparison: (1) Intracompany, which compares an item or financial relationship with other data within a company. (2) Industry, which compares company data with industry averages. (3) Intercompany, which compares an item or financial relationship of a company with data of one or more competing companies.
2. **Identify the tools of financial statement analysis.** Financial statements can be analyzed horizontally, vertically, and with ratios.
3. **Explain and apply horizontal (trend) analysis.** Horizontal analysis is a technique for evaluating a series of data over a period of time to determine the increase or decrease that has taken place, expressed as either an amount or a percentage.
4. **Describe and apply vertical analysis.** Vertical analysis is a technique that expresses each item within a financial statement in terms of a percentage of a relevant total or a base amount.
5. **Identify and compute ratios, and describe their purpose and use in analyzing a firm's liquidity, profitability, and solvency.** The formula and purpose of each ratio was presented in Illustration 15-27.
6. **Understand the concept of earning power, and indicate how material items not typical of regular operations are presented.** Earning power refers to a company's ability to sustain its profits from operations. "Irregular items"—discontinued operations, extraordinary items, and changes in accounting principles—are presented net of tax below income from continuing operations to highlight their unusual nature.
7. **Recognize the limitations of financial statement analysis.** The usefulness of analytical tools is limited by the use of estimates, the cost basis, the application of alternative accounting methods, atypical data at year-end, and the diversification of firms.

THE NAVIGATOR

GLOSSARY

Acid-test (quick) ratio A measure of a company's immediate short-term liquidity; computed by dividing the sum of cash, short-term investments, and net receivables by current liabilities. (p. 696).

Asset turnover A measure of how efficiently a company uses its assets to generate sales; computed by dividing net sales by average assets. (p. 700).

Change in accounting principle The use of a principle in the current year that is different from the one used in the preceding year. (p. 709).

Comprehensive income Includes all changes in stockholders' equity during a period except those resulting from investments by stockholders and distributions to stockholders. (p. 710).

Current ratio A measure used to evaluate a company's liquidity and short-term debt-paying ability; computed by dividing current assets by current liabilities. (p. 695).

Debt to total assets ratio Measures the percentage of total assets provided by creditors; computed by dividing total debt by total assets. (p. 703).

Discontinued operations The disposal of a significant segment of a business. (p. 706).

Earnings per share (EPS) The net income earned on each share of common stock; computed by dividing net income by the number of weighted average common shares outstanding. (p. 701).

Extraordinary items Events and transactions that are unusual in nature and infrequent in occurrence. (p. 707).

Horizontal analysis A technique for evaluating a series of financial statement data over a period of time, to determine the increase (decrease) that has taken place, expressed as either an amount or a percentage. (p. 689).

Inventory turnover A measure of the liquidity of inventory; computed by dividing cost of goods sold by average inventory. (p. 698).

Leverage See Trading on the equity.

Liquidity ratios Measures of the short-term ability of the enterprise to pay its maturing obligations and to meet unexpected needs for cash. (p. 695).

Payout ratio Measures the percentage of earnings distributed in the form of cash dividends; computed by dividing cash dividends by net income. (p. 702).

Price-earnings (P-E) ratio Measures the ratio of the market price of each share of common stock to the earnings per share; computed by dividing the market price of the stock by earnings per share. (p. 702).

Profit margin Measures the percentage of each dollar of sales that results in net income; computed by dividing net income by net sales. (p. 699).

Profitability ratios Measures of the income or operating success of an enterprise for a given period of time. (p. 699).

Ratio An expression of the mathematical relationship between one quantity and another. The relationship may be expressed either as a percentage, a rate, or a simple proportion. (p. 694).

Ratio analysis A technique for evaluating financial statements that expresses the relationship between selected financial statement data. (p. 694).

Receivables turnover A measure of the liquidity of receivables; computed by dividing net credit sales by average net receivables. (p. 697).

Return on assets An overall measure of profitability; computed by dividing net income by average assets. (p. 700).

Return on common stockholders' equity Measures the dollars of net income earned for each dollar invested by the owners; computed by dividing net income by average common stockholders' equity. (p. 700).

Solvency ratios Measures of the ability of the enterprise to survive over a long period of time. (p. 703).

Times interest earned Measures a company's ability to meet interest payments as they come due; computed by dividing income before interest expense and income taxes by interest expense. (p. 704).

Trading on the equity (leverage) Borrowing money at a lower rate of interest than can be earned by using the borrowed money. (p. 701).

Vertical analysis A technique for evaluating financial statement data that expresses each item within a financial statement as a percent of a base amount. (p. 692).

SELF-STUDY QUESTIONS

Self-Study/Self-Test

www.wiley.com/college/weygandt

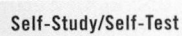

Answers are at the end of the chapter.

(SO 1) **1.** Comparisons of data within a company are an example of the following comparative basis:
a. Industry averages.
b. Intracompany.
c. Intercompany.
d. Both (b) and (c).

(SO 3) **2.** In horizontal analysis, each item is expressed as a percentage of the:
a. net income amount.
b. stockholders' equity amount.
c. total assets amount.
d. base year amount.

(SO 4) **3.** In vertical analysis, the base amount for depreciation expense is generally:
a. net sales.
b. depreciation expense in a previous year.
c. gross profit.
d. fixed assets.

(SO 4) **4.** The following schedule is a display of what type of analysis?

	Amount	Percent
Current assets	$200,000	25%
Property, plant, and equipment	600,000	75%
Total assets	$800,000	

a. Horizontal analysis.
b. Differential analysis.
c. Vertical analysis.
d. Ratio analysis.

(SO 3) **5.** Sammy Corporation reported net sales of $300,000, $330,000, and $360,000 in the years, 2004, 2005, and 2006, respectively. If 2004 is the base year, what is the trend percentage for 2006?
a. 77%.
b. 108%.
c. 120%.
d. 130%.

6. Which of the following measures is an evaluation of a firm's ability to pay current liabilities? (SO 5)
a. Acid-test ratio.
b. Current ratio.
c. Both (a) and (b).
d. None of the above.

7. A measure useful in evaluating the efficiency in managing inventories is: (SO 5)
a. inventory turnover.
b. average days to sell inventory.
c. Both (a) and (b).
d. None of the above.

8. In reporting discontinued operations, the income statement should show in a special section: (SO 6)
a. gains and losses on the disposal of the discontinued segment.
b. gains and losses from operations of the discontinued segment.
c. Both (a) and (b).
d. Neither (a) nor (b).

9. Scout Corporation has income before taxes of $400,000 and an extraordinary loss of $100,000. If the income tax rate is 25% on all items, the income statement should show income before extraordinary items and extraordinary items, respectively, of: (SO 6)
a. $325,000 and $100,000.
b. $325,000 and $75,000.
c. $300,000 and $100,000.
d. $300,000 and $75,000.

10. Which of the following is generally *not* considered to be a limitation of financial analysis? (SO 7)
a. Use of estimates.
b. Use of ratio analysis.
c. Use of cost.
d. Use of alternative accounting methods.

THE NAVIGATOR

QUESTIONS

1. (a) Alan Rodriquez believes that the analysis of financial statements is directed at two characteristics of a company: liquidity and profitability. Is Alan correct? Explain.
   (b) Are short-term creditors, long-term creditors, and stockholders interested primarily in the same characteristics of a company? Explain.
2. (a) Distinguish among the following bases of comparison: (1) intracompany, (2) industry averages, and (3) intercompany.
   (b) Give the principal value of using each of the three bases of comparison.
3. Two popular methods of financial statement analysis are horizontal analysis and vertical analysis. Explain the difference between these two methods.
4. (a) If Roberts Company had net income of $480,000 in 2006 and it experienced a 24.5% increase in net income for 2007, what is its net income for 2007?
   (b) If six cents of every dollar of Roberts revenue is net income in 2006, what is the dollar amount of 2006 revenue?
5. What is a ratio? What are the different ways of expressing the relationship of two amounts? What information does a ratio provide?
6. Name the major ratios useful in assessing (a) liquidity and (b) solvency.
7. Angeles Ochoa is puzzled. His company had a profit margin of 10% in 2006. He feels that this is an indication that the company is doing well. Celia Cruz, his accountant, says that more information is needed to determine the firm's financial well-being. Who is correct? Why?
8. What do the following classes of ratios measure? (a) Liquidity ratios. (b) Profitability ratios. (c) Solvency ratios.
9. What is the difference between the current ratio and the acid-test ratio?
10. Bloom Company, a retail store, has a receivables turnover of 4.5 times. The industry average is 12.5 times. Does Bloom have a collection problem with its receivables?
11. Which ratios should be used to help answer the following questions?
    (a) How efficient is a company in using its assets to produce sales?
    (b) How near to sale is the inventory on hand?
    (c) How many dollars of net income were earned for each dollar invested by the owners?
    (d) How able is a company to meet interest charges as they fall due?
12. The price-earnings ratio of **General Motors** (automobile builder) was 8, and the price-earnings ratio of **Microsoft** (computer software) was 38. Which company did the stock market favor? Explain.
13. What is the formula for computing the payout ratio? Would you expect this ratio to be high or low for a growth company?
14. Holding all other factors constant, indicate whether each of the following changes generally signals good or bad news about a company.
    (a) Increase in profit margin.
    (b) Decrease in inventory turnover.
    (c) Increase in the current ratio.
    (d) Decrease in earnings per share.
    (e) Increase in price-earnings ratio.
    (f) Increase in debt to total assets ratio.
    (g) Decrease in times interest earned.
15. The return on total assets for Wyeth Corporation is 7.6%. During the same year Wyeth's return on common stockholders' equity is 12.8%. What is the explanation for the difference in the two rates?
16. Which two ratios do you think should be of greatest interest to:
    (a) A pension fund considering the purchase of 20-year bonds?
    (b) A bank contemplating a short-term loan?
    (c) A common stockholder?
17. Why must preferred stock dividends be subtracted from net income in computing earnings per share?
18. (a) What is meant by trading on the equity?
    (b) How would you determine the profitability of trading on the equity?
19. Jackson Inc. has net income of $210,000, weighted average shares of common stock outstanding of 50,000, and preferred dividends for the period of $40,000. What is Jackson's earnings per share of common stock? Kate Jackson, the president of Jackson Inc., believes the computed EPS of the company is high. Comment.
20. Why is it important to report discontinued operations separately from income from continuing operations?
21. You are considering investing in Cederno Transportation. The company reports 2006 earnings per share of $6.50 on income before extraordinary items and $4.75 on net income. Which EPS figure would you consider more relevant to your investment decision? Why?
22. MCE Inc. reported 2005 earnings per share of $3.20 and had no extraordinary items. In 2006, EPS on income before extraordinary items was $2.99, and EPS on net income was $3.49. Is this a favorable trend?
23. Indicate which of the following items would be reported as an extraordinary item in Weiland Corporation's income statement.
    (a) Loss from damages caused by volcano eruption.
    (b) Loss from sale of short-term investments.
    (c) Loss attributable to a labor strike.
    (d) Loss caused when manufacture of a product was prohibited by the Food and Drug Administration.
    (e) Loss from flood damage. (The nearby Black River floods every 2 to 3 years.)
    (f) Write-down of obsolete inventory.
    (g) Expropriation of a factory by a foreign government.

24. When studying for an accounting test, a fellow student says, "Changes in accounting principle are reported in the retained earnings statement." Is your friend correct, or should he study harder?
25. Identify and briefly explain five limitations of financial analysis.
26. Explain how the choice of one of the following accounting methods over the other raises or lowers a company's net income during a period of continuing inflation.
    (a) Use of FIFO instead of LIFO for inventory costing.
    (b) Use of a 6-year life for machinery instead of a 9-year life.
    (c) Use of straight-line depreciation instead of accelerated declining-balance depreciation.

BRIEF EXERCISES*

Prepare horizontal analysis.
(SO 3)

BE15-1 Using the following data from the comparative balance sheet of Jane Hull Company, illustrate horizontal analysis.

	December 31, 2007	December 31, 2006
Accounts receivable	$ 540,000	$ 400,000
Inventory	$ 840,000	$ 600,000
Total assets	$ 3,640,000	$2,800,000

Prepare vertical analysis.
(SO 4)

BE15-2 Using the same data presented above in BE15-1 for Jane Hull Company, illustrate vertical analysis.

Calculate percentage of change.
(SO 3)

BE15-3 Net income was $500,000 in 2005, $400,000 in 2006, and $508,000 in 2007. What is the percentage of change from **(a)** 2005 to 2006 and **(b)** 2006 to 2007? Is the change an increase or a decrease?

Calculate net income.
(SO 3)

BE15-4 If Alana Company had net income of $650,000 in 2007 and it experienced a 30% increase in net income over 2006, what was its 2006 net income?

Calculate change in net income.
(SO 4)

BE15-5 Vertical analysis (common size) percentages for Osborne Company's sales, cost of goods sold, and expenses are shown below.

Vertical Analysis	2007	2006	2005
Sales	100.0	100.0	100.0
Cost of goods sold	59.2	62.4	64.5
Expenses	25.0	26.6	27.5

Did Osborne's net income as a percent of sales increase, decrease, or remain unchanged over the 3-year period? Provide numerical support for your answer.

Calculate change in net income.
(SO 3)

BE15-6 Horizontal analysis (trend analysis) percentages for Klamoth Company's sales, cost of goods sold, and expenses are shown below.

Horizontal Analysis	2007	2006	2005
Sales	96.2	106.8	100.0
Cost of goods sold	102.0	97.0	100.0
Expenses	109.6	98.4	100.0

Did Klamoth's net income increase, decrease, or remain unchanged over the 3-year period?

*Follow the rounding procedures used in the chapter.

BE15-7 Selected condensed data taken from a recent balance sheet of Kutenai Inc. are as follows.

Calculate liquidity ratios.
(SO 5)

KUTENAI INC.
Balance Sheet (partial)

Cash	$ 8,041,000
Short-term investments	1,947,000
Accounts receivable	12,545,000
Inventories	14,814,000
Other current assets	5,571,000
Total current assets	$42,918,000
Total current liabilities	$40,644,000

What are the **(a)** working capital, **(b)** current ratio, and **(c)** acid-test ratio?

BE15-8 Augusta Corporation has net income of $11.44 million and net revenue of $88 million in 2006. Its assets are $14 million at the beginning of the year and $18 million at the end of the year. What are **(a)** Augusta's asset turnover and **(b)** profit margin?

Calculate profitability ratios.
(SO 5)

BE15-9 The following data are taken from the financial statements of Abbado Company.

Evaluate collection of accounts receivable.
(SO 5)

	2007	2006
Accounts receivable (net), end of year	$ 550,000	$ 520,000
Net sales on account	3,850,000	3,100,000

Terms for all sales are 1/10, n/60.

(a) Compute for each year (1) the receivables turnover and (2) the average collection period. At the end of 2005, accounts receivable (net) was $490,000.
(b) What conclusions about the management of accounts receivable can be drawn from these data?

BE15-10 The following data are from the income statements of Kristi Thomas Company.

Evaluate management of inventory.
(SO 5)

	2007	2006
Sales	$6,420,000	$6,240,000
Beginning inventory	960,000	860,000
Purchases	4,540,000	4,661,000
Ending inventory	1,020,000	960,000

(a) Compute for each year (1) the inventory turnover and (2) the average days to sell the inventory. **(b)** What conclusions concerning the management of the inventory can be drawn from these data?

BE15-11 Watson Company has stockholders' equity of $400,000 and net income of $54,000. It has a payout ratio of 20% and a rate of return on assets of 15%. How much did Watson pay in cash dividends, and what were its average assets?

Calculate profitability ratios.
(SO 5)

BE15-12 An inexperienced accountant for Omar Corporation showed the following in the income statement: income before income taxes and extraordinary item $400,000, and extraordinary loss from flood (before taxes) $70,000. The extraordinary loss and taxable income are both subject to a 25% tax rate. Prepare a correct income statement starting with income before income taxes.

Prepare income statement including extraordinary items.
(SO 6)

BE15-13 On June 30, Tanner Corporation discontinued its operations in Mexico. During the year, the operating loss was $300,000 before taxes. On September 1, Tanner disposed of the Mexico facility at a pretax loss of $160,000. The applicable tax rate is 30%. Show the discontinued operations section of the income statement.

Prepare discontinued operations section of income statement.
(SO 6)

BE15-14 On January 1, 2006, Ramirez Inc. changed from the straight-line method of depreciation to the declining-balance method. The cumulative effect of the change was to increase prior years' depreciation by $60,000 and 2006 depreciation by $8,000. Show the change in accounting principle section of the 2006 income statement, assuming the tax rate is 30%.

Prepare change in accounting principle section of income statement.
(SO 6)

EXERCISES*

Prepare horizontal analysis.
(SO 3)

E15-1 Financial information for Marysara Inc. is presented below.

	December 31, 2007	December 31, 2006
Current assets	$125,000	$100,000
Plant assets (net)	380,000	330,000
Current liabilities	91,000	70,000
Long-term liabilities	140,000	95,000
Common stock, $1 par	135,000	115,000
Retained earnings	139,000	150,000

Instructions

Prepare a schedule showing a horizontal analysis for 2007 using 2006 as the base year.

Prepare vertical analysis.
(SO 4)

E15-2 Operating data for Jessi Corporation are presented below.

	2007	2006
Sales	$800,000	$600,000
Cost of goods sold	472,000	390,000
Selling expenses	120,000	72,000
Administrative expenses	76,000	54,000
Income tax expense	33,000	21,000
Net income	99,000	63,000

Instructions

Prepare a schedule showing a vertical analysis for 2007 and 2006.

Prepare horizontal and vertical analyses.
(SO 3, 4)

E15-3 The comparative balance sheets of Ramsey Corporation are presented below.

RAMSEY CORPORATION
Comparative Balance Sheets
December 31

	2007	2006
Assets		
Current assets	$ 76,000	$ 80,000
Property, plant, and equipment (net)	99,000	90,000
Intangibles	25,000	40,000
Total assets	$200,000	$210,000
Liabilities and stockholders' equity		
Current liabilities	$ 40,800	$ 48,000
Long-term liabilities	143,000	150,000
Stockholders' equity	16,200	12,000
Total liabilities and stockholders' equity	$200,000	$210,000

Instructions

(a) Prepare a horizontal analysis of the balance sheet data for Ramsey Corporation using 2006 as a base.

(b) Prepare a vertical analysis of the balance sheet data for Ramsey Corporation in columnar form for 2007.

*Follow the rounding procedures used in the chapter.

E15-4 The comparative income statements of Accra Corporation are shown below.

Prepare horizontal and vertical analyses.

(SO 3, 4)

ACCRA CORPORATION
Comparative Income Statements
For the Years Ended December 31

	2007	2006
Net sales	$600,000	$500,000
Cost of goods sold	480,000	420,000
Gross profit	120,000	80,000
Operating expenses	57,200	44,000
Net income	$ 62,800	$ 36,000

Instructions

(a) Prepare a horizontal analysis of the income statement data for Accra Corporation using 2006 as a base. (Show the amounts of increase or decrease.)

(b) Prepare a vertical analysis of the income statement data for Accra Corporation in columnar form for both years.

E15-5 **Nordstrom, Inc.** operates department stores in numerous states. Selected financial statement data for the year ending January 31, 2002, are as follows.

Compute liquidity ratios and compare results.

(SO 5)

NORDSTROM

NORDSTROM, INC.
Balance Sheet (partial)

(in millions)	End-of-Year	Beginning-of-Year
Cash and cash equivalents	$ 331	$ 25
Receivables (less allowance of $23 and $17)	699	722
Merchandise inventory	888	946
Prepaid expenses	37	29
Other current assets	102	91
Total current assets	$2,057	$1,813
Total current liabilities	$ 950	$ 951

For the year, net sales were $5,634, and cost of goods sold was $3,766.

Instructions

(a) Compute the four liquidity ratios at the end of the current year.

(b) Using the data in the chapter, compare Nordstrom's liquidity with (1) that of **Sears, Roebuck and Co.**, and (2) the industry averages for department stores.

E15-6 Seliz Incorporated had the following transactions occur involving current assets and current liabilities during February 2006.

Perform current and acid-test ratio analysis.

(SO 5)

Feb.	3	Accounts receivable of $15,000 are collected.
	7	Equipment is purchased for $28,000 cash.
	11	Paid $3,000 for a 3-year insurance policy.
	14	Accounts payable of $12,000 are paid.
	18	Cash dividends of $5,000 are declared.

Additional information:

1. As of February 1, 2006, current assets were $140,000, and current liabilities were $50,000.
2. As of February 1, 2006, current assets included $15,000 of inventory and $2,000 of prepaid expenses.

Instructions

(a) Compute the current ratio as of the beginning of the month and after each transaction.

(b) Compute the acid-test ratio as of the beginning of the month and after each transaction.

Compute selected ratios.
(SO 5)

E15-7 Marcus Company has the following comparative balance sheet data.

MARCUS COMPANY
Balance Sheets
December 31

	2006	2005
Cash	$ 15,000	$ 30,000
Receivables (net)	70,000	60,000
Inventories	60,000	50,000
Plant assets (net)	200,000	180,000
	$345,000	$320,000
Accounts payable	$ 40,000	$ 60,000
Mortgage payable (15%)	100,000	100,000
Common stock, $10 par	140,000	120,000
Retained earnings	65,000	40,000
	$345,000	$320,000

Additional information for 2006:

1. Net income was $25,000.
2. Sales on account were $420,000. Sales returns and allowances were $20,000.
3. Cost of goods sold was $198,000.
4. The allowance for doubtful accounts was $2,500 on December 31, 2006, and $2,000 on December 31, 2005.

Instructions

Compute the following ratios at December 31, 2006.

(a) Current.
(b) Acid-test.
(c) Receivables turnover.
(d) Inventory turnover.

Compute selected ratios.
(SO 5)

E15-8 Selected comparative statement data for Crimson Tide Products Company are presented below. All balance sheet data are as of December 31.

	2007	2006
Net sales	$800,000	$720,000
Cost of goods sold	480,000	440,000
Interest expense	7,000	5,000
Net income	60,000	42,000
Accounts receivable	120,000	100,000
Inventory	85,000	75,000
Total assets	580,000	500,000
Total common stockholders' equity	430,000	325,000

Instructions

Compute the following ratios for 2007.

(a) Profit margin.
(b) Asset turnover.
(c) Return on assets.
(d) Return on common stockholders' equity.

E15-9 The income statement for Nancy Kwan, Inc., appears below.

Compute selected ratios.
(SO 5)

NANCY KWAN, INC.
Income Statement
For the Year Ended December 31, 2006

Sales	$400,000
Cost of goods sold	230,000
Gross profit	170,000
Expenses (including $16,000 interest and $24,000 income taxes)	100,000
Net income	$ 70,000

Additional information:

1. The weighted average common shares outstanding in 2006 were 30,000 shares.
2. The market price of Nancy Kwan, Inc. stock was $13 in 2006.
3. Cash dividends of $23,000 were paid, $5,000 of which were to preferred stockholders.

Instructions
Compute the following ratios for 2006.

(a) Earnings per share.
(b) Price-earnings.
(c) Payout.
(d) Times interest earned.

E15-10 Sosa Corporation experienced a fire on December 31, 2007, in which its financial records were partially destroyed. It has been able to salvage some of the records and has ascertained the following balances.

Compute amounts from ratios.
(SO 5)

	December 31, 2007	December 31, 2006
Cash	$ 30,000	$ 10,000
Receivables (net)	72,500	126,000
Inventory	200,000	180,000
Accounts payable	50,000	90,000
Notes payable	30,000	60,000
Common stock, $100 par	400,000	400,000
Retained earnings	113,500	101,000

Additional information:

1. The inventory turnover is 3.2 times.
2. The return on common stockholders' equity is 22%. The company had no additional paid-in capital.
3. The receivables turnover is 8.4 times.
4. The return on assets is 20%.
5. Total assets at December 31, 2006, were $605,000.

Instructions
Compute the following for Sosa Corporation.

(a) Cost of goods sold for 2007.
(b) Net sales (credit) for 2007.
(c) Net income for 2007.
(d) Total assets at December 31, 2007.

Prepare a correct income statement.
(SO 6)

E15-11 For its fiscal year ending October 31, 2006, Moreno Corporation reports the following partial data.

Income before income taxes	$540,000
Income tax expense (30% × $440,000)	132,000
Income before extraordinary items	408,000
Extraordinary loss from flood	100,000
Net income	$308,000

The flood loss is considered an extraordinary item. The income tax rate is 30% on all items.

Instructions

(a) Prepare a correct income statement, beginning with income before income taxes.
(b) Explain in memo form why the income statement data are misleading.

Prepare income statement.
(SO 6)

E15-12 Servia Corporation has income from continuing operations of $240,000 for the year ended December 31, 2006. It also has the following items (before considering income taxes).

1. An extraordinary loss of $80,000.
2. A gain of $30,000 on the discontinuance of a division.
3. A cumulative change in an accounting principle that resulted in an increase in prior years' depreciation of $40,000.
4. A correction of an error in last year's financial statements that resulted in a $10,000 understatement of 2005 net income.

Assume all items are subject to income taxes at a 30% tax rate.

Instructions

(a) Prepare an income statement, beginning with income from continuing operations.
(b) Indicate the statement presentation of any item not included in (a) above.

PROBLEMS*

Prepare vertical analysis and comment on profitability.
(SO 4, 5)

P15-1 Comparative statement data for Rocking Company and Rolling Company, two competitors, appear below. All balance sheet data are as of December 31, 2007, and December 31, 2006.

	Rocking Company		Rolling Company	
	2007	**2006**	**2007**	**2006**
Net sales	$1,549,035		$339,038	
Cost of goods sold	1,080,490		241,000	
Operating expenses	292,275		79,000	
Interest expense	8,980		2,252	
Income tax expense	44,500		6,650	
Current assets	325,975	$312,410	83,336	$ 79,467
Plant assets (net)	521,310	500,000	139,728	125,812
Current liabilities	70,325	75,815	35,348	30,281
Long-term liabilities	108,500	90,000	29,620	25,000
Common stock, $10 par	500,000	500,000	120,000	120,000
Retained earnings	168,460	146,595	38,096	29,998

Instructions

(a) Net income (Rocking) 7.9%; (Rolling) 3.0%

(a) Prepare a vertical analysis of the 2007 income statement data for Rocking Company and Rolling Company in columnar form.
(b) Comment on the relative profitability of the companies by computing the return on assets and the return on common stockholders' equity ratios for both companies.

*Follow the rounding procedures used in the chapter.

P15-2 The comparative statements of Taylor Tool Company are presented below.

Compute ratios from balance sheet and income statement.

(SO 5)

TAYLOR TOOL COMPANY
Income Statement
For the Year Ended December 31

	2006	2005
Net sales	$1,818,500	$1,750,500
Cost of goods sold	1,011,500	996,000
Gross profit	807,000	754,500
Selling and administrative expense	506,000	479,000
Income from operations	301,000	275,500
Other expenses and losses		
Interest expense	18,000	14,000
Income before income taxes	283,000	261,500
Income tax expense	84,000	77,000
Net income	$ 199,000	$ 184,500

TAYLOR TOOL COMPANY
Balance Sheets
December 31

Assets	2006	2005
Current assets		
Cash	$ 60,100	$ 64,200
Short-term investments	69,000	50,000
Accounts receivable (net)	107,800	102,800
Inventory	133,000	115,500
Total current assets	369,900	332,500
Plant assets (net)	600,300	520,300
Total assets	$970,200	$852,800
Liabilities and Stockholders' Equity		
Current liabilities		
Accounts payable	$160,000	$145,400
Income taxes payable	43,500	42,000
Total current liabilities	203,500	187,400
Bonds payable	200,000	200,000
Total liabilities	403,500	387,400
Stockholders' equity		
Common stock ($5 par)	280,000	300,000
Retained earnings	286,700	165,400
Total stockholders' equity	566,700	465,400
Total liabilities and stockholders' equity	$970,200	$852,800

All sales were on account. The allowance for doubtful accounts was $3,200 on December 31, 2006, and $3,000 on December 31, 2005.

Instructions

Compute the following ratios for 2006. (Weighted average common shares in 2006 were 57,000.)

(a) Earnings per share.
(b) Return on common stockholders' equity.
(c) Return on assets.
(d) Current.
(e) Acid-test.
(f) Receivables turnover.
(g) Inventory turnover.
(h) Times interest earned.
(i) Asset turnover.
(j) Debt to total assets.

Perform ratio analysis, and evaluate financial position and operating results.

(SO 5)

P15-3 Condensed balance sheet and income statement data for Jeff Malone Corporation appear below.

JEFF MALONE CORPORATION
Balance Sheets
December 31

	2007	2006	2005
Cash	$ 25,000	$ 20,000	$ 18,000
Receivables (net)	50,000	45,000	48,000
Other current assets	90,000	95,000	64,000
Investments	75,000	70,000	45,000
Plant and equipment (net)	400,000	370,000	358,000
	$640,000	$600,000	$533,000
Current liabilities	$ 75,000	$ 80,000	$ 70,000
Long-term debt	80,000	85,000	50,000
Common stock, $10 par	340,000	310,000	300,000
Retained earnings	145,000	125,000	113,000
	$640,000	$600,000	$533,000

JEFF MALONE CORPORATION
Income Statement
For the Year Ended December 31

	2007	2006
Sales	$740,000	$700,000
Less: Sales returns and allowances	40,000	50,000
Net sales	700,000	650,000
Cost of goods sold	420,000	400,000
Gross profit	280,000	250,000
Operating expenses (including income taxes)	232,000	218,000
Net income	$ 48,000	$ 32,000

Additional information:

1. The market price of Malone's common stock was $4.00, $5.00, and $8.00 for 2005, 2006, and 2007, respectively.
2. All dividends were paid in cash.

Instructions

(a) Compute the following ratios for 2006 and 2007.
  (1) Profit margin.
  (2) Asset turnover.
  (3) Earnings per share. (Weighted average common shares in 2007 were 32,000 and in 2006 were 31,000.)
  (4) Price-earnings.
  (5) Payout.
  (6) Debt to total assets.

(b) Based on the ratios calculated, discuss briefly the improvement or lack thereof in financial position and operating results from 2006 to 2007 of Jeff Malone Corporation.

P15-4 Financial information for Fat Cat Company is presented below.

Compute ratios, and comment on overall liquidity and profitability.

(SO 5)

FAT CAT COMPANY
Balance Sheets
December 31

Assets	**2007**	**2006**
Cash	$ 70,000	$ 65,000
Short-term investments	52,000	40,000
Receivables (net)	94,000	90,000
Inventories	129,000	125,000
Prepaid expenses	29,000	23,000
Land	130,000	130,000
Building and equipment (net)	180,000	175,000
	$684,000	$648,000
Liabilities and Stockholders' Equity		
Notes payable	$100,000	$100,000
Accounts payable	48,000	42,000
Accrued liabilities	50,000	40,000
Bonds payable, due 2010	150,000	150,000
Common stock, $10 par	200,000	200,000
Retained earnings	136,000	116,000
	$684,000	$648,000

FAT CAT COMPANY
Income Statement
For the Years Ended December 31

	2007	**2006**
Sales	$850,000	$790,000
Cost of goods sold	620,000	575,000
Gross profit	230,000	215,000
Operating expenses	194,000	180,000
Net income	$ 36,000	$ 35,000

Additional information:

1. Inventory at the beginning of 2006 was $118,000.
2. Receivables (net) at the beginning of 2006 were $88,000. The allowance for doubtful accounts was $4,000 at the end of 2007, $3,800 at the end of 2006, and $3,700 at the beginning of 2006.
3. Total assets at the beginning of 2006 were $630,000.
4. No common stock transactions occurred during 2006 or 2007.
5. All sales were on account.

Instructions

(a) Indicate, by using ratios, the change in liquidity and profitability of Fat Cat Company from 2006 to 2007. (*Note*: Not all profitability ratios can be computed.)

(b) Given below are three independent situations and a ratio that may be affected. For each situation, compute the affected ratio (1) as of December 31, 2007, and (2) as of December 31, 2008, after giving effect to the situation. Net income for 2008 was $45,000. Total assets on December 31, 2008, were $700,000.

Situation	Ratio
(1) 18,000 shares of common stock were sold at par on July 1, 2008.	Return on common stockholders' equity
(2) All of the notes payable were paid in 2008. The only change in liabilities was that the notes payable were paid.	Debt to total assets
(3) Market price of common stock was $9 on December 31, 2007, and $12.80 on December 31, 2008.	Price-earnings ratio

Compute selected ratios, and compare liquidity, profitability, and solvency for two companies.

(SO 5)

P15-5 Selected financial data of **Target** and **Wal-Mart** for 2001 are presented here (in millions).

	Target Corporation	Wal-Mart Stores, Inc.
	Income Statement Data for Year	
Net sales	$39,176	$217,799
Cost of goods sold	27,246	171,562
Selling and administrative expenses	9,962	36,173
Interest expense	464	1,326
Other income (expense)	712	2,013
Income tax expense	842	3,897
Net income	$ 1,374	$ 6,854
	Balance Sheet Data (End of Year)	
Current assets	$ 9,648	$ 28,246
Noncurrent assets	14,506	55,205
Total assets	$24,154	$ 83,451
Current liabilities	$ 7,054	$ 27,282
Long-term debt	9,240	21,067
Total stockholders' equity	7,860	35,102
Total liabilities and stockholders' equity	$24,154	$ 83,451
	Beginning-of-Year Balances	
Total assets	$19,490	$78,130
Total stockholders' equity	6,519	31,343
Current liabilities	6,301	28,949
Total liabilities	12,971	46,787
	Other Data	
Average net receivables	$1,916	$ 1,884
Average inventory	4,349	22,028
Net cash provided by operating activities	1,992	10,260

Instructions

(a) For each company, compute the following ratios.

(1) Current.
(2) Receivables turnover.
(3) Average collection period.
(4) Inventory turnover.
(5) Days in inventory.
(6) Profit margin.
(7) Asset turnover.
(8) Return on assets.
(9) Return on common stockholders' equity.
(10) Debt to total assets.
(11) Times interest earned.

(b) Compare the liquidity, solvency, and profitability of the two companies.

Compute numerous ratios.

(SO 5)

P15-6 The comparative statements of Enis Company are presented below.

ENIS COMPANY
Income Statement
For Year Ended December 31

	2007	2006
Net sales (all on account)	$600,000	$520,000
Expenses		
Cost of goods sold	415,000	354,000
Selling and administrative	123,800	114,800
Interest expense	7,800	6,000
Income tax expense	18,000	14,000
Total expenses	564,600	488,800
Net income	$ 35,400	$ 31,200

ENIS COMPANY
Balance Sheets
December 31

Assets	2007	2006
Current assets		
Cash	$ 21,000	$ 18,000
Short-term investments	18,000	15,000
Accounts receivable (net)	92,000	74,000
Inventory	84,000	70,000
Total current assets	215,000	177,000
Plant assets (net)	423,000	383,000
Total assets	$638,000	$560,000

Liabilities and Stockholders' Equity	2007	2006
Current liabilities		
Accounts payable	$122,000	$110,000
Income taxes payable	23,000	20,000
Total current liabilities	145,000	130,000
Long-term liabilities		
Bonds payable	120,000	80,000
Total liabilities	265,000	210,000
Stockholders' equity		
Common stock ($5 par)	150,000	150,000
Retained earnings	223,000	200,000
Total stockholders' equity	373,000	350,000
Total liabilities and stockholders' equity	$638,000	$560,000

Additional data:

The common stock recently sold at $19.50 per share.
The year-end balance in the allowance for doubtful accounts was $3,000 for 2007 and $2,400 for 2006.

Instructions

Compute the following ratios for 2007.

(a) Current.
(b) Acid-test.
(c) Receivables turnover.
(d) Inventory turnover.
(e) Profit margin.
(f) Asset turnover.
(g) Return on assets.
(h) Return on common stockholders' equity.
(i) Earnings per share.
(j) Price-earnings.
(k) Payout.
(l) Debt to total assets.
(m) Times interest earned.

Compute missing information given a set of ratios.
(SO 5)

P15-7 Presented below is an incomplete income statement and an incomplete comparative balance sheet of Sulu Corporation.

SULU CORPORATION
Income Statement
For the Year Ended December 31, 2007

Sales	$11,000,000
Cost of goods sold	?
Gross profit	?
Operating expenses	1,204,600
Income from operations	?
Other expenses and losses	
Interest expense	?
Income before income taxes	?
Income tax expense	560,000
Net income	$?

SULU CORPORATION
Balance Sheets
December 31

Assets	**2007**	**2006**
Current assets		
Cash	$ 450,000	$ 249,000
Accounts receivable (net)	?	1,076,000
Inventory	?	1,720,000
Total current assets	?	3,045,000
Plant assets (net)	4,912,500	3,955,000
Total assets	$?	$7,000,000
Liabilities and Stockholders' Equity		
Current liabilities	$?	$ 825,000
Long-term notes payable	?	2,800,000
Total liabilities	?	3,625,000
Common stock, $1 par	3,000,000	3,000,000
Retained earnings	400,000	375,000
Total stockholders' equity	3,400,000	3,375,000
Total liabilities and stockholders' equity	$?	$7,000,000

Additional information:

1. The receivables turnover for 2007 is 10 times.
2. All sales are on account.
3. The profit margin for 2007 is 11.5%.
4. Return on assets is 16% for 2007.
5. The current ratio on December 31, 2007, is 3.0.
6. The inventory turnover for 2007 is 3.8 times.

Instructions

Compute the missing information given the ratios above. Show computations. (*Note*: Start with one ratio and derive as much information as possible from it before trying another ratio. List all missing amounts under the ratio used to find the information.)

P15-8 Clinton Corporation owns a number of cruise ships and a chain of hotels. The hotels, which have not been profitable, were discontinued on September 1, 2006. The 2006 operating results for the company were as follows.

Prepare income statement with discontinued operations and extraordinary loss.

(SO 6)

Operating revenues	$12,850,000
Operating expenses	8,700,000
Operating income	$ 4,150,000

Analysis discloses that these data include the operating results of the hotel chain, which were: operating revenues $2,500,000 and operating expenses $3,000,000. The hotels were sold at a gain of $200,000 before taxes. This gain is not included in the operating results. During the year, Clinton suffered an extraordinary loss of $600,000 before taxes, which is not included in the operating results. In 2006, the company had other revenues and gains of $100,000, which are not included in the operating results. The corporation is in the 30% income tax bracket.

Instructions

Prepare a condensed income statement.

P15-9 The ledger of Iceland Corporation at December 31, 2006, contains the following summary data.

Prepare income statement with nontypical items.

(SO 6)

Net sales	$1,700,000	Cost of goods sold	$1,100,000
Selling expenses	120,000	Administrative expenses	130,000
Other revenues and gains	20,000	Other expenses and losses	28,000

Your analysis reveals the following additional information that is not included in the above data.

1. The entire puzzles division was discontinued on August 31. The income from operations for this division before income taxes was $20,000. The puzzles division was sold at a loss of $70,000 before income taxes.
2. On May 15, company property was expropriated for an interstate highway. The settlement resulted in an extraordinary gain of $90,000 before income taxes.
3. During the year, Iceland changed its depreciation method from double-declining-balance to straight-line. The cumulative effect of the change on prior years' net income was an increase of $80,000 before taxes. (Assume that depreciation under the new method is correctly included in the ledger data.)
4. The income tax rate on all items is 30%.

Instructions

Prepare an income statement for the year ended December 31, 2006. Use the format illustrated in Demonstration Problem 2 (p. 714).

BROADENING YOUR PERSPECTIVE

Financial Reporting and Analysis

FINANCIAL REPORTING PROBLEM: PepsiCo

BYP15-1 Your parents are considering investing in **PepsiCo, Inc.** common stock. They ask you, as an accounting expert, to make an analysis of the company for them. Fortunately, excerpts from a current annual report of PepsiCo are presented in Appendix A of this textbook. Note that all dollar amounts are in millions.

Instructions

(Follow the approach in the chapter for rounding numbers.)

(a) Make a 5-year trend analysis, using 1999 as the base year, of (1) net sales and (2) net income. Comment on the significance of the trend results.

(b) Compute for 2003 and 2002 the (1) profit margin, (2) asset turnover, (3) return on assets, and (4) return on common stockholders' equity. How would you evaluate PepsiCo's profitability? Total assets at December 29, 2001, were $21,695,000,000, and total stockholders' equity at December 29, 2001, was $8,766,000,000.

(c) Compute for 2003 and 2002 the (1) debt to total assets ratio and (2) times interest earned. How would you evaluate PepsiCo's long-term solvency?

(d) What information outside the annual report may also be useful to your parents in making a decision about PepsiCo, Inc.?

■ COMPARATIVE ANALYSIS PROBLEM: PepsiCo vs. Coca-Cola

BYP15-2 **PepsiCo**'s financial statements are presented in Appendix A. **Coca-Cola Company**'s financial statements are presented in Appendix B.

Instructions

(a) Based on the information contained in these financial statements, determine each of the following for each company.

  (1) The percentage increase (decrease) in (i) net sales and (ii) net income from 2002 to 2003.

  (2) The percentage increase in (i) total assets and (ii) total common stockholders' (shareholders') equity from 2002 to 2003.

  (3) The basic earnings per share and price-earnings ratio for 2001. Coca-Cola's common stock had a market price of $50.75 at the end of fiscal-year 2003.

(b) What conclusions concerning the two companies can be drawn from these data?

■ RESEARCH CASE

BYP15-3 The October 15, 2002, issue of the *Wall Street Journal* included an article by Jesse Drucker titled "**Motorola**'s Profit: 'Special' Again?"

Instructions

Read the article and answer the following questions.

(a) For how many consecutive quarters, including the quarter anticipated in the article, has Motorola reported a "special" item on its income statement? What is the total amount of these special charges over this period?

(b) What justification does Motorola give for reporting these charges as special items on its income statement, rather than reporting them as ordinary expenses?

(c) In the second quarter of 2002, what was Motorola's pro forma income, and what was its net income according to generally accepted accounting principles (GAAP)?

(d) According to the article, do Wall Street analysts give more attention to GAAP income or pro forma income? Do analysts agree on how to treat special charges, such as those of Motorola?

■ INTERPRETING FINANCIAL STATEMENTS

BYP15-4 **Manitowoc Company** and **Caterpillar, Inc.** are both producers and sellers of large fixed assets. Caterpillar is substantially larger than Manitowoc. Financial information taken from each company's financial statements is provided below.

	Caterpillar (in millions)		**Manitowoc (in thousands)**	
Financial Highlights	**Current Year**	**Prior Year**	**Current Year**	**Prior Year**
Cash and short-term investments	$ 638	$ 419	$ 16,635	$ 16,163
Accounts receivable	4,285	4,290	51,011	29,500
Inventory	1,921	1,835	52,928	36,793
Other current assets	803	865	14,571	14,082
Current assets	7,647	7,409	135,145	96,538
Total assets	16,830	16,250	324,915	159,465
Current liabilities	6,049	5,498	110,923	54,064
Total liabilities	13,442	13,339	243,254	84,408
Total stockholders' equity	3,388	2,911	81,661	75,057
Sales	15,451		313,149	
Cost of goods sold	12,000		237,679	
Interest expense	191		1,865	
Income tax expense	501		8,551	
Net income	1,136		14,569	

Instructions

(a) Calculate the following liquidity ratios for the current year, and discuss the relative liquidity of the two companies.
  (1) Current ratio.
  (2) Acid-test (quick) ratio.
  (3) Receivables turnover.
  (4) Inventory turnover.

(b) Calculate the following profitability ratios for the current year, and discuss the relative profitability of the two companies.
  (1) Asset turnover.
  (2) Profit margin.
  (3) Return on assets.
  (4) Return on common stockholders' equity.

(c) Calculate the following solvency ratios for the current year, and discuss the relative solvency of the two companies.
  (1) Debt to total assets.
  (2) Times interest earned.

■ A GLOBAL FOCUS

BYP15-5 The use of railroad transportation has changed dramatically around the world. Attitudes about railroads and railroad usage differ across countries. In England, the railroads were run by the government until recently. Five years ago, **Railtrack Group PLC** became a publicly traded company. The largest railroad company in the United States is **Burlington Northern Santa Fe Railroad Company**. The following data were taken from the 2001 financial statements of each company.

	Railtrack Group (pounds in millions)		Burlington Northern Santa Fe (dollars in millions)	
Financial Highlights	**2001**	**2000**	**2001**	**2000**
Total current assets	£ 602	£ 1,177	$ 723	$ 976
Accounts receivable (net)	428	834	172	314
Total assets	9,443	11,484	24,721	24,375
Current liabilities	2,517	1,314	2,161	2,186
Total liabilities	6,795	8,411	16,872	16,895
Total stockholders' equity	2,648	3,073	7,849	7,480
Sales	2,476		9,208	
Operating costs and other	2,188		7,563	
Interest expense	89		463	
Income tax expense (credit)	(53)		445	
Net income	252		737	

Instructions

(a) Calculate the following 2001 liquidity ratios and discuss the relative liquidity of the two companies.
  (1) Current ratio.
  (2) Receivables turnover.

(b) Calculate the following 2001 solvency ratios and discuss the relative solvency of the two companies.
  (1) Debt to total assets.
  (2) Times interest earned.

(c) Calculate the following 2001 profitability ratios and discuss the relative profitability of the two companies.
  (1) Asset turnover.
  (2) Profit margin.
  (3) Return on assets.
  (4) Return on common stockholders' equity.

(d) What other issues must you consider when comparing these two companies?

■ EXPLORING THE WEB

BYP15-6 The Management Discussion and Analysis section of an annual report addresses corporate performance for the year, and sometimes uses financial ratios to support its claims.

Address: www.ibm.com/financialguide, or go to www.wiley.com/college/weygandt

Steps

1. From IBM's Financial Guide, choose **Getting Started**.
2. Choose **What's an Annual Report**.
3. Choose **Anatomy of an Annual Report**.

Instructions

Using the information from the above site, answer the following questions.

(a) What are the optional elements that are often included in an annual report?
(b) What are the elements of an annual report that are required by the SEC?
(c) Describe the contents of the Management Discussion.
(d) Describe the contents of the Auditors' Report.
(e) Describe the contents of the Selected Financial Data.

Critical Thinking

■ GROUP DECISION CASES

BYP15-7 As the CPA for Roenick Manufacturing Inc., you have been asked to develop some key ratios from the comparative financial statements. This information is to be used to convince creditors that the company is solvent and will continue as a going concern. The data requested and the computations developed from the financial statements follow.

	2004	2003
Current ratio	3.1 times	2.1 times
Acid-test ratio	.8 times	1.4 times
Asset turnover	2.8 times	2.2 times
Net income	Up 32%	Down 8%
Earnings per share	$3.30	$2.50
Book value per share	Up 8%	Up 11%

Instructions

With the class divided into groups, answer the following.

(a) Roenick Manufacturing Inc. asks you to prepare a list of brief comments stating how each of these items supports the solvency and going-concern potential of the business. The company wishes to use these comments to support its presentation of data to its creditors. You are to prepare the comments as requested, giving the implications and the limitations of each item separately. Then prepare a collective inference that may be drawn from the individual items about Roenick's solvency and going-concern potential.
(b) What warnings should you offer these creditors about the limitations of ratio analysis for the purpose stated here?

BYP15-8 General Dynamics develops, produces, and supports innovative, reliable, and highly sophisticated military and commercial products. In July of a recent year, the corporation announced that its Quincy Shipbuilding Division (Quincy) will be closed following the completion of the Maritime Prepositioning Ship construction program.

Prior to discontinuance, the operating results of Quincy were net sales $246.8 million, income from operations before income taxes $28.3 million, and income taxes $12.5 million. The corporation's loss on disposition of Quincy was $5.0 million, net of $4.3 million income tax benefits.

From its other operating activities, General Dynamics' financial results were net sales $8,163.8 million, cost of goods sold $6,958.8 million, and selling and administrative expenses $537.0 million. In addition, the corporation had interest expense of $17.2 million and interest revenue of $3.6 million. Income taxes were $282.9 million.

General Dynamics had an average of 42.3 million shares of common stock outstanding during the year.

Instructions

With the class divided into groups, answer the following.

(a) Prepare the income statement for the year, assuming that the year ended on December 31, 2006. Show earnings per share data on the income statement. All dollars should be stated in millions, except for per share amounts. (For example, $8 million would be shown as $8.0)

(b) In the preceding year, Quincy's earnings were $51.6 million before income taxes of $22.8 million. For comparative purposes, General Dynamics reported earnings per share of $0.61 from discontinued operations for Quincy in the preceding year.

(1) What was the average number of common shares outstanding during the preceding year?

(2) If earnings per share from continuing operations was $7.47, what was income from continuing operations during the preceding year? (Round to two decimals.)

COMMUNICATION ACTIVITY

BYP15-9 Dawn Flutie is the CEO of Tomorrow's Electronics. Flutie is an expert engineer but a novice in accounting. She asks you to explain (1) the bases for comparison in analyzing Tomorrow's financial statements, and (2) the limitations, if any, in financial statement analysis.

Instructions

Write a letter to Dawn Flutie that explains the bases for comparison and the limitations of financial statement analysis.

ETHICS CASE

Accounting Matters!

BYP15-10 Mike Singletary, president of Singletary Industries, wishes to issue a press release to bolster his company's image and maybe even its stock price, which has been gradually falling. As controller, you have been asked to provide a list of twenty financial ratios along with some other operating statistics relative to Singletary Industries' first quarter financials and operations.

Two days after you provide the ratios and data requested, Curtis Conway, the public relations director of Singletary, asks you to prove the accuracy of the financial and operating data contained in the press release written by the president and edited by Curtis. In the news release, the president highlights the sales increase of 25% over last year's first quarter and the positive change in the current ratio from 1.5:1 last year to 3:1 this year. He also emphasizes that production was up 50% over the prior year's first quarter.

You note that the press release contains only positive or improved ratios and none of the negative or deteriorated ratios. For instance, no mention is made that the debt to total assets ratio has increased from 35% to 55%, that inventories are up 89%, and that while the current ratio improved, the acid-test ratio fell from 1:1 to .5:1. Nor is there any mention that the reported profit for the quarter would have been a loss had not the estimated lives of Singletary's plant and machinery been increased by 30%. Curtis emphasized, "The prez wants this release by early this afternoon."

Instructions

(a) Who are the stakeholders in this situation?

(b) Is there anything unethical in president Singletary's actions?

(c) Should you as controller remain silent? Does Curtis have any responsibility?

CONTINUING COOKIE CHRONICLE

Accounting Matters!

(Note: This is a continuation of the Cookie Chronicle from Chapters 1 through 14.)

BYP15-11 The comparative balance sheet of Cookie & Coffee Creations Inc. at October 31, 2008, for the years 2008 and 2007, and the income statements for the years ended October 31, 2007 and 2008, are presented on the following page.

COOKIE & COFFEE CREATIONS INC.
Balance Sheet
October 31

Assets	**2008**	**2007**
Cash	$ 34,324	$13,050
Accounts receivable	3,250	2,710
Inventory	7,897	7,450
Prepaid expenses	6,300	6,050
Equipment	96,500	75,500
Accumulated depreciation	(25,200)	(9,100)
Total assets	$123,071	$95,660
Liabilities and Stockholders' Equity		
Accounts payable	$ 3,650	$ 2,450
Income taxes payable	10,251	11,200
Dividends payable	28,000	25,000
Salaries payable	2,250	1,280
Interest payable	188	0
Note payable—current portion	3,000	0
Note payable—long-term portion	4,500	0
Preferred stock, no par, $6 cumulative—3,000 and 2,500 shares issued, respectively	15,000	12,500
Common stock, $1 par—23,180 shares issued	23,180	23,180
Additional paid in capital—Treasury stock	250	250
Retained earnings	32,802	19,800
Total liabilities and stockholders' equity	$123,071	$95,660

COOKIE & COFFEE CREATIONS INC.
Income Statement
Year Ended October 31

	2008	**2007**
Sales	$485,625	$462,500
Cost of goods sold	222,694	208,125
Gross profit	262,931	254,375
Operating expenses		
Depreciation expense	17,850	9,100
Salaries and wages expense	147,979	146,350
Other operating expenses	43,186	42,925
Total operating expenses	209,015	198,375
Income from operations	53,916	56,000
Other expenses		
Interest expense	413	0
Loss on sale of computer equipment	2,250	0
Total other expenses	2,663	0
Income before income tax	51,253	56,000
Income tax expense	10,251	11,200
Net income	$ 41,002	$ 44,800

Additional information:
Natalie and Curtis are thinking about borrowing an additional $20,000 to buy more kitchen equipment. The loan would be repaid over a 4-year period. The terms of the loan provide for equal semi-annual payments of $2,500 on May 1 and November 1 of each year, plus interest of 5% on the outstanding balance.

Instructions

(a) Calculate the following ratios for 2007 and 2008.

1. Current ratio
2. Debt to total assets
3. Gross profit rate
4. Profit margin
5. Return on assets (Total assets at November 1, 2006, were $33,180.)
6. Return on common stockholders' equity (Total common stockholder's equity at November 1, 2006, was $23,180.)
7. Payout ratio

(b) Prepare a horizontal analysis of the income statement for Cookie & Coffee Creations Inc. using 2007 as a base year.

(c) Prepare a vertical analysis of the income statement for Cookie & Coffee Creations Inc. for 2008 and 2007.

(d) Comment on your findings from parts (a) to (c).

(e) What impact would borrowing an additional $15,000 to buy more equipment have on each of the ratios in (a) above, assuming that no changes are expected on the income statement and balance sheet? Comment on your findings.

(f) What would justify a decision by Cookie & Coffee Creations Inc. to buy the additional equipment? What alternatives are there instead of bank financing?

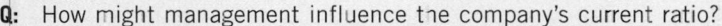

Answers to Accounting Matters! Questions

Accounting Matters!

p. 696

Q: How might management influence the company's current ratio?

A: Management can affect the current ratio by speeding up or withholding payments on accounts payable just before the balance sheet date. Management can alter the cash balance by increasing or decreasing long-term assets or long-term debt, or by issuing or purchasing equity shares.

p. 703

Q: Why would you purchase the stock of a company that has never paid a dividend?

A: Many companies pay little or no dividend, but instead put their earnings back into the business. Their shares sell at high prices or multiples because of their growth and earnings potential (their underlying value) and their financial ability either to pay a cash dividend in the future or to reward stockholders with a higher stock price in the future.

p. 704

Q: If you want to keep current with the financial and operating developments of a company in which you own shares, what are some ways you can do so?

A: You can obtain current information on your investments through a company's Web site, financial magazines and newspapers, CNBC television programs, investment letters, and a stockbroker.

p. 707

Q: If a company takes a large restructuring charge, what is the effect on the company's current income statements versus its future ones?

A: The current period's net income can be greatly diminished by a large restructuring charge, while the net income in future periods can be enhanced because they are relieved of costs (i.e., depreciation and labor expenses) that would have been charged to them.

Answer to PepsiCo Review It Question 4, p. 694

PepsiCo presents horizontal analyses in its Financial Highlights section and in its Management's Discussion and Analysis section. Vertical analysis is used in discussions presented in the Management's Discussion and Analysis section.

Answers to Self-Study Questions

1. b **2.** d **3.** a **4.** c **5.** c **6.** c **7.** c **8.** c **9.** d **10.** b

REMEMBER to go back to the Navigator box on the chapter-opening page and check off your completed work.

Specimen Financial Statements: PepsiCo, Inc.

THE ANNUAL REPORT

Once each year a corporation communicates to its stockholders and other interested parties by issuing a complete set of audited financial statements. The **annual report**, as this communication is called, summarizes the financial results of its operations for the year and its plans for the future. Many annual reports have become attractive, multicolored, glossy public relations pieces containing pictures of corporate officers and directors as well as photos and descriptions of new products and new buildings. Yet the basic function of every annual report is to report **financial information**, almost all of which is a product of the corporation's accounting system.

The content and organization of corporate annual reports have become fairly standardized. Excluding the public relations part of the report (pictures and products), the following items are the traditional financial portions of the annual report:

Financial Highlights
Letter to the Stockholders
Auditor's Report
Management's Responsibility for Financial Statements
Management Discussion and Analysis
Financial Statements and Accompanying Notes
Five- or Ten-Year Summary

In this appendix we illustrate current financial reporting with a comprehensive set of corporate financial statements. They have been prepared in accordance with generally accepted accounting principles and audited by an international independent certified public accounting firm. We are grateful for permission to use the actual financial statements and other accompanying financial information from the annual report of a large, publicly held company, **PepsiCo, Inc.**

The financial information herein is reprinted with permission from the PepsiCo, Inc. 2003 Annual Report. The complete financial statements are available through a link at the book's companion Web site and with new copies of the textbook.

Financial Highlights

The financial highlights section is usually presented inside the front cover or on the first two pages of the annual report. This section generally reports the total or per share amounts for five to ten financial items for the current year and one or more previous years. Financial items from the income statement and the balance sheet that typically are presented are sales, income from continuing operations, net income, net income per share, dividends per common share, and the amount of capital expenditures. The financial highlights section from PepsiCo's Annual Report is shown below.

Financial Highlights

PepsiCo 2003 and 2002

($ in millions except per share amounts; all per share amounts assume dilution)

	2003	2002	%Chg[(a)]
Summary of Operations			
Division net revenue	**$26,969**	$24,978	8
Total net revenue	**$26,971**	$25,112	7
Division operating profit	**$5,813**	$5,308	10
Total operating profit	**$4,781**	$4,295	11
Net income	**$3,568**	$3,000	19
Net income per common share	**$2.05**	$1.68	22
Other Data			
Management operating cash flow[(b)]	**$3,032**	$3,279	(7)
Net cash provided by operating activities	**$4,328**	$4,627	(6)
Capital spending	**$1,345**	$1,437	(6)
Common share repurchases	**$1,929**	$2,158	(11)
Dividends paid	**$1,070**	$1,041	3
Long-term debt	**$1,702**	$2,187	(22)

(a) Percentage changes above and in text are based on unrounded amounts.

(b) Excludes net capital spending. For additional information see "Our Liquidity and Capital Resources" in Management's Discussion and Analysis.

As shown above, PepsiCo chose also to present the percent change from last year to the current year for each of the reported items.

Letter to the Stockholders

Nearly every annual report contains a letter to the stockholders from the Chairman of the Board or the President (or both). This letter typically discusses the company's accomplishments during the past year. It also highlights significant events such as mergers and acquisitions, new products, operating achievements, business philosophy, changes in officers or directors, financing commitments, expansion plans, and future prospects. The letter to the stockholders signed by Steve Reinemund, President and Chief Executive Officer of PepsiCo, is shown on pages A3–A5.

PEPSICO

Dear Fellow Shareholders:

Growth and trust at PepsiCo are integrally connected, and we are proud of that.

They are at the core of our heritage, and together form the cornerstone for our future success. We are so confident of this connection that we chose to highlight it on our cover, and to share our 2003 performance in the context of our culture. We're focused squarely on a commitment to deliver *sustained growth* through *empowered people* acting with *responsibility* and building *trust*. Put simply, this commitment represents our priorities in the pursuit of creating value.

Steve Reinemund
Chairman and Chief Executive Officer

This isn't just corporate speak. It's how our 143,000 associates do business. It enables us to deliver our annual results, to plan for our future and to address challenges opportunistically. To help show how, we've included in this publication a Corporate Social Responsibility Report for the first time in our company's history. I encourage you to read this special report, as it provides a clear line of sight into how we're operating responsibly, and building trust along the way.

Through growth and trust, your company consistently delivers industry leading performance. Over the past four years, we've grown faster than both the S&P 500 and our industry group. We improved on that strong record in 2003:

- Volume grew 5%.
- Division net revenue grew 8%.
- Division operating profit grew 10%.
- Total return to shareholders was 12%.
- Earnings per share grew 22%.
- Cash flow from operations was $4.3 billion and management operating cash flow was more than $3 billion.

Our leading brands, unparalleled distribution systems, and vibrant pipeline of innovation continued to drive that performance, and serve as strong platforms for future growth. We're proud of all these tools, and continue to invest in them. But at the heart of our capabilities is a culture committed to growth.

A commitment to sustained growth

It's not just any kind of growth. Just about any way you look at our businesses, we're producing solid, balanced growth. Our health and wellness brands are growing, as are our fun-for-you businesses. We've achieved solid growth rates in snacks as well as beverages, within our North American as well as international operations. Our top-line and bottom-line growth rates are in step, as are our short-term and long-term growth prospects.

Our businesses are strong. We rank fourth among the largest food and beverages companies in the world. We have 6 of the 15 largest-selling brands in U.S. supermarkets. And, around the world, 16 of our brands sell more than one billion dollars each at retail. Our products are enjoyed by people of all ages, at all times of day.

There's no better time to invest for future growth than when things are going well, and that's exactly what we did in 2003. Specifically, we streamlined our North American beverage operations, retired old snack assets, and restructured our international businesses. And we're investing in new business processes that will yield funds to reinvest back into our businesses. Those dollars will enhance our capabilities and advantages; for example, driving product innovation and exercising marketing muscle across the globe.

People make the difference

Just as growth is part of PepsiCo's DNA, so is the idea of personal ownership. Our people have a long history of thinking and acting like they own their businesses, which is a reflection of their passion and ability to make a difference in their work. The associates who make, move and sell our products, and their colleagues who support them, understand that even the greatest brands and plans in the world won't succeed without empowered people to steer those capabilities and resources in meaningful ways.

That has never been more true or necessary than today. The need for personal ownership is more compelling than ever as we face three inescapable realities:

- A rapidly consolidating customer base that expects us to operate efficiently and effectively to meet their needs.
- A changing consumer with increasingly different needs, and a desire and expectation for choices.
- Increasingly sophisticated competitors who understand that convenient foods and beverages, our "sweet spot," also represent an opportunity for growth.

To successfully address these challenges and meet our growth goals, the importance of ownership is clear. It's a long-standing strength we will continue to build upon, as we change and adapt to these market conditions. And we are changing ourselves.

First and foremost, we've taken the best of what we've done historically — managing each independent and successful business vertically — and added a new dimension: managing across all our businesses horizontally to maximize PepsiCo's muscle. Whether that means purchasing boxes for everything from cereals to juices, or manufacturing and selling across a broader array of product lines, we're pushing ourselves to operate faster and smarter than ever before. And we're doing it from a position of strength and success. In essence, we're building on how we've managed best.

In this new environment of vertical and horizontal management, PepsiCo associates are empowered to innovate not only across our brands, but through virtually any business process they touch. They're using their diverse experiences to develop new product platforms, to power up our existing big brands with big ideas, and to find new ways to enhance our effectiveness through deeper collaboration. For example, in Mexico our Sabritas and Gamesa businesses have joined together to share services such as accounting, audit, legal, fleet operations and warehousing to take advantage of their combined scale and create major efficiencies. Strong and successful businesses in their own right, Sabritas and Gamesa have discovered they can be even greater together.

Working together has also created success in the marketplace. Under our continuing "Power of One" initiative, we've adopted a horizontal management perspective with our customers — with great results. In 2003, we created dedicated sales teams to represent and sell our entire portfolio of brands to our major retail customers. Today, we have 20 teams that market our products to more than 35 of our largest partners: mass merchandisers, club, supermarket and convenience stores, drug and dollar stores, and foodservice accounts. We've learned that we can do much more together than any one of our divisions or business units can do alone. This approach increases our in-store presence — and boosts sales and profits for our customers. In fact, our brands drive nearly as much sales and profit growth and cash flow for major U.S. retailers as all five of our next largest competitors combined.

Empowerment helps drive success, and with success comes rewards. Last year, we redesigned our compensation system for executives, and our SharePower stock option program for PepsiCo associates. Our new compensation designs provide industry leading pay for industry leading performance, and provide strong incentives for superior performance. Related to these compensation changes, we began expensing stock options at the end of 2003, ahead of the expected requirement to do so — something that will make financial performance comparisons easier in years to come.

No discussion of empowered people would be complete without mentioning two important PepsiCo leadership milestones. Rogelio Robelledo, president and CEO of our Frito-Lay International business, and Peter Thompson, president and CEO of our PepsiCo Beverages International business, have chosen to retire. With more than 40 years of PepsiCo leadership experience between them, they have left an inspiring legacy for our company, for which we are extremely grateful. While these seasoned leaders are leaving PepsiCo, I'm particularly pleased that Rogelio Robelledo has taken a new leadership role with The Pepsi Bottling Group as president and CEO of PBG Mexico. His track record for driving growth will serve PBG and PepsiCo well.

Doing it the right way

From product quality to environmental stewardship, regulatory compliance to corporate governance, we have a broad range of constituents who need to understand, support and trust our businesses and the way we operate them. Consumers need to trust that our products are high quality and that they are safe. Our shareholders and government agencies need to fully understand how our businesses are performing. Our communities need to know that we are actively involved in the issues and challenges of the times. We need to demonstrate what we are doing to be responsible stewards of the environment we all share. For these reasons, and many more, we have a responsibility to do things the right way, and we take it seriously.

We take pride in providing transparency in reporting financial and operating performance, in running our businesses responsibly, and in building trust with our constituents. Those efforts are being recognized. Institutional Shareholder Services in 2003 reviewed and rated our corporate governance programs. PepsiCo outscored 100% of all other food, beverage and tobacco companies and 96% of the S&P 500 companies.

The enclosed Corporate Social Responsibility report begins to share more insight into just how we're accomplishing our work along these lines. You'll find details on our approach to managing our economic, environmental and social responsibilities.

It works

To see how growth and trust work together to create value for you, consider how PepsiCo is taking action to address the issue of health and wellness.

You can't read a newspaper without finding a story on obesity in the United States and other countries, and its related health consequences. As a result, consumers want more choices of convenient foods and beverages that are healthier.

We started balancing PepsiCo's portfolio in the 1990s by adding some of the world's most recognizable better-for-you brands to our lineup of successful base brands — literally retooling our company for future growth. Bringing the Tropicana, Quaker Oats and Gatorade brands to PepsiCo dramatically increased our ability to provide more choices for consumers. We led the U.S. food and beverage industry as the first major company to eliminate trans fats from its salty snack brands, and we committed to driving 50% of innovation to better-for-you and good-for-you products. We exceeded that goal in 2003.

And that's just the beginning. We've engaged leading health and nutrition experts and formed a Blue Ribbon Health and Wellness Advisory Board to help us identify consumer nutrition needs. Our Advisory Board is made up of medical, nutrition, fitness and public policy professionals. Its role is not to endorse our actions or speak on our behalf — only to advise us objectively and candidly on how we can improve the healthfulness of existing products, develop new better-for-you products and encourage more active lifestyles. It has been invaluable in helping us create a strong health and wellness agenda.

We are adopting scientifically accepted standards for nutritious foods and beverages — those based on guidelines from the National Academy of Sciences and the U.S. Food and Drug Administration — to better assess our product portfolio. We've expanded product choices through trusted brands like Quaker, Tropicana, Gatorade, Diet Pepsi, Lay's and Aquafina. We've identified many opportunities for other product improvements, and we're aggressively pursuing new product platforms like low-carbohydrate chips and reduced-calorie orange juice.

Importantly, we're looking at health and wellness globally, and working hard to understand unique nutritional needs in different parts of the world. For example, whereas calcium consumption is a concern in developed markets, iron deficiency is a problem in developing countries. A global business must be sensitive to local needs, and that's just what we intend to be.

Another example of turning challenge into opportunity is in the area of diversity. PepsiCo is addressing rapidly changing consumer product needs with an aggressive focus on diversity and inclusion, both inside and outside the company. And we've been doing it for years. We understand that consumers — particularly those in urban markets — have diverse product needs. The first company to "crack the code" for those needs will win in the marketplace.

That's why we have goals for recruiting a diverse workforce to help us better serve our changing, more diverse consumer base. It's also why we've set aggressive plans in action to nurture an inclusive work environment — one that assures all employees feel welcome and captures the best of diverse thinking. That focus is paying off with an array of new products and promotions for urban markets. Whether it's Gatorade Xtremo!, Quaker Oatmeal Breakfast Squares or guacamole-flavored Lay's potato chips, new products are reaching and connecting with urban and ethnic consumers in meaningful ways.

Two additional critical resources we're tapping to stay connected with our consumers are our Ethnic Advisory Boards. Our African American and Latino/Hispanic Advisory Boards comprise leading influencers and thought leaders in these rapidly growing ethnic segments of the population. They further enable us to keep pace with — if not lead — the trends that our consumers are following.

Our approach to health and wellness — and to diversity — is about acting responsibly, and delivering products consumers trust in a range of convenient food and beverage choices.

Riding the wave

Our good news is that PepsiCo finished 2003 with industry leading results, strong momentum, a highly complementary stable of growing businesses, and a pipeline full of innovation.

We've opportunistically invested in ways designed to capture costs and reinvest them into our growing businesses. We've further strengthened a culture focused squarely on delivering sustained growth with empowered people, and new compensation programs that rewards industry leading performance.

We're also doing things the right way. Acting with responsibility and building trust are hallmarks of our commitment to corporate social responsibility, and we're more committed than ever to delivering results that we're proud to call our own, and proud to deliver to you. We welcome your thoughts and reactions, and look forward to updating you on our continued progress.

Steve Reinemund
Chairman of the Board and
Chief Executive Officer

Independent Auditor's Report

All publicly held corporations, as well as many other enterprises and organizations (both profit and not-for-profit, large and small) engage the services of independent certified public accountants who will provide an objective, expert report on their financial statements. Based on a comprehensive examination of the company's accounting system and records, and of the financial statements, the outside CPA issues the auditor's report.

The standard auditor's report consists of three pieces of information, expressed in separate sentences or paragraphs: (1) a responsibilities statement, (2) a scope statement, and (3) the opinion. In the **responsibilities statement**, the auditor identifies who and what was audited and indicates the responsibilities of management and the auditor relative to the financial statements. In the **scope statement**, the auditor states that the audit was conducted in accordance with generally accepted auditing standards and discusses the nature and limitations of the audit. In the **opinion statement**, the auditor expresses an informed opinion as to (1) the fairness of the financial statements and (2) their conformity with generally accepted accounting principles. The **Report of KPMG, Independent Public Accountants**, appearing in PepsiCo's Annual Report is shown below.

Independent Auditors' Report

PEPSICO

Board of Directors and Shareholders
PepsiCo, Inc.:

We have audited the accompanying Consolidated Balance Sheet of PepsiCo, Inc. and Subsidiaries as of December 27, 2003 and December 28, 2002 and the related Consolidated Statements of Income, Cash Flows and Common Shareholders' Equity for each of the years in the three-year period ended December 27, 2003. These consolidated financial statements are the responsibility of PepsiCo, Inc.'s management. Our responsibility is to express an opinion on these consolidated financial statements based on our audits.

We conducted our audits in accordance with auditing standards generally accepted in the United States of America. Those standards require that we plan and perform the audit to obtain reasonable assurance about whether the financial statements are free of material misstatement. An audit includes examining, on a test basis, evidence supporting the amounts and disclosures in the financial statements. An audit also includes assessing the accounting principles used and significant estimates made by management, as well as evaluating the overall financial statement presentation. We believe that our audits provide a reasonable basis for our opinion.

In our opinion, the consolidated financial statements referred to above present fairly, in all material respects, the financial position of PepsiCo, Inc. and Subsidiaries as of December 27, 2003 and December 28, 2002, and the results of their operations and their cash flows for each of the years in the three-year period ended December 27, 2003, in conformity with accounting principles generally accepted in the United States of America.

As discussed in Note 6 to the consolidated financial statements, in 2003 PepsiCo, Inc. adopted the fair value method of accounting for employee stock options by retroactively restating all periods presented as described in the Financial Accounting Standards Board's Statement of Financial Accounting Standards No. 148, "Accounting for Stock Based Compensation — Transition and Disclosure." Furthermore, as discussed in Note 4 to the consolidated financial statements, in 2002 PepsiCo, Inc. adopted the provisions of the Financial Accounting Standards Board's Statement of Financial Accounting Standards No. 142, "Goodwill and Other Intangible Assets."

KPMG LLP

KPMG LLP
New York, New York
February 9, 2004

The auditor's report issued on PepsiCo's financial statements is **unqualified** or "clean." That is, it contains no qualifications or exceptions. The auditor conformed completely with generally accepted auditing standards in performing the audit, and the financial statements conformed in all material respects with generally accepted accounting principles.

When the financial statements do not conform with generally accepted accounting principles, the auditor must issue a **qualified** opinion and describe the exception. If the lack of conformity with GAAP is sufficiently material, the auditor is compelled to issue an **adverse** or negative opinion. An adverse opinion means that the financial statements do not present fairly the company's financial condition and/or the results of the company's operations at the dates and for the periods reported.

In circumstances where the auditor is unable to perform all the auditing procedures necessary to reach a conclusion as to the fairness of the financial statements, a **disclaimer** must be issued. In these rare instances, the auditor must report the reason for failure to reach a conclusion on the fairness of the financial statements.

Companies strive to obtain an unqualified auditor's report. Hence, only infrequently are you likely to encounter anything other than this type of opinion on the financial statements.

Management's Responsibility for Financial Statements

A relatively recent addition to corporate annual reports is the statement made by management about its role in and responsibility for the accuracy and integrity of the financial statements. PepsiCo's management letter is entitled **Management's Responsibility for Financial Statements**. In it, the Chairman of the Board along with the President and Chief Financial Officer, and Senior Vice President and Controller on behalf of management, do the following: They (1) assume primary responsibility for the financial statements and the related notes, (2) declare the financial statements in conformity with generally accepted accounting principles, (3) comment on the audit by the certified public accountant, (4) outline and assess the company's internal control system, and (5) disclose the composition and role of the Audit Committee of the Board of Directors. PepsiCo's management report is presented on the next page.

PEPSICO

To Our Shareholders:

At PepsiCo, our actions — the actions of all our associates — are governed by our Worldwide Code of Conduct. This code is clearly aligned with our stated values — a commitment to sustained growth, through empowered people, operating with responsibility and building trust. Both the code and our core values enable us to operate with integrity — both within the letter and the spirit of the law. Our Code of Conduct is reinforced consistently at all levels and in all countries. We have maintained strong governance policies and practices for many years.

The management of PepsiCo is responsible for the objectivity and integrity of our consolidated financial statements. The Audit Committee of the Board of Directors has engaged independent auditors, KPMG LLP, to audit our consolidated financial statements and they have expressed an unqualified opinion. We are committed to providing timely, accurate and understandable information to investors.

This encompasses:

Maintaining a strong internal control environment with a focus on financial stewardship. Our system of internal controls includes written policies and procedures, segregation of duties and the careful selection and development of employees. The system is designed to provide reasonable assurance that transactions are executed as authorized and accurately recorded; that assets are safeguarded; and that accounting records are sufficiently reliable to permit the preparation of financial statements that conform in all material respects with accounting principles generally accepted in the United States of America. We maintain disclosure controls and procedures designed to ensure that information required to be disclosed in reports under the Securities Exchange Act of 1934 is recorded, processed, summarized and reported within the specified time periods. We monitor these internal controls through self-assessments and an ongoing program of internal audits. Our internal controls are reinforced through our Worldwide Code of Conduct, which sets forth our commitment to conduct business with integrity, and within both the letter and the spirit of the law.

Exerting rigorous oversight of the business. We continuously review our business results and strategies. This encompasses financial discipline in our strategic and daily business decisions. Our Executive Committee is actively involved — from understanding strategies and alternatives to reviewing key initiatives and financial performance. The intent is to ensure we remain objective in our assessments, constructively challenge our approach to potential business opportunities and issues, and monitor results and controls.

Engaging strong and effective Corporate Governance from our Board of Directors. We have an active, capable and diligent Board that meets the required standards for independence, and we welcome the Board's oversight as a representative of our shareholders. Our Audit Committee comprises independent directors with the financial knowledge and experience to provide appropriate oversight. We review our critical accounting policies, financial reporting and internal control matters with them and encourage their direct communication with KPMG LLP, our independent auditors and with our General Auditor.

Providing investors with financial results that are complete, transparent and understandable. The consolidated financial statements and financial information included in this report are the responsibility of management. This includes preparing the financial statements in accordance with accounting principles generally accepted in the United States of America, which require estimates based on management's best judgment.

PepsiCo has a strong history of doing what's right. We realize that great companies are built on trust, strong ethical standards and principles. Our financial results are delivered from that culture of accountability, and we take responsibility for the quality and accuracy of our financial reporting.

Peter Bridgman

Peter A. Bridgman
Senior Vice President and Controller

Indra K. Nooyi
President and Chief Financial Officer

Steven S Reinemund
Chairman of the Board and Chief Executive Officer

Management's Discussion and Analysis

The **management's discussion and analysis (MD&A)** section typically covers three financial aspects of a company: its results of operations, its ability to pay near-term obligations, and its ability to fund operations and expansion. Management must highlight favorable or unfavorable trends and identify significant events and uncertainties that affect these three aspects. This discussion obviously involves a number of subjective estimates and opinions. The MD&A section of PepsiCo's annual report is 20 pages in length and covers many company features, including its operations, customers, distribution network, competition, market risks, critical accounting policies, and financial results. To save pages, we have chosen to include here only coverage of "Items Affecting Comparability," "Results of Operations—Consolidated Review," and "Our Liquidity and Capital Resources." To read the topics not printed here, see PepsiCo's hard-copy 2003 Annual Report or an online version at the textbook's Web site.

Our Financial Results

PEPSICO

Items Affecting Comparability

The year-over-year comparisons of our financial results are affected by the following items:

	2003	2002
Operating profit		
Impairment and restructuring charges	**$(147)**	–
Merger-related costs	**$(59)**	$(224)
Net income		
Impairment and restructuring charges	**$(100)**	–
Merger-related costs	**$(42)**	$(190)
Net tax benefit	**$109**	–
Net income per common share — diluted		
Impairment and restructuring charges	**$(0.06)**	–
Merger-related costs	**$(0.02)**	$(0.11)
Net tax benefit	**$0.06**	–

For the items and accounting changes affecting our 2001 results, see Note 1 to our consolidated financial statements and our 2002 Annual Report.

Impairment and Restructuring Charges and Merger-Related Costs

In the fourth quarter of 2003, we incurred a restructuring charge of $147 million in conjunction with the streamlining of our North American divisions and PepsiCo International. Also, during 2003 and 2002, we incurred costs associated with our merger with The Quaker Oats Company (Quaker). For additional information, see Note 3 to our consolidated financial statements.

Net Tax Benefit

At the end of 2003, we entered into agreements with the IRS for open tax years through 1997. As part of these agreements, we also resolved the treatment of certain other issues related to future tax years. These agreements resulted in a tax benefit of $109 million. For additional information, see "Note 5—Income Taxes" and "Our Liquidity and Capital Resources."

Accounting Changes

See "Note 6—Stock Compensation" on the adoption of fair value accounting for stock options. There are no recently issued accounting standards that we have not yet adopted that are expected to have a material impact on our consolidated financial statements.

Results of Operations – Consolidated Review

In the discussions of net revenue and operating profit below, effective net pricing reflects the year-over-year impact of discrete pricing actions, sales incentive activities and mix resulting from selling varying products in different package sizes and in different countries.

Servings

Since our divisions each use different measures of physical unit volume (i.e., kilos, pounds and case sales), a common servings metric is necessary to reflect our consolidated physical unit volume. Our divisions' physical volume measures are converted into servings based on U.S. Food and Drug Administration guidelines for single-serving sizes of our products.

Total servings increased 5% in 2003 compared to 2002 as servings for snacks worldwide and beverages worldwide each grew 5%. PI, PBNA and FLNA contributed to the total servings growth. Total servings increased 4% in 2002 compared to 2001 primarily due to contributions across our divisions, led by beverage growth.

Net Revenue and Operating Profit

				Change	
	2003	2002	2001	**2003**	2002
Division net revenue	**$26,969**	$24,978	$24,045	**8%**	4%
Divested businesses	**2**	134	173		
SVE consolidation	**–**	–	(706)		
Total net revenue	**$26,971**	$25,112	$23,512	**7%**	7%
Division operating profit	**$5,813**	$5,308	$4,774	**10%**	11%
Corporate unallocated	**(852)**	(812)	(756)	**5%**	7%
Merger-related costs	**(59)**	(224)	(356)		
Impairment and restructuring charges	**(147)**	–	(31)		
Divested businesses	**26**	23	39		
Other reconciling items	**–**	–	(34)		
Total operating profit	**$4,781**	$4,295	$3,636	**11%**	18%
Division operating profit margin	**21.6%**	21.2%	19.9%	**0.4**	1.3
Total operating profit margin	**17.7%**	17.1%	15.5%	**0.6**	1.6

2003

Net revenue increased 7%. Division net revenue increased 8%, primarily due to the strong volume which contributed 4 percentage points of growth. Favorable product and country mix, as well as North American snack and concentrate price increases, contributed over 2 percentage points to the growth. Favorable foreign currency movements contributed nearly 1 percentage point to the net revenue growth.

Total operating profit increased 11% and margin increased 0.6 percentage points. Division operating profit increased 10% and division margin increased 0.4 percentage points. These gains were driven by the strong volume and higher effective net pricing. Cost of sales increased 8% reflecting increased commodity costs, particularly corn oil and natural gas. Selling, general and administrative expenses increased 6% driven by higher selling costs primarily reflecting the increased volume and increased fuel costs. Unfavorable foreign currency reduced operating profit growth by nearly 1 percentage point. In addition, total operating profit reflects the benefit from lower merger-related costs, offset by the 2003 impairment and restructuring charges of $147 million.

2002

Net revenue increased 7%. Division net revenue increased 4% driven by volume gains across all divisions, higher concentrate pricing and favorable mix. These gains were partially offset by increased promotional spending at PepsiCo Beverages North America and Frito-Lay North America, and net unfavorable foreign currency movement. The consolidation of SVE increased total net revenue growth by 3 percentage points, and net unfavorable foreign currency reduced the growth by 1 percentage point.

Total operating profit increased 18% and margin increased 1.6 percentage points. Division operating profit increased 11% and margin increased 1.3 percentage points. These gains were driven by the net revenue growth. In addition, total operating profit benefited from Quaker merger-related synergies of approximately $250 million, lower merger-related costs and productivity. Total operating profit growth improved 6 percentage points from the impact of lower merger-related costs, the absence of other impairment and restructuring costs and the adoption of SFAS 142. Operating profit growth was not materially affected by foreign currency movements.

Corporate Unallocated Expenses

Corporate unallocated expenses include the costs of our corporate headquarters, centrally managed initiatives, unallocated insurance and benefit programs, foreign exchange transactions gains and losses and certain other items. In the fourth quarter, we voluntarily elected to expense stock options. As a result, corporate unallocated expenses also include stock compensation expense of $407 million in 2003, $435 million in 2002 and $385 million in 2001.

For 2003, corporate unallocated expenses increased 5% primarily reflecting our 2003 investment in the Business Process Transformation initiative as discussed in "Our President and CFO Perspective." Higher employee-related costs, including deferred compensation, and corporate departmental costs also contributed to the increase. The increase in the deferred compensation costs is partially offset in net interest expense as described below. Corporate departmental expenses increased 5% reflecting staffing and other costs related to our health and wellness initiatives.

For 2002, corporate unallocated expenses increased 7% due to higher employee-related expenses partially offset by lower net foreign exchange transaction losses. Corporate departmental expenses declined 2%.

Other Consolidated Results

				% Change	
	2003	2002	2001	**2003**	2002
Bottling equity income	**$323**	$280	$160	**16**	75
Interest expense, net	**$(112)**	$(142)	$(152)	**(21)**	(6)
Annual tax rate	**28.5%**	32.3%	34.1%		
Net income	**$3,568**	$3,000	$2,400	**19**	25
Net income per common share — diluted	**$2.05**	$1.68	$1.33	**22**	27

Bottling equity income includes our share of the net income or loss of our non-controlled bottling affiliates as described in "Our Customers." Our interest in these bottling investments may change from time to time. Any gains or losses from these changes, as well as other transactions related to our bottling investments, are also included on a pre-tax basis.

2003

Bottling equity income increased 16%. This increase primarily reflects a favorable comparison to the impairment charge taken in 2002 on a Latin American bottling investment, and increased earnings from PBG and PAS in 2003.

Net interest expense declined 21% primarily due to a gain of $22 million on investments used to economically hedge a portion of our deferred compensation liability versus losses of $18 million in the prior year. The offsetting increase in deferred compensation costs is reported in corporate unallocated expenses within selling, general and administrative expenses. This net gain was partially offset by lower investment rates.

The annual tax rate decreased 3.8 percentage points compared to the prior year. At the end of 2003, we entered into agreements with the IRS. These agreements resulted in a tax benefit of $109 million, reducing our tax rate by over 2 percentage points. The resolution of certain issues is also expected to lower our future tax rate. Lower taxes on foreign results, including the impact of our new concentrate operations, also reduced our tax rate by nearly 2 percentage points. The impact of lower nondeductible merger-related costs contributed 0.9 percentage points to the decrease.

Net income increased 19% and the related net income per common share increased 22%. These increases primarily reflect the solid operating profit growth, our lower annual tax rate and increased bottling equity income. The benefit of lower merger-related costs was largely offset by the impairment and restructuring charges. Net income per common share also reflects the benefit of a reduction in average shares outstanding primarily as a result of share buyback activity.

2002

Bottling equity income increased 75%. This increase primarily reflects the adoption of SFAS 142, improved performance of our international bottling investments, and contributions from our North American anchor bottlers. The impact of impairment charges of $35 million relating to a Latin American bottling investment was more than offset by the settlement of issues upon the sale of our investment in Pepsi-Gemex, our Mexican bottling affiliate, and the absence of 2001 unusual items.

Net interest expense declined 6% primarily due to lower average debt levels, partially offset by increased losses of $10 million on investments used to economically hedge a portion of our deferred compensation liability. Decreases in borrowing rates were offset by decreases in investment rates.

The annual tax rate decreased 1.8 percentage points compared to prior year. The adoption of SFAS 142 reduced the rate by 0.9 percentage points. The impact of nondeductible merger-related costs decreased from 2.5 percentage points in 2001 to 1.0 percentage point in 2002.

Net income increased 25% and the related net income per common share increased 27%. These increases primarily reflect the solid operating profit growth, lower merger-related costs and the adoption of SFAS 142. Net income per common share also reflects the benefit of a reduction in average shares outstanding primarily as a result of increased share buyback activity.

Our Liquidity and Capital Resources

Our strong cash-generating capability and financial condition give us ready access to capital markets throughout the world. Our principal source of liquidity is operating cash flows, which are derived from net income. This cash-generating capability is one of our fundamental strengths and provides us with substantial financial flexibility in meeting operating, investing and financing needs. In addition, we have revolving credit facilities that are further discussed in Note 9 to our consolidated financial statements.

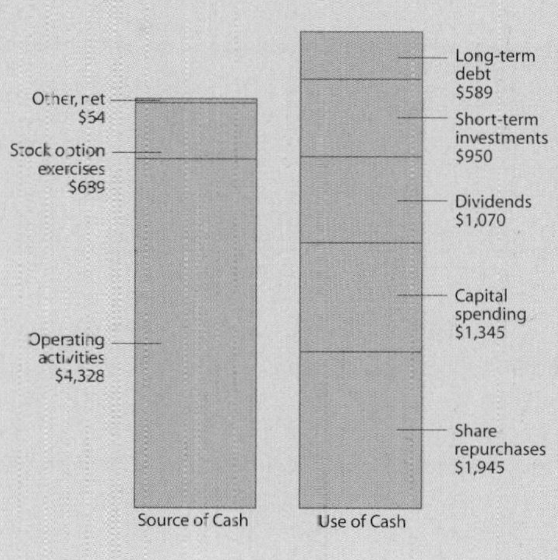

Operating Activities
In 2003, our operations provided $4.3 billion of cash reflecting our solid business results, net of pension plan contributions of $535 million of which $500 million was discretionary, and a $250 million tax payment related to our IRS agreements. In 2002, net cash provided by operating activities of $4.6 billion reflected our business results, pension plan contributions of $820 million of which $750 million was discretionary, and a net tax refund of approximately $250 million related to prior years. The year-over-year decline in cash flows from operations is primarily attributable to the higher net tax payments, partially offset by lower pension contributions in 2003.

In the first half of 2004, we will make an additional tax payment of approximately $750 million as a result of the IRS agreements. A portion of this payment represents deductible interest, which will lower our estimated tax payments during the second half of 2004 by a total of approximately $150 million. Due to the tax payment and the current market environment, we expect to issue medium-term debt of up to $500 million in the first half of 2004. We estimate our 2004 discretionary pension contributions will be approximately $400 million.

Investing Activities
In 2003, we used $2.3 billion for investing, primarily reflecting capital spending of $1.3 billion and short-term investments of $1.0 billion. In 2002, we used $0.5 billion for investing, primarily reflecting capital spending of $1.4 billion and the acquisition of the Wotsits brand in the United Kingdom, partially offset by short-term investment maturities and proceeds from the Pepsi-Gemex transaction.

We expect capital spending to continue at a rate of approximately 5% to 5.5% of net revenue in 2004.

Financing Activities
In 2003, we used $2.9 billion for financing, primarily reflecting share repurchases at a cost of $1.9 billion and dividend payments of $1.1 billion. This compares to $3.2 billion used for financing in 2002 for share repurchases of $2.2 billion and dividend payments of $1.0 billion.

In 2002, our Board of Directors authorized a share repurchase program of up to $5 billion over a three-year period. Since inception of the program, we have repurchased $4.1 billion of shares, leaving $0.9 billion of remaining authorization. Our current dividend policy is to pay approximately one-third of our previous year's net income in dividends.

Each spring we review our capital structure with our Board. Our discussion covers our dividend policy and share repurchase activity.

Management Operating Cash Flow
We focus on management operating cash flow as a key element in achieving maximum shareholder value and it is the primary measure we use to monitor cash flow performance. However, it is not a measure provided by accounting principles generally accepted in the United States. Since net capital spending is essential to our product innovation initiatives and maintaining our operational capabilities, we believe that it is a recurring and necessary use of cash. As such, we believe investors should also consider net capital spending when eval-

Management operating cash flow was $3.0 billion in 2003.

Net cash provided by operating activities was $4.3 billion in 2003.

uating our cash from operating activities. The table below reconciles the net cash provided by operating activities as reflected in our Consolidated Statement of Cash Flows to our management operating cash flow.

	2003	2002	2001
Net cash provided by operating activities	**$4,328**	$4,627	$3,820
Capital spending	**(1,345)**	(1,437)	(1,324)
Sales of property, plant and equipment	**49**	89	–
Management operating cash flow	**$3,032**	$3,279	$2,496

Management operating cash flow was used primarily to repurchase shares and pay dividends. We expect management operating cash flow in 2004 to grow by 10% or more reflecting our underlying business growth. We currently expect to continue to return approximately all our management operating cash flows to our shareholders through dividends and share repurchases. However, see "Cautionary Statements" for certain factors that may impact our operating cash flows.

Credit Ratings

Our debt ratings of Aa3 from Moody's and A+ from Standard & Poor's contribute to our ability to access global capital markets. We have maintained healthy investment grade ratings for over a decade. Standard & Poor's rating reflects an upgrade from A to A+ during 2003 and Moody's rating reflects an upgrade from A1 to Aa3 in 2004 due to the strength of our balance sheet and cash flows. Each rating is considered strong investment grade and is in the first quartile of their respective ranking systems. These ratings also reflect the impact of our anchor bottlers' cash flows and debt.

Credit Facilities and Long-Term Contractual Commitments

See Note 9 to our consolidated financial statements for a description of our credit facilities and long-term contractual commitments.

Off-Balance Sheet Arrangements

It is not our business practice to enter into off-balance sheet arrangements nor is it our policy to issue guarantees to our bottlers, noncontrolled affiliates or third parties. However, certain guarantees were necessary to facilitate the separation of our bottling and restaurant operations from us. As of year-end 2003, we believe it is remote that these guarantees would require any cash payment. See Note 9 to our consolidated financial statements for a description of our off-balance sheet arrangements.

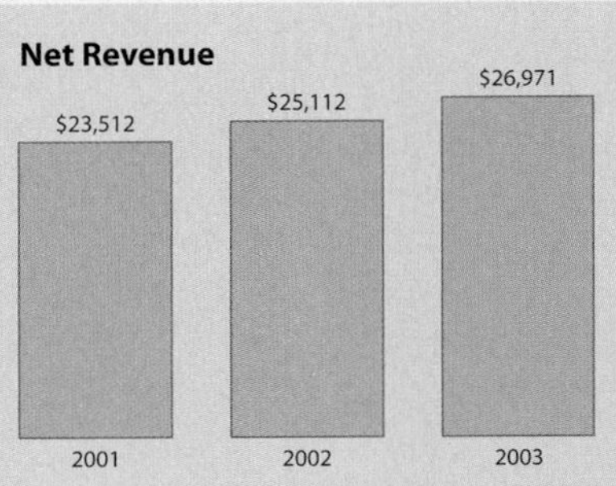

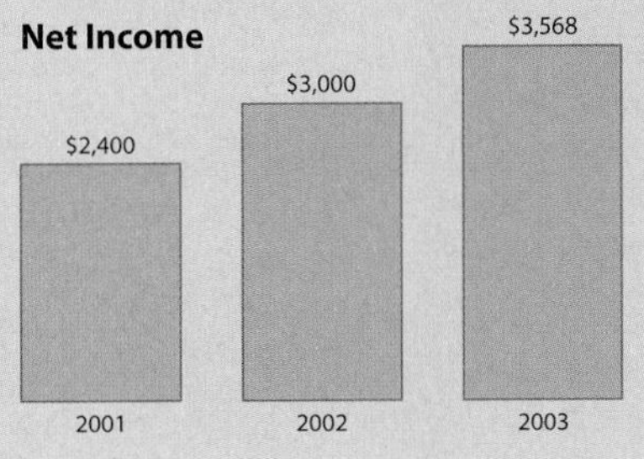

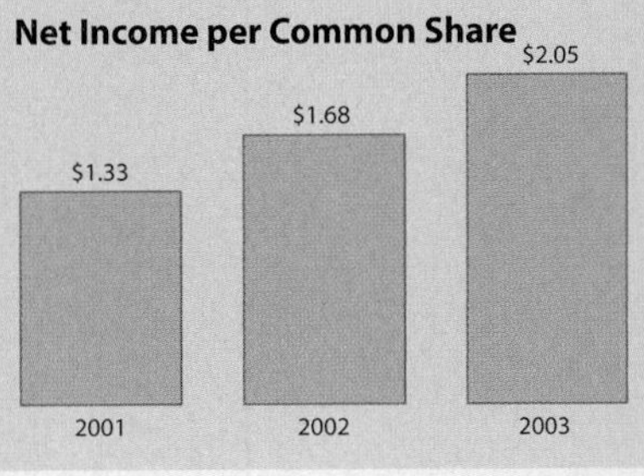

Financial Statements and Accompanying Notes

The standard set of financial statements consists of: (1) a comparative statement of income (statement of operations) for three years, (2) a comparative balance sheet for two years, (3) a comparative statement of cash flows for three years, (4) a statement of stockholders' (or shareholders') equity for three years, and (5) a set of accompanying notes that are considered an integral part of the financial statements. The auditor's report, unless stated otherwise, covers the financial statements and the accompanying notes. The financial statements and accompanying notes plus some supplementary data for PepsiCo, Inc. appear on the following pages.

Consolidated Statement of Income

PEPSICO

PepsiCo, Inc. and Subsidiaries
Fiscal years ended December 27, 2003, December 28, 2002 and December 29, 2001

(in millions except per share amounts)	2003	2002	2001
Net Revenue	**$26,971**	$25,112	$23,512
Cost of sales	**12,379**	11,497	10,750
Selling, general and administrative expenses	**9,460**	8,958	8,574
Amortization of intangible assets	**145**	138	165
Merger-related costs	**59**	224	356
Impairment and restructuring charges	**147**	–	31
Operating Profit	**4,781**	4,295	3,636
Bottling equity income	**323**	280	160
Interest expense	**(163)**	(178)	(219)
Interest income	**51**	36	67
Income Before Income Taxes	**4,992**	4,433	3,644
Provision for Income Taxes	**1,424**	1,433	1,244
Net Income	**$ 3,568**	$ 3,000	$ 2,400
Net Income per Common Share			
Basic	**$2.07**	$1.71	$1.36
Diluted	**$2.05**	$1.68	$1.33

See accompanying notes to consolidated financial statements.

Consolidated Statement of Cash Flows

PEPSICO

PepsiCo, Inc. and Subsidiaries
Fiscal years ended December 27, 2003, December 28, 2002 and December 29, 2001

(in millions)	2003	2002	2001
Operating Activities			
Net income	**$ 3,568**	$ 3,000	$ 2,400
Adjustments to reconcile net income to net cash provided by operating activities			
Depreciation and amortization	**1,221**	1,112	1,082
Stock compensation expense	**407**	435	385
Merger-related costs	**59**	224	356
Impairment and restructuring charges	**147**	–	31
Cash payments for merger-related costs and restructuring charges	**(109)**	(123)	(273)
Pension plan contributions	**(535)**	(820)	(446)
Bottling equity income, net of dividends	**(276)**	(222)	(103)
Deferred income taxes	**(323)**	174	45
Other noncash charges and credits, net	**415**	263	257
Changes in operating working capital, excluding effects of acquisitions and dispositions			
Accounts and notes receivable	**(220)**	(260)	7
Inventories	**(49)**	(53)	(75)
Prepaid expenses and other current assets	**23**	(78)	(6)
Accounts payable and other current liabilities	**(11)**	426	(236)
Income taxes payable	**182**	270	389
Net change in operating working capital	**(75)**	305	79
Other	**(171)**	279	7
Net Cash Provided by Operating Activities	**4,328**	4,627	3,820
Investing Activities			
Capital spending	**(1,345)**	(1,437)	(1,324)
Sales of property, plant and equipment	**49**	89	–
Acquisitions and investments in noncontrolled affiliates	**(71)**	(351)	(432)
Divestitures	**46**	376	–
Short-term investments, by original maturity			
More than three months — purchases	**(981)**	(62)	(2,537)
More than three months — maturities	**6**	833	2,078
Three months or less, net	**25**	(14)	(41)
Snack Ventures Europe consolidation	**–**	39	–
Net Cash Used for Investing Activities	**(2,271)**	(527)	(2,256)
Financing Activities			
Proceeds from issuances of long-term debt	**52**	11	324
Payments of long-term debt	**(641)**	(353)	(573)
Short-term borrowings, by original maturity			
More than three months — proceeds	**88**	707	788
More than three months — payments	**(115)**	(809)	(483)
Three months or less, net	**40**	40	(397)
Cash dividends paid	**(1,070)**	(1,041)	(994)
Share repurchases — common	**(1,929)**	(2,158)	(1,716)
Share repurchases — preferred	**(16)**	(32)	(10)
Quaker share repurchases	**–**	–	(5)
Proceeds from reissuance of shares	**–**	–	524
Proceeds from exercises of stock options	**689**	456	623
Net Cash Used for Financing Activities	**(2,902)**	(3,179)	(1,919)
Effect of exchange rate changes on cash and cash equivalents	**27**	34	–
Net (Decrease)/Increase in Cash and Cash Equivalents	**(818)**	955	(355)
Cash and Cash Equivalents, Beginning of Year	**1,638**	683	1,038
Cash and Cash Equivalents, End of Year	**$ 820**	$ 1,638	$ 683

See accompanying notes to consolidated financial statements.

Consolidated Balance Sheet

PEPSICO

PepsiCo, Inc. and Subsidiaries
December 27, 2003 and December 28, 2002

(in millions except per share amounts)	2003	2002
ASSETS		
Current Assets		
Cash and cash equivalents	$ 820	$ 1,638
Short-term investments, at cost	1,181	207
	2,001	1,845
Accounts and notes receivable, net	2,830	2,531
Inventories	1,412	1,342
Prepaid expenses and other current assets	687	695
Total Current Assets	6,930	6,413
Property, Plant and Equipment, net	7,828	7,390
Amortizable Intangible Assets, net	718	801
Goodwill	3,796	3,631
Other nonamortizable intangible assets	869	787
Nonamortizable Intangible Assets	4,665	4,418
Investments in Noncontrolled Affiliates	2,920	2,611
Other Assets	2,266	1,841
Total Assets	$25,327	$23,474
LIABILITIES AND SHAREHOLDERS' EQUITY		
Current Liabilities		
Short-term obligations	$ 591	$ 562
Accounts payable and other current liabilities	5,213	4,998
Income taxes payable	611	492
Total Current Liabilities	6,415	6,052
Long-Term Debt Obligations	1,702	2,187
Other Liabilities	4,075	4,226
Deferred Income Taxes	1,261	1,486
Total Liabilities	13,453	13,951
Preferred Stock, no par value	41	41
Repurchased Preferred Stock	(63)	(48)
Common Shareholders' Equity		
Common stock, par value $1^2/_3$¢ per share (issued 1,782 shares)	30	30
Capital in excess of par value	548	207
Retained earnings	15,961	13,489
Accumulated other comprehensive loss	(1,267)	(1,672)
	15,272	12,054
Less: repurchased common stock, at cost (77 and 60 shares, respectively)	(3,376)	(2,524)
Total Common Shareholders' Equity	11,896	9,530
Total Liabilities and Shareholders' Equity	$25,327	$23,474

See accompanying notes to consolidated financial statements.

PEPSICO

Consolidated Statement of Common Shareholders' Equity

PepsiCo, Inc. and Subsidiaries
Fiscal years ended December 27, 2003, December 28, 2002 and December 29, 2001

(in millions)	2003		2002		2001	
	Shares	**Amount**	Shares	Amount	Shares	Amount
Common Stock						
Balance, beginning of year	**1,782**	**$ 30**	1,782	$ 30	2,029	$ 34
Stock option exercises	**–**	**–**	–	–	9	–
Shares issued to effect merger	**–**	**–**	–	–	(256)	(4)
Balance, end of year	**1,782**	**30**	1,782	30	1,782	30
Capital in Excess of Par Value						
Balance, beginning of year		**207**		115		375
Stock compensation expense		**407**		435		385
Stock option exercises [(a)]		**(66)**		(339)		77
Reissued shares		**–**		–		150
Shares issued to effect merger		**–**		–		(873)
Other		**–**		(4)		1
Balance, end of year		**548**		207		115
Deferred Compensation						
Balance, beginning of year		**–**		–		(21)
Net activity		**–**		–		21
Balance, end of year		**–**		–		–
Retained Earnings						
Balance, beginning of year		**13,489**		11,535		16,510
Net income [(b)]		**3,568**		3,000		2,400
Shares issued to effect merger		**–**		–		(6,366)
Cash dividends declared — common		**(1,082)**		(1,042)		(1,005)
Cash dividends declared — preferred		**(3)**		(4)		(4)
Other		**(11)**		–		–
Balance, end of year		**15,961**		13,489		11,535
Accumulated Other Comprehensive Loss						
Balance, beginning of year		**(1,672)**		(1,646)		(1,374)
Currency translation adjustment [(b)]		**410**		56		(218)
Cash flow hedges, net of tax [(b)]		**(12)**		18		(18)
Minimum pension liability adjustment, net of tax [(b)]		**7**		(99)		(38)
Other [(b)]		**–**		(1)		2
Balance, end of year		**(1,267)**		(1,672)		(1,646)
Repurchased Common Stock						
Balance, beginning of year	**(60)**	**(2,524)**	(26)	(1,268)	(280)	(7,920)
Share repurchases	**(43)**	**(1,946)**	(53)	(2,192)	(35)	(1,716)
Stock option exercises	**26**	**1,096**	19	931	20	751
Reissued shares	**–**	**–**	–	–	13	374
Shares issued to effect merger	**–**	**–**	–	–	256	7,243
Other	**–**	**(2)**	–	5	–	–
Balance, end of year	**(77)**	**(3,376)**	(60)	(2,524)	(26)	(1,268)
Total Common Shareholders' Equity		**$11,896**		$ 9,530		$ 8,766

(a) Includes total tax benefit of $340 million in 2003, $136 million in 2002 and $207 million in 2001.
(b) Combined, these amounts represent total comprehensive income of $3,973 million in 2003, $2,974 million in 2002 and $2,128 million in 2001.
See accompanying notes to consolidated financial statements.

Notes to Consolidated Financial Statements

Note 1 — Basis of Presentation and Our Divisions

Basis of Presentation
Our financial statements include the consolidated accounts of PepsiCo, Inc. and the affiliates that we control. In addition, we include our share of the results of certain other affiliates based on our ownership interest. We do not control these other affiliates, as our ownership in these other affiliates is generally less than fifty percent. Our share of the net income of noncontrolled bottling affiliates is reported in our income statement as bottling equity income. See Note 8 for additional information on our noncontrolled bottling affiliates. Our share of other noncontrolled affiliates is included in division operating profit. Intercompany balances and transactions are eliminated.

The preparation of our consolidated financial statements in conformity with generally accepted accounting principles requires us to make estimates and assumptions that affect reported amounts of assets, liabilities, revenues, expenses and disclosure of contingent assets and liabilities. Actual results could differ from these estimates.

Impairment and restructuring charges and merger-related costs (described in Note 3), the net tax benefit (described in Note 5), the adoption of SFAS 142 (described in Note 4) and the consolidation of Snack Ventures Europe (SVE) affect the comparability of our consolidated results. See "Our Divisions" below and for additional unaudited information on these items, see "Items Affecting Comparability" in Management's Discussion and Analysis.

Tabular dollars are in millions, except per share amounts. All per share amounts reflect common per share amounts, assume dilution unless noted, and are based on unrounded amounts. Certain reclassifications were made to prior year amounts to conform to the 2003 presentation.

Our Divisions

We manufacture or use contract manufacturers, market and sell a variety of salty, sweet and grain-based snacks, carbonated and non-carbonated beverages, and foods through our North American and international business divisions. Our North American divisions include the United States and Canada. The accounting policies for the divisions are the same as those described in Note 2.

Division results are based on how our Chairman and Chief Executive Officer manages our divisions. Beginning in 2003, we combined our North American beverage businesses as PepsiCo Beverages North America and our international snack, beverage and food businesses as PepsiCo International to reflect operating management changes. Prior year results have been restated to reflect this change. In addition, division results exclude significant restructuring and impairment charges, merger-related costs and divested businesses and have been adjusted to reflect the adoption of SFAS 142 and consolidation of SVE. For additional unaudited information on our divisions, see "Our Operations" in Management's Discussion and Analysis.

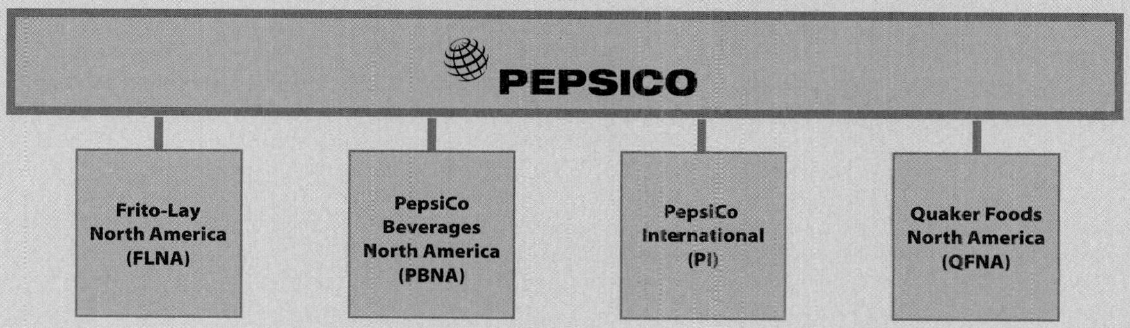

	2003	2002	2001	**2003**	2002	2001
	Net Revenue			**Operating Profit**		
FLNA	**$ 9,091**	$ 8,565	$ 8,216	**$2,366**	$2,216	$2,056
PBNA	**7,733**	7,200	6,888	**1,775**	1,577	1,466
PI	**8,678**	7,749	7,504	**1,186**	1,042	863
QFNA	**1,467**	1,464	1,437	**486**	473	389
Total division	**26,969**	24,978	24,045	**5,813**	5,308	4,774
Divested businesses	**2**	134	173	**26**	23	39
Corporate	**–**	–	–	**(852)**	(812)	(756)
	26,971	25,112	24,218	**4,987**	4,519	4,057
Impairment and restructuring charges	**–**	–	–	**(147)**	–	(31)
Merger-related costs	**–**	–	–	**(59)**	(224)	(356)
Other	**–**	–	–	**–**	–	2
SVE consolidation	**–**	–	(706)	**–**	–	(13)
SFAS 142 adoption	**–**	–	–	**–**	–	(23)
Total	**$26,971**	$25,112	$23,512	**$4,781**	$4,295	$3,636

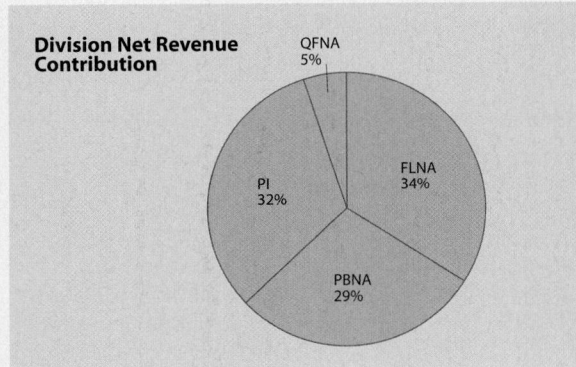

Division Net Revenue Contribution

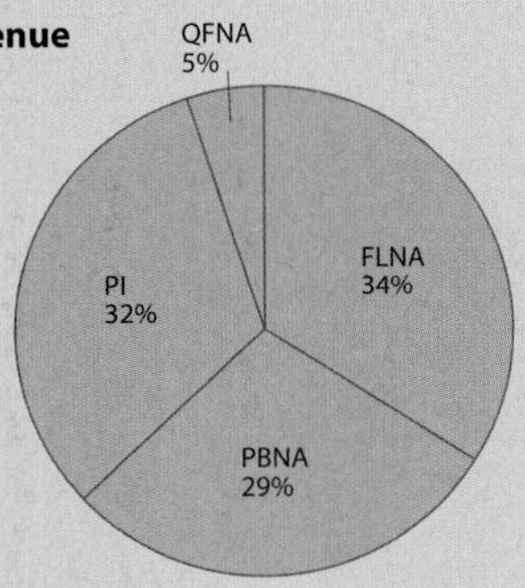

Division Operating Profit Contribution

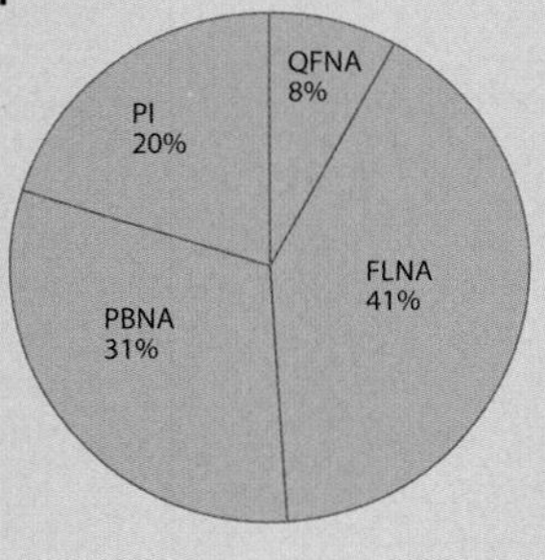

Divested Businesses — During 2003, we sold our Quaker Foods North America Mission pasta business. As a result, net revenue of $27 million in 2002 and $29 million in 2001 and operating profit of $8 million in 2002 and $10 million in 2001 have been reclassified to divested businesses. During 2002, we sold our Quaker Foods North America bagged cereal business and our PepsiCo International food businesses in Colombia and Venezuela.

Corporate — Corporate includes costs of our corporate headquarters, centrally managed initiatives, unallocated insurance and benefit programs, foreign exchange transaction gains and losses and certain other charges. We voluntarily elected to expense stock options and, as a result, corporate unallocated expenses also reflect stock compensation expense for all years presented. See Note 6, and for additional unaudited information, see "Our Critical Accounting Policies" in Management's Discussion and Analysis.

Impairment and Restructuring Charges and Merger-Related Costs — See Note 3.

The following items are necessary to reconcile division results to consolidated results since, as noted above, division results are presented as managed.

SVE Consolidation — As a result of changes in the operations of our European snack joint venture (SVE), we determined that effective in 2002, consolidation was required.

SFAS 142 Adoption — In 2002, we adopted SFAS 142, *Goodwill and Other Intangible Assets*, which eliminated amortization of goodwill and perpetual brands, and resulted in an acceleration of the amortization of certain of our other intangibles. See Note 4 for additional information, and the after-tax impact.

Other Division Information

Total Assets

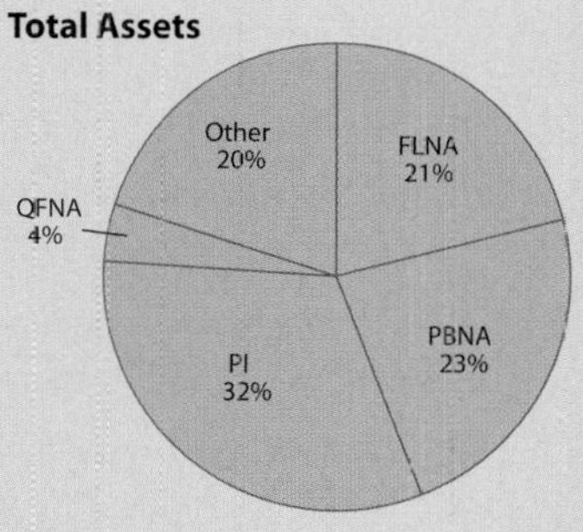

Capital Spending

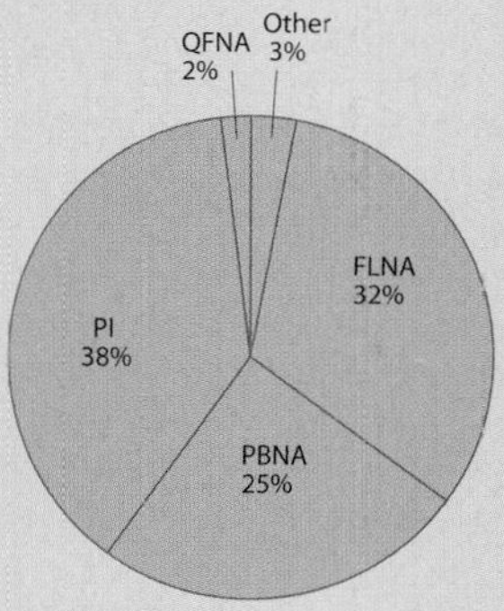

Net Revenue

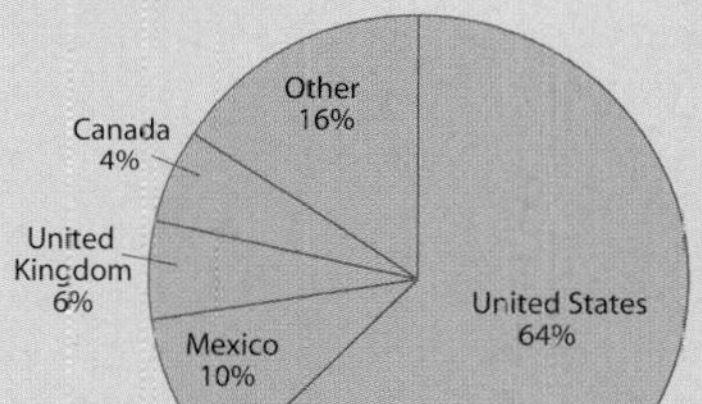

Long-Lived Assets

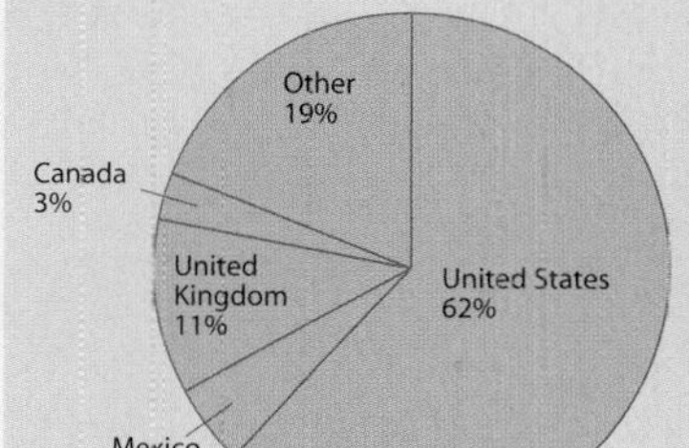

	2003	2002	2001	**2003**	2002	2001
	Total Assets			**Capital Spending**		
FLNA	**$ 5,332**	$ 5,099	$ 4,623	**$ 426**	$ 523	$ 514
PBNA	**5,856**	5,691	5,403	**332**	367	359
PI (a)	**8,109**	7,275	6,359	**521**	473	385
QFNA	**995**	1,001	878	**32**	50	55
Total division	**20,292**	19,066	17,263	**1,311**	1,413	1,313
Divested businesses	**–**	–	58	**–**	1	3
Corporate (b)	**2,384**	2,072	1,927	**34**	23	8
Investments in bottling affiliates	**2,651**	2,336	2,447	**–**	–	–
	$25,327	$23,474	$21,695	**$1,345**	$1,437	$1,324

	2003	2002	2001	**2003**	2002	2001
	Amortization of Intangible Assets			**Depreciation and Other Amortization**		
FLNA	**$ 3**	$ 3	$ 7	**$ 416**	$399	$377
PBNA	**75**	70	69	**245**	206	193
PI	**66**	64	68	**350**	300	310
QFNA	**1**	1	1	**36**	37	41
Total division	**145**	138	145	**1,047**	942	921
Divested businesses	**–**	–	–	**–**	3	4
Corporate	**–**	–	–	**29**	29	18
SVE consolidation	**–**	–	(3)	**–**	–	(26)
SFAS 142 adoption	**–**	–	23	**–**	–	–
	$145	$138	$165	**$1,076**	$974	$917

	2003	2002	2001	**2003**	2002	2001
	Net Revenue			**Long-Lived Assets(c)**		
United States	**$17,377**	$16,588	$15,976	**$ 9,907**	$ 9,767	$ 9,439
Mexico	**2,642**	2,686	2,609	**869**	764	1,065
United Kingdom	**1,510**	1,106	954	**1,724**	1,529	1,104
Canada	**1,147**	967	896	**508**	410	375
All other countries	**4,295**	3,765	3,077	**3,123**	2,750	2,605
	$26,971	$25,112	$23,512	**$16,131**	$15,220	$14,588

(a) PepsiCo International assets include investments in noncontrolled affiliates, principally Productos SAS, of $153 million in 2003, $145 million in 2002 and $155 million in 2001.

(b) Corporate assets consist principally of cash and cash equivalents, short-term investments primarily held outside the United States and property, plant and equipment.

(c) Long-lived assets represent net property, plant and equipment, nonamortizable and net amortizable intangible assets and investments in noncontrolled affiliates.

Note 2 — Our Significant Accounting Policies

Revenue Recognition

We recognize revenue upon delivery to our customers in accordance with written sales terms that do not allow for a right of return. However, our policy for direct-store-delivery and chilled products is to remove and replace out-of-date products from store shelves to ensure that our consumers receive the product quality and freshness that they expect. Similarly, our policy for warehouse distributed products is to replace damaged and out-of-date products. Based on our historical experience with this practice, we have reserved for anticipated damaged and out-of-date product. For additional unaudited information on our revenue recognition and related policies, including our policy on bad debt, see "Our Critical Accounting Policies" in Management's Discussion and Analysis. We are exposed to concentration of credit risk by our customers, PBG and Wal-Mart, as each represents approximately 10% of our net revenue. We have not experienced credit issues with these customers.

Sales Incentives and Other Marketplace Spending

We offer sales incentives through various programs to our customers and consumers. Sales incentives are accounted for as a reduction to revenue and totaled $6.0 billion in 2003, $5.5 billion in 2002 and $4.7 billion in 2001. Most of these incentive arrangements have terms of no more than one year. However, we have arrangements, such as fountain pouring rights, which may extend up to 15 years. Costs incurred to obtain these arrangements are expensed over the contract period and the remaining balance of $359 million at December 27, 2003 and $349 million at December 28, 2002 is included in other assets in our Consolidated Balance Sheet. For additional unaudited information on our sales incentives, see "Our Critical Accounting Policies" in Management's Discussion and Analysis.

Other marketplace spending includes the costs of advertising and other marketing activities and is reported as selling, general and administrative expenses. Advertising expenses were $1.6 billion in 2003, $1.5 billion in 2002 and $1.7 billion in 2001. Deferred advertising costs are not expensed until the year first used and consist of:

- media and personal service prepayments,
- promotional materials in inventory, and
- production costs of future media advertising.

Deferred advertising costs of $137 million at year-end 2003 and $147 million at year-end 2002 are classified as prepaid expenses in the Consolidated Balance Sheet.

Distribution Costs

Distribution costs, including the costs of shipping and handling activities, are reported as selling, general and administrative expenses for direct-store-delivery distribution systems. For our other distribution systems, these costs are reported in cost of sales. Shipping and handling expenses classified as selling, general and administrative expenses were $3.0 billion in 2003, $2.8 billion in 2002 and $2.6 billion in 2001.

Cash Equivalents

Cash equivalents are investments with original maturities of three months or less.

Commitments and Contingencies

We are subject to various claims and contingencies related to lawsuits, taxes and environmental matters, as well as commitments under contractual and other commercial obligations. We recognize liabilities for contingencies and commitments when a loss is probable and estimable. For additional information on our commitments, see Note 9.

Other Significant Accounting Policies

Our other significant accounting policies are disclosed as follows:

- *Property, Plant and Equipment and Intangible Assets* — Note 4 and, for additional unaudited information on brands and goodwill, see "Our Critical Accounting Policies" in Management's Discussion and Analysis.
- *Income Taxes* — Note 5 and, for additional unaudited information, see "Our Critical Accounting Policies" in Management's Discussion and Analysis.
- *Stock Compensation Expense* — Note 6 and, for additional unaudited information, see "Our Critical Accounting Policies" in Management's Discussion and Analysis.
- *Pension, Retiree Medical and Savings Plans* — Note 7 and, for additional unaudited information, see "Our Critical Accounting Policies" in Management's Discussion and Analysis.
- *Risk Management* — Note 10 and, for additional unaudited information, see "Our Market Risks" in Management's Discussion and Analysis.

Recent Accounting Changes

As further discussed in Note 6, we voluntarily adopted the fair value method of accounting for stock options at the end of 2003. We selected the retroactive method as described in SFAS 148, *Accounting for Stock-Based Compensation — Transition and Disclosure*, to adopt this accounting and restated our results.

The Financial Accounting Standards Board issued Interpretation No. 46 (FIN 46), *Consolidation of Variable Interest Entities.* This interpretation requires consolidation of existing noncontrolled affiliates if the affiliate is unable to finance its operations without investor support, or where the other investors do not have exposure to the significant risks and rewards of ownership. We do not expect our significant noncontrolled affiliates to require consolidation under FIN 46. The Emerging Issues Task Force (EITF) issued EITF 01-8, *Determining Whether an Arrangement Contains a Lease.* EITF 01-8 did not have a significant impact on our financial statements.

Note 3 — Impairment and Restructuring Charges and Merger-Related Costs

Impairment and Restructuring Charges

In the fourth quarter of 2003, we incurred a charge of $147 million ($100 million after-tax or $0.06 per share) in conjunction with actions taken to streamline our North American divisions and PepsiCo International. These actions are intended to increase focus and eliminate redundancies at PBNA and PI, and improve the efficiency of the supply chain at FLNA. Of this charge, $81 million related to impairment, reflecting $57 million for the closure of a snack plant in Kentucky, the retirement of snack manufacturing lines in Maryland and Arkansas and $24 million for the closure of a PBNA office building in Florida. The remaining $66 million includes employee-related costs of $54 million and facility and other exit costs of $12 million. Employee-related costs primarily reflect the termination costs for approximately 850 sales, distribution, manufacturing, research and marketing employees. As of December 27, 2003, approximately 140 terminations have occurred. The majority of the remaining terminations are expected to occur in the first quarter of 2004. Through December 27, 2003, we have paid $9 million leaving a remaining accrual of $57 million. This accrual is included in other current liabilities.

In 2001, we incurred other impairment and restructuring costs for Quaker's supply chain reconfiguration and manufacturing and distribution optimization project initiated in 1999.

Merger-Related Costs

On August 2, 2001, we completed our merger with Quaker and accounted for it as a pooling-of-interests. We recognized the following costs associated with our merger with Quaker:

	2003	2002	2001
Transaction costs	$ –	$ –	$117
Integration and restructuring costs	59	224	239
Total merger-related costs	$59	$224	$356
After-tax	$42	$190	$322
Per share	$ 0.02	$ 0.11	$0.18

Transaction costs were incurred to complete the merger. Integration and restructuring costs represent incremental one-time merger-related costs. Such costs include consulting fees and expenses, employee-related costs, information system integration costs, asset impairments and other costs related to the integration of Quaker. Employee-related costs include retirement and other benefits, severance costs and expenses related to change-in-control provisions of pre-merger employment contracts.

Merger-related integration and restructuring reserves are as follows:

	Integration	Employee Related	Asset Impairment	Facility and Other Exit	Total
Reserves, December 29, 2001	$ 22	$51	$ –	$ 4	$ 77
2002 costs	90	53	56	25	224
Cash payments	(62)	(43)	–	(13)	(118)
Reclassification to retiree medical/postemployment liabilities	(7)	(9)	–	–	(16)
Other noncash utilization	–	(4)	(56)	(10)	(70)
Reserves, December 28, 2002	43	48	–	6	97
2003 costs	**46**	**10**	–	**3**	**59**
Cash payments	**(63)**	**(33)**	–	**(4)**	**(100)**
Reclassification to retiree medical/postemployment liabilities	–	**(3)**	–	–	**(3)**
Other noncash utilization	**4**	–	–	**(2)**	**2**
Reserves, December 27, 2003	**$30**	**$22**	**$ –**	**$ 3**	**$55**

The remaining integration and severance accruals at December 27, 2003 are included within other current liabilities in the Consolidated Balance Sheet.

Note 4 — Property, Plant and Equipment and Intangible Assets

	Useful Life	2003	2002	2001
Property, plant and equipment, net				
Land and improvements		**$ 557**	$ 504	
Buildings and improvements	20 – 40 yrs.	**3,449**	3,119	
Machinery and equipment, including fleet	5 – 15	**10,170**	9,005	
Construction in progress		**579**	767	
		14,755	13,395	
Accumulated depreciation		**(6,927)**	(6,005)	
		$ 7,828	$ 7,390	
Depreciation expense		**$1,020**	$929	$843
Amortizable intangible assets, net				
Brands	5 – 40	**$ 985**	$ 938	
Other identifiable intangibles	3 – 15	**212**	203	
		1,197	1,141	
Accumulated amortization		**(479)**	(340)	
		$ 718	$ 801	
Amortization expense		**$145**	$138	$165

Depreciation and amortization are recognized on a straight-line basis over an asset's estimated useful life. Land is not depreciated and construction in progress is not depreciated until ready for service. Amortization for each of the next five years, based on existing intangible assets and 2003 foreign exchange rates, is expected to be $147 million in 2004, $139 million in 2005, $138 million in 2006, and $22 million in 2007 and thereafter.

Depreciable and amortizable assets are only evaluated for impairment upon a significant change in the operating or macroeconomic environment. In these circumstances, if an evaluation of the undiscounted cash flows indicates impairment, the asset is written down to its estimated fair value, which is generally based on discounted future cash flows. Useful lives are periodically evaluated to determine whether events or circumstances have occurred which indicate the need for revision. No impairment charges resulted from the adoption of SFAS 144, *Accounting for the Impairment or Disposal of Long-Lived Assets* in 2002. For additional unaudited information on our amortizable brand policies, see "Our Critical Accounting Policies" in Management's Discussion and Analysis.

Nonamortizable Intangible Assets

Perpetual brands and goodwill are assessed for impairment at least annually to ensure that future cash flows continue to exceed the related book value. A perpetual brand is impaired if its book value exceeds its fair value. Goodwill is evaluated for impairment if the book value of its reporting unit exceeds its fair value. A reporting unit can be a division or business within a division. If the fair value of an evaluated asset is less than its book value, the asset is written down based on its discounted future cash flows to fair value. No impairment charges resulted from the required impairment evaluations. The change in the book value of nonamortizable intangible assets during 2003 is as shown.

	Balance, Beginning of Year	Acquisitions	Translation and Other	Balance, End of Year
Frito-Lay North America				
Goodwill	$ 109	$ –	$ 21	**$ 130**
PepsiCo Beverages North America				
Goodwill	2,149	–	8	**2,157**
Brands	59	–	–	**59**
	2,208	–	8	**2,216**
PepsiCo International				
Goodwill	1,186	24	124	**1,334**
Brands	720	–	88	**808**
	1,906	24	212	**2,142**
Quaker Foods North America				
Goodwill[(a)]	187	–	(12)	**175**
Corporate				
Pension intangible	8	–	(6)	**2**
Total goodwill	3,631	24	141	**3,796**
Total brands	779	–	88	**867**
Total pension intangible	8	–	(6)	**2**
	$ 4,418	$ 24	$ 223	**$4,665**

(a) Activity reflects the sale of our Mission pasta business.

We adopted SFAS 142, *Goodwill and Other Intangible Assets*, in 2002. Prior to the adoption of SFAS 142, our nonamortizable intangible assets had useful lives ranging from 20 to 40 years. The following table provides pro forma disclosure for 2001 of the elimination of goodwill and perpetual brands amortization and the acceleration of certain other amortization as if SFAS 142 had been adopted in 2001:

	Net Income	Earnings per common share Basic	Earnings per common share Diluted
Reported	$ 2,400	$ 1.36	$ 1.33
Cease goodwill amortization	112	0.06	0.06
Adjust brands amortization	(67)	(0.03)	(0.03)
Cease equity investee goodwill amortization	57	0.03	0.03
Adjusted	$ 2,502	$ 1.42	$ 1.39

For additional unaudited information on our goodwill and nonamortizable brand policies, see "Our Critical Accounting Policies" in Management's Discussion and Analysis.

Note 5 — Income Taxes

	2003	2002	2001
Income before income taxes			
U.S.	**$3,267**	$3,178	$2,580
Foreign	**1,725**	1,255	1,064
	$4,992	$4,433	$3,644
Provision for income taxes			
Current: U.S. Federal	**$1,326**	$ 948	$ 921
Foreign	**341**	256	226
State	**80**	55	53
	1,747	1,259	1,200
Deferred: U.S. Federal	**(274)**	146	46
Foreign	**(47)**	11	(8)
State	**(2)**	17	6
	(323)	174	44
	$1,424	$1,433	$1,244
Tax rate reconciliation			
U.S. Federal statutory tax rate	**35.0%**	35.0%	35.0%
State income tax, net of U.S. Federal tax benefit	**1.0**	1.0	1.0
Lower taxes on foreign results	**(5.5)**	(3.5)	(4.3)
Settlement of prior years audit	**(2.2)**	–	–
Merger-related costs and impairment and restructuring charges	**0.1**	1.0	2.5
Other, net	**0.1**	(1.2)	(0.1)
Annual tax rate	**28.5%**	32.3%	34.1%
Deferred tax liabilities			
Investments in noncontrolled affiliates	**$ 792**	$ 753	
Property, plant and equipment	**806**	746	
Pension benefits	**512**	327	
Intangible assets other than nondeductible goodwill	**146**	127	
Safe harbor leases	**33**	57	
Zero coupon notes	**53**	61	
Other	**199**	342	
Gross deferred tax liabilities	**2,541**	2,413	
Deferred tax assets			
Net carryforwards	**535**	504	
Stock compensation	**332**	232	
Retiree medical benefits	**343**	315	
Other employee-related benefits	**333**	228	
Various current and noncurrent liabilities	**482**	414	
Gross deferred tax assets	**2,025**	1,693	
Valuation allowances	**(438)**	(487)	
Deferred tax assets, net	**1,587**	1,206	
Net deferred tax liabilities	**$ 954**	$1,207	
Included within:			
Prepaid expenses and other current assets	**$307**	$279	
Deferred income taxes	**$1,261**	$1,486	

Operating loss carryforwards totaling $3.5 billion at year-end 2003 are being carried forward in a number of foreign and state jurisdictions where we are permitted to use tax operating losses from prior periods to reduce future taxable income. These operating losses will expire as follows: $0.2 billion in 2004, $2.8 billion between 2005 and 2023 and $0.5 billion may be carried forward indefinitely. In addition, certain tax credits generated in prior periods of approximately $74 million are available to reduce certain foreign tax liabilities through 2011. We establish valuation allowances for our deferred tax assets when the amount of expected future taxable income is not likely to support the use of the deduction or credit.

We have not recognized any United States tax expense on undistributed international earnings since we have the intention to reinvest the earnings outside the United States for the foreseeable future. These undistributed earnings are approximately $8.8 billion at December 27, 2003.

Analysis of valuation allowances:

	2003	2002	2001
Balance, beginning of year	**$487**	$511	$ 813
(Benefit)/provision	**(52)**	(22)	(300)
Other additions/(deductions)	**3**	(2)	(2)
Balance, end of year	**$438**	$487	$ 511

For additional unaudited information on our income tax policies, see "Our Critical Accounting Policies" in Management's Discussion and Analysis.

Note 6 — Stock Compensation

Our stock option program is a broad-based program designed to attract and retain employees while also aligning employees' interests with the interests of our shareholders. Employees at all levels participate in our stock option program. In addition, members of our Board of Directors receive stock options and restricted stock units for their service on our Board. Stock options are granted to employees under the 2003 Long-Term Incentive Plan (LTIP), our only active plan. At year-end 2003, 72 million shares were available for future executive and SharePower grants. For additional unaudited information on our stock option program, see "Our Critical Accounting Policies" in Management's Discussion and Analysis.

SharePower Grants

SharePower options are awarded under our 2003 LTIP to all eligible employees. Options become exercisable after three years, have a 10-year term, and through 2003, were based on annual earnings and tenure. In 2003, SharePower grants represented approximately 23% of our annual employee option grants.

Executive Grants

All senior management and certain middle management are awarded 2003 LTIP executive grants which, through 2003, were generally based on a multiple of base salary. LTIP executive grants generally become exercisable at the end of three years and have a 10-year term.

Fair Value Method of Accounting

Historically, we have accounted for our employee stock options using the intrinsic value method. This method measures stock compensation expense as the amount by which the market price of the stock exceeds the exercise price on the date of grant. We did not recognize any stock compensation expense under this method because we grant our stock options at the current stock price. At the end of 2003, we voluntarily adopted the fair value method of accounting for stock options. We selected the retroactive restatement method as described in SFAS 148, *Accounting for Stock-Based Compensation — Transition and Disclosure*, to adopt this accounting. Under this method, we have restated our 2003, 2002 and 2001 results to recognize stock compensation expense as if we had always applied the fair value method to account for our unvested stock options in the years presented. The impact of the restatement is as follows:

	2003	2002	2001
Income before income taxes			
Income before income taxes,			
before restatement	**$5,399**	$ 4,868	$ 4,029
Stock compensation expense	**(407)**	(435)	(385)
Restated income before income taxes	**$4,992**	$ 4,433	$ 3,644
Net income			
Net income, before restatement	**$3,861**	$3,313	$ 2,662
Stock compensation expense	**(293)**	(313)	(262)
Restated net income	**$3,568**	$3,000	$ 2,400
Net income per common share — basic			
Net income per common share,			
before restatement	**$ 2.25**	$ 1.89	$ 1.51
Stock compensation expense	**(0.18)**	(0.18)	(0.15)
Restated net income per common share	**$ 2.07**	$ 1.71	$ 1.36
Net income per common share — diluted			
Net income per common share,			
before restatement	**$ 2.21**	$ 1.85	$ 1.47
Stock compensation expense	**(0.16)**	(0.17)	(0.14)
Restated net income per common share	**$ 2.05**	$ 1.68	$ 1.33

Our Assumptions

Under the fair value method of accounting, we measure stock compensation expense at the date of grant using a Black-Scholes valuation model. Our weighted-average Black-Scholes fair value assumptions include:

	2003	2002	2001
Expected life	**6 yrs.**	6 yrs.	5 yrs.
Risk free interest rate	**3.1%**	4.4%	4.8%
Expected volatility	**27%**	27%	29%
Expected dividend yield	**1.15%**	1.14%	0.98%

Our Stock Option Activity [a]:

	2003		2002		2001	
	Options	**Average Price[b]**	Options	Average Price[b]	Options	Average Price[b]
Outstanding at beginning of year	**190,432**	**$36.45**	176,922	$32.35	170,640	$28.08
Granted	**41,630**	**39.89**	37,376	48.75	40,432	43.53
Exercised	**(25,833)**	**26.74**	(19,558)	23.32	(29,064)	21.59
Forfeited/expired	**(8,056)**	**43.56**	(4,308)	39.01	(5,086)	34.83
Outstanding at end of year	**198,173**	**38.12**	190,432	36.45	176,922	32.35
Exercisable at end of year	**97,663**	**$32.56**	82,620	$30.14	83,521	$26.32
Weighted average fair value of options granted		**$11.21**		$15.20		$13.53

Stock options outstanding and exercisable at December 27, 2003 [a]:

	Options Outstanding			Options Exercisable	
Range of Exercise Price	Options	Average Life[c]	Average Price[b]	Options	Average Price[b]
$13.72 to $21.31	6,683	1.20 yrs.	$16.42	6,365	$16.31
$21.36 to $38.25	72,455	4.52	31.57	71,035	31.62
$38.50 to $51.50	119,030	8.00	43.42	20,263	41.51
	198,173	6.41	38.12	97,663	32.56

(a) Options are in thousands and include options granted under Quaker plans.
(b) Weighted average exercise price.
(c) Weighted average contractual life remaining in years.

Note 7 — Pension, Retiree Medical and Savings Plans

Our pension plans cover full-time employees in the United States and certain international employees. Benefits are determined based on either years of service or a combination of years of service and earnings. U.S. retirees are also eligible for medical and life insurance benefits (retiree medical) if they meet age and service requirements. Generally, our retiree medical costs are capped at a specified dollar amount, with retirees contributing the remainder. We use a September 30 measurement date. The cost or benefit of plan changes which increase or decrease benefits for prior employee service (prior service cost) is included in expense on a straight-line basis over the average remaining service period of employees expected to receive benefits.

Our 2003 disclosures do not reflect any impact of the Medicare Prescription Drug, Improvement and Modernization Act of 2003 (the Act) signed into law in December 2003, as it occurred after the measurement date for our plans. For 2004, we will account for the effect of the Act. We expect our 2004 retiree medical costs to be between $5 million and $10 million lower as a result of the Act and expect our liability to be reduced by approximately $50 million. These amounts are based on preliminary estimates that are dependent on interpretative regulations not yet available, and therefore, subject to change.

For additional unaudited information on our pension and retiree medical plans and related accounting policies and assumptions, see "Our Critical Accounting Policies" in Management's Discussion and Analysis.

	2003	2002	2001
Weighted average pension assumptions			
Liability discount rate	**6.1%**	6.7%	7.4%
Expense discount rate	**6.7%**	7.4%	7.7%
Expected return on plan assets	**8.2%**	9.1%	9.8%
Rate of salary increases	**4.4%**	4.4%	4.6%
Components of pension expense			
Service cost	**$ 178**	$156	$127
Interest cost	**284**	265	233
Expected return on plan assets	**(359)**	(329)	(301)
Amortization of prior service cost	**6**	6	8
Amortization of experience loss/(gain)	**48**	4	(11)
Pension expense	**157**	102	56
Special termination benefits	**4**	9	27
Total	**$ 161**	$111	$ 83
Weighted average retiree medical assumptions			
Liability discount rate	**6.1%**	6.7%	7.5%
Expense discount rate	**6.7%**	7.5%	7.8%
Components of retiree medical expense			
Service cost	**$ 33**	$ 25	$ 20
Interest cost	**73**	66	63
Amortization of prior service benefit	**(3)**	(7)	(12)
Amortization of experience loss	**13**	3	–
Retiree medical expense	**116**	87	71
Special termination benefits	**–**	1	1
Total	**$ 116**	$ 88	$ 72

	2003	2002	2003	2002
	Pension		Retiree Medical	
Change in projected benefit liability				
Liability at beginning of year	**$ 4,324**	$ 3,556	**$1,120**	$ 911
Service cost	**178**	156	**33**	25
Interest cost	**284**	265	**73**	66
Plan amendments	**5**	12	**(63)**	(25)
Participant contributions	**6**	6	**–**	–
Experience loss	**541**	514	**171**	205
Benefit payments	**(208)**	(234)	**(70)**	(63)
Special termination benefits	**4**	9	**–**	1
Foreign currency adjustment	**80**	40	**–**	–
Liability at end of year	**$5,214**	$ 4,324	**$1,264**	$1,120
Liability at end of year for service to date	**$4,350**	$ 3,678		

	2003	2002	2003	2002
	Pension		Retiree Medical	
Change in fair value of plan assets				
Fair value at beginning of year	**$3,537**	$ 3,129	**$ –**	$ –
Actual return on plan assets	**281**	(221)	**–**	–
Employer contributions/funding	**552**	820	**70**	63
Participant contributions	**6**	6	**–**	–
Benefit payments	**(208)**	(234)	**(70)**	(63)
Foreign currency adjustment	**77**	37	**–**	–
Fair value at end of year	**$4,245**	$ 3,537	**$ –**	$ –
Funded status as recognized in the Consolidated Balance Sheet				
Funded status at end of year	**$ (969)**	$ (787)	**$(1,264)**	$(1,120)
Unrecognized prior service cost/(benefit)	**44**	44	**(83)**	(23)
Unrecognized experience loss	**2,207**	1,607	**434**	275
Fourth quarter benefit payments	**6**	23	**19**	19
Net amounts recognized	**$1,288**	$ 887	**$ (894)**	$ (849)
Net amounts as recognized in the Consolidated Balance Sheet				
Other assets	**$1,581**	$1,097	**$ –**	$ –
Intangible assets	**2**	8	**–**	–
Accrued benefit liability	**(334)**	(283)	**(894)**	(849)
Accumulated other comprehensive income	**39**	65	**–**	–
Net amounts recognized	**$1,288**	$ 887	**$(894)**	$(849)
Components of increase in unrecognized experience loss				
Decrease in discount rate	**$ 446**	$ 369	**$ 60**	$ 79
Employee-related assumption changes	**(6)**	53	**80**	76
Liability-related experience different from assumptions	**100**	89	**32**	50
Actual asset return different from expected return	**78**	550	**–**	–
Amortization of losses	**(48)**	(4)	**(13)**	(3)
Other, including foreign currency adjustments	**30**	16	**–**	–
Total	**$ 600**	$1,073	**$159**	$202
Selected information for plans with liability for service to date in excess of plan assets				
Liability for service to date	**$(383)**	$(419)	**$(1,264)**	$(1,120)
Projected benefit liability	**$(727)**	$(656)	**$(1,264)**	$(1,120)
Fair value of plan assets	**$123**	$182	**–**	–

Of the total projected pension benefit liability at year-end 2003, $535 million relates to plans that we do not fund because of unfavorable tax treatment.

Our estimated future benefit payments are as follows:

	2004	2005	2006	2007	2008	2009-13
Pension	$190	$190	$200	$215	$225	$1,385
Retiree medical	$75	$80	$85	$90	$95	$515

These benefit payments include payments made from both funded and unfunded pension plans. The above payments exclude any discretionary contributions we may make. We expect such contributions to be approximately $400 million in 2004.

Pension Assets

The expected return on pension plan assets is based on our historical experience, our pension plan investment guidelines, and our expectations for long-term rates of return. Our pension plan investment guidelines are established based upon an evaluation of market conditions, tolerance for risk and cash requirements for benefit payments. Our target allocation for 2004 and actual pension plan asset allocation at year-end 2003 and 2002 are as follows:

	Target Allocation	Actual Allocation	
Asset Category	2004	2003	2002
Equity securities	60%	57%	48%
Debt securities	40%	34%	29%
Other, primarily cash	–	9%	23%
Total	100%	100%	100%

Pension assets include approximately 5.5 million shares of PepsiCo common stock with a market value of $251 million in 2003, and 5.5 million shares with a market value of $202 million in 2002. Our investment policy limits the investment in PepsiCo stock at the time of investment to 10% of the fair value of plan assets.

Retiree Medical Cost Trend Rates

An average increase of 12% in the cost of covered retiree medical benefits is assumed for 2004. This average increase is then projected to decline gradually to 5% in 2010 and thereafter. These assumed health care cost trend rates have an impact on the retiree medical plan expense and liability. However, the cap on our share of retiree medical costs limits the impact. A 1 percentage point change in the assumed health care trend rate would have the following effects:

	1% Increase	1% Decrease
2003 service and interest cost components	$4	$(4)
2003 benefit liability	$45	$(35)

Savings Plan

Our U.S. employees are eligible to participate in 401(k) savings plans, which are voluntary defined contribution plans. The plans are designed to provide employees with retirement savings and strengthen their incentive to build shareholder value. Beginning in 2004, we will make matching contributions with PepsiCo stock for a portion of eligible pay based on years of service.

Note 8 — Noncontrolled Bottling Affiliates

Our most significant noncontrolled bottling affiliates are The Pepsi Bottling Group (PBG) and PepsiAmericas (PAS). Approximately 10% of our net revenue reflects sales to PBG.

The Pepsi Bottling Group

In addition to approximately 41% of PBG's outstanding common stock that we own at year-end 2003, we own 100% of PBG's class B common stock and approximately 7% of the equity of Bottling Group, LLC, PBG's principal operating subsidiary. This gives us economic ownership of approximately 45% of PBG's combined operations. PBG's summarized financial information is as follows:

	2003	2002
Current assets	**$ 3,039**	$ 1,737
Noncurrent assets	**8,505**	8,306
Total assets	**$11,544**	$10,043
Current liabilities	**$2,478**	$1,248
Noncurrent liabilities	**6,789**	6,623
Minority interest	**396**	348
Total liabilities	**$9,663**	$8,219
Our investment	**$1,353**	$1,107

	2003	2002	2001
Net revenue	**$10,265**	$9,216	$8,443
Gross profit	**$5,050**	$4,215	$3,863
Operating profit	**$956**	$898	$676
Net income	**$416**	$428	$305

In December 2002, PBG acquired Pepsi-Gemex, a franchise bottler in Mexico, in which we previously held a 34% ownership interest. The table above includes the results of Pepsi-Gemex from the transaction date forward.

Our investment in PBG was $240 million higher than our ownership interest in their net assets at year-end 2003. Based upon the quoted closing price of PBG shares at year-end 2003, the calculated market value of our shares in PBG, excluding our investment in Bottling Group, LLC, exceeded our investment balance by approximately $1.6 billion.

PepsiAmericas

At year-end 2003, we owned approximately 40% of PepsiAmericas and their summarized financial information is as follows:

	2003	2002
Current assets	**$ 560**	$ 550
Noncurrent assets	**3,022**	3,013
Total assets	**$3,582**	$3,563
Current liabilities	**$ 599**	$ 698
Noncurrent liabilities	**1,418**	1,416
Total liabilities	**$2,017**	$2,114
Our investment	**$847**	$782

	2003	2002	2001
Net revenue	**$3,237**	$3,240	$3,144
Gross profit	**$1,360**	$1,272	$1,232
Operating profit	**$316**	$301	$268
Income from continuing operations	**$158**	$136	$90
Net income	**$158**	$130	$19

Our investment in PAS was $230 million higher than our ownership interest in their net assets at year-end 2003. Based upon the quoted closing price of PAS shares at year-end 2003, the calculated market value of our shares in PepsiAmericas exceeded our investment balance by approximately $136 million.

Related Party Transactions

Our significant related party transactions involve our noncontrolled bottling affiliates. We sell concentrate to these affiliates that is used in the production of carbonated soft drinks and non-carbonated beverages. The sale of concentrate is reported net of bottler funding. We also sell certain finished goods to these affiliates and we receive royalties for the use of our trademarks for certain products. For further unaudited information on these bottlers, see "Our Customers" in Management's Discussion and Analysis. These transactions with our bottling affiliates are reflected in our consolidated financial statements as follows:

	2003	2002	2001
Net revenue	**$3,699**	$3,455	$2,262
Selling, general and administrative expenses	**$128**	$105	$ 75
Accounts and notes receivable	**$158**	$126	
Accounts payable and other current liabilities	**$138**	$122	

Such amounts are settled on terms consistent with other trade receivables and payables. See Note 9 regarding our guarantee of certain PBG debt.

In addition, we coordinate, on an aggregate basis, the negotiation and purchase of sweeteners and other raw materials requirements for certain of our bottlers with suppliers. Once we have negotiated the contracts, the bottlers order and take delivery directly from the supplier and pay the suppliers directly. Consequently, these transactions are not reflected in our consolidated financial statements. As the contracting party, we could be liable to these suppliers in the event of any nonpayment by our anchor bottlers, but we consider this exposure to be remote.

Note 9 — Debt Obligations and Commitments

	2003	2002
Short-term debt obligations		
Current maturities of long-term debt	**$446**	$485
Other borrowings (5.1% and 5.7%)	**520**	452
Amounts reclassified to long-term debt	**(375)**	(375)
	$591	$562
Long-term debt obligations		
Short-term borrowings, reclassified	**$ 375**	$ 375
Notes due 2004-2026 (5.7% and 4.0%)	**1,186**	1,716
Zero coupon notes, $575 million due 2004-2012 (13.5%)	**330**	338
Other, due 2004-2015 (6.4% and 7.6%)	**257**	243
	2,148	2,672
Less: current maturities of long-term debt obligations	**(446)**	(485)
	$1,702	$2,187

The interest rates in the above table reflect weighted average rates.

Short-term borrowings are reclassified to long-term when we have the intent and ability, through the existence of the unused lines of credit, to refinance these borrowings on a long-term basis. At year-end 2003, we maintained $750 million in corporate lines of credit subject to normal banking terms and conditions. These credit facilities support short-term debt issuances and remained unused at year-end 2003. Of the $750 million, $375 million expires in June 2004 with the remaining $375 million expiring in June 2008. Upon consent of PepsiCo and the lenders, these facilities can be extended an additional year. In addition, $395 million of our debt was outstanding on various lines of credit maintained for our international divisions. These lines of credit are subject to normal banking terms and conditions and are committed to the extent of our borrowings.

Long-Term Contractual Commitments and Off-Balance Sheet Arrangements

		Payments Due by Year			
	Total	Less Than 1 Year	1-3 Years	3-5 Years	More Than 5 Years
Long-term contractual commitments [(a)]					
Long-term debt obligations [(b)]	$1,702	$ –	$ 274	$ 902	$ 526
Non-cancelable operating leases	610	154	209	99	148
Purchasing commitments [(c)]	3,363	844	1,070	565	884
Marketing commitments	584	218	290	63	13
Other commitments	44	27	13	2	2
	$6,303	$1,243	$1,856	$1,631	$1,573

(a) Reflects non-cancelable commitments as of December 27, 2003 based on year-end foreign exchange rates.
(b) Excludes current maturities of long-term debt of $446 million which are classified within current liabilities.
(c) Includes approximately $50 million of long-term commitments which are reflected in other liabilities in our Consolidated Balance Sheet.

Most long-term contractual commitments, except for our long-term debt obligations, are not recorded in our Consolidated Balance Sheet. Non-cancelable purchasing and marketing commitments are in the normal course of our business for our projected needs. As bottler funding is negotiated on an annual basis, these commitments are not reflected in our long-term contractual commitments. See Note 7 regarding our pension and retiree medical obligations and discussion below regarding our commitments to noncontrolled bottling affiliates and former restaurant operations.

Off-Balance Sheet Arrangements

It is not our business practice to enter into off-balance sheet arrangements nor is it our policy to issue guarantees to our bottlers, noncontrolled affiliates or third parties. However, certain guarantees were necessary to facilitate the separation of our bottling and restaurant operations from us. In connection with these transactions, we have guaranteed $2.3 billion of Bottling Group, LLC's long-term debt through 2012 and $57 million of YUM! Brands, Inc. (YUM) outstanding obligations, primarily property leases. The terms of our Bottling Group, LLC debt guarantee are intended to preserve the structure of PBG's separation from us and our payment obligation would be triggered if Bottling Group, LLC failed to perform under these debt obligations or the structure significantly changed. Our guarantees of certain obligations ensured YUM's continued use of certain properties. These guarantees would require our cash payment if YUM failed to perform under these lease obligations.

Note 10 — Risk Management

We are exposed to the risk of loss arising from adverse changes in:

- commodity prices, affecting the cost of our raw materials and fuel;
- foreign exchange risks;
- stock prices; and
- discount rates, affecting the measurement of our pension and retiree medical liabilities.

In the normal course of business, we manage these risks through a variety of strategies, including the use of derivative instruments designated as cash flow and fair value hedges. See "Our Market Risks" in Management's Discussion and Analysis for further unaudited information on our risks.

For cash flow hedges, changes in fair value are generally deferred in accumulated other comprehensive loss within shareholders' equity until the underlying hedged item is recognized in net income. For fair value hedges, changes in fair value are recognized immediately in earnings, consistent with the underlying hedged item. Hedging transactions are limited to an underlying exposure. As a result, any change in the value of our derivative instruments would be substantially offset by an opposite change in the value of the underlying hedged items. Hedging ineffectiveness and a net earnings impact occur when the change in the value of the hedge does not offset the change in the value of the underlying hedged item. We do not use derivative instruments for trading or speculative purposes and we limit our exposure to individual counterparties to manage credit risk.

Commodity Prices

We are subject to commodity price risk because our ability to recover increased costs through higher pricing may be limited in the competitive environment in which we operate. This risk is managed through the use of fixed-price purchase orders, pricing agreements, geographic diversity and cash flow hedges. We use cash flow hedges, with terms of no more than two years, to hedge price fluctuations related to a portion of our anticipated commodity purchases, primarily for corn, natural gas and oats. Any ineffectiveness is recorded immediately. However, our commodity hedges have not had any significant ineffectiveness. We classify both the earnings and cash flow impact from these hedges consistent with the underlying hedged item. During the next 12 months, we expect to reclassify gains of approximately $1 million from accumulated other comprehensive loss into net income.

Foreign Exchange

Our operations outside of the United States generated approximately 35% of our net revenue of which Mexico, the United Kingdom and Canada contributed nearly 20%. As a result, we are exposed to foreign currency risks from unforeseen economic changes and political unrest. On occasion, we enter into hedges, primarily forward contracts with terms of no more than two years, to reduce the effect of foreign exchange rates. Ineffectiveness on these hedges was not material to our results of operations. In 2002, we hedged 2.1 billion Mexican pesos related to our net investment in Pepsi-Gemex which resulted in a $5 million gain upon our disposal of Pepsi-Gemex described in Note 8.

Stock Prices

The portion of our deferred compensation liability that is based on certain market indexes and on our stock price is subject to market risk. We hold mutual fund investments and prepaid forward contracts to manage this risk. Changes in the fair value of these investments and contracts are recognized immediately in earnings and are offset by changes in the related compensation liability.

Fair Value

All derivative instruments are recognized in our Consolidated Balance Sheet at fair value. The fair value of our derivative instruments is generally based on quoted market prices. Book and fair values of our derivative and financial instruments are as follows:

	2003		2002	
	Book Value	**Fair Value**	Book Value	Fair Value
Assets				
Cash and cash equivalents	**$820**	**$820**	$1,638	$1,638
Short-term investments [(a)]	**$1,181**	**$1,181**	$207	$207
Forward exchange contracts [(b)]	**$3**	**$3**	$2	$2
Commodity contracts [(b)]	**$4**	**$4**	$6	$6
Prepaid forward contracts [(b)]	**$107**	**$107**	$96	$96
Liabilities				
Forward exchange contracts [(c)]	**$33**	**$33**	$3	$3
Commodity contracts [(c)]	**–**	**–**	$2	$2
Debt obligations	**$2,293**	**$2,569**	$2,749	$3,134

Included in the Consolidated Balance Sheet under the captions noted above or as indicated below.

(a) Includes $103 million at December 27, 2003 and $82 million at December 28, 2002 of mutual fund investments used to manage a portion of market risk arising from our deferred compensation liability.

(b) Included within prepaid expenses and other current assets.

(c) Included within accounts payable and other current liabilities.

This table excludes guarantees, including our guarantee of $2.3 billion of Bottling Group, LLC's long-term debt. The guarantee had a fair value of $35 million at December 27, 2003 and December 28, 2002 based on an external estimate of the cost to us of transferring the liability to an independent financial institution. See Note 9 for additional information on our guarantees.

Note 11 — Net Income per Common Share

Basic net income per common share is net income available to common shareholders divided by the weighted average of common shares outstanding during the period. Diluted net income per common share is calculated using the weighted average of common shares outstanding adjusted to include the effect that would occur if in-the-money employee stock options were exercised and preferred shares were converted into common shares. Options to purchase 49.0 million shares in 2003, 37.9 million shares in 2002 and 0.3 million shares in 2001 were not included in the calculation of diluted earnings per common share because these options were out-of-the-money.

The computations of basic and diluted net income per common share are as shown.

	2003		2002		2001	
	Income	**Shares(a)**	Income	Shares(a)	Income	Shares(a)
Net income	**$3,568**		$3,000		$2,400	
Preferred shares:						
Dividends	**(3)**		(4)		(4)	
Redemption	**–**		–		(1)	
Net income available for common shareholders	**$3,565**	**1,718**	$2,996	1,753	$2,395	1,763
Basic net income per common share	**$ 2.07**		$1.71		$1.36	
Net income available for common shareholders	**$3,565**	**1,718**	$2,996	1,753	$2,395	1,763
Dilutive securities:						
Stock options	**–**	**17**	–	25	–	37
ESOP convertible preferred stock	**3**	**3**	3	3	3	4
Unvested stock awards	**–**	**1**	–	1	–	1
Diluted	**$3,568**	**1,739**	$2,999	1,782	$2,398	1,805
Diluted net income per common share	**$2.05**		$1.68		$1.33	

(a) Weighted average common shares outstanding.

Note 12 — Preferred and Common Stock

As of December 27, 2003, there were 3.6 billion shares of common stock and 3 million shares of convertible preferred stock authorized. The preferred stock was issued only for an employee stock ownership plan (ESOP) established by Quaker and these shares are redeemable by the ESOP participants. The preferred stock accrues dividends at an annual rate of $5.46 per share. At year-end 2003, there were 803,953 preferred shares issued and 531,453 shares outstanding. Each share is convertible at the option of the holder into 4.9625 shares of common stock. The preferred shares may be called by us upon written notice at $78 per share plus accrued and unpaid dividends.

As of December 27, 2003, 0.5 million outstanding shares of preferred stock with a fair value of $123 million and 21 million shares of common stock were held in the accounts of ESOP participants. Quaker made the final award to its ESOP plan in June 2001.

	2003		2002		2001	
	Shares	**Amount**	Shares	Amount	Shares	Amount
Preferred stock						
Balance, beginning of year	**0.8**	**$41**	0.8	$41	1.3	$100
Adjustment to effect merger	**–**	**–**	–	–	(0.5)	(59)
Balance, end of year	**0.8**	**$41**	0.8	$41	0.8	$ 41
Repurchased preferred stock						
Balance, beginning of year	**0.2**	**$48**	0.1	$15	0.5	$ 51
Redemptions	**0.1**	**15**	0.1	33	0.1	23
Adjustment to effect merger	**–**	**–**	–	–	(0.5)	(59)
Balance, end of year	**0.3**	**$63**	0.2	$48	0.1	$ 15

Note 13 — Accumulated Other Comprehensive Loss

Comprehensive income is a measure of income which includes both net income and other comprehensive income or loss. Other comprehensive loss results from items deferred on the balance sheet in shareholders' equity. Other comprehensive income was $405 million in 2003 and other comprehensive loss was $26 million in 2002 and $272 million in 2001. The accumulated balances for each component of other comprehensive loss were as shown.

	2003	2002	2001
Currency translation adjustment	**$(1,121)**	$(1,531)	$(1,587)
Cash flow hedges, net of tax [(a)]	**(12)**	–	(18)
Minimum pension liability adjustment [(b)]	**(135)**	(142)	(43)
Other	**1**	1	2
Accumulated other comprehensive loss	**$(1,267)**	$(1,672)	$(1,646)

(a) Includes a $8 million gain in 2003, a $4 million loss in 2002 and a $7 million loss in 2001 for our share of our equity investees' accumulated derivative activity. In addition, 2001 includes a $3 million gain related to the cumulative effect of adopting SFAS 133.

(b) Net of taxes of $67 million in 2003, $72 million in 2002 and $22 million in 2001. Also, includes $110 million in 2003, $99 million in 2002 and $29 million in 2001 for our share of our equity investees' minimum pension liability adjustments.

Note 14 — Supplemental Financial Information

	2003	2002	2001
Accounts receivable			
Trade receivables	**$2,309**	$ 1,924	
Other receivables	**626**	723	
	2,935	2,647	
Allowance, beginning of year	**116**	121	$ 126
Charged to expense	**32**	38	41
Other additions [(a)]	**–**	3	2
Deductions [(b)]	**(43)**	(46)	(48)
Allowance, end of year	**105**	116	$ 121
Net receivables	**$2,830**	$ 2,531	
Inventory[(c)]			
Raw materials	**$ 618**	$ 525	
Work-in-process	**160**	214	
Finished goods	**634**	603	
	$1,412	$ 1,342	
Accounts payable and other liabilities			
Accounts payable	**$1,638**	$ 1,543	
Accrued marketplace spending	**1,243**	1,240	
Accrued compensation and benefits	**851**	806	
Dividends payable	**274**	259	
Insurance accruals	**151**	168	
Other current liabilities	**1,056**	982	
	$5,213	$ 4,998	
Other liabilities [(d)]	**$4,075**	$ 4,226	
Other supplemental information			
Rent expense	**$231**	$194	$165
Interest paid	**$175**	$119	$159
Income taxes paid	**$1,580**	$1,056	$857
Acquisitions[(e)]			
Fair value of assets acquired	**$178**	$626	$604
Cash paid and debt issued	**(71)**	(351)	(432)
Liabilities assumed	**$107**	$275	$172

(a) Includes acquisitions and currency translation effects.

(b) Includes accounts written off and currency translation effects.

(c) Inventories are valued at the lower of cost or market. Cost is determined using the average, first-in, first-out (FIFO) or last-in, first-out (LIFO) methods. Approximately 10% in 2003 and 19% in 2002 of the inventory cost was computed using the LIFO method. The differences between LIFO and FIFO methods of valuing these inventories are not material.

(d) Includes reserves for tax positions when, despite our belief that our position is fully supportable, we believe that our position is likely to be challenged and that we may not succeed.

(e) Includes our acquisition of the Wotsits brand in the United Kingdom for $228 million in 2002 and the SoBe brand in the United States for $337 million in 2001.

Five- or Ten-Year Summary

Usually presented in close proximity to the audited financial statements is a five- or ten-year summary of selected financial data. From such a summary, one can determine trends and growth patterns over a fairly long period of time. PepsiCo presents five years of selected financial data that includes operating data, financial position data, and selected statistics and ratios.

Selected Financial Data

(in millions except per share amounts, unaudited)

PEPSICO

FIVE-YEAR SUMMARY	2003	2002	2001	2000	1999
Net revenue	**$26,971**	25,112	23,512	22,337	22,183
Net income	**$ 3,568**	3,000	2,400	2,543	2,505
Income per common share — basic	**$ 2.07**	1.71	1.36	1.45	1.41
Income per common share — diluted	**$ 2.05**	1.68	1.33	1.42	1.38
Cash dividends declared per common share	**$ 0.630**	0.595	0.575	0.555	0.535
Total assets	**$25,327**	23,474	21,695	20,757	19,948
Long-term debt	**$ 1,702**	2,187	2,651	3,009	3,527

As a result of the adoption of SFAS 142 and the consolidation of SVE in 2002, the bottling deconsolidation in 1999 and items identified below, the data provided above is not comparable.

• Includes Quaker merger-related costs of:

	2003	2002	2001
Pre-tax	**$59**	$224	$356
After-tax	**$42**	$190	$322
Per share	**$0.02**	$0.11	$0.18

• Includes restructuring and impairment charges of:

	2003	2001	2000	1999
Pre-tax	**$147**	$31	$184	$73
After-tax	**$100**	$19	$111	$45
Per share	**$0.06**	$0.01	$0.06	$0.02

• The 2000 fiscal year consisted of fifty-three weeks compared to fifty-two weeks in our normal fiscal year. The 53rd week increased 2000 net revenue by an estimated $294 million and net income by an estimated $44 million (or $0.02 per share).

• In 1999, includes a net gain on bottling transactions of $1.0 billion ($245 million after-tax or $0.14 per share) and a Quaker favorable tax adjustment of $59 million (or $0.03 per share).

• In 2003, we voluntarily adopted the fair value method of accounting for stock options. We selected the retroactive restatement method as described in SFAS 148, *Accounting for Stock-Based Compensation — Transition and Disclosure*, to adopt this accounting. Under this method we have restated our 2003, 2002 and 2001 results to recognize stock compensation expense as follows:

	2003	2002	2001
Pre-tax	**$407**	$435	$385
After-tax	**$293**	$313	$262
Per share	**$0.16**	$0.17	$0.14

Fiscal years 2000 and 1999 have not been restated for this adoption.

• Cash dividends per common share are those of pre-merger PepsiCo prior to the effective date of the merger.

QUARTERLY	2003	2002	2003	2002	2003	2002	2003	2002
	First Quarter		Second Quarter		Third Quarter		Fourth Quarter	
Net revenue	**$5,530**	5,311	**6,538**	6,119	**6,830**	6,300	**8,073**	7,382
Gross profit	**$2,996**	2,881	**3,546**	3,343	**3,714**	3,427	**4,336**	3,964
Merger-related costs	**$ 11**	36	**11**	65	**9**	33	**28**	90
Net income								
As reported	**$777**	689	**1,009**	875	**1,077**	953		
Stock compensation expense	**(79)**	(87)	**(65)**	(67)	**(65)**	(69)		
As restated	**$ 698**	602	**944**	808	**1,012**	884	**914**	706
Stock price per share (a)								
High	**$44.06**	51.48	**45.11**	53.50	**47.98**	52.00	**48.88**	45.30
Low	**$36.24**	47.43	**38.06**	49.88	**43.10**	35.01	**44.11**	34.00
Close	**$41.50**	50.90	**44.74**	50.90	**44.33**	37.99	**46.47**	41.67

(a) Represents the composite high and low sales price and quarterly closing prices for one share of PepsiCo common stock. Pre-merger amounts are those of PepsiCo prior to the effective date of the merger.

Specimen Financial Statements: The Coca-Cola Company

CONSOLIDATED STATEMENTS OF INCOME

The Coca-Cola Company and Subsidiaries

Year Ended December 31. (In millions except per share data)	2003	2002	2001
NET OPERATING REVENUES	**$ 21,044**	$ 19,564	$ 17,545
Cost of goods sold	**7,762**	7,105	6,044
GROSS PROFIT	**13,282**	12,459	11,501
Selling, general and administrative expenses	**7,488**	7,001	6,149
Other operating charges	**573**	—	—
OPERATING INCOME	**5,221**	5,458	5,352
Interest income	**176**	209	325
Interest expense	**178**	199	289
Equity income—net	**406**	384	152
Other income (loss)—net	**(138)**	(353)	39
Gains on issuances of stock by equity investees	**8**	—	91
INCOME BEFORE INCOME TAXES AND CUMULATIVE EFFECT OF ACCOUNTING CHANGE	**5,495**	5,499	5,670
Income taxes	**1,148**	1,523	1,691
NET INCOME BEFORE CUMULATIVE EFFECT OF ACCOUNTING CHANGE	**4,347**	3,976	3,979
Cumulative effect of accounting change for SFAS No. 142, net of income taxes:			
Company operations	—	(367)	—
Equity investees	—	(559)	—
Cumulative effect of accounting change for SFAS No. 133, net of income taxes	—	—	(10)
NET INCOME	**$ 4,347**	$ 3,050	$ 3,969
BASIC NET INCOME PER SHARE:			
Before accounting change	**$ 1.77**	$ 1.60	$ 1.60
Cumulative effect of accounting change	—	(0.37)	—
	$ 1.77	$ 1.23	$ 1.60
DILUTED NET INCOME PER SHARE:			
Before accounting change	**$ 1.77**	$ 1.60	$ 1.60
Cumulative effect of accounting change	—	(0.37)	—
	$ 1.77	$ 1.23	$ 1.60
AVERAGE SHARES OUTSTANDING	**2,459**	2,478	2,487
Effect of dilutive securities	**3**	5	—
AVERAGE SHARES OUTSTANDING ASSUMING DILUTION	**2,462**	2,483	2,487

Refer to Notes to Consolidated Financial Statements.

The financial information herein is reprinted with permission from The Coca-Cola Company 2003 Annual Report. The accompanying Notes are an integral part of the consolidated financial statements. The complete financial statements are available through a link at the book's companion Web site.

CONSOLIDATED BALANCE SHEETS

The Coca-Cola Company and Subsidiaries

December 31, (In millions)	2003	2002
ASSETS		
CURRENT		
Cash and cash equivalents	**$ 3,362**	$ 2,260
Marketable securities	**120**	85
	3,482	2,345
Trade accounts receivable, less allowances of $61 in 2003 and $55 in 2002	**2,091**	2,097
Inventories	**1,252**	1,294
Prepaid expenses and other assets	**1,571**	1,616
TOTAL CURRENT ASSETS	**8,396**	7,352
INVESTMENTS AND OTHER ASSETS		
Equity method investments:		
Coca-Cola Enterprises Inc.	**1,260**	972
Coca-Cola Hellenic Bottling Company S.A.	**941**	872
Coca-Cola FEMSA, S.A. de C.V.	**674**	347
Coca-Cola Amatil Limited	**652**	492
Other, principally bottling companies	**1,697**	2,054
Cost method investments, principally bottling companies	**314**	254
Other assets	**3,322**	2,694
	8,860	7,685
PROPERTY, PLANT AND EQUIPMENT		
Land	**419**	385
Buildings and improvements	**2,615**	2,332
Machinery and equipment	**6,159**	5,888
Containers	**429**	396
	9,622	9,001
Less allowances for depreciation	**3,525**	3,090
	6,097	5,911
TRADEMARKS WITH INDEFINITE LIVES	**1,979**	1,724
GOODWILL	**1,029**	876
OTHER INTANGIBLE ASSETS	**981**	858
TOTAL ASSETS	**$ 27,342**	$ 24,406
LIABILITIES AND SHARE-OWNERS' EQUITY		
CURRENT		
Accounts payable and accrued expenses	**$ 4,058**	$ 3,692
Loans and notes payable	**2,583**	2,475
Current maturities of long-term debt	**323**	180
Accrued income taxes	**922**	994
TOTAL CURRENT LIABILITIES	**7,886**	7,341
LONG-TERM DEBT	**2,517**	2,701
OTHER LIABILITIES	**2,512**	2,260
DEFERRED INCOME TAXES	**337**	304
SHARE-OWNERS' EQUITY		
Common stock, $0.25 par value		
Authorized: 5,600,000,000 shares;		
issued: 3,494,799,258 shares in 2003 and 3,490,818,627 shares in 2002	**874**	873
Capital surplus	**4,395**	3,857
Reinvested earnings	**26,687**	24,506
Accumulated other comprehensive income (loss)	**(1,995)**	(3,047)
	29,961	26,189
Less treasury stock, at cost (1,053,267,474 shares in 2003; 1,019,839,490 shares in 2002)	**(15,871)**	(14,389)
	14,090	11,800
TOTAL LIABILITIES AND SHARE-OWNERS' EQUITY	**$ 27,342**	$ 24,406

Refer to Notes to Consolidated Financial Statements.

CONSOLIDATED STATEMENTS OF CASH FLOWS

The Coca-Cola Company and Subsidiaries

Year Ended December 31, (In millions)	2003	2002	2001
OPERATING ACTIVITIES			
Net income	**$ 4,347**	$ 3,050	$ 3,969
Depreciation and amortization	**850**	806	803
Stock-based compensation expense	**422**	365	41
Deferred income taxes	**(188)**	40	56
Equity income or loss, net of dividends	**(294)**	(256)	(54)
Foreign currency adjustments	**(79)**	(76)	(60)
Gains on issuances of stock by equity investees	**(8)**	—	(91)
(Gains) losses on sales of assets, including bottling interests	**(5)**	3	(85)
Cumulative effect of accounting changes	**—**	926	10
Other operating charges	**330**	—	—
Other items	**249**	291	(17)
Net change in operating assets and liabilities	**(168)**	(407)	(462)
Net cash provided by operating activities	**5,456**	4,742	4,110
INVESTING ACTIVITIES			
Acquisitions and investments, principally trademarks and bottling companies	**(359)**	(544)	(651)
Purchases of investments and other assets	**(177)**	(141)	(456)
Proceeds from disposals of investments and other assets	**147**	243	455
Purchases of property, plant and equipment	**(812)**	(851)	(769)
Proceeds from disposals of property, plant and equipment	**87**	69	91
Other investing activities	**178**	159	142
Net cash used in investing activities	**(936)**	(1,065)	(1,188)
FINANCING ACTIVITIES			
Issuances of debt	**1,026**	1,622	3,011
Payments of debt	**(1,119)**	(2,378)	(3,937)
Issuances of stock	**98**	107	164
Purchases of stock for treasury	**(1,440)**	(691)	(277)
Dividends	**(2,166)**	(1,987)	(1,791)
Net cash used in financing activities	**(3,601)**	(3,327)	(2,830)
EFFECT OF EXCHANGE RATE CHANGES ON CASH AND CASH EQUIVALENTS	**183**	44	(45)
CASH AND CASH EQUIVALENTS			
Net increase during the year	**1,102**	394	47
Balance at beginning of year	**2,260**	1,866	1,819
Balance at end of year	**$ 3,362**	$ 2,260	$ 1,866

Refer to Notes to Consolidated Financial Statements.

CONSOLIDATED STATEMENTS OF SHARE-OWNERS' EQUITY

The Coca-Cola Company and Subsidiaries

Year Ended December 31, (In millions except per share data)	2003	2002	2001
NUMBER OF COMMON SHARES OUTSTANDING			
Balance at beginning of year	**2,471**	2,486	2,485
Stock issued to employees exercising stock options	**4**	3	7
Purchases of stock for treasury[1]	**(33)**	(14)	(6)
Adoption of SFAS No. 123	—	(4)	—
Balance at end of year	**2,442**	2,471	2,486
COMMON STOCK			
Balance at beginning of year	**$ 873**	$ 873	$ 870
Stock issued to employees exercising stock options	**1**	1	2
Restricted stock and other stock plans, less cancellations	—	—	1
Adoption of SFAS No. 123	—	(1)	—
Balance at end of year	**874**	873	873
CAPITAL SURPLUS			
Balance at beginning of year	**3,857**	3,520	3,196
Stock issued to employees exercising stock options	**105**	111	162
Tax benefit from employees' stock option and restricted stock plans	**11**	11	58
Stock-based compensation	**422**	365	—
Restricted stock and other stock plans, less amortization and cancellations	—	—	132
Unearned restricted stock adjustment	—	—	(28)
Adoption of SFAS No. 123	—	(150)	—
Balance at end of year	**4,395**	3,857	3,520
REINVESTED EARNINGS			
Balance at beginning of year	**24,506**	23,443	21,265
Net income	**4,347**	3,050	3,969
Dividends (per share—$0.88, $0.80 and $0.72 in 2003, 2002 and 2001, respectively)	**(2,166)**	(1,987)	(1,791)
Balance at end of year	**26,687**	24,506	23,443
OUTSTANDING RESTRICTED STOCK			
Balance at beginning of year	—	(150)	(195)
Adoption of SFAS No. 123	—	150	—
Restricted stock and other stock plans, less cancellations	—	—	(24)
Amortization of restricted stock	—	—	41
Unearned restricted stock adjustment	—	—	28
Balance at end of year	—	—	(150)
ACCUMULATED OTHER COMPREHENSIVE INCOME (LOSS)			
Balance at beginning of year	**(3,047)**	(2,638)	(2,527)
Net foreign currency translation adjustment	**921**	(95)	(207)
Cumulative effect of adoption of SFAS No. 133	—	—	50
Net gain (loss) on derivatives	**(33)**	(186)	92
Net change in unrealized gain (loss) on available-for-sale securities	**40**	67	(29)
Net change in minimum pension liability	**124**	(195)	(17)
Net other comprehensive income adjustments	**1,052**	(409)	(111)
Balance at end of year	**(1,995)**	(3,047)	(2,638)
TREASURY STOCK			
Balance at beginning of year	**(14,389)**	(13,682)	(13,293)
Purchases of treasury stock	**(1,482)**	(707)	(277)
Restricted stock and other stock plans, less cancellations	—	—	(112)
Balance at end of year	**(15,871)**	(14,389)	(13,682)
TOTAL SHARE-OWNERS' EQUITY	**$ 14,090**	$ 11,800	$ 11,366
COMPREHENSIVE INCOME			
Net income	**$ 4,347**	$ 3,050	$ 3,969
Net other comprehensive income adjustments	**1,052**	(409)	(111)
TOTAL COMPREHENSIVE INCOME	**$ 5,399**	$ 2,641	$ 3,858

[1] Common stock purchased from employees exercising stock options numbered 0.4 million, 0.2 million and 0.3 million shares for the years ended December 31, 2003, 2002 and 2001, respectively.

Refer to Notes to Consolidated Financial Statements.

Appendix C

Time Value of Money

STUDY OBJECTIVES

After studying this appendix, you should be able to:

1. Distinguish between simple and compound interest.
2. Solve for future value of a single amount.
3. Solve for future value of an annuity.
4. Identify the variables fundamental to solving present value problems.
5. Solve for present value of a single amount.
6. Solve for present value of an annuity.
7. Compute the present value of notes and bonds.

Would you rather receive $1,000 today or a year from now? You should prefer to receive the $1,000 today because you can invest the $1,000 and earn interest on it. As a result, you will have more than $1,000 a year from now. What this example illustrates is the concept of the **time value of money**. Everyone prefers to receive money today rather than in the future because of the interest factor.

THE NATURE OF INTEREST

STUDY OBJECTIVE 1

Distinguish between simple and compound interest.

Interest is payment for the use of another person's money. It is the difference between the amount borrowed or invested—called the **principal**—and the amount repaid or collected. The amount of interest to be paid or collected is usually stated as a rate over a specific period of time. The rate of interest is generally stated as an annual rate.

The amount of interest involved in any financing transaction is based on three elements:

1. **Principal (p):** The original amount borrowed or invested.
2. **Interest rate (i):** An annual percentage of the principal.
3. **Time (n):** The number of years that the principal is borrowed or invested.

Simple Interest

Simple interest is computed on the principal amount only. It is the return on the principal for one period. Simple interest is usually expressed as shown in Illustration C-1 (next page).

Illustration C-1
Interest computation

Interest	=	**Principal**	×	**Rate**	×	**Time**
		p		*i*		*n*

For example, if you borrowed $5,000 for 2 years at a simple interest rate of 12% annually, you would pay $1,200 in total interest, computed as follows:

$$\begin{aligned}\text{Interest} &= p \times i \times n\\ &= \$5{,}000 \times .12 \times 2\\ &= \$1{,}200\end{aligned}$$

Compound Interest

Compound interest is computed on principal **and** on any interest earned that has not been paid or withdrawn. It is the return on (or growth of) the principal for two or more time periods. Compounding computes interest not only on the principal but also on the interest earned to date on that principal, assuming the interest is left on deposit.

To illustrate the difference between simple and compound interest, assume that you deposit $1,000 in Bank One, where it will earn simple interest of 9 percent per year, and you deposit another $1,000 in City Corp, where it will earn compound interest of 9 percent per year compounded annually. Also assume that in both cases you will not withdraw any interest until 3 years from the date of deposit. The computation of interest to be received and the accumulated year-end balances are indicated in Illustration C-2.

Illustration C-2
Simple vs. compound interest

Bank One

Simple Interest Calculation	Simple Interest	Accumulated Year-end Balance
Year 1 $1,000.00 × 9%	$ 90.00	$1,090.00
Year 2 $1,000.00 × 9%	90.00	$1,180.00
Year 3 $1,000.00 × 9%	90.00	$1,270.00
	$ 270.00	

City Corp.

Compound Interest Calculation	Compound Interest	Accumulated Year-end Balance
Year 1 $1,000.00 × 9%	$ 90.00	$1,090.00
Year 2 $1,090.00 × 9%	98.10	$1,188.10
Year 3 $1,188.10 × 9%	106.93	$1,295.03
	$ 295.03	

$25.03 Difference

Note in the illustration above that simple interest uses the initial principal of $1,000 to compute the interest in all 3 years. Compound interest uses the accumulated balance (principal plus interest to date) at each year-end to compute interest in the succeeding year—which explains why your compound interest account is larger.

Obviously if you had a choice between investing your money at simple interest or at compound interest, you would choose compound interest, all other things—especially risk—being equal. In the example, compounding provides $25.03 of additional interest income. For practical purposes, compounding assumes that unpaid interest earned becomes a part of the principal, and the accumulated balance at the end of each year becomes the new principal on which interest is earned during the next year.

As can be seen in Illustration C-2, you should invest your money at City Corp, which compounds interest annually. Compound interest is used in most business situations. Simple interest is generally applicable only to short-term situations of one year or less.

SECTION 1 FUTURE VALUE CONCEPTS

Future Value of a Single Amount

STUDY OBJECTIVE 2

Solve for future value of a single amount.

The **future value of a single amount** is the value at a future date of a given amount invested assuming compound interest. For example, in Illustration C-2, \$1,295.03 is the future value of the \$1,000 at the end of 3 years. The \$1,295.03 could be determined more easily by using the following formula.

$$\mathbf{FV} = p \times (1 + i)^n$$

where:

$$\begin{aligned} \text{FV} &= \text{future value of a single amount} \\ p &= \text{principal (or present value)} \\ i &= \text{interest rate for one period} \\ n &= \text{number of periods} \end{aligned}$$

The \$1,295.03 is computed as follows.

$$\begin{aligned} \text{FV} &= p \times (1 + i)^n \\ &= \$1{,}000 \times (1 + i)^3 \\ &= \$1{,}000 \times 1.29503 \\ &= \$1{,}295.03 \end{aligned}$$

The 1.29503 is computed by multiplying ($1.09 \times 1.09 \times 1.09$). The amounts in this example can be depicted in the following time diagram.

Illustration C-3
Time diagram

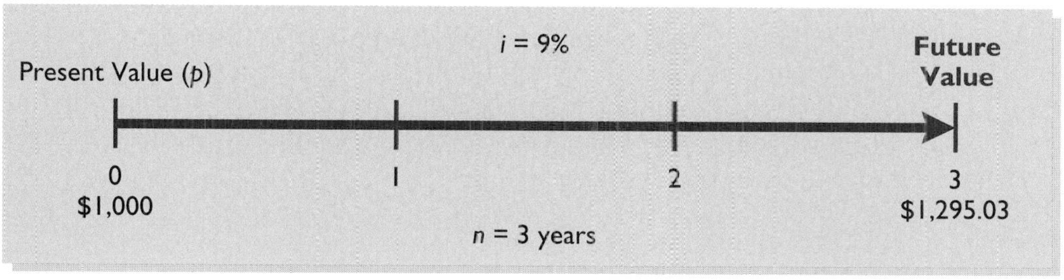

Another method that may be used to compute the future value of a single amount involves the use of a compound interest table. This table shows the future value of 1 for *n* periods. Table 1, shown below, is such a table.

TABLE 1
Future Value of 1

(*n*) Periods	4%	5%	6%	8%	9%	10%	11%	12%	15%
1	1.04000	1.05000	1.06000	1.08000	1.09000	1.10000	1.11000	1.12000	1.15000
2	1.08160	1.10250	1.12360	1.16640	1.18810	1.21000	1.23210	1.25440	1.32250
3	1.12486	1.15763	1.19102	1.25971	1.29503	1.33100	1.36763	1.40493	1.52088
4	1.16986	1.21551	1.26248	1.36049	1.41158	1.46410	1.51807	1.57352	1.74901
5	1.21665	1.27628	1.33823	1.46933	1.53862	1.61051	1.68506	1.76234	2.01136
6	1.26532	1.34010	1.41852	1.58687	1.67710	1.77156	1.87041	1.97382	2.31306
7	1.31593	1.40710	1.50363	1.71382	1.82804	1.94872	2.07616	2.21068	2.66002
8	1.36857	1.47746	1.59385	1.85093	1.99256	2.14359	2.30454	2.47596	3.05902
9	1.42331	1.55133	1.68948	1.99900	2.17189	2.35795	2.55803	2.77308	3.51788
10	1.48024	1.62889	1.79085	2.15892	2.36736	2.59374	2.83942	3.10585	4.04556
11	1.53945	1.71034	1.89830	2.33164	2.58043	2.85312	3.15176	3.47855	4.65239
12	1.60103	1.79586	2.01220	2.51817	2.81267	3.13843	3.49845	3.89598	5.35025
13	1.66507	1.88565	2.13293	2.71962	3.06581	3.45227	3.88328	4.36349	6.15279
14	1.73168	1.97993	2.26090	2.93719	3.34173	3.79750	4.31044	4.88711	7.07571
15	1.80094	2.07893	2.39656	3.17217	3.64248	4.17725	4.78459	5.47357	8.13706
16	1.87298	2.18287	2.54035	3.42594	3.97031	4.59497	5.31089	6.13039	9.35762
17	1.94790	2.29202	2.69277	3.70002	4.32763	5.05447	5.89509	6.86604	10.76126
18	2.02582	2.40662	2.85434	3.99602	4.71712	5.55992	6.54355	7.68997	12.37545
19	2.10685	2.52695	3.02560	4.31570	5.14166	6.11591	7.26334	8.61276	14.23177
20	2.19112	2.65330	3.20714	4.66096	5.60441	6.72750	8.06231	9.64629	16.36654

In Table 1, *n* is the number of compounding periods, the percentages are the periodic interest rates, and the 5-digit decimal numbers in the respective columns are the future value of 1 factors. In using Table 1, the principal amount is multiplied by the future value factor for the specified number of periods and interest rate. For example, the future value factor for two periods at 9 percent is 1.18810. Multiplying this factor by $1,000 equals $1,188.10, which is the accumulated balance at the end of year 2 in the CityCorp example in Illustration C-2. The $1,295.03 accumulated balance at the end of the third year can be calculated from Table 1 by multiplying the future value factor for three periods (1.29503) by the $1,000.

The following demonstration problem illustrates how to use Table 1.

Illustration C-4
Demonstration Problem—
Using Table 1 for FV of 1

John and Mary Rich invested $20,000 in a savings account paying 6% interest at the time their son, Mike, was born. The money is to be used by Mike for his college education. On his 18th birthday, Mike withdraws the money from his savings account. How much did Mike withdraw from his account?

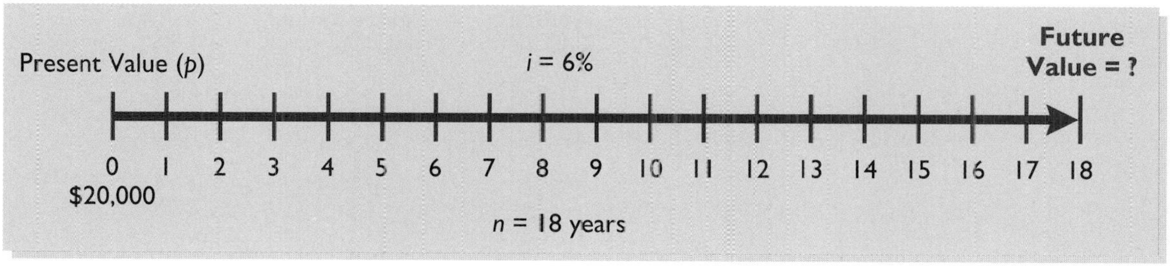

Answer: The future value factor from Table 1 is 2.85434 (18 periods at 6%). The future value of $20,000 earning 6% per year for 18 years is **$57,086.80** ($20,000 × 2.85434).

Future Value of an Annuity

STUDY OBJECTIVE 3

Solve for future value of an annuity.

The preceding discussion involved the accumulation of only a single principal sum. Individuals and businesses frequently encounter situations in which a series of equal dollar amounts are to be paid or received periodically, such as loans or lease (rental) contracts. Such payments or receipts of equal dollar amounts are referred to as **annuities**. The **future value of an annuity** is the sum of all the payments (receipts) plus the accumulated compound interest on them. In computing the future value of an annuity, it is necessary to know (1) the interest rate, (2) the number of compounding periods, and (3) the amount of the periodic payments or receipts.

To illustrate the computation of the future value of an annuity, assume that you invest $2,000 at the end of each year for 3 years at 5 percent interest compounded annually. This situation is depicted in the time diagram in Illustration C-5.

Illustration C-5
Time diagram for a 3-year annuity

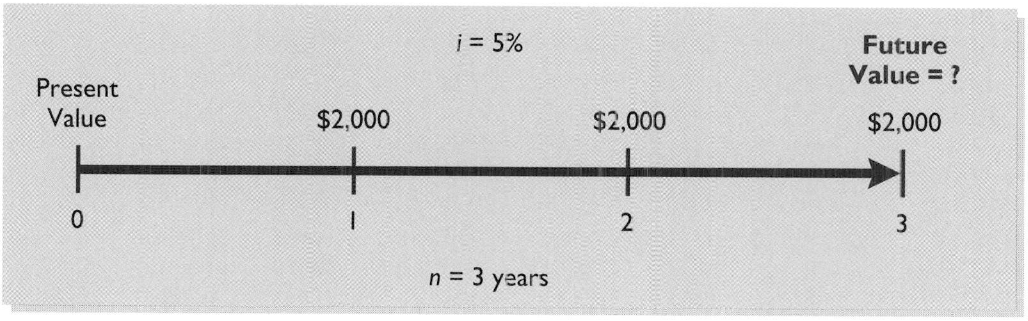

As can be seen in Illustration C-5, the $2,000 invested at the end of year 1 will earn interest for 2 years (years 2 and 3), and the $2,000 invested at the end of year 2 will earn interest for 1 year (year 3). However, the last $2,000 investment (made at the end of year 3) will not earn any interest. The future value of these periodic payments could be computed using the future value factors from Table 1 as shown in Illustration C-6.

Illustration C-6
Future value of periodic payments

Year Invested	Amount Invested	×	Future Value of 1 Factor at 5%	=	Future Value
1	$2,000	×	1.10250	=	$2,205
2	$2,000	×	1.05000	=	2,100
3	$2,000	×	1.00000	=	2,000
			3.15250		**$6,305**

The first $2,000 investment is multiplied by the future value factor for two periods (1.1025) because 2 years' interest will accumulate on it (in years 2 and 3). The second $2,000 investment will earn only one year's interest (in year 3) and therefore is multiplied by the future value factor for one year (1.0500). The final $2,000 investment is made at the end of the third year and will not earn any interest. Consequently, the future value of the last $2,000 invested is only $2,000 since it does not accumulate any interest.

This method of calculation is required when the periodic payments or receipts are not equal in each period. However, when the periodic payments (receipts) are the same in each period, the future value can be computed by using a future value of an annuity of 1 table. Table 2, shown below, is such a table.

TABLE 2
Future Value of an Annuity of 1

(*n*) Periods	4%	5%	6%	8%	9%	10%	11%	12%	15%
1	1.00000	1.00000	1.00000	1.00000	1.00000	1.00000	1.00000	1.00000	1.00000
2	2.04000	2.05000	2.06000	2.08000	2.09000	2.10000	2.11000	2.12000	2.15000
3	3.12160	3.15250	3.18360	3.24640	3.27810	3.31000	3.34210	3.37440	3.47250
4	4.24646	4.31013	4.37462	4.50611	4.57313	4.64100	4.70973	4.77933	4.99338
5	5.41632	5.52563	5.63709	5.86660	5.98471	6.10510	6.22780	6.35285	6.74238
6	6.63298	6.80191	6.97532	7.33592	7.52334	7.71561	7.91286	8.11519	8.75374
7	7.89829	8.14201	8.39384	8.92280	9.20044	9.48717	9.78327	10.08901	11.06680
8	9.21423	9.54911	9.89747	10.63663	11.02847	11.43589	11.85943	12.29969	13.72682
9	10.58280	11.02656	11.49132	12.48756	13.02104	13.57948	14.16397	14.77566	16.78584
10	12.00611	12.57789	13.18079	14.48656	15.19293	15.93743	16.72201	17.54874	20.30372
11	13.48635	14.20679	14.97164	16.64549	17.56029	18.53117	19.56143	20.65458	24.34928
12	15.02581	15.91713	16.86994	18.97713	20.14072	21.38428	22.71319	24.13313	29.00167
13	16.62684	17.71298	18.88214	21.49530	22.95339	24.52271	26.21164	28.02911	34.35192
14	18.29191	19.59863	21.01507	24.21492	26.01919	27.97498	30.09492	32.39260	40.50471
15	20.02359	21.57856	23.27597	27.15211	29.36092	31.77248	34.40536	37.27972	47.58041
16	21.82453	23.65749	25.67253	30.32428	33.00340	35.94973	39.18995	42.75328	55.71747
17	23.69751	25.84037	28.21288	33.75023	36.97351	40.54470	44.50084	48.88367	65.07509
18	25.64541	28.13238	30.90565	37.45024	41.30134	45.59917	50.39593	55.74972	75.83636
19	27.67123	30.53900	33.75999	41.44626	46.01846	51.15909	56.93949	63.43968	88.21181
20	29.77808	33.06595	36.78559	45.76196	51.16012	57.27500	64.20283	72.05244	102.44358

Table 2 shows the future value of 1 to be received periodically for a given number of periods. You can see from Table 2 that the future value of an annuity of 1 factor for three periods at 5 percent is 3.15250. The future value factor is the total of the three individual future value factors as shown in Illustration C-6. Multiplying this amount by the annual investment of $2,000 produces a future value of $6,305.

The demonstration problem in Illustration C-7 illustrates how to use Table 2.

Illustration C-7
Demonstration Problem—
Using Table 2 for FV of an annuity of 1

Henning Printing Company knows that in four years it must replace one of its existing printing presses with a new one. To insure that some funds are available to replace the machine in 4 years, the company is depositing $25,000 in a savings account at the end of each of the next four years (4 deposits in total). The savings account will earn 6% interest compounded annually. How much will be in the savings account at the end of 4 years when the new printing press is to be purchased?

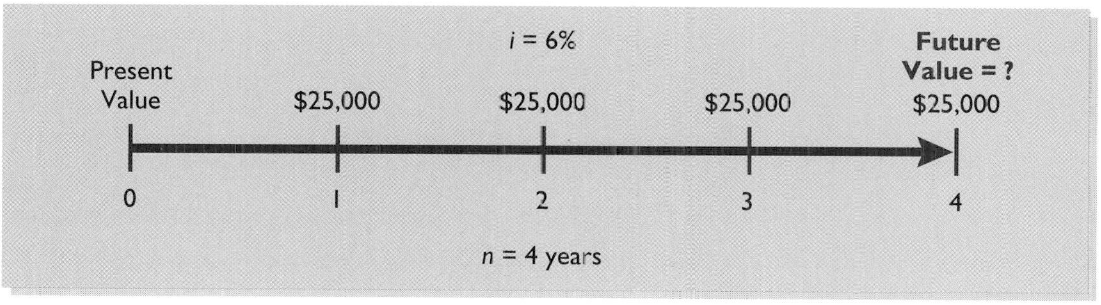

Answer: The future value factor from Table 2 is 4.37462 (4 periods at 6%). The future value of $25,000 invested at the end of each year for 4 years at 6% interest is **$109,365.50** ($25,000 × 4.37462).

Section 2 Present Value Concepts

Present Value Variables

STUDY OBJECTIVE 4

Identify the variables fundamental to solving present value problems.

The **present value** is the value now of a given amount to be invested or received in the future, assuming compound interest. Like the future value, present value is based on three variables: (1) the dollar amount to be received (future amount), (2) the length of time until the amount is received (number of periods), and (3) the interest rate (the discount rate). The process of determining the present value is referred to as **discounting the future amount.**

Present Value of a Single Amount

STUDY OBJECTIVE 5

Solve for present value of a single amount.

To illustrate present value concepts, assume that you are willing to invest a sum of money that will yield \$1,000 at the end of one year. In other words, what amount would you need to invest today to have \$1,000 one year from now? If you want a 10 percent rate of return, the investment or present value is \$909.09 (\$1,000 ÷ 1.10). The computation of this amount is shown in Illustration C-8.

Illustration C-8
Present value computation—\$1,000 discounted at 10% for 1 year

$$\textbf{Present Value} = \text{Future Value} \div (1 + i)^1$$
$$PV = FV \div (1 + 10\%)^1$$
$$PV = \$1{,}000 \div 1.10$$
$$\mathbf{PV = \$909.09}$$

The future amount (\$1,000), the discount rate (10 percent), and the number of periods (1) are known. The variables in this situation can be depicted in the following time diagram.

Illustration C-9
Finding present value if discounted for one period

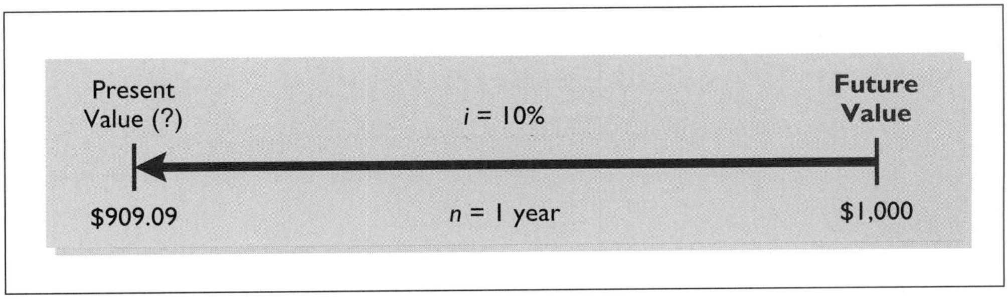

If the single amount of \$1,000 is to be received **in 2 years** and discounted at 10 percent [$PV = \$1{,}000 \div (1 + 10\%)^2$], its present value is \$826.45 [(\$1,000 ÷ 1.10) ÷ 1.10], depicted as follows.

Illustration C-10
Finding present value if discounted for two periods

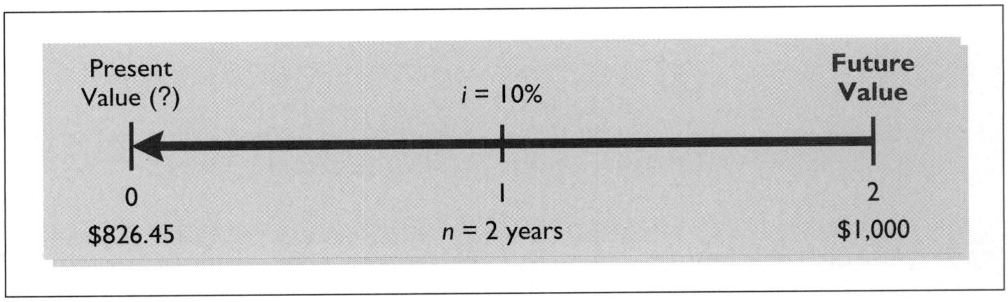

The present value of 1 may also be determined through tables that show the present value of 1 for n periods. In Table 3, n is the number of discounting periods involved. The percentages are the periodic interest rates or discount rates, and the 5-digit decimal numbers in the respective columns are the present value of 1 factors.

TABLE 3
Present Value of 1

(*n*) Periods	4%	5%	6%	8%	9%	10%	11%	12%	15%
1	.96154	.95238	.94340	.92593	.91743	.90909	.90090	.89286	.86957
2	.92456	.90703	.89000	.85734	.84168	.82645	.81162	.79719	.75614
3	.88900	.86384	.83962	.79383	.77218	.75132	.73119	.71178	.65752
4	.85480	.82270	.79209	.73503	.70843	.68301	.65873	.63552	.57175
5	.82193	.78353	.74726	.68058	.64993	.62092	.59345	.56743	.49718
6	.79031	.74622	.70496	.63017	.59627	.56447	.53464	.50663	.43233
7	.75992	.71068	.66506	.58349	.54703	.51316	.48166	.45235	.37594
8	.73069	.67684	.62741	.54027	.50187	.46651	.43393	.40388	.32690
9	.70259	.64461	.59190	.50025	.46043	.42410	.39092	.36061	.28426
10	.67556	.61391	.55839	.46319	.42241	.38554	.35218	.32197	.24719
11	.64958	.58468	.52679	.42888	.38753	.35049	.31728	.28748	.21494
12	.62460	.55684	.49697	.39711	.35554	.31863	.28584	.25668	.18691
13	.60057	.53032	.46884	.36770	.32618	.28966	.25751	.22917	.16253
14	.57748	.50507	.44230	.34046	.29925	.26333	.23199	.20462	.14133
15	.55526	.48102	.41727	.31524	.27454	.23939	.20900	.18270	.12289
16	.53391	.45811	.39365	.29189	.25187	.21763	.18829	.16312	.10687
17	.51337	.43630	.37136	.27027	.23107	.19785	.16963	.14564	.09293
18	.49363	.41552	.35034	.25025	.21199	.17986	.15282	.13004	.08081
19	.47464	.39573	.33051	.23171	.19449	.16351	.13768	.11611	.07027
20	.45639	.37689	.31180	.21455	.17843	.14864	.12403	.10367	.06110

When Table 3 is used, the future value is multiplied by the present value factor specified at the intersection of the number of periods and the discount rate. For example, the present value factor for one period at a discount rate of 10 percent is .90909, which equals the $909.09 ($1,000 × .90909) computed in Illustration C-8. For two periods at a discount rate of 10 percent, the present value factor is .82645, which equals the $826.45 ($1,000 × .82645) computed previously.

Note that a higher discount rate produces a smaller present value. For example, using a 15 percent discount rate, the present value of $1,000 due one year from now is $869.57 versus $909.09 at 10 percent. It should also be recognized that the further removed from the present the future value is, the smaller the present value. For example, using the same discount rate of 10 percent, the present value of $1,000 due in **5** years is $620.92 versus $1,000 due in **1** year is $909.09.

The following two demonstration problems (Illustrations C-11, C-12) illustrate how to use Table 3.

Illustration C-11
Demonstration Problem—
Using Table 3 for PV of 1

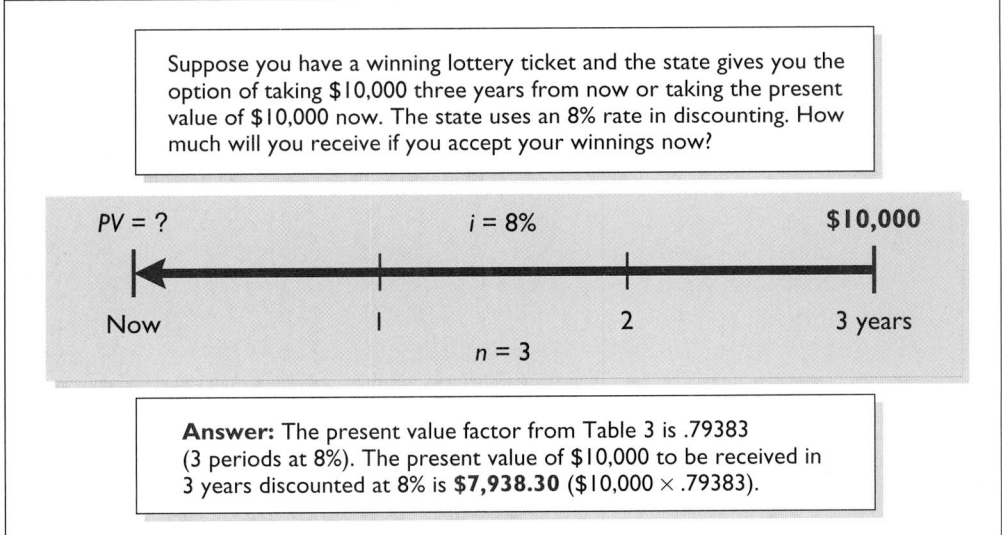

Suppose you have a winning lottery ticket and the state gives you the option of taking $10,000 three years from now or taking the present value of $10,000 now. The state uses an 8% rate in discounting. How much will you receive if you accept your winnings now?

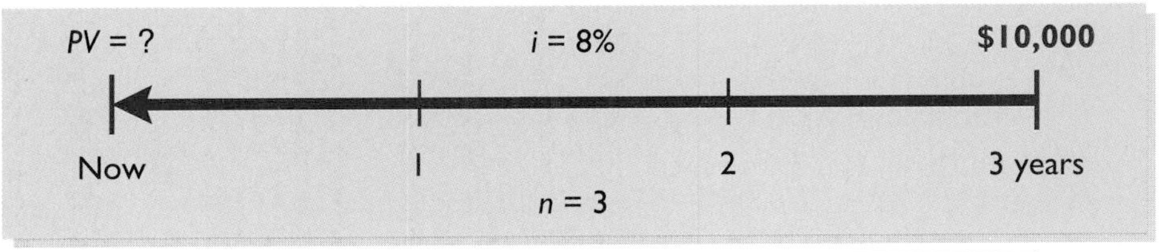

Answer: The present value factor from Table 3 is .79383 (3 periods at 8%). The present value of $10,000 to be received in 3 years discounted at 8% is **$7,938.30** ($10,000 × .79383).

Illustration C-12
Demonstration Problem—
Using Table 3 for PV of 1

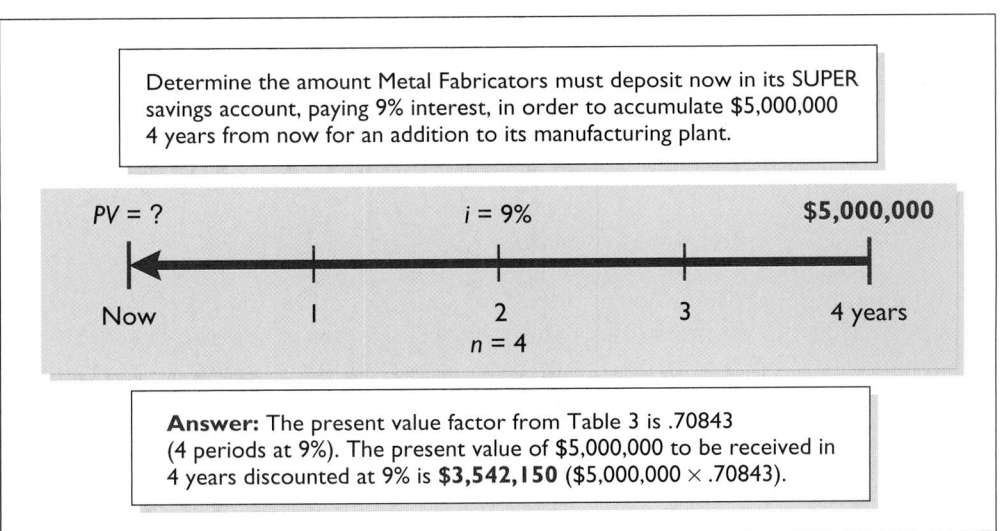

Determine the amount Metal Fabricators must deposit now in its SUPER savings account, paying 9% interest, in order to accumulate $5,000,000 4 years from now for an addition to its manufacturing plant.

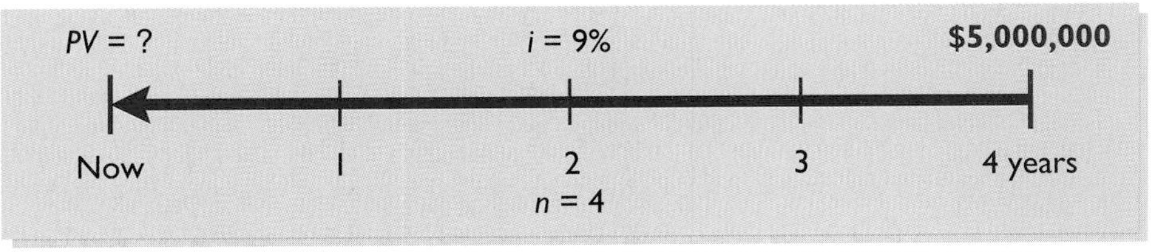

Answer: The present value factor from Table 3 is .70843 (4 periods at 9%). The present value of $5,000,000 to be received in 4 years discounted at 9% is **$3,542,150** ($5,000,000 × .70843).

Present Value of an Annuity

STUDY OBJECTIVE 6

Solve for present value of an annuity.

The preceding discussion involved the discounting of only a single future amount. Businesses and individuals frequently engage in transactions in which a series of equal dollar amounts are to be received or paid periodically. Examples of a series of periodic receipts or payments are loan agreements, installment sales, mortgage notes, lease (rental) contracts, and pension obligations. These series of periodic receipts or payments are called **annuities**. The **present value of an annuity** is a series of future receipts or payments discounted to their values now, assuming compound interest. To compute the present value of an annuity, it is necessary to know (1) the discount rate, (2) the number of discount periods, and (3) the amount of the periodic receipts or payments.

To illustrate the computation of the present value of an annuity, assume that you will receive $1,000 cash annually for 3 years at a time when the discount rate is 10 percent. This situation is depicted in the time diagram in Illustration C-13.

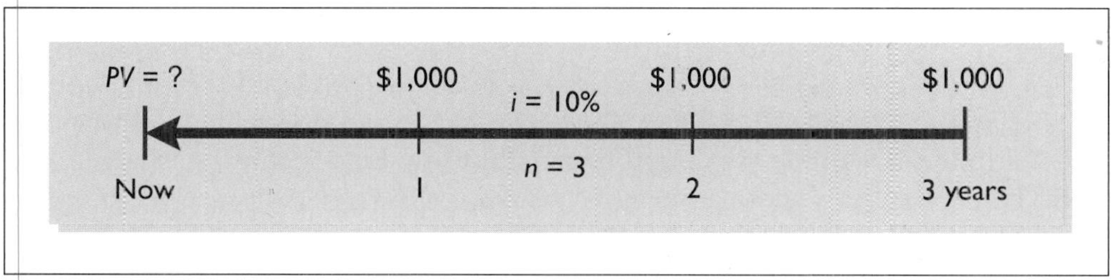

Illustration C-13
Time diagram for a 3-year annuity

The present value in this situation may be computed as follows.

Illustration C-14
Present value of a series of future amounts computation

Future Amount	×	Present Value of 1 Factor at 10%	=	Present Value
$1,000 (1 year away)	×	.90909	=	$ 909.09
1,000 (2 years away)	×	.82645	=	826.45
1,000 (3 years away)	×	.75132	=	751.32
		2.48686		**$2,486.86**

This method of calculation is required when the periodic cash flows are not uniform in each period. However, when the future receipts are the same in each period, there are two other ways to compute present value. First, the annual cash flow can be multiplied by the sum of the three present value factors. In the previous example, $1,000 × 2.48686 equals $2,486.86. Second, annuity tables may be used. As illustrated in Table 4 below, these tables show the present value of 1 to be received periodically for a given number of periods.

TABLE 4
Present Value of an Annuity of 1

(*n*) Periods	4%	5%	6%	8%	9%	10%	11%	12%	15%
1	.96154	.95238	.94340	.92593	.91743	.90909	.90090	.89286	.86957
2	1.88609	1.85941	1.83339	1.78326	1.75911	1.73554	1.71252	1.69005	1.62571
3	2.77509	2.72325	2.67301	2.57710	2.53130	2.48685	2.44371	2.40183	2.28323
4	3.62990	3.54595	3.46511	3.31213	3.23972	3.16986	3.10245	3.03735	2.85498
5	4.45182	4.32948	4.21236	3.99271	3.88965	3.79079	3.69590	3.60478	3.35216
6	5.24214	5.07569	4.91732	4.62288	4.48592	4.35526	4.23054	4.11141	3.78448
7	6.00205	5.78637	5.58238	5.20637	5.03295	4.86842	4.71220	4.56376	4.16042
8	6.73274	6.46321	6.20979	5.74664	5.53482	5.33493	5.14612	4.96764	4.48732
9	7.43533	7.10782	6.80169	6.24689	5.99525	5.75902	5.53705	5.32825	4.77158
10	8.11090	7.72173	7.36009	6.71008	6.41766	6.14457	5.88923	5.65022	5.01877
11	8.76048	8.30641	7.88687	7.13896	6.80519	6.49506	6.20652	5.93770	5.23371
12	9.38507	8.86325	8.38384	7.53608	7.16073	6.81369	6.49236	6.19437	5.42062
13	9.98565	9.39357	8.85268	7.90378	7.48690	7.10336	6.74987	6.42355	5.58315
14	10.56312	9.89864	9.29498	8.24424	7.78615	7.36669	6.98187	6.62817	5.72448
15	11.11839	10.37966	9.71225	8.55948	8.06069	7.60608	7.19087	6.81086	5.84737
16	11.65230	10.83777	10.10590	8.85137	8.31256	7.82371	7.37916	6.97399	5.95424
17	12.16567	11.27407	10.47726	9.12164	8.54363	8.02155	7.54879	7.11963	6.04716
18	12.65930	11.68959	10.82760	9.37189	8.75563	8.20141	7.70162	7.24967	6.12797
19	13.13394	12.08532	11.15812	9.60360	8.95012	8.36492	7.83929	7.36578	6.19823
20	13.59033	12.46221	11.46992	9.81815	9.12855	8.51356	7.96333	7.46944	6.25933

You can see from Table 4 that the present value of an annuity of 1 factor for three periods at 10 percent is 2.48685.[1] This present value factor is the total of the three individual present value factors as shown in Illustration C-14. Applying this amount to the annual cash flow of $1,000 produces a present value of $2,486.85.

The following demonstration problem (Illustration C-15) illustrates how to use Table 4.

Illustration C-15
Demonstration Problem—
Using Table 4 for PV of an annuity of 1

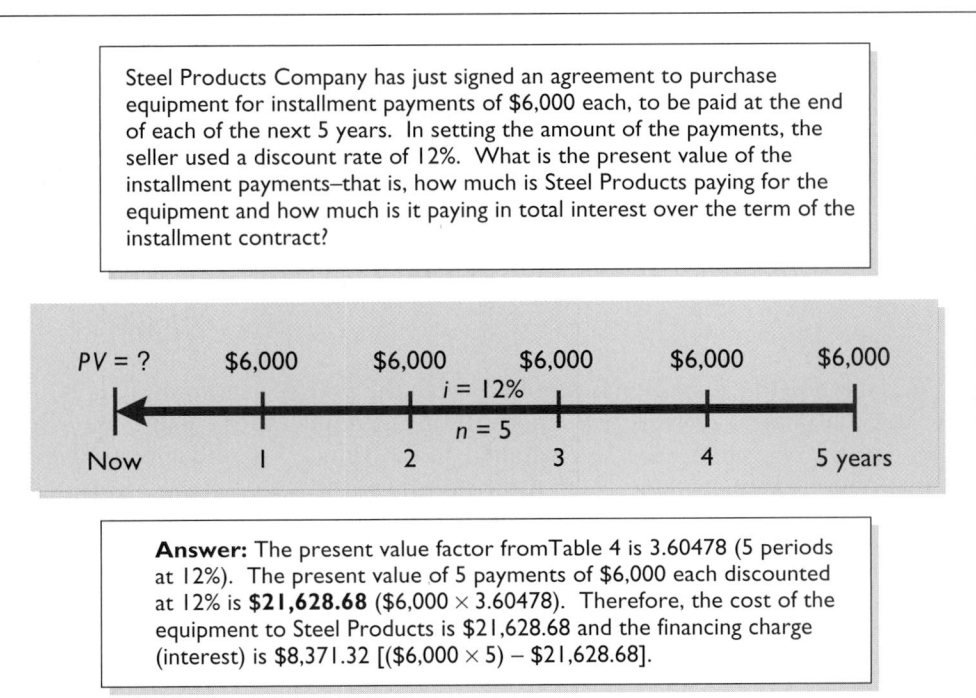

Steel Products Company has just signed an agreement to purchase equipment for installment payments of $6,000 each, to be paid at the end of each of the next 5 years. In setting the amount of the payments, the seller used a discount rate of 12%. What is the present value of the installment payments–that is, how much is Steel Products paying for the equipment and how much is it paying in total interest over the term of the installment contract?

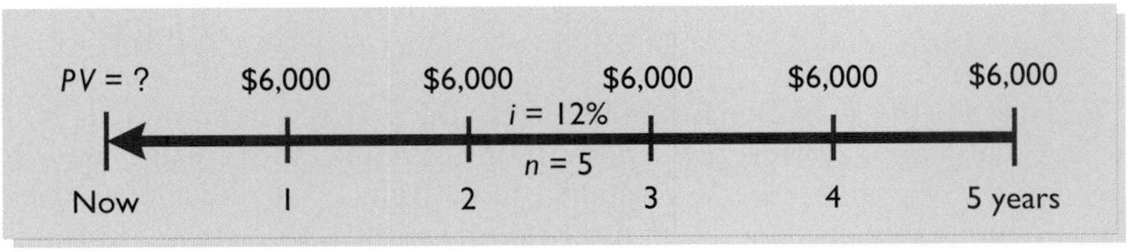

Answer: The present value factor fromTable 4 is 3.60478 (5 periods at 12%). The present value of 5 payments of $6,000 each discounted at 12% is **$21,628.68** ($6,000 × 3.60478). Therefore, the cost of the equipment to Steel Products is $21,628.68 and the financing charge (interest) is $8,371.32 [($6,000 × 5) – $21,628.68].

Time Periods and Discounting

In the preceding calculations, the discounting has been done on an annual basis using an annual interest rate. Discounting may also be done over shorter periods of time such as monthly, quarterly, or semiannually. When the time frame is less than one year, it is necessary to convert the annual interest rate to the applicable time frame.

Assume, for example, that the investor in Illustration C-14 received $500 **semiannually** for 3 years instead of $1,000 annually. In this case, the number of periods becomes 6 (3 × 2), the discount rate is 5 percent (10% ÷ 2), the present value factor from Table 4 is 5.07569, and the present value of the future cash flows is $2,537.85 (5.07569 × $500). This amount is slightly higher than the $2,486.86 computed in Illustration C-14 because interest is computed twice during the same year. That is, interest is earned on the first half year's interest.

[1]The difference of .00001 between 2.48686 and 2.48685 is due to rounding.

Computing the Present Value of a Long-Term Note or Bond

STUDY OBJECTIVE 7

Compute the present value of notes and bonds.

The present value (or market price) of a long-term note or bond is a function of three variables: (1) the payment amounts, (2) the length of time until the amounts are paid, and (3) the discount rate. Our illustration uses a 5-year bond issue.

The first variable (dollars to be paid) is made up of two elements: (1) a series of interest payments (an annuity) and (2) the principal amount (a single sum). To compute the present value of the bond, both the interest payments and the principal amount must be discounted—two different computations. The time diagrams for a bond due in 5 years are shown in Illustration C-16.

Illustration C-16
Present value of a bond time diagram

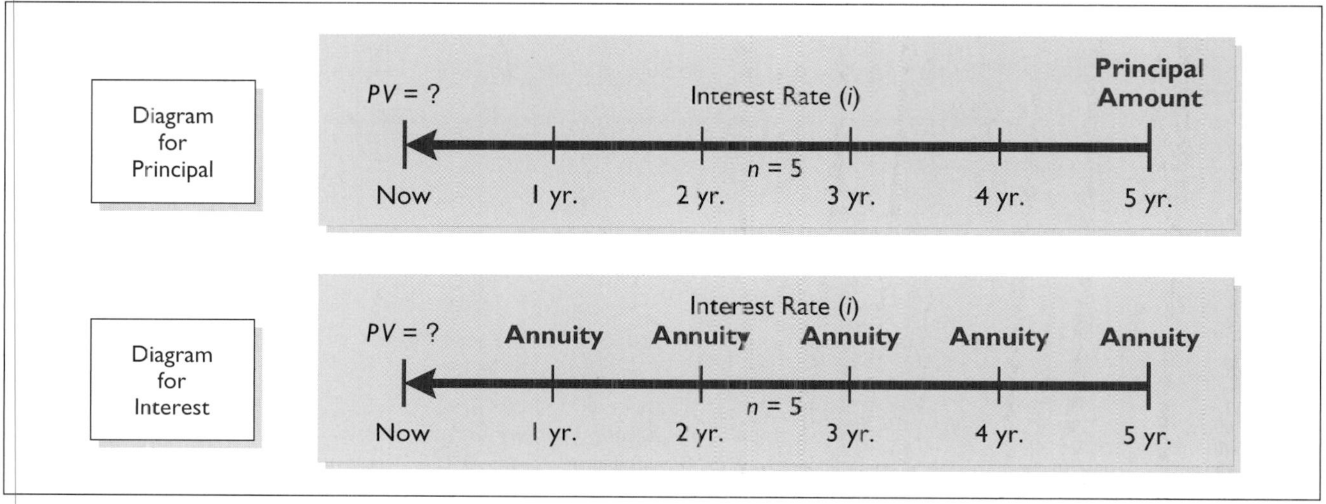

When the investor's discount rate is equal to the bond's contractual interest rate, the present value of the bonds will equal the face value of the bonds. To illustrate, assume a bond issue of 10%, 5-year bonds with a face value of $100,000 with interest payable **semiannually** on January 1 and July 1. If the discount rate is the same as the contractual rate, the bonds will sell at face value. In this case, the investor will receive (1) $100,000 at maturity and (2) a series of ten $5,000 interest payments [($100,000 × 10%) ÷ 2] over the term of the bonds. The length of time is expressed in terms of interest periods (in this case, 10) and the discount rate per interest period (5%). The following time diagram (Illustration C-17) depicts the variables involved in this discounting situation.

Illustration C-17
Time diagram for present value of a 10%, 5-year bond paying interest semiannually

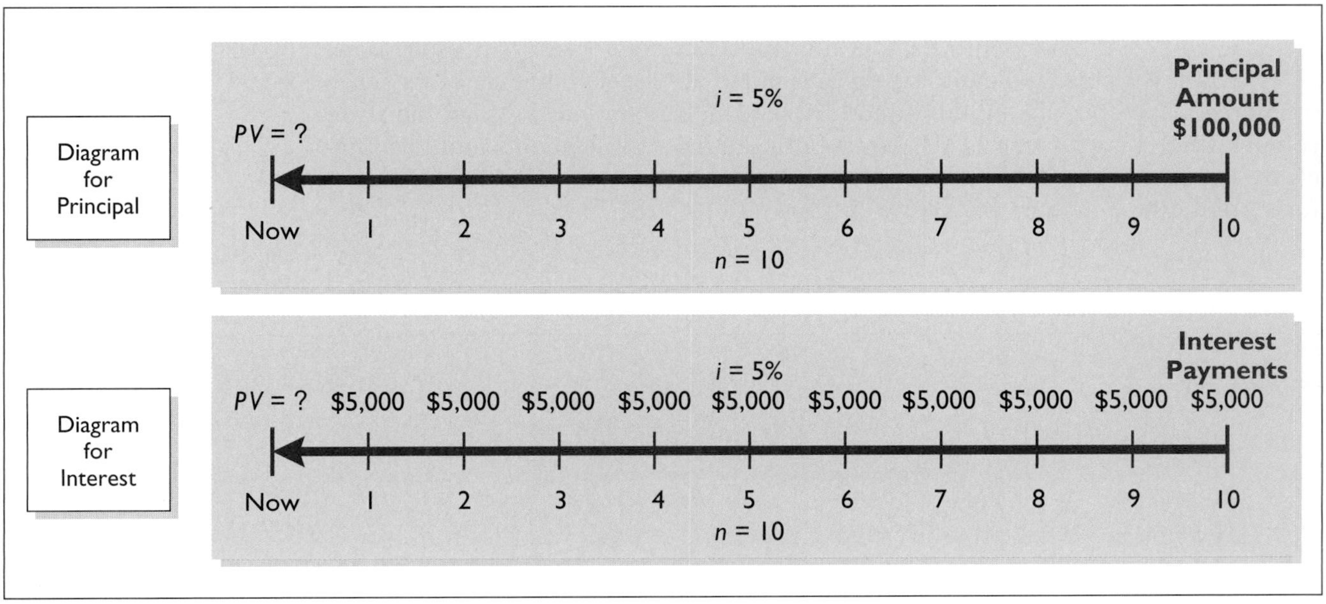

The computation of the present value of these bonds is shown below.

Illustration C-18
Present value of principal and interest—face value

Bonds Trading at Face Value
10% Contractual Rate—10% Discount Rate

Present value of principal to be received at maturity	
$100,000 × PV of 1 due in 10 periods at 5%	
$100,000 × .61391 (Table 3)	$ 61,391
Present value of interest to be received periodically over the term of the bonds	
$5,000 × PV of 1 due periodically for 10 periods at 5%	
$5,000 × 7.72173 (Table 4)	38,609*
Present value of bonds	**$100,000**

*(Rounded).

Now assume that the investor's required rate of return is 12 percent, not 10 percent. The future amounts are again $100,000 and $5,000, respectively, but now a discount rate of 6 percent (12% ÷ 2) must be used. The present value of the bonds is $92,639, as computed below.

Illustration C-19
Present value of principal and interest—discount

Bonds Trading at a Discount
10% Contractual Rate—12% Discount Rate

Present value of principal to be received at maturity	
$100,000 × .55839 (Table 3)	$55,839
Present value of interest to be received periodically over the term of the bonds	
$5,000 × 7.36009 (Table 4)	36,800
Present value of bonds	**$92,639**

Conversely, if the discount rate is 8 percent and the contractual rate is 10 percent, the present value of the bonds is $108,111, computed as follows.

Illustration C-20
Present value of principal and interest—premium

Bonds Trading at a Premium 10% Contractual Rate—8% Discount Rate	
Present value of principal to be received at maturity	
$100,000 × .67556 (Table 3)	$ 67,556
Present value of interest to be received periodically over the term of the bonds	
$5,000 × 8.11090 (Table 4)	40,555
Present value of bonds	**$108,111**

As discussed in this appendix, the selling price of the bonds can be determined via present value formulas. Many computer spreadsheets and computer programs can perform the discounting functions given the basic information of the situation.

SUMMARY OF STUDY OBJECTIVES

1. **Distinguish between simple and compound interest.** Simple interest is computed on the principal only, whereas compound interest is computed on the principal and any interest earned that has not been withdrawn.
2. **Solve for future value of a single amount.** Prepare a time diagram of the problem. Identify the principal amount, the number of compounding periods, and the interest rate. Using the future value of 1 table, multiply the principal amount by the future value factor specified at the intersection of the number of periods and the interest rate.
3. **Solve for future value of an annuity.** Prepare a time diagram of the problem. Identify the amount of the periodic payments, the number of compounding periods, and the interest rate. Using the future value of an annuity of 1 table, multiply the amount of the payments by the future value factor specified at the intersection of the number of periods and the interest rate.
4. **Identify the variables fundamental to solving present value problems.** The following three variables are fundamental to solving present value problems: (1) the future amount, (2) the number of periods, and (3) the interest rate (the discount rate).
5. **Solve for present value of a single amount.** Prepare a time diagram of the problem. Identify the future amount, the number of discounting periods, and the discount (interest) rate. Using the present value of 1 table, multiply the future amount by the present value factor specified at the intersection of the number of periods and the discount rate.
6. **Solve for present value of an annuity.** Prepare a time diagram of the problem. Identify the future amounts (annuities), the number of discounting periods, and the discount (interest) rate. Using the present value of an annuity of 1 table, multiply the amount of the annuity by the present value factor specified at the intersection of the number of periods and the interest rate.
7. **Compute the present value of notes and bonds.** To determine the present value of the principal amount: Multiply the principal amount (a single future amount) by the present value factor (from the present value of 1 table) intersecting at the number of periods (number of interest payments) and the discount rate. To determine the present value of the series of interest payments: Multiply the amount of the interest payment by the present value factor (from the present value of an annuity of 1 table) intersecting at the number of periods (number of interest payments) and the discount rate. Add the present value of the principal amount to the present value of the interest payments to arrive at the present value of the note or bond.

GLOSSARY

Annuity A series of equal dollar amounts to be paid or received periodically. (p. C5)

Compound interest The interest computed on the principal and any interest earned that has not been paid or received. (p. C2)

Discounting the future amount(s) The process of determining present value. (p. C7)

Future value of a single amount The value at a future date of a given amount invested assuming compound interest. (p. C3)

Future value of an annuity The sum of all the payments or receipts plus the accumulated compound interest on them. (p. C5)

Interest Payment for the use of another's money. (p. C1)

Present value The value now of a given amount to be invested or received in the future assuming compound interest. (p. C7)

Present value of an annuity A series of future receipts or payments discounted to their value now assuming compound interest. (p. C10)

Principal The amount borrowed or invested. (p. C1)

Simple interest The interest computed on the principal only. (p. C1)

BRIEF EXERCISES*

Compute the future value of a single amount.
(SO 2)

BEC-1 Russ Holub invested $4,000 at 5% annual interest, and left the money invested without withdrawing any of the interest for 10 years. At the end of the 10 years, Russ withdrew the accumulated amount of money.

(a) What amount did Russ withdraw assuming the investment earns simple interest?
(b) What amount did Russ withdraw assuming the investment earns interest compound annually?

Use future value tables.
(SO 2, 3)

BEC-2 For each of the following cases, indicate (1) to what interest rate columns and (2) to what number of periods you would refer in looking up the future value factor.

1. In Table 1 (future value of 1):

	Annual Rate	Number of Years Invested	Compounded
(a)	8%	5	Annually
(b)	5%	3	Semiannually

2. In Table 2 (future value of an annuity of 1):

	Annual Rate	Number of Years Invested	Compounded
(a)	5%	10	Annually
(b)	4%	6	Semiannually

Compute the future value of a single amount.
(SO 2)

BEC-3 Racine Company signed a lease for an office building for a period of 10 years. Under the lease agreement, a security deposit of $10,000 is made. The deposit will be returned at the expiration of the lease with interest compounded at 4% per year. What amount will Racine receive at the time the lease expires?

Compute the future value of an annuity.
(SO 3)

BEC-4 Chaffee Company issued $1,000,000, 10-year bonds and agreed to make annual sinking fund deposits of $75,000. The deposits are made at the end of each year into an account paying 6% annual interest. What amount will be in the sinking fund at the end of 10 years?

Compute the future value of a single amount and of an annuity.
(SO 2, 3)

BEC-5 Wayne and Brenda Anderson invested $5,000 in a savings account paying 5% compound annual interest when their daughter, Sue, was born. They also deposited $1,000 on each of her birthdays until she was 18 (including her 18th birthday). How much will be in the savings account on her 18th birthday (after the last deposit)?

---

*Use tables to solve the Exercises.

BEC-6 Ty Ngu borrowed $20,000 on July 1, 2000. This amount plus accrued interest at 6% compounded annually is to be repaid on July 1, 2006. How much will Ty have to repay on July 1, 2006?

Compute the future value of a single amount.
(SO 2)

BEC-7 For each of the following cases, indicate (a) to what interest rate columns and (b) to what number of periods you would refer in looking up the discount rate.

Use present value tables.
(SO 5, 6)

1. In Table 3 (present value of 1):

	Annual Rate	Number of Years Involved	Discounts Per Year
(a)	12%	6	Annually
(b)	10%	15	Annually
(c)	8%	10	Semiannually

2. In Table 4 (present value of an annuity of 1):

	Annual Rate	Number of Years Involved	Number of Payments Involved	Frequency of Payments
(a)	8%	20	20	Annually
(b)	10%	5	5	Annually
(c)	12%	4	8	Semiannually

BEC-8 **(a)** What is the present value of $20,000 due 8 periods from now, discounted at 8%? **(b)** What is the present value of $20,000 to be received at the end of each of 6 periods, discounted at 9%?

Determine present values.
(SO 5, 6)

BEC-9 Gonzalez Company is considering an investment that will return a lump sum of $500,000 5 years from now. What amount should Gonzalez Company pay for this investment in order to earn a 10% return?

Compute the present value of a single-sum investment.
(SO 5)

BEC-10 Lasorda Company earns 9% on an investment that will return $875,000 8 years from now. What is the amount Lasorda should invest now in order to earn this rate of return?

Compute the present value of a single-sum investment.
(SO 5)

BEC-11 Bosco Company is considering investing in an annuity contract that will return $30,000 annually at the end of each year for 15 years. What amount should Bosco Company pay for this investment if it earns a 6% return?

Compute the present value of an annuity investment.
(SO 6)

BEC-12 Modine Enterprises earns 11% on an investment that pays back $120,000 at the end of each of the next 4 years. What is the amount Modine Enterprises invested to earn the 11% rate of return?

Compute the present value of an annuity investment.
(SO 6)

BEC-13 Midwest Railroad Co. is about to issue $100,000 of 10-year bonds paying a 10% interest rate, with interest payable semiannually. The discount rate for such securities is 8%. How much can Midwest expect to receive from the sale of these bonds?

Compute the present value of bonds.
(SO 5, 6, 7)

BEC-14 Assume the same information as in BEC-13 except that the discount rate is 10% instead of 8%. In this case, how much can Midwest expect to receive from the sale of these bonds?

Compute the present value of bonds.
(SO 5, 6, 7)

BEC-15 Lounsbury Company receives a $50,000, 6-year note bearing interest of 8% (paid annually) from a customer at a time when the discount rate is 9%. What is the present value of the note received by Lounsbury Company?

Compute the present value of a note.
(SO 5, 6, 7)

BEC-16 Hartzler Enterprises issued 8%, 8-year, $2,000,000 par value bonds that pay interest semiannually on October 1 and April 1. The bonds are dated April 1, 2006, and are issued on that date. The discount rate of interest for such bonds on April 1, 2006, is 10%. What cash proceeds did Hartzler receive from issuance of the bonds?

Compute the present value of bonds.
(SO 5, 6, 7)

Compute the value of a machine for purposes of making a purchase decision.
(SO 7)

BEC-17 Vinny Carpino owns a garage and is contemplating purchasing a tire retreading machine for $16,280. After estimating costs and revenues, Vinny projects a net cash flow from the retreading machine of $3,000 annually for 8 years. Vinny hopes to earn a return of 11% on such investments. What is the present value of the retreading operation? Should Vinny Carpino purchase the retreading machine?

Compute the present value of a note.
(SO 5, 6)

BEC-18 Rodriguez Company issues a 10%, 6-year mortgage note on January 1, 2006, to obtain financing for new equipment. Land is used as collateral for the note. The terms provide for semiannual installment payments of $56,413. What were the cash proceeds received from the issuance of the note?

Compute the maximum price to pay for the equipment.
(SO 7)

BEC-19 Goltra Company is considering purchasing equipment. The equipment will produce the following cash flows: Year 1, $30,000; Year 2, $40,000; Year 3, $50,000. Goltra requires a minimum rate of return of 12%. What is the maximum price Goltra should pay for this equipment?

Compute the interest rate on a single sum.
(SO 5)

BEC-20 If Maria Sanchez invests $3,152 now, she will receive $10,000 at the end of 15 years. What annual rate of interest will Maria earn on her investment? (*Hint:* Use Table 3.)

Compute the number of periods of a single sum.
(SO 5)

BEC-21 Lori Burke has been offered the opportunity of investing $42,410 now. The investment will earn 10% per year and at the end of that time will return Lori $100,000. How many years must Lori wait to receive $100,000? (*Hint:* Use Table 3.)

Compute the interest rate on an annuity.
(SO 6)

BEC-22 Nancy Burns purchased an investment for $12,462.21. From this investment, she will receive $1,000 annually for the next 20 years, starting one year from now. What rate of interest will Nancy's investment be earning for her? (*Hint:* Use Table 4.)

Compute the number of periods of an annuity.
(SO 6)

BEC-23 Betty Estes invests $7,536.08 now for a series of $1,000 annual returns, beginning one year from now. Betty will earn a return of 8% on the initial investment. How many annual payments of $1,000 will Betty receive? (*Hint:* Use Table 4.)

Payroll Accounting

STUDY OBJECTIVES

After studying this appendix, you should be able to:

1. Discuss the objectives of internal control for payroll.
2. Compute and record the payroll for a pay period.
3. Describe and record employer payroll taxes.

Payroll and related fringe benefits often make up a large percentage of current liabilities. Employee compensation is often the most significant expense that a company incurs. For example, **General Motors** recently reported total employees of 386,000 and labor costs of $21.6 billion. Add to labor costs such fringe benefits as health insurance, life insurance, disability insurance, and so on, and you can see why proper accounting and control of payroll are so important.

Payroll accounting involves more than paying employees' wages. Companies are required by law to maintain payroll records for each employee, file and pay payroll taxes, and comply with numerous state and federal tax laws related to employee compensation. Accounting for payroll has become much more complex due to these regulations.

PAYROLL DEFINED

The term "payroll" pertains to both salaries and wages. Managerial, administrative, and sales personnel are generally paid **salaries**. Salaries are often expressed in terms of a specified amount per month or per year rather than an hourly rate. For example, the faculty and administrative personnel at the college or university you are attending are paid salaries. In contrast, store clerks, factory employees, and manual laborers are normally paid **wages**. Wages are based on a rate per hour or on a piecework basis (such as per unit of product). Frequently, the terms "salaries" and "wages" are used interchangeably.

The term "payroll" does not apply to payments made for services of professionals such as certified public accountants, attorneys, and architects. Such professionals are independent contractors rather than salaried employees. Payments to them are called **fees**, rather than salaries or wages. This distinction is important because government regulations relating to the payment and reporting of payroll taxes apply only to employees.

INTERNAL CONTROL OF PAYROLL

STUDY OBJECTIVE 1

Discuss the objectives of internal control for payroll.

Internal control was introduced in Chapter 8. As applied to payrolls, the objectives of internal control are (1) to safeguard company assets against unauthorized payments of payrolls, and (2) to ensure the accuracy and reliability of the accounting records pertaining to payrolls.

Irregularities often result if internal control is lax. Overstating hours, using unauthorized pay rates, adding fictitious employees to the payroll, continuing terminated employees on the payroll, and distributing duplicate payroll checks are all methods of stealing from a company. Moreover, inaccurate records will result in incorrect paychecks, financial statements, and payroll tax returns.

Payroll activities involve four functions: hiring employees, timekeeping, preparing the payroll, and paying the payroll. For effective internal control, these four functions should be assigned to different departments or individuals. To illustrate these functions, we will examine the case of Academy Company and one of its employees, Michael Jordan.

Hiring Employees

Hiring Employees

Human Resources department documents and authorizes employment.

The human resources (personnel) department is responsible for posting job openings, screening and interviewing applicants, and hiring employees. From a control standpoint, this department provides significant documentation and authorization. When an employee is hired, the human resources department prepares an authorization form. The one used by Academy Company for Michael Jordan is shown in Illustration D-1.

The authorization form is sent to the payroll department, where it is used to place the new employee on the payroll. A chief concern of the human resources department is ensuring the accuracy of this form. The reason is quite simple: one of the most common types of payroll frauds is adding fictitious employees to the payroll.

The human resources department is also responsible for authorizing changes in employment status. Specifically, they must authorize (1) changes in pay rates and (2) terminations of employment. Every authorization should be in writing, and a

Illustration D-1
Authorization form prepared by the human resources department

ACADEMY COMPANY

Employee Name Jordan, (LAST) Michael (FIRST) (MI) Starting Date 9/01/04

Classification Skilled-Level 10 Social Security No. 329-36-9547

Department Shipping Division Entertainment

NEW HIRE	Classification Clerk Salary Grade Level 10 Trans. from Temp. ☐ Rate $ 10.00 per hour Bonus N/A Non-exempt ☒ Exempt ☐
RATE CHANGE	New Rate $ 12.00 Effective Date 9/1/05 Present Rate $ 10.00 Merit ☒ Promotion ☐ Decrease ☐ Other ____ Previous Increase Date None Amount $ ____ per ____ Type ____
SEPARATION	Resignation ☐ Discharge ☐ Retirement ☐ Reason ____ Leave of absence ☐ From ____ to ____ Type ____ Last Day Worked ____
APPROVALS	BEW — BRANCH OR DEPT. MANAGER; 9/1/05 — DATE; EMW — DIVISION V.P.; 9-1-05 — DATE James E. Speer — PERSONNEL DEPARTMENT

copy of the change in status should be sent to the payroll department. Notice in Illustration D-1 that Jordan received a pay increase of $2 per hour.

Timekeeping

Another area in which internal control is important is timekeeping. Hourly employees are usually required to record time worked by "punching" a time clock. Times of arrival and departure are automatically recorded by the employee by inserting a **time card** into the clock. Michael Jordan's time card is shown in Illustration D-2.

Timekeeping

Supervisors monitor hours worked through time cards and time reports.

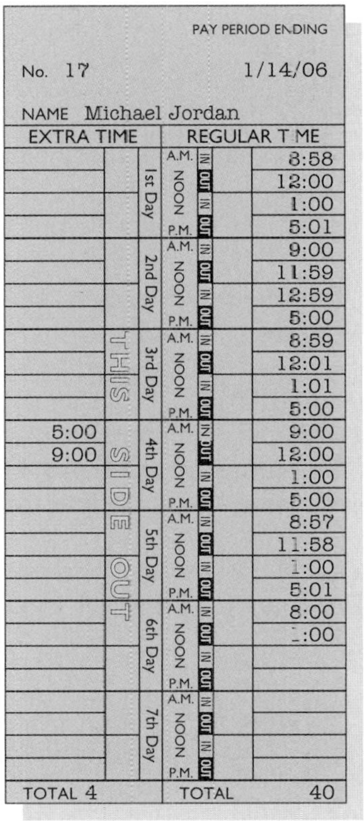

PAY PERIOD ENDING

No. 17 1/14/06

NAME Michael Jordan

Day		EXTRA TIME	REGULAR TIME
1st Day	A.M. IN		8:58
	NOON OUT		12:00
	NOON IN		1:00
	P.M. OUT		5:01
2nd Day	A.M. IN		9:00
	NOON OUT		11:59
	NOON IN		12:59
	P.M. OUT		5:00
3rd Day	A.M. IN		8:59
	NOON OUT		12:01
	NOON IN		1:01
	P.M. OUT		5:00
4th Day	A.M. IN	5:00	9:00
	NOON OUT	9:00	12:00
	NOON IN		1:00
	P.M. OUT		5:00
5th Day	A.M. IN		8:57
	NOON OUT		11:58
	NOON IN		1:00
	P.M. OUT		5:01
6th Day	A.M. IN		8:00
	NOON OUT		:00
	NOON IN		
	P.M. OUT		
7th Day	A.M. IN		
	NOON OUT		
	NOON IN		
	P.M. OUT		
		TOTAL 4	TOTAL 40

THIS SIDE OUT

Illustration D-2
Time card

In large companies, time clock procedures are often monitored by a supervisor or security guard to make sure an employee punches only one card. At the end of the pay period, each employee's supervisor approves the hours shown by signing the time card. When overtime hours are involved, approval by a supervisor is usually mandatory. This guards against unauthorized overtime. The approved time cards are then sent to the payroll department. For salaried employees, a manually prepared weekly or monthly time report kept by a supervisor may be used to record time worked.

Preparing the Payroll

Preparing the Payroll

Two (or more) employees verify payroll amounts; supervisor approves.

The payroll is prepared in the payroll department on the basis of two inputs: (1) human resources department authorizations and (2) approved time cards. Numerous calculations are involved in determining gross wages and payroll deductions. Therefore, a second payroll department employee, working independently, verifies all calculated amounts, and a payroll department supervisor then approves the payroll. The payroll department is also responsible for preparing (but not signing) payroll checks, maintaining payroll records, and preparing payroll tax returns.

Paying the Payroll

Treasurer signs and distributes checks.

Paying the Payroll

The payroll is paid by the treasurer's department. **Payment by check minimizes the risk of loss from theft, and the endorsed check provides proof of payment.** For good internal control, payroll checks should be prenumbered, and all checks should be accounted for. All checks must be signed by the treasurer (or a designated agent). Distribution of the payroll checks to employees should be controlled by the treasurer's department. Many employees have their pay credited electronically to their bank accounts. To control these disbursements, receipts detailing gross pay deductions and net pay are provided to employees.

Occasionally the payroll is paid in currency. In such cases it is customary to have a second person count the cash in each pay envelope. The paymaster should obtain a signed receipt from the employee upon payment.

Determining the Payroll

STUDY OBJECTIVE 2

Compute and record the payroll for a pay period.

Determining the payroll involves computing three amounts: (1) gross earnings, (2) payroll deductions, and (3) net pay.

Gross Earnings

Gross earnings is the total compensation earned by an employee. It consists of wages or salaries, plus any bonuses and commissions.

Total **wages** for an employee are determined by multiplying the hours worked by the hourly rate of pay. In addition to the hourly pay rate, most companies are required by law to pay hourly workers a minimum of $1\frac{1}{2}$ times the regular hourly rate for overtime work in excess of 8 hours per day or 40 hours per week. In addition, many employers pay overtime rates for work done at night, on weekends, and on holidays.

Michael Jordan's time card shows that he worked 44 hours for the weekly pay period ending January 14. The computation of his gross earnings (total wages) is as follows.

Illustration D-3
Computation of total wages

Type of Pay	Hours	×	Rate	=	Gross Earnings
Regular	40	×	$12.00	=	$480.00
Overtime	4	×	18.00	=	72.00
Total wages					**$552.00**

This computation assumes that Jordan receives $1\frac{1}{2}$ times his regular hourly rate ($12.00 × 1.5) for his overtime hours. Union contracts often require that overtime rates be as much as twice the regular rates.

ETHICS NOTE

Bonuses often reward outstanding individual performance; but successful corporations also need considerable teamwork. A challenge is to motivate individuals while preventing an unethical employee from taking another's idea for his or her own advantage.

The **salary** for an employee is generally based on a monthly or yearly rate. These rates are then prorated to the payroll periods used by the company. Most executive and administrative positions are salaried. Federal law does not require overtime pay for employees in such positions.

Many companies have **bonus** agreements for management personnel and other employees. A recent survey found that over 94% of the largest U.S. manufacturing companies offer annual bonuses to their key executives. Bonus arrangements may be based on such factors as increased sales or net income. Bonuses may be paid in cash and/or by granting executives and employees the opportunity to acquire shares of company stock at favorable prices (called stock option plans).

Payroll Deductions

As anyone who has received a paycheck knows, gross earnings are usually very different from the amount actually received. The difference is due to **payroll deductions**. Such deductions do not result in payroll tax expense to the employer. The employer is merely a collection agent, and subsequently transfers the amounts deducted to the government and designated recipients. Payroll deductions may be mandatory or voluntary. Mandatory deductions are required by law and consist of FICA taxes and income taxes. Voluntary deductions are at the option of the employee. Illustration D-4 summarizes the types of payroll deductions.

Illustration D-4
Payroll deductions

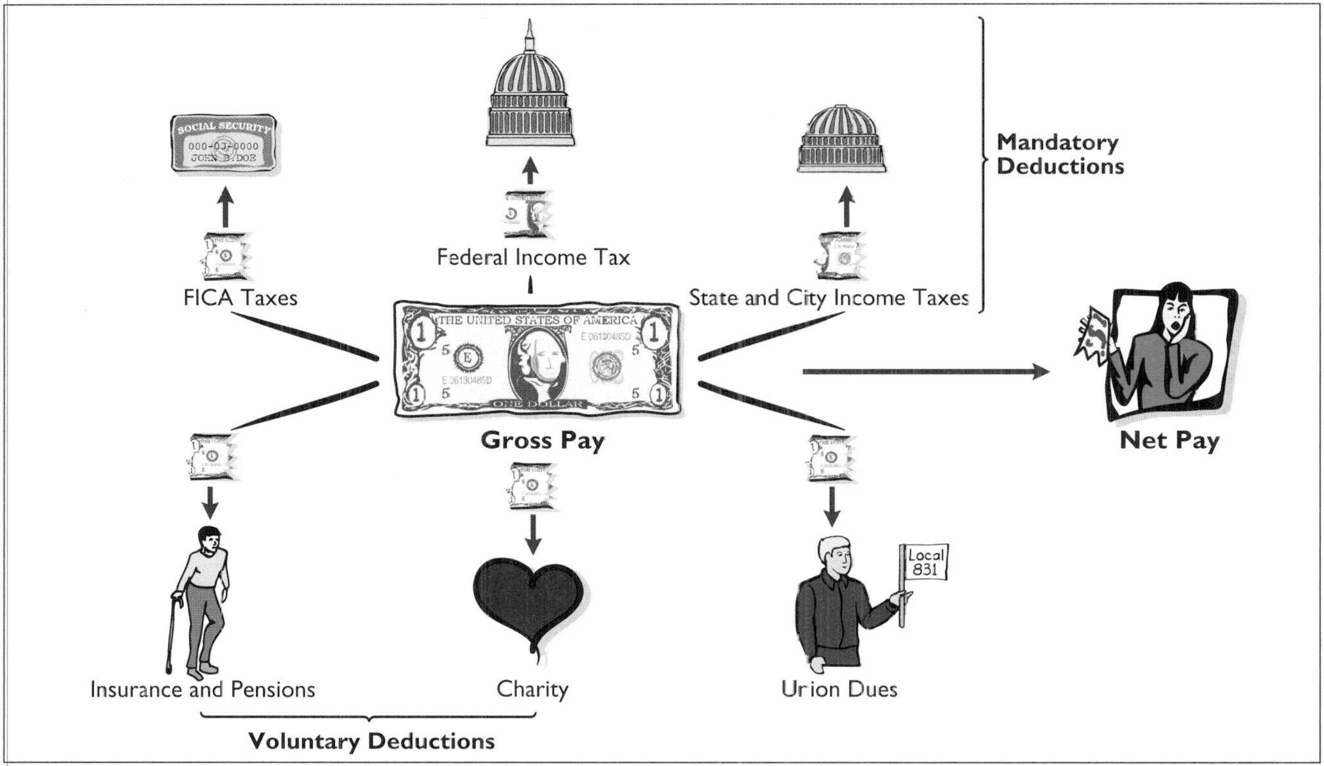

FICA Taxes

In 1937 Congress enacted the Federal Insurance Contribution Act (FICA). **FICA taxes are designed to provide workers with supplemental retirement, employment disability, and medical benefits.** In 1965, benefits were expanded to include Medicare for individuals over 65 years of age. The benefits are financed by a tax levied on employees' earnings. FICA taxes are commonly referred to as **Social Security taxes.**

The tax rate and the tax base for FICA taxes are set by Congress. When FICA taxes were first imposed, the rate was 1% on the first $3,000 of gross earnings, or a maximum of $30 per year. The rate and base have changed dramatically since that time! In 2003, the rate was 7.65% (6.2% Social Security plus 1.45% Medicare) on the first $87,900 of gross earnings for each employee.[1] For purpose of illustration in this chapter, we will assume a rate of 8% on the first $87,900 of gross earnings, or a maximum of $7,032. Using the 8% rate, the FICA withholding for Jordan for the weekly pay period ending January 14 is $44.16 ($552 × 8%).

Income Taxes

Under the U.S. pay-as-you-go system of federal income taxes, employers are required to withhold income taxes from employees each pay period. The amount to be withheld is determined by three variables: (1) the employee's gross earnings; (2) the number of allowances claimed by the employee; and (3) the length of the pay

[1]The Medicare provision also includes a tax of 1.45% on gross earnings in excess of $87,900. In the interest of simplification, we ignore this 1.45% charge in our end-of-chapter assignment material. We assume zero FICA withholdings on gross earnings above $87,900.

period. The number of allowances claimed typically includes the employee, his or her spouse, and other dependents. **To indicate to the Internal Revenue Service the number of allowances claimed, the employee must complete an Employee's Withholding Allowance Certificate (Form W-4).** As shown in Illustration D-5, Michael Jordan claims two allowances on his W-4.

Illustration D-5
W-4 form

Form **W-4** — Department of the Treasury, Internal Revenue Service

Employee's Withholding Allowance Certificate

► For Privacy Act and Paperwork Reduction Act Notice, see page 2.

OMB No. 1545-0010 — **2006**

1 Type or print your first name and middle initial: Michael — Last name: Jordan — 2 Your social security number: 329-36-9547

Home address (number and street or rural route): 2345 Mifflin Ave.

3 ☐ Single ☒ Married ☐ Married, but withhold at higher Single rate.
Note: *If married, but legally separated, or spouse is a nonresident alien, check the Single box.*

City or town, State, and ZIP code: Hampton, MI 48292

4 If your last name differs from that on your social security card, check here and call 1-800-772-1213 for a new card . . . . . ► ☐

5 Total number of allowances you are claiming (from line H above or from the worksheet on page 2 if they apply) . . . 5 | 2
6 Additional amount, if any, you want withheld from each paycheck . . . 6 | $
7 I claim exemption from withholding for 2006, and I certify that I meet BOTH of the following conditions for exemption:
• Last year I had a right to a refund of ALL Federal income tax withheld because I had NO tax liability AND
• This year I expect a refund of ALL Federal income tax withheld because I expect to have NO tax liability.
If you meet both conditions, enter "Exempt" here . . . . . ► 7

Under penalties of perjury, I certify that I am entitled to the number of withholding allowances claimed on this certificate or entitled to claim exempt status.

Employee's signature ► *Michael Jordan* — Date ► September 1, 20 06

8 Employer's name and address (Employer: Complete 8 and 10 only if sending to the IRS) — 9 Office code (optional) — 10 Employer identification number

Cat. No. 102200

Withholding tables furnished by the Internal Revenue Service indicate the amount of income tax to be withheld. Withholding amounts are based on gross wages and the number of allowances claimed. Separate tables are provided for weekly, biweekly, semimonthly, and monthly pay periods. The withholding tax table for Michael Jordan (assuming he earns $552 per week) is shown in Illustration D-6. For a weekly salary of $552 with two allowances, the income tax to be withheld is $49.

Illustration D-6
Withholding tax table

MARRIED Persons — **WEEKLY** Payroll Period
(For Wages Paid in 2006)

If the wages are –		And the number of withholding allowances claimed is –										
At least	But less than	0	1	2	3	4	5	6	7	8	9	10
		The amount of income tax to be withheld is –										
490	**500**	56	48	40	32	24	17	9	1	0	0	0
500	**510**	57	49	42	34	26	18	10	3	0	0	0
510	**520**	59	51	43	35	27	20	12	4	0	0	0
520	**530**	60	52	45	37	29	21	13	6	0	0	0
530	**540**	62	54	46	38	30	23	15	7	0	0	0
540	**550**	63	55	48	40	32	24	16	9	1	0	0
550	**560**	65	57	**49**	41	33	26	18	10	2	0	0
560	**570**	66	58	51	43	35	27	19	12	4	0	0
570	**580**	68	60	52	44	36	29	21	13	5	0	0
580	**590**	69	61	54	46	38	30	22	15	7	0	0
590	**600**	71	63	55	47	39	32	24	16	8	1	0
600	**610**	72	64	57	49	41	33	25	18	10	2	0
610	**620**	74	66	58	50	42	35	27	19	11	4	0
620	**630**	75	67	60	52	44	36	28	21	13	5	0
630	**640**	77	69	61	53	45	38	30	22	14	7	0
640	**650**	78	70	63	55	47	39	31	24	16	8	0
650	**660**	80	72	64	56	48	41	33	25	17	10	2
660	**670**	81	73	66	58	50	42	34	27	19	11	3
670	**680**	83	75	67	59	51	44	36	28	20	13	5
680	**690**	84	76	69	61	53	45	37	30	22	14	6

Most states (and some cities) also require **employers** to withhold income taxes from employees' earnings. As a rule, the amounts withheld are a percentage (specified in the state revenue code) of the amount withheld for the federal income tax. Or they may be a specified percentage of the employee's earnings. For the sake of simplicity, we have assumed that Jordan's wages are subject to state income taxes of 2%, or $11.04 (2% × $552) per week.

There is no limit on the amount of gross earnings subject to income tax withholdings. In fact, the higher the earnings, the higher the amount of taxes withheld.

Other Deductions

Employees may voluntarily authorize withholdings for charitable, retirement, and other purposes. All voluntary deductions from gross earnings should be authorized in writing by the employee. The authorization(s) may be made individually or as part of a group plan. Deductions for charitable organizations, such as the United Fund, or for financial arrangements, such as U.S. savings bonds and repayment of loans from company credit unions, are made individually. Deductions for union dues, health and life insurance, and pension plans are often made on a group basis. We will assume that Jordan has weekly voluntary deductions of $10 for the United Fund and $5 for union dues.

ALTERNATIVE TERMINOLOGY

Net pay is also called *take-home pay.*

Net Pay

Net pay is determined by subtracting payroll deductions from gross earnings. For Michael Jordan, net pay for the pay period is $432.80, computed as follows.

Illustration D-7
Computation of net pay

Gross earnings		$552.00
Payroll deductions:		
FICA taxes	$44.16	
Federal income taxes	49.00	
State income taxes	11.04	
United Fund	10.00	
Union dues	5.00	119.20
Net pay		**$432.80**

Assuming that Michael Jordan's wages for each week during the year are $552, total wages for the year are $28,704 (52 × $552). Thus, all of Jordan's wages are subject to FICA tax during the year. Let's assume that Jordan's department head earns $1,800 per week, or $93,600 for the year. Since only the first $87,900 is subject to FICA taxes, the maximum FICA withholdings on the department head's earnings would be $7,032 ($87,900 × 8%).

Recording the Payroll

Recording the payroll involves maintaining payroll department records, recognizing payroll expenses and liabilities, and recording payment of the payroll.

Maintaining Payroll Department Records

To comply with state and federal laws, an employer must keep a cumulative record of each employee's gross earnings, deductions, and net pay during the year. The record that provides this information is the **employee earnings record**. Michael Jordan's employee earnings record is shown in Illustration D-8 below.

Illustration D-8
Employee earnings record

ACADEMY COMPANY
Employee Earnings Record
For the Year 2006

Name Michael Jordan **Address** 2345 Mifflin Ave.
Hampton, Michigan 48292
Social Security Number 329-36-9547
Date of Birth December 24, 1962 **Telephone** 555-238-9051
Date Employed September 1, 2004 **Date Employment Ended** ______
Sex Male **Exemptions** 2
Single ______ **Married** x

2006 Period Ending	Total Hours	Gross Earnings				Deductions						Payment	
		Regular	Overtime	Total	Cumulative	FICA	Fed. Inc. Tax	State Inc. Tax	United Fund	Union Dues	Total	Net Amount	Check No.
1/7	42	480.00	36.00	516.00	516.00	41.28	43.00	10.32	10.00	5.00	109.60	406.40	974
1/14	**44**	**480.00**	**72.00**	**552.00**	**1,068.00**	**44.16**	**49.00**	**11.04**	**10.00**	**5.00**	**119.20**	**432.80**	**1028**
1/21	43	480.00	54.00	534.00	1,602.00	42.72	46.00	10.68	10.00	5.00	114.40	419.60	1077
1/28	42	480.00	36.00	516.00	2,118.00	41.28	43.00	10.32	10.00	5.00	109.60	406.40	1133
Jan. Total		1,920.00	198.00	2,118.00		169.44	181.00	42.36	40.00	20.00	452.80	1,665.20	

A separate earnings record is kept for each employee. It is updated after each pay period. The cumulative payroll data on the earnings record are used by the employer to: (1) determine when an employee has earned the maximum earnings subject to FICA taxes, (2) file state and federal payroll tax returns (as explained later in the appendix), and (3) provide each employee with a statement of gross earnings and tax withholdings for the year. Illustration D-12 on page D13 shows this statement.

In addition to employee earnings records, many companies find it useful to prepare a **payroll register**. This record accumulates the gross earnings, deductions, and net pay by employee for each pay period. It provides the documentation for preparing a paycheck for each employee. Academy Company's payroll register is presented in Illustration D-9 on page D9. It shows the data for Michael Jordan in the wages section. In this example, Academy Company's total weekly payroll is $17,210, as shown in the gross earnings column.

Note that this record is a listing of each employee's payroll data for the pay period. In some companies, a payroll register is a journal or book of original entry. Postings are made from it directly to ledger accounts. In other companies, the payroll register is a memorandum record that provides the data for a general journal entry and subsequent posting to the ledger accounts. At Academy Company, the latter procedure is followed.

Illustration D-9
Payroll register

ACADEMY COMPANY
Payroll Register
For the Week Ending January 14, 2006

		Earnings			Deductions						Paid		Accounts Debited	
Employee	**Total Hours**	**Regular**	**Over-time**	**Gross**	**FICA**	**Federal Income Tax**	**State Income Tax**	**United Fund**	**Union Dues**	**Total**	**Net Pay**	**Check No.**	**Office Salaries Expense**	**Wages Expense**
Office Salaries														
Arnold, Patricia	40	580.00		580.00	46.40	61.00	11.60	15.00		134.00	446.00	998	580.00	
Canton, Matthew	40	590.00		590.00	47.20	63.00	11.80	20.00		142.00	448.00	999	590.00	
Mueller, William	40	530.00		530.00	42.40	54.00	10.60	11.00		118.00	412.0	1000	530.00	
Subtotal		5,200.00		5,200.00	416.00	1,090.00	104.00	120.00		1,730.00	3,470.00		5,200.00	
Wages														
Bennett, Robin	42	480.00	36.00	516.00	41.28	43.00	10.32	18.00	5.00	117.60	398.40	1025		516.00
Jordan, Michael	**44**	**480.00**	**72.00**	**552.00**	**44.16**	**49.00**	**11.04**	**10.00**	**5.00**	**119.20**	**432.80**	**1028**		**552.00**
Milroy, Lee	43	480.00	54.00	534.00	42.72	46.00	10.68	10.00	5.00	114.40	419.60	1029		534.00
Subtotal		11,000.00	1,010.00	12,010.00	960.80	2,400.00	240.20	301.50	115.00	4,017.50	7,992.50			12,010.00
Total		16,200.00	1,010.00	17,210.00	1,376.80	3,490.00	344.20	421.50	115.00	5,747.50	11,462.50		5,200.00	12,010.00

Recognizing Payroll Expenses and Liabilities

From the payroll register in Illustration D-9, a journal entry is made to record the payroll. For the week ending January 14 the entry is:

Jan. 14	Office Salaries Expense	5,200.00	
	Wages Expense	12,010.00	
	FICA Taxes Payable		1,376.80
	Federal Income Taxes Payable		3,490.00
	State Income Taxes Payable		344.20
	United Fund Payable		421.50
	Union Dues Payable		115.00
	Salaries and Wages Payable		11,462.50
	(To record payroll for the week ending January 14)		

A	=	L	+	SE
		+1,376.80		−5,200.00 Exp
		+3,490.00		−12,010.00 Exp
		+344.20		
		+421.50		
		+115.00		
		+11,462.50		

Cash Flows
no effect

Specific liability accounts are credited for the mandatory and voluntary deductions made during the pay period. In the example, debits to Office Salaries and Wages Expense are used for gross earnings because office workers are on a salary and other employees are paid on an hourly rate. In other companies, there may be debits to other accounts such as Store Salaries or Sales Salaries. The amount credited to Salaries and Wages Payable is the sum of the individual checks the employees will receive.

Recording Payment of the Payroll

Payment by check is made either from the employer's regular bank account or a payroll bank account. Each paycheck is usually accompanied by a detachable **statement of earnings** document. This shows the employee's gross earnings, payroll deductions, and net pay for the period and for the year-to-date. The Academy Company uses its regular bank account for payroll checks. The paycheck and statement of earnings for Michael Jordan are shown in Illustration D-10 (on page D10).

Illustration D-10
Paycheck and statement of earnings

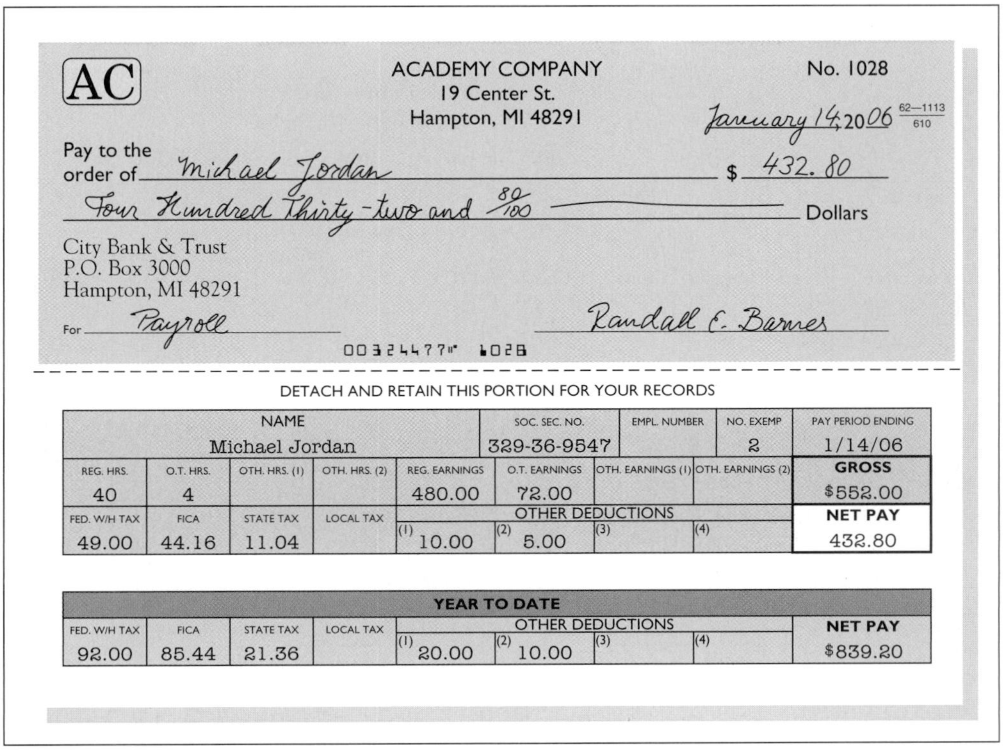
AC

ACADEMY COMPANY
19 Center St.
Hampton, MI 48291

No. 1028

January 14, 2006 62—1113/610

Pay to the order of Michael Jordan $ 432.80

Four Hundred Thirty-two and 80/100 Dollars

City Bank & Trust
P.O. Box 3000
Hampton, MI 48291

For Payroll

Randall E. Barnes

003244771⑈ 1028

DETACH AND RETAIN THIS PORTION FOR YOUR RECORDS

NAME				SOC. SEC. NO.	EMPL. NUMBER	NO. EXEMP	PAY PERIOD ENDING
Michael Jordan				329-36-9547		2	1/14/06

REG. HRS.	O.T. HRS.	OTH. HRS. (1)	OTH. HRS. (2)	REG. EARNINGS	O.T. EARNINGS	OTH. EARNINGS (1)	OTH. EARNINGS (2)	GROSS
40	4			480.00	72.00			$552.00

FED. W/H TAX	FICA	STATE TAX	LOCAL TAX	OTHER DEDUCTIONS (1)	(2)	(3)	(4)	NET PAY
49.00	44.16	11.04		10.00	5.00			432.80

YEAR TO DATE

FED. W/H TAX	FICA	STATE TAX	LOCAL TAX	OTHER DEDUCTIONS (1)	(2)	(3)	(4)	NET PAY
92.00	85.44	21.36		20.00	10.00			$839.20

HELPFUL HINT

Do any of the income tax liabilities result in payroll tax expense for the employer?

Answer: No. The employer is acting only as a collection agent for the government.

Following payment of the payroll, the check numbers are entered in the payroll register. The entry to record payment of the payroll for Academy Company is as follows.

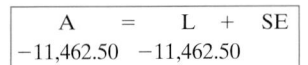

A	=	L	+	SE
−11,462.50		−11,462.50		

Cash Flows
−11,462.50

Jan. 14	Salaries and Wages Payable	11,462.50	
	Cash		11,462.50
	(To record payment of payroll)		

When currency is used in payment, one check is prepared for the payroll's total amount of net pay. This check is then cashed, and the coins and currency are inserted in individual pay envelopes for disbursement to individual employees.

BEFORE YOU GO ON...

Review It

1. Identify two internal control procedures that apply to each payroll function.
2. What are the primary sources of gross earnings?
3. What payroll deductions are (a) mandatory and (b) voluntary?
4. What account titles are used in recording a payroll, assuming only mandatory payroll deductions are involved?

Do It

Your cousin Stan is establishing a house-cleaning business and will have a number of employees working for him. He is aware that documentation procedures are an important part of internal control. But he is confused about the difference between an employee earnings record and a payroll register. He asks you to explain the principal differences, because he wants to be sure that he sets up the proper payroll procedures.

ACTION PLAN

- Determine the earnings and deductions data that must be recorded and reported for each employee.
- Design a record that will accumulate earnings and deductions data and will serve as a basis for journal entries to be prepared and posted to the general ledger accounts.
- Explain the difference between the employee earnings record and the payroll register.

SOLUTION An employee earnings record is kept for *each* employee. It shows gross earnings, payroll deductions, and net pay for each pay period. It provides cumulative payroll data for that employee. In contrast, a payroll register is a listing of *all* employees' gross earnings, payroll deductions, and net pay for each pay period. It is the documentation for preparing paychecks and for recording the payroll. Of course, Stan will need to keep both documents.

Related exercise material: *BED-1, BED-3, and ED-3.*

Employer Payroll Taxes

STUDY OBJECTIVE 3

Describe and record employer payroll taxes.

Payroll tax expense for businesses results from three taxes **levied on employers** by governmental agencies. These taxes are: (1) FICA, (2) federal unemployment tax, and (3) state unemployment tax. These taxes plus such items as paid vacations and pensions (discussed in Appendix F) are collectively referred to as **fringe benefits**. As indicated earlier, the cost of fringe benefits in many companies is substantial.

FICA Taxes

We have seen that each employee must pay FICA taxes. An employer must match each employee's FICA contribution. The matching contribution results in **payroll tax expense** to the employer. The employer's tax is subject to the same rate and maximum earnings applicable to the employee. The account, FICA Taxes Payable, is used for both the employee's and the employer's FICA contributions. For the January 14 payroll, Academy Company's FICA tax contribution is $1,376.80 ($17,210.00 × 8%).

Federal Unemployment Taxes

HELPFUL HINT

FICA taxes are paid by both the employer and employee. Federal unemployment taxes and (in most states) the state unemployment taxes are borne entirely by the employer.

The Federal Unemployment Tax Act (FUTA) is another feature of the federal Social Security program. **Federal unemployment taxes** provide benefits for a limited period of time to employees who lose their jobs through no fault of their own. Under provisions of the Act, the employer is required to pay a tax of 6.2% on the first $7,000 of gross wages paid to each employee during a calendar year. The law allows the employer a maximum credit of 5.4% on the federal rate for contributions to state unemployment taxes. Because of this provision, state unemployment tax laws generally provide for a 5.4% rate. The effective federal unemployment tax rate thus becomes 0.8% (6.2% − 5.4%). This tax is borne **entirely by the employer**. There is no deduction or withholding from employees.

The account Federal Unemployment Taxes Payable is used to recognize this liability. The federal unemployment tax for Academy Company for the January 14 payroll is $137.68 ($17,210.00 × 0.8%).

State Unemployment Taxes

All states have unemployment compensation programs under state unemployment tax acts (SUTA). Like federal unemployment taxes, **state unemployment taxes** provide benefits to employees who lose their jobs. These taxes are levied on employers.[2] The basic rate is usually 5.4% on the first $9,800 (in Illinois) of wages paid to an employee during the year. The basic rate is adjusted according to the employer's experience rating: Companies with a history of unstable employment may pay more than the basic rate. Companies with a history of stable employment may pay less than 5.4%. Regardless of the rate paid, the credit on the federal unemployment tax is still 5.4%.

The account State Unemployment Taxes Payable is used for this liability. The state unemployment tax for Academy Company for the January 14 payroll is $929.34 ($17,210.00 × 5.4%).

Illustration D-11 summarizes the types of employer payroll taxes.

Illustration D-11
Employer payroll taxes

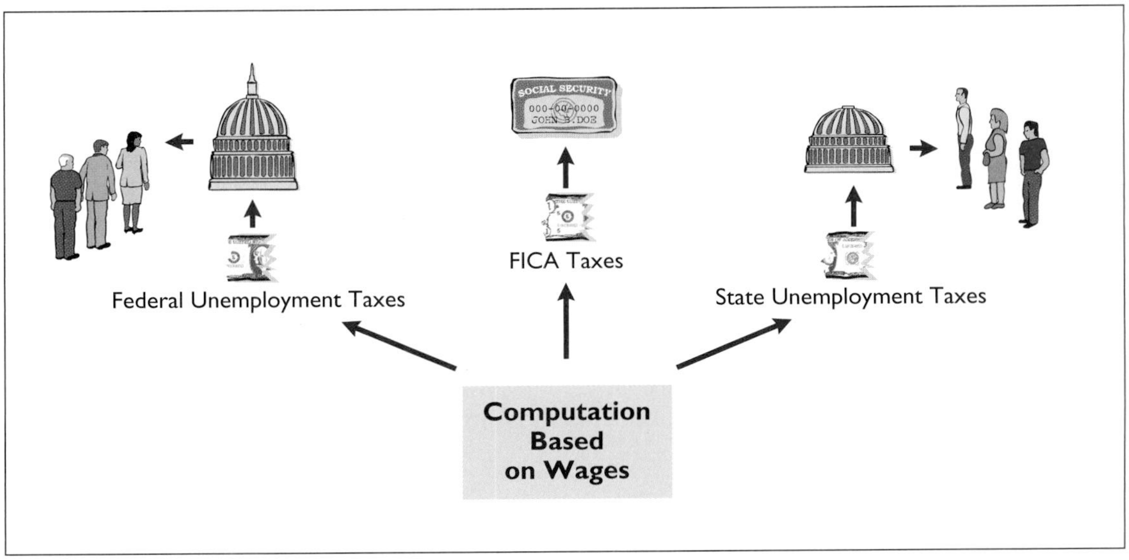

Recording Employer Payroll Taxes

Employer payroll taxes are usually recorded at the same time the payroll is journalized. The entire amount of gross pay ($17,210.00) shown in the payroll register in Illustration D-9 is subject to each of the three taxes mentioned above. Accordingly, the entry to record the payroll tax expense associated with the January 14 payroll is:

A	= L	+ SE
	+1,376.80	−2,443.82 Exp
	+137.68	
	+929.34	

Cash Flows
no effect

Jan. 14	Payroll Tax Expense	2,443.82	
	FICA Taxes Payable		1,376.80
	Federal Unemployment Taxes Payable		137.68
	State Unemployment Taxes Payable		929.34
	(To record employer's payroll taxes on January 14 payroll)		

Separate liability accounts are used instead of a single credit to Payroll Taxes Payable. Why? Because these liabilities are payable to different taxing authorities at different dates. The liability accounts are classified in the balance sheet as current

[2] In a few states, the employee is also required to make a contribution. In this textbook, including the homework, we will assume that the tax is only on the employer.

liabilities since they will be paid within the next year. Payroll Tax Expense is classified on the income statement as an operating expense.

Filing and Remitting Payroll Taxes

Preparation of payroll tax returns is the responsibility of the payroll department. Payment of the taxes is made by the treasurer's department. Much of the information for the returns is obtained from employee earnings records.

For purposes of reporting and remitting to the IRS, FICA taxes and federal income taxes that were withheld are combined. **The taxes must be reported quarterly**, no later than one month following the close of each quarter. The remitting requirements depend on the amount of taxes withheld and the length of the pay period. Remittances are made through deposits in either a Federal Reserve bank or an authorized commercial bank.

Federal unemployment taxes are generally filed and remitted **annually** on or before January 31 of the subsequent year. Earlier payments are required when the tax exceeds a specified amount. State unemployment taxes usually must be filed and paid by the **end of the month following each quarter**. When payroll taxes are paid, payroll liability accounts are debited, and cash is credited.

The employer is also required to provide each employee with a **Wage and Tax Statement (Form W-2)** by January 31 following the end of a calendar year. This statement shows gross earnings, FICA taxes withheld, and income taxes withheld for the year. The required W-2 form for Michael Jordan, using assumed annual data, is shown in Illustration D-12.

Illustration D-12
W-2 form

Form **W-2 Wage and Tax Statement** — Calendar Year **2006**

1 Control number		OMB No. 1545-0008	
2 Employer's name, address and ZIP code: Academy Company, 19 Center St., Hampton, MI 48291		3 Employer's identification number: 36-2167852	4 Employer's State number
		5 Stat. employee ☐ Deceased ☐ Legal rep. ☐ 942 emp. ☐ Subtotal ☐ Void ☐	
		6 Allocated tips	7 Advance EIC payment
8 Employee's social security number: 329-36-9547	9 Federal income tax withheld: $2,248.00	10 Wages, tips, other compensation: $26,300.00	11 Social security tax withheld: $2,104.00
12 Employee's name, address, and ZIP code: Michael Jordan, 2345 Mifflin Ave., Hampton, MI 48292		13 Social security wages: $26,300.00	14 Social security tips
		16	

17 State income tax: $526.00	18 State wages, tips, etc.	19 Name of State: Michigan
20 Local income tax	21 Local wages, tips, etc.	22 Name of locality

The employer must send a copy of each employee's Wage and Tax Statement (Form W-2) to the Social Security Administration. This agency subsequently furnishes the Internal Revenue Service with the income data required.

BEFORE YOU GO ON...

Review It

1. What payroll taxes are levied on employers?
2. What accounts are involved in accruing employer payroll taxes?

Do It

In January, the payroll supervisor determines that gross earnings in Halo Company are $70,000. All earnings are subject to 8% FICA taxes, 5.4% state unemployment taxes, and 0.8% federal unemployment taxes. You are asked to record the employer's payroll taxes.

ACTION PLAN

- Compute the employer's payroll taxes on the period's gross earnings.
- Identify the expense account(s) to be debited.
- Identify the liability account(s) to be credited.

SOLUTION The entry to record the employer's payroll taxes is:

Payroll Tax Expense	9,940	
FICA Taxes Payable ($70,000 × 8%)		5,600
Federal Unemployment Taxes Payable ($70,000 × 0.8%)		560
State Unemployment Taxes Payable ($70,000 × 5.4%)		3,780
(To record employer's payroll taxes on January payroll)		

Related exercise material: *BED-2, BED-3, BED-4, ED-1, ED-2, ED-3, ED-4, and ED-5.*

DEMONSTRATION PROBLEM

Indiana Jones Company had the following selected transactions.

Feb. 1 Signs a $50,000, 6-month, 9%-interest-bearing note payable to CitiBank and receives $50,000 in cash.

10 Cash register sales total $43,200, which includes an 8% sales tax.

28 The payroll for the month consists of Sales Salaries $32,000 and Office Salaries $18,000. All wages are subject to 8% FICA taxes. A total of $8,900 federal income taxes are withheld. The salaries are paid on March 1.

28 The following adjustment data are developed.
1. Interest expense of $375 has been incurred on the note.
2. Employer payroll taxes include 8% FICA taxes, a 5.4% state unemployment tax, and a 0.8% federal unemployment tax.

Instructions

(a) Journalize the February transactions.
(b) Journalize the adjusting entries at February 28.

SOLUTION TO DEMONSTRATION PROBLEM

(a) Feb. 1	Cash	50,000	
	Notes Payable		50,000
	(Issued 6-month, 9%-interest-bearing note to CitiBank)		
10	Cash	43,200	
	Sales ($43,200 ÷ 1.08)		40,000
	Sales Taxes Payable ($40,000 × 8%)		3,200
	(To record sales and sales taxes payable)		
28	Sales Salaries Expense	32,000	
	Office Salaries Expense	18,000	
	FICA Taxes Payable (8% × $50,000)		4,000
	Federal Income Taxes Payable		8,900
	Salaries Payable		37,100
	(To record February salaries)		
(b) Feb. 28	Interest Expense	375	
	Interest Payable		375
	(To record accrued interest for February)		
28	Payroll Tax Expense	7,100	
	FICA Taxes Payable		4,000
	Federal Unemployment Taxes Payable (0.8% × $50,000)		400
	State Unemployment Taxes Payable (5.4% × $50,000)		2,700
	(To record employer's payroll taxes on February payroll)		

ACTION PLAN

- To determine sales, divide the cash register total by 100% plus the sales tax percentage.
- Base payroll taxes on gross earnings.

SUMMARY OF STUDY OBJECTIVES

1. **Discuss the objectives of internal control for payroll.** The objectives of internal control for payroll are (1) to safeguard company assets against unauthorized payments of payrolls, and (2) to ensure the accuracy and reliability of the accounting records pertaining to payrolls.
2. **Compute and record the payroll for a pay period.** The computation of the payroll involves gross earnings, payroll deductions, and net pay. In recording the payroll, Salaries (or Wages) Expense is debited for gross earnings, individual tax and other liability accounts are credited for payroll deductions, and Salaries (Wages) Payable is credited for net pay. When the payroll is paid, Salaries and Wages Payable is debited, and Cash is credited.
3. **Describe and record employer payroll taxes.** Employer payroll taxes consist of FICA, federal unemployment taxes, and state unemployment taxes. The taxes are usually accrued at the time the payroll is recorded by debiting Payroll Tax Expense and crediting separate liability accounts for each type of tax.

GLOSSARY

Bonus Compensation to management personnel and other employees, based on factors such as increased sales or the amount of net income. (p. D4)

Employee earnings record A cumulative record of each employee's gross earnings, deductions, and net pay during the year. (p. D8)

Employee's Withholding Allowance Certificate (Form W-4) An Internal Revenue Service form on which the employee indicates the number of allowances claimed for withholding federal income taxes. (p. D6)

Federal unemployment taxes Taxes imposed on the employer that provide benefits for a limited time period to employees who lose their jobs through no fault of their own. (p. D11)

FICA taxes Taxes designed to provide workers with supplemental retirement, employment disability, and medical benefits. (p. D5)

Gross earnings Total compensation earned by an employee. (p. D4)

Net pay Gross earnings less payroll deductions. (p. D7)

Payroll deductions Deductions from gross earnings to determine the amount of a paycheck. (p. D4)

Payroll register A payroll record that accumulates the gross earnings, deductions, and net pay by employee for each pay period. (p. D8)

Salaries Specified amount per month or per year paid to managerial, administrative, and sales personnel. (p. D1)

Statement of earnings A document attached to a paycheck that indicates the employee's gross earnings, payroll deductions, and net pay. (p. D9)

State unemployment taxes Taxes imposed on the employer that provide benefits to employees who lose their jobs. (p. D12)

Wage and Tax Statement (Form W-2) A form showing gross earnings, FICA taxes withheld, and income taxes withheld which is prepared annually by an employer for each employee. (p. D13)

Wages Amounts paid to employees based on a rate per hour or on a piece-work basis. (p. D1)

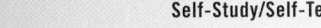

SELF-STUDY QUESTIONS

Self-Study/Self-Test

Answers are at the end of the appendix.

(SO 1) **1.** The department that should pay the payroll is the:
- **a.** timekeeping department.
- **b.** human resources department.
- **c.** payroll department.
- **d.** treasurer's department.

(SO 2) **2.** J. Barr earns $14 per hour for a 40-hour week and $21 per hour for any overtime work. If Barr works 45 hours in a week, gross earnings are:
- **a.** $560.
- **b.** $630.
- **c.** $650.
- **d.** $665.

3. Employer payroll taxes do not include: (SO 3)
- **a.** federal unemployment taxes.
- **b.** state unemployment taxes.
- **c.** federal income taxes.
- **d.** FICA taxes.

QUESTIONS

1. You are a newly hired accountant with Schindlebeck Company. On your first day, the controller asks you to identify the main internal control objectives related to payroll accounting. How would you respond?
2. What are the four functions associated with payroll activities?
3. What is the difference between gross pay and net pay? Which amount should a company record as wages or salaries expense?
4. Which payroll tax is levied on both employers and employees?
5. Are the federal and state income taxes withheld from employee paychecks a payroll tax expense for the employer? Explain your answer.
6. What do the following acronyms stand for: FICA, FUTA, and SUTA?
7. What information is shown on a W-4 statement? On a W-2 statement?
8. Distinguish between the two types of payroll deductions and give examples of each.
9. What are the primary uses of the employee earnings record?
10. (a) Identify the three types of employer payroll taxes. (b) How are tax liability accounts and Payroll Tax Expense classified in the financial statements?

BRIEF EXERCISES

Identify payroll functions. (SO 1)

BED-1 Hernandez Company has the following payroll procedures.

(a) Supervisor approves overtime work.
(b) The human resources department prepares hiring authorization forms for new hires.
(c) A second payroll department employee verifies payroll calculations.
(d) The treasurer's department pays employees.

Identify the payroll function to which each procedure pertains.

Compute gross earnings and net pay. (SO 2)

BED-2 Sandy Teter's regular hourly wage rate is $16, and she receives an hourly rate of $24 for work in excess of 40 hours. During a January pay period, Sandy works 45 hours. Sandy's federal income tax withholding is $95, and she has no voluntary deductions. Compute Sandy Teter's gross earnings and net pay for the pay period.

Record a payroll and the payment of wages. (SO 2)

BED-3 Data for Sandy Teter are presented in BED-2. Prepare the journal entries to record **(a)** Sandy's pay for the period and **(b)** the payment of Sandy's wages. Use January 15 for the end of the pay period and the payment date.

Record employer payroll taxes. (SO 3)

BED-4 In January, gross earnings in Yoon Company totaled $90,000. All earnings are subject to 8% FICA taxes, 5.4% state unemployment taxes, and 0.8% federal unemployment taxes. Prepare the entry to record January payroll tax expense.

EXERCISES

Compute net pay and record pay for one employee. (SO 2)

ED-1 Betty Williams' regular hourly wage rate is $14.00, and she receives a wage of 1½ times the regular hourly rate for work in excess of 40 hours. During a March weekly pay period Betty worked 42 hours. Her gross earnings prior to the current week were $6,000. Betty is married and claims three withholding allowances. Her only voluntary deduction is for group hospitalization insurance at $15.00 per week.

Instructions

(a) Compute the following amounts for Betty's wages for the current week.
   (1) Gross earnings.
   (2) FICA taxes. (Assume an 8% rate on maximum of $87,900.)
   (3) Federal income taxes withheld. (Use the withholding table in the text, page D6.)
   (4) State income taxes withheld. (Assume a 2.0% rate.)
   (5) Net pay.
(b) Record Betty's pay, assuming she is an office computer operator.

Compute maximum FICA deductions. (SO 2)

ED-2 Employee earnings records for Brantley Company reveal the following gross earnings for four employees through the pay period of December 15.

C. Mays	$83,500	D. Delgado	$86,100
L. Jeter	$85,600	T. Rolen	$87,000

For the pay period ending December 31, each employee's gross earnings is $3,000. The FICA tax rate is 8% on gross earnings of $87,900.

Instructions

Compute the FICA withholdings that should be made for each employee for the December 31 pay period. (Show computations.)

Prepare payroll register and record payroll and payroll tax expense. (SO 2, 3)

ED-3 Canseco Company has the following data for the weekly payroll ending January 31.

	Hours							Federal	
							Hourly	Income Tax	Health
Employee	**M**	**T**	**W**	**T**	**F**	**S**	**Rate**	**Withholding**	**Insurance**
M. Hindi	8	8	9	8	10	3	$11	$34	$10
E. Benson	8	8	8	8	8	2	13	37	15
K. Estes	9	10	8	8	9	0	14	58	15

Employees are paid 1½ times the regular hourly rate for all hours worked in excess of 40 hours per week. FICA taxes are 8% on the first $87,900 of gross earnings. Canseco Company is subject to 5.4% state unemployment taxes on the first $9,800 and 0.8% federal unemployment taxes on the first $7,000 of gross earnings.

Instructions

(a) Prepare the payroll register for the weekly payroll.
(b) Prepare the journal entries to record the payroll and Canseco's payroll tax expense.

Compute missing payroll amounts and record payroll.
(SO 2)

ED-4 Selected data from a February payroll register for Landmark Company are presented below. Some amounts are intentionally omitted.

Gross earnings:		State income taxes	$(3)
Regular	$8,900	Union dues	100
Overtime	(1)	Total deductions	(4)
Total	(2)	Net pay	$7,215
Deductions:		Accounts debited:	
FICA taxes	$ 760	Warehouse wages	(5)
Federal income taxes	1,140	Store wages	$4,000

FICA taxes are 8%. State income taxes are 3% of gross earnings.

Instructions

(a) Fill in the missing amounts.
(b) Journalize the February payroll and the payment of the payroll.

Determine employer's payroll taxes; record payroll tax expense.
(SO 3)

ED-5 According to a payroll register summary of Cruz Company, the amount of employees' gross pay in December was $850,000, of which $70,000 was not subject to FICA tax and $760,000 was not subject to state and federal unemployment taxes.

Instructions

(a) Determine the employer's payroll tax expense for the month, using the following rates: FICA 8%, state unemployment 5.4%, federal unemployment 0.8%.
(b) Prepare the journal entry to record December payroll tax expense.

PROBLEMS: SET A

Identify internal control weaknesses and make recommendations for improvement.
(SO 1)

PD-1A The payroll procedures used by three different companies are described below.

1. In Brewer Company each employee is required to mark on a clock card the hours worked. At the end of each pay period, the employee must have this clock card approved by the department manager. The approved card is then given to the payroll department by the employee. Subsequently, the treasurer's department pays the employee by check.
2. In Hilyard Computer Company clock cards and time clocks are used. At the end of each pay period, the department manager initials the cards, indicates the rates of pay, and sends them to payroll. A payroll register is prepared from the cards by the payroll department. Cash equal to the total net pay in each department is given to the department manager, who pays the employees in cash.
3. In Hyun-chan Company employees are required to record hours worked by "punching" clock cards in a time clock. At the end of each pay period, the clock cards are collected by the department manager. The manager prepares a payroll register in duplicate and forwards the original to payroll. In payroll, the summaries are checked for mathematical accuracy, and a payroll supervisor pays each employee by check.

Instructions

(a) Indicate the weakness(es) in internal control in each company.
(b) For each weakness, describe the control procedure(s) that will provide effective internal control. Use the following format for your answer:

(a) Weaknesses	(b) Recommended Procedures

PD-2A Graves Drug Store has four employees who are paid on an hourly basis plus time-and-a-half for all hours worked in excess of 40 a week. Payroll data for the week ended February 15, 2006, are presented below.

Prepare payroll register and payroll entries.

(SO 2, 3)

Employees	Hours Worked	Hourly Rate	Federal Income Tax Withholdings	United Fund
L. Leiss	39	$14.00	$?	$-0-
S. Bjork	42	$12.00	?	5.00
M. Cape	44	$12.00	61	7.50
L. Wild	48	$12.00	52	5.00

Leiss and Bjork are married. They claim 2 and 4 withholding allowances, respectively. The following tax rates are applicable: FICA 8%, state income taxes 3%, state unemployment taxes 5.4%, and federal unemployment 0.8%. The first three employees are sales clerks (store wages expense). The fourth employee performs administrative duties (office wages expense).

Instructions

(a) Prepare a payroll register for the weekly payroll. (Use the wage-bracket withholding table in the text for federal income tax withholdings.)

(b) Journalize the payroll on February 15, 2006, and the accrual of employer payroll taxes.

(c) Journalize the payment of the payroll on February 16, 2006.

(d) Journalize the deposit in a Federal Reserve bank on February 28, 2006, of the FICA and federal income taxes payable to the government.

(a) Net pay $1,786.32; Store wages expense $1,614.00
(b) Payroll tax expense $317.79

PD-3A The following payroll liability accounts are included in the ledger of Eikleberry Company on January 1, 2006.

Journalize payroll transactions and adjusting entries.

(SO 2, 3)

FICA Taxes Payable	$ 662.20
Federal Income Taxes Payable	1,254.60
State Income Taxes Payable	102.15
Federal Unemployment Taxes Payable	312.00
State Unemployment Taxes Payable	1,954.40
Union Dues Payable	250.00
U.S. Savings Bonds Payable	350.00

In January, the following transactions occurred.

Jan. 10 Sent check for $250.00 to union treasurer for union dues.
12 Deposited check for $1,916.80 in Federal Reserve bank for FICA taxes and federal income taxes withheld.
15 Purchased U.S. Savings Bonds for employees by writing check for $350.00.
17 Paid state income taxes withheld from employees.
20 Paid federal and state unemployment taxes.
31 Completed monthly payroll register, which shows office salaries $17,600, store wages $27,400, FICA taxes withheld $3,600, federal income taxes payable $1,770, state income taxes payable $360, union dues payable $400, United Fund contributions payable $1,800, and net pay $37,070.
31 Prepared payroll checks for the net pay and distributed checks to employees.

At January 31, the company also makes the following accrual for employer payroll taxes: FICA taxes 8%, state unemployment taxes 5.4%, and federal unemployment taxes 0.8%.

Instructions

(a) Journalize the January transactions.

(b) Journalize the adjustments pertaining to employee compensation at January 31.

(b) Payroll tax expense $6,390.00

Prepare entries for payroll and payroll taxes; prepare W-2 data.

(SO 2, 3)

PD-4A For the year ended December 31, 2006, R. Visnak Company reports the following summary payroll data.

Gross earnings:	
Administrative salaries	$180,000
Electricians' wages	320,000
Total	$500,000
Deductions:	
FICA taxes	$ 35,200
Federal income taxes withheld	153,000
State income taxes withheld (2.6%)	13,000
United Fund contributions payable	25,000
*Hospital insurance premiums	15,800
Total	$242,000

R. Visnak Company's payroll taxes are: FICA 8%, state unemployment 2.5% (due to a stable employment record), and 0.8% federal unemployment. Gross earnings subject to FICA taxes total $440,000, and unemployment taxes total $110,000.

(a) Wages Payable $258,000
(b) Payroll tax expense $38,830

Instructions

(a) Prepare a summary journal entry at December 31 for the full year's payroll.
(b) Journalize the adjusting entry at December 31 to record the employer's payroll taxes.
(c) The W-2 Wage and Tax Statement requires the following dollar data.

Wages, Tips, Other Compensation	Federal Income Tax Withheld	State Income Tax Withheld	FICA Wages	FICA Tax Withheld

Complete the required data for the following employees.

Employee	Gross Earnings	Federal Income Tax Withheld
R. Lopez	$60,000	$27,500
K. Kirk	27,000	11,000

PROBLEMS: SET B

Identify internal control weaknesses and make recommendations for improvement.

(SO 1)

PD-1B Selected payroll procedures of Wallace Company are described below.

1. Department managers interview applicants and on the basis of the interview either hire or reject the applicants. When an applicant is hired, the applicant fills out a W-4 form (Employee's Withholding Allowance Certificate). One copy of the form is sent to the human resources department, and one copy is sent to the payroll department as notice that the individual has been hired. On the copy of the W-4 sent to payroll, the managers manually indicate the hourly pay rate for the new hire.
2. The payroll checks are manually signed by the chief accountant and given to the department managers for distribution to employees in their department. The managers are responsible for seeing that any absent employees receive their checks.
3. There are two clerks in the payroll department. The payroll is divided alphabetically; one clerk has employees A to L and the other has employees M to Z. Each clerk computes the gross earnings, deductions, and net pay for employees in the section and posts the data to the employee earnings records.

Instructions

(a) Indicate the weaknesses in internal control.
(b) For each weakness, describe the control procedures that will provide effective internal control. Use the following format for your answer:

(a) Weaknesses	(b) Recommended Procedures

PD-2B Lee Hardware has four employees who are paid on an hourly basis plus time-and-a half for all hours worked in excess of 40 a week. Payroll data for the week ended March 15, 2006, are presented below.

Prepare payroll register and payroll entries.

(SO 2, 3)

Employee	Hours Worked	Hourly Rate	Federal Income Tax Withholdings	United Fund
Joe Coomer	40	$15.00	$?	$5.00
Mary Walker	42	13.00	?	5.00
Andy Dye	44	13.00	60	8.00
Kim Shen	48	13.00	67	5.00

Coomer and Walker are married. They claim 0 and 4 withholding allowances, respectively. The following tax rates are applicable: FICA 8%, state income taxes 3%, state unemployment taxes 5.4%, and federal unemployment 0.8%. The first three employees are sales clerks (store wages expense). The fourth employee performs administrative duties (office wages expense).

Instructions

(a) Prepare a payroll register for the weekly payroll. (Use the wage-bracket withholding table in the text for federal income tax withholdings.)

(b) Journalize the payroll on March 15, 2006, and the accrual of employer payroll taxes.

(c) Journalize the payment of the payroll on March 16, 2006.

(d) Journalize the deposit in a Federal Reserve bank on March 31, 2006, of the FICA and federal income taxes payable to the government.

(a) Net pay $1,910.37; Store wages expense $1,757

(b) Payroll tax expense $345.48

PD-3B The following payroll liability accounts are included in the ledger of Nordlund Company on January 1, 2006.

Journalize payroll transactions and adjusting entries.

(SO 2, 3)

FICA Taxes Payable	$760.00
Federal Income Taxes Payable	1,204.60
State Income Taxes Payable	108.95
Federal Unemployment Taxes Payable	288.95
State Unemployment Taxes Payable	1,954.40
Union Dues Payable	870.00
U.S. Savings Bonds Payable	360.00

In January, the following transactions occurred.

Jan. 10 Sent check for $870.00 to union treasurer for union dues.

12 Deposited check for $1,964.60 in Federal Reserve bank for FICA taxes and federal income taxes withheld.

15 Purchased U.S. Savings Bonds for employees by writing check for $360.00.

17 Paid state income taxes withheld from employees.

20 Paid federal and state unemployment taxes.

31 Completed monthly payroll register, which shows office salaries $21,600, store wages $28,400, FICA taxes withheld $4,000, federal income taxes payable $1,958, state income taxes payable $414, union dues payable $400, United Fund contributions payable $1,888, and net pay $41,340.

31 Prepared payroll checks for the net pay and distributed checks to employees.

At January 31, the company also makes the following accrued adjustment for employer payroll taxes: FICA taxes 8%, federal unemployment taxes 0.8%, and state unemployment taxes 5.4%.

Instructions

(a) Journalize the January transactions.

(b) Journalize the adjustments pertaining to employee compensation at January 31.

(b) Payroll tax expense $7,100

Prepare entries for payroll and payroll taxes; prepare W-2 data.

(SO 2, 3)

PD-4B For the year ended December 31, 2006, Niehaus Electrical Repair Company reports the following summary payroll data.

Gross earnings:	
Administrative salaries	$180,000
Electricians' wages	370,000
Total	$550,000
Deductions:	
FICA taxes	$ 38,000
Federal income taxes withheld	168,000
State income taxes withheld (2.6%)	14,300
United Fund contributions payable	27,500
*Hospital insurance premiums	17,200
Total	$265,000

Niehaus Company's payroll taxes are: FICA 8%, state unemployment 2.5% (due to a stable employment record), and 0.8% federal unemployment. Gross earnings subject to FICA taxes total $475,000, and unemployment taxes total $125,000.

Instructions

(a) Wages payable $285,000
(b) Payroll tax expense $42,125

(a) Prepare a summary journal entry at December 31 for the full year's payroll.
(b) Journalize the adjusting entry at December 31 to record the employer's payroll taxes.
(c) The W-2 Wage and Tax Statement requires the following dollar data.

Wages, Tips, Other Compensation	Federal Income Tax Withheld	State Income Tax Withheld	FICA Wages	FICA Tax Withheld

Complete the required data for the following employees.

Employee	Gross Earnings	Federal Income Tax Withheld
Anna Hashmi	$59,000	$28,500
Sharon Bishop	26,000	10,200

BROADENING YOUR PERSPECTIVE

Financial Reporting and Analysis

■ EXPLORING THE WEB

www.wiley.com/college/weygandt

BYPD-1 The Internal Revenue Service provides considerable information over the Internet. The following demonstrates how useful one of its sites is in answering payroll tax questions faced by employers.

Address: www.irs.ustreas.gov/formspubs/index.html, or go to www.wiley.com/college/weygandt

Steps

1. Go to the site shown above.
2. Choose **Publications Online**.
3. Choose **Publication 15, Circular E, Employer's Tax Guide**.

Instructions

Answer each of the following questions.

(a) How does the government define "employees"?
(b) What are the special rules for Social Security and Medicare regarding children who are employed by their parents?
(c) How can an employee obtain a Social Security card if he or she doesn't have one?
(d) Must employees report to their employer tips received from customers? If so, what is the process?
(e) Where should the employer deposit Social Security taxes withheld or contributed?

Critical Thinking

GROUP DECISION CASE

BYPD-2 Summerville Processing Company provides word-processing services for business clients and students in a university community. The work for business clients is fairly steady throughout the year. The work for students peaks significantly in December and May as a result of term papers, research project reports, and dissertations.

Two years ago, the company attempted to meet the peak demand by hiring part-time help. However, this led to numerous errors and considerable customer dissatisfaction. A year ago, the company hired four experienced employees on a permanent basis instead of using part-time help. This proved to be much better in terms of productivity and customer satisfaction. But, it has caused an increase in annual payroll costs and a significant decline in annual net income.

Recently, Valarie Flynn, a sales representative of Davidson Services Inc., has made a proposal to the company. Under her plan, Davidson Services will provide up to four experienced workers at a daily rate of $80 per person for an 8-hour workday. Davidson workers are not available on an hourly basis. Summerville Processing would have to pay only the daily rate for the workers used.

The owner of Summerville Processing, Nancy Bell, asks you, as the company's accountant, to prepare a report on the expenses that are pertinent to the decision. If the Davidson plan is adopted, Nancy will terminate the employment of two permanent employees and will keep two permanent employees. At the moment, each employee earns an annual income of $22,000. Summerville Processing pays 8% FICA taxes, 0.8% federal unemployment taxes, and 5.4% state unemployment taxes. The unemployment taxes apply to only the first $7,000 of gross earnings. In addition, Summerville Processing pays $40 per month for each employee for medical and dental insurance.

Nancy indicates that if the Davidson Services plan is accepted, her needs for workers will be as follows.

Months	Number	Working Days per Month
January–March	2	20
April–May	3	25
June–October	2	18
November–December	3	23

Instructions

With the class divided into groups, answer the following.

(a) Prepare a report showing the comparative payroll expense of continuing to employ permanent workers compared to adopting the Davidson Services Inc. plan.

(b) What other factors should Nancy consider before finalizing her decision?

COMMUNICATION ACTIVITY

BYPD-3 Ivan Blanco, president of the Blue Sky Company, has recently hired a number of additional employees. He recognizes that additional payroll taxes will be due as a result of this hiring, and that the company will serve as the collection agent for other taxes.

Instructions

In a memorandum to Ivan Blanco, explain each of the taxes, and identify the taxes that result in payroll tax expense to Blue Sky Company.

ETHICS CASE

Accounting Matters!

BYPD-4 Johnny Fuller owns and manages Johnny's Restaurant, a 24-hour restaurant near the city's medical complex. Johnny employs 9 full-time employees and 16 part-time employees. He pays all of the full-time employees by check, the amounts of which are determined by Johnny's public accountant, Mary Lake. Johnny pays all of his part-time employees in cash. He computes their wages and withdraws the cash directly from his cash register.

Mary has repeatedly urged Johnny to pay all employees by check. But as Johnny has told his competitor and friend, Steve Hill, who owns the Greasy Diner, "First of all, my part-time employees prefer the cash over a check, and secondly I don't withhold or pay any taxes or workmen's compensation insurance on those wages because they go totally unrecorded and unnoticed."

Instructions

(a) Who are the stakeholders in this situation?
(b) What are the legal and ethical considerations regarding Johnny's handling of his payroll?
(c) Mary Lake is aware of Johnny's payment of the part-time payroll in cash. What are her ethical responsibilities in this case?
(d) What internal control principle is violated in this payroll process?

Answers to Self-Study Questions

1. d **2.** d **3.** c

Appendix E

Subsidiary Ledgers and Special Journals

STUDY OBJECTIVES

After studying this appendix, you should be able to:

1. Describe the nature and purpose of a subsidiary ledger.
2. Explain how special journals are used in journalizing.
3. Indicate how a multi-column journal is posted.

SECTION 1 EXPANDING THE LEDGER—SUBSIDIARY LEDGERS

NATURE AND PURPOSE OF SUBSIDIARY LEDGERS

STUDY OBJECTIVE 1

Describe the nature and purpose of a subsidiary ledger.

Imagine a business that has several thousand charge (credit) customers and shows the transactions with these customers in only one general ledger account—Accounts Receivable. It would be virtually impossible to determine the balance owed by an individual customer at any specific time. Similarly, the amount payable to one creditor would be difficult to locate quickly from a single Accounts Payable account in the general ledger.

Instead, companies use subsidiary ledgers to keep track of individual balances. A **subsidiary ledger** is a group of accounts with a common characteristic (for example, all accounts receivable). The subsidiary ledger frees the general ledger from the details of individual balances. A subsidiary ledger is an addition to, and an expansion of, the general ledger.

Two common subsidiary ledgers are:

1. The **accounts receivable** (or **customers'**) **subsidiary ledger**, which collects transaction data of individual customers.
2. The **accounts payable** (or **creditors'**) **subsidiary ledger**, which collects transaction data of individual creditors.

In each of these subsidiary ledgers, individual accounts are usually arranged in alphabetical order.

The detailed data from a subsidiary ledger are summarized in a general ledger account. For example, the detailed data from the accounts receivable subsidiary ledger are summarized in Accounts Receivable in the general ledger. The general ledger account that summarizes subsidiary ledger data is called a **control account**. An overview of the relationship of subsidiary ledgers to the general ledger is shown in Illustration E-1 on page E2. The general ledger control accounts are shown in a pink color, and subsidiary ledger accounts are shown in a green color. Note that Cash and Common Stock in this illustration are not control accounts because there are no subsidiary ledger accounts related to these accounts.

Each general ledger control account balance must equal the composite balance of the individual accounts in the related subsidiary ledger at the end of an accounting period. For example, the balance in Accounts Payable in Illustration E-1 must equal the total of the subsidiary balances of Creditors X + Y + Z.

Illustration E-1
Relationship of general ledger and subsidiary ledgers

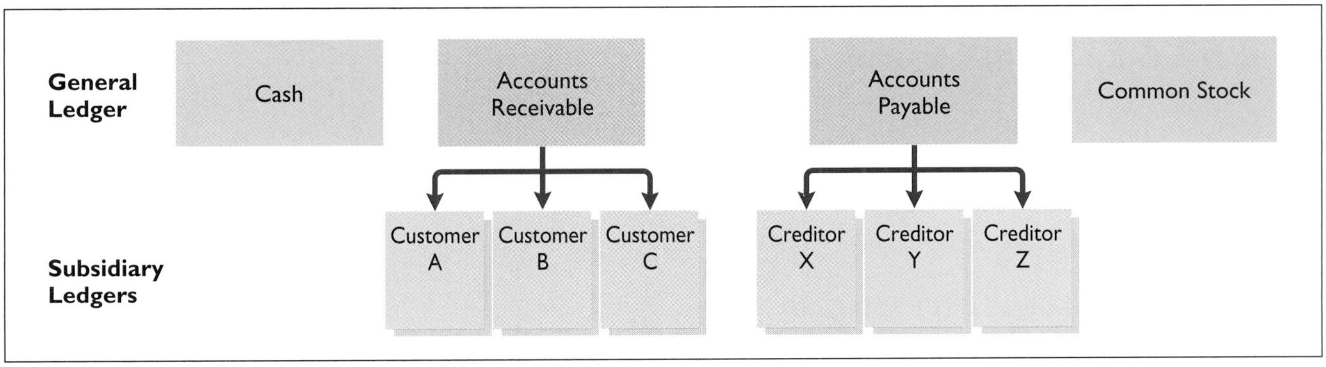

Example

An example of a control account and subsidiary ledger for Larson Enterprises is provided in Illustration E-2. (The explanation column in these accounts is not shown in this and subsequent illustrations due to space considerations.)

Illustration E-2
Relationship between general and subsidiary ledgers

ACCOUNTS RECEIVABLE SUBSIDIARY LEDGER

Aaron Co.

Date	Ref.	Debit	Credit	Balance
2006				
Jan 10		6,000		6,000
19			4,000	**2,000**

Branden Inc.

Date	Ref.	Debit	Credit	Balance
2006				
Jan 12		3,000		3,000
21			3,000	------

Caron Co.

Date	Ref.	Debit	Credit	Balance
2006				
Jan 20		3,000		3,000
29			1,000	**2,000**

GENERAL LEDGER

Accounts Receivable **No. 112**

Date	Ref.	Debit	Credit	Balance
2006				
Jan 31		12,000		12,000
31			8,000	**4,000**

The subsidiary ledger is separate from the general ledger.

Accounts Receivable is a control account.

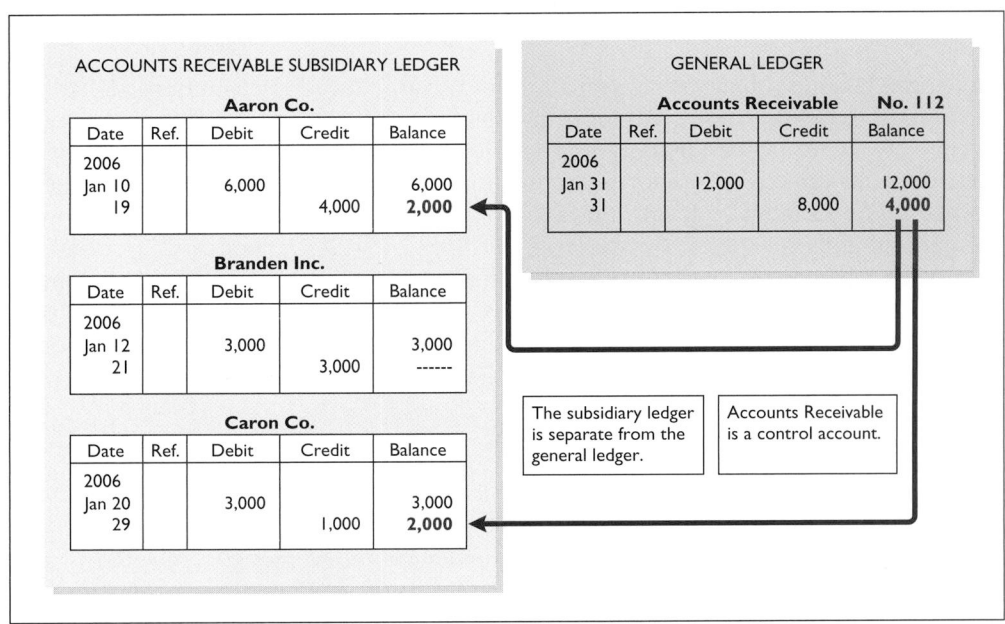

The example is based on the transactions listed below.

Illustration E-3
Sales and collection transactions

Credit Sales			**Collections on Account**		
Jan. 10	Aaron Co.	$ 6,000	Jan. 19	Aaron Co.	$ 4,000
12	Branden Inc.	3,000	21	Branden Inc.	3,000
20	Caron Co.	3,000	29	Caron Co.	1,000
		$12,000			$ 8,000

The total debits ($12,000) and credits ($8,000) in Accounts Receivable in the general ledger are reconcilable to the detailed debits and credits in the subsidiary accounts. Also, the balance of $4,000 in the control account agrees with the total of the balances in the individual accounts (Aaron Co. $2,000 + Branden Inc. $0 + Caron Co. $2,000) in the subsidiary ledger.

As shown, postings are made monthly to the control accounts in the general ledger. This practice allows monthly financial statements to be prepared. Postings to the individual accounts in the subsidiary ledger are made daily. Daily posting ensures that account information is current. This enables the company to monitor credit limits, bill customers, and answer inquiries from customers about their account balances.

Advantages of Subsidiary Ledgers

Subsidiary ledgers have several advantages. They:

1. **Show transactions affecting one customer or one creditor in a single account,** thus providing up-to-date information on specific account balances.
2. **Free the general ledger of excessive details.** As a result, a trial balance of the general ledger does not contain vast numbers of individual account balances.
3. **Help locate errors in individual accounts** by reducing the number of accounts in one ledger and by using control accounts.
4. **Make possible a division of labor** in posting. One employee can post to the general ledger while someone else posts to the subsidiary ledgers.

BEFORE YOU GO ON...

Review It

1. What is a subsidiary ledger, and what purpose does it serve?
2. What is a control account, and what purpose does it serve?
3. Name two general ledger accounts that may act as control accounts for a subsidiary ledger. Can you think of a third control account?

Do It

Presented below is information related to Sims Company for its first month of operations. Determine the balances that appear in the accounts payable subsidiary ledger. What Accounts Payable balance appears in the general ledger at the end of January?

Credit Purchases			Cash Paid		
Jan. 5	Devon Co.	$11,000	Jan. 9	Devon Co.	$7,000
11	Shelby Co.	7,000	14	Shelby Co.	2,000
22	Taylor Co.	14,000	27	Taylor Co.	9,000

ACTION PLAN

- Subtract cash paid from credit purchases to determine the balances in the accounts payable subsidiary ledger.
- Sum the individual balances to determine the Accounts Payable balance.

SOLUTION Subsidiary ledger balances: Devon Co. $4,000 ($11,000 − $7,000); Shelby Co. $5,000 ($7,000 − $2,000); Taylor Co. $5,000 ($14,000 − $9,000). General ledger Accounts Payable balance: $14,000 ($4,000 + $5,000 + $5,000).

Related exercise material: *BEE-1, BEE-2, EE-1, EE-2, EE-3, EE-4, EE-5, and EE-9.*

SECTION 2 EXPANDING THE JOURNAL—SPECIAL JOURNALS

STUDY OBJECTIVE 2

Explain how special journals are used in journalizing.

So far you have learned to journalize transactions in a two-column general journal and post each entry to the general ledger. This procedure is satisfactory in only the very smallest companies. To expedite journalizing and posting, most companies use special journals **in addition to the general journal.**

A **special journal** is used to record similar types of transactions. Examples would be all sales of merchandise on account, or all cash receipts. What special journals a company uses depends largely on the types of transactions that occur frequently. Most merchandising enterprises use the journals shown in Illustration E-4 to record transactions daily.

Illustration E-4
Use of special journals and the general journal

Sales Journal	Cash Receipts Journal	Purchases Journal	Cash Payments Journal	General Journal
Used for: All sales of merchandise on account	Used for: All cash received (including cash sales)	Used for: All purchases of merchandise on account	Used for: All cash paid (including cash purchases)	Used for: Transactions that cannot be entered in a special journal, including correcting, adjusting, and closing entries

If a transaction cannot be recorded in a special journal, it is recorded in the general journal. For example, if you had special journals only for the four types of transactions listed above, purchase returns and allowances would be recorded in the general journal. So would sales returns and allowances. Similarly, **correcting, adjusting, and closing entries are recorded in the general journal**. Other types of special journals may sometimes be used in some situations. For example, when sales returns and allowances are frequent, special journals may be used to record these transactions.

Special journals **permit greater division of labor** because several people can record entries in different journals at the same time. For example, one employee may journalize all cash receipts, and another may journalize all credit sales. Also, the use of special journals **reduces the time needed to complete the posting process**. With special journals, some accounts may be posted monthly, instead of daily, as will be illustrated later in the chapter.

Sales Journal

HELPFUL HINT

Postings are also made daily to individual ledger accounts in the inventory subsidiary ledger to maintain a perpetual inventory.

The **sales journal** is used to record sales of merchandise on account. Cash sales of merchandise are entered in the cash receipts journal. Credit sales of assets other than merchandise are entered in the general journal.

Journalizing Credit Sales

Karns Wholesale Supply uses a **perpetual inventory** system. Under this system, each entry in the sales journal results in one entry **at selling price** and another entry at cost—a debit to Accounts Receivable (a control account) and a credit of equal amount to Sales. The entry **at cost** is a debit to Cost of Goods Sold and a credit of equal amount to Merchandise Inventory (a control account). A sales journal with two amount columns can show on only one line a sales transaction at both selling price and cost. The two-column sales journal of Karns Wholesale Supply is shown in Illustration E-5, using assumed credit sales transactions (for sales invoices 101–107).

Illustration E-5
Journalizing the sales journal—perpetual inventory system

Karns Wholesale Supply
SALES JOURNAL **S1**

Date	Account Debited	Invoice No.	Ref.	Accts. Receivable Dr. Sales Cr.	Cost of Goods Sold Dr. Merchandise Inventory Cr.
2006					
May 3	Abbot Sisters	101		10,600	6,360
7	Babson Co.	102		11,350	7,370
14	Carson Bros.	103		7,800	5,070
19	Deli Co.	104		9,300	6,510
21	Abbot Sisters	105		15,400	10,780
24	Deli Co.	106		21,210	15,900
27	Babson Co.	107		14,570	10,200
				90,230	62,190

The reference (Ref.) column is not used in journalizing. It is used in posting the sales journal, as explained in the next section. Also, note that, unlike the general journal, an explanation is not required for each entry in a special journal. Finally, note that each invoice is prenumbered to ensure that all invoices are journalized.

Posting the Sales Journal

Postings from the sales journal are made **daily to the individual accounts receivable** in the subsidiary ledger. Posting **to the general ledger** is made **monthly**. Illustration E-6 (on page E6) shows both the daily and monthly postings.

A check mark (✓) is inserted in the reference posting column to indicate that the daily posting to the customer's account has been made. A check mark (✓) is used in this illustration because the subsidiary ledger accounts are not numbered. At the end of the month, the column totals of the sales journal are posted to the general ledger. Here, the column totals are a debit of \$90,230 to Accounts Receivable (account No. 112), a credit of \$90,230 to Sales (account No. 401), a debit of \$62,190 to Cost of Goods Sold (account No. 505), and a credit of \$62,190 to Merchandise Inventory (account No. 120). Insertion of the account numbers below the column total indicates that the postings have been made. In both the general ledger and subsidiary ledger accounts, the reference **S1** indicates that the posting came from page 1 of the sales journal.

Proving the Ledgers

The next step is to "prove" the ledgers. To do so, we must determine two things: (1) The total of the general ledger debit balances must equal the total of the general ledger credit balances. (2) The sum of the subsidiary ledger balances must equal the balance in the control account. The proof of the postings from the sales journal to the general and subsidiary ledger is shown in Illustration E-7 (on page E7).

Illustration E-6
Posting the sales journal

Karns Wholesale Supply
SALES JOURNAL
S1

Date	Account Debited	Invoice No.	Ref.	Accts. Receivable Dr. Sales Cr.	Cost of Goods Sold Dr. Merchandise Inventory Cr.
2006					
May 3	Abbot Sisters	101	√	10,600	6,360
7	Babson Co.	102	√	11,350	7,370
14	Carson Bros.	103	√	7,800	5,070
19	Deli Co.	104	√	9,300	6,510
21	Abbot Sisters	105	√	15,400	10,780
24	Deli Co.	106	√	21,210	15,900
27	Babson Co.	107	√	14,570	10,200
				90,230	62,190
				(112) / (401)	(505) / (120)

Totals are posted at the end of the accounting period to the general ledger.

Individual amounts are posted daily to the subsidiary ledger.

ACCOUNTS RECEIVABLE SUBSIDIARY LEDGER

Abbot Sisters

Date	Ref.	Debit	Credit	Balance
2006				
May 3	S1	10,600		10,600
21	S1	15,400		26,000

Babson Co.

Date	Ref.	Debit	Credit	Balance
2006				
May 7	S1	11,350		11,350
27	S1	14,570		25,920

Carson Bros.

Date	Ref.	Debit	Credit	Balance
2006				
May 14	S1	7,800		7,800

Deli Co.

Date	Ref.	Debit	Credit	Balance
2006				
May 19	S1	9,300		9,300
24	S1	21,210		30,510

GENERAL LEDGER

Accounts Receivable **No. 112**

Date	Ref.	Debit	Credit	Balance
2006				
May 31	S1	90,230		90,230

Merchandise Inventory **No. 120**

Date	Ref.	Debit	Credit	Balance
2006				
May 31	S1		62,190	62,190[1]

Sales **No. 401**

Date	Ref.	Debit	Credit	Balance
2006				
May 31	S1		90,230	90,230

Cost of Goods Sold **No. 505**

Date	Ref.	Debit	Credit	Balance
2006				
May 31	S1	62,190		62,190

The subsidiary ledger is separate from the general ledger.

Accounts Receivable is a control account.

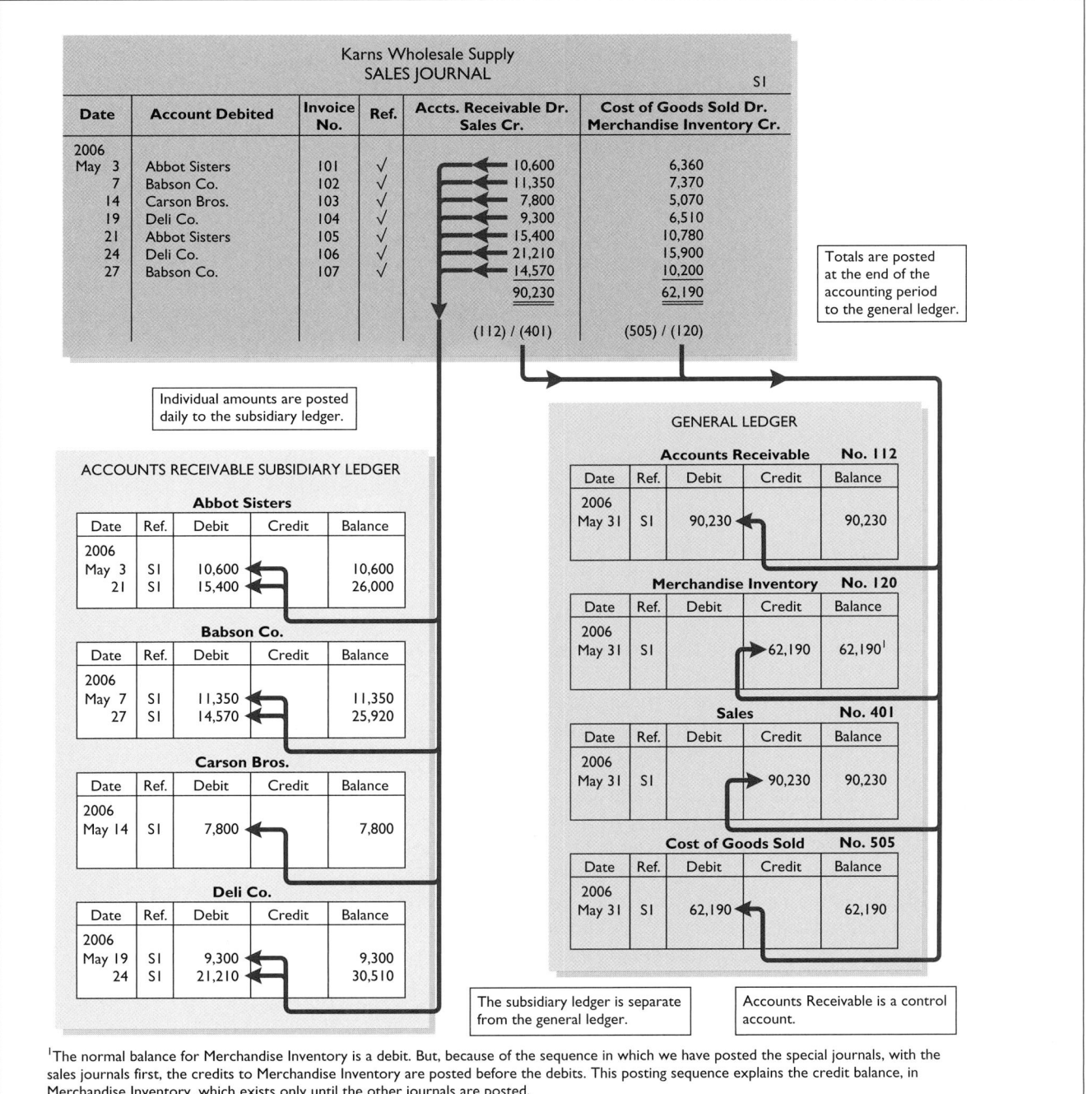

[1]The normal balance for Merchandise Inventory is a debit. But, because of the sequence in which we have posted the special journals, with the sales journals first, the credits to Merchandise Inventory are posted before the debits. This posting sequence explains the credit balance, in Merchandise Inventory, which exists only until the other journals are posted.

Advantages of the Sales Journal

The use of a special journal to record sales on account has a number of advantages. First, the one-line entry for each sales transaction **saves time**. In the sales journal, it is not necessary to write out the four account titles for each transaction. Second, only totals, rather than individual entries, are posted to the general ledger. This **saves posting time and reduces the possibilities of errors in posting**. Finally, **a division of labor results**, because one individual can take responsibility for the sales journal.

Illustration E-7
Proving the equality of the postings from the sales journal

Postings to General Ledger

General Ledger

Credits	
Merchandise Inventory	$62,190
Sales	90,230
	$152,420

Debits	
Accounts Receivable	$90,230
Cost of Goods Sold	62,190
	$152,420

Debit Postings to the Accounts Receivable Subsidiary Ledger

Subsidiary Ledger

Abbot Sisters	$26,000
Babson Co.	25,920
Carson Bros.	7,800
Deli Co.	30,510
	$90,230

Cash Receipts Journal

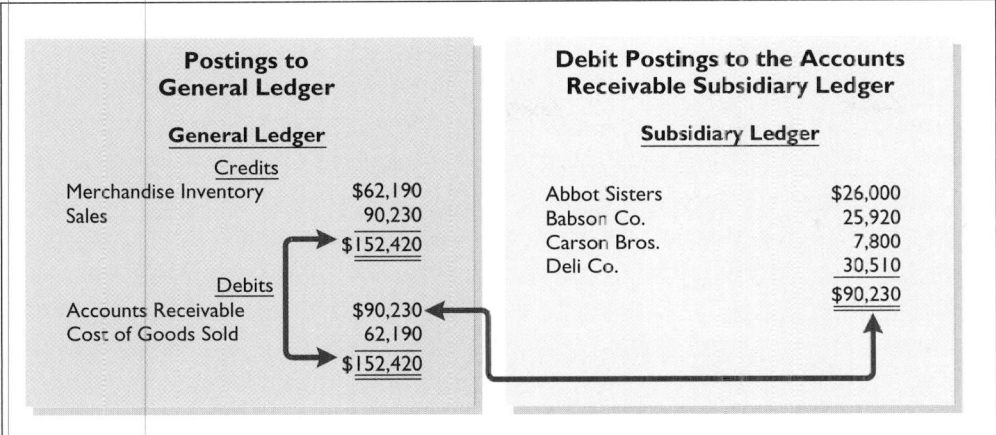

All receipts of cash are recorded in the **cash receipts journal**. The most common types of cash receipts are cash sales of merchandise and collections of accounts receivable. Many other possibilities exist, such as receipt of money from bank loans and cash proceeds from disposal of equipment. A one- or two-column cash receipts journal would not have space enough for all possible cash receipt transactions. Therefore, a multiple-column cash receipts journal is used.

Generally, a cash receipts journal includes the following columns: debit columns for cash and sales discounts; and credit columns for accounts receivable, sales, and "other" accounts. The Other Accounts category is used when the cash receipt does not involve a cash sale or a collection of accounts receivable. Under a perpetual inventory system, each sales entry is accompanied by another entry that debits Cost of Goods Sold and credits Merchandise Inventory for the cost of the merchandise sold. This entry may be recorded separately. A six-column cash receipts journal is shown in Illustration E-8 (on page E8).

Additional credit columns may be used if they significantly reduce postings to a specific account. For example, a loan company, such as **Household International**, receives thousands of cash collections from customers. A significant saving in posting would result from using separate credit columns for Loans Receivable and Interest Revenue, rather than using the Other Accounts credit column. In contrast, a retailer that has only one interest collection a month would not find it useful to have a separate column for Interest Revenue.

Journalizing Cash Receipts Transactions

To illustrate the journalizing of cash receipts transactions, we will continue with the May transactions of Karns Wholesale Supply. Collections from customers relate to the entries recorded in the sales journal in Illustration E-5. The entries in the cash receipts journal are based on the following cash receipts.

May 1 Stockholders invest $5,000 in the business.
7 Cash sales of merchandise total $1,900 (cost, $1,240).
10 A check for $10,388 is received from Abbot Sisters in payment of invoice No. 101 for $10,600 less a 2% discount.
12 Cash sales of merchandise total $2,600 (cost, $1,690).
17 A check for $11,123 is received from Babson Co. in payment of invoice No. 102 for $11,350 less a 2% discount.
22 Cash is received by signing a note for $6,000.

Illustration E-8
Journalizing and posting the cash receipts journal

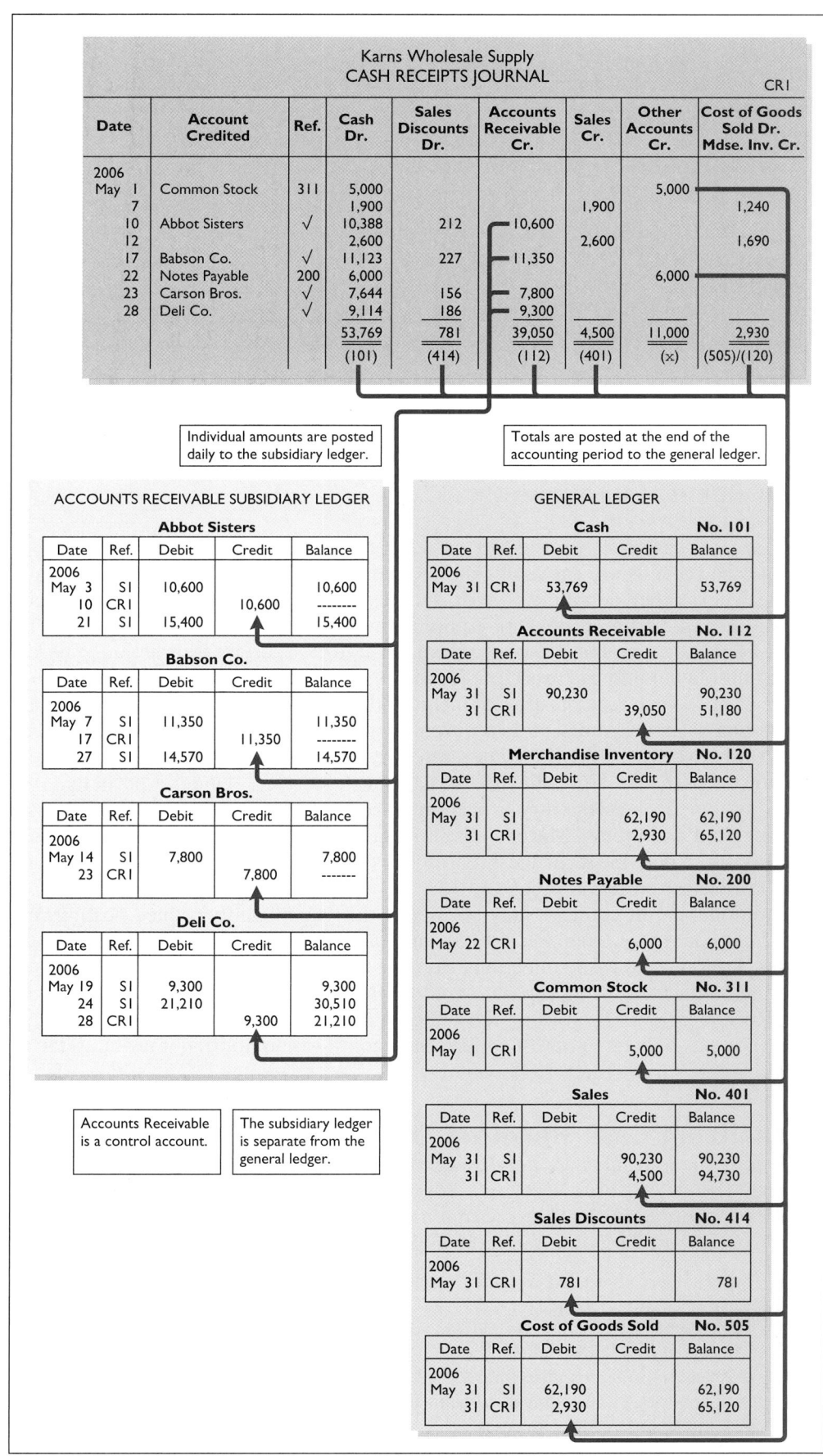

Karns Wholesale Supply
CASH RECEIPTS JOURNAL

CR1

Date	Account Credited	Ref.	Cash Dr.	Sales Discounts Dr.	Accounts Receivable Cr.	Sales Cr.	Other Accounts Cr.	Cost of Goods Sold Dr. Mdse. Inv. Cr.
2006								
May 1	Common Stock	311	5,000				5,000	
7			1,900			1,900		1,240
10	Abbot Sisters	√	10,388	212	10,600			
12			2,600			2,600		1,690
17	Babson Co.	√	11,123	227	11,350			
22	Notes Payable	200	6,000				6,000	
23	Carson Bros.	√	7,644	156	7,800			
28	Deli Co.	√	9,114	186	9,300			
			53,769	781	39,050	4,500	11,000	2,930
			(101)	(414)	(112)	(401)	(x)	(505)/(120)

Individual amounts are posted daily to the subsidiary ledger.

Totals are posted at the end of the accounting period to the general ledger.

ACCOUNTS RECEIVABLE SUBSIDIARY LEDGER

Abbot Sisters

Date	Ref.	Debit	Credit	Balance
2006				
May 3	S1	10,600		10,600
10	CR1		10,600	--------
21	S1	15,400		15,400

Babson Co.

Date	Ref.	Debit	Credit	Balance
2006				
May 7	S1	11,350		11,350
17	CR1		11,350	--------
27	S1	14,570		14,570

Carson Bros.

Date	Ref.	Debit	Credit	Balance
2006				
May 14	S1	7,800		7,800
23	CR1		7,800	-------

Deli Co.

Date	Ref.	Debit	Credit	Balance
2006				
May 19	S1	9,300		9,300
24	S1	21,210		30,510
28	CR1		9,300	21,210

Accounts Receivable is a control account.

The subsidiary ledger is separate from the general ledger.

GENERAL LEDGER

Cash **No. 101**

Date	Ref.	Debit	Credit	Balance
2006				
May 31	CR1	53,769		53,769

Accounts Receivable **No. 112**

Date	Ref.	Debit	Credit	Balance
2006				
May 31	S1	90,230		90,230
31	CR1		39,050	51,180

Merchandise Inventory **No. 120**

Date	Ref.	Debit	Credit	Balance
2006				
May 31	S1		62,190	62,190
31	CR1		2,930	65,120

Notes Payable **No. 200**

Date	Ref.	Debit	Credit	Balance
2006				
May 22	CR1		6,000	6,000

Common Stock **No. 311**

Date	Ref.	Debit	Credit	Balance
2006				
May 1	CR1		5,000	5,000

Sales **No. 401**

Date	Ref.	Debit	Credit	Balance
2006				
May 31	S1		90,230	90,230
31	CR1		4,500	94,730

Sales Discounts **No. 414**

Date	Ref.	Debit	Credit	Balance
2006				
May 31	CR1	781		781

Cost of Goods Sold **No. 505**

Date	Ref.	Debit	Credit	Balance
2006				
May 31	S1	62,190		62,190
31	CR1	2,930		65,120

23 A check for $7,644 is received from Carson Bros. in full for invoice No. 103 for $7,800 less a 2% discount.

28 A check for $9,114 is received from Deli Co. in full for invoice No. 104 for $9,300 less a 2% discount.

Further information about the columns in the cash receipts journal (see Illustration E-8) is listed below.

Debit Columns:

1. **Cash.** The amount of cash actually received in each transaction is entered in this column. The column total indicates the total cash receipts for the month.
2. **Sales Discounts.** Karns includes a Sales Discounts column in its cash receipts journal. By doing so, it is not necessary to enter sales discount items in the general journal. As a result, the collection of an account receivable within the discount period is expressed on one line in the appropriate columns of the cash receipts journal.

Credit Columns:

3. **Accounts Receivable.** The Accounts Receivable column is used to record cash collections on account. The amount entered here is the amount to be credited to the individual customer's account.
4. **Sales.** The Sales column records all cash sales of merchandise. Cash sales of other assets (plant assets, for example) are not reported in this column.
5. **Other Accounts.** The Other Accounts column is used whenever the credit is other than to Accounts Receivable or Sales. For example, in the first entry, $5,000 is entered as a credit to Common Stock. This column is often referred to as the sundry accounts column.

Debit and Credit Column:

6. **Cost of Goods Sold and Merchandise Inventory.** This column records debits to Cost of Goods Sold and credits to Merchandise Inventory.

In a multi-column journal, generally only one line is needed for each entry. Debit and credit amounts for each line must be equal. When the collection from Abbot Sisters on May 10 is journalized, for example, three amounts are indicated. Note also that the Account Credited column is used to identify both general ledger and subsidiary ledger account titles. General ledger accounts are illustrated in the May 1 and May 22 entries. A subsidiary account is illustrated in the May 10 entry for the collection from Abbot Sisters.

When the journalizing of a multi-column journal has been completed, the amount columns are totaled, and the totals are compared to prove the equality of debits and credits. The proof of the equality of Karns's cash receipts journal is as follows.

HELPFUL HINT

When is an account title entered in the "Account Credited" column of the cash receipts journal? Answer: A *subsidiary ledger* title is entered there whenever the entry involves a collection of accounts receivable. A *general ledger* account title is entered there whenever the entry involves an account that is not the subject of a special column (and an amount must be entered in the Other Accounts column). No account title is entered there if neither of the foregoing applies.

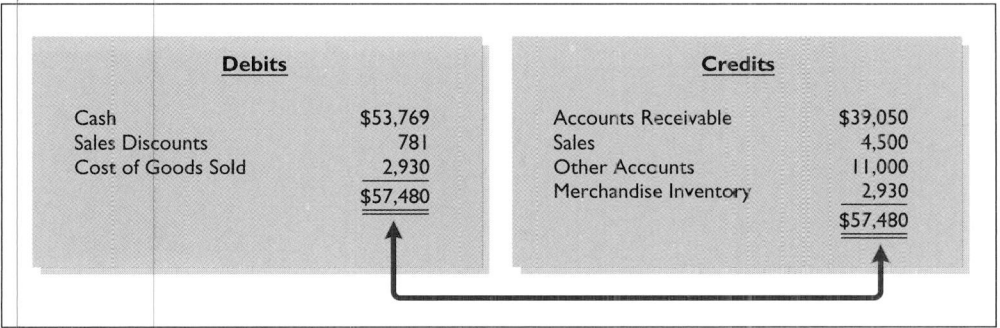

Illustration E-9
Proving the equality of the cash receipts journal

Debits	
Cash	$53,769
Sales Discounts	781
Cost of Goods Sold	2,930
	$57,480

Credits	
Accounts Receivable	$39,050
Sales	4,500
Other Accounts	11,000
Merchandise Inventory	2,930
	$57,480

Totaling the columns of a journal and proving the equality of the totals is called **footing** and **cross-footing** a journal.

Posting the Cash Receipts Journal

Posting a multi-column journal involves the following steps.

STUDY OBJECTIVE 3

Indicate how a multi-column journal is posted.

1. All column totals except for the Other Accounts total are posted **once at the end of the month** to the account title(s) specified in the column heading (such as Cash or Accounts Receivable). Account numbers are entered below the column totals to show that they have been posted. Cash is posted to account No. 101, accounts receivable to account No. 112, merchandise inventory to account No. 120, sales to account No. 401, sales discounts to account No. 414, and cost of goods sold to account No. 505.
2. The **individual amounts comprising the Other Accounts total are posted separately** to the general ledger accounts specified in the Account Credited column. See, for example, the credit posting to Common Stock. The total amount of this column is not posted. The symbol (X) is inserted below the total to this column to indicate that the amount has not been posted.
3. The individual amounts in a column, posted in total to a control account (Accounts Receivable, in this case), are posted **daily to the subsidiary ledger** account specified in the Account Credited column. See, for example, the credit posting of $10,600 to Abbot Sisters.

The symbol **CR** is used in both the subsidiary and general ledgers to identify postings from the cash receipts journal.

Proving the Ledgers

After posting of the cash receipts journal is completed, it is necessary to prove the ledgers. As shown in Illustration E-10, the general ledger totals are in agreement. Also, the sum of the subsidiary ledger balances equals the control account balance.

Illustration E-10
Proving the ledgers after posting the sales and the cash receipts journals

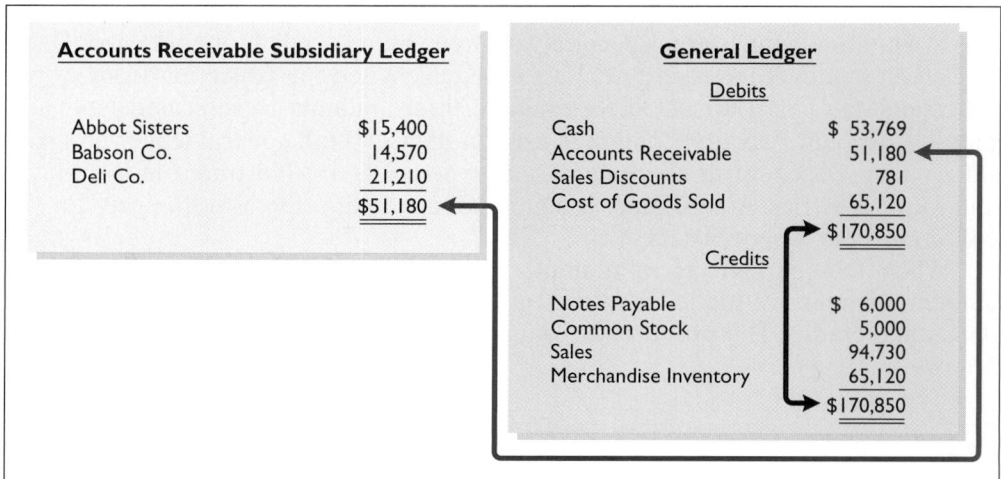

Accounts Receivable Subsidiary Ledger

Abbot Sisters	$15,400
Babson Co.	14,570
Deli Co.	21,210
	$51,180

General Ledger

Debits	
Cash	$ 53,769
Accounts Receivable	51,180
Sales Discounts	781
Cost of Goods Sold	65,120
	$170,850
Credits	
Notes Payable	$ 6,000
Common Stock	5,000
Sales	94,730
Merchandise Inventory	65,120
	$170,850

Purchases Journal

All purchases of merchandise on account are recorded in the **purchases journal**. Each entry in this journal results in a debit to Merchandise Inventory and a credit to Accounts Payable. When a one-column purchases journal is used (as in Illustration E-11, on page E11), other types of purchases on account and cash purchases cannot be journalized in it. For example, credit purchases of equipment or supplies must be recorded in the general journal. Likewise, all cash purchases are entered in the cash payments journal. As illustrated later, where credit purchases for items other than merchandise are numerous, the purchases journal is often expanded to a multi-column format. The purchases journal for Karns Wholesale Supply is shown in Illustration E-11.

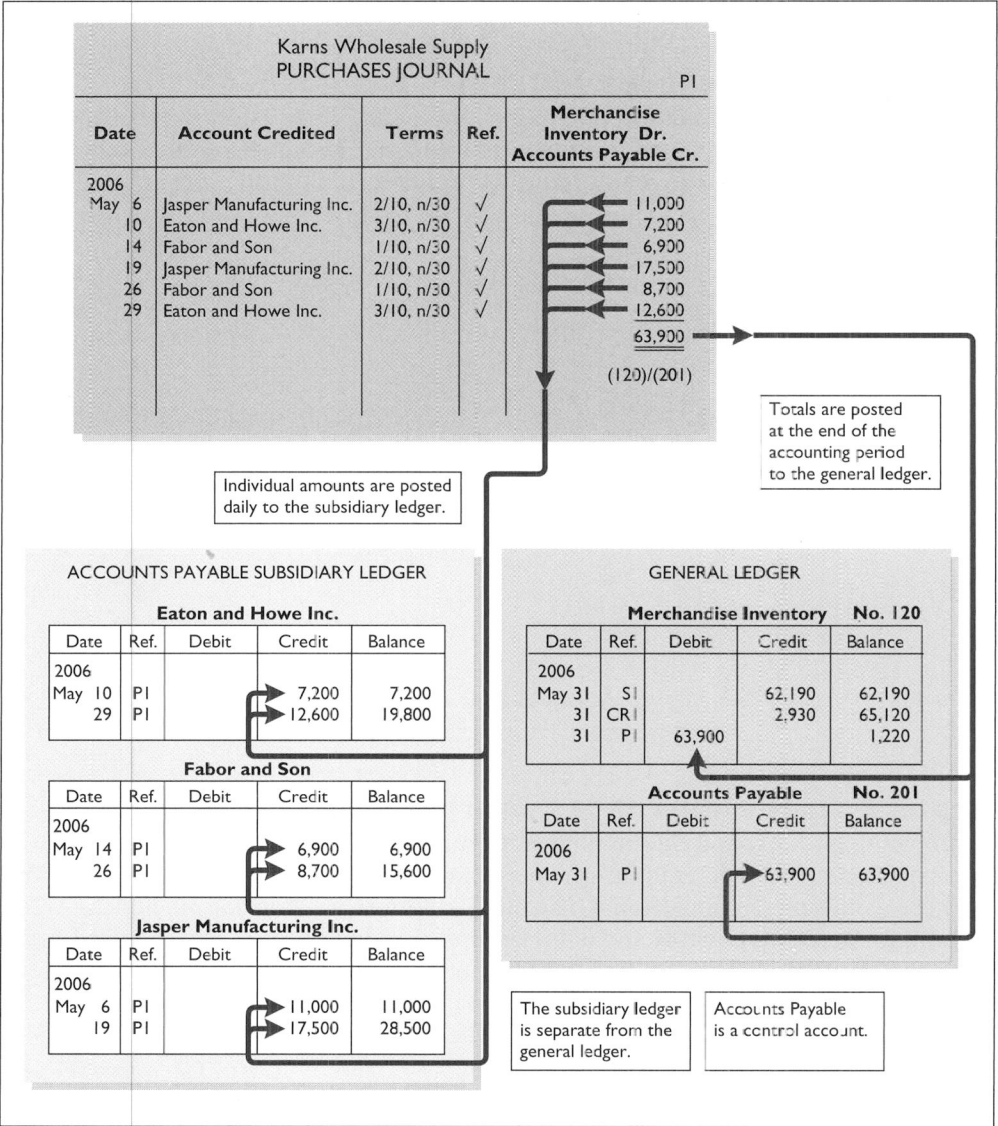

Illustration E-11
Journalizing and posting the purchases journal

Karns Wholesale Supply
PURCHASES JOURNAL
P1

Date	Account Credited	Terms	Ref.	Merchandise Inventory Dr. Accounts Payable Cr.
2006				
May 6	Jasper Manufacturing Inc.	2/10, n/30	√	11,000
10	Eaton and Howe Inc.	3/10, n/30	√	7,200
14	Fabor and Son	1/10, n/30	√	6,900
19	Jasper Manufacturing Inc.	2/10, n/30	√	17,500
26	Fabor and Son	1/10, n/30	√	8,700
29	Eaton and Howe Inc.	3/10, n/30	√	12,600
				63,900
				(120)/(201)

Totals are posted at the end of the accounting period to the general ledger.

Individual amounts are posted daily to the subsidiary ledger.

ACCOUNTS PAYABLE SUBSIDIARY LEDGER

Eaton and Howe Inc.

Date	Ref.	Debit	Credit	Balance
2006				
May 10	P1		7,200	7,200
29	P1		12,600	19,800

Fabor and Son

Date	Ref.	Debit	Credit	Balance
2006				
May 14	P1		6,900	6,900
26	P1		8,700	15,600

Jasper Manufacturing Inc.

Date	Ref.	Debit	Credit	Balance
2006				
May 6	P1		11,000	11,000
19	P1		17,500	28,500

GENERAL LEDGER

Merchandise Inventory No. 120

Date	Ref.	Debit	Credit	Balance
2006				
May 31	S1		62,190	62,190
31	CR1		2,930	65,120
31	P1	63,900		1,220

Accounts Payable No. 201

Date	Ref.	Debit	Credit	Balance
2006				
May 31	P1		63,900	63,900

The subsidiary ledger is separate from the general ledger.

Accounts Payable is a control account.

HELPFUL HINT

A single-column purchases journal needs only to be footed to prove the equality of debits and credits.

Journalizing Credit Purchases of Merchandise

Entries in the purchases journal are made from purchase invoices. The journalizing procedure is similar to that for a sales journal. In contrast to the sales journal, the purchases journal may not have an invoice number column, because invoices received from different suppliers will not be in numerical sequence. To assure that all purchase invoices are recorded, some companies consecutively number each invoice upon receipt and then use an internal document number column in the purchases journal.

The entries for Karns Wholesale Supply are based on the following assumed credit purchases.

Illustration E-12
Credit purchases transactions

Date	Supplier	Amount
5/6	Jasper Manufacturing Inc.	$11,000
5/10	Eaton and Howe Inc.	7,200
5/14	Fabor and Son	6,900
5/19	Jasper Manufacturing Inc.	17,500
5/26	Fabor and Son	8,700
5/29	Eaton and Howe Inc.	12,600

HELPFUL HINT

Postings to subsidiary ledger accounts are done daily because it is often necessary to know a current balance for the subsidiary accounts.

Posting the Purchases Journal

The procedures for posting the purchases journal are similar to those for the sales journal. In this case, postings are made **daily** to the **accounts payable ledger** and **monthly** to Merchandise Inventory and Accounts Payable in the general ledger. In both ledgers, P1 is used in the reference column to show that the postings are from page 1 of the purchases journal.

Proof of the equality of the postings from the purchases journal to both ledgers is shown by the following.

Illustration E-13
Proving the equality of the purchases journal

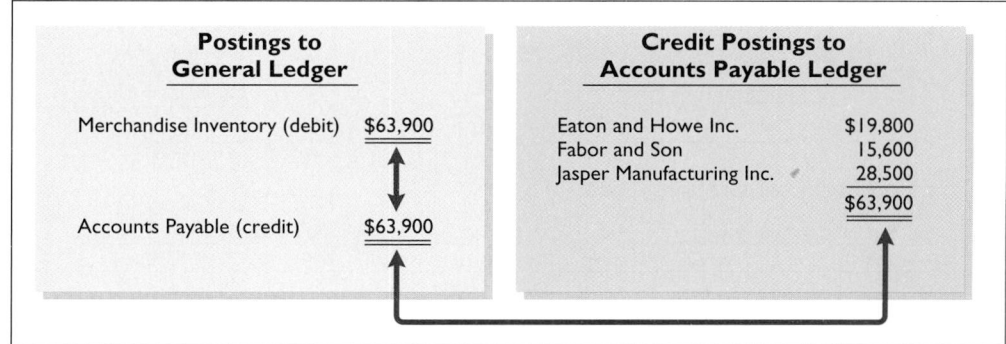

Postings to General Ledger	
Merchandise Inventory (debit)	$63,900
Accounts Payable (credit)	$63,900

Credit Postings to Accounts Payable Ledger	
Eaton and Howe Inc.	$19,800
Fabor and Son	15,600
Jasper Manufacturing Inc.	28,500
	$63,900

Expanding the Purchases Journal

Some companies expand the purchases journal to include all types of purchases on account. Instead of one column for merchandise inventory and accounts payable, they use a multiple-column format. The multi-column format usually includes a credit column for accounts payable and debit columns for purchases of merchandise, of office supplies, of store supplies, and other accounts. Illustration E-14 is an example of a multi-column purchases journal for Hanover Co. The posting procedures are similar to those illustrated earlier for posting the cash receipts journal.

Illustration E-14
Columnar purchases journal

Hanover Co.
PURCHASES JOURNAL **P1**

Date	Account Credited	Ref.	Account Payable Cr.	Merchandise Inventory Dr.	Office Supplies Dr.	Store Supplies Dr.	Other Accounts Dr. Account	Other Accounts Dr. Ref.	Other Accounts Dr. Amount
2006									
June 1	Signe Audio	✓	2,000		2,000				
3	Wight Co.	✓	1,500	1,500					
5	Orange Tree Co.	✓	2,600				Equipment	157	2,600
30	Sue's Business Forms	✓	800			800			
			56,600	43,000	7,500	1,200			4,900

Cash Payments Journal

All disbursements of cash are entered in a **cash payments journal**. Entries are made from prenumbered checks. Because cash payments are made for various purposes, the cash payments journal has multiple columns. A four-column journal is shown in Illustration E-15.

ALTERNATIVE TERMINOLOGY

The cash payments journal is sometimes called the *cash disbursements journal.*

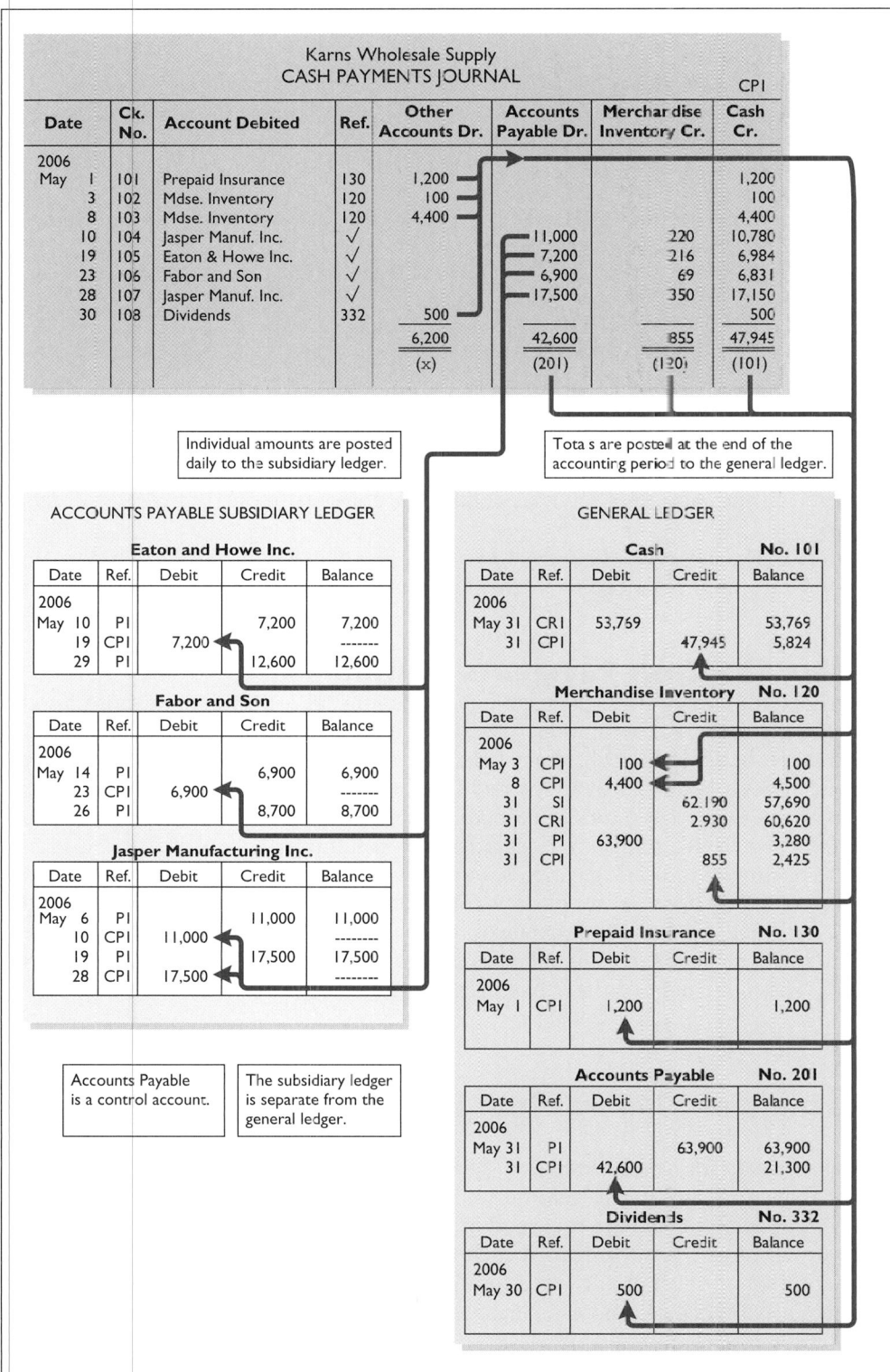

Illustration E-15
Journalizing and posting the cash payments journal

Karns Wholesale Supply
CASH PAYMENTS JOURNAL
CPI

Date	Ck. No.	Account Debited	Ref.	Other Accounts Dr.	Accounts Payable Dr.	Merchandise Inventory Cr.	Cash Cr.
2006							
May 1	101	Prepaid Insurance	130	1,200			1,200
3	102	Mdse. Inventory	120	100			100
8	103	Mdse. Inventory	120	4,400			4,400
10	104	Jasper Manuf. Inc.	√		11,000	220	10,780
19	105	Eaton & Howe Inc.	√		7,200	216	6,984
23	106	Fabor and Son	√		6,900	69	6,831
28	107	Jasper Manuf. Inc.	√		17,500	350	17,150
30	108	Dividends	332	500			500
				6,200	42,600	855	47,945
				(x)	(201)	(120)	(101)

Individual amounts are posted daily to the subsidiary ledger.

Totals are posted at the end of the accounting period to the general ledger.

ACCOUNTS PAYABLE SUBSIDIARY LEDGER

Eaton and Howe Inc.

Date	Ref.	Debit	Credit	Balance
2006				
May 10	PI		7,200	7,200
19	CPI	7,200		-------
29	PI		12,600	12,600

Fabor and Son

Date	Ref.	Debit	Credit	Balance
2006				
May 14	PI		6,900	6,900
23	CPI	6,900		-------
26	PI		8,700	8,700

Jasper Manufacturing Inc.

Date	Ref.	Debit	Credit	Balance
2006				
May 6	PI		11,000	11,000
10	CPI	11,000		--------
19	PI		17,500	17,500
28	CPI	17,500		--------

GENERAL LEDGER

Cash No. 101

Date	Ref.	Debit	Credit	Balance
2006				
May 31	CR1	53,769		53,769
31	CPI		47,945	5,824

Merchandise Inventory No. 120

Date	Ref.	Debit	Credit	Balance
2006				
May 3	CPI	100		100
8	CPI	4,400		4,500
31	SI		62,190	57,690
31	CRI		2,930	60,620
31	PI	63,900		3,280
31	CPI		855	2,425

Prepaid Insurance No. 130

Date	Ref.	Debit	Credit	Balance
2006				
May 1	CPI	1,200		1,200

Accounts Payable No. 201

Date	Ref.	Debit	Credit	Balance
2006				
May 31	PI		63,900	63,900
31	CPI	42,600		21,300

Dividends No. 332

Date	Ref.	Debit	Credit	Balance
2006				
May 30	CPI	500		500

Accounts Payable is a control account.

The subsidiary ledger is separate from the general ledger.

Journalizing Cash Payments Transactions

The procedures for journalizing transactions in this journal are similar to those described earlier for the cash receipts journal. Each transaction is entered on one line, and for each line there must be equal debit and credit amounts. The entries in the cash payments journal in Illustration E-15 are based on the following transactions for Karns Wholesale Supply.

May 1 Check No. 101 for $1,200 issued for the annual premium on a fire insurance policy.
3 Check No. 102 for $100 issued in payment of freight when terms were FOB shipping point.
8 Check No. 103 for $4,400 issued for the purchase of merchandise.
10 Check No. 104 for $10,780 sent to Jasper Manufacturing Inc. in payment of May 6 invoice for $11,000 less a 2% discount.
19 Check No. 105 for $6,984 mailed to Eaton and Howe Inc. in payment of May 10 invoice for $7,200 less a 3% discount.
23 Check No. 106 for $6,831 sent to Fabor and Son in payment of May 14 invoice for $6,900 less a 1% discount.
28 Check No. 107 for $17,150 sent to Jasper Manufacturing Inc. in payment of May 19 invoice for $17,500 less a 2% discount.
30 Check No. 108 for $500 issued to stockholders as a dividend.

Note that whenever an amount is entered in the Other Accounts column, a specific general ledger account must be identified in the Account Debited column. The entries for checks No. 101, 102, and 103 illustrate this situation. Similarly, a subsidiary account must be identified in the Account Debited column whenever an amount is entered in the Accounts Payable column. See, for example, the entry for check No. 104.

After the cash payments journal has been journalized, the columns are totaled. The totals are then balanced to prove the equality of debits and credits.

Posting the Cash Payments Journal

The procedures for posting the cash payments journal are similar to those for the cash receipts journal. The amounts recorded in the Accounts Payable column are posted individually to the subsidiary ledger and in total to the control account. Merchandise Inventory and Cash are posted only in total at the end of the month. Transactions in the Other Accounts column are posted individually to the appropriate account(s) affected. No totals are posted for this column.

The posting of the cash payments journal is shown in Illustration E-15. Note that the symbol **CP** is used as the posting reference. After postings are completed, the equality of the debit and credit balances in the general ledger should be determined. In addition, the control account balances should agree with the subsidiary ledger total balance. The agreement of these balances is shown in Illustration E-16 (page E15).

Effects of Special Journals on General Journal

Special journals for sales, purchases, and cash substantially reduce the number of entries that are made in the general journal. **Only transactions that cannot be entered in a special journal are recorded in the general journal.** For example, the general journal may be used to record such transactions as granting of credit to a customer for a sales return or allowance, granting of credit from a supplier for purchases returned, acceptance of a note receivable from a customer, and purchase of equipment by issuing a note payable. Also, correcting, adjusting, and closing entries are made in the general journal.

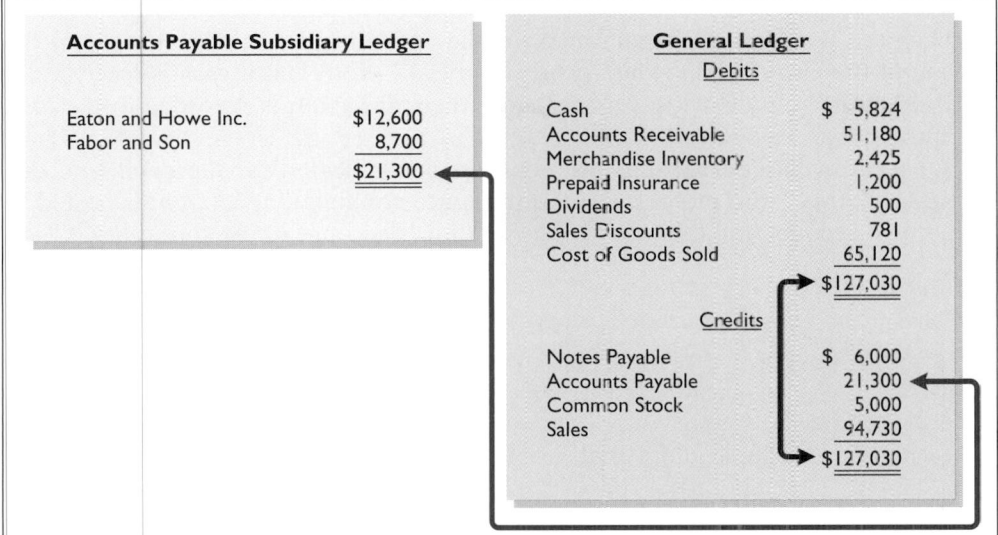

Illustration E-16
Proving the ledgers after postings from the sales, cash receipts, purchases, and cash payments journals

Accounts Payable Subsidiary Ledger

Eaton and Howe Inc.	$12,600
Fabor and Son	8,700
	$21,300

General Ledger

Debits	
Cash	$ 5,824
Accounts Receivable	51,180
Merchandise Inventory	2,425
Prepaid Insurance	1,200
Dividends	500
Sales Discounts	781
Cost of Goods Sold	65,120
	$127,030
Credits	
Notes Payable	$ 6,000
Accounts Payable	21,300
Common Stock	5,000
Sales	94,730
	$127,030

The general journal has columns for date, account title and explanation, reference, and debit and credit amounts. When control and subsidiary accounts are not involved, the procedures for journalizing and posting of transactions are the same as those described in earlier chapters. When control and subsidiary accounts are involved, two changes from the earlier procedures are required:

1. In **journalizing**, both the control and the subsidiary accounts must be identified.
2. In **posting**, there must be a **dual posting**: once to the control account and once to the subsidiary account.

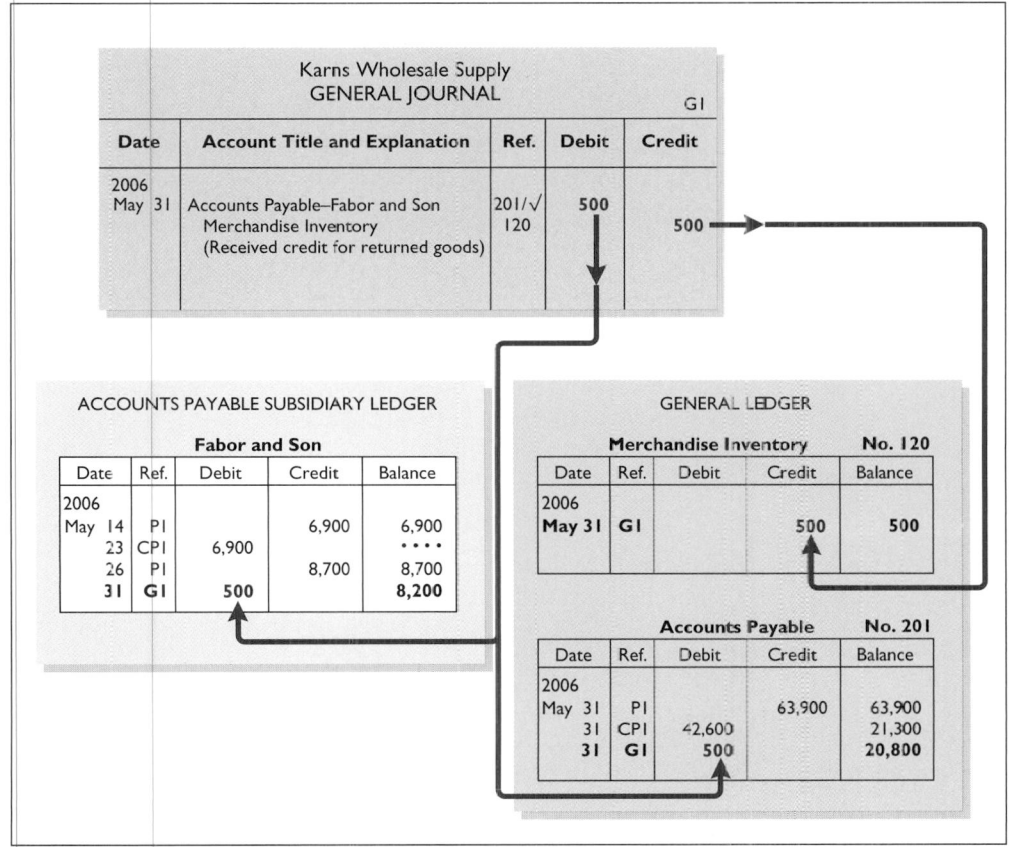

Illustration E-17
Journalizing and posting the general journal

Karns Wholesale Supply
GENERAL JOURNAL — G1

Date	Account Title and Explanation	Ref.	Debit	Credit
2006 May 31	Accounts Payable–Fabor and Son	201/√	500	
	Merchandise Inventory	120		500
	(Received credit for returned goods)			

ACCOUNTS PAYABLE SUBSIDIARY LEDGER

Fabor and Son

Date	Ref.	Debit	Credit	Balance
2006				
May 14	P1		6,900	6,900
23	CP1	6,900		••••
26	P1		8,700	8,700
31	**G1**	**500**		**8,200**

GENERAL LEDGER

Merchandise Inventory — **No. 120**

Date	Ref.	Debit	Credit	Balance
2006				
May 31	**G1**		**500**	**500**

Accounts Payable — **No. 201**

Date	Ref.	Debit	Credit	Balance
2006				
May 31	P1		63,900	63,900
31	CP1	42,600		21,300
31	**G1**	**500**		**20,800**

To illustrate, assume that on May 31, Karns Wholesale Supply returns $500 of merchandise for credit to Fabor and Son. The entry in the general journal and the posting of the entry are shown in Illustration E-17. Note that if cash is received instead of credit granted on this return, then the transaction is recorded in the cash receipts journal.

Observe in the journal that two accounts are indicated for the debit, and two postings ("201/✓") are indicated in the reference column. One amount is posted to the control account and the other to the creditor's account in the subsidiary ledger.

BEFORE YOU GO ON...

Review It

1. What types of special journals are frequently used to record transactions? Why are special journals used?
2. Explain how transactions recorded in the sales journal and the cash receipts journal are posted.
3. Indicate the types of transactions that are recorded in the general journal when special journals are used.

DEMONSTRATION PROBLEM

Peachtree

www.wiley.com/college/weygandt

Celine Dion Company uses a six-column cash receipts journal with the following columns: Cash (Dr.), Sales Discounts (Dr.), Accounts Receivable (Cr.), Sales (Cr.), Other Accounts (Cr.), and Cost of Goods Sold (Dr.) and Merchandise Inventory (Cr.). Cash receipts transactions for the month of July 2006 are as follows.

July	3	Cash sales total $5,800 (cost, $3,480).
	5	A check for $6,370 is received from Jeltz Company in payment of an invoice dated June 26 for $6,500, terms 2/10, n/30.
	9	An additional investment of $5,000 in cash is made in the business by stockholders.
	10	Cash sales total $12,519 (cost, $7,511).
	12	A check for $7,275 is received from R. Eliot & Co. in payment of a $7,500 invoice dated July 3, terms 3/10, n/30.
	15	A customer advance of $700 cash is received for future sales.
	20	Cash sales total $15,472 (cost, $9,283).
	22	A check for $5,880 is received from Beck Company in payment of $6,000 invoice dated July 13, terms 2/10, n/30.
	29	Cash sales total $17,660 (cost, $10,596).
	31	Cash of $200 is received on interest earned for July.

Instructions

(a) Journalize the transactions in the cash receipts journal.

(b) Contrast the posting of the Accounts Receivable and Other Accounts columns.

ACTION PLAN

- Record all cash receipts in the cash receipts journal.
- The "account credited" indicates items posted individually to the subsidiary ledger or general ledger.
- Record cash sales in the cash receipts journal—not in the sales journal.
- The total debits must equal the total credits.

SOLUTION TO DEMONSTRATION PROBLEM

(a)

Celine Dion Company
CASH RECEIPTS JOURNAL — CR1

Date	Account Credited	Ref.	Cash Dr.	Sales Discounts Dr.	Accounts Receivable Cr.	Sales Cr.	Other Accounts Cr.	Cost of Goods Sold Dr. Mdse. Inv. Cr.
2006								
7/3			5,800			5,800		3,480
5	Jeltz Company		6,370	130	6,500			
9	Common Stock		5,000				5,000	
10			12,519			12,519		7,511
12	R. Eliot & Co.		7,275	225	7,500			
15	Unearned Revenue		700				700	
20			15,472			15,472		9,283
22	Beck Company		5,880	120	6,000			
29			17,660			17,660		10,596
31	Interest Revenue		200				200	
			76,876	475	20,000	51,451	5,900	30,870

(b) The Accounts Receivable column total is posted as a credit to Accounts Receivable. The individual amounts are credited to the customers' accounts identified in the Account Credited column, which are maintained in the accounts receivable subsidiary ledger.

The amounts in the Other Accounts column are only posted individually. They are credited to the account titles identified in the Account Credited column.

SUMMARY OF STUDY OBJECTIVES

1. **Describe the nature and purpose of a subsidiary ledger.** A subsidiary ledger is a group of accounts with a common characteristic. It facilitates the recording process by freeing the general ledger from details of individual balances.
2. **Explain how special journals are used in journalizing.** A special journal is used to group similar types of transactions. In a special journal, generally only one line is used to record a complete transaction.
3. **Indicate how a multi-column journal is posted.** In posting a multi-column journal:
   (a) All column totals except for the Other Accounts column are posted once at the end of the month to the account title specified in the column heading.
   (b) The total of the Other Accounts column is not posted. Instead, the individual amounts comprising the total are posted separately to the general ledger accounts specified in the Account Credited (Debited) column.
   (c) The individual amounts in a column posted in total to a control account are posted daily to the subsidiary ledger accounts specified in the Account Credited (Debited) column.

GLOSSARY

Accounts payable (creditors') subsidiary ledger A subsidiary ledger that contains accounts of individual creditors. (p. E1).

Accounts receivable (customers') subsidiary ledger A subsidiary ledger that contains individual customer accounts. (p. E1).

Cash payments journal A special journal used to record all cash paid. (p. E13).

Cash receipts journal A special journal used to record all cash received. (p. E7).

Control account An account in the general ledger that controls a subsidiary ledger. (p. E1).

Purchases journal A special journal used to record all purchases of merchandise on account. (p. E10).

Sales journal A special journal used to record all sales of merchandise on account. (p. E4).

Special journal A journal that is used to record similar types of transactions, such as all credit sales. (p. E4).

Subsidiary ledger A group of accounts with a common characteristic. (p. E1).

SELF-STUDY QUESTIONS

Self-Study/Self-Test

Answers are at the end of the appendix.

(SO 1) **1.** Which of the following is *incorrect* concerning subsidiary ledgers?
  a. The purchases ledger is a common subsidiary ledger for creditor accounts.
  b. The accounts receivable ledger is a subsidiary ledger.
  c. A subsidiary ledger is a group of accounts with a common characteristic.
  d. An advantage of the subsidiary ledger is that it permits a division of labor in posting.

(SO 2) **2.** A sales journal will be used for:

	Credit Sales	Cash Sales	Sales Discounts
a.	no	yes	yes
b.	yes	no	yes
c.	yes	no	no
d.	yes	yes	no

(SO 2) **3.** Which of the following statements is correct?
  a. The sales discount column is included in the cash receipts journal.
  b. The purchases journal records all purchases of merchandise whether for cash or on account.
  c. The cash receipts journal records sales on account.
  d. Merchandise returned by the buyer is recorded by the seller in the purchases journal.

(SO 3) **4.** Which of the following is *incorrect* concerning the posting of the cash receipts journal?
  a. The total of the Other Accounts column is not posted.
  b. All column totals except the total for the Other Accounts column are posted once at the end of the month to the account title(s) specified in the column heading.
  c. The totals of all columns are posted daily to the accounts specified in the column heading.
  d. The individual amounts in a column posted in total to a control account are posted daily to the subsidiary ledger account specified in the Account Credited column.

5. Postings from the purchases journal to the subsidiary ledger are generally made: (SO 3)
  a. yearly.
  b. monthly.
  c. weekly.
  d. daily.

6. Which statement is *incorrect* regarding the general journal? (SO 2)
  a. Only transactions that cannot be entered in a special journal are recorded in the general journal.
  b. Dual postings are always required in the general journal.
  c. The general journal may be used to record acceptance of a note receivable in payment of an account receivable.
  d. Correcting, adjusting, and closing entries are made in the general journal.

7. When special journals are used: (SO 2)
  a. all purchase transactions are recorded in the purchases journal.
  b. all cash received, except from cash sales, is recorded in the cash receipts journal.
  c. all cash disbursements are recorded in the cash payments journal.
  d. a general journal is not necessary.

8. If a customer returns goods for credit, an entry is normally made in the: (SO 2)
  a. cash payments journal.
  b. sales journal.
  c. general journal.
  d. cash receipts journal.

QUESTIONS

1. What are the advantages of using subsidiary ledgers?
2. (a) When are postings normally made to (1) the subsidiary accounts and (2) the general ledger control accounts? (b) Describe the relationship between a control account and a subsidiary ledger.
3. Identify and explain the four special journals discussed in the chapter. List an advantage of using each of these journals rather than using only a general journal.
4. Tom Wetzel Company uses special journals. A sale made on account to R. Janine for $435 was recorded in a sales journal. A few days later, R. Janine returns $70 worth of merchandise for credit. Where should Tom Wetzel Company record the sales return? Why?
5. A $500 purchase of merchandise on account from Brim Company was properly recorded in the purchases journal. When posted, however, the amount recorded in the

subsidiary ledger was $50. How might this error be discovered?

6. Why would special journals used in different businesses not be identical in format? Can you think of a business that would maintain a cash receipts journal but not include a column for accounts receivable?

7. The cash and the accounts receivable columns in the cash receipts journal were mistakenly overadded by $4,000 at the end of the month. (a) Will the customers' ledger agree with the Accounts Receivable control account? (b) Assuming no other errors, will the trial balance totals be equal?

8. One column total of a special journal is posted at month-end to only two general ledger accounts. One of these two accounts is Accounts Receivable. What is the name of this special journal? What is the other general ledger account to which that same month-end total is posted?

9. In what journal would the following transactions be recorded? (Assume that a two-column sales journal and a single-column purchases journal are used.)
   (a) Recording of depreciation expense for the year.
   (b) Credit given to a customer for merchandise purchased on credit and returned.
   (c) Sales of merchandise for cash.
   (d) Sales of merchandise on account.
   (e) Collection of cash on account from a customer.
   (f) Purchase of office supplies on account.

10. In what journal would the following transactions be recorded? (Assume that a two-column sales journal and a single-column purchases journal are used.)
   (a) Cash received from signing a note payable.
   (b) Investment of cash by the owner of the business.
   (c) Closing of the expense accounts at the end of the year.
   (d) Purchase of merchandise on account.
   (e) Credit received for merchandise purchased and returned to supplier.
   (f) Payment of cash on account due a supplier.

11. What transactions might be included in a multiple-column purchases journal that would not be included in a single-column purchases journal?

12. Give an example of a transaction in the general journal that causes an entry to be posted twice (i.e., to two accounts), one in the general ledger, the other in the subsidiary ledger. Does this affect the debit/credit equality of the general ledger?

13. Give some examples of appropriate general journal transactions for an organization using special journals.

BRIEF EXERCISES

Identify subsidiary ledger balances. (SO 1)

BEE-1 Presented below is information related to Holloway Company for its first month of operations. Identify the balances that appear in the accounts receivable subsidiary ledger and the accounts receivable balance that appears in the general ledger at the end of January.

Credit Sales				Cash Collections		
Jan. 7	Duffy Co.	$8,000		Jan. 17	Duffy Co.	$7,000
15	Hanson Co.	6,000		24	Hanson Co.	4,000
23	Lewis Co.	9,000		29	Lewis Co.	9,000

Identify subsidiary ledger accounts. (SO 1)

BEE-2 Identify in what ledger (general or subsidiary) each of the following accounts is shown.

1. Rent Expense
2. Accounts Receivable—Char
3. Notes Payable
4. Accounts Payable—Thebeau

Identify special journals. (SO 2)

BEE-3 Identify the journal in which each of the following transactions is recorded.

1. Cash sales
2. Payment of dividends
3. Cash purchase of land
4. Credit sales
5. Purchase of merchandise on account
6. Receipt of cash for services performed

Identify entries to cash receipts journal. (SO 2)

BEE-4 Indicate whether each of the following debits and credits is included in the cash receipts journal. (Use "Yes" or "No" to answer this question.)

1. Debit to Sales
2. Credit to Merchandise Inventory
3. Credit to Accounts Receivable
4. Debit to Accounts Payable

Indicate postings to cash receipts journal. (SO 3)

BEE-5 Henning Computer Components Inc. uses a multi-column cash receipts journal. Indicate which column(s) is/are posted only in total, only daily, or both in total and daily.

1. Accounts Receivable
2. Sales Discounts
3. Cash
4. Other Accounts

Identify transactions for special journals.
(SO 2)

BEE-6 Hitache Co. uses special journals and a general journal. Identify the journal in which each of the following transactions is recorded.

(a) Purchased equipment on account.
(b) Purchased merchandise on account.
(c) Paid utility expense in cash.
(d) Sold merchandise on account.

Identify transactions for special journals.
(SO 2)

BEE-7 Identify the special journal(s) in which the following column headings appear.

1. Sales Discounts Dr.
2. Accounts Receivable Cr.
3. Cash Dr.
4. Sales Cr.
5. Merchandise Inventory Dr.

EXERCISES

Determine control account balances, and explain posting of special journals.
(SO 1, 2)

EE-1 Maureen Company uses both special journals and a general journal as described in this chapter. On June 30, after all monthly postings had been completed, the Accounts Receivable control account in the general ledger had a debit balance of $320,000; the Accounts Payable control account had a credit balance of $87,000.

The July transactions recorded in the special journals are summarized below. No entries affecting accounts receivable and accounts payable were recorded in the general journal for July.

Sales journal	Total sales $161,400
Purchases journal	Total purchases $56,400
Cash receipts journal	Accounts receivable column total $141,000
Cash payments journal	Accounts payable column total $47,500

Instructions

(a) What is the balance of the Accounts Receivable control account after the monthly postings on July 31?
(b) What is the balance of the Accounts Payable control account after the monthly postings on July 31?
(c) To what account(s) is the column total of $161,400 in the sales journal posted?
(d) To what account(s) is the accounts receivable column total of $141,000 in the cash receipts journal posted?

Explain postings to subsidiary ledger.
(SO 1)

EE-2 Presented below is the subsidiary accounts receivable account of Nathan Ross.

Date	Ref.	Debit	Credit	Balance
2006				
Sept. 2	S31	61,000		61,000
9	G4		14,000	47,000
27	CR8		47,000	—

Instructions

Write a memo to Barb Murphy that explains each transaction.

Post various journals to control and subsidiary accounts.
(SO 1, 2)

EE-3 On September 1 the balance of the Accounts Receivable control account in the general ledger of Welter Company was $11,960. The customers' subsidiary ledger contained account balances as follows: Jana $2,440, Kingston $2,640, Cavanaugh $2,060, Bickford $4,820. At the end of September the various journals contained the following information.

Sales journal: Sales to Bickford $800; to Jana $1,260; to Iman $1,030; to Cavanaugh $1,100.
Cash receipts journal: Cash received from Cavanaugh $1,310; from Bickford $2,300; from Iman $380; from Kingston $1,800; from Jana $1,240.
General journal: An allowance is granted to Bickford $220.

Instructions

(a) Set up control and subsidiary accounts and enter the beginning balances. Do not construct the journals.
(b) Post the various journals. Post the items as individual items or as totals, whichever would be the appropriate procedure. (No sales discounts given.)
(c) Prepare a list of customers and prove the agreement of the controlling account with the subsidiary ledger at September 30, 2006.

Record transactions in sales and purchases journals.
(SO 1, 2)

EE-4 Sing Tao Company uses special journals and a general journal. The following transactions occurred during September 2006.

Sept. 2 Sold merchandise on account to T. Mephisto, invoice no. 101, $520, terms n/30. The cost of the merchandise sold was $300.
10 Purchased merchandise on account from L. Fantasia $600, terms 2/10, n/30.
12 Purchased office equipment on account from R. Press $6,500.
21 Sold merchandise on account to P. Shinhan, invoice no. 102 for $800, terms 2/10, n/30. The cost of the merchandise sold was $480.
25 Purchased merchandise on account from W. Manion $810, terms n/30.
27 Sold merchandise to S. Miller for $700 cash. The cost of the merchandise sold was $400.

Instructions

(a) Draw a sales journal (see Illustration E-6) and a single-column purchases journal (see Illustration E-11). (Use page 1 for each journal.)
(b) Record the transaction(s) for September that should be journalized in the sales journal and the purchases journal.

Record transactions in cash receipts and cash payments journals.
(SO 1, 2)

EE-5 Svenska Co. uses special journals and a general journal. The following transactions occurred during May 2006.

May 1 I. Svenska invested $60,000 cash in the business in exchange for common stock.
2 Sold merchandise to B. Sherrick for $6,300 cash. The cost of the merchandise sold was $4,200.
3 Purchased merchandise for $8,200 from J. Rome using check no. 101.
14 Paid salary to H. Potter $700 by issuing check no. 102.
16 Sold merchandise on account to K. Denmark for $900, terms n/30. The cost of the merchandise sold was $630.
22 A check of $9,000 is received from M. Irish in full for invoice 101; no discount given.

Instructions

(a) Draw a multiple-column cash receipts journal (see Illustration E-8) and a multiple-column cash payments journal (see Illustration E-15). (Use page 1 for each journal.)
(b) Record the transaction(s) for May that should be journalized in the cash receipts journal and cash payments journal.

Explain journalizing in cash journals.
(SO 2)

EE-6 Dodi Company uses the columnar cash journals illustrated in the textbook. In April, the following selected cash transactions occurred.

1. Made a refund to a customer for the return of damaged goods.
2. Received collection from customer within the 3% discount period.
3. Purchased merchandise for cash.
4. Paid a creditor within the 3% discount period.
5. Received collection from customer after the 3% discount period had expired.
6. Paid freight on merchandise purchased.
7. Paid cash for office equipment.
8. Received cash refund from supplier for merchandise returned.
9. Paid cash dividends to stockholders.
10. Made cash sales.

Instructions
Indicate **(a)** the journal, and **(b)** the columns in the journal that should be used in recording each transaction.

Journalize transactions in general journal and post.
(SO 1, 2)

EE-7 Argentina Company has the following selected transactions during March.

Mar. 2 Purchased equipment costing $7,400 from Chile Company on account.
5 Received credit memorandum for $410 from Lyden Company for merchandise damaged in shipment to Argentina.
7 Issued a credit memorandum for $400 to Higley Company for merchandise the customer returned. The returned merchandise had a cost of $260.

Argentina Company uses a one-column purchases journal, a sales journal, the columnar cash journals used in the text, and a general journal.

Instructions
(a) Journalize the transactions in the general journal.
(b) In a brief memo to the president of Argentina Company, explain the postings to the control and subsidiary accounts from each type of journal.

Indicate journalizing in special journals.
(SO 2)

EE-8 Below are some typical transactions incurred by Peru Company.

1. Payment of creditors on account.
2. Return of merchandise sold for credit.
3. Collection on account from customers.
4. Sale of land for cash.
5. Sale of merchandise on account.
6. Sale of merchandise for cash.
7. Received credit for merchandise purchased on credit.
8. Sales discount taken on goods sold.
9. Payment of employee wages.
10. Payment of cash dividend to stockholders.
11. Depreciation on building.
12. Purchase of office supplies for cash.
13. Purchase of merchandise on account.

Instructions
For each transaction, indicate whether it would normally be recorded in a cash receipts journal, cash payments journal, sales journal, single-column purchases journal, or general journal.

Explain posting to control account and subsidiary ledger.
(SO 1, 3)

EE-9 The general ledger of Bolivia Company contained the following Accounts Payable control account (in T-account form). Also shown is the related subsidiary ledger.

GENERAL LEDGER

Accounts Payable

Feb. 15	General journal	1,400	Feb. 1	Balance	26,025
28	?	?	5	General journal	265
			11	General journal	550
			28	Purchases	13,900
			Feb. 28	Balance	10,200

ACCOUNTS PAYABLE LEDGER

Perez

	Feb. 28	Bal. 4,600

Fernando

	Feb. 28	Bal. ?

Lucia

	Feb. 28	Bal. 2,300

Instructions
(a) Indicate the missing posting reference and amount in the control account, and the missing ending balance in the subsidiary ledger.
(b) Indicate the amounts in the control account that were dual-posted (i.e., posted to the control account and the subsidiary accounts).

EE-10 Selected accounts from the ledgers of Rockford Company at July 31 showed the following.

Prepare purchases and general journals.
(SO 1, 2)

GENERAL LEDGER

Store Equipment — No. 153

Date	Explanation	Ref.	Debit	Credit	Balance
July 1		G1	3,900		3,900

Merchandise Inventory — No. 120

Date	Explanation	Ref.	Debit	Credit	Balance
July 15		G1	400		400
18		G1		100	300
25		G1		200	100
31		P1	8,800		8,900

Accounts Payable — No. 201

Date	Explanation	Ref.	Debit	Credit	Balance
July 1		G1		3,900	3,900
15		G1		400	4,300
18		G1	100		4,200
25		G1	200		4,000
31		P1		8,800	12,800

ACCOUNTS PAYABLE LEDGER

Adam Equipment Co.

Date	Explanation	Ref.	Debit	Credit	Balance
July 1		G1		3,900	3,900

Dan Co.

Date	Explanation	Ref.	Debit	Credit	Balance
July 14		P1		1,100	1,100
25		G1	200		900

Brian Co.

Date	Explanation	Ref.	Debit	Credit	Balance
July 3		P1		2,400	2,400
20		P1		700	3,100

Erik Co.

Date	Explanation	Ref.	Debit	Credit	Balance
July 12		P1		500	500
21		P1		600	1,100

Colleen Corp

Date	Explanation	Ref.	Debit	Credit	Balance
July 17		P1		1,400	1,400
18		G1	100		1,300
29		P1		2,100	3,400

Grace Inc.

Date	Explanation	Ref.	Debit	Credit	Balance
July 15		G1		400	400

Instructions

From the data prepare:

(a) the single-column purchases journal for July.
(b) the general journal entries for July.

EE-11 Canada Products uses both special journals and a general journal as described in this chapter. Canada also posts customers' accounts in the accounts receivable subsidiary ledger. The postings for the most recent month are included in the subsidiary T accounts below.

Determine correct posting amount to control account.
(SO 3)

Brynn

	Debit	Credit
Bal.	340	250
	200	

Marcus

	Debit	Credit
Bal.	150	150
	290	

Carol

	Debit	Credit
Bal.	–0–	145
	145	

Paul

	Debit	Credit
Bal.	120	120
	190	
	150	

Instructions

Determine the correct amount of the end-of-month posting from the sales journal to the Accounts Receivable control account.

PROBLEMS: SET A

Journalize transactions in cash receipts journal; post to control account and subsidiary ledger.
(SO 1, 2, 3)

Peachtree

PE-1A Lewis Company's chart of accounts includes the following selected accounts.

101 Cash	401 Sales
112 Accounts Receivable	414 Sales Discounts
120 Merchandise Inventory	505 Cost of Goods Sold
311 Common Stock	

On June 1 the accounts receivable ledger of Lewis Company showed the following balances: Bernard & Son $3,500, Farley Co. $1,900, Grinnell Bros. $1,600, and Maquoketa Co. $1,300. The June transactions involving the receipt of cash were as follows.

June 1 Stockholders invested $10,000 additional cash in the business, for common stock.
3 Received check in full from Maquoketa Co. less 2% cash discount.
6 Received check in full from Farley Co. less 2% cash discount.
7 Made cash sales of merchandise totaling $6,135. The cost of the merchandise sold was $4,090.
9 Received check in full from Bernard & Son less 2% cash discount.
11 Received cash refund from a supplier for damaged merchandise $320.
15 Made cash sales of merchandise totaling $4,800. The cost of the merchandise sold was $3,200.
20 Received check in full from Grinnell Bros. $1,600.

Instructions

(a) Balancing totals $29,555

(a) Journalize the transactions above in a six-column cash receipts journal with columns for Cash Dr., Sales Discounts Dr., Accounts Receivable Cr., Sales Cr., Other Accounts Cr., and Cost of Goods Sold Dr./Merchandise Inventory Cr. Foot and crossfoot the journal.
(b) Insert the beginning balances in the Accounts Receivable control and subsidiary accounts, and post the June transactions to these accounts.
(c) Prove the agreement of the control account and subsidiary account balances.

Journalize transactions in cash payments journal; post to the general and subsidiary ledgers.
(SO 1, 2, 3)

PE-2A Congo Company's chart of accounts includes the following selected accounts.

101 Cash	157 Equipment
120 Merchandise Inventory	201 Accounts Payable
130 Prepaid Insurance	332 Dividends

On November 1 the accounts payable ledger of Congo Company showed the following balances: A. Hess & Co. $4,500, C. Pillsbury $2,350, G. Saeman $1,000, and Wex Bros. $1,900. The November transactions involving the payment of cash were as follows.

Nov. 1 Purchased merchandise, check no. 11, $1,140.
3 Purchased store equipment, check no. 12, $1,700.
5 Paid Wex Bros. balance due of $1,900, less 1% discount, check no. 13, $1,881.
11 Purchased merchandise, check no. 14, $2,000.
15 Paid G. Saeman balance due of $1,000, less 3% discount, check no. 15, $970.
16 Paid a cash dividend in the amount of $500, check no. 16.
19 Paid C. Pillsbury in full for invoice no. 1245, $1,150 less 2% discount, check no. 17, $1,127.
25 Paid premium due on one-year insurance policy, check no. 18, $3,000.
30 Paid A. Hess & Co. in full for invoice no. 832, $2,800, check no. 19.

Instructions

(a) Balancing totals $15,190

(a) Journalize the transactions above in a four-column cash payments journal with columns for Other Accounts Dr., Accounts Payable Dr., Merchandise Inventory Cr., and Cash Cr. Foot and crossfoot the journal.
(b) Insert the beginning balances in the Accounts Payable control and subsidiary accounts, and post the November transactions to these accounts.
(c) Prove the agreement of the control account and the subsidiary account balances.

PE-3A The chart of accounts of Dutch Company includes the following selected accounts.

Journalize transactions in multi-column purchases journal; post to the general and subsidiary ledgers.

(SO 1, 2, 3)

112 Accounts Receivable	401 Sales
120 Merchandise Inventory	412 Sales Returns and Allowances
126 Supplies	505 Cost of Goods Sold
157 Equipment	610 Advertising Expense
201 Accounts Payable	

In May the following selected transactions were completed. All purchases and sales were on account except as indicated. The cost of all merchandise sold was 65% of the sales price.

May 2 Purchased merchandise from Van Houk Company $9,500.
3 Received freight bill from Ruden Freight on Van Houk purchase $360.
5 Sales were made to Ellie Company $1,980, Cornelis Bros. $2,700, and Jan Company $1,500.
8 Purchased merchandise from Tulip Company $8,000 and Zeider Company $8,700.
10 Received credit on merchandise returned to Zeider Company $500.
15 Purchased supplies from Sandvoort Supply $900.
16 Purchased merchandise from Van Houk Company $4,500, and Tulip Company $7,200.
17 Returned supplies to Sandvoort Supply, receiving credit $100. (*Hint*: Credit Supplies.)
18 Received freight bills on May 16 purchases from Ruden Freight $500.
20 Returned merchandise to Van Houk Company receiving credit $300.
23 Made sales to Cornelis Bros. $2,400 and to Jan Company $3,100.
25 Received bill for advertising from Amster Advertising $900.
26 Granted allowance to Jan Company for merchandise damaged in shipment $200.
28 Purchased equipment from Sandvoort Supply $250.

Instructions

(a) Journalize the transactions above in a purchases journal, a sales journal, and a general journal. The purchases journal should have the following column headings: Date, Account Credited (Debited), Ref., Other Accounts Dr., Merchandise Inventory Dr., and Accounts Payable Cr.

(b) Post to both the general and subsidiary ledger accounts. (Assume that all accounts have zero beginning balances.)

(c) Prove the agreement of the control and subsidiary accounts.

(a) Purchases journal—Accounts Payable, Cr. $40,810
Sales journal total $11,680
(c) Accounts Receivable $11,480
Accounts Payable $39,910

PE-4A Selected accounts from the chart of accounts of Jolie Company are shown below.

Journalize transactions in special journals.

(SO 1, 2, 3)

101 Cash	201 Accounts Payable
112 Accounts Receivable	401 Sales
120 Merchandise Inventory	414 Sales Discounts
126 Supplies	505 Cost of Goods Sold
140 Land	610 Advertising Expense
145 Buildings	

The cost of all merchandise sold was 70% of the sales price. During October, Jolie Company completed the following transactions.

Oct. 2 Purchased merchandise on account from Angelina Company $18,500.
4 Sold merchandise on account to Drew Co. $8,700. Invoice no. 204, terms 2/10, n/30.
5 Purchased supplies for cash $80.
7 Made cash sales for the week totaling $9,160.
9 Paid in full the amount owed Angelina Company less a 2% discount.
10 Purchased merchandise on account from Diez Corp. $3,500.
12 Received payment from Drew Co. for invoice no. 204.
13 Issued a debit memorandum to Diez Corp. and returned $210 worth of damaged goods.
14 Made cash sales for the week totaling $8,180.
16 Sold a parcel of land for $27,000 cash, the land's book value.
17 Sold merchandise on account to G. Paltrow & Co. $5,350, invoice no. 205, terms 2/10, n/30.
18 Purchased merchandise for cash $2,125.
21 Made cash sales for the week totaling $8,200.
23 Paid in full the amount owed Diez Corp. for the goods kept (no discount).

25 Purchased supplies on account from Robinson Co. $260.
25 Sold merchandise on account to Hunt Corp. $5,220, invoice no. 206, terms 2/10, n/30.
25 Received payment from G. Paltrow & Co. for invoice no. 205.
26 Purchased for cash a small parcel of land and a building on the land to use as a storage facility. The total cost of $35,000 was allocated $21,000 to the land and $14,000 to the building.
27 Purchased merchandise on account from Kudro Co. $8,500.
28 Made cash sales for the week totaling $8,540.
30 Purchased merchandise on account from Angelina Company $14,000.
30 Paid advertising bill for the month from the *Gazette*, $400.
30 Sold merchandise on account to G. Paltrow & Co. $4,600, invoice no. 207, terms 2/10, n/30.

Jolie Company uses the following journals.

1. Sales journal.
2. Single-column purchases journal.
3. Cash receipts journal with columns for Cash Dr., Sales Discounts Dr., Accounts Receivable Cr., Sales Cr., Other Accounts Cr., and Cost of Goods Sold Dr./Merchandise Inventory Cr.
4. Cash payments journal with columns for Other Accounts Dr., Accounts Payable Dr., Merchandise Inventory Cr., and Cash Cr.
5. General journal.

(b) Sales journal $23,870
Purchases journal $44,500
Cash receipts journal—Cash, Dr. $74,849
Cash payments journal, Cash, Cr. $59,025

Instructions

Use the selected accounts provided to do the following.

(a) Record the October transactions in the appropriate journals.
(b) Foot and crossfoot all special journals.
(c) Show how postings would be made by placing ledger account numbers and check marks as needed in the journals. (Actual posting to ledger accounts is not required.)

Journalize in purchases and cash payments journals; post; prepare a trial balance; prove control to subsidiary; prepare adjusting entries; prepare an adjusted trial balance.

(SO 1, 2, 3)

PE-5A Presented below are the sales and cash receipts journals for Zamtel Co. for its first month of operations.

SALES JOURNAL **S1**

Date	Account Debited	Ref.	Accounts Receivable Dr. Sales Cr.	Cost of Goods Sold Dr. Merchandise Inventory Cr.
Feb. 3	S. Appel		5,500	3,630
9	C. Boyd		6,500	4,290
12	F. Catt		8,000	5,280
26	M. Dogg		6,000	3,960
			26,000	17,160

CASH RECEIPTS JOURNAL **CR1**

Date	Account Credited	Ref.	Cash Dr.	Sales Discounts Dr.	Accounts Receivable Cr.	Sales Cr.	Other Accounts Cr.	Cost of Goods Sold Dr. Merchandise Inventory Cr.
Feb. 1	Common Stock		30,000				30,000	
2			6,500			6,500		4,290
13	S. Appel		5,445	55	5,500			
18	Merchandise Inventory		150				150	
26	C. Boyd		6,500		6,500			
			48,595	55	12,000	6,500	30,150	4,290

In addition, the following transactions have not been journalized for February 2006.

Feb.	2	Purchased merchandise on account from J. Zea for $4,600, terms 2/10, n/30.
	7	Purchased merchandise on account from P. Kneiser for $30,000, terms 1/10, n/30.
	9	Paid cash of $1,250 for purchase of supplies.
	12	Paid $4,508 to J. Zea in payment for $4,600 invoice, less 2% discount.
	15	Purchased equipment for $8,000 cash.
	16	Purchased merchandise on account from J. Lakota $2,400, terms 2/10, n/30.
	17	Paid $29,700 to P. Kneiser in payment of $30,000 invoice, less 1% discount.
	20	Paid a cash dividend of $1,100.
	21	Purchased merchandise on account from G. Reedy for $5,800, terms 1/10, n/30.
	28	Paid $2,400 to J. Lakota in payment of $2,400 invoice.

Instructions

(a) Open the following accounts in the general ledger.

101 Cash	311 Common Stock
112 Accounts Receivable	332 Dividends
120 Merchandise Inventory	401 Sales
126 Supplies	414 Sales Discounts
157 Equipment	505 Cost of Goods Sold
158 Accumulated Depreciation—Equipment	631 Supplies Expense
201 Accounts Payable	711 Depreciation Expense

(b) Journalize the transactions that have not been journalized in a one-column purchases journal and the cash payments journal (see Illustration E-15).

(b) Purchases journal total $42,800
Cash payments journal—Cash, Cr. $46,958

(c) Post to the accounts receivable and accounts payable subsidiary ledgers. Follow the sequence of transactions as shown in the problem.

(d) Post the individual entries and totals to the general ledger.

(e) Prepare a trial balance at February 28, 2006.

(e) Totals $68,300

(f) Determine that the subsidiary ledgers agree with the control accounts in the general ledger.

(g) The following adjustments at the end of February are necessary.

(1) A count of supplies indicates that $300 is still on hand.

(2) Depreciation on equipment for February is $200.

Prepare the adjusting entries and then post the adjusting entries to the general ledger.

(h) Prepare an adjusted trial balance at February 28, 2006.

(h) Totals $68,500

Journalize in special journals; post; prepare a trial balance.

(SO 1, 2, 3)

PE-6A The post-closing trial balance for Bedazzle Co. is as follows.

BEDAZZLE CO.
Post-Closing Trial Balance
December 31, 2006

	Debit	Credit
Cash	$ 41,500	
Accounts Receivable	15,000	
Notes Receivable	45,000	
Merchandise Inventory	23,000	
Equipment	6,450	
Accumulated Depreciation—Equipment		$ 1,500
Accounts Payable		43,000
Common Stock		86,450
	$130,950	$130,950

The subsidiary ledgers contain the following information: (1) accounts receivable—J. Balton $2,500, F. Cone $7,500, T. Dudley $5,000; (2) accounts payable—J. Feeney $10,000, D. Goodman $18,000, and K. Hollis $15,000. The cost of all merchandise sold was 60% of the sales price.

The transactions for January 2007 are as follows.

Jan. 3 Sell merchandise to M. Sanford $4,000, terms 2/10, n/30.
5 Purchase merchandise from E. Westphal $3,000, terms 2/10, n/30.
7 Receive a check from T. Dudley $3,500.
11 Pay freight on merchandise purchased $300.
12 Pay rent of $1,000 for January.
13 Receive payment in full from M. Sanford.
14 Post all entries to the subsidiary ledgers. Issue a credit memo to acknowledge receipt of damaged merchandise of $500 returned by J. Balton.
15 Send K. Hollis a check for $14,850 in full payment of account, discount $150.
17 Purchase merchandise from G. Louis $1,600, terms 2/10, n/30.
18 Pay sales salaries of $2,800 and office salaries $1,500.
20 Give D. Goodman a 60-day note for $18,000 in full payment of account payable.
23 Total cash sales amount to $9,100.
24 Post all entries to the subsidiary ledgers. Sell merchandise on account to F. Cone $7,400, terms 1/10, n/30.
27 Send E. Westphal a check for $950.
29 Receive payment on a note of $40,000 from B. Lemke.
30 Return merchandise of $500 to G. Louis for credit.

Post all journals to the subsidiary ledger.

Instructions

(a) Open general and subsidiary ledger accounts for the following.

101 Cash	311 Common Stock
112 Accounts Receivable	401 Sales
115 Notes Receivable	412 Sales Returns and Allowances
120 Merchandise Inventory	414 Sales Discounts
157 Equipment	505 Cost of Goods Sold
158 Accumulated Depreciation—Equipment	726 Sales Salaries Expense
200 Notes Payable	727 Office Salaries Expense
201 Accounts Payable	729 Rent Expense

(b) Sales journal $11,400
Purchases journal $4,600
Cash receipts journal (balancing) $56,600
Cash payments journal (balancing) $21,550
(d) Totals $139,600

(b) Record the January transactions in a sales journal, a single-column purchases journal, a cash receipts journal (see Illustration E-8), a cash payments journal (see Illustration E-15), and a general journal.

(c) Post the appropriate amounts to the general ledger.

(d) Prepare a trial balance at January 31, 2007.

(e) Determine whether the subsidiary ledgers agree with controlling accounts in the general ledger.

PROBLEMS: SET B

Journalize transactions in cash receipts journal; post to control account and subsidiary ledger.
(SO 1, 2, 3)

PE-1B Iqbal Company's chart of accounts includes the following selected accounts.

101 Cash	401 Sales
112 Accounts Receivable	414 Sales Discounts
120 Merchandise Inventory	505 Cost of Goods Sold
311 Common Stock	

On April 1 the accounts receivable ledger of Iqbal Company showed the following balances: Naper $1,550, Chelsea $1,200, Finlandia Co. $2,900, and Baez $1,400. The April transactions involving the receipt of cash were as follows.

Apr. 1 Stockholders invested $7,200 additional cash in the business, for common stock.
4 Received check for payment of account from Baez less 2% cash discount.
5 Received check for $620 in payment of invoice no. 307 from Finlandia Co.
8 Made cash sales of merchandise totaling $7,245. The cost of the merchandise sold was $4,347.
10 Received check for $600 in payment of invoice no. 309 from Naper.

11 Received cash refund from a supplier for damaged merchandise $740.
23 Received check for $1,500 in payment of invoice no. 310 from Finlandia Co.
29 Received check for payment of account from Chelsea.

Instructions

(a) Journalize the transactions above in a six-column cash receipts journal with columns for Cash Dr., Sales Discounts Dr., Accounts Receivable Cr., Sales Cr., Other Accounts Cr., and Cost of Goods Sold Dr./Merchandise Inventory Cr. Foot and crossfoot the journal.

(a) Balancing totals $20,505

(b) Insert the beginning balances in the Accounts Receivable control and subsidiary accounts, and post the April transactions to these accounts.

(c) Prove the agreement of the control account and subsidiary account balances.

(c) Accounts Receivable $1,730

Journalize transactions in cash payments journal; post to control account and subsidiary ledgers.

(SO 1, 2, 3)

PE-2B Mann Company's chart of accounts includes the following selected accounts.

101 Cash	201 Accounts Payable
120 Merchandise Inventory	332 Dividends
130 Prepaid Insurance	505 Cost of Goods Sold
157 Equipment	

On October 1 the accounts payable ledger of Mann Company showed the following balances: Bovary Company $1,700, Magic Co. $2,500, Pyron Co. $1,800, and Tess Company $3,700. The October transactions involving the payment of cash were as follows.

Oct. 1 Purchased merchandise, check no. 63, $300.
3 Purchased equipment, check no. 64, $800.
5 Paid Bovary Company balance due of $1,700, less 2% discount, check no. 65, $1,666.
10 Purchased merchandise, check no. 66, $2,250.
15 Paid Pyron Co. balance due of $1,800, check no. 67.
16 Paid cash dividend of $400, check no. 68.
19 Paid Magic Co. in full for invoice no. 610, $1,600 less 2% cash discount, check no. 69, $1,568.
29 Paid Tess Company in full for invoice no. 264, $3,100, check no. 70.

Instructions

(a) Journalize the transactions above in a four-column cash payments journal with columns for Other Accounts Dr., Accounts Payable Dr., Merchandise Inventory Cr., and Cash Cr. Foot and crossfoot the journal.

(a) Balancing totals $11,950

(b) Insert the beginning balances in the Accounts Payable control and subsidiary accounts, and post the October transactions to these accounts.

(c) Prove the agreement of the control account and the subsidiary account balances.

(c) Accounts Payable $1,500

Journalize transactions in multi-column purchases journal; post to the general and subsidiary ledgers.

(SO 1, 2, 3)

PE-3B The chart of accounts of Odeon Company includes the following selected accounts.

112 Accounts Receivable	401 Sales
120 Merchandise Inventory	412 Sales Returns and Allowances
126 Supplies	505 Cost of Goods Sold
157 Equipment	610 Advertising Expense
201 Accounts Payable	

In July the following selected transactions were completed. All purchases and sales were on account. The cost of all merchandise sold was 70% of the sales price.

July 1 Purchased merchandise from Gucci Company $5,000.
2 Received freight bill from Wayward Shipping on Gucci purchase $400.
3 Made sales to Marion Company $1,300, and to Wayne Bros. $1,500.
5 Purchased merchandise from Lee Company $3,200.
8 Received credit on merchandise returned to Lee Company $300.
13 Purchased store supplies from Boyd Supply $720.
15 Purchased merchandise from Gucci Company $3,600 and from Anton Company $3,300.
16 Made sales to Rowen Company $3,450 and to Wayne Bros. $1,570.
18 Received bill for advertising from Lynda Advertisements $600.
21 Sales were made to Marion Company $310 and to Haddad Company $2,300.
22 Granted allowance to Marion Company for merchandise damaged in shipment $40.
24 Purchased merchandise from Lee Company $3,000.
26 Purchased equipment from Boyd Supply $600.
28 Received freight bill from Wayward Shipping on Lee purchase of July 24, $380.
30 Sales were made to Rowen Company $5,600.

(a) Purchases journal—
Accounts Payable
$20,800
Sales journal $16,030
(c) Accounts Receivable
$15,990
Accounts Payable
$20,500

Instructions

(a) Journalize the transactions above in a purchases journal, a sales journal, and a general journal. The purchases journal should have the following column headings: Date, Account Credited (Debited), Ref., Other Accounts Dr., Merchandise Inventory Dr., and Accounts Payable Cr.
(b) Post to both the general and subsidiary ledger accounts. (Assume that all accounts have zero beginning balances.)
(c) Prove the agreement of the control and subsidiary accounts.

Journalize transactions in special journals.
(SO 1, 2, 3)

PE-4B Selected accounts from the chart of accounts of Alpine Company are shown below.

101 Cash	401 Sales
112 Accounts Receivable	412 Sales Returns and Allowances
120 Merchandise Inventory	414 Sales Discounts
126 Supplies	505 Cost of Goods Sold
157 Equipment	726 Salaries Expense
201 Accounts Payable	

The cost of all merchandise sold was 60% of the sales price. During January, Alpine completed the following transactions.

Jan.	3	Purchased merchandise on account from Vanessa Co. $12,000.
	4	Purchased supplies for cash $80.
	4	Sold merchandise on account to Niki $7,250, invoice no. 371, terms 1/10, n/30.
	5	Issued a debit memorandum to Vanessa Co. and returned $300 worth of damaged goods.
	6	Made cash sales for the week totaling $3,150.
	8	Purchased merchandise on account from Marti Co. $4,500.
	9	Sold merchandise on account to Connor Corp. $6,400, invoice no. 372, terms 1/10, n/30.
	11	Purchased merchandise on account from Betz Co. $3,700.
	13	Paid in full Vanessa Co. on account less a 2% discount.
	13	Made cash sales for the week totaling $6,260.
	15	Received payment from Connor Corp. for invoice no. 372.
	15	Paid semi-monthly salaries of $14,300 to employees.
	17	Received payment from Niki for invoice no. 371.
	17	Sold merchandise on account to Andrews Co. $1,200, invoice no. 373, terms 1/10, n/30.
	19	Purchased equipment on account from Murphy Corp. $5,500.
	20	Cash sales for the week totaled $3,200.
	20	Paid in full Marti Co. on account less a 2% discount.
	23	Purchased merchandise on account from Vanessa Co. $7,800.
	24	Purchased merchandise on account from Forgetta Corp. $5,100.
	27	Made cash sales for the week totaling $3,730.
	30	Received payment from Andrews Co. for invoice no. 373.
	31	Paid semi-monthly salaries of $13,200 to employees.
	31	Sold merchandise on account to Niki $9,330, invoice no. 374, terms 1/10, n/30.

Anton Company uses the following journals.

1. Sales journal.
2. Single-column purchases journal.
3. Cash receipts journal with columns for Cash Dr., Sales Discounts Dr., Accounts Receivable Cr., Sales Cr., Other Accounts Cr., and Cost of Goods Sold Dr./Merchandise Inventory Cr.
4. Cash payments journal with columns for Other Accounts Dr., Accounts Payable Dr., Merchandise Inventory Cr., and Cash Cr.
5. General journal.

(a) Sales journal $24,180
Purchases journal $33,100
Cash receipts journal
balancing total $31,190
Cash payments journal
balancing total $43,780

Instructions

Use the selected accounts provided to do the following.
(a) Record the January transactions in the appropriate journal noted.
(b) Foot and crossfoot all special journals.
(c) Show how postings would be made by placing ledger account numbers and checkmarks as needed in the journals. (Actual posting to ledger accounts is not required.)

Journalize in sales and cash receipts journals; post; prepare a trial balance; prove control to subsidiary; prepare adjusting entries; prepare an adjusted trial balance.

(SO 1, 2, 3)

PE-5B Presented below are the purchases and cash payments journals for Scott Co. for its first month of operations.

PURCHASES JOURNAL P1

Date	Account Credited	Ref.	Merchandise Inventory Dr. Accounts Payable Cr.
July 4	G. Bashful		6,800
5	A. Doc		8,100
11	J. Happy		3,920
13	C. Sleepy		15,300
20	M. Sneezy		7,900
			42,020

CASH PAYMENTS JOURNAL CP1

Date	Account Debited	Ref.	Other Accounts Dr.	Accounts Payable Dr.	Merchandise Inventory Cr.	Cash Cr.
July 4	Store Supplies		600			600
10	A. Doc			8,100	81	8,019
11	Prepaid Rent		6,000			6,000
15	G. Bashful			6,800		6,800
19	Dividends		2,500			2,500
21	C. Sleepy			15,300	153	15,147
			9,100	30,200	234	39,066

In addition, the following transactions have not been journalized for July. The cost of all merchandise sold was 65% of the sales price.

July 1	The founder, D. Scott, invests $80,000 in cash in exchange for common stock.
6	Sell merchandise on account to Dopey Co. $6,200 terms 1/10, n/30.
7	Make cash sales totaling $4,000.
8	Sell merchandise on account to S. Beauty $3,600, terms 1/10, n/30.
10	Sell merchandise on account to W. Queen $4,900, terms 1/10, n/30.
13	Receive payment in full from S. Beauty.
16	Receive payment in full from W. Queen.
20	Receive payment in full from Dopey Co.
21	Sell merchandise on account to H. Prince $4,000, terms 1/10, n/30.
29	Returned damaged goods to G. Bashful and received cash refund of $420.

Instructions

(a) Open the following accounts in the general ledger.

101 Cash	332 Dividends
112 Accounts Receivable	401 Sales
120 Merchandise Inventory	414 Sales Discounts
127 Store Supplies	505 Cost of Goods Sold
131 Prepaid Rent	631 Supplies Expense
201 Accounts Payable	729 Rent Expense
311 Common Stock	

(b) Journalize the transactions that have not been journalized in the sales journal, the cash receipts journal (see Illustration E-8), and the general journal.

(c) Post to the accounts receivable and accounts payable subsidiary ledgers. Follow the sequence of transactions as shown in the problem.

(d) Post the individual entries and totals to the general ledger.

(e) Prepare a trial balance at July 31, 2006.

(f) Determine whether the subsidiary ledgers agree with the control accounts in the general ledger.

(b) Sales journal total $18,700
Cash receipts journal balancing totals $99,120

(e) Totals $114,520

(f) Accounts Receivable $4,000
Accounts Payable $11,820

(g) The following adjustments at the end of July are necessary.
(1) A count of supplies indicates that $140 is still on hand.
(2) Recognize rent expense for July, $500.
Prepare the necessary entries in the general journal. Post the entries to the general ledger.

(h) Totals $114,520

(h) Prepare an adjusted trial balance at July 31, 2006.

COMPREHENSIVE PROBLEM: APPENDIX E AND CHAPTERS 3 TO 7

Raymond Company has the following opening account balances in its general and subsidiary ledgers on January 1 and uses the periodic inventory system. All accounts have normal debit and credit balances.

General Ledger

Account Number	Account Title	January 1 Opening Balance
101	Cash	$33,750
112	Accounts Receivable	13,000
115	Notes Receivable	39,000
120	Merchandise Inventory	20,000
125	Office Supplies	1,000
130	Prepaid Insurance	2,000
157	Equipment	6,450
158	Accumulated Depreciation	1,500
201	Accounts Payable	35,000
311	Common Stock	70,000
320	Retained Earnings	8,700

Accounts Receivable Subsidiary Ledger

Customer	January 1 Opening Balance
R. Draves	$1,500
B. Jacovetti	7,500
S. Kysely	4,000

Accounts Payable Subsidiary Ledger

Creditor	January 1 Opening Balance
S. Liazuk	$ 9,000
R. Mikush	15,000
D. Nguyen	11,000

The following transactions occurred in January.

Jan. 3 Sell merchandise on credit to B. Soto $3,100, invoice no. 510, and J. Ebel $1,800, invoice no. 511.
5 Purchase merchandise from S. Welz $3,000 and D. Laux $2,700.
7 Receive checks for $4,000 from S. Kysely and $2,000 from B. Jacovetti.
8 Pay freight on merchandise purchased $180.
9 Send checks to S. Liazuk for $9,000 and D. Nguyen for $11,000.
9 Issue credit memo for $300 to J. Ebel for merchandise returned.
10 Summary cash sales total $15,500.
11 Sell merchandise on credit to R. Draves for $1,900, invoice no. 512, and to S. Kysely $900, invoice no. 513.
Post all entries to the subsidiary ledgers.
12 Pay rent of $1,000 for January.
13 Receive payment in full from B. Soto and J. Ebel.
15 Pay cash dividend in amount of $800.
16 Purchase merchandise from D. Nguyen for $15,000, from S. Liazuk for $13,900, and from S. Welz for $1,500.
17 Pay $400 cash for office supplies.
18 Return $200 of merchandise to S. Liazuk and receive credit.
20 Summary cash sales total $17,500.
21 Issue $15,000 note to R. Mikush in payment of balance due.
21 Receive payment in full from S. Kysely.
Post all entries to the subsidiary ledgers.

22 Sell merchandise on credit to B. Soto for $1,700, invoice no. 514, and to R. Draves for $800, invoice no. 515.
23 Send checks to D. Nguyen and S. Liazuk in full payment.
25 Sell merchandise on credit to B. Jacovetti for $3,500, invoice no. 516, and to J. Ebel for $6,100, invoice no. 517.
27 Purchase merchandise from D. Nguyen for $14,500, from D. Laux for $1,200, and from S. Welz for $2,800.
28 Pay $200 cash for office supplies.
31 Summary cash sales total $19,920.
31 Pay sales salaries of $4,300 and office salaries of $2,600.

Instructions

(a) Record the January transactions in the appropriate journal—sales, purchases, cash receipts, cash payments, and general.

(b) Post the journals to the general and subsidiary ledgers. New accounts should be added and numbered in an orderly fashion as needed.

(c) Prepare a trial balance at January 31, 2006, using a work sheet. Complete the work sheet using the following additional information.
- **(1)** Office supplies at January 31 total $700.
- **(2)** Insurance coverage expires on October 31, 2006.
- **(3)** Annual depreciation on the equipment is $1,500.
- **(4)** Interest of $30 has accrued on the note payable.
- **(5)** Merchandise inventory at January 31 is $16,000.

(c) Trial balance totals $193,820; Adj. T/B totals $193,975

(d) Prepare a multiple-step income statement and a retained earnings statement for January and a classified balance sheet at the end of January.

(d) Net income $4,685 Total assets $123,315

(e) Prepare and post the adjusting and closing entries.

(f) Prepare a post-closing trial balance, and determine whether the subsidiary ledgers agree with the control accounts in the general ledger.

(f) Post-closing T/B totals $124,940

BROADENING YOUR PERSPECTIVE

Financial Reporting and Analysis

FINANCIAL REPORTING PROBLEM—Mini Practice Set

BYPE-1 (The working papers that accompany this textbook are needed in order to work this mini practice set.)

Cedzo Co. uses a perpetual inventory system and both an accounts receivable and an accounts payable subsidiary ledger. Balances related to both the general ledger and the subsidiary ledger for Cedzo are indicated in the working papers. Presented below are a series of transactions for Cedzo Co. for the month of January. Credit sales terms are 2/10, n/30. The cost of all merchandise sold was 60% of the sales price.

Jan. 3 Sell merchandise on credit to B. Stahre $4,100, invoice no. 510, and to J. Eppler $1,800, invoice no. 511.
5 Purchase merchandise from S. Wong $3,000 and D. Lynch $2,200, terms n/30.
7 Receive checks from S. LaDew $4,000 and B. Garcia $2,000 after discount period has lapsed.
8 Pay freight on merchandise purchased $235.
9 Send checks to S. Jung for $9,000 less 2% cash discount, and to D. Norby for $11,000 less 1% cash discount.
9 Issue credit memo for $300 to J. Eppler for merchandise returned.
10 Summary daily cash sales total $15,500.
11 Sell merchandise on credit to R. Dvorak $1,600, invoice no. 512, and to S. LaDew $900, invoice no. 513.
12 Pay rent of $1,000 for January.
13 Receive payment in full from B. Stahre and J. Eppler less cash discounts.

15 Pay an $800 cash dividend.
15 Post all entries to the subsidiary ledgers.
16 Purchase merchandise from D. Norby $16,000, terms 1/10, n/30; S. Jung $14,200, terms 2/10, n/30; and S. Wong $1,500, terms n/30.
17 Pay $400 cash for office supplies.
18 Return $200 of merchandise to S. Jung and receive credit.
20 Summary daily cash sales total $18,100.
21 Issue $15,000 note to R. Moses in payment of balance due.
21 Receive payment in full from S. LaDew less cash discount.
22 Sell merchandise on credit to S. Stahre $2,700, invoice no. 514, and to R. Dvorak $800, invoice no. 515.
22 Post all entries to the subsidiary ledgers.
23 Send checks to D. Norby and S. Jung in full payment less cash discounts.
25 Sell merchandise on credit to B. Garcia $3,500, invoice no. 516, and to J. Eppler $6,100, invoice no. 517.
27 Purchase merchandise from D. Norby $14,500, terms 1/10, n/30; D. Lynch $1,200, terms n/30; and S. Wong $5,400, terms n/30.
27 Post all entries to the subsidiary ledgers.
28 Pay $200 cash for office supplies.
31 Summary daily cash sales total $21,300.
31 Pay sales salaries $4,300 and office salaries $2,800.

Instructions

(a) Record the January transactions in a sales journal, a single-column purchases journal, a cash receipts journal as shown on page E8, a cash payments journal as shown on page E13, and a two-column general journal.

(b) Post the journals to the general ledger.

(c) Prepare a trial balance at January 31, 2006, in the trial balance columns of the work sheet. Complete the work sheet using the following additional information.

(1) Office supplies at January 31 total $900.
(2) Insurance coverage expires on October 31, 2006.
(3) Annual depreciation on the equipment is $1,500.
(4) Interest of $50 has accrued on the note payable.

(d) Prepare a multiple-step income statement and retained earnings statement for January and a classified balance sheet at the end of January.

(e) Prepare and post adjusting and closing entries.

(f) Prepare a post-closing trial balance, and determine whether the subsidiary ledgers agree with the control accounts in the general ledger.

Critical Thinking

■ GROUP DECISION CASE

BYPE-2 Manion & Roben is a wholesaler of small appliances and parts. Manion & Roben is operated by two owners, Andy Manion and Lorelei Roben. In addition, the company has one employee, a repair specialist, who is on a fixed salary. Revenues are earned through the sale of appliances to retailers (approximately 75% of total revenues), appliance parts to do-it-yourselfers (10%), and the repair of appliances brought to the store (15%). Appliance sales are made on both a credit and cash basis. Customers are billed on prenumbered sales invoices. Credit terms are always net/30 days. All parts sales and repair work are cash only.

Merchandise is purchased on account from the manufacturers of both the appliances and the parts. Practically all suppliers offer cash discounts for prompt payments, and it is company policy to take all discounts. Most cash payments are made by check. Checks are most frequently issued to suppliers, to trucking companies for freight on merchandise purchases, and to newspapers, radio, and TV stations for advertising. All advertising bills are paid as received. Andy and Lorelei each receive a monthly dividend. The salaried repairman is paid twice monthly. Manion & Roben currently has a manual accounting system.

Instructions

With the class divided into groups, answer the following.

(a) Identify the special journals that Manion & Roben should have in its manual system. List the column headings appropriate for each of the special journals.

(b) What control and subsidiary accounts should be included in Manion & Roben's manual system? Why?

■ COMMUNICATION ACTIVITY

BYPE-3 Kris Leask, a classmate, has a part-time bookkeeping job. She is concerned about the inefficiencies in journalizing and posting transactions. Jon Breiwa is the owner of the company where Kris works. In response to numerous complaints from Kris and others, Jon hired two additional bookkeepers a month ago. However, the inefficiencies have continued at an even higher rate. The accounting information system for the company has only a general journal and a general ledger. Jon refuses to install a computerized accounting system.

Instructions

Now that Kris is an expert in manual accounting information systems, she decides to send a letter to Jon Breiwa explaining (1) why the additional personnel did not help and (2) what changes should be made to improve the efficiency of the accounting department. Write the letter that you think Kris should send.

■ ETHICS CASE

Accounting Matters!

BYPE-4 Teofilo Products Company operates three divisions, each with its own manufacturing plant and marketing/sales force. The corporate headquarters and central accounting office are in Teofilo, and the plants are in Freeport, Rockport, and Bayport, all within 50 miles of Teofilo. Corporate management treats each division as an independent profit center and encourages competition among them. They each have similar but different product lines. As a competitive incentive, bonuses are awarded each year to the employees of the fastest growing and most profitable division.

Ismael Soto is the manager of Teofilo's centralized computer accounting operation that keyboards the sales transactions and maintains the accounts receivable for all three divisions. Ismael came up in the accounting ranks from the Bayport division where his wife, several relatives, and many friends still work.

As sales documents are keyboarded into the computer, the originating division is identified by code. Most sales documents (95%) are coded, but some (5%) are not coded or are coded incorrectly. As the manager, Ismael has instructed the keyboard operators to assign the Bayport code to all uncoded and incorrectly coded sales documents. This is done he says, "in order to expedite processing and to keep the computer files current since they are updated daily." All receivables and cash collections for all three divisions are handled by Teofilo as one subsidiary accounts receivable ledger.

Instructions

(a) Who are the stakeholders in this situation?

(b) What are the ethical issues in this case?

(c) How might the system be improved to prevent this situation?

Answers to Self-Study Questions

1. a **2.** c **3.** a **4.** c **5.** d **6.** b **7.** c **8.** c

Appendix F

Other Significant Liabilities

STUDY OBJECTIVES

After studying this appendix, you should be able to:

1. Describe the accounting and disclosure requirements for contingent liabilities.
2. Contrast the accounting for operating and capital leases.
3. Identify additional fringe benefits associated with employee compensation.

In addition to the current and long-term liabilities discussed in Chapter 11, several more types of liabilities may exist that could have a significant impact on a company's financial position and future cash flows. These other significant liabilities will be discussed in this appendix. They are: (a) contingent liabilities, (b) lease liabilities, and (c) additional liabilities for employee fringe benefits (paid absences and postretirement benefits).

CONTINGENT LIABILITIES

STUDY OBJECTIVE 1

Describe the accounting and disclosure requirements for contingent liabilities.

With notes payable, interest payable, accounts payable, and sales taxes payable, we know that an obligation to make payment exists. But suppose that your company is involved in a dispute with the Internal Revenue Service (IRS) over the amount of its income tax liability. Should you report the disputed amount as a liability on the balance sheet? Or suppose your company is involved in a lawsuit which, if you lose, might result in bankruptcy. How should this major contingency be reported? The answers to these questions are difficult, because these liabilities are dependent—contingent—upon some future event. In other words, a **contingent liability** is a potential liability that may become an actual liability in the future.

How should contingent liabilities be reported? Guidelines have been adopted that help resolve these problems. The guidelines require that:

1. If the contingency is **probable** (if it is likely to occur) **and** the amount can be **reasonably estimated**, the liability should be recorded in the accounts.
2. If the contingency is only **reasonably possible** (if it could happen), then it need be disclosed only in the notes that accompany the financial statements.
3. If the contingency is **remote** (if it is unlikely to occur), it need not be recorded or disclosed.

Recording a Contingent Liability

Product warranties are an example of a contingent liability that should be recorded in the accounts. Warranty contracts result in future costs that may be incurred in replacing defective units or repairing malfunctioning units. Generally, a manufacturer, such as **Black & Decker**, knows that some warranty costs will be incurred. From prior experience with the product, the company usually can reasonably estimate the anticipated cost of servicing (honoring) the warranty.

The accounting for warranty costs is based on the matching principle. **The estimated cost of honoring product warranty contracts should be recognized as an expense in the period in which the sale occurs.** To illustrate, assume that in 2006 Denson Manufacturing Company sells 10,000 washers and dryers at an average price of $600 each. The selling price includes a one-year warranty on parts. It is expected that 500 units (5%) will be defective and that warranty repair costs will average $80 per unit. In 2006, warranty contracts are honored on 300 units at a total cost of $24,000.

At December 31, it is necessary to accrue the estimated warranty costs on the 2006 sales. The computation is as follows.

Illustration F-1
Computation of estimated product warranty liability

Number of units sold	10,000
Estimated rate of defective units	× 5%
Total estimated defective units	500
Average warranty repair cost	× $80
Estimated product warranty liability	**$40,000**

The adjusting entry, therefore, is:

A	=	L	+	SE
		+40,000		−40,000 Exp

Cash Flows
no effect

Dec. 31	Warranty Expense	40,000	
	Estimated Warranty Liability		40,000
	(To accrue estimated warranty costs)		

The entry to record those repair costs incurred in 2006 to honor warranty contracts on 2006 sales is shown below.

A	=	L	+	SE
−24,000		−24,000		

Cash Flows
no effect

Jan. 1– Dec. 31	Estimated Warranty Liability	24,000	
	Repair Parts		24,000
	(To record honoring of 300 warranty contracts on 2006 sales)		

Warranty expense of $40,000 is reported under selling expenses in the income statement. Estimated warranty liability of $16,000 ($40,000 − $24,000) is classified as a current liability on the balance sheet.

In the following year, all expenses incurred in honoring warranty contracts on 2006 sales should be debited to Estimated Warranty Liability. To illustrate, assume that 20 defective units are replaced in January 2007, at an average cost of $80 in parts and labor. The summary entry for the month of January 2007 is:

A	=	L	+	SE
−1,600		−1,600		

Cash Flows
no effect

Jan. 31	Estimated Warranty Liability	1,600	
	Repair Parts		1,600
	(To record honoring of 20 warranty contracts on 2006 sales)		

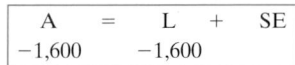

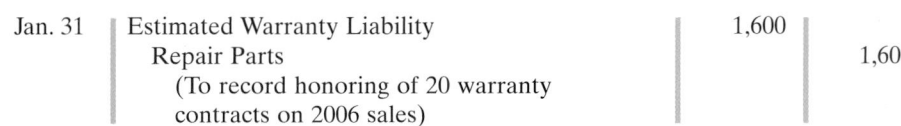

Disclosure of Contingent Liabilities

When it is probable that a contingent liability will be incurred but the amount cannot be reasonably estimated, or when the contingent liability is only reasonably possible, only disclosure of the contingency is required. Examples of contingencies that may require disclosure are pending or threatened lawsuits and assessment of additional income taxes pending an IRS audit of the tax return.

The disclosure should identify the nature of the item and, if known, the amount of the contingency and the expected outcome of the future event. Disclosure is usually accomplished through a note to the financial statements, as illustrated by the following.

Illustration F-2
Disclosure of contingent liability

USAIRWAYS
Notes to the Financial Statements

Legal Proceedings

The Company and various subsidiaries have been named as defendants in various suits and proceedings which involve, among other things, environmental concerns about noise and air pollution and employment matters. These suits and proceedings are in various stages of litigation, and the status of the law with respect to several of the issues involved is unsettled. For these reasons the outcome of these suits and proceedings is difficult to predict. In the Company's opinion, however, the disposition of these matters is not likely to have a material adverse effect on its financial condition.

Lease Liabilities

STUDY OBJECTIVE 2

Contrast the accounting for operating and capital leases.

A **lease** is a contractual arrangement between a lessor (owner of the property) and a lessee (renter of the property). It grants the right to use specific property for a period of time in return for cash payments. Leasing is big business. An estimated $125 billion of capital equipment was leased in a recent year. This represents approximately one-third of equipment financed that year. The two most common types of leases are operating leases and capital leases.

Operating Leases

The renting of an apartment and the rental of a car at an airport are examples of operating leases. **In an operating lease the intent is temporary use of the property by the lessee. The lessor continues to own the property.** The lease (or rental) payments are recorded as an expense by the lessee and as revenue by the lessor. For example, assume that a sales representative for Western Inc. leases a car from Hertz Car Rental at the Los Angeles airport and that Hertz charges a total of $275. The entry by the lessee, Western Inc., is:

Car Rental Expense	275	
Cash		275
(To record payment of lease rental charge)		

A	=	L	+	SE
−275				−275 Exp

Cash Flows
−275

The lessee may incur other costs during the lease period. For example, in the case above, the lessee may pay for gas and oil. These costs are also reported as an expense.

HELPFUL HINT

A capital lease situation is one that, although legally a rental case, is *in substance* an installment purchase by the lessee. Accounting standards require that substance over form be used in such a situation.

Capital Leases

In most lease contracts, a periodic payment is made by the lessee and is recorded as rent expense in the income statement. But, in some cases, the lease contract transfers substantially all the benefits and risks of ownership to the lessee. Such a lease is in effect a purchase of the property. This type of lease is called a **capital lease**. Its name comes from the fact that the present value of the cash payments for the lease is capitalized and recorded as an asset. Illustration F-3 indicates the major difference between an operating and a capital lease.

Lessor has substantially all of the benefits and risks of ownership

Lessee has substantially all of the benefits and risks of ownership

Illustration F-3
Types of leases

The lessee must record a lease **as an asset**—that is, as a capital lease—if **any one** of the following conditions exists:

1. **The lease transfers ownership of the property to the lessee.** *Rationale:* If during the lease term the lessee receives ownership of the asset, the leased asset should be reported as an asset on the lessee's books.
2. **The lease contains a bargain purchase option.** *Rationale:* If during the term of the lease the lessee can purchase the asset at a price substantially below its fair market value, the lessee will exercise this option. Thus, the lease should be reported as a leased asset on the lessee's books.
3. **The lease term is equal to 75% or more of the economic life of the leased property.** *Rationale:* If the lease term is for much of the asset's useful life, the asset should be recorded by the lessee.
4. **The present value of the lease payments equals or exceeds 90% of the fair market value of the leased property.** *Rationale:* If the present value of the lease payments is equal to or almost equal to the fair market value of the asset, the lessee has essentially purchased the asset. As a result, the leased asset should be recorded on the books of the lessee.

To illustrate, assume that Gonzalez Company decides to lease new equipment. The lease period is 4 years; the economic life of the leased equipment is estimated to be 5 years. The present value of the lease payments is $190,000, which is equal to the fair market value of the equipment. There is no transfer of ownership during the lease term, nor is there any bargain purchase option.

In this example, Gonzalez has essentially purchased the equipment. Conditions 3 and 4 have been met. First, the lease term is 75% or more of the economic life of the asset. Second, the present value of cash payments is equal to the equipment's fair market value. The entry to record the transaction is as follows.

Leased Asset—Equipment	190,000	
Lease Liability		190,000
(To record leased asset and lease liability)		

A	=	L	+	SE
+190,000		+190,000		

Cash Flows
no effect

The leased asset is reported on the balance sheet under plant assets. The lease liability is reported on the balance sheet as a liability. **The portion of the lease liability expected to be paid in the next year is reported as a current liability. The remainder is classified as a long-term liability.**

Most lessees do not like to report leases on their balance sheets. Why? Because the lease liability increases the company's total liabilities. This, in turn, may make it more difficult for the company to obtain needed funds from lenders. As a result, companies attempt to keep leased assets and lease liabilities off the balance sheet by not meeting any of the four conditions mentioned above. The practice of keeping liabilities off the balance sheet is referred to as **off-balance-sheet financing**.

Additional Liabilities for Employee Fringe Benefits

STUDY OBJECTIVE 3
Identify additional fringe benefits associated with employee compensation.

In addition to the three payroll tax fringe benefits discussed in Appendix D (FICA taxes and state and federal unemployment taxes), employers incur other substantial fringe benefit costs. Indeed, fringe benefits have been growing faster than pay. In a recent year, benefits equaled 38 percent of wages and salaries. While vacations and other forms of paid leave still take the biggest bite out of the benefits pie, as shown in Illustration F-4, medical costs are the fastest-growing item.

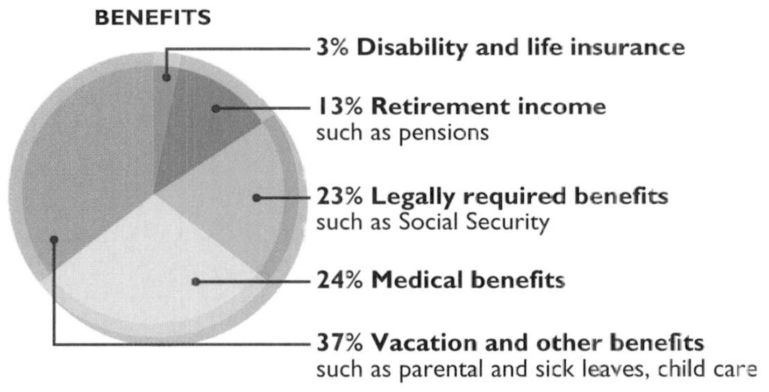

Illustration F-4
The fringe benefits pie

We discuss two of the most important fringe benefits—paid absences and postretirement benefits—in this section.

Paid Absences

Employees often are given rights to receive compensation for absences when certain conditions of employment are met. The compensation may be for paid vacations, sick pay benefits, and paid holidays. When the payment for such absences is **probable** and the amount can be **reasonably estimated**, a liability should be accrued for paid future absences. When the amount cannot be reasonably estimated, the potential liability should be disclosed. Ordinarily, vacation pay is the only paid absence that is accrued. The other types of paid absences are only disclosed.[1]

To illustrate, assume that Academy Company employees are entitled to one day's vacation for each month worked. If 30 employees earn an average of $110 per day in a given month, the accrual for vacation benefits in one month is $3,300. The liability is recognized at the end of the month by the following adjusting entry.

A	=	L	+	SE
		+3,300		−3,300 Exp

Cash Flows
no effect

Jan. 31	Vacation Benefits Expense	3,300	
	Vacation Benefits Payable		3,300
	(To accrue vacation benefits expense)		

This accrual is required by the matching principle. Vacation Benefits Expense is reported as an operating expense in the income statement, and Vacation Benefits Payable is reported as a current liability in the balance sheet.

Later, when vacation benefits are paid, Vacation Benefits Payable is debited and Cash is credited. For example, if the above benefits for 10 employees are paid in July, the entry is:

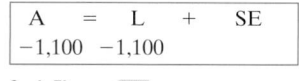

A	=	L	+	SE
−1,100		−1,100		

Cash Flows
−1,100

July 31	Vacation Benefits Payable	1,100	
	Cash		1,100
	(To record payment of vacation benefits)		

The magnitude of unpaid absences has gained employers' attention. Consider the case of an assistant superintendent of schools who worked for 20 years and rarely took a vacation or sick day. A month or so before she retired, the school district discovered that she was due nearly $30,000 in accrued benefits. Yet the liability had never been accrued.

Postretirement Benefits

Postretirement benefits are benefits provided by employers to retired employees for (1) health care and life insurance and (2) pensions. For many years the accounting for postretirement benefits was on a cash basis. Now, both types of postretirement benefits are accounted for on the accrual basis.

Postretirement Health Care and Life Insurance Benefits

Providing medical and related health care benefits for retirees was at one time an inexpensive and highly effective way of generating employee goodwill. This practice has now turned into one of corporate America's most worrisome financial problems. Runaway medical costs, early retirement, and increased longevity are sending the liability for retiree health plans through the roof.

Many companies began offering retiree health care coverage in the form of Medicare supplements in the 1960s. Almost all plans operated on a pay-as-you-go basis. The companies simply paid for the bills as they came in, rather than setting aside funds to meet the cost of future benefits. These plans were accounted for on the cash basis. But, the FASB concluded that shareholders and creditors should know the amount of the employer's obligations. As a result, employers must now use the **accrual basis** in accounting for postretirement health care and life insurance benefits.

[1] The typical U.S. company provides an average of 12 days of paid vacation for its employees, at an average cost of 5% of gross earnings.

Pension Plans

A **pension plan** is an agreement whereby an employer provides benefits (payments) to employees after they retire. Over 50 million workers currently participate in pension plans in the United States. The need for good accounting for pension plans becomes apparent when one appreciates the size of existing pension funds. Most pension plans are subject to the provisions of ERISA (Employee Retirement Income Security Act), a law enacted to curb abuses in the administration and funding of such plans.

Three parties are generally involved in a pension plan. The **employer** (company) sponsors the pension plan. The **plan administrator** receives the contributions from the employer, invests the pension assets, and makes the benefit payments to the **pension recipients** (retired employees). Illustration F-5 indicates the flow of cash among the three parties involved in a pension plan.

Illustration F-5
Parties in a pension plan

An employer-financed pension is part of the employees' compensation. ERISA establishes the minimum contribution that a company must make each year toward employee pensions. The company records the pension costs as an expense while the employees are working because that is when the company receives benefits from the employees' services. Generally the pension expense is reported as an operating expense in the company's income statement.

Frequently, the amount contributed by the company to the pension plan is different from the amount of the pension expense. A **liability** is recognized when the pension expense to date is **more than** the company's contributions to date. An **asset** is recognized when the pension expense to date is **less than** the company's contributions to date. Further consideration of the accounting for pension plans is left for more advanced courses.

The two most common types of pension arrangements for providing benefits to employees after they retire are defined contribution plans and defined benefit plans.

DEFINED CONTRIBUTION PLAN. In a **defined contribution plan**, the employer's contribution to the plan is defined by the terms of the plan. That is, the employer agrees to contribute a certain sum each period based on a formula.

The accounting for a defined contribution plan is straightforward: The employer simply makes a contribution each year based on the formula established in the plan. As a result, the employer's obligation is easily determined. It follows that **the amount of the contribution required each period is reported as pension expense. A liability is reported by the employer only if the contribution has not been made in full.**

To illustrate, assume that Alba Office Interiors Corp. has a defined contribution plan in which it contributes $200,000 each year to the pension fund for its employees. The entry to record this transaction is:

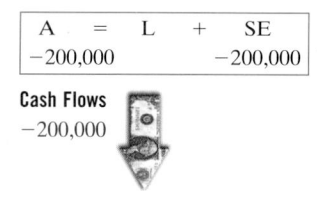

A	=	L	+	SE
−200,000				−200,000

Cash Flows
−200,000

Pension Expense	200,000	
Cash		200,000
(To record pension expense and contribution to pension fund)		

To the extent that Alba did not contribute the $200,000 defined contribution, a liability would be recorded. Pension payments to retired employees are made from the pension fund by the plan administrator.

DEFINED BENEFIT PLAN. In a **defined benefit plan**, the benefits that the employee will receive at the time of retirement are defined by the terms of the plan. Benefits are typically calculated using a formula that considers an employee's compensation level when he or she nears retirement and the employee's years of service. Because the benefits in this plan are defined in terms of uncertain future variables, an appropriate funding pattern is established to ensure that enough funds are available at retirement to meet the benefits promised. This funding level depends on a number of factors such as employee turnover, length of service, mortality, compensation levels, and investment earnings. **The proper accounting for these plans is complex and is considered in more advanced accounting courses.**

Postretirement Benefits as Long-term Liabilities

While part of the liability associated with (1) postretirement health care and life insurance benefits and (2) pension plans is generally a current liability, the greater portion of these liabilities extends many years into the future. Therefore, many companies are required to report significant amounts as long-term liabilities for postretirement benefits.

BEFORE YOU GO ON...

Review It

1. What is a contingent liability?
2. How are contingent liabilities reported in financial statements?
3. What accounts are involved in accruing and paying vacation benefits?
4. What basis should be used in accounting for postretirement benefits?

SUMMARY OF STUDY OBJECTIVES

1. **Describe the accounting and disclosure requirements for contingent liabilities.** If it is probable that the contingency will happen (if it is likely to occur) and the amount can be reasonably estimated, the liability should be recorded in the accounts. If the contingency is only reasonably possible (it could occur), then it should be disclosed only in the notes to the financial statements. If the possibility that the contingency will happen is remote (unlikely to occur), it need not be recorded or disclosed.
2. **Contrast the accounting for operating and capital leases.** For an operating lease, lease (or rental) payments are recorded as an expense by the lessee (renter). For a capital lease, the lessee records the asset and related obligation at the present value of the future lease payments.
3. **Identify additional fringe benefits associated with employee compensation.** Additional fringe benefits associated with wages are paid absences (paid vacations, sick pay benefits, and paid holidays), postretirement health care and life insurance, and pensions. The two most common types of pension arrangements are a defined contribution plan and a defined benefit plan.

GLOSSARY

Capital lease A contractual arrangement that transfers substantially all the benefits and risks of ownership to the lessee so that the lease is in effect a purchase of the property. (p. F4).

Contingent liability A potential liability that may become an actual liability in the future. (p. F1).

Defined benefit plan A pension plan in which the benefits that the employee will receive at retirement are defined by the terms of the plan. (p. F8).

Defined contribution plan A pension plan in which the employer's contribution to the plan is defined by the terms of the plan. (p. F7).

Operating lease A contractual arrangement giving the lessee temporary use of the property, with continued ownership of the property by the lessor. (p. F3).

Pension plan An agreement whereby an employer provides benefits to employees after they retire. (p. F7).

Postretirement benefits Payments by employers to retired employees for health care, life insurance, and pensions. (p. F6).

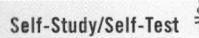

SELF-STUDY QUESTIONS

Self-Study/Self-Test

Answers are at the end of the appendix.

(SO 1) **1.** A contingency should be recorded in the accounts when:
- **a.** It is probable the contingency will happen but the amount cannot be reasonably estimated.
- **b.** It is reasonably possible the contingency will happen and the amount can be reasonably estimated.
- **c.** It is reasonably possible the contingency will happen but the amount cannot be reasonably estimated.
- **d.** It is probable the contingency will happen and the amount can be reasonably estimated.

(SO 1) **2.** At December 31, Anthony Company prepares an adjusting entry for a product warranty contract. Which of the following accounts are included in the entry?
- **a.** Warranty Expense.
- **b.** Estimated Warranty Liability.
- **c.** Repair Parts/Wages Payable.
- **d.** Both (a) and (b).

(SO 2) **3.** Lease A does not contain a bargain purchase option, but the lease term is equal to 90 percent of the estimated economic life of the leased property. Lease B does not transfer ownership of the property to the lessee by the end of the lease term, but the lease term is equal to 75 percent of the estimated economic life of the lease property. How should the lessee classify these leases?

	Lease A	Lease B
a.	Operating lease	Capital lease
b.	Operating lease	Operating lease
c.	Capital lease	Capital lease
d.	Capital lease	Operating lease

4. Which of the following is *not* an additional fringe benefit? (SO 3)
- **a.** Salaries.
- **b.** Paid absences.
- **c.** Paid vacations.
- **d.** Postretirement pensions.

QUESTIONS

1. What is a contingent liability? Give an example of a contingent liability that is usually recorded in the accounts.
2. Under what circumstances is a contingent liability disclosed only in the notes to the financial statements? Under what circumstances is a contingent liability not recorded in the accounts nor disclosed in the notes to the financial statements?
3. (a) What is a lease agreement? (b) What are the two most common types of leases? (c) Distinguish between the two types of leases.
4. Orbison Company rents a warehouse on a month-to-month basis for the storage of its excess inventory. The company periodically must rent space when its production greatly exceeds actual sales. What is the nature of this type of lease agreement, and what accounting treatment should be accorded it?
5. Costello Company entered into an agreement to lease 12 computers from Estes Electronics Inc. The present value of the lease payments is $186,300. Assuming that this is a capital lease, what entry would Costello Company make on the date of the lease agreement?
6. Identify three additional types of fringe benefits associated with employees' compensation.
7. Often during job interviews, the candidate asks the potential employer about the firm's paid absences policy. What are paid absences? How are they accounted for?

8. What are the two types of postretirement benefits? During what years does the FASB advocate expensing the employer's costs of these postretirement benefits?

9. What basis of accounting for the employer's cost of postretirement health care and life insurance benefits has been used by most companies, and what basis does the FASB advocate in the future? Explain the basic difference between these methods in recognizing postretirement benefit costs.

10. Identify the three parties in a pension plan. What role does each party have in the plan?

11. Brenna Ottare and Caitlin Wilkes are reviewing pension plans. They ask your help in distinguishing between a defined contribution plan and a defined benefit plan. Explain the principal difference to Brenna and Caitlin.

BRIEF EXERCISES

Prepare adjusting entry for warranty costs.
(SO 1)

BEF-1 On December 1, Viná Company introduces a new product that includes a 1-year warranty on parts. In December 1,000 units are sold. Management believes that 5% of the units will be defective and that the average warranty costs will be $60 per unit. Prepare the adjusting entry at December 31 to accrue the estimated warranty cost.

Prepare entries for operating and capital leases.
(SO 2)

BEF-2 Prepare the journal entries that the lessee should make to record the following transactions.

1. The lessee makes a lease payment of $80,000 to the lessor in an operating lease transaction.
2. Zander Company leases a new building from Joel Construction, Inc. The present value of the lease payments is $900,000. The lease qualifies as a capital lease.

Record estimated vacation benefits.
(SO 3)

BEF-3 In Alomar Company, employees are entitled to 1 day's vacation for each month worked. In January, 50 employees worked the full month. Record the vacation pay liability for January assuming the average daily pay for each employee is $120.

EXERCISES

Record estimated liability and expense for warranties.
(SO 1)

EF-1 Boone Company sells automatic can openers under a 75-day warranty for defective merchandise. Based on past experience, Boone Company estimates that 3% of the units sold will become defective during the warranty period. Management estimates that the average cost of replacing or repairing a defective unit is $15. The units sold and units defective that occurred during the last 2 months of 2006 are as follows.

Month	Units Sold	Units Defective Prior to December 31
November	30,000	600
December	32,000	400

Instructions

(a) Determine the estimated warranty liability at December 31 for the units sold in November and December.

(b) Prepare the journal entries to record the estimated liability for warranties and the costs (assume actual costs of $15,000) incurred in honoring 1,000 warranty claims.

(c) Give the entry to record the honoring of 500 warranty contracts in January at an average cost of $15.

Prepare the current liabilities section of the balance sheet.
(SO 1)

EF-2 Larkin Online Company has the following liability accounts after posting adjusting entries: Accounts Payable $63,000, Unearned Ticket Revenue $24,000, Estimated Warranty Liability $18,000, Interest Payable $8,000, Mortgage Payable $120,000, Notes Payable $80,000, and Sales Taxes Payable $10,000. Assume the company's operating cycle is less than 1 year, ticket revenue will be earned within 1 year, warranty costs are expected to be incurred within 1 year, and the notes mature in 3 years.

Instructions

(a) Prepare the current liabilities section of the balance sheet, assuming $40,000 of the mortgage is payable next year.

(b) Comment on Larkin Online Company's liquidity, assuming total current assets are $300,000.

Prepare journal entries for operating lease and capital lease.

(SO 2)

EF-3 Presented below are two independent situations.

1. Speedy Car Rental leased a car to Rundgren Company for 1 year. Terms of the operating lease agreement call for monthly payments of $500.
2. On January 1, 2006, Miles Inc. entered into an agreement to lease 20 computers from Halo Electronics. The terms of the lease agreement require three annual rental payments of $40,000 (including 10% interest) beginning December 31, 2006. The present value of the three rental payments is $99,474. Miles considers this a capital lease.

Instructions

(a) Prepare the appropriate journal entry to be made by Rundgren Company for the first lease payment.

(b) Prepare the journal entry to record the lease agreement on the books of Miles Inc. on January 1, 2006.

Prepare adjusting entries for fringe benefits.

(SO 3)

EF-4 Bunill Company has two fringe benefit plans for its employees:

1. It grants employees 2 days' vacation for each month worked. Ten employees worked the entire month of March at an average daily wage of $80 per employee.
2. It has a defined contribution pension plan in which the company contributes 10% of gross earnings. Gross earnings in March were $30,000. The payment to the pension fund has not been made.

Instructions

Prepare the adjusting entries at March 31.

PROBLEMS: SET A

Prepare current liability entries, adjusting entries, and current liabilities section.

(SO 1)

PF-1A On January 1, 2006, the ledger of Shumway Software Company contains the following liability accounts.

Accounts Payable	$42,500
Sales Taxes Payable	5,800
Unearned Service Revenue	15,000

During January the following selected transactions occurred.

Jan.	1	Borrowed $15,000 in cash from Amsterdam Bank on a 4-month, 8%, $15,000 note.
	5	Sold merchandise for cash totaling $10,400 which includes 4% sales taxes.
	12	Provided services for customers who had made advance payments of $9,000. (Credit Service Revenue.)
	14	Paid state treasurer's department for sales taxes collected in December 2005 ($5,800).
	20	Sold 700 units of a new product on credit at $52 per unit, plus 4% sales tax. This new product is subject to a 1-year warranty.
	25	Sold merchandise for cash totaling $12,480, which includes 4% sales taxes.

Instructions

(a) Journalize the January transactions.

(b) Journalize the adjusting entries at January 31 for (1) the outstanding notes payable, and (2) estimated warranty liability, assuming warranty costs are expected to equal 5% of sales of the new product.

(c) Prepare the current liabilities section of the balance sheet at January 31, 2006. Assume no change in accounts payable.

Analyze three different lease situations and prepare journal entries.

(SO 2)

PF-2A Presented below are three different lease transactions in which Ortiz Enterprises engaged in 2006. Assume that all lease transactions start on January 1, 2006. In no case does Ortiz receive title to the properties leased during or at the end of the lease term.

	Lessor		
	Schoen Inc.	Casey Co.	Lester Inc.
Type of property	Bulldozer	Truck	Furniture
Bargain purchase option	None	None	None
Lease term	4 years	6 years	3 years
Estimated economic life	8 years	7 years	5 years
Yearly rental	$13,000	$15,000	$4,000
Fair market value of leased asset	$80,000	$72,000	$27,500
Present value of the lease rental payments	$48,000	$62,000	$12,000

Instructions

(a) Identify the leases above as operating or capital leases. Explain.
(b) How should the lease transaction with Casey Co. be recorded on January 1, 2006?
(c) How should the lease transactions for Lester Inc. be recorded in 2006?

PROBLEMS: SET B

Prepare current liability entries, adjusting entries, and current liabilities section.
(SO 1)

PF-1B On January 1, 2006, the ledger of Zaur Company contains the following liability accounts.

Accounts Payable	$52,000
Sales Taxes Payable	7,700
Unearned Service Revenue	16,000

During January the following selected transactions occurred.

Jan. 5 Sold merchandise for cash totaling $17,280, which includes 8% sales taxes.
12 Provided services for customers who had made advance payments of $10,000. (Credit Service Revenue.)
14 Paid state revenue department for sales taxes collected in December 2005 ($7,700).
20 Sold 600 units of a new product on credit at $50 per unit, plus 8% sales tax. This new product is subject to a 1-year warranty.
21 Borrowed $18,000 from UCLA Bank on a 3-month, 9%, $18,000 note.
25 Sold merchandise for cash totaling $12,420, which includes 8% sales taxes.

Instructions

(a) Journalize the January transactions.
(b) Journalize the adjusting entries at January 31 for (1) the outstanding notes payable, and (2) estimated warranty liability, assuming warranty costs are expected to equal 7% of sales of the new product. (*Hint:* Use one-third of a month for the UCLA Bank note.)
(c) Prepare the current liabilities section of the balance sheet at January 31, 2006. Assume no change in accounts payable.

Analyze three different lease situations and prepare journal entries.
(SO 2)

PF-2B Presented below are three different lease transactions that occurred for Milo Inc. in 2006. Assume that all lease contracts start on January 1, 2006. In no case does Milo receive title to the properties leased during or at the end of the lease term.

	Lessor		
	Gibson Delivery	Eller Co.	Louis Auto
Type of property	Computer	Delivery equipment	Automobile
Yearly rental	$ 8,000	$ 4,200	$ 3,700
Lease term	6 years	4 years	2 years
Estimated economic life	7 years	7 years	5 years
Fair market value of leased asset	$44,000	$19,000	$11,000
Present value of the lease rental payments	$41,000	$13,000	$6,400
Bargain purchase option	None	None	None

Instructions

(a) Which of the leases above are operating leases and which are capital leases? Explain.
(b) How should the lease transaction with Eller Co. be recorded in 2006?
(c) How should the lease transaction for Gibson Delivery be recorded on January 1, 2006?

BROADENING YOUR PERSPECTIVE

Financial Reporting and Analysis

FINANCIAL REPORTING PROBLEMS

BYPF-1 Refer to the financial statements of **PepsiCo** and the Notes to Consolidated Financial Statements in Appendix A to answer the following questions about contingent liabilities, lease liabilities, and pension costs.

PEPSI.

(a) Where does PepsiCo report its contingent liabilities?
(b) What is management's opinion as to the ultimate effect of the "various claims and legal proceedings" pending against the company?
(c) Where did PepsiCo report the details of its lease obligations? What amount of rent expense from operating leases did PepsiCo incur in 2003? What was PepsiCo's total future minimum annual rental commitment under noncancelable operating leases as of December 27, 2003?
(d) What type of employee pension plan does PepsiCo have?
(e) What is the amount of postretirement benefit expense (other than pensions) for 2003?

BYPF-2 Presented below is the lease portion of the notes to the financial statements of CF Industries, Inc.

CF INDUSTRIES, INC.
Notes to the Financial Statements

Leases The present value of future minimum capital lease payments and the future minimum lease payments under noncancelable operating leases at December 31, 2005, are:

	(in millions)	
	Capital Lease Payments	**Operating Lease Payments**
2006	$ 7,733	$3,067
2007	6,791	2,052
2008	6,730	1,056
2009	6,788	918
2010	6,785	86
Thereafter	13,441	6
Future minimum lease payments	48,268	$7,185
Less: Equivalent interest	11,391	
Present value	36,877	
Less: Current portion	5,570	
	$31,307	

Rent expense for operating leases was $7.0 million for the year ended December 31, 2005, $5.3 million for 2004, and $5.6 million for 2003.

Instructions

What type of leases does CF Industries, Inc. use? What is the amount of the current portion of the capital lease obligation?

Critical Thinking

■ GROUP DECISION CASE

BYPF-3 Presented below is the condensed balance sheet for Express, Inc. as of December 31, 2006.

EXPRESS, INC.
Balance Sheet
December 31, 2006

Current assets	$ 800,000	Current liabilities	$1,200,000
Plant assets	1,600,000	Long-term liabilities	700,000
		Common stock	400,000
		Retained earnings	100,000
Total	$2,400,000	Total	$2,400,000

Express has decided that it needs to purchase a new crane for its operations. The new crane costs $900,000 and has a useful life of 15 years. However, Express's bank has refused to provide any help in financing the purchase of the new equipment, even though Express is willing to pay an above-market interest rate for the financing.

The chief financial officer for Express, Lisa Colder, has discussed with the manufacturer of the crane the possibility of a lease agreement. After some negotiation, the crane manufacturer agrees to lease the crane to Express under the following terms: length of the lease 7 years; payments $100,000 per year. The present value of the lease payments is $548,732.

The board of directors at Express is delighted with this new lease. They reason they have the use of the crane for the next 7 years. In addition, Lisa Colder notes that this type of financing is a good deal because it will keep debt off the balance sheet.

Instructions

With the class divided into groups, answer the following.

(a) Why do you think the bank decided not to lend money to Express, Inc.?
(b) How should this lease transaction be reported in the financial statements?
(c) What did Lisa Colder mean when she said "leasing will keep debt off the balance sheet"?

Answers to Self-Study Questions

1. d **2.** d **3.** c **4.** a

PHOTO CREDITS

Chapter 1 Opener: Courtesy Pepsi-Cola North America. Page 7: Hai Wen China Tourism Press/The Image Bank/Getty Images. Page 8: Jean Miele/Corbis Stock Market. Page 24: Will Crocker/The Image Bank/Getty Images. Page 30: Mike Cressy/ Stock Illustration Source/Images.com. Page 42: Coutesy Nestlé S.A.

Chapter 2 Opener: Rod Long/Stone/Getty Images. Page 51: ©AP/Wide World Photos. Page 54: PhotoDisc, Inc./Getty Images. Page 58: Mike Stewart/Corbis Sygma. Page 60: Joe Bator/Corbis Stock Market.

Chapter 3 Opener: T. Kevin Smyth/Corbis Stock Market. Page 94: Chris Bell/Taxi/Getty Images. Page 95: ©AP/Wide World Photos. Page 99: Jeff Greenberg/PhotoEdit. Page 102: Illustration Works/Getty Images. Page 107: Peter Poulides/ Stone/Getty Images.

Chapter 4 Opener: Matthias Kulka/Corbis Stock Market. Page 145: William Whitehurst/Corbis Stock Market. Page 150: Keith Dannemiller/SABA. Page 152: M. Tcherevkoff/The Image Bank/Getty Images. Page 157: Miguel S. Salmeron/FPG International/Getty Images. Page 159 (top): Courtesy United Airlines. Page 159 (bottom): Reproduced with permission of Yahoo! Inc. ©1999 by Yahoo! Inc. YAHOO! and the YAHOO! logo are trademarks of YAHOO! Inc. Page 160 (top): John Fiordalisi/SUPERSTOCK. Page 160 (bottom): Digital Vision/ Getty Images. Page 161 (top): Courtesy Deckers Outdoor Corporation. Page 161 (bottom): Zigy Kaluzny/Stone/Getty Images. Page 162: Courtesy Dell Computer Corporation.

Chapter 5 Opener: Artville/Getty Images. Page 193: Michael Simpson/Taxi/Getty Images. Page 197: Ed Honowitz/ Stone/Getty Images. Page 199: Grant V. Faint/The Image Bank/Getty Images. Page 205: Dennis Galante/Stone/Getty Images.

Chapter 6 Opener: Chris Noble/Stone/Getty Images. Page 243: John Turner/Stone/Getty Images. Page 244: Tom Tracey/ Taxi/Getty Images. Page 253: PhotoDisc, Inc./Getty Images. Page 255: Jose Luis Pelaez, Inc/Corbis Images. Page 257: Courtesy Wal-Mart Stores, Inc. Page 284: Fuji and FujiFilm are registered trademarks of Fuji Film Co., Ltd. Page 285: Courtesy Eastman Kodak Company.

Chapter 7 Page 290: Artville/Getty Images. Page 298: Doug Armand/Stone/Getty Images. Page 299: Barbara Nessim/Stock Illustration Source/Images.com. Page 307: Steve Forney/ SUPERSTOCK. Page 309: Olney Vasan/Stone/Getty Images.

Chapter 8 Opener: Robert Stanton/Stone/Getty Images. Page 336: Corbis Digital Stock. Page 338: Gianni Dagli Orti/ Corbis Images. Page 341: Sean Kane/Stock Illustration Source/ Images.com. Page 346: SUPERSTOCK. Page 351: Miachel A. Keller/Corbis Stock Market. Page 357: Courtesy Eastman Kodak Company. Page 374 (top): PhotoDisc, Inc./Getty Images. Page 374 (bottom): Oracle is a registered trademark of the Oracle Corporation and/or its affiliates.

Chapter 9 Opener: PhotoDisc, Inc./Getty Images. Page 383: David Gould/The Image Bank/Getty Images. Page 388: ©Zefa/Index Stock. Page 397: EyeWire, Inc./Getty Images.

Chapter 10 Opener: Image State. Page 427: Greg Probst/ Stone/Getty Images. Page 433: AFP/Corbis Images. Page 440: David McNew/Getty Images News and Sport Services. Page 442 (bottom): Courtesy Owens-llinois. Page 442 (top): Courtesy of The Proctor and Gamble Company. Page 462: Courtesy Bob Evans.

Chapter 11 Opener: John Turner/Stone/Getty Images. Page 471: Pamela Hamilton/The Image Bank/Getty Images. Page 475: Courtesy Caterpillar Inc. Page 478: ©AP/Wide World Photos. Page 488: Andy Levine/Stock Illustration Source/ Images.com. Page 521: Courtesy Apache Corporation.

Chapter 12 Opener: David Young-Wolf/PhotoEdit. Page 530: Reuters NewMedia Inc/Corbis Images. Page 532: ©AP/ Wide World Photos. Page 535: Susan Van Etten/PhotoEdit. Page 541: Alex Fevzer/Corbis Images. Page 546: Atsushi Tsunoda/Imagina/Alamy Images. Page 551: PhotoDisc, Inc./ Getty Images. Page 553: David Madison/Stone/Getty Images. Page 554: Information courtesy of Tektronix, Inc. Page 558: KELLOGG'S® is a registered trademark of Kellogg Company. All rights reserved. Used with permission.

Chapter 13 Opener: Getty Images News and Sport Services. Page 592: D. Boone/Corbis.

Chapter 14 Opener: John Lund/Stone/Getty Images. Page 632: Darren McCollester/Getty Images News and Sport Services. Page 635: William Whitehurst/Corbis Images. Page 654: PhotoDisc, Inc./Getty Images. Page 681: Courtesy Élan Corporation.

Chapter 15 Opener: Jerry Driendl/Taxi/Getty Images. Page 689: Courtesy Sears, Roebuck and Co. Page 696: Nora Good/ Masterfile. Page 703: ©Eric Sander. Page 704: Royalty-Free/ Corbis Images. Page 707: Andy Sacks/Stone/Getty Images. Page 712: Jan Cobb /The Image Bank/Getty Images. Page 713: Jan Cobb /The Image Bank/Getty Images. Page 721: Courtesy Nordstrom.

Appendix F Page F3: ©The Image Bank/Getty Images.

COMPANY INDEX

SUBJECT INDEX

RAPID REVIEW

Weygandt, Kieso, Kimmel

Financial Accounting, Fifth Edition

FINANCIAL STATEMENTS

Order of Preparation	Date
1. Income statement	For the period ended
2. Retained earnings statement	For the period ended
3. Balance sheet	As of the end of the period
4. Statement of cash flows	For the period ended

Income Statement (perpetual inventory system)

Name of Company Income Statement For the Period Ended		
Sales revenues		
Sales	$ X	
Less: Sales returns and allowances	X	
Sales discounts	X	
Net sales		$ X
Cost of goods sold		X
Gross profit		X
Operating expenses		
Selling expenses		
(Examples: store salaries, advertising, delivery)	X	
Administrative expenses		
(Examples: rent, depreciation, utilities, insurance)	X	X
Income from operations		X
Other revenues and gains		
(Examples: interest, gains)	X	
Other expenses and losses		
(Examples: interest, losses)	X	X
Net income		$ X

Income Statement (periodic inventory system)

Name of Company Income Statement For the Period Ended			
Sales revenues			
Sales		$ X	
Less: Sales returns and allowances		X	
Sales discounts		X	
Net sales			$ X
Cost of goods sold			
Beginning inventory		X	
Purchases	$ X		
Less: Purchase returns and allowances	X		
Net purchases	X		
Add: Freight in	X		
Cost of goods purchased		X	
Cost of goods available for sale		X	
Less: Ending inventory		X	
Cost of goods sold			X
Gross profit			X
Operating expenses			
Selling expenses			
(Examples: store salaries, advertising, delivery)		X	
Administrative expenses			
(Examples: rent, depreciation, utilities, insurance)		X	X
Income from operations			X
Other revenues and gains			
(Examples: interest, gains)		X	
Other expenses and losses			
(Examples: interest, losses)		X	X
Net income			$ X

Retained Earnings Statment

Name of Company Retained Earnings Statement For the Period Ended	
Retained earnings, beginning of period	$ X
Add: Net income (or deduct net loss)	X
	X
Deduct: Dividends	X
Retained earnings, end of period	$ X

STOP AND CHECK: Net income (loss) presented on the retained earnings statement must equal the net income (loss) presented on the income statement.

Balance Sheet

Name of Company Balance Sheet As of the End of the Period			
Assets			
Current assets			
(Examples: cash, short-term investments, accounts receivable, merchandise inventory, prepaids)			$ X
Long-term investments			
(Examples: investments in bonds, investments in stocks)			X
Property, plant, and equipment			
Natural resources		$ X	
Buildings and equipment	$ X		
Less: Accumulated depreciation	X	X	X
Intangible assets			X
Total assets			$ X
Liabilities and Stockholders' Equity			
Liabilities			
Current liabilities			
(Examples: notes payable, accounts payable, accruals, unearned revenues, current portion of notes payable)			$ X
Long-term liabilities			
(Examples: notes payable, bonds payable)			X
Total liabilities			X
Stockholders' equity			
Common stock			X
Retained earnings			X
Total liabilities and stockholders' equity			$ X

STOP AND CHECK: Total assets on the balance sheet must equal total liabilities and stockholders' equity; and, ending retained earnings on the balance sheet must equal ending retained earnings on the retained earnings statement.

Statement of Cash Flows

Name of Company Statement of Cash Flows For the Period Ended	
Cash flows from operating activities	
Note: May be prepared using the direct or indirect method	
Cash provided (used) by operating activities	$ X
Cash flows from investing activities	
(Examples: purchase/sale of long-term assets)	
Cash provided (used) by investing activities	X
Cash flows from financing activities	
(Examples: issue/repayment of long-term liabilities, issue of stock, payment of dividends)	
Cash provided (used) by financing activities	X
Net increase (decrease) in cash	X
Cash, beginning of the period	X
Cash, end of the period	$ X

STOP AND CHECK: Cash, end of the period, on the statement of cash flows must equal cash presented on the balance sheet.